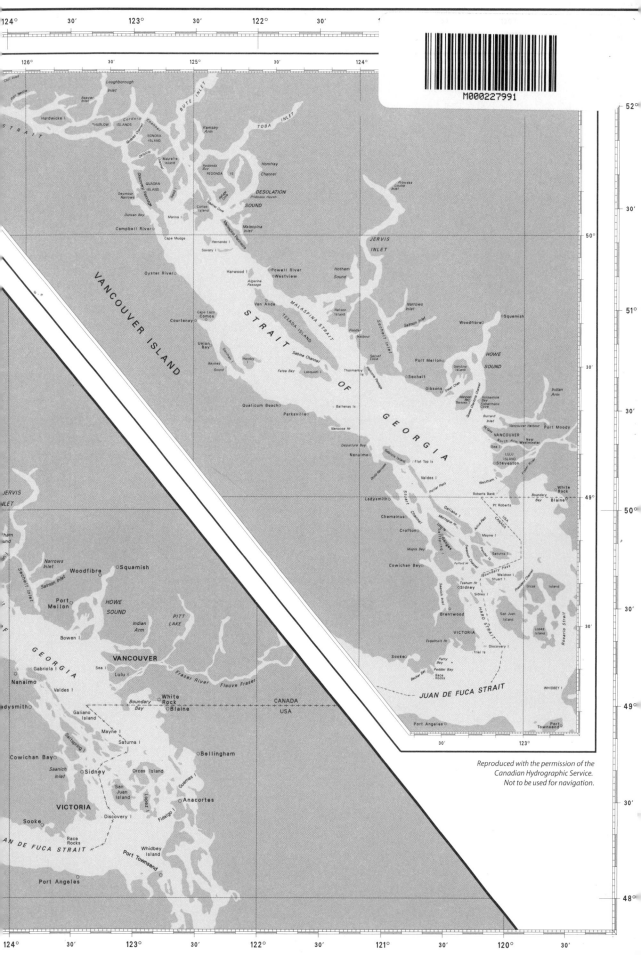

Reproduced with the permission of the
Canadian Hydrographic Service.
Not to be used for navigation.

M000227991

The Encyclopedia of
RAINCOAST PLACE NAMES
A Complete Reference to Coastal British Columbia

The Encyclopedia of

RAINCOAST
PLACE NAMES

A Complete Reference to Coastal British Columbia

Andrew Scott

Harbour Publishing

In
memory
of

JACK DAVID SCOTT
(1915–2007)

PAMELA MILDRED SCOTT
(1921–2009)

Table of Contents

FOREWORD

It is a testament to the excellence of *British Columbia Coast Names* by Captain John T. Walbran, first published in 1909, that it has taken exactly 100 years for anyone to get up the nerve to attempt a sequel. The magnificent obsession of an old salt who poured into it everything he had learned during lengthy service on the BC coast, Walbran's book has served as a de facto maritime history of the province and remains a staple on coastal bookshelves to this day. As a publisher of things coastal I had been flirting with the idea of a Walbran update for several decades, not because of any lack of regard for the original, but because, as Philip Akrigg noted in his introduction to the 1971 reprint by the Vancouver Public Library, "time has left it out of date."

It would make a good story to claim that the appearance of this book precisely on the 100th anniversary of its predecessor was the result of uncanny long-range planning by the publisher, but the truth is that it might have come out years earlier if it hadn't taken so long to find an author who was up to the daunting task of reconsidering all that has happened in coastal toponymy since 1909. Several well-qualified candidates initially showed interest but retreated after getting a close look at the vastness of the wordscape unfolding before them. It occurred to me that Andrew Scott would be a prime candidate after witnessing his work on the *Encyclopedia of British Columbia*, for which he provided the exemplary coverage of small communities, but my growing appreciation of the task made me wary of approaching one who seemed to be already making such full use of his time. The resources available were so insignificant in proportion to the undertaking that it could only be contemplated as a labour of love, and it is normally advisable to let others choose their own labours of love.

Normally, yes. But this turned out to be a glorious exception. Scott took to the project like he was born to do it. In many ways I suppose he was. A veteran journalist who has published some 1,000 articles as well as having edited and produced several substantial magazines himself, he combines prodigious energy with the fastidiousness of a philatelist, which he also is. His specialization is in BC postal history, which gave him a longstanding fascination with the province's less-known nooks and crannies. Additionally, he is an avid kayaker and coastal explorer, having written two of his five previous books about visiting the less inhabited reaches of BC's "Secret Coastline." Once he got started there was no holding him back, and I could only nod and smile as his time and space estimates extended, then extended again. Walbran reportedly worked on his opus for ten years and produced some 1,500 entries. Scott worked on his for three years and produced 4,000 entries. In terms of sheer magnitude it stands as one of the remarkable achievements of coastal literature. But it is so much more than that. Like Walbran, Scott brings a lifetime's fascination with the province and its people to his work. He is less given to digression than the master but he, too, has the storyteller's gift and uses it on every page. In one sense, *The Encyclopedia of Raincoast Place Names* is a long-overdue update of coastal toponymy. In another, it is a chronicle of the BC coast in digest form.

Howard White, CM, OBC
Harbour Publishing, Madeira Park, BC
July 2009

INTRODUCTION

I pressed on, taking fresh trouble for granted.
—Juan Francisco de la Bodega y Quadra, from the journal of
his 1775 voyage on the *Sonora*

W e navigate the world with names. Names familiarize the world, make it intelligible to us, help us live in it. As humans began to occupy what is now the coast of British Columbia, they must have applied the forerunners of today's names, and those names must have changed as the people changed. The place names we have today—the official names that are listed in gazetteers and appear on our maps and charts—bear no resemblance to the names that might have existed here in 1750, before the appearance of European visitors.

Because this book examines mainly official names, and because those names resulted from a long period of European exploration and colonization, the years between 1774

Potlatch dancers arriving at a coastal village. *Gordon Miller painting*

and 1945 are the primary focus of the text. There are, of course, hundreds of names on the coast with First Nation origins. Most of these, unfortunately, were applied by officials with European backgrounds and no knowledge whatsoever of aboriginal culture and language. They were approximations and best guesses and are often completely wrong. Nevertheless, they are the official names. For now, anyway. Today's First Nation treaties are adding a new generation of names to the gazetteer and correcting an old era of misunderstandings and errors. Sometime in the future, when the coastal aboriginal cultures are fairly and accurately reflected on our maps, a companion volume to this book may be required.

In the meantime, these pages honour those who came before, First Nation and not. The entries form a remembrance of sorts, touching briefly on past lives. They marvel at the stamina and courage of the pioneers, their daring and determination, and shudder at the sufferings they endured. They commemorate the officers and officials and chiefs who always get their names on maps, of course, but also recall a host of more modest characters on the frontier's broad stage—gold seekers, sealers, fishers, merchants, homesteaders and seamen.

The heroes of the book, surely, are the surveyors. Not the traders, who mainly went where profits could be found, nor even the ship captains, who tried to travel the safest waterways possible (though both these categories are well represented in the chapters that follow). It was the marine surveyors who explored and named every corner of the coast, who bumped their ships' small boats over rocks and reefs, in all kinds of weather. This was their job. And it was the hydrographers, as the surveyors are more properly called, who applied the bulk of the place names. Thus it is only fair that dozens of them are celebrated here, along with their associates and co-workers who crewed the hydrographic vessels.

The *Lady Washington* trading at Ninstints in 1791. *Gordon Miller painting*

Top: Victoria's Empress Hotel, on James Bay, opened in 1908. *John Lund*
Bottom: Brokers Bay in Vancouver's False Creek. *John Lund*

Introduction

SO IMPORTANT IS THE HISTORY of surveying to toponymy (the study of place names) that a brief sketch of that history may help put BC's coastal geography in perspective. Many of the individuals and ships mentioned in this introduction have places named after them in BC; additional biographical and historical information can often be found by consulting the appropriate entry.

Most early European visitors to the Pacific Northwest in the late 18th century made surveys of one kind or another. Because the prevailing winds were largely from the west, the first explorers—Juan José Pérez Hernandez in 1774, Bruno de Hezeta and Juan Francisco de la Bodega y Quadra in 1775, James Cook in 1778—kept well off the dangerous, unknown coastline for the most part and only came close to shore at certain specific sites. Their charts are thus extremely localized and sketchy.

The early fur traders made charts as well, as knowledge of the coast was almost as valuable a commodity as the sea otter skins that motivated their journeys. James Hanna, James Strange, George Dixon and Nathaniel Portlock, Charles Duncan and James Colnett, John Kendrick and Robert Gray, John Meares, Charles Barkley and others all contributed bits and pieces to the jigsaw puzzle of coastal knowledge that was slowly forming.

It was not until the early 1790s, however, that serious survey efforts got underway. The

Spanish hydrographers—among them José Maria Narváez, Manuel Quimper, Francisco de Eliza y Reventa, Dionisio Alcalá-Galiano and Cayetano Valdés y Flores—made detailed studies of southern BC, and Jacinto Caamaño explored farther north, around Dixon Entrance. Then, of course, came George Vancouver, who conducted comprehensive surveys of the BC and Alaska mainland coasts between 1792 and 1794 (and also charted the US coastline south of BC). Vancouver incorporated information into his charts from the earlier surveys of Cook, the Spanish, Russian colonists (in Alaska) and the fur traders, as well. And he put to final rest the long-lasting myth that a navigable waterway—the fabled Northwest Passage or Strait of Anián or Strait of Fonte—existed across North America and might provide a shortcut connecting Europe to the Far East.

The Royal Navy established a hydrographic office in 1795 and began collecting and co-ordinating navigational data from around the world. Regular Admiralty chart publication began in 1800. But for decades after Vancouver's visit, little hydrographic work was done in BC. Hudson's Bay Company officers surveyed the lower Fraser River in the 1820s, and Sir Edward Belcher charted Friendly Cove at Nootka Sound in 1837, but it was not until the mid-1840s that a resurgence in survey activity took place.

In 1843, anticipating that the British-US border in the Pacific Northwest might

Left: The old North Pacific Cannery on Inverness Passage is now a historic site and tourist attraction. *Andrew Scott*
Above: Telegraph Cove, once a sawmill site, now attracts tourists. *Rachel Talibart*

soon run along the 49th parallel, at least on the mainland, the Hudson's Bay Company established Fort Victoria on the southern tip of Vancouver Island. After the Oregon Treaty was signed in 1846, confirming the boundary we know today, the company moved its headquarters to the new post from Fort Vancouver on the Columbia River. The dispute over the border had prompted the Royal Navy to station several warships in the region, and their commanders began to use Esquimalt Harbour as an anchorage. Two of them, Henry Kellett of HMS *Herald* and James Wood of HMS *Pandora*, surveyed the south coast of Vancouver Island from Port San Juan to Victoria Harbour in 1846–47. The Admiralty charts that resulted (#1897, 1901 and 1910) were the first for the BC coast. Wood also wrote the first sailing directions for the region.

Over the next decade only a few local surveys were conducted, mostly by Royal Navy vessels on general patrol. The officers of HMS *Daphne* and *Daedalus*, for instance, did some work at the northern end of Vancouver Island in 1850–51 while punishing members of the Nahwitti First Nation for the alleged murders of three Hudson's Bay Company deserters. In 1852 and 1853, Augustus Kuper of HMS *Thetis* and James Prevost of the *Virago*, sent to keep the peace in the Queen Charlotte Islands in the wake of BC's first gold rush, produced surveys of Houston Stewart Channel and the north coast of Graham Island, as well as of Port Simpson and Nanaimo Harbour.

HMS *Plumper*, a specially fitted survey ship, arrived on the BC coast in 1857, under George Richards, who had been appointed one of the British officials on the Canada-US boundary commission. He began his work by determining where the 49th parallel crossed the northwest coastline and then surveyed the entire region around the south end of the Strait of Georgia, including the lower Fraser River and Burrard Inlet. Richards transferred to a larger vessel, HMS *Hecate*, in 1861, and before returning to England at the end of 1862 had more or less completed a detailed survey of the BC coast south of Queen Charlotte Sound, including all of Vancouver Island. He also wrote the first two editions of *Vancouver Island Pilot*.

Beachcombers stroll the sandy strand on Sidney Island. *Andrew Scott*

His assistant, Daniel Pender, took over the hydrographic work, and the ancient Hudson's Bay Company paddle steamer *Beaver* was hired for Pender's use. He continued charting the coast until 1870, reaching the south end of Alaska and the heads of Portland Canal and Observatory Inlet. Between them, Richards and Pender made a massive contribution to our knowledge of coastal waters and allowed relatively safe commercial navigation to become a reality.

Between 1870 and 1898, marine surveying came almost to a standstill. BC was now part of Canada, and the Royal Navy wanted to reduce its presence on the Pacific coast. The crews of HMS *Boxer* and *Daring* produced some charts of northern BC in the 1870s while helping search for potential sites for a Pacific railroad terminus. In 1898, however,

Top: Fishboats at Queen Charlotte City on Graham Island. *John Alexander*
Bottom: Cow Bay and Prince Rupert's new cruise ship centre. *John Alexander*

Britain agreed to again station a dedicated survey vessel, HMS *Egeria*, in BC waters. Coastal traffic was increasing, and larger-scale charts were needed. The Klondike gold rush was on, new settlers were arriving and taking up land, mines and salmon canneries were opening: BC was enjoying a boom.

In 1910 the *Egeria* was decommissioned, and the Canadian Hydrographic Service took over responsibility for Pacific surveys and chart production. A survey vessel, CGS *Lillooet*, was based on the BC coast, and Philip Musgrave became the first regional hydrographer, serving until 1919. His successor, Henri Parizeau, was in charge until 1946 and had a great influence on the evolution of coastal place names during that period, as we shall see.

By then, of course, the coast was charted. A small article buried in the *Victoria Times* of Oct 19, 1954, reported that BC officials hoped to "fill in the last blank spots on survey maps of the province" late the next year. Surveys would continue, however. When new technologies (aerial photography, for instance, or depth sounders or global positioning systems) allow for more refined measurements, charts must be corrected and upgraded. Shifting river channels and estuaries need constant checking. Larger ships with deeper drafts need more detailed charts, as do new ports and the approaches to new industrial and residential developments. As R W "Sandy" Sandilands, who spent 30 years as a marine surveyor on the BC coast, has noted, "the work of the hydrographer is never ending."

Above: The BC coast is laced with hard-flowing tidal rapids. Sechelt Rapids, located in Skookumchuck Narrows at the north end of Sechelt Inlet, is reputed to be the fastest-flowing of all. "Skookumchuck" means "strong water" in Chinook jargon. *Peter Vassilopoulos*
Right: The Cape Beale lighthouse, built in 1874, was the first on Vancouver Island's rugged west coast. *Russ Heinl*

NEW PLACE NAMES CONTINUE to be added to the BC coast, though not very often. BC's Geographical Names Office, in its document on naming principles, points out, quite firmly, that "not all features need a name at this time," and that "the opportunity and privilege to name landscape features" must be available to future generations, as well. The office establishes naming policies and procedures: names cannot be bought or sold, for instance; corporate, commercial, discriminatory or derogatory names are certainly not permitted; "ownership of land does not confer the right or entitlement to name a geographical feature."

The most acceptable new names are ones with a long history of local use. Failing that, the following sources for names are considered: historical events that occurred in the area, unique natural features, associated First Nation names, early residents from the vicinity, and those who died during war service.

Place name trends have changed dramatically over the years. The earliest official names mainly celebrate the heroes of the Old World. British explorers often selected naval and political names; Vancouver also bestowed names of "particular friends," family members and the officers of his two ships. The Spanish seemed to prefer religious ones, though they honoured naval figures as well. Dozens of Spanish place names, fortunately, have been preserved on the BC coast, although many were added at a later time to recognize the major contributions made by early Spanish explorers.

Richards and Pender, who had to come up with hundreds of place names but knew little about the history and culture of the area, relied heavily on their Royal Navy heritage. Virtually every ship and officer that served on the BC coast before 1870 is honoured with one or more names. As few of them had lasting connections with the area, these names seem startlingly irrelevant today. But at least the hydrographers chose to pay tribute to individuals who had actually been in BC waters. Many played important, if

Above: The *City of Nanaimo* at the Texada Island mining settlement of Van Anda, 1908. *Author's collection*
Left: Stanley Park's Siwash Rock stands sentinel over English Bay. *David Nunuk*

brief, historic roles on the coast, either as administrators or by taking part in gunboat actions designed to subdue and punish unruly First Nation groups. Colonial officials and visiting celebrities were also commemorated. Minor features, however, were given bland and forgettable names; Bare Islet and Steep Bluff, for instance, were favourites. Perhaps Richards and Pender had neither the time nor the inclination to come up with distinctive labels. It didn't really matter, because Henri Parizeau changed most of these names in the 1920s and '30s.

Fewer place names were added in the turn-of-the-century *Egeria* era, and the ship's commanders—Morris Smyth, Cortland Simpson, John Parry, Frederick Learmonth and John Nares—who were mainly re-surveying heavily used areas, often chose names that were related to those that already existed. The captain of CGS *Quadra*, the federal lighthouse tender on the Pacific coast, also did a fair amount of survey work in BC at this time. This was John Walbran, who applied many names related to his family history and many that were designed to please senior officials in the Department of Fisheries and Marine. He later wrote a seminal book on coast place names.

Regional hydrographer Henri Parizeau was interested in toponymy and spent much time in the archives researching BC's pioneer history. He believed fervently that place names should reflect local history and not be imported from other countries and cultures. He was also determined to eliminate duplicated names, which he considered dangerous, as place names were used to give bearings and distances for navigation and, especially, in rescues and other emergencies.

Sawmill and company houses at Queen Charlotte City about 1910. *Author's collection*

Hundreds of early BC settlers had geographical features named for them by Parizeau. He commemorated the Royal Engineers, who had come to BC as a contingent in 1858 and 1859, laid out townsites and constructed roads. He honoured merchant mariners, especially the skippers of Victoria's sealing schooners and the masters of the coastal steamships. Dozens of pioneers attending the 1924 old-timers' reunion in Victoria found their names on coastal charts, as did many men and women who crewed under Parizeau on the west coast survey vessels *Lillooet* and *William J Stewart*. When World War II began, he developed patriotic themes: Victoria Cross winners, naval officers serving at Esquimalt, famous warships and combat aircraft.

Parizeau's wholesale naming and name-changing alarmed property owners (who were rarely consulted) and disturbed bureaucrats. The Geographic Board of Canada had the final say on place names, and the board's members adhered to certain strongly held principles. One of them was that "old historic names, firmly established by time," should not be altered. Battles took place over names, and lengthy correspondence ensued. Parizeau had to back down in some instances, which he did not do gracefully, but he still managed, over the course of his lengthy tenure, to rewrite most charts and forever alter the history of coastal nomenclature.

(The Geographic Board of Canada, established in 1897, changed its name to the Canadian Board on Geographic Names in 1948. In 1961, responsibility for place names was transferred to the provinces, and the board, now an advisory body with provincial representation, became the Canadian Permanent Committee on Geographical Names. In

Sturdies Bay, Galiano Island, in the 1940s. *Author's collection*

2000 its name changed again, to the Geographical Names Board of Canada.)

The coastal place names of BC have certain obvious biases and deficiencies. Upper-middle-class white European males predominate as source material. Ethnic groups that made important contributions to Canadian history—especially Chinese and Japanese immigrants—are almost completely ignored. Although an effort was obviously made by some officials to include First Nation and female names, relatively few were approved.

Victoria and its citizens are far better represented by coastal names than other areas of the province (Vancouver, by comparison, received short shrift when place names were assigned). Victoria is BC's oldest city. "The congregation here," wrote George Hills, the colony's first Anglican bishop, in 1860, "contains a larger proportion of shrewd, thrifty, intelligent, educated gentlemen than any in England outside London." In the 19th century, Victoria was the commercial, administrative and cultural centre of the entire region, as well as the provincial capital. The hydrographic service had its main Pacific office nearby. Provincial government departments and officials that might have influenced place naming were all located in Victoria. The BC Archives, where Parizeau went to research pioneer names, is in Victoria, of course, and its holdings are especially reflective of 19th-century Victoria.

There are an amazing number of errors in BC's place names—mostly small spelling mistakes in people's surnames. Many of these are understandable; in the 18th and early 19th centuries, for instance, consistency in spelling was not considered as important as it is today. People often changed the way they spelled their names (*see* Blackney Channel) or spelled them several different ways (*see* Mackenzie Sound). Immigrants with unusual names (by British standards) made alterations in order to conform to British spellings. Some had their names written down wrongly by government officials or employers (*see* Work Channel) and decided that life would be simpler if they just went on with the new name rather than trying to change it back. But so many mistakes were made that one can only suspect that a certain amount of plain old carelessness was also involved in the recording and transferring of names.

BC's coastal place names may not be representative of all the province's citizens, but they do tell a complex, exciting story. The intricate, convoluted shorelines of the coast, which would stretch more than 27,000 kilometres if one could unroll them like a skein of wool into one long, straight thread, were not easy to investigate. The maze of channels and the 7,000 islands did not give up their secrets easily. BC was the last part of the non-polar world to be surveyed and charted, and it frustrated early visitors, who followed the great inlets that penetrate the mainland, hoping to discover a route across North America, only to have their journeys dead-end beneath the gleaming snowfields of a mountain range. Fierce tidal rapids suddenly grabbed their vessels and swung them on the rocks, and hundreds of hidden shoals and reefs constantly threatened their progress. Many vessels met their ends on these shores, and many travellers lost their lives bringing the province's heady possibilities—part promise, part danger—to our attention.

This book is a testament to their efforts and dreams.

USER'S GUIDE

Of the nearly 42,000 place names in the British Columbia gazetteer, about 9,000 are associated with the coast. This book deals, in 4,000 entries, with approximately 5,200 of those coastal names. So what is *not* included?

Roughly 1,500 names for which I have been able to find no data at all have been omitted. I've left out another 1,200 or so because they are purely descriptive or generic. It seems pointless, for instance, to include entries for West Island, Rugged Point and Gull Rock (unless something of particular interest took place there). The remaining omissions concern names with available source information that is so inadequate or unreliable or conflicting that to include an entry would just add to the confusion.

With very few exceptions, only official or "gazetted" names have entries. Important alternative, obsolete and locally used names are listed alphabetically but then cross-referenced to the current, gazetted form of the name, where they may be discussed in more detail. When a historically significant individual is commemorated with many place names, these are usually all dealt with in a single entry. Colonial governor James Douglas, for instance, gave his name to James Bay and James Island as well as to Douglas Channel and Douglas Point. In such instances, the basic biographical entry will always be associated with the surname; a smaller entry for the James names is cross-referenced to the main Douglas entry.

This book is principally about the history of the place names, not the places themselves. For that I refer you to the *Encyclopedia of British Columbia*. However, a brief historical overview of a place is sometimes included as background for the reader. Additional information, often quite detailed, may also be present for obscure but interesting sites, especially if it is not readily available elsewhere.

Early aerial view of Campbell River and district, with Discovery Passage and Quadra Island in the distance. *Courtesy Tim Woodland*

The letter-by-letter, "dictionary" style of alphabetization is used instead of the more common word-by-word format. Occasional awkwardness occurs as a result: Beechey Head, for instance, goes before Beech Island, and Ball Point comes after Ballingall Islets. But if applied "to the letter," this system of alphabetization is infallible. If you don't see a name where you intuitively expect to find it, just apply the letter-by-letter principle. Names that begin with "Cape," "Mount," "Point" and "Port" are listed under "C," "M" and "P."

Geographic references and coordinates are included for each coastal place name. If coordinates are not listed, then they are the same as those for the other features in the entry. References are given in relation to major features or communities (Port Hardy, for instance, or Queen Charlotte Strait or Princess Royal Island) that most readers will know. Basic maps are included to aid readers unfamiliar with the BC coast. References are given from the perspective of a mariner: the "west entrance" to a bay or cove, for example, is the point (rock, cliff, etc.) at the west side of its mouth; the "west approach" to a bay is farther out to sea than the west entrance but in the same general area.

Coastal features, such as islands, channels, coves and bays, points and peninsulas, are those that can be viewed from a passing boat. Rivers and mountains may be coastal as well, depending on how visible they are from the water. And rocks, shoals, reefs and banks, while not always visible, are certainly important aspects of coastal geography. If a geographic feature is listed in *Sailing Directions*, the comprehensive guide to coastal navigation published and regularly updated by the Canadian Hydrographic Service, then it qualifies, in my view, as coastal. In this book, coastal features are boldfaced, spelled without abbreviations and given geographic co-ordinates when they are the subjects of entries. Non-coastal BC geographic features, while frequently mentioned and discussed, are not given this treatment.

Sailing Directions covers the lower reaches of the Fraser River, to Pitt Lake and Harrison Lake; this work does not. I only include place names from the mouths or estuaries of the major rivers, which, in the case of the Fraser, stops just short of New Westminster.

This book is written for a general audience and for contemporary sensibilities. The text, at the risk of annoying some nautical friends and colleagues, does not adopt all aspects of naval and marine terminology—no matter how deeply held such language may be. Thus vessels in this book have no gender, the names of warships are often prefixed by the article "the" (frowned upon by naval personnel) and mariners serve "on" a ship more often than they do "in" one.

SOURCES

This book, perhaps more than most books, builds on the work of previous authors and reporters. It extends and updates prior efforts in the field and could not exist without the contributions of earlier writers. Sources include nearly every useful book written on the history of the BC coast; for this reason, a bibliography has not been included. Sources are discussed here only in general terms, and for this I will no doubt be criticized. But to have added source information to every entry would have greatly lengthened what is already a very long book and made it needlessly repetitive and formal. And in many cases it would have been pointless.

This is partly because a major primary source for BC's place names is the province's Geographical Names Office, located in Victoria and directed, in my day, by provincial toponymist Janet Mason. I was fortunate enough, while researching this book, to be able to spend two months working at the names unit, which was at that time (and may still be) part of the Integrated Land Management Bureau and the Ministry of Agriculture and Lands. I was allowed complete access to the office's century-old archives, and for this privilege I am very grateful indeed.

The archives were, in the early 2000s, a delightful anachronism in a digital world. A solid set of steel drawers held about 60,000 four-by-six-inch file cards and were backed by three bookshelf-sized cabinets with a century's worth of correspondence and supporting documents. All around spread the cubicles and large-screened computers of a branch

Bathing pool on Hotspring Island, east of Moresby Island and Juan Perez Sound. *John Alexander*

Ladysmith became an important sawmill centre in the mid-1930s. *Courtesy Tim Woodland*

of government that specializes in highly technical mapping services. Each official place name in the province, however, whether current or obsolete, still had an ancient file card, and that card had, over the decades, been faithfully marked up with relevant information by generations of geographers and related specialists.

The information on the cards has gradually been making its way to the BC Geographical Names Information System (BCGNIS), an internet database located at *www.ilmb.gov. bc.ca/bcnames*. This wonderful project, which was only about 30 percent finished in 2009, when this book was published, allows users to search for and sort a wealth of place name data. The site has many other useful features as well, including a downloadable digital gazetteer and an illustrated, audio-assisted section on place names introduced by the Nisga'a First Nation treaty. It is part of an internet portal for provincial geographic services named GeoBC and is a necessary bookmark for anybody interested in the history of BC's place names.

The Geographical Names Office, of course, is not infallible. Its data is often of uncertain or unknown origin (and clearly marked as such). In the study of toponymy, weasel words like "probably," "possibly" and "presumably" are encountered on a regular basis, and you will find them in this book, as well. Definitive explanations can be elusive when it comes to names, and hundreds of meanings and origins will forever remain partly obscured or hidden. Varying theories have been put forward over the years to explain many names, and those theories can conflict. Sometimes there are no obvious answers.

Genealogical data from BC Archives (birth, death and marriage records) have been essential to my research, as have census and voters lists, various early directories and, of course, BC's historical newspaper of record, the Victoria *Colonist* (originally known as the *British Colonist* and later as the *Times Colonist*).

Certain texts have been so valuable that, at the end of many entries, I refer readers to them for additional information with a *D*, *E* or *W*. These letters refer to Kathleen

E Dalzell's *The Queen Charlotte Islands: Places and Names*; the *Encyclopedia of British Columbia*, edited by Daniel Francis; and Captain John T Walbran's *British Columbia Coast Names 1592–1906: Their Origin and History*. For readers in search of additional intelligence on the Queen Charlotte Islands, Dalzell's exhaustively researched works are the ultimate guide. The *Encyclopedia*, meanwhile, is a fabulous resource for background information on communities, geographical features, First Nations and all major historical figures (and much else).

John Walbran needs a more extensive tribute, as he is the foundation upon which all coastal place name research must be based. He was a mariner as well as a writer, master of the lighthouse tender *Quadra* at the turn of the 19th century, and his information about the coast was based on direct observation and on personal contact with the pioneers and naval personages whose names inform today's charts. His anecdotal style and lengthy historical digressions have endeared him to generations of readers. Thousands of names have been added to the charts since his *Coast Names* was published in 1909, however, and much of his data, while accurate at the time (for the most part), is now sadly out of date. This present book, which appears exactly one century after his and seeks in some ways to supersede Walbran as a guide and a reference work, continues to celebrate his remarkable contribution.

A number of authors have been especially helpful to my understanding of coastal history. Barry Gough, for starters, is a master at unravelling the complexities of the coastal fur trade. His *Gunboat Frontier: British Maritime Authority and the Northwest Coast Indians, 1846–90*, in particular, is essential reading. Many coastal names in BC are linked to skirmishes between First Nation groups and the Royal Navy, and though these incidents may seem minor and inconsequential, they say a great deal about Britain's gradual conquest of the region. Gough excels at detailing the conflicts and putting them in a historical context.

W Kaye Lamb's outstanding, five-volume edition of George Vancouver's *A Voyage of Discovery to the North Pacific Ocean and Round the World, 1791–95*, has been a constant research companion, as has the erudite *Cartography of the Northwest Coast of America to the Year 1800*, by Henry Wagner. I have also found several books by Victoria writer Peter

First Nation funeral procession crossing bridge from Port Simpson to Rose Island. *Author's collection*

Murray tremendously useful, including works on the sealing industry (*The Vagabond Fleet*), the history of the Gulf Islands (*Homesteads and Snug Harbours*) and missionary activity in northern BC (*The Devil and Mr Duncan*).

We are blessed in BC with remarkable books on the nautical history of the coast. I referred regularly to *Macdonald's Steamboats and Steamships of the Pacific Northwest*, by Joseph F Macdonald (two volumes); *Lewis and Dryden's Marine History of the Pacific Northwest*, edited by E W Wright; *The H W McCurdy Marine History of the Pacific Northwest*, edited by Gordon Newell; *Whistle up the Inlet: The Union Steamship Story*, by

Gerald Rushton; and *The Princess Story: A Century and a Half of West Coast Shipping*, by Norman Hacking and W Kaye Lamb.

Other works and authors I owe a particular debt to include *British Columbia Place Names*, by G P V and Helen B Akrigg; *North Coast Odyssey* and *Cannery Village: Company Town*, by Kenneth Campbell; *A Traveller's Guide to Aboriginal BC*, by Cheryl Coull; *The Greater Vancouver Book*, edited by Chuck Davis; *Working in the Woods: A History of Logging on the West Coast*, by Ken Drushka; *A History of Victoria 1842–1970*, by Harry Gregson; *Norwegians in the Northwest*, by Eric Faa; *Kanaka: The Untold Story of Hawaiian Pioneers in British Columbia and the Pacific Northwest*, by Tom Koppel; and the several *Cruising Guides to British Columbia*, by Bill Wolferstan.

A host of BC books cover specific geographical areas. I found the following of particular use: *Nootka Sound Explored: A Westcoast History*, by Laurie Jones; *Salt Spring: The Story of an Island*, by Charles Kahn; *Tidal Passages: A History of the Discovery Islands*, by Jeanette Taylor; *Voices from the Sound: Chronicles of Clayoquot Sound and Tofino 1899–1929*, by Margaret Horsfield; *Kwakwaka'wakw Settlements, 1775–1920: A Geographical Analysis and Gazetteer*, by Robert Galois; *The Quatsino Chronicle 1894–1995*, by Gwen Hansen; *Bright Seas, Pioneer Spirits: The Sunshine Coast*, by Betty C Keller and Rosella M Leslie; *Sunny Sandy Savary: A History of Savary Island 1792–1992*, by Ian Kennedy; *Bowen Island 1872–1972*, by Irene Howard; *The Skeena: River of Destiny*, by R Geddes Large; *Haida Monumental Art: Villages of the Queen Charlotte Islands*, by George F MacDonald; *Lasqueti Island: History and Memory*, by Elda Copley Mason; *Full Moon, Flood Tide*, by Bill Proctor and Yvonne Maximchuk; *Barkley Sound: A History of the Pacific Rim National Park Area*, by R Bruce Scott; *Notes and Quotes: A Brief Historical Record of Southern Vancouver Island*, by Dorothy Stranix; *Esquimalt Naval Base: A History of Its Work and Its Defenses*, by F V Longstaff; and *Bella Coola*, by Cliff Kopas.

Finally, we come to the internet, which many historians seem leery of but which has developed into an important contemporary source of historical information. The internet has its limitations, certainly, and like other sources must be treated cautiously and confirmed independently wherever possible. But surely no one can deny its usefulness. Many works no longer under copyright are now fully available (and searchable) online, including Vancouver's *Voyage of Discovery* and *Lewis and Dryden's Marine History*, both mentioned above. An extraordinary quantity of genealogical data can now be explored, and many excellent sites deal in great depth with aspects of marine and military history. Of particular interest is the BC History Digitization Program at the University of BC, which promotes free online access to an ever-increasing range of historical materials. Go to *www.ikebarberlearningcentre.ubc.ca/ps/BCDigitInfo.html* to find the latest completed and planned BC digitization projects.

The downside of the internet, of course, is its instability. As a researcher, you are at its mercy. You never know when there's going to be a power outage or a circuit collapse. Sites suddenly disappear when domain registrations expire or service providers go bankrupt. Web pages change without notice, instantly becoming more useful or (often) completely useless as proprietors make "improvements." There's still nothing like a solid, reliable book. Nevertheless, without the internet this book would have taken ten years to complete instead of three. Listed below are some recommended digital resources.

www.bcarchives.bc.ca The genealogical indexes are pure gold, but general searches can also turn up much that is intriguing and unexpected. The visual records are extraordinary.

www.rootsweb.ancestry.com/~canbc A website devoted to 19th-century records about Victoria and Vancouver Island: voters lists, census lists, directories, obituaries, civil service and land grant lists and more. The 1901 Victoria census (which covers the area from Port Renfrew to the Gulf Islands) has had a great deal of material added from other sources, making it one of the most useful databases of its kind.

www.britishcolonist.ca An exemplary research site for anyone wishing to explore Victoria's *Colonist* newspaper in detail. See also *web.uvic.ca/~lang02/timescol/search.php*

www.royalengineers.ca Everything you ever wanted to know about the Royal Engineers and Royal Marines who served in BC.

www.gov.mb.ca/chc/archives/hbca/biographical Surprisingly forthright biographical entries on employees of the Hudson's Bay Company, created from the company's archives.

www.canfoh.org A specialized but very informative website on the personnel, vessels and history of the Canadian Hydrographic Service.

www.biographi.ca The Dictionary of Canadian Biography Online has authoritative articles on major BC historical figures, complete with source information.

www.abcbookworld.com Extensive data on BC writers and books about the province.

www.vpl.ca/bccd A comprehensive collection of searchable BC city directories dating between 1860 and 1901—one of many digital resources provided by the Vancouver Public Library.

www.canadiana.org A wide range of early Canadian books can be viewed here in their entirety. See also *www.nosracines.ca* and *www.gutenberg.org*.

web.viu.ca/black/amrc The Alejandro Malaspina Research Centre, operated by Vancouver Island University, is a fine source of biographical data on the Spanish explorers of the Pacific Northwest.

pages.quicksilver.net.nz/jcr This extraordinary site, the work of New Zealand historian John Robson, is dedicated to James Cook, George Vancouver and other 18th-century explorers and traders who were active in the Pacific Northwest.

www.em.gov.bc.ca/Mining/Geolsurv/Publications The annual reports of BC's Ministry of Energy, Mines and Petroleum Resources, from 1874 to 2000 (including indexes), are all available online.

www.ageofnelson.org A formidable and extensive site dealing with the officers, ships and history of the Royal Navy in the 18th and 19th centuries. See also the equally astonishing *www.pbenyon.plus.com/Naval.html* and *www.pdavis.nl/Selecter.php*.

www.rcnvr.com Detailed biographical data on Royal Canadian Navy personnel who received awards between 1910 and 1968.

airforce.ca Similarly detailed information on Royal Canadian Air Force personnel who served during World War II.

ACKNOWLEDGMENTS

Many people have helped with this book, in many different ways. I particularly want to thank provincial toponymist Janet Mason of BC's Geographical Names Office, who made space and resources available for me to work in Victoria and who patiently answered many questions. This book could really not have been completed without the co-operation of Janet and other members of the provincial government's Base Mapping and Geomatic Services Branch (which has since been reorganized). Thanks also to Kate Russell and her knowledgeable staff of reference librarians at Special Collections, my home away from home at the central branch of the Vancouver Public Library.

From 2006 to 2008 I wrote a column on coastal place names, called "Coastlines," for *Pacific Yachting* magazine, and this employment helped finance my research. I'm grateful to Peter A. Robson, the magazine's editor at the time, for this opportunity, and also to the other staff members I worked with, especially Hilary Henegar, Wendy Bone, Dale Miller and Jocelyn Cooper.

Over the course of my research I received assistance from staff members and volunteers at many museums, archives, libraries and other institutions. Special thanks to Denis D'Amours, director (Pacific), Canadian Hydrographic Service; Michael Ward of the Canadian Hydrographic Service; David Hill-Turner of the Underwater Archaeological Society of BC; Richard MacKenzie of the Maritime Museum of BC; Harold E Wright of New Brunswick's Heritage Resources; Joyce Austin, manager of the Rossland Museum;

Boat day at Bella Coola always brought out a crowd. Most of the community's vehicles showed up as well. *Harbour Publishing collection*

Matt Cavers and Reana Mussato at the Sunshine Coast Museum & Archives; Ann Watson, archivist at Sechelt Community Archives; Jean Eiers-Page of Prince Rupert City & Regional Archives; Leila Muldrew of the Victoria Genealogical Society; Clare Sugrue, administrative assistant and webmaster, and Lt Cdr (retired) David J Freeman, naval historian and volunteer, both at CFB Esquimalt Naval & Military Museum; Daniel A Haskins, archives records manager at the Archdiocese of Portland, Oregon; Victoria Ertelt, library administrator, and Suzanne McKenzie, volunteer archivist, both at Mount Angel Abbey, St Benedict, Oregon; Jamie Purves, education and programming co-ordinator at the Vancouver Maritime Museum; Lisa Mitchell, information and privacy coordinator for the New Westminster Police; and Linda Sawyer, executive director, BC/ Yukon Command, for the Royal Canadian Legion.

I have benefited hugely, as always, from the generous support and enthusiasm of my friends and family. Tracy Cooper and Gary Little made many helpful suggestions. Tim Woodland lent postcard images and scarce books. Theresa Kishkan alerted me to the existence of the Douglas maple, thus saving me the embarrassment of claiming that northern BC was maple-free. Gray Scrimgeour, Bob Smith, Bill Topping, John Keenlyside and Peter Jacobi shared their expert knowledge of BC history. My partner, Katherine Johnston, especially, encouraged me to stay the long course and endured, with her usual kindly grace and wisdom, the monomania that inevitably results from such a fixed, intense focus.

The following individuals all provided useful information, often about family members. Many of them responded to emails out of the blue. Indeed, the open and friendly answers I received from total strangers was most inspiring. My heartfelt thanks to Andrew Loveridge and Charles Dodwell of Pender Island; Kim Dodwell from Shrewsbury; Kris and John Stevens Lovekin of Riverside, California; Tahirah Shadforth; Ron Beaumont; Davis Bigelow, who grew up at Pointer Island lighthouse; Dawn Turner of Comox and Dave Lemkay of Douglas, Ontario, for information on John Young Rochester (Rochester Island); Jim Shaw on Bowen Island; Victor G Wiebe, librarian emeritus at the University of Saskatchewan; Brian Lee, editor and publisher of Pender Harbour's *Harbour Spiel*; and June Cameron, author of *Destination Cortes Island*. Many entries in the book have benefited from the helpful suggestions of BC historian Jean Barman.

I am grateful to my editor, Audrey McClellan, for correcting and improving this text. The errors that remain are mine alone. It has been a great pleasure to work with the passionate, capable staff at Harbour Publishing. I feel very fortunate to have had the opportunity to steep myself so purposefully in the culture and history of the BC coast.

ABBREVIATIONS

Adm	Admiral	Gov	Governor	OBE	Order of the British Empire
AFC	Air Force Cross	GPS	Global Positioning System	Oct	October
AFM	Air Force Medal	GTP	Grand Trunk Pacific Railway	Ont	Ontario
Apr	April	ha	hectare, hectares	PEI	Prince Edward Island
Assoc	Association	HBC	Hudson's Bay Company	PGE	Pacific Great Eastern Railway
Aug	August	Hbr	Harbour (only in geographical	PM	Prime Minister
b	born (only in reference to birth/		names)	PNW	Pacific Northwest
	death dates)	HMCS	His/Her Majesty's Canadian	QCI	Queen Charlotte Islands (Haida
BC	British Columbia		Ship(s)		Gwaii)
BNA	British North America	HMNZS	His/Her Majesty's New Zealand	Que	Quebec
Bros	Brothers		Ship(s)	qv	which see (quod vide)
c	circa or about (only in reference	HMS	His/Her Majesty's Ship(s)	R	River (only in geographical
	to birth/death dates)	Hon	Honourable		names)
Capt	Captain	hp	horsepower	RCAF	Royal Canadian Air Force
CB	Companion of the Order of the	HQ	headquarters	RCMP	Royal Canadian Mounted Police
	Bath	Hts	Heights (only in geographical	RCN	Royal Canadian Navy
CBE	Companion of the Order of the		names)	RCNR	Royal Canadian Navy Reserve
	British Empire	Hwy	Highway	RCNVR	Royal Canadian Navy Volunteer
Cdr	Commander	I, Is	Island, Islands (only in		Reserve
CFB, CFS	Canadian Forces Base,		geographical names)	Rd	Road
	Canadian Forces Station	It, Its	Islet, Islets (only in geographical	RE	Royal Engineer(s)
CGS	Canadian Government Ship		names)	Rev	Reverend
CHS	Canadian Hydrographic Service	Jan	January	Rk, Rks	Rock, Rocks (only in geographical
Ck	Creek (only in geographical	Jr	Junior		names)
	names)	KCB	Knight Commander of the Order	RN	Royal Navy
CMG	Companion of the Order of St		of the Bath	RNR	Royal Navy Reserve
	Michael and St George	km, km/h	kilometre, kilometres; kilometres	RNVR	Royal Navy Volunteer Reserve
CMS	Church Missionary Society		per hour	Rwy	Railway (in proper names only)
CNR	Canadian National Railways	LA	Los Angeles	S	south (usually spelled out in
Co	Company (only in business	Lk, Lks	Lake, Lakes (only in geographical		proper names)
	names)		names)	Sask	Saskatchewan
CO	Commanding Officer	Lt	Lieutenant	Sd	Sound (only in geographical
Col	Colonel	Ltd	Limited (only in business names)		names)
Corp	Corporation	m	metre, metres	SE	southeast (usually spelled out in
Cpl	Corporal	Maj	Major		proper names)
CPN	Canadian Pacific Navigation	Mar	March	Sept	September
	Company	MC	Military Cross	Sgt	Sergeant
CPR	Canadian Pacific Railway	MCR	Museum at Campbell River	sp	species
CVA	City of Vancouver Archives	MIT	Massachusetts Institute of	SS	Steamship
d	died (only in reference to birth/		Technology	St	Street, Saint (in proper names
	death dates)	MLA	Member of Legislative Assembly		only)
D	See additional information in		(provincial)	Str	Strait (only in geographical
	The Queen Charlotte Islands:	MM	Military Medal		names)
	Places and Names, by	MP	Member of Parliament (federal or	Sub-Lt	Sub-Lieutenant
	Kathleen E Dalzell		British)	SW	southwest (usually spelled out in
DC	District of Columbia	Mt, Mtn	Mount, Mountain (only in		proper names)
Dec	December		geographical names)	TB	tuberculosis
Dept	Department	MW	megawatts	UBC	University of British Columbia
DFC	Distinguished Flying Cross	N	north (usually spelled out in	UK	United Kingdom
DFM	Distinguished Flying Medal		proper names)	Univ	University
DSC	Distinguished Service Cross	NB	New Brunswick	US	United States
DSO	Distinguished Service Order	NCO	Non-commissioned officer	UVic	University of Victoria
E	east (usually spelled out in proper	NE	northeast (usually spelled out in	VC	Victoria Cross
	names)		proper names)	VMM	Vancouver Maritime Museum
E	See additional information in the	Nfld	Newfoundland	VPL	Vancouver Public Library
	Encyclopedia of British	Nov	November	W	west (usually spelled out in proper
	Columbia, edited by Daniel	NS	Nova Scotia		names)
	Francis	NW	northwest (usually spelled out in	*W*	See additional information in
E&N	Esquimalt & Nanaimo Railway		proper names)		Capt John T Walbran's *British*
Feb	February	NWC	North West Company		*Columbia Coast Names*
Fr	Father (for religious titles only)	NWT	Northwest Territories (earlier		*1592–1906*
Ft	Fort (only in geographical names)		spelled North-West)	WWI,	
GB	Great Britain	NY	New York	WWII	World War I, World War II
Gen	General	NZ	New Zealand		

Aberdeen Point (54°13'00" 129°53'00" N side of Skeena estuary, opposite Port Essington). Named by the hydrographic service in 1950 after the Aberdeen Cannery, established by Robert Draney for the Windsor Canning Co in 1878 at the mouth of Aberdeen Ck. William Dempster was manager. Aberdeen was the second salmon cannery built on the N coast and, with its post and telegraph office and store, also served as a trading centre for miners heading up the Skeena R. In 1889 the operation was sold to the BC Canning Co. Aberdeen was rebuilt in 1895 after a major fire, but after it burned again in 1902, the company abandoned the plant and built Oceanic Cannery instead on Smith I the following year.

Abraham Point (52°28'10" 131°27'20" S end of Werner Bay, SE side of Moresby I, QCI). After the influential German geologist and teacher Abraham Werner, who died in 1817. *See* Werner Bay.

Abrams Island (52°32'00" 128°50'00" W of Swindle I, NW of Bella Bella). James Atkinson Abrams (1845–1914) was born at Napanee, Ont. He came to Victoria in 1867, then moved to Nanaimo, where he became president of the Nanaimo Tanning Co and, from 1878 to 1882, the MLA for the area. He was appointed a justice of the peace in 1890. Abrams, his US-born wife Georgina Elizabeth (1861–1925) and their family later moved to Cumberland. Formerly known as Double I but renamed in 1927.

Absalom Island (53°51'00" 130°36'00" SE of Porcher Peninsula, W of Kitkatla, S of Prince Rupert). After mariner and fisherman Absalom Freeman, founder of the Canadian Fishing Co in 1905. *See* Cape Freeman.

Achilles Bank (49°33'00" 124°30'00" E of Hornby I, Str of Georgia). Named in 1945 after HMNZS *Achilles*, a British *Leander*-class light cruiser built 1932 and on loan to the NZ navy. The ship joined RN cruisers *Exeter* and *Ajax* to overcome the German pocket battleship *Admiral Graf Spee* in the 1939 Battle of the River Plate. The *Graf Spee* retreated to the neutral harbour of Montevideo, Uruguay,

where it was scuttled and destroyed by members of its crew. In 1948 the 169-m, 6,594-tonne *Achilles* was sold to India. It was refitted in 1955, renamed the *Delhi* and decommissioned in 1978.

Acland Islands (48°49'00" 123°23'00" SW of Prevost I, Gulf Is). These islands were probably named after British politician, businessman and philanthropist Sir Thomas Dyke Acland (1787–1871), who was MP for Devon for many years. It is possible, however, that they commemorate Lt Edward Ackland instead, an RN officer who served on the *Orestes, Thalie, Impregnable* and *Insolent* in the early 1800s and with the Coast Guard, 1831–34. The name first appears on an 1861 Admiralty chart.

Acland Rock (49°39'00" 124°09'00" E side of Malaspina Str, S of Nelson I). Pilot Officer Ion Hugh Acland of the RCAF, from Saltspring I, was killed on active service Mar 18, 1941, aged 26. Prior to enlisting, he had been a seaman aboard Canadian survey vessel *William J Stewart*. Acland is buried at Andover Cemetery, Hampshire, UK.

Actaeon Sound (50°57'00" 127°06'00" N side of Drury Inlet, N of Port McNeill). Named by RN surveyor Lt Daniel Pender after HMS *Actaeon*, a 16-gun, 562-tonne frigate engaged in survey duties off the coast of China, 1856–62. William Blakeney, a member of Pender's crew, had served on this vessel and suggested the name. The *Actaeon* was built in 1831, became a hospital ship in 1866 and was broken up in 1889. *W*

Active Islet (52°12'31" 128°09'55" Entrance to Kynumpt Hbr, N end of Campbell I, just N of Bella Bella). The hydrographic service designated this feature in 1925 to keep alive an early name for Kynumpt Hbr (qv). HBC fur trader William Fraser Tolmie had described the harbour as Active's Cove in his 1834–35 diaries, written while he was stationed at Fort McLoughlin, located farther S on the E side of Campbell I.

A

Active Pass, with Village Bay on Mayne Island to the right. *Peter Vassilopoulos*

Active Pass (48°52'00" 123°18'00" Between Galiano I and Mayne I, Str of Georgia). The 52-m, 678-tonne paddleboat *Active*, a US revenue and survey vessel under Lt Cdr James Alden, was the first naval steamer to use this passage, in 1855. The vessel, built in NY in 1849 as the *Gold Hunter*, was brought to San Francisco, renamed and at first carried freight between California and Oregon. The US government acquired the *Active* about 1853. Active Pass was known before 1858 as Plumper Pass, after HMS *Plumper*, an RN hydrographic vessel that worked with the *Active* in 1857 to survey the boundary between BC and Washington. In 1859 the *Active* was involved in the US-British standoff over the San Juan Is, known today as the Pig War. It returned to merchant service in the 1860s, running passengers and mail between San Francisco and Portland, Puget Sd and Victoria, with side trips to Alaska, and was sold to Mexican owners about 1871. Today Active Pass is an important shipping route (and site of regular marine accidents), with currents of up to 7 knots (13 km/h) and abundant marine life. *W*

Adam River (50°28'00" 126°17'00" Flows N into Johnstone Str, NW of Sayward, Vancouver I). An early name, appearing on Admiralty charts from 1867. The mouth of the river, where a breakwater has been constructed, has long been the site of a logging camp and booming ground. According to historians Philip and Helen Akrigg, the First Nation name for the river is He-la-de, meaning "land of plenty" in Kwakwala and referring to the abundance of berries, birds, animals and salmon in the area. The river's main tributary is named Eve.

Adams Bay (52°56'00" 128°59'00" E side of Surf Inlet, Princess Royal I). John B Adams (1876–1964), a long-time Victoria resident, participated in that city's famous old-timers' reunion in 1924. This event, the first large-scale get-together of its kind in the province, was sponsored by the BC Historical Society and required considerable preparations. Seven hundred BC pioneers known to be resident in the province in the 1870s or earlier were invited, and 300 accepted. They were received at Government House, toured through the city in a grand cavalcade and entertained at a fine banquet and dance held at the Empress Hotel. The banquet table settings, which featured gold-rush scenes and models of sternwheelers and fur-trading forts, were so elaborate that the general public was invited to view them before dinner for a small fee. By all accounts the reunion was a huge success, and newspaper coverage was widespread. Downtown store windows displayed period clothes and historical photos. Sourdoughs from the Klondike rubbed shoulders with survivors of the Boer War. On the final evening, while the old-timers were being fêted at the legislature in the plush rooms of the Legislative Library, an upper storey caught on fire and several hundred people had to be evacuated. "'Tain't everybody who would burn down their parliament buildings to give a kick to the entertainment," one wag was reported as saying. "Or perhaps they set them on fire to get rid of us." On the suggestion of regional hydrographer Henri Parizeau, the surnames of many pioneers in attendance were adopted in 1926 as place names on the BC coast. Nearby Adams Point is named for a different old-timer.

Adams Harbour (51°41'05" 128°06'50" NW tip of Calvert I, Hakai Passage, S of Bella Bella). Rear Adm Kenneth Frederick Adams (1903–84), born at Victoria, was a cadet at the Royal Naval College of Canada in 1919, while it was briefly (1918–22) located at Esquimalt Dockyard after the calamitous Halifax Hbr explosion of 1917. He was master of one of the luxurious CNR *Prince* ships on the BC coast in the 1920s but rejoined the RCN in 1928. From 1939 to 1951 he commanded numerous RCN vessels, including the minesweeper *Nootka*, armed merchant cruisers *Prince David* and *Prince Henry*, destroyers *Assiniboine*, *Ottawa* and *Iroquois*, cruiser *Uganda* and aircraft carrier *Magnificent*, by which point he had been promoted commodore and was senior Canadian naval officer afloat. He ended his career in 1958 as CO naval divisions and then worked for Canadian Westinghouse as western regional manager after retiring from the RCN. Adams Hbr, named in 1944, is still known locally as Welcome Hbr, its former name, which first appeared on an Admiralty chart dated 1872.

Adams Island (52°59'00" 129°36'00" Head of Gillen Hbr, N side of Caamaño Sd). Named in 1926 for George D Adams of Langley Prairie, who participated in the Victoria old-timers' reunion of May 1924 (*see* Adams Bay).

Adamson Rocks (48°54'00" 125°09'00" E side of Imperial Eagle Channel, Barkley Sd, W side of Vancouver I). Capt John William Adamson, in command of the British ship *Jenny*, left Bristol in 1793 and traded very successfully between Oregon and Alaska the following summer, getting most of his 2,000 pelts in the QCI and travelling part of the distance with a Haida chief from Langara I named Kow. Adamson was an experienced mariner, having sailed with John Meares and also served as 2nd mate on the Boston-based brigantine *Hancock*, under Capt Samuel Crowell, which traded in the QCI in 1791. (The crew of the *Hancock* built a sloop on Graham I that July, the first European-style vessel built in the QCI, and Adamson had charge of it for the season.) After meeting Capt George Vancouver at Nootka Sd in Sept 1794, Adamson took the *Jenny* back to England via Canton in 1795, circumnavigating the globe in only 22 months—a remarkable feat considering the navigation standards of the era.

Adams Point (52°57'00" 128°59'00" N side of Adams Bay, Surf Inlet, Princess Royal I). William Frederick Adams (1866–1943) was born at Victoria and married Norah Bessie Craig (1866–1931) there in 1894. She was born in Scotland and had come to Canada in 1884. William worked for the Victoria Gas Co and eventually became chief clerk of the BC Electric Rwy Co. He and Norah participated in the grand Victoria old-timers' reunion of 1924 (*see* Adams Bay).

Ada Shoal (52°16'00" 128°30'00" W entrance to Seaforth Channel, Milbanke Sd, NW of Bella Bella). Ada Skinner was a member of a prominent pioneer family that arrived in Ft Victoria from England in 1853. Her father, Thomas Skinner, was hired as the bailiff, or manager, of Oaklands, also known as Constance Cove Farm—one of four farms established near Victoria by the Puget's Sd Agricultural Co, a subsidiary of the HBC. He was appointed a justice of the peace and elected to Vancouver I's initial legislative assembly in 1856. Ada first married Joseph Mason, MLA for Cariboo, and later became the wife of John Stevenson.

Addenbroke Island (51°36'00" 127°51'00" Entrance to Fish Egg Inlet, Fitz Hugh Sd, E of Calvert I), **Addenbroke Point** (51°32'00" 127°47'00" N entrance to Darby Channel, Fitz Hugh Sd), **Mount Addenbroke** (50°14'00" 124°41'00" E side of E Redonda I, at entrance to Toba Inlet, NE of Campbell R and Desolation Sd). Capt George Vancouver named Point Addenbrooke in 1792 after Lt Peter Puget and Joseph Whidbey, master of HMS *Discovery*, examined this portion of the coast in small boats. It is not known who Vancouver wished to honour with this name—possibly Dr John Addenbrooke (1680–1719), the founder of Addenbrooke's Hospital at Cambridge. The Geographic Board of Canada changed the spelling and form of the name to Addenbroke Point. A lighthouse was constructed on Addenbroke I in 1914; keeper Ernie Maynard was murdered there in 1928, a crime that was never conclusively resolved. Much of Mt Addenbroke, which rises straight from the ocean to 1,591 m, was named BC's second ecological reserve in 1971 in order to protect a unique ecosystem in which five different biogeoclimatic subzones are represented. Addenbroke was long thought to be the highest mountain in BC not on the mainland or on Vancouver I, but an unnamed peak on King I is now known to be 1,679 m high.

Addenbroke lighthouse was erected in 1914. *Peter Vassilopoulos*

Adeane Point (50°44'00" 125°41'00" E side of Knight Inlet, N of Glendale Cove). After a pony belonging to Elizabeth "Lillie" Blakeney, daughter of Capt James Murray Reid of Victoria, a veteran employee of the HBC (*see* Reid Passage *and* Reid I). Nearby Kitty Cone is named for the pony belonging to her husband, William Blakeney, an RN officer who also spelled his name Blackney. *See* Blackney Channel. *W*

Adelaide Point (51°19'00" 127°22'00" Junction of Naysash Inlet and Smith Inlet, S of entrance to Rivers Inlet). Catherine Adelaide Horsfall (1841–67) was the youngest daughter of Rev Thomas Horsfall, vicar of Cundall, Yorkshire. She was an aunt of Capt John Walbran, BC mariner and author, who named the point after her in 1903. *W*

A

Admiral Group (52°02'00" 128°17'00" E side of Tide Rip Passage, SW of Bella Bella). Named in 1944 after RCN officers Victor Brodeur, George Jones and Percy Nelles, appointed to the rank of adm between 1938 and 1942. *See* Brodeur I, Jones I *and* Nelles I for individual biographies.

Admiral Island. *See* Saltspring I.

Admiralty Point (49°18'00" 122°55'00" SE entrance to Indian Arm, Burrard Inlet, E of Vancouver). This area, part of Belcarra Regional Park, was reserved by naval surveyors in the 19th century because it would have been a useful site for a fort to protect Port Moody, proposed terminus of the CPR. It was known locally as the "Admiralty reserve." The name was suggested in 1940 by Maj J S Matthews of Vancouver City Archives.

Adventure Cove (49°12'00" 125°51'00" E side of Lemmens Inlet, Meares I, Clayoquot Sd, W side of Vancouver I), **Adventure Point** (49°26'00" 126°15'00" SW entrance to Holmes Inlet, NW of Tofino, Clayoquot Sd). Boston fur trader Robert Gray, capt of the *Columbia Rediviva* (first US ship to sail round the world), overwintered at Adventure Cove in 1791. He and his crew erected a defensive log structure they named Ft Defiance, refitted the *Columbia* and constructed the 40-tonne sloop *Adventure* (third European vessel built on the BC coast, after John Meares's *North West America* and the Spanish *Santa Saturnina*). According to a journal kept by John Boit, 5th mate of the *Columbia*, the local Tla-o-qui-aht people "appear'd to be highly pleas'd with the Idea of our tarrying among them through the Cold Season." On Christmas Day, the crew decorated fort and ship and invited their First Nation neighbours for a feast, followed by carol singing. The guests reciprocated with dancing and drumming performances. In Mar 1792, on hearing that the Tla-o-qui-aht had turned against them and were planning an attack,

Adventure Cove on Meares Island was the site of Fort Defiance, established by Robert Gray in 1791. *Elsie Hulsizer*

Gray ordered the nearby village of Opitsaht—"the Work of Ages," according to Boit, and "by no means inelegant"—burned to the ground. This hostile act, committed as Gray left his winter quarters, set relations in the region back for years. The *Adventure* was commanded that summer by Robert Haswell, the *Columbia*'s 1st mate, then sold to the Spanish at Nootka Sd for 80 prime sea otter skins and renamed the *Orcasitas*. Knowledge of the location of Ft Defiance slipped from memory after Gray's departure—until 1966, that is, when Tofino historian Ken Gibson, guided by a detailed painting made by George Davidson, the *Columbia*'s carpenter, uncovered bricks and other artifacts at the site. Adventure Cove is now protected as an archeological reserve; its name was officially adopted in 1975.

Aero (53°03'05" 131°57'35" N side of Gillatt Arm, Cumshewa Inlet, NE side of Moresby I, QCI). A P Allison established the QCI's only railway logging camp here in 1936. It became an important supplier of Sitka or "airplane" spruce and was taken over during WWII by a Crown corporation named Aero Timber. The Powell R Co acquired the operation after the war at a giveaway price and ran the railway until 1955. The camp was abandoned by 1967, and all that remained by the 1990s were the ruins of a wharf.

Agamemnon Bay (49°45'00" 123°59'00" N end of Agamemnon Channel), **Agamemnon Channel** (49°42'00" 124°04'00" Between Nelson I and Sechelt Peninsula, SE of Powell R, NW of Vancouver). HMS *Agamemnon* was the first ship of the line commanded by British naval hero Adm Lord Nelson. The 64-gun vessel was launched in 1781 and took part in the 1805 Battle of Trafalgar, but ran aground in 1809 at the River Plate in Uruguay and was destroyed. Agamemnon Channel was named Boca de Moniño, after the family name of statesman Count Floridablanca, by Spanish naval officer José Narváez on his historic 1791 exploration of the Str of Georgia. It received its current name in 1860 from Capt George Richards of the survey vessel *Plumper*. The Sechelt First Nation name for the channel is Lílkw̓émin.

Agassiz Banks (53°05'00" 130°03'00" W of Estevan Group, Hecate Str). Lewis Nunn Agassiz (1827–80) was born in Essex, England, and immigrated to PEI after retiring as an officer from the British Army. He moved to Ont with his wife, Mary Caroline Schram (1829–1921, *see* Schram Rks), and children, then left them to chase gold in California and BC. The family reunited at Victoria in 1862 and lived for a time at Hope and then Yale, where Agassiz was constable and postmaster. In 1862 he pre-empted land in the eastern Fraser Valley, where he and his family took up residence in 1867, calling their home Ferney Coombe. Agassiz left Canada again in 1875 to embark on a solo world tour, dying in Constantinople while visiting his brother. After the arrival of the CPR in 1885, a community grew up around Ferney Coombe and the name was changed to Agassiz. Root crops, hops, corn, and dairy and beef farming have all been important to this rural farming district. Agassiz Banks was named by regional hydrographer Henri Parizeau in 1926. *See also* Goodfellow Point.

Agnes Point (52°22'00" 128°23'00" NE end of Lady Douglas I, Milbanke Sd). Agnes Douglas (1841–1928), born at Ft Vancouver in what is now Washington state, was the fourth daughter of BC colonial gov James Douglas and Amelia Douglas. She was the boldest and perhaps the wildest of the Douglas offspring and in 1862 married Arthur Thomas Bushby, an HBC employee who became secretary to Chief Justice Matthew Baillie Begbie. Bushby was later appointed registrar gen and acting postmaster gen of the colony of BC, during which time he and Agnes lived at New Westminster. Agnes spent time in England, where three of her five children (one died in infancy) attended school, and in California. After Bushby's death in 1875, she lived at Victoria and San Francisco, and moved eventually to England to be with her youngest daughter. The point was named by regional hydrographer Henri Parizeau in 1929.

Agnew Bank (54°11'00" 130°19'00" SW entrance to Porpoise Channel, S of Prince Rupert). Named by the hydrographic service in 1945 after Augustus W Agnew, a native of eastern Canada, who was one of the original GTP surveyors at Prince Rupert (1906–14). He served in WWI as a maj with the Canadian Pioneers, was wounded in action and died Sept 17, 1916, at Amiens, France, aged 35, leaving a wife, Martha (1881–1967), and two children. He is buried at Contay British Cemetery, Somme, France.

Agnew Islet (52°06'00" 128°24'00" W entrance to Seaforth Channel, Milbanke Sd, NW of Bella Bella). Commodore Ronald Ian Agnew, OBE (1895–1949), born at Toronto, was a cadet at the Royal Naval College of Canada in 1911. In his early career he was in charge of the destroyers *Patrician* (1926–28), *Vancouver* (1928) and *Saguenay* (1934–36) and served as CO at Esquimalt in 1931. During WWII he commanded the Canadian armed merchant cruiser *Prince Henry* (1940–41) and the British aircraft carrier *Atheling* (1943) and also held senior staff appointments at HMCS *Naden* (1945) and in the UK (1942, 1947–49) and Washington (1946). The feature was named in 1944 by regional hydrographer Henri Parizeau.

Agnew Passage (49°46'45" 123°59'30" Between Captain I and Nelson I at entrance to Jervis Inlet, NW of Vancouver). Private Frank Agnew, of Vancouver, was killed in action on Oct 16, 1944, aged 26. He served in the N Shore (NB) Regiment of the Royal Canadian Infantry Corps and is buried at Adagem Canadian War Cemetery in Belgium.

Aguilar Point (48°50'00" 125°08'00" N end of Mills Peninsula, E side of Trevor Channel, Barkley Sd, W side of Vancouver I). Named in 1861 by RN surveyor Capt George Richards after Henry Aguilar, 2nd master and navigating officer aboard HMS *Grappler*, a gunboat that served on the BC coast from 1860 to 1863. Aguilar retired with the rank of lt in 1874 and died in 1902. The point was once the site of a Huu-ay-aht (Ohiaht) First Nation village named Tsa-he-tsa. Today a lodge, Aguilar House, is located there. *W*

Ahlstrom Point (49°47'00" 124°08'00" N side of lower Jervis Inlet, S of Lois Lk, NW of Vancouver). Private Knute Emanuel Ahlstrom, of Vancouver, with the 1st Battalion, Canadian Scottish Regiment, Royal Canadian Infantry Corps, was killed in action in Normandy on June 9, 1944, aged 22. He is buried at Bretteville-sur-Laize Canadian War Cemetery, Calvados, France.

Ahmah Island (48°57'00" 125°05'00" NW of Tsartus I, Barkley Sd, W side of Vancouver I). Ahmah has been translated as meaning "large grey river" in the language of the Nuu-chah-nulth First Nation. Formerly known as Davies I or Davis I but renamed by the hydrographic service in 1945.

First Nation village of Ahousat on Flores Island. *Peter Vassilopoulos*

Ahousat (49°17'00" 126°04'00" SE end of Flores I, NW of Tofino, Clayoquot Sd, W side of Vancouver I). This is the principal village of the Ahousaht First Nation, which is part of the Nuu-chah-nulth Tribal Council. The Ahousahts are fishers and once were whalers; they formerly lived at Ahous Bay on Vargas I, and their name has been translated (in 2003, in the Nuu-chah-nulth newspaper *Ha-shilth-sa*) as "people living with their backs to the land and mountains." Over 150 years ago, they proved victorious in a long war against the Otsosaht, a neighbouring tribe, and took control of their territory and salmon-bearing rivers, including this site. The residential area on the E side of Matilda Inlet is known as Marktosis (qv), while the name Ahousat refers specifically to the commercial settlement on the W side of the inlet or,

A

more generally, to the combined community. In 1864, a notorious incident took place in the inlet, when the crew of the schooner *Kingfisher*, engaged in the seal oil trade, were killed by the Ahousahts and their vessel burned. British warships shelled villages in the region, resulting in a number of deaths, and took prisoners, who were tried but later acquitted for lack of evidence. In the late 1800s a Presbyterian mission and school were established at Ahousat. From 1918 to the 1930s, it was the base for the family logging business of Gordon Gibson, famed "Bull of the Woods." *E W*

Ahous Bay (49°11'00" 126°01'00" W side of Vargas I, NW of Tofino, Clayoquot Sd, W side of Vancouver I), **Ahous Point** (49°10'00" 126°01'00" S side of Ahous Bay). Ahous was the name of an Ahousaht First Nation village once located on the bay—the original abode of the inhabitants of nearby Ahousat (qv) on Flores Island.

Aikman Passage (53°05'00" 129°07'00" Between Borde I and W side of Princess Royal I). James Allan Todd Aikman (1871–1925) was born at Victoria and married Christine Aurora M Neal at Vancouver in 1922. He was the son of Hugh Bowlsby Willson Aikman (1837–1904), the first Canadian law student to receive his diploma in BC and a former BC registrar gen (1871). James, listed as a law student in the 1892 Victoria directory, followed in his father's footsteps and practised law in the Yukon in the early 1900s. He is believed to have taken part in the festivities at the Victoria old-timers' reunion of 1924 (*see* Adams Bay). The passage was named in 1925 by regional hydrographer Henri Parizeau.

Ainslie Point (48°45'44" 123°15'16" W side of S Pender I, Gulf Is). Gilbert Herbert Ainslie (b 1861) immigrated to Canada from England in 1895 and pre-empted land at Winter Cove on Saturna I in 1896. In 1900, after being issued a Crown grant, he sold his property and moved to S Pender I. He is noted for persuading the navy to help dismantle his log home on Saturna and reassemble it on S Pender—a project that was accomplished in a mere 36 hours. Ainslie later sold out to Capt Ernest Beaumont, after whom nearby Beaumont Provincial Marine Park is named. The name was suggested in 1969 by the Gulf Is Branch of the BC Historical Assoc.

Aiskew Island, **Aiskew Point** (55°23'00" 129°46'00" W side of Observatory Inlet, S of Alice Arm). Named in 1922 after Sir Thomas Aiskew Larcom (1801–79), who was the father of RN officer Thomas Henry Larcom, who served on the BC coast (*see* Larcom I). Trained as a military surveyor, Sir Thomas occupied a number of significant roles in the British administration of Ireland, becoming permanent undersecretary (1853–68), and was widely respected for his impartiality and competence.

Aitken Islands (52°37'00" 128°48'00" S of Princess Royal I in approach to Laredo Inlet). George Griffith Aitken (1884–1955) was appointed chief geographer for BC in 1912. He later sat on the Geographic Board of Canada as the BC member (1924–39 and 1943–45). He served in both world wars, achieving the rank of maj in the first and lt col in the second. Aitken Ck, a tributary of the Blueberry R in the Peace R district, is also named after him. Formerly known as the South Bay Is, these geographical features were renamed by the hydrographic service in 1925.

Aitken Point (48°50'52" 123°14'43" E side of Mayne I, Gulf Is). John Aitken (1873–1959) was born at Lanark, Scotland. He came to BC in 1881 and logged, prospected and beachcombed, then landed on the Gulf Is, where he worked as a farmhand on Moresby I and also for Max Enke on Galiano I. Aitken bought a home and store at Miners Bay on Mayne I in 1908 and was postmaster from 1912 to 1916. In 1920 he acquired George Paddon's Horton Bay farm, where he raised sheep and prize flowers. According to historian and journalist Peter Murray, Aitken's ox, named William, was an island icon, pulling ploughs and carts for nearly four decades. Aitken retired in 1946 and his farm was taken over by his son Roy. The name was suggested in 1969 by the Gulf Is Branch of the BC Historical Assoc.

Ajax Bank (49°39'00" 124°43'00" E of Comox Hbr, Str of Georgia). Named by regional hydrographer Henri Parizeau in 1945 after the *Leander*-class light cruiser *Ajax*, under Capt Charles Woodhouse, which joined HMS *Exeter* and HMNZS *Achilles* to ultimately destroy German pocket battleship *Admiral Graf Spee* in the Battle of the River Plate, at Montevideo, Uruguay, in 1939. The 169-m, 6,549-tonne *Ajax*, launched in 1934, spent most of the rest of WWII in the Mediterranean. It was decommissioned in 1948. The town of Ajax, Ont, is also named for this vessel.

Akam Point (50°53'00" 127°12'00" N side of Queen Charlotte Str, SE of Blunden Hbr). Chief Engine Room Artificer Thomas Akam, of Victoria, was killed in action while serving aboard the RCN destroyer *Margaree*. HMCS *Margaree* sank on convoy duty after colliding with a merchant vessel in the N Atlantic on Oct 22, 1940; 142 hands were lost. Akam was born at Tottenham, England, in 1906 and joined the RCNVR in 1926 at Hamilton. He is commemorated on the Halifax Memorial.

Akre Rocks (50°32'00" 127°38'00" N of Drake I, Quatsino Sd, N Vancouver I). The correct spelling of this Quatsino pioneer's name is Ole Aakre (1865–1932), though Akre appears on his official land documents and on his death certificate. He was from Norway, one of a group of Scandinavian colonists who settled on Quatsino Sd in 1895 and received Crown grants there (his are dated 1901 and 1916). Aakre joined the Klondike gold rush, earning his living transporting miners' supplies across Chilkoot Pass, then returned to Quatsino, built and rented out a number of cabins and, in 1919, opened a store. His property was known as Aakreville. According to Quatsino historian Gwen Hansen, he also owned a fish packer named *Avro* for a while. His nephew, Knute Aakre, joined him from Norway in 1930 and ran the store and cabins until about 1950. The rocks were named by regional hydrographer Henri Parizeau in 1926.

Ala Narrows (53°31'00" 129°54'00" E side of Anger I, W of Pitt I), **Ala Passage** (53°31'30" 129°53'00" Between Anger I and Pitt I). The *Ala* was a small vessel used in this region in 1921 by a coastal triangulation party under Alfred Wright, a surveyor with the BC Lands Service.

Alan Reach (53°28'00" 128°38'00" Between Walkem Point and Kiltuish Inlet, Gardner Canal). After Adm Lord Alan Gardner, a British naval officer who was a friend and mentor of Capt George Vancouver. *See* Gardner Canal. Named in 1907 by Capt Frederick Learmonth of the RN survey vessel *Egeria*.

Alarm Cove (52°07'00" 128°06'00" W side of Denny I, SW of Bella Bella). Named about 1866 by Lt Daniel Pender of the hired survey vessel *Beaver* after the 15-tonne coastal trading schooner *Alarm*, built at Victoria in 1860. Capt William Ettershanks was master in the mid-1860s, trading and carrying freight between Victoria and Nanaimo.

Alarm Rock (48°57'00" 123°41'00" In Stuart Channel, W of Kuper I, Gulf Is). The frigate *Alarm*, 26 guns and 827 tonnes, was built at Sheerness dockyard, Kent, in 1845 and spent much time over the next seven years in the W

Indies, seeing action in Nicaragua in 1848 after several British citizens were abducted by the Nicaraguan army. The vessel was posted to the Pacific Station, under Capt Douglas Curry, from 1855 to 1858. It was converted to a coal hulk in 1860 and spent 40 years in that capacity before being turned into a landing stage in 1900 and then broken up in 1904. Named by RN surveyor Capt George Richards in 1859.

Alberni Inlet (49°05'00" 124°49'00" Extends NE from head of Barkley Sd, Vancouver I), **Port Alberni** (49°14'30" 124°48'00" Head of Alberni Inlet). Pedro de Alberni (1747–1802), an infantry capt in the Spanish army, was in command of a squadron of 76 soldiers attached to Lt Francisco Eliza's 1790 expedition to the BC coast. Eliza and Alberni reoccupied the Spanish base at Nootka that Estéban Martínez had abandoned the year before and re-

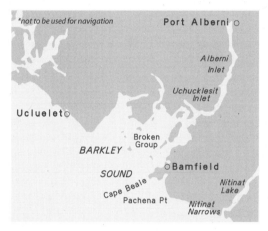

Alberni Inlet. *Reproduced with the permission of the Canadian Hydrographic Service*

View of Canadian Pacific Lumber Co's mill at Port Alberni, dated about 1914. *Courtesy Tim Woodland*

established Spanish authority in the region; Eliza named the inlet after his colleague in 1791. Alberni oversaw much of the garrison work, constructing buildings and fortifications, installing wells and a bakery, raising animals, successfully growing a range of vegetables and developing good relations with his First Nation neighbours. He left Nootka in 1792 and was later in charge of Spain's military posts in California. It is not known if he ever visited Alberni Inlet, at the head of which was established, in 1860, BC's first export sawmill and the earliest farm N of Victoria. From such modest beginnings emerged the city of Port Alberni, the main forest products centre on Vancouver I and BC's third-largest port. Alberni Inlet was officially known as Alberni Canal until 1945, when the name was changed on the recommendation of regional hydrographer Henri Parizeau, who felt that the word "canal" would raise the spectre of "fees for pilotage, canal dues, extra insurance and so forth" in the minds of foreign shipping executives, to the future detriment of Port Alberni. *E W*

Albert Head (48°23'00" 123°29'00" SW edge of Royal Roads, W of Victoria). Named in 1846 by Capt Henry Kellett of HMS *Herald* after Prince Albert, Queen Victoria's husband, because the settlement on the other side of the bay, Ft Victoria, had been named for the queen. Prince Albert of Saxe-Coburg and Gotha (1819–61) was the second son of Ernest, Duke of Saxe-Coburg and Gotha, and married Queen Victoria in 1840. Spanish explorer Manuel Quimper landed at Albert Head in 1790, while making the first European exploration of Juan de Fuca Str, and claimed Vancouver I for Spain. The headland was the site of BC's first steam sawmill, 1853–59, though it seems only a small quantity of lumber was cut there before the mill was destroyed by fire. A quarantine station (later moved to William Head) operated at Albert Head (1883–93), and the promontory was fortified to guard Esquimalt Hbr during WWII. A Dept of National Defence training centre is currently located there. The Songhees First Nation name for Albert Head was Tleepet. *E*

Albert Islet (52°18'05" 127°55'55" E side of Johnson Channel off NE end of Cunningham I, NE of Bella Bella). After coastal steamship *Prince Albert*, formerly the *Bruno*, built in 1892 in England. In 1910, as the first vessel in the GTP Coast Steamship Co fleet (later part of the CNR), it was put on the QCI run. Capt Cecil Wearmouth was the first master, followed by Capt Duncan Mackenzie. Only 63 m in length, and with little in the way of luxury, the *Prince Albert* had a daredevil life, running aground on Butterworth Rks near Prince Rupert in 1914 and colliding with the *Prince John* near Skidegate Inlet in 1920. It became a mothership for the rum-running trade in 1925 and was noted for managing to break the Pacific telegraph cable. Converted to a tug in 1933 and renamed the *J R Morgan*, it towed Davis rafts from Haida Gwaii to the mainland. In

1950, after another conversion—this time to a log barge—the vessel finally foundered off Vancouver I.

Dionisio Alcalá-Galiano (1760–1805). *Archivo General de la Nacion, Mexico City*

Alcala Point (49°00'00" 123°35'00" W side of Galiano I near N end, Gulf Is). Dionisio Alcalá-Galiano (1760–1805), from Córdoba, was a Spanish naval officer and experienced cartographer who was a member of Alejandro Malaspina's 1789–94 round-the-world voyage (though he did not go to Alaska and Nootka Sd with Malaspina in 1791). He had studied under Vicente Tofiño, Spain's legendary chief hydrographer, and also participated in Antonio de Córdoba's journey to survey the Str of Magellan in 1785 aboard the *Santa María de la Cabeza*. In 1792 he and Cayetano Valdés left Malaspina's expedition at Mexico (New Spain) and were dispatched instead to BC to continue the Spanish search for the NW Passage. Alcalá-Galiano, in command of the *Sutil*, and Valdés, in the smaller *Mexicana*, charted the coast from Rosario Str to Queen Charlotte Sd and made a historic circumnavigation of Vancouver I. En route, they encountered Capt George Vancouver off Point Grey and explored with him for several weeks. Alcalá-Galiano's excellent charts were used by Vancouver, and the normally reticent Spanish government published an account of his explorations in 1802 to offset works by Vancouver and Lapérouse. He died at the Battle of Trafalgar while commanding the *Bahama*. The point was named by Cdr John Parry of the RN survey vessel *Egeria* while re-surveying Porlier Pass in 1905. *See also* Galiano Bay. *E*

Aldrich Point (52°20'00" 128°37'00" SE side of Price I, NW of Bella Bella). Sub-Lt Pelham Aldrich (1844–1930) served under Capt John Price aboard HMS *Scout*, which was based at the RN's Pacific Station in Esquimalt, 1865–68. From 1872 to 1875 he was with Capt George Nares aboard HMS *Challenger* on the Royal Society's round-the-world oceanographic expedition, and he transferred with Nares to HMS *Alert* for the British Arctic expedition of 1875–76. Aldrich led a sledge party that managed to map more than 350 km of Ellesmere I's previously unexplored coastline. He was promoted to capt in 1883 and pursued survey work in China, S Africa, Australia and the Mediterranean. In 1896 he became inspecting capt of boys' training ships and in 1902, as a rear adm, superintendent of Portsmouth dockyard. He retired from the RN in 1908 with the rank of adm. The point was named by RN surveyor Lt Daniel Pender in 1866.

Aldridge Point (48°46'03" 123°15'30" E side of N Pender I, Gulf Is). Dr and Mrs Augustus Aldridge retired to the Pender Is in the early 1900s, and Dr Aldridge died at Sidney in 1951, aged 77. The name was adopted in 1969 after being suggested by the Gulf Is Branch of the BC Historical Assoc.

Alec Islet (52°21'00" 128°23'00" Off E side of Lady Douglas I, NW of Bella Bella). Alec Douglas, born in 1831 at Ft Vancouver on the Columbia R, was the eldest son of BC colonial gov James Douglas and Amelia Douglas. Named after Alexander, James Douglas's older brother, he died at age three after a tragic accident. The islet was named in 1929 by regional hydrographer Henri Parizeau.

Alert Bay (50°35'00" 126°56'00" S side of Cormorant I, Broughton Str, N end of Johnstone Str), **Alert Island** (52°07'00" 128°07'00" Off W side of Denny I, W of Bella Bella), **Alert Rock** (50°35'00" 126°57'00" S of Cormorant I), **Alert Rock** (54°11'00" 132°58'00" E end of Solide Passage, Langara I, QCI). HMS *Alert*, a 17-gun screw corvette, was built at Pembroke in 1856 and based at Esquimalt, 1858–61 (under Cdr William Pearse) and 1865–69 (under Cdr Arthur Innes). Its crew did survey work in the QCI in 1860 and re-surveyed Alert Bay in 1867. The 681-tonne ship had a historic career. It was converted for Arctic exploration in 1874 and commanded by Capt George Nares on the 1875–76 British Arctic expedition, during which crew members reached a new record latitude of 83°20'26". Nares was also cdr of this vessel on his 1878–79 survey of Magellan Str. In 1884 the *Alert* was loaned to the US Navy and helped rescue the Adolphus Greeley polar expedition. The following year it was transferred to Canada and conducted a survey of Hudson Bay, then was used as a lighthouse supply ship and buoy tender in NS and the Gulf of St Lawrence. It was broken up in 1894. The fishing village of Alert Bay is now the main population centre of the Kwakwaka'wakw First Nation, home to a hospital and

Alert Bay in the early 1900s. *Author's collection*

an array of marine facilities. The community, known for its totem poles and for an important collection of masks and other artifacts at the U'mista Cultural Centre, also attracts a growing number of tourists. According to the Museum at Campbell R, the Kwakwala name for the village, 'Yalis, means "spread-leg beach" (ie, a bay bounded by narrow points on either side). RN surveyor Capt George Richards of HMS *Plumper* named Alert Bay in 1860. *D E*

Alert Point (49°59'51" 127°27'20" W side of Lookout I, Kyuquot Sd). Named in 1947 after one of the first sealing schooners to operate on the BC coast, owned by Capt Hugh McKay and Capt William Spring. McKay arrived in Victoria in 1848; Spring in 1853. These pioneer coastal traders specialized first in cured and salted salmon, then entered the sealing business with several vessels in the late 1860s. They acquired the *Alert* in 1864. The vessel sank on Great Bear Reef in Barkley Sd in 1880, carrying, according to the Victoria *Colonist*, a "cargo of oil and skins ... valued at about $7,000." The crew of six managed to escape in canoes. This geographic feature appears on early (1866) Admiralty charts as Nob Point.

Alexander Inlet (52°38'00" 128°37'00" SE end of Princess Royal I, NW of Bella Bella). Harold Rupert Leofric George Alexander (1891–1969), 1st Earl Alexander of Tunis, became Canada's 17th gov gen in 1946. He was a WWII military leader, serving in Burma, the Middle East and Italy and becoming, in 1944, Supreme Allied Cdr Mediterranean, with the rank of field marshal. Alexander was the last British gov gen of Canada—an active, popular appointee who travelled widely, visiting BC in 1946, where he was made an honorary chief of the Kwakwaka'wakw First Nation. He returned to England in 1952 to become minister of defence in Winston Churchill's government, then retired in 1954. Nearby Tunis Point is also named for him. *See* Errigal Point, as well.

Alexander Islands (52°57'22" 129°18'30" Off S tip of Campania I, Caamaño Sd). David Alexander was born in Australia of Scottish descent, immigrated with his wife

A

and children to Cowichan Bay in 1862 and settled on the E side of Somenos Lk on a homestead known as Oak Bank Farm. The Alexanders were well-known pioneers in the district, and David, who retired to Duncan, is believed to have been a participant at the Victoria old-timers' reunion of 1924 (*see* Adams Bay). The islands were formerly known as the Eclipse Is but were renamed in 1926.

Alexander Point (49°44′00″ 124°14′00″ W side of Hardy I, entrance to Jervis Inlet). After both Rear Adm Sir Alexander John Ball and the 74-gun ship of the line HMS *Alexander*, which he commanded at the 1798 Battle of the Nile. *See* Ball Point.

Alexander Rock (50°34′00″ 126°41′00″ E side of Hanson I, Blackney Passage, N end of Johnstone Str). Boatswain George Hamilton Alexander was assigned to surveying duties on the BC coast from 1900 to 1903 aboard HMS *Egeria*, under Cdr Cortland H Simpson. In 1904 he was appointed to HMS *Sealark*. The feature was also known for several years as Davis Rk.

Alexander Shoal (53°33′00″ 130°08′00″ In Principe Channel between Banks I and S end of McCauley I). Named in 1950 after Squadron Leader Edward Sudbury Alexander of the RCAF, who was born in England but raised in Montreal and Vancouver. He was awarded the DFM in 1942, while flying with No 419 Squadron, after skilfully navigating a damaged bomber back to the UK from Europe. The DFC came in 1944 while Alexander was with No 156 Squadron, flying Lancasters; he had at that time completed 51 bombing sorties against heavily defended targets in Europe and "displayed high skill, fortitude and devotion to duty." He was killed in action on Jan 14, 1944, and is buried at Bergen-op-Zoom War Cemetery, Netherlands.

Alford Reefs (54°18′00″ 130°30′00″ S of Tugwell I, Chatham Sd, W of Prince Rupert). Rev Charles Richard Alford was principal of the Church Missionary Society college at Highbury, London, 1854–64. The name was suggested by William Duncan, founder of the famous mission at Metlakatla, who trained at Highbury for two years. Alford, born in 1816, was also Bishop of Victoria, Hong Kong, 1867–72.

Alfred Point (52°53′00″ 131°47′00″ S end of Louise I opposite Selwyn Inlet). After geologist Alfred Selwyn, a 19th-century director of the Geological Survey of Canada. *See* Selwyn Inlet.

Algerine Island (52°10′00″ 127°56′00″ In Gunboat Passage between Cunningham I and Denny I E of Bella Bella), **Algerine Passage** (49°49′00″ 124°38′00″ Between Harwood I and Texada I, Str of Georgia). HMS *Algerine* (later HMCS *Algerine*), a sloop-of-war launched in

The sloop-of-war *Algerine* in Esquimalt Harbour. *BC Archives A-00203*

England in 1895, saw action in China before being based in Esquimalt, 1908–18. The 57-m vessel, sixth to bear its name in the RN, was steel-hulled, with a clipper bow, barque-rigged for sail but also with twin steam engines that gave it a speed of almost 13 knots. Its duties included sealing patrols in the Bering Sea (1908–13) and acting as Esquimalt Naval Base depot ship (1914–18). Purchased by the Pacific Salvage Co in 1919, it ran aground on Brodie Rk in Principe Channel in 1923 and was towed to Victoria and sold for scrap in 1924. Algerine I was formerly known as Julia I but was renamed by regional hydrographer Henri Parizeau in 1925; the passage was named in 1945.

Alice Arm (55°27′00″ 129°33′00″ E arm of Observatory Inlet, S of Stewart), **Alice Rock** (55°25′00″ 129°40′00″ NE of Liddle I, Alice Arm). Alice Mary Woods (1851–1933) was the second daughter of Richard Woods, registrar of the Supreme Court of BC, 1862–75. She was born in Ireland but grew up in Victoria and was married there, in 1868, to Rev Robert Tomlinson (*see* Mt Tomlinson), who had charge of the Church Missionary Society post at Kincolith on Nass Bay, 1867–79. Immediately after the wedding she travelled to Kincolith by Haida canoe, a journey of more than 1,000 km that took 24 days. She spent most of her life on the N coast, assisting her husband's missions at Kincolith, Ankitlast (near Kispiox), Metlakatla, New Metlakatla (in SE Alaska) and Meanskinisht, a non-sectarian establishment founded by Robert Tomlinson at Cedarvale, where she died. The arm was named by RN surveyor Lt Daniel Pender in 1868. The village of Alice Arm sprang up in 1916 to serve the rich mining region to the N, in the Kitsault R (qv) valley—especially the famous Dolly Varden silver mine. The mine only lasted until 1921, but a small prospecting community lingered on for many years; Alice Arm post office did not close until 1987. According to the Nisga'a Tribal Council, the First Nation name for Alice Arm is Ts'im Gits'oohl ("inside, in behind"). *E*

All Alone Stone (52°29′00″ 131°24′00″ Juan Perez Sd, E side of Moresby I, QCI). A rounded, forested islet about

40 m in height, named in 1878 by Dr George M Dawson of the Geological Survey of Canada because it, along with Monument Rk, were thought to be useful landmarks for vessels entering Burnaby Str. A local literary periodical chose this name in the 1970s as a title and symbol of Haida Gwaii itself.

Allatt Point (53°06'00" 129°09'00" SE end of Gil I, Caamaño Sd). Frederick Richard Allatt (1853–1930) was born at Sydney, Australia, and moved to Victoria with his family in 1858. His father, Thomas Smith Allatt (1818–80), became a well-established house builder and general contractor in the city. Fred took up carpentry and joined the Deluge Co, one of three competing fire brigades in Victoria in the days when firefighting was a private enterprise (and the various companies weren't above sabotaging each other's efforts, often by disconnecting their rivals' hoses). The firemen were noted for their parades—and for the prodigious amounts of alcohol they consumed at social functions. It wasn't until 1886 that fire services were taken over by the city and paid for with tax monies. Allatt married Margaret Jane Reid at Victoria in 1881 (they later divorced) and took part in the Victoria old-timers' reunion of 1924 (*see* Adams Bay). The point was formerly marked on Admiralty charts as Turn Point but was renamed by regional hydrographer Henri Parizeau in 1926.

Allcroft Point (53°36'00" 130°04'00" SE entrance to Petrel Channel between McCauley I and Pitt I). Flying Officer Frederick Charles Allcroft, from Lund, was killed in action on Jan 3, 1944, aged 20. He was awarded the DFC in 1943, while serving with the RCAF No 61 Squadron, for making successful bombing runs on targets at Essen and Dortmund despite the fact that his aircraft had suffered substantial damage from enemy gunfire. Allcroft is buried at the Berlin 1939–1945 War Cemetery, Germany. (His surname was an alias; the family name was Hewett. Frederick was probably underage when he enlisted.)

Alldridge Point (48°19'00" 123°38'00" W entrance to Becher Bay, S end of Vancouver I). Lt George Manly Alldridge was an officer in the RN's surveying branch. He was promoted cdr in 1855 and took on special surveying duties at HMS *Fisgard*, Woolwich, England. He retired with the rank of capt in 1864 and died in 1905. Named in 1846 by Capt Henry Kellett of HMS *Herald*, who undertook early surveying duties around the S end of Vancouver I.

Allen Point (53°26'30" 128°24'10" S shore of Europa Reach, Gardner Canal, SE of Kitimat). Cdr Allen Thomas Hunt (1866–1943) entered the RN in 1879, took part in the Anglo-Egyptian War of 1882 and the Boer War, and was in charge of HMS *Shearwater* on the BC coast, 1904–6. The sloop *Shearwater* had a lengthy history as an Esquimalt-based naval vessel (*see* Shearwater I). Hunt went on to an important RN career, commanding a light cruiser

squadron in WWI, becoming a vice adm in 1922 and, in 1924, a knight. This geographic feature was formerly known as Hunt Point but was renamed in 1952 to avoid confusion with Hunt Point on Porcher I.

Allen Rocks (52°33'00" 129°27'00" NW of Conroy I off W side of Aristazabel I). Sapper Frederick Allen served with the Columbia detachment of Royal Engineers, on duty in BC from 1858 to 1863. Virtually nothing, unfortunately, is known about him. The feature was named in 1928 by regional hydrographer Henri Parizeau.

Allerton Passage (53°30'00" 130°27'00" Entrance to Kingkown Inlet, NW side of Banks I). The *Allerton* was an early sailing vessel on the BC coast. Charles Goring of Victoria was the master.

Alleviation Rock (50°55'00" 127°37'00" Just NW of Redfern I, Gordon Channel, off NE end of Vancouver I). This name was adopted in 1947 to keep alive a historical reference from 1792. James Johnstone, master of HMS *Chatham*, had finally obtained a clear view of the Pacific Ocean from this vicinity while travelling in the ship's cutter—thus proving the insularity of Vancouver I and "alleviating" Capt George Vancouver's concern about reaching open water. In his journal, Vancouver named a feature in the area Alleviation I, but the name did not appear on his chart, and it is no longer known which island he was referring to. Redfern I (qv) and Pine I (qv) are the most logical candidates.

Alleyne Island (52°05'00" 128°20'00" S of Stryker I, SW of Bella Bella). Cdr Victor Percy Alleyne (1887–1952), born at London, England, was a retired RN officer living on Vancouver I when WWII began. He had married Elizabeth Helen Wace at Shawnigan Lk in 1929. Alleyne re-enlisted with the RCN and was placed in charge at HMCS *Givenchy*, part of the naval station at Esquimalt. In 1939 he served as commodore of the first merchant marine convoy to leave Canada for Britain and was in charge of Canadian N Atlantic convoys, 1939–41, for which role he was awarded the OBE. Alleyne was CO of the shore establishment HMCS *Shelburne* in NS, 1941–42. He died at Saanich. Alleyne I was formerly known as Entrance I.

Allies Island (50°12'00" 124°48'00" In Waddington Channel between E Redonda I and W Redonda I, NE of Campbell R). Originally known by the name Prussian I, which can be found on pre-WWI charts and was in local use until at least the 1960s. Prussian I was officially changed to Allies I sometime during WWI, probably as a result of patriotic pressure. The first appearance of the new name was on a chart dated 1919.

Alliford Bay (53°12'15" 131°59'30" SE side of Skidegate Inlet, NE Moresby I, QCI). William Alliford was

The wharf at Alliford Bay. *Harbour Publishing collection*

quartermaster on the HBC steamship *Beaver* after it was hired as a survey vessel by the RN in 1863. He was coxswain of the ship's boat used to sound this bay during the survey of Skidegate Inlet in 1866, and Lt Daniel Pender named it after him. The bay was chosen as the site of a "model cannery town" in 1911 but the scheme came to nothing. In WWII, a 700-man seaplane base operated here. For many years the bay has been the terminus for ferry service between Moresby I and Graham I. Alliford Ck flows NW into Alliford Bay. *D E*

Allison Cone (51°01'00" 127°31'00" Just S of Allison Hbr), **Allison Harbour** (51°03'00" 127°30'00" E of Bramham I, NW side of Queen Charlotte Str), **Allison Reefs** (51°02'00" 127°31'00" Entrance to Allison Hbr). Ambrose P Allison (1883–1947) was the owner of A P Allison Logging, an important independent forestry company on the BC coast. He was born in the UK, came to Canada in 1892 and got his first job at a mill in Chemainus in 1900. Allison worked his way up, running a railway logging camp and shingle mill at Greene Point Rapids in 1908 and managing operations in the Allison Hbr area for Smith-Dollar Lumber Co in the 1920s. He later established railway camps at Homathko R, and at Cumshewa Inlet in the QCI; the latter produced "airplane" spruce and was taken over by the federal government during WWII and renamed Aero Timber. Allison started a sawmill in N Vancouver after the war and was president of the Truck Loggers' Assoc at the time of his death, after which his sons took over the company and logged for many years on Johnstone Str. Allison Hbr, named about 1922, was formerly known as False Bay and False Schooner Passage. Allison Reefs were named by the hydrographic service in association with the harbour in 1946, Allison Cone in 1958. *E*

Alman Island (52°31'00" 129°03'00" Off Weeteeam Bay, SW side of Aristazabal I). Sapper Daniel D Alman arrived in BC with the Columbia detachment of the Royal Engineers, which served in the province 1858–63, but later deserted. Named in 1927 by regional hydrographer Henri Parizeau.

Alma Russell Islands (48°57'00" 125°12'00" NW side of Imperial Eagle Channel, Barkley Sd, W side of Vancouver I). Formerly known as Narrow Is and Julia Is, these features were renamed by regional hydrographer Henri Parizeau in 1935. Alma Russell (1873–1964), born at Douglastown, NB, moved with her family to Victoria in the 1880s. Trained at the Pratt Institute of Library Science, Brooklyn, NY, she was BC's first professional female librarian and served as assistant provincial archivist and librarian, 1897–1933. In the 1930s she presided over the BC Historical Assoc and in 1939 co-founded the Society for Furtherance of BC Indian Arts and Crafts.

Alpha Bay (53°52'00" 130°16'00" NW end of Pitt I, S of Prince Rupert), **Alpha Islet** (48°26'00" 123°14'00" N of Discovery I off Oak Bay, SE end of Vancouver I), **Alpha Passage** (48°55'00" 125°32'00" S of Ucluelet Inlet, Barkley Sd, W coast of Vancouver I), **Alpha Point** (53°52'00" 130°17'00" E side of Ogden Channel, NW end of Pitt I). In 1859, the 53-tonne trading schooner *Alpha* was the first vessel built at Nanaimo—hence the name. It assisted the owners of the *Florencia*, wrecked near Ucluelet in 1861, by bringing the doomed ship's cargo to Nanaimo. In Feb 1863, under Capt William McCulloch, the *Alpha* ran aground on the islet that now bears its name (formerly Seabird I); although the incident occurred in the middle of the night, and in a blinding snowstorm, the heavily laden vessel was only slightly damaged and its eight passengers quite unhurt. It acquired new owners and sailed from Victoria in 1868, bound for Honolulu with a cargo of lumber, but was driven onto Flores I in a winter gale and totally destroyed. The crew persuaded the island's First Nation inhabitants to take them to Barkley Sd, and from there, with great difficulty, they hiked to Nanaimo. The passage was named by RN surveyor Capt George Richards in 1861, the islet and bay by Lt Daniel Pender in 1863 and 1867 respectively. *W*

Alston Cove (52°45'00" 128°45'00" E side of Laredo Inlet, Princess Royal I). Edward Graham Alston (1832–72), a lawyer and pioneer resident of Victoria, was appointed registrar of titles for colonial Vancouver I and BC, 1861–71, and was very briefly attorney gen of the colony of BC in 1871. He was one of three commissioners who drew up BC's *Consolidated Statutes*. Alston immigrated from

England to Victoria in 1859 and was married twice, to Elizabeth Caroline Abbott (d 1865) and then to Anna Maria Trizo. As was common in the smaller British colonies, Alston wore a number of civil service hats: he was a member of the legislative council of Vancouver I (1861–62), the board of education and the legislative council of BC (1868–71); he also served as an Indian reserve commissioner, commissioner of savings banks, justice of the peace, registrar of joint stock companies and inspector gen of schools. He and his wife lived at Broome Cottage on Fort St, which was later the site of Pentrelew, the Italianate home and social gathering spot of BC attorney gen Henry Crease and his family. Alston was no fan of responsible government, believing that when BC joined Canada, "all vacancies will be filled by the political friends of the ministry of the day." He left Victoria in 1871 to take up a senior civil service position in Sierra Leone. Unfortunately, he caught an African fever the following year and died there. Alston Cove was named in 1928 by regional hydrographer Henri Parizeau. Mt Alston and Alston Ck on Vancouver I are also named for him and recall his participation in an 1868 expedition that crossed the island from Nootka Sd to the E coast.

Ambrosia Bay (50°12'00" 127°49'00" N side of Brooks Peninsula, S of Quatsino Sd, NW side of Vancouver I). Named after the plant *Ambrosia chamissonis*, or silver bursage, which grows in abundance on the beach here. The name was suggested by members of the provincial museum's 1981 Brooks Peninsula expedition.

Amelia Island (49°18'00" 124°09'00" S side of Ballenas Channel, N of Nanoose Hbr, Str of Georgia). After Lady Amelia Douglas (née Connolly), wife of Vancouver I and BC gov Sir James Douglas. *See* Douglas I.

Amethyst Rock (52°46'00" 131°58'00" NE of Botany I, Tasu Sd, E side of Moresby I, QCI). Named in 1962 for the *Amethyst*, a copper-fastened ship of all trades built of live oak in Boston in 1821. It started life as a packet on the Boston–Liverpool run, then served as a whaler for 20 years, a coal ship on the eastern seaboard, a coaster in the China trade and, in the 1870s, a lumber carrier on the Pacific coast. The indefatigable *Amethyst* put in a final, Victoria-based stint of whaling and sealing in the 1880s before meeting with a fatal disaster off the coast of Siberia.

Amor Point (50°32'00" 124°59'00" W side of Bute Inlet, SW of Clipper Point). Named by RN surveyor Capt George Richards in 1862 in association with nearby Cosmos Heights, after newspaperman and politician Amor de Cosmos, BC's second premier, 1872–74. *See* DeCosmos Lagoon.

Amos Passage (53°50'00" 128°43'00" Douglas Channel, E side of Coste I, S of Kitimat). Named by the hydrographic

service in 1953 after the well-known Kitamaat First Nation chief Charlie Amos (1843–91), whose traditional name was Waks Gamalayu (Wahuksqumalayou). He travelled to Victoria in the mid-1870s, found work at a sawmill and was converted to Christianity by Rev William Pollard. On his return to Kitamaat about 1877, Amos built a log church and held prayer meetings. Several First Nation missionaries, trained at Port Simpson by Thomas Crosby, came to Kitamaat in the next few years and helped establish a Methodist mission there. Amos married a Kitamaat woman named Gwunta'laks, raised a family and spent many years on the N BC coast as a lay preacher.

Amphitrite Point lighthouse station. *Peter Vassilopoulos*

Amphitrite Point (48°55'17" 125°32'23" S point of Ucluth Peninsula, Ucluelet, W coast of Vancouver I). HMS *Amphitrite*, a 24-gun, 967-tonne corvette, was built of teak at Bombay in 1816 and served on the BC coast from 1851 to 1857, initially under Capt Charles Frederick and then under Capt Richard Burridge. The ship, originally constructed as a 46-gun frigate, was obsolete by 1840 and decommissioned. In 1846 it was modernized by cutting it down one deck, turning it into what was known as a "razee" corvette, and sent out to the W coast of Africa to combat the slave trade. The *Amphitrite* brought gold, silver and jewels worth almost $2 million—the property of merchants made nervous by civil unrest—from Mexico to England in 1850. The vessel was broken up in 1875. Amphitrite Point was the site of a terrible shipwreck in 1905 when the 2,000-tonne *Pass of Melfort*, under Capt Harry Scougall, was driven ashore on Christmas night, with the loss of at least 36 lives. Named about 1859 by RN surveyor Capt George Richards.

Amur Point (52°42'00" 131°45'00" W side of Darwin Sd, E side of Moresby I, QCI), **Amur Rock** (52°50'00" 131°52'00" Pacofi Bay, E side of Moresby I). The CPR steamer *Amur* was a well-known sight in the QCI, 1908–12, under Capt Louis P Locke, who was involved in many aspects of the early development of Haida Gwaii. A 66-m British coaster built in 1890, the *Amur* was brought to the BC coast in 1898 for the Klondike gold rush and then sold a year later to the Canadian Pacific Navigation Co. With a speed of

A

12 knots and accommodation for 60 passengers, the vessel had a useful career on the BC and Alaska coasts, running aground several times but never injuring anyone. In 1906 it carried a relief cargo to San Francisco after the great earthquake and fire. The *Amur* was sold in 1912, refitted and used as an ore carrier between Tacoma, Britannia Beach and Anyox. Sold again in 1924 and renamed *Famous*, it was wrecked on the Skeena R in 1926, salvaged, abandoned near Vancouver in 1928 and scuttled in Indian Arm a few years later. The name itself refers to one of Russia's major rivers.

Amyes Island (50°36'00" 126°16'00" In Chatham Channel, E of Minstrel I at entrance to Knight Inlet). Electrical Artificer Alfred William Amyes, of Victoria, was killed in action at age 28 while serving aboard the RCN destroyer HMCS *Margaree*, which was on merchant marine convoy duty in the N Atlantic on Oct 22, 1940, when it collided with a freighter and sank with the loss of 142 lives. His name is inscribed on the Halifax Memorial.

Anacla. *See* Pachena Bay.

Anderson Islands (52°45'00" 129°22'00" Off NW side of Aristazabal I). Victoria pioneer James Robert Anderson (1841–1930) was born at Fort Nisqually in what is now Washington state. He was the son of HBC explorer and chief trader Alexander Caulfield Anderson (1814–84) and lived at Victoria from 1850 to 1852 to attend school and again from 1858 until his death. James worked in the colonial customs and post office depts, became an accountant and businessman, and was BC deputy minister of agriculture, 1894–1908. A keen naturalist and amateur historian, he was a guest of honour at the Victoria old-timers' reunion of 1924 (*see* Adams Bay), as he had at that time been resident in the city longer than any other living person. In the 1840s his father blazed the Coquihalla and Douglas trails through BC's coastal mountains—vital routes used by early HBC fur brigades. In 1858–59, A C Anderson held important posts in the colonial government of Vancouver I, including collector of customs, treasurer and postmaster gen. He has several geographical features in BC named after him, including Anderson Lk and Anderson R, though none on the coast. The Anderson Is were named by the hydrographic service in 1926. *E*

Anderson Passage (53°08'00" 129°32'00" N entrance to Weinberg Inlet, Campania I, NE Estevan Sd). Named in 1944 by regional hydrographer Henri Parizeau after John Anderson, who was quartermaster aboard the Canadian survey vessel *William J Stewart* in the early 1940s.

Anderson Point (49°39'00" 126°28'00" S entrance to Muchalat Inlet, Nootka Sd, W side of Vancouver I). William Anderson (1750–78), from Scotland, was the surgeon and naturalist aboard HMS *Resolution*, which was refitted at Nootka Sd in 1778 during the third great expedition of Capt James Cook. He had also sailed on Cook's second voyage, 1772–75, as a surgeon's mate. Anderson wasn't trained in the natural sciences but nevertheless made a valuable collection of specimens during the voyage and also an important study of S Pacific languages. He died of tuberculosis aboard the *Resolution* in the Bering Sea. Cook had "a very great regard" for Anderson and wrote that "he was a sensible young man, an agreeable companion, well skilled in his profession." Named in 1862 by Capt George Richards. *W*

Anderson Point (53°39'00" 128°50'00" E shore of Devastation Channel, S of Kitimat). Lt Col William Patrick Anderson (1851–1927) was chief engineer of Canada's Dept of Marine and Fisheries and gen superintendent of lighthouses from 1880 until the early 20th century. During his tenure, over 500 lighthouses were built and thousands of aids to navigation installed. He made numerous tours of inspection on the BC coast, and in 1898 was aboard CGS *Quadra* in Devastation Channel when the vessel's master, Capt John T Walbran, named this feature. A powerful, influential administrator with many accomplishments to his name, Anderson is nevertheless pilloried in Donald Graham's two-volume history of BC lighthouses as a heartless bureaucrat, intent on imposing low pay and poor working conditions on station staff while cultivating a reputation as a genius of lighthouse construction. The Haisla First Nation name for Anderson Point is Hukwalinuxw. *W*

Anderson Rock (53°35'00" 130°34'00" In Rawlinson Anchorage, W of Banks I). Robert Anderson (1824–83) was born at Edinburgh and immigrated to Victoria in 1853, where he worked for many years as a building contractor. He established Lochend Farm, well known in its time, at the head of the Gorge. Formerly known as Brown Rk but renamed in 1926.

Andrew Point (52°35'00" 131°22'00" NE point of Ramsay I, Juan Perez Sd, E side of Moresby I, QCI). After 19th-century Scottish geologist Sir Andrew Ramsay, director gen of the British Geological Survey. *See* Ramsay I.

Andys Bay (49°29'00" 123°27'00" W side of Gambier I, Howe Sd, NW of Vancouver). Capt Rasmus Andreas "Andy" Johnson (1871–1953) arrived on the BC coast in 1895 and lived at Vancouver. He eventually, after serving as mate, skipper and part owner, became sole owner of the tug *St Clair*, with which he towed logs from coastal camps to mills in the Vancouver area. The McLeod Timber and Logging Co ran a railroad logging show on Gambier, 1918–24, and other logging companies also operated in the area. In the 1950s a large-scale log-sorting operation took place in this bay.

Annacis Channel (49°11'00" 122°57'00" Lower Fraser R, between Annacis I and Lulu I), **Annacis Island** (49°10'00" 122°57'00" E of Lulu I). Francis Noel Annance, born in 1789 at St Francis, Que, was a fur trader of mixed Abenaki descent who joined the NWC in 1818 and worked as a trapper in the Columbia district. When the company merged with the HBC, he stayed on as a clerk and interpreter. In 1824 the literate, multilingual Annance accompanied James McMillan on a survey of the lower Fraser R, and in 1827, aboard *Cadboro*, he helped McMillan establish Ft Langley. Annance worked at Ft Simpson on the Mackenzie R, 1833–34, and then, frustrated at the HBC's refusal to promote mixed-race employees (and in trouble over an affair he'd had with the wife of his superior, John Stuart), left the company and moved back to Que, where he farmed, taught school and lived until at least the late 1860s. An early map correctly identifies the island as Annance's I, but a cartographic error crept into the 1858 Admiralty chart of the area and the name was misspelled Annacis. It was also known in the 1860s as Murphy I or Innish Murphy after Patrick O'Brian Murphy, a squatter. For most of its life, Annacis has actually been two islands; the NE part was once separate—known, after its owner, as Robson I. John Robson (1824–92) pre-empted this piece of land in 1861, the same year he founded the *British Columbian*, the oldest newspaper on the BC mainland. He went on to become the province's premier, 1889–92. Several other places are named for him, including the community of Robson near Castlegar. When Annacis was developed as an industrial park in 1954, the channel between the two islands was filled in. The name Robson I was officially cancelled in 1957. *E*

Annesley Point (53°01'42" 132°29'54" S entrance to Kitgoro Inlet, NW side of Moresby I, QCI). After Annesley Denham, a midshipman aboard HMS *Thetis*, on the Pacific Station, 1851–53. *See* Denham Point.

Annette Inlet (48°50'00" 123°23'00" W side of Prevost I, E of Saltspring I, Gulf Is), **Annette Island** (52°09'00" 131°04'00" Between Kunghit I and Moresby I in Houston Stewart Channel, QCI), **Annette Point** (48°50'00" 123°24'00" W side of Prevost I). Annette Prevost was a daughter of Capt James Prevost, an RN officer based on the Pacific Station, 1850–54 and 1857–60. As British boundary commissioner, Prevost played an important if unsuccessful role in settling the San Juan Is boundary dispute (also known as the Pig War) between BC and the US. He enjoyed a significant career in the RN and rose in rank to adm (*see* Prevost I). Prevost himself named Annette I in 1853. The inlet was originally called Annette Ck ("creek" being an old hydrographic term for a narrow, drying inlet) in 1859 by Capt George Richards. Its Hul'qumi'num' (Coast Salish) name is Hwtl'uquyxum, meaning "whirlpool place." The hydrographic service named the point in 1946.

Annie Point (53°26'00" 129°51'00" S of Mink Trap Bay, W side of Pitt I). Anne Douglas Savage (1896–1971) was a Montreal-born artist and teacher who studied with William Brymner and Maurice Cullen, maintained a lengthy correspondence with A Y Jackson and had close ties with Emily Carr and other well-known Canadian artists. She was a central figure in the early Canadian modernist movement and a founding member of the Beaver Hall Hill group and the Canadian Group of Painters. She taught at Montreal's Baron Byng High School, 1922–48. In 1928, sponsored by the National Gallery, Savage, anthropologist Marius Barbeau and sculptor Florence Wyle travelled to the upper Skeena R area to record totem poles. Concordia Univ owns an important collection of her work. The name Mavis Point—referring to the wife of Robert Young, senior assistant hydrographer on the BC coast at the time—was rejected for this feature in 1944 by federal surveyor gen Frederic Peters. One of his aides wrote to BC regional hydrographer Henri Parizeau that "it is felt that too many names of your office staff and of the ship's crew have been used without reasonable discretion."

Annieville Channel (49°11'00" 122°55'00" SW Fraser R, SE side of Annacis I). The N Delta community of Annieville was supposedly named for Annie Symes, who waded ashore there in 1871 while searching, with her husband James Symes, for a good site for a salmon cannery. One of the earliest canneries on the Fraser R was subsequently built at this location on a very ancient First Nation village site. Another source claims that the Annie in question was Annie Laidlaw (later Annie Behrill or Birrell), wife of one of the cannery's early owners. Also known as Gunderson Slough. *E*

Annis Point (52°01'00" 130°59'00" E side of Kunghit I off S end of Moresby I, QCI). John Annis was a boatswain on Capt John Kendrick's first fur-trading voyage to the BC coast aboard the *Columbia Rediviva* in 1788. In 1789, while trading near Anthony I at the S end of the QCI, Kendrick seized and humiliated Chief Koya, head of the Kunghit Haida, over a pilfering dispute, causing a vengeful Koya to attack other trading vessels and turn the region into a war zone (*see* Koya Bay). Named by the hydrographic service in 1948.

Anthony Island (52°05'44" 131°13'12" W of Kunghit I, S of Moresby I, QCI). Venerable Anthony Denny, the archdeacon of an Irish diocese who knew nothing of BC, had his name attached to this important Haida site because his son, Edward Denny, happened to be a midshipman aboard HMS *Virago* on an 1853 survey of the region (*see* Denny Rocks). Known as SGang Gwaay (Skung'wai), or Red Cod I, to the Haida people, it is a UNESCO World Heritage Site and home to the last best Haida memorial and mortuary poles still at their original location. This was where Capt John Kendrick's assault on

Naming Rocks the Hard Way

Having a coastal feature named for you is normally a great honour. Having a rock or reef named for you, however, can be somewhat of a disgrace. According to nautical tradition, if you manage to wreck your boat on an uncharted rock, that rock is named for you—or, more commonly, for your vessel. But this really only happens if your boat is quite large or if you are important enough for notoriety to ensue. Usually the rock or reef in question has already been named for some unfortunate earlier wreckee.

The BC coast is littered with rocks that commemorate marine mishaps and enshrine the shame of certain skippers. At the entrance to Mantrap Inlet in Fitz Hugh Sound is Barracuda Rock, where the survey launch *Barracuda* came to grief. The British merchant steamer *Benmohr* "grazed" Ben Mohr Rock in Trincomali Channel west of Galiano Island, and the *Wellington* did the same to Wellington Rock in Seaforth Channel. The venerable Union steamship *Cutch*, originally built as a pleasure craft for an Indian maharaja, had the dubious honour in 1899 of christening Cutch Rock in Metlakatla Bay near Prince Rupert. The steamship *Danube* crashed into Danube Rock in Skidegate Inlet, and later, renamed the *Salvor*, became a specialist in salvaging wrecks on reefs. The list goes on and on.

Most ships with rocks named for them survive their fraught encounters. They are refloated by rising tides or pulled off by tugs and taken to drydock for repair. Many go on to give long and eventful service. The 40-metre patrol boat *Armentières*, for instance, spent much of its life on the BC coast. In 1925 it struck unreported Armentières Rock in Pipestem Inlet and sank, but was raised, towed to Victoria and refitted. Forty years later it was still at work, though under a different name.

Other reef-bound vessels are less fortunate and suffer tremendous damage. Consider the USS *Suwanee*, an iron sidewheeler that had been built during the US Civil War for river use, with a shallow draft and front-and-rear rudders. On its way to Alaska in 1868, the warship became firmly grounded on an unmarked rock (known today, of course, as Suwanee Rock) in Shadwell Passage off the north end of Vancouver Island. As the tide dropped, the ship broke in half and was utterly destroyed. The crew survived, and salvage operations retrieved the guns, ammunition and machinery. The wreck has been a popular dive site for years, and artifacts from the *Suwanee* adorn the homes and gardens of several recreational divers.

If you're a ship captain, a far easier method of attaching your name to a dangerous rock or reef is to discover the threat *without* getting wrecked and then report it to the Coast Guard. Thus we have Marchant Rock in Hecate Strait, spotted in 1869 by master George Marchant while he was ashore enjoying breakfast on dry land. Hewitt Rock in Finlayson Channel and McCulloch Rock in Dixon Entrance received their names after captains James Hewitt and William McCulloch, respectively, located these menaces and described them to naval officials.

It is possible, should you end up on some reef, to avoid having your name, or your vessel's name, printed on the charts for fellow mariners to chuckle over until the end of time. Just blame the person who sent you on your journey! The success of this strategy can be seen in the name of a rock in Trincomali Channel. HMS *Plumper* was anchored at Nanaimo in 1859 when its master, Captain George Richards, received an urgent order from Governor James Douglas to return to Victoria. En route, at full speed, the *Plumper* hit a rock where there weren't supposed to be any. Damage was negligible, fortunately. Richards and his officers felt that it was Douglas who had ordered the voyage, and Douglas, not them, who should forever be associated with the site of the accident. They named the hazard Governor Rock.

The steamship *Danube* at Port Essington, circa 1898. *BC Archives D-01382*

The poles at SG̲ang Gwaay on Anthony Island. *Author's collection*

Chief Koya had such disastrous consequences (*see* Koya Bay). The name of Chief Ninstints (Nan Stins, "he who is two"), prominent here in the mid-1800s, is also strongly associated with the area.

Anthony Point (52°10'00" 127°58'00" N end of Denny I, E of Bella Bella). Lt Cdr D'Arcy Anthony Denny was in command of the RN gunboat *Forward* on the BC coast, 1866–68. *See* Denny I *and* Forward Bay.

Anthracite Point (53°12'00" 132°14'00" Between Long Inlet and Kagan Bay at W side of Skidegate Inlet, QCI). This feature was formerly known as South Point but was renamed by the hydrographic service in 1945. Coal was found in the area in 1859, and some work was done at the Cowgitz Mine, 1865–72. The coal was found to be of poor quality and insufficient quantity, however, and the operation was later abandoned.

Antiquary Bay (52°55'20" 132°20'30" S of Englefield Bay, NW Moresby I, QCI). Sir Henry Charles Englefield, a scientific writer and antique collector, was a "much esteemed" friend of Capt George Vancouver. *See* Englefield Bay.

Antle Islands (53°29'00" 130°27'00" In Kingkown Inlet, W side of Banks I). Rev John Antle (1865–1949) was born and raised in Nfld, where he worked in remote communities as a teacher and Anglican missionary. He moved to Washington state in 1897 and to Vancouver two years later. In 1904, after exploring the coast in the *Laverock*, a tiny boat, he established the Columbia Coast Mission. Under Antle's supervision, the mission constructed numerous vessels (mostly named *Columbia*), churches and hospitals, and ministered to the pastoral and medical needs of those living in the remote First Nation villages, logging camps and other settlements on the southern BC coast. After retirement in 1936, Antle lived aboard his yacht *Reverie* and, at the age of 73, sailed it across the Atlantic. *E*

Antonio Point (50°14'00" 125°09'00" S point of Maurelle I, NE of Quadra I, N of Str of Georgia). After Spanish naval officer Francisco Antonio Maurelle, who explored the BC coast in 1775 and 1779. *See* Maurelle I.

Anvil Island (49°32'00" 123°18'00" NE of Gambier I in Howe Sd, NW of Vancouver). Named for its shape by Capt George Vancouver in 1792. He was able to observe a latitude in this vicinity and later noted that "Passage and Anvil islands in one" provided an ideal line for staying safely W of the mud flats at the mouth of the Fraser R. He also named Anvil's highest point Leading Peak because, in line with Passage I, it was "a most excellent leading mark." The S end of Anvil I was first settled in 1874 and still has a summer community. The area was found to have valuable clay deposits; a brick factory operated there, 1897–1917, and a post office, 1896–1950.

The *Prince Rupert* at the Anyox waterfront. *Author's collection*

Anyox Rock (55°24'00" 129°47'00" SE of Granby Point, Observatory Inlet). The town of Anyox on Granby Bay was the site of a smelter and one of the largest and most productive copper mines in N America, established in 1912 by the Granby Consolidated Mining, Smelting and Power Co. Abandoned in 1942 after a major fire, Anyox had a population of 2,700 at its peak. The name is a derivation of a Tsimshian First Nation name for Granby Bay and may mean "place of hiding." *E*

Apodaca Cove (49°21'00" 123°20'00" E side of Bowen I, Howe Sd, NW of Vancouver). Named in 1954 to keep alive a reference to the survey work of Spanish navigator José Narváez, who explored this area in 1791 in the *Santa Saturnina*. Narváez gave the name Islas de Apodaca to Bowen I and Keats I, in honour of Sebastián Ruiz de Apodaca (1747–1818), a notable Spanish adm. Apodaca began his career at Cadiz with the coast guard in 1760 and served throughout the Spanish empire. In 1796 he was sent to the W Indies to defend the island of Trinidad but was blockaded by a much larger British fleet and forced to destroy his vessels, an action for which he was first demoted and imprisoned, then exonerated and reinstated. In 1814 he was appointed lt gen, the highest Spanish rank at the time.

A

Appleby Island (53°36'00" 130°33'00" In Griffith Hbr, NW end of Banks I). Named by the hydrographic service in 1926 after W Appleby, a seaman on the survey vessel *Lillooet* in the early 1920s.

Arachne Reef (48°41'00" 123°18'00" Off S side of Moresby I, Prevost Passage, Gulf Is). In Greek legend, Arachne, a skilful weaver, unwisely challenged the goddess Athena to a weaving contest. For such presumption, Athena destroyed the mortal's work and loom, after which Arachne hung herself in despair. The goddess then resurrected Arachne as a spider. Arachnids (from *arakhne*, the Greek word for spider) are a class of invertebrates including spiders, scorpions, mites and ticks. The name appears on an Admiralty chart published in 1861.

Arakun Islands (49°11'00" 125°53'00" S end of Lemmens Inlet, Meares I, Clayoquot Sd, W side of Vancouver I). The word "raccoon" is derived from the Virginia Algonquian First Nation word for this animal—*arakun* or *aroughcun*—which means "he scratches with his hands." These geographic features were formerly known as the Raccoon Is, but were changed by the hydrographic service in 1947 to avoid duplication.

Aranzazu Banks (52°52'00" 129°40'00" S of Estevan Group at entrance to Caamaño Sd), **Aranzazu Point** (54°37'18" 131°05'33" NW end of Zayas I, NW of Prince Rupert). The Spanish corvette *Nuestra Señora de Aránzazu* (named for a Spanish shrine), built at Cavite in the Philippines, made several trips to the BC coast in the late 18th century, mostly as a storeship. In 1789 it came to Nootka Sd under José de Canizares, then returned the following year. In 1792, under Lt Cdr Jacinto Caamaño, it was part of Juan Francisco de la Bodega y Quadra's 1792 Nootka expedition. Bodega met Capt George Vancouver there in an attempt to settle the details of the Nootka Sd Convention, which eventually ended Spanish control of the PNW coast. He also sent Caamaño and the *Aránzazu* to survey the coastline N and S of Dixon Entrance, where they laid to rest the myth that a navigable sea passage (the fictitious Str of Fonte) crossed N America at that latitude. The *Aránzazu*, under José Tobar y Tamariz, made two more trips to Nootka Sd in 1794, carrying supplies. Aranzazu Point was named by Capt Frederick Learmonth of HMS *Egeria* while re-surveying Zayas I in 1908.

Arbutus Bay (49°20'00" 123°22'00" S side of Bowen I, W of Cowan Point, Howe Sd, NW of Vancouver). A number of BC coastal features draw their names from the distinctive arbutus tree, *Arbutus menziesii*, with its peeling red-brown bark, white flowers and red berries. This name was bestowed by lawyer George Cowan and his wife in 1907 after the grove of trees beside their Bowen I home. It was formerly known as Wilson Bay after early Bowen summer holidayers Dr David Wilson and his wife.

Archer Islets (52°31'20" 129°01'45" Off SW side of Aristazabal I). Sapper Samuel Archer came to BC with the Columbia detachment of Royal Engineers, which served there from 1858 to 1863. He stayed on, working as a miner at Lightning Ck (1876–77), Granite Ck (1893) and Lytton (1900–1907), and as a shoemaker in New Westminster about 1908–9. He received a Crown grant for land in New Westminster land district in 1893. Archer attended a reunion held at New Westminster in 1909 to honour the 12 members of the Columbia detachment who still remained in BC.

Archer Point (52°58'00" 132°16'00" S side of Hibben I, W of Moresby I, QCI). Archibald Leslie Archer, MD, was assistant surgeon aboard HMS *Thetis*, based at Esquimalt 1851–53. In 1852 the *Thetis* surveyed this part of the QCI and preserved order during the short-lived QCI gold frenzy; the ship's master, George Moore, is believed to have named this feature. Archer served on HMS *Nile*, 1854–56, during the war with Russia. He was eventually promoted to staff surgeon and retired to Devonport, England. Nearby Leslie Point also commemorates him.

Archibald Point (52°08'00" 128°08'00" W side of Denny I, SE of Bella Bella). After HBC fur trader Archibald Napier, in charge of the Bella Bella post, 1867–71. *See* Napier Point.

Archie Rock (53°37'00" 130°35'00" Off NW end of Banks I). Probably named for Lt Archibald Bell, who served aboard HMS *Egeria* while it was on survey duty in this region, 1908–10. It was previously known as Archibald I and Archie It but was renamed by the hydrographic service in 1954.

Arden Islet (48°20'00" 123°36'00" N side of Becher Bay at S tip of Vancouver I). William Arden (1837–1935) and his wife Hannah (1850–1926) came to Ont from England in the late 1860s and bought property in the Metchosin area about 1890. They were pioneer homesteaders, and their land was known as Alvany Farm. One of their 10 children, Eustace T Arden (1882–1962), became the keeper at nearby Sheringham Point lighthouse from the time the station opened in 1912 until 1946. Before that he drove the mail stage to Sooke. Eustace married Ann Sanderson (1882–1967) at Victoria in 1909. Formerly known as White I.

Ardmillan Bay (52°11'00" 128°07'00" NE side of Campbell I, at Bella Bella). Named about 1867 by RN surveyor Lt Daniel Pender after James Crawford, Lord Ardmillan (1805–76), a celebrated justice. He was appointed sheriff of Perthshire in 1849 and solicitor gen for Scotland in 1853. *W*

Argonaut Point (49°43'00" 126°29'00" SW entrance to Hisnit Inlet, NW side of Tlupana Inlet, Nootka Sd, W side of Vancouver I). The *Argonaut*, a British trading vessel under the command of James Colnett (*see* Colnett Point), arrived at Nootka Sd in the spring of 1789. After quarrelling with Estéban José Martínez, the Spanish commander established in the area, Colnett was arrested and sent to Mexico, and his ships were impounded—acts that helped bring Spain and England to the brink of war. He won his release in July 1790 and sailed the *Argonaut* back to the W coast of Vancouver I for continued trading until Feb 1791, then went on to the Hawaiian Is and China. Colnett later served in both the merchant marine and the RN before retiring in 1805. Named by the hydrographic service in 1934. *W*

Argyh Cove (52°54'00" 129°02'00" S side of Surf Inlet, W side of Princess Royal I). Named in 1926 after Albert Argyh, who was born at New Westminster in 1863 and is believed to have taken part in the Victoria old-timers' reunion of 1924 (*see* Adams Bay).

Argyle Islet (48°19'00" 123°36'00" E side of Becher Bay, S end of Vancouver I). Thomas Argyle (1840–1919), born at Birmingham, England, joined the Royal Engineers and came to BC with the Columbia detachment, which served in the province 1858–63. He was the company armourer and had the rank of sapper (or private). When the detachment left, he stayed on, married Mary Ellen Tufts (1837–1923) from Halifax in 1863, received a grant of land at Rocky Point in Metchosin and raised a large family. Argyle served as lighthouse keeper at Race Rks, 1867–88. In 1874 he rescued two men clinging to logs; they turned out to be RN deserters, however, and he was fined $100 for "aiding and abetting" criminals. He was noted for his swimming and diving prowess in the dangerous currents that swirled around the lighthouse—activity he engaged in partly to collect seafood and partly to retrieve objects from the many wrecks in the area. He appears to have been lucky in his treasure hunting; an 1885 newspaper story reported that for many years he paid for provisions in Victoria with a seemingly endless supply of mysterious gold sovereigns. After retiring from the lighthouse station, he and his wife owned and operated the Willows Hotel on Cadboro Bay Rd. He built a home in the area, which still stands on the Lansdowne campus of Camosun College. Argyle attended a reunion held at New Westminster to honour the 12 members of the Columbia detachment remaining in BC in 1909. In 2001 his great-grandson, Barry Fisher, president of the Vancouver I Brewery, introduced a new brand, Thomas Argyle's Best British Ale, in the pioneer's honour. Argyle It was formerly known as the Surf Its, then as the Argyle Its.

Arichika Island (52°28'00" 131°20'00" NE of Huxley I, off SE side of Moresby I, QCI), **Arichika Shoal** (52°28'00" 131°21'00" Just NW of Arichika I). Arichika Ikeda owned the Ikeda Bay Mines in the QCI. *See* Ikeda Cove.

Ariel Rock (52°48'00" 132°03'00" NE of Shearer Point, Tasu Sd, Moresby I, QCI). Two different sealing schooners named *Ariel* operated from the W coast in the 1880s. The earlier one, which sailed out of San Francisco, distinguished itself by catching 131 fur seals in a single day in 1881. The second *Ariel* was brought out from Halifax in 1888 by Capt John McLeod for its new owner, Samuel Bucknam of Victoria, former master of the *Sardonyx*. It was boarded and seized off Copper I in 1892 by Russian authorities and taken to Petropavlovsk. According to QCI historian Kathleen Dalzell, James Prevost—son of Capt James Prevost of the RN, who served on the BC coast in the 1850s—also owned the *Ariel* at one time.

Aristazabal Island (52°38'00" 129°05'00" SW of Princess Royal I). Named by Lt Cdr Jacinto Caamaño, on his 1792 exploration of the N BC coast with the *Aránzazu*, for Gabriel de Aristazábal (1743–1805), a celebrated Spanish adm he had served under. Aristazábal was born at Madrid and entered the navy in 1760, serving on both the Atlantic and the Pacific, but especially in the Philippines, where he commanded a Spanish naval base in the 1770s. He gained distinction as a frigate capt in the early 1780s in the American Revolutionary War and was promoted to executive rank about 1882 and to lt gen (equivalent to vice adm) in 1791. In 1795, as cdr of Spain's large W Indies fleet, he oversaw the handover of Santo Domingo to France in the Peace of Basel and the removal of Christopher Columbus's remains to Havana. After further campaigns in New Spain, Aristazábal returned home in 1800 and was appointed capt gen of Cadiz in 1802. The name of the island is pronounced *a-REES-ta-bal* by local mariners. Capt George Vancouver misspelled it "Aristizable" on his chart. At 425 sq km, it is BC's 10th-largest island, a remote wilderness area and a traditional hunting and fishing territory of the Kitasoo First Nation, which is based today at Klemtu.

Armentières Channel (53°07'00" 132°24'00" Between Moresby I and Chaatl I, QCI), **Armentières Rock** (49°01'00" 125°18'00" N of Bazett I in Pipestem Inlet, SW of Port Alberni, W side of Vancouver I). HMCS *Armentières*, a 40-m *Battle*-class trawler (357 tonnes, top speed 10 knots), was built by Canadian Vickers Ltd in Montreal and launched in 1917 as a patrol boat and minesweeper. The ship spent much of its life on the BC coast and was stationed at Bamfield in winter to assist vessels in distress. In 1925, under Lt Colin Donald, it struck this previously uncharted rock in Pipestem Inlet and sank, but was refloated, towed to Victoria and repaired. In 1935, now under the command of Lt Cdr Harry Soulsby, the *Armentières* anchored in this channel (formerly known as Canoe Pass) while assisting CGS *William J Stewart* with QCI survey operations. The trawler also served as a training ship, a fisheries patrol boat and, during WWII, an examination vessel at Prince Rupert. After the war it was renamed *Polaris* and renovated at Everett as a timber

HMCS *Armentières*, a *Battle*-class trawler. *BC Archives A-00213*

Arnet Island was named after Jacob and Johanna Arnet, shown here in 1938 at their home in Tofino. *Courtesy Dorothy Arnet*

survey vessel for use in Alaska (under Capt Walter Davis). Subsequent owners included Coastal Towing (1949, renamed *A G Garrish*), Arctic Shipping (1958, renamed *Arctic Rover*), Vancouver Tug Boat (renamed *La Force*) and Seaspan International. Armentières, site of several WWI battles, is a French town near the Belgian border.

Armstrong Point (48°40'00" 123°24'00" SE point of Tsehum Hbr, NE side of Saanich Peninsula, N of Victoria). Named in 1934 after Wilson Joseph Armstrong (1828–1917), who was born in Que and moved W to California in the 1850s in search of gold. His wife Letitia (1830–1905, née Breaky) and their children followed at a later date. Armstrong was a wheelwright by trade and worked in San Francisco and, later, Victoria as a carriage maker. In 1875 he purchased land in N Saanich from Donald McDonald and developed a farm named the Maples. He also constructed many of the area's early farm wagons and helped build the first Methodist church in the region. His son William Robert Armstrong, a farmer as well, was appointed justice of the peace for the area and served as reeve of the municipality of N Saanich in 1910. The Armstrong family lived on the N Saanich Peninsula for many years.

Armstrong Rock (51°16'00" 127°49'00" W of Table I at entrance to Smith Sd, NW of Port Hardy). George Thomas Armstrong pre-empted the S half of nearby Table I in 1914 and received a Crown grant to his property in 1919. Formerly known as Bare Rk but renamed by the hydrographic service in 1948.

Arnet Island (49°09'00" 125°54'00" N of Tofino, Clayoquot Sd, W side of Vancouver I). Jacob Hendrick Arnet (1869–1941) pre-empted 80 ha at Tofino in 1893 and carved out a homestead. He married Johanna Johnson (1867–1942) in 1896 and worked as the watchman for the sawmill at Mosquito Hbr in the early 1900s. Arnet was coxswain on the local lifeboat and served as Tofino's first mayor, 1932–35. Arnet I was also known as Tibb's I, Castle I and Dream I after the unusual residence built there by one-time owner Frederick Gerald Tibbs, who died in 1921. Tibbs left the trunk of an isolated 30-m tree standing on his heavily logged property, which he named Dreamisle, then built a ladder up it and a viewing platform on the very top, where he would sometimes sit and play the cornet. In his will he bequeathed the island to Jacob Arnet's daughter Alma (later Alma Sloman). There are numerous descendants of Jacob and his three brothers in BC.

Arnold Point (52°06'00" 131°08'00" W side of Kunghit I, off SW end of Moresby I, QCI). Nathan Arnold was bosun's mate on the first fur-trading voyage of the *Columbia Rediviva*, under Capt John Kendrick (and later Capt Robert Gray), to the BC coast in 1788. Arnold joined the *Columbia* in Boston in 1787 and remained on it for three years. He and bosun John Annis (*see* Annis Point) were each paid two pounds five shillings per month. Named by the hydrographic service in 1948.

Arrandale (54°58'40" 130°00'30" S entrance to Nass Bay, NE of Portland Inlet, N of Prince Rupert). This salmon cannery was built by John Wallace in 1905 with machinery moved from Pacific Northern Cannery on Observatory Inlet. He named it after his Isle of Arran birthplace, sold it in 1911 to the Anglo-BC Packing Co and moved on to build Butedale cannery (qv), also named after his Scottish homeland. The federal fisheries and immigration office was located at Arrandale, also the BC Provincial Police station and a post office (1903–54, originally called Port Nelson). The cannery operated until 1942. Then the site served as a gillnet camp until the late 1950s, when it was abandoned. Only pilings remained in the early 2000s.

Leaving Arrandale dock, about 1910. *Author's collection*

Arran Point (50°25'00" 125°08'00" N end of Stuart I, W entrance to Bute Inlet), **Arran Rapids** (Between N end of Stuart I and the mainland). The rapids were named by Admiralty surveyors about 1862 because of their proximity to Bute Inlet (qv). Bute and Arran are the two main islands in Scotland's Firth of Clyde; until 1975, when the region was reorganized for administrative purposes, they formed the local county of Buteshire. The point was named in 1955 in association with the rapids, which can produce currents of 9 knots (17 km/h) at large tides. Dionisio Alcalá-Galiano and Cayetano Valdés were the first Europeans to pass this way, in 1792.

Arriaga Islands (52°31'00" 129°05'00" W of Weeteeam Bay, Aristazabal I). Juan Pantoja y Arriaga was 1st pilot to Spanish naval officer Lt Cdr Jacinto Caamaño, who named and charted Aristazabal I in 1792. Caamaño had helped establish the Spanish settlement in Nootka Sd in 1790 and returned to the BC coast as part of Juan Francisco de la Bodega y Quadra's 1792 expedition to Nootka. *See* Pantoja Is for a more detailed biography.

Arrow Passage (50°43'00" 126°39'00" Between Bonwick I and Mars I, SE of Broughton I, E Queen Charlotte Str). The British trading schooner *Arrow* operated on the BC coast in 1862. Named by Lt Daniel Pender aboard the *Beaver* about 1867.

Arthur Island (54°04'00" 130°36'00" NW of Porcher I, S of Prince Rupert), **Arthur Passage** (54°02'00" 130°15'00" E of Porcher I). Named in the late 1860s by Lt Daniel Pender after Sir Arthur Edward Kennedy, third gov of the colony of Vancouver I, 1864–66. *See* Kennedy R.

Artillery Islets (50°26'00" 125°59'00" S of Yorke I, Johnstone Str). Named in 1951 by the hydrographic service in association with the WWII fortifications on nearby Yorke I (qv).

Ascroft Islet (53°18'00" 129°25'00" Between Farrant I and SE end of Pitt I). James Ascroft was chief engineer on the Canadian government survey vessel *Lillooet* and, later,

from 1932 to 1945, on CGS *William J Stewart*. Named by the hydrographic service in 1944.

Ashby Point (50°56'00" 127°55'00" N side of Hope I, off NE Vancouver I). James William Murray Ashby was a naval paymaster who rose to the rank of paymaster in chief in 1878. He was secretary to Vice Adm Sir James Hope, cdr-in-chief of the RN's N America and W Indies stations, 1864–67. Ashby, who assisted a number of senior RN officers, was made a CB in 1867 and knighted in 1902. The point was named by Capt George Richards, the RN's chief hydrographer, in 1864. Nearby Secretary Point is also named for Ashby.

Ashdown Island (53°04'00" 129°13'00" S of Gil I, W of Princess Royal I). Civil engineer and land surveyor Ashdown Henry Green (1840–1927) was born at London, England, and immigrated to Victoria in 1862, where he was appointed city surveyor. He worked all over BC: in the Selkirk Mtns in 1865 as part of the Columbia R Exploring Party, for the CPR in the early 1870s, on Saltspring I in 1874. In 1880 he joined the federal Indian dept as a surveyor. Green bought a farm in the Cowichan Valley, near Somenos Lk, in 1865. The first Cowichan Indian Agricultural Exhibition was held on his land, and in 1874 he was elected to the N Cowichan council. A keen naturalist and former president of the Victoria Natural History Society, he was the designer of a well-known fishing fly, the Ashdown Green, and discovered nine fish new to science; two—*Couesius plumbeus greeni* (a subspecies of lake chub) and *Liparis greeni* (the lobefin snailfish)—are named after him. Green's 1893 residence on the Cowichan R, named Kilninta, was a much-modified part of the Silver Bridge Inn at Duncan in the early 2000s and home to the Anglers Tavern. Ashdown I was formerly known as Passage I but was renamed by regional hydrographer Henri Parizeau in 1926.

Ashe Head (48°26'00" 123°26'00" E side of Esquimalt Hbr, S Vancouver I). Named in 1847 after Lt Edward David Ashe (d 1895), who served in BC waters aboard HMS *Fisgard*, under Capt John Duntze, and was based on the Pacific Station, 1844–47. He retired in 1866 with the rank of cdr. The area around Ashe Head, known to the Songhees people as Eyellnuk, meaning "clear" or "open field," is now a Songhees First Nation reserve. *W*

Ashlar Cove (50°16'00" 125°21'00" NW side of Quadra I, N end of Str of Georgia). Ashlar is dressed stone, square or rectangular in shape and evenly faced, used in masonry. Ashlar blocks usually have a rough finish and in the past were frequently used for walls and the exteriors of buildings. Today ashlar is more commonly used as a facing. Rock formations in this area have broken up in rectangular patterns reminiscent of ashlar and were often used as building materials. The name was adopted, along with nearby Ashlar Lk and Ashlar Ck, in 1975.

A

Ashworth Point (49°58'00" 124°55'00" S end of Hernando I, N Str of Georgia). Newspaperman and real-estate promoter George Johnston Ashworth (1863–1937) was a long-time resident of Savary I. He was born at Newmarket, Ont, and served as an officer with the Queen's York Rangers during the 1885 Riel Rebellion. After moving to Vancouver in 1909, he became a crime reporter for the Vancouver *Province* and visited Savary I in 1910 to write an article about a notorious murder that had been committed there in 1893. Excited about the island's potential as a summer vacation spot, he formed a business partnership that purchased, subdivided and developed much of Savary and promoted it widely as the "Catalina of the North." In 1928 he opened the Royal Savary Hotel on the island and operated it until he died. Ashworth Point was formerly known as Boulder Point.

Askew Islands (53°35'00" 130°33'00" In Millar Bay, off NW Banks I). S H Askew, after returning from active service in Europe in WWI, was assistant steward on board Canadian government survey vessel *Lillooet* in 1921.

Asman Point (50°24'00" 125°09'00" NW side of Stuart I in entrance to Bute Inlet). Frank N Asman pre-empted land in this area in 1911 and received a Crown grant in 1920. The feature was formerly known as Steep Point. Nearby Big Bay was originally called Asman Bay, but the name was changed in 1962 to reflect established local usage.

Assits Island (48°56'00" 125°02'00" NE side of Trevor Channel at entrance to Alberni Inlet, W side of Vancouver I). *Assits* is the Nuu-chah-nulth First Nation word for wasp, as listed in Gilbert Sproat's *Scenes and Studies of Savage Life* (1868), which included a Nuu-chah-nulth vocabulary. Formerly known as Turn I and Assists I.

Aster Bay (50°12'00" 127°49'00" NE side of Brooks Peninsula, NW Vancouver I). Douglas's aster (*Aster subspicatus*) grows on the beach here, as it does widely along the coast of BC. The name was submitted in 1984 by the provincial museum's 1981 Brooks Peninsula Expedition.

Astrolabe Rock (54°11'00" 133°00'00" S side of Parry Passage, NW end of Graham I, QCI). The *Astrolabe*, a 41-m, 500-tonne frigate (formerly the storeship *Autruche*) commanded by Capt Paul-Antoine-Marie Fleuriot de Langle, was dispatched on a round-the-world scientific journey by France in 1785. The expedition was led by Capt Jean-François de Galaup, Comte de Lapérouse, aboard the *Boussole*. After seeking the NW Passage off Alaska in July 1786, the vessels passed down the BC coast, sighting Haida Gwaii and naming several features en route. De Langle and 11 of his men were killed at Tutuila in Samoa in 1787 during a fight with native inhabitants. After leaving Australia in 1788, both ships ran aground on Vanikoro I in Vanuatu (or

the New Hebrides). The loss, however, was not confirmed until 1827, when wreckage and artifacts were discovered; the fate of the crews was never determined. An astrolabe is an instrument that was once used to make astronomical observations as an aid to marine navigation. The rock was named by Admiralty surveyors in the early 1900s.

Atchison Island (50°35'00" 126°13'00" N of entrance to Call Inlet, E side of Broughton Archipelago, E of Port McNeill). Named in 1860 by RN surveyor Capt George Richards after James Atchison, MD (1803–62), from County Tyrone, Ireland. He was the surgeon aboard HMS *Havannah*, under Capt Thomas Harvey, on the Pacific Station, 1855–59.

Athabaskan Island (52°03'00" 128°18'00" W side of Tide Rip Passage, SW of Bella Bella). HMCS *Athabaskan* was a *Tribal*-class destroyer (115 m, 2270 tonnes, top speed 36 knots), built in Britain and launched in 1943. In Apr 1944 it encountered four German *E*-class destroyers while patrolling the western approaches to the English Channel with a sister vessel, HMCS *Haida*. After an hour-long engagement, the *Athabaskan* was struck by a torpedo and sank, with the loss of 111 men including its capt, Lt Cdr John Stubbs. Two other RCN destroyers have also borne this name: a second *Tribal*-class ship, launched in 1948 and sold in 1969, and an *Iroquois*-class vessel, launched in 1972. The island was named by regional hydrographer Henri Parizeau in 1944.

Athlone Island (52°11'00" 128°26'00" One of the Bardswell Group, S side of Seaforth Channel, W of Bella Bella). The 1st Earl of Athlone, Sir Alexander Augustus Frederick William Alfred George Cambridge (1874–1957), was sworn in as Canada's 16th gov gen in 1940 and served until 1946. A British Army officer who attained the rank of maj gen, he was the uncle of King George VI and a former gov gen of S Africa (1924–31). Athlone hosted the Quebec Conferences of 1943–44, which mapped out Allied strategies for the duration of WWII. The island was formerly known as Smyth I but was renamed by the hydrographic service in 1944. Princess Alice I (qv), just S of Athlone I, is named for his wife.

Athlow Bay (53°38'00" 132°59'00" S of Port Louis, W side of Graham I, QCI). Adapted from At-loo, the ancient Haida name for nearby Port Chanal. The name was adopted in 1933.

Atkinson Island (50°53'00" 126°51'00" N side of N Broughton I, NE of Port McNeill). Thomas Hall Atkinson was assistant surgeon aboard HMS *Sutlej*, the flagship of Rear Adm Joseph Denman, who was cdr-in-chief of the RN's Pacific Station, 1864–66, and based at Esquimalt. Atkinson assisted with the surveying efforts on the BC coast by becoming the acting surgeon on the hired vessel

Beaver, under Lt Daniel Pender, in the late 1860s. Atkinson was promoted to staff surgeon in 1876 and fleet surgeon in 1884; in 1890–91 he served as fleet surgeon for the Channel squadron on HMS *Howe*, after which he retired. The nearby Surgeon Its are also named for him.

Atrevida Point (49°39'00" 126°26'00" N entrance to Muchalat Inlet, Nootka Sd, W side of Vancouver I), **Atrevida Reef** (49°55'00" 124°40'00" Near E end of Savary I, Str of Georgia). The 36-m *Atrevida* (meaning "audacious"), a Spanish naval corvette under the command of Capt José Bustamente y Guerra, was one of the two vessels in the 1791 expedition to the BC coast of Alejandro Malaspina. The ships visited Nootka Sd that Aug and made a survey of the PNW coast while on a round-the-world scientific expedition for Spain. Bustamente was later appointed gov of Paraguay in 1796, and capt-gen of Guatemala, 1810–19. The reef was named by Capt John Walbran in 1902, the point by the hydrographic service in 1935.

Auchterlonie Point (48°48'10" 123°16'22" E side of N Pender I, Gulf Is). Lawrence Auchterlonie (1839–1917) and his family emigrated from Scotland to N Pender I in the early 1880s and established a farm. Lawrence's son James (1867–1912) took over as soon as he was old enough and raised sheep, pigs and Jersey cows. Lawrence is listed as Pender I postmaster 1901–4 (at Hope Bay, named after David Hope, his brother-in-law), though it is believed that his son ran the office. James became a justice of the peace, a member of Pender I's first school board and one of the initial trustees of the Pender I cemetery, where he is buried. His youngest son, Lawrence, operated the Auchterlonie farm for many years.

Augustine Islands (50°54'00" 127°16'00" S of Bradley Lagoon in Blunden Hbr, NE of Port Hardy). After Lt John Augustine Edgell, who served in BC on the survey vessel *Egeria*, 1903–6. *See* Edgell I. Formerly known as the Bonwick Is after RN officer Charles Bonwick, engineer aboard the *Beaver* while it was hired as a survey vessel in the 1860s (*see* Bonwick I), but renamed in 1903 by Cdr John Parry.

Augustus Point (48°57'00" 123°39'00" S side of Kuper I, E of Chemainus, Gulf Is), **Augustus Rock** (53°00'00" 132°23'00" Off W side of Hibben I, NW Moresby I, QCI). Capt Augustus L Kuper surveyed the NW coast of Moresby I aboard HMS *Thetis* in 1852, and named Augustus Rk at that time. Cdr John Parry, of the survey vessel *Egeria*, named Augustus Point after Kuper in 1905. *See* Cape Kuper.

Aurelia Rock (52°21'00" 128°28'00" W entrance to Moss Passage, Milbanke Sd, NW of Bella Bella). Aurelia Yale (1837–1931) was born at or near Ft Langley, where her father, James Murray Yale, was the HBC's chief trader, 1834-60, and her mother a Fraser Valley First Nation woman. She went to school in Victoria, and in 1857, at Ft Langley, she married John Duncan Manson, son of chief trader Donald Manson, who had a long career with the HBC and was superintendent of the New Caledonia district, 1844–57. John Manson became HBC chief trader at Fort Fraser, 1858–63. The Mansons settled in Victoria in 1864 and later built a home at Saanich. The feature was formerly known as Bird Rk but was renamed by the hydrographic service in 1929.

Auseth Islet (49°11'00" 125°39'00" Tofino Inlet, E of McCaw Peninsula, Clayoquot Sd, W side of Vancouver I), **Auseth Point** (49°07'00" 125°48'00" SE point of Meares I, Clayoquot Sd). Named by the hydrographic service in 1934 after Bernt Auseth, who pre-empted land at nearby Grice Bay in 1896 and received a Crown grant in 1900.

Awaya Point (52°18'00" 131°08'00" S entrance to Ikeda Cove, SE side of Moresby I, QCI). Named for one of the principals of the Japanese fishing firm Awaya, Ikeda and Co, active in BC in the early 1900s. Arichika Ikeda, the other company owner, found copper ore near here in 1906 and established a profitable mine at Ikeda Cove.

Awun Bay (53°40'00" 132°31'00" SW side of Masset Inlet, Graham I, QCI). According to Haida leader Reynold Russ, interviewed in 1996, *awun* can be translated as "something precious over on the other side." The bay was named by Lt Cdr Philip Musgrave, the regional hydrographer, in 1910. He conducted a survey of Masset Inlet that year with CGS *Lillooet* after the Graham Steamship, Coal & Lumber Co announced plans to open a sawmill at this site. The mill was never built. Nearby Awun R and Awun Lk derive their names from the same source.

Azimuth Island (53°32'00" 129°59'00" W end of Evinrude Passage, off N side of Anger I, W side of Pitt I). A 1921 coast triangulation party under Alfred Wright, a surveyor with the BC Lands Service, applied a number of surveying-related place names to this region. Associated names, including this one, were added by the hydrographic service in the early 1950s. The concept of an azimuth—a horizontal angle measured clockwise from any fixed reference plane—has found use in navigation, astronomy and other fields, as well as in surveying. *See also* Cosine Bay, Logarithm Point, Sine I *and* Tangent I.

B

Babbage Island (52°35'00" 129°09'00" Entrance to Clifford Bay, SW side of Aristazabal I). Sapper Richard Babbage came to BC with the Columbia detachment of Royal Engineers, which served in the province 1858–63. Little seems to be known about him, unfortunately. The name was adopted in 1927, as suggested by W coast hydrographic officials.

Bacchante Bay (49°27'00" 126°02'00" NE end of Shelter Inlet, NE of Flores I, Clayoquot Sd, W side of Vancouver I). HMS *Bacchante*, a screw steam frigate of 3,746 tonnes, with 51 guns, was a frequent visitor to Esquimalt in the early 1860s, under Capt Donald Mackenzie. It was the flagship of Rear Adm Sir Thomas Maitland, cdr-in-chief of the RN's Pacific squadron, 1860–62. The 72-m vessel was launched at Portsmouth dockyard in 1859 and had a complement of 560 men.

Bacon Cove (54°20'00" 130°19'00" Tsimpsean Peninsula, N side of Prince Rupert Hbr), **Bacon Point** (54°20'00" 130°19'00" N side of Prince Rupert Hbr), **Bacon Rock** (54°13'00" 130°20'00" W side of Ridley I, SE of entrance to Prince Rupert Hbr). James H Bacon, born in the eastern US and a graduate of Harvard Univ, was the engineer responsible, in 1903–4, for choosing Kaien I as the site for the western terminus of the GTP. He later served as harbour engineer for the new town of Prince Rupert. The central downtown portion of Prince Rupert, in fact, was known as Baconville in its early days. All three of these features were named about 1907.

Baeria Rocks (48°57'00" 125°09'00" Near N end of Imperial Eagle Channel, Barkley Sd, W side of Vancouver I). These rocks were originally called the Bird Is during an 1861 Admiralty survey but were renamed by the hydrographic service in 1934 to avoid duplication with other Bird Is. Naturalist and ethnologist Charles Newcombe claimed that *Baeria coronaria* (now called *Lasthenia coronaria*), or royal goldfields—an uncommon yellow annual plant more usually found in southern California—was growing at this site.

Baile Island (52°57'00" 129°08'00" Entrance to Kiln Bay, Chapple Inlet, W side of Princess Royal I). Unity Theodora Jeffreys Baile was a junior member of the Canadian Hydrographic Service staff in Victoria in the early 1940s. A 1944 proposal to label additional geographic features with her first three names was rejected as injudicious by senior CHS staff in Ottawa, who wanted to see "not more than one feature named after any one person" and nothing named after "[survey vessel] crew members who have only been on the ship for one season."

Bailey Point (52°20'00" 128°20'00" SE side of Lady Trutch Passage, E of Milbanke Sd). Sarah Margaret Bailey (1838–1924) was born Sarah Patterson at Hobart, Tasmania. Her father, a mariner, brought his family to California in 1849 on his own vessel. Sarah married Benjamin Bailey (1827–98), from Maine, in 1855 and in 1861 moved to Yale, where her husband operated a store and hotel. In 1882 the Baileys and their children came to live in Victoria. William, their eldest son (of 15 children), established the pioneer Ashcroft merchant firm of Harvey, Bailey & Co. The point was named in 1929 on the suggestion of the hydrographic service.

Bain Point (54°02'00" 132°35'00" W side of Naden Hbr, N end of Graham I, QCI). Named for Archibald Bain (d 1890), chief engineer of the RN paddle sloop *Virago*, under Cdr James Prevost, during a survey of N Graham I in 1853. Bain accompanied the *Virago*'s master, George Inskip, in the ship's boat for an initial examination of Virago Sd and Naden Hbr. Inskip named nearby Isabella Point after Bain's wife at the same time. Bain left the RN in 1874 but remained on navy lists and reached the rank of fleet engineer, retired, in 1886.

Bajo Point (49°37'00" 126°49'00" W side of Nootka I, W side of Vancouver I), **Bajo Reef** (49°34'00" 126°49'00" S of Bajo Point). Bajo, which means "under" or "beneath" in Spanish, can also be translated as "shoal" or "sandbank." The dangerous reef here, where the British vessel *King David* was wrecked in Dec 1905, with the loss of seven lives, was noted by Capt James Cook in 1778 and first named by Alejandro Malaspina in 1791. Bajo Point was the site of an ancient Mowachaht First Nation summer camp. Sea otters, hunted to near extinction in the early 1900s, have been successfully reintroduced to the Bajo Point area. *W*

Baker Bay (49°55'00" 124°02'00" Head of Hotham Sd, N of lower Jervis Inlet, NW of Vancouver), **Baker Island** (50°45'00" 126°35'00" W side of Gilford I, NE of Port McNeill). Lt Joseph Baker (1767–1817) was with Capt George Vancouver on his historic exploration of the BC coast, starting the voyage as 3rd lt of HMS *Discovery* and ending it as 1st lt. He was responsible for drawing the principal charts made on the journey and also for keeping the ship's log. Baker had met Vancouver in 1786, when both were serving aboard HMS *Europa*. In 1799, as a cdr, Baker was in charge of HMS *Calypso*, and in 1805, by now a capt, he commanded the frigate *Castor*. His next command, in 1808, was HMS *Tartar*, which he managed to wreck in 1811 on a sandbar in the Baltic. Although he was absolved of any wrongdoing, this incident ended his active naval career. Baker ran a prison near Bristol, 1812–14, then retired. One of his sons became an RN adm, another an Indian Army gen and a knight. Baker I is definitely named for him (as are Mt Baker in Washington state and several features in Alaska); the attribution for Baker Bay, formerly known as West Bay, is less certain but still probable. *W*

Baker Point (52°48'00" 129°13'00" NE side of Aristazabal I). James Baker (1854–1929) was born at London, Ont, and migrated with his parents to Victoria in 1867. His wife, Clara (1848–1902), came to Canada from Germany in 1862. James became a well-established building contractor in the city and is believed to have taken part in the famous Victoria old-timers' reunion of 1924 (*see* Adams Bay). Formerly known as Sandspit Point but renamed by the hydrographic service in 1926.

Baker Rock (50°06'00" 127°42'00" In Checleset Bay, E side of Brooks Peninsula, NW side of Vancouver I). Capt Wentworth E Baker (b 1862), from Yarmouth, Maine, was an active participant in the early Victoria-based sealing industry. He came out from Halifax on the *Viva* in 1886 and began sealing on that vessel, then crewed on the *C H Tupper*. Later he was master of the *Pioneer*, *Allie I Alger* and *Tupper*. On this last vessel, in 1892, he was boarded by the Russian cruiser *Zabiaka* for sealing in waters claimed by Russia but was set free for lack of incriminating evidence. His record haul was 3,642 seal skins in 1889. Baker Rk was formerly known as Mile Rk.

Baker Shoal (52°31'00" 129°27'00" E of Aristazabal I, Hecate Str). 2nd Cpl John S Baker came to BC with the Columbia detachment of Royal Engineers, which served

in the province 1858–63. He arrived with the main contingent of men aboard the *Thames City* in 1859, and in 1861 was appointed chief constable at Rock Ck, where he attempted to bring order to that tumultuous boomtown during its short-lived gold rush. In 1862, tragically, Baker drowned in the Harrison R.

Balagny Passage (52°17'00" 128°22'00" Between Watch I and SW tip of Don Peninsula, Milbanke Sd). Louise L'Hôtelier, whose stage and maiden name was Louise Balagny, was a native of France and a star of the Paris Grande Opera. In 1858, with her Chilean second husband and her son Charles Lombard (born of her first marriage), she moved to Victoria for a number of years, where Mr L'Hôtelier went into business as a coffee merchant. She died at Lima, Peru, in 1873. Her son stayed in Victoria and became a well-known local resident (*see* Lombard Point).

Balaklava Island (50°50'57" 127°37'32" E of Nigei I, Goletas Channel, Queen Charlotte Str). Named by Lt Daniel Pender in Oct 1863, on the ninth anniversary of the famous Charge of the Light Brigade at the Battle of Balaklava in the Crimea. The cavalry charge, led by Lord Cardigan against a much stronger, artillery-supported Russian force, resulted in heavy British losses. Several other features in the vicinity—Cardigan Rks, Lucan Is, Nolan 'Point, Raglan Point—are also named for British Army officers associated with this military blunder. *W*

Balch Islands (53°14'00" 132°05'00" N of Maude I, Skidegate Inlet, QCI). Lafayette Balch (1825–62), a native of Maine, founded the Washington state community of Steilacoom in 1850 and established a brisk trade shipping lumber to San Francisco. In Jan 1852, with the schooner *Demaris Cove*, he rescued the crew and passengers of the schooner *Georgianna* in Skidegate Inlet. Both ships were US-based and had travelled to Haida Gwaii late in 1851 to investigate rumours of gold. The *Georgianna* was wrecked in a storm and its occupants held (whether as "guests" or prisoners depends on who is telling the story) for eight weeks by the Haida. A plea for help to the HBC at Ft Simpson produced no action, as the company viewed the QCI as its private preserve and the Americans as foreign invaders. Eventually Capt Balch, who had returned to the US and heavily armed his vessel when the *Georgianna* failed to rendezvous with him, managed to safely ransom all the detainees. The Balch Is were formerly known as the Channel Is but were renamed by the hydrographic service in 1945. *D*

Balcom Inlet (52°06'00" 131°01'00" E side of Kunghit I, S of Moresby I, QCI), **Balcom Point** (50°01'00" 127°11'00" E point of Whitely I, Kyuquot Sd, W side of Vancouver I). Members of Victoria's Balcom family were pioneers in the W coast sealing and whaling industries. Capt George W Sprott Balcom (1851–1925), of NS, first brought a

B

sealing schooner round Cape Horn to Victoria in 1892. In the course of an eventful career he was arrested by the Russian navy for sealing too close to the Kuril Is and imprisoned near Petropavlovsk, then escaped to Japan. These experiences, which were later related to Rudyard Kipling when the famous author visited Victoria, form the background to the story "The Devil and the Deep Sea," according to Balcom family lore. Sprott Balcom founded the Pacific Whaling Co in 1905 with Capt William Grant and ran a fleet of vessels from stations at Sechart in Barkley Sd, Cachalot in Kyuquot Sd, Departure Bay near Nanaimo, and Rose and Naden harbours in the QCI. His brother Reuben (1855–1929), Reuben's son Willis (1881–1945) and other Balcoms were also part of the business, which operated until 1943. Balcom Point is named after Sprott Balcom, while Balcom Inlet apparently commemorates both Sprott and Reuben. *E*

The Ballenas Islands, site of an early lighthouse. *Peter Vassilopoulos*

Ballenas Channel (49°20'00" 124°10'00" W side of Str of Georgia, E of Parksville), **Ballenas Islands** (49°21'00" 124°09'00"), **Ballenas Trough** (49°15'00" 123°43'00" N of Gabriola I). *Ballenas* is the Spanish word for whales. The islands were named in 1791 during an exploration of the SW Str of Georgia by Spanish pilot José Narváez in the *Santa Saturnina*. A lighthouse was built on the S island in 1900, then transferred to the N island in 1912. Both channel and islands were long shown incorrectly on charts as "Ballinac." Ballenas Trough, an underwater feature, was named in 1980. *W*

Ballet Bay (49°43'00" 124°11'00" S side of Blind Bay, Nelson I, entrance to Jervis Inlet). This year-round safe anchorage was named in 1941 by Nelson I residents Harry and Margery "Midge" Thomas, in honour of their daughter Audree, who joined the Ballet Russe de Monte Carlo at age 14. She danced under the stage name Anna Istomina.

Ballingall Islets (48°54'00" 123°28'00" Trincomali Channel, off NE Saltspring I, Gulf Is). Alexander Campbell

Ballingall served as 2nd lt aboard HMS *Trincomalee*, a 24-gun frigate based at Esquimalt, 1853–56, under Capt Wallace Houstoun. The islets were formerly known as the Twin Is but were renamed in 1905 by Cdr John Parry of HMS *Egeria*.

Ball Point (49°45'00" 124°13'00" NW point of Hardy I, Jervis Inlet). Named about 1860 by RN surveyor Capt George Richards after Sir Alexander John Ball (1757–1809), a British rear adm, former commissioner of the navy at Gibraltar and first civil commissioner of the island of Malta (1801–9). As a capt, in command of HMS *Alexander*, he fought at the 1798 Battle of the Nile. Ball was a close friend of Adm Lord Nelson, whose flagship, HMS *Vanguard*, he once towed to safety after it had been dismasted in a fierce storm. He was responsible for the naval blockade of Malta and for its capture from the French in 1800. *W*

Bamfield (48°50'00" 125°08'00" On Bamfield Inlet), **Bamfield Inlet** (48°49'00" 125°08'00" E of Trevor Channel and Mills Peninsula, SE side of Barkley Sd, W side of Vancouver I). Bamfield is a corruption of the name of William Eddy Banfield, who arrived in BC in 1846 as a carpenter aboard HMS *Constance*. He left the RN in 1849, became a trader on the W coast of Vancouver I and was the first white settler at Barkley Sd. Banfield explored widely and collected ethnographic data on local First Nation groups, and in 1861 was appointed Indian agent for the region. His death in 1862, supposedly by drowning, was suspicious; it is believed that he was stabbed to death by Klatsmick, a Huu-ay-aht (Ohiaht) chief, who was taken to Victoria for trial but released for lack of reliable evidence. Bamfield was chosen in 1902 as the terminus of a trans-Pacific telegraph cable. A post office was established in 1903, with cancelling equipment that read "Bamfield" and was never corrected. The misspelled form of the name eventually became standard usage. The cable station, designed by noted architect Francis Rattenbury, operated until 1959 (the site later became home to a marine sciences facility), and the village was not connected to the wider world by road until 1963. The inlet was formerly identified on charts as Banfield Ck ("creek" being a 19th-century term for a narrow tidal inlet), then Banfield Inlet, and was not officially changed to Bamfield Inlet until 1951, when all attempts to hang on to the correct spelling of a historical name were finally abandoned.

Bamfield Islands (54°04'00" 130°18'00" Off NE coast of McMicking I, S of Prince Rupert). Samuel Bamfield was assistant surgeon aboard HMS *Malacca*, based at Esquimalt, 1865–68, under Capt Radulphus Oldfield. He was promoted to fleet surgeon in 1882 and went on to achieve the rank of deputy inspector-gen, hospitals and fleets (retired), in 1892, the year he died. Named by surveyor Lt Daniel Pender of the *Beaver* in 1867.

Cases of Mistaken Identity

"Truth is uniform and narrow," wrote Benjamin Franklin. "But error is endlessly diversified.... In this field the soul has room enough to expand herself, to display all her boundless faculties, and all her beautiful and interesting extravagancies and absurdities." So it is, certainly, with geographical place names. Mistakes in translating and transcribing names; errors in hearing, attributing and understanding names; spelling and punctuation mistakes—all have subtly distinguished our coastal heritage.

The range and quantity of errors is quite amazing. Some are mundane but still manage to leave a distinct impression in the fabric of coastal history. The west coast hamlet of Bamfield, for example, was named after early trader William Banfield, first white settler at Barkley Sound. A post office was established in 1903 with cancelling equipment that read "Bamfield" and was never corrected. The hydrographic service kept the name Banfield Inlet alive on charts until 1951, when all attempts to hang on to the true spelling of a historical name were abandoned and the feature officially became Bamfield Inlet. Dozens of other BC place names have suffered similar minor mishaps.

By contrast, there are names such as Caulfeild in West Vancouver, commemorating British land developer Francis Caulfeild, which appear to be misspelled but are, in fact, accurate. No doubt many attempts have been made over the years to "correct" this odd, old-fashioned name.

Numerous coastal names show the effect of what we might call "variable" spelling. Writers in the past did not have the same fixation on exact spelling that we do and were often quite content to spell the same word differently—even in the same sentence. Mackenzie Sound, for instance, north of Kingcome Inlet, is named for Kenneth McKenzie, bailiff of Craigflower Farm in the 1850s. Either spelling suited him. Corporal James Duffy of the Royal Engineers also spelled his name Duffey. Thus Duffy Rock and Duffey Lake both refer to the same person. Hudson's Bay Company official John Wark got listed by mistake on company records as John Work and decided to just stick with the new name rather than face the bureaucratic nightmare of trying to get it changed back. Five coastal features named Blackney all refer to Royal Navy paymaster William Blakeney, who altered his name for reasons unknown after serving on the BC coast in the 1860s. A long list of comparable examples could be drawn up.

Early chart-makers had a difficult time with names from unfamiliar languages. The Ballenas Islands in the Strait of Georgia, christened with the Spanish word for whales, were shown on charts for many years as "Ballinac." Gabriola Island is a misnomer. The actual name, applied by Spanish navigators in the early 1790s, was Gaviola, which may refer to a 17th-century Spanish naval officer. Gaviola was sometimes written Gabiola (which is pronounced similarly in Spanish), and a British cartographer managed to slip in an errant "r," probably in the mid-1800s. Now we're stuck with Gabriola. (The same cartographer also misspelled the name Porlier, with the result that Portier Pass appeared on Gulf Island charts for half a century until changed back to its original form.)

Historians make mistakes as well. Henry Wagner, the foremost authority on 19th-century Pacific Northwest map-making, known for his scrupulous accuracy, was nevertheless convinced that José Narváez, first Spanish explorer to see Gabriola, named the island's eastern point Gaviota, Spanish for seagull. But there is no documentary evidence for this claim whatsoever.

First Nation terms, naturally, bedevilled pioneer carto-graphers. All kinds of huge mistakes were made over them. The name of Nootka Sound itself, the main site of early contact and exchange between European and First Nation cultures, is the most famous booboo. Captain James Cook reported in 1778 that the inlet was named Nootka by its inhabitants. But what he probably heard when asking, no doubt with many hand gestures, for the name of the place was advice on where to anchor his vessels: *nootka-a*, meaning "go around." This minor mix-up resulted in one of our most significant place names.

No doubt there are other mysterious naming blunders out there on the coast waiting to be unravelled and put to rights.

The picturesque west coast village of Bamfield, named for William Banfield. *Peter Vassilopoulos*

B

Bancroft Point (52°41'00" 128°26'00" S entrance to Watson Bay, NW end of Roderick I, N of Bella Bella). Hubert Howe Bancroft (1832–1918) was a San Francisco bookseller and publisher who produced (and partly wrote) an important 39-volume history of western N and Central America. The three volumes on BC and the PNW, issued 1884–87 and among the earliest histories of the region, are still considered useful reference works. Bancroft's archives at the Univ of California are a valuable repository of source materials on BC's early days. In 1948 a number of points on Roderick I were named by the hydrographic service for BC historians. *E*

Banfield Creek, Banfield Inlet. *See* Bamfield.

Banks Island (53°25'00" 130°10'00" Between Hecate Str and Principe Channel), **Banks Reef** (50°05'00" 127°51'00" S end of Brooks Peninsula, NW side of Vancouver I). Sir Joseph Banks (1743–1820), one of the most significant men of science of his era, was president of the Royal Society, Britain's national academy of science, from 1778 until his death. He was born in London to a wealthy family, educated at Harrow, Eton and Cambridge, and accompanied Capt James Cook aboard *Endeavour* on Cook's first expedition to the S Pacific (1768–71), serving as botanist and naturalist. Banks had considerable

influence over the outfitting and itinerary for Capt George Vancouver's PNW expedition, appointing Archibald Menzies, the voyage's botanist, and receiving detailed reports from him. Banks introduced numerous exotics to Europe, including the eucalyptus, acacia and mimosa; the genus *Banksia* is named for him, as are about 80 plant species, Banks I in the Arctic and numerous place names in NZ and Australia. Remote and unpopulated, Banks is BC's sixth-largest island (855 sq km) and is part of the traditional territory of the Gitxaala (Kitkatla) First Nation. It was named in 1788 by fur trader Charles Duncan, capt of the *Princess Royal*; Banks Reef was named by RN surveyor Capt George Richards of HMS *Plumper* in 1860. *W*

Barba Point (52°16'00" 127°46'00" At the junction of Cousins Inlet and Dean Channel, SW of Ocean Falls). Named in 1953 for the pioneer steamer *Barbara Boscowitz*. *See* Boscowitz Rk.

Barber Island (49°06'00" 123°06'00" In the Fraser R's S Arm, just W of Ladner and S of Vancouver). The brothers Alfred B and Charles E Barber of Ladner acquired this island in 1888 from Henry Hicks and James Moran, who had received a Crown grant for the property—and for several other islands in the mouth of the Fraser—in 1885. The name appears on a geological survey map of the

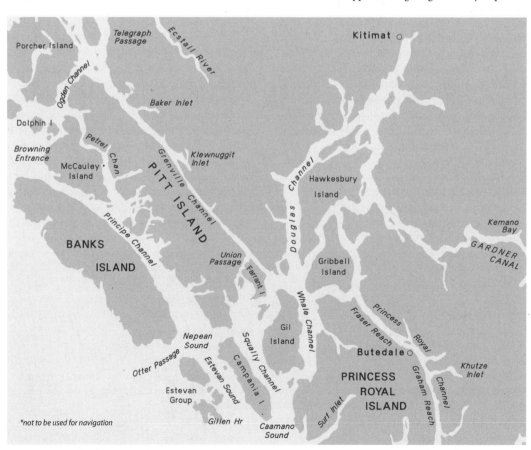

Banks and Pitt islands and the north-central coast. *Reproduced with the permission of the Canadian Hydrographic Service*

Fraser delta in 1923 and was adopted by the hydrographic service in 1936.

Barber Passage (50°24'00" 125°09'00" Between Jimmy Judd I and Stuart I at entrance to Bute Inlet). The name was adopted by the hydrographic service in 1955 for Alec Barber, an early settler in the area, who operated a small mine on Sonora I and drowned in this channel.

Barclay Sound. *See* Barkley Sd.

Barfleur Passage (49°23'00" 123°28'00" Between Keats I and Pasley I, W of Bowen I in entrance to Howe Sd). HMS *Barfleur* was a 98-gun, 1,766-tonne ship of the line, built at Chatham in 1768. It had a crew of 758 men. After seeing action in the W Indies, it took part, under Capt Cuthbert Collingwood, in Adm Earl Howe's 1794 victory over the French in the English Channel engagement known as the Glorious First of June. The passage was one of many features Capt George Richards named to commemorate this battle when he surveyed Howe Sd in 1859–60. The *Barfleur* was also present in 1797 at the Battle of Cape St Vincent and later had a long career with the Channel and Mediterranean fleets. The vessel was broken up in 1819.

Bargain Bay (49°37'00" 124°02'00" E side of Malaspina Str, S of Pender Hbr, SE of Powell R), **Bargain Narrows** (N end of Bargain Bay). The bay was originally named Bargain Hbr, probably by RN surveyor Capt George Richards about 1860. The name's meaning has unfortunately been lost, and it is not known if the location of a Sechelt First Nation reserve right next to the narrows has any bearing on its origin. The local name for the narrows has long been Canoe Pass; the Sechelt First Nation name of Sálálus (Salaloose), meaning "little pass," is now applied more generally to the nearby community of Madeira Park. The Sechelt name for the harbour is P'úḵwp'aḵwem.

Barge Point (53°02'00" 131°57'00" S entrance to Gillatt Arm, Cumshewa Inlet, NE Moresby I, QCI). John L Barge, a carpenter, was lured to Haida Gwaii in 1908 by newspaper advertisements and settled, with his family, at Queen Charlotte City. He contributed much to the community, serving at various times as government agent, mining recorder, road superintendent and undertaker. Named by regional hydrographer Henri Parizeau in 1926. *D*

Barkley Sound (48°51'00" 125°23'00" SE of Clayoquot Sd, W side of Vancouver I). Charles William Barkley (1759–1832), formerly with the E India Co, arrived as an independent British trader at Nootka Sd in June 1787 aboard the *Imperial Eagle*. He was accompanied by his young bride, Frances Hornby Trevor (1769–1845, *see* Trevor Channel). With the help of the unfortunate John McKay—who had been living at Nootka for over a year,

Pocket beaches on Benson Island in Barkley Sound. *Elsie Hulsizer*

having been left there by an earlier expedition in order to learn the customs of the Nuu-chah-nulth people (*see* McKay Passage)—Barkley was able to purchase numerous sea otter furs. He explored and named Barkley Sd, charted the entrance to Juan de Fuca Str and then proceeded to China, after which he became embroiled in legal disputes arising from the voyage. The Barkleys made another trading voyage together, this time to the Alaska coast in 1792 in the *Halcyon* (also later plagued with business problems), then more or less disappeared from the historical record. Frances Barkley, whose journal was published in 1978, is believed to have been the first European woman to see the BC coast. Barkley Sd was erroneously spelled Barclay on early charts. The Spanish knew it as Baia de Carrasco, named in 1789 by José Narváez after the naval officer Juan Carrasco, who participated in several important voyages of exploration on BC's S coast. *E W*

Barnard Harbour (53°05'00" 129°07'00" NW side of Princess Royal I, S end of Whale Channel). Francis Jones Barnard (1829–89), from Quebec City, married Ellen Stillman in 1853 and came to BC for the 1859 gold rush. He and his family settled at Yale, and Barnard began carrying mail—by foot at first—to the Cariboo. In 1862 he founded the BC and Victoria Express Co and won a contract to deliver mail, by pony, from Yale to Williams Ck. By 1864 he was running stagecoaches and carrying large quantities of gold, and by 1867 Barnard's Express & Stage Line (later the BC Express Co) controlled much of the transport business between Victoria and Barkerville. His stage line was, for a time, the longest in N America and used hundreds of horses bred at his Okanagan BX Ranch. Barnard became a member of BC's legislative council, 1867–69, and was MP for Yale, 1879–87. His sons were also successful—George Henry became a senator, and Francis Stillman a knight and lt gov of BC (*see below*)—while his daughter Alice Telfer married businessman and politician John Andrew Mara. *E*

Barnard Island (53°02'00" 129°38'00" Between Dewdney I and Trutch I, Estevan Group, SE of Banks I). Sir Francis

B

Stillman Barnard (1856–1936) was born at Toronto, the son of express operator Francis Jones Barnard (*see* Barnard Hbr). He married Martha Amelia Sophia Loewen (1865–1942) at Victoria in 1883. Frank Barnard expanded his father's stage-line business into shipping, mining, ranching, railways and land development and became one of BC's richest men—a founder and first managing director of the BC Electric Rwy Co, a Victoria city councillor, 1886–87, and a Conservative MP for the Cariboo, 1888–96. He was eventually appointed lt gov of BC, 1914–19. Mt Barnard on the BC-Alberta boundary is also named for him. The island was formerly known as West I but was renamed by the hydrographic service in 1950 to avoid duplication. *E*

Barnes Shoal (53°42'00" 132°58'00" At entrance to Port Louis, NW Graham I, QCI). Master mariner Charles Barnes (1860–1926), from England, worked on the BC coast for Canada's Dept of Marine and Fisheries and served on a series of lighthouse tenders. He married Rose Pfeiffer (1865–1935), a native of Germany, at Victoria in 1892. Barnes was 2nd officer on CGS *Quadra* and then capt of CGS *Newington*, acquired in 1908. He was also the first skipper of CGS *Estevan*, built in 1912. The shoal was named by regional hydrographer Henri Parizeau in 1926.

Barney Rocks (49°21'00" 126°17'00" W of entrance to Hot Springs Cove, between Nootka Sd and Clayoquot Sd, W side of Vancouver I). "Barney" was the nickname of the unfortunate Peter Cornelius, a Maltese trader who worked at Kyuquot as a storekeeper for pioneer merchants William Banfield and Peter Francis. In 1855, while travelling by canoe to Clayoquot Sd, he and several of his Ka:'yu:'K't'h (Kyuquot) First Nation companions were murdered by rival tribe members off Estevan Point. Formerly known as Canoe Reef and Canoe Rocks but renamed by the hydrographic service in 1946 to avoid duplication.

Barnsley Shoal (50°16'00" 125°12'00" In Okisollo Channel, E of the N end of Quadra I, N of Campbell R). John Barnsley (1860–1924), from Birmingham, UK, a gunsmith by trade, immigrated to BC in 1881 and established a sporting goods store in Victoria with John R Collister. In 1887, at Victoria, he married his partner's sister, Elizabeth Jane Collister (1867–1952), who was born in Australia and came to Canada with her family in 1875. Barnsley later worked in the cannery trade and became secretary-manager of the Boscowitz Steamship Co. When the Union Steamship Co bought out Boscowitz in 1911, he was named Union's agent at Prince Rupert. He moved up to assistant manager in 1919, gen manager in 1920 and managing director in 1922, serving as the company's senior executive until his sudden death. Barnsley was issued BC's first auto licence, in 1904 (he drove a primitive vehicle known as a Waltham Orient Buckboard), and kept licence plate #1 until he died. Barnsley Shoal was named by the hydrographic service in 1924.

Baron Island (54°27'55" 130°49'19" One of the Dundas Is, W side of Chatham Sd, off Prince Rupert). Named after Henry Dundas, Viscount Melville and Baron Dunira, British navy treasurer, 1783–1801. *See* Dundas I.

Baron Point (53°52'00" 130°03'00" E shore of Grenville Channel, N of Kumealon Inlet). Named in 1947 after Baron Grenville (William Wyndham Grenville), British PM in 1806–7. *See* Grenville Channel.

Barracuda Rock (51°36'15" 127°45'15" S side of Fish Egg Inlet, Fitz Hugh Sd, W of Rivers Inlet). The Canadian Hydrographic Service named this hazard in 1980 after the government survey launch *Barracuda*, which ran aground on the isolated, dangerous rock.

Barrat Shoal (54°38'00" 130°29'00" Off NW end of Tsimpsean Peninsula, N of Prince Rupert). Elizabeth June Barrat, born at Winnipeg in 1907, was a nurse-in-training at Port Simpson Gen Hospital at the time this feature was named, in 1927. She married Bernard Cyril "Flicky" Doyle (1904–89) at New Westminster in 1935 and died at Vancouver about 1996. Doyle played lacrosse for the New Westminster Salmonbellies and was a member of the team that won the gold medal at the 1928 Olympics.

Barrett Rock (54°15'00" 130°21'00" S entrance to Prince Rupert Hbr). According to BC's Geographical Names Office, this feature commemorates a coxswain named Barrett who was a member of the staff of the hydrographic service in 1906. The feature was named the following year.

Barrie Point (52°53'00" 128°07'00" S side of Mussel Inlet, Sheep Passage, N of Don Peninsula and Bella Bella), **Barrie Reach** (53°28'00" 128°16'00" Between Europa Reach and Whidbey Reach, Gardner Canal, SE of Kitimat). Robert Barrie (1774–1841), born in Florida, joined the RN in 1788 as a midshipman on HMS *Europa*, the flagship of his uncle, Commodore Alan Gardner, cdr-in-chief of the W Indies Station. There he met George Vancouver, a lt on the *Europa*. Gardner was Vancouver's friend and mentor, and recommended him as cdr of the historic expedition to the PNW in 1791, which Barrie also joined as a midshipman on HMS *Discovery*. In 1793, Barrie helped Joseph Whidbey explore Gardner Canal, and when the region was re-surveyed in 1907, Capt Frederick Learmonth of HMS *Egeria* named Barrie Reach in his honour. Barrie Point, named in 1965, commemorates the fact that the young officer was in this area also, surveying with James Johnstone and the ships' boats, when several seamen took ill after eating tainted mussels; one of them, John Carter, died. Barrie went on to a respected career in the RN, capturing several French privateers and numerous merchant vessels while in command of HMS *Pomone*, 1806–11. He was noted for his service in the War of 1812, where, as capt of HMS *Dragon*, he led a blockade of Chesapeake Bay and successfully attacked forts and harbours on the US E coast. In 1819 he was appointed commissioner of Kingston dockyard in Upper Canada and, as senior naval officer for the Canadian colonies, oversaw marine surveys of the Great Lks and the St Lawrence R, and the building of the Rideau and Welland canals. Barrie returned to England in 1834, was knighted and promoted rear adm in 1837. The Ont communities of Barrie and Barriefield are also named for him, as is Barrie I in Lk Huron.

Barry Inlet (52°34'00" 131°49'00" Between Mike Inlet and Pocket Inlet, W side of Moresby I, QCI), **Barry Island** (53°37'00" 132°56'00" Just outside Port Chanal, Athlow Bay, W Graham I, QCI). According to QCI historian Kathleen Dalzell, both features were named by Capt Absalom Freeman in the early 1910s after Capt B Barry, Freeman's former mate on the *Flamingo* and later skipper of the Canadian Fishing Co trawler *Celestial Empire*.

Barugh Shoal (51°19'00" 128°14'00" NW of Virgin Rocks in the Sea Otter Group, Smith Sd). Named by the hydrographic service in 1948 to honour Walter Bird Barugh of Victoria, a wireless operator on the W coast survey vessels *William J Stewart* and *Alberni*, who had died the previous year at the tender age of 23.

Bassett Point (50°20'00" 125°07'00" SE point of Sonora I, N of Campbell R). George Bassett (1872–1943), an early settler in the area, lived within sight of this point and also owned land near Hole in the Wall. Apparently his descendants were still residing in the region many years later. The name was adopted by the hydrographic service in 1954.

Batchelor Cove (49°22'00" 123°17'00" SE of White Cliff Point, W Vancouver), **Batchelor Point** (49°21'00" 123°17'00" W of Fishermans Cove, S of Batchelor Cove, W Vancouver). Capt Robert Alexander Batchelor (1872–1934) was senior pilot with the Empire Steamship Co and a founder of the Vancouver Pilotage Assoc. He was first appointed a pilot at Vancouver in 1905, the year he married Helen Broomhead Clark. Batchelor Cove, adopted in 1929, was formerly known as Fishermans Cove (qv). Batchelor Point was named in 1949; before that, for many years, it was called Bridgman Point.

Batchelor Point (49°11'00" 123°55'00" NE point of Protection I, Nanaimo Hbr, off E side of Vancouver I). Named in 1853 by George Inskip, master of HMS *Virago* and in charge of survey duties. A seaman named Batchelor was apparently a member of the boat crew that sounded Nanaimo Hbr and Departure Bay that year.

Bate Passage (50°54'00" 127°49'00" Between Nigei I and Hope I off N end of Vancouver I). Capt William Thornton

Bate (1820–57) was a noted RN surveying officer who was never in BC but spent most of his career in Asia, charting the coast of China with HMS *Royalist* and *Bittern*. He captured the port of Canton during the 2nd Anglo-Chinese War, while in command of HMS *Actaeon*, but was killed while storming the walls of Guangzhou itself. The passage was named by RN surveyor Capt George Richards about 1861; Mt Bate on Vancouver I also commemorates him. *W*

Bate Point (49°10'45" 123°56'00" S point of Newcastle I, Nanaimo Hbr). Mark Bate (1837–1927) was born at Birmingham, UK, and arrived in 1857 on the BC coast, where he began working for the HBC at Nanaimo as a cashier. He joined the Vancouver Coal Co when it purchased the HBC's Nanaimo holdings in 1862, and served as manager, 1869–84. From 1886 to 1913 he was government agent for Nanaimo. Bate was elected the first mayor of Nanaimo in 1875 and served as mayor in 1875–79, 1881–86, 1888–89 and 1898–1900. He was appointed a justice of the peace in 1873 and held many other civic posts, both administrative and cultural, over the course of his career. Mark Bay (Newcastle I) and Mt Mark (N of Horne Lk, Vancouver I) are also named after him. Bate Point was formerly known as Reef Point but was renamed by the hydrographic service in 1939.

Batt Bluff (50°37'00" 126°20'00" NE of Turnour I, Knight Inlet). David Batt was master of HMS *Clio*, a 22-gun screw corvette, under Capt Nicholas Turnour, and was based at Esquimalt, 1864–68. He retired as a lt in 1870 and died in 1886. Named by RN surveyor Lt Daniel Pender in 1865.

Batt Rock (48°49'00" 123°25'00" SE entrance to Ganges Hbr, Saltspring I, Gulf Is). Robert Barrie Batt (1823–86) was master of HMS *Ganges* and served on the Pacific Station, 1857–60, under Capt John Fulford. The 84-gun vessel—the last active line-of-battle sailing ship on foreign service in the RN—was the flagship of Rear Adm Robert Baynes, the station's cdr-in-chief. Batt was promoted to cdr in 1864 and capt in 1868. He retired in 1882 and died in NW Kent. The rock, formerly known as One Fathom Patch, was renamed by Cdr John Parry of HMS *Egeria* while re-surveying Ganges Hbr in 1905. *W*

Baudre Point (53°05'00" 128°32'00" Entrance to Khutze Inlet, E of Princess Royal I). Rev Julien Michel Baudre, a French Canadian missionary and member of the Oblates of Mary Immaculate (OMI), was the first principal of the Roman Catholic boys' school established in Victoria in 1858. This institution later became St Louis College, which opened in a new building in 1864 with 40 pupils. Baudre had come W in the mid-1850s from Galveston, Texas, where he had completed construction of a seminary and college, and served as its founding principal. In 1877 he was in the Okanagan Valley, conducting an OMI First

Nations census. By 1887 he had been appointed superior at the St Eugene Mission in the E Kootenays.

Bauza Cove (50°33'00" 126°49'00" S side of Johnstone Str, SE of Beaver Cove), **Bauza Islet** (50°33'00" 126°48'00" In entrance to Bauza Cove). Spanish naval officer Felipe Bauzá y Cañas, born at Palma, Majorca, studied under hydrographer Vicente Tofiño and taught at the naval academy in Cadiz. He was chosen as the chief cartographer on the historic 1789–94 expedition of Alejandro Malaspina. Bauzá later surveyed and charted the S American coastline between Santiago and Buenos Aires under José de Espinosa y Tello. In 1815 he became director of the Spanish hydrographic office. He went into politics and was elected to the Spanish parliament in 1820, but was forced to flee to England in 1823 as a result of his liberal views. He died there in 1834. These features were probably named by explorer Dionisio Alcalá-Galiano (as was Puerto de Bauzá, now Beaver Cove) and adopted by Capt George Richards in 1860.

Bawden Bay (49°17'00" 126°01'00" E side of Millar Channel, Clayoquot Sd, W side of Vancouver I), **Bawden Point** (49°18'00" 126°01'00" At junction of Herbert Inlet and Millar Channel, E of Flores I, Clayoquot Sd). Charles Bawden (d 1876) was master of HMS *Bacchante*, the 51-gun flagship of Rear Adm Sir Thomas Maitland. He served on the Pacific Station, 1860–63, having previously seen action in China, Borneo and the Bering Str, and retired in 1870 with the rank of cdr. Bawden Bay was named in 1861 by Donald Mackenzie, capt of the *Bacchante*. Bawden Point was formerly known as Charles Point (also after Charles Bawden) but was renamed in 1934; nearby Bawden Ck is also named for this naval officer. *W*

Baxter Shoal (50°45'00" 126°30'00" W side of Baker I, E end of Queen Charlotte Str, NE of Port McNeill). Petty Officer Richard Alexander Baxter, of Vancouver, was killed in action June 25, 1940, aboard HMCS *Fraser*. The RCN destroyer sank after accidentally colliding with a British cruiser, HMS *Calcutta*, during attempts to evacuate refugees on France's SW coast near Bayonne; 47 lives were lost on *Fraser* and 19 on *Calcutta*. Baxter's name is inscribed on the Halifax Memorial.

Baylee Bay (53°01'00" 132°19'00" N side of Inskip Channel, Moresby I, QCI), **Baylee Bluff** (52°59'00" 132°12'00" S shore of Hibben I, off NW Moresby I). Rev William Cecil Percy Baylee was a popular RN chaplain and instructor aboard HMS *Thetis* during Capt Augustus Kuper's 1852 survey of this area. Nearby Instructor I and Percy Point are also named for him.

Bayly Point (51°45'00" 128°01'00" NE entrance to Hakai Passage, S of Bella Bella). William Bayly (1737–1810), a self-taught British astronomer and mathematician,

became an assistant at the Royal Observatory, Greenwich, after first working as a schoolteacher. In 1769 he sailed to Norway with Jeremiah Dixon to observe the transit of Venus. He served as astronomer on Capt James Cook's second and third voyages of discovery, 1776–80, and his observations were published at London in 1777 and 1782. Later he was headmaster at Portsmouth's Royal Naval Academy, 1785–1807. The point was named by the hydrographic service in 1944.

Baynes Sound is known for its oyster production. *Rob Morris*

Baynes Channel (48°27'00" 123°16'00" Between Chatham Is and Cadboro Point, E of Victoria), **Baynes Peak** (48°48'05" 123°31'02" Highest point on Mt Maxwell, W Saltspring I, Gulf Is), **Baynes Sound** (49°29'00" 124°45'00" Between Denman I and Vancouver I, Str of Georgia). Rear Adm Robert Lambert Baynes (1796–1869) served as cdr-in-chief of the Pacific Station, 1857–60, based at Valparaiso, Chile, and ended his distinguished RN career as a knight and an adm. He came to BC in his flagship, HMS *Ganges*, in order to preserve stability and British rule during the 1858 gold rush, and recommended that the RN move its Pacific HQ N to Esquimalt, which it did in 1862. During the 1859 squabble over the ownership of the San Juan Is (popularly known as the "Pig War"), Baynes made a show of force with his warships but refused to authorize an actual invasion, as demanded by Gov James Douglas. His tact and caution allowed the dispute to eventually enjoy a political resolution. In 1859, RN hydrographer Capt George Richards changed the name of Saltspring I to Admiral I in honour of Baynes (it was changed back in 1905) and named the island's high point Mt Baynes. This was also changed, in 1911, to Mt Maxwell, after rancher John Maxwell, one of Saltspring's first residents, though the name Baynes Peak was retained for the apex. Richards also named the channel and sound about 1859. Baynes Sd is particularly rich in marine life and produces roughly half of BC's cultured oysters and manila clams. *W*

Bazan Bay (48°38'00" 123°24'00" E side of Saanich Peninsula, S of Sidney). Antonio Valdés y Bazán (1744–1816) was a celebrated Spanish naval officer who became capt-gen and minister of the navy. He put much effort into improving the education of Spanish naval officers and promoted a number of scientific maritime expeditions, including that of Alejandro Malaspina to the Pacific. The bay was named by Juan Pantoja y Arriga, one of the pilots of Spanish cdr Francisco Eliza, who explored the region in 1791 along with José Narváez.

Beacon Hill (48°24'38" 123°21'54" S side of Victoria, SE end of Vancouver I). Named in the 1840s by HBC officials after two beacons were installed—one on the hill and one on the shoreline—so that, when they were aligned, mariners could avoid running aground on dangerous offshore Brotchie Ledge when entering Victoria Hbr. The feature appears as Mt Beacon on an early Admiralty chart published in 1847, but the name Beacon Hill was well established by 1864. The area around the hill was reserved as a public park by Gov James Douglas in the 1850s. The traditional Songhees First Nation name for the area is Mee-a-can or Meeqan, meaning "warmed by the sun." Two ancient villages were located on Finlayson Point and Clover Point; their inhabitants would harvest edible bulbs in the camas meadows around the hill and play a game there that resembled field hockey.

Beadle Rocks (53°34'00" 130°34'00" W side of Rawlinson Anchorage, W of Banks I). Named by the hydrographic service in 1926 after Alfred or Arthur Beadle, who worked as a fireman aboard CGS *Lillooet* in the early 1920s, after serving overseas during WWI.

Beal Cove (54°11'00" 132°59'00" S side of Langara I, NW of Graham I, QCI). Canton and Macao merchant Daniel Beale (d about 1842), a former E India Co employee, was one of the partners in the Merchant Proprietors, an 18th-century fur-trading company formed by John Meares, which owned the vessels *Felice Adventurer* and *Iphigenia Nubiana*. Beale was also involved with its successor company, the Associated Merchants Trading to the NW Coast of America, which dispatched the *Argonaut* and *Princess Royal* to Nootka Sd in 1789. Beale, who doubled as Prussia's consul at Canton (a position that protected his trading activities), left Asia about 1797 for London, where he and Francis Magniac formed a jewellery and watch business. He was later involved with the building of London's St Pancras church. Beale's main associate in Asia was John Henry Cox (*see* Cox Bay), and after many changes of partnership the firm Cox & Beale, founded in 1787, became the famous mercantile house Jardine Matheson & Co. Beal Cove is shown on early charts as Beale's Hbr, the name given it in 1789 by William Douglas, master of the *Iphigenia*, who is said to have stepped ashore here and thus become the second white man (after Robert Haswell) to set foot on Haida Gwaii. Somewhere along the line the name Beale lost its second "e." **D**

Beales Bay (52°10'35" 127°58'40" S shore of Cunningham I, E of Bella Bella), **Beale Cove** (49°42'00" 124°34'00" SE of Welcome Bay, W side of Texada I, Str of Georgia), **Beales Lagoon** (52°10'55" 127°59'05" Just NW of Beales Bay). Francis "Fred" Joseph Beale (1885–1965) arrived in BC from Auckland, NZ, in 1910 and worked as a tug and scow operator for Whalen Pulp & Paper. The Whalen mills needed lime for making both pulp and paper, and Beale was put in charge of producing it. The first limestone deposits he developed were on the Redonda Is. In 1923 he established a large quarry and camp, complete with a school, on Cunningham I and went into business as Beale Quarries Ltd. Ruined scows, used to supply the pulp mill at Ocean Falls, littered the shoreline there for decades. In 1931, Beale set up his camp and kilns on Texada I, where rich mineral resources are found, and produced lime for the nearby Powell R mill. His Texada holdings were purchased in 1940 by Balfour Guthrie Ltd, which sold them in 1956 to Lafarge Cement, a company that still maintains an enormous industrial presence on the island. The cove was named in 1974, the bay and lagoon in 1992.

Beard Islands (51°59'00" 128°16'00" In Queens Sd, NW of Hunter I, S of Bella Bella). Named in 1944 after Cdr Charles Taschereau Beard (1890–1950), who was born at Ottawa and began his long naval career, during which he served on 30 different ships, in Britain. He joined the RCN in 1910 and by 1922 was senior naval officer at Esquimalt. In 1940 he came out of retirement to command HMCS *Prince Robert*, a former passenger vessel converted to an auxiliary cruiser, and captured the German merchant vessel *Weser* off Mexico. Beard served as Esquimalt's MLA, 1945–50. Beard Lk near Port Hardy is named after his son, Midshipman Thomas Norman Kemp Beard of the RCN, who was killed in action in May 1941, aged 20, during HMS *Hood*'s disastrous engagement with the German battleship *Bismarck*. Cdr Beard died at Esquimalt.

Bear River. *See* Bedwell Bay.

Beatrice Shoal (52°50'00" 131°51'00" N entrance to Dana Passage, between Talunkwan I and Moresby I, QCI). SS *Princess Beatrice*, a modest little vessel built for the CPR at Esquimalt in 1903 by the BC Marine Rwy Co, was designed for work in Alaska and on the BC N coast. The single-screw wooden ship, 60 m long and 1,170 tonnes, could manage 13 knots and carry 350 passengers. *Beatrice* operated in the QCI, 1907–12, and also on the Victoria–Seattle route. In 1929 it was sold, gutted and used as a floating cannery on Vancouver I's W coast.

Beattie Anchorage (53°02'00" 131°54'00" At entrance to Carmichael Passage, Cumshewa Inlet, QCI), **Beattie Point** (53°15'00" 132°04'00" N shore of Bearskin Bay, Skidegate Inlet, QCI). Newspaper ads attracted George DeWitt Beattie (1877–1946) to Queen Charlotte City, where he served as the first postmaster (1909–40), operated the islands' first drugstore, married fellow islander Azeline Girard in 1914 and became a lifelong resident. The anchorage was the site of a steamer landing for many years and was also used as a log-rafting area. *D*

Beauchemin Channel (52°37'00" 129°15'00" W side of Aristazabal I). Joseph Ulric Beauchemin, a graduate of Montreal's École Polytechnique, worked for the Canadian Hydrographic Service, 1912–47. While most of his career took place in Atlantic Canada, in 1922 he participated in a survey of Hecate Str and was placed in charge of a survey camp at Borrowman Bay on Aristazabal I. For many years he was officer in charge of CGS *Acadia*, involved in oceanographic surveys off Nfld and NS, in Hudson Bay and in the Gulf of St Lawrence. The channel was named in 1926. Ulric Point at the N end of Aristazabal I also commemorates him.

Beaumont Island (52°17'00" 127°57'00" NE of Cunningham I, NE of Bella Bella). Named by the hydrographic service in 1925 after R Beaumont, who was a senior official with GTP Coast Steamships Co (later Canadian National Steamships Ltd) in the early 1920s.

Beaumont Shoal (48°27'00" 123°12'00" In Haro Str, NE of Chatham Is, E of Victoria). Ernest Godfrey Beaumont (1874–1967) was born at London, UK, and educated at Cambridge. He immigrated to Victoria, bought land on S Pender I and married Constance Ida Hay Currie (1874–1952) about 1921. In 1918 he bought half of Discovery I, just E of Victoria, from the estate of Warburton Pike and lived there for almost half a century. Beaumont owned and operated numerous vessels, including the beautiful 15-m *Discovery Isle*, built in Hong Kong in 1925, which he wrecked on the Trial Is in 1950. He willed his Discovery I property to the Boy Scouts of Canada when he died, and it was later turned into a provincial marine park. Other Beaumont land donations—on S Pender I and at Fraser Lk—also became provincial parks. Griffin I, just N of Discovery I, was once named for him as well, but was changed in 1934.

Beaven Islands (52°47'00" 129°23'00" Off NW Aristazabal I). Charles Frederick Beaven (1845–1926) was born at Charlottetown, PEI, and moved in 1870 to Victoria and went into business as a carriage builder. He married the widowed Mary Helen Bowden (1846–1900, née Moody), a native of Maine, in 1877. (Mary Moody, incidentally, was a sister of Sewell Prescott Moody, pioneer BC lumberman and founder of the Moodyville sawmill on Burrard Inlet.) After Mary's death, Charles married Hattie Anna Gray (1857–1929, née Smith), also a widow, in 1908. He and Hattie are believed to have participated in the grand Victoria old-timers' reunion of 1924 (*see* Adams Bay).

The historic steamship *Beaver* in Burrard Inlet, photographed by H T Devine about 1888, just before it was wrecked on Prospect Point. *BC Archives A-00009*

Beaver Cove (50°32'00" 126°51'00" NE side of Vancouver I, at junction of Broughton Str and Johnstone Str), **Beaver Harbour** (50°42'00" 127°24'00" Just E of Port Hardy, Vancouver I), **Beaver Inlet** (50°30'00" 125°37'00" SW side of Loughborough Inlet, N of Johnstone Str), **Beaver Island** (49°37'00" 124°03'00" E side of Malaspina Str, S of Pender Hbr), **Beaver Passage** (53°44'00" 130°22'00" Between Spicer I and McCauley I, S of Porcher I), **Beaver Point** (48°46'00" 123°22'00" SE side of Saltspring I, Gulf Is), **Beaver Rock** (50°20'00" 125°26'00" Off Chatham Point, at junction of Discovery Passage and Johnstone Str, NW of Campbell R), **Beaver Rock** (54°21'00" 130°42'00" Off SE Melville I, NW of Prince Rupert). The HBC's *Beaver*, built in 1835 in London, UK, of oak and elm, was the first steamship on the NW coast and inspired numerous BC place names. The 31-m, 98-tonne vessel sailed around Cape Horn in 1836 and arrived at Ft Vancouver on the Columbia R, where its side paddles, boiler and twin 35-hp engines were installed, giving it a top speed of almost 10 knots. The *Beaver* had a long and useful career supplying HBC posts, carrying furs and transporting dignitaries between Victoria and the mainland, including to Ft Langley, where the colony of BC was proclaimed in 1858. Hired by the RN and equipped with small brass cannons, it performed invaluable coastal survey work under Lt Daniel Pender, 1863–70. After being sold to a Victoria company in 1874, it towed barges and carried freight until 1888, when it was wrecked and remained for years on the rocks at Prospect Point in Vancouver Hbr. Many relics from the *Beaver* are displayed at the Vancouver Maritime Museum. Beaver Cove was originally named Puerto de Bauzá, after Felipe Bauzá, Alejandro Malaspina's cartographer (*see* Bauza Cove), by Spanish explorer Dionisio Alcalá-Galiano, who anchored there in 1792. Beaver Inlet was first known as Beaver Ck. Beaver I is not an official name as this feature is technically a peninsula (Francis Peninsula) at low tide. *E W*

Beavis Islets (53°45'00" 133°02'00" W entrance to Otard Bay, NW Graham I, QCI), **Beavis Point** (Just N of Beavis Its). After attending HMS *Conway*, a UK maritime training facility, Lancelot R W Beavis (1864–1940) began his career in 1878 as an apprentice on the *Star of France*, a jute clipper. By 1893 he was master on the *Micronesia*, a globe-trotting square-rigger, always vying for a record passage. His sailing career came to an abrupt end in 1897 when the *Micronesia*, under tow off the English coast, was destroyed by fire, and Beavis was forced to turn to steamships, which he despised. He worked on Atlantic cattle carriers, on CGS *Lillooet* (doing survey work in the QCI, 1912–15), at HMCS *Naden* during WWI, and for W Vancouver's ferries, leaving the sea in 1930 to retire to Vancouver I and write *Passage from Sail to Steam*, his memoirs. The point, known to the Haida as Koot-tellgas-kwoon ("Eagle Nest Point"), was named about 1914, in recognition of Beavis's contributions as a surveyor; the islets were named in 1946.

Beazley Islands (52°15'00" 128°12'00" S of Dearth I, Seaforth Channel, NW of Bella Bella), **Beazley Passage** (50°13'35" 125°08'50" Between Quadra I, Read I and Maurelle I, NE of Campbell R). Ernest H Beazley (1876–1920), born at Birkenhead, UK, came to Vancouver in 1911 to direct the Union Steamship Co after Liverpool's J H Welsford & Co acquired control. He was a successful manager, taking the company into the profitable tourist excursion business and becoming president of the Ship Owners Assoc of BC before his untimely death in an airplane accident. The Beazley Is were formerly known as the Jumble Is but were renamed in 1925; Beazley Passage (originally Beazley Pass) had been named the year before.

Becher Bay (48°20'00" 123°37'00" S end of Vancouver I, between Sooke Hbr and Pedder Bay). Alexander Bridport Becher (1796–1876) was an RN hydrographer who began his career helping chart lakes in eastern Canada in 1814–17. He worked as a surveyor in the N Atlantic, was promoted to capt in 1856 and served as an assistant at the Admiralty's hydrographic office for more than three decades. Becher wrote numerous books on navigation and marine history, edited the *Nautical Magazine* and made improvements to the sextant, inventing an artificial horizon in 1834. He reached the rank of rear adm, retired, in 1874. Capt Henry Kellett of HMS *Herald* named this feature in 1846 while doing survey work off S Vancouver I. Mt Becher and Becher Lk W of Comox also commemorate him. Becher Bay is often misspelled Beecher, a possible confusion with nearby Beechey Head, named after a different RN officer. *W*

Becker Point (53°28'00" 129°55'00" S entrance of Ala Passage, W side of Pitt I). Named in 1944 after G Becker, who was a watchman aboard the survey vessel *William J Stewart* in the early 1940s.

Beddis Rock (48°46'00" 123°18'00" Off Boat Nook, SW of N Pender I, Gulf Is). Samuel John Beddis (1850–93) was born in England and arrived in Victoria with his wife, Emily Adelaide (1852–1919), and their five children in 1884 after living in the US. Saltspring I pioneer Henry Ruckle persuaded them to homestead on Saltspring, and they settled on the E coast, near the mouth of Cusheon Ck, where one of the island's nicest beaches is named after the family. Samuel developed a fine apple orchard, and he and his son Charles (b 1873) built many heritage structures in the Gulf Is, including Saltspring's first real school, at Beaver Point (1885), and the interior of St Mark's Church. Beddis Rk was formerly known as Black Rk but was renamed by the hydrographic service in 1936 to avoid duplication.

Bedford Island (53°57'00" 130°09'00" One of the Gibson Group, N entrance to Grenville Channel, S of Prince Rupert). William Orlebar Bedford, born in Ireland about 1849, was on the RN's Pacific Station, based at Esquimalt, 1869–72. At that time he was assistant paymaster aboard HMS *Scylla*, under Capt Frederick A Herbert. He became chief paymaster in 1905. Named in 1869 by Lt Daniel Pender on the *Beaver*. *W*

Bedford Islands (48°19'00" 123°36'00" E entrance to Becher Bay, S end of Vancouver I). Historian Capt John Walbran suggests that RN surveyor Capt Henry Kellett may have named this feature in 1846 after Bedford C T Pim, at that time a midshipman aboard Kellett's survey vessel *Herald*, because Bedford was already a famous name in hydrographic circles. Two brothers, Rear Adm George A Bedford (1809–69) and Vice Adm Edward J Bedford (1810–87), had been associated with the RN's surveying branch for their entire careers (neither were related to Pim). Pim himself ultimately became a rear adm (*see* Pim Head). *W*

Bedingfield Bay (49°21'00" 125°59'00" W side of Herbert Inlet, Clayoquot Sd, W side of Vancouver I). After Charles Bedingfield Wood, RN surgeon aboard HMS *Plumper*, 1860–62. *See* Wood Cove. The Bedingfield Range, N of Tofino on Vancouver I, is also named for him.

Bedwell Bay (49°19'00" 122°55'00" E side of Indian Arm, NE of Vancouver Hbr), **Bedwell Harbour** (48°45'00" 123°15'00" Between N Pender I and S Pender I, Gulf Is), **Bedwell Islands** (50°29'00" 127°54'00" N side of Quatsino Sd, NW end of Vancouver I), **Bedwell Point** (50°54'00" 127°03'00" N side of Drury Inlet, N of Port McNeill), **Bedwell River** (49°22'00" 125°46'00" Flows SW into head of Bedwell Sd), **Bedwell Sound** (49°17'00" 125°49'00" N of Meares I, Clayoquot Sd, W side of Vancouver I). Edward Parker Bedwell (1834–1919) was born at Jersey and joined the RN in 1848. He came to the PNW in 1857 as 2nd master of the survey vessel *Plumper*, under Capt George Richards, who named all these features except the Bedwell

Poets Cove Resort at Bedwell Harbour in the Gulf Islands. *John Lund*

R, which was known for many years as the Bear R. Bedwell was promoted to master in 1860 aboard HMS *Hecate*, which took over from the *Plumper* that Dec as the main survey vessel on the BC coast. He was a talented artist, and several of his drawings and paintings of the BC coast have been preserved at the BC Archives. He also did extensive survey work in Australia—especially on the Queensland coast, where he married Emily Harrison (1840–1909, née Ackerley), a widow, in 1877—before retiring in England with the rank of cdr. Bedwell Lk on Vancouver I is named for him as well. Bedwell Hbr's Hul'qumi'num (Coast Salish) name is Ste'yus, meaning "wind drying." *W*

Beechey Head (48°19'00" 123°39'00" S tip of Vancouver I, W of Becher Bay). Rear Adm Frederick William Beechey (1796–1856) was a prominent RN navigator and geographer. In 1818 he served under Lt John Franklin (the future famed Arctic explorer) on Capt David Buchan's expedition to Spitsbergen. In 1819–20 he accompanied Lt William Edward Parry on his successful exploration of parts of the NW Passage in HMS *Hecla*. Beechey was present for important surveys of the Mediterranean coast of Africa (1821–22), Bering Str and W Arctic (1825–28), S America (1835–36) and Ireland (1837–47). An accomplished artist and author of several books, he was elected president of the Royal Geographical Society, 1855–56. Named in 1846 by Capt Henry Kellett. *W*

Beech Islet (52°02'00" 128°17'00" SE of Athabaskan I, SW of Bella Bella). Commodore William James Robert Beech (1895–1975) was born on Saltspring I, enrolled as a cadet at the Royal Naval College of Canada in 1912 and first served on submarines, becoming cdr of HMS *L-1* in 1920. He married Beatrice Annie Wolfenden (1902–87) at Esquimalt in 1924. Beech commanded a number of RCN vessels, including the trawler *Thiepval* (1924) and the destroyers *Patrician* (1924–26) and *Saguenay* (1936–38). In 1931 he was CO at Esquimalt naval base and from 1940–43 was appointed CO for the Pacific Coast. He concluded

his distinguished career as chief of staff to the cdr-in-chief NW Atlantic and was awarded the US Legion of Merit in 1946, the year after he retired from the RCN and settled at Victoria. The islet was named by the hydrographic service in 1944.

Beeton Point (52°12'00" 128°28'00" W side of Athlone I, W of Bella Bella). Ann Beeton (1804–84) was the first white woman to settle in the Metchosin district, W of Victoria. She and her husband, Thomas Blinkhorn (1806–56), arrived in BC in 1851 with her teenaged niece, Martha Cheney. In partnership with Capt James Cooper, a trader, they established 160-ha Bilston Farm. After Thomas's death, Ann lived at Victoria with Martha and her husband, Henry Ella. Formerly known as Ledge Point but renamed by regional hydrographer Henri Parizeau in 1929. *See also* Blinkhorn Peninsula, Cheney Point *and* Cooper Inlet.

Begg Point (52°33'00" 128°26'00" SW end of Roderick I, opposite Klemtu Passage, NW of Bella Bella). Born in Scotland, journalist Alexander Begg (1825–1905) became an immigration commissioner for Ont and, later, BC and influenced many of his countrymen to head W. While his overly ambitious colonization schemes failed (as did his attempts to influence the boundary dispute between Canada and Alaska), he did manage to write *History of British Columbia from Its Earliest Discovery to the Present Time* in 1894. It was the second history of BC, after Hubert Howe Bancroft's three groundbreaking volumes on the PNW (1884–87). Begg is not to be confused with another Alexander Begg (1839–97), also a journalist and immigration agent, who was an early historian of Manitoba. The hydrographic service named several features on Roderick I after BC historians in 1948.

Belcarra Bay (49°19'00" 122°55'00" SE side of Indian Arm, NE of Vancouver). Belcarra is from the Irish Gaelic and can be translated as "a lovely land that the sun shines on." The name was bestowed in the 1880s by New Westminster lawyer and judge William Norman Bole, who was from Ireland, naturally, and who obtained a large piece of land in the area in a somewhat unusual way. He defended the previous owner, an Irish horticulturist named John Hall, against a charge of murder and got the charge reduced to manslaughter. Hall, unable to pay Bole, was forced to sign his land over to his lawyer, who sold part of it on Hall's behalf so he would have money on his release from prison, kept part of it as a family summer retreat and sold the rest much later for residential development. An important Tsleil-Waututh First Nation winter village, Tum-tay-whuen-ton, was once situated on the bay; its name means "end of the wind," as the westerlies that blow up Burrard Inlet seem to rise there and pass over the land. The contemporary suburban village of Belcarra, now site of a large regional park, is part of Greater Vancouver Regional District.

Belcher Point (49°25'00" 126°04'00" S side of Shelter Inlet, NE of Flores I, Clayoquot Sd, W side of Vancouver I). RN officer Sir Edward Belcher (1799–1877) was born at Halifax, grandson of Jonathan Belcher, who was a lt gov of NS. Edward was assistant surveyor on Frederick Beechey's Pacific voyages in the 1820s and '30s. As cdr of HMS *Sulphur*, he visited and took observations at Nootka Sd in 1837 as part of a six-year assignment to chart the W coasts of N and S America (*see* Sulphur Passage). In 1852, as a capt, Belcher commanded an infamous Arctic expedition in search of Sir John Franklin. After two unsuccessful years, he abandoned four vessels in the pack ice (against the urgent advice of his subordinates) and returned home. One of the ships, HMS *Resolute*, was later found by whalers, quite intact. Belcher faced a court martial for this action but was acquitted. He published several narratives of his voyages, as well as a standard treatise on nautical surveying, and attained the rank of adm, retired, in 1872. Mt Belcher on Saltspring I is also named for him. *W*

Belize Inlet (51°08'00" 127°09'00" N of Seymour Inlet and Queen Charlotte Str). Named in 1865 by Lt Daniel Pender of the *Beaver* in honour of Frederick Seymour, gov of BC, 1864–69, who had previously been gov of British Honduras and lived at Belize, its capital. *See* Seymour Inlet. *E*

Beljay Bay (52°42'00" 131°38'00" In Atli Inlet, N side of Lyell I, E of Moresby I, QCI), **Beljay Point** (52°42'00" 131°37'00" W entrance to Beljay Bay). Beljay was the telegraph code name for B L Johnson, Walton Co Ltd, gen shipping agents for Kelley Logging, which had its HQ at Atli Inlet for many years. Thomas A Kelley, a civil engineer from the US, became active in the QCI prior to WWI and ended up running one of the largest logging operations on the islands, providing wood to the Whalen Pulp & Paper Co mill at Swanson Bay and to the Powell River Co, which eventually took over his business interests about 1945. Beljay Bay was formerly known as Centre Bay but was renamed sometime before 1930. *D*

Bella Bella (52°09'43" 128°08'42" On NE Campbell I and W Denny I on either side of Lama Passage, NE of Queens Sd), **Bella Bella Islands** (52°10'00" 128°07'00" Off NW Denny I). Bella Bella is an adaptation of the name of the Heiltsuk First Nation settlement originally established at McLoughlin Bay, where the HBC had a post, Fort McLoughlin, 1833–45. The name appears in the 1834 journal of HBC trader and medical officer William Fraser Tolmie as Bilbilla. Historians Philip and Helen Akrigg have suggested that the name may derive from a word meaning "flat point," describing the location of the village site; another explanation is that it represents the Heiltsuk pronunciation of Milbanke (the name of a nearby sound) re-assimilated into English. Bolstered by a new HBC store and a Methodist mission and school, Bella Bella village

Postcard of Bella Bella from the early 1900s. *Author's collection*

moved farther N, to its present location on Campbell I, in the 1890s and grew to become the main Heiltsuk centre and an important central-coast community. It was sometimes referred to as New Bella Bella, but since 1974 the post office name has been Waglisla (qv). The non-Native part of Bella Bella, on Denny I, once boasted a major cannery and used to be known as Old Bella Bella (or E Bella Bella). A marina and resort named Shearwater, on the site of a WWII seaplane base, just N of the abandoned cannery, later became the heart of the Denny I community. *E W*

Bella Coola (52°23'00" 126°45'00" Head of N Bentinck Arm, E of Burke Channel and Bella Bella), **Bella Coola River** (Flows W into N Bentinck Arm). Bella Coola is a Heiltsuk First Nation name for the aboriginal inhabitants of the area, who call themselves the Nuxalk people, after their term for the Bella Coola valley. The name appears as Billichoola in the 1834 journal of HBC trader and medical officer William Fraser Tolmie, and it has also been recorded as Bellaghchoola, Bellichoola, Belhoola and Bi'lxula. The main Nuxalk village, Q'umquots (Komkotes), has long been located at the site of Bella Coola, near the mouth of the Bella Coola R. Alexander Mackenzie arrived at this spot in 1793 to become the first white person to cross N America N of Mexico; he referred to the community as Rascal's Village after surviving an altercation with the local residents. Members of Capt George Vancouver's expedition also arrived that year, from the sea. The HBC had a post here, 1868–82, later purchased by its former manager, trader John Clayton. A colony of Norwegian settlers arrived in the valley in 1894 and farmed, while several salmon canneries operated on the waterfront. The community of Bella Coola, with a population of almost 1,000 in the early 2000s, was not linked to the rest of BC by road until 1953. *E W*

Belle Chain Islets (48°50'00" 123°11'00" N of Saturna I, Gulf Is). Isabel Gertrude "Belle" Nagle (b 1846) was the youngest daughter of Capt Jeremiah Nagle (1800–82), who was Victoria harbourmaster in the 1860s and '70s, and an important landowner in the capital city. She was born in NZ and migrated with her family to California in

B

the 1850s, arriving at Victoria in 1859. In 1865 she married Philip J Hankin, a former RN officer on the BC coast who later held various positions in the BC colonial service, including superintendent of police (1864–66) and colonial secretary (1869–71). He also served as colonial secretary of British Honduras, 1866–68, and Sierra Leone, 1868–69 (*see* Hankin Cove). W

Belleisle Sound (50°53'00" 126°25'00" S side of Kingcome Inlet, N of W Johnstone Str). Named in 1864 by Lt Daniel Pender of the hired survey vessel *Beaver*, in association with Kingcome Inlet. Cdr John Kingcome had been in command of HMS *Belleisle*, a 20-gun troopship, in China in the 1840s. In 1863–64, as a rear adm, he was cdr-in-chief of the RN's Pacific Station, based at Esquimalt. The 1,547-tonne *Belleisle* was launched in 1819, converted to a hospital ship in 1854 and broken up in 1872. W

Belle Point (53°13'00" 132°03'00" N end of Maude I, Skidegate Inlet, QCI). Marie Isabella "Belle" Gillatt was a daughter of Capt James Gillatt (*see* Gillatt Arm), a retired British Army officer and Boer War veteran. The Gillatt family were pioneer settlers at Sandspit, moving there from Port Simpson in 1911 and building a large home and ranch. Belle took over her father's tidewatching duties for the hydrographic service while he was in hospital at Prince Rupert. She married William Henry G Brandon (1903–47) in 1926 and moved to Victoria. D

Bellhouse Bay (48°52'16" 123°18'37" SE end of Galiano I, Gulf Is). John Wortley Bellhouse (1862–1921) and his large family arrived in BC from Manitoba in 1907. He purchased the Galiano I farm that Robert Grubb had established about 1890, built up Grubb's Jersey herd and dairy business, raised flocks of poultry and developed an apple orchard. The cattle, apparently named after characters from the novels of Charles Dickens, won prizes at all the local fairs. His son, Leonard Thorneycroft Bellhouse (1894–1968), whose wife Jessie was a granddaughter of BC attorney gen Henry Crease, took over the property in 1921 and turned his old home into the Farmhouse Inn. He donated the land to BC in 1964 as a provincial park. The name was adopted in 1969 after being submitted the year before by the Gulf Is Branch of the BC Historical Assoc.

Bell Point (52°58'00" 132°14'00" Entrance to Douglas Inlet, W side of Moresby I, QCI). John Bell was the paymaster aboard HMS *Thetis* and served on the Pacific Station, 1851–53, under Capt Augustus Kuper. Kuper named this feature in 1852 while the *Thetis* patrolled and surveyed the area as a preventative measure during the short-lived QCI gold rush.

Belmont Point (49°48'00" 126°56'00" E entrance to Port Langford, Nuchatlitz Inlet, W side of Vancouver I). Named in 1862 by RN surveyor Capt George Richards after

Belmont, the Esquimalt Hbr residence of David Cameron, brother-in-law of Gov James Douglas and chief justice of the colony of Vancouver I, 1853–65. Cameron named his home after his former estate in British Guiana (Guyana). Belmont was eventually dismantled when Fort Rodd Hill was developed but still lends its name to the neighbouring area, Belmont Park, a suburb of the city of Colwood. *See also* Cameron Rks. W

Belvedere Rock (49°20'00" 122°53'00" N of Bedwell Bay, E side of Indian Arm, NE of Vancouver). The rock is in Farrer Cove (qv), just off Belvedere Landing, one of the many summer recreation areas on Indian Arm that used to be served by vessels of the Harbour Navigation Co. A belvedere, from the Italian for "beautiful view," is a lookout tower on the roof of a building. The name was suggested by the hydrographic service and adopted in 1948.

Bendickson Harbour (50°24'53" 125°55'21" S side of Hardwicke I, N side of Johnstone Str opposite Sayward). Hans Andreas Bendickson (1878–1952) arrived in BC from Norway in 1901 and became a logger, working first in Howe Sd and on Broughton I. He established his own logging operations, complete with floating camps, at Port Moody, Quadra I, Pitt Lk and Britannia Beach, then settled with his wife, Gjertrud (1881–1969), née Andersdatter), and their seven children on Hardwicke I in 1918. The family raised vegetables and livestock, and their company, Bendickson Logging, built a breakwater and safe harbour at Earl Ledge in 1950 and maintained the island wharf. Several family members still live on Hardwicke. The harbour name was endorsed by local residents and adopted in 2000 to acknowledge the family's contributions in the region.

Benjamin Point (52°13'00" 131°00'00" Extreme SE point of Moresby I, QCI). After 19th-century British naturalist and author William Benjamin Carpenter. *See* Carpenter Bay. Formerly known as Islet Point but renamed by the hydrographic service in 1946.

Ben Mohr Rock (48°51'00" 123°23'00" In Trincomali Channel, off SW Galiano I, Gulf Is). Named in the early 1900s for the 3,000-tonne Scottish steamer *Benmohr*, under Capt A Wallace, which "grazed" this rock in 1900 after leaving Ladysmith with a load of coal. Two years later it collided with the *Banffshire* off England's Thames estuary, spilling a cargo of cement-filled barrels along the shoreline. The *Benmohr*, which was built at Glasgow in 1893 and owned by the Ben Line of Leith, was sold to Japanese interests in 1911 and renamed the *Nippo Maru*. It was scrapped in Japan in 1927.

Bennett Bay (48°51'00" 123°14'00" E side of Mayne I, Gulf Is). The Bennett family, whose members homesteaded and farmed beside the bay, were Mayne I pioneers,

The wharf at Bennett Bay on Mayne Island, looking out to Georgeson Island. *Kevin Oke*

arriving about 1880. Thomas Bennett (1845–1924), a native of Ireland, and his Scottish wife, Elsie (1846–1926), immigrated to Canada with two children in 1878. From 1895 to 1900 they were the proprietors of the Point Comfort Hotel (later the Cherry Tree Inn), a Mayne I landmark until 1958, when it was torn down. Elsie Bennett also served as a Gulf Is midwife for many years. Bennett Bay was submitted by the Public Works dept in 1939 as a well-established name and adopted by the hydrographic service in 1951.

Bennett Islet (53°35'00" 130°34'00" W side of Rawlinson Anchorage, off NW Banks I). Named by regional hydrographer Henri Parizeau in 1921 after James Bennett, who was a quartermaster aboard the survey vessel *Lillooet* in the early 1920s.

Benney Islets (52°35'00" 129°10'00" Off Clifford Bay, SW side of Aristazabal I). Sapper Henry J Benney came to BC with the Columbia detachment of Royal Engineers, which served in the province 1858–63. He arrived in 1859 on *Thames City* with the main body of men and participated in the amateur theatricals that passengers put on to pass the time. Benney, in fact, wore women's attire to play the role of Estelle de Burgh in a production of *Crossing the Line*, and was roundly teased for it in *The Emigrant Soldier's Gazette & Cape Horn Chronicle*, published on board during the voyage. He stayed on in BC after the detachment was disbanded, building a home in New Westminster that was destroyed by fire in 1864.

Benn Point (52°17'00" 127°45'00" E side of Cousins Inlet, SW of Ocean Falls). Sir Ion Hamilton Benn (1863–1961), Conservative MP for Greenwich, England, 1910–22, and also a former mayor of Greenwich, was one of the promotors of the original Ocean Falls Co, which went bankrupt in 1913. He visited the area in 1908. Benn, who

was born in Ireland, was the chairman of Price & Pierce Ltd, a leading British timber company. He saw notable service during WWI as part of the RNVR, leading a flotilla of raiders along the Belgian coast, receiving the DSO and being appointed a CB in 1918. He was also chairman of Greenwich's Dreadnought Hospital for seamen for many years. Benn Point was adopted by the hydrographic service in 1925.

Benrot Island (52°21'20" 127°43'25" NW side of Cousins Inlet, W of Ocean Falls). Capt J Benrot worked as a ship's master for the HBC and was also a pilot at Nanaimo. The names Price I and Finmore I (after Walter Finmore, a storekeeper at Esquimalt dockyard) had originally been suggested for this feature, but Benrot I was chosen by the hydrographic service in 1925.

Bensins Island (52°13'00" 126°55'00" In S Bentinck Arm, SW of Bella Coola). The name is a corruption of the surname of Archibald Menzies, the RN assistant surgeon and naturalist who accompanied Capt George Vancouver on his 1792–94 PNW explorations (*see* Menzies Bay). Fur trader Alexander Mackenzie reported in his journal that when he arrived at this location, at the end of his historic 1793 overland journey, he was told by the First Nation inhabitants of the area that white men had recently visited by boat—Bensins (Menzies) and Macubah (Vancouver), in particular. Named in 1924 on the suggestion of BC's surveyor gen.

Benson Island (48°53'00" 125°23'00" In the Broken Group, Barkley Sd, W side of Vancouver I). John Webb Benson (1850–1913), a native of Maine, pre-empted land on this island in 1893 and built a rustic hotel there, Barclay House. Benson was a local character; he reportedly hitched a pair of oxen to his boat and had them swim from place to place, towing him behind. A series

B

of women, ordered through a marriage bureau, appeared on the island as prospective brides, only to discover that their real purpose was to serve as unpaid hotel employees. The ninth of these unfortunates, Ella Matilda, did indeed marry Benson; she bought the entire island in 1911 for $600 and ran the resort for several years after his death. The property changed owners several times before becoming part of Pacific Rim National Park Reserve in 1970. No trace remains of Barclay House, and there are only a few signs of the pasturage and gardens created by Benson and his successors. This feature appears as Hawkins I on an Admiralty chart published in 1865 but was changed by the hydrographic service in 1934.

Benson Point (49°47'00" 126°53'00" N side of Nuchatlitz Inlet, Nootka I, W side of Vancouver I). Probably named by RN surveyor Capt George Richards after his friend Dr Alfred Robson Benson, who was employed as the medical officer at Nanaimo by the HBC, 1857–62, and then by the Vancouver Coal Co, 1862–64. Lt Charles Wilson, secretary of the N American Boundary Commission, visited Nanaimo in 1858 and described Benson as "a great character, never seen without a pipe in his mouth, and his rooms are crowded with Indian curiosities, bird skins, geological specimens, books and tobacco in the most inextricable confusion." Benson was returning officer in Vancouver I's colonial legislative election of 1859, when there was only one qualified voter at Nanaimo, Capt Charles Stuart, who nevertheless elected the candidate, Capt John Swanson, by a majority of one. Mt Benson and Benson Ck, both on Vancouver I, are also named for him.

Bent Harbour (52°31'00" 129°03'00" N side of Weeteeam Bay, SW side of Aristazabal I). Reginald Whitman Bent (1882–1962) served as a junior hydrographer on the 1926 survey of this part of the BC coast. He began working for the Canadian Hydrographic Service in 1915 and served mostly on the E coast, especially on the St Lawrence R and Gulf of St Lawrence, and in NS and NB. In 1931, Bent was officer in charge of CGS *Cartier*, after which he was reassigned to Ottawa, where he was made responsible for many of the service's publications, particularly *Sailing Directions*. He retired in 1944.

Bentinck Island (48°19'00" 123°32'00" Between Race Rks and extreme S tip of Vancouver I). This feature may have been named after Lord George Bentinck (1802–48), a British Conservative politician and racehorse owner, and a grandson of William Cavendish-Bentinck, 3rd Duke of Portland (*see* Bentinck Narrows). The island, reserved in 1860 for a lighthouse that was never built, replaced D'Arcy I as Canada's only leprosy colony on the W coast. Between 1924 and 1956, when the leprosarium was closed, 22 patients lived on the island in 15 private cottages. Two larger buildings housed nurses and caretakers. Most patients were of Asian heritage, although one, the only woman, was a Caucasian missionary who had contracted the disease in Africa. Since 1962 the island has been used intermittently as an RCN demolition range. Vestiges of gardens, maintained by the former inhabitants, remain, as does a cemetery, where 13 patients are buried.

Bentinck Narrows (51°59'00" 126°41'00" Near the head of S Bentinck Arm), **North Bentinck Arm** (52°22'00" 126°53'00" Between the mouth of the Bella Coola R and Burke Channel), **South Bentinck Arm** (52°10'00" 126°50'00" S of N Bentinck Arm and Bella Coola). William Henry Cavendish-Bentinck (1738–1809), 3rd Duke of Portland, was a Tory statesman who served as PM of Britain in 1783 and 1807–9. The N and S Bentinck arms were named by Capt George Vancouver in 1793 after Lt James Johnstone had explored the area in HMS *Chatham*, the smaller of Vancouver's two vessels. Bentinck Narrows was named by the hydrographic service in 1958. **W**

Bentley Rock (50°18'00" 125°14'00" Upper Rapids, Okisollo Channel, NE of Quadra I, N of Campbell R). Herbert Bentley (1866–1928) and his wife, Rolla, were early settlers at Waiatt Bay on the NE end of Quadra I, where they ran a small store and post office, 1916–28 (the post office name was spelled Wyatt Bay). Herbert had apparently been a railroad engineer in England and worked on logging railways on the BC coast before becoming a storekeeper. The rock was named by the hydrographic service about 1924.

Berens Island (48°25'00" 123°24'00" W side of Victoria Hbr, SE end of Vancouver I). Named by the officers of Ft Victoria after the father and son duo of Joseph Berens (1774–1853) and Henry Hulse Berens (1804–83). Joseph, a lawyer, was deputy gov of the HBC, 1807–12, and gov, 1812–22. His son Henry Hulse was deputy gov, 1856–58, and gov, 1858–63. Henry was also a director of the Bank of England. A lighthouse was built on the island in 1874 but was converted to an automated beacon in 1925. The name was adopted by Capt Henry Kellett of the RN on his 1846 survey of the area. **W**

Beresford Bay (54°03'00" 133°06'00" NW side of Graham I, QCI). William Beresford was assistant trader, cargo officer and purser aboard Capt George Dixon's merchant vessel *Queen Charlotte*. In 1787, Dixon made a historic fur-trading journey around much of the QCI and was the first European to realize that the islands were an archipelago. Beresford kept a journal of the voyage and in 1789 wrote *A Voyage Round the World; but more Particularly to the North-West Coast of America*, published by Dixon. The bay was named by Capt Frederick Learmonth of HMS *Egeria*, who surveyed this area in 1907. Nearby Beresford Ck is named after the bay. The Scott Is off Cape Scott were originally called Beresford's Is by George Dixon.

Beresford Inlet (52°37'00" 131°36'00" SW end of Lyell I, E of Moresby I, QCI). According to QCI historian Kathleen Dalzell, this feature, formerly known as Beresford Arm, was named after Henry Lawry "Charlie" Beresford, an early prospector in the QCI and sub-mining recorder at Lockeport, 1908–12. "Even when on a drunk," a Dalzell source reported, Beresford "was always very much a gentleman" and was nicknamed "The Admiral," after a supposed connection with British politician and adm Lord Charles Beresford (*see below*). He returned to England at the beginning of WWI. A record at BC's Geographical Names Office, however, suggests that the inlet may in fact have been named after William Beresford of Beresford Bay (qv). *D*

Beresford Island (50°47'26" 128°46'22" One of the Scott Is, off NW tip of Vancouver I). Charles William de la Poer Beresford (1846–1919), 1st Baron Beresford, was a British adm and politician. He was a junior officer aboard HMS *Clio*, *Tribune* and *Sutlej* on the Pacific Station (based at Esquimalt), 1864–67, and later had a distinguished naval career, serving as cdr of several warships and as naval aide-de-camp to the Prince of Wales. Beresford was promoted rear adm and deputy cdr of the Mediterranean fleet in 1897, adm and cdr of the Channel fleet in 1902 and cdr of the Mediterranean fleet in 1905–7. He was a Conservative MP in 1875–80, 1885–88, 1897–1900, 1902–6 and 1909–16. Beresford I was formerly known as E Haycock I but was renamed by the hydrographic service in 1946.

Berge Islet (49°43'17" 124°10'20" In Blind Bay, S entrance to Jervis Inlet, NW of Vancouver). Stoker 1st Class Olaf Elmer Berge, of Vancouver, was killed in action Apr 16, 1945, aged 20, while serving aboard HMCS *Esquimalt*. The minesweeper was torpedoed near Halifax Hbr by the German submarine *U-190*, with the loss of 44 hands. Berge is buried at Mountainview Cemetery, Vancouver. This is a relatively recent place name addition, adopted in 1990.

Bernard Point (50°19'00" 125°07'00" N tip of Maurelle I, N of Campbell R). Named by the hydrographic service in 1954 after Trafford Bernard, a well-known local resident and railway logger who operated in the Hole in the Wall and Port Neville areas, and at Orford Bay on Bute Inlet. His companies—Southgate Logging, Homalco Logging and Bernard Timber & Logging—were major employers in the region in the 1920s; the Orford Bay camp alone was home to three locomotives and a 600-man crew. Bernard's descendants still live in the district. He died at Alert Bay in 1938.

Berryman Cove (49°09'00" 125°40'00" S side of Tofino Inlet, Clayoquot Sd, W side of Vancouver I), **Berryman Point** (49°09'00" 125°41'00" E side of Tofino Inlet, S of McCaw Peninsula). Harry Berryman (1872–1932), a native of Quebec City, was manager of the salmon cannery at Kennfalls for many years. Located at the outlet of Kennedy Lk, site of the region's main sockeye run, the facility was operated from 1899 to about 1930 by the Clayoquot Sd Canning Co, which also co-owned and ran a fleet of seiners manned by local crews. The two geographical names were adopted in 1977.

Berry Point (49°18'00" 122°59'00" S side of Vancouver Hbr, E of Second Narrows). Coastal historian John Walbran says that the point commemorates Rear Adm Sir Edward Berry (1768–1831), but it's possible that it was simply named (by Capt George Richards, about 1860) after a profusion of berry bushes. Berry was a follower of Adm Lord Nelson and served as his flag capt on HMS *Vanguard* at the Battle of the Nile in 1798. He was also present at the famous naval battles of St Vincent (1797) and Trafalgar (1805). *W*

Bessborough Bay (50°29'00" 125°47'00" N of Hardwicke I and Johnstone Str). Named by Admiralty surveyors in 1865 after the earls of Bessborough, a powerful Irish family. Edward Ponsonby (1851–1920), an RN midshipman who served for a time on the BC coast, was a nephew of John George Brabazon Ponsonby (1809–80), the 5th Earl of Bessborough. In 1906, Edward inherited the title himself. He left the RN as a lt in 1876, became a lawyer, civil servant and businessman, and held numerous ceremonial offices in Ireland over the course of his life. *W*

Best Point (49°23'00" 122°53'00" W side of Indian Arm, NE of Vancouver). Named by the hydrographic service in 1966 after Private Wilfred Marshall Best, from Deep Cove, who was killed in action Sept 17, 1944, aged 37, while serving with the Seaforth Highlanders in Italy. He is buried at Coriano Ridge War Cemetery on the Adriatic coast.

Betteridge Inlet (53°06'00" 129°30'00" W side of Campania I, Caamaño Sd). Ernie Betteridge had a lengthy career aboard CGS *William J Stewart*, serving as a boatswain in the early 1940s and as 1st officer by 1964. Named by the hydrographic service in 1944.

Betton Rocks (53°15'00" 129°29'00" SE side of Pitt I). Roderick Betton, a native of Glasgow, born about 1766, was a sailmaker's mate aboard HMS *Discovery* during Capt George Vancouver's 18th-century exploration of the PNW coast. The name was adopted by the hydrographic service in 1950. Betton was seriously wounded at Escape Point in SE Alaska in 1793 when a survey party under Vancouver's command was attacked by Tlingit First Nation warriors. Vancouver did not normally name geographical features after his seamen: only officers and gentlemen were so honoured. He made an exception with Betton, however (and with John Carter; *see* Carter Bay), and named Betton I in Behm Canal after this "unfortunate shipmate."

B

Bickle Passage (51°34'00" 127°34'00" N side of Walbran I, Rivers Inlet). According to BC historians Helen and Philip Akrigg, Eddie Bickle was working as the laundryman at Dr George Darby's Rivers Inlet hospital at the time a new coastal survey was being conducted in the late 1930s. The name was adopted by the hydrographic service in 1947.

Big Bay (50°24'00" 125°08'00" W side of Stuart I, mouth of Bute Inlet). This small logging and fishing community, also known as Yaculta Landing in its early days, became established after the arrival of early settler Anderson Secord in 1907. A school operated in the late 1920s. When residents lobbied for a post office in the 1960s, they argued that the established local name was Big Bay, not Asman Bay as the feature had previously been marked on charts (*see* Asman Point). In the early 2000s, a store, marina and resort were operating there. *E*

Big Bay on west side of Stuart Island. *Peter Vassilopoulos*

Bigsby Inlet (52°37'00" 131°45'00" W side of Darwin Sd, E side of Moresby I, QCI), **Bigsby Point** (52°36'00" 131°40'00" S entrance to Bigsby Inlet). Dr John Jeremiah Bigsby (1792–1881), an English physician and geologist, joined the British Army medical service and was stationed in Canada, 1818–27. He prepared a report on the geology of Upper Canada and in 1822 was appointed British secretary and medical officer to the International Boundary Commission. He returned to England to practise medicine and to write, mostly about geology and paleontology. He was elected a member of the Royal Society and the Geological Society of London. A two-volume memoir of his time in Canada, *The Shoe and Canoe*, appeared in 1850. The inlet was named by George M Dawson of the Geological Survey of Canada in 1878. The point was named in association with the inlet by the hydrographic service in 1962. Nearby Jeremiah Point is also named for this scientist. *W*

Billard Rock (50°26'00" 127°58'00" Entrance to Quatsino Sd, W of Harvey Cove, NW end of Vancouver I). George Lewis Billard (1898–1987) was the coxswain of CGS

Restless, a sounding launch used during the 1921 survey of Quatsino Sd. He was born at Victoria, where his father, a Nfld native, worked for the sealing industry. From 1945 to 1959, Billard served as capt and sailing master of the survey vessel *William J Stewart*, working especially in the QCI, Hecate Str and Queen Charlotte Sd, but also in many other parts of BC. The rock was named by the hydrographic service in 1927.

Billings Bay (49°42'00" 124°12'00" NW side of Nelson I, mouth of Jervis Inlet, NW of Vancouver), **Billings Point** (Just NE of Billings Spit), **Billings Spit** (48°22'00" 123°41'00" NE end of Sooke Hbr, between Sooke Hbr and Sooke Basin, S end of Vancouver I). William Thomas Billings served as assistant surgeon aboard HMS *Herald* in 1846 when that vessel, under Capt Henry Kellett, surveyed Victoria Hbr and the adjacent waters of Juan de Fuca Str. Billings retired in 1874 as a staff surgeon. Billings Point was also known in the 1920s and '30s as Jackson's Point. Billings Bay, where Union steamships once served a floating freight shed and post office, was a focal point for many Nelson I settlers in the 1950s and '60s.

Billington Rocks (52°10'00" 131°20'00" SE of Nagas Point, SW end of Moresby I, QCI). Capt Billington was master of the Pacific Whaling Co's tender *Gray* in the early 1920s. The vessel carried supplies and whaling products between the company's five whaling stations and W coast ports, 1910–39, and was also chartered out to various shipping firms. Named in 1962 by the hydrographic service.

Bilton Island (51°27'00" 127°40'00" S of Ripon I, mouth of Rivers Inlet), **Bilton Point** (49°01'00" 124°52'00" W side of Alberni Inlet, Vancouver I). Tasmania-born Henry Reginald Bilton (1874–1959) was a veteran mariner on the BC coast. He served his apprenticeship aboard the *Thermopylae*, which was one of the fastest and most famous "clipper" ships in the tea trade before being reduced to transporting rice, coal and lumber between China and the PNW. Bilton worked on coastal steamships in the early 1900s before becoming master of CGS *Newington*, a lighthouse supply vessel and buoy tender. He was best known as skipper of the much larger CGS *Estevan*, the main lighthouse tender on the BC S coast, a position he held from 1922 to 1944. He was a long-time Victoria resident. Both features were named by the hydrographic service in 1946–47.

Bingham Narrows (52°38'00" 128°37'00" In Alexander Inlet, Princess Royal I, NW of Bella Bella). Named in 1948 after Lady Margaret Diana Bingham (1905–77), the popular wife of Harold R L G Alexander, 1st Earl of Tunis and 17th gov gen of Canada, 1946–52. She was the second daughter of the Earl of Lucan and married Lord Alexander in 1931. They had four children, including one adopted during their stay in Canada.

B

Binnington Bay (50°20'00" 125°19'00" Just W of Cameleon Hbr, W side of Sonora I, N of Campbell R). William Binnington served as 2nd lt aboard HMS *Cameleon*, a 17-gun sloop based at Esquimalt on the Pacific Station, 1863–65. (The *Cameleon* was also stationed on the BC coast in 1867–69 and 1870–74, but without Binnington.) He was present in 1863 when several RN warships, including the *Cameleon*, searched for the murderers of a Saturna I family, a pursuit that eventually resulted in the shelling and destruction of a Lamalcha First Nation village on Kuper I (*see* Lamalchi Bay). RN surveyor Lt Daniel Pender commemorated the event by naming a number of features around Cameleon Hbr after the warship's officers in 1863.

Binns Island (49°20'00" 125°57'00" E side of Herbert Inlet, Clayoquot Sd, W side of Vancouver I). Charles Carlyle "Cap" Binns (1873–1939), a pioneer prospector on the W coast of Vancouver I, was listed as a farmer on the 1898 BC voters list. He was the original discoverer of placer gold in the beach sand at Florencia Bay, near Tofino, in the late 1890s. The sands were worked for several years by the Ucluelet Placer Co but eventually proved uneconomical. In 1933, Binns and two others found gold at the head of Herbert Inlet and sold their claims (the Big Boy group) to Herbert Arm Gold Mines of Vancouver. Named by the hydrographic service in 1934.

Birch Point (53°36'00" 130°33'00" S side of Griffith Hbr, NW Banks I, S of Prince Rupert). Named in 1926 by regional hydrographer Henri Parizeau after R Birch, who was a seaman serving aboard W coast survey vessel *Lillooet* in the early 1920s.

Birkby Point (51°18'00" 127°35'00" NW side of Greaves I, Smith Sd, N of Port Hardy). Named by coastal mariner and historian John T Walbran in 1903 after the farm and homestead of Birkby Nab in Yorkshire, ancient abode of the Greaves family, who were ancestors of Walbran's wife, Anne. Nearby Nab Patch is also named for this British locality. *W*

Birnie Island (54°35'46" 130°27'34" Entrance to Port Simpson, N of Prince Rupert). James Birnie (c 1800–64), born at Aberdeen, Scotland, came to Canada in 1816. Two years later he joined the NWC as a clerk at Ft Spokane, and after that company amalgamated with the HBC in 1821, he was sent to Ft George (now Astoria) on the Pacific coast. He served at a number of inland posts, including Ft Colville, Ft Okanogan and Ft Umpqua, and assisted Dr John McLoughlin with the establishment of Ft Vancouver on the Columbia R in 1824. Birnie was dispatched to Ft Simpson in northern BC in 1831 and helped relocate that trading post farther S in 1834, after which he returned to Oregon about 1838 to take charge of Ft George. He retired in 1845 and settled at Cathlamet, Washington, where, not surprisingly, he opened a store. Birnie I was named by

HBC officials about 1836. A lighthouse was located there, 1905–17. *W*

Bischof Islands (52°34'00" 131°33'00" Off SW end of Lyell I, QCI). German chemist and geologist Karl Gustav Bischof (1792–1870) was a professor at Bonn Univ. He was noted for his work on the inflammable power of gas and the role of water in geological processes. Named by George Dawson of the Geological Survey of Canada in 1878.

Bishop Bay (53°28'00" 128°53'00" Extends NE from Ursula Channel, E of Gribbell I, N of Princess Royal I, S of Kitimat). According to anthropologist Jay Powell, this bay is known to the Haisla First Nation as Giltu'yis (pronounced *GILL-tsoo-weez*), meaning "long inlet." Gilttoyees Inlet (qv) has the same Haisla name. The popular hot springs at the head of Bishop Bay is called Kukwsta. A floating logging camp was located on the bay in the 1930s, complete with a general store and post office (open 1933–38). The significance of the name is not known.

Bishop Island (54°14'00" 130°20'00" Just SW of Kaien I and Prince Rupert). Named in 1907 in association with nearby Ridley I (qv). William Ridley was the first Anglican bishop of the northern BC diocese of Caledonia.

Bishop Point (50°15'00" 124°48'00" NE side of W Redonda I, entrance to Toba Inlet, NE of Campbell R). Bishop Point and nearby Church and Dean points all resulted from a binge of ecclesiastical naming, probably by Capt George Richards in 1862 or Lt Daniel Pender in 1864.

Bishop Rock (52°20'00" 131°09'00" Entrance to Skincuttle Inlet, SE side of Moresby I, QCI). Charles Bishop (c 1765–1810), from Hampshire, was a former RN midshipman who was employed as a ship's capt by Bristol merchant Sidenham Teast. He worked off the W Africa coast, 1792–94, then was given command of the *Ruby*, a small vessel that traded in the QCI in 1795. Fearing that the 100-tonne *Ruby* had been damaged by grounding on a ledge, Bishop cut short his BC voyage and headed S to spend the winter on the Columbia R, further wrecking his ship on the notorious Columbia bar. In retrospect, these mishaps turned out to be fortunate, as Bishop later learned that, had he stayed in the QCI, Koya, the renegade Haida chief (*see* Koya Bay), was planning to attack him. He managed to sail the *Ruby* to China, where he sold it and bought the *Nautilus*, in which he traded around the S Pacific and Australasia, 1797–99. Back in England, Bishop went into partnership with explorer and surgeon George Bass. The pair bought the ship *Venus*, sailed back to Australia in 1801 and resumed trading in the region. Bass and the *Venus* famously disappeared in 1803, and Bishop farmed near Sydney until developing dementia and returning to England in 1809. Bishop Rk was named by the hydrographic service about 1962. *D*

Bjerre Rock

Bjerre Rock (50°18'00" 125°19'00" Okisollo Channel, N of Quadra I and Campbell R), **Bjerre Shoal** (49°34'00" 124°02'00" E side of Malaspina Str, S of Pender Hbr, SE of Powell R). August Jorgen Bjerre (1864–1921) emigrated from Denmark about 1880 and became a master mariner and pilot on the BC coast. He married Ellen Pederson (1866–1945) at Vancouver in 1890. In 1904 he was master of the tug *Active*. He died in Hecate Str aboard the tug *Commodore*. Both names appear to have been applied in the late 1890s.

Blackburn Peninsula (52°06'00" 131°00'00" NE side of Kunghit I, S of Moresby I, QCI). Capt David O "Lucky" Blackburn, originally from NS, became a fisherman on the Columbia R and then a master and owner of ships. According to QCI historian Kathleen Dalzell, he had a reputation as a risk taker, someone who might overload his vessel or leave the safety of port in all kinds of rough weather. During a terrible storm off Juan de Fuca Str in Dec 1894, Blackburn's luck ran out. In command of the coal carrier *Montserrat*, he went to the assistance of the foundering *Keeweenah*, also a coaler, but both ships sank, with the loss of all hands. Six months later and 600 km to the NW, debris from the two vessels was found at the S end of Moresby I. The name, formerly Blackburn Point, was adopted in 1962. *D*

Black Creek (49°50'00" 125°08'00" Between Courtenay and Campbell R, E side of Vancouver I). The actual creek that gives this community its name appears on Admiralty charts as Black Ck as early as 1865. The source of the name is not known. The village of Black Ck got its start in the 1930s after a group of Mennonites settled there to farm. A post office opened in 1936, and the community gradually became a service centre for the region; its population in the early 21st century was about 2,000. Logging and tourism have also become important in this area. *E*

Blackie Spit (49°04'00" 122°53'00" E side of Boundary Bay at mouth of Nickomekl R, S of Vancouver). Walter Blackie (1824–1902) was the first blacksmith at New Westminster and a city councillor. Of Scottish descent, he arrived from Australia in the early 1860s and bought land at Crescent Beach in 1871. He purchased the 2.6-hectare spit in 1875, for $6.50 ($1 an acre), and added more adjacent land in 1878. He eventually moved to California but returned to BC on his wife's death. Blackie died in New Westminster, leaving a substantial estate to a remote relative in Scotland.

Blackney Channel (51°19'00" 127°40'00" N side of Smith Sd, N of Port Hardy), **Blackney Island** (51°29'00" 128°06'00" Off SW side of Calvert I, S of Bella Bella), **Blackney Passage** (50°34'00" 126°41'00" Between Hanson I and Harbledown I, W entrance to Johnstone Str), **Blackney Point** (50°55'00" 127°06'00" N side of Drury Inlet, N of Queen Charlotte Str), **Port Blackney** (52°19'00" 128°21'00" SW side of Don Peninsula, NW of Bella Bella). William Blakeney (d about 1911) was an RN paymaster who spelled his name Blackney at the time these features were named. He served in BC, 1863–65, as assistant surveying officer aboard the *Beaver*, an HBC vessel hired by the RN for survey duties and commanded by Lt Daniel Pender. Blakeney married Elizabeth Reid (d 1873), youngest daughter of early HBC master mariner Capt James Murray Reid (*see* Reid Passage). Back in England, he was appointed secretary (naval assistant) to the RN's head hydrographer and retired in 1882 with the rank of chief paymaster. *W*

Blair Inlet (52°17'00" 128°23'00" SW side of Don Peninsula, NW of Bella Bella). David Blair was apparently a Victoria businessman at the time this inlet was first surveyed, by Lt Daniel Pender in 1867. There are no references to him, however, in early Victoria directories or voters lists.

Blanche Point (50°29'00" 125°42'00" N side of Forward Hbr, E of Hardwicke I, N of Johnstone Str). Lady Blanche Emma Lascelles (1837–63) was a sister of Lt Horace Lascelles, who was in command of the RN gunboat *Forward* on the BC coast, 1861–65 (*see* Lascelles Point). She became the Countess of Shannon by marrying Henry Boyle (1833–90), the 5th Earl of Shannon, in 1859. Lascelles was also a British aristocrat, a son of the Earl of Harewood, and Admiralty surveyors in the 1860s named many features in the vicinity of Forward Hbr after his family, including four points that commemorate his sisters.

Bland Island (50°30'00" 127°40'00" W of Brockton I, Buchholz Channel, Quatsino Sd, NW side of Vancouver I). Named by the hydrographic service in 1927 to commemorate the Bland family. Charles Loftus Bland (1882–1973), a native of Jersey in the Channel Is, spent more than 65 years on Quatsino Sd. He homesteaded on the S side of the sound, near Kewquodie Ck, in 1907, and with his second wife, Mary, raised five children there. According to regional historian Gwen Hansen, Charles was a follower of the Christian anarchist theories of Russian novelist Leo Tolstoy. He apparently spent decades writing a book called *The Principle of Unity* but was unable to finish it before he died.

Bland Point (53°02'00" 132°21'00" N side of Englefield Bay, NW Moresby I, QCI). Nathaniel Bland Herbert was 2nd master aboard HMS *Thetis*, 1851–53. *See* Herbert Head. Named by the hydrographic service about 1946.

Bland Rocks (53°02'00" 129°43'00" Off Oswald Bay in the Estevan Group, SE of Banks I, N of Caamaño Sd). James William Bland (1853–1921) was born in Peru and moved in 1859 with his family to Victoria, where his parents established an early Esquimalt hotel, the well-known

Halfway House. Bland worked as an usher at the Supreme Court of BC for 31 years, retiring in 1919. The feature was named in 1926 by hydrographer Henri Parizeau.

Blenkinsop Bay (50°29'00" 126°00'00" N side of Johnstone Str between Port Neville and Sunderland Channel, N of Sayward). George Blenkinsop (1822–1904), born in Cornwall, UK, joined the HBC in 1840. He was posted to Ft Stikine in northern BC, then helped establish Ft Rupert on N Vancouver I in 1850, working there until 1856. Blenkinsop was married twice: to Helen McNeill, one of the many daughters of pioneer HBC shipmaster William McNeill, and to Emma Oteokorie, of Iroquois and Kwakwaka'wakw descent, in 1884. After a stint at Ft Colville on the Columbia R, he took charge of Ft Langley, 1860–61, but left the HBC to unsuccessfully pursue private business opportunities. In 1874 he joined the Dept of Indian Affairs, where he set up reserves and made the first census of aboriginal people in BC. Blenkinsop ended his career as the Indian agent at Ft Rupert and is noted for the information he provided to anthropologists and government officials about First Nation culture. Blenkinsop Lk, N of Victoria, and Point George at the W entrance to Blenkinsop Bay are named for him as well. His name is sometimes incorrectly spelled Blinkinsop. *See also* Charlie Is, Dennie Point *and* Jesse I. *E W*

Blenkinsop Islet (53°17'00" 129°19'00" NW of Gil I, Wright Sd, entrance to Douglas Channel, SW of Kitimat). Squadron Leader Edward "Teddy" Weyman Blenkinsop, DFC, Croix de Guerre (Belgium), died at Bergen-Belsen concentration camp on Jan 23, 1945, aged 24. He was born at Williams Lk and educated at Victoria as a chartered accountant. After his Lancaster bomber was shot down over Belgium in 1944, he joined the local resistance but was captured by the Gestapo and imprisoned. Blenkinsop is commemorated on the Runnymede Memorial, Surrey, UK. He was a grandson of Capt Cyril Neroutsos (*see* Neroutsos Inlet).

Bligh Island (49°39'15" 126°31'15" NE of mouth of Nootka Sd, W side of Vancouver I). William Bligh (1754–1817) served as master (the warrant officer in charge of navigation) of HMS *Resolution* on Capt James Cook's third voyage of discovery to the S Pacific. In 1778, while visiting Nootka Sd, Cook refitted his vessel at Resolution Cove on this island. Bligh was later promoted to lt and earned a reputation as a fine surveyor but a harsh, bad-tempered cdr. He was chosen to lead an expedition to transplant breadfruit from Tahiti to the W Indies aboard HMS *Bounty* in 1787, and it was on this voyage that his crew famously mutinied, setting him adrift, with 18 followers, in a small open boat that he sailed nearly 6,000 km to safety. In 1791, as a capt, "Breadfruit" Bligh succeeded in transferring a second load of plants to their intended destination. In 1805 he became gov of New S Wales but so upset local sensibilities with his authoritarian behaviour that he was deposed and confined for two years. Bligh ended his career as a vice adm. *W*

Blind Bay (49°44'00" 124°11'00" W side of Nelson I, mouth of Jervis Inlet). It was at the Battle of Copenhagen in 1801 that Adm Horatio Nelson put his blind eye to his telescope and was thus unable to see his superior's signal recalling him (*see* Telescope Passage). In 1860, Capt George Richards named several features in this vicinity in Lord Nelson's honour, including Blind Bay, which faces Telescope Passage and lies between Nelson I and Hardy I (qv). A far less plausible explanation for the name is that, from some angles, the bay is partly hidden from view. The Sechelt First Nation name for the bay is Saugh-wáh-ten.

Blind Bay in the mouth of Jervis Inlet. *Peter Vassilopoulos*

Blind Channel (50°25'00" 125°30'00" E side of W Thurlow I, on Mayne Passage, NW of Campbell R). Capt George Vancouver missed the fact that Thurlow I is actually two islands, and Blind Channel may be an early local name for the body of water that separates them (now Mayne Passage). It has also been suggested that the small community of Blind Channel got its name because it is tucked into a cove and cannot easily be seen by passing boat traffic. A village sprang up there in the early 1900s around a sawmill, and about 1918 a salmon cannery was established by W E Anderson, who also owned a cannery at Quathiaski Cove. Anderson and his partner, Frank Allen, built a shingle mill beside their canning plant, and Blind Channel also attracted a boatbuilder and a marine repair facility. It was a busy place in the 1920s, with a school, dance hall and steamship landing. But the mill burned down, twice, and the cannery was sold, converted to a saltery about 1935, then closed when its Japanese proprietors were interned at the beginning of WWII. In 1970, Edgar and Annemarie Richter developed a marine resort at Blind Channel with cabins, a store and post office, a restaurant called the Cedar Post Inn, laundromat, showers and water-taxi service. The industrial buildings were dismantled in 1976. *E*

B

Blinkhorn Peninsula (50°33'00" 126°47'00" Just E of Telegraph Cove, NE side of Vancouver I). Thomas Blinkhorn (1806–56), from Huntingdonshire, arrived in BC from England in 1851 on the HBC supply ship *Tory*. His wife, Ann (1804–84, née Beeton), and teenaged niece Martha Cheney accompanied him. Together with trader Capt James Cooper, they established 160-ha Bilston Farm at Metchosin. Blinkhorn had raised stock in Australia before coming to N America and was reported to have helped rescue famed Arctic explorer Sir John Franklin—at that time gov of Van Diemen's Land (Tasmania)—from a grim fate while lost in the bush. Lady Jane Franklin, Sir John's widow, apparently visited Ann Blinkhorn in Victoria in 1861 while touring BC. Thomas was appointed a justice of the peace at Metchosin and also managed Cloverdale, the large Saanich farm of HBC officer William Fraser Tolmie, before falling ill and dying at age 51. Mt Blinkhorn and Blinkhorn Lk, SW of Victoria, are named for this pioneering family. *See* Beeton Point, Cheney Point *and* Cooper Inlet for additional details. W

Bliss Landing (50°02'00" 124°49'00" NW side of Malaspina Peninsula, NW of Powell R). Originally known as Bishop Landing, after early settler and postmaster Peter W Bishop, this small settlement and steamship stop was formed at the end of WWI. In 1923 the post office name was changed to Bliss Landing, which is believed to commemorate Joe Blissto, a pioneer handlogger who operated in the area in the early 1900s. A private marina was located at the landing in the early 2000s.

Bloedel (50°07'00" 125°23'00" In Menzies Bay, N of Campbell R, E side of Vancouver I). The namesake of this logging camp, terminus of a major railway operation, was Julius Harold Bloedel (1864–1957), a Wisconsin-born lumberman who came to BC in 1911 and formed Bloedel, Stewart & Welch Ltd. In 1951, BS&W merged with the H R MacMillan Export Co to form MacMillan Bloedel Ltd, BC's largest forestry company. The community of Bloedel was active from 1925 until about 1960 and at its peak had a population of 400. It was named in 1925 by Sidney Garfield Smith, BS&W's managing director. E

Blowhole Bay (49°50'00" 126°40'00" NE side of Nootka I, facing Tahsis Inlet, W side of Vancouver I). A strong crosswind hits Tahsis Inlet at this spot, funnelling down through the only gap in the high country to the W. A dryland log sort is located beside the bay, as well as a dock used by coastal freighter *Uchuck III*. Nearby Blowhole Ck is named after the bay. Both features were named by the hydrographic service about 1946.

Bloxam Flat (53°56'00" 130°07'00" Off E side of Gibson I, near Bloxam I), **Bloxam Island** (53°55'00" 130°08'00" One of the Gibson Group, head of Grenville Channel, S of Prince Rupert), **Bloxam Passage** (54°02'00" 130°16'00"

Between Arthur Passage and Kelp Passage, NE of Porcher I), **Bloxam Point** (51°17'00" 127°38'00" E end of Indian I, Takush Hbr, Smith Sd, N of Port Hardy). Cecil Robert Bloxam (d 1870) was an RN midshipman aboard HMS *Malacca*, under Capt Radulphus Oldfield, on the BC coast in 1866–67. He probably also served temporarily on the *Beaver* with Lt Daniel Pender, who surveyed and named Bloxam I and Bloxam Passage in 1867. Cecil Patch, NE of Porcher I, is also named for him.

1930s view of limestone and logging operations at Blubber Bay.
BC Archives A-04516

Blubber Bay (49°48'00" 124°37'00" N end of Texada I, Str of Georgia), **Blubber Point** (49°48'00" 124°38'00" W entrance to Blubber Bay). The tip of Texada was a gathering spot for early whalers. Capt Elijah John Fader and his brother Silas Fader set up a primitive whale-oil rendering operation on the beach here in the 1880s, where the Sliammon First Nation village of Tah-lahk-natch was once located. The bay, named about 1874, is the site of a small community, a large and very visible limestone quarry, and the terminus for a ferry to Powell R. Blubber Ck flows into and takes its name from the bay. The point first appears on a 1913 Admiralty chart. E

Blunden Bay (51°11'00" 127°46'00" N of Cape Caution, Queen Charlotte Sd), **Blunden Harbour** (50°54'00" 127°17'00" NE side of Queen Charlotte Str, N of Port Hardy), **Blunden Island** (49°11'00" 126°03'00" W of Vargas I, Clayoquot Sd, W side of Vancouver I), **Blunden Islet** (48°45'00" 123°10'00" Off SE end of Pender I, Gulf Is), **Blunden Passage** (50°44'00" 126°36'00" Between Eden I and Insect I, E end of Queen Charlotte Str), **Blunden Point** (49°15'00" 124°05'00" S entrance to Nanoose Hbr, NW of Nanaimo, E side of Vancouver I), **Blunden Rock** (49°00'00" 125°01'00" Uchucklesit Inlet, head of Barkley Sd, Vancouver I). Edward Raynor Blunden, born about 1842 in Ireland, near Cork, was a master's assistant aboard the RN survey vessel *Hecate* in 1861, under Capt George Richards. In 1863 he was 2nd master with Lt Daniel Pender on the *Beaver*, hired from the HBC for survey duties.

The number of features named for him suggests that he covered a great deal of coastline in a short period of time (the Raynor Group and Raynor Point also commemorate Blunden). He left the RN in 1864. Blunden Hbr was an important Kwakwaka'wakw First Nation village until the 1960s, when it was abandoned in favour of Port Hardy. *E*

Boas Islet (51°41'00" 128°05'00" N end of Kwakshua Channel, between Hecate I and Calvert I, S of Bella Bella). Franz Boas (1858–1942), a German-born geographer, was so intrigued by a Nuxalk First Nation group from Bella Coola, which visited Germany in 1885, that he became an anthropologist instead. He made seven trips to BC between 1886 and 1897, collecting artifacts and information—especially on the Kwakwaka'wakw First Nation—and published widely on PNW aboriginal culture. After becoming a US citizen and Columbia Univ professor, Boas developed the first PhD program in anthropology in America and, along with his students, profoundly influenced the direction of the discipline. He wrote such seminal works as *The Mind of Primitive Man* (1911) and *Race, Language and Culture* (1940). Boas Ck NE of Lac la Hache is also named for him. *E*

Boat Basin. *See* Rae Basin.

Boca del Infierno Bay (49°37'00" 126°38'00" SE side of Nootka I, W side of Vancouver I). In a 1933 memo, Henri Parizeau, chief hydrographer on Canada's Pacific coast, wrote that "whilst the name translated means Bay of Fury or Bay of Hell, and therefore is objectionable, being in a foreign language its objection is not so apparent." Boca del Infierno, bestowed by 18th-century Spanish explorers based at Nootka Sd, was allowed to stand. It likely refers to the reversing tidal rapids at the mouth (*boca* in Spanish) of the bay. The area was preserved in 1996 as a provincial marine park.

Bockett Islets (Just SE of Bockett Point), **Bockett Point** (50°32'00" 126°14'00" S side of E Cracroft I, Havannah Channel, N of Johnstone Str). William Charles Bockett died in 1859 while assistant surgeon aboard HMS *Havannah*, under Capt Thomas Harvey. He served on the Pacific Station, 1855–59. The islets were named by Capt George Richards in 1860 while on survey duties with HMS *Plumper*; the point was named in 1955.

Bocking Peninsula (55°22'00" 129°47'00" E of Granby Peninsula, Observatory Inlet). Charles S Bocking, born in Missouri in 1876, became gen manager of the Granby Consolidated Mining, Smelting & Power Co in 1925. For 10 years before that he was vice-president of another large mining company, Butte and Superior, in Montana. Granby operated an enormous copper mine and smelter at Anyox on Observatory Inlet, 1912–35, and ran other major copper-producing facilities elsewhere in BC.

Bodega Anchorage (50°17'00" 125°13'00" Okisollo Channel, NE side of Quadra I, N of Campbell R), **Bodega Hill** (48°57'42" 123°31'43" N of Quadra Hill, Galiano I, Gulf Is), **Bodega Island** (49°44'00" 126°38'00" N end of Kendrick Inlet, E of Nootka I, off W side of Vancouver I), **Bodega Point** (50°15'00" 125°22'00" S entrance to Kanish Bay, W side of Quadra I). Naval officer Juan Francisco de la Bodega y Quadra (1744–94), born in Peru and trained in Spain, arrived in Mexico in 1774. He joined an important PNW coastal expedition in 1775, under the command of Bruno de Hezeta in the *Santiago*, to investigate Russian activity in Alaska. Quadra, cdr of the tiny schooner *Sonora*, became separated from Hezeta (who only got as far as Vancouver I before returning to Mexico) and reached the Glacier Bay region of Alaska, the farthest N that any Spanish explorer had been at that time. In 1779, Quadra (aboard the *Favorita*) and Ignacio de Arteaga charted the S coast of Alaska to Cook Inlet. He was then posted to Cuba and Spain but returned to Mexico in 1789 to take command of the Spanish naval base at San Blas, where he assisted Malaspina and others searching for the NW Passage. In 1792 he sailed to Nootka Sd to meet Capt George Vancouver and, as Spanish commissioner to the Nootka Sd Convention, arrange British access to the PNW and restore confiscated British property. He and Vancouver were not able to come to terms but established a firm friendship and agreed to give the name Quadra and Vancouver's I to the large body of land that Vancouver had just circumnavigated. It was only later that this name was shortened to Vancouver I. Quadra, unwell, returned to Monterey and died not long after at Mexico City. Francisco I, Francisco Point, Quadra Hill (qv), Quadra Island and Quadra Saddle are also named for him. *E*

Captain George Vancouver meeting Spanish naval officer Juan Francisco de la Bodega y Quadra at Nootka Sound in 1792. Pen and colour wash by Robert John Banks. *BC Archives PDP00480*

Boit Rock (50°08'00" 127°40'00" E of Jackobson Point, Nasparti Inlet, NW side of Vancouver I). John Boit (1774–1829) was 5th mate aboard the *Columbia Rediviva* on Capt Robert Gray's 1791–92 trading expedition to the PNW. A native of Boston, he was a brother-in-law of one of the ship's merchant owners. His journal or logbook is the most complete surviving record of this historic voyage. In 1794–96, as capt of the merchant vessel *Union*, Boit circumnavigated the globe on a second trading journey and kept another important log. While in the QCI in 1795, the crew of the *Union* repulsed a Haida attack and killed Koya, the renegade chief who had been a scourge of foreign traders to the region (*see* Koya Bay). Scholarly editions of both Boit's logbooks have been published. The name Boit Rk was adopted in 1982.

Bold Point (50°10'00" 125°10'00" S end of Bold I, NE of Village Bay, Quadra I). This fishing community and Union Steamship Co landing got its start when Moses Ireland, a renowned timber cruiser, established a small hotel and ranch there in 1901. A store followed, and a post office in 1911. Ireland came to BC for gold, went into business with Sewell Moody, who started Burrard Inlet's first sawmill (and first industry), logged in the Cortes I area and ran a freight business on the Skeena R. Bold Point lost its steamship service in 1952, its post office in 1960 and in the early 2000s was slumbering in rural peace. The name appears on an Admiralty chart published in 1867. *E*

Bolin Bay (52°50'14" 128°12'41" NW side of Sheep Passage, E of Princess Royal I). Able Seaman Walter Gordon Bolin, from Vancouver, was killed in action Mar 29, 1945, aged 21. He was serving with the RCNVR aboard HMCS *Teme* when the frigate was torpedoed and irreversibly damaged by a U-boat while escorting a coastal convoy in the English Channel. His name is inscribed on the Halifax Memorial.

Bolivar Islet (51°34'00" 128°07'00" Off NW Calvert I, S of Bella Bella), **Bolivar Passage** (50°54'00" 127°33'00" In the Walker Group, entrance to Queen Charlotte Str, N of Port Hardy). After the US brig *Bolivar*, which operated on the BC coast in the 1840s, competing with the HBC's *Lama* in the fur-transport business.

Bolkus Islands (52°20'00" 131°16'00" In Skincuttle Inlet, off SE Moresby I, QCI). According to a Haida First Nation legend, these islands were the first part of Haida Gwaii to rise from the waters following the great flood and are thus sacred. An important village, Hagi (Xaagyah), was once located there. The 1862 map of engineer Francis Poole, who spent several years in this area in an unsuccessful attempt to mine copper, shows the feature as Balkus I. Geologist George M Dawson modified the name to Bolkus in 1878. Fur trader Joseph Ingraham referred to them in 1791 as Needham's Isles. *D*

Bolt Point (52°41'00" 128°22'00" N side of Watson Bay, NW tip of Roderick I, N of Bella Bella). The name, adopted in 1948, refers to a bolt that serves as a benchmark here, placed during a hydrographic survey.

Bone Anchorage (52°51'00" 129°01'00" Head of Racey Inlet, Caamaño Sd), **Bone Islet** (53°36'00" 130°33'00" W side of Griffith Hbr, NW of Banks I), **Bone Point** (53°00'00" 132°23'00" NW tip of Hibben I, off NW Moresby I, QCI). William Henry Bone (1855–1946), born at Bowmanville, Ont, arrived in Victoria with his family in 1863. After working his way up from messenger boy, he became a partner in T N Hibben & Co, the city's pioneer stationer and bookseller, and also a landlord; his Hibben-Bone building on Government St, for instance, later destroyed by fire, was where the Victoria *Colonist* was printed in the 1880s, and then became the Churchill Hotel. In the 1940s, as one of Victoria's oldest long-time residents, Bone was a familiar sight at historical dedications and plaque unveilings. T N Hibben & Co was an early publisher of maps, brochures and much else and was well known to mariners as the agent for Admiralty charts.

The ruins of the old Bones Bay salmon cannery. *Peter Vassilopoulos*

Bones Bay (50°35'00" 126°21'00" N side of W Cracroft I, N of Johnstone Str). Named along with nearby Minstrel I, Negro Rk and Sambo Point after a troupe of amateur performers aboard HMS *Amethyst*, which carried Lord Dufferin, the gov gen, and Lady Dufferin on a cruise to Metlakatla in 1876. These entertainers put on minstrel shows, based on black cultural stereotypes, in which "Mr Bones" and "Sambo" were stock characters. Presumably, such a show was staged in the vicinity for the vice-regal couple. Much later, about 1920, the Canadian Fishing Co built a large salmon cannery at Bones Bay. It operated until the early 1950s. A settlement of sorts lingered on for another decade, but only pilings remained at the site by the early 2000s. Bones Ck flows NW into Bones Bay.

Bonilla Island (53°30'00" 130°37'00" W of northern Banks I), **Bonilla Point** (48°36'00" 124°43'00" At NW entrance to Juan de Fuca Str), **Bonilla Rocks** (53°26'00" 130°36'00" S of

Bonilla I). Antonio Bonilla, a senior administrator in New Spain from the 1770s to the early 1800s, also compiled one of the first histories of Texas. Carmanah Point on the W coast of Vancouver I was originally named Punta Bonilla by Spanish naval officer Manuel Quimper in 1790, when he was surveying Juan de Fuca Str aboard the *Princesa Real* (the captured British fur-trading vessel *Princess Royal*). In the mid-1800s, however, Bonilla was misapplied by British Admiralty surveyors to the next point to the east—a much less prominent feature—and there it stayed. Bonilla I was named in 1792 by naval officer Jacinto Caamaño, another Spanish explorer, who made an important survey of the BC N coast in the *Aránzazu*. This name was retained in 1793 by Capt George Vancouver, who had a copy of Caamaño's chart. Bonilla Ck is named for Bonilla Point. Bonilla Arm is an old name for Kingkown Inlet.

Bonner Islet (50°15'00" 127°47'00" N side of Klaskish Inlet and Brooks Peninsula, NW side of Vancouver I). Frank Richard Bonner was a seaman aboard CGS *William J Stewart*, which was conducting survey work in this area in 1937. After suffering a severe attack of appendicitis, Bonner died aboard ship on Aug 11 of that year, aged 23.

Bonson Rock (52°39'00" 129°15'00" NW of Clifford Bay, W side of Aristazabal I). Sgt Lewis F Bonson (1831–1917) was a member of the Columbia detachment of Royal Engineers, which served in BC 1858–63. He was born in Peebleshire, Scotland, apprenticed as a furniture maker and wheelwright, then served in Turkey, Gibraltar and Central America before returning to England, marrying Jemima Urquhart and volunteering for service in BC. He was senior NCO of the first group to reach Victoria, via Panama, under Capt Robert Parsons, in Nov 1858. His wife and children arrived with the main body of men in Apr 1859. Mrs Bonson was later hired as a cook by Mary Moody, wife of Col Richard Moody, head of the detachment. The family remained in BC after the engineers were disbanded, and Bonson became a contractor and builder at New Westminster. In 1871 he bought the London Arms, a local hotel, and also served as provincial road superintendent, 1876–80. From 1892 to 1905 he farmed in the Port Hammond area, where he had taken up the free land grant given to those sappers who stayed on in BC. Bonson retired to New Westminster, where he was one of 12 surviving Royal Engineers honoured at a 1909 reunion attended by BC premier Richard McBride.

Bonwick Island (50°42'00" 126°39'00" W of Gilford I, E end of Queen Charlotte Str), **Bonwick Point** (53°51'00" 130°04'00" NE side of Pitt I). Charles Bonwick, born about 1830 in Surrey, England, was assistant engineer on the RN gunboat *Grappler* in 1860, then became chief engineer, under Lt Daniel Pender (who applied these names), aboard the historic paddle steamship *Beaver*, which was hired by the RN for survey duties on the BC coast, 1863–

70. He was married at Esquimalt in 1870 to Isabella Munro (née Austin), a widow, and is believed to have remained in BC and worked on CPR surveys. Mt Bonwick on Dundas I, NW of Prince Rupert, is also named for him, as were the Bonwick Is, near Blunden Hbr, before they were given their current name, the Augustine Is, in 1903.

Boom Islet (49°45'00" 123°54'00" Sechelt Rapids, mouth of Sechelt Inlet, NW of Vancouver). Named by the hydrographic service about 1950 for the log booms that often scrape past this obstruction while being towed out of Sechelt Inlet.

Booth Bay (48°52'00" 123°34'00" NW side of Saltspring I, Gulf Is), **Booth Inlet** (48°52'00" 123°32'00" Extends E from Booth Bay). These features were almost certainly named after John Patton Booth, the prominent, lifelong politician from Saltspring, who pre-empted land on both sides of Booth Inlet shortly after his arrival on the island in 1860—and not after Eric A Booth, who was one of the original 1859 group of black settlers on the island. John Booth (1838–1902) was born in the Orkney Is. He came to Canada in 1842 and Victoria in 1859. In 1879 he married Elizabeth Griffiths, a widow, who ran Fernwood, a large nursery and orchard at the N end of the island. Booth then moved to Fernwood and sold his land on Booth Inlet. When BC joined Canada in 1871, he won one of the 25 seats in the new legislature, serving as an MLA in 1871–75 and 1894–1902 and also as speaker of the assembly, 1898–1902. He was a dedicated public servant: officer of the Salt Spring I Agricultural Assoc, road commissioner, school board trustee and reeve of the short-lived township of Salt Spring I (the name of the island was usually divided into two words in the old days). In 1947, Acland's Resort opened at Booth Bay; it was renamed Booth Bay Resort in 1961 and closed in the 1990s. Booth Inlet was formerly known as Booth Canal. The names appear on an Admiralty chart published in 1907.

Borde Island (53°05'00" 129°07'00" Off W side of Princess Royal I, S end of Whale Channel). Hippolyte Borde (1856–1942) was born in California and came to Victoria with his family in 1859. He and his brother Auguste (1854–1919) opened a restaurant, the Louvre, in Seattle in 1889 but continued to live in Victoria, where Auguste was a volunteer fire chief and, for 28 years, the city's water rates collector. Hippolyte is believed to have taken part in the great Victoria old-timers' reunion of 1924 (*see* Adams Bay). Formerly known as Trouble I but renamed by the hydrographic service in 1926.

Bordelais Islets (48°49'07" 127°13'47" SW side of Trevor Channel, Barkley Sd, W side of Vancouver I). The 200-tonne *Bordelais*, under Lt Camille de Roquefeuil (1781-1831), was an early visitor to Barkley Sd. Roquefeuil circumnavigated the globe in 1816–19 on a trading

B

voyage, attempting to find new markets for France. He spent two weeks in Barkley Sd, mostly in Grappler Inlet, in Sept 1817, then returned to the Alaska and BC coasts the following year, passing time in Haida Gwaii and with Chief Maquinna at Nootka Sd. Roquefeuil's account of his voyage, published in 1823, provides a detailed European view of early First Nation life on the BC coast. The islets were formerly thought to be one land mass and were shown on Admiralty charts as Ship It until 1934, when they were renamed.

Borg Point (52°17'00" 127°38'00" N side of Dean Channel near its entrance, NE of Bella Bella). Peter Borg (1839–1932) was one of the original group of Norwegian pioneers who settled in the Bella Coola valley in 1894. The name was adopted in 1953, as suggested by the hydrographic service.

Borrowman Bay (52°44'00" 129°17'00" NW side of Aristazabal I), **Borrowman Group** (53°36'00" 130°34'00" N side of Griffith Hbr, W side of Banks I), **Borrowman Shoals** (53°44'00" 132°14'00" Off E side of Masset Inlet, Graham I, QCI). Andrew R Borrowman (1865–1935) was born in Devon, England, and arrived in Victoria in 1898. He went N to the Klondike, where he served as an engineer aboard several Yukon R vessels, and later was a partner in a sawmill at the entrance to Douglas Channel. He installed the engines on CGS *Lillooet*, then became its 2nd engineer, 1908–11, and chief engineer, 1911–32. Borrowman Bay, known locally as Scow Bay, was renamed by the hydrographic service in 1926.

Borthwick Rock (52°56'00" 129°31'00" S of Estevan Group, Caamaño Sd). Ralph Borthwick (1838–1921) was a well-known Victoria pioneer and old-timer. He was born at Manchester, UK, and arrived in Victoria when he was 20. In 1863 he married Isabella Keir (1849–1880), who died of TB, leaving four children; his second wife, Phoebe (1840–1907), was born in Kent, UK, and came to Canada in 1877. Borthwick was listed as a gold miner in the 1881 census. In 1890 he purchased the Palace Saloon, which he had previously been leasing, for $25,000. The rock was named in 1926.

Boscowitz Point (52°16'00" 127°47'00" W entrance to Cousins Inlet, Dean Channel, SW of Ocean Falls). This feature was supposedly named because the *Venture*, a vessel owned by the Boscowitz Steamship Co, was thought to be the first steamer to enter Cousins Inlet. It arrived in 1906, bringing timber cruiser Mark Smaby and a crew of 25 men to begin clearing the townsite of Ocean Falls, where a gigantic pulp and paper mill would soon rise. *See also* Boscowitz Rk. Regional hydrographer Henri Parizeau had wanted to name the feature after James Herbert Delves (1882–1967), victualling officer at Esquimalt's HMCS *Dockyard* in 1924, but this suggestion was rejected. It was formerly known as Walker Point.

Boscowitz Rock (49°01'00" 123°35'00" Porlier Pass, N of Galiano I, Gulf Is). After the *Barbara Boscowitz*, an early steamship on the BC coast, built at Victoria in 1883 for fur dealers Joseph Boscowitz (1835–1923) and James Warren (*see* Warren Rks). These pioneer coastal entrepreneurs would later become embroiled in legal and financial disagreements, but for a time they operated a successful fleet of sealing schooners out of Victoria. Another of Joseph's business partners was his brother Leopold, also a fur trader, who went on to play a major role in forming the Alaska Commercial Co. In 1899, Joseph founded the Boscowitz Steamship Co, which operated several coastal passenger and cargo vessels, including the 37-m *Boscowitz*, named for its owner's daughter Barbara. The wooden, sail-assisted "Barbara Biscuit-Box," as it was known, had few creature comforts. It worked mainly on the N coast, serving canneries and other small communities, carrying mail and developing a reputation for hitting reefs. In 1904, in thick fog at Harbledown I, it ran aground for the last time. Three children died when a lifeboat tipped during the ship's evacuation. Its machinery was later salvaged, the hull towed to Esquimalt and left to decay on the beach. In 1911, Boscowitz Steamship was sold to the Union Steamship Co for $160,000. Barba Point is also named for this vessel.

Boston Point (49°39'40" 126°36'44" E side of Nootka I, off W side of Vancouver I). The 28-m, 244-tonne *Boston* was a US trading vessel under Capt John Salter that arrived on the W coast of Vancouver I in Mar 1803. After 10 peaceful days in Nootka Sd, Salter managed to deeply insult Maquinna, the powerful local Mowachaht First Nation chief, who attacked the ship with a group of warriors, killing 25 of the 27 crew members. John Jewitt and John Thompson, the survivors, were held captive for nearly three years until rescued by Capt Samuel Hill of the brig *Lydia*. The *Boston* was beached and later accidentally burned. Jewitt published his Nootka Sd journal in 1807 and then, with Richard Alsop, produced a more detailed narrative of his captivity, *The Adventures and Sufferings of John R Jewitt*, which appeared in 1815 to great success. *See also* Jewitt Cove. This feature was formerly known as Rough Point but was renamed in 1934.

Boswell Inlet (51°22'00" 127°30'00" NE continuation of Smith Sd, S of Rivers Inlet). Named in 1903 by Capt John Walbran after Hazel and Olive Boswell, the granddaughters of Sir Henri-Gustave Joly de Lotbinière, lt gov of BC, 1900–1906. Their father, St George Boswell, served as Que's harbour engineer. Walbran was making a preliminary survey of Smith and Boswell inlets at the time; nearby Hazel I and Olive Point—and Hazel Point on Smith I—also commemorate the two sisters. A sockeye salmon cannery was built on Boswell Inlet in 1926 by the Gosse Packing Co and owned by BC Packers, 1928–36. The site was used as a fishing camp until the mid-1950s.

Botanical Beach (48°32'00" 124°26'00" Between Port Renfrew and Sooke, SW side of Vancouver I). A marine outpost, complete with a large log-cabin lodge and two laboratories, was established here in the early 1900s by Dr Josephine Tildon of the Univ of Minnesota. In order to study the abundant intertidal life, students and researchers travelled by steamship from Victoria to Port Renfrew and then reached the beach by foot. A road in, though promised, was never built, and the station closed in 1907 due to the difficult access and a lack of financial support. Virtually nothing remained of the facility by the early 2000s. The beach, now part of Juan de Fuca Provincial Park, is still visited by biology students wishing to study the rich ecosystem. The well-established local name was officially adopted in 1978.

Botel Islet (50°30'00" 127°50'00" E side of Koprino Hbr, Quatsino Sd, NW end of Vancouver I). Named for John Christian Botel, one of 14 children of Martha (1888–1956) and Claus Botel (1868–1953), who emigrated from Germany to Canada in 1913. The family settled first at Topknot Point on the W coast of Vancouver I, S of Cape Scott, then moved to Winter Hbr in 1918 and later to Julian Cove in Quatsino Sd. John (1897–1982) built a home at Hecate Cove in 1927 and married Doris Warren in 1930. Martha and Claus moved to Hecate Cove in 1940 after their last children had moved out. Botel It was formerly known as Burnt It but was renamed in 1927. Botel Lk, SE of Winter Hbr, commemorates one of John's brothers, Max Botel (1903–83), a logger, fisherman and prominent resident of the area.

Bottle Inlet (52°55'00" 132°17'00" NW side of Moresby I, QCI), **Bottle Point** (52°54'00" 132°20'00" S entrance to Bottle Inlet). According to QCI historian Kathleen Dalzell, thick kelp beds on either side of the inlet's entrance leave only a cramped navigable passage, causing early fish-boat skippers to refer to the narrow indentation as Bottleneck Hbr. A constriction at the entrance to **Bottleneck Inlet** (52°42'00" 128°24'00" NW side of Roderick I, NW of Bella Bella) is responsible for the similar name of a geographic feature farther S.

Boughey Bay (50°31'00" 126°11'00" E side of Havannah Channel, E of Cracroft Is, N of Johnstone Str), **Boughey Shoal** (50°32'00" 126°11'00" Havannah Channel). Charles Fenton Fletcher Boughey (1823–94), from Staffordshire, UK, was 1st lt aboard HMS *Havannah*, under Capt Thomas Harvey, and served on the Pacific Station, 1855–59. He was promoted to capt in 1866 and rose to the rank of vice-adm, retired, in 1888. The bay was named by Capt George Richards, who surveyed this region from HMS *Plumper* with the assistance of several officers from the *Havannah*. The shoal was named by the hydrographic service in 1955, in association with the bay.

Boukind Bay (52°27'20" 127°56'05" N end of Florence Peninsula, NW of Ocean Falls), **Boukind Bluff** (52°27'00" 127°55'00" N side of Roscoe Inlet, NW of Ocean Falls). Peter Boukind was one of the original Norwegian settlers to colonize the Bella Coola valley in 1894. He served as the colony's vice-president, and on the death of its leader, Christian Saugstad, in 1897, briefly acted as president until Christian Carlson took over. Boukind was listed as a farmer in the 1898 BC voters list. Both features were named by the hydrographic service in 1957.

Boundary Bay (49°02'00" 122°56'00" On the US-Canadian border between White Rk and Tsawwassen), **Boundary Bluff** (49°00'09" 123°05'25" S of Tsawwassen Beach, SW of Vancouver). Named in the 1860s because of the international boundary, which passes through the bay and just S of the bluff. On their 1792 expedition to the PNW, Spanish explorers Dionisio Alcalá-Galiano and Cayetano Valdés called this bay Ensenada del Engaño, or Gulf of Deception, perhaps because of its shallowness. Thousands of years ago the mouth of the Fraser R emptied into the bay; today the estuary has shifted N and W, and the flat marshy wetlands around the bay provide critical feeding and resting places for migrating waterfowl. *E*

Bourke Rock (52°01'00" 128°27'00" NW of Goose I, Golby Passage, SW of Bella Bella). Cdr Rowland Richard Louis Bourke (1885–1958) was born at Kensington, UK, and by 1902 had immigrated to Crescent Bar, near Nelson, BC, where his family operated a fruit farm. He returned to England, enlisted in the RNVR in 1915 and, as a lt in charge of motor launch *ML276*, was awarded the DSO for bravery during the Apr 1918 British raid on the German U-boat base at Ostend, Belgium. A month later, promoted to lt cdr, Bourke received the VC after a second raid on Ostend, where he rescued badly wounded crew members from HMS *Vindictive* despite heavy fire that practically destroyed his launch. (The ancient cruiser *Vindictive* had been scuttled in an unsuccessful attempt to block the harbour entrance.) He was also made a Chevalier of the Légion d'honneur by France. He returned to his Kootenay Lk orchards after the war, married Rosalind Thelma Barnet (1894–1971) in 1919, then moved to Victoria in 1932 to work at HMCS *Dockyard* as a civilian clerk. In WWII, Bourke helped organize the W coast Fishermen Reserve Service and worked as a recruiting officer. In 1941 he rejoined the RCNVR and became cdr of naval shore establishments at Esquimalt and Vancouver. Bourke died at Esquimalt and is buried at Royal Oak Cemetery. Mt Bourke on Vancouver I is also named for him.

Boussole Rock (53°58'00" 133°09'00" NE of Frederick I, NW side of Graham I, QCI). The 41-m, 500-tonne frigate *Boussole* (formerly the storeship *Portefaix*) was commanded by Capt Jean-François de Galaup, Comte de Lapérouse, who was in charge of a scientific expedition

B

sent by France in 1785 to circumnavigate the globe and find the NW Passage. Lapérouse and his fellow capt, Paul-Antoine-Marie Fleuriot de Langle, commanding the *Astrolabe*, sailed along the BC coast in 1786 and named many features in the QCI, which Lapérouse suspected were an archipelago and not part of the mainland. In 1788, after crossing the Pacific, exploring the NE coast of Asia and visiting Australia, both vessels were wrecked in Vanuatu (formerly the New Hebrides), a loss not confirmed until 1827, when artifacts from the ships were found by Irish sea capt Peter Dillon. No one knows what became of the crew members. *Boussole* is French for "marine compass."

Bowden Islands (52°34'00" 129°13'00" Off Clifford Bay, SW side of Aristazabal I). Cpl William Bowden (1830–79) was a member of the Columbia detachment of Royal Engineers, which served in BC 1858–63. Born in Belfast, Ireland, he enlisted in the Royal Artillery at age 18, serving as a gunner and, later, a bombardier. He was posted to Halifax, 1853, and to Bermuda, 1853–57, after which he volunteered to go to BC. He sailed with his wife, Amelia, on the *Euphrates*, arriving at Victoria in June 1859. In 1861 he became Gov James Douglas's orderly. Bowden remained in BC when the detachment disbanded. He received—as did all sappers who stayed—a 60-ha land grant, which he apparently took in the New Westminster area in 1870. He and his family lived in Victoria, however, where Bowden became a sgt in the police dept in 1867, rising to inspector in 1870, the year Amelia died. (Bowden married Kate Longfellow later that same year.) In 1876 he was appointed

a superintendent in the provincial police force, known at the time as the BC Constabulary. Two years later he was demoted for the alleged mismanagement of the Victoria jail and police barracks.

Bowen Bay (49°22'00" 123°25'00" W side of Bowen I), **Bowen Island** (49°23'00" 123°22'00" Entrance to Howe Sd, NW of Vancouver). James Bowen (1751–1835) had an illustrious career with the RN, which he entered in the late 1770s as a master (a senior non-commissioned rank) after commanding vessels in the merchant marine. He was master of HMS *Queen Charlotte*, Adm Lord Howe's flagship, during the 1794 defeat of the French fleet off Brittany in the battle known as the Glorious First of June. Bowen soon became a capt and served as a commissioner of the RN in 1816. He retired in 1825 with the rank of rear adm. In 1791, explorer José Narváez gave the name Islas de Apodaca to Bowen I and neighbouring Keats I, after Spanish naval officer Sebastian Ruiz de Apodaca; RN surveyor Capt George Richards applied Bowen's present name in 1860. The island, once a popular destination for holiday steamship excursions, has long been a bedroom suburb of Vancouver, served by ferry from Horseshoe Bay. *E W*

Bowers Islands (50°35'00" 126°13'00" E side of Cracroft Is, Chatham Channel, N of Johnstone Str). Clyde Bowers, who died at Alert Bay in 1939, aged 58, operated BC's first blue-fox farm on the main island in this small archipelago for 11 years. Formerly known as Low I but renamed by the hydrographic service in 1948.

The landmark Union Steamship Company Marina at Snug Cove, Bowen Island. *Peter Vassilopoulos*

Bowles Point (52°04'00" 131°07'00" W side of Kunghit I, SE of Moresby I, QCI). William Bowles was a mariner and fur trader who spent much time in the QCI in the late 18th century. He sailed with Capt Robert Gray on the first voyage of the *Columbia Rediviva*, 1787–90, and later became mate of the *Sea Otter*, under Capt Stephen Hill. When Hill and two other crew members were killed in 1796 during a skirmish with the Haida, Bowles took command of the vessel and completed the trading mission, much to the satisfaction and profit of the ship's Boston owners, who appointed him capt of the *Alert* for two more successful voyages to the PNW between 1798 and 1801. *D*

Bowyer Island (49°25'30" 123°16'00" Howe Sd, NE of Bowen I, NW of Vancouver). Sir George Bowyer (1740–1800) had a significant career with the RN. During the American Revolution (1775–83) he commanded first HMS *Burford* and then HMS *Albion*, and after the war was in charge of HMS *Boyne*. In 1794, as a rear adm, with HMS *Barfleur* as his flagship, he lost a leg (but gained a pension) in the naval victory over the French known as the Glorious First of June. (Capt George Richards, doing survey work aboard HMS *Plumper* in 1860, named many features in Howe Sd after participants in that battle.) Bowyer had attained the rank of adm by the time of his death. The island was purchased by Herbert Bingham in 1926 as a recreational property and continues to be privately owned, though extensively subdivided, with the S part still held by Bingham's descendants. *W*

Boxer Cliff (53°06'00" 128°26'00" N side of Khutze Inlet, opposite Princess Royal I), **Boxer Reach** (53°30'00" 128°59'00" NE side of Gribbell I, SW of Kitimat). HMS *Boxer* was a twin-screw gunboat (four guns) of 422 tonnes, built at Devonport, UK, in 1867 and launched the following year. It was based at Esquimalt (HQ of the RN's Pacific Station), 1869–75, and was often used to investigate or settle incidents of First Nation unrest. In 1872, for instance, the *Boxer*'s officers were mediating between white and aboriginal belligerents at the mouth of the Skeena R. The following year the vessel carried Rear Adm Arthur Farquhar, cdr-in-chief of the Pacific Station, on a fact-finding mission to Metlakatla and the N coast. Dr Israel Wood Powell, BC's first superintendent of Indian Affairs, also made an extensive inspection of coastal First Nation villages aboard the *Boxer* in 1874. The vessel was eventually sold for scrap in 1887. Its capts in BC were Lt Cdr Frederick Egerton (1869–72), Lt Cdr William Fitzgerald (1872–73) and Lt Cdr William Collins (1873–75). Collins Point, Moody Point, Riordan Point and Tomkinson Point (qv) are all named after officers serving on the *Boxer*.

Boxer Point (50°50'00" 127°39'00" SE end of Nigei I, N of Vancouver I). Alexander Fraser Boxer, born about 1830,

was master of 17-gun HMS *Alert*, under Cdr William Pearse, and served on the BC coast, 1858–61. He had been active during the Crimean War aboard HMS *Beagle* and went on to command the storeship HMS *Hesper* in 1862. Boxer retired from the RN as a lt in 1870. The point was named by RN surveyor Capt George Richards in 1860; nearby Fraser I and Port Alexander also commemorate this officer. *W*

Boyko Rock (53°10'00" 129°34'00" NW side of Campania I, NE Estevan Sd, E of Hecate Str). Named by regional hydrographer Henri Parizeau in 1944 after Steve Boyko, who served as a coxswain aboard the survey vessel *William J Stewart* in the 1940s.

Boyle Island (50°51'00" 127°33'00" N of Hurst I, Gordon Channel, NW of Port Hardy), **Boyle Point** (49°28'00" 124°41'00" SE end of Denman I, Str of Georgia), **Boyle Rocks** (51°28'00" 128°02'00" Off Stafford Point, SW side of Calvert I, W of Rivers Inlet). David Boyle (1833–1915) served on the BC coast in 1859–60 as 1st lt of HMS *Tribune*, under Capt Geoffrey Hornby. He had previously seen action in the Crimean War (1854–55) and the 2nd Anglo-Chinese War (in 1857). In 1874, Boyle was cdr of HMS *Niobe*, which was wrecked off Miquelon I; an official inquiry exonerated him of any blame. He retired from the RN as a capt in 1878 and in 1890 succeeded his cousin as the 7th Earl of Glasgow. Boyle became gov of New Zealand, 1892–97, and was named president of the Institute of Naval Architects in 1905. While the point and rocks are known to be named after him (as is Mt Boyle, W of Loughborough Inlet), the attribution of Boyle I, according to BC's Geographical Names Office, is less certain and can only be presumed. *W*

Boyles Point (50°49'00" 127°01'00" W entrance to Wells Passage, Queen Charlotte Str, N of Malcolm I). Capt Charles Boyles (1756–1816) achieved much acclaim as an RN officer. In 1794, as cdr of HMS *Swiftsure*, he captured the French frigate *L'Atalante* and its famous cdr, Charles-Alexandre Durand, Compte de Linois. As cdr of HMS *Windsor Park*, Boyles played important roles in Sir Robert Calder's 1805 battle off Finisterre and in Sir John Duckworth's forcing of the Dardanelles in 1807. He died with the rank of vice adm. Named in 1792 by Capt George Vancouver. *W*

Brabant Channel (49°12'00" 126°04'00" NW of Vargas I and Tofino, Clayoquot Sd, W side of Vancouver I), **Brabant Islands** (48°56'00" 125°19'00" Part of the Broken Group, Barkley Sd, W side of Vancouver I). Pioneer Roman Catholic missionary Augustin Joseph Brabant (1845–1912) was born and educated in Belgium. He came to Victoria in 1869 and in 1875 established the first mission on the W coast of Vancouver I, at Hesquiat, N of Clayoquot Sd, where he worked for 33 years. Brabant

B

compiled a dictionary of the Nuu-chah-nulth language and published an important history, *Vancouver Island and Its Missions*, in 1900, the same year he helped found the Christie residential school at Kakawis. In 1908 he became administrator of the diocese of Vancouver I. Brabant Channel was formerly known as Ship Channel but was renamed in 1934; the Brabant Is, originally thought to be a single feature, had their name changed from Pender I in 1924. *E W*

Brackett Cove (48°46'45" 123°16'20" NE of Hamilton Cove, Port Browning, N Pender I, Gulf Is). The Brackett family pioneered here in the 1890s. James Alexander Brackett (1860–1929) and his wife, Margaret (1864–1945), moved from Dresden, Ont, to New Westminster to live and also bought property on N Pender I. While staying on Pender in Sept 1898, the great New Westminster fire destroyed all their possessions, so they decided to remain and become permanent residents. Their house, built in 1896, was expanded as more children arrived and was eventually replaced in the 1960s. The Bracketts farmed and found various employments around the Gulf Is. They were notorious for a huge I-beam gong—"Brackett's Bell"—that hung by chains from two front-yard firs and was struck by a sledgehammer to announce the noon hour and to call various family members. Apparently it could be heard for miles around. The name was submitted in 1968 by the Gulf Is Branch of the BC Historical Assoc. *See also* Hamilton Beach.

Brackman Island (48°43'00" 123°23'00" W of Portland I, N of Sidney, Gulf Is). After participating in the Cariboo gold rush, Henry Brackman (1832–1903) built a a small gristmill on Tsehum Hbr (formerly Shoal Bay) near Sidney in 1878. Four years later, David Russell Ker (*see* Ker I) became a partner, and in the 1890s the Brackman-Ker Milling Co built a bigger mill at the entrance to Victoria Hbr and produced flour and all kinds of animal feeds. It also owned a large building in downtown Victoria. The business expanded and became very successful, eventually operating warehouses, mills and elevators throughout BC and Canada. Before 1935, Brackman I was known as Black I, after RN assistant surgeon Alexander Black of HMS *Monarch*, who served on the BC coast, 1854–57. The 5-ha feature was named an ecological reserve in 1989. Its Sencoten (Coast Salish) name is Xexecoten, meaning "little dry mouth."

Bramham Island (51°04'00" 127°34'00" Between Slingsby Channel and Schooner Channel, N entrance to Queen Charlotte Sd, N of Port Hardy), **Bramham Point** (51°03'00" 127°36'00" SW side of Bramham I). Bramham I was named by Lt Daniel Pender about 1866 after Bramham Park, the Yorkshire residence of noted English sportsman George Lane Fox (1810–96), in association with nearby Fox Is. A small community existed here early in the 20th

century, and a post office, misspelled Branham I, was open in 1917–18. Bramham Point, formerly known as Cust Point, was renamed by the hydrographic service in 1949 in association with the island. *W*

Brandon Islands (49°12'00" 123°57'00" In Departure Bay, at Nanaimo, E side of Vancouver I), **Brandon Point** (50°54'00" 127°16'00" N side of Robinson I, Blunden Hbr, Queen Charlotte Str, N of Port Hardy), **Brandon Rock** (50°53'00" 127°15'00" SE of Blunden Hbr). Lt Vivian Roland Brandon, aboard the RN survey vessel *Egeria*, under Cdr John Parry, helped chart Nanaimo and Blunden harbours in 1903–4. He was promoted to cdr in 1914, then imprisoned at Colditz Castle during WWI for allegedly spying off the N Sea coast. He was awarded a CBE and retired with the rank of capt.

Branks Islet (52°17'00" 128°23'00" In Blair Inlet, off SW tip of Don Peninsula, NW of Bella Bella). Kate and Jennie (Jane) Branks were sisters, daughters of Robert and Catherine Branks of Scotland. The Branks family immigrated to NZ, where Jennie was born, then moved to California in 1851. Both sisters married prominent BC men. Jennie (1845–1928), after visiting a family member who had moved to Victoria, became the wife of Dr Israel Wood Powell, BC's first superintendent of Indian Affairs (*see* Powell R), in 1865. In 1877, Kate married Forbes George Vernon, who ranched in the Okanagan, gave his name to the city of Vernon and was BC's chief commissioner of Lands and Works for many years. He also served as an MLA, 1875–82 and 1886–94, and as BC's agent gen in London, 1895–98. Regional hydrographer Henri Parizeau named the feature, apparently after Kate Branks, in 1929, perhaps because of its proximity to Powell Anchorage.

Brant Bay (53°15'00" 129°22'00" W side of Fin I, near entrance to Douglas Channel, SW of Kitimat). The *Brant* was one of the launches carried by CGS *William J Stewart*, which surveyed these waters in 1949. The bay was named by the hydrographic service in 1950.

Brant Point (49°19'00" 124°16'00" S of Parksville, E side of Vancouver I). This name was suggested by BC Parks and adopted in 1975. The point, in Rathtrevor Beach Provincial Park, is a favourite gathering spot for brant geese (*Branta bernicla*), which use the beaches here as staging and feeding zones when migrating to northern Canada and Alaska each spring.

Brasseau Bay (50°24'00" 125°58'00" At Sayward, Vancouver I, S side of Johnstone Str). Named about 1938 after Pete Brasseau, a fisherman and logger who lived at this site for two years before settling on Quadra I. He applied for water rights on the creek that flows into the bay.

B

Bray Island (52°16'03" 128°42'30" W of S end of Price I, NW of Bella Bella). Marshall Bidwell Bray (1840–1912) was born at Halton, Ont, and came to the Cariboo in 1862 in search of gold. He settled at Nanaimo in 1876, where he worked as a carpenter and at James Abrams's general store, and was appointed government agent in 1880, a position he held for 30 years. In 1883 he married Sarah Randle (1858–1939). Bray wore numerous local civil service hats during his career: registrar of the supreme and county courts; gold commissioner; registrar of births, deaths and marriages; assistant commissioner of Lands and Works. He was also a founding board member of the Nanaimo Hospital Assoc (1881) and became a police magistrate in 1909. Named by the hydrographic service in 1927.

Braza Island (50°40'00" 126°15'00" Off SE end of Gilford I, Knight Inlet). Named to recall the original Spanish name for Knight Inlet—Brazo de Vernaci—bestowed by the explorers Dionisio Alcalá-Galiano and Cayetano Valdés in 1792 during their historic circumnavigation of Vancouver I. *Brazo* is the Spanish word for "arm." Juan Vernaci y Retamal, of Italian heritage, was 1st lt aboard the *Mexicana* under Valdés (though some reports describe him as the pilot of Galiano's ship, the *Sutil*) and made a reconnaissance of Knight Inlet. Earlier in his career he had worked on surveys of the Spanish and Argentine coasts, and later he would do the same in Central America. In 1804 the Royal Philippines Co sent him to Manila. Vernaci died about 1810. Formerly known as Martin I but renamed in 1949. *See also* Vernaci I.

Breadner Group (51°48'00" 128°14'00" S of Spider I, Queens Sd, S of Bella Bella), **Breadner Point** (51°51'00" 128°16'00" W end of Spider I). RCAF officer Lloyd Samuel Breadner, CB, DSC (1894–1952), was born at Carleton Place, Ont. He was a fighter pilot in France in WWI, then joined the Canadian Air Board as a licence examiner, moving to Camp Borden training base in 1924 as CO. Breadner was appointed director of the RCAF, 1928–36, chief of air staff in 1940 and RCAF overseas air officer cdr-in-chief in 1944. The following year, upon retirement, he was promoted to air chief marshal—one of only two officers to ever hold this rank. A substantial WWII radar station was built at Breadner Point in 1942–43; its remains were still visible in the early 2000s. The station closed in 1945, but a small radio post remained in operation there for several more years. Both geographical features were named by the hydrographic service in 1944.

Breakenridge Point (52°31'00" 129°02'00" N side of Weeteeam Bay, SW side of Aristazabal I). Sapper Archibald T Breakenridge was a surveyor and a member of the Columbia detachment of Royal Engineers, which served in BC 1858–63. He was with Lt Henry Palmer's party during an 1859 reconnaissance of the country between the N end of Harrison Lk and Four Mile House on the Lillooet

R. Little else seems to be known about his life. The point was named by the hydrographic service about 1927. Mt Breakenridge, N of Harrison Lk, also commemorates him.

Brecciated Point (49°56'10" 127°13'13" S of Rugged Point, NW of Bamfield, Barkley Sd, W side of Vancouver I). Breccia, found at this site, is a visually striking rock composed of angular fragments cemented in a fine-grained matrix such as sand or clay. The point was named in 1950. Breccia Mtn and Breccia Glacer in the Coast Mtns also take their names from this rock, as does Breccia Peak in northern BC.

Brechin Point (49°11'00" 123°57'00" In Nanaimo, facing Newcastle I, E side of Vancouver I). Brechin was a miners' residential community that became a suburb of Nanaimo. It was named after the nearby Brechin (or No 4) coal mine, which was named, in turn, after a town on the E coast of Scotland. The mine was opened in 1904 and operated until about 1913. The name of the point was adopted in 1949.

Brem Bay (50°26'00" 124°40'00" N side of Toba Inlet at mouth of the Brem R, NE of Campbell R). The meaning of Brem is uncertain, though the Klahoose First Nation name for the bay is Kw'ikw'tichenam, meaning "having lots of pink (humpback) salmon." A Klahoose village was located there and abandoned in the late 1920s. The area is known locally as Salmon Bay.

Bremner Bay (51°51'00" 128°07'00" SE end of Hunter I, S of Bella Bella). Named in 1944 after T S Bremner, who was hired by the Canadian Hydrographic Service in 1938, the year he graduated from UBC with a civil engineering degree. He worked on a survey in Malaspina Str, 1939–40, then resigned.

Bremner Islet (51°06'00" 127°41'00" Just W of Bremner Point), **Bremner Point** (51°06'00" 127°40'00" S end of Burnett Bay, SE of Cape Caution, Queen Charlotte Sd). John Bremner (1837–98), a native of Caithness, Scotland, was an RN paymaster at the naval dockyard in Esquimalt in the 1860s. In 1865 he married Annie Louise Skinner, a daughter of Thomas Skinner, manager of Constance Cove Farm, one of four farms established around Victoria by the Puget's Sd Agricultural Co, an HBC subsidiary. Bremner worked as a naval storekeeper at Hong Kong, 1874–84, was promoted to fleet paymaster in 1886 and then served as a district paymaster in SW England, 1890–94. He died on the China Station, aboard HMS *Centurion*.

Brent Island (50°17'00" 125°20'00" Okisollo Channel, N of Quadra I and Str of Georgia). The British shipyard Randall & Brent, on the Thames R at Rotherhithe in SE London, built more than 60 vessels between 1770 and 1803, including, in 1789, HMS *Discovery*, which Capt George Vancouver sailed to the PNW in 1791. One of London's main private shipbuilding firms, originally established by John Randall and John Brent (1729–1812) on Lower Queen St, it mainly produced ships for the RN, HBC and E India Co. John Brent's sons, Samuel (1760–1814) and Daniel (1764–1834), eventually took the company over and ran it under various names—S & D Brent, Brent & Co, Daniel Brent & Co—until 1828, when it went out of business. The company had three separate yards and could construct 74-gun ships of the line—the largest vessels built at that time outside the naval dockyards. The name Brent I was adopted in 1924.

Brentwood Bay on the east side of Saanich Inlet. *John Lund*

Brentwood Bay (48°35'00" 123°28'00" E side of Saanich Inlet, NW of Victoria). When the BC Electric Rwy's Saanich line was completed in 1913, the interurban station (and powerhouse) here was named Brentwood, after the Essex, UK, town where Robert M Horne-Payne, chairman of the railway's board of directors, had just built a lavish country house called Merrymeade. Before that time, this part of Saanich was known as Sluggett Bay, after John Sluggett, who settled in the area in the 1870s and farmed (*see* Sluggett Point). Gradually, the name Brentwood found favour. The post office was renamed Brentwood Bay in 1925, and the name of the bay itself was changed in 1934. By the early 2000s the area was mainly residential and suburban, with ferry service across Saanich Inlet to Mill Bay. *E*

Brentzen Rock (53°52'00" 128°43'00" NE side of Douglas Channel, S of Kitimat). Fridjof "Fritz" Brentzen (1866–1946) was a teacher at Kitamaat Mission around the turn of the 19th century and helped found the mission's well-known brass band. His father, Hans Peter Brentzen, from Oslo, had originally come to BC in the mid-1850s to work for the HBC but became an independent fur trader at Kitimat. In 1874, Hans married Catherine, a First Nation woman, at Port Simpson. Fritz died at Vancouver. The rock was named by the hydrographic service about 1953.

Brethour Island (48°41'00" 123°19'00" W side of Prevost Passage, NE of Sidney, Gulf Is). Samuel Brethour (1818–1877), a native of Ireland and for many years resident at N York, Ont, came to Victoria in 1873 with his wife, Margaret (1829–1883, née St John), and their large family and purchased 200 ha of land in the N Saanich area. His four adult sons—John (1847–1923), Julius (1850–1934), Henry (1853–1938) and James Westley (1856–1917)—inherited the property, which was officially incorporated as the township of Sidney in 1891. Julius Brethour was president of the Victoria & Sidney Rwy, completed in 1895. Brethour I (34 ha) has had a series of owners since 1886, when James Forest received a Crown grant for it. In 1902, John Muir bought the island for $1,100; his family owned it for 25 years and made many improvements. From 1927 onward it has had mostly US absentee owners, including, from 1940 to 1956, Hollywood travelogue producer James A Fitzpatrick. It was originally known as Hill I but was renamed by regional hydrographer Henri Parizeau in 1935.

Breton Islands (50°07'00" 125°11'00" E of Open Bay, Quadra I, N of Str of Georgia). Named sometime prior to 1919, possibly after Dr William Edward Breton (d 1914), an RN surgeon who served on the BC coast in the late 1870s with HMS *Opal* and retired in 1908.

Brew Bay (49°46'00" 124°23'00" N side of Malaspina Str, SE of Powell R). Thomas W Brew pre-empted land in the area in 1895. He later drowned off this bay. Formerly known as Douglas Bay but renamed before 1923.

Brew Island (52°57'00" 128°40'00" Head of Laredo Inlet, Princess Royal I). Chartres Brew (1815–70), a veteran of the Crimean War and former inspector in the Royal Irish Constabulary at Cork, Ireland, was appointed the first inspector of police in the new colony of BC in 1858. A year later he was also chief gold commissioner and chief magistrate at New Westminster. Brew was one of BC's most important colonial officials, involved in all the major events of the time, and had a reputation for competence and impartiality. He was colonial treasurer, 1862–64, and a legislative council member, 1864–68. He ended his career as county court judge at Richfield in the Cariboo gold district, where he oversaw the reconstruction of Barkerville after a disastrous fire. In 1864, during the so-called Chilcotin War, when Tsilhqot'in warriors killed a number of settlers and roadbuilders, Brew led a party to capture the offenders. To commemorate the pursuit, Brew Ck, which flows into the Homathko R NW of Bute Inlet, was named for him. Two mountains also bear his surname, one on the N side of Quesnel Lk, the other just S of Lillooet.

Brew Point (52°20'00" 128°22'00" SW end of Lake I, W of Don Peninsula, NW of Bella Bella). Jane Augusta Brew

(1827–89) was the sister of Chartres Brew (*see* Brew I). She followed her brother out from Ireland and in 1861 married Augustus Frederick Pemberton (1808–91), who had followed his better-known nephew—politician and colonial surveyor gen Joseph Despard Pemberton—to Victoria in 1855. After farming for several years, Augustus became a police commissioner, magistrate and coroner in Victoria. (The Pemberton Hills, N of Holberg Inlet on Vancouver I, are named for him.)

Bribery Islet (54°06'00" 130°19'00" Off NE side of Porcher I, S of Prince Rupert). Named in association with nearby Lawyer Is and Client Reefs during Lt Daniel Pender's survey of 1867 or 1869.

Bridgeman Rock (52°38'00" 129°17'00" Off W side of Aristazabal I, NW of Bella Bella). Sgt Richard Bridgman (apparently the correct spelling of his name is without an "e") was a member of the Columbia detachment of Royal Engineers, which served in BC 1858–63. He sailed to Victoria in 1859 on *Thames City* with the main body of men, accompanied by his pregnant wife and young son. Sadly, the boy, Richard, died on the journey; five days later, his wife gave birth. At the Sapperton camp, Bridgman was appointed postmaster sgt, in charge of the royal mails. He was able to take early discharge from the detachment, and in Sept 1863 he and Sapper John Smith purchased Hick's Hotel in New Westminster.

Brigade Bay (49°29'00" 123°20'00" E side of Gambier I, Howe Sd, NW of Vancouver). The Boy's Brigade, an international non-denominational Christian youth organization, camped on this bay in the 1930s and '40s and tried, unsuccessfully, to purchase the site as a permanent retreat. The name was suggested in 1945 by Vancouver city archivist Maj J S Matthews and adopted the following year.

Briggs Inlet (52°22'00" 128°00'00" Between Florence Peninsula and Coldwell Peninsula, N of Bella Bella). Thomas Lasher Briggs (1839–1920), of New Westminster, was a business associate of Capt John Irving, the dominant steamship operator on the Fraser R in the 19th century. He was also Irving's brother-in-law, having married Mary Irving (1852–1931) in 1874. When Irving's Pioneer Line was merged with the HBC's fleet of steamers in 1883 to form the Canadian Pacific Navigation Co, Briggs was one of the shareholders and also acted as the company's New Westminster agent. By 1901, when taken over by the CPR, the CPN was operating 14 vessels. Briggs Inlet was formerly known as Sisters Inlet but was renamed in 1925.

Brig Rock (50°47'00" 126°54'00" Off SW end of the Polkinghorne Is, W of Broughton I, NE side of Queen Charlotte Str). Named about 1865 by Lt Daniel Pender of the *Beaver* in association with the Polkinghorne Is (qv) and Fantome Point (qv). Charles Polkinghorne had been master of the brig *Fantome*, under Cdr John Gennys, on the RN's Australian Station, 1850–56.

Britannia Beach (49°38'00" 123°12'00" E side of Howe Sd, S of Squamish). The community of Britannia Beach was named after the Britannia Mine, which operated at this site from 1905 to 1974 and was the largest copper mine in the British Commonwealth in the 1920s. The mine, in turn, commemorates the mountains that loom above it, the Britannia Range, named after HMS *Britannia*, a 100-gun ship of the line, built in 1762, that participated in many important campaigns, including the battles of St Vincent and Trafalgar. Nearby Britannia Ck is also named for this vessel. By the early 2000s, Britannia Beach was a national historic site and home to the BC Museum of Mining. The abandoned mine became a serious source of toxic effluent into Howe Sd after it closed, eventually requiring a major environmental cleanup. *E W*

British Columbia. *See* Columbia Cove.

Brittain River (50°00'00" 124°01'00" Flows SE into Princess Royal Reach, Jervis Inlet, E of Powell R). Named in 1922 after Rowland Brittain (1857–1926), BC's first patent attorney, who owned land at the mouth of the river in 1901–2. He was born in England and immigrated to Victoria in 1888, moving to Vancouver about a decade later. The name first appears on charts as Britain R but was changed in 1950 to Brittain, the correct spelling of the family name. Slhílhem, one of the winter villages of the Sechelt First Nation, was located at the mouth of the river and abandoned before 1860.

Brock Islands (53°42'00" 132°59'00" E approach to Kiokathli Inlet, Port Louis, W side of Graham I, QCI). Geologist Reginald Walter Brock (1874–1935) was born at Perth, Ont. He taught at Queens Univ, 1902–7, before becoming director of the Geological Survey of Canada, 1907–14, and deputy minister of Mines in 1914. After service in WWI he worked at UBC as dean of applied science until 1935, when he and his wife were killed in an aircraft accident. Named during or just after James D MacKenzie's 1913–14 geological survey of Graham I.

Brockton Island (50°29'00" 127°46'00" W of Drake I, Quatsino Sd, N end of Vancouver I), **Brockton Point** (49°18'00" 123°07'00" E point of Stanley Park, W side of Vancouver Hbr). Francis Brockton was chief engineer of the survey vessel *Plumper* under Capt George Richards, who explored Burrard Inlet in 1859 and named Brockton Point and nearby Coal Hbr (qv). Brockton, much to the RN's delight, found a coal seam just S of the area that would become Stanley Park in 1887. He retired in 1879 and died in 1898. Brockton Point was the site of a well-established—and often controversial—community that got its start in the 1860s and lasted until the 1950s. A lighthouse (replaced

Brockton Point in 1914 showing the old fog bell and the new lighthouse tower under construction. *BC Archives A-00184*

by the current tower in 1914) was built at the point in 1902 as an aid to shipping in Vancouver Hbr. By the early 2000s this area had become one of the most popular in Stanley Park, home to the Brockton Oval playing field, totem poles and a visitor centre. *E*

Brodeur Island (52°01'00" 128°17'00" In the Admiral Group, SW of Bella Bella). Rear Adm Victor Gabriel Brodeur (1892–1976) was born at Beloeil, Que. He was among the first group of cadets to graduate from the Royal Naval College of Canada in 1911, and he commanded a number of RCN destroyers over his career, including the *Champlain* (1929–30), *Skeena* (1931–32, 1937–38), *Fraser* (1937) and *Ottawa* (1938). Brodeur was CO at Naden and Esquimalt, 1932–34, and CO Pacific coast, 1938–40 and 1943–46. He was promoted to commodore in 1940 and rear adm in 1942, and he spent three years in Washington as naval attaché and RCN representative on the Canadian Joint Staff. As well as the CB and CBE, he was also awarded the US Legion of Merit and the French Légion d'honneur and Croix de Guerre. Brodeur I was named by the hydrographic service in 1944.

Brodie Island (51°19'00" 127°45'00" N entrance to Smith Sd, E of Queen Charlotte Sd), **Brodie Point** (53°24'00" 129°16'00" W side of Promise I, entrance to Douglas Channel, SW of Kitimat), **Brodie Rock** (48°24'10" 123°17'00" E of Trial Is, SE of Gonzales Point and Victoria), **Mount Brodie** (53°23'11" 129°14'31" On Promise I). RN officer George Staunton Brodie (d 1901) served on the BC coast, 1865–70. From 1867 to 1870 he was aboard the historic steamship *Beaver*, initially as 2nd master, then as navigating lt. The vessel was hired from the HBC for survey work, under Lt Daniel Pender, 1863–70. Brodie retired in 1876 and concentrated on writing; he published at least six books of poetry and drama between 1876 and 1898, often illustrated by his own artwork. Staunton Shoal in Smith Sd is also named for him. Brodie Point was formerly known as Hall Point.

Brokers Bay (49°16'00" 123°08'00" In False Ck, Vancouver). Boats are sold here by brokerage companies. The name was submitted by J Keith King of Foreshore Projects Ltd, endorsed by False Ck Development Group and the City of Vancouver, and adopted in 1984.

Bromley Island (53°35'00" 130°33'00" In Rawlinson Anchorage, off W side of Banks I). William John Bromley (1900–81), of Victoria, went to sea at the age of 16, working on whaling ships out of Naden Hbr in the QCI. In the early 1920s he was quartermaster aboard CGS *Lillooet*, the W coast survey vessel. After a stint in the towboating business he went N as 2nd mate of the *Canadian*, a sternwheeler owned by the British Yukon Navigation Co (a division of the White Pass & Yukon Route). Bromley spent the next 31 years on the Yukon R, 17 of them in command of the sternwheeler *Klondike* (which has been turned into a museum at Whitehorse), running between Dawson City and Whitehorse. The island was named in 1926.

Looking south to Brooks Peninsula from Lawn Point. *Greg Shea*

Brooks Bay (50°13'00" 127°53'00" N side of Brooks Peninsula), **Brooks Peninsula** (50°10'00" 127°45'00" Between Kyuquot Sd and Quatsino Sd, NW side of Vancouver I). In 1785 a British syndicate, the King George's Sd Co (also known as Richard Cadman Etches & Co, after its main investor), was formed to trade to Nootka Sd. The company employed James Colnett, aboard the *Prince of Wales*, and Charles Duncan, on the *Princess Royal*, for a fur-trading voyage to the BC coast the following year. In Aug 1787, on their way N from Nootka Sd, Colnett and Duncan visited Nasparti Inlet, S of Brooks Peninsula, which Colnett named Port Brooks, either after Robert Hanning Brooks, who once had a wine-and-tea-importing partnership with Etches, or Mary Camilla Brooks, Robert's wife and one of the backers of the King George's Sd Co. Later maps incorrectly assigned Port Brooks to the N side of Brooks Peninsula, and this error was perpetuated by several historians (e g, Walbran, Howay and Wagner), who located it at Klaskish Inlet. Capt George Richards, surveying the region in 1862, named Brooks Peninsula—

and Brooks Bay on its N side—to keep alive the old Port Brooks designation. He also named Nasparti Inlet and Klaskish Inlet, an easterly arm of Brooks Bay. Brooks Peninsula became a Class A provincial park in 1996, protected for its unusual ecology and rich biodiversity; it partly escaped the last glaciation and thus formed a rare refuge for plant and animal species. *E*

Brotchie Ledge (48°24'00" 123°23'00" In Juan de Fuca Str, S of Victoria Hbr and Victoria). Capt William Brotchie (1799–1859), from Scotland, was on the Pacific coast as early as 1831 as a seaman aboard the HBC brig *Dryad*. From 1835 onward he was master of several HBC vessels, including the *Cadboro* (1835–38), *Nereid* (1839), *Cowlitz* (1841) and *Beaver* (1842–43). In 1849 he travelled to Vancouver I from London via Sydney, Australia, aboard the *Albion*, under Capt Richard Hinderwell; despite Brotchie's experienced advice, this vessel struck the reef, thus giving it its name. From 1849 to 1855, Brotchie had a licence to cut and export spars from Vancouver I. The business apparently failed because of the difficulties arranging transport for such magnificent timbers, the largest of which stretched 35 m in length. Gov James Douglas appointed Brotchie harbourmaster for Vancouver I in 1858. Many years later, Dr John Helmcken described Brotchie in the Victoria *Daily Colonist* as "a character, genial, heavy, fat, with a twinkling humour." In 1891 the US steamer *San Pedro* grounded on Brotchie Ledge and remained there for six years. The ledge was formerly known as Buoy Rk. *W*

Brothers Islands (48°25'00" 123°26'00" Off Esquimalt, NW of Saxe Point, S end of Vancouver I). RN personnel were buried on the main island in the 1850s and '60s, and it was known as Deadmans I for many years. When a gun emplacement was erected there in the 1890s, the human remains were reinterred at the naval and military cemetery next to Gorge Vale golf course. The origin of the current name is unknown.

Brougham Point (50°22'00" 125°23'00" SE side of E Thurlow I, N of Campbell R). Loughborough Inlet and the adjacent Thurlow Is were named in 1792 by Capt George Vancouver after lord chancellors of England. Capt George Richards continued this theme on his 1860 survey of the area, naming Chancellor Channel to the N of W Thurlow I. Richards also named Brougham Point and Mt Brougham on E Thurlow I at this time, so they presumably refer to jurist and politician Henry Peter Brougham (1778–1868, pronounced *broom*), from Edinburgh, who was appointed chancellor, 1830–34. A liberal and a keen supporter of the Slavery Abolition Act, he introduced important legal, educational and parliamentary reforms and helped found the Univ of London. He was raised to the peerage as Baron Brougham and Vaux in 1830.

Broughton Archipelago (50°40'00" 126°30'00" E end of Queen Charlotte Str, NE side of Vancouver I), **Broughton Island** (50°49'00" 126°45'00" In NW Broughton Archipelago), **Broughton Lagoon** (50°50'00" 126°41'00" N side of Broughton I), **Broughton Peaks** (48°59'45" 125°13'31" N of the Broken Group, Barkley Sd, W side of Vancouver I), **Broughton Point** (50°50'00" 126°48'00" S side of N Broughton I), **Broughton Strait** (50°37'00" 127°03'00" Separates NE Vancouver I from Malcolm I and Cormorant I), **North Broughton Island** (50°51'00" 126°48'00" N of Broughton I). Lt William Robert Broughton (1762–1821) accompanied Capt George Vancouver on his historic 1791 voyage to the PNW as cdr of the armed tender HMS *Chatham*. In Jan 1793 he carried official papers back to England, travelling overland from California, while *Chatham* was taken over by Lt Peter Puget. Two years later, Broughton returned to BC as cdr of HMS *Providence* but found that Vancouver had finished his work and gone home. He then surveyed the coast of Asia for four years, publishing the history of his voyage in 1804 and later serving in India and Indonesia, rising to the rank of commodore. He was created a CB in 1812. Broughton Archipelago, Broughton I and Broughton Str were all named by Capt Vancouver in 1792; Broughton Lk on Broughton I is also named for him. The archipelago covers the southern extremity of what geologists refer to as the Hecate Depression; it includes Broughton, Gilford, E and W Cracroft, and the smaller islands in between, many of which became part of Broughton Archipelago Marine Provincial Park in 1992. *E W*

Aerial view of the Broughton Archipelago. *Peter Vassilopoulos*

Brown Bank (51°21'00" 127°51'00" W of Kelp Head, entrance to Fitz Hugh Sd). Named about 1946 by regional hydrographer Henri Parizeau "after a surveyor aboard surveying vessel *William J Stewart*," possibly J A Brown, who participated in surveys of the Inside Passage (1946–50) and was officer in charge of CGS *Parry* (1947–52 and 1962–64). Brown was also officer in charge of CGS *Marabell* (1953–57), after which he suffered a mild stroke and spent 1957–61 writing sailing directions.

B

Brown Channel (50°00'00" 127°26'00" NW entrance to Kyuquot Sd, NW side of Vancouver I). Sealer and master mariner George D Brown (1834–1914), a native of Liverpool, went to sea as a 13-year-old boy, working on clipper ships and for the Cunard Line. After first visiting Victoria in 1852 on the *Annie Moore*, Brown settled there about 1870 and married Clara Ann Unsworth Crowther (1856–1946) in 1874. He worked for many years for the fur dealers Joseph Boscowitz and James Warren, prominent players in the Victoria-based pelagic fur seal industry and also successful coastal traders. Brown was skipper of the sealing schooner *Anna Beck* and managed Warren's trading posts at Nootka Sd and Kyuquot. Later in his career he joined the Canadian Pacific Navigation Co and its successor, the CPR's BC Coast Steamship Service, serving on the *Princess* ships and as master of the steamer *Maude* on the W Vancouver I run. This feature was known for many years as Halibut Channel but was renamed by officials of the hydrographic service about 1947. *See also* Crowther Channel.

Brown Cove (52°41'00" 128°34'00" N entrance to Meyers Passage, SE side of Princess Royal I). Able Seaman David Edgar Brown, of Richmond, a member of the RCNVR, was killed in action May 7, 1944, aged 19, while serving aboard HMCS *Valleyfield*. The frigate was returning from convoy duty to St John's, Nfld, when it was torpedoed off Cape Race by a U-boat and sank, with the loss of 125 lives. Brown's name is inscribed on the Halifax Memorial.

Browne Rock (50°44'00" 126°34'00" S of Baker I, E end of Queen Charlotte Str). Lt Rodney James Browne, from W Vancouver, was killed in action June 16, 1942, aged 32, while serving with the RCNVR aboard the British light cruiser *Hermione*, which was torpedoed by a German submarine in the Mediterranean and sank, with the loss of 87 lives. He is buried at the Alexandria (Hadra) War Memorial Cemetery in Egypt.

Browning Channel (51°18'00" 127°38'00" S of Barrier Group, Smith Sd, S of Rivers Inlet), **Browning Entrance** (53°44'00" 130°31'00" N of Banks I, S of Prince Rupert), **Browning Inlet** (50°30'00" 128°04'00" W of Winter Hbr, Quatsino Sd, NW side of Vancouver I), **Browning Islands** (50°54'00" 127°20'00" SW of Blunden Hbr, N side of Queen Charlotte Str), **Browning Passage** (50°51'30" 127°38'45" Between Nigei I and the Balaklava Is, off NE side of Vancouver I), **Browning Rock** (50°33'00" 126°12'00" Havannah Channel, E of Cracroft Is, N of Johnstone Str), **Port Browning** (48°46'00" 123°16'00" E side of N Pender I, Gulf Is). George Alexander Browning (1838–1913), a native of Cornwall, was Lt Daniel Pender's assistant surveying officer aboard the *Beaver*, 1863–68, which the RN had hired from the HBC for coastal duties. Previously, he had been 2nd master on HMS *Hecate*, under Capt George Richards, 1861–62. Browning obviously explored

a great deal of the BC coast during his eight-year stint as a surveyor, and Pender must have had a good deal of confidence in his deputy to have named so many features for him. Back in England he was a naval assistant in the hydrographic office for many years and retired in 1893 with the rank of capt.

Browning Passage (49°08'00" 125°52'00" Between Meares I and Esowista Peninsula, SE of Tofino, Clayoquot Sd). Rev Arthur Browning (b 1830) was a British Methodist missionary who came out to Victoria in 1859 and was posted first to Nanaimo and then to Ft Hope (where he married Mary Ann Orchard in 1861), New Westminster (1863–64 and 1868) and Victoria (1865–67). He returned to England in 1870.

Brown Passage (54°20'00" 130°53'00" Between Tree Nob Group and Melville I, N of Stephens I, W of Prince Rupert). Capt William Brown (d 1795) of the *Butterworth*, accompanied by two small tenders, the *Prince Leboo* and the *Jackal*, was a British trader and former Greenland whaler present on the BC coast in 1792–94. His expedition—the first to investigate the prospects of whaling, as well as fur trading, in the region—was financed by a group of London businessmen led by William Curtis, an alderman and whaling merchant. The passage was named by Capt George Vancouver, who encountered Brown at the N end of Stephens I in 1793 (and also several times in 1794) and was led by him to a safe anchorage in stormy weather. Brown briefed Vancouver about the region and allowed the sloop *Prince Leboo* to guide the British survey ships on their exploration of Portland Canal and Observatory Inlet. Mt Brown, on the NE side of Portland Canal, is also named for this experienced mariner, and the original name Vancouver gave to Portland Inlet was Brown Inlet. It was one of Brown's vessels that accidentally killed the US fur trader John Kendrick at Hawaii by saluting him with a loaded cannon in 1794; Brown himself died there the following year while repulsing an attack on his ship by Hawaiian islanders. *W*

Brown Rock (50°27'00" 127°59'00" Entrance to Quatsino Sd, NW end of Vancouver I). Named by the hydrographic service in 1927 after H Brown, who served as a coxswain aboard the survey vessel *Restless* while it was working in Quatsino Sd in 1921.

Bruce Bight (48°46'00" 123°08'00" S end of Saturna I, Gulf Is), **Bruce Peak** (48°46'01" 123°30'27" W side of Fulford Hbr, SW Saltspring I, Gulf Is). Rear Adm Henry William Bruce (1792–1863) was cdr-in-chief on the Pacific Station, 1854–57, with HMS *Monarch* as his flagship. He entered the RN in 1803, was present at the 1805 Battle of Trafalgar and also saw action during the War of 1812. After being promoted to capt in 1821 he had several important commands, including HMS *Britannia*, *Agincourt* and

Queen, and was commodore of an RN squadron off W Africa in 1851 before becoming a rear adm the following year. After his Pacific posting, Bruce served as cdr-in-chief at Portsmouth, with his flag in HMS *Victory*. He was knighted in 1861 and reached the rank of adm in 1863. Bruce Bight, formerly known as Open Bight, was renamed in association with Monarch Head by Cdr John Parry of HMS *Egeria* while re-surveying the region in 1905. **W**

Bruce Islet (52°30'00" 129°02'00" Weeteeam Bay, SW side of Aristazabal I). Henry Bruce (1832–1910), a carpenter by trade, was a sapper with the Columbia detachment of Royal Engineers, which served in BC 1858–63. He saw action in the Crimea in 1854, then travelled to BC on the *Arato* with Capt John Grant's small group in 1858. Bruce stayed on after the detachment disbanded, taking up the free 60-ha land grant—offered to all Royal Engineers who remained in the colony—in the New Westminster area. According to the *British Colonist*, he "lost every article he possessed in the world" in a serious fire in 1864 that damaged parts of New Westminster.

Bruce Point (50°21'00" 125°19'00" N entrance to Cameleon Hbr, Sonora I, N of Campbell R). John Bruce was 1st lt aboard HMS *Cameleon*, which was on the Pacific Station, based at Esquimalt, 1863–65, 1867–69 and 1870–74. Many features in Cameleon Hbr were named after officers who served on the vessel in 1863 during the naval pursuit of a First Nation group from Lamalchi Bay on Kuper I, suspected of murdering two Gulf Is settlers (*see* Lamalchi Bay). **W**

Bruin Bay (54°10'00" 132°59'00" NW side of Graham I, opposite Langara I, QCI). Named by officers of HMS *Virago*, on survey duty in these waters in 1853, after a large bear that came down to the beach opposite their ship. Crew members tried to shoot the animal but were unsuccessful.

Brunswick Point (49°32'00" 123°16'00" E side of Montagu Channel, Howe Sd, NW of Vancouver). The point was named in 1950 in association with nearby Brunswick Mtn, NE of Lions Bay. In 1859–60, RN surveyor Capt George Richards named the mountain and many other features in Howe Sd after the officers and ships involved in the great British naval victory known as the Glorious First of June, which took place in the English Channel in 1794. HMS *Brunswick*, a 74-gun, 1,665-tonne ship of the line, built at Deptford dockyard and launched in 1790, participated in that battle. Its cdr, Capt John Harvey, lost a limb there and died soon after. The vessel went on to serve in the W Indies, 1794–1803, then underwent repairs at Portsmouth and joined the Baltic fleet. It ended its career as a prison ship and powder magazine before being broken up in 1826. **W**

Bryant Islands (48°57'00" 125°22'00" N end of Loudoun Channel, Barkley Sd, W side of Vancouver I). William C Bryant pre-empted land in this vicinity, W of Macoah Passage, in 1892. William Cullen Bryant (1871–1922) and his father, William Charles Bryant (1838–1895), are listed in early census and voters lists as Victoria farriers. The islands were formerly thought to be a single feature and were known as Table It and Table I before being renamed by the hydrographic service in 1934.

Bryant Point (52°53'00" 129°06'00" E of entrance to Racey Inlet, Caamaño Sd). John Dart Bryant (1835–1922) was born in Lincolnshire, UK, and arrived in Victoria in 1865. He and his wife, Betsy (Elizabeth Jane, 1837–1923), established a showcase farm, Rosedale, in the central Saanich area. Bryant served as president of the N and S Saanich Agricultural Society and the Saanich Fair. The point was named by the hydrographic service in 1926.

Bryden Bay (48°40'30" 123°24'28" N side of Tsehum Hbr, just N of Sidney, Saanich Peninsula, S Vancouver I). James Bryden (1825–87), a native of Scotland, was a farmer and miller and one of the first landowners in N Saanich, purchasing 65 ha at Canoe Cove in the late 1860s or early '70s. He helped Henry Brackman start his pioneer flour mill in 1878 at nearby Tsehum Hbr. The name was adopted in 1965 after a submission by local residents.

The sandy beach at Buccaneer Bay Provincial Park. *John Alexander*

Buccaneer Bay (49°30'00" 123°59'00" Between N and S Thormanby Is, NW of Sechelt, Str of Georgia). Many features around the Thormanby Is (qv) were named in 1860 by RN surveyor Capt George Richards after the Epsom Derby, won that year by racehorse Thormanby. Buccaneer was one of the favourites but faded in the stretch and ended well back in the pack. He won the Royal Hunt Cup at Ascot, however, the following year. The bay is home to tiny but popular Buccaneer Bay Provincial Park, established in 1989, and one of the nicest beaches N of Vancouver. The Sechelt First Nation name for the bay is Klay-ah-kwohss.

Buchan Inlet (53°23'00" 129°46'00" N of Port Stephens, SW side of Pitt I). Sir John Buchan, 1st Baron Tweedsmuir of Elsfield (1875–1940), was gov gen of Canada, 1935–40. A poet and prolific author of both histories (*The Marquis of Montrose, Augustus*) and novels (*The Thirty-Nine Steps, Greenmantle*), Buchan created the Gov Gen's Literary Awards in 1936. He also served the British government in S Africa and France, was newspaper tycoon Lord Beaverbrook's director of information, 1917–18, and became a Scottish Unionist politician in 1927. The inlet was named in 1944. Other features that commemorate him in BC include nearby Tweedsmuir and Elsfield points, Tweedsmuir Provincial Park and Buchan Ck, NW of Quesnel.

Buchholz Channel (50°30'00" 127°38'00" S side of Drake I, Quatsino Sd, NW side of Vancouver I), **Buchholz Rock** (50°29'00" 127°34'00" Entrance to Neroutsos Inlet, Quatsino Sd). Capt Otto Franz Carl Buchholz (1864–1935), a native of Germany, was a sealer early in his deep-sea career. In 1892, as master of the *Sea Lion*, he defied US attempts to seize his vessel in Alaska for alleged illegal hunting and set an armed US marshal adrift in a small boat. The protests of Buchholz and other Canadian sealers against attempts by the US government and the Alaska Commercial Co to forcibly control the seal trade eventually resulted in the 1911 N Pacific Fur Seal Convention, which ended the pelagic hunt. Buchholz was the first keeper, in 1909, at Estevan lighthouse, which he helped build. In 1920–21 he became pilot and marine superintendent for Whalen Pulp & Paper at the company's Port Alice mill. By 1924 he was living on Quatsino Sd at Hecate Cove with his wife, Nellie, and two adopted daughters and operating the tug *Canpac*. Both geographical features were named by the hydrographic service about 1927.

Buck Channel (53°06'00" 132°28'00" Between Chaatl I and NW Moresby I, QCI), **Buck Point** (53°06'00" 132°34'00" NW tip of Moresby I). Buck Point was named in 1793 by Capt George Vancouver on his way S to California and Hawaii after concluding his season's work in the PNW. It is believed to commemorate the prominent Buck family of Norwich, who lived not far from where Vancouver himself was raised, at King's Lynn, Norfolk. Buck Channel, shown as Canoe Pass and Douglas Inlet on early maps, was named in association with the point and appears on Capt Absalom Freeman's 1912–16 sketch map of the area. According to ethnologist Dr Charles Newcombe, the Haida First Nation name for the point was Sta'nlengesalskun. *D*

Buckle Point (53°16'00" 129°23'00" W side of Fin I, SE of Pitt I). Named in 1950 after Wing Cdr Arthur Buckle, of Victoria, who died in a flying accident on Nov 23, 1944, at the age of 44. He was the RCAF's senior personnel staff officer at No 3 Training Command HQ, Montreal, and was awarded the MBE posthumously in 1945. Buckle is buried at St Stephen's Cemetery in Saanichton, N of Victoria.

Buckley Bay (49°31'00" 124°51'00" W side of Baynes Sd, S of Courtenay, E side of Vancouver I). The origin of the name is uncertain, though a Samuel Buckley is listed in the 1898 BC voters list as a farmer residing at nearby Union Bay. The Coast Salish name for the bay is Tamxwayksen. A terminus for a ferry to Denman I was established at this location in 1952.

Buckley Cove (53°43'00" 132°27'00" N side of Masset Inlet, Graham I, QCI). Frank L Buckley, a native of Iowa, was managing director of the Masset Timber Co, which built a large mill here in 1918 to saw Sitka or "aeroplane" spruce, a light, strong wood used to build Mosquito fighter-bombers and other planes. After WWI the demand for spruce declined. The LA Lumber Co bought the mill in 1922 and closed it two years later. The long-deserted site was originally known as Buckley Bay, and a post office by that name operated there, 1918–34; Buckley Cove was adopted by the hydrographic service in 1948 to recall the historical post office name. Frank Buckley was also involved in raising produce and beef on N Graham I for sale to QCI logging camps. He built a handsome mansion in Vancouver's Shaughnessy district in 1913 (called Iowa, at 3498 Osler), where he lived with his family until 1939. *D*

Buckley Head (52°29'00" 128°17'00" NE of Dowager I, N of Bella Bella). Rev Arthur Buckley was an RN chaplain and instructor aboard HMS *Scout*, under Capt John Price, and served on the BC coast, 1865–68. He was later transferred to HMS *Lord Warden* on the Mediterranean Station. Lt Daniel Pender named the feature Buckley Point in 1867, but it was changed by the hydrographic service to Buckley Head in 1948.

Buckley Point (53°56'00" 130°06'00" E side of Telegraph Passage, S of mouth of Skeena R, SE of Prince Rupert). Capt Cecil William Buckley, VC (1830–1872), was on the BC coast in 1868–69 as cdr of the 17-gun HMS *Pylades*. He won his VC in 1855 in the Crimean War by twice landing and, under heavy enemy fire, setting important Russian stores ablaze and destroying them. The point was named by RN hydrographer Lt Daniel Pender in 1868. Cecil Point, just N of Pitt I, is also named for him. *W*

Bughouse Bay (50°54'00" 126°59'00" NW of Broughton I, N side of Drury Inlet, N of Port McNeill). Named in 1958 after a demented settler who occupied a cabin on the shore here. Nearby Bughouse Lk also honours him. Another Bughouse Bay, located on Shushwap Lk, plus Bugcamp Ck in the Kamloops district, suggest that mad pioneers, perhaps deranged by solitude and isolation, were not all that uncommon in BC.

Bullen Rock (52°15'00" 128°17'00" Off SE tip of Don Peninsula, NW of Bella Bella). William Fitzherbert Bullen (1860–1921) was born near London, Ont, arrived in Victoria in 1878 and became manager of the Albion Iron Works. In 1893, with his brother Harry Bullen and brother-in-law George Bushby, he founded the Esquimalt Marine Rwy Co (later BC Marine Rwys Co), a pioneer shipyard and repair facility. Bullen's, as it was known, built several steamships, including *Princess Beatrice*, *Princess Royal* and *Princess Maquinna* for the CPR; the sternwheeler *Casca* for the Klondike trade; and the survey vessel *Lillooet*. The Bullens founded the BC Salvage Co in 1896, established a shipyard in Vancouver in 1898 and then sold out to Yarrows Ltd in 1913. William Bullen married Annie Amelia Bushby (1863–1956, *see* Bushby Rk), daughter of BC colonial official and judge Arthur Bushby (and granddaughter of BC gov Sir James Douglas), at Victoria in 1884. Bullen Rk, formerly known as Mark Rk, was renamed by the hydrographic service in 1925.

Bulley Bay (52°28'00" 128°19'00" N side of Dowager I, NW of Bella Bella). Frederick Augustus Bulley (b 1832) served on the Pacific Station, 1865–68, based at Esquimalt, as chief engineer aboard HMS *Scout*. He was chief engineer on HMS *Asia* in 1870 and on the battleship *Iron Duke* in 1875. The name appears on an Admiralty chart published in 1874.

Bull Harbour (50°54'00" 127°56'00" S side of Hope I, off N end of Vancouver I). This very old name was known to HBC officers as early as 1840 and likely refers to the many huge and cantankerous adult male sea lions found in the area. HBC gov Sir George Simpson visited in 1841 and mentions both harbour and sea lions in his 1847 book *Journey Round the World*. The harbour was the site of Humdaspe, the principal Nahwitti First Nation settlement after the Tlatlasikwala and Nakumgilisala tribes merged and moved from Nahwitti (qv) village at Cape Sutil. A Coast Guard search and rescue station was located at this site in the early 2000s.

Bull Island (E end of Bull Passage), **Bull Passage** (49°29'00" 124°12'00" Between Lasqueti I and Jedediah I, S of Texada I in Str of Georgia). John Augustus Bull was master of HMS *Plumper*, 1857–60, and senior survey assistant to Capt George Richards, who named the passage after him about 1860. He died suddenly in Nov of that year at Esquimalt, aged 27, only nine months after marrying Emma Langford, third daughter of Edward Langford (*see* Langford), BC's first settler. Langford was manager of Colwood Farm, one of four farms set up around Victoria by the Puget's Sd Agricultural Co, an HBC subsidiary. Bull was buried in Victoria's old Quadra St cemetery.

Bunsby Islands (50°06'00" 127°30'00" E side of Checleset Bay, NW of Kyuquot Sd, NW side of Vancouver I). Capt John Bunsby, cdr of the brig *Cautious Clara*, is a character in *Dombey and Son*, an 1848 novel by Charles Dickens. According to his friend Capt Edward Cuttle, Bunsby "was beat in his apprenticeship, for three weeks (off and on), about the head with a ring-bolt. And yet a clearer-minded man don't walk." During an 1862 survey aboard HMS *Hecate*, Capt George Richards named several local features after aspects of the novel, including the Cuttle Its, Cautious Point and Clara It. Gay Passage, also associated with *Dombey and Son*, was added later.

Buntzen Bay (49°23'00" 122°52'00" E side of Indian Arm, W of Buntzen Lk, NE of Vancouver). Danish lawyer Johannes Buntzen (1859–1922) had worked in three different countries by the time he was 23: he was an English shipping company employee in 1878, an immigration agent at Winnipeg in 1881 and, from 1882 to 1889, a journalist in Copenhagen, where he married Marie Wendrich. The Buntzens came to Vancouver about 1890. Johannes joined Vancouver Loan and Trust as an accountant and then became manager of the Vancouver Electric Light and Rwy Co. Eight years later he was appointed the BC Electric Rwy Co's first gen manager. In 1903 a BCER subsidiary, the Vancouver Power Co, built a hydroelectric project NE of Vancouver that would eventually send water from Coquitlam Lk to Buntzen Lk by tunnel, then transfer it via penstocks to two power plants on Indian Arm, just S of Buntzen Bay. Buntzen moved to London, England, in 1905 to become BCER chairman. He resigned in 1909 and died at Copenhagen. Buntzen Lk and Buntzen Ck are also named for him.

Burdwood Bay (50°10'05" 125°05'25" W side of Read I, NE of Campbell R), **Burdwood Group** (50°48'00" 126°28'00" Between Gilford I and Broughton I, E of Queen Charlotte Str), **Burdwood Point** (49°35'00" 126°34'00" E entrance to Nootka Sd, W side of Vancouver I). As master of HMS *Persian* in 1842, John Burdwood helped capture a slaver in the Bight of Benin. He became an assistant in the RN's hydrographic dept, 1847–69, and compiled azimuth tables for part of the northern hemisphere. Burdwood was promoted staff cdr in 1863. He never served in BC waters. *W*

Burgess Cove (49°26'00" 123°27'00" SW side of Gambier I, Howe Sd, NW of Vancouver). Thomas Henry "Harry" Burgess (1868–1961), a native of Wiltshire, England, joined the *Empress of China* as an engineer in 1893 and was eventually marine superintendent of engineering for the CPR, 1922–31. He married Jean Allan at Vancouver in 1898. According to his obituary, Burgess was an amateur heavyweight boxing champion in his youth, a founder of the Vancouver Rowing Club and the initial president of the Vancouver Game Assoc. He installed the machinery in an early Hawaiian sugar mill and was responsible for drawing up the plans for the first Capilano suspension bridge. The

B

Burgess family bought property on Gambier I in 1908. The name was submitted by Vancouver city archivist Maj J S Matthews in 1938.

Burgoyne Bay (48°48'00" 123°32'00" W side of Saltspring I, Gulf Is). Cdr Hugh Talbot Burgoyne, VC (1833–70), born at Dublin, was an officer aboard HMS *Ganges*, flagship of Rear Adm Robert Baynes, under Capt John Fulford, and served on the BC coast, 1857–60. He was the son of Field Marshal Sir John Fox Burgoyne, a prominent officer in the 1808–14 Peninsular War. Burgoyne won his VC during the Crimean War when, in 1855, under perilous conditions, he and two other men landed and managed to destroy Russian stores and ammunition dumps. Burgoyne had the misfortune to be the first cdr of HMS *Captain*, a new (and faulty) design of masted warship with rotating turrets, which turned turtle and sank off Cape Finisterre in 1870, with the loss of about 480 lives, including those of its cdr and the vessel's designer, Capt Cowper Phipps Coles. Burgoyne Bay was the site of an early cattle ranch (1860) and home to a post office, 1880–1900. Saltspring I's main log sort was later located there. *E W*

Burgoyne Bay on Saltspring Island. *Peter Vassilopoulos*

Burke Channel (51°55'00" 127°53'00" Separates King I and the mainland, E of Bella Bella). Edmund Burke (1729–97), statesman, orator, author, political theorist and philosopher, was born at Dublin and educated at Trinity College. He was a Whig MP for many years, a leader of the party's conservative faction—well known for his support of the dissident American colonies and his ardent opposition to the French Revolution. Burke published works on anarchy, aesthetics, history and politics, including his famous *Reflections on the Revolution in France*, and founded a political review named the *Annual Register*. He is often considered the philosophical founder of modern political conservatism. Burke Channel was named by Capt George Vancouver in 1793. Edmund Point, at the mouth of the channel, is also named for him, as is Mt Burke, E of Coquitlam.

Burleith Arm (49°00'00" 123°48'00" E side of Woods I, Ladysmith Hbr, E side of Vancouver I). Named in 1904 by Cdr John Parry of HMS *Egeria* after the stately Victoria residence of James Dunsmuir, the BC industrialist who served as premier of the province, 1900–1902, and lt gov, 1906–9. Dunsmuir named his home after the birthplace of his father, Robert Dunsmuir, also a BC industrialist and politician, in Ayrshire, Scotland. James would go on in 1908 to build a far more ostentatious mansion, Hatley Castle, designed by leading architect Samuel Maclure and, since 1996, part of Esquimalt's Royal Roads Univ. Burleith, built about 1900, deteriorated after the Dunsmuirs sold it in 1909 and was destroyed by fire in 1931. Its gatehouse still stands.

Burly Bay (50°55'00" 126°47'00" S side of Mackenzie Sd, N of Broughton I, E end of Queen Charlotte Str). William Blair McKenzie (1850–1901), known to his intimates as "Burly," was born in Scotland and died in Spokane. He was the son of Kenneth McKenzie, manager of Craigflower Farm, one of the large farms established in the 1850s near Victoria by the Puget's Sd Agricultural Co, an HBC subsidiary. A large logging camp operated here from about 1900 to 1930; it had a Chinese owner at first but was then taken over by Japanese loggers. The bay was named by Admiralty surveyors in 1865.

Burnaby Island (52°23'00" 131°19'00" Between Skincuttle Inlet and Juan Perez Sd, off SE Moresby I, QCI), **Burnaby Shoal** (49°18'00" 123°07'00" Vancouver Hbr, SE of Brockton Point), **Burnaby Strait** (52°22'00" 131°21'00" Between Burnaby I and Moresby I). Robert Burnaby (1828–78) was a British civil servant who came to Victoria in 1858 and found a position as secretary to Col Richard Moody, BC's lt gov and commissioner of Lands and Works. He assisted with the laying out of New Westminster, tried his hand as a coal merchant, became a commission agent and ended up a prominent Victoria businessman and Freemason, first grand master of the Grand Lodge of BC and Yukon. Burnaby was elected to Vancouver I's legislative assembly, 1860–65. The city of Burnaby, E of Vancouver, is also named for him, as are Burnaby Lk, Mt Burnaby and

Burnaby Strait off Moresby Island is famed for its rich subtidal life.
John Alexander

the **Burnaby Range** (53°32'00" 129°36'00") on SE Pitt I. Burnaby I was named by mining engineer Francis Poole in 1862. The Haida people know it as Skwa'i Kungwa'i. *E W*

Burnes Passage (53°05'00" 129°06'00" Campania Sd, NW side of Princess Royal I). Named in 1926 after Robert Edward Burnes, who was born at Victoria in 1873 and married Sophia E Pears (1882–1955) there in 1907. He was a son of Irishman Thomas J Burnes (1833–1915), who arrived in BC in 1858 and married Katherine E McCloy (1836–1919), from NY, in 1862. Thomas built and operated the American Hotel and Burnes House, worked for the Victoria customs dept for many years and was also a well-known city fire chief and fundraiser for public charities. In turn-of-the-century lists and directories, Robert is described as a dry goods clerk; he was working for W & J Wilson, pioneer Victoria clothiers, in 1912. He is believed to have taken part in the city's famous old-timers' reunion of 1924 (*see* Adams Bay).

Burnett Bay (51°07'00" 127°41'00" NW of Bramham I, NW side of Queen Charlotte Str). Stoker John Henry Burnett, from Victoria, was killed in action Oct 22, 1940, aged 20, while serving aboard HMCS *Margaree*. The RCN destroyer sank in the N Atlantic while on convoy escort duty after colliding with the freighter *Port Fairy*; 142 crew members were lost with the ship. Burnett's name is inscribed on the Halifax Memorial.

Burns Bay (53°28'00" 129°50'00" N part of Mink Trap Bay, W side of Pitt I). Named by the hydrographic service in 1944 after B Burns, who was chief cook aboard CGS *William J Stewart* in the early 1940s.

Burns Point (49°18'00" 122°55'00" N entrance to Port Moody, Burrard Inlet, E of Vancouver). Kenneth Jardine Burns (1878–1966) was born in Ont and went to sea at the age of 20 as 2nd purser on the *Empress of China*. He worked for the CPR and the Great Northern Rwy, then in 1918 was appointed BC manager of the Canadian Robert Dollar Co, which ran steamships between Vancouver and Asia. Burns served as superintendent and gen manager for the port of Vancouver, 1924–47, a period in which the city's shipping volume tripled. The name was submitted by Vancouver city archivist Maj J S Matthews in 1940.

Burnt Island (53°13'00" 132°10'00" In Kagan Bay, Skidegate Inlet, QCI). QCI historian Kathleen Dalzell describes a gory incident that took place on this fortified island when the family of a Haida woman insulted by a suitor named Batons murdered the man's relatives in revenge and held Batons as a slave. Other relatives then murdered a member of the insulted woman's family; in retaliation, the miserable Batons was bisected with a crosscut saw on nearby Torrens I. Burnt I was named in 1866 by RN surveyor Lt Daniel Pender. *D*

Burrard Inlet, looking west toward Stanley Park and First Narrows.
Courtesy Port Metro Vancouver

Burrard Inlet (49°18'00" 123°12'00" Just N of Vancouver). Capt George Vancouver explored the inlet in 1792 and named it Burrard's Channel after his friend Capt Sir Harry Burrard (1765–1840), who had served with him as a lt on HMS *Europa* in the W Indies in 1785. Burrard, who took the surname Burrard-Neale after his 1794 marriage to Grace Neale, had an important naval career, becoming cdr-in-chief on the Mediterranean Station, 1823–26, and a full adm in 1830. He was also a British MP for 40 years. In 1791, Spanish explorer Francisco Eliza named this body of water Brazo de Floridablanca, after the famous Spanish statesman José Moñino y Redondo, the Count of Floridablanca; the following year, Dionisio Alcalá-Galiano and Cayetano Valdéz also examined it, marking the feature on one of their charts as Canal de Sasamat, which they understood to be the original First Nation name. Today, of course, the inlet forms Vancouver's waterfront and is a major port for freighters, cruise ships and smaller craft. A long-standing tradition of the Burrard family holds that the inlet was named after Sir Harry Burrard's uncle, the 1st baronet, whose name was also Sir Harry Burrard (1707–91) and whom Vancouver knew as well, but this supposition was convincingly refuted in a 1946 scholarly article by historian W Kaye Lamb. *E W*

Burrill Point (48°52'00" 123°19'00" S of Sturdies Bay, SE side of Galiano I, Gulf Is). Joseph Burrill (1870–1957), from Yorkshire, came to Galiano I in 1896 and farmed on the island's SE corner. Frederick James Burrill (1867–1952), his older brother, arrived in 1899. They opened a general store in 1903, which they expanded and owned until 1947. Joe ran the store and Fred the farm, and the two bachelors became a local island institution, with Joe especially well known as a musician and singer. The point was named in 1904 by Cdr John Parry of the RN survey vessel *Egeria*.

Burrowes Island (54°19'00" 130°22'00" Entrance to Russell Arm, Prince Rupert Hbr). Gilbert Burrowes was a leveller with the 1906 GTP party that surveyed Prince Rupert for the railroad. (A leveller used an optical instrument with a spirit level to measure grades and elevations.) The name was adopted by the Geographic Board of Canada in 1917.

Burr Rock (52°52'00" 128°42'00" Off Fifer Cove, Laredo Inlet, Princess Royal I). Joseph Burr spent 21 years in Ireland as a soldier with the British Army (62nd Regiment) and was discharged with the rank of sgt-maj. He immigrated to eastern Canada with his wife Elizabeth and family, then managed to secure a position as schoolmaster at Yale, 1866–67. In 1869 he was appointed Yale's chief constable and postmaster. The actor Raymond Burr, born at New Westminster in 1917, was probably his great-grandson. The rock was named by the hydrographic service in 1928.

Burt Point (50°50'00" 126°40'00" N side of Broughton I, E end of Queen Charlotte Str). James Burt (1869–1956) was a Nflder and a veteran of the W coast pelagic sealing industry, where he worked as a hunter on the schooner *Mermaid*. He was later employed by the Canadian Pacific Navigation Co and Island Tug & Barge. In the 1901 Victoria census, Burt is listed as a winch driver aboard CPN's *Amur*. He died at Victoria. The point was formerly known as Hall Point, a name that appears on an 1867 Admiralty chart.

Bushby Rock (50°33'00" 128°16'00" Off Commerell Point, S of San Josef Bay, NW end of Vancouver I). Annie Amelia Bushby (1863–1956) was a niece of Adm Sir John Commerell, who is commemorated on nearby Commerell Point (qv). She was also a daughter of BC colonial official and judge Arthur Bushby and a granddaughter of BC gov Sir James Douglas. Annie married Esquimalt shipyard pioneer William Bullen (*see* Bullen Rk) in 1884. Named about 1940 by regional hydrographer Henri Parizeau.

Butchart Cove (48°34'00" 123°28'00" E side of Tod Inlet, W side of Saanich Inlet, NW of Victoria). Butchart, adopted as a well-established local name in 1981, commemorates the adjacent Butchart Gardens, which were named for cement tycoon Robert Pim Butchart (1856–1943) and his wife, Jeanette Foster Kennedy Butchart (1868–1950), both from Ont. The Butcharts came to BC in 1903, and Robert, who had cement interests across N America, established a plant at Tod Inlet; during WWI he also ran the Imperial Munitions Board's W coast shipbuilding operations. The Butcharts constructed a home at Tod Inlet, called Benvenuto, and in about 1909, Jeanette transformed an abandoned quarry into the famous 20-ha gardens, which opened to the public in 1915 and soon became a major tourist attraction. Nearby Butchart Lk derives its name from the same source. *E*

Aerial view of Butedale cannery in the mid-1930s. *Author's collection*

Butedale (53°09'00" 128°42'00" NE side of Princess Royal I), **Butedale Passage** (53°10'00" 128°40'00" S end of Fraser Reach, between Work I and Princess Royal I). John and Peter Wallace were natives of the Isle of Arran, just SW of the Isle of Bute. They immigrated to Astoria in the 1880s and, after spending time in the Columbia R sturgeon business, moved to BC, formed Wallace Bros Fisheries Ltd and became successful curers and canners of salmon. They went their separate ways in 1910 but remained in the canning industry. John sold his Nass Bay Arrandale operation in 1911 and immediately built a cannery on Princess Royal I that he called Butedale, thus commemorating both the Scottish islands he had known best as a child. The Canadian Fishing Co acquired Butedale in 1923, enlarged it and added cold-storage and reduction plants before closing the cannery in 1950 and the reduction facility in 1962. The site continued as a supply centre for passing vessels until the mid-1980s but grew increasingly derelict. New owners were attempting to revitalize the ruins in the early 2000s. The Haisla First Nation name for Butedale, according to anthropologist Jay Powell, is C'idexs, which means "diarrhea" and likely refers to the consequences of overindulging in the area's abundant berries. Nearby Butedale Ck, Butedale Falls and Butedale Lk are all named after the cannery. *E*

Bute Inlet (50°21'00" 125°06'00" Between Toba Inlet and Loughborough Inlet, NE of Campbell R). Capt George Vancouver named this feature in 1792 after John Stuart, 3rd Earl of Bute (1713–92), a Scottish nobleman and British PM, 1762–63. He was a close associate of Frederick, Prince of Wales, and his son, the future King George III, who later turned against him. Bute was keener on botany than politics; he wrote about British plants and was an important patron of literature and art. Mt Bute and Bute Glacier, near the head of the inlet, are also named for him, as is Stuart I (qv) at the inlet's mouth. Bute Inlet, one of BC's largest fjords, juts 66 km into the Coast Mtns. It is notorious for its strong outflow winds and for "Bute wax," an oily material that sometimes appears on the inlet's surface. In 1862, entrepreneur Alfred Waddington attempted to build a road to the BC Interior from its head. This unsuccessful incursion into Tsilhqot'in First Nation territory led to the so-called Chilcotin War, in which a number of settlers, road workers and Tsilhqot'in died. The inlet was the Brazo de Quintano of Spanish explorer Dionisio Alcalá-Galiano, which was probably named after Fernando Quintano, one of Alejandro Malaspina's officers on the *Descubierta*. *E W*

Bute Island (48°59'45" 123°47'30" In Ladysmith Hbr, E side of Vancouver I). The name was proposed in 1963 by the island's owner, H W McCurdy of Seattle, after the ancestral home of the McCurdy clan on the Isle of Bute in Scotland's Firth of Clyde. Formerly known as Island No 3.

Butler Cove (54°07'00" 130°40'00" SE side of Stephens I, SW of Prince Rupert). John William Butler (1868–1924), a native of Nfld, worked for the New England Fish Co in Hecate Str, 1896–97, as capt of the steamer *Thistle*. The company had a fish-packing facility in the cove at that time. In the 1901 census he is listed as master of the giant tug *Lorne*. The cove was named by Capt John Walbran in 1897 while surveying the area with CGS *Quadra*.

Butler Rock (53°34'00" 130°33'00" In Rawlinson Anchorage, off W side of Banks I). Ann Jane Bates (1846–1930) was born at Manchester, UK, and immigrated to Victoria in 1863. In 1867, at Sapperton, she married Robert Butler, a printer, who had come to BC with the Columbia detachment of the Royal Engineers (*see* Butler Shoal, *below*). She is believed to have participated in the Victoria old-timers' reunion held in 1924 (*see* Adams Bay). The feature was formerly known as Hunt Rk but was renamed by regional hydrographer Henri Parizeau in 1926.

Butler Shoal (52°38'00" 129°14'00" In Beauchemin Channel, off W side of Aristazabal I). Sapper Robert Butler (1842–1917), born at Manchester, UK, was part of the Columbia detachment of Royal Engineers, which served in BC 1858–63. He was the detachment bugler—a boy soldier—and only 17 when he and two other sappers helped capture a notorious fugitive who had robbed and killed at least eight gold miners. Butler married Ann Bates in 1867 (*see above*), moved to Victoria about 1868 and had a large family. He worked for half a century at the Government Printing Office, was active with the local rifle corps, both in New Westminster and Victoria, and was honoured at the 1909 reunion held for the last 12 sappers still living in BC.

Butterworth Rocks (54°14'00" 130°59'00" NW of Stephens I, W of Prince Rupert). The 356-tonne *Butterworth*, a former 30-gun French frigate captured by the RN, was put into service as a British trading vessel and sent to the PNW under Capt William Brown. Brown traded successfully on the BC N coast in the summers of 1792 and 1793; he also spent much time at Hawaii, where he was killed in an attack by islanders in 1795. He encountered Capt George Vancouver several times in BC and helped him find safe anchorage at the N end of Stephens I in a storm in 1793 (*see* Brown Passage). The *Butterworth* returned to England via Cape Horn with a large cargo of seal skins and whale oil, and may have later been refitted to operate as a whaling vessel in the S Pacific.

Butze Point (Just S of Butze Rapids), **Butze Rapids** (54°18'00" 130°15'00" Between Fern Passage and Morse Basin, E side of Kaien I and Prince Rupert). Both names were adopted in 1908–10 by the Geographic Board of Canada after A Butze, who was a GTP purchasing agent in 1906, when Prince Rupert was established as the railroad's western terminus. A railway station in Alberta was named for him also. The rapids, according to *Sailing Directions*, "are dangerous and, at times, spectacular."

Byers Bay (53°31'14" 130°22'36" N side of Kingkown Inlet, NW end of Banks I), **Byers Passage** (48°40'00" 123°23'00" Between Little Shell I and Ker I, NE of Sidney, Gulf Is). Capt William Douglas Byers (1863–1944), a native of NS, became involved in the W coast pelagic fur seal industry after sailing round Cape Horn to Victoria in 1888. In 1893, as master of *Carlotta G Cox*, he outdid all other sealing schooners off the Japanese coast, securing a total of 2,766 skins. *Geneva* was another of his vessels. After his wife Emma died in 1906, aged 31, Byers married Mary Elizabeth Harrison (1885–1935) in 1909. He settled in Sidney, became a member of the local board of trade and operated a boat service to the Gulf Is until 1918. Byers Cone on the W side of Vancouver I is also named for him. Byers Bay was named by the hydrographic service in the 1940s; Byers Passage was adopted in 1965 after a submission by local residents.

Byers Islands (52°34'00" 129°24'00" W side of Beauchemin Channel, off W side of Aristazabal I). Nothing seems to be known about Lance Cpl William Byers, who was a member of the Columbia detachment of Royal Engineers, which served in BC 1858–63. Formerly known as the Middle Gander Is but renamed by regional hydrographer Henri Parizeau in 1927.

Caamaño Passage (54°35'00" 131°00'00" Between Dundas I and Zayas I, NW of Prince Rupert), **Caamaño Sound** (52°54'00" 129°15'00" Between Estevan Group and Aristazabal I, W side of Princess Royal I). Jacinto Caamaño, born at Madrid in 1759, was a Spanish naval officer, sent to Mexico in 1789 to join the San Blas naval dept. As cdr of the *Princesa*, he helped found Spain's Nootka Sd settlement in 1790. Two years later he came N again as part of Juan Francisco de la Bodega y Quadra's squadron and, aboard the *Aránzazu*, surveyed the N BC coast on either side of Dixon Entrance and searched for the fictitious Str of Fonte, a navigable sea passage that supposedly crossed N America at that latitude. Caamaño also kept an early and important journal describing his encounters with First Nation groups. He served in the Philippines and Mexico, as well, and died sometime after 1820, in Equador, where he was capt of the port of Guayaquil. Jacinto Is and Jacinto Point are named for him, as are several features in Puget Sd in Washington state, which was earlier named Ensenada de Caamaño (by Manuel Quimper), then Boca de Caamaño (by Francisco Eliza). *E*

Cachalot Inlet (50°00'00" 127°09'00" E side of Kyuquot Channel, SE side of Kyuquot Sd, NW side of Vancouver I). *Cachalot* is the French word for sperm whale. A whaling station by this name—operated here from 1907 to 1924 by Sprott Balcom and the Pacific Whaling Co—was the most productive in BC in terms of numbers of whales landed. In 1926, Wallace Bros acquired the property, converted it to a reduction plant for pilchards and ran it for another decade. Cachalot post office was open from 1918 to 1935. The remains of the station and plant were still visible in the early 2000s. The inlet used to be known as Narrow Gut Ck.

Cadboro Bay (48°27'00" 123°17'00" SE side of District of Saanich, N of Victoria), **Cadboro Point** (48°27'00" 123°15'52" E of Cadboro Bay). The HBC brigantine *Cadboro* was the first regular trading and supply ship on the BC coast. The historic vessel, only 17 m in length and 63 tonnes, was built in England in 1824 and arrived at Ft Vancouver on the Columbia R three years later. Sporting

six guns, and with a picked crew of 35 men, it was the first ship to enter the Fraser R (in 1827, under Capt Aemilius Simpson) and to explore Victoria Hbr and Cadboro Bay (in 1842, under Capt James Scarborough). Sold in 1860 to Capt Edward Howard, the *Cadboro* was wrecked near Port Angeles in a gale while carrying lumber from Puget Sd to Victoria in 1862. The bay—named by the officers of the HBC about 1842—was known to Songhees First Nation members as Sungayka, meaning "snow patches"; it was an important early village site. The point was named by RN surveyor Capt George Richards in 1858. *E W*

Cadman Island (53°17'00" 132°39'00" S side of Kano Inlet, SW side of Graham I, QCI), **Cadman Point** (52°10'00" 131°13'00" E side of Louscoone Inlet, QCI). After Richard Cadman Etches, the main investor in the 18th-century King George's Sd Co. *See* Etches Point.

Caesar Cove (49°45'35" 124°33'50" S side of Sturt Bay, E side of Texada I, Str of Georgia). Whoever named the cove was perhaps reminded of sculptures of Caesar by the light-coloured marble found in the limestone formations here. Caesar Cove appears on Admiralty charts starting about 1913; before then this feature was known as Marble Bay or Marble Cove.

Caffery Point (48°20'00" 123°36'00" N side of Becher Bay, S end of Vancouver I). Mary Ann Caffery (1853–1936) and her seven children moved to E Sooke from Prevost I in 1888 after the death of her sea capt husband, Thomas Caffery. They were a pioneer farming family, and the Caffery House, built by James Caffery (1874–1938) in the 1890s, is one of the district's heritage homes. James and his younger brother Joseph Peter (1882–1918) are listed as sealers in the 1901 census. Frank Caffery (1888–1940) received a Crown grant of land in E Sooke in 1912. Caffery Point was named about 1934; before that it was known as Bluff Point.

Cain Peninsula (48°53'00" 123°19'00" SE side of Galiano I, Gulf Is), **Cain Point** (N end of Cain Peninsula). William

The Ships and Skippers of the Hudson's Bay Company

The Hudson's Bay Company, Canada's oldest corporation, relied heavily on what it called its "marine service." The names of its early vessels—and those who commanded them—now adorn a slew of geographic features on the BC coast. And the marine service itself, through a series of business acquisitions and mergers, metamorphosed into the steamship line that operated the famous *Princess* vessels in BC.

It all began on the Columbia River with the brigantine *Cadboro*. The Hudson's Bay Company decided to get into the coastal fur trade, and it needed something small to set up trading posts and transport furs and supplies. The historic *Cadboro*, built in England for £800, was small indeed, only 17 metres long and about 60 tonnes. It was the first European ship to enter the Fraser River, in 1827, when Aemilius Simpson and his crew of 35 sailed cautiously upstream and established Fort Langley.

The HBC also had a small fleet to ply back and forth between England and its far-flung posts. The captains employed on these long journeys, some of whom also worked on the BC coast, could be something of a trial. Governor George Simpson wrote of James Davidson, for instance, master of the 185-tonne *Dryad*, that he knew nothing of his "talent as a Navigator ... but his talent as a Grog Drinker I understand is without parallel." Chief factor John McLoughlin commented that L J Hayne of the *Ganymede* was "so much addicted to Liquor I conceive it would be hazarding the safety of the Vessel to give him charge of her. I have several times perceived he made free with Liquor before Breakfast." Hayne went mad en route to England and sailed his ship to Tasmania instead.

The *Cadboro* proved too small for safety. "There are hundreds of War Canoes on the coast longer and higher out of the water than she is," exclaimed Simpson. Larger vessels were sought. The 175-tonne *Eagle*, under John Grave, helped determine the site of Fort Nass in 1830. The *Lama*, under William McNeill, an experienced, sober trader, brought materials to Bella Bella in 1833 to build the trading post of Fort McLoughlin.

The most famous of the HBC's coastal vessels was the *Beaver*, which arrived in 1836 to become the first steamship on the BC coast. With its side paddlewheels and a top speed of almost 10 knots, the *Beaver* had a long and honourable career on the coast. It was hired by the Royal Navy from 1863 to 1870 and performed invaluable survey work under Lt Daniel Pender before being wrecked in 1888 at Prospect Point in Vancouver Harbour.

The *Beaver* had many skippers. One was William Brotchie, who had also been in charge of the *Cadboro*. A portly, good-natured fellow, Brotchie left Hudson's Bay service in 1849 and got a licence from the Royal Navy to cut and export spars. His business was a total failure, though, as the prodigious masts and yards he felled in the forest and shipped out proved too large and magnificent for practical use. Another competent

captain, Charles Dodd, had charge of the *Beaver* from 1852 to 1856 and went on to become a senior Hudson's Bay officer.

Many other HBC vessels and skippers added their names to the coast as the years went by. The *Otter*, the first propeller-driven steamer in the Pacific Northwest, is commemorated by almost as many place names as the *Beaver*. The *Labouchere* and the *Enterprise* both have stories to tell. Willie Mitchell and the *Una* set off the Queen Charlotte Islands gold rush in 1852.

The *Cadboro*, as painted by R. Boyd MacGill. *BC Archives A-00278*

Charles Stuart of the *Beaver* has five places named for him, as does the reliable John Swanson, who had a 30-year career with the company.

The Hudson's Bay Company dominated BC's coastal shipping until 1883, when it merged with the Pioneer Line, which had equal dominance over BC's riverboats. Pioneer, with its fleet of shallow-draft sternwheelers, had been founded in 1862 by William Irving and operated since 1872 by his son John Irving. The combined operation, known as the Canadian Pacific Navigation Co, was taken over in 1901 by the Canadian Pacific Railway, which called its new subsidiary the BC Coast Steamship Service. The CPR invested heavily in a series of new and elegant *Princess* ships, and any lingering trace of the old fur-trading marine department soon disappeared.

C

Cain (1847–1928) came to Canada from England in 1867 and lived on Mayne I as well as Galiano I. A carpenter and cabinetmaker by trade, he built a home on Galiano in 1894 that featured elaborate, hand-carved woodwork. Cain also built the Church of St Mary Magdalene, still standing on Mayne I, in 1897, much of it in native Garry oak. He died at Victoria. Cain Point appears on an Admiralty chart published in 1907.

Calamity Bay (53°10'00" 129°51'00" S end of Banks I), **Calamity Harbour** (53°10'00" 129°47'45" Just E of Calamity Bay). Capt James Colnett, with the *Prince of Wales*, and Capt Charles Duncan, in the *Princess Royal*, led an early fur-trading expedition to the BC coast under the auspices of the King George's Sd Co. In late autumn of 1787 they were forced to spend two and a half months repairing the *Prince of Wales* at a secluded anchorage on Banks I. The vessel was unloaded and the main mast replaced, but during the relaunch the keel was damaged and further repairs required. Relations with the local Tsimshian people, positive at first, soon degenerated into a series of desperate skirmishes, culminating with the theft of a longboat and anchor, and several First Nation deaths. Colnett named this anchorage Port Ball, but the crew called it Calamity Hbr and the latter name stuck. On the 1870 Admiralty chart of the area, the name of the harbour was inadvertently transferred to a more open body of water due W and changed to Calamity Bay. It was not until 2003, on the recommendation of historian and author Richard E Wells, that Calamity Hbr was officially restored. Now both names are in use.

Caldwell Island (49°45'00" 124°03'00" NW side of Agamemnon Channel, mouth of Jervis Inlet, N of Pender Hbr). Capt Benjamin Caldwell (1739–1820) was the first cdr of the 64-gun ship of the line *Agamemnon*, launched in 1781. He was promoted to capt in 1765 and spent much of his career on the N American and W Indies stations, becoming a rear adm in 1793. Caldwell was also an MP, 1776–90. He commanded HMS *Impregnable* at the 1794 battle known as the Glorious First of June but was overlooked in the dispatches of the cdr-in-chief, Lord Howe, a snub that infuriated Caldwell. He was briefly appointed cdr-in-chief of the W Indies Station but was replaced and left the RN in high dudgeon, refusing to serve at sea again. He rose automatically to the rank of adm, retired, in 1799 and was knighted in 1820. The island was named by the hydrographic service in 1945.

Call Bight (50°06'05" 124°42'00" E side of Desolation Sd, N of Gifford Peninsula, N end of Str of Georgia). Petty Officer George E Call, who joined the RCN at Esquimalt in 1927, was a stoker aboard the destroyer *Fraser*, which collided with the British cruiser *Calcutta* and sank while participating in an evacuation of French refugees in June 1940. Call died on July 4, 1940, aged 33, one of 64 men to lose their lives in this tragic accident, and is buried at Plymouth Cemetery, Devon, UK.

Call Inlet (50°36'30" 126°04'30" E of E Cracroft I, N of Johnstone Str), **Call Shoal** (50°35'00" 126°08'00" N side of Call Inlet). Sir John Call (1732–1801) was a military engineer with the British E India Co and rose to the rank of chief engineer. He helped the company capture the well-defended Indian fortresses of Pondicherry and Vellore. He later became a British MP and founded a London banking house, Call, Marten & Co. The inlet was originally named Call Canal in 1792 by Lt William Broughton, who was with Capt George Vancouver as cdr of the tender *Chatham*, and was later changed to Call Ck ("creek" being an old hydrographic term for a narrow tidal inlet). *W*

Calmus Passage (49°13'00" 126°00'00" N side of Vargas I, Clayoquot Sd, W side of Vancouver I). Ildephonse Calmus (1885–1959) was a Benedictine missionary and principal of the Christie residential school at Kakawis, in Clayoquot Sd, 1922–29. He then moved to Salem, Oregon, where he became chaplain of the Chemawa Indian School. This feature was originally named Hecate Passage by Admiralty surveyors, then changed to Maurus Passage in 1933 and Calmus Passage in 1947 by the hydrographic service.

Calver Point. *See* Cape Calver.

Calvert Island, looking north across Kwakshua Channel, with Hecate Island upper right. *James and Jennifer Hamilton*

Calvert Island (51°35'00" 128°03'00" W of entrance of Rivers Inlet), **Cape Calvert** (51°25'00" 127°54'00" S tip of Calvert I). Rugged Calvert I was named by fur trader Capt Charles Duncan of *Princess Royal*, who spent 10 days at Safety Cove, on Calvert's E coast, in 1788, cleaning his vessel's hull. The name, retained by Capt George Vancouver in 1792, probably refers to the barons of Baltimore, an Irish title originally granted to George Calvert (c 1580–1632), who established a Catholic colony on Nfld's Avalon Peninsula in 1627. His son Cecil Calvert (1605–75) was the first gov of Maryland. Safety Cove (qv) was the site of a logging community and post office in the 1910s. *E*

Calvert Point (53°53'00" 130°07'00" NE side of Pitt I, S of Prince Rupert). Calvert was the original surname of Sir Harry Verney (1801–94), a British peer and long-time Liberal MP who inherited the estates of the Verney family in 1827. He was a close friend of Lord Palmerston, the English PM, an outspoken abolitionist, an evangelical member of the Church Missionary Society and supporter of nurse Florence Nightingale, who was the sister of his second wife, Frances Parthenope Nightingale. George Hills, BC's first Anglican bishop, 1859–92, was his cousin. A son from his first marriage (to Eliza Hope, daughter of an RN adm) was Lt Cdr Edmund Verney, who served on the BC coast, 1862–65. Verney Jr, much influenced by his father's views, became a strong promoter of female immigration to BC (*see* Mt Verney). Mt Calvert, a different Mt Verney and the Sir Harry Range, all on the N side of Queen Charlotte Str, are also named for Verney Sr. *W*

Cameleon Harbour (50°20'30" 125°18'20" SW side of Sonora I, N of Campbell R). The 17-gun HMS *Cameleon*, a 1,238-tonne, 57-m wooden steam corvette, was launched in 1860. It spent four periods on the Pacific Station, largely based at Esquimalt: 1861–63, under Cdr Edward Hardinge; 1863–66, under Cdr Theodore Jones; 1867–70, under Cdr William Annesley; and 1870–74, under Cdr Josiah Hatchard, Cdr Karl Mainwaring and Cdr Andrew Kennedy. In 1863 the vessel investigated the seizure at Nootka Sd, by members of the Mowachaht First Nation, of the schooner *Trader* and was also involved in the pursuit of the Lamalcha, a Kuper I group suspected of murdering two Gulf Is settlers (*see* Lamalchi Bay). A number of the harbour's features were named in 1863 by Lt Daniel Pender after officers who served aboard the *Cameleon* during the Lamalcha incident. The ship was sold in 1883. *W*

Camel Rock (49°41'10" 126°30'00" E side of Tlupana Inlet at junction with Hanna Channel, Nootka Sd, W side of Vancouver I). The rock supposedly looks like a Bactrian (twin-humped) camel drinking from the water. Adopted in 1991 as a well-established local name.

Cameron Cove (53°04'00" 129°07'00" In Barnard Hbr, NW side of Princess Royal I). William George Cameron (1854–1930) was born in California and came to Victoria with his family in 1860. He married Rhoda Partridge (1860–1942) in 1884 and ran a city clothing store. A long-serving alderman (1895–96, 1899–1903, 1908, 1916–19) and a Liberal MLA (1903–7), he participated in the 1924 Victoria old-timers' reunion (*see* Adams Bay). His sister, Agnes Deans Cameron, became a teacher and one of Canada's best-known journalists.

Cameron Point (52°17'00" 128°24'00" S end of Cecilia I, NW of Bella Bella). Cecilia Eliza Douglas (1812–59) was born in British Guiana (today's Guyana), the sister of James Douglas, future colonial gov of Vancouver I and the BC mainland. After apparently being deserted by her first husband, named Cowan, she married David Cameron,

manager of a sugar-cane plantation (*see below*), and in 1853 came to BC, where her husband went to work for her brother and eventually became chief justice of Vancouver I. The feature was named in 1929 by regional hydrographer Henri Parizeau.

Cameron Rocks (49°46'00" 126°55'00" Nuchatlitz Inlet, W side of Nootka I, off W side of Vancouver I). David Cameron (1804–72), first chief justice of Vancouver I, was born in Scotland and became a cloth merchant in Perth before moving to British Guiana (Guyana) in 1830 to run a sugar-cane plantation. There he married Cecilia Douglas (*see* Cameron Point), sister of James Douglas, who later, after becoming gov of Vancouver I, arranged an HBC job for Cameron in Nanaimo. Soon, despite a lack of legal training, he was named a judge. In 1856 he resigned from the HBC and was appointed chief justice of the Supreme Court, serving until 1865, a stormy period in which Cameron was steadily attacked by reformist politicians and journalists who objected to his lack of qualifications and the nepotistic ties between the judicial and executive branches of the colonial government. He was also a member of Vancouver I's legislative council, 1859–63. Cameron Lk and Cameron R on Vancouver I are named for him as well, as is Justice Rk off Nootka I. Belmont Point, near Justice Rk and Cameron Rks, is named after the Cameron family residence on Esquimalt Hbr. *W*

Campania Island (53°05'00" 129°25'00" Between Squally Channel and Estevan Sd, N of Caamaño Sd, W of Princess Royal I), **Campania Sound** (53°00'00" 129°15'00" Between Campania I and Princess Royal I). Both features were named Compañía by Spanish naval officer Jacinto Caamaño, who explored this area in 1792 aboard *Aránzazu*, looking for (and disproving the existence of) a navigable passage across N America that the mythical Bartholomew de Fonte was supposed to have found in 1640. The significance of the name is unknown, though *compañía* is Spanish for "company" or "fellowship."

Camp Bay (48°44'00" 123°11'00" SE end of S Pender I, Gulf Is). Local lore has it that a campsite was established at this location in the old days by island sheep owners and sometimes used by sheep thieves. The name appears on an Admiralty chart dated 1859, however, so it is more likely that the camp was associated with early RN surveyors or a First Nation group.

Campbell Bay (48°51'45" 123°15'40" E side of Mayne I, Gulf Is), **Campbell Point** (48°51'00" 123°15'00" SE entrance to Campbell Bay). Samuel Campbell (1832–1910), a native of Ireland and graduate of the Univ of Glasgow, was assistant surgeon aboard RN survey vessels *Plumper* and *Hecate*, under Capt George Richards, on the BC coast, 1857–62. He was also in charge of Esquimalt's rudimentary naval hospital. Campbell accompanied

C

fellow officer Lt Richard Mayne on an overland journey from Jervis Inlet to Lillooet in 1859 to investigate potential access routes to the goldfields. He was appointed to the Royal Marine Infirmary at Woolwich in 1864 and went on to serve in other survey vessels: HMS *Nassau*, which charted the Strs of Magellan, 1867–69 (Mayne was the ship's capt), and HMS *Sylvia*, employed off the coast of China, 1870–72. He retired from the RN in 1877 with the rank of fleet surgeon. Samuel I in the Gulf Is is also named for him, and it is probable that **Campbell Island** (52°07'00" 128°12'00" N of Hunter I, Queens Sd), Campbell Lk (on Vancouver I), **Campbell Point** (50°37'00" 125°32'00" N of Johnstone Str, E side of Loughborough Inlet) and **Campbell River** (50°01'00" 125°14'30" NW of Courtenay, E side of Vancouver I) are as well. Campbell R has grown to become Vancouver I's third-largest centre, with a large pulp mill, a mine and extensive hydroelectric and forestry operations nearby. It is known as BC's sport-fishing capital.

Campbell Cove (48°20'00" 123°38'00" W side of Becher Bay, S end of Vancouver I). This feature, originally known by local residents as Browns Cove and Frenchmans Cove, may have been named after Hugh Campbell, who preempted land in the Muir Ck area at Shirley, W of Sooke, and was one of the earliest settlers in the district. He is probably the same Hugh Campbell who died at Sooke Lk in 1927, aged 89; in 1915 he donated land, now a park, for a school. Then again, the name may predate this era, as it appears on an Admiralty chart from the 1870s.

Camp Point (53°59'00" 132°08'00" NE side of Masset Sd, Graham I, QCI). According to QCI historian Kathleen Dalzell, surveyors may have used this point as their camp. A kelp-processing plant was built near here in 1969 but never went into operation. The name was adopted in 1948.

Canaveral Passage (53°34'00" 130°08'00" Between Squall I and McCauley I, Principe Channel, S of Prince Rupert), **Canaveral Rock** (53°33'00" 130°09'00" In Port Canaveral), **Port Canaveral** (53°34'00" 130°08'59" Off SW end of McCauley I). Spanish explorer Lt Cdr Jacinto Caamaño, aboard *Aránzazu*, originally applied the name Puerto del Cañaveral to the S entrance of Petrel Channel, W of Pitt I, on his 1792 survey of the N coast. Capt George Vancouver retained the name when passing through the following year but apparently used it to describe a different feature nearby. The significance of the name is unknown, though *cañaveral* is a Spanish word for a canebrake or a piece of land thickly overgrown with cane or reed. Canaveral Rk, adopted in 1950, was formerly known as Harbour Rk.

Cane Rock (55°23'00" 129°48'00" Off E side of Granby Peninsula, N end of Observatory Inlet, S of Stewart). Named by the hydrographic service in 1968 after Norman Cane, who apparently filed a mining claim in this area in the early 1900s.

Canned Cod Bay (48°44'22" 123°10'58" NE side of S Pender I, Gulf Is). Many years ago a crate of canned codfish was found washed up in this bay. The name was submitted about 1968 by the Gulf Is Branch of the BC Historical Assoc.

Cannery Bay (48°41'00" 124°51'00" Near mouth of Nitinat R, SE of Barkley Sd, W side of Vancouver I). The Nitinat Cannery was built here, just inside the Nitinat Narrows, by the Lummi Bay Packing Co about 1917. The operation changed hands several times and was owned by Nitinat Packers Ltd in 1924, Gosse Packing Co in 1927 and BC Packers Ltd in 1928. The plant was closed in 1931 and abandoned three years later. The name, which appears on a sketch map of the area dated 1920, was not officially adopted until 1979.

Cannery Bay (49°08'30" 125°40'00" E side of Tofino Inlet, Clayoquot Sd, W side of Vancouver I). Clayoquot Sd Cannery, built in 1895 by Thomas Earle and the Clayoquot Fishing & Packing Co, was located at the mouth of the Kennedy R, site of the region's main sockeye run. Also known as the Kennfalls Cannery, it was taken over by the Clayoquot Sd Canning Co in 1902 and operated until the 1940s. The company also co-owned and ran a fleet of locally crewed seiners. The bay was formerly known as Kennedy Cove but officially renamed in 1986. (Kennedy Cove now refers only to a small bay on the Kennedy R at the Okeamin First Nation reserve.)

Cannery Channel (49°07'00" 123°10'00" Mouth of the Fraser R, between Steveston I and Lulu I). In 1895, when Steveston was the "salmon capital of the world," a dozen canneries lined the S shore of Lulu I: Atlas, Gulf of Georgia, Star, Steveston, Lulu I, Brunswick, Imperial, Phoenix, Britannia, Pacific Coast, Beaver and Canadian Pacific. Between the early 1880s and the end of the 20th century, 20 different operations started up and then fell silent. Today the Gulf of Georgia Cannery remains as a national historic site. The channel is a recent feature, having formed, along with Steveston I, only since the early 1900s; a rock jetty, constructed in 1955, trained the buildup and expansion of the island to the W and also lengthened the channel.

Canniff Point (51°27'00" 127°38'00" SE point of Ripon I, Rivers Inlet). According to BC historians Helen and Philip Akrigg, Canniff was the name of a young nurse working at Dr George Darby's Rivers Inlet hospital at the time a new coastal survey was being conducted in the late 1930s. The name was adopted in 1947.

Cann Inlet (52°33'00" 128°41'00" Kitasu Bay, W side of Swindle I, Laredo Sd). George Cann, born about 1810 in Middlesex, UK, was a cpl in the Crimean War before being promoted sgt maj and joining the Columbia detachment of Royal Engineers, which served in BC

The Cape Beale lighthouse, 1981. *Jim Ryan*

1858–63. His wife accompanied him to Victoria in the *Thames City*. Cann participated in the long voyage's theatrical events; according to the ship's newspaper he narrated "a lovely episode in the life of a broom-seller" to "rapturous" applause. In BC he played a major role in the construction of the Cariboo Rd, supervising the blasting out of a route through the mountains at Yale. Gov James Douglas himself noted the "highly creditable" manner in which Cann had completed "the arduous part of this undertaking." Although he purchased land in BC, Cann and his wife appear to have returned to England in 1863, where he was still alive, though widowed, in 1881.

Canoe Passage (49°04'00" 123°08'00" Mouth of Fraser R, S of Westham I). Named for the hundreds of hopeful gold miners who took this route, many of them in canoes, during the 1858 Fraser R gold rush. Their purpose in doing so was to avoid the checkpoint at the mouth of the river's main channel, where the purchase of a $5 mining licence was enforced, as was the payment of a stiff 10 percent customs duty on all imported goods. The passage was originally named South Channel by Capt George Richards in 1860.

Cape Anne (51°18'00" 127°23'00" E end of Greaves I, Smith Inlet, S of Rivers Inlet). Anne Mary Walbran (1849–1907), born at Ripon, Yorkshire, was married to mariner John Thomas Walbran, author of the classic *British Columbia Coast Names 1592–1906*, published in 1909. *W*

Cape Beale (48°47'00" 125°13'00" SE entrance to Barkley Sd, W coast of Vancouver I). John Beale, purser in the fur-trading vessel *Imperial Eagle*, under Capt Charles Barkley, was killed along with several other crew members in a 1787 First Nation attack at the Hoh R, on the W coast of the Olympic Peninsula in Washington. Trader John Meares claimed to have named this cape in 1788 and suggested that the Beale in question was Canton merchant Daniel Beale, his partner and a backer of early fur-trading expeditions (including that of Barkley). But Frances Barkley, who travelled with her husband aboard the *Imperial Eagle*, indicated in her memoir that her husband had named this feature after John Beale the previous year. It appears on 18th-century Spanish charts as Punta de Alegria. An early BC lighthouse was built here in 1874, the first on the treacherous W coast of Vancouver I. *W*

Cape Calver (48°19'30" 123°32'15" S side of Pedder Bay, S end of Vancouver I). Edward Killwick Calver (1813–92) was an RN surveying specialist and master of HMS *Fisgard*, 1851–56, though he was probably never present in BC waters. He wrote *The Conservation and Improvement of Tidal Rivers* in 1853 and commanded HMS *Porcupine* on several surveys off Ireland and Scotland in 1869, during which a group of scientists made the deepest dredges of the ocean floor ever achieved at that time. To celebrate this accomplishment, Calver had a number of deep-sea inverterbrates named after him. He retired with the rank of staff capt. The cape was named in 1846 by his colleague Capt Henry Kellett of the survey vessel *Herald*. Presumably, **Calver Point** (52°09'00" 128°02'00" N side of Denny I, E of Bella Bella) also commemorates him.

Cape Calvert. *See* Calvert I.

C

Cape Caution (51°10'00" 127°47'00" NW entrance to Queen Charlotte Str, N of Vancouver I). Capt George Vancouver named this point in 1793 for "the dangerous navigation in its vicinity." The previous year his ship, HMS *Discovery*, was almost wrecked on a rock about 25 km SE of the cape.

Cape Chroustcheff (53°13'00" 131°47'00" NE side of Moresby I, QCI). This name, which is also spelled Chroutschoff and Khrushchoff in various documents, refers to the cdr of the Russian naval sloop *Apollo*, who was in these waters in 1821 and whose account of his voyage was published at St Petersburg in 1847. The name first appears on an 1856 Admiralty chart that was prepared from Capt George Vancouver's 1792 chart, with corrections from 1849 Russian charts. Russian vessels, manned with Aleut hunters, used to travel to the QCI in the early 1800s to hunt for sea otters. *D*

Cape Cockburn (49°40'00" 124°12'00" Just S of Cockburn Bay), **Cockburn Bay** (49°41'00" 124°12'00" SW side of Nelson I, entrance to Jervis Inlet, NW of Vancouver). RN officer George Cockburn (1772–1853) was a friend of Adm Lord Nelson and his flag capt aboard HMS *Minerve*, 1796–97. He was later knighted and reached the rank of adm himself. As deputy cdr of naval forces during the War of 1812, Cockburn spearheaded the attack on Washington in 1814 that led to its capture and burning. The following year he conveyed Napoleon Bonaparte to exile at St Helena and acted as gov of that remote colony until 1816. He was appointed cdr-in-chief of the N American and W Indies stations, 1832–37, and served several terms as 1st Lord of the Admiralty and as a Tory MP. Cockburn Lk is also named for him. *W*

Cape Cook (50°08'00" 127°55'00" NW end of Brooks Peninsula, NW side of Vancouver I), **Cape Cook Lagoon** (50°12'00" 127°48'00" N side of Brooks Peninsula near Klaskish Inlet), **Cook Bank** (50°57'00" 128°26'00" N of Scott Channel, off NW tip of Vancouver I), **Cook Channel** (49°38'00" 126°36'00" S of Boston Point, W side of Nootka Sd, W side of Vancouver I). James Cook (1728–79), "the father of British hydrography," was born in Yorkshire and worked on merchant vessels before joining the RN as a seaman in 1755. He rose to the rank of master and made a name for himself in the Seven Years' War, where, in 1759, his charts of the St Lawrence R helped the British capture Que. Cook's fine charts of the Nfld coast, surveyed 1762–67, made him the leading hydrographer of the day—and he wasn't even a commissioned officer. He was soon promoted to lt, however, then chosen to command HMS *Endeavour* on a scientific mission to the S Pacific (1768–71), during which the coasts of NZ and Australia were partly mapped. On another S Pacific voyage (1772–75) he delved far into Antarctic waters. A third expedition (1776–80), with HMS *Resolution* and *Discovery*, took Cook, now a capt, up the PNW coast to Nootka Sd, where he became the first British navigator to visit BC and the first white man to set foot there. He spent Apr 1778 at Nootka, restocking and repairing his vessels and trading with the Nuu-chah-nulth. From BC he sailed N to the Alaska coast, then returned to Hawaii, where he was killed in a fracas with the local inhabitants. The publication of Cook's journals (1784–85) revealed the extravagant prices his men had received in China for sea otter furs and helped precipitate a rush of fur-trading expeditions to the PNW. Cape Cook was named in 1860 by Capt George Richards; Cook had called the promontory Woody Point. George Vancouver was a midshipman on Cook's second and third voyages (though technically listed on the second voyage as an able-bodied seaman).

Cape Edensaw (54°06'00" 132°26'00" E side of Virago Sd, N shore of Graham I, QCI). Gwaayang Gwanhlin (c 1810–94), whose Haida name can be translated as "the man who rests his head on an island," was a prominent, wealthy chief of the Sta'stas Eagle lineage. Edensaw—or Edenshaw, as the name is more commonly spelled—is an anglicized form of his hereditary title, Eda'nsa or Idansaa ("melting ice from a glacier"). Born near Cape Ball, he lived at Kiusta and Kung before moving to Masset in the early 1870s. He led HBC officials to gold in the QCI in 1850 and played an ambiguous role in the affair of the *Susan Sturgis*, which was plundered near Masset in 1852 while Edensaw was acting as pilot. (Some accounts claim that he saved the lives of the crew, others that he helped plan the attack and shared in the loot; *see* Susan Bank.) In 1884, when converting to Christianity, he chose as his personal names those of the man he considered his peer: Albert Edward, Queen Victoria's son and heir. RN officer James Prevost called him "the most advanced Indian I have met on the Coast: quick, cunning, ambitious, crafty and, above all, anxious to obtain the good opinion of the white men." The cape was named by George Inskip in 1853 while on survey duty in this area with HMS *Virago*. *W*

Cape Freeman (52°09'00" 131°19'00" SE of Flamingo Inlet, SW end of Moresby I, QCI), **Freeman Island** (53°36'00" 132°56'00" Entrance to Port Chanal, W side of Graham I, QCI), **Freeman Passage** (53°50'00" 130°36'30" Between Goschen I and Porcher Peninsula, SW of Prince Rupert), **Freeman Rock** (53°26'00" 132°56'00" W of Rennell Sd, W side of Graham I, QCI). Capt Absalom Freeman (1867–1930), a native of Trinity, Nfld, first fished on the Grand Banks and off Labrador. He came to BC in 1890, chartered the *Capilano* from the Union Steamship Co and ran it as a halibut boat for the Boston-based New England Fish Co. In 1905 he helped found the Canadian Fishing Co, which became a New England subsidiary. Master of many vessels over the years, including the *Coquitlam*,

New England, *Flamingo* and *Celestial Empire*, Freeman worked mostly in Hecate Str and off the W coast of the QCI, where his detailed notes and sketch maps proved useful to government hydrographers. New England Fish had a halibut-packing station in Freeman Passage in the 1890s, later moved to Butler Cove. Freeman, believed to have introduced otter trawling to BC waters, also worked for the Union Steamship Co in its pioneer days. Absalom I in Freeman Passage is named for him as well. *D*

Cape George (53°51'00" 130°42'00" SW coast of Porcher Peninsula, Porcher I, SW of Prince Rupert). After 19th-century British parliamentarian and naval official George Joachim Goschen. *See* Goschen I.

Cape Henry (52°56'00" 132°22'00" Between Bottle Inlet and Kuper Inlet, Moresby I, QCI). After Capt George Vancouver's friend, the antiquary and scientific writer Sir Henry Englefield. *See* Englefield Bay.

Cape Keppel (48°43'00" 123°29'00" S end of Saltspring I, Gulf Is). Sir Henry Keppel, GCB (1809–1904), was known as the "father of the British navy" and attained the rank of adm of the fleet in 1877. He was active in the Crimean War, leading the assault on Sevastopol and its capture, and also spent much time off Asia and Africa, serving as cdr-in-chief of the RN's Cape Station, 1860–61, and China Station, 1867–69. Keppel wrote several books, including his 1899 three-volume memoir, *A Sailor's Life under Four Sovereigns*. The cape was named by Capt George Richards in 1859. *W*

Cape Knox (54°11'00" 133°05'00" NW end of Graham I, QCI), **Knox Bay** (50°23'23" 125°36'44" S side of W Thurlow I, Johnstone Str), **Knox Point** (54°35'00" 130°28'00" S end of Birnie I, N of Prince Rupert). Sub-Lt Henry Needham Knox (1831–1916) served on the BC coast aboard HMS *Virago*. In 1853 he assisted George Inskip with surveys of Port Simpson and the QCI (Virago Sd and northern Graham I, and Houston Stewart Channel) and made the survey of Knox Bay himself. He retired from the RN in 1873 with the rank of cdr. Nearby Knox Hill is also named for him, as is Needham Point at the entrance to Knox Bay. *W*

Cape Kuper (52°58'17" 132°20'40" SW side of Hibben I, W side of Moresby I, QCI), **Kuper Inlet** (52°59'00" 132°10'00" E of Englefield Bay, W side of Moresby I), **Kuper Island** (48°58'00" 123°39'00" NW of Saltspring I, Gulf Is). Capt Augustus Leopold Kuper (1809–85) served on the Pacific Station, 1851–53, as cdr of HMS *Thetis*. He and his crew were sent to the NW coast of Moresby I in 1852 to conduct a survey of the area and maintain a naval presence after the discovery of gold in the vicinity. He had served earlier in Australia and by 1861 was in command of the China Station, in which capacity, as a rear adm, he led

Kuper Island's Penelakut Spit with Thetis Island at right. *Kevin Oke*

several major naval actions against Japan. He was knighted in 1864 and promoted adm in 1872. Kuper I is home to the Penelakut, a Coast Salish First Nation group, and was the site of a Roman Catholic residential school, 1890–1978. In 1863, in an incident that brought early First Nation treaty negotiations to a standstill in BC, an RN gunboat shelled a Lamalcha village on the SW end of the island as part of a massive campaign to pursue and apprehend those believed responsible for the murder of white settlers (*see* Lamalchi Bay). Four men from the village were later tried and hanged for the crimes. In Haida Gwaii, Augustus Rk and the Leopold Is are named for Adm Kuper, as is Augustus Point in the Gulf Is. Kuper Inlet was formerly known as Port Kuper. *W*

Cape Lazo, just east of Courtenay. *Peter Vassilopoulos*

Cape Lazo (49°42'00" 124°52'00" NE of Comox Hbr, Str of Georgia). In his 1791 exploration of the Str of Georgia, Spanish naval officer José Narváez, aboard *Santa Saturnina*, named this feature Punta de Lazo de la Vega. While historian Capt John Walbran speculated that the name was somehow based on the appearance of the cape (*lazo* being a Spanish word for trap, and *vega* meaning "plain"), it seems more likely that Narváez was referring to a person. A number of officials in New Spain were named Lazo de la Vega, including a viceroy of Peru, a gov of Yucatan and a bishop of Cuba. Lazo is also the name of the agricultural district to the W of the cape.

C

Cape Mark (52°09'00" 128°32'00" On an island off SW end of Athlone I, W of Bella Bella, Milbanke Sd). After Vice Adm Mark Milbanke, RN officer and former gov of Nfld. *See* Milbanke Sd *and* Cape Swaine.

Cape McKay (52°24'00" 127°25'00" S end of Cascade Inlet, Dean Channel, NE of Bella Bella), **McKay Bay** (52°24'00" 127°26'00" N side of Dean Channel). Alexander McKay (c 1770–1811), who also signed his name MacKay, was a fur trader and explorer who served as Alexander Mackenzie's deputy on his historic overland journey to the Pacific coast in 1793. He continued to work for the NWC until 1808, becoming a partner in 1800. In 1810, McKay joined with John Jacob Astor to found the trading post of Ft Astoria at the mouth of the Columbia R. He was killed the following year at Clayoquot Sd aboard the *Tonquin*, when most members of the ship's crew were massacred during a Tla-o-qui-aht (Clayoquot) First Nation attack. The rest, along with more than 100 of the attackers, probably died when the vessel was blown up by the wounded ship's clerk (*see* Tonquin I).

A number of mariners have perished off Cape Mudge, where dangerous waves form when strong winds oppose the tide. *Alan Haig-Brown*

Cape Mudge (50°00'00" 125°11'00" S end of Quadra I, N Str of Georgia). The cape, known for its treacherous offshore conditions, was named after Zachary Mudge (1770–1852), 1st lt on Capt George Vancouver's HMS *Discovery* in 1792. Vancouver and naturalist Archibald Menzies, who left a detailed description, visited a village on the cape—Tsqulotn or Tsa-kwa-luten, meaning "playing field"—that was occupied at that time by the Coast Salish people. Mudge returned to England that year, from Nootka Sd via China, with official dispatches, but was back on the BC coast in 1795 as 1st lt to Capt William Broughton in HMS *Providence*. In 1805, as cdr of HMS *Blanche*, he surrendered to a French squadron after his vessel had been badly damaged in a skirmish, an act for which he was honourably acquitted of blame at a court martial. He attained the rank of adm in 1849. Mudge Inlet (qv) was named for his grandson, Henry Colton Mudge. Dionisio Alcalá-Galiano and Cayetano Valdés named this

feature Punta de Magallanes on their 1792 exploration of the Str of Georgia. Cape Mudge village, now the main community of the We-wai-kai people, a branch of the Lekwiltok (Kwakwaka'wakw) First Nation, is known today as Yaculta (qv). A lighthouse station was built on the cape in 1898. *E W*

Cape Naden (54°07'00" 132°34'00" W entrance to Virago Sd, N end of Graham I, QCI), **Naden Harbour** (54°00'00" 132°36'00" S of Virago Sd), **Naden River** (53°56'50" 132°40'10" Flows N into Naden Hbr). Naden is a Haida name adopted by Raven crest members who lived at the mouth of the Naden R; they were the Ne dan xada i, part of the Ecetas family. A whaling station, operated by the Pacific Whaling Co, was located in the harbour, 1911–42, and also a cannery, which processed salmon, clams and crab intermittently from 1910 to '40. A small schooner named *Naden*, built in N Vancouver in 1913 for the federal hydrographic service, was loaned in WWI to the RCN at Esquimalt for training purposes. It became the depot ship for the naval shore facility, which was commissioned as HMCS *Naden* in 1922 and later developed into the RCN's main training centre on the Pacific coast. Naden Mtn, S of the Homathko R, is named after HMCS *Naden*. The Haida people know Naden Hbr as Ow'way, meaning "many sandbanks." *W*

Cape North. *See* Langara I *and* St Margaret Point.

Cape Palmerston (50°36'00" 128°18'00" S of San Josef Bay, NW end of Vancouver I). Henry John Temple, 3rd Viscount Palmerston (1784–1865), was one of Britain's most famous statesmen. He served as an MP for 58 continuous years and was foreign secretary (1830–51), home secretary (1852–55) and PM (1855–58 and 1859–65). Although liberal in many of his attitudes and a supporter of technological progress, he remained deeply opposed to democratic parliamentary reforms. Palmerston is primarily remembered for an aggressive, imperialistic foreign policy that took advantage of British naval supremacy to settle controversies and disputes. The "gunboat diplomacy" practised on the BC coast during this era was very much in keeping with the views of his government. Mt Palmerston and Palmerston Ck on NE Vancouver I are also named for him. *W*

Cape Parkins (50°27'00" 128°03'00" N entrance to Quatsino Sd, W of Kains I, NW end of Vancouver I), **Parkins Rock** (50°26'00" 128°03'00" SW of Cape Parkins). Capt James Hanna of the *Sea Otter*, the first European fur trader to arrive in BC waters, named this cape in 1786—an early date for a BC place name. Unfortunately, it is not known who Parkins was.

Cape Roger Curtis (49°20'00" 123°26'00" SW end of Bowen I, Howe Sd, NW of Vancouver). British naval

C

officer Sir Roger Curtis (1746–1816) saw action in the 1794 naval victory over the French known as the Glorious First of June. He was flag capt to Adm Lord Howe, aboard HMS *Queen Charlotte*, at the time, and later that year was also created a baronet and rear adm. In 1799, as a vice adm, Curtis was appointed cdr-in-chief of the Cape Station. He was promoted to adm in 1803 and ended his career as cdr-in-chief at Portsmouth in 1809. *W*

Cape Russell (50°41'00" 128°22'00" Between Lowrie Bay and Sea Otter Cove, NW end of Vancouver I). British Liberal politician John Russell, 1st Earl Russell, was PM of England, 1846–52 and 1865–66. A reformer and campaigner for religious freedom, he was an MP for 48 years and held many important cabinet positions, including home secretary (1835–39), war secretary (1839–41), colonial secretary (1855) and foreign secretary (1852–53, 1859–65). Russell's record was marred by his government's inadequate response to the Irish potato famine, which only served to intensify that disaster. He was the grandfather of philosopher Bertrand Russell. Russell I (qv) off Saltspring I may also be named for him. *W*

Cape St James (51°56'00" 131°01'00" S end of St James I), **St James Island** (S of Kunghit I, QCI). Cape St James was named by early fur trader Capt George Dixon of the *Queen Charlotte*, who rounded this headland on the holy day of St James, July 25, 1787. It was the Cap Hector of French explorer Jean-François de Galaup, Comte de Lapérouse, and appears on an early US chart as Cape Haswell. The Haida First Nation name for the cape is Rangxiid Kun. An important lighthouse and meteorological station were built there in 1913–14, and a WWII radar facility at the isolated cape required a staff of 65 men. The station was automated in 1992. Bare, grassy St James I was formerly known as Hummock I. *D*

Cape Scott (50°47'00" 128°26'00" NW tip of Vancouver I), **Scott Channel** (50°47'00" 128°28'00" Between Cape Scott and Cox I), **Scott Islands** (50°48'00" 128°50'00" W of Cape Scott). David Scott (1746–1805) was a Bombay merchant who financed one of the earliest fur-trading voyages to the BC coast—that of James Strange, with the *Captain Cook* and *Experiment* (1785–86). Scott was later chairman of the powerful E India Co (1796–97, 1801), though at the time of Strange's expedition he was an independent entrepreneur who was apparently trying to loosen the company's monopoly on trade. The cape, named by the expedition's cdrs after their patron, was later the site of an unsuccessful colonization attempt by Danish settlers. One of BC's last lighthouse stations was built there in 1959, and a wilderness provincial park established in 1973. The park, which incorporates the ruins of the Danish colony as well as a rocky, exposed coastline interspersed with spectacular beaches, is reached by a historic 24-km hiking trail from San Josef Bay (which Strange had named Scott's

The lighthouse station at Cape Scott was built in 1959. *Greg Shea*

Bay). The Scott Is were originally named Lance's Is by early fur trader James Hanna (*see* Lanz I) and Beresford's Is by trader George Dixon (*see* Beresford Bay). They were once home to the Yutlinuk, a Kwakwaka'wakw First Nation that succumbed to European diseases and died out in the early 1800s. *E W*

Cape Sutil (50°53'00" 128°03'00" N tip of Vancouver I), **Sutil Channel** (50°08'00" 125°04'00" Between Cortes I and Quadra I, N end of Str of Georgia), **Sutil Mountain** (48°52'12" 123°22'42" SW Galiano I, Gulf Is), **Sutil Point** (50°01'00" 124°59'00" S end of Cortes I). Spanish naval officer Dionisio Alcalá-Galiano, cdr of the *Sutil*, made a historic circumnavigation of Vancouver I in 1792 while surveying the BC coast with his subordinate, Cayetano Valdés, aboard the *Mexicana*. En route, they unexpectedly met Capt George Vancouver in English Bay and travelled in convoy with his two ships for several weeks. The 16-m, 41-tonne *Sutil* was schooner-rigged, with five guns and a crew of 19. Vancouver wrote this description of the officers' quarters: "Their apartments just allowed room for sleeping places on each side with a table in the intermediate space, at which four persons with some difficulty could sit, and were in all other respects the most ill calculated and unfit vessels that could possibly be imagined for such an expedition." Cape Sutil (Spanish for "subtle") was the site of the historic fortified First Nation village of Nahwitti (qv). It was named by the Spanish explorers in 1792, then renamed Cape Commerell by Capt George Richards in 1862. The original name was restored by the Geographic Board of Canada in 1906; Commerell was commemorated with a feature on the NW end of Vancouver I instead (*see* Commerell Point). The Subtle Islands in Sutil Channel also honour this vessel. Sutil Point was formerly known as Reef Point. *W*

C

Cape Swaine (52°14'00" 128°26'00" NW tip of Athlone I, W of Bella Bella), **Swaine Point** (50°31'00" 126°34'00" S side of W Cracroft I, Johnstone Str), **Swaine Point** (54°45'00" 130°26'00" E side of Wales I, NW entrance to Portland Inlet). Capt George Vancouver named the cape in 1793 after Spelman Swaine (1769–1848), HMS *Discovery*'s 3rd lt. Swaine, who had influential friends (*see* Hardwicke I), started the voyage as a master's mate but was twice promoted for his competent survey work. After returning to England he served as a lt on HMS *Spitfire* and *Princess Charlotte*, became cdr of the RN sloop *Raven* in 1802 and attained the rank of capt with the 38-gun frigate *Statira* in 1814. In 1834, Swaine was appointed chief bailiff of the Isle of Ely. He was made a rear adm, retired, in 1846. Cape Swaine was mislabelled (and misspelled Cape Swain) on Lt Daniel Pender's 1866–69 chart and placed off the SW end of Athlone I, where Cape Mark is today, while today's Cape Swaine was incorrectly named Sound Point by Pender. Swaine Point off W Cracroft I commemorates an early examination of Johnstone Str by Swaine and James Johnstone, master of HMS *Chatham*. Capt Vancouver named the point off Wales I because Swaine assisted him with his exploration of Portland Inlet. *W*

Cap Rocks (48°41'00" 123°23'00" Off SW side of Coal I and NE Saanich Peninsula, N of Victoria). The name, adopted by the hydrographic service in 1965 as a well-established term, refers to Capt Frederick Lewis, who purchased Coal I in 1939 and used the rocks as a lookout to watch for vessels coming up John Passage. *See* Lewis Bay.

Captain Cove (53°49'00" 130°12'00" NW side of Pitt I, S of Prince Rupert), **Captain Point** (53°49'00" 130°13'00" S entrance to Captain Cove). After Union Steamship capt and fisheries protection officer Holmes Newcomb (whose name was often misspelled Newcombe). *See* Newcombe Hbr.

Captain Island (49°47'00" 123°59'00" NE of Nelson I in Jervis Inlet, NW of Vancouver). The 74-gun *Captain*, built in 1787, was the ship in which Commodore Horatio Nelson, at the 1797 Battle of Cape St Vincent, disregarded the orders of his cdr, Sir John Jervis, and altered course to prevent the Spanish fleet from escaping, thus winning the day for Britain (and setting in motion his legendary career). It was from the *Captain* that Nelson accomplished one of his most daring feats: boarding the *San Nicolas* and then, from the *San Nicolas*, the *San Josef*, and capturing both. The *Captain* was destroyed by fire in 1813. Capt George Richards bestowed a number of Nelson-related place names in this vicinity in 1860. The Sechelt First Nation name for the island is Stá'als. *W*

Captain Passage (48°49'00" 123°25'00" Between Saltspring I and Prevost I, Gulf Is). Named for Capt John Fulford, who commanded HMS *Ganges*, the flagship of Rear Adm Robert Baynes, on the Pacific Station, 1857–60. Capt George Richards named several features on and around Saltspring I in association with Baynes in 1859. *See* Baynes Channel *and* Fulford Hbr. *W*

Cardena Bay (53°59'00" 130°10'00" S end of Kennedy I, S of Prince Rupert). Named after García López de Cárdenas, deputy to the Spanish conquistador Francisco Vásquez de Coronado, leader of a disastrous expedition to the SW US in 1540–42. Cardenas is said to have been the first white man to see the Grand Canyon; he was later tried in Spain for various genocidal crimes against First Nation groups and imprisoned. The Union steamship *Cardena* was named after the bay, not vice versa, as the name appears on an Admiralty chart published in 1867.

Cardigan Rocks (50°53'00" 127°39'00" Just NW of Balaklava I, Queen Charlotte Str, NW of Port Hardy). James Thomas Brudenell (1797–1868), the 7th Earl of Cardigan, rose in the British Army mainly by using his wealth to purchase commissions. During the Crimean War he led the infamous 1854 Charge of the Light Brigade against superior Russian forces at Balaklava. His troops were decimated, though he himself received only a slight wound. He went on to become a lt gen, a knight and the army's inspector-gen of cavalry. The cardigan sweater was named for him. Lt Daniel Pender applied a number of names in the vicinity in 1863–64 to commemorate this notorious military disaster.

Carew Bay (53°17'00" 132°38'00" Kano Inlet, W side of Graham I, QCI), **Carew Rock** (54°10'00" 133°07'00" W of Lepas Bay, NW side of Graham I). John Ewen Carew was 1st mate aboard the *Queen Charlotte* on George Dixon's historic fur-trading expedition of 1785–88. Dixon, in 1787, was the first European to trade extensively in the QCI, which he named after his vessel. He was also the first to realize that Haida Gwaii was an archipelago and not part of the BC mainland.

Carey Group (50°36'00" 126°37'00" Between Crease I and Harbledown I, E end of Queen Charlotte Str). Charles James Carey (1836–91) was 1st lt aboard HMS *Clio*, under Capt Nicholas Turnour, and was based on the BC coast at Esquimalt, 1865–68. In 1865 he led an unsuccessful negotiation with Chief Jim, of Ku-Kultz village outside Ft Rupert, over the surrender of three suspected murderers. The chief and his followers defied the RN, refusing to give up the suspects, and the *Clio* retaliated by completely destroying the village and its 50 large canoes. Carey retired from the RN as a capt in 1883.

Carlos Island (49°10'00" 123°42'00" One of the Flat Top Is, E of Gabriola I, Gulf Is). After the Spanish naval vessel *San Carlos*. *See* San Carlos Point. Formerly known as Bare I but renamed by the hydrographic service in 1944.

C

Carlsen Islet (49°43'17" 124°10'30" In Blind Bay, S entrance to Jervis Inlet, N of Malaspina Str). Stoker 1st-class Harvey Morris Carlsen, from Vancouver, was killed in action Apr 16, 1945, aged 19, while serving with the RCNVR aboard HMCS *Esquimalt*. The minesweeper (and last Canadian vessel lost in WWII) was torpedoed by a German U-boat and sunk off Halifax, with a loss of 44 lives. Carlsen is buried at Forest Lawn Memorial Park in Burnaby. The feature was named quite recently, in 1990.

Carlson Inlet (52°34'00" 127°14'00" SW of Skowquiltz Bay, W side of Dean Channel, NE of Ocean Falls). The hydrographic service named this feature about 1958 after "C Carlson, early settler in the Bella Coola area," without providing any further details. The reference, however, is probably to Christian Carlson (1854–1917), whose name was often spelled "Carlsen." In 1897 he became president of the group of Norwegian immigrants who colonized the Bella Coola valley in 1894. His 1895 marriage to Ovidia Baarli (1872–1933) was the first wedding of settlers in the region.

Carlson Islets (55°27'00" 129°46'00" Hastings Arm, Observatory Inlet, S of Stewart). Ernest Carlson (1881–1918) first staked the Dolly Varden claims near the head of Alice Arm in 1910, along with three other Scandinavian prospectors: Ole Evindsen, Ole Pearson and Karl Ludwig Eik. In 1915 the quartet sold their find to Chicago investors, who went on to develop a narrow-gauge mining railway and a rich but ultimately unsuccessful silver mine in 1919–21. The discoverers got $10,000 each. Carlson died at Anyox Hospital during the 1918 influenza epidemic. The name was adopted in 1970. *See also* Eik Rk *and* Pearson Point.

Carlson Point (49°31'57" 123°47'23" SW side of Sechelt Inlet, NW of Vancouver). Herman (1845–1910) and Otilie Carlson and their five sons—Ellis, Ivar, Eric, Gustaf and Axel—pre-empted land at the mouth of nearby Carlson Ck (also named for them) in 1909. They homesteaded there, clearing 6 ha and building workshops, storerooms, stables and barns. All the Carlson boys were noted for their carpentry and boatbuilding skills. When conscription was introduced during WWI, the family left for the US.

Carmanah Point (48°37'00" 124°45'00" Between Nitinat Lk and Port San Juan, SW side of Vancouver I). Carmanah is an adaptation of the name of a Ditidaht (Nuu-chah-nulth) village that used to be located on the E side of the promontory. It can be translated as "canoe landing in front." The headland was named Punta Bonilla by Spanish naval officer Manuel Quimper in 1790, but subsequent British charts misapplied Bonilla to the next point to the E. Carmanah lighthouse was established in 1891 and in 1907 became one of the stations on the W Coast Lifesaving Trail. The point was named by Admiralty surveyors about 1860. *E W*

Carmelo Point (49°27'00" 123°24'00" On Gambier I, between Centre Bay and West Bay, Howe Sd). Spanish naval officer José Narváez, the first European to explore the Str of Georgia, gave the name Bocas del Carmelo to Howe Sd in 1791, no doubt on or about July 16, the saint day of Our Lady of Mt Carmel. This title for Mary, the mother of Jesus, is associated with the Roman Catholic Carmelite order, originally founded in the 12th century on Mt Carmel, a mountain range in northern Israel. The feature appears as Gordon Point on an Admiralty chart published in 1863 but was renamed by the hydrographic service in 1945 to avoid confusion with other Gordon names and to keep alive a historic reference.

Carmichael Passage (52°59'00" 131°55'00" Between Louise I and NE side of Moresby I, QCI). Provincial assayer Herbert Carmichael, travelling by canoe with hired Haida paddlers, examined Cumshewa Inlet and the surrounding area for the BC Ministry of Mines in 1901. He had been sent to investigate the "bituminous matter" that oozed between rocks on the Tar Is and elsewhere but was unable to determine its commercial value. Originally named Carmichael Arm by the hydrographic service in 1926. *D*

Carmichael Point (52°28'00" 128°13'00" SW side of Salmon Bay, W side of Don Peninsula, N of Bella Bella). William Carmichael was assistant surgeon aboard HMS *Scout*, under Capt John Price, and served on the BC coast, based at Esquimalt, 1865–68. Named by Lt Daniel Pender in 1867.

Carne Bay (52°52'00" 129°02'00" E side of Racey Inlet, W side of Princess Royal I), **Carne Island** (52°59'00"

The Carmanah Point lighthouse station in 1978. *Jim Ryan*

C

129°36'00" Head of Gillen Hbr, Estevan I, N side of Caamaño Sd), **Carne Rock** (52°18'00" 128°22'00" Reid Passage, NW of Bella Bella). Named after members of Victoria's pioneer Carne family. Frederick Carne (1829–1904), born in Cornwall, UK, came to eastern Canada in the 1850s as a miner. He married Harriet Richards (1833–1931), also from Cornwall, at Sault Ste Marie in 1853, then followed the gold rush to California and BC, arriving in Victoria in 1858. Harriet returned to England in 1855, then rejoined her husband in Victoria in 1864. About 1876, Frederick left the Cariboo gold mines, and the Carnes bought the Angel Hotel, which they ran as a temperance establishment for decades. Harriet, known for her social work, was a founder of the Victoria Aged Women's Home. Frederick Jr, born in England in 1856, married Agnes M Gowan in 1885 and became a Victoria grocer. He also owned three sealing schooners. Several family members participated in the 1924 Victoria old-timers' reunion (*see* Adams Bay). Carne Bay was named for Agnes, Carne I for the younger Fred and Carne Rk, formerly known as Flatfish Rk, for Harriet.

Carney Point (48°41'00" 123°23'00" NE entrance to John Passage, W side of Coal I, NE of Sidney). Alexander Carney or Kâné (b 1845), a Kanaka or pioneer of Hawaiian descent, pre-empted the W half of Coal I and received a Crown grant for the land in 1886. The other half of the island was settled by the Kanaka family of Kama and Mary Kamai (*see* Kamai Point), who pre-empted their property as early as 1873. Carney married Kamai's oldest daughter, also Mary, in 1870 and was still farming on Coal I in the 1890s.

Carolina Channel (48°55'15" 125°31'50" S of Ucluelet, Barkley Sd, W side of Vancouver I), **Carolina Islands** (54°20'00" 130°25'00" Venn Passage, just E of Metlakatla, NW of Prince Rupert), **Carolina Reef** (48°26'00" 123°16'00" Just N of Chain Its, off Oak Bay, SE end of Vancouver I). The 14-m, 50-tonne schooner *Carolina* was built by Franklin Sherman, a Port Townsend shipwright. Known for its speed, the vessel made several record journeys under Capt Jemmy Jones, carrying coal and other goods between Victoria, Nanaimo and ports on Puget Sd. In 1863 it was bought for $1,500 by missionary William Duncan and plied between Victoria and Metlakatla with furs, produce and supplies. Duncan sold the ship for $1,000 in 1868 to trader and sealer Capt William Spring, who rebuilt it and sold it, in turn, to the Dept of Marine and Fisheries in 1873 as Victoria's pilot boat. The next owner was Capt William Munsie, who sent it sealing again to the Bering Sea, where it was seized in 1886 by a US revenue cutter and left to rot on the shore at Unalaska. Its name is sometimes spelled *Carolena* or *Caroline*. W

Carpenter Bay (52°14'00" 131°07'00" S of Collison Bay, SE end of Moresby I, QCI). William Benjamin Carpenter,

CB (1813–85), an English physician and noted biologist and author, was appointed professor of physiology at the Royal Institution in 1844. He then served as registrar of the Univ College of London, 1856–79. Carpenter's ideas on the unconscious and the important role it played in ordinary life were influential. He also took a great interest in marine zoology and oceanography, developing theories on oceanic temperature gradients and circulation, and was a leading promoter of the 1872–76 HMS *Challenger* expedition, which undertook the first scientific study of deep-ocean activity. Carpenter Bay was named in 1878 by George M Dawson of the Geological Survey of Canada. W

Car Point. *See* Carr I.

Carraholly Point (49°18'00" 122°55'00" N side of Port Moody, Burrard Inlet, E of Vancouver). The Johnston family homesteaded at this location in the early 1900s, building resort cottages and a boat landing. The name was supposedly devised by New Westminster lawyer and judge William Norman Bole, an Irishman who owned much land in the Belcarra area. He cobbled together the Gaelic word *carra*, meaning "fair land," with "holly," several of which had been planted on the property.

Carrington Bay (50°09'00" 125°00'00" W side of Cortes I, NE of Campbell R), **Carrington Lagoon** (50°07'00" 124°59'00" SE extension of Carrington Bay). Capt George Richards, in charge of the RN's marine surveys of the BC coast for many years, was appointed the navy's chief hydrographer in 1864 and moved back to England. In honour of the occasion, Lt Daniel Pender, who took over the BC survey, named a number of features after employees of the hydrographic dept, most of whom had never been anywhere near the PNW. Draftsman (1st class) Robert C Carrington, who retired in 1875, was one of them. **Carrington Reef** (51°31'00" 128°06'00" SW side of Calvert I, W of Rivers Inlet) is presumed to be named for him as well.

Carr Island (54°20'00" 130°28'00" Metlakatla Bay, W of Prince Rupert). Anthony Carr, who died in 1854, was an Anglican clergyman from Beverley, Yorkshire, and a father figure to young William Duncan, later to find fame as a missionary on the N BC coast. Capt George Richards used a number of names associated with the Metlakatla mission and its supporters, all supplied by Duncan, in his 1862 survey of the area with HMS *Hecate*. **Car Point** (55°20'25" 130°00'10" NW of Belle Bay, E side of Portland Canal on the BC-Alaska border) and **Carr Point** (55°29'00" 129°44'00" E side of Hastings Arm, N end of Observatory Inlet, S of Stewart) may also be named for this person. It is not known how the "r" got dropped on one of the names. Walbran incorrectly gives Anthony's name as Edward Carr.

Carse Point (52°55'00" 128°07'00" N side of Mussel Inlet, N of Mathieson Channel and Bella Bella). Stoker James Gilbert Carse, from Vancouver, was killed in action Oct 22, 1940, aged 21, while serving aboard HMCS *Margaree*. The RCN destroyer sank on convoy duty in the N Atlantic after colliding with the merchant freighter *Port Fairy*; 142 crew members were lost. Carse's name is inscribed on the Halifax Memorial.

Carswell Island (53°01'00" 132°25'00" Entrance to Inskip Channel, NW side of Moresby I, QCI). James Carswell and Thomas Hibben established an early Victoria book and stationery shop in 1858 (after buying out Kierski's bookstore). Carswell married Elizabeth Ferguson of Glasgow in 1860. In 1866, Hibben bought him out, and two years later Carswell was listed in the Victoria directory as the owner of a "provision store" at Cowichan. T N Hibben & Co became well known to seafaring types as the local agent for Admiralty charts; several other features in the vicinity were named by the hydrographic service in association with this pioneer business. Carswell I was formerly known as Cliff I.

Carter Bay (52°49'00" 128°23'00" N side of Sheep Passage at junction with Finlayson Channel, N of Bella Bella), **Carter Point** (52°49'08" 128°23'29" E entrance to Carter Bay), **Carter River** (52°50'00" 128°22'00" Flows S into Carter Bay). John Carter, a 24-year-old native of Surrey, England, was an able seaman aboard Capt George Vancouver's HMS *Discovery*. In June 1793, while surveying Mussel Inlet in two of the ship's boats, several crew members became very ill with paralytic shellfish poisoning after eating tainted mussels for breakfast at what came to be known as Poison Cove. "After pulling his oar to the last" (according to Capt John Walbran), John Carter died in the early afternoon and was buried at the first appropriate stopping place, which Vancouver named Carter's Bay. After seeing his fate, the other men drank hot seawater as an emetic, which they had resisted despite their officers' urging, and recovered. Vancouver normally only named places after officers and "gentlemen," but he made an exception in poor John Carter's case. Carter Point, formerly known as East Point, and the Carter R were named by the hydrographic service about 1949.

Carter Rocks (52°40'00" 129°30'00" W side of Moore Is, W of Aristazabal I). William Oliver Carter (c 1857–1934) was born at London, Ont. In 1862 he moved with his family to Victoria, where he married Hattie Collins (1875–1960), a native of NS, in 1897. The 1901 census lists his occupation as office clerk. The Carters took part in the Victoria old-timers' reunion of 1924 (*see* Adams Bay). The feature was named about 1926.

Carthew Point (54°10'00" 129°56'00" E side of mouth of Ecstall R, Skeena R, opposite Port Essington). John

Alexander Carthew (1857–1914) was born in NS and became a successful BC cannery owner. In 1885 he opened the Comox Hotel, and three years later he married Carrie Eliza Pratt (1859–1937), a native of Illinois, at Victoria. He ran the Wannock Cannery at Rivers Inlet 1887–88, then built the N Pacific Cannery, producer of the Walrus brand of salmon, at Inverness on the Skeena R in 1889. The following year he sold out to Henry Bell-Irving's Anglo-British Columbia Packing Co for $40,000. Carthew went on to build and manage Claxton Cannery (1891–94) and Carlisle Cannery (1894–97), both located at the mouth of the Skeena R. He died at Prince Rupert and on his death certificate was listed as a millwright. Carthew Ck and Mt Carthew were also named for him.

Cartwright Rocks (53°02'00" 129°27'00" Off SW side of Campania I, Caamaño Sd). William Cartwright (1841–1923) was born in England and immigrated to Victoria in 1862. His wife, Mary Finlay (1854–1927), was from Nanaimo. The Cartwrights pre-empted land at E Sooke in 1875, raising a family and farming there for many years before moving to Victoria (there is also an 1878 land pre-emption record in William's name for Thetis I). The rocks were shown on Admiralty charts as the Guano Rks as early as 1872 but were renamed by the hydrographic service about 1926.

Cartwright Sound (53°12'00" 132°40'00" Between Tcenakun Point and Hunter Point, SW side of Graham I, QCI). Capt George Vancouver named this feature in 1793, at the end of the season's exploration of the BC coast, after English political reformer John Cartwright (1740–1824). He originally served in the RN and spent five years in Nfld before returning home and joining the Nottinghamshire Militia as a maj. His many writings and speeches argued for universal suffrage, regular elections, a secret ballot and equal electoral districts, notions we now take for granted.

Casanave Passage (53°04'00" 129°11'00" Between Ashdown I and NW side of Princess Royal I, Caamaño Sd). Alexis Carni Casanave (1845–1928), a rancher and miner, was born in Basses-Pyrénées, France, and came to Victoria in 1862 after spending several years in San Francisco. He wandered the province for gold, then bought 4 ha of John Tod's Oak Bay property in 1875 and turned his hand to dairy and mixed farming. In 1884, at Victoria, he married Elizabeth Coigdarripe (1861–1931), who had come to BC from France the previous year. The Casanaves, whose surname appears in the 1901 census as Casanava, are believed to have participated in Victoria's grand old-timers' reunion of 1924 (*see* Adams Bay). The family farm was located beside Bowker Ck, where Oak Bay High School now stands, and their farmhouse survived on the property until 1967. A large sequoia tree, planted as a seed by Alexis, grows there today.

C

Cascade Bluff (52°25'00" 127°24'00" E entrance to Cascade Inlet), **Cascade Inlet** (52°30'00" 127°30'00" NW side of Dean Channel, W of Bella Coola). The inlet was named in 1793 by Capt George Vancouver, who wrote in his journal that the waterfalls "were extremely grand, and by much the largest and most tremendous of any we had ever beheld." It was in this area that Alexander Mackenzie ended his unprecedented overland journey from the Canadian interior, marking a rock with his name and the date of July 22, 1793. He had missed encountering Vancouver by a mere six weeks. *W*

Casey Cove (54°17'00" 130°23'00" E side of Digby I, just W of Prince Rupert), **Casey Point** (54°16'00" 130°21'00" W end of Kaien I, Prince Rupert). Maj William Archer Casey was born in Ont and graduated from Upper Canada College. He became a topographical engineer for the GTP, camping on Casey Point in 1906 while doing preliminary survey work for the railway terminus. A member of the BC Regiment in WWI, Casey was killed in action at the Somme on Sept 8, 1916, aged 29, and is buried in France at the Albert Communal Cemetery. The Digby I wireless station was located in Casey Cove. Casey Point was named in 1906 by hydrographer G B Dodge, while Casey Cove appeared on maps in 1916 and was adopted the following year by the Geographic Board of Canada.

Caspaco (54°11'00" 130°11'00" N side of Inverness Passage, just NW of mouth of the Skeena R and just SE of Prince Rupert). The name is an abbreviation and acronym for the Cassiar Packing Co, which built a cannery at this location in 1903. John Macmillan gained control of the company in 1910, and his son, Ewen Macmillan, grandson of pioneer cannery owner Alexander Ewen (*see* Ewen Slough), managed the plant for many years. A large cold-storage facility was added in 1979. The Cassiar cannery closed in 1983 after eight decades of continuous operation, a record for the BC coast, and the site was sold to Ocean Fisheries Ltd, which uses it for storage and transport. Caspaco post office was open from 1916 to 1954. Caspaco Ck, which flows S into Inverness Passage here, is named after the cannery.

Caswell Point (54°03'00" 133°04'00" N end of Beresford Bay, NW side of Graham I, QCI). Joshua Caswell (1765–91) was 2nd mate of the fur-trading vessel *Columbia Rediviva*, under Capt Robert Gray, on its second voyage to the PNW in 1791–92. He and two other crew members, while off fishing in a small boat and out of sight of *Columbia*, were murdered on the E side of Prince of Wales I in SE Alaska. Caswell "was a man of mild and gentle temper, a complete Seaman," according to John Boit, 5th mate of *Columbia*, whose log of the voyage was published in a scholarly edition. "In Mr Caswell I lost a firm and steady friend." *D*

Catala Island (49°50'15" 127°03'10" Entrance to Esperanza Inlet, W side of Vancouver I), **Catala Passage** (52°16'00" 128°43'00" Between Bray I and McInnes I, SW of Price I, Milbanke Sd). Magin Catalá (1761–1830), an energetic Franciscan monk with a reputation for saintliness, served as chaplain at Spain's Nootka Sd establishment in 1793–94. He was born in Spain and arrived in Mexico in 1786. After Nootka he lived at Santa Clara Mission in California, where he was noted for miracles and prophecies. Catala I was shown on Alejandro Malaspina's 1791 chart and named on the 1792 chart of Dionisio Alcalá-Galiano. Many years later, in 1925, the Union Steamship Co named its new 1,338-tonne passenger and cargo vessel after the island. Catala Passage, in turn, received its name from the ship, the first large steamer to pass through this rock-infested area. *Catala* had a long career on the BC coast, running first from Vancouver to Prince Rupert and Stewart, then to Rivers Inlet, Bella Coola and Ocean Falls. In 1927 it required major repairs after hitting a reef; it was also damaged by grounding in 1937. During WWII the vessel was employed by the US Navy as an armed merchant ship. It was sold to Northland Navigation Co in 1959, then spent a few years as a floating hotel before being dismantled in 1965.

Cates Bay (49°25'00" 123°19'00" NE side of Bowen I, Howe Sd, NW of Vancouver). Capt John Andrew "Jack" Cates (1862–1942) was one of five seafaring brothers, all of whom influenced BC marine history. Born in Maine, Jack arrived in Vancouver in 1886, worked on coastal vessels, bought the tugs *Swan* and *Lois*, then joined the Klondike gold rush, where he earned enough to buy a steamer, the *Defiance*, and begin a ferry service in Howe Sd. In 1900 he purchased the old Mannion estate on Bowen I and turned it into a holiday destination for picnickers and vacationers. His Terminal Steam Navigation Co ran a number of small vessels, including the *Britannia*, on freight and passenger routes in Burrard Inlet and Howe Sd. Cates sold out to the Union Steamship Co in 1920 and turned to ranching and mining in the BC Interior, then came back to the coast to operate more tugboats and a hotel at Crescent Beach. His brother Charles Cates (1859–1938) founded C H Cates and Sons Ltd, a major Vancouver tugboat company. *E*

Catface Range (49°16'00" 125°58'00" N of Vargas I, NW of Tofino, Clayoquot Sd, W side of Vancouver I). This formation was named in 1861 by RN surveyor Capt George Richards after a large mineral deposit that can be seen from the water and gives the side of the principal mountain the appearance of a cat's face.

Cathcart Island (51°18'00" 127°40'00" Part of the Barrier Group, Smith Sd, S of Rivers Inlet). Henry Cathcart (1869–1961) was born in Ireland and came to Canada with his family about 1873. He married Annie Isabelle Harrison at Victoria in 1909. Cathcart worked for the BC government for over 60 years, starting as a clerk and retiring in 1944 as deputy minister of Lands. Formerly known as Long I but renamed by the hydrographic service about 1948.

Caulfeild Cove in West Vancouver. *Peter Vassilopoulos*

Caulfeild Cove (49°20'00" 123°15'00" Just NE of Point Atkinson, in W Vancouver). Francis William Caulfeild (1840–1934) was a British land developer, born at London, who visited the BC coast and purchased a large chunk of real estate in W Vancouver in 1899. He laid out his property in the style of an English village, with house lots, broad winding footpaths (now roads), an Anglican church (St Francis-in-the-Wood) and a waterfront park, all contoured to the slopes of the land. Caulfeild never actually lived in BC, but he visited often. His English surname is a very old one, dating to the 16th century, and has so far resisted many recent local attempts to "correct" it to Caulfield. This site was known in the early 1900s as Skunk Cove.

Cautious Point (50°05'00" 127°33'00" Bunsby Is, Checleset Bay, NW of Kyuquot Sd, NW side of Vancouver I). *Cautious Clara* was a fictional brig commanded by Capt Jack Bunsby, a character in *Dombey and Son*, an 1848 novel by Charles Dickens. *See* Bunsby Is.

Cavin Cove (52°11'00" 128°08'00" NE side of Campbell I, N of Bella Bella). Probably named for George W Cavin (1849–1930), master of the *Beaver* and other early HBC vessels on the BC coast. Possibly after John Cavin (1852–1924), also a master mariner and tugboat capt. The two men were brothers and came to BC from NB along with a third brother, Robert Samuel Cavin (1855–1933), who farmed at Saanich and Cobble Hill. John's son Ellice Martin Cavin (1889–1975) was also a pioneer tugboat capt. Formerly known as Rock Ck ("creek" being an early Admiralty term for a small inlet that dried at low tide).

Cayetano Point (49°01'00" 123°36'00" SW point of Valdes I, Gulf Is). After Spanish naval officer and explorer Cayetano Valdés. *See* Valdes Bay.

Cecil Cove (52°51'00" 131°52'00" W end of Selwyn Inlet, E side of Moresby I, QCI). Named for geologist Alfred Richard Cecil Selwyn of the Geological Survey of Canada. *See* Selwyn Inlet.

Cecilia Island (52°18'00" 128°23'00" Off SW side of Don Peninsula, Milbanke Sd). Cecilia Douglas (1834–65) was the eldest daughter of James Douglas, colonial gov of Vancouver I and BC, and his wife Amelia. She was born at Ft Vancouver and went to boarding school in Oregon City. At Ft Victoria she acted as her father's private secretary. In 1852, Cecilia married John Helmcken (1824–1920), HBC surgeon and a noted BC politician during the colonial era. She had seven children, only four of whom survived, before her premature death from pneumonia. This feature was formerly known as Mary I but renamed by the hydrographic service about 1929.

Cecil Patch (54°03'00" 130°16'00" NE of Porcher I, junction of Arthur Passage and Malacca Passage, S of Prince Rupert). After Cecil Bloxam, an RN midshipman on the BC coast, 1866–67. *See* Bloxam Flat.

Cecil Point (53°57'00" 130°08'00" SE side of Marrack I, Telegraph Passage, just N of Pitt I, S of Prince Rupert). After Capt Cecil Buckley, VC, cdr of HMS *Pylades* on the BC coast, 1868–69. *See* Buckley Point.

Ceepeecee (49°52'00" 126°42'00" N side of Hecate Channel, SW of Tahsis, W side of Vancouver I). The name of this former fish-processing community comes from the initials of the Canadian Packing Corp, a subsidiary of the California Packing Corp, which built a pilchard-reduction plant there in 1926. Nelson Bros Fisheries bought the operation in 1934 and expanded it with a cannery in 1938. Fire destroyed most of the site in 1954, and only a small boat ways remained by the early 2000s. Ceepeecee post office was open 1926–60. Nearby Ceepeecee Lk takes its name from the settlement. *E*

Celestial Bluff (53°36'00" 132°54'00" N side of Port Chanal, W side of Graham I, QCI), **Celestial Reef** (54°31'10" 131°28'00" W of Dundas I, NW of Prince Rupert). Capt Absalom Freeman made surveys of both these areas aboard the iron-hulled fishing vessel *Celestial Empire* in 1912. This 37-m, 185-tonne, steam halibut trawler, built in 1897 to work in the N Sea, was owned by the Canadian Fishing Co. In the 1920s it was renamed the *Cape Scott* by Capt Barney Jones and used to tow logs across Hecate Str. After a stint with the Pacific Coyle Navigation Co, the vessel was broken up in 1946. Celestial Bluff was formerly known as Bluff Point.

Cerantes Rocks (48°32'00" 124°28'00" Off S entrance to Port San Juan, SW side of Vancouver I). Antonio Serantes (as his name is more commonly spelled) was a Spanish pilot who made several voyages to the PNW coast aboard the *Princesca*. He was in Alaska with Estéban Martínez

C

in 1788 and again with Salvador Fidalgo in 1790. He and Fidalgo were at Nootka Sd with the *Princesca* in 1792 as part of Juan Francisco de la Bodega y Quadra's small fleet. Later that year, at Puerto de Nuñez Gaona (Neah Bay) in Washington state, Serantes was murdered, and Fidalgo retaliated by killing the inhabitants of a passing canoe. The situation seemed likely to escalate, with local chiefs threatening a coordinated attack on all European fur traders, but it was defused by the diplomacy of Bodega y Quadra and the Nuu-chah-nulth leader Maquinna. Formerly known as Observatory Rk.

Cessford Islands (53°51'00" 130°30'00" Between Goschen I and Porcher I, SW of Prince Rupert). James Cessford (1865–1944) was born in NB and came to Victoria with his family at the age of three. He had a diverse career, serving aboard the *Mary Ellen* in the pelagic fur seal trade and then joining the Klondike gold rush in 1897. On the 1898 BC voters list his occupation is described as "hack-driver," while for the 1901 census he is listed as a miner. Cessford married Florence Grace Campbell (1874–1960), a native of Ont, in 1893, but they separated. He died at Seattle, his wife at Quesnel.

Chaatl Island (53°07'00" 132°28'00" W end of Skidegate Channel, between Graham I and Moresby I, QCI), **Chaatl Narrows** (53°06'00" 132°24'00" SE side of Chaatl I). Chaatl (Ts'aa'ahl), on the island's S shore, was a major Haida First Nation village in ancient times. In the 1830s, John Work, HBC trader at Port Simpson, estimated that over 550 people lived there, in 35 houses, but most had moved to Skidegate Inlet by 1870. *D*

Chads Island (48°44'00" 123°22'00" Between Saltspring I and Portland I, Gulf Is), **Chads Point** (52°48'00" 132°14'00" Just NW of Tasu Sd, W side of Moresby I, QCI). Capt Henry Chads (1819–1906) served on the Pacific Station, 1850–53, as cdr of HMS *Portland*, the flagship of Rear Adm Fairfax Moresby. He was a founder of the Royal Sailors Home in Portsmouth, capt-superintendent of Deptford dockyard, 1863–66, deputy cdr of the Channel fleet, 1869–70, and he ended his career in 1876–77 as cdr-in-chief at the Nore (responsible for protecting the entrance to the port of London, where the Nore sandbank is located). Chads reached the rank of adm in 1877 and was knighted in 1887. Chads I was first acquired by Frank Norris in 1910. Real-estate speculators have bought and sold it numerous times since then, driving the price from about $4,000 to $80,000 in the mid-1960s. *W*

Chain Islets (48°25'00" 123°16'00" Between Discovery I and Oak Bay, off SE tip of Vancouver I). The purely descriptive name of Chain Is was given by Capt Henry Kellett of HMS *Herald* in 1847, while surveying the area. It was changed to Chain Its in 1934. These rocky features figure in Songhees First Nation creation myths. During

the great flood, a single, very high island reportedly stood at this location, and the local people tied their canoes to it as the waters rose. After the flood, the island collapsed into many smaller islets, hence its Songhees name Thleethlayakw, meaning "broken in pieces."

Chalk Island (48°55'00" 125°19'00" NW end of the Broken Group, Barkley Sd, W side of Vancouver I). William Max Chalk, from New Westminster, was a clerk-stenographer with the Canadian Hydrographic Service. The feature was formerly known as Price I, probably after Capt John Price of HMS *Scout*, but was changed to Chalk I in 1945.

Chalmers Anchorage (54°03'00" 130°16'00" N side of Elliott I, Malacca Passage, S of Prince Rupert). Francis Chalmers (not Chalmer, as the name is spelled in Walbran's *Coast Names*) was on the BC coast in the mid-1860s as a midshipman aboard HMS *Malacca*. A good draftsman, he was placed temporarily (1866–67) on the *Beaver*, which the RN hired from the HBC as a survey vessel for a number of years. He retired from the navy in 1872 with the rank of lt. Nearby Francis Point is also named for him.

Chanal Point (53°43'00" 132°59'00" N entrance to Port Louis, W side of Graham I, QCI), **Chanal Reef** (54°11'00" 133°02'00" SE side of Parry Passage, between Langara I and Graham I), **Chanal Rock** (53°35'00" 132°50'00" Head of Port Chanal), **Port Chanal** (53°36'00" 132°54'00" SE part of Athlow Bay, W side of Graham I). Capt Prosper Chanal, a retired French naval officer and hydrographer, served as deputy cdr, under Capt Etienne Marchand, of *La Solide*. This well-equipped, 275-tonne vessel was built by the wealthy House of Baux in Marseilles to make a voyage around the world in search of scientific knowledge and commercial opportunity. It anchored in the QCI at Cloak Bay for several weeks in 1791. Chanal and Lt Louis Marchand, the capt's brother, took a longboat and charted the NW coast of Graham I S to Hippa I; several of the names he applied are still in use. Chanal's journal of the voyage of *La Solide* contains useful accounts of visits to Haida villages in the vicinity of Parry Passage. *D*

Chancellor Channel (50°25'00" 125°42'00" N of W Thurlow I, Johnstone Str). Named by Capt George Richards in 1860 because of its adjacency to the Thurlow Is and Loughborough Inlet, both named by Capt George Vancouver in 1792 after lord chancellors of England. This was the Ensenada de Viana of Spanish explorer Dionisio Alcalá-Galiano, named for Francisco Xavier Viana, one of Alejandro Malaspina's officers in the *Descubierta*.

Chandler Rocks (53°36'00" 130°35'00" SW of Parlane Point, W side of Banks I). George Chandler returned from overseas action in WWI to serve as an oiler aboard CGS *Lillooet* in the early 1920s. Named in 1926 by regional hydrographer Henri Parizeau.

Chapman Islet (50°28'00" 127°52'00" Koskimo Bay, S side of Quatsino Sd, NW side of Vancouver I). Nellie Chapman obtained a Crown grant for land in this vicinity in 1897. Formerly known as Canoe It but renamed by the hydrographic service in 1927 to avoid duplication.

Chapman Point (54°20'00" 130°31'00" N end of Tugwell I, W of Prince Rupert). Rev John Chapman (1814–63) was secretary to the Anglican Church Missionary Society for many years. He was educated at Cambridge and worked in India, 1840–53, as superintendent of theological colleges in Travancore (now Kerala) and Madras. The name was adopted in 1862 by RN surveyor Capt George Richards, on the recommendation of William Duncan, who was trained by the society and whose "model Christian village" of Metlakatla, founded in 1862, was located nearby.

Chapple Inlet (52°56'00" 129°08'00" N of entrance to Surf Inlet, W side of Princess Royal I). W coast hydrographer Cdr John Knight named this feature in 1914 after the district's fish and game warden, a man named Chapple. Before that it was known as N Surf Inlet.

Chaputs Passage (48°59'00" 124°59'00" Entrance to Uchucklesit Inlet, S end of Alberni Inlet, W side of Vancouver I). Chaputs is an approximation of the Nuu-chah-nulth First Nation word for canoe. The feature appears on early Admiralty charts as Steamer Passage but was renamed by the hydrographic service about 1945.

Character Cove (48°53'00" 125°03'00" NE of Bamfield, Barkley Sd, W side of Vancouver I). UVic students made up a facetious catchphrase—"oceanography builds character"—during intensive research projects undertaken in this cove. The name was adopted in 1985 after being proposed by a student group working at Bamfield Marine Station.

Charles Head (52°35'00" 128°17'00" S end of Pooley I, E of Roderick I, N of Bella Bella). After BC colonial civil servant, lawyer and politician Charles Edward Pooley. *See* Pooley I.

Charles Islands (52°09'00" 131°03'00" E entrance to Houston Stewart Channel, S of Moresby I, QCI), **Charles Rocks** (48°50'40" 123°22'30" In Trincomali Channel, off N side of Prevost I, Gulf Is). After James Charles Prevost, British boundary commissioner and RN officer, who served on the BC coast in 1857–60. *See* Prevost I.

Charles Narrows (52°30'40" 128°25'15" Between Nowish I and Susan I, Finlayson Channel, SE of Klemtu). After HBC mariner Capt Charles Dodd. *See* Dodd Islets.

Charles Reef (49°19'00" 122°54'00" NW entrance to Bedwell Bay, Indian Arm, NE of Vancouver). After Charles Hibbert Tupper, lawyer and politician, who moved to BC in 1897. *See* Tupper Rk.

Charlie Islands (50°44'00" 127°23'00" N side of Beaver Hbr, just E of Port Hardy, NE side of Vancouver I). These islands were originally named The Two Charlies in 1851 by Lt George Mansell of HMS *Daphne*. Charley Beardmore and Charley Blenkinsop were the young sons of HBC officers stationed at Ft Rupert in the 1850s (*see* Blenkinsop Bay for more on George Blenkinsop). Capt George Richards amended the name to its present form on his 1860 plan of Beaver Hbr.

Charmer Point (48°41'00" 123°21'00" E side of Coal I, off NE Saanich Peninsula, N of Victoria). The passenger steamship *Charmer* had an eventful if accident-prone career on the PNW coast. It was originally built as the *Premier* in San Francisco in 1887 for Capt John Irving's Canadian Pacific Navigation Co. The 980-tonne, 61-m vessel ran between Vancouver, Seattle and Tacoma until 1894, when it suffered a collision with the *Willamette* in which four people died. US salvage efforts failed, but Irving, in the dead of night, managed to refloat the steamer and tow it to Esquimalt, where it was rebuilt and renamed the *Charmer*. For the next 30 years the CPR's BC Coast Steamship Service ran the ship between Victoria and Vancouver, and then on Nanaimo, Comox, Powell R and Gulf Is routes. It survived several more pileups and managed to sink the lighthouse tender *Quadra* in Nanaimo Hbr in 1917. The first vessel on the BC coast with electric lights, the *Charmer* could handle 500 passengers and was converted to carry autos in 1923. After a long and useful life (3,000 voyages as early as 1902) it was turned into a floating summer-resort hotel at Newcastle I for two years before being scrapped in 1935.

Chasina Island (50°17'00" 125°13'00" Okisollo Channel, between Quadra I and Maurelle I, N of Campbell R). This First Nation name, its meaning unknown, was chosen by the Union Steamship Co, which often used Okisollo Channel, for one of its vessels. The *Chasina* was originally built at Glasgow in 1881 as the *Santa Cecilia*, private pleasure craft of Sir Henry Paget, 4th Marquis of Anglesey. Stories abound of mad parties aboard the yacht and excessive behaviour; Prince Albert Edward, the future King Edward VII, was a guest, as was actress Lily Langtry. In 1910 the ship was purchased by the All Red Line, renamed *Selma* and run between Vancouver and Powell R until 1917, when the Union Steamship Co acquired All Red's assets. As *Chasina*, the 234-tonne, 43-m vessel operated on the Howe Sd and Sunshine Coast routes for six years, then was sold and became a rum-runner until 1928. In 1931, en route to Macao from Hong Kong, the vessel and its crew of 11 disappeared forever.

C

Chassepot Rock (54°14'00" 130°24'00" Off S end of Digby I, just W of Prince Rupert). A chassepot, invented about 1866 by Antoine Alphonse Chassepot, was a breech-loading rifle that fired a paper cartridge. It became the standard service weapon for the French army until 1874 and greatly outperformed German army rifles in the Franco-Prussian War of 1870–71. The rock was given this name prior to 1916, though it is not known why.

Chatfield Island (52°16'00" 128°04'30" Between Cunningham I and Yeo I, N of Bella Bella). RN officer Alfred John Chatfield, CB (1831–1910), served on the BC coast, 1875–78. He was capt of HMS *Amethyst* when that vessel hosted the Earl of Dufferin, gov gen of Canada, and the Countess of Dufferin on their summer tour of BC's N coast in 1876, during which the vice-regal couple bestowed names on many geographic features. Chatfield also saw action in the Crimean War and off NW Africa. He was promoted to rear adm in 1886 and reached the rank of adm, retired, in 1897. His son, Adm Sir Alfred Ernle Montacute Chatfield, later Baron Chatfield, was one of Britain's most famous naval officers and the Admiralty's 1st Sea Lord in 1933–38. Chatfield I was formerly known as Sunday I.

Chatham Channel (50°35'00" 126°15'00" NE of E Cracroft I, between Knight Inlet and Call Inlet), **Chatham Islands** (48°26'00" 123°15'00" Off Oak Bay, E of Victoria), **Chatham Point** (50°20'00" 125°26'00" NW end of Discovery Passage, NW of Campbell R). HMS *Chatham*, the 122-tonne brig that accompanied HMS *Discovery* on Capt George Vancouver's 1791–95 expedition to the PNW, was named after the Earl of Chatham (*see below*), 1st Lord of the Admiralty when Vancouver left England. This small armed tender, with its four three-pounders and six swivel guns, was built at Dover and carried a crew of 55. On its way to the PNW it became separated from the *Discovery* and inadvertently encountered an island archipelago (now the Chatham Is) off NZ, the first European vessel to do so. In 1792 the *Chatham* made a side trip to explore the Columbia R. Lt William Broughton was in command until he returned to England in 1793 with official dispatches, after which Lt Peter Puget of the *Discovery* took over. Chatham Channel was named about 1866 by Lt Daniel Pender to commemorate Broughton's earlier exploration of the area. BC's Chatham Is were named in association with Discovery I, probably during the 1845–46 surveys of Capt Henry Kellett and Lt Cdr James Wood. Vancouver named Chatham Point after his consort vessel in 1792. The *Chatham* was renovated on its return to England and eventually sold in Jamaica in 1830. The Songhees First Nation name for the Chatham Is was Stsnaang.

Chatham Sound (54°22'00" 130°35'00" Between Dundas Is, Stephens I and the mainland W of Prince Rupert). John Pitt, the 2nd Earl of Chatham (1756–1835), was 1st Lord of the British Admiralty, 1788–94, in the cabinet of his younger brother, PM William Pitt. He was from a famous family: his father, William Pitt the elder, was also a British PM. John Pitt went on to serve as Lord Privy Seal and Lord President of the Privy Council before rejoining the army, his first career, and rising to the rank of gen. He was gov of Gibralter, 1820–35. Chatham Sd was named in 1788 by Capt Charles Duncan of the fur-trading vessel *Princess Royal*; the name was retained by Vancouver. Chatham Reach on the Pitt R is also named for him, while the Pitt R itself is named for his brother William. **Pitt Shoal** (54°11'00" 130°30'00") in Chatham Sd probably commemorates John as well. *W*

Chearnley Islet (54°26'00" 130°59'00" SW of S end of Dundas I, NW of Prince Rupert), **Chearnley Passage** (54°02'00" 130°41'00" Between Henry I and William I, off NW Porcher I, SW of Prince Rupert). Lt Cecil P Chearnley served on the BC coast, 1907–9, aboard HMS *Egeria* during the survey of Browning Entrance N of Banks I.

Checleset Bay (50°06'00" 127°40'00" E side of Brooks Peninsula, NW side of Vancouver I). The Che:K'tles7et'h' (Checleset, Cheklesaht) First Nation is positioned on the frontier between Nuu-chah-nulth- and Kwakwala-speaking territories, and its members traditionally spoke both languages. They once occupied the shores of Checleset Bay but moved to nearby Mission I in the 1950s. Today they live at Houpsitas on Kyuquot Sd, a village they share with the Ka:'yu:'K't'h' (Kyuquot) people, having formally amalgamated with that group in 1963. Both First Nations belong to the Nuu-chah-nulth Tribal Council. In 2003 the Nuu-chah-nulth official newspaper, *Ha-shilth-sa*, translated the name Checleset as "people from the place where you gain strength." The bay was named by the hydrographic service in the 1930s.

Cheeseman Rock (52°10'00" 128°33'00" SW entrance to Milbanke Sd, SW of Bardswell Group, W of Bella Bella). Named for Jane Cheeseman (1832–97, née Dyke), who arrived in Victoria in 1853 from England aboard the HBC supply ship *Norman Morison*. Her husband, Richard (c 1820–62), who had worked for the HBC at Victoria since 1850 but returned to the UK to marry, accompanied her. Jane gave birth to her first child, Mary, on the voyage while rounding Cape Horn. Richard left the HBC, and the Cheesemans settled on the Saanich Peninsula, where they established the Royal Oak Hotel. Jane supposedly chose the hotel name, applied afterwards to the district, after a particularly large local Garry oak (though the name of her birthplace, Sevenoaks, may also have influenced her). After Richard's untimely death in a freak horse-team accident, she married James Bailey of Rose Hill Farm, who died in 1871, and then John Durrance of Spring Valley Farm. Jennie Cheeseman (1857–1947), one of Jane's five daughters, and her husband, Louis Joseph Napoleon

Duval (1849–1933), continued to run the pioneer hotel, rebuilding it in 1890 after it burned down.

Cheeyah Island (48°59'00" 124°59'00" Entrance to Uchucklesit Inlet, SW end of Alberni Inlet, W side of Vancouver I). The island was used by the Nuu-chah-nulth First Nation for drying chum salmon in the fall. The name is a reference to splitting salmon for drying. The feature was formerly known as Harbour I but was renamed by the hydrographic service in 1931.

Marina at Chemainus on a calm day. *John Lund*

Chemainus (48°55'00" 123°43'00" Between Duncan and Ladysmith, SE side of Vancouver I), **Chemainus Bay** (48°55'00" 123°42'00" Just E of Chemainus). The district was named in the 1850s after its First Nation inhabitants, who, in turn, derived their name from the horseshoe shape of the bay. This shape suggested the bite mark that a shaman might leave on a tribe member during a ritual performance, and Chemainus is an adaptation of an Island Halkomelem phrase meaning "bitten breast." The **Chemainus River** (48°54'00" 123°41'00"), which flows into Stuart Channel, S of Chemainus, and Chemainus Lk also take their names from this source. The bay was formerly known as Horseshoe Bay. The town of Chemainus became an important forestry centre in the late 19th century, and when that industry faltered, it resurrected itself as a tourist destination with a series of innovative outdoor murals. *See also* Kulleet Bay. *E W*

Cheney Point (52°12'24" 128°28'01" W side of Athlone I, Milbanke Sd, W of Bella Bella). Martha Beeton Cheney (1835–1911) arrived at Victoria from England in 1851 with her aunt and uncle, Ann and Thomas Blinkhorn (*see* Beeton Point, Blinkhorn Peninsula). Together with Capt James Cooper they established Metchosin's pioneer Bilston Farm. In 1855, Cheney married Capt Henry Ella (1826–73), a master mariner with the HBC and later a coastal pilot (*see* Ella Point). They settled at Victoria and raised a large family. Martha kept a valuable diary of colonial life on Vancouver I that was edited by James Nesbitt and published in 1949 in the *BC Historical Quarterly*.

Cherry Islets (53°14'00" 129°29'00" Off SE side of Pitt I). Cpl Frank A Cherry, from Penticton, was killed in action Apr 10, 1945, aged 21, while serving in Europe with the Canadian Scottish Regiment. He is buried at the Holten Canadian War Cemetery in the Netherlands. The name was adopted by the hydrographic service in 1950.

Cherry Point (48°43'00" 123°33'00" SE of Cowichan Bay, SE side of Vancouver I). Named sometime prior to 1913 for the native bitter cherry tree, *Prunus emarginata*, which used to flourish at this location.

Chesterman Beach (49°07'00" 125°53'00" Just S of Tofino, W side of Vancouver I). John Phillip Chesterman (1867–1913) received Crown land grants on the Esowista Peninsula, opposite Chesterman Beach, in 1900 and 1912. His wife, Elizabeth Ann Adams, whom he married at Victoria in 1901, also acquired Crown grants in the area in 1915 and 1917. The Chestermans farmed, and John served as coxswain of the Tofino lifeboat. He tried to develop the Kallapa Mine, a copper and gold deposit on Meares I, and managed to ship some ore in 1913 before he died.

Chettleburgh Point (52°57'00" 129°09'00" W side of Chapple Inlet, Caamaño Sd). Kathleen Ursula Chettleburgh became a junior (student) draftsperson at the Victoria offices of the Canadian Hydrographic Service in 1942. A proposal to mark additional geographic features with her Christian and middle names was rejected in 1944 by senior mandarins in Ottawa on the grounds that too many staff names had "been used without reasonable discretion."

Chic Chic Bay (51°28'00" 128°01'00" SW side of Calvert I, S of Bella Bella). *Chikchik* was the word for a wheel or any wheeled vehicle in Chinook jargon, the pidgin language used on the W coast by First Nation groups and early traders and settlers. It is not known how the name relates to the bay (or to Chic Chic Lk, also on SW Calvert I). Franz Arthur Heinrich had built a cabin near the lake by 1913 and cleared land for a garden and chicken run. Chic Chic Bay was formerly known as Rocky Bay.

Chief Point (53°50'00" 130°30'00" S side of Porcher I, S of Prince Rupert). After Chief William Ewart Gladstone Shakes of the Kitkatla First Nation, in association with nearby Ewart I, Gladstone Is and Shakes Is. *See* Shakes Is.

Chimmin Point (48°57'00" 125°03'00" E end of Tzartus I, NE Barkley Sd, W side of Vancouver I). After a Nuu-chah-nulth First Nation term for a wooden halibut hook. The name of this geographic location, shown on early Admiralty charts as Limestone Point, was changed by the hydrographic service about 1945 to avoid duplication. Chimmin is not necessarily a traditional First Nation name for this particular feature.

China Beach (48°25'00" 124°05'00" SE of Port Renfrew, SW side of Vancouver I). This well-established local name, adopted in 1976, recalls the former name of Uglow Ck, which enters the ocean here and was known to pioneer loggers as China Ck. (Uglow Ck, in turn, is named after W Lawrence Uglow, a UBC geologist who did work in the area about 1920 in association with the adjacent Uglow mining claim.)

Allen and Sharie Farrell's junk, *China Cloud*. www.hiddenplaces.net

China Cloud Bay (49°29'38" 124°20'55" E side of False Bay, Lasqueti I, Str of Georgia). *China Cloud* is a triple-masted junk, handcrafted by boatbuilder Allen Farrell (1912–2002), that was moored in the bay for many winters. Allen and Sharie Farrell (1907–96) lived on Lasqueti I for nearly 30 years, about half that time aboard *China Cloud*. They were well known for their unusual way of life and were the subjects of numerous books, articles and documentaries. A group of Japanese families had a canning and fishing operation here in the 1920s and '30s. Formerly known as Mud Bay.

China Hat. *See* Klemtu.

Chisholm Island (48°48'00" 123°36'00" In Birds Eye Cove, Maple Bay, SE side of Vancouver I). A man named Chisholm was reportedly the earliest resident of this area. He lived just S of the head of Birds Eye Cove and worked as a land inspector. (This is probably either Joseph Chisholm or William Chisholm, both of whom are described in the 1898 BC voters list as farmers at Maple Bay. Other Chisholms lived at Quamichan and Genoa Bay.)

Chismore Passage (54°03'00" 130°19'00" Off NE Porcher I, SW of Prince Rupert). Dr George Chismore (1840–1906), a native of NY state, studied medicine in California

then joined the Western Union Telegraph Co, 1865–67, as medical officer of an expedition that surveyed an overland telegraph route through northern BC. (The project was cancelled after a cable was successfully laid across the Atlantic.) He then joined the US Army, serving on Tongass I, Alaska, in 1868, as well as in Arizona, Washington, Nevada and California. In 1873 he set up a practice in San Francisco. The Chismore Range and Chismore Ck are also named for him.

Chittenden Point (53°58'00" 132°38'00" Head of Naden Hbr, N side of Graham I, QCI). Capt Newton Henry Chittenden (1840–1925), a native of Connecticut, had been a lawyer and a Union cavalry officer in the Civil War before migrating W in search of adventure. He was hired by the BC government to prepare an extensive report on the QCI, which was published in 1884 (and reprinted a century later). The Victoria *Colonist* noted that he was "a man of remarkable energy and endurance" and "a total abstainer," who had "traversed from Mexico to Alaska more extensively than any other man living." Chittenden donated his collection of First Nation artifacts to the BC provincial museum. Newton Point on Skidegate Channel is also named for him. His grandson Wilfred W "Curley" Chittenden (1913–95), a logger turned conservationist, helped save the Canadian side of the Skagit R valley from being flooded and co-wrote two illustrated histories of Fraser Valley logging. According to QCI historian Kathleen Dalzell, the Haida name for this feature, Ke As Kwoon, means "sunlight point."

Chivers Point (48°57'00" 123°34'00" N tip of Wallace I, off NE end of Saltspring I, Gulf Is). Jeremiah "Jack" Chivers (1838–1927) came to Canada from Scotland aboard the *Cyclone* in 1862 and spent many years in the goldfields, travelling to the Cariboo, Cassiar and Omineca districts. In 1889 he received a Crown grant for the southern two-thirds of 80-ha Wallace I (then known as Narrow I) and was listed in the 1901 census as a fisherman. He cleared land, planted a large orchard and lived there alone for 28 years.

Cholberg Point (50°55'00" 127°44'00" E entrance to Cascade Hbr, Nigei I, off N end of Vancouver I). Seaman and shipbuilder Christian Cholberg (1884–1952) was born in Norway, immigrated to Oregon in the early 1900s and worked in the cannery business in Alaska. With his wife, Astrid Torp, and sons, he came to Victoria about 1912 and built some of BC's last four-masted windjammers, including the *Seiki Maru* and *S F Tolmie*, at Cholberg Shipyard before going bankrupt in 1922. After operating Venus Cannery in Vancouver until it, also, went bankrupt, in 1929, Cholberg moved to remote Cascade Hbr on Nigei I and re-entered the boat business, building and restoring a number of small fishing vessels. About 1940 he and his wife, who died in 1942, bought the store and hotel at Shushartie Bay at the N end of Vancouver I. Chris Cholberg died at New Westminster.

Chonat Bay (50°18'00" 125°18'00" NW end of Quadra I, N of Campbell R), **Chonat Point** (50°18'00" 125°19'00" N entrance to Chonat Bay). Chonat is the traditional First Nation name for this bay. According to historians Helen and Philip Akrigg, the word is Kwakwala for "where coho salmon are found." The bay and point were named by Capt John Walbran of CGS *Quadra* about 1904. Chonat Lk was named later, in association with the other features. Chonat Bay was formerly known as Lake Bay.

Christensen Point (50°50'00" 128°13'00" NE of Cape Scott, N end of Vancouver I). Soren Christensen (1844–1915), a native of Denmark (whose name is sometimes spelled Christiansen), settled E of this point, beside the mouth of the Strandby R, about 1894. He was joined in 1903 by his sister Marie. Nearby Soren Hill is also named for him. A small community that later formed on adjacent Shuttleworth Bight had disappeared by the 1920s.

Christian Rock (52°07'00" 130°59'00" SE of High I, NE side of Kunghit I, QCI). The name was adopted by the hydrographic service in 1962 after master mariner Lars Christian. He was skipper of the whaling ship *Germania*, which was active in these waters in the early 1900s, working out of Rose Hbr for the Pacific Whaling Co.

Christiansen Point (52°14'00" 128°11'00" SW tip of Chatfield I, N side of Seaforth Channel, just N of Bella Bella). Capt James Christiansen (1840–1927), born in Denmark, arrived at Victoria in 1864 on a Liverpool cargo ship and soon secured a job as mate of Capt William Spring's trading schooner *Surprise*. He also worked on the *Alert*, another trading schooner. In 1868, as skipper of the *Surprise*, he was one of the first to try a new method of sealing: taking First Nation hunters aboard ship with their canoes, then setting them loose far offshore to pursue their prey. Christiansen brought the initial news of the US barque *John Bright* to Victoria in 1869. (This unhappy vessel struck a reef off Vancouver I; those crew members who made it to shore were allegedly murdered by certain residents of Hesquiat, two of whom were later convicted and hanged.) He spent much time commanding tugs, including the *Pilot*, *Alexander* and *Lorne*, then became a Victoria and Nanaimo district pilot, a position he held until he was 80. He was the pilot aboard the steamship *San Pedro* when it was wrecked on Brotchie Ledge off Victoria in 1891. His son, also James Christiansen (b 1870), followed in his father's footsteps as skipper of the *Lorne* and was master of other tugs at Victoria until 1894, when he and seven crew members died after the *Estelle* foundered off Cape Mudge. The family name is often spelled Christensen. Christiansen Point was formerly known as Angle Point, then as Beard Point (after Cdr Charles Beard, *see* Beard Is).

Christie Islands (53°44'00" 130°25'00" S entrance to Schooner Passage, S of Porcher I and Prince Rupert), **Christie Passage** (50°50'00" 127°36'00" Between Hurst I and Balaklava I, NW of Port Hardy), **Christie Rock** (53°43'53" 130°25'32" Just W of Christie Is). George Christie was master of HMS *Sparrowhawk*, under Cdr Edwin Porcher, and served on the BC coast 1866–69, based in Esquimalt. He left the RN in 1875. **Christie Bay** (53°12'00" 132°13'00" SW part of Kagan Bay, Skidegate Inlet, QCI) is believed to be named for him as well. The islands, passage and bay were all named about 1866 by RN surveyor Lt Daniel Pender.

Christie Islet (49°30'00" 123°18'00" S of Anvil I, Howe Sd, NW of Vancouver). This bird sanctuary was originally known as Centre I. To avoid confusion with other Centre islands, the name was changed in 1945 to Cynthia I, after the Union Steamship Co vessel *Lady Cynthia*, which operated in Howe Sd. In 1948, for reasons unknown, the name was changed again, to Christie It, but the significance of this last name has not been recorded.

Christie Point (48°27'00" 123°25'00" S side of Portage Inlet, NW of Victoria Hbr). John Christie owned historic Craigflower Farm near Victoria in the 1930s and '40s. While he did accomplish some restoration of the heritage 1856 manor house and its furnishings, he also imposed numerous indignities on the site, leasing parts of it as a service station and Big Ben's Burger House, demolishing old outbuildings and erecting a motel. Bruce McKelvie, writing in the Victoria *Colonist* in 1937, reported that Christie was creating a bathing beach, importing electric motorboats, laying out a "small" golf course and "working to make Craigflower as famous in this age for its comfort and hospitality as it was in the brave days of old."

Christie Shoal (52°37'00" 129°23'00" Between Moore Is and Byers Is, W of Aristazabal I). 2nd Cpl William Christie was a member of the Columbia detachment of Royal Engineers, which served in BC 1858–63. Little is known about him, though a bag containing his personal belongings—including a pair of moleskin trousers and $16 in cash—fell off a mule while he was working on the Cariboo Rd in 1863 and tumbled into the Thompson R. An archival letter from Lt Henry Palmer asks Col Richard Moody, cdr of the detachment, about the "propriety" of remunerating Christie for his loss.

Christmas Point (48°31'00" 123°33'00" W side of Finlayson Arm, Saanich Inlet, NW of Victoria). Anglican clergyman Frederick Granville Christmas (1854–1931) was born in Jersey, Channel Is, and married May Flora Elton (1857–1943) in 1880. They moved to Canada in 1887. Granville, who enjoyed being called Father Christmas and developed quite a reputation as a poultry breeder, was minister of St Stephen's in Saanichton, 1890–1901, and

C

long owned a waterfront cottage on Saanich Inlet. He also served at St George's in Banff and in the communities of Cedar, Cumberland and Duncan. Formerly known as Emily Point but renamed in 1934.

Chrome Island (49°28'00" 124°41'00" Off S end of Denman I, Str of Georgia). The light-coloured rocks of this geographical feature originally inspired the name Yellow I, bestowed by Admiralty surveyors about 1860. BC's chief geographer, "presuming the 'yellow' to be a descriptive name," authorized the change to Chrome I in 1923, pointing out that "there are three others of the same name [Yellow] in BC." A lighthouse was established on the E end of the island in 1891 as an aid to navigating the narrow S entrance to Baynes Sd. Sadly, it did not assist the steamship *Alpha*, which was wrecked on Chrome I in 1900, with the loss of nine lives. The island is well known for its outstanding First Nation petroglyphs.

The lighthouse at Chrome Island off Denman Island. *Peter Vassilopoulos*

Chrow Islands (48°54'26" 125°28'15" NE end of Felice Channel, W side of Barkley Sd, W side of Vancouver I). William Chrow (1859–1905) received a Crown grant of land on the N side of Barkley Sd in 1892. He married Jean Simson (1864–1948) in 1895 at Victoria and is listed in the 1898 BC voters list as a clerk at Victoria. Both William and Jean died at Vancouver. Formerly shown on early Admiralty charts as Double Is and renamed about 1936.

Chum Point (49°39'00" 123°38'00" S side of Salmon Inlet, E of Sechelt Inlet, NW of Vancouver). Named by the hydrographic service in 1949 for a species of salmon, *Oncorhynchus keta*, also known as dog salmon.

Chup Point (48°57'20" 125°01'37" N entrance to Alberni Inlet, head of Barkley Sd, W side of Vancouver I). Chup, an adaptation of the Nuu-chah-nulth First Nation word for tongue, is descriptive of the shape of the point. It was shown on early Admiralty charts as Nob Point but was changed by the hydrographic service in 1931.

Church Cove (48°48'30" 123°11'51" NW side of Saturna I, Gulf Is). Saturna I's first church was located here in 1899. A log cabin that had been used by Japanese fishermen as

a boathouse was converted to a church by Rev Hubert St John Payne and George Bradley-Dyne. Called St Christopher's but never consecrated, the building was still standing as a private chapel in the early 2000s. A more modern St Christopher's Anglican church was built and dedicated elsewhere on Saturna in 1963.

The abandoned village of Church House in 2001. *Peter A. Robson*

Church House (50°20'00" 125°04'00" NE side of Calm Channel, entrance to Bute Inlet). This abandoned Homalco First Nation community was the site of an early Roman Catholic mission, established about 1900 after an earlier village site, Múushkin, located on the W side of Calm Channel, was damaged by a severe storm. A church, built in 1918, was still standing, barely, until 2007, when it collapsed. Church House had a population of more than 100 in 1966 and was sporadically occupied until the early 1990s. The original Homalco name for the site was Lhílhukwem, meaning "basin shaped."

Church Island (48°18'30" 123°35'10" SE of Becher Bay, off S tip of Vancouver I), **Church Point** (48°19'00" 123°35'00" Between Becher Bay and Whirl Bay). Cdr William Harvey Church was an RN surveying officer, but it is unlikely that he was ever present in BC waters. Both features were named by Capt Henry Kellett of HMS *Herald* in 1846, while making a survey of Becher Bay. Church Point was originally called Church Cape. Nearby Church Hill is also named for him.

Church Point (50°11'00" 124°46'00" E side of W Redonda I, entrance to Toba Inlet, NE of Campbell R). Church Point and nearby Bishop and Dean points were all named in a fit of ecclesiastical enthusiasm, probably by Capt George Richards in 1862 or Lt Daniel Pender in 1864.

Cia Rock (48°50'00" 125°11'00" E side of Diana I, Trevor Channel, E side of Barkley Sd, W side of Vancouver I). Cia, a secondary chief of the Huu-ay-aht (Ohiaht) First Nation, was described in the published account of Capt Camille de Roquefeuil of the *Bordelais*, who visited this area in 1817 (*see* Bordelais Its). Cia had apparently been hospitable, but Roquefeuil noted that many of the presents given him

C

ended up as the possessions of Nanat, a more important chief, who treated Cia poorly. The feature appears on early Admiralty charts as Todd Rk but was renamed in 1934.

Cinque Islands (50°18'00" 125°24'00" Off SW side of Sonora I, N end of Discovery Passage, N of Campbell R). Named after the Cinque Ports, a string of seaport towns on the Kent and Sussex coasts in SE England, which were granted special privileges about 1150–1550 in return for providing coastal defence services. The original Cinque ports were Dover, Sandwich, Hastings, New Romney and Hythe, though other, smaller places became associated with them in a confederation that eventually included 42 communities.

Clanninick Cove (50°02'00" 127°24'00" Just NW of Kyuquot, NW side of Vancouver I). Clanninick (or Kai-ne-nitt) was a Kyuquot First Nation chief at Aktis on Village I near the entrance to Kyuquot Sd. In 1862 he helped Lt Philip Hankin (*see* Hankin I) and Dr Charles Wood of HMS *Hecate*, who had been instructed by Capt George Richards to explore N Vancouver I on foot. Through Clanninick's good graces, the duo hired seven Aktis men to carry their gear and accompany them to the mouth of the Nimpkish R on the E side of the island that June. Clanninick Ck is named after the cove. *W*

Clapp Basin (53°18'00" 132°26'00" S end of Shields Bay, Rennell Sd, W side of Graham I, QCI), **Clapp Islands** (53°19'00" 132°26'00" In Shields Bay). Geologist Charles Horace Clapp (1883–1935) surveyed this area in 1912 for the Geological Survey of Canada. Educated at MIT and Harvard, he was an instructor at the Univ of N Dakota, 1905–7, before leaving to work in Canada, where he also surveyed the lower Sooke watershed on Vancouver I. He went on to teach at the Univ of Arizona and the Montana State School of Mines at Butte, where he served as president, 1918–21. Clapp was also president of the State Univ of Montana at Missoula, 1921–35. Clapp Ck on Vancouver I is named for him too.

Clapp Passage (50°39'00" 126°15'00" Between SE Gilford I and Shewell I, entrance to Knight Inlet). Possibly named after Navigating Lt Edward Scobell Clapp, who was based at Esquimalt in 1871–73 aboard HMS *Scout*, under Capt Ralph Cator. He later served in Bermuda and was inspector of lighthouses for the Bahamas in 1889. Clapp retired from the RN in 1890 with the rank of staff cdr and died in 1902. This name, however, may predate Clapp's presence on the BC coast.

Clara Islet (50°04'00" 127°35'00" SW of Bunsby Is, Checleset Bay, NW side of Vancouver I). *Cautious Clara* was a fictional brig commanded by Capt Jack Bunsby, a character in *Dombey and Son*, an 1848 novel by Charles Dickens. *See* Bunsby Is.

Clarke Cove (52°58'00" 129°11'00" N of Chapple Inlet, W side of Princess Royal I). Capt Charles Edward Clarke (1854–1925) was born in Somerset, UK, and came to BC about 1874. He was master of the coastal steamers *Juanita* and *Alert* before joining the sealing fleet in 1889. Clarke later served for many years as Victoria's harbourmaster and port warden. In 1906 he married Ont native Georgina Barbara Potts (1872–1947) at Victoria. The cove appears on early Admiralty charts as Hole-in-the-Wall.

Clarke Island (48°53'00" 125°23'00" W side of Broken Group, Barkley Sd, W side of Vancouver I). Named in 1933 for William R Clarke, who obtained a Crown grant for land on Uchucklesit Inlet in 1893. The island, which appears on early Admiralty charts as Quoin I, was pre-empted in 1911 by Harry Schwarzer of Ucluelet, who received a Crown grant for it in 1914.

Clark Island (49°55'00" 127°14'00" S end of Barrier Is, entrance to Kyuquot Sd, NW side of Vancouver I). Benjamin C Clark was apparently the original owner, in 1911, of the property facing this island. The feature was shown as One Tree I on early Admiralty charts. Clark I was adopted in 1946 on the suggestion of the hydrographic service.

Clark Islet (53°39'00" 129°56'00" Head of Hevenor Inlet, Pitt I, S of Prince Rupert). Flight Lt Donald Hartford Clark, a native of Winnipeg who was living at New Westminster and enlisted at Vancouver, died Feb 7, 1944, aged 25, in a collision over the Gulf of Mexico with a US Navy training plane. He was awarded the DFC in 1943 for displaying "courage, determination and cool judgment" while flying Consolidated PBY Catalina bombers on anti-submarine patrol for No 210 Squadron. Clark is buried at Ocean View Burial Park, Burnaby.

Claudet Island (53°13'00" 132°09'00" In Kagan Bay, Skidegate Inlet, QCI), **Claudet Point** (53°05'00" 129°07'00" W entrance to Barnard Hbr, NW side of Princess Royal I). Metallurgist and amateur photographer Francis George Claudet (1837–1906) was born at London, England, youngest son of inventor and pioneer photographer Antoine Claudet. He arrived in BC in 1860 as superintendent of the colonial assay office at New Westminster, and the following year was sent to San Francisco to buy equipment for minting coins. The BC mint never got off the ground; only a handful of $10 and $20 gold pieces were produced, and they now rank among the world's rarest coins. On the strength of Claudet's assays of coal samples from the QCI, the Cowgitz Mine on Kagan Bay was established in the mid-1860s. He married Frances Fleury (1836–99) at Victoria in 1863 but returned to the UK with his family in 1873 and worked for various London chemical and metallurgical firms. His sons eventually made their way back to Canada and settled in BC. Claudet I was formerly known as Wedge I.

C

Claxton (54°05'00" 130°05'00" E side of Telegraph Passage, S entrance to the Skeena R, SE of Prince Rupert). Claxton cannery and sawmill were built by the Royal Canadian Packing Co in 1892 and sold to the Victoria Canning Co in 1898. They were named after Frederick J Claxton (b 1857), a Victoria realtor and insurance agent, originally from California, who was one of Royal Canadian's trustees. For many years the operation was run by the Wallace brothers, John and Peter, who purchased it in 1900. Peter Wallace later bought his brother out and owned the plant under the name Wallace Fisheries Ltd until his firm was acquired by BC Packers Ltd in 1926. A cold-storage plant, added in 1900, burned down in 1934 and was not rebuilt. The cannery closed in 1945 and was used as a net loft until 1949, then dismantled. Its ruins were still visible in the early 2000s. Nearby Claxton Ck was named after the cannery and Claxton post office, which was open 1893–1945. *E*

Claydon Bay (50°56'00" 126°54'00" W side of Grappler Sd, N of N Broughton I and E Queen Charlotte Str). Claydon House, Buckinghamshire, was the residence of British peer and long-time MP Sir Harry Verney (1801–94), whose son, Lt-Cdr Edmund Hope Verney, commanded the gunboat *Grappler* on the BC coast, 1862–65. Named by Lt Daniel Pender in 1865 along with a related suite of nearby names: Calvert Point (qv), Mt Calvert, Mt Verney, Sir Harry Range, Mt Florence and Mt Nightingale (the latter two named for the legendary British nurse and reformer, who was a sister of Sir Harry's second wife). *See also* Verney Passage. The bay was the site of a steamship landing in the 1940s; a large truck-logging camp operated there, with a floating school and hospital. *W*

Clayoquot (49°10'00" 125°56'00" E side of Stubbs I, just off Tofino, Clayoquot Sd), **Clayoquot Sound** (49°12'00" 126°06'00" Between Barkley Sd and Nootka Sd, W side of Vancouver I). Named after the resident Tla-o-qui-aht First Nation, whose members are part of the Nuu-chah-nulth Tribal Council. The word is sometimes translated as "people of other tribes" and was spelled many different ways by early traders, including Clioquatt, Clayocuat, Klaooquat and Klahoquaht. In 1787, Capt Charles Barkley

Clayoquot Sound from north side of Vargas Island. *Andrew Scott*

of *Imperial Eagle* called this Wickaninnish's Sd after the hereditary name of the region's principal chief. The Clayoquot spelling appears on Capt George Vancouver's 1792 chart. The community of Clayoquot on Stubbs I (qv, also known locally as Clayoquot I) grew from a modest trading post, established in the 1850s, into a small but vibrant commercial settlement, complete with store, hotel, post office, school and police constable. Nearby Tofino, which has road access to the rest of Vancouver I, eventually overtook Clayoquot as the regional centre, but the old hotel and pub kept operating until 1964. Stubbs I was privately owned in the early 2000s. Clayoquot Lk, Clayoquot R and Clayoquot Arm on Kennedy Lk are also named for the Tla-o-qui-aht people. *E W*

Clayton Island (52°02'00" 127°57'00" W side of Fisher Channel, off NE end of Hunter I, SE of Bella Bella), **Clayton Passage** (52°09'00" 128°05'00" W side of Kliktsoatli Hbr, NW side of Denny I, E of Bella Bella). John Clayton (1842–1910), originally from Leicester, England, came to the BC coast in 1873 and found employment with the HBC, first at Bella Coola (1874–77) and then at Fort McLoughlin, just S of Bella Bella (1878–82). Chief Factor William Charles described him as "a good occupant, though uncertain, never knows how long he wants to remain, steady and sober." In 1882, Clayton bought both posts from the HBC, as well as considerable property, and operated independently. He and Tom Draney built the first cannery in the Bella Coola area in 1900. His wife, Elizabeth Orten (1861–1941), whom he married in 1890, ran the Bella Coola store after he died at San Diego. He'd travelled there with his son, seeking relief from respiratory ailments. Storyteller Clayton Mack was the grandson of John Clayton and Q'uit, the Nuxalk woman the trader had lived with before his marriage to Orten. Clayton Falls Ck, W of Bella Coola, is also named for him. Clayton Passage was formerly known as Steamer Passage.

Cleland Island (49°10'00" 126°05'00" SW of Blunden I, W of Vargas I, Clayoquot Sd, W side of Vancouver I). Fletcher Henderson Cleland obtained a Crown grant for land on the W side of Vargas I in 1916. Cleland I, 7.7 ha, was one

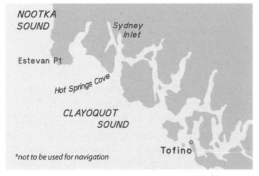

NOOTKA SOUND

Sydney Inlet

Estevan Pt

Hot Springs Cove

CLAYOQUOT SOUND

Tofino

*not to be used for navigation

Clayoquot Sound. *Reproduced with the permission of the Canadian Hydrographic Service*

C

of BC's first ecological reserves, established in 1971, and is closed to the public. It protects major breeding colonies of Leach's storm petrel, black oystercatcher, tufted puffin, rhinoceros auklet and other seabirds. It was formerly known as Bare I and renamed in 1934.

Clement Rapids (53°13'00" 129°03'00" Entrance to Cornwall Inlet, NW side of Princess Royal I). After lawyer and politician Clement Francis Cornwall, lt gov of BC, 1881–87. *See* Cornwall Inlet.

Clerke Islet (50°12'00" 127°50'00" Brooks Bay, NE of Cape Cook, NW side of Vancouver I), **Clerke Peninsula** (49°37'00" 126°31'00" SW extension of Bligh I, Nootka Sd, W side of Vancouver I), **Clerke Point** (50°05'00" 127°48'00" SW corner of Brooks Peninsula, SE of Cape Cook), **Clerke Reefs** (50°13'00" 127°52'00" NW of Clerke It). Cdr Charles Clerke (1741–79) was present on all three of Capt James Cook's voyages of discovery. He entered the RN about 1755 and was a midshipman on the survey vessel *Dolphin* during Commodore John Byron's 1764–66 circumnavigation of the globe. On Cook's first journey, Clerke served as master's mate and was promoted to lt. On the second trip he was 2nd lt of HMS *Resolution*. He commanded HMS *Discovery* on the final voyage, during which they visited Nootka Sd and the PNW coast in 1778, then took charge of *Resolution* and the entire expedition upon Cook's death in Hawaii the following year. His own demise, from TB, occurred later in 1779, however, and he was buried at Kamchatka. Lt John Gore then brought the two vessels successfully back to England. *W*

Cleve Island (51°29'00" 127°45'00" Off SW Penrose I, Schooner Retreat, N entrance to Rivers Inlet). This geographical feature was formerly known as Cliff I, but to avoid confusion with other "Cliff" names it was changed in 1949 to Cleve, a long-obsolete Middle English word meaning "cliff" or "steep slope or hillside" (from the Old English *cleofu*, "cliff").

Client Reefs (54°06'00" 130°19'00" Between Marcus Passage and Malacca Passage, just NE of Porcher I, S of Prince Rupert). Named during Lt Daniel Pender's survey of 1867 or 1869 in association with nearby Lawyer Is and Bribery It. The significance of the names is not recorded.

Cliffe Point (50°28'00" 127°56'00" S entrance to Quatsino Sd, NW side of Vancouver I). Capt Thomas Cliffe (1886–1947) served with the CPR's BC Coast Steamship Service as master of the *Princess Elaine* and *Princess Charlotte*. He was born and died at Comox (*see* Cliffe Rock *and also* Harmston I) and married Annie Sewell Palmer (1890–1973) in 1913 at New Westminster. The point was formerly known as Bold Bluff but was renamed by the hydrographic service in 1927.

Cliffe Rock (52°50'00" 129°28'00" Just W of Rennison I, entrance to Caamaño Sd). After Comox valley pioneer Florence Mary Cliffe, whose family name was Harmston. *See* Harmston I. She was the mother of steamship capt Thomas Cliffe (*see* Cliffe Point). Formerly known as Surprise Rk and renamed in 1926.

Clifford Bay (52°36'00" 129°08'00" W side of Aristazabal I). Frank Clifford Goulding Smith (1890–1983) assisted with Pacific coastal surveys aboard CGS *Lillooet* in 1925 as a junior hydrographer. He was born in Montreal and joined the Canadian Hydrographic Service in 1914. In the 1920s he worked mainly in the Gulf of St Lawrence, then became officer-in-charge of the Hudson Str survey, 1931–35. Smith was appointed superintendent of charts, 1937–52, and served as dominion hydrographer, 1952–57, managing a major post-war expansion of the CHS and an increased focus on charting the Arctic. Nearby Clifford Ck is also named for him.

Clifford Point (49°17'00" 126°02'00" SW end of Bawden Bay, E of Flores I, Clayoquot Sd, W side of Vancouver I). Clifford Bawden was the son of RN officer Charles Bawden, after whom Bawden Bay (qv) is named. Clifford, also an RN officer, entered the navy in 1863 and served on the BC coast, based at Esquimalt, 1890–93, where he was staff cdr aboard the cruiser *Warspite*, under Capt Hedworth Lambton. The *Warspite* was the flagship of Rear Adm Charles Hotham, cdr-in-chief of the Pacific Station. In 1902, Clifford Bawden was a staff capt and harbourmaster of Devonport dockyard at Plymouth. *W*

Clifford Rocks (53°05'00" 129°30'00" Off Betteridge Inlet, W side of Campania I, Estevan Sd, N of Caamaño Sd). Named in 1944 by regional hydrographer Henri Parizeau after Cecil Clifford, who was a driver aboard the W coast survey vessel *William J Stewart* in the early 1940s.

Clio Bay (53°54'00" 128°41'00" N of Coste I, Kitimat Arm, S of Kitimat), **Clio Channel** (50°35'00" 126°24'00" Between W Cracroft I and Turnour I, Johnstone Str), **Clio Island** (49°23'38" 126°11'02" Shelter Inlet, N of George

A drawing of HMS *Clio*, about 1860. *BC Archives A-00217*

C

Is, Clayoquot Sd, W side of Vancouver I), **Clio Island** (49°43'08" 124°11'24" S side of Blind Bay, NW side of Nelson I, entrance to Jervis Inlet, NW of Vancouver), **Clio Point** (53°55'00" 128°42'00" W entrance to Clio Bay). HMS *Clio* was a 61-m, 400-hp screw corvette, built at Sheerness dockyard in 1857 and armed with 21 guns. It spent two intervals on the BC coast—1859–62, under Capt Thomas Miller, and 1864–68, under Capt Nicholas Turnour—and saw much action there, especially during the latter period. In 1865, for instance, the *Clio* destroyed Ku-Kultz, a Kwakwaka'wakw village outside Ft Rupert, when three suspected murderers were not given up. That year it also went to northern BC (during which voyage Clio Bay was named by the ship's officers) to curtail an illegal traffic in liquor. Three traders and their vessels were captured, and William Duncan, the whisky-loathing missionary and magistrate from Metlakatla, penalized them severely to set an example. On appeal, however, his heavy sentences were reduced by Judge Matthew Baillie Begbie. The *Clio* went on to serve on the Australia Station, 1870–74, and then became a training ship on the coast of N Wales until 1919, when the 1,984-tonne vessel was sold for scrap and broken up. *W*

Clitheroe Island (52°13'00" 127°51'00" W side of Fisher Channel, NE of Bella Bella). Clitheroe is a town in Lancashire, situated in the Ribble Valley on the S edge of the Yorkshire Dales. It apparently had ancestral associations for the family of BC master mariner and historian John Walbran. However, James King, a great friend of Capt George Vancouver, with whom Vancouver had served on Cook's third voyage of discovery (*see* King I *and* Dean Channel), also had a connection to this town: he was born there, and his father had been the curate of Clitheroe. The name was adopted in 1925, on the suggestion of William Stewart, Canada's chief hydrographer.

Clive Island (48°42'00" 123°24'00" Off SE Piers I, NE of Saanich Peninsula, N of Victoria). Sir Edward Clive Oldnall Long Phillipps-Wolley (1854–1918) was an early owner of Piers I. He was supposedly a direct descendant of Robert Clive, the soldier of fortune who amassed great wealth while establishing British military and commercial supremacy in India. Phillipps-Wolley was an army officer, investor and lawyer who first came to BC in the 1880s on big-game hunting expeditions, which he adored. He returned with his family in 1890, built a large house on an estate, Woodhall, in Oak Bay and twice ran unsuccessfully as a federal Conservative candidate. He moved to Piers I in 1901 and built a fine country home there too, which burned down in 1913. By then Phillipps-Wolley had sold Piers (in 1909 to James Harvey for $18,000) and moved to the Duncan area, where he spent the rest of his life. Phillipps-Wolley was a well-known writer of travel books, poetry and novels for both adults and young people. He was knighted in 1915 for founding the Navy League in

western Canada. Clive I appears on early charts as Hood I; the current name was proposed by the hydrographic service and adopted in 1933. *E*

Cloak Bay (54°11'00" 133°01'00" W side of Langara I, off NW end of Graham I, QCI). Named in 1787 by Capt George Dixon of the *Queen Charlotte*, the first European trader in these waters, after the large number of superb sea otter cloaks he was able to obtain there from the Haida. Two years later, Capt Robert Gray, with the *Lady Washington*, also received hundreds of prime skins at this spot, trading for one crude iron chisel each, a bargain he boasted about repeatedly. However, the resentment of the Haida when they realized they'd been exploited set back trading relations for years and led to a number of hostile incidents. *D*

Cloake Hill (48°41'27" 123°27'01" W of Swartz Bay, N end of Saanich Peninsula, N of Victoria). After Isaac Cloake, a pioneer farmer at nearby Deep Cove, who, along with a partner, William Towner (*see* Towner Bank), was one of the region's first hop growers. He died in 1876 in a mysterious house fire. The feature, known earlier as Saddle Hill and Arbutus Hill, was officially named in 1934.

Clonard Bay (53°21'00" 132°30'00" S side of Rennell Sd, W side of Graham I, QCI), **Clonard Point** (53°26'00" 132°40'00" N side of Rennell Sd, entrance to Tartu Inlet). Baie de Clonard was the name that Capt Jean-François de Galaup, Comte de Lapérouse, gave to Rennell Sd in 1786, after the 1st lt on his ship, the *Boussole*. Lapérouse was in charge of a scientific expedition sent by France in 1785 to circumnavigate the globe and find the NW Passage. Clonard Bay and Clonard Point were named by the hydrographic service in the late 1940s to recall this historic footnote.

Clo-oose (48°39'00" 124°49'00" Just SW of W end of Nitinat Lk, SW side of Vancouver I), **Clo-oose Bay** (48°40'00" 124°49'00" S of Nitinat Lk). Although many different meanings (and spellings) have been put forward for this name over the years, it most likely is derived from the Ditidaht First Nation term for a beach campsite. Before the main Ditidaht village was established at Clo-oose, the site was apparently a halibut fishing station. A trading post was established there in the late 19th century, and a Methodist mission and school opened in 1894. A post office operated from 1911 until the mid-1960s, when the Ditidaht moved to a new reserve on Nitinat Lk. According to BC historians Philip and Helen Akrigg, a pre-WWI Victoria realtor sold land at Clo-oose to some affluent British families, and a few fine cottages were built. The newcomers disliked the First Nation name and petitioned unsuccessfully to have it changed to Clovelly. Nearby Clo-oose Ck and Clo-oose Lk are also named after the former village. *E*

Clotchman Island (49°37'00" 126°34'00" One of the Spanish Pilot Group, SW of Bligh I, Nootka Sd, W side of Vancouver I). Clotchman is a variation of *klootchman*, the Chinook jargon word for woman or female. Chinook was a pidgin language used on the W coast by First Nation groups and early traders and settlers. In 1934, regional hydrographer Henri Parizeau attempted to change this name to Carrasco I, after the Spanish pilot Juan Carrasco, who sailed with both Manuel Quimper in 1790 and José Narváez in 1791 on their historic surveys of Juan de Fuca and Georgia straits. Carrasco was the first European to explore the entrance to Puget Sd. Parizeau was making a great many name changes at the time, and there was bureaucratic resistance to some of his proposals, including this one (*see* Spanish Pilot Group). His recommendation was rejected, and Clotchman I, a long-established local name, was retained.

Clover Point (48°24'00" 123°21'00" Southernmost tip of Victoria, SE Vancouver I). Named by the HBC's James Douglas in 1842 after a species of red clover (*Trifolium*) that grew here in abundance. According to Douglas's grandson, this was the spot where the future gov of Vancouver I first stepped ashore from the *Cadboro* to make a detailed survey of the shoreline and decide on the best site for a new post. Ft Victoria would become the HBC headquarters on Canada's W coast and the future capital of BC.

Clute Point (52°10'05" 127°57'35" N side of Gunboat Passage, E of Bella Bella). John Stilwell Clute (1840–1929) was born at Kingston, Ont, came to Victoria in 1862 and joined the Cariboo gold rush. He operated a clothing store with C C Major in New Westminster, 1863–70, married Jennie Clarkson (1847–1925) at New Westminster in 1866, was mayor of that city in 1867 and also served as a councillor. Clute moved to Missouri, 1870–75, to work with his brother. Returning to New Westminster in 1878, he set up as a general merchant and druggist, and later was appointed a justice of the peace and collector of customs. Clute Point was formerly known as Steep Point. Clute Ck and Clute Lk near Kootenay Lk are named for Clute's son, also John Stilwell (1867–1924), who became a lawyer in New Westminster, his birthplace, then moved to Rossland in 1895, where he was alderman, 1898–1901, mayor in 1902 and 1904, and also a justice of the peace.

Cluxewe River (50°37'00" 127°10'00" Flows NW into Broughton Str, just W of Port McNeill). This Kwakwala name, which also appears in historic documents as Kliksiwi, Klucksiwi and Lex'si'we, has two meanings: "place of the changing river mouth" and "place of refuge." The Cluxewe Resort, owned by Ft Rupert's Kwakiutl First Nation band, is today located at the mouth of the river on the Klickseewy reserve, once an ancient village site. Nearby Cluxewe Mtn is named after the river.

Overlooking Vancouver's Coal Harbour in 1910. *Courtesy Tim Woodland*

Coal Harbour (49°17'30" 123°07'20" W end of Vancouver Hbr). Seams of coal were discovered here in 1859 by Francis Brockton, chief engineer of HMS *Plumper*, during a survey of Burrard Inlet by Capt George Richards. In fact, on his 1860 chart of the region, Richards gave the name Coal Peninsula to the entire body of land occupied today by Stanley Park and downtown Vancouver. The coal turned out to be of poor quality and was never mined, but the harbour soon became a centre for shipbuilding, sawmilling and other industries. These were cleared away in the 1960s, replaced by the luxurious Bayshore Inn and extensive marinas.

Coal Harbour (50°36'00" 127°35'00" N side of Holberg Inlet, Quatsino Sd, S of Port Hardy, NW Vancouver I). Coal was discovered at this location in the 1850s by a geologist working on the HBC's pioneer steamship *Beaver*. Numerous attempts were made over the next 40 years to develop the deposits (the crew of a British warship took on coal from this site in the early 1860s), but the seams were small and inferior, and a viable industry never evolved. An old trail connected Port Hardy to Coal Hbr, providing access to Quatsino Sd from the E coast of Vancouver I. When the trail was improved, about 1915, one of the coal-mining buildings was turned into a "roadhouse" for travellers. The Hole family acquired this operation in the 1920s, put in a dock and settled in the area. An RCAF flying-boat station was established on the harbour during WWII. This base was converted for whaling, 1947–67, and after that the residents of the area survived mainly from fishing. Coal Hbr was formerly known as Stephens Bay.

Coal Island (48°41'00" 123°22'00" Off NE end of Saanich Peninsula, N of Victoria). Joseph Pemberton, who worked as a surveyor for the HBC in the early 1850s and later became surveyor gen of the colony of Vancouver I, produced an early map of S Vancouver I in 1855 that named this island and identified coal on its E side. In the 1940s and '50s the property was owned by Capt Fred Lewis (*see* Lewis Bay).

C

Coburg Peninsula (48°25'00" 123°28'00" W side of Royal Roads, just SW of Victoria). Named after Queen Victoria's husband, Prince Albert of Saxe-Coburg and Gotha. Coburg is a city in Bavaria, Germany. In the 17th century it was the capital of the duchy of Saxe-Coburg; later it became one of the two capitals of the duchy of Saxe-Coburg and Gotha. Lt Cdr James Wood of HMS *Pandora*, who surveyed this area in 1847, also named nearby Saxe Point and Gotha Point. Albert Head, just to the S, had already been named the year before by Capt Henry Kellett of HMS *Herald*.

Cochrane Islands (50°03'00" 124°46'00" E side of Malaspina Peninsula, N end of Str of Georgia). Possibly named after Adm of the Fleet Sir Thomas John Cochrane (1789–1872), the unpopular first resident gov of Nfld, 1825–34, who was cdr-in-chief of the RN's China Station in the 1840s and cdr-in-chief for Portsmouth, 1852–55. He is not believed to have ever visited the BC coast, however. Another RN adm of this name, Rear Adm Arthur Auckland Pedro Cochrane (1824–1905), did serve as cdr-in-chief of the Pacific Station from 1873 to 1876, with his flag in HMS *Repulse*.

Cockatrice Bay (50°48'00" 126°50'00" SW side of Broughton I, NE end of Queen Charlotte Str). HMS *Cockatrice* was a 6-gun brigantine of 165 tonnes, designed by famous naval architect Sir Richard Seppings and built at Pembroke in 1832. The gunboat was stationed in S America in the 1830s and '40s and served as a tender to the flagships of the Pacific Station, 1848–57, before being decommissioned in 1858. It operated in BC waters in 1851–52 under master William Dillon.

Cockburn Bay. *See* Cape Cockburn.

Codville Hill (52°02'00" 127°53'00" Just SW of Codville Lagoon), **Codville Island** (52°03'00" 127°51'00" In Codville Lagoon), **Codville Lagoon** (52°03'00" 127°50'00" SW side of King I, SE of Bella Bella). James Codville (1837–1917), of Woodstock, Ont, came to BC in 1858 for the gold rush but found no wealth. Almost 30 years later he returned, with his wife, Fanny (1842–1931), and son, Benjamin (1881–1969), and worked for the Dept of Marine and Fisheries on the Skeena and Nass rivers. In 1894 he unwisely bought land and settled at Evans Inlet on remote King I, believing the spot would be named the GTP railroad terminus, but was saved from ruin when nearby Pointer I (qv) lighthouse was built in 1899, and he was hired as keeper. After his death, Ben took over the station and stayed until 1945, assisted by his wife, Annie Slade (1885–1968). Pointer I lighthouse was dismantled in 1989. Codville Lagoon became a 440-ha provincial marine park in 1965. Codville Hill was formerly known as Bare Hill.

Coffin Island (Just E of Coffin Point), **Coffin Point** (48°59'00" 123°45'00" W side of Stuart Channel at N entrance to Ladysmith Hbr, SE side of Vancouver I). Coffin Point was the site of a Chemainus First Nation village known as Kumalockasun. The area somehow was not included with the main Chemainus reserve, just to the NW, when the reserves were laid out in 1913. Coffin I is an old name, appearing on an Admiralty chart published in 1863. Coffin Point was named in association with the island by Cdr John Parry of HMS *Egeria* while conducting a survey of the area in 1903–4.

Coffin Island Point (48°26'00" 123°23'00" N side of Victoria Hbr, W of Lime Bay, SE end of Vancouver I). First Nation people in the vicinity had used Coffin I, named on Capt Henry Kellett's 1847 chart, as a cemetery for many years. Bodies were left there in wooden boxes but not buried, sometimes attracting relic hunters, vandals and arsonists. A lurid Victoria *Colonist* account of an 1867 fire mentions rats, "disturbed in the midst of their horrid meal," leaping into the water and swimming to the nearest shore. An 1889 article describes a brush fire "playing around the whitening bones, and shining through the sockets of the empty skulls." In the 1960s and '70s, landfills so altered the shoreline that the island became joined to the mainland, and in 1976 the name was changed to Coffin I Point.

Coghlan Anchorage (53°23'00" 129°16'00" W side of Promise I, junction of Grenville Channel and Douglas Channel, SW of Kitimat), **Coghlan Rock** (48°24'00" 123°28'00" S end of Royal Roads, just N of Albert Head, SW of Victoria), **Coghlan Rock** (54°26'30" 130°41'25" E of Moffat Is, Chatham Sd, NW of Prince Rupert). Lt James Edmond "Jerry" Coghlan was assistant surveying officer, 1868–70, aboard the *Beaver*, a historic paddle steamer the RN hired from the HBC for survey duties on the BC coast. In later years Coghlan participated in or led surveys of Mauritius (1876–78), W Australia (1882–87) and England (1887–92, with HMS *Triton*). He was promoted to staff cdr in 1879 and reached the rank of capt, retired, in 1897. RN surveyor Lt Daniel Pender named these features about 1869. *W*

Colburne Passage (48°42'00" 123°25'00" Between Piers I and NE end of Saanich Peninsula, N of Victoria). Edward S Colburne (d 1863) served aboard HMS *Hawke* in 1855 and was promoted to 2nd master in 1857. The name was adopted in 1910.

Cole Island (48°27'00" 123°27'00" N end of Esquimalt Hbr, just W of Victoria). Edmund Picoti Cole was master aboard HMS *Fisgard*, under Capt John Duntze, and served on the Pacific Station from 1843 to 1847. He retired in 1858 with the rank of staff cdr and died in 1877. Lt Cdr James Wood of HMS *Pandora* named numerous features in Esquimalt Hbr after the officers of *Fisgard* during his

1847 survey. The tiny, 1,500-sq-m island was the site of Esquimalt's main RN magazine or ammunition depot from 1859 to 1905, by which time wooden walkways led to more than a dozen thick-walled brick buildings. The RCN also used the island for storage until WWII. Attempts to sell the property were abandoned in the early 1960s, and Cole I, though derelict and heavily vandalized, is now a national historic site. Five of the largest buildings are still standing. It is also known as Magazine I.

Cole Rock (50°01'00" 127°27'00" W of McLean I, Kyuquot Sd, NW side of Vancouver I). Frederick Cole, a native of Nfld, was born in 1854 and came to BC in 1890 with his wife, Emma (1857–1932), and family. He worked as a sealing capt during the Victoria-based pelagic fur seal hunt aboard the *Penelope* (1892–93), in which he was the first to seal on the Japanese coast, and the *Dora Sieward* (1894). In 1901 he had command of the *Aurora*. Named about 1937 by regional hydrographer Henri Parizeau.

Coles Bay (48°38'00" 123°28'00" W side of Saanich Peninsula, N of Victoria). John Coles (1832–1910), born at London, England, was a midshipman aboard HMS *Thetis*, under Capt Augustus Kuper, on the Pacific Station, 1851–53. He retired from the RN after the Crimean War, returned to BC in 1857, took up land and farmed near the bay now named for him, marrying Mary Harcus at Victoria in 1860. Coles represented Saanich in Vancouver I's legislative assembly, 1860–63. In 1866 he went back to the UK, claiming that the land on Vancouver I was not even good enough for growing potatoes. He later became map curator of the Royal Geographical Society, 1877–1900, and travel editor of *Field* magazine. Named in 1860 by RN surveyor Capt George Richards of HMS *Plumper*. *W*

Collingwood Channel (49°23'00" 123°25'00" Entrance of Howe Sd, between Bowen I and Keats I, NW of Vancouver), **Collingwood Point** (50°32'00" 126°00'00" N side of Port Neville, N side of Johnstone Str). Capt Cuthbert Collingwood (1750–1810) of HMS *Barfleur* was present at Adm Lord Howe's 1794 victory over a French fleet in the English Channel, known as the Glorious First of June. He also participated at the Battle of St Vincent as cdr of HMS *Excellent*. By 1805 he was a vice adm and second-in-command to Adm Lord Nelson at the Battle of Trafalgar aboard HMS *Royal Sovereign*. After this victory he was named Baron Collingwood and commanded the RN's Mediterranean squadron until his death. Cuthbert Rk and Collingwood Mtn are also named for him, as is the town of Collingwood in Ont. *W*

Collins Bay (53°33'00" 128°44'00" Just inside the entrance of Gardner Canal, S of Kitimat), **Collins Point** (53°32'00" 128°45'00" W entrance to Collins Bay). Lt Cdr William Collins served on the BC coast, 1873–75, in command of HMS *Boxer*, based at Esquimalt. In 1876 he was directed by the Admiralty to report on the suitability of various BC inlets, including Gardner Canal, as possible termini for the CPR. He eventually achieved the rank of rear adm, retired, in 1901. Named about 1875 by members of the CPR survey. *W*

Collinson Point (48°52'00" 123°21'00" SW point of Galiano I, Gulf Is). William Tonkins "Tom" Collinson (1840–1911), a native of Yorkshire, arrived in BC in 1858 in pursuit of gold. In the 1870s he moved to Mayne I, where he opened a store at Miners Bay, was appointed postmaster and magistrate, and farmed. He and his wife, Mary Olifers (whom he married at Victoria in 1884, his first wife, also Mary, having died the year before), turned their home into a boarding house in 1895. His daughter Emma and her husband, Brooke Naylor, expanded this business after Collinson's death and named it Grandview Lodge; in the early 2000s it was still operating as the Springwater Lodge, one of BC's oldest inns. Named by Cdr John Parry of HMS *Egeria*, who re-surveyed Active Pass in 1904. *W*

Collins Shoal (48°59'00" 123°46'00" In Evening Cove, N side of entrance to Ladysmith Hbr, SE side of Vancouver I). L Collins was a petty officer aboard HMS *Egeria*, under Cdr John Parry, during Str of Georgia surveys in 1903–4. The name was adopted by the Geographic Board of Canada in 1924.

Collishaw Point (49°33'00" 124°41'00" NW side of Hornby I, Str of Georgia). Raymond Collishaw (1893–1976) was born and raised at Nanaimo and found his first job on a fisheries patrol boat, then took flying lessons and became a pilot with the Royal Naval Air Service. He shot down 60 enemy aircraft in WWI—the third-highest total on the Allied side and fifth-highest overall—and was awarded the DSC, DSO and DFC. He stayed with the RAF, flying and fighting in Russia and Iraq, and in WWII commanded the Egypt Group (Desert Air Force), which overwhelmed the Italian air force in N Africa. He was promoted air vice-marshal in 1941 but retired two years later after disagreements with superiors and returned to BC, where he co-owned a mine near Barkerville. Formerly known as Boulder Point. *E*

Collison Bay (52°17'00" 131°08'00" SE of Skincuttle Inlet, SE end of Moresby I, QCI), **Collison Point** (53°47'00" 132°13'00" SW side of Masset Sd, entrance to Masset Inlet, Graham I, QCI). William Henry Collison (1847–1922), from Ireland, graduated from the Church Missionary College in London and came with his wife, nurse Marion M Goodwin (1850–1919), to William Duncan's Anglican mission at Metlakatla in 1873. In 1876 the couple established the first mission to the Haida; two years later, Collison was ordained. He returned to Metlakatla in 1879 and transferred to Kincolith, on Nass Bay, in 1884. He was based there until his death, becoming one of the longest-

C

serving missionaries on the N coast. Marion provided vital medical services to the region, and Collison, who made himself fluent in Tsimshian, Haida and Nisga'a, translated many Christian texts into Native languages. He also published a memoir, *In the Wake of the War Canoe*, in 1915; it was reprinted, edited by Charles Lillard, in 1981. *E W*

Colnett Point (53°59'00" 132°40'00" Head of Naden Hbr, N end of Graham I, QCI), **Mount Colnett** (49°10'28" 125°50'14" E side of Meares I, Clayoquot Sd, W side of Vancouver I). James Colnett (1753–1806) was one of the earliest British fur traders to appear on the BC coast. A former RN officer who had served on Capt James Cook's second S Pacific expedition, 1772–75, he was sent to the PNW by Richard Etches and the King George's Sd Co in 1786, in command of the *Prince of Wales* and the smaller *Princess Royal* (under Charles Duncan). In 1789, as part of a new expedition organized by John Meares, Colnett returned with the *Argonaut* and the *Princess Royal* (now under Thomas Hudson) to Nootka Sd, where he was arrested by Spanish cdr Estéban José Martínez. The vessels and crews were seized and sent to Mexico, an act that brought England and Spain close to war. After his release, Colnett continued to trade and to serve with the RN and also wrote an account of his travels. Two scholarly editions of his important PNW journals have been published. *E W*

Colston Cove (48°48'39" 123°16'45" E side of N Pender I, Gulf Is), **Colston Islet** (52°30'00" 129°02'00" Entrance to Weeteeam Bay, SW end of Aristazabal I). Sapper Robert W Colston, from Scotland, was a member of the Columbia detachment of Royal Engineers, which served in BC 1858–63. He and his wife, Frances (1836–1918, née Christie), arrived in the colony in 1859 on the *Thames City*. Permanent damage to his hand, caused by a rock slide when he was working on the Cariboo Rd, did not appear to hamper his acting career with the Royal Engineers' Dramatic Club. His 1863 role "as a ballet girl created perhaps more laughter than anything else in the evening," according to the *British Colonist*. "The real excellencies of his dancing may not have been quite appreciated." Colston later became secretary to BC gov Frederick Seymour and moved with his family to Victoria. His son Robert Christie Colston (1860–1953), born at Sapperton, farmed on Galiano and Mayne islands before buying land on N Pender I in 1890 with his brother Sweany (1868–1949). His widowed mother, sister Florence Maria Phelps (1864–1949) and her four children joined him there. Robert Jr also farmed at Ladner and Langley Prairie in later years but always returned to Pender. Colston Cove is named for him while Colston It is named for his father.

Colton Islet (52°58'00" 132°09'00" Entrance to Mudge Inlet, Moresby I, QCI), **Colton Point** (52°59'00" 132°09'00" Just N of Colton It). Lt Henry Colton Mudge of HMS *Thetis* was in this area in 1852. *See* Mudge Inlet.

Columbia Cove (50°08'00" 127°41'00" W side of Nasparti Inlet, SE of Brooks Peninsula, NW side of Vancouver I), **Columbia Islet** (49°12'00" 125°51'00" E side of Lemmens Inlet, Clayoquot Sd, W side of Vancouver I). The *Columbia Rediviva*, only 25 m long and 192 tonnes, was built at Plymouth, Massachusetts, probably in 1773. It left Boston in 1787 under Capt John Kendrick and reached Nootka Sd the following year in company with the smaller *Lady Washington*, under Capt Robert Gray. In 1789, Gray took the fur-laden *Columbia* back to Boston, via China, making it the first US vessel to circumnavigate the globe. On its second voyage to the PNW, with Gray in command, *Columbia* traded in the QCI before spending the winter of 1791–92 at Adventure Cove (qv). Gray then sailed S and became the first white explorer to enter the mouth of the Columbia R, which he named for his ship. After another summer's trading on the BC coast, Gray sold his furs in China and returned to Boston in 1793. All the BC names that derive from the Columbia R (including Columbia Lk, Columbia Mtns, Columbia Icefield, Mt Columbia and the province of British Columbia itself) are indirectly named for Gray's vessel. Presumably **Columbia Beach** (49°21'00" 124°23'00" N of Qualicum Beach, E side of Vancouver I) and **Columbia Point** (55°25'00" 130°00'55" E side of Portland Canal, S of Stewart) are too. The origin of the name *Columbia Rediviva* itself is uncertain. *Rediviva* means "revived" in Spanish and may indicate that the ship had been rebuilt. Columbia, a poetic word for America, is derived from Christopher Columbus. Some historians suggest that the vessel was named for Columba (Latin for dove), the 6th-century Irish saint who converted the Picts to Christianity and founded the Scottish monastery of Iona. The historic ship was decommissioned in 1806.

Columbine Bay (49°25'00" 123°19'00" N end of Bowen I, Howe Sd, NW of Vancouver). Possibly named after the red columbine, *Aquilegia formosa*, which grows widely throughout BC. Columbine Peak in northern BC is also named for this delicate plant.

Colvile Island (48°26'00" 123°23'00" W side of Victoria Hbr, NE of Work Point). British merchant Andrew Wedderburn Colvile (1779–1856) owned sugar plantations in Jamaica and was a shrewd and practical businessman. He first acquired stock in the HBC in 1809 after his brother-in-law Thomas Douglas, 5th Earl of Selkirk and founder of the Red River Colony, became a shareholder. Colvile served as HBC deputy gov, 1839–52, and gov, 1852–56. His son Eden Colvile was also an HBC gov. The name of Colvile I, bestowed by HBC officers at Ft Victoria and often misspelled Colville, was adopted by Capt Henry Kellett when he surveyed Victoria Hbr in 1846. Colvile Town was an early name for Nanaimo. The Colville Range, N of E Queen Charlotte Str, is named for Andrew Colville McKenzie, whose father (*see* Mackenzie Sd) ran Victoria's pioneer Craigflower Farm. However, Andrew's middle name honours the HBC gov (and the farm was named after Colvile's English estate).

Colwood (48°26'00" 123°29'00" W of Victoria, S end of Vancouver I), **Colwood Rocks** (49°48'00" 126°56'00" Entrance to Port Langford, NW Nootka I, W side of Vancouver I). Capt Edward Langford (*see* Langford) and his family were among the first immigrants to the colony of Vancouver I, arriving in 1851. Langford had been hired to manage one of four farms operated by the Puget's Sd Agricultural Co, a subsidiary of the HBC, and he named his farm, just W of Esquimalt Hbr, after his family's estate of Colwood in Sussex, UK. Though still a residential suburb of Victoria, Colwood became a separate city in 1985 and is home to the historic sites of Ft Rodd Hill and Fisgard Lighthouse, as well as Royal Roads Univ and some RCN facilities. Colwood Ck and Colwood Lk also derive their names from Colwood Farm. *E*

Commander Point (52°25'00" 131°34'00" Just W of Soulsby Cove, Gowgaia Bay, W side of Moresby I, QCI). After artist and RCN officer Cdr Henry Soulsby, who spent much of his career on the BC coast and anchored here in 1935 with HMCS *Armentières*. See Soulsby Cove.

Commerell Point (50°34'00" 128°15'00" S entrance to Raft Cove, S of San Josef Bay, NW end of Vancouver I). Adm Sir John Edmund Commerell, GCB, VC (1829–1901), had an esteemed career in the RN. He won his VC during the Crimean War for a daring commando attack on a Russian supply depot. Over the years he served in S America, China and W Africa and was cdr-in-chief at Portsmouth in 1888–91. He was a lord of the Admiralty, 1879–80, an MP, 1885–88, and a great favourite of Queen Victoria. The northernmost point of Vancouver I was named after him by Capt George Richards in 1862, but its Spanish name, Cape Sutil, was restored in 1906. Commerell Point was

adopted in 1910. Edmund Rk off Cape Sutil is also named for him. *W*

Commodore Passage (49°09'00" 123°40'00" E of Gabriola I, Gulf Is). Named in 1944 in honour of the Royal Vancouver Yacht Club, which has a facility near here on the SW side of Tugboat I. The senior official of a yacht club often sports the nominal title Commodore.

Commodore Point (48°25'00" 123°14'00" S point of Discovery I, off Oak Bay and SE tip of Vancouver I). The 1,071-tonne, 65-m sidewheeler *Commodore* was built at NY in 1851 and ran on the San Francisco–Portland route. In 1859, during the Fraser R gold rush, it ferried thousands of miners from Victoria to Ft Hope. Purchased by the California Steam Navigation Co and renamed *Brother Jonathan*, the steamer ran between San Francisco and Portland, Puget Sd and Victoria until 1865, when it struck a reef off N California in a gale and went to pieces, with the loss of 166 lives. Named in 1858 by RN surveyor Capt George Richards. *W*

Comox (49°40'59" 124°56'05" Just SE of Courtenay, E side of Vancouver I), **Comox Bar** (49°39'00" 124°54'00" SE of Comox Hbr), **Comox Harbour** (49°40'00" 124°57'00" Just SW of Comox, Str of Georgia). The name is an abbreviation of a Lekwiltok (Kwakwaka'wakw) First Nation term meaning "abundance" or "plenty"; the spellings Komous, Comuck and Comax have also been recorded. Comox Ck, Comox Lk, Comox Gap and Comox Glacier all have the same origin. The first white settlers moved to the area in 1862, and the agricultural community of Comox developed from about 1874. CFB Comox, home to air-sea rescue and maritime patrol aircraft, was established in 1942. Comox Hbr was formerly known as Port Augusta, while Comox Bar was identified on earlier charts as Kelp Bar. *E W*

Comox's marinas and public wharf sit safely behind extensive stone breakwaters. *Peter Vassilopoulos*

C

Compton Island (50°35'00" 126°41'00" S of Swanson I, Blackfish Sd, SE end of Queen Charlotte Str), **Compton Point** (50°53'00" 126°53'00" NW entrance to Wells Passage, NE Queen Charlotte Str). Pym Nevins Compton (1838–79) was born in Essex, England, and came to Victoria in 1859 as purser on the HBC ship *Labouchere*. He was aboard this vessel when it was seized (and later released) by a Tlingit group on an 1862 trading voyage to Alaska. He was later stationed at Ft Simpson and by 1865 was in charge of the HBC post at Ft Rupert. Compton returned to England the following year but came W again, to California, and died in Victoria, as did his wife, Catherine (1848–80). He was a talented artist and linguist; his paintings of northern BC, many of which are at BC Archives, are of much historical interest. *W*

Comrie Head (53°49'00" 130°17'00" NW side of Pitt I, S of Prince Rupert). Peter Comrie was the surgeon on HMS *Sparrowhawk*, under cdrs Edwin Porcher and Henry Mist, and served on the BC coast, 1865–70, based at Esquimalt. In 1869 he examined the mangled bodies of the crew of the *John Bright*, found at Hesquiat near the wreck of their vessel, and testified at the trial of several accused Nuu-chah-nulth men, two of whom were found guilty of murdering the seamen and hanged. He also attended the final illness of BC gov Frederick Seymour, who died at Bella Coola in 1869 aboard *Sparrowhawk*. Comrie himself died in 1882. *W*

Concepcion Point (49°40'00" 126°29'00" E tip of Bligh I, Nootka Sd, W side of Vancouver I). The Spanish naval vessel *Concepcion*, commanded by Francisco Eliza, was one of the ships sent from Mexico in 1790 to re-establish the garrison at Nootka Sd.

Conconi Reef (48°49'00" 123°17'00" In Navy Channel, between N Pender I and Mayne I, Gulf Is). Thomas David Conconi (b 1829), from Margate, Kent, was a paymaster aboard HMS *Pylades*, under Capt Michael De Courcy, and served on the Pacific Station, 1859–60. Named by RN surveyor Capt George Richards of HMS *Plumper* about 1860.

Coneehaw Rock (54°10'00" 132°56'00" Off Gunia Point, NW side of Graham I, QCI). Blakow-Coneehaw and Gunia are both corruptions of the name of the head chief of Kiusta village at the time of initial European contact. William Douglas of the *Iphigenia Nubiana*, sent to the QCI by John Meares in 1788, was the first fur trader to encounter this powerful figure; the two men exchanged names in a complex Haida ceremony. The chief became well known to visitors, some of whom referred to Parry Passage, where Kiusta was located, as Cunneyah's Strs (there are many spellings of this name). He later migrated to the Prince of Wales Archipelago in SE Alaska with most of the members of his tribe. *D*

Conglomerate Point (53°04'00" 131°51'00" N shore of Cumshewa Inlet, NE side of Moresby I, QCI). Named for its mineralogical characteristics by George M Dawson of the Geological Survey of Canada on an 1878 field trip. Conglomerate is a sedimentary rock made up of small individual stones cemented together. Conglomerate Bluff, Conglomerate Ck and Conglomerate Mtn in northern BC are presumably all named for the same substance. The Haida First Nation name for the point is Q'ayraan T'iis Kun.

Connel Islands (54°25'00" 130°56'00" In Hudson Bay Passage, S of Dundas I, just NW of Prince Rupert). The name, which appears on an Admiralty chart dated 1912, may come from a Gaelic word meaning "fury" or "uproar" and could refer to the strong currents that swirl around these small islands and reefs. Connel Ck, which flows into Anderson Lk, W of Lillooet, has a similar derivation. It was, in fact, chosen to replace an older name, Roaring Ck, which was duplicated elsewhere.

Connis Cove (53°45'12" 130°17'30" NW side of McCauley I, S of Porcher I and Prince Rupert), **Connis Islet** (53°45'00" 130°19'00" In Beaver Passage, between McCauley I and Spicer I), **Connis Point** (50°18'00" 124°55'00" NW side of W Redonda I, NE of Campbell R), **Connis Rocks** (54°34'00" 130°37'00" In Chatham Sd, between Dundas I and N end of Tsimpsean Peninsula, NW of Prince Rupert). Connis was the name of a Skye terrier that accompanied its owner, Lt Daniel Pender, master of the hired RN survey vessel *Beaver*, on his hydrographic journeys along the BC coast, 1863–70. *W*

Connolly Point (50°54'00" 126°47'00" N side of Sutlej Channel, N of N Broughton I and E end of Queen Charlotte Str). Cdr Matthew Connolly (1817–1901) served on the Pacific Station, 1854–57, with HMS *Monarch*, flagship of Rear Adm Henry Bruce. He was leader of an 1856 military expedition to the Cowichan Valley that captured a First Nation man suspected of shooting and attempting to kill a British settler. Connolly was back on the BC coast in 1863–64 with the rank of capt, in command of HMS *Sutlej*, flagship of Rear Adm John Kingcome. During his RN career he also had command of HMS *Hannibal* and *Pallas* and eventually reached the rank of vice adm, retired, in 1880. The nearby Matthew Range and Mt Connolly are named for him as well. *W*

Conover Cove (48°56'00" 123°33'00" SW side of Wallace I, NE of Saltspring I, Gulf Is). Photographer David B Conover (1919–83) and his first wife, Jeanne, purchased Wallace I for $18,000 in 1946, after his discharge from the US Army, and together built a rustic summer resort there. David, from LA, wrote several books about his Gulf Is experiences and also about his role in the "discovery" of actress Marilyn Monroe and his friendship with her (he had been commissioned in 1945 by his CO, Ronald

Conover Cove, part of Wallace Island Marine Provincial Park, is a popular Gulf Islands anchorage. *Kevin Oke*

Reagan, to take promotional photos of women working for the US war effort; one of them was Marilyn). The Conovers bought and logged other nearby islands, including Secret I (qv), to keep their resort business going. They separated in 1967, and most of Wallace I was sold to a group of teachers from Seattle for $240,000. David, who remarried twice, retained 4.4 ha and his house and remained on the island until the year he died. Wallace I became a provincial marine park in 1990.

Conroy Island (52°31'00" 129°24'00" Off SW side of Aristazabal I). Virtually nothing is known about Sapper James Conroy, who was a member of the Columbia detachment of Royal Engineers, which served in BC 1858–63. The island was formerly known as S Gander I but was renamed by the hydrographic service in 1927.

Constance Bank (48°21'00" 123°21'00" In Juan de Fuca Str, S of Victoria), **Constance Cove** (48°26'00" 123°26'00" E side of Esquimalt Hbr, just W of Victoria). HMS *Constance*, a 50-gun frigate, was a presence on the Pacific Station from 1846 to 1849, under Capt George Courtenay. The 78-m, 1,927-tonne ship spent much time in Mexican ports, loading gold and silver that foreign merchants wished to remove from Mexico during that country's war with the US (1846–48). In 1848 it became one of the first RN vessels to anchor in Esquimalt Hbr. The *Constance* was converted to steam in 1862 and served on the N America and W Indies stations until 1868; it was sold and broken up in 1875. A farm established in the early 1850s near Esquimalt Hbr by Puget's Sd Agricultural Co, an HBC subsidiary, was named after Constance Cove. Managed by pioneer settler Thomas Skinner, it was also known as Oaklands. Both cove and bank were named in 1847 by

Lt Cdr James Wood, an early surveyor of the S end of Vancouver I with HMS *Pandora*. The cove was shown as Village Bay on Joseph Pemberton's historic 1855 map of SE Vancouver I. *See* Courtenay for additional information.

Conuma Peak (49°49'53" 126°18'36" E of the Conuma R, NW of Gold R, central Vancouver I), **Conuma River** (49°48'00" 126°26'00" Flows S into Moutcha Bay, Tlupana Inlet, Nootka Sd, W side of Vancouver I). Conuma Peak (1,481 m), with its sharp pinnacle, is the most conspicuous mountain visible from Nootka Sd and was a landmark for all early visitors to the region. On Dionisio Alcalá-Galiano's early chart it was marked Pico de Tasis, after Chief Maquinna's principal village at Tahsis. On later charts the name was altered to Conuma, the Nuu-chah-nulth First Nation word for a high or rocky peak (also spelled Konoomah). According to Alcalá-Galiano's journal, "the corpses of the chiefs are borne up in pomp by the common people, with continuous lamentations, to the slopes [of this peak], and are wrapped in splendid robes of sea otter, placed in wooden boxes in a sitting posture and hung up in the branches of trees." The river, of course, takes its name from the mountain. *W*

Coode Island (50°02'00" 124°45'00" Off N end of Coode Peninsula), **Coode Peninsula** (50°01'00" 124°44'00" Malaspina Inlet, E side of Malaspina Peninsula, NE end of Str of Georgia). Capt Trevenen Penrose Coode served on the Pacific Station, 1864–66, based at Esquimalt, as cdr of HMS *Sutlej*, flagship of Rear Adm Joseph Denman, the station's cdr-in-chief. He participated in the punitive 1864 campaign against the Ahousaht First Nation in Clayoquot Sd—a response to the killing of the crew of the trading schooner *Kingfisher*—during which nine villages were shelled and burnt (*see* Denman I). Coode attained the rank of vice adm, retired, in 1884. Nearby Trevenen Bay and Penrose Bay are also named for him.

Cook Bank, Cook Channel. *See* Cape Cook.

Cook Bay (49°33'00" 124°15'00" SW side of Texada I, Str of Georgia). Ezra S Cook obtained a Crown grant of land on this bay in 1890. In 1893 he married Louise McCutcheon at Nanaimo, where he was listed as a farmer on the 1898 BC voters list. In 1902, Cook also received Crown grants in the New Westminster land district. Cook Ck on Texada is named for him as well.

Cook Cove (48°55'10" 123°24'14" N of Montague Hbr, NE side of Galiano I, Gulf Is). John (c 1865–1955) and Mary Cook (b 1865) were early Galiano settlers who farmed at this location. According to author and historian Peter Murray, John's father, Nicholas Cook (1832–70), was one of Mayne I's earliest settlers. When he was about three, John was apparently kidnapped from Mayne by Haida paddlers and spent 10 years in the QCI as a slave. One year, while accompanying his captors on their annual voyage to Victoria, he recognized his former home and managed to escape and find his mother, Kitty, a Cowichan woman, who had remarried after his father died. John worked on a Saanich farm and later took up land on Galiano I, where he married, raised a family and grew apples. He also laboured on other island farms and was noted for his excellent split-rail fences.

Cook Island (50°35'00" 126°32'00" In Beware Passage, N of Harbledown I and W Johnstone Str). Lance Cpl Edwin Victor Cook, from Alert Bay, was killed in action on Sept 30, 1944, while serving in the Netherlands with the Calgary Highlanders, Royal Canadian Infantry Corps. He is buried at Bergen-op-Zoom Canadian War Cemetery, NW of Antwerp.

Cook Point (49°46'40" 124°03'15" NE side of Nelson I, Jervis Inlet, NW of Vancouver). Named in 1999 after Flying Officer Roy James Cook, who was killed Jan 28, 1944, when his Lancaster bomber was shot down near Bazencourt, France, after a bombing mission (his 15th) over Berlin with No 625 Squadron. He was born at Toronto in 1921 and moved with his family to Victoria in 1933. Cook travelled to England to enlist with the RAF in 1941 and was awarded the DFM in 1943 after completing a successful bombing raid over Frankfurt despite being forced to fly at a low elevation due to engine damage. He is buried at Marissel French National Cemetery in Oise.

Cook Point (53°48'00" 132°12'00" NW side of Masset Sd, Graham I, QCI). Brothers Jack and Bill Cook were townsite managers for the Anchor Investment Co, which promoted and developed a new community in 1909, originally called Graham City, adjacent to the ancient Haida village of Masset. Graham City is now known as Masset, while the historic Haida village is usually called Old Masset. The name of the point was adopted in 1948.

Coolidge Point (52°21'00" 127°43'00" E side of Cousins Inlet, Dean Channel, W of Ocean Falls). H H Coolidge was chief engineer for Pacific Mills Ltd at the Ocean Falls pulp and paper mill from 1916 until at least 1922. The feature was formerly known as David Point but was renamed by regional hydrographer Henri Parizeau in 1924.

Coomes Bank (49°13'00" 126°00'00" Calmus Passage, N side of Vargas I, Clayoquot Sd, W side of Vancouver I). Ferzando E Coomes pre-empted land at Long Beach in 1896 and received a Crown grant in 1912. Coomes Bank was formerly known as North Bank but was renamed in 1933 by regional hydrographer Henri Parizeau.

Cooper Cove (48°23'00" 123°39'00" N side of Sooke Basin, S end of Vancouver I). Edward James Lloyd Cooper (1814–52) was 3rd lt aboard the RN survey vessel *Herald*, under Capt Henry Kellett (who named this feature), and served on the BC coast in 1846. He took part in the search for Sir John Franklin's missing Arctic expedition in 1849–51 as a lt on HMS *Plover*, spending two winters in the far N, at Kotzebue Sd and Port Clarence. *W*

Cooper Inlet (52°04'00" 128°05'00" N side of Hunter I, SE of Bella Bella). Capt James Cooper, born in England in 1821, entered the marine service of the HBC in 1844. He was in command of the *Mary Dare* in 1846 and the *Columbia* in 1849. He resigned from the HBC in 1849 to become an early independent settler on Vancouver I at Metchosin, where, in 1851, he established Bilston Farm, managed by Thomas Blinkhorn (*see* Blinkhorn Peninsula). Cooper brought out from England, in pieces, a small iron vessel, the 41-tonne *Alice*, which he used on trading ventures between the PNW and Hawaii and San Francisco. These enterprises threatened the HBC's monopoly on trade, and he was thwarted by HBC officials at every turn, causing him to become a vocal opponent of the company and its stifling influence on the colony. As a member of the three-man council appointed to advise the gov of Vancouver I, Cooper was in regular conflict with James Douglas. He was appointed harbourmaster at Victoria in 1859 and helped select the site for Race Rks lighthouse. From 1860 to 1868 he served as New Westminster's harbourmaster, then was BC's first agent for the federal Dept of Marine and Fisheries from 1872 until 1879, when he was charged with fraud, skipped bail and fled the country with his family to California. Named in 1866 by RN surveyor Lt Daniel Pender of the hired HBC vessel *Beaver*. *W*

Cooper Island (48°52'00" 125°21'00" In the Broken Group, Barkley Sd, W side of Vancouver I). Named about 1934 after George A Cooper, who obtained a Crown grant of land at the entrance to Uchucklesit Inlet in 1892. This was the same year that the Barclay Sd Land & Improvement Co announced that it would be developing a new town named Barclay on the inlet. The remote location was "the natural terminus for the coming transcontinental line," according to the company's advertisements, and its harbour had been "recommended to the Imperial government for the naval station and drydock." Nothing ever came of the scheme, of course. A real-estate broker named George Arthur Cooper, baptized in New Westminster in 1864, appears in the 1892 Victoria directory and on the 1898 BC voters list.

Cooper Reach (50°41'00" 125°28'00" Head of Loughborough Inlet, N of E Johnstone Str). Lt Henry Towry Miles Cooper (1839–1877) of the Royal Marines, born in Berkshire, UK, served in China, 1856–59, and was involved in the capture of Canton. He was part of a volunteer group of about 165 marines sent from China to BC in HMS *Tribune* in 1859. Most of the men went to New Westminster, but Cooper and 24 others remained at Esquimalt for duty in the Victoria area. A dispute arose that year between GB and the US over the ownership of the San Juan archipelago, and Cooper spent the next seven years with the joint military force that occupied San Juan I (after which the disagreement was settled politically). In 1864 he also served as aide-de-camp to BC gov Frederick Seymour during the so-called Chilcotin War, when Tsilhqot'in warriors killed a number of BC settlers and roadbuilders, and a military force was sent to capture them. He retired from the Royal Marines in 1872 and was appointed collector of customs at Bathurst, Gambia, W Africa, where he died. Nearby Towry Head also commemorates him, as do Towry Point and Miles Point on Seymour Inlet. Mt Cooper, just S of Miles Point, is probably named for this officer as well.

Coopte Point (49°42'00" 126°35'00" SE entrance to Tahsis Inlet, Nootka Sd, W side of Vancouver I). Coopte was the name of a long-abandoned winter village on this site belonging to the Mowachaht people, who are members of the Nuu-chah-nulth First Nation. José Mariano Moziño, the scientist on Juan Francisco de la Bodega y Quadra's 1792 expedition to Nootka Sd, left a description of a potlatch at Coopte, held in honour of the coming of age of Chief Maquinna's daughter. It was published in his *Noticias de Nutka*, which has been translated in a scholarly edition by Iris Higbie Wilson. The name of the point was adopted in 1935, as submitted by the hydrographic service.

Copeland Islands (50°00'00" 124°48'00" Off Malaspina Peninsula, NE end of Str of Georgia). Joe Copeland was a well-known handlogger and trapper who came to the Desolation Sd area around 1900 and lived at Portage Cove. He had been a bugler in the US Civil War and then joined a gang that robbed stagecoaches before he escaped to Canada one step ahead of the law. He carried a Luger pistol and, according to coastal pioneer Jim Spilsbury, "used to meet the steamboat dressed in a full Confederate Army uniform, complete with the little cap that kind of folded in the middle." The Copelands, formerly known as the

The Copeland Islands off Malaspina Peninsula. *Peter Vassilopoulos*

Ragged Is but renamed by the hydrographic service about 1945, became a provincial marine park in 1971.

Copper Bay (53°10'00" 131°47'00" NE side of Moresby I, QCI). George M Dawson of the Geological Survey of Canada named this site in 1878 to recognize the 1862 mining efforts of English prospector Edmund Cosworth Waddington. Waddington, who was related to BC entrepreneur Alfred Waddington (*see* Waddington Bay), had come to Victoria for the Cariboo gold rush but ended up in the QCI instead, lured by earlier discoveries of copper in the area. He hired a crew and sank a 60-m shaft with two crosscuts, then gave the project up and left the country. Nearby Copper Ck is named after the bay. *D*

Copper Island (49°45'25" 124°09'30" W of Nelson I, entrance to Jervis Inlet). Two possible explanations for this name have been advanced: a narrow vein of copper supposedly runs across Nelson I; and in the 1940s local residents would careen their boats there and copperpaint them. The name was adopted in 1991 for use on large-scale hydrographic charts.

Copper Islands (52°21'00" 131°13'00" Off entrance to Skincuttle Inlet, SE side of Moresby I, QCI). While George M Dawson of the Geological Survey of Canada appears to have named this island group in 1878, the individual islands, including E Copper I, were named by Francis Poole in 1862. The QCI had seen a short-lived gold rush in 1851–53; subsequent mining surveys in 1859 by William Downie and Capt Robert Torrens indicated the presence of copper and coal. Poole, a young mining engineer with the Queen Charlotte Mining Co of Victoria, spent 1862–64 searching for copper on and around nearby Burnaby I. His labours were unrewarding (and it appears that he helped spread the annihilating scourge of smallpox among the Haida), but he fell in love with the archipelago and wrote an early, if unremarkable, book about the area, published in 1872. *D*

Copp Island (50°03'00" 127°11'00" Entrance to Dixie Cove, E side of Hohoae I, Kyuquot Sd, NW side of

C

Vancouver I). William Harvey Copp (1842–1928), from NB, was active in the pelagic sealing industry in the late 19th century. He was one of the few Vancouver-based sealers (most were from Victoria), arriving in that city in 1887. He built the schooner *Vancouver Belle* and sealed off Russia in 1891, but the following year he was boarded by the crew of a Russian warship, the *Zabiaka*, and taken to Petropavlovsk. Copp's ship and cargo were seized, and he and his crew were given another confiscated Victoria schooner, the worn-out, unseaworthy *Rosie Olsen*, to make their way home in. After this money-losing experience he retired from the marine trade and became a stevedore. Formerly known as Gun I.

Cordero Channel north of Sonora Island. *Peter Vassilopoulos*

Coquitlam Island (53°51'00" 130°35'00" Between Goschen I and W side of Porcher I, SW of Prince Rupert). The 230-tonne *Coquitlam* was a small steel freighter built at Glasgow in 1891 and assembled at Vancouver for the Union Steamship Co. In 1892 it was chartered by the Victoria Sealing Co to carry supplies to its schooners in the Gulf of Alaska and bring back their skins but was seized by a US revenue cutter for allegedly operating in US territorial waters. Taken to Sitka and later released under bond, the vessel was the cause of a long-running international legal dispute that was not completely settled until 1931. In 1894 the *Coquitlam* was chartered by the New England Fish Co, which had a halibut-packing station near Coquitlam I. The 39-m ship was rebuilt in 1897 with more passenger amenities and ran to mostly northern ports, including Alaska during the Klondike gold rush, until sold in 1923 and renamed the *Bervin*. During WWI it operated as HMCS *Hespeler*. After further adventures, this pioneer vessel's hull was turned into a herring barge in 1950 and eventually became part of the breakwater at Sointula on Malcolm I in 1959. The Kwayhquitlam or Coquitlam people, part of the Coast Salish First Nation, are associated with the area around the Coquitlam R, just E of Vancouver. Their name, which comes from a Salishan term for "small red salmon," has also been applied to Coquitlam Mtn, Coquitlam Lk, another Coquitlam I in the lake and the Lower Mainland communities of Coquitlam and Port Coquitlam. *E*

Corbett Point (53°17'00" 129°23'00" NW tip of Fin I, off S end of Pitt I). Pilot Officer Edward Salter Corbett was born at Ganges on Saltspring I and enlisted in the RCAF at Vancouver in 1940. He was awarded the AFM for making 66 operational flights and inspiring other personnel. According to his citation, "during a period of intense enemy activity he cheerfully accepted more than his share of the extra duties imposed on his squadron." Corbett was killed on Dec 9, 1942, aged 21, when his Catalina crashed on takeoff at Dartmouth, NS. He was a member of Eastern Air Command's No 116 Bomber Reconnaissance Squadron and is buried at Ft Massey Cemetery, Halifax.

Cordero Channel (50°26'00" 125°33'00" N side of E Thurlow I and Sonora I, N of Campbell R), **Cordero Islands** (50°26'00" 125°30'00" In Cordero Channel, off NE side of W Thurlow I), **Cordero Point** (49°07'42" 123°42'08" NE tip of Valdes I, Str of Georgia). Manuel José Antonio Cardero, born in 1766 in Spain, was a cabin boy on Alejandro Malaspina's round-the-world voyage of 1789–92. In Mexico he was reassigned to Dionisio Alcalá-Galiano's 1792 survey of the BC coast as artist, draftsman ("dibuxante") and pilot. His drawings and paintings, made at Nootka Sd in 1791 and along the Inside Passage in 1792, mark him as one of the PNW's most significant early visual chroniclers. Cardero was also probably the primary author of the account of the 1792 expedition, published in 1802 under Alcalá-Galiano's name. He died in Spain some time after 1810. His artworks are at the Museo de América and Museo Naval in Madrid. Canal de Cardero was spelled correctly on the original Spanish charts but somehow became changed to Cordero. Dibuxante Point and Josef Point in the Gulf Is are also named for him. *E W*

Cordova Bay (48°30'00" 123°20'00" E side of Saanich Peninsula, just N of Victoria), **Cordova Channel** (48°36'00" 123°22'00" Between Saanich Peninsula and James I), **Cordova Spit** (48°36'00" 123°22'00" NE side of Saanichton Bay, Cordova Channel). Puerto de Cordova was the original name given to Esquimalt Hbr by Spanish naval officer Manuel Quimper in 1790 to honour the viceroy of Mexico, Antonio Maria Villacis y Cordova. The officers of the HBC transferred the name E to the current Cordova Bay about 1842. Capt Henry Kellett then charted the feature in 1846 as Cormorant Bay, after the RN steam sloop *Cormorant*, which had towed his survey vessel, HMS *Herald*, to anchorage there on a windless day. In 1905 the Geographic Board of Canada restored the name Cordova Bay. *W*

Corlett Peninsula (52°45'15" 131°59'20" Tasu Sd, E side of Moresby I, QCI). Named in 1971 for James Emery Corlett, managing director of the Moresby Lumber Co mill at Queen Charlotte City. From about 1908 to 1915 he also owned a number of mining claims in the area.

C

Cormorant Channel (50°36'00" 126°54'00" Between Cormorant I and Malcolm I), **Cormorant Island** (50°35'00" 126°55'00" SE end of Queen Charlotte Str), **Cormorant Point** (48°30'00" 123°19'00" SE point of Cordova Bay, SE side of Saanich Peninsula, just N of Victoria), **Cormorant Rock** (50°43'00" 127°25'00" SW of Cattle Is, Beaver Hbr, just E of Port Hardy). HMS *Cormorant*, a 6-gun, 1,251-tonne paddle sloop built in 1842 at Sheerness dockyard, served on the Pacific Station, 1844–49, under Cdr George Gordon. It was the first naval steam vessel in BC waters and carried a crew of 145 men. The gunboat went on to capture several notorious slave ships on the E coast of S America before being broken up in 1853. Another HMS *Cormorant* served on the BC coast in the late 1880s under Cdr J E T Nicholls and was sent to Metlakatla when the schism between missionary William Duncan and Bishop William Ridley turned ugly (*see* Duncan I). The features listed above, however, are all named for the earlier ship. The fishing village of Alert Bay on Cormorant I, site of a museum and a fine collection of memorial poles, is the main community of the Kwakwaka'wakw First Nation. *E W*

Corney Cove (52°37'00" 128°43'00" SW end of Princess Royal I, near W entrance to Meyers Passage). Peter Corney was a British mariner and adventurer who worked intermittently for the NWC and HBC between 1813 and 1836, when he died aboard the HBC barque *Columbia*. In 1821 he wrote a series of articles on the PNW for the *London Gazette*, pointing out "the vast trade that is being carried on ... by the Americans and the Russians while an English flag is rarely to be seen." His collected journalism appeared in 1896 under the title *Early Voyages in the N Pacific* and was republished in 1965. Corney, who married Frances Loder in 1820 at Cork, Ireland, was something of a mercenary; in 1818, at Hawaii, he joined the fleet of Argentine privateer Hippolyte de Bouchard as cdr of the captured corvette *Santa Rosa* and was apparently present at the sacking of Monterey and other Spanish settlements along the California coast later that year.

Cornwall Inlet (53°10'49" 128°59'06" E of River Bight, NW side of Princess Royal I), **Cornwall Point** (53°28'00" 128°22'00" At W entrance to Barrie Reach, Gardner Canal, SE of Kitimat). Lawyer and politician Clement Francis Cornwall (1836–1910) was lt gov of BC in 1881–87. He was born at Gloucester, England, and educated at Cambridge Univ, then came to BC in 1862 with his brother Henry Pennant Cornwall. They established a ranch near Ashcroft that was run like an English country estate, complete with racehorses and fox hunts (Ashcroft Manor, their home, is an important heritage site). Clement also practised law and was appointed a justice of the peace in 1864. He married Charlotte Pemberton (1851–1930) at Victoria in 1871. A member of the colonial legislative council (1864–70) and assembly (1870–71), he became one of BC's three federal senators (1871–81) when the colony joined Confederation and was later appointed a judge. Nearby Clement Rapids is also named for him, as are Cornwall Ck and Cornwall Hills in the Ashcroft area. Cornwall Point was formerly known as Douglas Point. *E*

Cortes Bay (50°04'00" 124°55'00" SE side of Cortes I), **Cortes Island** (50°07'00" 124°59'00" Between Quadra I and W Redonda I, N end of Str of Georgia). Cortes I was named after Hernán Cortés (1485–1547), the conqueror of

Cortes Bay on the southeast side of Cortes Island is home to a marine resort and a government wharf. *Peter Vassilopoulos*

C

Mexico, by Spanish naval officers Dionisio Alcalá-Galiano and Cayetano Valdes in 1792. Associated features in the vicinity (Hernando I, Marina I, qv) were named at the same time. By the early 2000s the island had a permanent population of about 600 and was served by ferry from Quadra I. Several small settlements (Mansons Landing, Whaletown) and a Klahoose First Nation reserve (Squirrel Cove) are supported by logging, farming and, increasingly, tourism. Cortes Bay was formerly known as Blind Ck ("creek" being an early Admiralty term for a small drying inlet or bay), and that name is still in occasional local usage. *E W*

Cort Rock (52°56'00" 129°30'00" Off SE side of Dewdney I, N entrance to Caamaño Sd). This rock was first noted in the early 1920s by Capt J J Moore of the government survey vessel *Lillooet* and named after his wife, whose maiden name was Cort, by regional hydrographer Henri Parizeau in 1924. *See also* Moore Is.

Cosine Bay (53°33'00" 129°59'00" W side of Cosine I), **Cosine Island** (53°33'00" 129°58'00" NW of Anger I, off W side of Pitt I), **Cosine Point** (W side of Cosine I). These features were named by members of a coast triangulation party under Alfred Wright, a surveyor with the BC Lands Service, in 1921. A cosine is a mathematical ratio between the sides of a right-angled triangle, used in surveying to measure gradients and distances. Other nearby features (Azimuth I, Logarithm Point, Sine I, Sine Point, Tangent I, Tangent Point) are also named after surveying terms.

Cosmos Heights (50°33'52" 125°02'01" W side of Bute Inlet, NE of Estero Basin and Campbell R). After newspaperman and politician Amor de Cosmos, BC's second premier, 1872–74. *See* DeCosmos Lagoon.

Coste Island (53°50'00" 128°45'00" Kitimat Arm, entrance to Kildala Arm, S of Kitimat), **Coste Point** (53°52'00" 128°44'00" N end of Coste I), **Coste Rocks** (53°48'00" 128°47'00" SW of Coste I, Douglas Channel). Louis Coste was chief engineer and, later, deputy minister of the Canadian Dept of Public Works in the 1890s and early 1900s. In 1905 he was appointed a member of the International Waterways Commission. Coste came to BC in 1898 and examined the heads of several inlets on BC's N coast, travelling aboard CGS *Quadra*. He was hoping to find a suitable terminus for a proposed railway to the Yukon. Capt John Walbran, the *Quadra*'s cdr, named Coste I after his distinguished guest.

Cosy Cove (49°20'00" 122°55'00" E side of Indian Arm, NE of Vancouver). The original 1909 owner of the waterfront at this location is said to have been a Vancouver customs official named Elridge, who sold it to UBC professor J D Davidson. The cove was an occasional stopping place in the 1920s and '30s for vessels of the Harbour Navigation Co, which served several cottages and a large cabin used in the summer by students of the Sprott-Shaw occupational-training schools.

Cottam Point (49°19'00" 124°13'00" NE entrance to Northwest Bay, just E of Parksville, E side of Vancouver I), **Cottam Reef** (49°19'00" 124°11'00" S side of Ballenas Channel, off Dorcas Point, E of Parksville). Lt George Frederick Cottam was an officer aboard HMS *Ganges*, the flagship of Rear Adm Robert Baynes. He served on the Pacific Station in 1857–60 and retired from the RN about 1870 with the rank of capt. Cottam Point was formerly known as Tongue Point.

Cotton Point (49°24'00" 123°26'00" E end of Keats I, Howe Sd, NW of Vancouver). Capt Charles Cotton (1753–1812), as cdr of HMS *Majestic*, was a participant in Adm Lord Howe's victory over a French fleet in the 1794 battle known as the Glorious First of June. In 1810, as an adm and a knight, he was appointed cdr-in-chief of the Mediterranean fleet. (Capt George Vancouver named Howe Sd in honour of Adm Howe, and Capt George Richards, doing survey work aboard HMS *Plumper* more than 65 years later, extended the honour by naming many features in the sound after participants in Howe's greatest triumph.) *W*

Counsel Point (52°36'00" 128°15'00" SE side of Pooley I, W of Don Peninsula, N of Bella Bella). Named in association with nearby Pooley I (qv) after BC lawyer and politician Charles Edward Pooley, who was appointed a Queen's Counsel in 1887.

Courageux Point (53°22'00" 128°03'00" E entrance to Chief Mathews Bay, Gardner Canal, S of Kitimat). In 1790, George Vancouver was a lt on the 74-gun HMS *Courageux*, flagship of Rear Adm Alan Gardner, his friend and mentor. Earlier, from 1784 to 1789, he had been a lt on HMS *Europa*, another of Gardner's flagships. Vancouver named Gardner Canal in his comrade's honour in 1793; in 1907, Capt Frederick Learmonth, aboard HMS *Egeria*, added other names associated with Gardner, including this one, during a detailed survey of the canal. The *Courageux*, which had been captured from the French in 1761 by HMS *Bellona*, was wrecked in 1796.

Courtenay (49°41'00" 124°59'00" Between Campbell R and Nanaimo, E side of Vancouver I), **Courtenay River** (Flows SE through Courtenay into Comox Hbr). Capt George William Conway Courtenay (c 1793–1863) was posted to the RN's Pacific Station, 1846–49, as cdr of the 50-gun frigate *Constance*, which was one of the first British naval vessels to anchor in Esquimalt Hbr. He had entered the RN in 1805 and spent much time in the W Indies, where, in addition to his naval duties, he was consul-gen of Haiti, 1832–42. He reached the rank of vice adm, retired,

C

Comox Glacier provides a scenic backdrop for the city of Courtenay.
Rob Morris

in 1861. In 1848, in order to quell unruliness among visiting First Nation groups at Ft Victoria, Courtenay landed 250 sailors and marines, complete with the ship's band, and performed weapons and marching drills outside the fort. A chief criticized the exercise, explaining to the capt that fighting from cover was preferable to doing so in the open. Roderick Finlayson, in charge of the HBC post, noted that while Courtenay was not pleased by these comments, the "display of arms from the *Constance* had a good effect on the natives, as they were evidently afraid to pick any quarrels with us for some time afterward." The community of Courtenay in the Comox valley got its start in the 1850s with the establishment of an HBC post. The first settlers arrived the following decade. The city of Courtenay, named after the river, was laid out in 1891 and is now the valley's commercial centre. *E W*

Cowans Point. *See* Point Cowan.

Cowards Cove (49°15'00" 123°16'00" N side of entrance to N Arm of Fraser R, S of Point Grey). So named in 1987 because it provides shelter for small craft trying to leave the N Arm of the Fraser R in lousy weather.

Cow Bay (54°19'00" 130°19'00" NW end of Kaien I, Prince Rupert). The name of this popular tourist and commercial district in Prince Rupert has a very uncertain derivation. It may have to do with the location of the pioneer Nehring Dairy. An oft-repeated legend tells that the first dairy herd was persuaded to jump into the water at this location and swim ashore as no dock had yet been built. The name Hill Cove, after A E Hill, a GTP engineer with the original 1906 Prince Rupert survey party, was adopted by the Geographic Board of Canada but then rejected. Cow Bay was Prince Rupert's main boatbuilding area from the 1910s to the '60s. A number of Japanese craftsmen were the first to locate their yards there, and scores of wooden fish boats of all types were constructed. The site was known locally

as Cameron Cove, and its upper reaches were called the Boneyard (also Cow Ck), as many ancient vessels were dumped there when their day was done.

Cowhoe Bay (53°38'00" 132°18'00" E side of Juskatla Inlet, Graham I, QCI). Haida Chief Kahu (1851–1889) was the eldest son of Chief Albert Edward Edensaw (or Gwaayang Gwanhlin, *see* Cape Edensaw). Cdr James Prevost, an ardent Christian and future adm, gave the two-year-old child a Bible during his 1853 survey of the QCI, in the hope, he said, that he was "casting bread upon the waters." About 1879, Kahu became the first Christian convert among the Masset Haida and the first teacher at the church school established by William Collison. He took the Christian name George Cowhoe but was also known as George Edensaw (or Edenshaw). He married Kitkune (b 1856). The name of this feature was adopted in 1953.

Cowichan Bay (48°45'00" 123°37'00" SE of Duncan, E side of Vancouver I), **Cowichan Head** (48°34'00" 123°22'00" N of Cordova Bay, E side of Saanich Peninsula, N of Victoria), **Cowichan River** (48°46'00" 123°38'00" Flows E into Cowichan Bay). The bay was named about 1850 by officers of the HBC for the powerful Coast Salish First Nation—the most populous in BC—that occupies this territory (and now spells its name Quw'utsun'). Cowichan

Cow Bay is home to Prince Rupert's cruise ship centre. *John Alexander*

C

Lk, Cowichan Station, the Cowichan Valley Regional District, etc, all derive their names from the same source. Cowichan is an adaptation of an Island Halkomelem term for "warming the back," which, in turn, refers to a bare, rocky formation on the side of Mt Tzouhalem, said to look like a frog sunning itself. There were many variants of this name in the old days, including Cowichin, Cowitchin, Cowitchan, K'au'itcin and Ka-way-chin. The earliest version recorded is probably that of HBC trader John Work, who mentioned the Coweechin in 1824. In fact, so many Quw'utsun' people migrated across the Str of Georgia each year to occupy summer village sites on the Fraser and harvest its great salmon runs that Work identified that river as the Coweechin. The Songhees First Nation name for Cowichan Head, the northern boundary of their territory, was Tiumalatchung. *E W*

Cowichan Gap. *See* Porlier Pass.

Cowley Islands (53°42'00" 132°22'00" Off S side of Masset Inlet, Graham I, QCI), **Cowley Rock** (53°41'00" 132°21'00" Just SE of the Cowley Is). Francis Penrose V Cowley (1887–1962), of Victoria, assisted with hydrographic surveys in northern BC, 1908–10. He was in charge of several shore parties and worked at Dixon Entrance and near the mouth of the Skeena R before resigning in 1910, the year after he married Sybil Frances Bagshawe (1891–1978) at Victoria.

Cox Bay (49°06'00" 125°53'00" W side of Esowista Peninsula facing Templar Channel, Clayoquot Sd, W side of Vancouver I), **Cox Island** (50°48'00" 128°36'00" One of the Scott Is, W of Cape Scott, off NW tip of Vancouver I), **Cox Island** (54°12'00" 133°01'00" Cloak Bay, W side of Langara I, QCI), **Cox Point** (49°06'00" 125°53'00" SW end of Cox Bay). John Henry Cox (1758–91) was a British merchant based in Asia who financed and organized the earliest fur-trading expeditions to the PNW. He came to Canton in 1781 on behalf of his father, James Cox, who was a leading maker of intricate mechanical toys (automatons), much loved by wealthy Chinese, and later went into the

opium trade. Cox, John Reid and Daniel Beale collaborated to acquire the tiny, 50-tonne brig *Harmon*, which they renamed the *Sea Otter* and put under the command of James Hanna. It sailed from Macao, where Cox lived part of the year, in 1785 under a Portuguese flag in order to avoid the trading monopolies of the British S Sea and E India companies. The following year Cox and his partners, along with associates in Bombay, formed the Bengal Fur Society, bought two more ships—the *Nootka* and another *Sea Otter*—and sent them, under John Meares and William Tipping, to the PNW. Cox also sent Hanna back on a second voyage (in yet another, different, vessel named *Sea Otter*) to the area in 1786, in a venture that may have been co-financed by David Lance (*see* Lanz I), another Canton trader. Cox may have had an interest in the *Imperial Eagle*, as well, which traded in PNW waters in 1787 under Charles Barkley. In 1788, Cox, Meares and Beale formed a trading alliance, Merchant Proprietors, and sent the *Felice Adventurer*, under Meares, and *Iphigenia Nubiana*, under William Douglas, to the PNW. The following year they merged with the King George's Sd Co, a British fur-trading consortium backed primarily by Richard Cadman Etches, and dispatched at least five vessels in search of sea otter furs. In 1789, Cox visited the Alaska coast with his own ship, the *Mercury* (which he renamed *Gustavus III* en route, as he had arranged to be sailing under a Swedish flag when he reached China). Cox managed to outfit two more trading expeditions before he died, and his company, after going through many changes of partnership, eventually metamorphosed into the famous mercantile house Jardine Matheson & Co. Meares named Port Cox, an anchorage in what is now Templar Channel, in honour of his partner in 1788; to keep this reference alive, the hydrographic service changed the name of nearby False Bay, S of Tofino, to Cox Bay in 1934. Hanna, thinking that the NW end of Vancouver I was a separate entity, named it Cox's I in 1786; Cox I now applies to the largest of the Scott Is. When Cox's Channel between Graham I and Langara I, named by William Douglas, was changed to Parry Passage, an island in Cloak Bay was named after Cox instead (*see* Coneehaw Rk). **Cox Point** (53°08'00" 129°45'00" NW end of Trutch I, S end of Banks I) presumably also commemorates this important but relatively unknown historical figure.

Cox Rocks (52°51'00" 129°02'00" In Racey Inlet, W side of Princess Royal I). Sapper John H Cox (1835–1926) was a member of the Columbia detachment of Royal Engineers, which served in BC 1858–63. He was born in Somerset, England, and arrived with the main body of men in 1959 aboard the *Thames City*. In 1863, at New Westminster, he married Minnie Gillan (1847–1911), who came from England in the *Tynemouth*, a so-called brideship. Cox was a jack of all trades. He served as a constable in the Cariboo, 1867–68, then cooked for Walter Moberly's CPR surveys E of Shuswap Lk, 1871–73. He and his family (13 children altogether) moved to Victoria, where he ran a grocery

Cox Island on the west side of Langara Island, Haida Gwaii. *Andrew Scott*

(which burned down), worked as a gardener and built bridges. He is listed in the 1901 census as a miner and a carpenter. Cox took part in the 1909 Royal Engineers reunion and the great old-timers' reunion held in 1924 in Victoria (*see* Adams Bay). Philip Jackman was the only BC member of the Columbia detachment to outlive John Cox, dying in 1927.

Crabapple Islets (50°11'00" 127°50'00" Brooks Bay, N of Brooks Peninsula, NW side of Vancouver I). Named by members of the Provincial Museum's 1981 Brooks Peninsula Expedition after the thick stands of Pacific crab apple (*Malus fusca*) found there. *E*

Cracroft Inlet (50°35'00" 126°18'00" Between E Cracroft I and W Cracroft I, entrance to Knight Inlet), **Cracroft Islands** (50°33'00" 126°20'00" E of Port McNeill, N side of Johnstone Str), **Cracroft Point** (50°33'00" 126°40'00" W end of W Cracroft I). Sophia Cracroft was a niece of Arctic explorer Rear Adm Sir John Franklin and lived with Lady Franklin as a secretary-companion for many years after Sir John's death in 1847. The two women visited N America in 1860–61, spending a month in Victoria and going up the Fraser R to Yale. The Sophia Is near W Cracroft are also named for her, while the Franklin Range on the S side of Johnstone Str is named for Sir John and his wife. Several RN officers and vessels active on the BC coast—including Capt Henry Kellett, who made three summer voyages to the Arctic, 1848–50, in HMS *Herald*, and Capt George Richards—were involved in the search for Franklin's lost expedition. The Cracroft Is were the site of a cannery, at Bones Bay; a hotel, at Port Harvey; and a large logging camp. *E*

Craft Bay (54°00'22" 132°34'11" E side of Naden Hbr, N end of Graham I, QCI). John Craft was 1st mate of the US trading brig *Hope* on its 1791 visit to the QCI. He died that fall while the ship was sailing to Hawaii to overwinter. The following season Joseph Ingraham, master of the *Hope*, named the body of water that would later become Virago Sd in his honour (Port Craft). The hydrographic service kept the reference alive with this current name. *D*

Craft Island (52°35'00" 129°08'00" In Clifford Bay, W side of Aristazabal I). Sapper Philip Craft (1828–74) was a member of the Columbia detachment of the Royal Engineers, which served in BC 1858–63. The correct spelling of his name seems to have been Crart. He came to BC in 1859 aboard *Thames City* with his wife, Elizabeth Herring, and family (which included two stepchildren) and served as orderly to Lt Arthur Lempriere. Later that year his wife, in a tragic fit of despondency, killed one of her children, wounded two others and committed suicide. The surviving children were apparently adopted by another soldier in the detachment, and the oldest, Sarah Sophia Hill, married Lance Cpl Henry Smith in 1860.

Sarah's stepbrother, Arthur Herring, married his cousin, BC novelist and journalist Frances Elizabeth Clarke Herring (1851–1916).

Craig Bay (49°18'00" 124°15'00" NW of Nanoose Bay, between Nanaimo and Parksville, E side of Vancouver I). James "Cougar" Craig (1864–1946) was an early sheep farmer, teamster and bounty hunter who settled in this area in 1887. When the E&N was extended N to Courtenay in 1914, his farm became a construction camp, and on completion of the railway line, Craig bought the project engineer's dwelling and converted it to a school. A station, siding and post office were soon built, and he served as Craigs Crossing postmaster, 1914–35. The site is now the location of Craig Heritage Park, which features a museum and a number of restored historical buildings, including Knox Heritage Church and the French Ck post office, built in the 1890s. Nearby Craig Ck is also named for James Craig.

Crane Bay (53°14'00" 129°18'00" W side of Gil I, between Pitt I and Princess Royal I). The name was adopted in 1950 after one of the small launches carried by survey vessel *William J Stewart*, the flagship of the Canadian Hydrographic Service on the BC coast, 1933–76.

Crane Point (48°50'32" 123°19'54" W side of Mayne I, Gulf Is). Engine Room Artificer Alan Creighton Crane, from S Pender I, was killed in action Oct 22, 1940, aged 24, while serving with the RCN aboard HMCS *Margaree*, under Lt Cdr Joseph Roy. The destroyer sank on convoy duty in the N Atlantic after colliding in rough weather with the *Port Fairy*, a merchant freighter; 142 crew members were lost. Crane's name is inscribed on the Halifax Memorial.

Cran Shoal (52°58'00" 129°45'00" On Cridge Banks, W of Dewdney I, Caamaño Sd). Mary Hills Cridge (1860–1941) was the eldest daughter of Victoria's pioneer Anglican cleric Edward Cridge. She married James Cran (1848–1920) in 1880; he worked for the Bank of BNA and managed branches at Ashcroft, Barkerville and Dawson City. Mary, who lived near Quamichan Lk for many years and died at Vancouver, took part in the grand old-timers' reunion held in Victoria in 1924 (*see* Adams Bay).

Cranston Island (53°18'00" 129°41'00" Entrance to Monckton Inlet, S of Port Stephens, SW side of Pitt I). After Lt Cdr Philip Cranston Musgrave, regional hydrographer on the Pacific coast, 1908–19. *See* Musgrave Peaks. Formerly known as Guide I.

Creak Islands (54°05'00" 130°29'00" Off N side of Porcher I, Chatham Sd, just S of Prince Rupert), **Creak Point** (54°05'00" 130°28'00" W of Hunt Inlet, N side of Porcher I). Capt Ettrick William Creak, CB (1835–1920), was never present on the BC coast. He joined the RN's

C

navigating branch about 1849 and was appointed to the hydrographic dept in 1868. For many years he served as superintendent of compasses, on which subject he wrote numerous technical papers. A fellow of the Royal and Royal Geographic societies, he retired in 1891. Nearby Ettrick Rk is also named for him.

Crease Island (50°37'00" 126°39'00" N of Harbledown I, E end of Queen Charlotte Str). Lawyer Henry Pering Pellew Crease (1823–1905), born in Cornwall, UK, first came to eastern Canada with his parents in 1849, then returned to England to manage a tin mine. In 1858 he was back, this time to Victoria, where he set up as the colony of Vancouver I's first barrister. He was elected to its legislative assembly in 1860 and the following year was appointed attorney gen, keeping the position when Vancouver I and BC united in 1866. A member of the BC Supreme Court, 1870–95, Crease was knighted on his retirement. His wife, Sarah Lindley (1826–1922), was a talented painter, and the couple's Victoria home, Pentrelew, became a social centre for the city's upper crust. Pering Its, next to Crease I, and Pering Point on Sarah I are also named for him; Crease Range in the QCI is believed to be as well. Crease I was formerly known as Lewis I. *E W*

Cree Island (48°51'00" 125°20'00" S side of Broken Group, Barkley Sd, W side of Vancouver I). Muriel Romala Cree (1882–1950, née Suddaby), of Kitchener, Ont, moved to Fernie about 1900 and married Arthur Cree (1861–1918), a member of the NW Mounted Police, in that city in 1907. The couple came to Victoria in 1912, and Muriel worked as a "custodian" and assistant archivist at BC's provincial library in the 1920s and '30s. She provided so much assistance to regional hydrographer Henri Parizeau in his place name research that he decided to honour her, as well.

Cree Point (52°09'00" 128°22'00" S end of Dufferin I, W of Bella Bella). Cdr C M Cree, a retired RN paymaster (now called a supply or logistics officer) living in the US before the start of WWII, re-enlisted at Halifax and became chief staff officer to the Pacific coast CO, 1940–43 (at HMCS *Burrard* in Vancouver). In 1943–44 he was CO of the shore establishment HMCS *Chatham* at Prince Rupert. Cree is identified in the 1929 RN list as an RNR paymaster at HMS *Vivid*, the barracks and depot ship located at Plymouth, England.

Creery Islands (52°04'00" 128°18'00" W side of Brown Narrows, S entrance to Raymond Passage, SW of Bella Bella). Wallace Bourchier Creery (1900–87), of Vancouver, graduated from RCN College in 1914 and married Monica Reid Hutchison (1900–81) in 1922. His first command, in 1928, was the trawler *Armentières*, and by 1934 he was CO of HMCS *Champlain*, a destroyer. After a stint as director of naval reserves (1935–37), he became cdr in charge at Halifax. In 1940, Creery was CO of the

destroyer *Fraser*, which was participating in an evacuation of French refugees when it collided with HMS *Calcutta*, a British cruiser, and sank, with the loss of 64 lives. He was promoted commodore in 1948 and made chief of naval personnel. Creery served in BC as CO of HMCS *Royal Roads* (1946) and flag officer Pacific coast (1950–53, with the rank of rear adm). He ended his career at naval HQ as vice-chief of naval staff. His awards include the CBE (1946) and Norway's Cross of Liberation (1949). Creery Is were formerly known as the William Is.

Crescent Inlet (52°46'00" 131°52'00" Head of Darwin Sd, Selwyn Inlet, NW side of Moresby I, QCI), **Crescent Point** (52°44'00" 131°48'00" S entrance to Crescent Inlet). Named in 1878 by George M Dawson, of the Geological Survey of Canada, after the shape of the inlet. Numerous copper claims were filed in the area in the early 1900s. Crescent Point was formerly known as Rock Point.

Crew Island (53°27'05" 128°40'55" Head of Triumph Bay, NW end of Gardner Canal, S of Kitimat). On Sept 27, 1995, seven employees of a Triumph Bay logging camp died, along with the pilot, when a Western Straits Air Otter crashed 15 km NE of Campbell R. Killed in the accident were pilot Dan White, 37; Gordon Tripple, 22; Ralph Holzer, 29; Thomas Hughes, 35; Joseph Ponton, 55; and David Snyder, 44, all from Campbell R; Kirby Folster, 30, from Black Ck; and Marlene Miller, 54, from Nanaimo. Leonard Brown from Campbell R and Charlotte Pfister from Quadra I survived the crash. A monument was erected on Crew I in 1996, and the name was officially adopted in 1999.

Crews Rock (53°09'00" 129°48'00" Between Trutch I and Banks I, SW of Kitimat). Arthur Crews was a midshipman aboard HMS *Discovery* on Capt George Vancouver's expedition to the PNW, 1791–95. The name was adopted in 1950, as submitted by the hydrographic service.

Creyke Point (48°20'00" 123°38'00" W side of Becher Bay, S end of Campbell Cove, S tip of Vancouver I). Named in 1846 by Capt Henry Kellett, who charted this area, after Lt Richard Boynton Creyke, an RN surveying officer who was never actually present on the BC coast. Creyke served in the Baltic Sea aboard survey vessel HMS *Merlin* during the Crimean War and retired from the RN in 1862 with the rank of capt.

Cridge Banks (52°58'00" 129°44'00" W of Dewdney I, entrance to Caamaño Sd), **Cridge Island** (54°17'00" 130°18'00" Off W side of Digby I, just W of Prince Rupert), **Cridge Lagoon** (53°20'00" 129°32'00" Head of Tuwartz Inlet, SE end of Pitt I), **Cridge Passage** (53°18'00" 129°22'00" Between Farrant I and Fin I, off SE end of Banks I). Edward Cridge (1817–1913), a native of Devon, England, graduated from Cambridge Univ and worked as an Anglican minister in London for a few years, marrying Mary Winmill (1837–1915) in 1854. He came to Victoria in 1855 as the HBC's chaplain and built the colony's first Anglican church the following year (it burned down in 1869). Cridge helped establish Victoria's first hospital and orphanage and was inspector of schools from 1856 to 1865. When bishop George Hills arrived in 1860, Cridge's church became Christ Church Cathedral and Cridge became dean of the diocese. He had a falling-out with his superior, however; Cridge was "low" Anglican and hated "ritualistic practices," while Hills was "high" church. He tried to get rid of Cridge, who wouldn't budge and even barred the bishop from the new cathedral, built in 1872. Hills eventually brought a lawsuit against his dean, which was decided in the bishop's favour by a reluctant Judge Matthew Baillie Begbie. Cridge left the Anglican church, along with many of his fellow Victorians, including Sir James Douglas; founded a Reformed Episcopal congregation; built a new house of worship in 1875 (the Church of Our Lord on Blanshard St); and became a bishop himself. Cridge Ck and Mt Cridge near Knight Inlet are also named for him. *E W*

Crippen Cove (54°19'00" 130°23'00" W of Grindstone Point, Digby I, entrance to Prince Rupert Hbr). Lionel Crippen (1875–1915), an early resident of the Prince Rupert area, came to Canada from Edinburgh and produced a delicacy named Crippen's Boneless Kippered Herring at his Digby I fish plant, 1913–14. He enlisted with the BC Regiment (7th Battalion) as a private in WWI and was killed in action on May 22, 1915. His name is inscribed on the Vimy Memorial, Pas de Calais, France.

Crispin Rock (48°48'00" 123°11'00" In Lyall Hbr, NW side of Saturna I, Gulf Is). Sub-Lt George Crispin Hammond served in BC, 1867–70, aboard the *Beaver*, hired by the RN as a coastal survey vessel. *See* Hammond Bay.

Croasdaile Island (54°07'00" 130°12'00" Off S side of Smith I, entrance to Skeena R, S of Prince Rupert). Henry Edward Croasdaile (1847–1915) served as an RN officer then immigrated to N America. By the mid-1870s he owned two sheep farms in Idaho that were destroyed in 1877 during conflicts with the Nez Perce First Nation. He came to Victoria with his wife, Ella Teresa Croasdaile (d 1913 in Guernsey), and became involved in several Nass Bay businesses, including canneries, a sawmill and an eulachon-processing plant. His paintings of the Stikine region during the Cassiar gold rush are held by the BC Archives. Croasdaile also speculated in Victoria real estate, successfully subdividing and developing property in the Mt Tolmie district. In the 1890s he moved to the W Kootenays, where he became gen manager of Hall Mines Ltd, which operated the short-lived but profitable Silver King and put Nelson on the map. Formerly known as Bay I but renamed in 1927.

A ferry service connects Crofton to Saltspring Island. *Kevin Oke*

Croft Island (52°38'00" 128°47'00" Just W of Hastings I, S entrance to Laredo Inlet, S end of Princess Royal I), **Crofton** (48°52'00" 123°39'00" N of Duncan, E side of Vancouver I). Henry "Harry" Croft (1856–1917), born at Sydney, Australia, and trained as an engineer, immigrated to BC in 1882 and became involved in the lumber industry at Chemainus. He married Mary Jean Dunsmuir (1862–1928), a daughter of industrialist Robert Dunsmuir, at Victoria in 1885 and served as MLA for Cowichan, 1886–94. In 1902 he built a smelter at what is now Crofton to process copper ore from the Lenora Mine on nearby Mt Sicker, which he had developed in 1898. Croft became enormously wealthy and built a huge mansion, Mt Adelaide, in Esquimalt (demolished in 1959). Crofton Lk on Vancouver I is also named for him. The town of Crofton declined after the Mt Sicker mines were worked out and the smelter closed, but recovered when a pulp mill was built in 1958. Today a ferry service operates between Crofton and Vesuvius Bay on Saltspring I. *E W*

Crofton. *See above.*

Croker Island (49°26'00" 122°52'00" N end of Indian Arm, Burrard Inlet, NE of Vancouver), **Croker Point** (48°47'00" 123°12'00" SW side of Saturna I, Gulf Is), **Croker Rock** (50°52'00" 127°38'00" N of Balaklava I, Gordon Channel, off NE side of Vancouver I). The island and point were probably named by Capt George Richards, who surveyed the BC coast with HMS *Plumper*, 1857–60 (and later with HMS *Hecate*), after James L Croker, assistant paymaster aboard the *Plumper* in 1860. The 63-ha island is the site of an old granite quarry that supplied stone for some of Vancouver's early buildings. Victoria lumberman Len Jones bought it in 1948 and sold it to real-estate investors Arvid and Walter Much in 1972.

Crombie Point (52°32'00" 131°23'00" SW tip of Ramsay I, E side of Moresby I, SE of Lyell I, QCI). After 19th-century Scottish geologist Andrew Crombie Ramsay. *See* Ramsay I.

Crosson Point (52°52'00" 128°10'00" SW side of Mussel Inlet, Matheson Channel, N of Bella Bella). Leading Coder Abraham Bullard Crosson, from Vancouver, was serving with the RCNVR aboard the minesweeper *Guysborough* when he was killed in action Mar 18, 1945, aged 31. *Guysborough* was escorting a convoy in the English Channel off Ushant when it was torpedoed and sunk by a U-boat, with the loss of 51 lives. Crosson's name is inscribed on the Halifax Memorial.

Crowell Point (53°59'00" 132°09'00" W side of Masset Sd, just SW of Masset, Graham I, QCI), **Crowell Rock** (52°14'00" 131°07'00" Carpenter Bay, SE end of Moresby I, QCI). Capt Samuel Crowell was master and part owner of the Boston-based brigantine *Hancock*, which made three fur-trading voyages to the QCI in 1790–93. The crew built a tender for their vessel on Maast I, near Crowell Point—the first European-style boat constructed in the archipelago—in the summer of 1791. During this time they were visited by the *Columbia*, under Capt Robert Gray. Crowell tried to explore S down Masset Sd with the *Hancock*, probably the first westerner to do so, but got stuck and abandoned the idea. Nearby Samuel Rk is also named for him, while Hancock Point (qv) and the Hancock R are named for his ship.

Crow Islet (50°05'00" 125°14'00" Gowlland Hbr, W side of Quadra I, N of Campbell R). Cdr Cortland Simpson, aboard the RN survey ship *Egeria* in 1900, named a series of islands and islets in Gowlland Hbr after native animals, including Stag, Fawn, Doe, Wren, Crow and Mouse.

Crowther Channel (50°02'00" 127°18'00" NW side of Union I, Kyuquot Sd, NW side of Vancouver I). Clara Ann Unsworth Crowther (1856–1946) was born at Liverpool, England, and came to Victoria with her family in 1862 aboard the *Rosedale*, which hit a rock in Juan de Fuca Str and had to be towed to Ross Bay and beached. In 1874 she married sealing capt George Brown (1834–1914, *see* Brown Channel) and from 1876 to 1882 lived at Kyuquot, the only white woman in the district, while her husband was in charge of a trading post established by sealer James Warren. After Brown's death she remarried twice, to John Garland (in 1915) and Henry Bailey (in 1924). Crowther Channel was formerly known as Blind Entrance and then as Blind Channel. Unsworth Point on Union I is also named for her.

Cruice Rock (54°07'00" 130°21'00" NW end of Lawyer Is, off NE side of Porcher I, just SW of mouth of Skeena R). William Henry Cruice was an RN surgeon aboard HMS *Malacca*, under Capt Radulphus Oldfield, and served on the BC coast, based at Esquimalt, in 1866–68. He reached the rank of deputy inspector of hospitals, retired, in 1883 and died in 1899. Named in 1867 by Lt Daniel Pender of the hired survey vessel *Beaver*.

Cudlip Point (48°19'00" 123°32'00" E side of Bentinck I, off S tip of Vancouver I). Named in 1846 by Capt Henry Kellett, who charted this area, after Lt Frederick Augustus Cudlip, an RN surveying officer who was never actually present on the BC coast. He visited Australia in 1829 as a midshipman aboard HMS *Sulphur* and drew a number of early charts of NZ harbours in 1834 while mate of HMS *Buffalo*. Cudlip participated in a survey of Baltic ports in 1854 as 1st lt of HMS *Lightning* and was eventually promoted to cdr.

Culloden Point (49°48'00" 124°05'00" N side of Jervis Inlet, S of St Vincent Bay, NW of Vancouver). HMS *Culloden* was a 74-gun, 1,486-tonne ship of the line built on the Thames R in 1783. Under Capt Thomas Troubridge it played an important role at the 1797 Battle of St Vincent, in which Adm Sir John Jervis's fleet achieved a victory over the Spanish navy W of Cadiz. The *Culloden* was also present at the Battle of the Nile in 1798. *W*

Cullum Point (52°36'00" 128°38'00" NW side of Meyers Passage, S end of Princess Royal I). Marine engineer William James Cullum (1867–1924), a native of Ireland, immigrated to Canada in 1884 and served as a federal steamship inspector in BC, 1908–24. He married Margaret Rosalina Burkholder (1878–1953), of Ont, at Victoria in 1897. Named in the early 1920s by regional hydrographer Henri Parizeau.

Culpepper Lagoon (52°44'00" 127°52'00" Extends SE from head of Kynoch Inlet, E of Mathieson Channel, N of Bella Bella). Petty Officer Stoker John Arthur Culpepper, of Victoria, was serving with the RCNVR aboard the corvette *Alberni* when he was killed in action Aug 21, 1944, aged 29. The *Alberni* was torpedoed and sunk by a U-boat (*U-480*) SE of the Isle of Wight, with the loss of 59 men. Culpepper's name is inscribed on the Halifax Memorial.

Cultus Sound (51°54'00" 128°13'00" W side of Hunter I, SW of Bella Bella). *Cultus* (or *kultus*) is a Chinook jargon word for "worthless" or "good for nothing." In its broadest sense it simply means "bad." (Chinook was a W coast lingua franca used by First Nation people and early traders and settlers.) The name presumably refers to the hazardous nature of the sound as an approach to Hunter Channel and Bella Bella. Many other geographical features in BC get their names from this word, including three creeks, two lakes, Kultus Cove and the Fraser Valley community of Cultus Lk.

C

Cumming Point (50°54'00" 126°59'00" N side of Drury Inlet, N of Queen Charlotte Str and Port McNeill). Adm Sir Arthur Cumming, KCB (1817–93), born at Nancy, France, was an RN officer who served extensively on the Mediterranean and N America stations. In 1842, as a lt on HMS *Frolic*, he and seven men, with the ship's pinnace, captured the much larger brigantine *Vincedora*, an illegal slaver, off the coast of S America. After long and conspicuous service as a cdr and capt, he was promoted to rear adm in 1870 and appointed cdr-in-chief of the E Indies Station, 1872–75. Cumming retired in 1882 and was knighted in 1887 on the occasion of Queen Victoria's golden jubilee. Cumming Point was named by RN hydrographer Capt George Richards about 1863, while Sir Arthur still had the rank of capt. Point Cumming (qv) in Douglas Channel is named for a different person.

Cummins Islet (52°29'09" 129°01'50" Entrance to Weeteeam Bay, SW end of Aristazabal I). Sapper Allan Cummins (1839–1911) was a member of the Columbia detachment of Royal Engineers, which served in BC 1858–63. His trade was listed as "nail maker," and he remained in BC when the corps disbanded, working as a blacksmith in New Westminster. Cummins was employed as an assistant steward at New Westminster's Royal Columbian Hospital, 1900–1907. He attended the 1909 reunion held in New Westminster to honour the 12 detachment members still alive in BC.

Cumshewa Head (53°02'00" 131°36'00" N entrance to Cumshewa Inlet), **Cumshewa Inlet** (53°03'00" 131°47'00" Between N side of Louise I and Moresby I, QCI), **Cumshewa Island** (53°02'00" 131°36'00" Off Cumshewa Head, entrance to Cumshewa Inlet), **Cumshewa Rocks** (53°01'00" 131°35'00" Entrance to Cumshewa Inlet). Cumshewa Inlet was named by early fur traders after Gumsiiwa or Gomshewah (transliterations vary widely), chief of the Xhiida Xhaaydaghaay (Eagle) lineage. He was also headman of the region's main village, known to the Haida as Hlqinul. George M Dawson of the Geological Survey of Canada appears to have been the first, in 1878, to use the current spelling, which came to refer also to the village site, now abandoned. It was probably Gumsiiwa—"an old man with authority"—who Capt George Dixon met on the W coast of Moresby I in July 1787 and gave a cavalry cap. A few days later, on the E side, Dixon met him again—*sans* cap—and discovered that in this area he was a chief of great importance. Gumsiiwa showed the mariner wounds he had suffered trying to retain possession of the treasured headpiece, and Dixon astutely found him another cap, which cemented the trading relationship and ensured a bounty of furs. While the Cumshewa people did not have a reputation for extreme aggression, several notorious attacks on trading vessels did occur in the inlet. In 1794, renegade chief Koya plundered and burned the *Resolution*,

killing most of its crew, and over the next two years the *Phoenix*, *Sea Otter* and *Alexander* all lost crew members in fights with Cumshewa warriors. Cumshewa Mtn was named after the inlet in 1984 when a decision was made to build a telecommunications facility on its summit. *D W*

Cundall Bay (52°09'00" 128°17'00" E side of Horsfall I, W of Bella Bella). Named in 1902 by Capt John Walbran, master of CGS *Quadra* for the federal Dept of Marine and Fisheries, 1891–1903, after a village in Yorkshire, England, where his grandfather, Rev Thomas Horsfall, was vicar, 1862–69. Walbran was author of the 1909 classic *British Columbia Coast Names*.

Cunningham Island (52°14'00" 127°59'00" Just N of Denny I, N of Bella Bella). Thomas Cunningham (1837–1916), a native of Ireland, came to Canada in 1853 and arrived at Victoria about six years later to join the gold rush. In 1861 he settled at New Westminster and opened a hardware store, then expanded his business to Nanaimo, buying the Vancouver Coal Co's general store there in 1864 and operating under the name Cunningham Bros with his brother James (1835–1925). In 1864 he married Emily Ann Woodman (1842–1921), who taught in New Westminster at the first BC mainland school; a year later, James married Emily's sister Mary Ann (1843–1930). Thomas was elected to Vancouver I's legislative assembly in 1865–66 as the Nanaimo representative. He moved to Oregon to manufacture farm vehicles for 15 years, then returned to New Westminster, established an urban farm (Pelham Gardens, noted for its fruit trees), served as a city councillor and BC MLA, 1889–90, and in 1892 built a house designed by noted architect Samuel Maclure. In 1900, as collector of votes, he refused to allow naturalized Japanese citizens to appear on the voters list, despite a legal challenge. He was later named provincial horticulturist, chief fruit inspector and president of the BC Agricultural Society. His brother James was mayor of New Westminster, 1873–74, MP, 1874–78, and MLA, 1884–86. Thomas's son James (1867–1945) was also a prominent city businessman.

Cunningham Passage (54°33'00" 130°27'00" Between Tsimpsean Peninsula and Finlayson I, N of Prince Rupert). Robert Cunningham (1837–1905) was born in Ireland and educated at the Anglican Church Missionary Society college in London. He arrived in BC in 1862 and joined William Duncan's mission at Metlakatla, but was dismissed about 1866 for being "easily led to sin." He married a Tsimshian woman, Elizabeth Ryan, and after working for the HBC, 1867–70, and briefly managing the Ft Simpson post, went into business with Thomas Hankin (*see* Hankin Reefs) and established stores at Port Essington and Hazelton on the Skeena R. Cunningham bought Hankin out in 1877 and settled at Essington, where he built a cannery in 1883, as well as a hotel, sawmill and dogfish-oil refinery. He also operated a number of sternwheeled riverboats and acquired much real estate. His wife drowned in a river accident in 1888, and in 1893 he married Florence F Bicknell. His son George carried on his business ventures until 1926. Nearby Cunningham Peak and Cunningham Lk are also named for him. *E W*

Curlew Bay (53°17'00" 129°19'00" N side of Fin I, entrance to Douglas Channel, SW of Kitimat). Named about 1950 for one of the small launches carried by federal government survey vessel *William J Stewart*, the flagship of the Canadian Hydrographic Service on the BC coast, 1933–76.

Curlew Island (48°50'00" 123°14'00" Off E side of Mayne I, Gulf Is), **Curlew Point** (51°28'00" 127°45'00" NW end of Ironside I, Schooner Retreat, N entrance to Rivers Inlet), **Curlew Rock** (54°27'00" 130°25'00" S side of Big Bay, Tsimpsean Peninsula, N of Prince Rupert). HMS *Curlew*, a 9-gun steam sloop launched at Deptford dockyard in 1854 and broken up in 1865, was stationed in the Mediterranean and off S America but never appeared in BC waters. In 1857, Cdr William Horton, a colleague of BC surveyor Capt George Richards, had charge of the 567-tonne vessel, and Richards presumably named Curlew I in the late 1850s along with nearby Horton Bay (qv). Curlew I was pre-empted in 1893 by James C Campbell (d 1933), who went on to become Vancouver Hbr's shipping master for 25 years and an alderman for six. It was owned in 1907 by Mary Watson and in 1910 by the Bjornsfelt family, one of whose members resided there, raised goats for many years and died on the island in 1931.

Curme Islands (50°07'00" 124°45'00" Between Otter I and Mink I, Desolation Sd, NE end of Str of Georgia). Capt Charles Thomas Curme (1827–92) was based at Esquimalt in 1872–73 as cdr of the RN battleship *Repulse*, flagship of Rear Adm Charles Hillyar. Nearby Mink I (qv) was renamed Repulse I in 1945 in association with the Curme Is, but in 1962, after a campaign against the change by the island's owner, the original name was restored. Curme was superintendent of Devonport dockyard in 1880, a vice adm in 1886 and cdr-in-chief at the Nore (responsible for protecting the entrance to the port of London, where the Nore sandbank is located) in 1890. The Curme Is were formerly known as the Broken Is.

Currie Islet (51°51'00" 128°27'00" S of Goose I, Queens Sd, SW of Bella Bella). Maj David Vivian Currie, VC (1912–86), born in Sask, fought with the S Alberta Regiment in WWII. He was awarded the VC for acts of bravery while blocking and holding one of the main German escape routes from the Falaise area of France during the Battle of Normandy in Aug 1944. After the war he worked in Que as a senior executive of paper and manufacturing companies.

He was appointed the House of Commons sgt-at-arms by PM John Diefenbaker in 1959. Nearby Vivian Rk is also named for him.

Curteis Point (48°40'29" 123°23'48" NE point of Tsehum Hbr, NE Saanich Peninsula, N of Victoria). Lt Col Cyril S S Curteis, CMG, DSO, was a retired British Royal Artillery officer who bought waterfront property about 1910 in N Saanich with his wife, Mabel Easton, of Bermuda. When the steamship *Iroquois*, which served the Gulf Is from Sidney and Nanaimo, sank in a storm in 1911, causing more than 20 deaths, the Curteis home was turned into a temporary hospital and morgue. The col rejoined the British Army in WWI and stayed in service afterwards, eventually retiring again, to Scotland.

Curwen Island (48°57'00" 125°22'00" SW end of David Channel, Barkley Sd, W side of Vancouver I). Charles Houston Curwen (1843–1927) immigrated to the US from England in 1868 and lived at Denver and New Orleans before ending up in Victoria with his wife, Laura Helena Wallace (b about 1843), whom he married in 1873. He received a Crown grant for land on the N side of Barkley Sd in 1892. Curwen was listed in the 1891 BC census as a goverment agent at Esquimalt and in later directories as an employee of F C Davidge & Co, a Victoria agency that represented various insurance and shipping firms. The island was formerly known as Gowlland I.

Cusheon Cove (48°48'00" 123°24'00" Just W of Yeo Point, SE side of Saltspring I, Gulf Is). John Ducie Cusheon (d 1874 in San Francisco) was a BC pioneer, operating the Union Hotel, 1858–61, in Victoria, where he married Margaret Hogg. He was one of the first landowners on Saltspring I, in 1860. Cusheon attempted to buy the pre-emptions of several other island settlers but was turned down by the government and purchased only 80 ha between Cusheon Lk (also named for him, as is Cusheon Ck) and Ganges Hbr. He had planned to raise cattle but left almost immediately, with his family, for the Cariboo gold rush. The Bulman sawmill was located at the cove about 1906–26, and an alternative community flourished there from 1972 to 1984.

Cust Point (50°29'00" 125°42'00" S side of Forward Hbr, E of Hardwicke I, N of Johnstone Str). Lady Florence Harriet Lascelles (1838–1901) was a sister of Lt Horace Lascelles, who was in command of HMS *Forward*, a gunboat on the BC coast, 1861–65 (*see* Lascelles Point). She married Lt Col John Francis Cust (1825–1903) in 1861. Nearby Florence Point is also named for her. Lascelles was a British aristocrat, a son of the 3rd Earl of Harewood, and in 1865, Lt Daniel Pender named many features in Forward Hbr after his family, including points commemorating his four sisters.

Cut, The. *See* The Cut.

The Union Steamship *Cutch*, sinking after hitting Horseshoe Reef, south of Juneau, Alaska, in 1900. *Harbour Publishing collection*

C

Cutch Rock (54°18'30" 130°29'06" Off Straith Point, Digby I, S entrance to Metlakatla Bay, just W of Prince Rupert). The *Cutch* was built at Hull, Yorkshire, in 1884 as a 294-tonne, 55-m pleasure craft for an Indian prince, the Maharaja of Cutch. He died soon after acquiring this toy, and the vessel was purchased by a group of local merchants and used in the Indian coastal trade. The next owner, the German government, employed it in E Africa, and in 1890 the Union Steamship Co bought it for service on the BC coast. The *Cutch* ran between Vancouver and Nanaimo until 1897. In 1892 its capt was found at fault for striking and severely damaging the steamship *Joan* in Nanaimo Hbr. The vessel was expensively remodelled in 1898 and put on the run to Skagway, Alaska. It "named" Cutch Rk, off Digby I, in 1899 but had a more serious accident the following year, when it was abandoned after running aground on Horseshoe Reef, S of Juneau. No lives were lost, fortunately, and the *Cutch* was salvaged and repaired by US interests. It ran briefly from Seattle to Alaska as the *Jessie Banning* before ending its days with the Colombian navy as the gunboat *Bogota*.

Cuthbert Rock (50°32'00" 125°59'00" In Port Neville, N side of Johnstone Str, NW of Sayward). After Vice Adm Lord Cuthbert Collingwood of the RN, a contemporary of Lord Nelson. *See* Collingwood Channel.

Cuttle Islets (50°06'00" 127°36'00" Entrance to Ououkinsh Inlet, Checleset Bay, S of Brooks Peninsula, NW side of Vancouver I). One-armed Capt Edward Cuttle is a comic character in the 1848 novel *Dombey and Son* by Charles Dickens. He is a great admirer of Capt Jack Bunsby, the oracular master of *Cautious Clara*, and a friend to Walter Gay, nephew of instrument maker Solomon Gills. During an 1862 survey of this area aboard HMS *Hecate*, Capt George Richards named several features after aspects of the novel. Sub-Lt Sydney Dickens, one of the famous writer's 10 children, served on the BC coast, 1868–70, aboard HMS *Pylades* and *Zealous* (*see* Dickens Point). **W**

Cyril Rock (49°48'21" 124°36'20" Off N end of Texada I, Str of Georgia). This feature is possibly named after Lt Col Cyril Houlton Neroutsos, DSO (1904–90), who commanded the Calgary Regiment in WWII. As a child he travelled on occasion with his father, Capt Cyril Demetrius Neroutsos (*see* Neroutsos Inlet), who became gen manager of the CPR's BC Coast Steamship Service. In 1913, young Cyril was told that the rock had been named for him. He later married Edythe Winter and moved to Montreal.

Cyrus Rocks (50°15'00" 125°12'00" Okisollo Channel, NE side of Quadra I, N of Campbell R). After politician and WWI hero Lt Col Cyrus Wesley Peck, VC. *See* Peck I.

D

Dacres Point (49°50'00" 123°56'00" N side of Goliath Bay, S end of Prince of Wales Reach, Jervis Inlet). Capt George Richards surveyed the area in HMS *Plumper* about 1860 and named a number of features in association with Adm Sir John Jervis, after whom the inlet had been named by Capt George Vancouver in 1792. Capt James Richard Dacres (1749–1810) was cdr of HMS *Barfleur*, flagship of Vice Adm William Waldegrave, at the 1797 Battle of St Vincent, Jervis's great victory. Dacres was soon a vice adm himself, and cdr-in-chief of the Jamaica Station, 1805–9. *W*

Daedalus Passage (50°44'00" 127°24'00" W side of Beaver Hbr, just E of Port Hardy, NE end of Vancouver I). HMS *Daedalus* was launched in 1826 as a 46-gun, 1,312-tonne frigate but was rebuilt in 1843 and reduced to 20 guns. It served on the Pacific Station in 1850–51 under Capt George Wellesley. In 1850 the vessel took Vancouver I gov Richard Blanshard to Fort Rupert on N Vancouver I to investigate the murder of three HBC deserters by members of the Nahwitti First Nation. When the suspects were not surrendered, armed boats from the *Daedalus* burned an abandoned Nahwitti encampment. The following year, Blanshard returned aboard HMS *Daphne* and ordered another village—possibly Nahwitti or Newitty on Cape Sutil—destroyed, after which the tribe killed three of its members and handed over their bodies. (*See* Daphne Point, Deserters Group *and* Nahwitti Bar for more details.) The *Daedalus* ended up as an RNR drill ship at Bristol in 1862 and was broken up in 1911. In Greek mythology, Daedalus was the craftsman who built the Cretan labyrinth and was then imprisoned by King Minos. He and his son, Icarus, escaped on handmade wings of feathers and wax, but Icarus flew too close to the sun and fell to his death when the wax melted. Daedalus Mtn, SE of Bella Coola, is named after the myth, not the ship. *W*

Daedalus Point (51°48'00" 128°00'00" N end of Nalau I, W side of Fitz Hugh Sd, S of Bella Bella). This *Daedalus* was a 317-tonne transport or storeship that rendezvoused with Capt George Vancouver at Nootka Sd late in 1792 in order to resupply him. The ship had stopped en route at Hawaii, with disastrous consequences: its cdr, Lt Richard Hergest, a friend of Vancouver, was killed by Hawaiian attackers, along with William Gooch, an astronomer coming to join HMS *Discovery*. Vancouver put Lt James Hanson, 1st lt of HMS *Chatham*, in command of the *Daedalus* (which was privately owned by Alexander Davison, Lord Nelson's agent) and sent the brig to Australia. In 1793 it resupplied Vancouver again, off San Francisco, and accompanied him to Hawaii, then returned to the UK, taking along some troublemakers from *Discovery* including the deranged midshipman Thomas Pitt, who later attacked his former capt on the streets of London.

Dakin Islets (52°16'00" 128°09'00" Spiller Channel, S of Yeo I, E of Milbanke Sd, N of Bella Bella). The name is a misspelling for William Philip Daykin (1842–1916), who came to Canada from England in 1886 with his wife, Helen (1843–1903, née Strelley), and family. He became a lighthouse keeper, first at Sand Heads, then at Race Rocks, 1888–91. In 1891 the Daykins were the first to reside at isolated Carmanah lighthouse on the W coast of Vancouver I, where they suffered great hardships. After Helen died, William married her sister Maria Elizabeth Strelley (1851–1937) in 1909. In 1912 he was finally given a less arduous posting, McLoughlin Point in Victoria Hbr, but his health, both physical and mental, was shattered by then and he died not long after at Esquimalt.

Dallain Point (52°39'00" 128°54'00" SW side of Princess Royal I, between Laredo Channel and Laredo Inlet). Capt Alphonsus John Dallain (1864–1942) was born in England and in 1895 came to Canada, where he married Helen Marion Downey (1876–1959) in 1902 at Victoria. He is identified as a clerk on the 1898 BC voters list, and as a clerk and master mariner in the 1901 census. He also served with the BC Battalion of Garrison Artillery. Dallain became an accountant with the federal Dept of Marine and Fisheries and died at Victoria. Formerly known as Steep Point.

Dallas Bank (48°26'00" 123°26'00" E side of Esquimalt Hbr, between Constance Cove and Ashe Head, just W of Victoria). Alexander Grant Dallas (1816–82), born in British Guiana (Guyana), was a director of the HBC and its representative in W Canada, 1857–62, gradually taking over responsibility for the company's affairs from Vancouver I gov James Douglas. He had begun his business life in Liverpool, England, and spent five years in China with the well-known trading company Jardine, Matheson. Dallas married Jane Douglas (1839–1909, *see below*), second daughter of James Douglas, in 1858 and built a home in Victoria. In 1862 he was appointed gov of Rupert's Land and moved to Ft Garry (now Winnipeg). He retired to his estates in Scotland in 1864 and served the HBC in an advisory capacity until 1866, though he took an active interest in BC politics for many years. Dallas Rd, along Victoria's S shoreline, is named for him and was the site of the three-storey brick Hotel Dallas, 1891–1928, once a distinguished city hostelry. *W*

Dallas Island (52°22'00" 128°28'00" Off SW side of Dowager I, Milbanke Sd, NW of Bella Bella). Jane Douglas (1839–1909) was born at Ft Vancouver in what is now Washington state, the second surviving daughter of HBC chief trader James Douglas and his wife, Amelia. She moved with her family in 1849 to Ft Victoria, where her father soon became gov of Vancouver I. Jane married wealthy businessman and HBC director Alexander Grant Dallas (1816–82, *see above*) in Victoria but spent most of her life in Britain. She had nine children, only seven of whom lived to adulthood. Dallas I (formerly known as Cliff I) was named in 1929 in association with nearby Lady Douglas I.

Dall Rocks (52°13'00" 128°09'00" Off N side of Campbell I, Seaforth Channel, N of Bella Bella). Capt Christopher C Dall ran the US sidewheel steamship *John L Stevens* onto these rocks in Oct 1867 while returning to the US from Alaska. He had been delivering troops and supplies to Sitka on the occasion of the US takeover of Alaska after its purchase from Russia. The vessel recovered and continued to operate between San Francisco, Portland and Alaska until the late 1870s. Dall was master over the years of a number of historic US sidewheelers, including the *California*, *Cortez*, *Oregon* and *Panama*. He worked for the Pacific Mail Line and for Holladay & Flint.

Dalton Point (53°57'00" 133°10'00" NE end of Frederick I, off W side of Graham I, QCI). William Dalton was the chief artificer engineer aboard the RN survey ship *Egeria* in 1907, when that vessel was working in this area. The point was named by Capt Frederick Learmonth, cdr of the *Egeria*.

Dana Inlet (52°48'00" 131°45'00" Between Tangil Peninsula and Talunkwan I, W of Laskeek Bay, E side of Moresby I, QCI), **Dana Passage** (52°50'00" 131°50'00" Between Talunkwan I and E side of Moresby I, S of Louise I, QCI). James Dwight Dana (1813–95), born at Utica, NY, was a prominent US geologist and zoologist and a long-time professor at Yale Univ. His most important contributions were in the fields of mountain building and volcanic activity. Dana was a member of the Wilkes Expedition of 1838–42, which explored the S Pacific region, and was editor of the *American Journal of Science and Arts* for many years. He received the Wollaston Medal in 1872 and the Copley Medal in 1877, the highest awards, respectively, of Britain's Geological Society and Royal Society. Named by George M Dawson of the Geological Survey of Canada in 1878, along with nearby Dwight Rk. *W*

Daniel Point (49°38'00" 124°04'00" SE entrance to Agamemnon Channel, W side of Sechelt Peninsula, Malaspina Str). Presumably named in association with nearby Pender Hbr after RN hydrographer Daniel Pender, who played an important role on the BC coast, 1857–71, as a marine surveyor. *See* Pender Canal. Nearby Mt Daniel, known to Sechelt First Nation members as Shélkém, is also named for him. Formerly known as Norman Point (a local name still in use in the 1990s).

Danube Rock (53°13'00" 132°12'00" Entrance to Kagan Bay, Skidegate Inlet, QCI). Named in 1891 when the merchant steamship *Danube*, under Capt William Meyer, struck this hazard. The 66-m, 805-tonne vessel had an adventurous life. It was built near Glasgow in 1869 for the Scottish Oriental Steamship Co and named *United Empire*. The Canadian Pacific Navigation Co (taken over by the CPR in 1903) purchased it in 1890. In 1891–92 the *Danube* carried British fur-seal-treaty commissioners to Alaska, and in 1893 it was impounded by US immigration officials while offloading 633 Asian passengers at Portland. The ship participated in the Klondike gold rush and was badly damaged in 1899 after running ashore on Denman I; in 1902 it struck an iceberg off Taku Inlet. The BC Salvage Co bought the *Danube* in 1905, converted it to a salvage vessel and renamed it the *Salvor*. Sold again in 1918 to a Montreal company, it operated as a tramp steamer, then as the Spanish iron-ore freighter *Nervion*, and was finally broken up in 1936. **Danube Bay** (53°35'00" 128°58'00" Verney Passage, E side of Hawkesbury I, S of Kitimat) is probably also named for this senior citizen of the seas. *W*

Daphne Point (50°45'00" 127°27'00" E entrance to Hardy Bay, Port Hardy, NE end of Vancouver I). HMS *Daphne*, an 18-gun corvette, was built at Pembroke in 1838 and sold in 1864; it was assigned to the Pacific Station on a number of occasions. In 1851, under Capt Edward Fanshawe, *Daphne* went to northern Vancouver I with colonial gov Richard Blanshard to continue investigations begun the previous year into the murders of three HBC deserters. Faced with

D

resistance from the Nahwitti First Nation, Blanshard ordered the destruction of a village—possibly Nahwitti or Newitty on Cape Sutil—after which, in return for 90 blankets, three suspects were killed and handed over to the RN. *See* Daedalus Passage, Deserters Group *and* Nahwitti Bar for more details. It was during this debacle that Lt George Mansell of the *Daphne* made the first survey of Beaver Hbr, just to the SE of Hardy Bay. Daphne Point was formerly known as Islet Point.

Darby Channel (51°31'00" 127°43'00" Entrance to Rivers Inlet, N of Penrose I). Dr George Elias Darby (1889–1962) was a Methodist medical missionary who served on the BC coast for 45 years. He was born in Ont and studied medicine at the Univ of Toronto, spending a summer in BC as a student in 1912. He interned at Vancouver in 1913 and the following year married Edna Matthews in Toronto. Together they moved to the central BC coast, where Darby ran a hospital at Bella Bella, had a summer hospital on Rivers Inlet and brought medical and religious services to surrounding First Nation communities. A Coast Guard vessel is named in his honour. Formerly known as Schooner Passage. *E*

Chinese Canadian lepers at D'Arcy Island in the 1890s. *BC Archives C-03858*

D'Arcy Island (48°34'00" 123°17'00" S of Sidney I, Haro Str, N of Victoria), **D'Arcy Shoals** (48°34'00" 123°18'00" W of D'Arcy I). Sub-Lt John D'Arcy (1831–84) was an officer aboard HMS *Herald* on its surveying expedition to the Pacific, 1852–54. He later commanded HMS *Osborne*, a paddle yacht (1865–69), and the troopships *Adventure* (1874) and *Jumna* (1875–78). D'Arcy was promoted capt in 1869. The 82-ha island was used as a leprosarium, 1891–1924, where Chinese lepers were quarantined and provisioned but left without medical care until 1906, when nurses were hired. The colony was moved to Bentinck I near Victoria in 1924. D'Arcy became a provincial marine park in 1961; the lepers' homes were burned, though some ruins are still visible. The island is now part of the Gulf Is National Park

Reserve. Its Sencoten (Coast Salish) name is Ctesu, meaning "just arrived." *E W*

D'Arcy Point (50°25'00" 125°43'00" Junction of Chancellor Channel and Wellbore Channel, N of W Thurlow I, Johnstone Str). After Lt D'Arcy Anthony Denny of the RN, who served on the BC coast, 1866–68. *See* Denny I.

Dare Beach (48°37'00" 124°46'00" N side of Carmanah Point, SW side of Vancouver I), **Dare Point** (48°39'00" 124°48'00" Between Carmanah Point and mouth of Nitinat R). The schooner *Dare*, under Capt F A Berry, was sailing from San Francisco to Tacoma in Dec 1890 when it was wrecked on Bonilla Point on the W coast of Vancouver I in thick fog. The crew reached shore safely, though the ship broke up in heavy seas. Its home port was North Bend, Oregon.

Daring Point (53°59'00" 130°09'00" SE end of Kennedy I, between Porcher I and mouth of the Skeena R). HMS *Daring*, launched in 1874, was a 4-gun steam sloop based at Esquimalt on the Pacific Station, 1875–78. The 811-tonne vessel surveyed the entrance to the Skeena R in 1877 under Cdr John Hanmer, who named a number of features in the vicinity after the ship and its officers. The *Daring* was broken up in 1889.

Darrell Bay (49°40'00" 123°10'00" NE side of Howe Sd, just S of Squamish, NW of Vancouver). Darrell B Burgess established a recreational fishing camp at this location in the 1940s. The site was formerly known as Shannon Bay, after William Shannon, who pre-empted land here in 1889, but Burgess requested the name change and it was granted. For many years a ferry ran from Darrell Bay across Howe Sd to the pulp mill at Woodfibre. Skxwúmish (Squamish) First Nation members harvested herring spawn in the bay, naming it Qu-tsa-tso-tsein, meaning "island in the mouth"—a reference to the islet at the entrance to the cove. They also met Capt George Vancouver in this vicinity in June 1792. He called it "a most uninhabitable place."

Darwin Point (52°34'00" 131°37'00" Entrance to Darwin Sd), **Darwin Sound** (52°40'00" 131°43'00" Between Moresby I and Lyell I, QCI). Named in 1878 by George M Dawson of the Geological Survey of Canada after Charles Robert Darwin (1809–82), the pre-eminent naturalist of the 19th century, whose groundbreaking theory of evolution was explained in an 1859 book, *On the Origin of Species*. Dawson named a number of features in the area after famous 19th-century scientists.

Dass Point (52°52'00" 131°41'00" SE point of Louise I, off NE Moresby I, QCI). Walter Leach Dass came to the archipelago in 1906 and first prospected in the Jedway area, then acquired a number of mining claims in the Selwyn Inlet region about 1910. He built and managed the first Jedway Hotel and later was skipper of several QCI vessels. In 1918 he married Flora Ellen Cook in Delta. He was still alive in Toronto about 1970. Dass Ck and Dass Lk are also named for him. *D*

Davey Islets (53°03'00" 131°59'00" Off N side of Gillatt Arm, Cumshewa Inlet, NE Moresby I, QCI). Cornishman "Cap" Davey was a notary public who ran the land office in Queen Charlotte City in the early days. He also ranched on Maude I and did his share of mining and prospecting. According to QCI historian Kathleen Dalzell, black oystercatchers were known locally for years as "Cap Daveys" because their long scarlet beaks reminded people of the capt's nose.

David Channel (48°59'30" 125°19'30" E of Stopper Is, N of Broken Group, Barkley Sd, W side of Vancouver I), **David Island** (48°58'00" 125°23'00" SW side of David Channel), **Mount David** (48°48'03" 123°09'58" Overlooking Lyall Hbr, Saturna I, Gulf Is). Dr David Lyall served in BC from 1857 to 1861, first as the surgeon of the RN survey vessel *Plumper* and then as a member of the N American Boundary Commission. *See* Lyall Hbr.

David Cove (48°51'58" 123°16'28" E side of Mayne I, Gulf Is). The Davids were an early farming family on Mayne I. Francis L David (1846–1909) came to Canada from France in 1887. He married Elizabeth Collinson (1866–1940), who was born at Sumas, BC, the daughter of Mayne I pioneer William Collinson (*see* Collinson Point), and they had a large family. The former local name for this feature was Hidden Cove.

David Ledge (52°01'00" 128°15'00" NW of the Prince Group, off SW end of Campbell I, SW of Bella Bella). The *Prince David* was one of three fast, luxurious liners built in the UK by the CNR for use on the BC coast. Put into service in 1930, they proved too cumbersome—and too expensive to operate in the Depression era—and the 109-m, 6,251-tonne *Prince David* was soon transferred to the W Indies as a cruise ship. In 1932 it was badly damaged after running aground at Bermuda. During WWII the *David* was converted to an armed merchant cruiser, serving in Bermuda and on the W and Alaska coasts, and participating as a landing ship on D-Day and at the liberation of Greece (where it struck a mine, ending its wartime service). In 1947 it was refitted in Britain for passenger service as the *Charlton Monarch*, but its first charter—transporting refugees from Europe to S America—was aborted, and it was scrapped in 1951, an "unlucky" vessel in many ways.

Davidson Bay (48°49'06" 123°17'54" N end of N Pender I, Gulf Is). Andrew Angus Davidson (1849–1928) was originally from Scotland and had lived for many years in Peru. He arrived on N Pender I in 1892, bought 120 ha at this bay (also known as Clam Bay) from an earlier settler, Washington Grimmer, and built a home for his wife, Margaret (1858–1944), and four children. Sons Andrew and Thomas farmed on Pender and served as early postmasters, but it appears that their father worked in Victoria as well, as a moulder at Spratt & Gray's Iron Works. Clam Bay Farm, somewhat reduced from its original size but with many buildings, was for sale in 2007 for $4.5 million.

Davidson Bay (49°08'00" 123°46'00" SE side of Mudge I, SE of Nanaimo, Gulf Is). Jim Davidson, a retired federal civil servant, and his wife, Jenny, moved permanently to Mudge I from Vancouver in the early 1970s. Their property on this bay, acquired about 1960, included Mudge's oldest remaining house, since restored by the Davidsons. The two-storey home was built before WWI by settlers John and Hazel Cox, who raised children and sheep, planted fruit trees and operated a sawmill. The bay's name was adopted in 1986 after being proposed the previous year by Mudge I residents.

Davidson Point (52°45'00" 132°07'00" N entrance to Tasu Sd, W side of Moresby I, QCI). A Dept of National Defence employee named Davidson was working aboard CGS *William J Stewart* in 1935 on topographical surveys. The name was adopted in 1946 after submission by the hydrographic service.

Davie Bay (49°36'00" 124°23'00" W side of Texada I, Str of Georgia), **Mount Davies** (49°35'54" 124°19'12" E of Davie Bay, Texada I). Both Davie Bay and Mt Davies may be corruptions of the surname of millwright John Coyne Davis (1842–1924), who was born in Ont and came to Nanaimo in 1875. He built a schooner on Texada I many years ago.

Davies Bay (54°19'00" 129°58'00" Head of Work Channel, E of Prince Rupert), **Davies Lagoon** (54°20'00" 129°59'00" Head of Davies Bay), **Davies Narrows** (54°19'00" 129°58'00" Head of Work Channel), **Davies Passage** (55°24'00" 129°41'00" Entrance to Alice Arm, between Liddle I and Davies Point, Observatory Inlet), **Davies Point** (55°24'00" 129°42'00" N entrance to Alice Arm), **Davies Rock** (55°24'00" 129°41'00" In Davies Passage). Lawyer and politician Sir Louis Henry Davies (1845–1924) was premier of PEI, 1876–79. He went into federal politics as a PEI MP, 1882–1901, and became a leading member of Sir Wilfrid Laurier's Liberal cabinet, serving as minister of Marine and Fisheries, 1896–1901. From 1901 until his death he was a judge of the Supreme Court of Canada, and chief justice from 1918. Davies Bay and Davies Point (formerly known as Way Point) were named in 1898 by Capt John Walbran, master of CGS *Quadra* and a Marine and Fisheries dept employee, who also named Gertrude Point and Helen Point (at the entrance to Kitkiata Inlet) and Ethel Rk (in Principe Channel) after the politician's daughters, and Ursula Rk off Texada I after his niece.

D

Davies Shoal (53°01'00" 131°44'00" SE of McLellan I, Cumshewa Inlet, NE Moresby I, QCI). Capt A M Davies was a frequent skipper of the *Prince John*, which operated in the QCI from 1911 to 1940 for the GTP Coast Steamship Co and Canadian National Steamships (and was then bought by the Union Steamship Co and renamed *Cassiar II*). In 1910 he also served aboard GTP's *Prince Rupert*. In the 1920s, Davies was an examiner for master's and mate's licences in Victoria.

Davy Ledge (54°04'00" 132°14'00" Off Westacott Point, entrance to Masset Hbr, N side of Graham I, QCI). Named by Capt Frederick Learmonth of the RN survey vessel *Egeria* after Lt Bishop O M Davy, who surveyed Masset Hbr in 1907, assisted by Lt James Troup and Lt James Harvey. In 1908, Davy was appointed cdr of HMS *Sealark* and conducted surveys off the coast of Ceylon (Sri Lanka). He had a long career as an RN hydrographer and is listed as co-author of the *Arctic Pilot* in 1931.

Dawes Point (54°19'00" 130°31'00" S end of Tugwell I, W side of Metlakatla Bay, W of Prince Rupert), **Dawes Rocks** (54°18'47" 130°31'38" Off S end of Tugwell I). According to Capt John Walbran, the missionary William Duncan named the point after "Gen Dawes," a retired British Army officer and important supporter of the Anglican Church Missionary Society in London about 1860. He was probably referring to William Dawes (1762–1836), an earlier figure, who was not a gen at all, but a lt. This Dawes was a marine, a scientist and an anti-slavery religious reformer who served in Australia and Sierra Leone (where he was gov of the Sierra Leone Co between 1792 and 1803). He was involved with the CMS from 1804 onwards, founding a training institute for missionaries in England and, in 1813, moving to the W Indies, where he established numerous CMS schools for the children of slaves. Capt George Richards, who surveyed Metlakatla Bay in HMS *Hecate* in 1862, adopted the names of both features.

Dawkins Point (55°16'00" 129°48'00" E side of Observatory Inlet, S of Stewart). Capt Richard Dawkins (d 1896) was cdr of HMS *Zealous*, based at Esquimalt as the flagship of Rear Adm Hon George Hastings, cdr-in-chief of the Pacific Station, 1866–69. Dawkins served in China and Indonesia in the 1840s, and in the Crimean War, and retired as a rear adm in 1878. Nearby Richards Point is also named for him. *W*

Dawley Passage (49°09'00" 125°48'00" S of Fortune Channel, E of Meares I, Clayoquot Sd, W side of Vancouver I). Walter Thomas Dawley (1860–1944), from Ont, was a trader at Clayoquot and also the region's first mining recorder from 1898 to the late 1930s. In 1891, with partner Thomas Stockham, he built a store from salvaged shipwreck lumber on Stockham I, opposite the Tla-o-qui-aht First Nation village of Opitsat on Meares I. The pair added a hotel in 1898, opened trading posts at Nootka and Ahousat, and took over the pioneer store on nearby Stubbs I in 1902. They expanded the hotel on Stubbs I, which was operated by Dawley's brother Clarence (1876–1957). Dawley bought out Stockham in 1904 and went on to become a justice of the peace, deputy returning officer and Clayoquot postmaster, 1902–37. At Victoria in 1905 the Dawley brothers married the Dennan sisters: Walter wed Rose Angela (1884–1950) and Clarence wed Mamie (1878–1954). When he retired in 1937, Walter gave Stubbs I to his daughter Madeline and her husband, Pierre Malon, as a wedding gift. Mt Dawley, NE of Ucluelet, is also named for him. Dawley Passage Provincial Park was established in 1995 to protect the area's rich marine ecosystem, which harbours a rare white hydrocoral (*Stylaster* species). Formerly known as Deception Pass.

Dawson Cove (53°03'00" 131°55'00" N side of Cumshewa Inlet, NE Moresby I, QCI), **Dawson Harbour** (53°10'00" 132°27'00" E side of Dawson Inlet), **Dawson Head** (53°20'00" 132°26'00" NE end of Shields I, Rennell Sd, SW Graham I, QCI), **Dawson Inlet** (53°11'00" 132°29'00" N side of Skidegate Channel, SW Graham I), **Dawson Islands** (53°43'00" 132°21'00" N side of Masset Inlet, Graham I), **Dawson Point** (53°25'00" 129°14'00" N end of Promise I, entrance to Douglas Channel, SW of Kitimat). Dr George Mercer Dawson, CMG (1849–1901), was a leading Canadian geologist and director of the Geological Survey of Canada, 1895–1901. A native of NS, he was appointed to the N American Boundary Commission in 1873 as geologist and naturalist. Three years later he joined the geological survey, and despite a severe spinal deformity caused by childhood TB, he undertook dozens of gruelling field trips in N and W Canada. In BC he made major studies of N Vancouver I, the QCI, the southern Interior and the Peace R district between 1875 and 1879. Dawson took many photographs, collected artifacts, published widely—on ethnology as well as geology—and was responsible for hundreds of BC place names, especially in the QCI. He became president of the Royal Society of Canada in 1893. Numerous other features in BC are named after this remarkable explorer, including the city of Dawson Ck, Dawson Glacier, Dawson Pks, Dawson Range, Dawson Ridge, Mercer Point and Mt Dawson. Dawson City in the Yukon also commemorates him. However, BC's Dawson Falls and Dawson R are named for George Herbert Dawson, the province's surveyor gen, 1912–17. *D E W*

Dawsons Landing (51°35'00" 127°35'00" N end of Darby Channel, NW side of Rivers Inlet). The federal Fisheries dept established a station at this sheltered location in 1924, in the heady, long-gone days of the great Rivers Inlet salmon boom. Years later, in quieter times, Jimmy and Jean Dawson established a store there; a post office was added in 1967. In the early 2000s the tiny floating

Dawsons Landing now caters mostly to tourists and sport fishers. *Andrew Scott*

community was the inlet's commercial heart—a regular floatplane stop and a fuel and supply centre for loggers, tourists and sport fishers.

Daybreak Point (49°31'00" 123°18'00" S end of Anvil I, Howe Sd, NW of Vancouver). Daybreak Point Bible Camp was located here, now run by Marineview Chapel, an independent community church in Vancouver. The name was adopted in 1955, as submitted by officials of the hydrographic service.

Dayman Island (48°58'20" 123°41'15" E side of Stuart Channel, SW of Thetis I, Gulf Is). Lt Joseph Dayman served aboard HMS *Thetis* on the Pacific Station, 1851–53, under Capt Augustus Kuper. From 1857 to 1860, as cdr of HMS *Cyclops*, *Gorgon* and *Firebrand*, he pioneered deep-sea sounding techniques in support of early cable-laying operations. He was appointed a capt in 1863. The 10-ha island has had a number of owners, but none so notorious as Alfred Matthew Hubbard (1902–82), Catholic mystic, electronics genius and secret service operative, who was also known as the "Johnny Appleseed of LSD." A native of rural Kentucky, he first took LSD in the early 1950s; later in the decade he helped Dr Ross MacLean use the psychedelic to treat alcoholics at New Westminster's Hollywood Hospital. Before hanging out with the likes of Timothy Leary and Aldous Huxley, Hubbard became rich chartering boats and mining uranium, but a personal financial crisis forced him to sell Dayman about 1968. In the 1970s, businessman Conn Andrie and his wife, Gay, bought the property and replaced Hubbard's dwelling with a fine new one. They apparently found a gallon jar of LSD capsules when they

rebuilt. The island, which was reportedly sold again in the mid-1990s for about $2.5 million, is said to be home to one of BC's largest arbutus trees.

Deadman Island (49°18'00" 123°07'00" Coal Hbr, Burrard Inlet, Vancouver). This 3-ha island was a former burial ground for Skxwúmish (Squamish) and X̱ʷmuzk̓ʷiʼum (Musqueam) First Nation groups using the Stanley Park area (its X̱ʷmuzk̓ʷiʼum name was Skwcàs, or "island")—and for the old community at Brockton Point. From the 1890s until 1931, as many as 150 squatters lived on the island. A Seattle lumberman, Theodore Ludgate, received a lease in 1898 to build a sawmill there, and violence ensued in the early 1900s when he tried to evict the unwanted dwellers. In 1918, still undeveloped, the island reverted to the government for unpaid taxes and was leased in 1931 by the city of Vancouver, which finally managed to remove the last 40 or so illegal residents. In WWII the Defence dept took the island over and in 1944 opened a naval cadet training school, HMS *Discovery*, which is connected to Stanley Park by a causeway. *E*

Dead Point (50°34'00" 126°34'00" N side of Harbledown I, Beware Passage, W end of Johnstone Str). This Kwakwaka'wakw reserve is the site of Tzatsisnukomi (T'sadzisnukwame̓) or New Vancouver, a community that was settled about 1891 by members of the Da'naxda'xw First Nation, who are an amalgamation of the Da'naxda'xw (Tenaktak) and Awaetlala people of Knight Inlet. Most residents moved away from the village to Ft Rupert and Alert Bay in the 20th century, but a settlement was in the process of being re-established on the reserve in the early 2000s. The name appears on an Admiralty chart published

D

in 1865 and was probably bestowed because of early burial grounds in the vicinity. Tzatsisnukomi has been translated as "eelgrass on the point" or "eelgrass in front."

Dean Channel (52°19'00" 127°31'00" From Fisher Channel NE to mouth of Dean R, W and N of Bella Coola), **Dean Island** (52°11'00" 127°52'00" Junction of Johnson Channel and Fisher Channel, SW of entrance to Dean Channel). Capt George Vancouver named "Dean's Canal" in 1793 in association with King I (qv) and Raphoe Point, after Rev James King (d 1795), dean of Raphoe, Ireland. The dean was the father of RN Capt James King, a great friend of Vancouver, with whom he had sailed on Capt James Cook's third expedition, 1776–80. The **Dean River** (52°48'00" 126°58'00" Flows W then SW into head of Dean Channel) is also named for him. *E W*

A re-creation of the message left by Alexander Mackenzie on a rock in Dean Channel in 1793. *BC Archives A-02312*

Dean Point (50°17'00" 124°47'00" NW tip of W Redonda I, entrance to Toba Inlet), **Dean Rock** (Just S of Dean Point). Dean Point and nearby Bishop and Church points were all named during the same survey, probably by Capt George Richards in 1862 or Lt Daniel Pender in 1864.

Deans Point (54°22'00" 130°42'15" SE end of Melville I, W of Prince Rupert). James Deans (1827–1905), born in Scotland, came to Victoria in 1853 aboard the *Norman Morison* and worked as a labourer on the HBC's Craigflower Farm. Four years later he was able to establish his own Oakvale Farm in the Mt Tolmie area, where his brother George Deans (1833–79) also settled. In 1864 he married Catherine Bullion, a fellow Scot, at Victoria. An amateur geologist and anthropologist, Deans became interested in BC's First Nation cultures and languages and made extensive trips to the N coast. In 1883 he accompanied James Swan to the QCI on an artifact-collecting journey for the Smithsonian Institution. He published a book, *Tales from the Totems of the Hidery*, in 1899, wrote ethnological articles for the *American*

Antiquarian and Oriental Journal (and many letters to the editor of Victoria's *Colonist* newspaper) and helped Haida artists prepare an elaborate exhibit, now at the Field Museum, for the 1893 Chicago World's Fair. *W*

Deans Rocks (53°36'00" 130°34'00" In Griffith Hbr, W side of Banks I). W Deans worked as 2nd cook aboard the W coast survey vessel *Lillooet* in the early 1920s on his return from overseas service in WWI. Named by Henri Parizeau of the hydrographic service and adopted in 1926.

Deas Island (49°07'00" 123°04'00" Fraser R estuary, between Lulu I and Delta), **Deas Slough** (Just S of Deas I). John Sullivan Deas (c 1838–80), from S Carolina, joined the California gold rush and came to Victoria about 1861. He married Fanny Harris there in 1862. He worked as a tinsmith and hardware dealer at Yale, 1866–68, and Victoria, 1868–71, and then began making tins for Capt Edward Stamp's salmon cannery at Sapperton. Deas, a mulatto, built his own substantial cannery on Deas I two years later and became a leader—and the only prominent black man—in the pioneer industry. He sold his business in 1878 and moved to Portland, where his wife had bought a rooming house. The 70-ha island is today a regional park with several fine preserved heritage buildings. Hwy 99 transects Deas I as it enters the George Massey Tunnel under the Fraser R. *E*

Deas Rock (52°38'00" 128°47'00" Off W side of Hastings I, Laredo Sd, NW of Bella Bella). Sapper William Deas was a member of the Columbia detachment of Royal Engineers, which served in BC 1858–63. He may not have joined the rest of the contingent until 1861. He remained in the colony after the engineers were disbanded and bought the Columbia Hotel in New Westminster ("the substantials and delicacies of the season will always be found on the table") with fellow sapper Samuel Dawson. In 1865 he was appointed a police constable at Ft Shepherd on the Columbia R in SE BC.

Deasy Island (53°40'00" 132°20'45" Entrance to Juskatla Inlet, S side of Masset Inlet, Graham I, QCI). Thomas Deasy (1857–1936) was the son of Daniel Deasy (*see below*), who came to BC in 1859 with the Royal Engineers. Thomas married Anne Elizabeth Smith (1862–1936) in Victoria in 1880 and for years was chief of the fire dept, first in Victoria and then in Nelson. In 1910, Deasy and his wife moved to Masset, where he became the Indian agent for the QCI.

Deasy Point (52°36'00" 129°07'00" E end of Clifford Bay, W side of Aristazabal I). Sapper Daniel Deasy (1826–95) was a member of the Columbia detachment of Royal Engineers, which served in BC 1858–63. He arrived at Esquimalt in 1859 aboard the *Euphrates* with his wife, Mary (1832–85), and children, and remained in the colony when the unit was

The Geographical Names Office

Every cove and creek mouth in BC may have already been explored and mapped, but the process of giving names to places continues. While all the major landmarks were tidied away nearly a century ago, names for minor features are still being considered and adopted. Naming procedures today are more highly regulated and not nearly as urgent as in the past, but each year several dozen BC place names are added to the gazetteer or have their credentials revised.

In the first half of 2009, nearly 30 names had been approved or updated. In 2008, another 28 new or altered names appeared on the list. What list is this? Well, in BC the Geographical Names Office is responsible for provincial place names; it maintains the BC Geographical Names Information System database, BCGNIS for short. The unit, with offices in Victoria, has a website (*www.ilmb.gov.bc.ca/bcnames*) where visitors can search a digital gazetteer by name or by area. Some searches produce fascinating data; others reveal nothing at all.

Many names listed in 2008 and 2009 reflect administrative changes. The Okanagan community of Westside, for instance, is now known as West Kelowna. A number of new water features were named, including evocative Moose Wallow Creek east of Prince George. But no coastal features appear on the list. In 2005, however, several new names were officially recognized on the west coast of Vancouver Island as a result of the approval in principle of the Maa-nulth Treaty with a group of five First Nations affiliated with the Nuu-chah-nulth Tribal Council. The names were required in order to establish water reserves for water-licensing purposes. Thus we now have St Pauls Dome Creek on Kyuquot Sound and Poett Creek on Barkley Sound. The names are adopted from other local landmarks and were chosen, somewhat unpoetically, by the Treaty Negotiations Office in order "to facilitate timely production of legal documents."

Getting a new place name on the books is no simple matter these days. As BC's Geographical Names Office makes very clear, "not all features need a name at this time." In other words, to keep the wilderness wild and to give future generations a chance to add a few names of their own, the government is in no rush to attach a label to every rock and puddle in the province. The names unit does not initiate new names; they have to come from the public. However, proponents must not only explain in detail the significance of the names being proposed but must also provide persuasive reasons why particular features need naming in the first place.

Names with a long history of local usage by the general public always take precedence in any new naming process. When no local name presents itself, other naming sources are considered: historical events that occurred in the area, unique descriptive terms, First Nation words associated with the area, early residents of the area, and persons who died during war service. You can't officially name a feature just because you own the land it's on or to commemorate a tragedy or the victim of an accident. Corporate or commercial names are not acceptable, and all names must, of course, be in good taste. Personal names are only considered after two or more years have elapsed since the death of the person in question.

The name Kebegwis, for example, was applied in 2005 to the south shore of Shuttleworth Bight on the northern tip of Vancouver Island. This First Nation word translates as "sandy beach" according to the Quatsino Band Council and Port Hardy Heritage Society. The name Third Beach was also adopted that year for a beach on the northwest coast of Nootka Island, off Vancouver Island. Bible camp leaders on Nuchatlitz Inlet came up with the name in the late 1940s; their "first" and "second" beaches were nearby, but they could only reach the "third" beach by boat. Today Third Beach marks the usual northern terminus of the rugged Nootka Trail. It was officially adopted as a "well-established local name," used by pilots and mariners, and identified on hiking maps.

So, while proposing a new BC coast name can be laborious, it's still possible. The place to start is the Geographical Names Office website, where you can download guidelines, or else write to PO Box 9355, Stn Prov Govt, Victoria, BC V8W 9M2.

Third Beach on Nootka Island is at the head of a popular wilderness hiking trail. *Peter A. Robson*

D

disbanded, receiving the 60-ha military land grant given to men who stayed on. Tragedy dogged the family: in 1864 they lost everything when fire at the engineers' Sapperton camp destroyed their home; one son died at 17 in a shooting accident; another died at 20. A third son, Thomas, was a fire chief and Indian agent (*see* Deasy I). Daniel, who also had two daughters, worked as a government messenger at New Westminster and, later, at Victoria, where he became caretaker of the legislative buildings.

DeCosmos Lagoon (51°56'00" 127°58'00" Just SW of DeCosmos Point), **DeCosmos Point** (51°57'00" 127°57'00" E side of Hunter I, Fisher Channel, SE of Bella Bella). Amor de Cosmos (1825–97) was born plain William Alexander Smith at Windsor, NS. He went to California at age 26, worked as a photographer and changed his name to "lover of the universe." Arriving in Victoria in 1858, he founded the *British Colonist*, BC's first newspaper, and as its editor became a constant irritant to Vancouver I gov James Douglas. De Cosmos was a member of BC's legislative council, 1867–71, and an advocate for union with Canada. He was BC's second premier, 1872–74, and a Victoria MP, 1871–72 and 1874–82, but his racist views lost him support, and late in life he degenerated into extreme eccentricity. Many other features in BC honour him, though the form of his name varies, as can be seen in the following list: Amor De Cosmos Ck, Amor Lk, Amor Point, Cosmos Heights and Mt DeCosmos. *E W*

De Courcy Group (49°06'00" 123°45'00" Between Stuart Channel and Pylades Channel, S of Gabriola I, Gulf Is),

De Courcy Island (One of the De Courcy Group, between Link I and Ruxton I). Capt Michael de Courcy served on the Pacific Station, 1859–60, as cdr of HMS *Pylades*. In 1866, as a commodore, he had command of the southern division of the Pacific Station, aboard HMS *Leander*. De Courcy retired from the RN in 1873 with the rank of vice adm. The notorious cult leader Edward Arthur Wilson, better known as Brother XII, based his operation at the S end of De Courcy I in the early 1930s; in 1966 the site became part of Pirates Cove Marine Provincial Park. The De Courcy Group contains Pylades, Ruxton, De Courcy, Link and Mudge islands and associated islets. *E W*

Deep Bay (49°28'00" 124°44'00" S end of Baynes Sd, NW of Bowser on E side of Vancouver I). There are many features in BC named Deep Bay. This one was a First Nation fishing site for thousands of years, then home to a Canadian Robert Dollar Co logging camp, 1917–31, and a fish-processing plant, 1917–51. In the early 2000s a small resort community flourished there. Formerly known as Lymn Bay.

Deep Cove (49°20'00" 122°56'00" SW side of Indian Arm, Burrard Inlet, N Vancouver). This summer recreation spot, with its dance hall, roller-skating rink and annual regatta, developed into a permanent residential community after WWII. In the early 2000s the suburb of Deep Cove, together with its neighbour Cove Cliff, had a population of about 3,500 and a busy boating scene. Capt George Richards bestowed its name in 1859 or 1860, though the post office here was originally named Deepwater, 1927–40. *E*

Kayakers at Deep Cove. *Duncan Rawlinson/www.thelastminuteblog.com*

Deer Island (50°43'00" 127°23'00" Entrance to Beaver Hbr, just E of Port Hardy, NE end of Vancouver I). The feature is known to the Kwakwaka'wakw people as Wazulis, a name translated by Franz Boas in the 1930s as "river on flat beach." It became a confrontation site in 1986 when local residents prevented a MacMillan Bloedel subcontractor from logging it. The island, site of an old village and graveyard, was used by Edward Curtis as the setting for his 1914 ethnographic film *In the Land of the War Canoes*.

Defence Islands (49°35'00" 123°17'00" NE of Anvil I, Howe Sd, NW of Vancouver). With these islands, 19th-century RN surveyor Capt George Richards continued his theme of naming features in Howe Sd after the 1794 English Channel victory known as the Glorious First of June, in which Adm Lord Howe triumphed over a French fleet. HMS *Defence*, under Capt James Gambier, had the "distinguished honour" of passing through the enemy's line first, a manoeuvre that dismasted the ship and resulted in heavy casualties. The 74-gun vessel, launched at Plymouth in 1763, also saw action at the battles of Trafalgar and the Nile, and was wrecked on the Jutland coast in 1811 when driven ashore in a gale, with the loss of almost 600 lives. *W*

Defender Shoal (50°07'00" 125°23'00" Menzies Bay, W side of Discovery Passage, N of Campbell R). The US yacht *Defender* won the America's Cup in 1895, beating British challenger *Valkyrie III*, owned by the Earl of Dunraven. The innovative vessel, designed by Nathanael Greene Herreshoff, used aluminum in its construction and was owned by William Vanderbilt, Edwin Morgan and Oliver Iselin. Named by Lt Bertram Chambers, who re-surveyed Menzies Bay that year from HMS *Nymph* and considered that the outline of the shoal at low water somewhat resembled the hull of a racing yacht. *W*

De Freitas Islets (52°27'00" 128°14'00" E side of Mathieson Channel, S of Salmon Bay, N of Bella Bella). Lt Cdr Percival Francis Mayow de Freitas, of Oak Bay, was killed in action Sept 20, 1943, aged 43, aboard HMCS *St Croix*. The destroyer was escorting a slow-moving convoy in the N Atlantic when it was torpedoed and sunk by a U-boat (*U-305*). De Freitas had previously commanded the corvette *Vancouver* on convoy duties off the Aleutian Is. He was the son of Sir Anthony de Freitas, OBE, of Barbados, who held a number of senior legal positions in the W Indies, and the brother of Geoffrey de Freitas, a British MP and diplomat. His name is inscribed on the Halifax Memorial.

Degnen Bay (49°08'00" 123°43'00" S end of Gabriola I, Gulf Is). The Degnen family farmed on Gabriola I for many years. Thomas Degnen (1832–1921), from Ireland, and his Cowichan First Nation wife, Jane Janimetga (1833–1919), were the original settlers, in the early 1860s, and many of their descendants stayed in the area.

Thomas's original surname seems to have been Dignol; a clerical error on a land pre-emption document resulted in Degnen, and rather than causing a lot of confusion by trying to change it back, he apparently just continued on with a new name. An immigrant to NY in 1849, he joined the US Army and served in the Oregon Territory, 1850–51, but became disillusioned by the brutal quelling of Native American uprisings and moved to Victoria in 1854. Degnen mined coal at Nanaimo before raising sheep and growing apples on Gabriola; he also operated a local boat service. The name of this geographical feature, adopted by the hydrographic service in 1944, may refer specifically to a later member of the Degnen clan, possibly Hannah Degnen (1860–1945), wife of James Degnen (1859–1921), Thomas and Jane's eldest son. There is a well-known petroglyph of a killer whale near the head of the bay.

De Horsey Island (54°08'00" 130°08'00" E of Smith I, mouth of Skeena R, SE of Prince Rupert), **De Horsey Passage** (54°08'00" 130°09'00" Between Smith I and De Horsey I). Rear Adm Algernon Frederick Rous de Horsey (1827–1922) was cdr-in-chief on the Pacific Station, 1876–79, based at Esquimalt, with his flag on HMS *Shah*. Earlier in his career, as cdr of HMS *Brisk*, he captured the famed Spanish slaver *Manuela*. He was senior RN officer during the Jamaican rebellion of 1865 and on Canada's Great Lks, 1866–67, during the Fenian uprising. De Horsey commanded the English Channel squadron, 1884–85. He was promoted to adm and made a KCB in 1893, the year after he retired from the RN. His grandson, Vice Adm Sir Thomas Phillips, was cdr-in-chief of the RN's Far East fleet in 1941 and died that year when his flagship, the new battleship *Prince of Wales*, was sunk, along with the battlecruiser *Repulse*, by Japanese torpedo bombers. De Horsey Passage is known locally as Osland Passage. *W*

De la Beche Inlet (52°32'00" 131°40'00" W end of Juan Perez Sd, E side of Moresby I, QCI), **De la Beche Island** (52°32'00" 131°37'00" Entrance to De la Beche Inlet). English geologist Sir Henry Thomas de la Beche (1796–1855) became the first director of the Geological Survey of Great Britain in 1835 and established the Museum of Practical Geology in London in 1851. Canadian geologist William Logan's maps of the Welsh coalfields impressed de la Beche, who recommended Logan as the first director of the Geological Survey of Canada, a position he held 1842–69. De la Beche published widely on geology and was also an important cartoonist. He was president of the Geological Society of London in 1848–49 and was awarded its highest honour, the Wollaston Medal, in 1855. These features were named in 1878 by George Dawson of the Geological Survey of Canada.

Delkatla Inlet (54°01'00" 132°08'00" Extends NE from Masset Hbr, N end of Graham I, QCI). The inlet is really a drying basin, known locally as Delkatla Slough. It is

D

bordered by grasslands (the Delkatla Flats) that were the site of the region's first farm, established in 1890 by Rev Charles Harrison, former Anglican missionary at Masset. Delkatla is also a part of Masset, on the SE side of the entrance to the inlet, where Charles Wilson first proposed a townsite in 1911. According to historian Kathleen Dalzell, the name comes from an old Haida description of the area meaning "water drifting in to the inside." The inlet and flats provide rich habitat for waterbirds. Delkatla Ck derives its name from the same source.

Delta (49°05'00" 123°05'00" S side of the mouth of the Fraser R, S of Vancouver). The first settlers to this rich farming area arrived in the 1860s and had to dike their lands before developing them. Agriculture is still important to the area, especially dairy farming, though the district municipality, formed in 1879, has seen rapid population growth since the George Massey Tunnel connected it to Richmond in 1958. Delta is now an important residential suburb of Vancouver with three population centres: Ladner, the business and administrative centre; Tsawwassen; and N Delta. The name, of course, refers to the estuary of the Fraser R.

Delusion Bay (54°16'00" 130°23'00" S end of Digby I, just SW of Prince Rupert). GTP assistant harbour engineer Joel Pillsbury gave the feature this name about 1908 after confidently setting up camp there at high tide. When he returned at low tide, he was surprised to find the bay, which had every appearance of a good anchorage, completely dry—hence the "delusion."

Demariscove Point (53°13'00" 132°23'00" E side of N entrance to Armentières Channel, Skidegate Inlet, QCI). The *Demaris Cove*, under Capt Lafayette Balch, voyaged to the QCI late in 1851 to investigate rumours of gold and rendezvous with the *Georgianna*, another US schooner. Balch discovered that the *Georgianna* had been wrecked in a storm and its occupants held (whether as "guests" or prisoners depends on who is telling the story) for two months by the Haida. He returned home, where the US government heavily armed his vessel, then sailed back to Haida Gwaii and was able to safely ransom all the detainees in Jan 1852. *D*

Denham Islet (50°26'00" 125°15'00" Off N end of Sonora I, Cordero Channel, N of Campbell R), **Denham Rock** (50°26'00" 125°14'00" Off NE side of Sonora I). Adm Sir Henry Mangles Denham (1800–87) was a prominent RN hydrographer. He assisted with surveys of the French coast (1827), Bristol Channel (1828–35) and Ireland (1842). As cdr of HMS *Avon*, he charted the W coast of Africa (1845–46). From 1852 to 1861 Denham made a major expedition to the S Pacific as capt of HMS *Herald*, surveying parts of Australia, New Caledonia, Fiji and many other islands, and making important contributions to botanical and

ornithological knowledge. Named by Lt Daniel Pender of the *Beaver* about 1864. *W*

Denham Point (52°57'00" 132°21'00" S entrance to Moore Channel, NW side of Moresby I, QCI), **Denham Shoals** (52°57'00" 132°27'00" Off Denham Point). Annesley Turner Denham was a midshipman aboard HMS *Thetis*, under Capt Augustus Kuper, and served on the Pacific Station, 1851–53. The son of Adm Sir Henry Denham (*see* Denham It), he assisted George Moore, master of the *Thetis*, in his survey duties of this area by taking charge of one of the ship's cutters. Denham retired from the RN in 1873 with the rank of cdr. Nearby Annesley Point is also named for him. *W*

Denise Inlet (54°17'00" 130°10'00" Just E of Prince Rupert). Denise Victoria Harris (1896–1948) of Victoria was a granddaughter of Sir James Douglas, BC colonial gov, and Lady Amelia Douglas. Her father was engineer and land surveyor Dennis Harris, who married Martha Douglas, youngest daughter of James and Amelia, at Victoria in 1878. Denise married Cdr John Eric Woodhouse Oland, DSC (1895–1948), at Victoria in 1919; he was a career RCN officer, born in NS, who served as CO of HMCS *Captor*, a naval base at St John, NB, during WWII and retired in 1945 (*see* Oland It). They died within three days of each other, both at St Joseph's Hospital in Victoria. *See also* Harris Point *and* Martha I. Denise Ck, flowing into the inlet, is named for her as well.

Denison Island (51°20'00" 127°33'00" Entrance to Boswell Inlet, Smith Sd, S of Rivers Inlet). Frank Napier Denison (1866–1946), from Ont, came to Victoria in 1898 as assistant Dominion meteorologist. He designed the observatory on Gonzales Hill, which was built in 1914, and lived there with his wife Ethel Margaret Elizabeth Walbran (1874–1945), whom he married at Victoria in 1904. Denison served as Victoria's chief seismologist and meteorologist, 1914–36, and provided regular forecasts and commentary for local newspapers. Ethel was the youngest daughter of BC historian Capt John Walbran, master of the lighthouse tender *Quadra*, who named Denison I, along with nearby Frank Rk and Napier I. *E*

Denman Island (49°32'45" 124°47'31" Between Hornby I and Vancouver I, W side of Str of Georgia), **Denman Point** (49°33'00" 124°51'00" W side of Denman I). Spanish explorer José Narváez named Denman I and Hornby I the Islas de Lerena, after Spanish politician and minister Pedro Lopez de Lerena (1734–92). Denman I received its current name from Capt George Richards about 1864. Rear Adm Joseph Denman (1810-74) was cdr-in-chief on the Pacific Station, 1864–66, based at Esquimalt on his flagship HMS *Sutlej*. He was the son of Lord Chief Justice Thomas Denman, a noted British opponent of slavery, and spent much time on the African coast attempting to eradicate the slave trade. According to historian Barry Gough, he "carried with him the reputation of being a ruthless fighter for just causes." In 1864, Denman took the *Sutlej* and *Devastation* to Clayoquot Sd to investigate the destruction of the trading sloop *Kingfisher* and the murder of its crew by Ahousaht warriors. His force shelled and burned nine First Nation villages but failed to capture Chapchah, the Ahousaht chief involved in the piracy. Denman retired from the RN in 1866 as a vice adm. Mt Denman, S of Toba Inlet, is also named for him. Denman I (50 sq km) was first settled in 1874; nearly 1,000 residents currently make a living from mixed farming, logging and tourism. Denman is connected to both Vancouver I and Hornby I by ferry. Denman Point was formerly known as Village Point. *E W*

Dennie Point (50°30'00" 126°00'00" N side of Blenkinsop Bay, Johnstone Str). Mary Dennie Blenkinsop (1861–90) was a daughter of HBC officer George Blenkinsop (*see* Blenkinsop Bay). In Oct 1885, at Victoria, she married John Hicks (1850–1885), from Cornwall, the bookkeeper at the Alert Bay cannery. Less than three weeks later he was killed in a bizarre incident at Victoria. A coroner's inquiry—the details of which filled the pages of the Victoria *Colonist* for weeks—found that Hicks had accidentally shot himself to death while trying to make it appear that he had been assaulted and robbed. Mary died at Rosebud, Alberta. Formerly known as Edward Point.

Denny Island (52°08'00" 128°00'00" At Bella Bella, just E of Campbell I), **Denny Point** (52°09'00" 127°55'00" NE side of Denny I, Gunboat Passage), **Denny Rock** (51°14'00" 127°50'00" SW of Egg I, entrance to Smith Sd). Lt D'Arcy Anthony Denny (d 1883) commanded the RN paddle gunboat *Coromandel* on the China Station in 1864 and the steam gunboat *Forward* on the Pacific Station, based at Esquimalt, 1866–68. In 1866, in an attempt to curb an illegal traffic in whisky, he took HMS *Forward* almost 20 km up the uncharted Nass R, a remarkable feat of navigation, to "show the flag" and threaten local chiefs with punishment if they didn't obey British laws. He was promoted to cdr in 1868 and put in charge of HMS *Dart*, a gun vessel on the SE coast of S America, 1872–76, after which he was appointed to Coast Guard service in England. D'Arcy Point (W Thurlow I) and Mt D'Arcy (Denny I) are also named for him. The eastern, non-Native part of Bella Bella, also called Shearwater, is located on the W side of Denny I.

Denny Rocks (52°10'00" 131°07'00" Entrance to Rose Inlet, S end of Moresby I, QCI). Edward Denny (d 1893) was on the BC coast in 1853 as a midshipman aboard HMS *Virago* under Capt James Prevost, who named this feature. The following year, Denny was present at the siege of Petropavlovsk on Russia's Kamchatka peninsula, and he also served in the Mediterranean before retiring from the RN as a lt in the mid-1860s. His grandfather was Sir Edward Denny, an Irish baronet; the important Haida site

of Anthony I (qv) was named after his clergyman father, the Venerable Anthony Denny. *W*

Denton Point (52°44'00" 128°27'00" N entrance to Wallace Bight, NW end of Roderick I, N of Bella Bella). In 1948, a number of points on Roderick I were named for BC historians. Vernon Llewellyn Denton (1881–1944) was principal of Victoria's Provincial Normal School and author of *The Far West Coast*, an account of BC coastal exploration published in 1924. He also wrote and edited history and geography textbooks for Canadian schools.

Departure Bay, now a BC Ferries terminal. *BC Archives I-12515*

Departure Bay (49°12'00" 123°57'00" Just NW of Nanaimo, E side of Vancouver I). Named by HBC surveyor Joseph Pemberton about 1853, supposedly because a First Nation group had recently left the bay and also for the fact that it was a good place for shipping to arrive and depart. Departure Ck, which flows into the bay, derives its name from the same source. George Inskip, master of HMS *Virago*, surveyed Nanaimo Hbr and Departure Bay in 1853. Spanish explorer José Narváez was the first European to note the entrance to Nanaimo, in 1791. He named the area Bocas de Winthuysen, presumably after Spanish naval officer Francisco Winthuysen, who was killed at the Battle of St Vincent in 1797. *W*

Derby Point (49°31'00" 123°59'00" N point of S Thormanby I, NW of Sechelt, E side of Str of Georgia). The Epsom Derby is a prestigious English horse race, established in 1780 by the Earl of Derby at Epsom Downs in Surrey. Capt George Richards and his officers, aboard RN survey vessel *Plumper*, gave the area many horse-racing names in 1860 after hearing happy news of that year's Derby.

Desbrisay Bay (52°47'00" 128°00'00" N side of Kynoch Inlet, E of Mathieson Channel, N of Bella Bella). Signalman Gordon Montgomery Des Brisay, from

D

Vancouver, was killed in action Sept 20, 1943, aged 19, while serving aboard HMCS *St Croix*. The destroyer was escorting a slow-moving convoy in the N Atlantic when it was torpedoed and sunk by a U-boat (*U-305*), with the loss of 65 lives. Tragically, all but one of the survivors from *St Croix* were killed two days later when their rescuer, HMS *Itchen*, was itself torpedoed and sunk. Des Brisay's name is inscribed on the Halifax Memorial.

Descanso Bay (49°11'00" 123°52'00" W end of Gabriola I, Gulf Is). In 1792, at the end of a long day of rough weather, the Spanish naval officers Dionisio Alcalá-Galiano and Cayetano Valdés—cdrs of the *Sutil* and *Mexicana*, respectively—named a safe anchorage at the W end of Gabriola I Cala del Descanso, or "cove of rest," in a gesture of appreciation. Descanso Bay was marked on early HBC maps, though an 1862 RN survey by Capt George Richards renamed it Rocky Bay. The Spanish name was restored in 1906 after a re-survey of the area by Cdr John Parry, but later research by historians John Kendrick and Nick Doe, based on cartographic sketches by Alcalá-Galiano only recently discovered in Spanish archives, has revealed that the *Sutil* and *Mexicana* actually anchored in nearby Pilot Bay and that the name Descanso had been applied to the wrong feature all along. *W*

Descubierta Point (49°41'00" 126°30'00" SE entrance to Tlupana Inlet, Nootka Sd, W side of Vancouver I). The three-masted corvette *Descubierta* (Spanish for "discovery") was especially built as the flagship of Capt Alejandro Malaspina's 1789–94 circumnavigation of the world. It was equipped (as was its sister vessel, *Atrevida*) with facilities for artists, naturalists, astronomers and surveyors; a library; and the latest navigational and hydrographic instruments. *See also* Malaspina Inlet.

Deserted Bay (50°05'30" 123°45'00" NE end of Princess Royal Reach, Jervis Inlet), **Deserted River** (50°05'30" 123°44'40" Flows SW into Deserted Bay). Ts'únay, one of the principal Sechelt First Nation winter villages, was located here but was abandoned after the smallpox epidemics of the 1860s. A Japanese fish saltery operated on the bay, 1904–39, and a Gustavson Bros railroad and truck-logging show, 1934–51. Slate quarrying dates back to 1890 (or much earlier, as the Sechelt people made spear points at this site for harpooning sea lions); flagstones and tiles were exported to California in the early 1900s and to Vancouver in 1957–58. Deserted Bay is still used as a summer camp by the Sechelt people and today is home to a Native environmental studies facility. The Sechelt name for the river is Tsooadie.

Deserters Group (50°53'00" 127°29'00" Off NE end of Vancouver I, in Ripple Passage, N of Port Hardy), **Deserters Island** (50°53'00" 127°28'00" One of the Deserters Group). The story of the Ft Rupert "deserters" and their grisly end has many versions, nearly all of which are jumbled and exaggerated. Historian Barry Gough untangles the threads most convincingly in his book *Gunboat Frontier: British Maritime Authority and NW Coast Indians, 1846–90*. The deserters in question, three in number, arrived at Ft Rupert, near Port Hardy, in 1850 on the trading barque *England*, which was taking on coal before heading to San Francisco. They were stowaway sailors from the HBC ship *Norman Morison*, seeking to escape binding employment contracts with

The mitre-shaped peak of Mount Denman looms over Desolation Sound. *Peter Vassilopoulos*

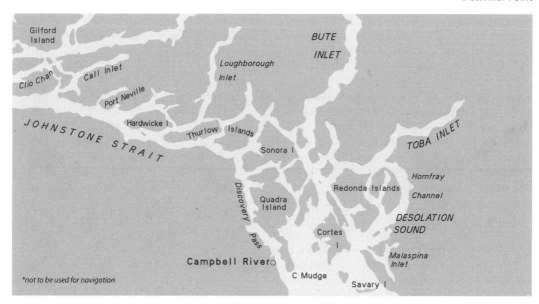

Desolation Sound, Campbell River and the Discovery Islands.
Reproduced with the permission of the Canadian Hydrographic Service

the company, which regarded them as outlaws. When the *Beaver*, another HBC vessel, appeared at Ft Rupert, the sailors panicked, left the *England* by canoe and headed down Goletas Channel, where they probably camped on Nigei I. When George Blenkinsop, the HBC officer in charge at Ft Rupert, heard about the deserters from a First Nation informant, he assumed they were Scottish miners and a blacksmith from the fort, who were dissatisfied with working conditions and had gone on strike, then decided to leave on the *England*. Blenkinsop promised a handsome reward for the recovery of these men, who were valuable indentured employees, but his offer was somehow translated to his informant as 30 blankets "per head" and may have been misconstrued as meaning "dead or alive," as Vancouver I gov Richard Blanshard later believed. The fleeing sailors were killed by members of the Nahwitti First Nation, an act that led to two attacks on Nahwitti settlements by British warships in 1850 and 1851 after the Nahwitti refused to surrender the killers. It is not likely that the sailors ever hid on the islands of the Deserters Group. *See* Daedalus Passage, Daphne Point, Nahwitti Bar, Willoughby Rks *and* Wishart I for more details of this incident and its consequences.

Desolation Sound (50°07'00" 124°47'00" E of Cortes I, at NE end of Str of Georgia). Capt George Vancouver anchored at nearby Teakerne Arm for three weeks in June and July 1792 and sent his boats out to survey the region. His mood could only be described as depressed. "Our situation here," he wrote, presented "as gloomy and dismal an aspect as nature could well be supposed to exhibit." Had it not been for the "agreeable society" of the Spanish explorers Dionisio Alcalá-Galiano and Cayetano Valdés, "our time would have passed infinitely

more heavily." As it was, he went on, "our residence here was truly forlorn; an awful silence pervaded the gloomy forests, whilst animated nature seemed to have deserted the neighbouring country, whose soil afforded only a few small onions, some samphire, and here and there bushes bearing a scanty crop of indifferent berries. Nor was the sea more favourable to our wants, the steep rocky shores prevented the use of the seine, and not a fish at the bottom could be tempted to take the hook." Vancouver's Desolation Sd included the channels that lead off to the N; today's sound, one of BC's most popular marine parks, is defined as the open entrance to those channels at the NE end of the Str of Georgia. *E W*

de Stein Point (54°19'00" 130°22'00" NW side of Prince Rupert Hbr). Joseph Nicholas de Stein (1880–1959) was a GTP engineer employed on early surveys of Prince Rupert and its harbour in 1906–8. His father had also been a railroad engineer and worked in Mexico and Russia, where Joseph was born. He received an engineering degree in Germany and had his first experience of railroad surveys in northern Egypt before coming to Canada in 1906. In 1912, still with the GTP, he was transferred to Regina and worked mostly in Sask and Manitoba. The following year de Stein married Elise Ilg. He left the railway in 1918 and set up a consulting engineering practice, which prospered until 1950, when he retired. He died at Regina.

Detwiller Point (49°03'00" 123°37'00" SE end of Valdes I, Gulf Is). In 1965, L F Detwiller of Victoria, owner of property at this location, applied successfully to have the point named in memory of his parents, Daniel Benjamin Detwiller (1879–1924) and Georgina Edith Wade Detwiller (1887–1939). Detwiller family members arrived in BC in 1924 and visited the Gulf Is on many occasions, becoming particularly attached to Valdes I.

D

Devastation Channel (53°40'00" 128°50'00" Between Hawkesbury I and the mainland, S of Kitimat), **Devastation Island** (54°19'00" 130°29'00" Metlakatla Bay, NW of Prince Rupert). HMS *Devastation*, a 6-gun, 960-tonne paddle sloop built at Woolwich in 1841 and decommissioned in 1867, was on the BC coast in 1862–65. The ship helped suppress numerous instances of First Nation unrest. In 1862, under Lt Charles Heysham, it was sent to the W coast of Vancouver I to inquire into complaints by early traders. It was back in 1864, under Cdr John Pike, to investigate the looting of the *Kingfisher* and slaughter of its crew, and to gather evidence in the suspected murder of Indian agent William Banfield. Along with HMS *Sutlej*, under Rear Adm Joseph Denman, it shelled and burned nine Ahousaht villages in Clayoquot Sd that year while hunting down pirates. Cdr Pike and his paddle steamer were busy policing the liquor trade in the Str of Georgia and northern BC in 1862–63, seizing vessels and destroying illicit cargoes. During the same period, *Devastation* also protected British miners headed for the Stikine gold rush and helped apprehend the killers of several Gulf Is settlers. Devastation Channel was formerly known as Pender Channel. *W*

Devlin Bay (53°04'00" 129°35'00" Between Trutch I and Prior I, facing Estevan Sd, SE of Banks I). Robert Beatty Devlin (1841–1925) was born at Toronto and moved to BC about 1862. He married Isabel Barlow at Victoria in 1888. A farmer and a miner, he took part in the 1924 old-timers' reunion held at Victoria (*see* Adams Bay). Named in 1926, as suggested by regional hydrographer Henri Parizeau.

Dewdney Island (52°59'00" 129°37'00" Southernmost of the Estevan Group, between Bank I and Aristazabal I). Engineer and politician Edgar Dewdney (1835–1916) was lt gov of BC, 1892–97. Born in England, he came to BC in 1859 and helped lay out the townsite of New Westminster. In 1860 he was awarded a contract to build a pack trail across southern BC from Hope. It reached the Wild Horse R, in the Kootenays, in 1865 and became known as the Dewdney Trail. Dewdney married Jane Shaw Moir (1842–1906) in 1864 at Hope and was named to BC's legislative council in 1868, representing Kootenay. He served as MP for Yale, 1872–79, before being appointed Indian commissioner of the NWT (which at that time comprised most of Canada between Ont and BC), 1879–88, and NWT lt gov from 1881 to 1888. He wielded great power in the NWT, where his generally repressive policies helped precipitate the NW Rebellion. Dewdney was elected MP for Assiniboia E, 1888–92, and immediately joined Sir John A Macdonald's Conservative cabinet as minister of the Interior and superintendent gen of Indian Affairs. As BC lt gov, he hosted the 1894–95 visits of Gov Gen Lord Aberdeen and Lady Aberdeen, and happily presided over Queen Victoria's diamond jubilee celebrations. After his first wife died, he married Blanche Elizabeth Plantagenet

Kemeys-Tynte (d 1936) in England in 1909. Dewdney Ck, Dewdney Flats, Dewdney Peak, Mt Dewdney and the community of Dewdney are also named for him. *E*

DeWolf Island (52°07'00" 128°18'00" S entrance to Raymond Passage, just SW of Bella Bella). Henry George DeWolf, CBE, DSO, DSC (1903–2000), was a celebrated RCN officer. Born in NS, he graduated from the Royal Naval College of Canada in 1918 and had his first command in 1920 on the patrol vessel *Festubert*. He commanded destroyers in WWII, including HMCS *St Laurent*, first Canadian warship to engage the enemy, and HMCS *Haida*, Canada's most successful warship, which sank or helped sink three German destroyers, two minesweepers and a U-boat on DeWolf's watch, earning its capt his DSO and DSC. DeWolf was promoted RCN assistant chief of naval staff in 1944. In 1947, as a commodore, he was CO of the aircraft carrier *Warrior*, and in 1948, now a rear adm, he became flag officer Pacific coast. He capped his career as chief of naval staff, 1956–61, with the rank of vice adm. His awards also included the Légion d'honneur and Croix de Guerre from France, Norway's King Haakan VII Cross, the US Legion of Merit and the 1998 Admirals' Medal. DeWolf I was formerly known as Mary I.

Diana Island (48°51'00" 125°11'00" W side of Trevor Channel, Barkley Sd, W side of Vancouver I). The *Diana* was a small steam schooner built as a launch in China in 1860 and brought to the US for the Pacific Mail Steamship Co. It was lengthened to 30 m in San Francisco, where its boiler exploded, causing two deaths. Capt Edward Stamp purchased the vessel about 1862 for his pioneer Port Alberni sawmill but sold it shortly after to Capt Thomas Wright, who rebuilt it for mail duty in the San Juan Is. The *Diana* was chartered for several trips to Ft Simpson and Sitka in 1867, when Alaska was purchased from Russia by the US. The following year it ran on San Francisco Bay for the Sausalito Ferry Co. The ship went aground and broke up on the NW Washington coast in 1874. Diana I was an important village site for the Huu-ay-aht (Ohiaht) First Nation and was also the location of an early trading post, built in the 1850s by Hugh McKay and William Spring. *W*

Dibrell Bay (54°14'00" 132°58'00" E side of Langara I, NW of Graham I, QCI). Capt Walter C Dibrell of the US Coast and Geodetic Survey vessel *Explorer* was charting S Alaskan waters in 1907 at the same time that Capt Frederick Learmonth, who named this feature, was doing survey work with HMS *Egeria*. Dibrell served as senior CO of the US Coast Guard & Lighthouse Service at Ketchikan, Alaska, 1913–39.

Dibuxante Point (49°07'31" 123°42'58" NW point of Valdes I, Gulf Is). *Dibuxante*—or its modern equivalent, *dibujante*—is Spanish for "draftsman" and was a subordinate rank on the early Spanish naval vessels that explored the BC coast in the late 18th century. This feature was named for Dibuxante Manuel José Antonio Cardero (often misspelled Cordero), who was a pilot, draftsman and artist on Dionisio Alcalá-Galiano's 1792 exploration of the Str of Georgia. *See* Cordero Channel. *W*

Dickens Point (55°09'00" 130°07'00" S of Stopford Point, SE side of Portland Canal, NW of Nass Bay). Sub-Lt Sydney Smith Haldimand Dickens (1847–72) served on the BC coast, 1868–70, aboard HMS *Zealous*, flagship of Rear Adm George Hastings, Pacific Station cdr-in-chief. He was the fifth son of the famed English novelist Charles Dickens and entered the navy as a 14-year-old. Promoted to lt in 1872 on HMS *Narcissus*, he became ill and died later that same year in Aden. Young Dickens was one of the main performers at a theatrical entertainment hosted by the RN in Esquimalt at Christmas 1868 and received a positive review in the Victoria *Colonist*. Dickens Point was named by Lt Daniel Pender, who probably attended the play. (Francis Jeffrey Dickens, the writer's third son, also had a brief career in Canada, as a North-West Mounted Police inspector, marked, according to the *Canadian Encyclopedia*, by "recklessness, laziness and heavy drinking.") *W*

Dickson Shoal (50°25'00" 125°42'00" In Chancellor Channel, between Hardwicke I and the mainland, NW of Campbell R). Cpl William Rodger Dickson of the RCAF, from Powell R, died on military service Aug 21, 1944, in England, aged 38. He is buried at Stonefall Cemetery, Surrey, UK.

Digby Island (54°17'00" 130°25'00" Between Chatham Sd and Prince Rupert Hbr). Lt Henry Almarus Digby was 2nd lt aboard HMS *Malacca*, under Capt Radulphus Oldfield, on the Pacific Station, 1866–68. He retired from the RN as a capt in 1894. RN surveyor Lt Daniel Pender named a number of geographical features in this area after the *Malacca* and its officers. Today the 34-sq-km island is the site of the Prince Rupert airport, opened in 1961 and reached from the city by vehicle ferry. Its traditional Tsimshian name is Ka'tat'nic. A small residential community with an interesting history is located at Dodge Cove (qv). *W*

Digby Point (48°48'27" 123°12'06" NW side of Saturna I, Gulf Is). Harold Digby Payne (1872–1954), a wealthy young Englishman, settled on Saturna about 1891 after following his older brothers Charles and Gerald out to the Gulf Is (*see* Payne Point). He built a store there and the island's first post office—originally called Pikes Landing, after early settler and adventurer Warburton Pike—and rowed across to Mayne I once a week to pick up mail. Harold raised sheep at Winter Cove and then, in 1898, went to the Stikine district with Pike and helped him operate a trading post at Telegraph Ck during the

Klondike gold rush. In 1907, after serving in the Boer War, he married Ruth Katinka Maude (1886–1914, *see* Ruth I), a member of the early Gulf Is family that owned Point Comfort Hotel on Mayne I. After her premature death, Payne married Jessie Catherine Ryle (1889–1964) in 1916 at Oak Bay, where the family eventually moved. Another move, to N Saanich, brought Harold closer to other Payne siblings, including his twin brother Rev Hubert St John Payne, who had come out to BC after him.

Digby Rock (52°30'08" 129°02'12" Entrance to Weeteeam Bay, SW side of Aristazabal I). Cpl James Digby (1833–60), born in Essex, England, was a member of the Columbia detachment of Royal Engineers, which served in BC 1858–63. He was killed in a hunting accident near the engineers' camp at Sapperton; his gravestone, now at Fraser Cemetery, is the oldest in the district. Digby's bricklayer brother Charles (1835–1907) was also with the detachment, as a sapper, and helped build the Cariboo Rd. He married Ann McMurphy, daughter of Sgt John McMurphy, another engineer, and became a steward at New Westminster's Royal Columbian Hospital.

Dillon Bay (53°13'00" 129°30'00" SE end of Pitt I, SW of Kitimat). Walter Dillon (b 1765) was an able seaman aboard HMS *Discovery* on Capt George Vancouver's 1791–95 voyage to the PNW. His claim to fame, unfortunately, is that he received three dozen lashes for drunkenness and two dozen for stealing liquor. The hydrographic service had first suggested the name Smart Bay for this feature in 1949, after Peter Smart, a student draftsman aboard CGS *William J Stewart* and later a hydrographic technician, but this was rejected.

Dillon Point (50°45'00" 127°24'00" W entrance to Beaver Hbr, just E of Port Hardy, NE end of Vancouver I), **Dillon Rock** (50°51'00" 127°51'00" S side of Goletas Channel, entrance to Shushartie Bay, N end of Vancouver I). William Ward Dillon made an 1850 sketch survey in the vicinity of Daedalus Passage and Shushartie Bay while temporarily serving as master of HMS *Daedalus*. He was also on the Pacific Station in command of RN flagship tender *Cockatrice*, 1851–52, and was promoted staff cdr in 1863.

Dimsey Point (51°27'00" 127°44'00" S end of Joachim I, entrance to Rivers Inlet). D G Dimsey was a civilian assistant at the Admiralty hydrographic dept, 1870–95, and never even glimpsed the BC coast. Named in 1871 by George Richards, who spent many years on BC coastal surveys but by this time was a rear adm and hydrographer of the RN.

Dingle Island (52°10'00" 127°57'00" In Gunboat Passage, N of Denny I, just W of Bella Bella). Named about 1925 by regional hydrographer Henri Parizeau for St Brendan of Clonfert (484–c 570), called "the Navigator," who sailed

D

from Dingle Bay on the SW coast of Ireland in the 6th century on an ambitious seven-year voyage of exploration in a small, skin-covered boat. Brendan, an early monastic priest, supposedly returned with his crew to tell of fiery oceanic mountains, floating palaces of crystal, cat-headed monsters with horns in their mouths and little furry men, which some have interpreted as volanoes, icebergs, walrus and Inuit. His legendary journey is described in the 9th-century *Voyage of St Brendan the Navigator*, which is as much a religious allegory and series of folk tales as it is travel literature.

Dionisio Point (49°01'00" 123°34'00" NE point of Galiano I, Gulf Is). After Spanish naval officer Dionisio Alcalá-Galiano, who visited this area with Cayetano Valdés—aboard the *Sutil* and *Mexicana*, respectively—during an important exploration of the BC coast in 1792. *See* Alcala Point. Named by Cdr John Parry of HMS *Egeria* while re-surveying Porlier Pass in 1905. Dionisio Point Provincial Park was established there in 1991.

Disappointment Inlet. *See* Lemmens Inlet.

Discovery Island (48°25'00" 123°14'00" Off Oak Bay, just E of Victoria), **Discovery Passage** (50°10'00" 125°21'00" Between Vancouver I and Quadra I, from Str of Georgia to Johnstone Str). HMS *Discovery* was the ship that took Capt George Vancouver on his journey of exploration to the PNW in 1791–95. The 303-tonne, 29-m sloop carried 10 four-pound guns, 10 swivel guns and a crew of 100, and was named after one of Capt James Cook's vessels (*see* Discovery Point). It was built in 1789 in SE London at the Rotherhithe shipyard of Randall & Brent and was originally to have been commanded by Capt Henry Roberts on a voyage to study the S Pacific whaling industry,

with Vancouver as 1st lt. Trouble with Spain cancelled that expedition, and Vancouver received a commission to chart the PNW coast and take possession of Nootka Sd from the Spanish. The *Discovery*, together with the armed tender *Chatham*, travelled S and E, doing survey work at Australia and NZ en route, and stopping at Tahiti and Hawaii. After three seasons in the PNW and two winters in Hawaii and S California, the ship and its crew headed home, stopping for repairs in Chile on the way. In 1797 the *Discovery* was converted to a bomb (or mortar) vessel and took part in the 1801 Battle of Copenhagen. It became an army hospital ship at Sheerness in 1807, a convict hulk at Woolwich in 1818 and Deptford in 1824, and was broken up in 1834. Port Discovery, an early stopping place of Vancouver on the S shore of Juan de Fuca Str in Washington state, is also named for the vessel. Discovery I, a former Songhees First Nation village site and now a provincial marine park, was probably named by Capt Henry Kellett of HMS *Herald*, who surveyed the area in 1846; Vancouver himself never examined this part of Vancouver I. W

Discovery Islands (N of Campbell R, NW of Str of Georgia). This name, while not official, is now widely used to describe the group of islands lying between the Str of Georgia and Johnstone Str. Quadra, Cortes, E and W Redonda, Read, Maurelle, Stuart, Sonora and E Thurlow are generally considered to be the main Discovery Is, but there is no consensus on the precise extent of the archipelago.

Discovery Point (49°35'00" 126°33'00" E entrance to Nootka Sd, W side of Vancouver I). This HMS *Discovery*, not to be confused with the one in the Discovery I entry, was consort to HMS *Resolution* on Capt James Cook's third great expedition, 1776–80. A refurbished 270-tonne

Discovery Island off Oak Bay and Victoria is part Songhees First Nation reserve and part provincial marine park. *Peter Vassilopoulos*

collier, built at Whitby as the *Diligence* in 1774, it sailed under Cdr Charles Clerke and, following Clerke's death, Lt John Gore, then Lt James King. It was on this trip, in 1778, that Cook visited Nootka Sd for almost a month and refitted his vessels. George Vancouver was a midshipman on *Discovery* and also served aboard *Resolution* on Cook's second expedition. After the voyage, the *Discovery* served as a transport until 1797, then was broken up.

Ditmars Point (52°44'00" 128°34'00" W side of Tolmie Channel, Princess Royal I). Lt Eric Soulis Ditmars, an RCNVR officer from Vancouver, was serving aboard HMS *Salvia* when he was killed in action, aged 26, on Dec 24, 1941. The corvette was torpedoed and sunk by a U-boat (*U-568*) in the Mediterranean off the coast of Egypt; 106 lives were lost (the ship was carrying survivors from another vessel). His name is inscribed on the Halifax Memorial.

Diver Islet (49°56'00" 127°15'00" SE end of Barrier Is, entrance to Kyuquot Sd, NW side of Vancouver I). The islet is a popular spot with cormorants (*Phalacrocorax* species), which are known locally as "divers."

Dixon Entrance (54°25'00" 132°00'00" N side of QCI), **Dixon Island** (53°34'00" 130°10'00" SW of McCauley I, Principe Channel, NE of Banks I, S of Prince Rupert). George Dixon (1748–95) was one of the earliest British fur traders on the BC coast. He and Nathaniel Portlock spent 1786–87 in the PNW—aboard the *Queen Charlotte* and *King George*, respectively—as part of a trading consortium known as the King George's Sd Co, formed in London in 1785. Both Dixon and Portlock had sailed on Capt James Cook's third expedition, which had visited Nootka Sd in 1778, and seen the profits to be made selling sea otter furs in China. (Dixon had been armourer and Portlock

master's mate on HMS *Discovery*; midshipman George Vancouver had been a shipmate.) Dixon named the QCI for his vessel after realizing they were not part of the mainland. Upon returning to England in 1788, he laid his manuscripts and charts before Sir Joseph Banks, the great scientist, and invited him to fill in a few place names. "He did me the honour to insert mine in the place you find it on the chart," Dixon wrote, referring to Dixon Entrance, after fellow trader John Meares belligerently claimed that he had named it first, after William Douglas, capt of one of his vessels. In 1789, Dixon and Portlock published *A Voyage Round the World; but more Particularly to the North-West Coast of America*, which was mainly written by William Beresford, purser and assistant trader on the voyage. *E W*

Dobbin Bay (50°47'00" 126°48'00" S side of Broughton I, NE end of Queen Charlotte Str). Thomas Sydney Dobbin (1836–1905) was a civilian clerk at the RN yard at Esquimalt, 1865–98. After his first wife, Alice Annie Dobbin (1840–80), died, he married Dorothea Bean McKenzie at Victoria in 1882. Originally from England, he became senior clerk in 1875 and returned to his birthplace after retirement.

Dobbs Islets (52°36'00" 129°09'40" Entrance to Clifford Bay, W side of Aristazabal I). Sapper George Dobbs was a member of the Columbia detachment of Royal Engineers, which served in BC 1858–63. He never reached the colony, however, as he apparently deserted en route at San Francisco in Oct 1858. Regional hydrographer Henri Parizeau named geographic features for dozens of Royal Engineers in the mid-1920s.

Dock Point (48°53'00" 123°35'00" Between Vesuvius Bay and Duck Bay, NW side of Saltspring I, Gulf Is). This

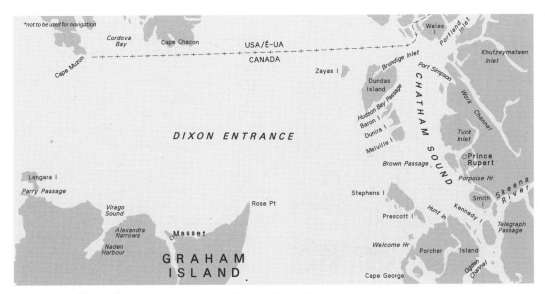

Dixon Entrance and Chatham Sound. *Reproduced with the permission of the Canadian Hydrographic Service*

D

feature, which has appeared as Dock Point on Admiralty charts since 1865, was apparently named in association with the adjacent bay, once known as Dock Bay. This latter name, however, somehow became corrupted over the years to Duck Bay (qv).

Dockrill Point (49°18'00" 122°52'00" NE side of Port Moody, Burrard Inlet, E of Vancouver). Joseph Dockrill (1838–1917), a farmer's son from Ont, married Maria Cathaline O'Gorman (1840–1909), from Ireland, at Florence, Ont, in 1858. They and their large family settled at this point in 1883, near the proposed terminus of the CPR. Joseph farmed and also operated a shingle mill. Dockrill's Landing became better known as Sunnyside Landing, and a nearby beach is still known as Sunnyside Beach. To commemorate the centenary of Joseph and Cathaline's arrival, their descendants, who still own land in the vicinity, held a "heritage" weekend celebration in 1983 and applied successfully to have this point named in the family's honour.

Dodd Islets (52°31'00" 128°26'00" Off entrance to Nowish Inlet, Finlayson Channel, NW of Bella Bella), **Dodd Narrows** (49°08'00" 123°49'00" Between Mudge I and Vancouver I, just SE of Nanaimo), **Dodd Passage** (54°34'00" 130°27'00" SW side of Port Simpson, Tsimpsean Peninsula, N of Prince Rupert), **Dodd Rock** (54°31'08" 130°28'07" Off S side of Finlayson I, Port Simpson). Capt Charles Dodd (1808–60), a native of Norwich, UK, came to Ft Vancouver on the Columbia R in 1835 as 2nd officer of HBC paddle steamer *Beaver*. For the next seven years he served as mate on various HBC vessels, then was capt of the *Beaver*, 1852–56. He was briefly in charge of the HBC post at Ft Stikine and later commanded the *Labouchere*, a larger HBC ship. At the time of his death, from a kidney infection, he was a chief factor in the company. Charles Narrows in Finlayson Channel is also named for him. Dodd Narrows, where the currents can run as fast as

9 knots (17 km/h), was formerly known as Nanaimo Narrows; the Dodd Its were called the Sisters Is. *E W*

Dodge Cove (54°17'00" 130°23'00" E side of Digby I, W end of Prince Rupert Hbr), **Dodge Island** (At Dodge Cove). George Blanchard Dodge (1874–1945), from Halifax, worked first as a federal hydrographer on Nfld and E coast surveys, then became head of special topographic surveys for the Dept of the Interior. He retired about 1932. He surveyed Prince Rupert Hbr in 1906, assisted by Philip Musgrave, Henri Parizeau and Louis Davies, all of whom would go on to respected hydrographic careers. During early WWII, Dodge was employed by Hughes-Owens Co, where he designed marine compasses for wartime merchant vessels. Mt Dodge, just S of the Skeena R mouth, is also named for him. An early Tsimshian First Nation village, supposedly the birthplace of Txamsem, the Tsimshian trickster figure, was located at the cove. In the early 1900s the cove was settled by fishermen, who called their community simply Norwegian Village. A Dept of Marine and Fisheries facility was built in 1912, along with a magnificent doctor's house connected by a wooden bridge to nearby Dodge I, where a three-storey quarantine hospital operated in 1912–14. (The expected influx of immigrants to Prince Rupert never happened.) In the late 1920s, Ed Wahl started Wahl Shipyards in the cove; he and his six sons built almost 1,100 vessels there and at a boatyard in Prince Rupert—mainly small fish boats for the salmon canneries—before shutting down in the 1970s. About 80 people still live at Dodge Cove. Dodge I was known locally as Hospital I.

Dodge Point (52°44'18" 131°29'18" NE side of Lyell I, off E side of Moresby I, QCI). Josiah Dodge was a seaman on the first voyage (1787–90) of early US fur-trading vessel *Columbia Rediviva*, under Capt John Kendrick and Capt Robert Gray. Named by the hydrographic service in 1948.

Dodger Channel (48°50'16" 125°12'00" W side of Diana I, between Trevor Channel and Imperial Eagle Channel, Barkley Sd, W side of Vancouver I). A small geographic feature at the N end of Diana I was named Dodger Cove in 1861 by RN surveyor Capt George Richards of HMS *Hecate* because it was a good place to "dodge" bad weather. He was referring more specifically to the schooner *Saucy Lass*, which dodged the weather there for several weeks that year with Capt Charles Stuart and Capt Edward King aboard. Stuart ran a trading post at Ucluelet and had unfairly claimed the wrecked vessel *Florencia* and its cargo; King had been sent by colonial authorities to take charge of the wreck. During his enforced sojourn on Diana I, King went deer hunting and was killed by the accidental discharge of his gun. *See also* Edward King I *and* Stuart Anchorage. Diana I and adjacent Haines I were important village sites for the Huu-ay-aht (Ohiaht) First Nation; the name Dodger Cove came to refer to a larger area on the

Dodd Narrows, with Nanaimo in the background. *Peter Vassilopoulos*

W side of Diana I and was renamed Dodger Channel in 1934. An early trading post was built on Diana I by Hugh McKay and William Spring in the 1850s. Roman Catholic and, later, Presbyterian missions operated there as well. *W*

Dodwell Island (52°00'00" 128°13'00" Off S side of Campbell I, just S of Bella Bella). Possibly named about 1944 after Harold W Dodwell, an RCNVR paymaster lt cdr, who enlisted for both World Wars. He was secretary to the CO at HMCS *Protector*, the naval base at Sydney, NS, 1939–43, and then came to BC to serve as paymaster and secretary to the CO at HMCS *Givenchy*, 1943–45. *Givenchy* was the name of the shore establishment at Esquimalt that administered reserve and auxiliary vessels and the dockyard.

Doe Islet (50°04'00" 125°13'00" Gowlland Hbr, W side of Quadra I, just N of Campbell R). Cdr Cortland Simpson of the RN survey vessel *Egeria* named a number of features in the vicinity after animals in 1900.

Doig Anchorage (52°55'00" 129°08'00" Entrance to Chapple Inlet, NW side of Princess Royal I). David Doig (1859–1929) was born in Scotland and immigrated to Canada in 1882 to work for the Bank of BNA in Montreal and Brantford, Ont. He arrived at Victoria two years later. In 1897 he was at the bank's Trail and Sandon offices, and the following year he opened its first branch at Dawson City—in a tent. Doig lived in style in the Yukon, according to his *Rootsweb* biography, dining on oysters and caviar, enjoying champagne for breakfast, playing the harmonium and bringing "a general air of sophistication to the community." He married Amelia Eliza Mary Powell (1872–1953) in 1914 at Victoria and served as manager of the bank's Victoria branch, 1907–21, overseeing its 1918 merger with the Bank of Montreal. Named by his friend Henri Parizeau of the hydrographic service.

Dollarton (49°19'00" 122°57'00" W side of entrance to Indian Arm, N Vancouver). Robert Dollar (1844–1932) owned the Canadian Robert Dollar Co, which, in turn, owned the community of Dollarton in its early days. Dollar moved from Scotland to Ottawa with his father and began working in the woods. He started up logging companies in Ont, Michigan and, in 1887, California; bought vessels to transport his logs; and then formed a shipping company in Victoria in 1911. In 1916 he acquired a sawmill in N Vancouver and laid out Dollarton as an employee village. From this base, Dollar set in motion a major trans-Pacific lumber trade. His empire dwindled under the direction of his son Melville and was sold in 1942, after which Dollarton developed as a residential suburb. The village of Dollarville, Michigan, also attests to Robert's restless entrepreneurial energy. The character Cappy Ricks, in the book of that name by Peter Kyne (also made into two films, the 1937 version with Walter Brennan), is supposedly based on Dollar. *E*

Dolphin Island (53°47'00" 130°26'00" S of Porcher I, Browning Entrance, SW of Prince Rupert), **Dolphin Lagoon** (53°47'00" 130°27'00" W side of Dolphin I). Lt Herbert Dolphin (1839–83) served on the Pacific Station, 1866–68, based at Esquimalt aboard HMS *Sparrowhawk*. Dolphin I is the site of the ancient Tsimshian First Nation fishing village Kitkatla.

Domett Point (49°34'00" 123°19'00" N tip of Anvil I, Howe Sd, NW of Vancouver). During his surveys of 1859–60, Capt George Richards of the RN named many features in Howe Sd after the vessels and heroes present at the Glorious First of June, a famous naval victory over the French. William Domett (1752–1828) participated in this 1794 English Channel battle as flag captain of the 110-gun HMS *Royal George*, under Adm Sir Alexander Hood, second-in-command to Adm Lord Howe. Domett was promoted to rear adm in 1804 and served as a lord of the Admiralty, 1808–13, after which he was appointed cdr-in-chief at Plymouth. He was knighted in 1815 and made a full adm in 1819. *W*

Domville Island (48°40'00" 123°19'00" S side of Prevost Passage, off NE side of Saanich Peninsula, N of Victoria), **Domville Point** (50°32'00" 126°17'00" SE entrance to Havannah Channel, N side of Johnstone Str). Rev David Edward Domville (1820–66) was vicar of St Ives and the chaplain on HMS *Satellite*, under Capt James Prevost, on the Pacific Station, 1857–59. He married a Nflder, Mary Jane Stubb (1824–78), in England in 1847. Domville came from a naval family; his father, James, was an RN surgeon and inspector-gen of hospitals and fleets, as was his brother Henry.

Donald Island (51°41'00" 128°06'00" Off NW tip of Calvert I, Hakai Passage). Capt Colin Degge Donald, OBE (1899–1974), was born in Chemainus and joined the RCN in 1917. He spent much of his career on the BC coast (part of it in charge of HMCS *Armentières; see* Armentières Channel) and was responsible for the formation of the Fishermen Reserve Service in BC in 1939. He later commanded the RCN destroyers *Annapolis* and *Ottawa*, then took charge of NS refitting base HMCS *Shelburn*, 1942–45. Donald ended his career as CO at Esquimalt and retired in 1947. This feature was formerly called Harbour I but was renamed in 1944.

Donald Islets (50°14'00" 127°48'00" W of McDougal I, Klaskish Inlet, S of Quatsino Sd, NW side of Vancouver I). Donald A McDougal was a wireless operator on W coast survey vessel *William J Stewart* in the late 1930s and one of regional hydrographer Henri Parizeau's survey assistants. Nearby McDougal I (qv) is also named for him. Formerly known as Surge Is.

D

Donald Point (52°18'00" 128°06'00" N entrance to Morehouse Bay, Chatfield I, N of Bella Bella). Daniel Donald was a long-time ship's capt on the BC coast and worked for both the Union Steamship Co and Canadian National Steamships. He was one of the *Prince Rupert's* regular masters throughout the 1920s and managed to run that vessel onto Ripple Rk in 1927. He was also in charge in 1931 when the *Rupert* sank at the Yarrows dock in Esquimalt; someone had left a porthole open during the annual overhaul. In 1925 he purchased the *Prince Charles* for the CNR from the Orkney & Shetland Steam Navigation Co and brought it to BC, where it operated for many years between Prince Rupert and the QCI.

Donaldson Island. *See* Secretary (Donaldson) I.

Donegal Head (50°38'00" 126°49'00" E end of Malcolm I, Queen Charlotte Str). HMS *Donegal*, under Capt Pulteney Malcolm, was a 74-gun ship of the line and a member of Adm Lord Nelson's fleet blockading the Spanish port of Cadiz prior to the 1805 Battle of Trafalgar. It was formerly the French vessel *Hoche*, taken as a prize of war, and saw action with the RN against a French fleet in the W Indies and off the French coast. *W*

Dong Chong Bay (50°34'40" 126°43'30" N side of Hanson I, E of Alert Bay, Queen Charlotte Str). Dong Chong (1906–91) ran a grocery store at Alert Bay from 1928 until he retired in 1965. In the 1940s, along with partners Harold Henderson and Don Mackie, he ventured into the logging business. This bay served as the booming area for the group's Hanson I operations. The name, though long established, was only recently adopted, in 1997.

Don Island (49°10'00" 122°59'00" In the Fraser R, W of Annacis I). The origin of this well-established local name is not recorded, though area residents have suggested that it may be a misspelling of Dawn, a woman's name. The island became the site of a Japanese colony in the early 1900s when Jinzaburo Oikawa built bunkhouses there to accommodate immigrant workers at nearby canneries. Eighty or more additional men and women arrived in 1906 aboard the schooner *Suian Maru*. Some families were still living on Don I in 1942 when Japanese nationals were forcibly relocated to the BC Interior and their possessions confiscated and sold.

Doolan Point (54°20'00" 130°29'00" S end of Tugwell I, off SW tip of Tsimpsean Peninsula, NW of Prince Rupert). Robert Reid Arthur Doolan was an Anglican missionary with the Church Missionary Society. A graduate of Cambridge Univ, he arrived on the N BC coast in 1864 as a deacon and was sent by William Duncan, founder of the "model Christian community" at Metlakatla, to establish a mission at a Nisga'a village about 15 km up the Nass R. He remained there until 1867, when he and Robert Tomlinson floated the mission house down the river on a raft to the present site of Gingolx (Kincolith). Discouraged at his inability to master a First Nation language, Doolan returned to England that year and became a priest. He later served as a chaplain at Seville, Spain, 1873–77. *W*

Doriston (49°43'00" 123°53'00" W side of Sechelt Inlet, NW of Sechelt and Vancouver). Doris Lloyd (1903–76) was the daughter of Samuel Lloyd, a British cabinetmaker who settled in this fishing and logging hamlet about 1913 and served as postmaster, 1918–23. Doris, who married Clifford Orestes Hammond (1895–1938) in 1923, was the oldest girl in the village when the post office was applied for, and the settlement was named after her. A sawmill operated there at the turn of the century, and a school from 1912 to 1939. An earlier post office at this spot was named Shaw Cove after the area's first resident, Austin Shaw. By the 1990s, Doriston was mostly a recreational community and only inhabited on a seasonal or irregular basis.

Dorman Bay (49°22'30" 123°19'34" E side of Bowen I, S of Snug Cove, Howe Sd, NW of Vancouver). Jacob Dorman (1858–1939) and his wife, Sarah (1862–1948), were Bowen I pioneers who first pre-empted land there in 1890. Jacob was born in Turkey, served in the Indian Army and in 1885 came from England to Canada, where he worked as a pipefitter for the CPR at Yale. Sarah, a strong Methodist, was born in London. The Dormans moved to Vancouver in the late 1880s, and Jacob ran the city's tiny steam electric plant. They sold their initial Bowen I land purchase to Royal City Planing Mills in the early 1890s and acquired the district lot between Dorman Bay and Snug Cove, then sold that lot when they moved back to the UK in 1895. They returned to BC in 1900, again bought land on Bowen and, in 1905, settled on Dorman Bay, which was formerly known as Salmon Bay. The extended Dorman family is well known on Bowen I.

Dorman Island (50°36'07" 126°20'12" S of Minstrel I, Clio Channel, N of Cracroft Is and Johnstone Str). John "Jack" Grandison Dorman (1889–1969) was born at Port Greville, NS. He came to Vancouver about 1910 and first operated a sawmill, then worked for various canneries on Vancouver I and the N coast. A colourful character known as "Johnny Bones," Dorman managed the Canadian Fishing Co cannery at Bones Bay on W Cracroft I from the 1920s until the mid-'50s, when it closed down—supposedly the only cannery operator never to have had a can rejected. Dorman I was marked on early charts as Double I.

Dorothy Island (53°39'20" 128°51'17" In Devastation Channel, S of Kitimat), **Dorothy Narrows** (53°39'00" 128°50'00" Between Dorothy I and the mainland). Dorothy Anderson was the daughter of Lt Col William Anderson, chief engineer of Canada's Dept of Marine and Fisheries and gen superintendent of lighthouses from 1880 until the early 20th century. He named these features in 1898 while examining Kitimat Arm aboard CGS *Quadra*, the W coast survey vessel commanded by Capt John Walbran. The Haisla First Nation name for Dorothy I is Tobexw.

Dorothy Rock (50°23'00" 125°46'00" Vere Cove, W end of W Thurlow I, Johnstone Str). Named in 1899, in association with Vere Cove, by Cdr Morris Smyth, in charge of survey duties on the BC coast with HMS *Egeria*, 1898–1900. Dorothy and Vera Thurlow were his nieces, the daughters of Maj Reginald Thurlow of the Royal Welsh Fusiliers. It is not known if there was a connection to Lord Edward Thurlow, the 18th-century British lord chancellor, after whom the Thurlow Is are named, or how Vera became changed to Vere. The detailed survey of the cove was done by Sub-Lt Horace Watson.

Dor Rock (54°10'16" 130°21'24" Between Greentop It and Kitson I, Chatham Sd, S of Prince Rupert). Named by G Blanchard Dodge, who surveyed Prince Rupert Hbr in 1906, after his daughter Dorothy. Dodge was head of the special surveys division in the federal Dept of the Interior. *See* Dodge Cove.

Dot Islet (50°37'26" 126°40'37" Off NW side of Crease I, N end of Swanson Passage, SE end of Queen Charlotte Str). This descriptive name for a very small, round geographic feature appears on a 1901 Admiralty chart.

Dougan Point (53°03'00" 129°19'00" SE Campania I, Caamaño Sd). James Dougan (1835–1915), born in Ireland, came to Cobble Hill in the Cowichan area in the late 1860s and farmed, eventually acquiring nearly 400 ha of land and running a large dairy herd. He also had a contract for many years to keep a section of the Goldstream Trail open. He had met his wife, Annie McGrath (1847–1922), in Australia while trying to strike it rich as a gold miner and had also visited the Cariboo goldfields in the early 1860s with his older brother Robert. James and Annie Dougan had many children—some of whom stayed and farmed in the S Cowichan district, where Dougan Lk is named for the family.

Douglas Bay (49°31'00" 123°21'00" NE side of Gambier I, Howe Sd, NW of Vancouver). A pioneer named Douglas logged this area with oxen in the late 1890s. The well-established local name was adopted in 1949.

Douglas Bay (50°28'57" 125°45'17" N side of Forward Hbr, E of Hardwicke I, N of Johnstone Str). After Lt Horace Douglas Lascelles, who served with the RN on the BC coast, 1860–65. *See* Lascelles Point.

Douglas Channel (53°40'00" 129°08'00" Between Wright Sd and Kitimat Arm, W side of Hawkesbury I), **Douglas Point** (54°20'00" 130°20'00" E of Melville Arm, N shore of

Remote Douglas Channel on the north BC coast. *pensondesignergems*

Prince Rupert Hbr). Sir James Douglas (1803–77), gov of Vancouver I, 1851–64, and of BC, 1858–64, was the pre-eminent figure in the province's colonial history. He was born in British Guiana (Guyana) of a Scottish merchant father and a Creole mother, educated in Scotland and apprenticed to the NWC in 1819. By 1825, after the company's merger with the HBC, he was stationed at Ft St James, where he married Amelia Connolly (1812–90), daughter of Chief Factor William Connolly (*see* Douglas I). In 1930 he was transferred to Ft Vancouver on the lower Columbia R, where he was promoted chief trader in 1834 and chief factor in 1839. Douglas selected the site for Ft Victoria and moved there in 1849 as head of the HBC's Columbia Dept. From 1851 he was both gov of Vancouver I and chief HBC officer in the region, but when he was also made gov of the mainland colony of BC in 1858, he resigned from the HBC. Douglas proved his mettle during the chaotic days of the Fraser R gold rush, managing to maintain order and British rule over a vast, virtually unknown territory. He created roads, made treaties with First Nations (on Vancouver I) and quelled uprisings. He was a fortunate choice as the region's chief executive: upright, impartial, prudent, brave, with sound judgment and great energy, though autocratic and hot-tempered (he was known, behind his back, as "Old Square-Toes"). BC could have suffered much worse. James Douglas was knighted in 1864, the year he retired. A number of other features in BC are also named for him, including Douglas I in the Fraser R, Mt Douglas N of Victoria, James Bay in Victoria Hbr and James I SE of Sidney. *E W*

Douglas Inlet (52°56'55" 132°12'47" S of Moore Channel, W of Mitchell Inlet, QCI). Dr John Douglas (d 1855) was the RN surgeon aboard HMS *Thetis* during its 1851–53 sojourn on the Pacific Station. The inlet was originally named Douglas Hbr in 1852 by Capt Augustus Kuper, cdr of the *Thetis*, which had been sent to the Charlottes to do survey work and maintain law and order in the wake of a minor gold discovery at Mitchell Inlet just to the E.

D

Douglas Island (49°18'40" 124°09'11" SW side of Ballenas Channel, E of Dorcas Point, Str of Georgia). Amelia Connolly (1812–90) was born at Ft Assiniboine, NW of Edmonton. Her father was William Connolly, an NWC fur trader, and her mother a Cree woman, Miyo Nipiy. Amelia was raised at various NWC and HBC trading posts before marrying James Douglas (1803–77), one of her father's clerks, in 1828, then moving with him to Ft Vancouver and Ft Victoria and bearing him many children. Although shy and known to avoid ceremony wherever possible, she eventually became a colonial gov's wife—and in 1864, when her husband was knighted, Lady Douglas. Amelia I, Dowager I and Lady Douglas I are named for her as well. *See also* Douglas Channel. *E*

Douglas Point (49°27'30" 124°16'30" S side of Lasqueti I, Str of Georgia). George and Mary Emma Douglas (née Purser) came to Lasqueti I in 1911 from Saltspring I with their five children in tow. They bought land overlooking this point and became an important part of the Lasqueti community. George logged and also operated a fish packer; Emma was an island midwife. Most of their children—Chester, Louise, Josie, Archy and Georgie—grew up and married on the island. The name was adopted in 1995, as proposed by the Lasqueti I Historical Society and endorsed by the Lasqueti Community Assoc.

Douglas Rock (54°10'00" 132°57'00" Off N shore of Graham I, QCI). The fur trader and mariner William Douglas made a number of early voyages to the PNW, 1788–91. He travelled to the QCI in 1788 as capt of the *Iphigenia Nubiana*, a ship belonging to John Meares and the Merchant Proprietors, and again the following year, though by this time the *Iphigenia* was owned by a larger consortium known as the Associated Merchants. In 1789, Douglas was detained at Nootka Sd by Spanish forces under Estéban Martínez but then released, perhaps because he was flying Portuguese colours. (Other vessels owned by Associated Merchants were seized and taken to Mexico, leading to the political skirmish known as the Nootka Sd Controversy.) Later that year, in the QCI, he had a historic meeting with Haida chief Blakow-Conneehaw of Kiusta, at which he exchanged names, with the result that Douglas has been an honoured Haida name in certain families for generations. By 1790, Douglas owned two small trading ships himself, the *Fairy* and the *Grace*, which he brought to the Charlottes, but he died in 1791 while returning to China aboard the *Grace*.

Dove Island (50°55'59" 127°08'36" N side of Drury Inlet, entrance to Actress Passage, N of Queen Charlotte Str, NE of Port Hardy), **Dove Point** (52°18'54" 128°11'48" SW side of Yeo I, opposite Don Peninsula, N of Bella Bella). Probably named after HMS *Dove*, a 210-tonne gunboat launched in 1855. It served as a tender, under Lt Cdr Charles James Bullock, to HMS *Actaeon*, which was engaged in survey work off China and in the E Indies, 1856–58. Actaeon Sd is just NE of Dove I.

Dowager Island (52°25'25" 128°22'13" Between Finlayson Channel and Mathieson Channel, W side of Don Peninsula, NW of Bella Bella). After Lady Amelia Douglas (née Connolly), who long outlived her husband, Sir James Douglas, who was knighted in 1864, the year he retired as gov of Vancouver I and BC. A number of features in this vicinity were named for members of the Douglas family. *See* Douglas I.

Downes Point (49°30'01" 124°38'02" E side of Hornby I, Str of Georgia). Edward D Panter Downes (1834–79), who entered the RN in 1847 and served in the Crimean War (1855–56) as a sub-lt on HMS *Duke of Wellington*, was 2nd lt aboard HMS *Tribune*, under Capt Geoffrey Hornby, on the Pacific Station in 1859–60. The frigate *Tribune* had been sent out from China with a force of Royal Marines to augment the British fleet when the dispute with the US over the San Juan Is threatened to become violent. Downes, who was promoted to cdr in 1864, was a talented artist, and his sketches and watercolours of the BC coast, some of which are held by BC Archives, form a vivid window on the colonial past. *W*

Downie Island (53°08'47" 132°21'35" W end of W Narrows, Skidegate Channel, QCI). "Major" William Downie (1819–94), originally from Scotland, worked as a sailor, logger and storekeeper before becoming a miner in California—and, in 1849, the founder of Downieville. He arrived in BC in 1858 and was commissioned by Gov James Douglas to investigate potential mining zones and routes, including in the Pemberton area, Jervis and Bute inlets, the Skeena R, Babine Lk and, in 1865, the Big Bend goldfields. In 1859, he and a crew explored the site of the 1851 gold strike at Mitchell Inlet in the QCI. Downie also prospected in nearby Douglas and Skidegate inlets but found only coal, a discovery that would, nevertheless, later result in the Cowgitz Mine. He married Adeline Davison (1828–1906) at Victoria in 1862. His 1893 book, *Hunting for Gold*, was ghostwritten by San Francisco journalist Chris Waage and reprinted in 1971. Downie died aboard the steamer *City of Puebla* en route to San Francisco. This feature was formerly known as Log I but the name was changed in 1946.

Drake Inlet (53°10'00" 128°59'00" S branch of Cornwall Inlet, Princess Royal I), **Drake Island** (50°30'00" 127°40'00" At junction of Quatsino Sd and Neroutsos Inlet, NW Vancouver I). Lawyer and politician Montague William Tyrwhitt-Drake (1830–1908) was born in England and came to BC in 1859 in unsuccessful pursuit of gold. He formed a law partnership in Victoria with colonial attorney gen George Cary, then founded Drake & Jackson (later Drake, Jackson & Helmcken), the city's most prominent early law firm, which survived until 1912. Drake married Joanna Tolmie (1835–1901), a native of Scotland, in 1862. He was a member of BC's legislative council, 1868–70, mayor of Victoria, 1876–77, Victoria MLA, 1882–86, president of the BC government's executive council, 1883–84, and a justice of the Supreme Court of BC, 1889–1904. He challenged the 1887 US seizure of Canadian sealing schooners at Sitka on behalf of the Canadian government, easing the way legally for an eventual Canadian court victory in 1893. Described as "somewhat dour of mien and reserved in manner" in *The Advocate*, BC's law society magazine, Drake was noted for the chilly welcome speech he made to a newly inducted lawyer. "You have taken a great many oaths. See that you keep them," was all he said. He was also known for his pro-US, anti-Confederation views and, while mayor, was forced to lower the "stars and stripes" he had raised on the city hall flagpole on July 4. Drake Inlet was formerly known as South Arm, Drake I as Limestone I.

Draney Inlet (51°27'00" 127°30'00" SE branch of Rivers Inlet), **Draney Narrows** (51°28'00" 127°33'00" Entrance to Draney Inlet), **Draney Point** (52°10'00" 127°56'00" S end of Cunningham I, just E of Bella Bella). Robert Draney (1852–1927), a blacksmith by vocation, came to BC from Ont in the early 1870s and found work in the cannery trade. He was on the Skeena R in 1876–79 at the Aberdeen and Inverness canneries, then built the first Rivers Inlet cannery in 1882. In 1893, Robert bought property at Namu from fur trader John Clayton and, with the help of his wife Kate (1851–1912) and other family members, established a large cannery there, adding a store and

sawmill as business prospered. He built another cannery at Kimsquit on Dean Channel in 1901. The family owned a fishing company as well; Draney Point marked one of the boundaries of its operating area. Draney Lks near Namu, and Robert Arm and Draney Ck on Draney Inlet, are also named after this enterprising canneryman, who sold his operations in 1912 to a business group led by Henry Doyle and retired to his farm in Langley Prairie. Doyle and fellow entrepreneur Richard Winch merged their cannery holdings as Northern BC Fisheries Ltd in 1918. *W*

Draper Islets (52°35'13" 128°45'31" Off NW side of Swindle I, Laredo Sd). James Nelson Draper (1834–98) was born at Woodstock, NB, and came to New Westminster in 1858. According to journalist Barry Mather, he erected the city's first office building and served as the representative of the Victoria lumber firm T G Jackson & Co. Draper married Katherine Vickery (1835–1917), of NB, in 1862 at Victoria. He was New Westminster's harbourmaster in 1890 and is listed as a clerk in that city on the 1898 BC voters list.

Drew Harbour (50°05'51" 125°11'40" E side of Quadra I, N end of Str of Georgia), **Drew Passage** (50°16'06" 125°03'20" Between Rendezvous Is and Read I, NE of Campbell R), **Drew Rock** (48°45'27" 123°15'43" Bedwell Hbr, W side of S Pender I). Charles Randolph Drew (d 1873) was on the BC coast, based at Esquimalt, from 1866 to 1871. He was assistant secretary to Rear Adm George Hastings, cdr-in-chief of the Pacific Station, and then paymaster aboard HMS *Pylades*, under Capt Cecil Buckley. In 1872 he was in Jamaica as secretary to Capt

A safe anchorage spot at the head of Draney Inlet, seen from the base of Caroline Lake falls. *James and Jennifer Hamilton*

D

Algernon de Horsey aboard HMS *Aboukir*. Drew Ck, which flows into Drew Hbr, is also named for him, as are, presumably, **Drew Islet** (50°49'00" 126°55'00" Off W end of Broughton I, N side of Queen Charlotte Str) and Mt Drew, near Sechelt Inlet. According to geographer Robert Galois, the original Kwakwaka'wakw First Nation name for Drew Hbr was Tsatsahesin, or "place with plenty of gravel." W

Drift Whale Bay (50°12'27" 127°47'52" W side of Brooks Peninsula, W side of Vancouver I). This translation of a local Nuu-chah-nulth First Nation name was provided by linguist R Levine of the BC Provincial Museum and submitted by members of the museum's 1981 Brooks Peninsula expedition. It was adopted in 1985.

Driver Point (49°26'43" 126°16'08" S entrance to Steward-son Inlet, Clayoquot Sd). HMS *Driver*, a 957-tonne paddlewheel gunboat built in 1841, was the RN vessel in which Richard Blanshard, unhappy first colonial gov of Vancouver I, was forced to live for several weeks upon arrival at Victoria in 1850. The 6-gun steamship, under Cdr Charles Johnson, had brought him on the Panama–Victoria portion of his long journey from England, but he was snubbed by James Douglas and the other HBC officers at Ft Victoria and provided with no assistance or accommodation. In Mar 1850, Blanshard went along with Johnson ("a nice man and uncommonly kind") to Ft Nisqually to fetch cattle and sheep for Ft Victoria, and to Ft Rupert on an inspection tour (where, according to Douglas, he was "over familiar" with the HBC's discontented coal miners and "supported all their demands"). The gov returned to N Vancouver I on different vessels twice more in the next 16 months and authorized BC's first naval attacks on First Nation villages. Three months later he resigned his post in disgust and retired to an English country estate. HMS *Driver* served in SE Asia, 1841–43, and was the first steam vessel in NZ in 1846. It was in the Baltic during the Crimean War and was wrecked at Mariguana I in the Bahamas in 1861.

Drumlummon Bay (53°46'02" 129°01'25" NW side of Douglas Channel, SW of Kitimat). Drumlummon Copper Mines Ltd owned a group of mineral claims in the early 1920s located on the N shore of this bay. The company took its name from a famous Montana gold mine of the 1880s and '90s. Formerly known as Mistatla Bay.

Drummond Bay (48°44'04" 123°11'27" S side of S Pender I, Gulf Is). The Drummond brothers—Arthur, Bertie and Walter—were pioneer residents of Saturna I and Pender I, descendants, supposedly, of a noble Scottish family. Walter, a fine violinist, operated a store on Saturna and was postmaster there, 1897–99. Arthur was appointed provincial police constable for the Gulf Is in 1894 and was based on Mayne, where a tiny jailhouse—still standing

and now a museum—was built at Miners Bay in 1896. Popular local crimes included theft, rustling, smuggling, bootlegging and illegal hunting, and Arthur attended to police business in his boat, the *Constable*.

Drummond Bay (53°05'01" 129°06'06" W side of Princess Royal I, on Whale Channel). James Drummond (b about 1754), from Edinburgh, was an able seaman on HMS *Discovery* during Capt George Vancouver's historic 1791–95 voyages to the PNW. The hydrographic service had originally submitted the name Ryan Bay for this feature, after a survey assistant on CGS *William J Stewart*, but that suggestion was rejected and Drummond Bay substituted in 1950.

Drury Inlet (50°54'00" 127°03'00" NW of Broughton I, NE of Port Hardy). Cdr Byron Drury (1815–88) took charge of HMS *Pandora* in 1848 after the survey vessel completed its work in southern BC under Lt Cdr James Wood. The *Pandora*, under Drury, served on the Australia Station, 1850–56. Drury had earlier been present on the BC coast as a lt aboard HMS *Herald*, under Capt Henry Kellett. He reached the rank of adm, retired, in 1885. A number of geographic features around Drury Inlet were named in 1865 by Lt Daniel Pender after RN officers serving on the *Pandora* with Drury. W

Historic Dryad Point lighthouse, built in 1899. *Andrew Scott*

Dryad Point (52°11'07" 128°06'43" NE side of Campbell I, NE of Bella Bella). The HBC brigs *Dryad* and *Lama* brought building materials and stores to Campbell I in 1833 from Ft Vancouver on the Columbia R. Their purpose was to construct and stock a new trading post, Ft McLoughlin, which was located just S of present-day Bella Bella until 1843. The 185-tonne *Dryad* was built on the Isle of Wight in 1825 and chartered, then purchased, by the HBC. Its master in 1825, Capt James Davidson, was "without parallel" as "a Grog Drinker," according to HBC gov George Simpson. Capt Thomas Minors, in charge in 1830, was another drunkard who pilfered the ship's stores and tried to organize a mutiny when ordered to relinquish the vessel. Capt Charles Kipling, who had earlier damaged the HBC schooner *Vancouver*, was its master in 1833. The following year the *Dryad* was sent to the Stikine R, where the Russians prevented the HBC from building a post; it then helped remove Ft Simpson from Nass Bay to a location nearer the Skeena R. The ship was sold in 1836. Dryad Point was formerly known as Turn Point, but when a lighthouse was built in 1899, its name was changed to avoid conflict with Turn Point lighthouse on Stuart I on the US side of Haro Str. *W*

Duck Bay (48°53'17" 123°34'43" N of Vesuvius Bay, NW side of Saltspring I). According to early Saltspring settler William Mouat, this feature was originally known as Dock Bay, named in association with adjacent Dock Point (qv), which has appeared on Admiralty charts since 1865. The bottom of the bay drops off so steeply that it gives the impression of a natural dock. The name, however, became corrupted to Duck Bay.

Duckers Islands (52°55'36" 129°11'34" N of entrance to Surf Inlet, W side of Princess Royal I). Esther Mary Duckers (1887–1961) emigrated from England to the US with her family in the early 1900s. Hettie, as she was known all her life, married Dr William Sager (*see* Sager Is) at Rhode I in 1914 and went with him to Hazelton, BC, where he worked at the Methodist hospital. He had planned to go to China as a medical missionary, but Hettie, with a young family, balked at the prospect, and the Sagers went to the remote Surf Inlet gold mines on Princess Royal I instead, where William worked as the company doctor and Hettie became the mother of the first child born at the site. William's medical career then took the family to Port Simpson, Port Coquitlam and Crescent Beach. Hettie died at Surrey. The Duckers Is were formerly known as the North Surf Is.

Duck Island (49°05'59" 123°07'18" Mouth of Fraser R between Westham I and Rose I). Named for its feathered inhabitants, which were especially valued as a never-ending supply of targets for hunters, such as businessman and former BC lt gov Eric W Hamber, president of the Duck Island Ranch Co, which leased the island as a shooting preserve for many years.

Dudevoir Passage (54°38'06" 130°26'22" Between Tsimpsean Peninsula and Maskelyne I, N of Prince Rupert). Alfred Dudoward (c 1849–1914), known as Skagwait (or Sgagweet), was the respected chief of the Gitando branch of the Tsimshian First Nation at Ft Simpson (Lax Kw'alaams). He was the son of a high-ranking Tsimshian mother, Elizabeth Diex (there are many variant spellings of her hereditary name). His father was Félix Dudoaire (Dudoire or Dudevoir), a French Canadian tailor at the HBC fort. After Félix's death, Alfred's surname was anglicized. In

1871, Alfred married Katherine Holmes, who also had a high-ranking Tsimshian mother and a white father. She had attended Anglican school in Victoria and been raised in a non-Native home. Following Elizabeth Diex's lead, the Dudowards became Methodists in 1873 while on a visit to Victoria. They persuaded Thomas Crosby to establish his Methodist mission at Ft Simpson in 1874, and both Alfred and Kate were deeply involved in mission activities. However, ongoing conflicts between Christian and traditional beliefs led the Dudowards to leave the church in the mid-1890s. The family operated a store at Ft Simpson and owned a trading sloop, the *Georgiana*, in the mid-1870s. Alfred and Kate's children included the well-known carver Charles Dudoward. Dudevoir Passage was formerly known as Canoe Pass.

Dudley Islet (51°20'08" 127°31'56" N entrance to Margaret Bay, Boswell Inlet, E of Smith Sd). Named in 1948 after Col Dudley Mills (d 1937), of the Royal Engineers, who married Ethel Joly de Lotbinière, daughter of Sir Henri-Gustave Joly de Lotbinière, lt gov of BC, 1900–1906 (*see* Lotbinière I). Formerly known as Green I.

Dufferin Island (52°12'25" 128°20'25" S side of Seaforth Channel, NW of Bella Bella, part of the Bardswell Group). Frederick Temple Blackwood, 1st Marquess of Dufferin and Ava (1826–1902), was Canada's third gov gen, 1872–78. Born at Florence, he was appointed a lord-in-waiting to Queen Victoria, wrote a popular book about his northern travels, *Letters from High Latitudes*, married Harriot Georgina Rowan-Hamilton (*see* Harriot I) in 1862, and served as undersecretary of state for India and undersecretary of war. He is best known as a diplomat, however. He was one of Canada's most politically active govs gen, proroguing parliament in 1873 and establishing an inquiry into the Pacific Scandal (in which bribes secured the transcontinental railway contract) that brought down Sir John A Macdonald's Conservative government. Lord and Lady Dufferin (who were an earl and a countess while in Canada, not being advanced to marquess and marchioness until 1888) visited every Canadian province and in 1876 made a tour of coastal BC on HMS *Amethyst*, during which many features were named, including this one. After Canada, Dufferin achieved the ultimate appointment—Viceroy of India (1884–88)—and was also an ambassador to Russia, the Ottoman Empire, Italy and France. The Countess of Dufferin Range and Harriot I E of Grenville Channel are named for Lady Dufferin. *See also* Bones Bay. *W*

Duffin Cove (49°09'03" 125°54'41" S of Grice Point at Tofino, Clayoquot Sd, W side of Vancouver I), **Duffin Passage** (49°09'07" 125°54'58" Between Felice I and Tofino). Robert Duffin was 1st mate of the *Felice Adventurer*, under John Meares, in summer 1788, when Meares visited the W coast of Vancouver I to establish a

D

trading post at Nootka Sd and build a 40-tonne schooner, the *North West America*, the first non-Native vessel constructed in the PNW. Duffin went with a longboat crew to examine the coast S of Barkley Sd and was wounded in a skirmish with Ditidaht warriors at Port San Juan. He was back to the PNW in 1789 as 1st mate of the *Argonaut*, under Capt James Colnett, and was arrested with other crew members by Spanish cdr José Martínez and taken to Mexico. Duffin was at Nootka again in 1792 as trader (or supercargo) on the Portuguese brig *Sao Jao y Fenix*. He met Capt George Vancouver there and took Lt Zachary Mudge back with him when he returned to China. In 1798 and 1799 he was on the BC coast in command of the British ship *Dove*, from Macao.

Duff Islet (50°45'00" 126°43'00" Off W side of Eden I), **Duff Point** (50°45'30" 126°42'50" NW end of Eden I, E end of Queen Charlotte Str). Duff Point was named in 1792 by Capt George Vancouver after his old friend and shipmate George Duff (1764–1804), who, as 1st lt of HMS *Europa*, was Vancouver's senior officer, 1786–89. Duff went to sea early, and by the age of 16 was a lt with 13 naval engagements under his belt. In 1792 he was a cdr and in charge of HMS *Martin*, a sloop of war stationed off Scotland. He was killed at the Battle of Trafalgar, while capt of HMS *Mars*, a 74-gun ship of the line. *W*

Duffy Rock (52°37'52" 128°49'05" Off entrance to Trahey Inlet, S end of Princess Royal I). James Duffy was a cpl in the Columbia detachment of Royal Engineers, which served in BC 1858–63. Trained as a surveyor, he arrived with the advance party and was stationed near Ft Langley at Derby, the first capital of the mainland colony of BC, until the main body of men arrived. In the summer of 1860 he laid out Cayoosh townsite (Lillooet). Then, at Gov James Douglas's direct request, he prepared a report on alternate routes up Cayoosh Ck and over the mountains to Lillooet Lk. (For this he was considered by his military superiors to have left his regular duties without authority and was reduced in rank to sapper.) Duffy was found frozen to death in 1861 on the Harrison–Lillooet trail. The route he reconnoitred along Cayoosh Ck is now Hwy 99, also known as the Duffey Lk Rd (his surname is spelled with and without an "e"). Duffey Ck on Aristazabal I is also named for him.

Duke Point (49°09'00" 123°53'00" Between Nanaimo Hbr and W side of Northumberland Channel). Named in association with Northumberland Channel (qv) by Cdr John Parry, who re-surveyed this area in 1903 in HMS *Egeria*. The channel, in turn, had been named by the officers of the HBC post at Nanaimo in 1853 because of the coal that had recently been discovered and was the reason for the establishment of a fort. The domain of Britain's Duke of Northumberland was, of course, famous for its coal. The tip of Duke Point once consisted of two fingers,

which were dredged and filled in the early 19th century; today the peninsula is known as Duke Point and the tip as Jack Point (qv).

Duncan Bay (50°04'39" 125°17'43" Between mouth of Campbell R and Menzies Bay, E coast of Vancouver I), **Duncan Bay** (54°21'21" 130°28'06" W side of Tsimpsean Peninsula, W of Prince Rupert). Capt Alexander Duncan, from Falkirk, Scotland, was an employee of the HBC maritime dept, which he joined in 1824, spending his early years on the *William and Ann* and the *Prince of Wales*. He was master of the *Dryad* on its 1834 voyage to the Stikine R, where the Russians prevented the HBC from building a post; on its return journey, the *Dryad* transferred the stores and employees of Ft Simpson, originally on Nass Bay, to a more permanent location N of Prince Rupert. Over the years, Duncan also had charge of the *Cadboro*, the second *Vancouver* (with which he helped build the HBC's Ft Durham, or Ft Taku, in 1840), the *Ganymede*, *Beaver* (1843–44), *Sumatra* and *Columbia* (1844–48). He retired in 1848 and moved with his wife, Ann (née Simpson, married in 1829), and family to a farm in the eastern US. The bay on Vancouver I, named by Capt George Richards about 1860, is the site of the enormous Elk Falls pulp and paper mill, which in 2008 was owned by Catalyst Paper Corp. The northern bay was named by HBC officials in the 1830s and adopted in 1862 by Richards, who felt, according to coastal historian John Walbran, that he was also honouring the missionary William Duncan (*see* Duncan I), who that year re-established the Tsimshian community of Metlakatla.

Duncan Bight (50°41'31" 125°42'05" NE of Glendale Cove, Knight Inlet), **Duncan Point** (50°40'57" 125°43'28" NE point of Glendale Cove). Named after Duncan Macdonald, a younger brother of former HBC officer William John Macdonald. William became a wealthy Victoria merchant and politician and was appointed a Conservative federal senator from BC, 1871–1915. *See* Macdonald Point. Several geographic features in this vicinity were named in 1865 by William Blakeney, assistant RN surveying officer aboard the *Beaver*, after Macdonald and his extended family. Duncan Bight was originally called Duncan Bay but was renamed in 1949 to avoid confusion with two other features on the BC coast named Duncan Bay.

Duncanby Landing (51°24'20" 127°38'43" E side of Goose Bay, S side of entrance to Rivers Inlet). James Graham built a wharf, store and fuel station at this spot about 1936 with the help of his father-in-law, cannery man Frank Inrig. According to Ken Campbell's *Cannery Village: Company Town*, Inrig wanted to call the location Duncan Bay after his friend Tom Duncan, who had worked for him at Port Essington as an engineer. The name was already in use, so Graham and Inrig settled for Duncanby Landing instead. James Graham and his wife, Jessie, added a restaurant

Duncanby Landing in Rivers Inlet. *Andrew Scott*

and persuaded Union steamships to stop at their popular landing, selling out in 1972.

Duncan Cove (49°38'00" 124°03'00" N side of Pender Hbr, between Garden Bay and Irvines Landing, NW of Sechelt). According to *The Sunshine Coast*, by writer and publisher Howard White, the cove was named after George Duncan, who set up a blacksmith shop there in the early 1900s.

Duncan Island (50°48'51" 127°33'06" SE of Hurst I, Goletas Channel, N shore of Vancouver I). William Duncan (1832–1918) was arguably BC's most famous missionary. He was an English leather salesman who was trained by the Church Missionary Society but not ordained as an Anglican clergyman, then sent via Victoria to Ft Simpson on the N BC coast in 1857. In 1862 he and 400 Tsimshians established Metlakatla, an old habitation site S of Ft Simpson, as a "model Christian village." Duncan safely vaccinated his followers against the virulent outbreak of smallpox that swept the coast that year and secured a reputation as a powerful leader and provider of spiritual and physical sanctuary. He was appointed a justice of the peace and moved quickly to make his new community self-sufficient. By the mid-1870s, Metlakatla was world-famous, with European-style homes, a tannery, cooperage, fire hall, sawmill, cannery, school, newspaper and the largest church W of Chicago and N of San Francisco (seating for 1,200). The village operated a store and trading schooner and began to monopolize the regional fur business. But Duncan's Anglican superiors grew dissatisfied with him; he modified church services and failed to train First Nation clergy. In 1879, Bishop William Ridley based his northern diocese at Metlakatla, and a feud arose between the two men that verged on

violence. In 1887, Duncan led more than 800 Tsimshians to Annette I in SE Alaska and founded New Metlakatla. His problems were not over, though. Divisions deepened between the leader, who could not relinquish control and whose attitudes were patronizing, and his flock, who understandably wished for education and economic growth. By the time of his death, Duncan was embittered and isolated, his noble efforts sabotaged by an unyielding personality. *E W*

Duncan Point (54°31'28" 130°27'41" SE side of Finlayson I, off NW side of Tsimpsean Peninsula, N of Prince Rupert). After senior HBC official Duncan Finlayson, who served on the BC coast in the 1830s. *See* Finlayson I.

Dundarave (49°20'12" 123°11'07" N shore of Burrard Inlet, at W Vancouver). This pleasant W Vancouver neighbourhood was named by an early landowner, Russell E Macnaughton (1861–1918), assistant professor of Greek at UBC. Dundarave Castle on Loch Fyne in Scotland was the ancestral home of the MacNaughtons. The name should rhyme with "have" and is Gaelic, apparently, for "castle of two oars," as you needed to row in order to reach it in the old days. Dundarave pier, built in 1914, has provided access over the years to a series of hotels and restaurants. A small commercial district developed around a PGE station that opened the same year.

Dundarave Beach at West Vancouver. *Kate Lore*

Dundas Island (54°33'47" 130°52'22" Largest of the Dundas Is), **Dundas Islands** (54°28'57" 130°56'22" W side of Chatham Sd, NW of Prince Rupert). The island group was named Dundas's I in 1793 by Capt George Vancouver, who thought he was looking at one solid land mass. Lawyer and politician Henry Dundas (1742–1811) was treasurer of the navy, 1782–1800, and held a number of other important offices under PM William Pitt the Younger, his great friend. He was an MP, solicitor gen for Scotland at the young age of 24, lord advocate in 1775, home secretary, 1791–94, and war secretary, 1794–1801. In 1804–5 he was 1st Lord of the Admiralty, and though noted for improving

D

the payment of seamen's wages, he became the subject of an inquiry into the misappropriation of public funds. While he was acquitted of any wrongdoing, a certain stigma of negligence stuck to him and he never held office again. In 1802, Dundas was created Viscount Melville and Baron Dunira. Baron, Dunira and Melville islands are also named for him, as are the town and county of Dundas, Ont, plus Dundas St in Toronto (his friend John Simcoe, lt gov of Upper Canada, bestowed these latter names). *W*

Dunira Island (54°26'30" 130°46'15" One of the Dundas Is, W side of Chatham Sd, NW of Prince Rupert). After Henry Dundas, Baron Dunira. *See* Dundas I.

Dunlap Island (49°13'07" 125°56'37" Between Vargas I and Meares I, Clayoquot Sd, W side of Vancouver I). Air Marshal Clarence "Larry" Rupert Dunlap, CBE (1908–2002), was a flight lt in 1930 when he took the first aerial photographs of the Pacific coast for the Canadian Hydrographic Service. Born at Sydney Mines, NS, he joined the RCAF in 1928 and was director of armament at RCAF HQ, Ottawa, by 1939. In WWII he served as CO of RAF Leeming, a UK bomber base; CO of No 331 Wing in Tunisia; and CO of No 139 Wing, which conducted daylight bombing raids from England against German V-1 launch sites. Dunlap personally flew 35 sorties. After the war he was CO of NW Air Command, Edmonton, then commandant of Canada's National Defence College, 1951–54, vice-chief of air staff, 1954–58, and chief of air staff, 1962–64. Canada's top air force officer retired in 1968 after a stint as deputy cdr-in-chief of NORAD, 1964–67.

Dunlop Point (49°30'35" 124°37'52" W entrance to Tribune Bay, Hornby I, Str of Georgia). Hamilton Dunlop (d 1900) served on the BC coast in 1859–60 as 4th lt of HMS *Tribune*, under Capt Geoffrey Hornby. He retired from the RN in 1883 with the rank of capt.

Dunn Bay (52°10'20" 127°58'13" S side of Cunningham I, just E of Bella Bella), **Dunn Point** (52°10'15" 127°58'25" Adjacent to Dunn Bay). John Dunn arrived from England about 1831 aboard the supply ship *Ganymede* to work for the HBC at Ft Vancouver and returned home about 1840. He was stationed at Ft McLoughlin as a trader and was later in charge of Ft George at Astoria. He also visited the QCI in 1836. In his book, *The Oregon Territory and the British North American Fur Trade*, which was published in several editions in the mid-1840s, Dunn supported British claims to the Oregon region, described the habits and practices of its inhabitants and gave an account of his sojourn in the PNW. Formerly known as Peel Bay and Peel Point, these features were renamed by the hydrographic service in 1924.

Dunn Passage (53°07'00" 129°32'00" S entrance to Weinberg Inlet, Campania I, NE Estevan Sd). Carl Dunn

was a quartermaster aboard the W coast survey vessel *William J Stewart* in the mid-1940s.

Dunns Nook (48°26'27" 123°27'05" W side of Esquimalt Hbr, S end of Vancouver I). Thomas Russell Dunn was an RN surgeon aboard HMS *Fisgard*, under Capt John Duntze, on the Pacific Station, 1843–47. By the time he retired, in 1861, he was an inspector-gen of hospitals and fleets (the RN's second-highest medical rank) and an honorary physician to Queen Victoria. The Nook has been much modified since it was named by Lt Cdr James Wood of HMS *Pandora*, who surveyed Esquimalt Hbr in 1847, and is now mostly drained. The area was an old Songhees First Nation village site; it was once known as Stchayak, meaning "mouldy beach"—a reference to the appearance of rocks turned over in the process of searching for food.

Dunsmuir Islands (48°59'31" 123°47'29" In Ladysmith Hbr, E side of Vancouver I). Industrialist and politician James Dunsmuir (1851–1920) founded the town of Ladysmith in 1901 as a residential community for the workers at his nearby Extension coal mine. Born at Ft Vancouver, he was the son of coal baron Robert Dunsmuir (1825–89), who became BC's wealthiest man on the strength of his Nanaimo mines and the Esquimalt & Nanaimo Rwy, which he built in 1883. Robert was also MLA for Nanaimo, 1882–89. His son James took over the family business on his father's death and was elected MLA for Comox in 1898. He was named premier of BC in 1900 but resigned in 1902; he also served as the province's lt gov, 1906–9. Both he and his father were legendary for their brutal opposition to organized labour, and their mines were exceedingly dangerous places to work. James sold his E&N holdings to the CPR in 1905 and the family collieries to railroad promoters Donald Mann and William Mackenzie in 1910. He lived out his days in extravagant style at Hatley Park, a Colwood mansion (now Royal Roads Univ). This geographical feature was formerly known as the Twin Is but was renamed in 1904 by Cdr John Parry of HMS *Egeria*. *E W*

Dunsterville Islet (50°08'43" 125°09'40" S end of Hoskyn Channel, N end of Str of Georgia), **Dunsterville Point** (50°08'54" 125°08'59" SW end of Read I, S end of Hoskyn Channel). Cdr Edward Dunsterville (d 1872) worked at the RN's hydrographic dept, 1842–70, and was in charge of supplying charts to naval vessels. He had served as an RN surveyor on the W Indies Station, 1826–37, and in the Mediterranean, as master of HMS *Cambridge*, 1840–42. Mt Dunsterville on Gilford I is also named for him. *W*

Duntze Head (48°25'52" 123°26'22" E entrance to Esquimalt Hbr, S end of Vancouver I). Capt John Alexander Duntze (1806–82) was cdr of HMS *Fisgard* on the Pacific Station, 1843–47. He went on to attain the rank of adm in 1865. Lt Cdr James Wood of HMS *Pandora*, who surveyed Esquimalt Hbr in 1847, named many of its features after the officers of the *Fisgard*, which was an occasional early visitor to the area. Esquimalt naval base's first buildings—three wooden huts to be used as a temporary hospital—were constructed on this point in 1855 by Gov James Douglas. They had been requested by Rear Adm Henry Bruce, cdr-in-chief of the Pacific Station, who expected casualties from an RN attack on Petropavlovsk, on the Kamchatka Peninsula, during the Crimean War. The Russian city had been evacuated by the time of the attack, however, and the Duntze Head hospital was scaled back to one hut; the others were used at various times as a stores depot, an RN surgeon's residence and an office for RN hydrographer Capt George Richards.

Dupont Island (52°56'23" 129°26'23" S entrance to Estevan Sd, Caamaño Sd). Businessman and investor Maj Charles Thomas Dupont (1837–1923) was born in Que and married Margaret Jessie Dupont (1819–1903) at Halifax in 1859. They arrived at Victoria about 1872 after spending some time in the Lk Superior region, where Dupont was an Indian agent. He was part of an 1884 syndicate, the Vancouver Improvement Co, that bought up a large amount of land in Vancouver with the foreknowledge that the CPR terminus would be there and not at Port Moody. He was also involved in the development of Oak Bay, as a shareholder in the Oak Bay Land and Improvement Co. After the death of his first wife, he married Mary L Wilmot, of Fredericton, NB, in 1906 and moved to England.

Dusenbury Island (49°37'19" 124°02'20" Gerrans Bay, Pender Hbr, NW of Vancouver). Ex-boxer and mechanical genius Hiram "Harry" Eugene Dusenbury (1873–1953) showed up at Pender Hbr in 1905, bought this island and built a machine shop and boat-repair business there. He was a major force behind the establishment of Pender Hbr's hospital. The island was home base for a sealing schooner he co-owned with a legendary character named Alex McLean (*see* McLean I), on whom Jack London was alleged to have modelled Wolf Larsen in his novel *The Sea Wolf*. Dusenbury drowned off his property at the age of 79.

Dusky Cove (50°41'35" 126°39'44" W side of Bonwick I, E end of Queen Charlotte Str). Named in 1865 by the officers of the *Beaver* because the cove was reached at twilight on a summer evening. The venerable paddle steamer was hired from the HBC by the RN for coastal survey work, 1863–70.

Duval Rock (53°03'23" 131°53'22" Off N shore of Cumshewa Inlet, QCI). Queen Charlotte City pioneer Archibald Arthur Duval (1878–1966) was a handlogger

and fisherman. Born in Ont, he worked as a carpenter in Revelstoke, Nelson and Vernon before reaching Haida Gwaii in 1908 and helping open up John McLellan's mining claims at Mitchell Inlet. Archie married Charlotte "Lottie" Matilda McCallum (1880–1957), a nurse at the Queen Charlotte City hospital, in 1911 at Prince Rupert. *D*

Du Vernet Point (54°19'00" 130°24'00" E side of Digby I, Prince Rupert Hbr). Frederick Herbert Du Vernet (1860–1924), from Que, was a pioneer Anglican clergyman on BC's N coast. Before arriving in BC he spent 12 years on the staff of Wycliffe College, Toronto. He became the second bishop of Caledonia in 1904, based at Metlakatla, though spending much of his time at newly founded Prince Rupert. To set an example to his staff, he rowed every week, until crippled by arthritis, from Prince Rupert to Metlakatla to hold services. In 1915 he was appointed the first metropolitan archbishop of BC. Du Vernet took a keen interest in mental telepathy, conducting experiments and writing extensively on "radio mind," as he called it. The terminus for the ferry linking Prince Rupert to the airport on Digby I occupies the point today.

Dwight Rock (52°49'26" 131°39'56" SE of Talunkwan I, QCI). Named after prominent US geologist James Dwight Dana in 1878 by George M Dawson of the Geological Survey of Canada. *See* Dana Inlet.

Dyer Cove (52°11'09" 128°28'16" W side of Athlone I, Milbanke Sd, W of Bella Bella), **Dyer Rocks** (48°37'33" 123°28'47" W side of Saanich Peninsula, S end of Vancouver I). Margaret Dyer (1841–1920) was the first white woman to settle on the Saanich Peninsula, in 1858. She was born in Scotland and came to Ft Victoria in 1853 with her mother and stepfather, Duncan Lidgate, an HBC carpenter. After marrying William Thomson (1829–1908, *see* Thomson Cove) at age 15, she moved to Bannockburn, the Thomson family farm, near Mt Newton and had 15 children. Many of her descendants still live in the district. Dyer Cove was formerly known as Anchor Bay, Dyer Rks as White Rks.

Dyke Point (48°26'56" 123°26'23" E side of Esquimalt Hbr, W of Thetis Cove, S end of Vancouver I). Charles Dyke was 2nd lt aboard HMS *Fisgard*, on the Pacific Station, 1843–47, under Capt John Duntze. He retired from the RN in 1864 with the rank of cdr. Lt Cdr James Wood of HMS *Pandora*, who surveyed Esquimalt Hbr in 1847, named many of its features after the officers of the *Fisgard*. Dyke Point was called White Lady Point by local residents around the turn of the 19th century, though it is not known why.

Eagle Bay (48°50'08" 125°08'41" W side of Bamfield facing Trevor Channel, Barkley Sd, W side of Vancouver I). This is a feeding and nesting area for bald eagles. The name was adopted in 1981 after being submitted by the owners of Aguilar House, Bamfield.

Eagle Bay (53°48'39" 128°42'31" SE side of Amos Passage, Kitimat Arm, S of Kitimat). The Haisla First Nation people know this bay as Toseqai'ya. Ironically, in their traditional ownership system, the area belongs to the Raven clan rather than the Eagle clan. A 2.5-ha Haisla reserve, Tosehka, is located on the E side of the bay.

Eagle Bight (54°32'03" 130°15'40" E side of Work Channel, N of Prince Rupert). Capt John Costello Grave, in the HBC brigantine *Eagle* (along with Capt Aemilius Simpson in the *Cadboro*), helped determine the site for Ft Nass on the Nass R in 1830. The trading post, later renamed Ft Simpson, was established the following year by Simpson in the *Cadboro*. The 175-tonne *Eagle* was built at Lynn in Norfolk, England, in 1824 and purchased by the HBC in 1827. It first arrived at Ft Vancouver on the Columbia R in 1828 but was mostly used as a supply ship between England and N America, travelling to Hudson Bay as well as the PNW. It was sold in 1837 after the company built larger supply vessels.

Eagle Harbour (49°21'06" 123°16'16" SE of Eagle I), **Eagle Island** (49°21'13" 123°16'26" E side of Queen Charlotte Channel, SE entrance to Howe Sd, W Vancouver). The name Eagle Hbr applies to the body of water SE of Eagle I, while the area to the NE is Fishermans Cove (qv). Apparently the whole embayment was once known locally as Eagle Hbr. The SE part had several old names, including Shelter Bay and Johnson Cove, after a Swedish-born tugboat capt who was appointed a Vancouver Hbr pilot in 1893. August Nelson pre-empted land there in the 19th century and started to build a sawmill, but the site was taken over by the Whiteside & Burnham cannery, which operated until about 1918. Eagle Hbr also refers to the adjacent residential suburb of W Vancouver, where a

yacht club was established in 1969. The small island 70 m offshore was the site of the Canessas fish smokehouse in 1890. It had long been known to nearby residents as Eagle I, but in order to avoid confusion with the five other Eagle islands on BC's S coast, it was officially named Abode I in 1929, after its many small summer cottages. There were protests at this move—W Vancouver municipal clerk Rupert Harrison noted in 1949 that it had only ever been known as Eagle I—and that year the name was officially changed to Eagle I to reflect entrenched local usage. For years residents got to their homes on a hand-cranked, chain-operated communal barge.

Eagle Harbour, West Vancouver, foreground, with Bowen Island in the background. *Peter Vassilopoulos*

Earl Ledge (50°24'47" 125°55'15" Extending S from SW side of Hardwicke I, Johnstone Str). Named by Cdr Cortland Simpson in association with nearby Hardwicke I, which had been named in 1792 by Capt George Vancouver after the Earl of Hardwicke. Simpson re-surveyed this area with HMS *Egeria* in 1901. In 1950 the Bendickson family, long-time Hardwicke I homesteaders, built a breakwater over Earl Ledge to create a boat harbour. *See* Bendickson Hbr and Hardwicke I for more information.

Earls Cove (49°45'12" 124°00'33" NE end of Agamemnon Channel, just S of Jervis Inlet). Thomas Egbert Earl, wounded in WWI, was recuperating at Shaughnessy Hospital in Vancouver when he met Nellie Youngblood (1889–1965), who had been living with her uncle on the N Sechelt Peninsula. They married in 1918 and settled on the cove, which in 1952 became the S terminus for a Black Ball ferry to Powell R. It was originally named Earl Cove but was changed to Earls Cove when the post office was established, in 1959, because another family named Earl also lived in the area. In 1972, BC's first aquaculture licence was issued nearby for an (unsuccessful) salmon-farming operation.

East Copper Island. *See* Copper Is.

East Cracroft Island. *See* Cracroft Is.

East Kinahan Island. *See* Kinahan Is.

East Redonda Island (50°14'32" 124°42'38" Entrance to Toba Inlet, NE of Campbell R). Spanish naval officers Dionisio Alcalá-Galiano and Cayetano Valdés named Isla Redonda (Spanish for "round") in 1792, not realizing that it was two islands. They anchored near Teakerne Arm at W Redonda I for several weeks with Capt George Vancouver's two vessels while exploring the region in small boats. E Redonda has one of the highest points in BC not on the mainland or Vancouver I: 1,591-m Mt Addenbroke (*see also* Addenbroke I). The elevation extremes on such a small island have created unusual ecosystems, and the E part of E Redonda I is protected as a large ecological preserve. Over the years the 280-sq-km Redondas have seen some mining (iron ore) and quarrying (limestone); a substantial salmon cannery; fruit, vegetable, hog, shellfish and fur farming; lots of logging; and tourism. A small but vibrant community used to exist at Redonda Bay (qv), while the one at Refuge Cove (qv) still thrives as a summer recreation retreat and marine supply centre. *E*

East Thurlow Island. *See* Thurlow Is.

Eaton Rock (52°34'25" 129°26'34" SE side of Wright Passage, W of Aristazabal I). Sapper George Eaton was a member of the Columbia detachment of Royal Engineers, which served in BC 1858–63. He stayed on after the corps disbanded and received a 60-ha military land grant in 1869 in the New Westminster land district. Earlier in the 1860s he was in the goldfields, serving as a temporary police constable at Richfield in 1866 and later as the Cariboo's mining recorder. In the 1875 and 1898 BC voters lists, George Eaton is described as a logger at Jervis and Malaspina inlets.

Eberts Cove (51°49'27" 127°21'35" E side of Moses Inlet, N of Rivers Inlet). Lawyer and politician David MacEwen Eberts (1850–1924) came to BC from Ont. In 1884, at Victoria, he married Mabel Hope Charles (1860–1931), who was born at Ft Hope, the daughter of HBC official William Charles. Eberts was elected a Conservative MLA for Victoria, 1890–1903, and Saanich, 1907–16, and served as BC's attorney gen in 1895–98 and 1900–1903. A 1901 editorial in the *Province* declared that "if he wasn't so confoundedly lazy he could be anything he cared to be." This reputation did not prevent him from becoming speaker of the legislative assembly, 1907–16, however—or, after retirement from politics, a judge on the BC court of appeal. The name Eberts Cove was suggested by members of the Law Society of BC and adopted in 1947. Nearby Eberts Ck is also named for him, as is the Eberts Range on Gil I. Mabel Lk in the Okanagan is named for Mabel Eberts.

Eburne (49°12'00" 123°08'00" E end of Sea I, between Richmond and Vancouver). William Henry "Harry" Eburne (1856–1924) came to BC in 1875 with his foster

Looking from Eburne on Sea Island toward Marpole (or Eburne Station) in south Vancouver, 1912. *BC Archives E-00145*

E

parents and worked for Fitzgerald McCleery, the first farmer in Vancouver, who cultivated the Southlands flats on the N shore of the Fraser R. Eburne opened a store in S Vancouver in 1881, then bought John Sexsmith's N Arm store and post office on Lulu I in 1885. In 1892 he married Rosamond Esther Bennett (1877–1953) at Vancouver and moved his operation to the E end of Sea I, renaming the post office Eburne. Bridges had been built connecting Sea I to Richmond and Vancouver, and after the Vancouver & Lulu I Rwy was completed in 1902, Eburne developed into a small but vigorous agricultural centre with a hotel, cannery and, later, a large sawmill. The district opposite, on the Vancouver side of the Fraser, was known as Eburne Station until 1916, when it was renamed Marpole.

Eby Rock (49°13'08" 126°01'17" Off NW tip of Vargas I, Clayoquot Sd, W side of Vancouver I). Jacob M Eby was an early settler on the N side of Vargas I, pre-empting land there in 1912 and receiving a Crown grant in 1917. This feature appeared on early Admiralty charts as Half-tide Rk but was renamed by the hydrographic service in 1934.

Echachis Island (49°07'39" 125°56'21" W side of Templar Channel, SW of Tofino, Clayoquot Sd, W side of Vancouver I). The name of the important former Tla-o-qui-aht (Clayoquot) First Nation summer village on this island has been translated as "land elevated above the surface of the ocean." Many spelling variations have been recorded, including Aachaches, Echachets and Ich'aachist. The site was used by the Tla-o-qui-aht as a major fishing station and whaling centre. *W*

Echinus Point (53°40'34" 132°17'31" S side of Masset Inlet, Graham I, QCI). *Echinus* is the generic name for the sea urchin, and the spiny sea creatures are abundant in this area. The point was named by George M Dawson of the Geological Survey of Canada in 1878.

Echo Bay (50°45'07" 126°29'48" W side of Gilford I, Broughton Archipelago, NE of Port McNeill). Echo Bay is an old name, applied by Admiralty surveyors in the early 1860s. On the N side of the bay, a 60-m cliff, marked with ancient pictographs, provides a fine surface for sounds to echo off. The Kwakwaka'wakw people once had a village on the bay but moved away during the smallpox epidemics of the mid-18th century. A non-Native floathouse community grew up in the early 1900s. Louie McKay opened a store in 1920, and a shingle mill operated in the 1930s. Fidel Laviolette started a hotel and pub in 1933, and the bay has been home to a floating fishing resort for many years. A BC Forest Service station was based there, 1951-68, on a site now occupied by Echo Bay Marine Provincial Park. The community's post office, confusingly, is called Simoom Sd (qv); it was opened on Simoom Sd in 1912, then moved to Gilford I in 1936 and to Echo Bay in 1973, but always retained its original name.

Ecoole (48°58'00" 125°03'30" S side of Seddall I, Barkley Sd, W side of Vancouver I). According to Nuu-chah-nulth First Nation writer and artist George Clutesi, the name of this ancient fishing village means "where vegetation reaches the water's edge." A different translation from the Nuu-chah-nulth is "bushes on a hill." Capt James Warren, a well-known sealer, operated a trading post there in the 19th century. Nelson Bros Fisheries built one of BC's largest pilchard-reduction plants in the 1920s and '30s and produced the Snow Cap brand of canned pilchards (which were never very popular as they were too oily). A fisheries camp lingered on at the abandoned plant for many years.

Ecstall Island (54°09'30" 129°57'19" At the mouth of the Ecstall R, SE of Prince Rupert), **Ecstall River** (Flows NW into the Skeena R near its mouth). Capt John Walbran reported that *ecstall* was a Tsimshian word for tributary—literally, "something from the side"—and referred to the Ecstall R, which enters the Skeena near its mouth. The word was used colloquially, as well, to mean "a side issue." Ecstall Lk is named after the river, which is also known locally as the Hocsall R; Ecstall I is known as Village I. *W*

Ede Island (52°30'00" 129°02'00" Entrance to Weeteeam Bay, W side of Aristazabal I). 2nd Cpl Charles Ede was a member of the Columbia detachment of the Royal Engineers, which served in BC 1858–63. He arrived at Esquimalt in 1858 with Capt John Grant's party and remained in the colony after the detachment was disbanded, though virtually nothing is known about his activities.

Eden Island (50°45'00" 126°40'00" S of Broughton I, NE end of Queen Charlotte Str). Adm Sir Charles Eden (1808–78) was comptroller-gen of the British Coast Guard in the late 1850s and a lord of the Admiralty, 1859–66. As capt of HMS *London* he took part in the shelling of Sebastopol during the Crimean War. Named by Lt Daniel Pender about 1864. *W*

Eden Point (50°24'00" 125°47'00" NW end of W Thurlow I, Johnstone Str). Adm Henry Eden (1797–1888) was a lord of the Admiralty, 1855–58. After serving as capt of HMS *Conway*, *Impregnable* and *Caledonia*, he was private secretary, 1846–48, to his politician cousin George Eden (1st Lord of the Admiralty, gov gen of India), and then superintendent of Woolwich dockyard, 1848–53. Named by Capt George Richards about 1860. *W*

Edgell Banks (49°16'00" 124°03'00" E of Maude I and Nanoose Hbr), **Edgell Island** (50°54'00" 127°16'00" S of Bradley Lagoon in Blunden Hbr, N side of Queen Charlotte Str), **Edgell Point** (Entrance to Blunden Hbr). Lt John Augustine Edgell (1880–1962) served on the BC coast aboard the survey vessel *Egeria* in 1903–6. He went on to command HMS *Mutine* in 1912, then became the

RN's superintendent of charts (1917–20 and 1923–25), assistant hydrographer (1928–32) and chief hydrographer (1932–45). He retired in 1945 as a vice adm and a knight. Edgell I and Edgell Banks were named by Cdr John Parry of HMS *Egeria* when he re-surveyed Blunden and Nanoose harbours in 1903. The nearby Augustine Is are also named for him.

Edith Point (48°51'00" 123°15'00" E side of Mayne I, Gulf Is). Edith Rebecca Cameron (1842–70) was the daughter of Chief Justice David and Cecilia Cameron, and niece of Sir James and Lady Douglas. In 1860 she married lawyer Henry Montagu Doughty (1841–1916), of Suffolk, England, who had served as an RN midshipman at Esquimalt and went on to write a number of books about travelling around Europe by boat. Her son, Lt Col Charles Doughty-Wylie, was awarded the VC at Gallipoli in WWI. *See also* Cameron Point *and* Cameron Rks.

Edmund Passage (51°28'00" 127°45'00" N of Ironside I, Schooner Retreat, entrance to Rivers Inlet). After Lt Cdr Edmund Hope Verney, who commanded the RN gunboat *Grappler* on the BC coast, 1862–65. *See* Verney Passage, which was the former name of this feature.

Edmund Point (51°54'00" 127°52'00" S entrance to Burke Channel, SE of Bella Bella). After 18th-century British parliamentarian and philosopher Edmund Burke. *See* Burke Channel.

Edmund Rock (50°53'00" 128°03'00" Off Cape Sutil, northernmost point of Vancouver I). After Adm Sir John Edmund Commerell, VC. *See* Commerell Point. Named by the Geographical Board of Canada in 1909 on the recommendation of Capt John Walbran.

Edna Mathews Island (51°35'00" 127°33'00" N of Walbran I, Rivers Inlet). Edna Mathews married fellow Univ of Toronto student George Darby in 1914 and moved with him to the central BC coast, where he became a well-known Methodist medical missionary based at Bella Bella. Edna played an important role in early mission activities but moved to Vancouver in 1923 for the Darby children's schooling. She returned to Bella Bella in 1948 until 1959, when the Darbys retired to Vancouver. *See also* Darby Channel.

Edward Channel (51°46'00" 128°04'00" Joins Hakai Passage and Nalau Passage, E side of Stirling I, S of Hunter I and Bella Bella). The early surveying firm of Underhill & Underhill conducted a number of land surveys on the mid-coast in the years following WWI. This feature was named after a member of one of the surveying parties.

Edward King Island (48°50'00" 125°12'00" W side of Trevor Channel, S of Diana I, Barkley Sd, W side of Vancouver I). Capt Edward Hammond King, born in

Devon, England, in 1832, accidentally shot and killed himself on this island in 1861 while taking his gun out of a boat to hunt deer. He had been sent by the BC government as a special constable to take charge of the wreck of the *Florencia* near Ucluelet and investigate the circumstances behind its sale to Ucluelet trader Charles Stuart. King and Stuart were returning to Victoria in the *Saucy Lass* when that vessel was forced to take shelter in nearby Dodger Channel. King had seen service in India and China with the British Army but retired in ill health in 1857 and moved with his family to BC two years later. He and a business partner published an official colonial gazette and two of BC's earliest and shortest-lived newspapers: the government-friendly *New Westminster Times* and *Victoria Gazette*. Edward King I was originally named King I in 1861 by Capt George Richards of HMS *Hecate* but was later changed to avoid confusion with similarly named features. Nearby Hammond Passage is also named for him. King Cove (qv) in Milbanke Sd is named for his wife.

Edward Point (50°21'00" 125°20'00" W side of Sonora I, S of Thurston Bay, N of Campbell R). After Cdr Edward Hardinge, who served with the RN on the BC coast in 1863. *See* Hardinge I.

Edwards Islet (53°20'00" 129°26'00" E of Hinton I, S of Union Passage and Pitt I). Mary Louise Edwards was a Victoria-based member of the Canadian Hydrographic Service staff in 1943, when this feature was named.

Edwards Point (52°09'00" 128°29'00" SW end of Athlone I, Milbanke Sd, W of Bella Bella). RCN officer John Crispo "Dutchie" Inglis Edwards, CBE (1896–1978), was born in NS and died at Sidney, BC. He graduated in the second class of the Royal Naval College of Canada in 1912, and his first command was HMCS *Festubert* in 1924. After commanding the destroyer *Champlain*, he was appointed assistant director naval reserves in 1931, then became CO of Esquimalt Barracks, 1936–39, and Halifax Barracks, 1939–41. In 1941–42, Edwards had charge of the armed merchant cruiser *Prince Henry*, patrolling S Atlantic and W coast waters and taking convoys to the Aleutian Is. His most challenging assignment was as CO of newly established HMCS *Cornwallis* in NS, the largest naval training base in the Commonwealth. He retired from the RCN in 1950 with the rank of commodore.

Edwin Point (54°02'00" 130°36'00" NW side of Porcher I, SW of Prince Rupert). After Cdr Edwin Augustus Porcher of the RN, who served on the BC coast in 1865–68. *See* Porcher I.

Edwin Reef (49°13'00" 126°05'00" SE of Bartlett I, Clayoquot Sd, W side of Vancouver I). Possibly named after the US barque *Edwin*, under Capt Hughes, which was wrecked in Hesquiat Hbr in Dec 1874. The vessel was

E

headed from Puget Sd to Australia when its cargo shifted and it drifted out of control and ran aground. Four people died in the incident, including the capt's wife and children. Chief Matlahaw of Hesquiat was afterwards awarded a silver medal by the Canadian government—and a cash award by the US—for organizing rescue parties and saving the rest of the crew. (Only five years earlier, two Hesquiat residents had been found guilty of murdering the crew of the *John Bright*, wrecked at the same location, and hanged.) Lumber from the *Edwin* was used to build Hesquiat's church.

Edye Passage (54°03'00" 130°37'00" NW side of Porcher I, SW of Prince Rupert). Capt William Henry Edye (1832–1910) arrived on the Pacific Station in 1869, aboard HMS *Satellite*. Earlier in his career he had been 2nd officer of HMS *Britannia*, 1862–65, when it was a cadet training vessel. Edye was inspector of RN training ships, 1874–78, then senior officer at Gibraltar. He rose to the rank of adm and retired from the RN in 1890. Nearby Henry I and William I are also named for him. *W*

Edye Point (48°19'00" 123°32'00" S side of Pedder Bay, S end of Vancouver I). Capt Adolphus George Edye (b 1815) was an RN hydrographer who came up with a number of improvements for marine surveying. He was awarded the silver medal of the Royal Society of Arts for inventing an instrument that registered the inclination and oscillations of a ship. He retired from the RN in 1863 and was appointed justice of the peace for the borough of Devonport. *W*

Eemdyk Passage (48°19'00" 123°33'00" Between Bentinck I and S end of Vancouver I). The freighter *Eemdyk*, purchased by the Holland-America Line in 1915, ran aground near here in Oct 1925 in dense fog. The vessel was refloated after its cargo was removed, but the old steam tug *Hope*, which was carrying longshoremen back and forth between Victoria and the salvage operation, became fouled on one of *Eemdyk*'s mooring cables, then, tragically, capsized and sank, with the loss of six lives.

Effingham Bay (48°53'00" 125°19'00" W side of Effingham I), **Effingham Inlet** (49°02'00" 125°09'00" NE of Barkley Sd), **Effingham Island** (48°52'00" 125°19'00" One of the Broken Group, Barkley Sd, W side of Vancouver I). The bay was named Port Effingham by British fur trader John Meares after Thomas Howard (1746–91), 3rd Earl of Effingham, deputy earl marshal of England, 1777–82, master of the mint, 1784–89, and a leading Freemason. Howard built Boston Castle at Rotherham in 1776 and named it in a gesture of sympathy to American republicans; he resigned his army commission rather than fight in the US Revolutionary War. Meares anchored at Port Effingham in *Felice Adventurer* for 10 days in July 1788; "we very sensibly enjoyed the benign influence

of the delightful season," he wrote, "in this calm and charming situation." Effingham I, former site of a large Nuu-chah-nulth settlement, was originally named Village I by Capt Charles Barkley, of the *Imperial Eagle*, in 1787 but was renamed in 1905 because of duplication with other Village islands. Meares and Barkley got into a bitter dispute over the latter's charts to the area, which Meares acquired—dishonestly according to some sources—through the *Eagle*'s agents. Effingham Lk and Effingham R are associated with the inlet, named in 1860 by Capt George Richards. *W*

The Royal Navy survey vessel *Egeria* firing a salute on the occasion of Queen Victoria's funeral, 1901. *BC Archives B-08462*

Egeria Bay (48°45'00" 123°14'00" W side of S Pender I, Gulf Is), **Egeria Bay** (54°13'00" 132°58'00" E side of Langara I, QCI), **Egeria Mountain** (53°55'04" 130°22'21" On SE Porcher I, S of Prince Rupert), **Egeria Reach** (53°18'00" 127°56'00" Head of Gardner Canal), **Egeria Rock** (54°21'00" 130°52'00" Brown Passage, W of Melville I and Prince Rupert), **Egeria Shoal** (50°38'00" 126°46'00" Between Malcolm I and Swanson I, SE end of Queen Charlotte Str). HMS *Egeria*, an 853-tonne, 48-m steam sloop with four guns, was the last RN ship stationed in BC waters. Built in 1873 at Pembroke, it took part, under Cdr Ralph Turton, in an 1875 expedition to Malaysia to punish the murderers of a British official. After being refitted for survey work in 1886 and sent to Australia and the S Pacific, *Egeria* arrived at Esquimalt in 1898, under Cdr Morris Smyth, to pick up where hydrographers Capt George Richards and Lt Daniel Pender had left off in 1870. It worked up and down the BC coast, especially in the N, until 1910, under Smyth (1898–1900), Cdr Cortland Simpson (1900–1903), Cdr John Parry (1903–6, 1909–10), Cdr Frederick Learmonth (1906–8) and Cdr John Nares (1910). The name *Egeria* was carved by crew members on a rock cliff next to the tidal benchmark left during the survey at S Pender I. The vessel was sold in 1911 by public auction at Esquimalt to the Navy League.

In Roman mythology, Egeria was a water nymph and wife of Numa Pompilius, second king of Rome, who dispensed prophecies and wisdom at her sacred grove.

Egerton Point (53°29'39" 128°58'30" E side of Ursula Channel, N of Bishop Bay, S of Kitimat), **Egerton Rock** (49°29'00" 123°57'00" Welcome Passage, E of S Thormanby I, W of Sechelt, Str of Georgia). Lt Cdr Frederick Wilbraham Egerton commanded the RN gunboat *Boxer* on the BC coast, 1869–72. Wilbraham Point, near Egerton Rk, is also named for him. To the Haisla people, Egerton Point is Wiilaxdels, meaning "high place to climb," according to former UBC anthropologist Jay Powell.

Egg Island (51°15'00" 127°50'00" S entrance to Smith Sd, S of Rivers Inlet). This isolated island is named for its prominent, rounded shape. A lighthouse was built here in 1898 to warn marine traffic headed to and from the Inside Passage of the deadly rocks of Smith Sd. It was a dangerous place to be stationed. Two replacement lighthouse keepers, Dan MacDonald and Jimmy Flewin, disappeared from Egg I in 1934, probably drowned while fishing. Their bodies were never found. In 1948 a tremendous winter storm destroyed the station, forcing the keeper, T R Wilkins, his wife and 10-year-old son to spend five days shivering in a chicken coop before they were rescued. The next keeper, Laurie Dupuis, committed suicide.

Egg Island, site of an isolated lighthouse. *Peter Vassilopoulos*

Egmont (49°45'00" 123°56'00" NW end of Sechelt Inlet, S side of Jervis Inlet, E of Powell R), **Egmont Point** (49°46'00" 123°57'00" NE end of Skookumchuck Narrows, NW of Egmont). HMS *Egmont*, a 74-gun ship of the line, took part in the 1797 Battle of Cape St Vincent, under Capt John Sutton. Sir John Jervis, the battle's champion, was created Earl St Vincent after his victory, and by naming Egmont Point in 1860, Capt George Richards continued a theme begun in 1792 when Capt George Vancouver named Jervis Inlet. The ship itself was named after John Perceval (1711–70), 2nd Earl of Egmont, who was 1st Lord of the Admiralty in 1763–66. The fishing village of Egmont, first settled in the late 1880s, was originally located on the N

side of the mouth of Sechelt Inlet but gradually moved over to the S side between the 1920s and '40s. The community was not connected by road until 1956. Nearby Egmont Ck takes its name from the village. The Sechelt First Nation name for Egmont Point is Selkant Kwátámus. *E*

Eik Rock (55°25'00" 129°40'00" N entrance to Alice Arm, Observatory Inlet, SE of Stewart). Karl Ludwig Eik and three other Scandinavian prospectors—Ole Evindsen, Ole Pearson and Ernest Carlson—first staked the Dolly Varden claims near the head of Alice Arm in 1910. Five years later they sold their shares for $10,000 each to Chicago investors, who went on to develop a narrow-gauge mining railway and a rich but ultimately unsuccessful silver mine, 1919–21. Eik later settled in Sask. *See also* Carlson Its *and* Pearson Point.

Ekins Point (49°32'00" 123°23'00" N end of Gambier I, Howe Sd, NW of Vancouver). Named by Capt George Richards in 1861, in association with the nearby Defence Is, after Charles Ekins (1768–1855), capt of HMS *Defence* in 1806–11. His first command was HMS *Ferret*, in 1795; he also commanded HMS *Echo*, *Amphitrite* and *Superb*, and was wounded aboard the latter at the 1816 bombardment of Algiers. Ekins achieved the rank of adm in 1841 and was knighted in 1852. He was a naval historian as well and wrote *The Naval Battles of Great Britain*, first published in 1824. *W*

Elephant Head Mountain (53°13'55" 128°51'16" NE end of Princess Royal I, S of Kitimat), **Elephant Head Point** (53°14'59" 128°50'45" NE side of Princess Royal I). According to *Sailing Directions*, it is the bold cliff face of the mountain, viewed from Fraser Reach, that resembles an elephant's head. Elephant Head Point is also a prominent landmark. These names were adopted in 1979.

Elephant Point (49°50'00" 124°02'00" W entrance to Hotham Sd, Jervis Inlet). HMS *Elephant*, a 74-gun ship of the line, was built in Hampshire, launched in 1786 and almost destroyed by lightning in Portsmouth hbr in 1790. It was Adm Horatio Nelson's flagship, under Capt John Foley, in the 1801 Battle of Copenhagen, where Nelson supposedly put a telescope to his blind eye to avoid seeing a signal ordering him to withdraw (*see* Telescope Passage). The vessel was reduced from 74 to 58 guns in 1818 and broken up in 1830. Elephant Point was formerly known as Berry Point (qv), after Rear Adm Sir Edward Berry.

Eliot Passage (50°37'00" 126°35'00" Between Village I and Indian Group, E end of Queen Charlotte Str). John Eliot served as 2nd lt aboard HMS *Clio*, on the BC coast 1859–62 and 1864–68. Named by Lt Daniel Pender in 1866.

Elizabeth Point (54°17'00" 130°22'00" E side of Digby I, just W of Prince Rupert). Elizabeth Parsons (1873–1934),

E

from W Virginia, married John W Moore (*see* Moore Pt) in 1893. He was a locating engineer for the GTP at the time this area was first surveyed in the early 1900s. Elizabeth accompanied her husband to Prince Rupert and lived in a "tent-house" on Centre St, 1906–8. The *Prince Rupert Empire* reported that she was "the first lady to make her home" in the newly established townsite.

Eliza Dome (49°53'10" 127°06'19" N side of entrance to Esperanza Inlet, between Nootka Sd and Kyuquot Sd, W side of Vancouver I), **Eliza Passage** (49°40'00" 126°35'00" E of Nootka I, S of Strange I, Nootka Sd), **Port Eliza** (49°53'00" 127°01'00" NW side of Esperanza Inlet). Francisco de Eliza y Reventa (1759–1825) was sent to Mexico in 1789 to bolster New Spain's San Blas naval station. In 1790, aboard the *Concepción*, he led an expedition to reoccupy Nootka Sd, where Estéban Martínez had established a Spanish base the year before. That summer Eliza sent Salvador Fidalgo, in the *San Carlos*, to explore the Alaska coast, and Manuel Quimper, in the *Princesa Real*, to survey Juan de Fuca Str. In 1791, Eliza and José Narváez, in the *San Carlos* and *Santa Saturnina*, respectively, became the first Europeans to see and explore the Str of Georgia. Eliza handed over control of Nootka Sd to Juan Francisco de la Bodega y Quadra in 1792 and returned to Mexico, where his reports added much to Spanish knowledge of BC's aboriginal people. He was in charge at San Blas from 1795 to 1801, but was posted to Cadiz, Spain, in 1803, where he continued to serve in the navy and also occupied several political positions from 1808 to 1814. Eliza Ears, near Port Eliza, is also named after this competent officer, and **Eliza Point** (48°22'00" 123°42'00" E side of Sooke Hbr, S end of Vancouver I) may be as well. *E*

Ella Point (50°33'00" 126°49'00" SW of Hanson I, S side of Johnstone Str). Henry Bailey Ella (1826–73) was born at London and went to sea at age 14, becoming a master mariner in 1853. He first arrived at Victoria in 1851 as a passenger in the HBC barque *Norman Morison* and later commanded such HBC vessels as the *Recovery* and the *Otter*. From the late 1850s onward he served as a coastal pilot and was often employed in this capacity in the RN survey ships *Plumper* and *Hecate*. Ella married another BC pioneer, Martha Cheney, at Victoria in 1855 (*see* Cheney Point) and built a family home there in 1862 that still stands (Wentworth Villa at 1156 Fort St). He drowned in a marine accident while on duty as a pilot in Vancouver Hbr. *W*

Ellard Rock (52°36'00" 128°46'00" W entrance to Meyers Passage, SW end of Princess Royal I). James Ellard (1836–78), born in England, was a sapper with the Columbia detachment of the Royal Engineers, which served in BC 1858–63. He stayed on after the detachment disbanded, married Emma Quinn in 1863 and leased, with fellow sapper Jonathan Brown, the Pioneer Billiard Saloon at New Westminster. Through "strict attention, the very best

quality of Liquors, and a comfortable and well-regulated Saloon," they hoped "to merit a share of the Public patronage" and provide "everything that can be desired for a quiet game." He later ran a dry goods store in the Royal City that, on his death, was taken over by James Harvey, who married Ellard's sister, Esther, and provided for his children. The Ellard Block, at 601 Columbia St, still occupied the store's former site in 2007.

Ellen Island (52°09'00" 131°06'00" In Houston Stewart Channel, between Moresby I and Kunghit I, QCI). Ellen Mary Moresby (b 1820) was the eldest daughter of Rear Adm Fairfax Moresby, cdr-in-chief of the RN's Pacific Station 1850–53. In 1842 she married James Charles Prevost (1810–91), who served on the Pacific Station in 1850–52 aboard HMS *Portland*, Moresby's flagship. Prevost named this feature in 1853 while surveying Houston Stewart Channel as cdr of the RN paddle sloop *Virago*. He served again on the BC coast, 1857–60, as cdr of HMS *Satellite* and chief British boundary commissioner. *See also* Prevost I *and* Moresby I.

Ellinor Rock (54°12'00" 130°23'00" E of Kinahan Is, just SW of Prince Rupert). Named by federal hydrographer G Blanchard Dodge (*see* Dodge Cove) in 1906 while surveying the area around Prince Rupert Hbr. The 635-tonne *Ellinor* was hired by the RN for survey work in eastern Canada in the early 1900s, then moved to the Caribbean in 1912. Dodge had served aboard the vessel as assistant surveying officer, under Capt William Tooker, on the Nfld coast in 1903.

Elliot Bluff (48°47'00" 123°13'00" W side of Saturna I, S of Payne Point, Gulf Is). Lt George Henry Elliot was a Royal Marines officer aboard HMS *Ganges*, flagship of Rear Adm Robert Baynes, on the Pacific Station in 1857–60. He was promoted to maj in 1879. Named by Capt George Richards of RN survey vessel *Plumper* in 1859.

Ellis Point (53°55'00" 133°10'00" S end of Frederick I, off W side of Graham I, QCI). Named in 1907 after the coxswain of one of the sounding boats carried aboard the RN survey vessel *Egeria*. Capt Frederick Learmonth and the crew of the *Egeria* made an extensive survey of Graham I that year, starting at Rose Point, the island's NE tip, and ending at Frederick I.

Ells Bay (53°19'00" 132°29'00" SW of Shields I, Rennell Sd, W side of Graham I, QCI), **Ells Point** (53°11'00" 132°34'00" E side of Tana Bay, Cartwright Sd, W side of Graham I), **Ells Rocks** (53°20'00" 132°29'00" Entrance to Ells Bay). Dr Robert Wheelock Ells (1845–1911), born in NS, was a prominent Canadian geologist who worked for the Geological Survey of Canada and the federal Department of Mines. Although he specialized in the geology of NB, and had a special interest in oil shales, Ells led a survey of much of Graham I in 1905, using a small Columbia R fish boat for transport. He and his crew rowed and sailed along the W and N coasts of the island and made a hazardous rounding of Rose Spit.

Elma Bay (49°51'00" 125°06'00" S of Kukushan Point, SE of Campbell R, E side of Vancouver I). Elizabeth Mary "Elma" Llewelyn (d 1969) was a long-time resident of the property adjacent to the bay. She was the daughter of Sir Robert Llewelyn, administrator of the colony of Gambia, 1891–1900, and later gov of the Windward Is in the W Indies. In 1919, Elma married Theed Pearse (1871–1971), a multi-term alderman and former mayor of Courtenay, who was also a noted naturalist and author of *Birds of the Early Explorers in the Northern Pacific*. Mt Elma in Strathcona Provincial Park, which she apparently ascended on horseback in 1930, is named for her as well. Pearse Lk on Forbidden Plateau is named for her husband.

Elsfield Point (53°22'00" 129°46'00" N entrance to Buchan Inlet, SW side of Pitt I). Sir John Buchan, 1st Baron Tweedsmuir of Elsfield, was gov gen of Canada, 1935–40. *See* Buchan Inlet.

Elsje Point (49°17'00" 123°09'00" English Bay, Vancouver). Elsje Armstrong (1918–81) was chair of the board of trustees of the Vancouver Museums and Planetarium Assoc and played a leading role in the development of the Vancouver Academy of Music. A talented pianist and daughter of former Vancouver Symphony Orchestra conductor Allard de Ridder, she was awarded the Order of Canada in 1977 and an honorary degree from Simon Fraser Univ in 1981. The point is actually an artificial breakwater in front of the Vancouver Maritime Museum. The name was adopted in 1984 after submission by officials from the museum.

Elswa Rock (52°19'00" 131°15'00" Skincuttle Inlet, SE side of Moresby I, QCI). Haida artist, guide and interpreter Johnny Kit Elswa, from Tanu, was active in the late 19th century. James Swan hired him on his 1883 artifact-collecting expedition to the Charlottes on behalf of the Smithsonian Institution. Elswa was noted as a carver and jeweller, and was also one of the first Haida artists to work in pen and watercolour on paper. A number of his pieces are in Yale Univ's Western Americana collection. *D*

Elworthy Island (50°11'50" 124°47'00" Between E and W Redonda Is, N of Desolation Sd, NE of Campbell R). Douglas Richard Elworthy was born at Cardiff, Wales, in 1918 and immigrated to Vancouver with his family in 1924. He and a partner operated a small gold mine in the BC Cariboo from 1936 until the outbreak of WWII, when he joined the merchant navy. Elworthy served as a pantryman aboard the *Empress of Asia*, which had been converted to a troopship, and was wounded when the

elderly passenger liner was destroyed by Japanese bombers near Singapore in Feb 1942. He died in hospital on Feb 10, the only crew member to perish (though 15 of the 2,235 British troops who embarked at Bombay were listed as missing after the attack). Elworthy is buried at Kranji War Cemetery, Singapore. The loss of the *Empress*, which was carrying vital war equipment as well as troops, had dire consequences for the Singapore garrison, which fell on Feb 15, 1942.

Embley Lagoon (50°57'00" 126°52'00" Head of Grappler Sd, NW of Broughton I, N of E Queen Charlotte Str). Embley Park, England, was the Hampshire home of William Nightingale, father of Florence Nightingale, the famed pioneer of modern nursing. Its connection with the BC coast is tenuous indeed: Florence Nightingale's sister, Parthenope, was the second wife of Sir Harry Verney, whose son (by his first wife) was Lt Cdr Edmund Verney, commander of RN gunboat *Grappler*, which was in BC waters in 1862–65. The lagoon was named by Lt Daniel Pender of the *Beaver* in 1865.

Emilia Island (53°45'00" 128°58'00" Off entrance to Gilttoyees Inlet, Douglas Channel, SW of Kitimat). Maria Emilia Tarte, of Montreal, was the eldest daughter of outspoken Que journalist and politician Joseph-Israël Tarte (1848–1907), who served as federal minister of Public Works, 1896–1902, in the Liberal cabinet of Sir Wilfrid Laurier.

Emily Carr in her Victoria studio, 1936. *BC Archives D-06009*

Emily Carr Inlet (52°55'00" 129°09'00" W of Chapple Inlet, W side of Princess Royal I). Victoria's Emily Carr (1871–1945) is BC's best-known artist. She studied at San Francisco, London and Paris and became fascinated with First Nation subjects, travelling extensively on the BC coast to paint at aboriginal villages. Carr taught art in Victoria and Vancouver but was unsuccessful in establishing herself professionally and stopped painting in 1913. For the next 15 years she kept a Victoria boarding house, but when some of her works were included in a 1927 National Gallery of Canada exhibition, she travelled to Ottawa and met members of the Group of Seven. Lawren Harris, particularly, encouraged her to resume painting, which she did, focusing on BC's overpowering coastal forests as subject matter and developing a national reputation in the 1930s. Carr was also a fine writer; a non-fiction book, *Klee Wyck* (her Nuu-chah-nulth nickname, which means "laughing one"), won a Gov Gen's Literary Award in 1941. The name Theodora Inlet, after Unity Theodora Jeffreys Baile, a junior member of the W coast hydrographic staff in 1943, was originally proposed for this geographic feature but was rejected as injudicious (*see* Baile I). *E*

Emily Islet (48°26'00" 123°17'00" E of Mary Tod I, Oak Bay, SE tip of Vancouver I). Emily Harris (1851–1922) was the youngest daughter of Thomas Harris (1817–84), first mayor of Victoria, 1862–65 (*see* Harris I). She was born at Liverpool in 1851 and came to Victoria with her family about 1860. In 1872 she married William Wilson (1843–1920)—listed as a "general dealer" in the 1881 census and employed at the land registry office in 1901—and raised a large family at Victoria. The 30-m towboat and coal carrier *Emily Harris*, built at Victoria in 1861, was named for her. This vessel ran between Victoria, Nanaimo and the Fraser R, but its boiler exploded in 1871, killing Capt James Frain and two crewmen. The Songhees First Nation name for the islet was Skwahanna.

Emmaline Bank (52°14'00" 128°30'00" W of NW Athlone I, Milbanke Sd). After Emmaline Jane Mohun (née Tod), a daughter of HBC fur trader John Tod. *See* Mohun Shoal.

Emmerson Point (54°16'00" 130°22'00" E side of Digby I, just W of Prince Rupert). Henry Robert Emmerson (1853–1914) was federal minister of Railways and Canals at the time Prince Rupert Hbr was surveyed in 1906. He was a native of NB and studied law at Boston Univ, graduating in 1877 and becoming an influential lawyer, businessman and politician in Moncton. In the 1890s he was appointed NB's chief commissioner of public works, sat on its legislative and executive councils, and served as premier of NB, 1897–1900. He then entered federal politics. Emmerson's stint as minister of Railways (1904–7) ended after his drinking and womanizing began to embarrass Sir Wilfrid Laurier, the Liberal PM. His constituents continued to re-elect him, however, and he remained an MP until his death.

Empire Anchorage (53°35'00" 132°54'00" S side of Port Chanal, W side of Graham I, QCI). Named by Capt Absalom Freeman in 1912 after an iron-hulled Canadian Fishing Co halibut trawler, the *Celestial Empire*. Freeman made a sketch survey of the area from this 37-m, 185-tonne vessel, which had been built in 1897 to work in the N Sea. It was renamed the *Cape Scott* by Capt Barney

Jones in the 1920s and used to tow logs across Hecate Str. After a stint with the Pacific Coyle Navigation Co, the ship was broken up in 1946. This anchorage was formerly known as Empire Hbr.

Emsley Cove (53°54'01" 128°46'49" W side of Kitimat Arm, Douglas Channel, S of Kitimat), **Emsley Point** (53°53'51" 128°46'09" E side of Emsley Cove). Emsley Raley was the first white boy raised in the Kitimat area, the youngest son of Rev George Raley, Methodist clergyman at Kitamaat Mission, 1893–1906, who named this cove (*see also* Raley Point). Emsley was educated at Toronto, won the Military Cross and was working for the Greater Vancouver civil defence authority in 1952. Emsley Ck, which runs into the cove, is also named for him. The Haisla name for this watershed and shoreline—and the nearby First Nation reserve—is Kitasa.

Engerbrightson Point (52°40'00" 127°01'00" W side of Dean Channel, opposite Swallop Ck). Ole E Engebretson was one of the Norwegian settlers who colonized the Bella Coola valley in the 1890s. He received a Crown land grant there in 1901 but later moved to the W Chilcotin. (Spellings of pioneer names can vary considerably: Engebretson appeared on the Crown land papers, Engelbretson on other early documents, and Engerbretson was used by the family's descendants.)

Englefield Bay (52°59'00" 132°25'00" W side of Hibben I, off NW Moresby I, QCI). Named in 1793 by Capt George Vancouver after his "much esteemed" friend, the antiquary and scientist Sir Henry Charles Englefield (1752–1822). Sir Henry was a fellow of the Royal Society and the Society of Antiquaries, which produced, under his direction, a series of engravings of English cathedrals. He carried on research in chemistry, mathematics, astronomy and geology, wrote widely and was prominent in Catholic affairs. Vancouver also named nearby Cape Henry for him. This area came to be known as Gold Hbr after the discovery of gold at Mitchell Inlet in 1851. The French explorer Lapérouse named it Baie de la Touche on his 1786 journey along the W coast of the QCI.

Englewood (50°32'00" 126°53'00" Head of Beaver Cove, W Johnstone Str, NE side of Vancouver I). The name of this former sawmill community came from the mill's owners, US lumbermen Edward G English (1851–1930) and Frederick J Wood (1869–1937), who formed Wood & English Ltd in order to log on Vancouver I. They were operating in the Nimpkish valley as early as 1917 and constructed the Englewood mill in 1924. It was taken over by Canadian Forest Products during WWII and has since been demolished. The region's logging rights—and Canada's last logging railroad—were purchased in 2006 by Western Forest Products.

Joe Fortes teaching swimmers at English Bay. *CVA 7-167*

English Bay (49°17'00" 123°10'00" S side of Burrard Inlet, W of False Ck, Vancouver), **English Bay Beach** (49°17'00" 123°09'00" E side of English Bay). These features and nearby Spanish Bank (qv) pay homage to the 1792 meeting off Point Grey of British explorer Capt George Vancouver and his Spanish counterparts Dionisio Alcalá-Galiano and Cayetano Valdés.

English Bluff (49°01'00" 123°05'22" N end of Tsawwassen Beach, S of Vancouver). The bluff got its name because it fell on the British side of the 49th parallel, as determined by the boundary commission of 1858–62. Tsawwassen First Nation members know the site as S'tlalep.

English Rock (53°35'00" 130°35'00" In Griffith Hbr, W side of Banks I). William English was 1st officer aboard the W coast survey vessel *Lillooet* from 1908 to 1910.

Enke Point (48°53'00" 123°19'00" SE end of Galiano I, Gulf Is). Max Enke (1884–1971), born at Manchester, UK, but of German heritage, moved to Belgium in the 1890s, where his family ran a rabbit-fur business. He came to Galiano in 1907—with 11 Belgian farm workers in tow—and bought Harry Clapham's Seabrook Farm, renaming it Valley Farm. Over the years he acquired several adjoining properties, at one point owning more than 530 ha, mostly at the S end of the island, where he raised sheep, pigs and pedigree Jersey cattle. Enke's wife, Marion (1880–1961), daughter of a wealthy English family, was driven around Galiano's rutted tracks in a fancy horse-drawn carriage. Ruth, their daughter (later Mrs L E Chambers), was supposedly the first white child born on the island, in 1910. Max, a great chess player, was BC champion in 1925 and 1927. The Enkes moved to a big Oak Bay home in 1913 and went back to Belgium in 1928 to run the family business. Max spent much of WWII in prisoner-of-war camps, where he met British novelist P G Wodehouse,

who modelled the character of Lord Uffenham (*Money in the Bank*, *Something Fishy*) on his fellow internee. After the war the Enkes retired to Victoria and in 1948 donated 37 ha of land above Georgeson Bay for Galiano's Bluffs Park.

Ensanada Islet (49°47'00" 126°58'00" N entrance to Nuchatlitz Inlet, off NW Nootka I, W side of Vancouver I). Ensenada de Ferrer (Ferrer's Inlet) appears on the chart Dionisio Alcalá-Galiano and Cayetano Valdés produced after their historic 1792 circumnavigation of Vancouver I. It presumably refers to what is today known as Nuchatlitz Inlet. In recognition of this older name, the S entrance to the inlet was designated Ferrer Point (qv) about 1860. The islet on the opposite side of Nuchatlitz, formerly known as Cliff It, was renamed (and misspelled) Ensanada in 1946. (This may have occurred because on the original chart Ensenada is abbreviated "Ens.a.")

Enterprise Channel (48°24'00" 123°18'00" Between SE Victoria and Trial Is, SE end of Vancouver I), **Enterprise Reef** (48°51'00" 123°21'00" Off NW end of Mayne I, Trincomali Channel, Gulf Is). Several vessels of this name operated in SW BC waters in the Victorian era. These geographic features recall the steamer *Enterprise* built in San Francisco in 1861 and run on Puget Sd until its purchase for $60,000 the following year by the HBC. The 41-m, 181-tonne sidewheeler was a mainstay on the Victoria–New Westminster route for years and became part of the Canadian Pacific Navigation Co's fleet in 1883. In 1888, under Capt George Rudlin, it suffered a fatal collision with the larger *R P Rithet*, under Capt Asbury Insley, off Cadboro Point. Two passengers died and both capts—but Insley especially—were censured for their lack of attention. *Enterprise* was beached at Cadboro Bay and stripped of its machinery; its timbers were visible for many years. Another well-known *Enterprise*, a 35-m, 176-tonne sternwheeler built in Oregon in 1855, operated on the Fraser R during the gold rush. Legend has it that owner and skipper Capt Thomas Wright once received $25,000

E

for a special run from Victoria to Murderer's Bar, below Ft Hope. This ship was wrecked and dismantled on the Chehalis R in 1862 and its machinery sent to China. *W*

Epper Passage (49°13'00" 125°58'00" N side of Morfee I, NW of Meares I, Clayoquot Sd, W side of Vancouver I). Frowin Epper (1865–1933), born in Switzerland, entered the Benedictine order in 1887 and was ordained as a Catholic priest in 1894. He immigrated to the US and studied science at the Univ of Washington (DC), moving later to Oregon where he became professor of science and museum curator at Mt Angel College. Epper served as principal of the Christie residential school at Kakawis on Meares I, 1911–16, after which he returned to teaching science at Mt Angel. In 1995, Epper Passage Provincial Park was established, primarily to protect an endangered marine organism, the purple lobular sea squirt, which inhabits the area's fast-water ecosystems. Formerly known as Deep Passage.

Epsom Point (49°30'00" 124°01'00" Westernmost point of N Thormanby I, Str of Georgia). The town of Epsom in Surrey is the site of Epsom Downs racecourse and one of England's most famous horse races. The Derby, established in 1780 by the Earl of Derby, is run each summer, along with the Oaks, another long-established race. Capt George Richards and his wager-loving officers aboard the RN survey vessel *Plumper* gave the area many horse-racing names in 1860 after hearing happy news of that year's Derby.

Equis Beach (48°58'00" 125°18'00" N side of Sechart Channel, E of Lyall Point, Barkley Sd, W side of Vancouver I). Equis is the original name of the abandoned First Nation village of Tseshaht (Sechart). It is also the name of the Nuu-chah-nulth reserve at this location. The Tseshaht people, who are part of the Nuu-chah-nulth Tribal Council and based today at Port Alberni, were once a whaling culture. BC's first whaling station, built by Pacific Whaling Co in 1905 on nearby Pipestem Inlet, was called Sechart.

Errigal Point (52°40'00" 128°34'00" Between Alexander Inlet and Meyers Passage, SE end of Princess Royal I). Named for part of one of the titles bestowed on Harold R L G Alexander, 1st Earl of Tunis and Canada's 17th gov gen (1946–52). Before he was created an earl (in 1952), his official title was 1st Viscount Alexander of Tunis, of Errigal, County Donegal. Errigal, at 751 m, is the highest peak in Donegal, Ireland, part of the Derryveagh Mtns. *See* Alexander Inlet.

Erskine Point (48°51'00" 123°34'00" SW of Booth Bay, W side of Saltspring I, Gulf Is). Named about 1859 by RN hydrographer Capt George Richards for Rear Adm John Elphinstone Erskine (1806–87), who at that time was second-in-command of the Channel squadron. He had served as senior officer on the Australia Station in 1848, then commanded HMS *Monarch* and *Orion* during the Crimean War. Erskine was an aide-de-camp to Queen Victoria, 1856–57; sat as a Liberal MP for Stirlingshire, 1865–74; and was promoted to adm in 1869 before retiring from the RN in 1876. He was also an author; *Journal of a Cruise among the Islands of the Western Pacific* was published in 1853. Saltspring's **Mount Erskine** (48°50'50" 123°32'59") is named for him as well.

Erwin Point (49°21'00" 123°16'00" E entrance to Howe Sd, N of Point Atkinson, NW of Vancouver). Walter Erwin (1853–1921), from Ont, was the third lighthouse keeper at Point Atkinson, arriving in 1880 with his wife, Jane Ternan (1845–1915). They had previously lived at Moodyville. It was on his watch that the station's first foghorn was installed, about 1889. He manned the lighthouse for 30 years, becoming firmly associated with it in the public mind. After ill health forced him to retire in 1910, he was given a glowing tribute—and the Imperial Service Medal—by Vancouver's mayor on the steps of city hall (but only paid a pension of $33 a month). Erwin was a pioneer of W Vancouver, pre-empting a large piece of land in what is now known as Cypress Park in 1891 and serving on the District of N Vancouver's first council that year. He married Rhoda Miles (1880–1930) in 1917.

Escalante Island (49°31'00" 126°34'00" S entrance to Nootka Sd, W side of Vancouver I), **Escalante Point** (49°32'00" 126°34'00" Just N of Escalante I), **Escalante Rocks** (49°32'00" 126°35'00" Just SW of Escalante Point). The name Punta e Islas ("point and islands") de Escalante appears on the charts of early Spanish explorers Francisco Eliza and Dionisio Alcalá-Galiano at this location and was probably applied by Eliza in 1791. Capt John Walbran has suggested that Escalante "is a Spanish word meaning climbing or scaling" and derives from the shapes of the rocks, which jut out from the shore like "a series of steps." The problem with this explanation is that *escalante*, while close to the Spanish words for "climbing" and "step," is not equivalent. It *is* a Spanish surname, however, and could refer to the Franciscan missionary Silvestre Velez de Escalante, who accompanied Fr Francisco Domínguez on his 1776 search for a route from Santa Fe to Monterey—the first European exploration of the Great Basin desert. Nearby Escalante R is named in association with these features. *W*

Esowista Peninsula (49°05'00" 125°50'00" S of Meares I, from Long Beach to Tofino, W side of Vancouver I). According to Eli Enns, a Tla-o-qui-aht political scientist and co-author of a 2008 Ecotrust Canada report on Nuu-chah-nulth governance structures, this name can be translated as "clubbed to death." It refers to a war in which scattered Tla-o-qui-aht groups first came together as a unified force to battle a neighbouring First Nation. The ancient whaling village of Esowista (Hisaawista) is located on the peninsula and is still occupied by the Tla-o-qui-aht people, who are members of the Nuu-chah-nulth Tribal Council. Formerly known as Low Peninsula.

Esperanza (49°52'00" 126°44'00" N side of Hecate Channel, SW of Tahsis), **Esperanza Inlet** (49°49'00" 126°56'00" NW side of Nootka I, W side of Vancouver I). In 1778, Capt James Cook gave the name Hope Bay to the large opening between Estevan Point and Cape Cook (he called the cape Woody Point); his "hope" was that there might be a good harbour there. The name on Cook's chart was translated by Spanish explorer Alejandro Malaspina in 1791 and applied to the inlet NW of Nootka I, which was investigated that summer by two of his officers, José Espinosa and Ciriaco Cevallos. Esperanza Inlet was the site of a major pilchard fishery, 1925–45, and has recently seen much logging and some tourism and aquaculture. The community of Esperanza got its start in 1937 when the Nootka Mission Hospital, now a camp and retreat centre, was built there by the Shantymen's Christian Assoc. An adjacent hotel, completed in 1938, burnt to the ground in 1960. *E W*

Aboard the *Uchuck III* in Esperanza Inlet. *Andrew Scott*

Espinosa Inlet (49°55'00" 126°56'00" N of Esperanza Inlet, W of Zeballos Inlet, W side of Vancouver I). José Espinosa y Tello (1763–1815) entered the Spanish Royal Navy in 1778 and studied cartography under Vicente Tofiño at the Cadiz observatory. He was assigned to join the scientific voyage of Alejandro Malaspina and was involved in its preparation but was unable to embark on the expedition because of ill health. Espinosa caught up with Malaspina in Acapulco in 1791 and accompanied him to the PNW that summer on a futile search for the NW Passage. Malaspina spent 15 days at Nootka Sd in Aug, during which time he assigned Lt Espinosa and Ciriaco Cevallos (after whom Zeballos is named) to examine Esperanza Inlet and other "interior canals" with the ships' boats. After his return to Spain, Espinosa became aide-de-camp to senior naval officer José de Mazarredo and, in 1797, director of the hydrographic

office at Madrid, where he published charts and accounts of Spanish explorations. He served the Council of the Admiralty as secretary until 1808 when, opposed to Joseph Bonaparte's reign as king of Spain, he moved to Seville and then England to continue his cartographic labours. In 1815, after Bonaparte's abdication, he returned to his position as Spain's director of hydrography but died shortly thereafter. Nearby Espinosa Ck and Mt Espinosa are also named for him. A pilchard-reduction plant was built on the inlet by the Canadian Fishing Co and operated 1928–38. *W*

HMS *Cormorant* in the Esquimalt drydock, late 1880s. *BC Archives F-08452*

Esquimalt (48°27'00" 123°25'00" Just W of Victoria, SE end of Vancouver I), **Esquimalt Harbour** (48°26'00" 123°26'00" W of Esquimalt), **Esquimalt Lagoon** (48°26'00" 123°28'00" W of Royal Roads, E of Colwood). Esquimalt is an adaptation of the Coast Salish name for the tidal flats at the head of the harbour and can be translated as "a place of gradually shoaling water." Esquimalt First Nation members long had a village site near Ashe Head on the E side of the harbour. In 1790, Spanish naval officer Manuel Quimper was the first European to enter this body of water, which he named Puerto de Cordova, after Mexican viceroy Antonio Villacis y Cordova (*see* Cordova Bay). HBC chief factor James Douglas examined the area in 1843 as a site for a trading post, Ft Victoria, which the company established on nearby Victoria Hbr, reserving the lands around Esquimalt for HBC farms. In a report to Dr John McLoughlin, Douglas spelled the name Is-whoy-malth. The RN was interested in the area from the mid-1840s, when its vessels first began to anchor there. Lt Cdr James Wood of HMS *Pandora* surveyed the harbour in 1847, naming many of its features after officers of HMS *Fisgard*, an occasional

E

early visitor. Hospital buildings erected on Duntze Head in 1855 were the modest beginnings of a naval yard, and by the mid-1860s Esquimalt had replaced Valparaiso, Chile, as HQ for the RN's Pacific Station. A major drydock was completed in 1887. In the 20th century, Esquimalt became the RCN's primary W coast base and training facility, a shipbuilding centre and an important residential suburb of Victoria. *E W*

Estero Basin (50°30'50" 125°11'00" Between N end of Frederick Arm and S end of Bute Inlet, N of Campbell R). Estero is Spanish for "tideland" or "estuary" and could also be translated as "lagoon." Frederick Arm was originally named Ensenada del Estero, or "Inlet of the Lagoon," by Dionisio Alcalá-Galiano and Cayetano Valdés during their expedition of 1792. The name of nearby Estero Peak, which is taken from the basin, was probably applied by Lt Daniel Pender in the 1860s. The Homalco First Nation people call it Pá'lhmin, or "place that grows"; it was this mountain that they tied their canoes to during the great flood.

Estevan Group (53°02'30" 129°37'30" W of Campania I, between Banks I and Aristazabal I), **Estevan Point** (49°23'00" 126°33'00" SW side of Hesquiat Peninsula, NW of Clayoquot Sd, W side of Vancouver I), **Estevan Reef** (52°58'00" 129°31'00" E of Dewdney I, Estevan Group), **Estevan Sound** (53°05'00" 129°32'00" Between Estevan Group and Campania I, N of Caamaño Sd). Spanish naval officer Estéban José Martínez (1742–98), born at Seville, was posted to San Blas naval base in Mexico. Although moody and irascible by most accounts, he nevertheless played a significant role in BC coastal history. He served as deputy cdr on the first documented journey by Europeans along the BC coast: the 1774 expedition of Juan Pérez and the *Santiago*. Pérez anchored off Estevan Point on Aug 7 and had contact with the Hesquiaht, the local First Nation inhabitants, but did not leave his ship (nor did he go ashore at Langara I in the QCI). He named his landfall Punta de San Estéban (St Stephen), whose feast day was Aug 3. Fr Juan Crespí, who accompanied Pérez as chaplain, claimed in his journal that the point was named after Martínez, but Pérez's diary states San Estéban, and this naming is consistent with the other names that Pérez bestowed on this voyage, all of which were for saints and none for crew members or officials. Martínez was in Mexico and California from 1775 until 1788, when he made a second voyage N to investigate Russian activity in Alaska, which he found to be substantial. It was on the basis of his reports that Mexican viceroy Manuel Antonio Flores (who may have been Martínez's uncle) decided to establish a fort at Nootka Sd in 1789, with Martínez as cdr. That summer he seized several British vessels at Nootka and sent them, with their imprisoned crews, to Mexico, thus sparking the Nootka Sd Controversy and threats of war between Britain and Spain. Martínez returned to Mexico in Dec 1789, was reproved for his actions by the new viceroy, the Conde de Revillagigedo, and sent back to Nootka temporarily (and unhappily) in a subordinate position. He spent the remainder of his career in Mexico and Spain. Estevan Point was named Breakers Point by Capt James Cook in 1778, but the Spanish name (without "San") was restored on the Admiralty chart of 1849 and has always—perhaps incorrectly—been associated by historians with

The Estevan Point lighthouse was reportedly shelled by a Japanese submarine during WWII. *Elsie Hulsizer*

Martínez. It is not the oldest surviving place name in BC of European origin, as is sometimes claimed (that honour belongs to the San Christoval Range on Moresby I, named by Pérez on July 23, 1774; *see also* St Margaret Point), but may well be second oldest. A lighthouse, built at Estevan Point in 1909, was shelled in 1941, allegedly by a Japanese submarine—the only instance of an enemy attack on Canada's W coast in WWII. Estevan I (later changed to Estevan Is, then Estevan Group) was named by Spanish explorer Jacinto Caamaño in 1792. *E W*

Estrado Lagoon (54°03'00" 132°12'00" N of Entry Point, Masset Hbr, Graham I, QCI). Spanish naval officer Nicolas Estrado was one of Lt Cdr Jacinto Caamaño's subordinates aboard *Aránzazu* in 1792. Caamaño, who had been sent N from Nootka Sd by Juan Francisco de la Bodega y Quadra to explore the coastlines in the area of Dixon Entrance, applied the name Puerto Estrado to the entrance to Masset Hbr. The following year, Capt George Vancouver adopted the name for the E entrance point to the harbour. In 1907, Capt Frederick Learmonth of the RN survey vessel *Egeria* changed Vancouver's Estrado Point to Entry Point, but more recently the hydrographic service has applied the name Estrado to the shallow waters behind a curved shingle spit that is growing N of Entry Point. *D*

Etches Point (52°09'00" 131°13'00" E side of Louscoone Inlet, SW Moresby I, QCI). British merchant Richard Cadman Etches (1744–1817) was the main investor in the King George's Sd Co (also known as Richard Cadman Etches & Co), which sent the *King George*, under Nathaniel Portlock, and the *Queen Charlotte*, under George Dixon, to the PNW coast in 1785 on one of the region's earliest fur-trading ventures. A second expedition was dispatched in 1786, under James Colnett, and in 1789 the company merged with the group of traders led by John Meares to form a new syndicate, the Associated Merchants of London and India Trading to the NW Coast of America. In the late 1780s, Etches, who was involved with numerous international trading schemes, lobbied the British government to found a convict colony on the BC coast (as it soon would do in Australia). Richard's brother John Cadman Etches sailed with Colnett in 1786–88 as a company official and trader (or supercargo) and helped negotiate the merger with Meares. A third brother, William Etches, was also involved in the business. Cadman Point on Graham I is named for Richard Etches as well. Juan Perez Sd in the QCI was known as Etches Sd by 18th-century fur traders.

Ethel Cove (51°20'00" 127°31'00" N of Margaret Bay, Smith Sd, N of Port Hardy). Ethel Joly de Lotbinière was a daughter of Sir Henri-Gustave Joly de Lotbinière, lt gov of BC in 1900–1906 (*see* Lotbinière I). She married Col Dudley Mills (d 1937) of the Royal Engineers (Dudley It is located nearby). Named by Capt John Walbran in 1903.

Ethel Island (51°33'00" 127°32'00" Between Ida I and Florence I, Rivers Inlet). Ethel Margaret Elizabeth Walbran (1874–1945) was the youngest daughter of Capt John Walbran, noted BC mariner and author of *British Columbia Coast Names 1592–1906*. She married Dominion meteorologist Frank Denison (1866–1946, *see* Denison I) in 1904, and together they lived at the observatory on Gonzales Hill in Victoria. The island was named by Walbran in 1890, when he was cdr of the Canadian Pacific Navigation Co steamship *Danube*.

Ethel Rock (53°34'00" 130°10'00" Off SW side of McCauley I, Principe Channel, between Banks I and Pitt I). Ethel Marion Davies (1877–1965) was born in PEI, daughter of lawyer and politician Sir Louis Henry Davies (1845–1924), who was premier of PEI in 1876–79 and federal minister of Marine and Fisheries, 1896–1901 (*see* Davies Bay). She married lawyer James Hyndman (1874–1971), also from PEI, who served many senior judicial roles in Alberta and Ottawa. Ethel Rk was named in 1901 by Capt John Walbran, master of CGS *Quadra* and a Dept of Marine and Fisheries employee.

The hard-working tugboat *Etta White*. *Courtesy Tim Woodland*

Etta Point (50°18'00" 125°13'00" W tip of Maurelle I, N of Campbell R). The historic 29-m tugboat *Etta White*, built in 1871 at Freeport, Washington, by Capt George White, operated on the mail route between Bellingham, Port Townsend and the San Juan Is under Capt Henry Smith. In 1875 it was bought by the Moodyville sawmill on Burrard Inlet, and by 1887 was working out of Victoria, still with Smith as master. The 88-tonne tug suffered several major mishaps, foundering on Tattenham Ledge, N of the Thormanby Is, in 1890 and catching fire in Vancouver's Coal Hbr. Both times it was repaired. The *Etta White's* long career came to an end in 1920, however, when it was totally destroyed by fire in Quatsino Sd.

Ettershank Islands (53°19'00" 129°42'00" Entrance to Port Stephens, SW side of Pitt I). Roy Hall "Etty" Ettershank (1896–1977) joined the Canadian Hydrographic Service

E

in 1927 as a junior hydrographer and retired in 1965, having worked on surveys of most parts of the BC coast. He also served aboard most of the W coast survey vessels, including CGS *Lillooet* and *William J Stewart* and the houseboats *Pender* and *Somass*. Ettershank was a specialist in marine architecture and the design and maintenance of ship machinery, and had a keen interest in echo sounders and other electrical and mechanical equipment. He was the son of pioneer Burrard Inlet pilot William Ettershank (*see below*). Nearby Roy I is also named for him.

Ettershank Point (52°19'00" 128°04'00" At junction of Return Channel and Bullock Channel, SE end of Yeo I, N of Bella Bella). Capt William Ettershank (1842–1926), son of an Aberdeen ship owner, visited Victoria in 1862 as 1st officer of the clipper *Cecelia*. He was 1st mate of the *Alpha* on its final, fatal 1868 voyage (*see* Alpha Bay) and later worked on the pioneer sidewheel steamers *Isabel*, built by Hastings Mill owner Edward Stamp, and *Emma*, built by Joseph Spratt of Victoria's Albion Iron Works. Ettershank married Claravilla Jean Glide (1863–85) at Victoria in 1880 and, after her early death, Sarah Anne Hall (1863–1954) at Vancouver in 1893. He became a fixture in Vancouver's marine trade—Burrard Inlet's first pilot, appointed in 1888, who specialized in guiding the giant CPR *Empress* ships—and lived at Skunk Cove (later known as Caulfeild Cove). His son Roy (*see* Ettershank Is) was a hydrographer on the W coast; another son, Joseph, served as an officer on the US W coast steamship *Beaver* (not the HBC paddlewheeler). The name of the point, formerly misspelled Ettershanks, was corrected in 1951. Ettershank Cove in W Vancouver, E of Caulfeild Cove, was officially designated in 1929, but the name was rescinded in 1949 in favour of Sandy Cove (qv), which had become well established locally.

Ettrick Rock (54°06'00" 130°29'00" NW of Creak Is, Chatham Sd, SW of Prince Rupert). After British RN compass specialist Capt Ettrick William Creak. *See* Creak Is.

Eucott Bay (52°27'00" 127°19'00" W shore of Dean Channel, opposite NE end of King I). The bay is home to a well-known hot springs. In the 1930s, cabins were available here for $2 a week so that visitors, mostly Ocean Falls residents, could receive treatment for rheumatism, arthritis and lumbago. The baths were attended and cost 10 cents a session. The Miracle Mineral Water Co sold heavily mineralized (sodium, calcium, sulphur) spring water in Vancouver and Victoria for $1.50 a gallon and also tried to market mud from the site as a skin rejuvenator. The origin of the name is not known.

Europa Passage (51°01'00" 127°43'00" S of Storm Is, Queen Charlotte Sd), **Europa Point** (53°26'00" 128°32'00" N side of Europa Reach), **Europa Reach** (53°27'00" 128°24'00" Between Alan Reach and Barrie Reach, Gardner Canal, SE of Kitimat). From 1784 to 1789, George Vancouver was a lt aboard the 50-gun HMS *Europa*, which spent most of this period on the W Indies Station, where it was the flagship of Commodore Alan Gardner, 1786–89. Many of the officers Vancouver later chose for his PNW expedition (Peter Puget, Zachary Mudge, Joseph Baker, Joseph Whidbey) served with him in the *Europa*. Gardner became his friend and mentor—and had Gardner Canal named in his honour by his protege in 1793. In 1907, Capt Frederick Learmonth, aboard HMS *Egeria*, added other names associated with Gardner, including Europa Reach, during a detailed survey of the canal. The 952-tonne *Europa*, built in 1783 at Woolwich, was converted to a troopship in 1798 and sold in 1814. Europa Ck and Europa Lk, near Europa Reach, are also named for this vessel.

Eussen Rock (48°55'00" 125°16'00" N of Dempster I in the Broken Group, Barkley Sd, W side of Vancouver I). Fr Louis Eussen, born in Limburg province, Netherlands, about 1853, and educated at Louvain College, Belgium, was a Roman Catholic missionary who arrived in BC in 1878. After 18 months in Victoria he replaced Fr Joseph Nicolaye at St Leo's, the Barkley Sd mission to the Huu-ay-aht (Ohiaht) First Nation on Numukamis Bay, in 1880. He returned to Holland in ill health shortly afterwards and died there about 1886. Formerly known as Channel Rk.

Evans Bay (50°11'00" 125°04'00" E side of Read I, NE of Campbell R). Capt Sir Frederick John Owen Evans (1815–85) was hydrographer of the RN, 1874–84. Unlike his predecessor, Rear Adm George Richards, he was never on the BC coast, but he did see much action in the field. He was master and assistant surveyor with HMS *Fly* in the New Guinea region, 1841–46, and also served in the *Acheron*, which charted the NZ coast, 1848–51. During the Crimean War, in 1854, he undertook secret survey work with HMS *Miranda* in the Gulf of Finland. Evans, who was also an excellent artist, was appointed superintendent of compasses in 1855 and wrote (with Archibald Smith) a standard text on compass deviations in 1862. He was made assistant hydrographer in 1865 and knighted in 1881. As chief RN hydrographer he helped prepare the 1875–76 Arctic expedition of Capt George S Nares and also supervised that officer's 1878–79 survey of the Strs of Magellan. Nearby Frederick Arm, Frederic Point and Owen Point also commemorate him. In the 1860s, Lt Daniel Pender named many geographic features in this area after RN officers who served under Richards in the hydrographic department. *W*

Evans Inlet (52°06'00" 127°47'00" W side of King I, E of Denny I and Bella Bella). Septimus Evans was RN surgeon in 1868–70 aboard the *Beaver*, which was hired from the HBC for survey duties. He joined the paddleship from HMS *Scout*, where he had been assistant surgeon. Later Evans served on HMS *Doris*, 1874–76, as surgeon. He died in 1881 when the magazine on HMS *Doterel* exploded in the Strs of Magellan, killing 143 crew members. Originally named Evans Arm by Lt Daniel Pender of the *Beaver* in 1867. Nearby Septimus Point is also named for him. *W*

Evans Rock (48°27'00" 123°16'00" S of Flower I, entrance to Cadboro Bay, Victoria). Rev Ephraim Evans (1804–92) was born in England and immigrated to Canada in 1820 with his father. He became a senior figure in Canadian Methodist circles: editor of the *Christian Guardian*, founder of the Upper Canada Anti-Slavery Society (1837), gov of Mt Allison Academy (1857–58) and a minister at Kingston, Niagara, Toronto, Hamilton, London, Halifax, Charlottetown and elsewhere. He married twice, to Charlotte Shaw in 1832 and Mary Gunn in 1874. In 1859, with the support of the British Wesleyan Church, he and three other Methodist missionaries—Arthur Browning, Edward White and Ebenezer Robson—and their families arrived at Victoria. Evans, the superintendent of Methodist missions on Vancouver I, led the first Methodist service in Victoria in Feb 1859. He was a scourge of Victoria's dance halls, which he described in a letter to the *Colonist* as "beds of vice and pollution," patronized by "crowds of depraved women." After the halls were closed at night, "the streets filled with hootings and blasphemies and ribald exclamations" as the patrons roamed at large in "drunken excitement," to the "demoralization of the settled population." He felt that it would "soon be the imperative duty of parents to hasten with their families from the town as they would from a pestilence." Evans himself moved to Nanaimo in 1868–69, then returned to Ont, where he continued to serve as a senior minister and as a delegate to early Methodist general conferences.

Evans Rock (52°50'00" 129°32'00" W of Rennison I, entrance to Caamaño Sd). David Evans (1843–1934), a native of Penthryn, Wales, immigrated in 1862 with his two brothers (John Newell and James) to Victoria, where he was employed by the HBC at Craigflower Farm. He was the first to take up land in the Cowichan Valley, in 1864, and was soon followed by his siblings; they farmed for many years in the Somenos area. David Evans married Margaret Nairn Mclay (1859–1934) at Victoria in 1878 and took part in the old-timers' reunion held at Victoria in 1924 (*see* Adams Bay).

Evenson Point (50°32'00" 127°36'00" NE entrance to Neroutsos Inlet, Quatsino Sd, NW end of Vancouver I). Eddijus "Ed" Evenson (1862–1946), born in Wisconsin, was part of the original group of Scandinavian settlers from the US Midwest that colonized Quatsino in 1894. His wife, Louise (1867–1951), five daughters and parents, Ellie and Even, arrived in 1896. Evenson received Crown grants for land in the area in 1901 and 1911, farmed, prospected

and served as mining recorder, district registrar and school trustee. He worked as a bookkeeper, operated the fuelling dock for many years and was Quatsino's postmaster, 1908–40. He and his wife also built the small Quatsino Hotel, which opened in 1912 and ran until 1958; in 2006 it had been renovated and reopened as Eagle Manor Resort, a fishing lodge.

Evinrude Inlet (52°48'00" 129°05'00" E side of Laredo Inlet, Princess Royal I). "Surveyed by Evinrude" was a notation occasionally found on blueprints for W coast nautical charts, especially in the 1940s. According to records at BC's Geographical Names Office, it meant that "a rough sketch" had been made in that area "from timing a rowboat powered by an Evinrude outboard engine." The name Evinrude Inlet was adopted in 1944. **Evinrude Passage** (53°32'00" 129°58'00" Between Cosine I and Anger I, W side of Pitt I), adopted 1949, probably derives its name from this technique as well.

Ewart Island (53°49'00" 130°26'00" Kitkatla Channel, S of Porcher I and Prince Rupert). William Ewart Gladstone Shakes was a late 19th-century chief of the Kitkatla people. *See* Shakes Is.

Ewen Slough (49°06'00" 123°10'00" Mouth of the Fraser R, SE of Reifel I). Alexander Ewen (1832–1907), born at Aberdeen, Scotland, was one of BC's earliest cannery owners. He had managed fishing stations on the Scottish coast and came to BC in 1864 to run a salmon-curing business on the Fraser R. Although mentioned on the 1875 BC voters list as a fishmonger, by 1871 he had become co-owner, with Alexander Loggie, of a pioneer cannery at Annieville. He married Mary Rogers (1845–1925) at New Westminster in 1876. By 1878 he was sole owner at Annieville and in 1884 built a much larger cannery on Lion I. In the 1890s, Ewen was an important independent figure in the competitive BC cannery industry. He merged his firm with the BC Packers Assoc in 1901 and served as association president until he died. Described by one account as "avaricious, erratic and stubborn, a diehard liberal and a notorious drinker," he accumulated large land holdings in Queensborough and sat on New Westminster city council. Ewen Slough was the site of an early fishing camp that supplied the Fraser R canneries. *E*

Ewin Inlet (49°38'00" 126°32'00" S end of Bligh I, Nootka Sd, W side of Vancouver I). William Ewin was a boatswain aboard HMS *Resolution*, which was refitted at Resolution Cove on Bligh I in the spring of 1778, during Capt James Cook's third scientific expedition. He also apparently served in the *Resolution* on Cook's second voyage, though with a lower rank. Named by Capt George Richards in 1862. Formerly known as Ewin Ck—a "creek" being an old Admiralty surveying term for a small drying inlet.

Changing Names

E

Words can carry many shades of meaning over the course of their careers. Everyone knows that a creek is a stream or brook, right? Something smaller than a river, preferably with rushing water? Well, everyone in North America knows it, as well as people in Australia and New Zealand. In Britain, however, a creek is a small harbour or a narrow coastal inlet, particularly one that dries at low tide. The word comes from *kriki*, Old Norse for "nook." And seeing that 19th-century British mariners provided the official names for many of BC's coastal features,

Gardner Canal, south of Kitimat. *Ian McAllister*

it should be no surprise that there were dozens of "creeks" on early charts, most of which have now been changed to "inlets" (Vancouver's False Creek is one exception).

Next, consider the word "canal." Most of us take it to mean an artificial waterway. But marine surveyors have also applied the term to long, narrow inlets that don't vary much in width—inlets that look, in other words, like artificial waterways. In BC, Alberni Inlet was known for decades as Alberni Canal. That name bothered certain people, though, and in 1945, on the recommendation of regional hydrographer Henri Parizeau, it was changed. Parizeau felt that the word "canal" would raise the spectre of "fees for pilotage, canal dues, extra insurance and so forth" in the minds of foreign shipping magnates, to the detriment of the future forestry centre of Port Alberni. Apparently, his argument was a convincing one.

In 1953 the hydrographic service also tried to change the name of Gardner Canal, south of Kitimat. This 192-kilometre inlet, the longest in BC, bores through the heart of the Coast Mountains and ends at the Kitlope Valley. En route, it passes Kemano Bay, downriver from the gigantic hydroelectric developments that power Alcan's Kitimat aluminum smelter. Again it was argued that by changing "canal" to "inlet," any potential misgivings on the part of shipping companies might be allayed. The Geographic Board of Canada wasn't buying the logic this time around, and the suggestion was rejected.

Changing the name of a geographical feature has become more difficult over the years, with the naming authorities sticking ever closer to "certain principles of nomenclature," one of which is that mere ownership of land is insufficient ground for an alteration. This principle is often challenged. In 1964, for instance, the new owner of Johnson Islet, off the northeast corner of Saanich Peninsula, petitioned the provincial government to change the name of his property to Rose Island. The original name, he reasoned, commemorated "a trapper" who owned the island from 1911 to 1928 but only lived there from time to time "as a bachelor ... and who is not remembered with any local significance." Rose Reid, by comparison, had owned the land for 30 years, since 1934, and her family had lived there all that time.

The head of BC's geographic division was not unsympathetic to the request but pointed out to the owner that as Johnson Islet had survived as an official name for over 50 years, "we would be loath to change that name without a very good reason." The regional hydrographer agreed that the change would create an "undesirable" precedent for other names in the area. The request was denied.

Hydrographers who worked on the Pacific coast, and who were obliged to come up with most new names for BC coastal features, on occasion ran afoul of their own superiors in Ottawa. In a 1944 memo to a Victoria-based underling, the chief of the hydrographic service expressed displeasure at a list of proposed new names, declaring that "too many names of your office staff and of the ship's crew have been used without reasonable discretion." Three junior female hydrographic employees appeared to be at the heart of the problem. These gals must have exerted quite a hypnotic appeal on their more senior male colleagues. Place names had been proposed based not only on the young women's surnames, but on their first and middle names as well. After much grumbling, the names were retracted and alternatives provided. Peace—and, presumably, discretion—descended once more on the Victoria hydrographic offices, and life returned to normal.

Exact Point (53°08'00" 132°24'00" NE side of Chaatl I, Skidegate Channel, QCI). When news leaked out in 1851 that gold-bearing quartz had been found at Mitchell Inlet on NW Moresby I, Capt Folger and the 22-m, 68-tonne schooner *Exact* rushed to the QCI from Portland, dropping off Seattle's founding settlers en route at Alki Point in Puget Sd. A large group of Haida had arrived at the gold site before Folger, though, and were demanding exorbitant prices for the ore. Folger and his companions, unused to the concept of bartering for minerals, abandoned the area but explored Haida Gwaii from Nov 1851 until Mar of the next year without finding any other signs of the coveted metal. *D*

Exeter Point (52°07'00" 127°51'00" W side of King I, E of Bella Bella). After Rev John Fisher, Bishop of Salisbury, 1807–25, and formerly Bishop of Exeter, 1803–7. *See* Fisher Channel.

Exeter Shoal (49°39'00" 124°39'00" NE of N end of Denman I, Str of Georgia). The *York*-class heavy cruiser *Exeter*, launched in 1929, was flagship of the British naval squadron commanded by Commodore Henry Harwood in the 1939 Battle of the River Plate, where the German pocket battleship *Admiral Graf Spee* was eventually destroyed at Montevideo, Uruguay. The 175-m, 7,610-tonne *Exeter* was badly damaged in the encounter, and 61 of her 630 crew members were killed. The ship was later sunk by Japanese forces in 1942 in the Battle of the Java Sea.

Expedition Islets (50°06'00" 127°14'00" Entrance to Kashutl Inlet, Kyuquot Sd, NW side of Vancouver I). Named for the three-week expedition that two officers from HMS *Hecate*, under Capt George Richards, made in 1862 from this vicinity to Ft Rupert on the E coast of Vancouver I. Lt Philip Hankin (*see* Hankin Cove) and Dr Charles Wood (*see* Wood Cove) left the Ka:'yu:'K't'h (Kyuquot) First Nation settlement of Aktis at Kyuquot Sd with six guides and hiked and canoed via Tahsish Inlet, Tahsish R, Atluck Lk, Hustan Lk and Nimpkish Lk to Queen Charlotte Str. They had to cross the lakes by building rafts, and ran somewhat short of food (at one point, according to Hankin, the guides were reduced to eating roots and ferns), but were the first Europeans to explore this part of Vancouver I. Hankin wrote a lengthy report of his journey for the Victoria *Colonist*.

Experiment Bight (50°47'00" 128°24'00" NW end of Vancouver I, just E of Cape Scott), **Experiment Point** (51°39'00" 127°58'00" SE tip of Hecate I, opposite Calvert I, Fitz Hugh Sd). The tiny 127-tonne *Experiment*, under Capt John Guise, and the 317-tonne *Captain Cook*, under Capt Henry Laurie, arrived at Nootka Sd in June 1786 from India. The two vessels, financed by Bombay merchant David Scott and under the overall command of E India Co factor James Strange, were the second fur-trading expedition to reach BC, after Capt James Hanna's *Sea Otter* the previous year. They also visited the Cape Scott area and the Alaska coast. Although the expedition was not successful financially, it left two valuable narratives, those of Strange and Alexander Walker, a friend of Guise who was in charge of a small force of soldiers aboard the *Experiment*. Walker had intended to build a post and overwinter at Nootka, but this idea was later abandoned. Another crew member from the *Experiment* was left at Nootka, however; surgeon's mate John McKay (*see* McKay Passage) volunteered to spend several months with the Nuu-chah-nulth, learning their customs and language and cultivating relationships. He was stuck there in great discomfort for over a year, though, until rescued by Capt Charles Barkley.

Explorer Bay (54°14'00" 132°58'00" NE side of Langara I, QCI). US coastal and geodetic survey vessel *Explorer*, under Capt Walter Dibrell, was charting S Alaskan waters in 1907 at the same time that Capt Frederick Learmonth, who named this feature, was doing survey work with HMS *Egeria*. The 41-m, 304-tonne *Explorer* was built at Wilmington, Delaware, in 1904 and suffered a bad collision with the *Indianapolis* in Seattle Hbr in 1907, in which two crew members were killed. In 1939, at the end of its survey career, the ship was sold, renamed the *Atkins* and continued to find employment in PNW waters for at least another decade.

F

Factor Islets (52°25'00" 128°26'00" Suzette Bay, S entrance to Finlayson Channel, N of Milbanke Sd). After fur trader Roderick Finlayson, an HBC chief factor at Ft Victoria and elsewhere. *See* Finlayson Arm.

Fairbairn Shoals (53°01'00" 131°41'00" Entrance to Cumshewa Inlet, NE Moresby I, QCI). William Howard Fairbairn (1881–1958) was a fisheries protection officer in Haida Gwaii for many years and named several features on the W coast of the QCI. He married Minnie Evelyn Graham (1885–1965) at Comox in 1907 and arrived in the Charlottes in 1911 as a handlogger. Together with partner and brother-in-law Clarence Johnston, he owned and operated the tugboats *Aimee* and *Edwin*. **D**

Fairchild Point (53°03'00" 129°37'00" S tip of Trutch I, Estevan Group, SE of Banks I). Named after an unknown model of Fairchild aircraft, which made the first photo flights over this area, probably in the 1930s. The Fairchild Aviation Corp was a US company, formed in 1925, that got its start manufacturing planes for aerial photography and went on to produce trainers, cargo planes and weapons during WWII. A Canadian subsidiary built several bush plane models designed for work in wilderness areas but went out of business in 1948.

Fairfax Inlet (52°45'00" 132°00'00" S side of Tasu Sd, W Moresby I, QCI). After Rear Adm Fairfax Moresby, cdr-in-chief on the RN's Pacific Station, 1850–53. *See* Moresby I. Fairfax Inlet was formerly known as Wright Inlet (qv), named in 1946 after BC land surveyor Alfred Wright, who made detailed triangulation studies of the entire NW part of Moresby I in 1918. It was changed in 1951 due to a duplication of names. In the early 1900s the shoreline of this inlet was almost entirely staked with mining claims.

Fairfax Island (52°09'00" 131°05'00" In Houston Stewart Channel, S of Moresby I, QCI). Lt Fairfax Moresby (1826–58) was the eldest son of Rear Adm Fairfax Moresby, cdr-in-chief on the RN's Pacific Station, 1850–53 (*see* Moresby

I), and served aboard his father's flagship, HMS *Portland*, on the BC coast. In 1856, as a cdr, he was in charge of HMS *Sappho*, a 12-gun brig assigned to suppress the slave trade on the W Africa coast. He seized several US vessels, including the *Panchita*, which caused a minor diplomatic furor when the ship's owner successfully brought a suit on the grounds of unlawful arrest. Moresby was drowned in Bass Str off Australia in 1858 when the *Sappho* and its crew of 140 went missing and were probably lost in a storm. Fairfax I was named by Cdr James Prevost, his brother-in-law, who was doing survey work in the QCI aboard HMS *Virago* in 1853. Point Fairfax in the Gulf Is may also be named for him (as well as for his father).

Fairlie Point (53°01'00" 132°21'00" N side of Inskip Channel, NW Moresby I, QCI). Named by the hydrographic service in 1946 in association with Inskip Channel (qv). George Inskip, responsible for surveying this area in 1853 as master of HMS *Virago*, spent his early nautical career, 1839–43, under Capt Edward Garrett on the 686-tonne *Fairlie*, a venerable merchant vessel that traded in the E Indies and carried passengers between England and Australia.

Fairweather Bay (49°20'00" 123°23'00" S side of Bowen I, Howe Sd, NW of Vancouver). The Cowan family, early landowners at the S end of Bowen I, originally called this little cove Winnipeg Bay in 1907, to honour nieces visiting from that city. One of George Cowan's daughters, Irene, married Ernest Rogers, a son of BC Sugar (now Rogers Sugar) owner Benjamin Rogers. Benjamin's widow, Vancouver philanthropist Mary Isabella Rogers, bought land at Winnipeg Bay from George Cowan and built a Bavarian-style lodge there that she called Fairweather. In 1976 the bay was renamed.

Falcon Rock (54°13'00" 130°22'00" S of Digby I, just SW of Prince Rupert). Named in 1907 by G Blanchard Dodge of the hydrographic dept, in association with Kestrel Rk (named for a sister ship), while surveying the approaches to Prince Rupert Hbr. CGS *Falcon* was a 24-m, 44-tonne fisheries patrol vessel, launched at Vancouver in 1902 for BC coastal service.

Falls River (53°49'00" 128°31'00" Flows NE into Kildala Arm, E side of Douglas Channel, S of Kitimat). The river tumbles over a 10-m-high precipice about 200 m before it enters Kildala Arm. The Haisla First Nation name for the river is Cinis (pronounced *TSEE-nees*), meaning "falls."

False Creek (49°17'00" 123°08'00" E of English Bay, Vancouver). Named by RN surveyor Capt George Richards in 1859 when he discovered that this waterway didn't lead anywhere. "Creek" was a common 19th-century Admiralty term for a small inlet that dried at low tide, and BC once had dozens of them. Their names have mostly been changed now to "inlets" or "coves" except this one, which remains as an example of an earlier nomenclature. False Ck used to be the industrial centre of Vancouver, and in the 1910s and '20s the extensive mud flats between Main St and Clark Dr were filled in and developed. In the 1970s, polluting mills and factories on the S shore of False Ck were replaced with townhomes and the urban renewal experiment of Granville I. The N shore, site of Expo 86, became a residential highrise community for 15,000 people in the 1990s. *E*

Fame Point (53°17'00" 132°42'00" S side of Kano Inlet, SW Graham I, QCI). Capt George Vancouver sailed past here in 1793 and named nearby Hunter Point (qv) after his friend Dr John Hunter, whom he had met at Jamaica while serving in 1782–83 as 4th lt aboard HMS *Fame*, under Capt George Wilson. The *Fame*, a 74-gun, 1,420-tonne ship of the line, was built at Deptford in 1759

and participated, just before Vancouver's transfer, in the Battle of the Isles des Saintes, in which the British won a decisive victory over the French in the Caribbean. It was converted to a prison ship in 1795, renamed *Guilford* and sold in 1814. The hydrographic service named this point in 1946 in association with Hunter Point.

Fane Island (48°48'00" 123°16'00" N of Hope Bay, NE side of N Pender I, Gulf Is). Charles George Fane (b 1837) was a sub-lt (or mate) aboard HMS *Ganges* while it was the flagship of Rear Adm Robert Baynes, cdr-in-chief of the Pacific Station, 1857–60. Fane also eventually reached the rank of rear adm, in 1890. Named by Capt George Richards of HMS *Plumper* in 1859.

Fannin Bay (53°12'00" 132°03'00" S side of Maude I, Skidegate Inlet, QCI). A type of ammonite fossil, genus *Fanninoceras*, is found at this bay. The fossil was named after naturalist John Fannin (1837–1904), who was appointed first curator of the BC Provincial Museum in 1886. He was born at Kemptville, Ont, and in 1862 went from Manitoba to the Cariboo with the Overlanders, a group of gold seekers who made an onerous trek across the Prairies by Red River cart and packhorse. Fannin later became a shoemaker at New Westminster and Burrard Inlet, and was also a hunting guide and taxidermist. There are a number of features in BC named after him, including Fannin Ck, Fannin Lk, Mt Fannin and the Fannin Range. *E*

Fanny Bay (49°30'25" 124°48'55" E side of Vancouver I, opposite Denman I). Various sources for this name have been proposed over the years, but none have been confirmed. It first appears on an 1862 Admiralty chart that was based on surveys conducted by Capt George Richards

Vancouver's False Creek, once an industrial zone, is now a prime downtown residential district. *Peter Vassilopoulos*

Vancouver Island's historic Fanny Bay Inn. *Rob Morris*

in 1860. Today the bay is the site of a small waterfront community, known for its oyster processing and the heritage Fanny Bay Inn. *E*

Fantome Point (50°47'00" 126°55'00" SE end of the Polkinghorne Is, W of Broughton I, NE side of Queen Charlotte Str, NE of Port McNeill). Named about 1865 by Lt Daniel Pender of the *Beaver* in association with Brig Rk and the Polkinghorne Is (qv). Charles Polkinghorne had been master of the brig *Fantome*, under Cdr John Gennys, on the Australian Station, 1850–56. The 438-tonne, 16-gun vessel, launched in 1839, saw service at the Cape of Good Hope, off W Africa and S America, and in the Mediterranean before being decommissioned in 1864.

Faraday Island (52°36'00" 131°29'00" Off SE side of Lyell I, QCI), **Faraday Passage** (52°37'00" 131°30'00" NW of Murchison I, N of Juan Perez Sd, QCI). English chemist and physicist Michael Faraday (1791–1867), a professor at the Royal Institution of Great Britain, was one of history's most influential scientists. His contributions were many; he was a brilliant experimentalist, discovering electromagnetic induction, electrolysis and chemical substances such as benzene, and he invented devices that would form the basis of electric motor technology. Named in 1878 by George M Dawson of the Geological Survey of Canada. *W*

Farewell Harbour (50°36'00" 126°40'00" Between Swanson I and Harbledown I, N of Blackfish Sd and Johnstone Str). Named in 1870 by Daniel Pender, who had recently been promoted cdr, and his officers because it was the last place they surveyed aboard the RN's trusty hired vessel, the *Beaver*, on the BC coast.

Farmer Islets (50°30'00" 127°39'00" W end of Buchholz Channel, Quatsino Sd, NW Vancouver I). Alexander Farmer supposedly received a Crown land grant near here in 1912, though government records do not show his name.

Farmer Point (52°04'00" 128°17'00" S side of Pinnington I, Queens Sd). Capt Donald William Farmer (1885–1972)

was head of the RCN's hydrographic division in the 1940s. He lived in BC for many years and died at N Vancouver. Formerly known as Henry Point (*see* Hand Bay).

Farrer Cove (49°20'00" 122°53'00" E side of Indian Arm, N of Bedwell Bay, NE of Vancouver). Lawyer George Edmund Farrer (1865–1957), born in the UK, owned 30 ha around the cove and retired to his property in the 1920s. This was the site of Belvedere Landing, one of many spots on Indian Arm served by vessels of the Harbour Navigation Co. Farrer raised fruit trees and chickens on his land and sold produce to local markets. After WWII, the YMCA bought his holdings for $7,500 and established Camp Howdy (since sold, in 2006, to the Evangelical Layman's Church). An outdoor theatre was built on Farrer's old house site.

Father Charles Channel (49°10'00" 125°57'00" E of Vargas I, Clayoquot Sd, W side of Vancouver I), **Father Charles Rock** (49°09'00" 125°57'00" S end of Father Charles Channel). After Charles Moser, pioneer Catholic missionary on the W coast. *See* Moser Point.

Father Point (54°39'00" 130°26'00" N entrance to Work Channel, N of Prince Rupert). William Hogan was a much-beloved Anglican missionary on the northern BC coast from 1893 to 1914. *See* Hogan I. Formerly known as Cook Point.

Favada Point (49°44'00" 124°38'00" W end of Texada I, Str of Georgia). There is confusion over the early naming of Lasqueti I and Texada I (qv). Spanish naval officer José Narváez was the first European to explore and chart the Str of Georgia, in 1791. According to Henry Wagner, an expert on the early cartography of the PNW, the chart prepared by Francisco Eliza, Narváez's superior—which Dionisio Alcalá-Galiano showed to Capt George Vancouver in 1792—labelled Isla de Texada in an unclear script. Vancouver mistakenly deciphered it as Favida or Fevada (both spellings appear in his journal). The correct Texada spelling prevailed, fortunately, and first appears on an Admiralty chart in 1862. Favada was adopted for this point by the hydrographic service in 1945 to keep alive a historical footnote.

Favourite Entrance (49°59'00" 127°23'00" S of Mission Group, Barrier Is, Kyuquot Sd, NW side of Vancouver I). The 72-tonne schooner *Favorite* (as it is more correctly spelled) was built at the Muir shipyard near Sooke in 1868 for pioneer sealers William Spring and Hugh McKay. It was used at first in the codfish trade and to carry freight to California, Mexico and Hawaii, but it joined the Victoria sealing fleet in 1873 and became one of the industry's most successful vessels. In the mid-1880s, Capt Alex McLean of the *Favorite* was the first to hire First Nation crews for the Bering Sea seal hunt and often returned to Victoria with the largest catch, consistently bringing back more than 2,000 skins a season. In the 1890s, Capt Laughlin McLean was in charge of the schooner. It was still in the sealing trade in the early 1900s but was later converted into a floating dormitory for female workers at George Heater's herring saltery on the W coast of Vancouver I (*see* Heater Hbr). The vessel sank about 1920 in Sydney Inlet after being badly damaged in a winter storm.

Fawcett Point (53°05'00" 129°17'00" S end of Gil I, between Pitt I and Princess Royal I). Edgar Fawcett (1847–1923) was born at Sydney, Australia, and arrived in Victoria, via San Francisco, about 1859 with his family. He worked in the family upholstery business at first but was later employed by the customs office, 1882–1910. In 1876 he married Myra Holden (1857–1933) at Nanaimo, where his father, Thomas Fawcett, had been appointed government agent. Fawcett family members were long-time residents of the James Bay district. Edgar's interest in history led him to become a founder of the Pioneers Society, write frequently for Victoria's newspapers and publish a book, *Some Reminiscences of Old Victoria*, in 1912.

Fawn Islet (50°05'00" 125°13'00" Gowlland Hbr, W side of Quadra I, just N of Campbell R). Cdr Cortland Simpson of the RN survey vessel *Egeria* named a number of features in the vicinity after animals in 1900.

Fearney Point (49°39'00" 124°06'00" SE tip of Nelson I, mouth of Jervis Inlet). William Fearney was one of Horatio Nelson's bargemen. At the 1797 Battle of St Vincent, when Nelson was a commodore, Fearney collected the swords of the Spanish officers after they surrendered, gathering them under his arm, according to Nelson, "with the greatest sang-froid." Capt George Richards, about 1860, named many features in the vicinity in association with Nelson and Vice Adm Sir John Jervis (Earl St Vincent). *W*

Fegen Islets (49°32'00" 124°23'00" Off NW side of Lasqueti I, Str of Georgia). Capt Edward Stephen Fogarty Fegen, VC (1891–1940), a native of Hampshire, was cdr of the armed merchant cruiser *Jervis Bay* when the N Atlantic convoy it was guarding was attacked in Nov 1940 by the pocket battleship *Admiral Scheer*. Without hesitation, the aging Australian liner, armed with obsolete six-inch guns, engaged the powerful German raider for all of 24 minutes before sinking. Its suicidal delaying tactic enabled most of the convoy's vessels to hide in the smoke and growing darkness and then escape. Fegen was one of 206 seamen to lose their lives in the ill-matched encounter and was awarded a posthumous VC for his actions. The misspelled name Fegan Its was adopted in 1945 but changed to its current, correct form in 1984. Shown on early charts as the Bare Its, these features are known locally as the Indian Is. *See also* Finnerty Is.

Felice Channel (48°54'00" 125°30'00" Entrance to Barkley Sd, W of Loudoun Channel, W side of Vancouver I), **Felice Island** (49°09'00" 125°55'00" Between Stubbs I and Tofino, Clayoquot Sd). John Meares was capt of the *Felice Adventurer*, on the BC coast in 1788 for the trading alliance Merchant Proprietors. The 209-tonne vessel, along with the *Iphigenia Nubiana*, under William Douglas, sailed from Macao under nominal Portuguese ownership to the PNW, where Meares spent the summer trading between Nootka Sd and the Oregon coast before returning to Asia. Felice Channel was formerly known as Ugly Channel, but the name was changed, according to the hydrographic service, because it was "objectionable and gives a false idea as to the safety of this important channel." Felice I was originally called Round I, a name that is still used locally on occasion.

Fellbrook Point (53°19'00" 128°59'00" S side of Gribbell I, N of Princess Royal I). John Fellbrook was a Royal Marines sgt aboard HMS *Chatham* on Capt George Vancouver's 1791–95 expedition to the PNW coast.

Fellowes Rock (52°23'00" 128°30'00" SW of Dowager I, Milbanke Sd). Eleanor Caroline Hill (1831–1926), born in Middlesex, was a daughter of Caroline Pearson and social and postal reformer Sir Rowland Hill. She came out to Victoria in 1862 after marrying hardware merchant Arthur Fellows (as the name is more commonly spelled) and had four children. The family settled first on Birdcage Walk (Government St) facing the old legislative buildings, then moved to Thetis Cottage in Esquimalt. They returned to the UK in 1869, where Caroline and Arthur later separated; she and her children were living in NS in 1882–83. In 1903 she became Mrs Smyth. Caroline was an artist, a fine singer and the author of numerous books and articles, including a biography of her famous father. Her memoirs reveal her as an unconventional woman, surprisingly liberal for her times and as interested in First Nation and non-British cultures as she was in "polite" colonial society.

Fell Point (52°31'00" 128°26'00" NW entrance to Nowish Inlet, Susan I, NW of Bella Bella). James Fell (1821–90) emigrated from England, where he was a tea merchant at Liverpool, to Victoria in 1858. He started up a spice and coffee business, and later a grocery, with John Finlayson, then took over the trade himself in 1868. Fell's reputation as an outspoken spiritualist did not prevent him from becoming mayor of Victoria, 1886–87, at which time he helped found the city's first public library.

Ferey Rock (50°07'26" 127°39'14" Entrance to Nasparti Inlet, Checleset Bay, NW side of Vancouver I). Capt George Ferey was born on the Channel Is in 1848. A globe-circling master mariner, he was based at Victoria in the 1880s and '90s, mainly as a sealing skipper. He was with the *W P Sayward* in 1887 when that sealer was seized in the Bering

F

Sea and taken to Sitka by a US revenue cutter. He also served on the sealers *Lottie Fairfield* and *Teresa*, sailed to China and Australia as mate of the barque *Nanaimo* and was master of the steamship *Hounslow*, which carried coal to San Diego. Formerly known as East Rk but renamed in the late 1930s.

Ferguson Bay (53°40'00" 132°17'00" S side of Masset Inlet, Graham I, QCI). Capt S Ferguson owned property on this bay. He planted fruit trees there and lived in a log cabin from 1912 until his 1920 death by drowning. Ferguson was best known as master of the BC Dept of Lands survey vessel *Polaris*. In the 1920s, Francis Millerd ran a cannery on the bay, using the hulk of the ancient sailing ship *Laurel Whalen* as part of his operation. *D*

Ferguson Cove (48°36'00" 123°23'30" W of Turgoose Point, Cordova Channel, Saanich Peninsula, N of Victoria). Arthur Ferguson (1877–1961) was born at Grand Bend, Ont, and came with his family in 1901 to Victoria, where they bought land and farmed in the Saanichton area.

Ferguson Point (49°18'00" 123°09'00" E side of English Bay, S of Siwash Rk, Vancouver). Civil engineer Alfred Graham Ferguson (c 1844–1903) came to Vancouver from the US and became wealthy as a tunnel contractor for the CPR. He built and owned several office buildings, including the Ferguson block at Hastings and Richards streets, which he actually built twice—once with wood and once, after the great 1886 fire, with brick. He was the first chairman, in 1888, of the Vancouver parks board (as a foreigner, his swearing-in ceremony was discreetly forgotten) and contributed much to the early development of Stanley Park. Ferguson died at San Francisco. The poet Pauline Johnson is buried at Ferguson Point, which was the site of a WWII gun battery and is today home to a popular restaurant.

Fernie Island (48°40'47" 123°23'38" E of Saanich Peninsula, N of Sidney). Peter Creeke Fernie (1830–1915) was a S Saanich pioneer. He came to Canada from England in 1862 after serving in the British Army, 1848–61, as a Royal Horse Artillery sgt and seeing service in the Crimean War and India. In BC he prospected and farmed and at one time owned a portion of the present Butchart Gardens property. In the 1880s, with his more famous brother William, after whom the BC town of Fernie is named (*see below*), he helped develop the coal deposits in the Elk R valley. Fernie Ridge in the Kootenays is named after both brothers. Peter died at Victoria. Fernie I was farmed in the 19th century by Tom Kamaree, a Hawaiian Islander or Kanaka, who received a Crown grant for it and adjacent Goudge I in 1889.

Fernie Point (52°39'00" 128°59'00" SE side of Aristazabal I). William Fernie (1837–1921), born at Kimbolton,

England, arrived in Victoria in 1860 after travelling widely. He prospected for gold at Revelstoke, the Cariboo and the Boundary district and worked on the Dewdney Trail. Fernie settled in the Kootenays, serving as government agent and mining recorder, 1876–82, then found coal in 1887 while prospecting on Michel Ck. With his brother Peter (*see* Fernie I), he discovered the extent of the huge coalfields of the Elk R valley and became a director of the Crows Nest Pass Coal Co. The town of Fernie is named for him, as is nearby Mt Fernie. William retired to Oak Bay in 1906 a wealthy man and built a mansion named Kimbolton. *E*

Fern Passage (54°19'00" 130°16'00" Between NE side of Kaien I and the mainland, Prince Rupert). The 15-tonne steam launch *Fern*, under Capt Robert Shears, was hired by surveyors in 1904–5 to help examine the area and find an acceptable terminus for the GTP. This narrow waterway, only navigable at high tide, was named by surveyor J Fred Ritchie.

Fernyhough Point (53°07'00" 129°25'00" E side of Campania I, between Pitt I and Princess Royal I). Pilot Officer Walter Fernyhough, a member of RCAF No 432 Squadron, was killed in action on June 29, 1944, aged 21. He was born at Clyde, Alberta, but was living in Victoria at the time he enlisted. Fernyhough was awarded the DFC after flying more than 30 bombing sorties, in which he "invariably displayed the utmost fortitude, courage and devotion to duty." He is buried at Creil Communal Cemetery in France.

Ferrer Point (49°45'00" 126°59'00" S entrance to Nuchatlitz Inlet, off NW Nootka I, W side of Vancouver I). The name Ensenada de Ferrer (Ferrer's Inlet) appears on the chart produced after the historic circumnavigation of Vancouver I by Dionisio Alcalá-Galiano and Cayetano Valdés in 1792. It refers to what is now known as Nuchatlitz Inlet. To keep a link alive with this older designation, the S entrance to Nuchatlitz was named Ferrer Point about 1860. Ferrer, a Catalan surname meaning "ironworker," could refer to any number of people, including Lorenzo Ferrer Maldonado, a pilot who, in 1588, launched the myth of the NW Passage (and whose claims were reluctantly investigated by Spanish explorer Alejandro Malaspina in 1791), or St Vincent Ferrer (1350–1419), a Dominican missionary and logician from Valencia. In *The Cartography of the NW Coast of America*, Henry Wagner suggests that Ensenada de Ferrer was not named by Alcalá-Galiano and Valdés but by José Espinosa and Ciriaco Cevallos, who explored Esperanza Inlet in the summer of 1791, when Malaspina visited Nootka Sd. According to Wagner, Spanish naval officer Vicente Ferrer, whose frigate was shipwrecked in 1793, may have been the source of the name (the Alcalá-Galiano chart is dated 1795). *See also* Ensanada It.

Fidalgo Passage (49°39'00" 126°34'00" W of Bligh I, Nootka Sd, W side of Vancouver I). Spanish naval officer Salvador Fidalgo (1757–1803), in command of the *San Carlos*, sailed north from Mexico in 1790 with Francisco Eliza, in the *Concepción*, to reoccupy Nootka Sd. Eliza, accompanied by Capt Pedro Alberni and a party of soldiers, fortified the Spanish settlement at Nootka that summer, while Fidalgo was ordered N to explore the coast of Alaska. He also travelled to Nootka in 1792, with the *Princesa*, in support of Francisco Bodega y Quadra, sent to negotiate the Nootka Sd Convention with Capt George Vancouver. Fidalgo spent most of that year establishing a Spanish post at Nuñez Gaona (Neah Bay) as a backup base for use after Nootka had been transferred to the British. He overwintered at Nootka in charge of the fort there, then returned to Mexico in 1793. Fidalgo made a final trip to Nootka in 1794 with the *Princesa* and Quadra's successor, José Manuel de Álava. Fidalgo I in the San Juan Is is also named for him.

Fifer Cove (52°52'00" 128°41'00" E side of Laredo Inlet, Princess Royal I). Dr Max William Fifer (1822–61) arrived at Ft Yale in 1858, where he was appointed HBC medical officer and later became chairman of the town council. He had earlier served in the US war with Mexico as a hospital steward, then made money as a gold miner before training as a doctor and setting up a practice in San Francisco. On July 5, 1861, he was murdered by Robert Wall, who held a grudge against Fifer over his treatment of Wall's venereal disease. Wall was convicted and sentenced to death that Aug by Judge Matthew Baillie Begbie.

Fife Rock (50°46'00" 126°34'00" E of Davies I, Fife Sd), **Fife Sound** (50°47'00" 126°38'00" S side of Broughton I, NE end of Queen Charlotte Str). James Duff, 2nd Earl of Fife (1729–1809), was a Scottish landowner who did a great deal to improve agricultural and cattle-breeding practices in his region, twice winning the gold medal of the Society for the Encouragement of Arts, Manufactures and Commerce. He was MP for Banffshire, 1754–84, and for Elginshire, 1784–90. Fife Sd was named by Capt George Vancouver in 1792. Fife Rock was formerly known as Gull Rock. *W*

Finisterre Island (49°25'00" 123°19'00" NE end of Bowen I, Howe Sd, NW of Vancouver). Named either after Finistère, the westernmost dept in France, or Cape Finisterre, one of Spain's most westerly headlands. The word derives from the Latin *finis terrae*, meaning "end of the earth," and was sometimes used on ancient maps to indicate land's end. The owners of the island, which is connected to Bowen at low tide, access their property through an artificial tunnel.

Finlayson Arm (48°30'00" 123°33'00" Head of Saanich Inlet, W of Victoria), **Finlayson Channel** (52°38'00"

Hudson's Bay Company fur trader Roderick Finlayson built Fort Victoria and became one of BC's wealthiest citizens. *BC Archives PDP02246*

128°28'00" N extension of Milbanke Sd, E of Swindle I and Sarah I), **Finlayson Head** (52°49'00" 128°26'00" E of S entrance to Hiekish Narrows, N end of Finlayson Channel), **Finlayson Point** (48°24'00" 123°22'00" S of Beacon Hill, Victoria). Fur trader Roderick Finlayson (1818–92) played a key role in the development of Victoria. He was born in Scotland and came to the US before joining the HBC as a clerk. In the early 1840s he worked at northern posts and was assigned in 1843 to yet-to-be-constructed Ft Victoria as deputy to Charles Ross. Ross died in 1844, and Finlayson was put in charge of Victoria until 1849, the year he married Sarah Work (1829–1906, after whom many BC features are also named; *see* Work Bay), at which time the fort became HQ for the Columbia district, and James Douglas was installed as chief officer. Finlayson—a "civil but hard Scot," according to RN capt William Courtenay—then held the position of chief accountant, 1849–62. He was a member of Vancouver I's colonial legislative council, 1851–63, and was made a chief factor in 1859. From 1862 until he retired in 1872, Finlayson was HBC superintendent in the BC Interior. He acquired much property in Victoria, and in 1890 the *Colonist* newspaper named him the wealthiest landowner in the city. After retirement he farmed and looked after his extensive business interests, serving as mayor of Victoria in 1878 and championing the construction of its city hall. Mt Finlayson at the head of Finlayson Arm is also named for him, as are the Factor Its, Roderick Cove, Roderick I and Roderick Lk in the Finlayson Channel area, and Finlayson Ck in the Cassiar region. Roderick I in the QCI is very likely named for him as well. *E W*

Finlayson Island (54°32'00" 130°28'00" S of entrance to Port Simpson, NW of Prince Rupert). Duncan Finlayson (c 1796–1862), from Scotland, joined the HBC in 1815 and worked as a supervisor in the Peace R and Red R districts in the 1820s. He was a chief factor on the PNW coast, 1831–37, under Dr John McLoughlin, with whom he did not get

F

along. Finlayson improved coastal trade and founded Ft McLoughlin on the central BC coast in 1833. In 1838 he married Isobel Simpson, cousin and sister-in-law of HBC gov George Simpson. He was appointed gov of Assiniboia district (Red River Colony) 1839–44. For the next 15 years, Finlayson lived in Que and England, supervising the HBC's Montreal Dept and acting as George Simpson's right-hand man. He died in England and left the bulk of his estate to the Anglican Church Missionary Society to be used for the benefit of First Nation groups. He was an uncle of Roderick Finlayson (*see* Finlayson Arm). Finlayson I was named by officers of the HBC about 1836. Duncan Point on the SE side of Finlayson I is also named for him.

Finlayson Peninsula (53°06'00" 129°32'00" NW side of Campania I, Estevan Sd, N of Caamaño Sd). Flight Lt Colin Gowans Finlayson, DFC (and bar), born in Alberta and raised at Victoria, was killed in action on Oct 18, 1944, aged 23. He was an observer with the RCAF's No 418 ("City of Edmonton") Squadron, equipped in 1943 with de Havilland Mosquito aircraft, and was decorated for displaying "the highest qualities of skill, bravery and devotion to duty." Finlayson was a veteran of numerous sorties and helped destroy five enemy aircraft. He is buried at the Belgrade War Cemetery, Serbia.

Finn Bay (51°30'00" 127°44'00" N side of Penrose I, Darby Channel, Rivers Inlet). A dozen families of Russian Finns homesteaded at this location about 1908 and earned their living from logging and fishing. The Millerd Packing Co established a fish saltery there in 1928. Floathouses are often moored in the bay, and a fuel station, small store and fishing lodge have all called Finn Bay home. Nearby Finn Ck and Finn Lk are named after the bay.

Finnerty Cove (48°28'00" 123°18'00" E side of Saanich Peninsula, N of Cadboro Bay and Victoria), **Finnerty Point** (53°04'00" 129°44'00" SW end of Nichol I, W of Trutch I, Estevan Group, N of Caamaño Sd). Michael Finnerty (1831–1930) was born at Mayo, Ireland, and came to Victoria in 1862 from the US, where he had found work in NY and Virginia. He joined the Cariboo gold rush and laboured on the Cariboo Rd, then bought land in S Saanich with his brother and was soon running a profitable market garden and feed business. He and his wife, Mary Ann (1849–1911), acquired more property between Gordon Head and Mt Tolmie (now the site of UVic) and became successful strawberry farmers. His name lingers on at UVic's Finnerty Gardens, especially in spring when the rhododendrons bloom. As Victoria's oldest surviving pioneer at age 94, Finnerty was a guest of honour at that city's great old-timers' reunion of 1924 (*see* Adams Bay).

Finnerty Islands (49°30'00" 124°24'00" Off NW side of Lasqueti I, Str of Georgia). In 1945 the hydrographic service successfully submitted Finnerty and Fegan as names for geographical features in this area. The intention was to honour Capt Edward Stephen Fogarty Fegen, who was awarded the VC in 1940 for his actions aboard HMS *Jervis Bay* (*see* Fegen Its). Unfortunately, the names submitted were in error. Fegan should have been Fegen and was afterwards corrected. Finnerty, however, which should have been Fogarty, was never changed, even though no other geographical feature in BC is called Fogarty and the name is thus theoretically available. The islands are known locally as the Flat Tops.

Finn Slough. *See* Gilmour Slough.

Burrard Inlet's First Narrows and the Lions Gate Bridge. *Peter Vassilopoulos*

First Narrows (49°19'00" 123°08'00" N of Prospect Point, Burrard Inlet, Vancouver). The entrance to Vancouver Hbr was named by RN surveyor Capt George Richards (as was Second Narrows) about 1859–60. Lions Gate, a more dramatic catchphrase drawn from The Lions—the twin guardian peaks that overlook the inlet from the N Shore—was suggested about 1890 by BC Supreme Court judge John Gray and later adopted as the name of the bridge across the narrows, completed in 1938. Both in name and design, the Lions Gate Bridge echoes San Francisco's longer Golden Gate Bridge, which had been finished a year earlier.

First Point (49°57'00" 124°48'00" N side of Savary I, Str of Georgia). Denotes the first point W of the government wharf. Adopted quite recently, in 1983, as a well-established name, along with Second Point.

Fisgard Island (48°26'00" 123°27'00" W entrance to Esquimalt Hbr, just W of Victoria). HMS *Fisgard* served on the Pacific Station, under Capt John Duntze, 1843–47, and was one of the first RN vessels to anchor in Esquimalt Hbr. Lt Cdr James Wood of HMS *Pandora*, who surveyed the harbour in 1847, named many of its features after the

F

Fisgard Island lighthouse station, built in 1860. *Andrew Scott*

Fisgard's officers. The 46-gun, 969-tonne frigate was built at Pembroke in 1819 and modelled on the French frigate *Leda*. For many years it was a guardship at Woolwich dockyard and was broken up in 1879. BC's first lighthouse was built on Fisgard I in 1860; the light, reached by an ornate iron spiral staircase, was automated in 1928. The station was connected to Esquimalt by a causeway in 1951 and named a national historic site in 1972. *E W*

Fish Bay (53°06'00" 129°16'00" S side of Gil I, between Pitt I and Princess Royal I). Robert Fish (1833–1927), born in Dorset, England, immigrated with his brother James to Victoria in 1851 aboard the *Tory* to work at the HBC's Craigflower Farm. His older brother Charles had come out the previous year. Having fulfilled their HBC contracts by 1856, Robert and James were able to buy 20 ha of land in Saanich. In 1862 they married two sisters, Ellen and Ann Morris. Robert and Ellen (1843–1921) later settled at Rock Bay on Victoria's Upper Hbr. He worked as a gardener and labourer and participated in the Victoria old-timers' reunion of 1924 (*see* Adams Bay).

Fisher Channel (52°08'00" 127°53'00" E of Hunter I, Denny I and Bella Bella, W of King I). Named in 1793 by Capt George Vancouver after his "much respected friend" Rev John Fisher (1748–1825). At that time, Fisher was vicar of Stowey and a teacher of Prince Edward Augustus, Queen Victoria's father. He also held an appointment as royal chaplain or "deputy clerk of the closet." Fisher became bishop of Exeter, 1803–7, and bishop of Salisbury, 1807–25, in which latter capacity he supervised the education of Princess Charlotte Augusta of Wales, at the time King George III's only legitimate grandchild. Vancouver also named nearby Port John for his friend. Exeter Point was named for him later, as were Salisbury Point and Salisbury Cone.

Fishermans Cove (49°21'25" 123°16'13" E side of Queen Charlotte Channel, SE entrance to Howe Sd, W Vancouver). With the encouragement of the BC government, a group of Nfld fishermen and their families settled here about 1888. It was formerly known as Robson Cove, after Capt Harry Robson Jones (1857–1933), a Vancouver Hbr pilot, 1892–1914, but the name was changed to Fisherman Cove in 1949 to conform to local usage, then to Fishermans Cove in 1961 (Batchelor Cove, just to the NW, was known as Fishermans Cove until 1929). Apparently the entire embayment, which now includes Fishermans Cove and Eagle Hbr, was once known as Eagle Hbr (qv). Today the cove is the site of a large marina, and the adjacent W Vancouver residential suburb is also known as Fishermans Cove.

Fisher Point (52°16'00" 128°21'00" S side of Don Peninsula, W end of Seaforth Channel, Milbanke Sd). Elizabeth Rich Morris (1840–1918) married William Fisher (1839–1924) in England and travelled with him from Falmouth to Victoria in 1864, accompanied by her widowed mother, also Elizabeth Morris. They settled at Metchosin, where young Elizabeth was appointed the first schoolteacher, and William farmed at Glen Lk. In 1872 they bought a 130-ha property overlooking Parry Bay that had formerly been owned by Gov James Douglas and used by him as a hunting preserve and summer residence. Elizabeth, who served as the local nurse, was noted for her musical abilities, while William, an enthusiastic horticulturist and beekeeper, developed a legendary orchard. They named their farm Ferncliffe.

Fishery Bay. *See* Ts'im K'ol'hl Da oots'ip.

Fishtrap Bay (53°33'14" 129°01'19" E side of Hawkesbury I, opposite N entrance to Ursula Channel, S of Kitimat). According to former UBC anthropologist Jay Powell, the bay takes its name from a fishtrap located at this site in the 1880s, built to provide fish for a nearby saltery at the mouth of the Crab R. Fishtraps were made illegal in BC in 1889, but the pilings in the bay were still visible until the 1940s. The Haisla First Nation name for this geographical feature is Neqetu, meaning "with the tops pulled down"; in former times, the Haisla people who lived in the area apparently demonstrated their strength by bending trees over.

Fitz Hugh Sound (51°40'00" 127°50'00" Between Calvert I and Hunter I and the mainland). William Fitzhugh was one of a group of British E India Co merchants living in Canton who also traded privately and were associates of John Cox and John Reid, the owners of the *Sea Otter*, Capt James Hanna's ship. Hanna sailed from Macao to Nootka Sd and back in 1785 and was thus the first fur trader on the BC coast. He returned the following year and ventured farther N to Queens Sd, naming a number of features

Pointer Island at the north end of Fitz Hugh Sound. *Peter Vassilopoulos*

en route, including Fitz Hugh Sd. Fitzhugh later became part of the syndicate that backed the 1789 expedition of Capt James Colnett; it included John Meares and Richard Cadman Etches and was somewhat laboriously known as the Associated Merchants of London and India Trading to the NW Coast of America. Fitz Hugh Sd is the S entrance to the Inside Passage. *E W*

Five Finger Island (49°14'00" 123°55'00" W side of Rainbow Channel, NE of Departure Bay, off E side of Vancouver I). This bare, rugged feature is so-named because, from certain angles, its five rocky hummocks look like the knuckles of a clenched fist.

Flamborough Head (48°27'00" 123°17'00" S side of Cadboro Bay, Victoria). Named for a famous geographical feature on the E coast of Yorkshire, England. The British Flamborough Head is a cave-ridden, 11-km-long chalk promontory and important seabird-breeding habitat. The tamer BC version is situated next door to the Royal Victoria Yacht Club.

Flamingo Inlet (52°13'00" 131°21'00" SW side of Moresby I, QCI), **Flamingo Rock** (53°38'00" 133°00'00" Athlow Bay, W side of Graham I, QCI). The 41-m, 241-tonne steam trawler *Flamingo*, built at Hull, England, in 1885, was owned by Capt Absalom Freeman, founder of the New England Fish Co (forerunner of the Canadian Fishing Co). He spent much time off the W coast of the QCI in the early 20th century and made important sketch maps of the area that were later used by the hydrographic service. Walter Dass (*see* Dass Point) was one of the *Flamingo's* skippers. The inlet was originally named Flamingo Hbr in 1912.

Fleet Point (49°15'00" 124°08'00" S side of Nanoose Hbr, E side of Vancouver I). Cdr Ernest James Fleet, in charge of the RN sloop-of-war *Icarus*, located and surveyed a dangerous rock in Nanoose Hbr in 1896 that had earlier been struck by HMS *Impérieuse*. That same year, in a splendid ceremony, he married Edythe Mary Macdonald, daughter of William J Macdonald, one of BC's three senators. In 1909, as a rear adm, Fleet recommended building up Canada's W coast naval presence with "one or more dirigible airships fitted for observation and scouting

and dropping high explosive bombs, to be worked by the Canadian navy and housed at Rodd Hill." Fleet Point was named in 1904 by Cdr John Parry of HMS *Egeria* while re-surveying the area.

Fleishman Point (53°13'00" 129°35'00" SW end of Pitt I, facing Nepean Sd). Flying Officer Edmund David Fleishman, AFM, from Vancouver, enlisted at Montreal and was posted to Saskatoon as a flying instructor before going overseas and joining RAF No 37 (Bomber) Squadron, which flew Vickers Wellingtons in WWII. He was reported missing on an air sortie over Kastelli Tediaga and was presumed killed in action Nov 23, 1942, aged 24. Fleishman is commemorated at Suda Bay War Cemetery on Crete.

Fleming Bay (48°25'00" 123°25'00" Just NW of Macaulay Point, Esquimalt, W of Victoria). Photographer Edgar Fleming (1860–1938) came to Victoria in 1887 from London, England, where he had worked for the London Stereoscopic and Photographic Co. In 1890 he married Catherine Robinson (1868–1948), who arrived in BC with her family in 1878, also from England. He set up a studio on Government St with Stanley Inchbold, an artist. Then in 1889 he joined his brother, Harold Fleming, to do primarily portrait and commercial work. Fleming Bros studio existed until 1934, when Harold died. In 1896, Edgar served as photographer on Rev William Bolton's second expedition to explore northern Vancouver I. He and his family lived at Esquimalt near Fleming Bay.

Fleming Bay (53°58'03" 130°05'40" SE end of Telegraph Passage, S of mouth of Skeena R), **Fleming Island** (48°53'00" 125°08'00" W side of Trevor Channel, Barkley Sd, W side of Vancouver I). Fleming Bay was named Port Fleming in 1879 by Capt J C Brundige, who was directed to search out potential sites for a railway terminus on BC's N coast. Brundige reported to civil engineer Sandford Fleming that this was the only place he could recommend "nearer the mouth of the Skeena River than Port Simpson" (Burrard Inlet, of course, eventually became the main terminus). Fleming (1827–1915) was born in Scotland and came to Canada in 1845. After he had served as chief engineer of the Northern and Intercolonial railways, the Canadian government appointed him to survey a route for a transcontinental railway, which occupied him from 1871 to 1880. Knighted in 1897, he was also a leading promoter of the Canada–Australia telegraph cable, advocate for international standard time and designer of Canada's first postage stamp. Sandford I, near Fleming I, is also named for him, as are the Sir Sandford Range and Mt Sir Sandford in the Rockies. *W*

Fleming Point (51°31'00" 127°40'00" N side of Darby Channel, Rivers Inlet). According to historians Helen and Philip Akrigg, Fleming was the name of a young nurse working at Dr George Darby's Rivers Inlet hospital at the time a new coastal survey was being conducted in the late 1930s. The name was adopted in 1947.

Flett Point (53°05'00" 129°06'00" N entrance to Barnard Hbr, NW side of Princess Royal I). Grocer and general merchant James Flett (1857–1940) was born at Victoria. His father, John Flett (1828–86), a cooper, had arrived there in 1849 from the Orkney Is to work for the HBC; in 1870, John moved to the Cowichan region to farm near Maple Bay. James, one of four brothers, married Henrietta Findlay (1866–1940) at Victoria in 1885. He and brother John William Flett operated a store in Victoria, and James later had a store in the Somenos area. His brothers farmed, and, between them, members of the Flett family played a significant role in the development of the Cowichan Valley. The Fletts are believed to have taken part in the Victoria old-timers' reunion of 1924 (*see* Adams Bay).

Fleurieu Point (54°05'00" 133°05'00" N of Beresford Bay, W side of Graham I, QCI). Charles Pierre Claret, Comte de Fleurieu (1738–1810), was an influential French naval officer and geographer who published a narrative of the 1790–92 round-the-world voyage of Capt Etienne Marchand. Marchand and *La Solide*, a well-built vessel equipped by private French interests for scientific inquiry and commercial trade, anchored at Cloak Bay for several weeks in 1791 and charted the NW QCI. Marchand died in 1792 and his papers were lost; Fleurieu based his account on the ship's log and diaries of other crew members. The count had a notable career. In 1768, on the *Isis*, he commanded an expedition to test the newly invented chronometer of Ferdinand Berthoud. He became inspector gen of ports and navy yards in 1776 and played a key role in France's naval involvement in the American Revolutionary War. Fleurieu occupied a number of senior government posts, including minister of the navy in 1790–91, and was the French official who signed the treaty ceding Louisiana to the US. He became a senator, an adm and gov of the Tuileries Palace, wrote numerous books and published a famous atlas. He is buried in the Pantheon. Fleurieu Point was named in 1907 by Capt Frederick Learmonth of the RN survey vessel *Egeria*.

Fleury Island (53°13'00" 132°07'00" S of Lina I, Maude Channel, between Graham I and Moresby I, QCI). Victoria pioneer Frances "Fanny" Fleury (1836–1899) married Francis Claudet, superintendent of BC's colonial assay office, in 1863. He assayed QCI coal samples from the Cowgitz Mine at Kagan Bay. The Claudets lived for 10 years at New Westminster, where Francis attempted, without success, to establish a mint for BC. The family then moved to London, England, but two sons returned and settled in BC in later years. Formerly known as Tuft I. Claudet I (qv) is nearby.

Flewett Point (49°06'00" 123°48'00" S entrance to Boat Hbr, SE of Cedar, E side of Vancouver I). William Minter Flewett (1832–1914) was born at London, England, and moved to NB in 1853, where he worked as a mining engineer. He married three times and had numerous children. In 1873 he arrived at Nanaimo and, in about 1881, married his third wife, Martha (1832–1915), who had come to Canada from Holland in 1875. After working in the coal mines, he bought an 8-m steam launch, the *Mercury*, which he renamed the *Nellie* and used to ferry passengers between Nanaimo and Departure Bay. By 1881, Flewett owned 130 ha on De Courcy I and was raising sheep for sale at Nanaimo's farmers' market. He and Martha lived at De Courcy for the rest of their lives, eventually owning the entire island (and Ruxton I to the S), rearing poultry and growing giant vegetables and fruits.

Flewin Point (54°37'00" 130°27'00" N entrance to Rushbrook Passage, N end of Tsimpsean Peninsula, N of Prince Rupert). John "Dashing Jack" Flewin (1857–1942) was born at Victoria, the son of Thomas Flewin (1832–1901), who had joined the HBC in 1852 and arrrived in BC from England the following year. John worked in the *Colonist* print room, then became a popular member of the provincial police force for many years. He married Helen Copeland (1864–1925) in 1881. As a police sgt he investigated two notorious BC murder cases: the 1886 killings of James Miller and William Dring at Cowichan, and those of four seamen aboard the schooner *Seabird* in 1887. He later led a contingent of 30 men to Hazelton to settle an uprising over the accidental death of a First Nation man at the hands of a police constable. Flewin was named co-respondent in a messy divorce case in 1886 and severely censured in court. The *Colonist* found him "not competent to fill such an office of trust and responsibility" and demanded his resignation, which he reluctantly offered, but the adulterous sgt got his job back three weeks later after 300 citizens signed a petition calling for his reinstatement. Flewin and his wife later moved to Port Simpson, where he served as the first gold commissioner, stipendiary magistrate and government agent in the Skeena district until 1907. He resided in northern BC for another 23 years but managed to get down to Victoria in 1924 to take in the famous old-timers' reunion held that year (*see* Adams Bay).

Flint Rock (50°29'00" 128°03'00" N side of North Hbr, Forward Inlet, Quatsino Sd, NW end of Vancouver I). Arthur St George Flint (1859–1918) received a Crown grant of land in this area. He was born in Ireland and came to Canada about 1886 with his wife, Mary Elizabeth Flint (1861–1940), and daughter. Flint worked in Victoria for over 30 years as an insurance and real-estate agent.

F

Flora Bank (54°11'00" 130°18'00" Between Lelu I and Kitson I, just S of Prince Rupert). Flora McDonald married Edward Horsey at Prince Rupert in 1909. Her father was manager of the Inverness Cannery in the early 1900s. *See* Horsey Bank.

Florence Island (51°32'00" 127°32'00" S of Ethel I, Rivers Inlet). Florence Horsfall Walbran (1873–1950), born in Lancashire, UK, was the eldest daughter of Capt John Walbran, noted mariner and author. She married Thomas Hugh Worthington, also from Lancashire, at Victoria in 1916. Capt Walbran named this feature in 1890 while making a survey of Rivers Inlet with the Canadian Pacific Navigation Co steamship *Danube*.

Florence Point (49°46'00" 126°55'00" S side of Nuchatlitz Inlet, NW Nootka I, W side of Vancouver I). Florence Isabella Langford was the fifth and youngest daughter of Flora and Edward Langford (*see* Langford), who came to Victoria in 1851 to manage Colwood Farm for the Puget's Sd Agricultural Co, an HBC subsidiary. In 1861, Capt Langford returned with his family to England, where Florence later married Charles Land Pugh. Florence Lk near Langford, W of Victoria, is possibly also named for her.

Florence Point (50°29'00" 125°43'00" S side of Forward Hbr, E of Hardwicke I, N of Johnstone Str). After Lady Florence Cust, a sister of Lt Horace Lascelles. Lascelles was in command of HMS *Forward*, an RN gunboat, on the BC coast from 1861 to 1865. *See* Cust Point.

Florencia Bay (48°59'00" 125°38'00" N of Barkley Sd, W side of Vancouver I), **Florencia Islet** (48°59'00" 125°39'00" In Florencia Bay). The 200-tonne *Florencia* was a Peruvian brigantine, under Capt J P de Echiandeia, that capsized off Vancouver I in a Nov 1860 storm. Four people died and the vessel was badly damaged, but it righted itself and drifted into Nootka Sd, where it was pumped out and found to be repairable. HMS *Forward* arrived from Esquimalt to tow the *Florencia* to Victoria but experienced engine trouble and had to cast the brigantine off. Several days later a gale blew up and the ship was wrecked in this bay (which was known as Wreck Bay prior to 1930). The *Forward* made repairs at Nootka Sd and eventually returned to Esquimalt in Jan 1861 after it had been searched for unsuccessfully and given up for lost. A minor gold rush was sparked at the turn of the 20th century when placer gold was discovered in Florencia Bay's black beach sands; despite great efforts, the elusive flakes defied economic extraction. *W*

Flores Island (49°20'00" 126°10'00" Between Sydney Inlet and Millar Channel, Clayoquot Sd, W side of Vancouver I). Manuel Antonio Flores (c 1722–1799) was the 51st viceroy of New Spain (or Mexico), 1787–89. He was responsible for establishing the Spanish fort at Nootka Sd

Flores Island, along the Wild Side Heritage Trail. *Andrew Scott*

and dispatched the 1788 and 1789 expeditions of Estéban Martínez (who may have been his nephew) to Alaska and Nootka Sd, respectively. Flores had been a senior Spanish naval officer and also spent five years as viceroy of New Granada (Colombia). **Mount Flores** (49°18'40" 126°09'48" NE of Rafael Point, Flores I) is named for him as well. Flores I, at 155 sq km, is home to the Nuu-chah-nulth community of Ahousat and the site of a well-known wilderness trail. Much of the island is a provincial marine park. *W*

Flyaway Islet (52°47'00" 131°59'00" SW entrance to Two Mtn Bay, Tasu Sd, Moresby I, QCI). The 7-tonne sloop *Flyaway* cruised 5,000 km in BC and Alaska waters while its master, Cape Breton native Capt Daniel McLean (b 1851), searched for mineral wealth and worked as a placer gold miner. He came to the W coast in 1880 and later, with his brother Capt Alex McLean, became involved in the sealing industry. Daniel was the first sealer, aboard the US schooner *City of San Diego*, to hunt in the Bering Sea, and he had command of various other vessels over the years, including the *Mary Ellen*, *Triumph* and *Edward E Webster*. He brought back 4,268 fur seal skins in 1886, the most ever secured in a season. *See* McLean I for more information.

Flynn Point (53°05'00" 129°45'00" W side of Trutch I, Estevan Group, SE of Banks I). Edward Flynn was a Royal Marines sgt aboard HMS *Discovery* on Capt George Vancouver's 1791–95 expedition to the PNW.

Foch Lagoon (53°48'00" 129°05'00" Extends NW of Drumlummon Bay, NW side of Douglas Channel, SW of Kitimat). French marshal and military theorist Ferdinand Foch (1851–1929) was one of France's most senior and successful army officers throughout WWI and was appointed supreme cdr of Allied forces in 1918. Nearby Foch Ck and Foch Lk are also named for him, as is Mt Foch on the BC-Alberta border. A settlement named Foch existed briefly in the 1910s and '20s at Olsen Lk, just E of Desolation Sd. According to UBC anthropologist Jay Powell, the Haisla First Nation term for Foch Lagoon is Mesgatli (also written as Miskatla or Misgatlee); somehow this name was applied by mistake to a nearby feature, now Miskatla Inlet, which the Haisla know as Kiyasa.

Foley Head (49°48'15" 123°58'05" Between Hotham Sd and Goliath Bay, N side of Jervis Inlet). Adm Sir Thomas Foley (1757–1833) had an illustrious career in the RN. In 1793, as flag capt of HMS *St George*, under Rear Adm John Gell, he was present at the capture of the Spanish treasure ship *St Jago*, the richest prize ever taken in British naval history. In 1797 he was flag capt of HMS *Britannia*, under Vice Adm Charles Thompson, and played a key role at the Battle of Cape St Vincent (Capt George Richards later named many features in Jervis Inlet after participants in this engagement). Foley was with Adm Lord Nelson at the Battle of the Nile, in HMS *Goliath*, and was Nelson's flag capt aboard HMS *Elephant* at the 1801 Battle of Copenhagen. He was buried in a coffin made of oak timbers from the *Elephant*, which was broken up in 1818. Nearby Mt Foley is also named for him. *W*

Folger Island (48°50'00" 125°15'00" In Folger Passage), **Folger Passage** (48°49'00" 125°16'00" E side of Imperial Eagle Channel, Barkley Sd, W side of Vancouver I). Henry Folger was 1st officer of the *Imperial Eagle* on Capt Charles Barkley's 1787 fur-trading expedition to the BC coast.

Foote Islets (52°16'00" 128°16'00" W entrance to Spiller Channel, NW of Bella Bella). Master mariner Hamilton R Foote (1858–1901) was born in Ireland and came to Canada in 1874. His wife, Edith Sophia Foote (1866–1947), was born at Toronto. Capt Foote had charge of several significant vessels in PNW waters, including the *Danube*, *Maude*, *Mischief* and *Willapa*, and was the first commodore of the NW International Yachting Assoc. He died, along with more than 40 others (the exact death toll was never determined), while master of the *Islander*, which sank off Alaska en route to Vancouver after striking an iceberg. Rumours spread that the vessel was carrying gold bullion, but when the *Islander* was finally salvaged in 1934, very little of value was found. Curiously, another master mariner named Foote—John Calvin Foote (1859–1949)—also served as captain of the *Islander* and was a pilot at Nanaimo until 1929, but he is not this feature's namesake. The Foote Its were formerly known as the Pitts Its, after Lt P Pitts, RNCVR 1914–18, but the name was changed in 1925.

Forbidden Plateau (49°41'00" 125°19'00" NW of Comox Lk, SW of Campbell R, Vancouver I). Several explanations have been put forward for the name of this feature, which is not really a plateau but a sloping terrain of ridges and open parkland. The area was supposedly shunned by local First Nations, either from a belief that it was haunted or because of bloody encounters between Comox, Cowichan and Nuu-chah-nulth hunting parties. One legend holds that a party of Comox women and children, sent to the

plateau during an enemy attack, suddenly vanished, the work of evil spirits. The plateau became Vancouver I's first popular skiing area in the 1920s. The name was submitted in 1935 and adopted in 1939. *E*

Ford Cove (49°30'00" 124°41'00" W side of Hornby I, Str of Georgia). George Ford (1831–99), from Devon, England, came to the Comox valley in 1862 with his friend Henry Maude. He was one of Hornby I's first settlers, arriving about 1869, followed shortly thereafter by Maude. Both men had First Nation wives, and Ford, in particular, raised so many children that he had to build them a school in 1880. By 1885 he owned 740 ha of fairly open land on the SW part of the island, where he ran cattle and planted fruit trees and vegetables. Maude also had large landholdings.

Ford Cove, west side of Hornby Island. *Peter Vassilopoulos*

Ford Rock (53°36'00" 130°32'00" In Griffith Hbr, W side of Banks I). A trimmer named A Ford—a "returned man" or WWI veteran who saw service in Europe—worked on board the W coast survey vessel *Lillooet* in the early 1920s. Trimmers were engine-room crewmen with the dirty, unenviable job of making sure that coal was evenly distributed in the bunkers and that the firemen were well supplied with fuel for stoking the boiler furnaces.

Forsyth Point (52°10'00" 131°04'00" N side of Houston Stewart Channel, between Moresby I and Kunghit I, QCI). William Codrington Forsyth was 1st lt on HMS *Virago*, under Cdr James Prevost, during its 1853 survey of Houston Stewart Channel. He served on the Pacific Station, 1852–55, and retired from the RN with the rank of capt in 1869.

Fort Defiance. *See* Adventure Cove.

Fort McLoughlin. *See* McLoughlin Bay *and* Bella Bella.

Fort Nass. *See* Fort Point, *below, and* Port Simpson.

Fort Point (54°59'00" 129°55'00" N side of Nass Bay, N of Prince Rupert). The HBC's Ft Nass was established near

F

this spot in 1831 by chief trader Capt Aemilius Simpson. He died there later that year, and the post was renamed Fort Simpson in his honour. It was soon found to be in an unsuitable spot—difficult to access and bitterly cold in winter—and was rebuilt at the present site of Port Simpson (qv), N of Prince Rupert, in 1834. After the old building had been stripped of useful materials and abandoned, local First Nation groups had such a Saturday night, according to Capt John Walbran's *British Columbia Coast Names*, as they had never had before: "The company had made them a parting present of a 25-gallon cask of rum, and with this aid to festivity the Indians duly celebrated the event. No sleep could be obtained on the *Dryad*, anchored a short distance from the shore, a drunken orgy of the wildest kind taking place, firearms were discharged and shrieks and yells filled the air. Among it all could be heard the ripping and hammering of timber, and when the short summer night was over the destruction of the fort was nearly complete." Simpson's body was taken south as well and reburied at the new post. *See also* Lax Kw'alaams.

Fort Rupert. *See* Rupert Inlet.

Fort Simpson. *See* Port Simpson.

Fort Victoria. *See* Victoria.

Forward Bay (50°31'00" 126°23'00" S side of W Cracroft I, Johnstone Str), **Forward Harbour** (50°29'00" 125°44'00" E of Wellbore Channel and Hardwicke I, NE of Sayward), **Forward Inlet** (50°30'00" 128°02'00" N side of entrance to Quatsino Sd, NW end of Vancouver I). HMS *Forward* was the quintessential W coast RN gunboat, especially designed for patrolling inshore waters and imposing law and order. Like its sister ship, HMS *Grappler*, it was a tiny 60-hp steam vessel of 211 tonnes, with two guns and a crew of 36. Built in 1855, it arrived at Esquimalt in 1860 and worked on the coast until 1869, attending to many emergencies and disturbances. In 1860, for instance, under Lt Charles Robson, the *Forward* assisted the disabled *Florencia* off Vancouver I's W coast and rescued the shipwrecked crew of the *Consort*, spending so long en route that it was feared, in Victoria, that the gunboat had been lost. In 1861 it attacked a camp of renegade Haida near Cape Mudge, made arrests and recovered property stolen from vessels and communities on the S coast. Under Lt Horace Lascelles, in 1863, the *Forward* destroyed a Lamalcha village on Kuper I while searching for the murderers of a Gulf Is family. The next cdr, Lt D'Arcy Denny, took it 20 km up the uncharted Nass R in 1866 to "show the flag." Lt Thomas Larcom was the gunboat's final RN cdr; after his stint it was auctioned off for $7,000 to the Mexican navy and shortly afterwards seized by rebels and burned. *W*

Fosbak Point (52°16'00" 127°37'00" E entrance to Jenny Inlet, King I, NE of Bella Bella). Engelbret Fosbak was a member of the original group of Norwegian colonists that established a community in the Bella Coola valley in 1894. He served as the colony's treasurer.

Foster Island (50°42'00" 126°50'00" Between Salmon Channel and George Passage, E end of Queen Charlotte Str). Maj George F Foster, a retired British Army officer, came to Victoria in 1859 and bought property on Esquimalt Hbr. He was named to Vancouver I's colonial legislative assembly of 1860–64, during which period he opposed the government of James Douglas and made controversial attempts to restrict borrowing and reduce the selling price of Crown land. He returned to England about 1870 and later was appointed to an official post at the British African colony of Gold Coast, where he died in 1887, according to Capt John Walbran. The Victoria *Colonist*, however, states that he died at Demerara (British Guiana). *W*

Foster Point (48°58'00" 123°40'00" S end of Thetis I, Gulf Is). Marine engineer and machinist Robert Foster (1857–1933) was born at NY and came to Victoria with his parents in 1860. He married Mary Jane McKinlay (1863–1918), from Ft Erie, Ont, at Victoria in 1883. Foster worked for BC Towing and Transportation Co and served on a number of historic vessels, including the *Beaver*, *Grappler*, *Pilot*, *Sardonyx*, *Cariboo and Fly*, *Gertrude* and *Joan*. He owned a quarry on this point from which stone was hauled by barge to his shipyard on Bay St in Victoria and used in the construction of the old post office and other city buildings.

Foster Rocks (51°42'00" 128°05'00" N end of Kwakshua Channel, S side of Hakai Passage, S of Bella Bella). William Wasborough "Billy" Foster, CMG (1875–1954), was a British engineer who came to Canada and worked for the CPR. In 1910 he was appointed BC's deputy minister of Public Works and in 1913 elected a Conservative MLA for Vancouver I. Foster was a brigadier in WWI (DSO with two bars, MC), then president of Pacific Engineers Ltd after the war. He was also appointed president of the Canadian Legion and the Canadian National Parks Assoc, and was an aide-de-camp to three govs gen. In 1935, in an attempt to control corruption, he was named Vancouver's police chief. During WWII, as a maj gen, Foster commanded defence projects in NW Canada. Later he became head of the BC Power Commission. He was also a keen mountaineer, involved in first ascents of Mt Robson (1913) and Mt Logan (1925), and president of the Alpine Club of Canada from 1920 to 1924. Foster Peak in Kootenay National Park and Mt Colonel Foster on Vancouver I are also named for him. *E*

Foucault Bluff (48°54'00" 125°05'00" SE side of Tzartus I, Barkley Sd, W side of Vancouver I). Named for the 1st mate of the French ship *Bordelais*, under Capt Camille de Roquefeuil, which visited Barkley Sd for two weeks in Sept 1817 while circumnavigating the globe on a trading voyage. Foucault, whose first name is unknown, had served as a lt in the French navy; on the BC coast he explored Bamfield and Grappler inlets with the ship's boats. Roquefeuil returned to the PNW the following year, visiting Nootka Sd and the QCI. *See also* Bordelais Its *and* Roquefeuil Bay.

Fougner Bay (51°54'17" 127°51'09" S entrance to Burke Channel, E of Bella Bella), **Fougner Point** (52°24'19" 127°22'46" S side of Dean Channel, E of Ocean Falls). Iver Fougner (1870–1947), born at Lillehammer, Norway, immigrated to Minnesota and worked as a teacher before joining the first group of Norwegians to settle in the Bella Coola valley in 1894. Articulate and intelligent, he served as the group's secretary and as a member of its managing committee. He was also the settlement's first schoolteacher. Fougner's writings are an important source of information about the colony. In 1901 he became the first person to receive a teacher's certificate at the old Vancouver Normal School; in 1909 he was named Indian agent for the Bella Coola region. Mt Fougner, S of Bella Coola, is also named for him.

Foul Bay. *See* Gonzales Bay.

Fox Islands (51°05'00" 127°37'00" Entrance to Slingsby Channel, NW side of Queen Charlotte Str). George Lane Fox (1810–96) was a member of an aristocratic Yorkshire family, occupants of Bramham Park estate. He was high sheriff of Leitrim in 1846 and high sheriff of the W Riding of Yorkshire in 1873. Lt Daniel Pender named several features in this vicinity after Yorkshire "sporting" families during his 1865 survey work. *W*

Fox Point (52°44'00" 129°16'00" NW side of Aristazabal I). George Thomas Fox (1868–1924) was born at Victoria, where his father, George Fox, was an early businessman. George Thomas operated a cutlery store there on Broad St for many years. He married Minnie Ellwood (1880–1960) at Victoria in 1894.

Frances Rock (52°27'00" 129°20'00" SE of Conroy I, off W side of Aristazabal I, Hecate Str). Named in 1927 by regional hydrographer Henri Parizeau after Frances Steele, wife of Alexander Johnston, deputy minister of Marine and Fisheries in the federal government, 1910–33. Johnston was a former Cape Breton newspaper publisher, MLA and MP (*see* Mt Johnston). Nearby Steele Rk is also named for her.

Francis Bay (52°22'00" 131°16'00" E side of Burnaby I, off SE Moresby I, QCI). After mining engineer Francis Poole, who found copper deposits in this part of the QCI in 1862. *See* Poole Inlet.

Francisco Island (50°17'00" 125°12'00" Okisollo Channel, S of Maurelle I, N end of Str of Georgia), **Francisco Point** (50°01'00" 125°09'00" SE end of Quadra I). After Spanish naval officer Juan Francisco de la Bodega y Quadra. *See* Bodega Anchorage.

Francis Island (48°55'00" 125°31'00" SE end of Ucluelet Inlet, Barkley Sd, W side of Vancouver I). Peter Francis (1826–85), a native of Jersey in the Channel Is, was owner of the sloop *Leonede* and an early trader in the Ucluelet area. He was a partner with William Banfield, first white settler on Barkley Sd in the late 1850s. After Banfield's suspicious death in 1862, Francis remained at Ucluelet, where he operated a trading post but joined forces with two other pioneer traders, William Spring and Hugh McKay of Victoria. In the 1870s he operated the schooner *Surprise*, and in 1874 took Bishop Charles Seghers and Fr Augustin Brabant along the W coast of Vancouver I in search of mission sites. The name was suggested in 1912 by Charles Spring, son of Capt William Spring. Formerly known as Round I.

Francis Peninsula (49°37'00" 124°03'00" E side of Malaspina Str, S of Pender Hbr), **Francis Point** (49°36'11" 124°03'28" SW end of Francis Peninsula). The name Francis Peninsula was adopted in the 1930 BC gazetteer, changed to Beaver I (qv) in 1945, then changed back again in 1972 to conform to local usage. This geographical feature is a peninsula at low tide and an island at high. Francis Point is a much older name and appears on Admiralty charts from 1863. The 82-ha Francis Point Provincial Park and Ecological Reserve was established in 2001 after funds were raised to acquire the property from its long-time private owners, the McQuarrie family. It is not known who Francis was.

Francis Point (54°03'00" 130°16'00" N end of Elliott I, Malacca Passage, S of Prince Rupert). After Midshipman Francis Chalmers, who served on the BC coast as an RN draftsman aboard the hired survey vessel *Beaver*, 1866–67. *See* Chalmers Anchorage.

Frankham Point (50°47'00" 127°35'00" Goletas Channel, S of Hurst I, N end of Vancouver I). Able Seaman David George Frankham, from Esquimalt, was killed in action on Oct 22, 1940, aged 19. He was serving aboard destroyer HMCS *Margaree*, which sank on convoy duty in the N Atlantic after colliding in rough weather with merchant freighter *Port Fairy*; 142 crew members were lost. His name is inscribed on the Halifax Memorial.

Franklin Glacier (51°16'00" 125°23'00" Head of the Franklin R, between head of Knight Inlet and Mt Waddington), **Franklin River** (51°05'00" 125°34'00" Flows S into head of Knight Inlet). Pioneer rancher Benjamin Franklin came to the Chilcotin region with his family

F

from Washington state in 1886 and bought land at the S end of Tatla Lk. In 1892 he explored a route from Tatla Lk down the Klinaklini R valley to the head of Knight Inlet as a possible shortcut for shipping his cattle to southern BC. Franklin sold out to Bob Graham in 1902 and moved to the Alexis Ck area.

Franklin Island (49°28'00" 123°55'00" Just W of Merry I, S entrance to Welcome Pass, Str of Georgia). Presumably named after Victoria-born William Thomas Franklin (1868–1955), first lighthouse keeper at Merry I, 1902–32. Will and his first wife, Mary Ann Clachar (1865–1941), pre-empted the rest of Merry I and did some modest farming. After Mary Ann's death, Will remarried and remained on Merry I until 1953.

Franklin River (49°06'00" 124°49'00" Flows W into Sproat Narrows, Alberni Inlet, S of Port Alberni, Vancouver I). This feature, originally called Franklin's R, was named in 1864 by members of the Vancouver I Exploring Expedition after Selim Franklin (1814–84). He and his brothers Lumley (Victoria's second mayor; d 1873) and Edward were members of a Jewish banking family from Liverpool who settled in California in 1849. Selim and Lumley joined the Fraser R gold rush, founded a Victoria auction house and land agency, and were appointed the colony's official auctioneers by James Douglas. Selim, an expert chess player, was elected to Vancouver I's legislative assembly, 1860–66, and was a prime backer of the Vancouver I expedition, which was organized primarily to search for gold and was led by botanist Robert Brown. Both brothers helped found the Victoria Philharmonic Society and both died at San Francisco, as did Edward Franklin. Franklin Camp, established near the river in 1934 by Bloedel, Stewart & Welch, was an important base for railway logging. The river's First Nation name was Owatchet.

Frank Rock (51°19'00" 127°33'00" Entrance to Margaret Bay, Smith Sd). After Victoria meteorologist Frank Napier Denison. *See* Denison I.

Fraser Island (50°51'00" 127°40'00" E side of Port Alexander, Nigei I, off NE Vancouver I). After RN officer Alexander Fraser Boxer. *See* Boxer Point.

Fraser Point (54°14'00" 130°23'00" S entrance to Tremayne Bay, S side of Digby I, just SW of Prince Rupert). Alexander Fraser was a chainman on the early GTP crews that surveyed this area after it had been selected as the railroad terminus. (Besides wielding the surveyor's measuring chain, the chainman also carried out numerous other survey duties and acted as assistant to the head of a survey party.)

Fraser Reach (53°14'00" 128°47'00" Between NE side of Princess Royal I and the mainland). Scottish lawyer and

journalist Donald Fraser (c 1811–1897) reached Victoria in 1858 after having travelled to California in 1849 to cover the gold rush as a special correspondent for the *Times* (London). He wrote about the BC gold rush as well and became a favourite of Gov James Douglas, who appointed him to Vancouver I's legislative council, 1858–62 and 1864–66. Fraser prospered at various business ventures and speculated in property, becoming a major landowner in Victoria. He returned to the UK about 1866 and sat on the self-styled London Committee for Watching the Affairs of British Columbia, an early lobby group opposed to the union of the colonies of Vancouver I and BC. Fraser returned to BC for six months in 1872 and spent much time visiting his old friend, now Sir James Douglas. The Haisla people know the N portion of this channel as P'nis (pronounced *puh-NEES*) and the S part as C'elitan (*tsuh-LEE-tuhn*). W

Fraser River (49°07'00" 123°11'00" Flows NW from the Rocky Mtns, then S and W to the Str of Georgia). Named in 1813 by David Thompson, fellow officer and fur trader with the NWC, after Simon Fraser (1776–1862), superintendent of the district of New Caledonia. Fraser was born in Vermont, joined the NWC in 1792 and was made a partner a decade later. Given the task of developing trade W of the Rocky Mtns, he established Ft McLeod, the first permanent European settlement in what is now BC, in 1805, then Ft St James, Ft Fraser and, in 1807, Ft George, near the present site of Prince George. In 1808 he and 23 others made a famously difficult journey to the mouth of the Fraser, discovering to their regret that it was neither navigable nor connected to the Columbia R. Fraser retired in 1818 to become a farmer at Cornwall, Ont. His river was known by many names: Tacoutche Tesse, Cowichans' R, Rio Floridablanca, New Caledonia R, Jackanet R. Dozens of non-coastal features and communities are named either for Simon Fraser or for the Fraser, which at 1,399 km is the longest river wholly within the province and contains in its basin 65 percent of BC's population. *E W*

Frazer Bay (50°43'00" 125°28'00" Head of Loughborough Inlet, just E of Knight Inlet), **Frazer Island** (48°20'00" 123°37'00" Becher Bay, S end of Vancouver I). RN surgeon Thomas Frazer, while never on the BC coast, was associated with those who were. He served aboard HMS *Herald*, off China, in the late 1830s and was with Lt Cdr Henry Kellett on HMS *Starling* during the 1st Anglo-Chinese War of 1840–41. He retired in 1866 as a deputy inspector-gen, hospitals and fleets. Kellett, as a capt, surveyed the S coast of Vancouver I with HMS *Herald* in 1846 and named Frazer I at that time. Frazer Bay was the site of a logging camp in the 1950s and '60s. Nearby Frazer Ck is named after Frazer Bay.

Freberg Islet (53°30'00" 130°01'00" W of Anger I, Principe Channel, E of Banks I). Flying Officer Philip Gustave R

The Fraser Estuary

The mouth of the Fraser River isn't high on the "must visit" lists of most recreational boaters. It is a fascinating place to explore, however, with lots of coastal history and some intriguing place names. As you might expect, the municipality of Delta is home to much of the Fraser estuary. The best access is through Ladner, BC's version of a bayou town, surrounded by marshes and backwaters.

William and Thomas Ladner were brothers, resilient Cornishmen who came west for gold in 1858 but ended up as farmers, businessmen and politicians. Their rich, well-diked lands became the nucleus of a riverside village called Ladners Landing. This was a busy part of the world a century ago. Ferries ran from the landing to New Westminster and across the Fraser's South Arm to Lulu Island. Just west along the riverbank at Port Guichon, named after another pioneer farming family, was an important embarkation point for Victoria. From 1903 to 1931 the Great Northern Railway had a spur line to the port and operated a railway ferry from there to Sidney on Vancouver Island.

The islands of the Fraser estuary are flat and fertile but not very stable. They shift and change shape constantly in response to both natural variations in water flow and a century and a half of diking and dredging. The largest of the islands, home to the city of Richmond, was named in 1862 after Lulu Sweet, a member of the first theatre group to perform in New Westminster. "Her conduct, acting and graceful manners gave great satisfaction," according to a newspaper account, and Col Richard Moody, BC's lieutenant-governor, was sufficiently smitten to name the prominent feature after the young actress.

Deas Slough and Deas Island, over which the George Massey Tunnel runs, were named for a South Carolina tinsmith, John Sullivan Deas, who, like so many others, followed the gold trail to California and BC. After establishing himself as a merchant in New Westminster, he built one of the Fraser's first salmon canneries, on Deas Island, in 1873 and became a leader—and the only prominent black man—in the industry.

West of Ladner Reach, in an overgrown muddle of wetlands, lies the heart of the estuary, a well-protected area where few boaters go because of the unpredictable shallows. Here rushes and cattails provide camouflage for many species of birds—loons and grebes, great blue herons, dabbling ducks of every description, shorebirds, even snow geese—and also for a handful of squatters in ramshackle houseboats. The swampy landscape is like a west-coast Everglades, pungent with decay but visceral and compelling. You half expect to see an alligator or python.

Many of the islands in these South Arm marshes—Kirkland, Gunn, Barber, Duck, Rose and Williamson—were also diked and farmed. Several became private shooting clubs, patronized by wealthy Vancouver industrialists such as H R MacMillan. Now they are managed as wildlife habitat. Most were named after early settlers in the region. John Kirkland, for instance, built many of Delta's early roads. Behind an artificial

training wall along the Fraser's main shipping channel, a new accretion, Woodward Island, is forming. It is named after Nathaniel Woodward, who settled on Lulu Island with his son Daniel in 1874.

Farther upstream is Annacis Island, which acquired its name as the result of a mix-up. In the 1860s it was known as Murphy Island after Patrick O'Brian Murphy, a squatter. Next it was called Annance's Island after Francis Noel Annance, a talented, multilingual fur trader of mixed Abenaki descent who joined the North West Company and worked as a trapper at Fort George, at the mouth of the Columbia River. When the North West and Hudson's Bay companies merged, he stayed on as a clerk and postmaster.

Aerial view of the Fraser River, looking east from the Port Mann Bridge.
Courtesy Port Metro Vancouver

In 1824, Annance accompanied James McMillan on a survey of the lower Fraser River and, three years later, helped him establish Fort Langley. In 1835, after a stint at Fort Simpson on the Mackenzie River, Annance left the company, frustrated by its refusal to promote mixed-race employees (and in trouble over an affair he'd had with the wife of his superior, John Stuart). Annance moved home to Quebec, where he farmed and taught school. Early Admiralty charts identify Annacis as Annance's Island, but an error crept into the 1858 edition and was never corrected, reminding us of the corruptibility of place names—and of words themselves.

Freberg, from New Westminster, was killed in action on Apr 11, 1943, when his Stirling heavy bomber, part of No 7 (RAF) Squadron, was shot down en route to Frankfurt. He was awarded the DFC in Sept 1942 when he survived the loss of another Stirling, parachuted into Holland and made his way back to Britain. He is buried at Hollerich Communal Cemetery in Luxembourg.

Frederick Arm (50°29'00" 125°16'00" Extends N from Cordero Channel, between Loughborough Inlet and Bute Inlet), **Frederic Point** (50°11'00" 125°03'00" E entrance to Evans Bay, Read I, NE of Campbell R). After Capt Sir Frederick Evans, hydrographer of the RN, 1874–84. *See* Evans Bay. It is not known how the "k" got dropped on Frederic Point, though the incorrectly spelled name appears on an Admiralty chart as early as 1862 (based on an 1860 survey by Capt George Richards). Frederick Arm was originally named Ensenada del Estero, or "Inlet of the Lagoon," by Dionisio Alcalá-Galiano and Cayetano Valdés during their expedition of 1792 (*see* Estero Basin).

Frederick Bay (51°02'00" 127°14'00" S side of Seymour Inlet, NW side of Queen Charlotte Str), **Frederick Sound** (51°01'00" 126°43'00" S of head of Seymour Inlet). After Frederick Seymour, gov of BC, 1864–69. *See* Seymour Inlet. **Frederick Islands** (51°02'00" 127°32'00" Entrance to Allison Hbr, NW side of Queen Charlotte Str) are probably named for him as well.

Frederick Island (53°56'00" 133°11'00" W side of Graham I, QCI). After Frederick Ingraham, nephew of Boston fur trader Joseph Ingraham of the *Hope* (*see* Ingraham Bay). Ingraham actually gave the name Young Frederick's I to Hippa I (qv), farther S, in 1791 or '92. In 1793, Capt George Vancouver changed that name back to Hippa and transferred Frederick's name to this feature, which was known to the Haida as Siscwai. *D*

Frederick Point (54°15'00" 130°22'00" SE side of Digby I, just E of Prince Rupert). After Frederick Lima, on the Pacific Station in 1866–67 as paymaster aboard HMS *Malacca*. *See* Lima Point. (Another source claims that this point was named for an instrument man on the first survey of Prince Rupert Hbr after it had been named as the terminus of the GTP.)

Frederic Point. *See* Frederick Arm.

Frederiksen Point (50°48'00" 128°21'00" N of head of Hansen Lagoon, E of Cape Scott, NW tip of Vancouver I). Theo Frederiksen was one of the original Danish settlers at Cape Scott, arriving in 1896 with wife Johanne and family. With a partner, Carl Rasmussen, he managed to transport a small, disassembled sawmill to the cape and produce lumber for housing and for the colony's boat, the *Cape Scott*. Frederiksen and N P Jensen set up driftwood fences

and planted clover to stabilize and reclaim the sand dunes between Guise Bay and Experiment Bight; then they raised dairy and beef cattle. Most of the colonists were gone by WWI, but members of the Frederiksen family were the last to leave, remaining until 1941.

Freeman Island, Freeman Passage, Freeman Rock. *See* Cape Freeman.

Freeman Point (52°33'00" 128°29'00" S end of Cone I, Klemtu, NW of Bella Bella). C A Freeman was chief engineer of the W coast survey vessel *Parry* in the late 1940s. Formerly known as Bare Point.

French Beach (48°23'00" 123°56'00" E of Point No Point, SW end of Vancouver I). British naturalist James George French (1865–1952) travelled the world to acquire exotic animals for zoos. He once brought home a small elephant. A brother of British WWI field marshal Sir John French, Earl of Ypres, he came to Canada in 1887, farmed at Swan Lk in Saanich and also pre-empted land at French Beach, eventually settling there with his animal menagerie. His wife, Jane Goudie (1884–1933), ran a rabbit farm. James was an early conservationist who also protected areas of wildlife habitat at Victoria and Sheringham Point. French Beach Provincial Park, 59 ha, was established in 1974.

Freshfield Point (52°58'00" 132°19'00" SW tip of Hibben I, off NW Moresby I, QCI). William Freshfield was assistant to master George Moore on HMS *Thetis*, under Capt Augustus Kuper. He played an active role in the 1852 survey of this area. In 1853 he transferred to HMS *Cockatrice*, aboard which he is believed to have died. *W*

Fresh Rock (50°36'00" 126°42'00" S side of Swanson I, SE end of Queen Charlotte Str). The name was suggested by the hydrographic service because the rock is located at the entrance to Freshwater Bay (*see below*). Formerly known as Bare Rk.

Freshwater Bay (50°36'00" 126°42'00" S side of Swanson I, Blackfish Sd, SE end of Queen Charlotte Str). European immigrants first settled at this ancient First Nation village site in the early 1900s. A man named Funkly established a floating fish-buying camp, the White Beach Trading Co, there, 1914–24, while ABC Packing Co ran a salmon saltery, 1919–28. A store and post office were located on the bay in the 1930s and '40s. The family of fisherman and author Bill Proctor acquired the store by 1940 and operated it, along with a fish-buying station, until 1962.

Friendly Cove (49°36'00" 126°37'00" SE end of Nootka I, W side of Vancouver I). Capt James Cook was the first European to reach this historic spot, in Apr 1778, calling it "a very snug harbour" with a large village. It was named in 1786 by James Strange, the British E India Co factor in

F

Historic Friendly Cove on Nootka Island. *Greg Shea*

charge of the second fur-trading expedition to reach the PNW coast, whose officers made a survey of the harbour. The name appears in the 1790 *Voyages* of John Meares. On Alejandro Malaspina's 1791 chart, the harbour is called Puerto de la Santa Cruz de Nuca. The Mowachaht (Nuu-chah-nulth) First Nation community located here was that of Chief Maquinna, and its name was Yuquot (qv), which can be translated as "windy place." Maquinna was well known to all the early visitors to the BC coast; he managed to control much of the fur business in the region and make Yuquot and Nootka Sd the main centre for trade. Friendly Cove was, in fact, the PNW's most important point of contact and interaction between First Nation and European cultures in the late 18th century. *W*

Frigon Islets (50°25'00" 127°29'00" E side of Neroutsos Inlet, N of Port Alice, NW Vancouver I). Edouard "Ned" Frigon (1834–1917), from Que, came W to BC in 1858 to follow the gold rush. He was one of the first white settlers on N Vancouver I and established trading posts at several locations, including Hope I off the N end of Vancouver I and Koprino Hbr in Quatsino Sd. He opened a store in 1895 on Limestone I, opposite Quatsino village, and built the Central Hotel there in 1909. Frigon eventually moved to the Port Alice area, where he had earlier obtained Crown grants of land. The Frigon Its were originally known as the Dog Its. *E*

Froek. *See* Frolander Bay (*below*).

Frolander Bay (49°45'00" 124°17'00" E side of Malaspina Str, NW of mouth of Jervis Inlet). Nils Frolander (1839–1908), a native of Sweden, established a fur-trading post and homestead at this location in the 1880s. He and his wife, Annie, also ran a post office there, named Froek, 1894–1902. Frolander was an early pre-emptor in W Vancouver as well, at Caulfeild, where he is listed on the application as a millwright; he sold this land as soon as he obtained a Crown grant for it.

Fulford Harbour (48°46'00" 123°26'00" SE side of Saltspring I, Gulf Is), **Fulford Reef** (48°27'00" 123°14'00" N of Chatham Is, W side of Haro Str, just E of Victoria). Capt John Fulford (1809–88) was in command of HMS

Ganges, the flagship of Rear Adm Robert Baynes on the Pacific Station, 1857–60. Before that he had been capt of HMS *Conway*. He reached the rank of rear adm himself in 1866 and was eventually promoted to adm, retired, in 1877. Nearby Fulford Ck also honours him, as does Captain Passage between Saltspring I and Prevost I. In 1859, RN surveyor Capt George Richards named several features on and around Saltspring I in association with Rear Adm Baynes. Today the pretty village of Fulford Hbr is a terminus for ferries to Vancouver I. *E W*

Postcard view of Fulford Harbour. *Author's collection*

Fuller Point (52°42'00" 131°26'00" E end of Lyell I, E of Moresby I, QCI). Jonathan Fuller was a seaman aboard the US vessel *Columbia Rediviva* on its first fur-trading voyage to the PNW, 1787–90, under Capt John Kendrick and Capt Robert Gray.

Fulton Passage (51°50'00" 128°15'00" S of Spider I, between Kildidt Sd and Queens Sd). Wing Cdr John "Moose" Fulton, DSO, DFC, AFC, was killed in action on July 29, 1942. He was born at Kamloops in 1912 and joined the RAF in 1934, becoming a pilot officer with a bomber transport group in Egypt. In WWII he flew Wellington bombers as cdr of RCAF No 419 Squadron and received his many awards for making more than 50 operational sorties, attacking industrial centres, dockyards, towns and airfields. Fulton is commemorated at the Runnymede Memorial, near Windsor, England. Fulton Passage, adopted in 1944, is one of many WWII aviation-related names in the area.

Funter Island (49°42'00" 126°38'00" In Kendrick Inlet, between Strange I and Nootka I, W side of Vancouver I), **Funter Point** (52°18'00" 131°13'00" S side of Skincuttle Inlet, SE Moresby I, QCI). Robert Funter was 2nd mate of the *Felice Adventurer* in 1788, under John Meares, and visited the PNW that summer to establish a fur-trading post at Nootka Sd and build the *North West America*, the first European vessel constructed on the BC coast. Funter was put in command of this 40-tonne schooner and took it to Hawaii for the winter. He returned in 1789 to Nootka, where Spanish naval officer Estéban Martínez seized his tiny ship and took it to Mexico, along with Funter and his crew, who were later released.

G

Gaarden Point (52°15'00" 127°22'00" SE side of King I, W side of Burke Channel, E of Bella Bella). Ole J Gaarden (1842–1914) was a blacksmith, one of the original Norwegian settlers who colonized the Bella Coola valley in 1894. He received a Crown land grant in the area in 1901.

Wave-eroded sandstone formations, such as this one on Gabriola Island, can also be found elsewhere in the Gulf Islands. *Kevin Oke*

Gabriola Island (49°10'00" 123°48'00" Just E of Nanaimo, W side of Str of Georgia), **Gabriola Passage** (49°07'45" 123°42'08" Between Valdes I and Gabriola I), **Gabriola Reefs** (49°09'00" 123°39'00" Off E end of Gabriola I), **Gaviola Island** (49°09'31" 123°41'18" One of the Flat Top Is, off E end of Gabriola I). The origin of the name Gabriola is uncertain. It is generally supposed that Spanish naval officer José Narváez, on his historic 1791 exploration of the Str of Georgia, gave the name Punta de Gaviola (Gaviola Point) to the E end of the 59-sq-km island. Gaviola was sometimes written Gabiola ("b"

and "v" are often pronounced similarly in Spanish), and became corrupted to Gabriola as the result of a mid-19th-century British mapping error. But what does Gaviola refer to? PNW cartography expert Henry Wagner claims that Narváez had actually named this point Gaviota, Spanish for seagull. More recent research by Nick Doe, of the Gabriola Historical & Museum Society, disputes this notion. Doe points out that Gaviola is an aristocratic Spanish family name and suggests that Simón de Gaviola y Zabala (born about 1577), paymaster of the Spanish naval fleet guarding trade routes to the Americas, was a likely candidate to be honoured with a geographic name. He also argues that it was probably applied by Juan Francisco de la Bodega y Quadra, not Narváez. Flat Top I was renamed Gaviola I in 1944 to recall the original Spanish designation. Gabriola I was first settled by coal miners from Nanaimo; it was the site of an early brickyard and a source of sandstone for building. In the early 2000s it had a year-round population of almost 3,000 and was popular as a recreation and boating destination. Currents in Gabriola Passage can exceed 8 knots (15 km/h). *E*

Gadu Point (54°46'55" 130°10'50" S entrance to Kwinamass Bay, Portland Inlet, N of Prince Rupert). This name may derive from a Tsimshian First Nation word meaning "prominent."

Galahad Point (50°04'00" 124°41'00" N side of Theodosia Inlet, E of Lancelot Inlet, NW of Powell R). Named in association with Lancelot Inlet after King Arthur's knights of the Round Table. Sir Galahad was the son of Sir Lancelot.

Galbraith Bay (49°24'00" 123°22'00" SW of Grafton Bay, W side of Bowen I, Howe Sd, NW of Vancouver). Edward Davidson Galbraith (1854–1912) pre-empted land here in 1900 and was issued a Crown grant in 1907. He was a former grocer who had been advised to get plenty of fresh air for the sake of his health. Edward and his wife, Mary Moore (1864–1942), a music teacher, were both of Irish heritage, born in Ont and strong Baptists. They hired Japanese workers to cut shingle bolts from the cedars on their property, cleared land, raised livestock and homesteaded.

Galiano Bay (49°42'00" 126°28'00" SE side of Tlupana Inlet, Nootka Sd, W side of Vancouver I), **Galiano Gallery** (49°11'29" 123°52'17" Just S of Malaspina Point, NW end of Gabriola I), **Galiano Island** (48°56'00" 123°27'00" NE of Saltspring I, SW Str of Georgia, Gulf Is). Galiano I was named in 1859 by RN surveyor Capt George Richards after Spanish naval officer Dionisio Alcalá-Galiano. *See* Alcala Point. Mt Galiano, on the S end of the island, is also named for him. The 57-sq-km island saw white settlement by the 1870s, and several small communities formed. Today it is a popular summer tourist destination, served by BC Ferries, and has a year-round population of about 1,000. Many artists and writers call Galiano home. Galiano Gallery is a dramatic overhanging sandstone formation noted by Alcalá-Galiano and sketched by the expedition's artist, Manuel José Cardero. A print loosely based on this drawing appeared in Alejandro Malaspina's *Voyages*, published posthumously in 1885. By this time the exact location of Malaspina's Gallery—as the feature was also known—had been forgotten, and it had to be "rediscovered" by local residents in the early 1900s. *E W*

Montague Harbour on Galiano Island. *Kevin Oke*

Gallows Point (49°10'00" 123°55'00" S end of Protection I, Nanaimo Hbr). Two Cowichan (Quw'utsun') First Nation men, Sque'is and Siam'a'sit, were hung here in 1853 after being found guilty of murdering an HBC shepherd at Lake Hill the previous Nov. The pursuit of the criminals, led by Gov James Douglas himself, was an early demonstration of British power. The steamship *Beaver* towed a string of smaller RN and HBC vessels filled with sailors and marines to Cowichan and Nanaimo. There, with threats

and a show of force, they coerced First Nation leaders into producing one suspect and captured the other in the forest. BC's first trial by jury took place aboard the *Beaver* and found the men guilty. Originally named Execution Point by HBC officials. *W*

G

Church camp, 1950s, Gambier Island. *Author's collection*

Gambier Harbour (49°26'00" 123°26'00" SW end of Gambier I), **Gambier Island** (49°29'35" 123°23'35" Howe Sd, NW of Vancouver), **Gambier Point** (49°27'00" 123°23'00" W entrance to Port Graves, Gambier I). RN officer John James Gambier (1756–1833) was born in the Bahamas, where his father was lt gov. He commanded HMS *Defence* in the 1794 British naval victory known as the Glorious First of June, from which many of Howe Sd's place names are drawn. Gambier was a lord of the Admiralty on several occasions between 1795 and 1807, and also gov of Nfld, 1802–4. As an adm and cdr-in-chief of the Baltic fleet, he captured the Danish navy at Copenhagen in 1807, for which he was named a baron. He is best known for a famous blunder: refusing to order the destruction of the French fleet—aground in the English Channel and vulnerable to British guns—during the Napoleonic Wars. In 1813, Lord Gambier helped negotiate the Treaty of Ghent between the UK and US. Gambier I is served from Langdale by passenger ferry. There are a number of recreational homes and church summer camps on the 58-sq-km island, and its shorelines are important log-booming grounds. Gambier Hbr, one of the island's two tiny communities, was formerly known as Grace Hbr (*see* Grace Is); a post office operated under this name in 1937–38 but was changed to Gambier I because of concerns that it might be confused with the Grace Hbr off Malaspina Inlet on Gifford Peninsula. Gambier Ck and Gambier Lk are named after Gambier I. *E W*

Gamble Point (54°06'00" 130°12'00" S end of Croasdaile I, Marcus Passage, just W of mouth of Skeena R). Thomas Gamble received Crown land grants in this area in 1890–91 and is described on the 1898 BC voters list as a farmer. Formerly known as Coffin Point.

G

Ganges (48°51'00" 123°30'00" E side of Saltspring I, Gulf Is), **Ganges Harbour** (48°51'00" 123°28'00" Just E of Ganges), **Ganges Shoal** (48°50'00" 123°27'00" W side of Ganges Hbr). HMS *Ganges*, under Capt John Fulford, was on the Pacific Station, 1857–60, as the flagship of Rear Adm Robert Baynes. This 84-gun, 2,039-tonne vessel was the last RN sailing ship of the line on active foreign service; it also had one of the longest careers of any RN ship, being launched at Bombay in 1821 and broken up in 1929, after serving for many years as a boys' training vessel at Falmouth and being renamed *Tenedos* (1906), *Indus* (1910) and *Impregnable* (1922). The shores of Ganges Hbr, which was previously known as Admiralty Bay, saw some of the earliest white settlement on Saltspring I, in 1859. Today Ganges is the commercial and service centre of the Gulf Is and their largest community, with a population of about 6,000. Ganges Ck takes its name from Ganges Hbr. *E W*

Gaowina Point (52°07'00" 131°01'00" Entrance to Heater Hbr, NE side of Kunghit I, QCI). QCI historian Kathleen Dalzell states that, according to a map made by ethnologist Charles Newcombe, the name comes from an ancient Haida site located farther NW on Kunghit I.

Garcin Rocks (52°13'00" 130°58'00" Off Benjamin Point, SE tip of Moresby I, QCI). Alpheus Dominic R "Alfus" Garcin (1879–1955), from Nfld, was the long-time gen manager of Consolidated Whaling Corp until 1947. He married May Dobinson (1883–1958) at Victoria in 1915. Consolidated purchased both QCI whaling stations, at Rose Hbr and Naden Hbr, in 1918. Formerly known as Danger Rks, the Garcins are an active sea-lion colony.

Garden Bay (49°38'00" 124°01'00" N side of Pender Hbr, NW of Sechelt), **Garden Peninsula** (49°38'00" 124°02'00" Just SW of Garden Bay). A provincial marine park and First Nation reserve dominate most of this bay. The rest of the shoreline, plus that of adjacent Hospital Bay, was purchased in 1892, along with Garden Peninsula, by realtor Henry Darling. Darling donated some of his land for the Sunshine Coast's first hospital, St Mary's. The claim, sometimes heard, that these features were named after a former BC surveyor gen cannot be correct, as there was never anyone in that position named Garden. The site may have simply been a good garden spot. Garden Bay Lk is named after Garden Bay. The Sechelt First Nation name for the bay is Séxw'ámin. *E*

Garden Island (54°19'00" 130°23'00" Between Digby I and Tsimpsean Peninsula, just outside Prince Rupert Hbr). The island was named for its appearance. It was formerly a Tsimshian First Nation reserve, then owned by the GTP, then by the city of Prince Rupert, which used it as the community's first cemetery about 1908–13. The name is an old one and may date back well into the 19th century.

Gardner Canal (53°27'00" 128°25'00" Extends SE from Devastation Channel, S of Kitimat), **Mount Gardner** (49°22'36" 123°23'27" W side of Bowen I, Howe Sd, NW of Vancouver). Adm Lord Alan Gardner (1742–1809) was a friend and mentor of Capt George Vancouver, who served under him as a lt on HMS *Europa*, 1784–89. As a lord of the Admiralty, 1790–95, Gardner strongly recommended Vancouver as cdr of the historic RN expedition to the PNW. He was cdr-in-chief on the Jamaica Station, 1786–89, and in 1794, as a rear adm, participated in the English Channel victory over the French fleet known as the Glorious First of June. Promoted to adm in 1795, he was named Baron Gardner of Uttoxeter in 1800 and appointed cdr-in-chief of the Channel fleet in 1807. Vancouver named Port Gardner (now Port Gardner Bay) in Puget Sd in 1792 and Gardner's Channel (now canal) in 1793. Joseph Whidbey, master of HMS *Discovery*, explored the 192-km canal in the ship's boats and reported to Vancouver that BC's longest inlet "was almost an entirely barren waste nearly destitute of wood and verdure." In the early 1950s, the Canadian Hydrographic Service tried to change the name from canal to inlet (as had been done earlier with Alberni Canal). It was feared that foreign shipping companies, assuming a "canal" to be an artificial feature with concomitant fees and costs, might avoid the area. The Geographic Board of Canada, however, rejected the CHS request. *E W*

Garnet Point (49°56'00" 124°47'00" SE side of Savary I, NE Str of Georgia). Garnets—deep red, semi-precious gemstones—can be found here. This well-established local name was adopted in 1983.

Garnier Bluff (53°08'00" 128°35'00" At mouth of Aaltanhash Inlet, E of Princess Royal I). John Miller Garnier (1774–1802) was a midshipman aboard HMS *Chatham* on Capt George Vancouver's 1791–95 expedition to the PNW coast. He was promoted capt of HMS *Hawke* in 1801 and participated in the British takeover of Dutch and Danish possessions in the W Indies, where he died shortly afterwards of yellow fever. His older brother, Thomas Garnier, was dean of Winchester, 1840–72.

Garrard Group (49°14'00" 126°07'00" N of Russell Channel, S of Flores I, Clayoquot Sd, W side of Vancouver I). Edward Burdett Garrard (1876–1917), from England, obtained Crown grants for the N end of Esowista Peninsula in 1911–12. He married Eleanor Mary Watson (1873–1955) at Victoria in 1900. Garrard was a farmer, prospector and early postmaster at Tofino and served as customs collector and telegraph agent at Port Alberni, 1902–16. He was one of several brothers who were active in the region, including Francis Charles Garrard (1863–1942)—lighthouse keeper at Lennard I, telegraph lineman and agent, and postmaster at Tofino—and William Burdett Garrard (1867–1924). The Garrards were also strongly associated with Port Alberni, and several family members pre-empted land on Clayoquot Sd, Barkley Sd and Alberni Inlet. Edward enlisted in the BC Regiment in WWI and served overseas, where he was killed in action in Belgium.

Garry Point (49°07'00" 123°12'00" N mouth of the Fraser R, SW tip of Lulu I). Nicholas Garry (c 1782–1856) was deputy gov of the HBC, 1822–35. Born in Surrey, UK, he became a merchant in London, trading initially with Russia. His stepfather, Thomas Langley, was an HBC director, and Garry was named a director also about 1817. In 1821 he played a key role in the NWC's merger with the HBC and was appointed president of the council of the HBC's northern dept. Garry Point was named by Capt Aemilius Simpson of the HBC schooner *Cadboro*, the first vessel to enter the Fraser R, in 1827. Ft Garry, the HBC post at what is now Winnipeg, was also named for him, as is the Garry oak, found in Canada only in SW BC.

Gartley Point (49°39'00" 124°55'00" S entrance to Comox Hbr, E side of Vancouver I). George Gartley (1842–1917), from NB, came to BC in 1872 with his wife, Margaret Jane Coburn (1845–1930), also a native of NB, and young son Ernest. They settled first on Burrard Inlet, where George logged for the Moodyville sawmill (he was a "spar-hewer and bull-puncher," according to Ernest's obituary). The family then crossed the Str of Georgia in a rowboat to Royston on Vancouver I and farmed the point of land now named for them. After a few years the Gartleys moved to Nanaimo and then back to the Vancouver area about 1905.

Garvey Point (52°46'00" 128°08'00" NE side of Mathieson Channel, E of Pooley I and Princess Royal I). Signalman William Garvey, of Vancouver, was killed in action Mar 18, 1945, aged 22. He was serving aboard HMCS *Guysborough*, a minesweeper torpedoed and sunk by a U-boat (*U-868*) while escorting a convoy in the Bay of Biscay, off France. Fifty-one crew members died. Garvey's name is inscribed on the Halifax Memorial.

Gatenby Rock (54°07'00" 133°08'00" NW of Sadler Point, off NW Graham I, QCI). John Gatenby was the boatswain aboard early fur-trading vessel *Queen Charlotte*, under Capt George Dixon, which visited the area in 1786–87. Named in 1907 by Capt Frederick Learmonth of the RN survey vessel *Egeria*.

Gaudin Islands (52°22'00" 128°29'00" W of Dowager I, Merilia Passage, Milbanke Sd). Named for Agnes Anderson (1849–1929), who married Capt James Gaudin (*see* Gaudin Passage) at Victoria in 1873. She was the second daughter of HBC explorer and chief trader Alexander Caulfield Anderson (*see* Anderson Is) and a true PNW pioneer, being born in Oregon Territory and raised as a child at Cathlamet on the lower Columbia R. The family moved to Victoria about 1858. When Agnes married, all the ships in Esquimalt Hbr were reported to have hung out flags that spelled the word "wedding" in order to commemorate the event.

Gaudin Passage (52°10'00" 131°06'00" N of Ellen I, Houston Stewart Channel, QCI), **Gaudin Point** (53°43'00" 128°50'00" NE end of Hawkesbury I, Devastation Channel, S of Kitimat), **Gaudin Rock** (52°36'00" 128°46'00" Off W entrance to Meyers Passage, S of Princess Royal I, Laredo Sd). Capt James Gaudin (1839–1913), a native of Jersey, crewed on E Indies- and Australia-bound trading vessels until 1865, when he became a ship's officer for the HBC, shuttling between London and Victoria. Gaudin married Agnes Anderson (1849–1929, *see* Gaudin Is) in Victoria in 1873 and settled there, working as a pilot and as owner of his own vessel, *Rover of the Seas*, until he joined the Dept of Marine and Fisheries in the 1880s. He served first as master of the lighthouse tender *Sir James Douglas*, then briefly as capt of CGS *Quadra* in 1892, during which time he struck an uncharted rock in Gaudin Passage and had to beach his vessel for repairs. Later that year he became the dept's Victoria agent, in charge of lighthouses, wrecks and any other federal marine business on the W coast. He remained in the post until 1911, a much-respected figure in BC nautical circles. Gaudin Point was named by Lt Col William Anderson, the dept's chief engineer, in 1898. *W*

Gaviola Island. *See* Gabriola I.

Gay Passage (50°06'00" 127°31'00" Entrance to Ououkinsh Inlet, Bunsby Is, off NW side of Vancouver I). Walter Gay is a character in *Dombey and Son*, an 1848 novel by Charles Dickens. Capt George Richards, who surveyed the area in 1862, named several features after aspects of this novel, including the Bunsby Is and Cuttle Is (qv). Gay Passage, though, was named much later by Capt John Walbran of the Dept of Marine and Fisheries, who examined the area in 1897. *W*

Gayward Rock (50°01'00" 127°23'00" NE of Aktis I, Kyuquot Sd, NW side of Vancouver I). Gayward Rk is believed to have been named after a Victoria-based sealing schooner, part of the large W coast sealing fleet that was active in the late 19th century. Formerly known as Channel Rk.

Geetla Inlet (51°30'00" 127°37'00" E side of Walbran I, Rivers Inlet), **Geetla Point** (51°29'00" 127°35'00" Entrance to Geetla Inlet). According to BC historians Helen and Philip Akrigg, when Rivers Inlet was re-surveyed in the late 1930s, a number of names were bestowed by the hydrographic service to honour the family of Methodist medical missionary Dr George Darby, who operated a summer hospital on the inlet for many years while based at Bella Bella. Geetla was a Heiltsuk First Nation nickname given to one of the Darby children.

G

Geneste Point (50°30'00" 125°51'00" SW entrance to Topaze Hbr, N side of Sunderland Channel, N of Johnstone Str). Louis Geneste (d 1872), from the Isle of Man, was 3rd lt aboard HMS *Topaze*, under Capt John Spencer, and served on the Pacific Station, 1859–63. He entered the RN in 1844, reached the rank of cdr in 1866 and was in command of gunboat *Torch* in the Mediterranean in 1871. Nearby Geneste Cone is also named for him.

Genn Islands (54°06'00" 130°17'00" Between Smith I and Porcher I, Marcus Passage, S of Prince Rupert). Edward Hawke Genn, from Falmouth, Cornwall, was a midshipman aboard HMS *Scout*, under Capt John Price, on the Pacific Station, 1865–68, where he temporarily served as a draftsman on the hired survey vessel *Beaver*, under Lt Daniel Pender. He was back on the BC coast as a sub-lt in 1870–71, based at Esquimalt with HMS *Scylla*, under Capt Frederick Herbert. He transferred to HMS *Daphne* on the E Indies Station and died at Calcutta in 1872. Named by Pender in 1867.

Genoa Bay (48°46'00" 123°36'00" N side of Cowichan Bay, SE end of Vancouver I). Probably named by early settler and trader Giovanni Baptiste Ordano (1838–1916) after his birthplace in Italy. Ordano travelled overland to California in 1856, then moved to BC and established the first store in the Cowichan district at Tzouhalem in 1858. He also had a store on San Juan I in the US and opened another branch at Cowichan Bay in 1868. Genoa Bay was the site of a large sawmill from the 1870s to 1925 and is today home to a marina and small residential community.

George Bay (52°18'00" 131°20'00" Head of Skincuttle Inlet, SE Moresby I, QCI), **George Island** (52°21'00" 131°13'00" One of the Copper Is, entrance to Skincuttle Inlet). Mining engineer Francis Poole gave the name George Hbr to the entrance to Slim Inlet, just S of today's George Bay, while prospecting in the area in 1862. George M Dawson of the Geological Survey of Canada changed Poole's name to George Bay in 1878. The hydrographic service later transferred the name to the current bay. Poole was referred to by the Haida as King-George-Tyee, or "important British person" ("King George" meant "British" in the Chinook jargon, a trade language used on the BC coast in the early days), and this is the probable source of the name. *D*

George Fraser Islands (48°54'00" 125°31'00" S of mouth of Ucluelet Inlet, W side of Vancouver I). George Fraser (1854–1944) came to Canada from Scotland in 1883 and arrived at Victoria in 1888. An experienced horticulturist, he played a key role in the establishment of Beacon Hill Park and also owned a farm in the Mt Tolmie area. He settled at Ucluelet in 1894 and operated a large nursery there—specializing in rhododendron hybrids, for which he was world renowned—until he was quite elderly. The village of Ucluelet holds an annual George Fraser Day and Heritage Fair in his honour each May. *E*

George Passage (50°41'00" 126°50'00" N side of Malcolm I, Queen Charlotte Str). Capt William E George (1834–1922), from London, UK, arrived on the BC coast about 1859, and from 1865 to 1868 was master of the trading schooner *Alpha*, the first vessel built at Nanaimo. After the wreck of the *Alpha* (see Alpha Bay), George worked for the Alaska Commercial Co as capt of the *Constantine* and then became a well-known Victoria-based pilot on both the BC and Alaska coasts. *W*

George Point (48°19'00" 123°32'00" S end of Bentinck I, SW of Victoria, S tip of Vancouver I). The origin of this name is uncertain. Before 1934, the feature was known as Tughope Point, after the tug *Hope*, which was assisting the grounded freighter *Eemdyk* in this vicinity when it capsized, with the loss of six lives (see Eemdyk Passage).

George Point (54°03'00" 132°34'00" E side of Alexandra Narrows, entrance to Naden Hbr, N side of Graham I, QCI). After George Inskip, master of HMS *Virago* on the Pacific Station, 1852–55. See Inskip Channel. The point was the site of an old Haida village named Skaos. A salmon cannery (1910–19) and crab cannery (1919–24, 1933–40) also operated there.

Georgeson Bay (48°51'51" 123°20'30" S end of Galiano I, Gulf Is), **Georgeson Island** (48°51'00" 123°14'00" E of Mayne I, SE of Campbell Point), **Georgeson Passage** (48°49'00" 123°14'00" SE end of Mayne I, between Mayne I and Samuel I). Henry "Scotty" Georgeson (1835–1927), a native of the Shetland Is, jumped ship at San Francisco and made his way to Victoria to join the Fraser R gold rush in 1858. He managed a hotel at Yale, then became one of Galiano I's first settlers in the early 1860s, pre-empting land in 1873 adjacent to what is now Georgeson Bay. After marrying his Lillooet First Nation spouse Sophy in 1881, he served as assistant keeper on the Sand Heads lightship at the mouth of the Fraser R, then was appointed the first keeper at the Georgina Point lighthouse on Mayne I in 1885. Henry worked at Georgina Point until 1921 and was succeeded as keeper by his son George Georgeson (1873–1949), who acquired Georgeson I in 1908. Other family members followed Henry to BC and became early homesteaders in the Gulf Is; several also worked in the lighthouse service or as pilots on the BC coast. Henry's brother James Georgeson (1849–1928), in particular, was a long-time keeper at the East Point lighthouse on Saturna I, succeeded by his son Peter Georgeson (1891–1968). Georgeson I's Sencoťen (Coast Salish) name is Tá'wen, meaning "coho salmon."

Georgetown Mills (54°28'00" 130°24'00" Head of Big Bay, N of Prince Rupert). Only ruins still exist of the historic, water-powered sawmill that operated on Big Bay from 1874 until the late 1960s. Methodist missionary Thomas Crosby encouraged its construction in order to provide lumber for new "Christian" homes at Port Simpson and to employ Tsimshian First Nation workers. A trail and telegraph line connected the community to the mill, which boasted its own post office (named Big Bay from 1910 to 1920 and Georgetown Mills, 1920–28) and a school (in 1928). Georgetown Ck, site of a 6-m waterfall and a dam just E of the ruins, takes its name from the mill, as does nearby Georgetown Lk, but the identity of the original George seems to have disappeared with time. The bay provides important habitat for waterfowl.

Georgianna Point (53°08'00" 132°29'00" N side of Skidegate Channel, SW Graham I, QCI). The *Georgianna*, under Capt William Rowland, sailed to the QCI from Puget Sd in Nov 1851 to investigate reports of gold. The 41-tonne US vessel was wrecked and driven ashore in Skidegate Inlet in a sudden storm, then pillaged by a hostile group of waiting Haida. The ship's 27 crew members and passengers were held by the Haida (whether as "guests" or prisoners

depends on who is telling the story) until ransomed eight weeks later by Capt Lafayette Balch of the *Demaris Cove*, who had returned to the US when the *Georgianna* failed to rendezvous with him, been heavily armed by the US government and sailed back to the QCI by early 1852. *D*

Georgia Rock (54°13'00" 130°22'00" S of Digby I, just SW of Prince Rupert). CGS *Georgia* was a small (31-tonne, 18-m) wooden steamer built at Victoria about 1900 as a fisheries patrol vessel. In 1912, after striking a rock in Mud Bay, Alaska, the ship was sold to private interests and eventually caught fire and sank off Bishop Cove in 1915. Nearby Falcon and Kestrel rks were also named, in 1906–7, after other early federal fisheries protection vessels working on the BC coast.

Georgia, Strait of (49°30'00" 124°00'00" Between Vancouver I and SW BC mainland, S of Quadra I). Capt George Vancouver called this vital inland sea, now at the heart of BC's most populous region, the Gulph of Georgia. The name honoured England's King George III (1738–1820) and was formally bestowed by Vancouver and his

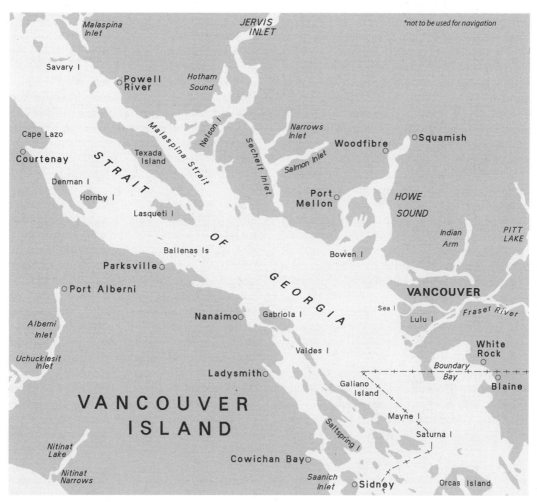

Strait of Georgia. *Reproduced with the permission of the Canadian Hydrographic Service*

officers on June 4, 1792, the king's birthday, at the same time that the navigator "took possession of the coast." The previous year, Spanish naval officers Francisco Eliza and José Narváez had been the first Europeans to explore the area, naming the strategic waterway the Gran Canal de Nuestra Señora del Rosario la Marinera. In 1858, RN surveyor Capt George Richards altered the form of the name from gulf to strait (though Gulf of Georgia is still in widespread use). In the early 2000s, a First Nations-backed initiative to change the name of the feature to the Salish Sea (qv) gained momentum. BC premier Gordon Campbell signalled acceptance of the idea in Mar 2008, saying that it was "really a matter of political respect and recognizing that the history of BC goes well beyond the history of Europeans coming to these shores." The strait extends 220 km from San Juan Is to Cape Mudge. *E W*

Georgina Point (48°52'00" 123°17'00" N tip of Mayne I, Gulf Is), **Georgina Shoals** (Just N of Georgina Point). Georgina Mary Berkeley (1793–1878) was the wife of Rear Adm Sir George Seymour, cdr-in-chief on the Pacific Station, 1844–46. They were married in 1811, when Seymour was a capt (*see also* Seymour Narrows). A boat party under Capt George Vancouver had camped in the vicinity of Georgina Point in 1792 while doing survey work; in 1881, Mayne I pioneer William Collinson found an English penny dated 1784 and the remains of a seaman's knife at this site. In 1885 a lighthouse was constructed there. *W*

Georgy Point (54°05'00" 130°11'00" N end of Kennedy I, S of Prince Rupert). Georgina "Georgy" Kennedy was the younger daughter of Arthur Kennedy, gov of Vancouver I in 1864–66 (*see* Arthur I). Lt Daniel Pender named this feature about 1866, at the same time that he named Elizabeth Peak on Kennedy I after Elizabeth Kennedy, the gov's older daughter (*see* Gilford Point). Pender presumably thought he was enhancing the association of Gov Kennedy with an island that many people, including Capt John Walbran, assumed was named for him. It was later discovered, however, that Kennedy I (qv) appeared on maps of the area well before Arthur Kennedy had arrived on the scene and was most likely named for Dr John Kennedy, an HBC chief trader at Port Simpson in the 1850s. *W*

Gerald Island (49°19'00" 124°10'00" Ballenas Channel, E of Dorcas Point, NW of Nanaimo, Str of Georgia), **Gerald Point** (52°26'00" 128°06'00" N end of Yeo I, N of Bella Bella). After British naval surgeon Gerald Yeo, who served on the Pacific Station, 1857–60. *See* Yeo Cove.

Germania Rock (52°07'00" 131°00'00" W of Rainy I, off E Kunghit I, QCI). The *Germania* was a 147-tonne whaler that operated in QCI waters in the early 1900s. Built at Oslo, Norway, about 1903 by the Aker shipbuilding company,

the 28.5-m steamship was originally employed in the Nfld whaling industry. It was purchased by the Pacific Whaling Co about 1907 and worked out of Rose Hbr, Naden Hbr and Sechart whaling stations until at least 1914. Germania Ck on Graham I is also named for this vessel.

German Point (52°05'00" 128°09'00" NE entrance to Hunter Channel, just S of Bella Bella). Capt Phillip Barry German was one of the first RCN officers to graduate from the new Royal Naval College of Canada, established at Halifax in 1911. He was a senior naval officer at Esquimalt in 1944, when this name was adopted.

Gertrude Point (53°38'00" 129°14'00" N entrance to Kitkiata Inlet, Douglas Channel, SW of Kitimat). Helen Gertrude Davies, born in PEI in 1873, was the eldest child of Sir Louis Davies, federal minister of Marine and Fisheries, 1896–1901. *See* Davies Bay. Capt John Walbran named this point and Helen Point opposite in 1898. He also named Ethel Rk in Principe Channel after Helen's sister.

Gertrude Rock (52°25'00" 129°23'00" SE of Conroy I, W of Aristazabal I, Hecate Str). Gertrude Gale (1877–1956) was married to Que-born Robert Henry Otley Gale (1878–1950), mayor of Vancouver in 1918–21 and also an alderman for three terms. Mayor Gale, a contractor and industrialist who failed twice in his efforts to become a Liberal MP, was an effective promoter of Vancouver as a major W coast port, especially for grain, following the opening in 1914 of the Panama Canal. The Gale family survived a murder attempt in 1933 when an intruder entered their home at night and turned on all the gas jets. Gertrude and Robert both died at Montreal.

Gibbons Point (53°33'00" 130°06'00" SW side of Wright I, Principe Channel, between Banks I and Pitt I). Flight Lt Noel James Gibbons, DFC, was killed in action Oct 22, 1944, aged 23, and is buried at Choloy War Cemetery in France. A talented athlete, he was born at Grande Prairie, Alberta, and grew up in W Vancouver. Gibbons was navigation leader for RCAF No 418 ("City of Edmonton") Squadron, which flew de Havilland Mosquito light bombers during WWII. He received his DFC (and bar) for making numerous sorties deep into enemy territory and for damaging or destroying more than 20 German aircraft.

Gibraltar Island (48°55'00" 125°15'00" Part of the Broken Group, Barkley Sd, W side of Vancouver I). Named in 1861 by Capt George Richards, of RN survey vessel *Hecate*, because it resembles a tiny Rock of Gibraltar when viewed from a particular perspective.

Gibson Cove (49°23'00" 125°56'00" E side of Herbert Inlet, Clayoquot Sd, W side of Vancouver I). William Fullerton Gibson (1869–1933) worked his way to BC as a carpenter and sawmill operator, and married Julia Earson Clark (1873–1964) at Vancouver in 1901. He was a gold miner during the Klondike rush, then worked at Vancouver's Hastings sawmill. In 1916, Gibson became a timber contractor at Clayoquot Sd, and at the end of WWI he built a small sawmill at Ahousat on Flores I. He and his four sons were Clayoquot entrepreneurs; they cut lumber and shingles, made boxes for canneries, fished, salted herring, operated boats, ran a general store and post office, and in the late 1920s constructed a number of pilchard-reduction plants, including their own at Ahousat. At the time of his death, William was trying to develop a gold mine at the head of Herbert Inlet. His sons—especially "Bull of the Woods" Gordon Gibson, later an outspoken MLA—became well known in the logging industry, building a large sawmill at Tahsis in 1945, which they sold to the E Asiatic Co in 1952. Much of Gibson Marine Provincial Park, established in 1967 on Flores I, was a gift from the Gibson family.

Gibson Group (53°57'00" 130°09'00" N of Pitt I, S of Kennedy I), **Gibson Island** (53°55'00" 130°10'00" Part of the Gibson Group). Lt Herbert William Sumner Gibson (1846–1923) served on the Pacific Station, based at Esquimalt, 1866–68. First he was on HMS *Topaze*, under Capt Richard Powell, and later on HMS *Sparrowhawk*. As an RN capt, Gibson had command of a number of vessels, including HMS *Wallaroo* (1891), *Curacoa* (1892), *Thunderer* (1896) and *Katoomba* (1897), and eventually rose to the rank of vice adm, in 1906. Named by Lt Daniel Pender in 1867. *W*

Gibson Point (52°04'00" 128°04'00" E entrance to Fannie Cove, Cooper Inlet, S of Bella Bella). Named after a clergyman on the BC coast, probably Rev W H Gibson, a missionary at Bella Coola (1907–21), but possibly Rev J B Gibson, who served at Anyox, then Smithers, and later became dean of Prince Rupert's Anglican cathedral in 1929 and bishop of Caledonia from 1945 until 1952, when he was killed in a car accident.

Gibsons (49°24'00" 123°30'00" W entrance to Howe Sd, NW of Vancouver). Retired RN officer George William Gibson (1829–1913) immigrated to Ont in 1878 and became a market gardener. He moved W with other family members and pre-empted land at this location in 1887. Gibson and his sons and son-in-law farmed and built a wharf for their vessel, *Swamp Angel*, then opened a general store in 1900. George was the community's first postmaster, 1892–1901 (the post office was originally called Howe Sd, then Gibsons Landing), and justice of the peace. Gibson Ck, which flows into Shoal Channel at this spot, is also named for him. The village of Gibsons, with almost 4,000 residents in 2007, got its first population boost in 1905, when a group of Finnish settlers arrived from the failed socialist utopian colony of Sointula on

The town of Gibsons on the Sunshine Coast. *Peter Vassilopoulos*

Malcolm I, and later became home to a large jam cannery. After WWII its economy depended on fishing, tourism and the pulp and paper mill at nearby Port Mellon. The Squamish First Nation term for the Gibsons area is Chekwelp, and a reserve by that name is located between Gibsons and Granthams Landing. *E*

Gikumi Point (51°18'00" 127°36'00" W end of Greaves I, Takush Hbr, Smith Sd). The 17-m *Gikumi* was built in Vancouver in 1954 for Fred Wastell, owner of the sawmill at Telegraph Cove on NW Vancouver I. It was originally constructed to tow logs for the mill but was also used as a pilot boat, harbour tug and cargo vessel. Stubbs I Whale Watching bought the *Gikumi* in 1980, and it became BC's earliest whale-watching craft. The name means "chief" in the Kwakwala language.

Gilbert Bay (52°02'00" 131°05'00" W side of Kunghit I, QCI). Jonathan Gilbert was a crewman aboard the early US fur-trading vessel *Columbia Rediviva* on its first visit to PNW waters in 1788–89.

Gildersleeve Bay (51°36'00" 127°46'00" S side of Fish Egg Inlet, E of Calvert I and Fitz Hugh Sd). George H "Doc" Gildersleve (1891–1956) came to BC from Oregon about 1918 with his wife, Amy Isadore Owens (1889–1955), and family. He worked as a handlogger on the central BC coast before founding Gilderslene Logging and building it into a substantial business. Doc supposedly got his nickname as a result of his midwifery skills; three of his six children were born at the family's isolated cabin on Burke Channel. He, his brother Bill Gilderslene (1889–1968) and other family members established the region's first truck-logging operations and had floating camps at Gardner Canal, Burke Channel, Smith Inlet, Rivers Inlet, S Bentinck Arm, Kimsquit, Draney Inlet and elsewhere. Confusion about this name has resulted in conflicting spellings; Gilderslene Bay and nearby Gilderslene Lk, for instance, both refer to the same family (as do Doc Ck and Amy Ck). Gilderslene is apparently the correct form.

Gilford Bay (50°40'00" 126°23'00" S side of Gilford I), **Gilford Island** (50°45'00" 126°20'00" Between Tribune Channel and Knight Inlet, E end of Queen Charlotte Str), **Gilford Rock** (50°40'00" 126°36'00" E of Bonwick I, off SW end of Gilford I). Capt Richard James Meade, Viscount Gilford (1832–1907), was cdr of HMS *Tribune* on the Pacific Station, 1862–64. He had served in the Crimean War and was badly wounded in the storming of Canton in 1857. Promoted to capt in 1859, he went on to a brilliant career: naval aide-de-camp to Queen Victoria (1872–76), lord of the Admiralty (1874–80), cdr-in-chief of the N America and W Indies stations (1885–86), cdr-in-chief at Portsmouth (1891–94) and adm of the fleet (1895). Meade became the 4th Earl of Clanwilliam in 1879 and was knighted in 1882. He retired from the RN in 1902. Nearby Gilford Ck and Gilford Lk are also named for him, as are Viscount I and Meade Bay. Gilford I, at 388 sq km, is the largest island in the Broughton Archipelago and the site of several small settlements, including Simoom Sd (Echo Bay) and the Kwakwaka'wakw First Nation village of Health Bay. Gilford Rk was formerly known as Whale Rk. *E*

Gilford Point (50°39'00" 126°26'00" S side of Gilford I, E end of Queen Charlotte Str). After Lady Elizabeth Henrietta Kennedy (d 1925), the eldest daughter of Arthur Kennedy, gov of Vancouver I, 1864–66. In 1867 she married the gallant Richard Meade, Viscount Gilford (*see above*), whom she met while he was based at Esquimalt in 1862–64 as cdr of HMS *Tribune*. In 1879, when her husband became an earl, she became the Countess of Clanwilliam. Nearby Port Elizabeth, Lady Is and Henrietta I are also named for her, as is Elizabeth Peak on Kennedy I (*see* Georgy Point).

Gil Island (53°12'00" 129°14'00" W side of Whale Channel, entrance to Douglas Channel, N of Caamaño Sd), **Gil Rock** (53°19'00" 129°12'00" Off N side of Gil I), **Mount Gil** (53°15'46" 129°11'50" NE side of Gil I). Spanish naval officer Jacinto Caamaño named Gil I in 1792 while charting BC's N coast in the *Aránzazu* and disproving the existence of the Str of Fonte, a mythical sea passage through N America. The derivation of the name is uncertain, though Capt John Walbran points out that Juan Gil was the ensign bearer aboard the *San Martin*, the Duke of Medina Sedonia's flagship, when the Spanish armada sailed against England in 1588. Juan Point on Gil I is also believed to be named for this figure. In Mar 2006 the *Queen of the North*, operated by BC Ferries, ran aground and sank off Gil I. Two passengers died. *W*

Gil Islet (52°43'00" 131°47'00" N entrance to Darwin Sd, off E side of Moresby I, QCI). QCI historian Kathleen Dalzell reports that this feature is named after James Gill, a broker who applied for a large timber licence in the region in 1907. It is not known how the spelling of his name became altered. The area was later the site of several copper claims.

Gillam Channel (49°48'00" 127°01'00" Entrance to Esperanza Inlet, W side of Vancouver I), **Gillam Islands** (50°27'00" 127°58'00" NW of Harvey Cove, entrance to Quatsino Sd, NW end of Vancouver I). Master mariner Edward Gillam (1864–1929) came W from NS in 1903, married Betty Buchholy (1869–1937) at Victoria in 1904 and spent many years with the CPR's BC Coast Steamship Service, becoming an authority on the W coast of Vancouver I. He was "a big, companionable man, kindly and firm, with great dignity and presence," according to W coast historian Margaret Horsfield, who "could control a group of drunken loggers with a glance." Gillam served as mate of the *Tees*, 1908–9, becoming skipper for 1909–13, then taking over as capt of *Princess Maquinna* and *Princess Mary* for the next 16 years. In 1929 he was named master of the CPR's newest steamship, the *Princess Norah*, but died suddenly as he was bringing that vessel into Tofino on its second voyage. Gillam Channel was named in 1929.

Gillan Point (53°38'00" 132°58'00" N of Port Chanal, W side of Graham I, QCI), **Gillen Harbour** (52°59'00" 129°36'00" S end of Dewdney I, Estevan Group, N of Caamaño Sd). William Hugh Gillen (1872–1930) began his life on the sea as a NS fisherman, then crewed out of Halifax to S America and the W Indies. He came to BC in 1895 and worked on sealers before being put in charge of the Bamfield lifeboat station in 1907, the year before he married Jessie Paterson Taylor (1882–1962) at Victoria. Gillen served on the CPR's *Empress of China*, on tugs in NY and the PNW, and with the five-masted schooner *Laurel Whalen* en route to Australia. In 1912 he was in the QCI as 1st mate of New England Fish Co's *Flamingo*. His charts of Athlow Bay and Port Chanal were used by company founder Capt Absalom Freeman and later proved helpful to government hydrographers. In 1928, Gillen took the *St Roch* from Burrard drydock, where it was built, to Herschel I in the Arctic (with Constable Henry Larsen, who would later command the RCMP patrol vessel on its historic voyages through the NW Passage, as 1st mate). Gillen was cdr of the HBC Arctic supply vessels *Nigalik* and *Old Maid No 2*, and it was from the deck of the latter ship that he mysteriously disappeared in Vancouver Hbr, his drowned body not found for a month. A typographical error presumably crept in to cause the misspelling of Gillan Point. *D*

Gillatt Arm (53°02'50" 131°59'00" Head of Cumshewa Inlet, NE side of Moresby I, QCI), **Gillatt Island** (53°15'00" 131°54'00" Off Shingle Bay, NE tip of Moresby I). Capt James Barratt Gillatt (1875–1947) was a retired Indian Army officer and Boer War veteran who was living with his family at Port Simpson in the early 1900s. Hearing laudatory accounts of the QCI, he moved to Sandspit in 1911, built a substantial home and established a farm, complete with cattle and riding ponies. Gillatt was a tide-watcher for the hydrographic service, a duty later taken

Master Mariners

As Patrick O'Brian wrote in the foreword to *Master and Commander*, the first of his legendary historic novels, 19th-century naval chronicles are filled with "actions that few men could invent," where "very often the improbable reality outruns fiction." On the BC coast it was not only navy men who led extraordinary lives. Many of the civilian seafarers whose names grace BC's geographic features had careers worthy of a thriller or adventure film.

Consider, for instance, the varied resumé of Captain William Gillen, of Wine Harbour, Nova Scotia. He started off as a fisherman, then crewed out of Halifax on merchant vessels bound for South America, Asia, Australia and the West Indies. Arriving in BC in 1895, he, like many other mariners, joined Victoria's sealing fleet. In 1907, Gillen was put in charge of the Bamfield lifeboat station, where he helped rescue the crew of the wrecked schooner *Soquel*. His sketch maps of the west coast of the Queen Charlotte Islands, made a few years later when he was mate of the New England Fish Company's *Flamingo*, form the basis of today's hydrographic charts. In 1928, Gillen took the historic RCMP patrol vessel *St Roch* from Burrard drydock, where it was built, to Herschel Island in the Arctic, and he later commanded Hudson's Bay Company Arctic supply ships. It was from the deck of one of these, in Vancouver Harbour, that he mysteriously disappeared in 1930. His drowned body was not found for a month.

What writer could have imagined the career of Captain Lancelot Beavis? After training at Britain's HMS *Conway* shore facility, he crewed on the great clipper ships that vied to make the fastest passage between Asia and Europe. By 1893 he was master of the *Micronesia*, a globe-trotting square-rigger, which he had the misfortune to watch burn to the waterline off the coast of England. Beavis loved the age of sail, but when that age was over he was forced to turn to steamships, which he despised. He worked on Atlantic cattle carriers, surveyed in the Queen Charlottes aboard CGS *Lillooet*, spent time on the training ship *Naden* at Esquimalt during World War I and ended up as a captain on the ferries that crossed to West Vancouver before the Lions Gate Bridge was built. After leaving the sea in 1930—reluctantly, no doubt—he retired to Vancouver Island and wrote his memoirs, *Passage from Sail to Steam*.

Captain Harry Burgess of Wiltshire, England, was another mariner with an exotic curriculum vitae. He had sailed as a young man on the *Empress of China* and was marine superintendent of engineering for Canadian Pacific in the 1920s. According to his obituary, however, these accomplishments were mere appetizers. He was an amateur heavyweight boxing champion, a founder of the Vancouver Rowing Club and the first president of the Vancouver Game Association. Burgess also installed machinery in Hawaii's early sugar mills and was responsible for designing the first Capilano suspension bridge.

Some of BC's master mariners may have actually found their way into literature. A rumour still circulates that sealing skipper Alex McLean, whose huge handlebar moustache could be tied behind his neck, was the model for Wolf Larsen in Jack London's famed 1904 novel *Sea Wolf* (both McLean and London denied that this was true).

"The Devil and the Deep Sea," a short story that Rudyard Kipling first published in 1898, was supposedly based on the exploits of two pioneer BC sealing captains, Sprott Balcom (later a whaler) and William Hughes. Balcom and Hughes were captured in 1892, along with their boats and crews, for alleged illegal hunting in Russian waters. After three weeks on a Russian cruiser, they were imprisoned for a further month in a roofless henhouse at Petropavlovsk. The Russian governor, deeply offended by the interest shown in his gold braid and brass buttons by First Nations crew members, stripped their vessels of every useful item, right down to the sailors' rubber boots. The two captains spent another month on another Russian warship before being released at Vladivostok and making their way to Japan, where an officious British consul tried to dock their future earnings in order to pay for their passage home. They finally arrived at Victoria eight months after leaving.

Today's marine vocations seem tame by comparison.

Captain William Gillen helped rescue the crew of the SS *Soquel* when it went aground on Seabird Rocks in Pachena Bay in 1909. *BC Archives B-00455*

G

over by his daughter Belle (*see* Belle Point). The Gillatts eventually moved to Victoria. Gillatt Arm was formerly known as West Arm. *D*

Gillen Harbour. *See* Gillan Point.

Gillespie Channel (53°03'00" 129°37'00" Between Trutch I and Prior I, Estevan Group, SE of Banks I). Flying Officer H V Gillespie navigated this channel in the *Sekani*, an RCAF supply vessel that was based at Western Air Command, Vancouver, during WWII. (The RCAF had a small fleet that assisted with flying-boat operations, searched for downed aircraft and helped supply and service its coastal bases. *See also* Sekani I.)

Gillies Bay on Texada Island. *Peter Vassilopoulos*

Gillies Bay (49°40'00" 124°29'00" W side of Texada I, Str of Georgia). A legend endures that Gillies Bay was named for a ship capt so relentlessly obnoxious that his crew threw him overboard there. Beyond that, little is known about the origin of the name. The community got its start with agriculture and logging, then expanded in the 1950s when its iron-ore deposits, which had been known about for years, were developed on a large scale. By the 2000s, retirees and tourists had become a mainstay of the local economy. *E*

Gilmour Island, Gilmour Slough (49°07'00" 123°07'00" Just S of Lulu I, N side of S Arm, Fraser R). These names are probably misspellings for James Gilmore (1864–1939), who acquired the island in 1906. He was born in Ireland and moved about 1883 to Sea I and then to Richmond, where he farmed, raised Holstein cattle and later served on the Richmond Police Commission, 1917–28. An elementary school is named for him. Gilmore married Nellie Dalziel (1874–1936), who had arrived in Canada about 1885; their children also farmed in the area. Gilmour I was formerly known as Whitworth I, after Isaac Whitworth (1865–1937), who owned it in 1890, and before that as Anderson I. Gilmour Slough is much better known locally as Finn Slough, named for a group of Finnish fishing families that began squatting here in the early 1900s, after moving from an earlier community nearby. It also used to be known as Tiffin Slough. By the early 2000s the residents of Finn Slough had successfully evaded eviction pressure from Richmond municipality for about a century and had turned their village into a heritage site and unique example of co-operative riverside anarchy.

Gilttoyees Inlet (53°50'09" 128°58'24" Extends N from Douglas Channel, SW of Kitimat). From the Haisla word *giltu'yis*, meaning "long inlet" (pronounced *GILL-tsoo-weez*). Bishop Bay (qv) has the same Haisla name. Nearby Gilttoyees Ck is named for the inlet. The S part of Gilttoyees Inlet (formerly spelled Cult-ta-yees) was known as Dawson Arm prior to 1946.

Gingolx (54°59'40" 129°57'15" N side of Nass Bay, NE of Prince Rupert). The Nisga'a First Nation village of Gingolx, long known by its anglicized spelling, Kincolith, was one of 34 place names adopted in 2000 as part of the Nisga'a Treaty. Gingolx means "place of scalps" and refers to a historic battle that took place there with the Haida, after which the scalps of the defeated were hung on poles as a warning. Nass Bay was such a vital source of seafood, especially of eulachon oil, a valuable trade good, that it was often raided by other tribes. The isolated community was founded in 1867 by Anglican missionaries and a breakaway group of Nisga'a from farther up the Nass R. The well-known missionary William Collison and his wife were based there, 1884–1922, and Kincolith was organized on the "model Christian village" style that had proved successful at Metlakatla. Numerous salmon canneries operated on Nass Bay between 1879 and 1942, providing economic stability. Gingolx, population about 300 and only recently connected to the wider world by highway, still makes its livelihood from fishing and still has a strong Anglican presence. Kincolith R (formerly Mission Ck), which flows through Mission Valley to enter Nass Bay here, is now known as Ksi Gingolx. *E W*

The village of Gingolx (Kincolith) is dominated by its community centre and historic Anglican church. *Andrew Scott*

Ginnard Point (49°08'00" 125°51'00" SW side of Meares I, SE of Tofino, Clayoquot Sd, W side of Vancouver I). A French settler named Ginnard is believed to have built a home on the point in the 1880s. Nearby Ginnard Ck, Tofino's backup water source, is named for the same person. The feature is known locally as Spittle Point or Spittle's Point after Bill Spittle, who squatted there in the 1910s and '20s with his dog, Joe Beef.

Girard Point (53°00'00" 131°40'00" NE side of Louise I, off NE Moresby I, QCI). Emmanuel Girard (1860–1943) was a pioneer resident of Queen Charlotte City. He arrived in the QCI about 1908 to take charge of the Moresby Lumber Co sawmill, bringing his wife and four daughters (a fifth daughter and her millwright husband arrived soon after). Girard was such an efficient manager that the lumber company's director, James Corlett, was able to indulge his passion for mining speculation on a full-time basis. Girard died at Maillardville, the French-speaking community in Coquitlam. *D*

Gits'oohl. *See* Kitsault.

Givenchy Anchorage (53°18'00" 132°33'00" Head of Kano Inlet, SW Graham I, QCI). HMCS *Givenchy*, launched in 1917, was one of 12 *Battle*-class trawlers used by the RCN. It served as a minesweeper in WWI, then was employed by the Fisheries Protection Branch on the BC coast from 1919 until WWII. Under Capt A M Anderson, the 40-m, 324-tonne vessel assisted the hydrographic service in surveying the inlets on the W coast of Graham I in the 1930s. HMCS *Givenchy* was later (1941–47) the name of a naval shore establishment at Esquimalt for reserve and auxiliary vessels and dockyard administration. *D*

Gladstone Islands (53°50'00" 130°26'00" N side of Kitkatla Channel, S of Porcher I and Prince Rupert). After Chief William Ewart Gladstone Shakes of the Kitkatla First Nation. *See* Shakes Is.

Glencoe Cove (48°29'00" 123°18'00" S of Gordon Head, Saanich Peninsula, just NE of Victoria). The cove was an ancient Lekwungen First Nation village site. In 1912, Victoria businessman Keith Wilson acquired the surrounding 5-ha property and named it Glencoe. Forty years and several owners later it was subdivided for residential development by Geoffrey Vantreight (*see* Vantreight Cove). Residents still sometimes refer to the area as the Glencoe estate (and, rarely, as Codfish Cove). The name Glencoe Cove was adopted in 1986, and in 1994 much of the area just N of the cove was preserved as Glencoe Cove-Kwatsech regional park.

Glendale Cove (50°40'00" 125°44'00" S side of Knight Inlet). Glendale was the ancestral home in Scotland of William Macdonald (1832–1916), a Victoria merchant

Glendale Cove, home to Knight Inlet Lodge. *Andrew Scott*

and politician who served as a BC senator, 1871–1915 (*see* Macdonald Point). William Blakeney, assistant surveying officer under Lt Daniel Pender aboard the *Beaver* in 1865, named a group of geographical features in this area after Macdonald and his family. Blakeney was Macdonald's brother-in-law; both men married daughters of early HBC master mariner James Murray Reid. Glendale Cove was later the site of an ABC Packing Co cannery, 1915–50 (which burned down in 1967), and a large logging camp. Since 1995 it has been home to Knight Inlet Lodge, one of BC's premier destinations for viewing grizzly bears. Nearby Glendale Ck and Glendale Lk are named after the cove. *W*

Glerup Rock (50°36'00" 127°40'00" E of Straggling Is, Holberg Inlet, NW end of Vancouver I). Peter Glerup was one of the Danish immigrants who settled Cape Scott in the late 1890s. When the colony failed, he and his family moved to Holberg and received Crown grants of land in that area in 1905 and 1911. Nearby Glerup Ck is also named for these pioneers.

Glide Islands (52°58'00" 129°29'00" E of Dewdney I, Estevan Group, Caamaño Sd). Henry Glide (1835–1921), born in Kent, England, came to Victoria in 1853 as a crew member aboard the HBC steamship *Otter*. He married Helen Lang (c 1845–97), who was from St Andrews, Scotland, at Victoria in 1861; she had come to BC in 1854 to join her father, Robert Lang. The Glides settled and raised a family at James Bay, and Henry worked for the HBC as a pilot. He is also described in various census and voters lists over the years as a labourer, drayman and packer. He later set up as a tobacconist and grocer with his son Andrew, and in 1916 was reported by the *Colonist* newspaper to be "an authority on the early history of Victoria."

Goat Harbour (53°21'00" 128°52'00" E side of Ursula Reach, just N of Princess Royal I). This harbour, a supply centre for a number of local logging operations in the 1920s, was probably named after the mountain goat (*Oreamnos americanus*). Capt George Vancouver's survey party noted a hot springs here. A floating post office opened briefly in the late 1930s.

Gobeil Bay (53°52'25" 128°40'28" N side of Kildala Arm, just inside entrance, S of Kitimat), **Gobeil Island** (53°51'54" 128°42'06" Entrance to Kildala Arm, NE side of Douglas Channel). Joseph E Gobeil was a government employee who accompanied Louis Coste (*see* Coste I), chief engineer of the federal Dept of Public Works, as private secretary on a W coast tour of inspection in 1898. They travelled on CGS *Quadra*, commanded by Capt John Walbran, who named Gobeil I. Nearby Loretta Channel and Loretta I are named for Gobeil's wife. The Haisla name for Gobeil I is Elsdem, meaning "place of graves," according to anthropologist Jay Powell.

Godfrey Rock (52°08'00" 128°30'00" W of Princess Alice I, SW of Athlone I, Milbanke Sd). Commodore Valentine Stuart Godfrey, OBE (1898–1968), born at London, UK, made his home at Victoria, where he married Margaret Horton Hardie (1899–1980) in 1924. He was an early graduate, in 1913, of the Royal Naval College of Canada and served on submarines, 1917–21. His first command was the destroyer *Champlain* in 1932. Godfrey served many roles in WWII: inspector of naval ordnance, Halifax (1937–41); CO of armed merchant cruiser *Prince David* and senior Canadian naval officer in the Alaska sector (1941–42); naval member of the Canadian Joint Staff Mission, Washington (1943, 1948); and CO of armed merchant cruiser *Prince Henry* (1943–45). He retired from the RCN in 1951 as chief officer for Nfld.

Godkin Point (50°54'00" 127°56'00" E entrance to Bull Hbr, Hope I, off N end of Vancouver I). Norman Godkin and his wife, Alice, were early pioneers in the Port Hardy area of N Vancouver I. Their daughter Eileen Excene Godkin (1903–83) married Jepther James Skinner (1868–1934) at Shushartie in 1921 (*see* Jepther Point). The couple operated the Shushartie Bay Trading Post. Eileen sold out about 1940 after the drowning death of her husband, moved to Vancouver and married Capt Ed Godfrey, skipper of the mission boat *Columbia* for many years. Nearby Norman I is named for Norman Godkin; Godkin Ck and Godkin Lk are also named for this family. Godkin Point was formerly known as Gallows Point.

Goepel Island (50°14'00" 125°08'00" Part of the Settlers Group, N end of Hoskyn Channel, S of Maurelle I, NE of Campbell R). Victoria pioneer Philip Dorset Goepel (1854–1932) came to Canada from England in 1875; his wife, Fanny (1858–1928), arrived in 1883. Philip was listed as a longshoreman in the 1891 census and as both a clerk at Victoria and a farmer on Mayne I in the 1901 version. He served as electoral returning officer for Saanich, 1909–16, and died at Qualicum Beach. His brother William Goepel (1857–1936) had an insurance business in Victoria, then

joined the BC civil service and became deputy minister of Finance.

Gogit Passage (52°40'00" 131°27'00" Between E side of Lyell I and Tar Is, QCI), **Gogit Point** (52°41'00" 131°26'00" E side of Lyell I). A *gogit* is a mythical Haida creature that harbours evil intentions and is often bent on injuring humans. The Haida also use this word to refer to a mad person or one afflicted with a serious physical deformity. It is sometimes encountered as a synonym for sasquatch or Bigfoot.

Golby Passage (52°01'00" 128°25'00" Between Goose Group and McMullin Group, Queens Sd, SW of Bella Bella). Lt Cdr Thomas Maitland Wake Golby, from Victoria, was born in Sussex, England, and came to Canada as a child in 1909. A member of the RCNR, he was in command of HMCS *Weyburn*, on convoy duty, when the corvette struck a mine off Cape Espartel, E of Gibraltar, and sank on Feb 22, 1943. Golby, aged 36, and six other members of the crew lost their lives. His name is inscribed on the Halifax Memorial. Hermit I in Howe Sd, formerly known as Golby I, also commemorated him at one time.

Golder Point (52°43'00" 128°26'00" S entrance to Wallace Bight, NW end of Roderick I, N of Bella Bella). In the 1940s the hydrographic service named several points on Roderick I after BC historians. Unfortunately, no details were provided. Most of the names (Bancroft, Denton, Howay) have obvious associations, but Golder does not. It could refer to Vancouver resident and philatelist Stephen Golder (1854–1934), who wrote books on cycling as well as articles for the Art, Historical and Scientific Assoc of Vancouver in the late 1920s and '30s. Or perhaps to Frank Alfred Golder (1877–1929), a Stanford Univ professor and author of definitive books on the Russian exploration and occupation of the N Pacific coast.

Gold Harbour. *See* Englefield Bay *and* Mitchell Inlet.

Gold River (49°41'00" 126°06'00" Flows S into Muchalat Inlet, Nootka Sd, W side of Vancouver I). The name appears on maps as early as 1869. A persistent rumour that gold was discovered here by the Spanish in the 1780s and then mined by Chinese workers brought to Nootka Sd in 1788 by fur trader John Meares has never been remotely proven. John Buttle, a former Royal Engineer and member of the 1864 Vancouver I Exploring Expedition, was the first to report gold in the river, in 1865, and likely applied the name, as well. A BC Dept of Mines report for 1895 mentions that Chinese placer miners found an undetermined (but probably small) amount of gold there, but it appears that no extensive mining was ever done in the area. The logging village of Gold R, established at Muchalat Inlet in 1955, was not connected to Campbell R by road until 1958. In 1965 a pulp mill was built and the village moved 12 km upriver. Since the mill's closure in 1999, Gold R has tried to reinvent itself as a recreational community. *E*

Goldstream Harbour (51°43'00" 128°00'00" NE end of Hecate I, S of Bella Bella). The 64-tonne trading schooner *Goldstream* was built at Alberni in 1864 and worked on the BC coast until taken to Hawaii and sold. Capt James Hewitt, in command of the vessel 1865–66, reported this harbour to Lt Daniel Pender of the RN, who surveyed and named it after the *Goldstream* in 1867. The ship was presumably named after the Goldstream R (*see below*).

The mouth of Goldstream River at Finlayson Arm. *Kevin Oke*

Goldstream River (48°29'00" 123°33'00" Flows SE and N into head of Finlayson Arm, Saanich Inlet, S Vancouver I). This waterway, originally known as Gold Ck or Gold Stream, experienced a minor gold rush in the mid-1860s after former Royal Engineer Peter John Leech (or Leach; *see* Leach It) of the Vancouver I Exploring Expedition found the precious metal there. As many as 300 men worked its gravels, which were soon played out. The river's Saanich First Nation name is usually spelled Sawluctus, meaning "fishing area tucked inside the arm." A hydroelectric facility was located on the Goldstream from 1897 to 1957; after it was dismantled, a 327-ha provincial park was established, and the river's spawning chum salmon now attract many visitors. Nearby Goldstream Lk takes its name from the river.

Goletas Channel (50°49'00" 127°44'00" Between NE end of Vancouver I and S side of Hope I and Nigei I). Spanish explorers Dionisio Alcalá-Galiano and Cayetano Valdés named this channel Salida de las Goletas, or Schooners Exit, in 1792. They were referring to their own vessels, the *Sutil* and *Mexicana*, as this was the way the expedition passed out to sea and returned to Nootka Sd on its historic circumnavigation of Vancouver I. The western "exit" to the channel is marked to the S by Cape Sutil and to the N by Mexicana Point.

Goliath Bay (49°50'00" 123°56'00" SW side of Prince of Wales Reach, Jervis Inlet, NW of Vancouver). Named after the 74-gun HMS *Goliath*, built at Deptford in 1781, because it took part, under Capt Sir Charles Knowles, in the 1797 Battle of Cape St Vincent and was thus associated with Rear Adm Sir John Jervis, after whom Jervis Inlet is named. Jervis, later Earl St Vincent, was leader of the British naval forces that triumphed that day over a much larger Spanish fleet. The 1,455-tonne *Goliath* was also involved, under Capt Thomas Foley, in the 1798 Battle of the Nile. *W*

Gona Point (52°17'00" 131°08'00" S side of Collison Bay, SE end of Moresby I, QCI). The name of Gona, a former Haida First Nation village located on Collison Bay, was taken from a map made by naturalist and ethnologist Dr Charles Newcombe, who contributed greatly to historical knowledge of the QCI.

Gonzales Bay, also known locally as Foul Bay. *Andrew Scott*

Gonzales Bay (48°24'36" 123°19'40" S side of Victoria, between Ross Bay and McNeill Bay), **Gonzales Hill** (48°24'48" 123°19'28" Just N of Gonzales Bay), **Gonzales Point** (48°24'43" 123°17'39" SE end of Oak Bay district municipality, E of Victoria). After Gonzales López de Haro, mate aboard the *Princesa Real*, the first European vessel to explore Juan de Fuca Str, in 1790. *See* Haro Str. Gonzales was also the name of the large estate of colonial surveyor gen Joseph Pemberton, located N of the bay. Gonzales Bay is still often referred to as Foul Bay, its official name from about 1847, when it was applied by Capt Henry Kellet or Lt James Wood during an early survey. The erroneous spelling "Fowl Bay" was also sometimes seen in the late 1800s, after

G

Isabella Ross's adjacent Fowl Bay Farm. By the 1920s the Foul Bay neighbourhood had grown from a collection of summer cottages into an upscale residential suburb. Local homeowners, ignorant of the original significance of the bay's name—which referred to its poor holding qualities as an anchorage—somehow became convinced that "foul" had to do with odour. Letters to the newspapers called the name "disgusting" and "vile" and argued that it subjected residents to ridicule, reduced the value of their homes and prevented "the proper development of the district." A decade-long war of words ensued. At first the Geographic Board of Canada and its allies resisted "any such change in old historic names, firmly established by time," which "carry with them the history, association and romance of the early days of the province." The constant battering of public opinion wore them down, however, and in 1934, after petitions and resolutions from Victoria and Oak Bay councils, the board finally relented and the name was changed to Gonzales Bay. To the confusion of tourists, the leafy boundary between Victoria and Oak Bay is still known as Foul Bay Rd. Gonzales Point was once the site of a Songhees First Nation village called Kukeeluk, meaning "place of war."

Gooch Island (48°39'50" 123°17'22" Haro Str, just E of Sidney, Gulf Is). Thomas Sherlock Gooch (1831–97) was 2nd lt aboard HMS *Satellite*, under Capt James Prevost, on the Pacific Station from 1857 to 1860. He achieved the rank of capt and retired in 1873. Gooch is an old English baronetcy with its seat at Benacre Hall, Suffolk. The island was named in 1859 by RN surveyor Capt George Richards, of HMS *Plumper*. For many years it was owned by Dan Martin, a car dealer and former US undersecretary of commerce, and his wife Charlotte. About 55 ha in size, it boasts an 11-bedroom lodge and has played host to such guests as John Wayne, US senator Henry Jackson and California gov Pat Brown. A destroyer escort, HMCS *Mackenzie*, was sunk just offshore in 1995 to create an artificial reef for sport divers. *W*

Goodacre Point (52°57'00" 129°33'00" SE tip of Dewdney I, Estevan Group, Caamaño Sd). Lawrence Goodacre (1840–1925) was born in England, migrated to Victoria in 1866 and set up in business as a butcher with partner John Stafford, who died in 1876. Goodacre married Stafford's widow, Maria (1846–1918, née Sketchly), in 1877. He was a six-term Victoria city councilor, 1889–1906, and, as chair of the parks committee, a force behind the zoo that once existed at Beacon Hill Park (he provided scraps from his butcher shop for the animals there for almost 20 years). The park's artificial Goodacre Lk is also named in his honour. He attended the famous old-timers' reunion held in the city in 1924 (*see* Adams Bay).

Goodfellow Point (53°04'00" 129°06'00" S side of Barnard Hbr, W side of Princess Royal I). Margaret Eliza Florence

Askin Goodfellow (1854–1940) was a daughter of Capt Lewis Agassiz (*see* Agassiz Banks) and Mary Caroline Schram (*see* Schram Rks). She was born at London, Ont, came to BC in 1862 and lived at Hope and then Yale, where her father was postmaster, before the family settled in 1867 at the Fraser Valley community named after them. Florence lived briefly in Victoria, 1868–69, to attend Angela College. She married John Goodfellow (1841–1912) at Agassiz in 1876 and moved with him to Victoria, where he was manager of the Bank of BNA. Goodfellow was transferred to Portland in 1880, and Florence, who bore 11 children over the years, died in Seattle and never did return to Canada. Her *Memories of Pioneer Life in BC* was published privately in 1941 and reprinted in 1958.

Gooding Cove (50°24'00" 127°57'00" S of Harvey Cove, N of Open Bay, Quatsino Sd, NW end of Vancouver I). C Gooding was a cook on the W coast survey vessel *Restless*, which charted Quatsino Sd in 1920–21 for the Canadian Hydrographic Service.

Good Point (49°10'00" 123°55'00" W point of Protection I, Nanaimo Hbr, E of Vancouver I). Henry Leslie Good (1864–1934), one of BC's longest-serving federal civil servants, was collector of national revenue and controller of Chinese immigration at Nanaimo for many years. He came to Canada from England with his father in 1866, was educated at Victoria's Collegiate School and joined the Dominion telegraph dept in 1881. In 1892 he married Mary Sirina Clarke at Nanaimo and in 1901 was appointed to the customs service there. Good retired in 1932.

Goodridge Islands (48°22'00" 123°39'00" SE Sooke Basin, S end of Vancouver I), **Goodridge Peninsula** (48°23'00" 123°39'00" N side of Sooke Basin). John Octavius Goodridge (c 1810–65) was the RN surgeon aboard HMS *Herald*, under Capt Henry Kellett, who surveyed these waters in 1846. He had been assistant surgeon on HMS *Starling* on the E Indies Station before coming to BC, and he later served with Kellett and the *Herald* in the Arctic, where they assisted in the futile search for missing explorer Sir John Franklin.

Goodwin Point (52°17'00" 131°05'00" S entrance to Collison Bay, SE side of Moresby I, QCI), **Goodwin Rock** (52°17'00" 131°04'00" E of Goodwin Point). After Marion M Goodwin (1850–1919), the first white woman to live on the QCI. A trained nurse with experience in the Franco-German War and Irish smallpox epidemics, she married Anglican missionary William Henry Collison (1847–1922, *see* Collison Bay) and travelled with him to BC in 1873. The couple were sent initially to Metlakatla, then in 1876 founded the first mission to the Haida. They later returned to Metlakatla before being transferred to Hazelton in 1880 and Kincolith in 1884, where they were based for the rest of their lives. Besides raising a large family, Marion worked steadily as a nurse, and Collison regarded her medical contributions as essential to the success of his mission. Nearby Marion Rk is also named for her. Goodwin Point was formerly known as Bluff Point, named in 1878 by geologist George Dawson. Goodwin Rk was formerly known as Bare Rk.

Goolden Islands (51°54'00" 128°13'00" SE of McNaughton Group, Cultus Sd, Queens Sd). Capt Massy Goolden (1887–1971) was an RN officer who served for many years in Canada at the Halifax shore base, HMCS *Stadacona*, and retired in 1927. He re-enlisted with the RCN in WWII and was appointed CO of *Stadacona* on a temporary basis, then CO of the Sydney, NS, shore base, HMCS *Protector*, in 1940–42. His next job was as CO of HMCS *Givenchy*, the shore establishment at Esquimalt for reserve and auxiliary vessels and dockyard administration. He was also naval officer-in-charge at Esquimalt until 1944, when he retired a second time. His wife, Alix, was one of the founders of the Victoria Conservatory of Music in 1964.

Islands of the Goose Group, Queens Sound. *James and Jennifer Hamilton*

Goose Group (51°57'00" 128°27'00" W of Hunter I, Queens Sd). All the islands in this beautiful beach-lined group—Goose, Gosling, Swan, Duck, Gull and Snipe—are named after marine or aquatic birds.

Gordon Bluff (50°34'00" 126°54'00" S end of Cormorant I, Broughton Str, E of Port McNeill), **Gordon River** (48°35'00" 124°25'00" Flows SW and S into Port San Juan, SW Vancouver I), **Gordon Rock** (50°35'00" 126°53'00" E of Cormorant I, Pearse Passage). Capt George Thomas Gordon (d 1887) served on the BC coast, 1846–50, as cdr of HMS *Cormorant*, the first steam naval vessel on the Pacific Station, and HMS *Driver*. At Victoria in 1850 he read out the commission of Richard Blanshard, Vancouver I's first colonial gov. Gordon was flag capt of HMS *Duke of Wellington* in 1854, under Vice Adm Sir Charles Napier, cdr-in-chief of the Baltic fleet. He was promoted to adm himself in 1877. Gordon R was named in 1847 by Lt Cdr James Wood of HMS *Pandora*. Gordon Bluff, formerly

known as Gordon Point, was named by Capt George Richards in 1860 in association with Cormorant I. *W*

Gordon Cove (53°02'00" 132°02'00" Head of Gillatt Arm, Cumshewa Inlet, E Moresby I, QCI). A J Gordon was a resident at Skidegate Landing in 1908. He was the first president of the Graham I Settlers' Assoc and took over the store at Skidegate oilery from William Leary. Gordon was active as a mining prospector and speculator into the mid-1930s. Named in 1926. *D*

Gordon Head (48°30'00" 123°18'00" E of Mt Douglas and Margaret Bay, N of Victoria), **Gordon Rock** (Just off Gordon Head). Capt John Gordon (1792–1869), whose brother George Hamilton-Gordon, 4th Earl of Aberdeen, served as a British foreign secretary and PM, was in PNW waters on "special service" with HMS *America*, 1845–46. Gordon was charged with preparing a report on the region's suitability for settlement and colonization, which he based on his own superficial opinions and a three-week survey of Puget Sd and Oregon by two of his officers. Although his views were unfavourable, it is unlikely that they influenced the boundary negotiations that culminated in the 1846 Oregon Treaty, in which Britain mostly abandoned its claims S of the 49th parallel. Gordon rose to the rank of adm in 1863. The farming and fruit-growing district of Gordon Head, now part of Saanich, has long been a residential suburb of greater Victoria. The Songhees First Nation name for Gordon Head was Kwatsech. *W*

Gordon Islands (52°06'00" 131°09'00" S entrance to Houston Stewart Channel, SW side of Moresby I, QCI), **Gordon Point** (54°34'00" 130°29'00" N end of Finlayson I, Port Simpson, N of Prince Rupert). William Ebrington Gordon (1831–97) was a mate or sub-lt in 1853 aboard HMS *Virago*, under Cdr James Prevost. He assisted George Inskip, the *Virago*'s master, in making surveys of Port Simpson and Houston Stewart Channel, and kept a useful journal of his travels, 1851–54, now owned by the State Library of New S Wales. Gordon went on to become a vice adm and superintendent of Portsmouth dockyard, 1888–91. *W*

Gordon Point (50°46'00" 126°44'00" S side of Broughton I, Fife Sd, NE end of Queen Charlotte Str). Capt George Vancouver named this point in 1792 after Sir Alexander Gordon, 4th Duke of Gordon (1743–1827), in association with Duff Point (qv) on the opposite side of Fife Sd. James Duff had been Vancouver's friend and shipmate aboard HMS *Europa*, 1786–89, and Gordon, a great landowner and leader of one of Scotland's most powerful families, had been Duff's patron, helping him gain promotion. Gordon is credited with developing the Gordon setter breed of dog. *W*

Gore Island (49°39'00" 126°24'00" Near W end of Muchalat Inlet, Nootka Sd, W side of Vancouver I). John

G

Gore (1730–90), a native of Virginia, had joined the RN as a midshipman by 1755. He was a junior officer on Capt James Cook's first voyage, in 1768, and served again, as 1st lt of HMS *Resolution*, on Cook's third voyage in 1776. He was thus present on the BC coast at Nootka Sd in 1778. When Cook was killed at Hawaii and Capt Charles Clerke became cdr, Gore took over HMS *Discovery*. After Clerke's death he became overall leader of the expedition and brought the two vessels safely back to Britain. In 1780 he was promoted capt and also appointed a capt of Greenwich seamen's hospital. Nearby Mt Gore is named for him as well. In 1862, Capt George Richards of RN survey vessel *Hecate* named several features in the vicinity after the *Resolution*'s officers. W

Gore-Langton Point (54°30'00" 130°53'00" SE side of Dundas I, NW of Prince Rupert), **Gore-Langton Rock** (54°05'00" 130°50'00" SW of Stephens I and Prince Rupert). Lt Evelyn Arthur Temple-Gore-Langton (1884–1972), son of the 4th Earl of Stowe, served aboard HMS *Egeria* on the BC coast, 1907–9. He assisted with the surveys of Dixon Entrance and Hecate Str, conducted under cdrs John Parry and Frederick Learmonth. Gore-Langton was later promoted to lt cdr.

Gorge Waters (48°26'52" 123°24'18" Between Chapman Point and Maple Point, Victoria Hbr, SE end of Vancouver I), **The Gorge** (48°27'00" 123°24'00" On Gorge Waters, between Portage Inlet and Selkirk Water). The Gorge Waters are part of Victoria Hbr. At the Gorge itself, the channel narrows to about 10 m in width. A reversing tidal rapids is formed there at full flood and ebb, when a foaming cascade of white water is squeezed through the narrow passage. Songhees First Nation members know the Gorge as Camossung (often spelled Camosack or Camosun) and consider it a sacred site for spirit quests.

Goring Reefs (53°30'00" 130°28'00" Entrance to Kingkown Inlet, NW side of Banks I). Charles Albert Goring (1875–1948), of Victoria, was capt of the sailing vessel *Allerton*, after which nearby Allerton Passage is named.

Gormely Point (50°50'00" 126°18'00" N side of Tribune Channel, N of Gilford I, between Kingcome Inlet and Knight Inlet). Marcus "Marc" William Gormely (1907–85) was the provincial forester for the Kingcome region at some point in his long career with the BC Forest Service. He was a member of the first council of the Assoc of BC Foresters in 1947 and its president in 1970. In 1983 he wrote a history of the association. Formerly known as Watson Point.

Goschen Island (53°49'00" 130°35'00" S of Porcher I and Prince Rupert), **Goschen Point** (53°47'00" 130°35'00" S side of Goschen I), **Goschen Spit** (53°47'00" 130°36'00" S of Goschen Point). British politician and naval official George Joachim Goschen (1831–1907) was born at London of German heritage. He was MP for several different constituencies (and for the Liberal, Liberal Unionist and Conservative parties) from 1863 to 1900 and held numerous cabinet positions, including paymaster-gen (1865–66), chancellor of the exchequer (1887–92) and 1st Lord of the Admiralty (1871–74, 1895–1900). Goschen was also gov of the HBC, 1874–80. He was raised to the peerage as Viscount Goschen in 1900 and wrote an influential book, *The Theory of the Foreign Exchanges*. Rear Adm George Richards, hydrographer of the RN, named Goschen I in 1871. Nearby Cape George, Viscount Point, Joachim Point, Joachim Rk and Joachim Spit are also named for him, as is Joachim I in the entrance to Rivers Inlet. W

Goski Bay (52°26'00" 131°33'00" N side of Gowgaia Bay, SW side of Moresby I, QCI), **Goski Islet** (52°25'00" 131°33'00" Entrance to Goski Bay). Goski comes from the Haida name for the village that once existed beside this bay. According to ethnologist Charles Newcombe, the Haida name for the bay itself is Gwa'kagwa. D

Gospel Island (53°23'00" 132°35'00" Rennell Sd, SW side of Graham I, QCI), **Gospel Point** (53°23'00" 132°32'00" E of Gospel I). Gospel I first appears on a sketch map prepared by Capt Absalom Freeman (*see* Cape Freeman) about 1912–16. The Gospel mineral claim was staked at Gospel Point after prospectors found signs there of iron and antimony. D

Gosse Bay (52°10'00" 127°56'00" N side of Gunboat Passage, NE of Bella Bella). Capt Richard Edward Gosse (1852–1927) was a Nfld sailor and sealer who moved to BC in 1887 and became a builder, especially of canneries. He bought his first cannery on Burrard Inlet in 1909. In 1913, with Francis Millerd, he formed Gosse-Millerd Packing Co (later Gosse-Millerd Ltd), which operated until 1926 and at one time was the second-largest salmon canner in BC. East Bella Bella cannery was purchased in 1915 but burned to the ground in 1923. The company also owned canneries at Namu and Kimsquit and on the Fraser R, Skeena R, Rivers Inlet and W coast of Vancouver I, as well as a can-making plant, sawmill and box factory. Millerd left the business about 1924 and Gosse reorganized in 1926 as the Gosse Packing Co, which merged with BC Packers Ltd after his death. His sons were prominent BC cannerymen too. *See also* Millerd Point. Gosse Bay was formerly known as Lucy Bay.

Gosse Passage (48°42'00" 123°24'00" Between Knapp I and Piers I, off N tip of Saanich Peninsula, N of Victoria), **Gosse Point** (49°18'00" 122°55'00" S of Admiralty Point, Burrard Inlet, just E of Vancouver). Capt Walter George Gosse (1900–1964), born at Vancouver but raised at Victoria, was a well-known pilot on the BC coast. He was the son of Capt Josiah Gosse (1865–1938), from Nfld, who came to the W coast about 1886, served on Skeena R steamers and other craft, then was employed for many years by the Canadian Pacific Navigation Co as BC's first licensed pilot. Walter Gosse married Violet Francis Keenan at Vancouver in 1925. He joined the BC Pilotage Assoc in 1937, became BC's senior pilot and president of the National Pilotage Assoc, and was a former president of the Canadian Merchant Seamen's Guild. He worked on the coast until his sudden death while returning home from a maritime conference in Nfld. *E*

Gosset Bay (53°12'00" 132°15'00" Between Anthracite Point and Josette Point, Skidegate Inlet, QCI). Capt William Driscoll Gosset (1822–99), born at London, graduated from the Royal Military Academy, Woolwich, as an engineer and became involved with survey projects in the UK and overseas. He married Helen Dorothea Gosset (1830–79), his cousin, in 1852, and in the mid-1850s was appointed surveyor gen of Ceylon (now Sri Lanka). Sent to BC in 1858 as colonial treasurer, he was soon acting as treasurer and postmaster gen of both BC and Vancouver I. The meticulous Gosset, full of costly, impractical ideas, was an ideal bureaucrat but a poor choice, perhaps, for those chaotic, underfunded colonies in their early days. He found much to disapprove of and soon became unpopular with Gov James Douglas. Relieved of his postal duties and transferred to New Westminster, Gosset nevertheless managed to persuade Douglas that BC should produce its own coinage. A used minting machine was acquired in San Francisco, dies were engraved (based on Gosset's own design of oak garland and crown) and a few samples struck off despite an injunction by Douglas to mint nothing until instructed to do so. Douglas lost interest in the project and nothing ever came of BC's mint; the handful of coins produced are now among the rarest in the world. In Nov 1861 the *British Columbian* reported that Gosset, "suffering from an attack of nervous debility, induced, we believe, by too close application to official duty," was visiting Victoria for "temporary relaxation from the harassing cares of official life." He returned to England on sick leave in Sept 1862, submitted his resignation the following year and never returned to BC, retiring in 1873 with the rank of maj gen.

Gossip Island (48°53'00" 123°19'00" Off SE side of Galiano I, Gulf Is), **Gossip Shoals** (48°53'00" 123°18'00" SE side of Gossip I). In a 1960 newspaper article, the *Vancouver Sun* suggested that Gossip I, surrounded as it was by promontories named after women (Mary Anne Point, Georgina Point, Helen Point, Edith Point), owed its name to the "sardonic humour" of certain anonymous mariners. All these names are old ones, dating from surveys made by Capt George Richards about 1860, so it is just possible that the *Sun's* uncharitable claim is correct. No evidence supports it, though. Gossip may also refer to the sounds of waves breaking on the shoreline or to the endless whispering of strong tides racing through nearby Active Pass. These currents, strangely, were not known to Capt I G Denroche, who in 1924 advertised furnished island bungalows in the pages of *The Square: A Magazine for Masons*. "The waters in these parts are well sheltered and absolutely safe for even the least experienced oarsman or woman," wrote Denroche, who was also promoting boat rentals. Each cabin had a private beach, fireplace and "large French windows opening on to spacious verandahs," and rented for $40 a month. Gossip Shoals was added to the charts by Cdr John Parry during his 1905 survey with HMS *Egeria*.

Gotha Point (48°26'00" 123°27'00" Tip of Coburg Peninsula, W entrance to Esquimalt Hbr, W of Victoria). Named after Queen Victoria's husband, Prince Albert of Saxe-Coburg and Gotha. Gotha is a town in Thuringia, Germany. In the 17th century it was the capital of the duchy of Saxe-Gotha; later it became one of the two capitals of the duchy of Saxe-Coburg and Gotha. Lt Cdr James Wood of HMS *Pandora*, who surveyed this area in 1847, also named nearby Saxe Point and Coburg Peninsula. Albert Head, just S, had been named the year before by Capt Henry Kellett of HMS *Herald*.

Gottlob Point (52°28'00" 131°28'00" S end of Werner Bay, SE side of Moresby I, QCI). After German geologist Abraham Gottlob Werner. *See* Werner Bay.

Goudge Island (48°41'00" 123°24'00" Just E of the N end of Saanich Peninsula, N of Victoria). The name first appears on a 1904 chart based on a 1902 survey by Cdr Cortland Simpson of HMS *Egeria*. The 13-ha island was farmed in the 19th century by Tom Kamaree, a Hawaiian Islander or Kanaka, who received a Crown grant for it and adjacent Fernie I in 1889. Goudge and Fernie were owned for many years by Nelson Paul Whittier (1904–91), a fabulously wealthy California oil tycoon, whose family founded Beverly Hills in 1906, built the Beverly Hills Hotel and went into dairy farming and land development. Whittier had a large interest in the Belridge Oil Co, which was sold to Shell in 1979 for $3.65 billion—one of the largest business transactions of its era. He was fascinated by aviation and boating, and built radio-controlled target drones for the US Army during WWII. It was at his factory that David Conover (*see* Conover Cove) "discovered" Marilyn Monroe. Whittier constructed a boatyard at Goudge I and at great expense rebuilt a Victorian steam yacht named the *Medea* there before donating it to the San Diego Maritime Museum. A pair of matching barges—the *Backenforth* and the *Forthenback*—provided access to this self-sufficient paradise. He and his second wife, Lucy, sold the island in 1979 and acquired recreational property at Friday Hbr on San Juan I instead.

G

Gould Rock (50°15'00" 127°50'00" NW of McDougal I, near entrance to Klaskish Inlet, Brooks Bay, NW side of Vancouver I). Capt Isaac Archibald Gould (1846–1938), from NS, came to Victoria in 1891 and entered the sealing trade in the schooner *Ariel*. He was master of the *E B Marvin* in 1893 and the *Katherine* in 1894–95, then spent a period as mate of the Canadian Pacific Navigation Co steamer *Willapa* before returning to the sealing grounds in 1906 in charge of the *Carrie C W*. Gould ended his career as superintendent of the Esquimalt dockyard from 1906 to at least 1913. He and his wife, Lauretta (1854–1936, née Bernard), lived at Metchosin.

Governor Rock (48°55'00" 123°30'00" Trincomali Channel, E of Saltspring I, Gulf Is). HMS *Plumper*, under Capt George Richards, was peacefully anchored at Nanaimo in 1859 when an urgent summons arrived from Gov James Douglas ordering him to Victoria. Richards sailed S as quickly as he could and ran his vessel full speed onto this unreported hazard. The *Plumper* eventually got free, and while valuable time was lost, little damage was suffered. Richards and his officers decided to name their embarrassment Governor Rk, as it was Douglas who had insisted they make this journey and Douglas's fault, clearly, that they had had such a regrettable accident. Rev Arthur Browning (*see* Browning Passage), who was along for a ride, received a great fright from this incident and, many years later, wrote a somewhat sensationalized account of it in the *Methodist Magazine and Review. W*

Governors Bar (54°59'00" 129°58'00" Off Gingolx, N shore of Nass Bay, NE of Prince Rupert). In 1869, BC colonial gov Frederick Seymour visited Gingolx (then known as Kincolith) aboard HMS *Sparrowhawk* to investigate a feud between Tsimshian and Nisga'a First Nations members that had resulted in the deaths of three men. He set off for shore in the ship's gig but became grounded on this sandbar and was unable to land. Kincolith's leaders had to come to him instead. Ninety-four years later it was the turn of Lt Gov George Pearkes to get stuck there, this time in a floatplane. Pearkes was making the first vice-regal visit to the region since Seymour's, and it was only with considerable rocking and pushing that his immobilized Beaver could be set free. This coincidental stranding of the only two govs to visit the area was deemed so unusual that Rear Adm William Landymore, senior naval officer on the Pacific coast, suggested that the offending feature—known locally as Canoe Flat or Kincolith Bar—be renamed. Governors Bar was officially adopted in 1965 after MLA Frank Calder, president of the Nisga'a Tribal Council, convened a village meeting at Kincolith at which the new name received unanimous endorsement.

Gowdas Islands (52°24'00" 131°36'00" Entrance to Gowgaia Bay, W side of Moresby I, QCI), **Gowdas Rocks** (52°23'00" 131°37'00" Just W of Gowdas Is). Named after the old Haida First Nation village of Gowdas (also spelled Ga'odas), which was located about 2 km to the S. The Gowdas Rks were formerly known as the Black Rks. *D*

Gower Point (49°23'00" 123°32'00" W entrance point to Howe Sd, NW of Vancouver). Adm Sir Erasmus Gower (c 1742–1814) was a member of two round-the-world voyages as a young officer, those of Cdr John Byron in HMS *Dolphin* (1764–66) and Capt Philip Carteret in HMS *Swallow* (1766–69). At the 1780 Battle of Cape St Vincent, as 1st lt of Adm Sir George Rodney's flagship HMS *Sandwich*, he was promoted directly to capt and put in charge of the captured Spanish vessel *Guipuzcoana*, which was later renamed HMS *Prince William*. Gower was flag capt at Nfld, 1786–89. He transported Earl Macartney's unsuccessful embassy to and from China in HMS *Lion*, 1793–94, and then joined the Channel fleet as cdr of HMS *Triumph* and *Neptune*. Gower was promoted to rear adm in 1799 and adm in 1809. Capt George Vancouver named Gower Point in 1792 and spent a night camping in the vicinity while surveying the region in his ships' boats. The Sechelt First Nation name for the area is Kwye-ahks. *W*

Gowgaia Bay (52°25'00" 131°35'00" W side of Moresby I, QCI), **Gowgaia Point** (52°24'00" 131°36'00" S entrance to Gowgaia Bay). This inlet was formerly known by the much-duplicated name Big Bay. Gowgaia, the Haida word for inlet, was adopted in 1947. There were no fewer than five Haida village sites on this body of water, with a sixth just S of the entrance. Fur trader Joseph Ingraham became very interested in the area in the 1790s; according to QCI historian Kathleen Dalzell, he set three pigs ashore there in the hope that, with few apparent predators, they might flourish. The unfortunate animals were never seen again. A WWII RCAF outpost was established near Gowgaia Point to watch for Japanese warships. The men who staffed the cabin had an excellent camping holiday during the war but did not see a single thing worth reporting. *D*

Gowing Island (52°46'00" 132°02'00" In Fairfax Inlet, Tasu Sd, W side of Moresby I, QCI). Prospector Arthur Gowing (1866–1914) came to the Tasu area about 1908 from Revelstoke and began staking mineral claims. One claim, initially investigated that year by the Elliott Mining Co, later became part of the large open-pit iron-ore operations of Wesfrob Mines Ltd, 1962–83. Wesfrob, a subsidiary of Falconbridge Nickel, built a modern, 400-resident townsite (since dismantled), complete with indoor swimming pool, on Gowing I. Gowing, in fact, is technically an island no longer, as a causeway now connects it with Moresby I. *D*

Gow Island (52°06'00" 128°17'00" N of Piddington I, Queens Sd, just SW of Bella Bella). Cdr Francis Robert William Roberts Gow, a native of NS who had moved to Victoria, was killed off Nfld in an air accident on Nov 8, 1942, aged 43. He was based at the RCN's Halifax shore establishment, HMCS *Stadacona*, and had served as an intelligence officer at Esquimalt, 1935–38. He is commemorated on the Halifax Memorial. His wife, Jean Donald Gow (1902–2005), established a program during WWII that still exists to distribute books and other reading material to naval personnel at sea. Her autobiography, *Alongside the Navy 1910–1950*, was published in 1999.

Gowlland Harbour, southwest Quadra Island. *Peter Vassilopoulos*

Gowlland Harbour (50°04'00" 125°13'00" SW side of Quadra I, N end of Str of Georgia), **Gowlland Island** (50°04'00" 125°14'00" In Gowlland Hbr), **Gowlland Rocks** (49°04'00" 125°51'00" Between Wickaninnish Bay and Templar Channel, Clayoquot Sd, W side of Vancouver I). John Thomas Gowlland (1838–74) was 2nd master aboard HMS *Plumper* and *Hecate*, under Capt George Richards, and involved in survey duties on the BC coast, 1857–62. He also assisted with surveys off Australia, 1865–74. In 1874 he was promoted staff cdr and was leading a survey party near Sydney when his small boat capsized on a submerged reef and he was drowned. Gowlland was a graduate of the Greenwich Royal Naval College and a fellow of the Royal Geographical Society. **Gowlland Point** (48°44'00" 123°11'00" S end of S Pender I, Gulf Is), the Gowlland Range and **Mount Gowlland** (52°12'52" 128°14'06" NE tip of Horsfall I, NW of Bella Bella) are probably named for him as well. According to geographer Robert Galois, Gowlland Hbr's First Nation name was Gwigwakulis, which has been translated, somewhat mysteriously, as "whale between the two."

Grace Harbour (50°02'55" 124°44'56" S side of Gifford Peninsula, facing Malaspina Peninsula, NW of Powell R). This major Sliammon First Nation winter village site, known as K'ák'ak'i, was also shared by the Klahoose and Homalco people. The name possibly derives from the word ḵ'iymtan, meaning "camping place."

Grace Islands (49°26'00" 123°27'00" S of SW Gambier I, Howe Sd, NW of Vancouver). Possibly named after Mary Grace Lett, wife of Charles Arthur Lett (1851–1923). The Letts were early settlers in the area, farming 5 ha on the SW shore of West Bay. In 1923 their home burned down, and Charles, trying to save some belongings, damaged his lungs so severely that he died. The next generation of Letts ran a store and post office at Gambier Hbr (qv), which was formerly named Grace Hbr. (Grace Hbr post office operated 1937–38 before its name was changed to Gambier I, 1938–41, and then again to Gambier Hbr.) The Grace Is are still referred to locally as Twin Is.

Grace Rock (54°10'22" 130°21'41" Between Greentop I and Kitson I, Chatham Sd, SW of Prince Rupert). Named by George Blanchard Dodge in 1906 after his wife, Grace (née Sample). Dodge was the federal government hydrographer in charge of surveying Prince Rupert Hbr that year, after it had been chosen as the terminus for the GTP (*see* Dodge Cove).

Graeme Point (50°38'00" 127°10'00" W end of Malcolm I, Broughton Str, NW of Port McNeill). Malcolm I (qv) was named after Adm Sir Pulteney Malcolm of the RN as early as 1846, and the spit at its SW end, where the lighthouse is now located, has long been known as Pulteney Point. In the early 1900s, though, the area was re-surveyed by Cdr Cortland Simpson of HMS *Egeria*; unaware of the origin of the name Malcolm, he renamed the spit after Graeme Malcolm, a figure in Sir Walter Scott's "Lady of the Lake," which Simpson happened to be reading at the time. His blunder was officially expunged in 1907 by the Geographic Board of Canada, mainly as a result of a letter by historian and master mariner John Walbran, who expressed "extreme regret" at the "incongruous" new name. Graeme Point had appeared on charts, however, and managed to establish itself. In 1947 it was adopted as the name for the W tip of Malcolm I, while Pulteney Point continued to refer to the SW end.

Grafton Bay (49°24'00" 123°22'00" W side of Bowen I, Howe Sd, NW of Vancouver). Caroline Susanna Grafton (1834–1914), who died in the tragic sinking of the *Empress of Ireland*, came to Ont from England with her daughter in the 1880s in order to join her three sons. Eldest son Thomas David Grafton (1866–1934) moved W and pre-empted land on Bowen I; the rest of the family soon joined him and acquired additional island property. Thomas was lighthouse keeper or assistant keeper at Point Atkinson from 1889 until he was killed while dynamiting fish. William Alfred Grafton (1868–1957) spent many years as a coast pilot, ran a ferry service on Howe Sd and later, after breaking his back in a logging accident, worked as a janitor in Vancouver. David Grafton (1871–1929) took part in the Klondike gold rush, then farmed on Bowen and served as foreman of the government road crew until he died in a hunting accident. Daughter Susan Caroline Grafton (1876–1904) married Frank Czar at Vancouver in 1898. Grafton Ck and Grafton Lk are also named for this pioneer family.

G

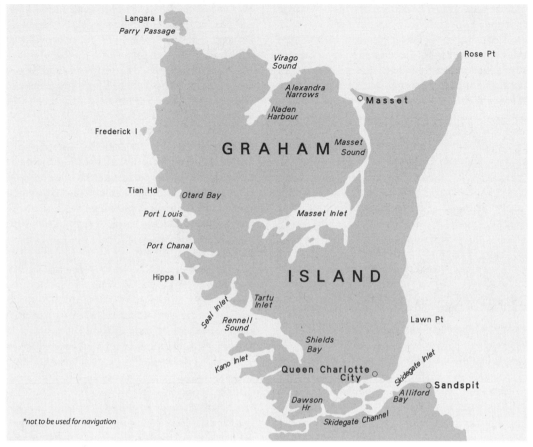

Graham Island, Queen Charlotte Islands. *Reproduced with the permission of the Canadian Hydrographic Service*

Graham Island (53°20'00" 132°25'00" Largest of QCI), **Graham Reach** (53°04'00" 128°34'00" Between Princess Royal I and the mainland). British statesman Sir James Robert Graham (1792–1861) was an important member of the reform party led by Lord Grey. A fine public speaker and capable administrator, he served as 1st Lord of the Admiralty, 1830–34 and 1852–55, and also as home secretary, 1841–46. Graham I, at 6,361 sq km, is the second-largest island in BC, after Vancouver I (and 22nd largest in Canada). It was named in 1853 by Cdr James Prevost, on Admiralty survey duty in the area with HMS *Virago*. W

Graham Rock (48°39'57" 123°23'31" Entrance to Roberts Bay, at Sidney, Saanich Peninsula, N of Victoria). Believed to be named after the capt of the first ferry to Denman I. He later moved to Sidney, where he kept his boat and scow at Roberts Bay and operated a freight service to the Gulf Is.

Grail Point (50°04'00" 124°42'00" E side of Lancelot Inlet, N of Theodosia Inlet, NW of Powell R). Named in association with Lancelot Inlet and Galahad Point after the knights of the Round Table, who vowed to search for the Holy Grail, the cup used by Jesus at the Last Supper and in which his blood was caught at the crucifixion.

Grainger Point (48°50'00" 123°14'00" N end of Samuel I, between Saturna I and Mayne I, Gulf Is). Martin Allerdale Grainger (1874–1941) was born at London, UK, lived in Australia as a child and graduated from Cambridge Univ in 1896. He first saw BC en route to the Klondike, then returned after service in the Boer War to work as a placer miner and logger. In 1908, back in London, he wrote *Woodsmen of the West*, a novel based on his BC experiences that has become a minor classic. He was appointed secretary of the 1910 Royal Commission on Forestry and became BC's deputy chief forester in 1915 and chief forester in 1916–20. In the 1920s and '30s he was involved in commercial forestry. Grainger, whose miscellaneous writings were published in 1995 as *Riding the Skyline*, was an important force behind the creation of Manning Provincial Park, established the year he died. The connection with Samuel I was through his wife, Mabel Florence Higgs, whom Martin married in 1908 on Mayne I. Mabel and her sister Winifred had come out from England to visit their brother Leonard Higgs, an early farmer on Saturna I and, later, S Pender. Winifred married Ralph Grey, who owned and farmed Samuel I, and lived there until 1910, accompanied much of the time by her sister Mabel. Grainger Ck in Manning Park is also named for Martin. *E*

Granby Bay (55°24'00" 129°49'00" W side of Observatory Inlet, W of Alice Arm, S of Stewart), **Granby Peninsula** (55°21'00" 129°49'00" Just E of Granby Bay), **Granby Point** (55°25'00" 129°47'00" N end of Granby Peninsula). The Granby Consolidated Mining, Smelting & Power Co operated a major copper mining and smelting operation here, 1912–35. At its peak the mine was one of the most productive in N America, and the nearby town of Anyox had a population of 2,700. The company was named after the Que hometown of its founder, Stephen Miner, who transformed a family tannery into a vast industrial empire. A copper smelter that operated at Grand Forks in the BC Interior, 1899–1919, gave its name to the Granby R. Granby Bay, formerly known as Goose Bay, was labelled Xschwan on an 1869 Admiralty chart based on surveys conducted by Lt Daniel Pender in 1868.

Henry Twidle's store and home at Granite Bay (about 1920). *MCR 7843*

Granite Bay (50°14'00" 125°19'00" SE of Kanish Bay, W side of Quadra I), **Granite Point** (50°17'00" 125°23'00" NW tip of Quadra I). Granite Bay was the site of a major railway-logging camp for BC Mills Timber & Trading Co from about 1890 to 1925. "Old Curly," an ancient CPR steam engine now on view at Burnaby Heritage Village, was used there. A group of Finns settled at the bay, and a small community grew up, complete with hotel, store, post office, school, brothel and steamship landing. The nearby Lucky Jim Mine produced copper, silver and gold ore, 1910–25. *E*

Grant Anchorage (52°29'00" 128°46'00" W entrance to Higgins Passage, Laredo Sd). Capt John Marshall Grant (1822–1902) was executive officer of the Columbia detachment of Royal Engineers, which served in BC 1858–63. He arrived at Esquimalt with his family in the *Arato* and, after a brief stop near Ft Langley, settled at New Westminster. He supervised the construction of the Cariboo Rd and also served as architect of historic Christ Church at Ft Hope. In 1863 the family returned to England, where Grant rose to the rank of col before retiring in 1882. He always maintained an interest in BC and held the land grant he received near New Westminster until his death. Captain Grant Ck, SE of Hope, is also named for him, as are, most likely, Grant Hill near Albion and Grant Narrows in Pitt Lk.

Grant Bank (52°07'00" 131°00'00" SE of High I, off E side of Kunghit I, QCI). Capt William Grant (1835–1916), from NS, married Helen Smith (1853–1943), a teacher, and travelled the world as a sailor, visiting Victoria and then settling there with his family in 1886. He was a founder and co-owner of the Victoria Sealing Co in 1899, and later, in 1905, joined with G W Sprott Balcom to form the Pacific Whaling Co. Helen worked in the business also, served on the Victoria school board and was a member of numerous women's organizations. The 28.5-m, 100-tonne *William Grant* was one of the steam whalers that operated out of Rose Hbr on Kunghit I and elsewhere in the QCI. Built at Victoria in 1910, it was used to hunt whales until 1942 and then saw service as a towboat until 1948. *E*

Grant Bay (50°28'00" 128°05'00" At N entrance to Quatsino Sd, SW of Winter Hbr, NW side of Vancouver I). William Grant and Thomas Sargent Lippy received Crown grants of land in this area in 1904–5. The feature is known locally as Open Bay.

Grant Bluff (49°45'00" 124°34'00" S side of Sturt Bay, NE Texada I, Str of Georgia). Presumably named after Alexander Grant (1847–1929), manager of the rich Marble Bay Mine at Van Anda for many years. The mine produced copper, gold and silver, and was purchased by the Tacoma Steel Co in 1902 from John Palmer, the original developer. It ceased operating in 1919. Grant was mine superintendent from 1904 to 1914 (and perhaps longer). Texada I's **Mount Grant** (49°36'50" 124°18'17") is likely named for him as well.

Granthams Landing (49°25'00" 123°30'00" SW side of Howe Sd, just NE of Gibsons, NW of Vancouver). Frederick Charles Grantham (1871–1954), from London, England, was a Vancouver juice and cider manufacturer. He bought recreational property at this location in 1909,

Granthams Landing about 1950. Photo by Harry Winn. *Author's collection*

G

Granville Island in 1917, its first year as an industrial site. *VPL 20405*

then subdivided his land, put in roads, wooden sidewalks, a water supply and a wharf, and sold cottage lots under the name of the Howe Sd Beach resort. Steamships stopped at his dock and a small community formed. Grantham, near Courtenay on Vancouver I, is named for the same family. *E*

Grant Island (49°31'00" 123°58'00" In Welcome Passage, between S Thormanby I and Sechelt Peninsula, Str of Georgia). Lt Alan F S Grant served on the BC coast aboard the hydrographic vessel *Egeria*, 1907–10. He was involved with surveys of Browning Entrance, Welcome Passage and other areas. Grant was also an officer on HMS *Cambrian*.

Grant Point (53°41'00" 129°05'00" W end of Maitland I, Douglas Channel, SW of Kitimat). Marine engineer Gordon Fraser Grant (1843–1908), from NS, arrived on the Pacific coast about 1868. He was originally employed by the federal Dept of Marine and Fisheries on the construction of the Esquimalt drydock, then became chief engineer of CGS *Sir James Douglas* and, in 1892, CGS *Quadra*. He retired in 1907. Named in 1908 by Louis Coste, chief engineer of Canada's Dept of Public Works. *W*

Grant Rocks (48°21'00" 123°42'00" Sooke Inlet, E of Whiffin Spit, S end of Vancouver I). Capt Walter Colquhoun Grant (1822–61), from Edinburgh, was the earliest colonist on Vancouver I who was not directly associated with the HBC. He sent eight settlers ahead of him, in 1848, to clear farmland in the Sooke area, and arrived himself the following year. Grant was hired by the HBC to survey and map Vancouver I, and he also built an early sawmill. After running short of funds he went to Oregon to prospect for gold, then sold his lands in 1853 to John Muir. He returned to his former career in the British Army and was serving in India when he died. Grant is infamous for introducing Scotch broom, an extremely invasive shrub, to BC. *E*

Granville Island (49°16'00" 123°08'00" False Ck, Vancouver). The island gets its name from its location: beneath the Granville St bridge. Granville was Vancouver's original townsite, laid out in 1870 on the S shore of Burrard Inlet, next to the Hastings sawmill. It was named for Granville Leveson-Gower, 2nd Earl Granville, the British colonial secretary at the time. This Liberal statesman held many important cabinet positions in his career, including foreign secretary (1851–52, 1870–74, 1880–85) and colonial secretary (1868–70, 1886). The island, a former sandbar and Squamish First Nation fishing spot, was created in 1916 with sediment dredged from False Ck. It became a busy industrial site but was redeveloped in the 1970s, with a large public market, art college, shops, theatres, restaurants and a hotel, as well as some of the original industries, and is often cited as one of Canada's most inspired examples of effective urban renewal. *E*

Granville Islands (51°55'00" 128°16'00" S end of Simonds Group, Queens Sd, SW of Bella Bella). After Canadian military leader Lt Gen Guy Granville Simonds. *See* Simonds Group.

Grappler Bight (52°15'00" 128°13'00" NW side of Dearth I, Seaforth Channel, N of Bella Bella), **Grappler Inlet** (48°50'00" 125°07'00" E of Bamfield Inlet, SE side of Barkley Sd, W side of Vancouver I), **Grappler Rock** (48°56'00" 123°36'00" Houston Passage, W of N end of Saltspring I, Gulf Is), **Grappler Sound** (50°55'00" 126°52'00" W side of Watson I, N of Wells Passage and NE Queen Charlotte Str). HMS *Grappler*, a 215-tonne gunboat, was launched in 1856 and operated on the BC coast from 1860 to 1868. It was a sister ship to HMS *Forward* and had a similarly adventurous career, investigating incidents of First Nation unrest at Alberni, Port Simpson and Clayoquot Sd, and helping pursue, under Lt Cdr Edmund Verney, a Lamalcha group suspected of murdering a Gulf Is family (*see* Lamalchi Bay). Unlike *Forward*, *Grappler* also had a lengthy post-navy career in BC. In 1868 it was sold for

The *Grappler* in the 1870s, after conversion to a freighter. *BC Archives G-06346*

$2,400 at public auction to Capt James Frain and converted to a coastal freighter. Over the next 15 years, under several owners, it ran between Victoria and Alaska before catching fire in a terrible accident near Seymour Narrows in 1883 en route to the N coast canneries. Eighty-eight passengers and crew lost their lives. Grappler Bight was formerly known as Bushby Bight, after George Bushby, owner of a Prince Rupert marine supply business in the 1920s. **W**

Grauer Beach (49°03'00" 123°02'00" W side of Boundary Bay, Delta, S of Vancouver). Jacob Grauer (1861–1936), a native of Württemberg, Germany, came to BC about 1883 after spending time in the US. He set up as a butcher in Vancouver in 1886, then moved in 1895 to a 120-ha farm on Sea I. About 1900 he also purchased 260 ha on Boundary Bay, where he grazed beef cattle and sheep, and grew feed for his Sea I dairy herds. Grauer's meat products were later marketed under the Frasea Farms label. His sons worked with him in the business, and several became prominent Vancouver-area citizens: George was said to be the first white boy born at Mt Pleasant; Rudolph was reeve of Richmond, 1930–49; and Albert ("Dal") was president of BC Electric and chancellor of UBC. Part of the Boundary Bay property was sold to a syndicate that developed Beach Grove Golf and Country Club.

Grautoff Point (52°20'00" 128°22'00" S end of Lake I, Mathieson Channel, Milbanke Sd). In 1864 the newly married Teresa Jane Pemberton (1843–1916, née Grautoff) accompanied her husband, Joseph Pemberton, from London, England, where she was wed, to Vancouver I, where Joseph had worked as the colony's surveyor gen since 1859. She was the daughter of London merchant Bernard Grautoff, originally from Lübeck in northern Germany. Pemberton was an engineer and HBC employee who played important roles in BC's early political and economic development (*see* Pemberton Bay). In 1909, Theresa donated the Pemberton Chapel, restored in 2003, to Victoria's Royal Jubilee Hospital.

Grave Bay (54°30'00" 130°14'00" E side of Work Channel, N of Prince Rupert). John Costello Grave, a former lt in

the RN, brought the brigantine *Eagle* from England to Ft Vancouver on the Columbia R in 1827 for the HBC. In 1830, as master of the *Eagle*, he helped select the first site of Ft Simpson (originally known as Ft Nass) on the Nass R.

Gravesend Reach (49°08'00" 123°02'00" Mouth of the Fraser R, between Lulu I and Tilbury I). In England, the towns of Gravesend and Tilbury are on opposite banks of the Thames R between Westminster and the sea. RN surveyor Capt George Richards gave this name to the branch of the Fraser R opposite Tilbury I (qv) between New Westminster and the Str of Georgia. Gravesend, Kent, was an early riverfront resort town and port of entry; today it is a city of over 50,000 with a large E Indian population.

Graveyard Bay (49°28'00" 124°16'00" S side of Lasqueti I, Str of Georgia). A grave marker beside the bay denotes the resting place of Maggie Richardson, who died on Lasqueti in 1899 at the age of two. She was a daughter of Thomas and Janet Richardson, who lived nearby while Tom worked as a shepherd for an early sheep-raising venture on the island. The family left Lasqueti for Nanaimo in the early 1900s. Nearby Richardson Cove (qv) is named after them.

Gray Peninsula (48°53'45" 123°24'24" W side of Galiano I, Gulf Is). John Lupton Gray (c 1849–1922) came to Canada from the US in 1886 and farmed on Galiano I. He opened a store at Montague Hbr about 1905, which was later run by his son Albert Edward Gray.

Gray Rock (51°51'00" 130°56'00" SE of Kerouard Is, off S tip of QCI), **Grays Cove** (52°06'00" 131°13'00" E side of Anthony I, off SW end of Moresby I, QCI). Capt Robert Gray (1755–1806) commanded the *Lady Washington*, one of the vessels in the first US fur-trading expedition to the PNW. He left Boston in 1787, arrived a year later at Nootka Sd and spent the summer of 1789 in the QCI. Exchanging ships with Capt John Kendrick, the expedition's leader, he then took the *Columbia Rediviva* back to Boston via China, thus becoming the first US mariner to circumnavigate the globe. Gray returned to BC in 1791 as cdr and part owner of the *Columbia* and again traded furs in the QCI before sailing S and overwintering at Adventure Cove (qv) in Clayoquot Sd. In 1792 he entered the lower Columbia R, the first non-Native to do so, then returned to the QCI and Nootka Sd, where he repaired his ship and became friends with Spanish naval officer Juan Francisco de la Bodega y Quadra, who was waiting to meet with Capt George Vancouver. Gray finally sailed back to Boston in 1793 via Hawaii and China. Gray Rk was discovered in 1792 in time-honoured fashion, with the keel of the *Columbia*, thus necessitating the Nootka Sd repairs; apparently Gray later reported the rock's location to Vancouver. Grays Cove is where he anchored the *Lady Washington* on his first trip to the QCI, in June 1789, and it was probably there that Robert Haswell, Gray's 2nd mate, became the

G

first white man to step ashore onto Haida Gwaii. Several other QCI features may also be named after Gray—**Gray Bay** (53°07'00" 131°41'00" Between Copper Bay and Cumshewa Inlet, NE side of Moresby I), **Gray Island** (53°43'00" 132°26'00" N side of Masset Inlet, Graham I) and **Gray Point** (53°06'00" 131°39'00" SE entrance to Gray Bay)—but this is not certain. *D*

Great Race Rock. *See* Race Passage.

Greaves Island (51°18'00" 127°30'00" In Smith Sd, N of Port Hardy). Richard Greaves (d 1868) of Ripon, Yorkshire, was the grandfather of Anne Walbran, wife of author and master mariner John Walbran. Capt Walbran had a long career on the BC coast with the federal Dept of Marine and Fisheries, and named this feature in 1903 while making a preliminary survey of the area in the government lighthouse tender *Quadra*.

Green Bay (52°20'00" 126°59'00" N of junction of S Bentinck Arm and N Bentinck Arm, W of Bella Coola). While the origin of the name Green Bay is uncertain, its former name, Porcupine Cove, was bestowed by the NWC's Alexander Mackenzie after his hungry party shot and gratefully consumed a porcupine at this spot in 1793. Mackenzie had just reached salt water on his historic overland journey from the interior and become the first white person to cross N America from coast to coast.

Green Cove (48°59'00" 124°59'00" E side of Uchucklesit Inlet, N side of Alberni Inlet, Vancouver I). This feature was formerly known as Elhlateese Cove, meaning "further down the beach," after the Nuu-chah-nulth First Nation village located at the head of Uchucklesit Inlet. The well-established local name of Green Cove was adopted in 1968.

Greene Point Rapids shingle mill. *Author's collection*

Greene Point (50°27'00" 125°31'00" NE tip of W Thurlow I, Johnstone Str, NW of Campbell R), **Greene Point Rapids** (50°26'00" 125°31'00" Off Greene Point). Named

in 1863 by Lt Daniel Pender after Molesworth Greene Jackson, 1st lt of HMS *Topaze*, who served on the Pacific Station, 1859–63. *See* Jackson Bay. A P Allison had a railway-logging camp here by 1908 that developed into one of the largest shingle mills on the BC coast.

Green Point (49°03'00" 125°43'00" E side of Wickaninnish Bay, Clayoquot Sd, W side of Vancouver I). One of the first non-Native residents in the Long Beach area lived near Combers Beach from 1880 to 1890 and was named A Green. His original house was burned by Parks Canada in 1973. Today the point is the site of a large Pacific Rim National Park campground.

Green Spit (53°05'00" 128°31'00" S shore of Khutze Inlet, E of Princess Royal I). This feature was formerly known as Ward Spit, after Ward B Smith, manager and mining engineer of the Western Copper Mine, located about 8 km up the Khutze valley from the head of the inlet. The mine was active prior to 1910 and again between 1925 and 1932. In 1923–24, before coming to the coast, Smith, from Spokane, was active in the W Kootenays with the Surprise Group of copper claims at Howser Lk. *See also* Pardoe Point. The origin of the current name is unknown.

Greenville. *See* Laxgalts'ap.

Greenwood Point (50°31'00" 128°02'00" W side of Winter Hbr, Quatsino Sd, NW side of Vancouver I). A Crown grant of land in this area was received in 1907 by a man named John Greenwood.

Greetham Point (50°20'00" 125°19'00" W side of Sonora I, SE of Bruce Point, N of Campbell R). Peter Greetham (1830–83), born at Flint, Wales, was an engineer aboard HMS *Cameleon*, under Cdr Edward Hardinge, and served on the Pacific Station, 1863–65. He entered the RN in 1854, became a chief engineer in 1872 and retired the following year. RN surveyor Lt Daniel Pender, in 1863, named a number of features in the area after those officers of the *Cameleon* who participated in a punitive expedition that same year against the Lamalcha, a Kuper I First Nation group suspected of murdering two Gulf Is settlers (*see* Lamalchi Bay).

Gregoire Point (49°54'00" 127°11'00" Between Esperanza Inlet and Kyuquot Sd, NW side of Vancouver I). Flying Officer Leo Joseph Robert Gregoire was killed in action Mar 3, 1945, aged 24. He was born in Alberta and was living at Vancouver, working as a plumber's assistant, at the time he enlisted. Gregoire, who was awarded the DFC after completing 26 sorties over Germany, often under fierce anti-aircraft fire, was a member of RAF No 153 Squadron, flying Lancaster heavy bombers, and is commemorated on the Runnymede Memorial in England.

Greig Island (48°41'00" 123°20'00" E of Coal I, off NE end of Saanich Peninsula, N of Victoria). A native of the Orkney Is, John Greig (1825–92) entered HBC service in 1844. At Ft Colville in the US he met his future wife, Margaret Goudie (1830–1914), daughter of HBC employee James Goudie and his First Nation wife, Catherine. The Greig family came to BC about 1852 and acquired land at Thetis Lk near Colwood, where John farmed, became a well-known fiddler and worked as a lime burner, selling his lime to the HBC. In 1869 he purchased property on Tod Inlet, in central Saanich, with better lime deposits. A quarry was developed there that eventually came under the control of cement tycoon Robert Butchart and was transformed in 1909 into the world-famous Butchart Gardens. Greig I was formerly known as Bird I.

Grenville Channel (53°37'00" 129°43'00" Between Pitt I and the mainland). Capt George Vancouver named this important leg of the Inside Passage in 1793 after William Wyndham Grenville, 1st Baron Grenville (1759–1834). Lord Grenville was a noted British Liberal statesman who held many cabinet positions, including home secretary (1789–91), foreign secretary (1791–1801) and PM (1806–7). He was chancellor of Oxford Univ, 1810–34. His wife, Anne Pitt (1773–1864), had a brother serving as a midshipman on HMS *Discovery*, Vancouver's vessel. This was the notorious Thomas Pitt, later Lord Camelford, who had to be discharged in Hawaii in 1794 for his insubordinate conduct. Vancouver had Pitt flogged, which was unusual for "gentlemen" and alienated some younger officers. It also filled Pitt with a raging desire for revenge. Back in London, he challenged Vancouver to a duel and even attacked him on the street, behaviour that was condoned, amazingly, by the press and by public opinion. In fact, Pitt's bad-mouthing helped gain Vancouver a reputation as a despot and bully that, at the time, partly

eclipsed his remarkable achievements. Pitt's subsequent career was marked by other violent acts, including an outright murder, though his wealth and exalted connections always allowed him to secure an acquittal or get off with a fine. He was finally killed in a duel, aged 29. According to the Earl of Rosebery, "his was a turbulent, rakehelly, demented existence.... Bull terriers, bludgeons, fighting of all kinds were associated with him; riots of all kinds were as the breath of his nostrils." *W*

Gribbell Island (53°24'15" 129°01'30" E of entrance to Douglas Channel, SW of Kitimat). RN surveyor Lt Daniel Pender named this island in 1867 after his future brother-in-law, Rev Francis Barrow Gribbell. Gribbell arrived at Victoria in 1865 as chaplain to Bishop George Hills and took charge of St John's Anglican church in 1868. A year later he became rector of St Paul's, Esquimalt, then principal of the Collegiate School in Victoria, 1870–75, after which he returned to England and served as vicar to various parishes in Kent. The island is part of the traditional territory of both the Haisla and Gitga'at First Nations and home to the highest known concentration of Kermode or "spirit" bears—black bears that, due to a genetic anomaly, have white or cream-coloured fur. As many as 30 percent of Gribbell's bears are white, raising the possibility that the recessive gene responsible for this variation originated on the island. Gribbell's mineral potential led several US companies to do much development work there in 1900–1905, hoping for rich copper, gold and silver strikes, but no commercial mining ever took place. The island was long considered to be part of Hawkesbury I.

Gribbell Islet (54°19'52" 130°26'47" Off Metlakatla in Venn Passage, just NW of Prince Rupert). According to Capt John Walbran, author of *British Columbia Coast Names*, this feature was named in 1868 by Lt Daniel Pender

Grenville Channel, 90 km long, is an important leg of the Inside Passage and much used by marine traffic. *John Alexander*

G

after Elizabeth Florence Isabel Gribbell (b 1866), the eldest daughter of Rev Francis Gribbell (*see* Gribbell I), rector of St John's church, Victoria. Later in his book, Walbran states, confusingly, that nearby Isabel It is named for Gribbell's wife. The wife, however, was named Elizabeth Mary Ann Gribbell. Pender married Frank Gribbell's sister, Amy Maria, at Esquimalt in 1869. The traditional Tsimshian First Nation name for this feature is Lac-skin-nee.

Grice Bay (49°06'00" 125°44'00" Entrance to Tofino Inlet, S of Indian I, Clayoquot Sd, W side of Vancouver I), **Grice Point** (49°09'00" 125°55'00" NW point of Esowista Peninsula, Tofino). John Grice (1850–1934), from Newcastle upon Tyne, England, became one of the Tofino district's first white settlers in 1891, pre-empting land at Grice Point. He learned to speak the Nuu-chah-nulth language and worked for the sealing industry, signing up First Nation hunters in the days when sealing was an important coastal industry. He later served as harbourmaster and justice of the peace. Grice and his wife, Jane West (1850–1934), whom he married in 1874, were cultured, educated English immigrants, highly esteemed in the community; they raised five children at Tofino and died within days of each other at the age of 84.

Grief Point (49°48'00" 124°31'00" NE side of Malaspina Str, at S end of city of Powell R). Named, according to historian Athelstan Harvey, because it is an exposed spot in a westerly wind, causing grief to many a mariner. The Sliammon First Nation name for this feature is Xákwuhem (Achquam), which refers to the cow parsnip that once grew here in abundance. The point, protected from SE winds, was a valued Sliammon camping and garden site.

Griffin Island (48°26'00" 123°14'00" Just N of Discovery I, off SE end of Vancouver I), **Griffin Point** (53°04'00" 128°33'00" E side of Graham Reach, opposite Princess Royal I, S of Khutze Inlet). Named after Capt Thomas Ormond Griffin (1858–1942), born at Liverpool, England, and a long-time Victoria resident. He arrived in BC in 1889, joined the Canadian Pacific Navigation Co as 1st officer of the *Islander* in 1891 and transferred to the CPR in 1901 when that company purchased the CPN fleet. In 1894, at Victoria, he married Jane Miriam Foster (1876–1935). Appointed a master in 1903, Griffin went on to become the senior skipper in the CPR's BC Coast Steamship Service, in command of *Princess Victoria* until 1908 and then *Princess Charlotte*, the flagship. Most of his service was on the Vancouver–Victoria–Seattle "triangle" route. He retired in 1924. Ormond Point in Kxngeal Inlet off Grenville Channel is also named for him. Before 1934, Griffin I was known as Beaumont I after Capt Ernest Beaumont, owner of Discovery I (*see* Beaumont Shoal).

Griffith Harbour (53°36'00" 130°32'00" NW side of Banks I). Frederick H Griffith (1871–1922), from NB, worked for the Canadian Pacific Navigation Co early in his career and was listed aboard the steamship *Amur* in the 1901 census. He served as sailing master of CGS *Lillooet*, 1908–22, and made a number of hydrographic surveys near the Skeena R before dying aboard ship while involved in a survey of Hecate Str. The name was adopted in 1926.

Griffon Point (53°49'00" 129°57'00" S entrance to Watts Narrows, Baker Inlet, opposite NE Pitt I). HMS *Griffon*, a 700-tonne steam-powered gunship, was the first command of Cdr Robert Watts Davies, who had served as a midshipman on the RN's Pacific Station, 1860–62. The vessel was launched in 1876 and posted to the N America Station, the E Indies and the E African coast, where it was involved in the suppression of the slave trade. *See also* Watts Narrows. A griffon, not to be confused with the mythical griffin or gryphon, is a small terrier dog originally bred for hunting.

Grilse Point (49°48'00" 124°36'00" NE end of Texada I, Malaspina Str). On the Pacific coast, grilse is the name given to immature salmon in their first year at sea. Presumably this is a good spot for catching them. On the E coast, where Atlantic salmon do not necessarily die after spawning, the word refers to small fish that are ready to enter a river and spawn after spending only one winter at sea.

Grimmer Bay (48°49'00" 123°19'00" W side of N Pender I, Gulf Is). After emigrating with his family from England to Australia, Washington Grimmer (1851–1930) travelled to Victoria in 1877 and sought gold in the Cariboo. In 1882 he bought the 600-ha N Pender I property of his brother Oliver Grimmer and put his Australian experience to good use by raising sheep. Three years later he married Elizabeth Brice Auchterlonie (1869–1945), another Pender I pioneer, at Victoria. His land, located where the community of Port Washington (also named for him) is today, became the site of the island's first wharf, school, hall and post office. Grimmer, naturally, was Pender's first postmaster (1891–93). His eldest son was born in the middle of Navy Channel as Elizabeth was being rapidly rowed to the midwife, who happened to live on Mayne I. As a result, the lad was burdened with the name Neptune Navy Grimmer (1889–1982), or "Nep" for short. After studies at Guelph's Ont Agricultural College, he took over the family farm and raised dairy and beef cattle. Washington, an avid musician and active participant in island life, turned his home into a guest house and built an oceanfront retirement cottage. He died at Ganges on Saltspring I and is buried in the Mayne I cemetery.

Grogan Island (50°35'00" 126°09'40" SW side of Call Inlet, N of Johnstone Str). Lt (Pilot) Jack Armstrong Grogan, of Victoria, was killed in action on May 19, 1945, aged 26. He was the son of Leo and Elza Grogan of Shawnigan Lk and is buried at Yeovilton churchyard in Somerset, England.

G

Grogan Rock (49°57'00" 127°14'00" S of Rugged Point, Kyuquot Sd, NW side of Vancouver I). Helen Aimee Grogan was an early owner of property on Rugged Point. In 1913 she married Frank Mortimer Kelly of Oak Bay, a poet and timber cruiser who spent much time on N Vancouver I.

Gross Point (49°57'15" 127°13'45" S of entrance to Kyuquot Channel, NW side of Vancouver I). Flight Lt Douglas Haig Gross, who enlisted in the RCAF at Vancouver, was killed in action Aug 18, 1944, aged 28, while serving with RAF No 184 Squadron. The squadron was equipped with Hawker Typhoon fighter-bombers and provided support for the Normandy invasion, attacking radar and communication sites and other specific ground targets. He is buried at the Bretteville-sur-Laize Canadian War Cemetery in France.

Growler Cove (50°32'00" 126°37'00" W end of W Cracroft I, NW entrance to Johnstone Str, E of Port McNeill). Possibly named after the *Growler*, a well-known Puget Sd schooner that left Victoria, under Capt Horace Coffin, for Sitka, Alaska, in 1868 and was wrecked "at the head of Vancouver's I," according to a contemporary report in the *NY Times*. None of the 13 crew or passengers were ever seen again. When the schooner *Nanaimo Packet* later reached the scene of the wreck and its crew members went ashore, they were attacked by a First Nation group and forced to leave. The *Growler* was built by John Izett in 1859, probably at Oak Hbr on Puget Sd, for Capt Ed Barrington. It was a frequent visitor to Victoria and the BC N coast and sailed on occasion as far S as San Francisco.

Guaquina Point (49°39'00" 126°06'00" S side of Muchalat Inlet, S of mouth of Gold R, W Vancouver I). This name recalls the fact that Muchalat Inlet was formerly known as Guaquina Arm. The derivation of Guaquina is uncertain. According to Fr Augustin Brabant, pioneer Roman Catholic missionary and historian, it is an adaptation of the name of a celebrated Muchalaht First Nation woman. Brabant's observation is repeated in Capt John Walbran's *British Columbia Coast Names*. However, on the 1791 chart of Spanish explorer Francisco Eliza, the inlet is shown as Fondo de Guicananish, while on Dionisio Alcalá-Galiano's 1792 chart, it is called Brazo de Guaquinaniz. Guaquina may have evolved from these names, which PNW cartography expert Henry Wagner suggests probably refer to the famous Nuu-chah-nulth chief Wickaninnish, even though his home territory was farther S, on Clayoquot Sd.

Guard Rock (51°00'00" 127°31'00" Part of the Southgate Group, NW Queen Charlotte Str). So named by Cdr John Parry, aboard the W coast survey vessel *Egeria* in 1903–6, because the rock guards the anchorage from the prevailing swell outside.

Guilliams Bay (50°10'00" 127°50'00" NW side of Brooks Peninsula and Vancouver I), **Guilliams Island** (50°11'00" 127°51'00" SE of Hackett I, Brooks Bay, off NW Brooks Peninsula). Rufus F Guilliams (1862–94), from Oregon, became involved in the Victoria sealing industry in the 1880s, working aboard the schooner *Kate and Anna*. He then moved to the trading vessels *George H Chance* and *Penelope*, and the sealer *Geneva*. In 1893 he became master of the sealing schooner *Louis Olsen* (the former British steamer *Dolphin*) and took that vessel to the Japanese coast, Aleutian Is and Bering Sea before returning in 1894 to Victoria, where he died suddenly.

Guillod Point (50°03'00" 127°16'00" S entrance to Chamiss Bay, Kyuquot Sd, NW side of Vancouver I). Harry Guillod (1838–1906) served for many years as Indian agent and justice of the peace in the Barkley Sd region and was a fluent speaker of the Nuu-chah-nulth language. He arrived at Victoria, via Panama and San Francisco, in 1862 from London, England, and tried his hand at mining in the Cariboo. He also acted as a lay Anglican teacher and missionary at Victoria, Alberni and Comox. Guillod was appointed an Indian agent in 1882, first at Ucluelet and then, from 1892 on, at Alberni, where he was church warden and raised three daughters with wife Kate Elizabeth Munro (1862–1949). In 1893 the Victoria *Colonist* noted that he was busy collecting First Nation artifacts for display at the Chicago World's Fair. Guillod was a talented musician and popular local resident—"a jolly fellow, good natured and true hearted," according to the *Colonist*—whose knowledge of medicine, the result of an apprenticeship as a pharmacist in England, was put to extensive use working with First Nation groups, especially during a W coast smallpox scare in 1892. But he also helped destroy those he was responsible for. "They are an impediment to the securing of local land by our people," Guillod wrote to his superiors in 1903, referring to the Ahousaht people. "Simple humanity requires the removal of the Indians who remain into the residential schools so that the ones who can be civilized can be won away from the corrupting influences of their parents and elders. This will undoubtedly mean that many of the children will die from the conditions in the schools, particularly the appalling incidence of tuberculosis. But such is in keeping with the existing practices, and I see no disadvantage to this Department to continue in this vein."

Guise Bay (50°46'00" 128°24'00" Just SE of Cape Scott, NW tip of Vancouver I), **Guise Point** (51°40'00" 127°58'00" E side of Hecate I, Fitz Hugh Sd, S of Bella Bella). Capt John Guise commanded the 127-tonne brig *Experiment* on James Strange's 1786 expedition to the BC coast. Together with the 317-tonne *Captain Cook*, under Capt Henry Laurie, Guise left Bombay and sailed to Nootka Sd via Java. Strange traded for sea otter furs at Nootka and left John McKay behind, at his own request,

The splendid beach at Guise Bay. *Greg Shea*

under Chief Maquinna's protection, to learn more about the Nuu-chah-nulth people (McKay, surgeon's mate on the *Experiment*, was eventually picked up in 1787 by Capt Charles Barkley). The ships then ventured N, naming Queen Charlotte Sd and several features around NW Vancouver I, and visited Alaska before returning to Asia. Guise Ck on Nootka I is probably also named for John Guise. (Guise's first name is often given as Henry, but his friend Alexander Walker, who accompanied the expedition and whose detailed journal of the voyage was finally published in 1982, distinctly refers to him as John.) *See* Experiment Bight *and* McKay Passage, as well.

Gulf Islands (48°57'00" 123°32'00" E of S end of Vancouver I). This geographical feature extends from D'Arcy I in the SW to the N end of Gabriola I and as far E as Saturna I; not included are Newcastle I, Protection I and other small islands off the coast of Nanaimo, nor any islands farther N, such as Texada and Denman. The terms Southern Gulf Is and Northern Gulf Is, though frequently encountered, are not official names. The Spanish naval officers Francisco Eliza and José Narváez were the first Europeans to explore the islands, in 1791. When Capt George Vancouver took formal "possession" of the BC coast on June 4, 1792, he referred to BC's inland sea as the Gulph of Georgia, in honour of King George III, whose birthday it was. Even though RN surveyor Capt George Richards changed gulf to strait in 1858, the name Gulf Is had become unalterably established. Now this scattered, sun-blessed archipelago, part of which is protected as a new national park, is a popular and increasingly expensive haven for holidaymakers, boaters, tourists and retirees. *E*

Gunboat Passage (52°10'00" 127°58'00" Between Cunningham I and Denny I, just E of Bella Bella). Named by Lt Daniel Pender in 1867 after HMS *Grappler* and *Forward*, which gave yeoman service on the BC coast as small, steam-powered naval gun vessels from 1860 to 1869. *See* Forward Bay *and* Grappler Bight for more detailed individual accounts.

Gunderson Slough. *See* Annieville Channel.

Gunia Point (54°10'00" 132°57'00" NW side of Graham I, QCI). After Haida chief Blakow-Coneehaw, or Gunia, of Kiusta village. *See* Coneehaw Rk.

Gunner Point (50°28'00" 125°57'00" N side of Sunderland Channel, N of Johnstone Str). Named in association with the WWII fortifications on nearby Yorke I (qv).

Guns Rock (52°17'00" 127°45'00" In Wallace Bay, E side of Cousins Inlet, NE of Bella Bella). Thomas Salter Guns (1868–1963) first saw Burrard Inlet in 1883, as an apprentice aboard the Scottish lumber barque *Highland Glen*. Five years later he returned, as quartermaster of the *Islander*, helping bring that newly constructed flagship of the Canadian Pacific Navigation Co from Glasgow to Victoria. Guns worked on a number of tugs and steamers for the CPN and CPR. In 1893 he was mate aboard the *Yosemite* when, in a fit of rage, Capt John Irving left his cargo on a Steveston dock—along with 14 seamen protesting that they had not been allowed a meal break

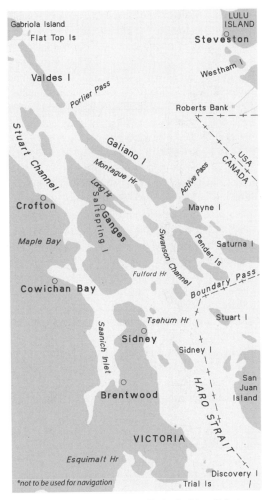

Gulf Islands. *Reproduced with the permission of the Canadian Hydrographic Service*

after working all night—and sailed to Victoria with a makeshift crew of stewards and Chinese mess boys. In 1897, Guns married Minnie Sparks (1871–1954), from Nfld, at Victoria. He later commanded the small steamship *Rainbow* (formerly the *Teaser*) and the large CPR tug *Nitinat*, then served as a BC coast pilot from 1916 until his retirement in 1935.

Gurd Inlet (53°53'00" 130°38'00" W side of Gurd I), **Gurd Island** (53°53'00" 130°37'00" In Kitkatla Inlet, SW of Porcher I and Prince Rupert), **Gurd Point** (53°55'00" 130°38'00" N end of Gurd I). Robert Winter Gurd (1856–1915), from Bristol, worked as a clerk before enrolling with the Anglican Church Missionary Society. He immigrated to BC in 1886 and married Eliza Hawley (1854–1935) at Victoria a year later. Gurd ministered primarily at Kitkatla, a Tsimshian First Nation community on Dolphin I on the N coast, where he arrived in 1894 and, with the support of Chief William Shakes, erected a small church in 1896. He also served at Claxton Cannery and Metlakatla, where he died. Nearby Robert I and Winter Rk are also named for him, as is, presumably, **Gurd Rock** (53°45'00" 130°19'00" In Beaver Passage, E of Spicer I, S of Porcher I). *W*

Gustavson Bay (49°39'30" 123°39'00" N side of Salmon Inlet, E of Sechelt Inlet, NW of Vancouver). Four Gustavson brothers came to BC from Sweden in 1914 and worked as loggers on Vancouver I and with N Vancouver's Capilano Timber Co. Two of them, Eric (d 1961) and Thure (1886–1967), became handloggers on Jervis and Sechelt inlets in the 1920s, and in 1929 took over the Regina Timber Co and its railway-logging operations at Misery Ck on Salmon Inlet, renaming the company Gustavson Bros Logging. The Gustavsons logged at Misery Ck until 1934, setting up a powerful "snubbing" engine to gingerly lower individual cars to the wharf, down the final 2 km of track, which at 45 degrees was too steep for locomotives. When their lease was logged off, they moved to the Stakawus

valley, SW of Deserted Bay on Jervis Inlet, and ran one of the last railway-logging shows on the BC mainland. The brothers shifted to truck logging in 1938 and sold out to N Shore Lumber in 1951.

Gust Point (54°09'00" 130°07'00" On N side of E entrance to Inverness Passage, SE of Prince Rupert). Gustavus Holmes, a hard-working Swedish fisherman who immigrated to Oregon, became co-owner of the British American Cannery on the Fraser R, built on the S shore of Lulu I. In 1883 he built and managed a cannery at Port Essington on the Skeena R, also called the British American, which First Nation workers referred to as Boston Cannery, "Boston" being the Chinook jargon word for American. In 1883, its poorest year, this operation produced 5,200 cases of salmon, employed 225 workers and owned 40 gillnet boats. In 1891, at which time Holmes acquired several Crown grants of land near Gust Point, it was sold to Henry Bell-Irving and the Anglo-BC Packing Co. Holmes had an interest in the Fidalgo I Packing Co, active in Washington and Alaska, as well. His 1890 home at 682 34th St, Astoria, Oregon, on what was once known as Holmes Hill, is a fine heritage example of the Queen Anne architectural style.

Gut, The. *See* The Cut.

Guy Island (51°58'00" 128°17'00" N end of Simonds Group, Queens Sd, SW of Bella Bella). After Canadian military leader Lt Gen Guy Granville Simonds. *See* Simonds Group.

Gypsy Shoal (50°18'00" 125°15'00" Lower Rapids, Okisollo Channel, between Quadra I and Okis I, N of Campbell R). Named in 1924 for the 25-tonne, 14-m tug *Gypsy*, built at Vancouver in 1905, which did considerable towing through these channels for BC Mills Timber & Trading Co, the province's largest early lumber manufacturer.

H

Haaksvold Point (51°58'00" 127°42'00" SE point of King I, Burke Channel, SE of Bella Bella). Simon L Haaksvold (1876–1955), from Norway, pre-empted land in this area in 1908 and acquired a Crown grant in 1911. He died at Bella Coola.

Haans Islet (53°02'00" 131°41'00" Off N side of Cumshewa Inlet, QCI). John George Haan (1871–1940), a native of Germany, was an experienced sealing skipper, 1896–1907, master of the *Labrador*, *Zilla May*, *Jessie* and, primarily, the *Umbrina*. He married Jane Miller Hall (1877–1971) at Victoria in 1902. After sealing, he joined the CPR briefly as capt of the powerful tug *Lorne*, which mostly towed sailing vessels from Cape Flattery to Victoria, then purchased the QCI dogfish oilery at Skidegate Landing in partnership with Simon Leiser. Haan's 26-m steam tug *Ranger* was used to tow small fishing boats to the best dogfish grounds. About 1911 the family moved to Sandspit, near Haans Ck, where the capt operated a charter boat, the *Wee Jeanie*. In later years, after a move to Queen Charlotte City, he ran the launch *Dot* for Pacific Mills. Haan's three sons, Jack, Peter and Charlie, all followed their father's lead and became master mariners as well. *D*

Hackett Bay (50°11'00" 127°50'00" W side of Brooks Peninsula, NW Vancouver I), **Hackett Island** (50°11'00" 127°52'00" SW of Orchard Point, Brooks Bay, off Brooks Peninsula). Charles Hackett (b 1849), from N Sydney, NS, arrived at Victoria in 1889 to participate in the sealing industry. He was skipper and owner of the successful sealing schooners *Annie C Moore* and *Libbie*, and in the mid-1890s established a store at Ahousat, on Clayoquot Sd, where he produced barrels of smoked codfish. Hackett replaced Capt John Walbran in 1903 as master of CGS *Quadra*, the government lighthouse tender on the BC coast. In December 1906 he orchestrated the rescue of the crew of the *Coloma*, an aged sailing vessel bound from Seattle to Australia with a cargo of lumber, which was wrecked off Cape Beale, on the W coast of Vancouver I, in a violent storm.

Haddington Island, site of an important granite quarry. *Andrew Scott*

Haddington Island (50°36'00" 127°01'00" S of Malcolm I, Broughton Str, just NE of Port McNeill), **Haddington Passage** (50°36'00" 127°00'00" Between Haddington I and Malcolm I), **Haddington Reefs** (50°37'00" 127°00'00" E of Haddington I). Named for Thomas Hamilton, 9th Earl of Haddington (1780–1858) and 1st Lord of the Admiralty, 1841–46. He was not very distinguished as a politician ("a man without shining or plausible qualities, interest or influence," according to the diarist Charles Greville) but managed to hold several significant positions, including lord lt of Ireland and lord privy seal—and even declined the important post of gov gen of India. Haddington I was the site of a quarry, from 1896 to 1966, that provided the andesite used to face many important buildings in Victoria and Vancouver, including the legislature, Empress Hotel, Hotel Vancouver, Vancouver courthouse (now Vancouver Art Gallery), several post offices, banks and offices. Demand for the fine-grained stone, which takes a sharp edge for carving, resulted in the reopening of the quarry in 2004. The *Queen of Prince Rupert*, a BC ferry, ran aground on Haddington I in 1967. *W*

Hagan Bight (48°35'00" 123°28'00" E side of Saanich Inlet, N of Victoria). Farmer James Hagan (1833–1913) emigrated from Ireland to the US in 1854 and ended up in BC about 1861. During the Cariboo gold rush he had some success at Lightning Ck and was able to buy a homestead in the Saanich district, on W Saanich Rd, in 1872. He was married twice, first to Rose Morris (1849–81) in the eastern US, and then, two years after her death, to Virginia Rey (c 1848–1919), at Victoria. Rey had come to Canada from France about 1870. A post office named Hagan was located on the family property, 1892–1913, with James as its only postmaster. Nearby Hagan Ck is also named for him. Hagan Bight is known to local anglers as Indian Bay.

Haggard Cove (48°58'00" 125°01'00" N entrance to Alberni Inlet, Barkley Sd, W side of Vancouver I). Lt William Alvin Haggard, DCM (1921–84), of Tisdale, Sask, served in the S Sask Regiment in WWII. As a private he participated in the disastrous raid on Dieppe, where he won distinction for taking charge of his platoon, whose leader had been wounded, and, with another soldier, orchestrating a successful attack on an enemy machine-gun position. Both were injured in the action. Haggard's portrait was painted by Lawren Harris, an official war artist, in 1942. The family moved to the US about 1950, and Haggard died in California. His brothers, residents of Port Alberni, suggested that a place be named after this war hero, and Haggard Cove was adopted in 1984. Nearby Haggard Lk is also named for him.

Hague Point (52°40'00" 128°50'00" S side of Princess Royal I, NW of Bella Bella). Henry Hague (1859–1945) was born at Victoria, in a tent. He learned the merchant's trade in the 1870s with Henry Saunders, a grocer on Johnson St, and married Lydia Heay (1863–1947), from Nebraska, in 1882. The couple moved to Ecoole in Barkley Sd, where James Warren operated a trading post, and then to Ucluelet, where he was employed at the store and sealing station owned by William Spring and Peter Francis. Over the next 20 years, Hague worked all over SW BC as a shopkeeper, spending time in Victoria (with Simon Leiser and John Weiler), Nanaimo, Chemainus, Vancouver (with Kelly, Douglas & Co) and Cumberland. He also tried his hand at fishing before finally pre-empting land and settling on Cortes I, where he homesteaded and served as postmaster, 1926–41. Hague described his beloved Cortes property as "scenic and secluded," with a safe anchorage, water power, lake frontage and "some good land sufficient for orchards and gardens." He took part in the old-timers' reunion held in Victoria in 1924 (*see* Adams Bay). Hague Lk on Cortes is also named for him.

Haida Gwaii. *See* Queen Charlotte Islands.

Haida Islands (52°03'00" 128°19'00" S of Stryker I, Queens Sd, SW of Bella Bella). Named in 1944 for HMCS *Haida*, a 1,995-tonne *Tribal*-class destroyer commissioned in 1943, which went on to achieve fame by sinking more enemy vessels—including two destroyers and a U-boat—than any other ship in the RCN. In 1950 the 115-m *Haida* was modernized as an anti-submarine escort and completed

two tours in Korea, 1952–54, before being taken out of service in 1963. Instead of being sold for scrap, it was purchased privately and turned into a naval museum and sea cadet training vessel at Toronto. HMCS *Haida* was named a national historic site in 1984 and berthed permanently at Hamilton in 2003. It is the only remaining example of the 27 *Tribal*-class destroyers built in England for the British, Canadian and Australian navies.

Haida Point (53°15'00" 132°01'00" N entrance to Skidegate Inlet, QCI), **Haida Rock** (52°25'00" 131°25'00" Entrance to Skaat Hbr, SW side of Moresby I, QCI). Haida Point was named in the early 1910s by Lt Cdr Philip Musgrave while conducting a survey of the region aboard CGS *Lillooet*. Haida Rk was named by the hydrographic service in 1962. Haida simply means "the people" in the Haida language; it is a nominalization of the verb *hata* or *hada*, "to be human, to be a Haida." Earlier spellings included Haidah, Hai-dai, Hydah and Hyder. The name Haida is also used to refer to Old Masset; it distinguishes the ancient village site from the newer white community to the SE, which was originally known as Graham City but usurped the traditional name Masset in order to more easily obtain a post office. *D*

Haig Rock (52°36'00" 128°55'00" Off E side of Aristazabal I). Sapper Andrew Haig was a member of the Columbia detachment of Royal Engineers that served in BC, 1858–63. He is believed to have died or left BC sometime prior to Nov 1907.

Haisla (53°58'50" 128°38'50" E side of Kitimat Arm, just S of Kitimat). This is the main community of the Haisla First Nation and is often called Kitamaat Village, its traditional name. In the Haisla (or Xaisla) language, the word *haisla* refers to "those living at the river mouth." The Haisla people comprise two main cultural groups that merged in the 1940s: the Kitamaat, from Douglas Channel, and the Henaaksiala (Kitlope), from Gardner Canal. Nearby Haisla Mtn is named for this First Nation as well. *See also* Kitimat. *E*

Hakai Passage (51°43'00" 128°04'00" Between Hecate I and Nalau I, S of Bella Bella). The name is believed to come from a Heiltsuk First Nation word meaning "wide passage." The waterway, renowned for its salmon fishing, is protected to the N and S by the 123,000-ha Hakai Conservation Study Area, home to at least 130 archeological sites and some of the province's finest wilderness kayaking opportunities. *E*

Hale Islet (53°05'00" 129°29'00" Entrance to Betteridge Inlet, Campania I, N of Caamaño Sd), **Hale Point** (53°20'00" 129°27'00" SW end of Hinton I, off SE Pitt I). Named in 1944 after Ray Samuel Hale, the radio operator aboard W coast survey vessel *William J Stewart* in 1943.

H

Halfmoon Bay in the 1930s. Helen McCall photo. *Author's collection*

Halfmoon Bay (49°30'00" 123°56'00" SW side of Sechelt Peninsula, NW of Vancouver). The original form of this name, Half-Moon Bay, appeared on a 1912 Admiralty chart, the result of a 1910 survey. It was descriptive of the shape of the bay. Another variation, Half Moon Bay, was also in common use in the early 20th century. The current spelling became established after the post office name of the small rural community at Priestland Cove (located on the bay) was changed from Welcome Pass to Halfmoon Bay in 1915. By the early 2000s the area was mostly residential and recreational, with a population of about 1,700. Sechelt First Nation members know the area as Hwail-kwai or Kwilkwil. There are several Halfmoon creeks and Halfmoon lakes in BC, as well as the **Half Moon Islets** (50°20'00" 127°53'00" S of Mayday I, N coast of Brooks Bay, NW side of Vancouver I). *E*

Halfway Islet (49°36'00" 123°49'00" W side of Sechelt Inlet, NW of Vancouver). So named because of its location on Sechelt Inlet, about halfway between the head of Porpoise Bay and the Skookumchuck Narrows. Nearby Halfway Beach is one of the six sites that form Sechelt Inlets Marine Provincial Park.

Halkett Bay (49°27'00" 123°20'00" SE end of Gambier I, Howe Sd, NW of Vancouver), **Halkett Head** (48°25'42" 123°22'12" NE point of Inner Hbr, under Johnson St bridge, Victoria), **Halkett Island** (48°26'20" 123°22'55" Selkirk Water, Victoria Hbr), **Halkett Point** (49°27'00" 123°19'00" SE point of Gambier I). Halkett was a well-known name in British naval circles. Adm Sir Peter Halkett (1765–1839) was cdr-in-chief of the N America & W Indies Station in 1836; his son Sir John Halkett (1805–47) was an RN cdr. Another family member, Capt

Peter Alexander Halkett (1820–85), served on the China Station, 1838–42, at the same time surveyor Capt George Richards was posted there. Peter was something of an inventor, and his inflatable cloth-and-rubber cloak, which converted into a boat, was taken to the Arctic by Sir John Franklin, as well as by later explorers, but never caught on with the general public. He also invented a new kind of inkstand, an apparatus for lifting heavy submerged objects and an improved method of cultivating land. Halkett Head and Halkett I were named by Capt Henry Kellett of HMS *Herald* on his 1846 survey of the S end of Vancouver I. Halkett Point was named about 1860 by Capt Richards. It has been claimed that Halkett Bay was named after Gordon Halkett (1885–1969), BC's superintendent of lights for 38 years. Government records, however, indicate that the bay was named in association with the point. In any case, the hydrographic service would hardly have named two adjacent features after two completely different Halketts. Halkett I was known at one time as Deadman's I and was an early First Nation burial ground. In 1867 the Victoria *Colonist* reported that two young men were arrested "for the desecration of Indian remains" after the island was accidentally set on fire. *W*

Hall Bank (50°29'00" 128°02'00" E of Browning Inlet, Quatsino Sd, NW Vancouver I). Alfred James Hall (1853–1918) was born in Surrey, England, and became an Anglican missionary, graduating from the Church Missionary College in Islington about 1874. He was posted to Metlakatla on the BC N coast in 1877, then sent to Ft Rupert, where he opened an unsuccessful school the following year. In 1879, at Victoria, he married Elizabeth M Thimbleby (d 1916), who had come out from England for the purpose. Hall moved his mission to Alert Bay in 1880 and found the local people more receptive to his teachings. He built a school and church there, and later a store and sawmill, and served the Kwakwaka'wakw community for more than 30 years. Hall translated the Anglican *Book of Common Prayer* and much of the New Testament into Kwakwala and also published *A Grammar of the Kwagiutl Language* in 1888, eventually receiving a divinity degree in 1894 in recognition of his literary efforts. He returned to England in 1911 and was appointed rector of a rural parish near Bristol.

Hallet Island (53°13'00" 132°14'00" Kagan Bay, S Graham I, QCI). Capt Hallet of the sloop *Random* brought a group of coal miners from New Westminster to the QCI in 1865 to develop the nearby Cowgitz Mine. He made a hydrographic survey of the area in order to determine the best anchorages and wharf sites for the operation, which was ultimately unsuccessful and more or less abandoned by 1872. *D*

The old Halliday ranch on Kingcome Inlet. *Andrew Scott*

Halliday Island (51°19'00" 127°38'00" W of Central I, Smith Sd, N of Port Hardy), **Halliday Point** (50°55'00" 126°18'00" S side of Kingcome Inlet, NE of E end of Queen Charlotte Str). William May Halliday (1867–1957) and Ernest Augustus Halliday (1868–1961) were brothers from Ont who moved to the head of Kingcome Inlet in 1895 and built up a remote cattle ranch that, despite its isolation, became a noted coastal landmark. Ernest married Elizabeth Lilly Kirby (1868–1955) at Comox in 1891; William married Jane Richmond (1862–1938) at Vancouver in 1896. Appointed the district's Indian agent in 1906, William presided over a famous 1922 trial that sent dozens of Kwakwaka'wakw First Nation potlatch participants to jail and confiscated their regalia. In his book *Potlatch and Totem: The Recollections of an Indian Agent*, published in 1935, he wrote that the potlatch was a "particularly wasteful and destructive custom" that "created ill-feeling, jealousy and in most cases great poverty." The Halliday family retained the Kingcome ranch until the 1990s. Halliday I is named for William, while Halliday Point commemorates both brothers. *E*

Hall Island (48°59'00" 123°36'00" Trincomali Channel, E of Kuper I, Gulf Is). Probably named after Richard Hall

(1877–1959) and his brothers Charles and Reginald, members of an affluent Cheshire family, who bought James I in the early 1900s. Richard, an educated agriculturalist, first settled in Sask and then migrated to Thetis I in search of a milder climate. After farming on James I he moved to Mayne I in 1910 and bought land at Point Comfort. Hall hired Asian labourers and specialized in growing tomatoes and daffodils in large greenhouses, shipping his goods to Vancouver by steamer. After serving overseas in WWI he expanded his hothouse operations by acquiring additional land at Miners Bay. In 1924 he married Galiano I resident Nesta Evelyn Steward (b 1895), a native of Muskoka, Ont.

Halsted Islet (50°51'00" 127°51'00" E entrance to Shushartie Bay, N tip of Vancouver I). Rev Frederick Charles Halsted (or Halstead, as some sources spell his name) was an RN chaplain aboard HMS *Daedalus*, under Capt George Wellesley, on the Pacific Station, 1850–53. The feature was named by William Dillon, who made a survey of Shushartie Bay in 1850 when he was temporarily master of the *Daedalus*.

Hamber Island (49°19'00" 122°56'00" W of Turtle Head, Indian Arm, NE of Vancouver). Named after businessman Eric Werge Hamber (1879–1960), lt gov of BC, 1936–41. He was born in Manitoba and moved to Vancouver in 1907 as a bank manager. In 1912, Hamber married Aldyen Irene Hendry (1885–1988), whose father, John Hendry, owned BC Mills Timber & Trading Co, the province's largest lumber manufacturer. Hamber was named president of BC Mills in 1916, after his father-in-law's death. An active sportsman, especially in horse racing and yachting, he also served as chancellor of UBC, 1944–51. Hamber Provincial Park on the BC-Alberta border is named for him as well. Hamber I and a small portion of adjacent Turtle Head, where the Hamber family had a summer home, were sold in May 2007 for nearly $3.5 million. *E*

Hamilton Beach (48°46'00" 123°16'00" Head of Port Browning, E side of N Pender I, Gulf Is), **Hamilton Cove** (48°46'40" 123°16'25" Just N of Hamilton Beach). Scottish stonecutter Alexander Hamilton (b about 1862) came to the US at the age of 20 and ended up at Victoria, where he carved gravestones at John Mortimer's stoneyard. Mortimer's quarry was near the isthmus between the two Pender Is, and Hamilton was so impressed with the area that he pre-empted land on N Pender in 1885 and built a summer retreat. In 1888 he returned from a visit to Scotland with a wife, Jeannie Torrance Leiper, and two younger brothers, Hugh (b about 1870) and Robert. Alex moved to New Westminster, where his home was destroyed in that city's great fire of 1898. The Hamiltons then settled permanently on N Pender, where the three brothers farmed. If extra money was needed, Alex worked in Victoria, cutting stone for the library, Empress Hotel and James Dunsmuir's residence at Hatley Park. Hamilton

H

Beach was named for Alexander. Hamilton Cove, named for Hugh, was originally known as Brackett Cove (qv), a name that was transferred in 1988 to the feature immediately to the NE.

Hamley Point (48°36'00" 123°16'00" E side of Sidney I, N of Victoria, Gulf Is). Wymond Thomas Ogilvy Hamley (1821–1907), born in Cornwall, came to New Westminster in 1859 as collector of customs for the colony of BC. The son of a British adm, he had served in the RN and the British civil service before receiving his post. Hamley arrived on the W coast aboard the *Thames City*, the same vessel that brought a large detachment of Royal Engineers to the new colony. He was a member of the colony of BC's legislative council, which first met in 1864, and when Victoria became the capital of the merged colonies in 1868, he moved there from New Westminster. After Confederation he continued as customs collector at Victoria for the federal government until the late 1880s. Nearby Wymond Point is also named for him.

Hammond Bay (49°14'00" 123°58'00" N of Nanaimo and Departure Bay, Str of Georgia), **Hammond Rocks** (48°32'00" 124°27'00" S side of Port San Juan, SW side of Vancouver I), **Hammond Rocks** (54°25'00" 130°40'00" SE of Moffat Is, Chatham Sd, NW of Prince Rupert). Sub-Lt George Crispin Hammond was Lt Daniel Pender's assistant aboard the sidewheel steamer *Beaver*, 1867–70, while it was leased from the HBC for survey work on the BC coast. He retired from the RN in 1888 with the rank of staff cdr. Crispin Rk off Saturna I is also named for him.

Hammond Passage (48°50'00" 125°14'00" E of Imperial Eagle Channel, Barkley Sd, W side of Vancouver I). Named after early Victoria resident and newspaper publisher Capt Edward Hammond King. *See* Edward King I.

Hanatsa Point (50°32'00" 125°59'00" S side of Port Neville, Johnstone Str). Located on and named after the 95-ha Hanatsa reserve, a traditional habitation site of the Matilpi people. In the early 1800s this Kwakwaka'wakw First Nation group moved to Havannah Channel and settled at Etsekin; in the 1890s they moved again, to Karlukwees (Qalogwis) on Turnour I, a village site they shared with the Tlawitsis people. Some Matilpi members continue to live there; others live at Alert Bay and Campbell R.

Hancock Point (52°14'00" 131°08'00" S side of Carpenter Bay, SE end of Moresby I, QCI). The 142-tonne, Boston-based brigantine *Hancock*, under Capt Samuel Crowell, made three fur-trading voyages to the QCI, 1790–93. In the summer of 1791 its crew built a tender for their vessel—the first European-style boat constructed in Haida Gwaii—on nearby Maast I. That year, to honour both his ship and John Hancock (gov of Massachusetts and a leader of the American Revolution), Crowell gave the name Hancock's

R to Masset Sd, the long, narrow entrance to Masset Inlet. In 1907, to keep this historic reference alive, Capt Frederick Learmonth named the present Hancock R, which flows NW into Masset Hbr. *See also* Crowell Point. D

Hand Bay (50°56'00" 127°05'00" S side of Actaeon Sd, N of Drury Inlet and Queen Charlotte Str), **Hand Island** (48°57'00" 125°19'00" Near NW end of the Broken Group, Barkley Sd, W side of Vancouver I). RN officer Henry Hand (d 1890) was 1st lt aboard HMS *Hecate*, the main survey vessel on the BC coast in 1861–62, under Capt George Richards. He had previously also served on the Pacific Station, 1854–56, as a sub-lt on HMS *Amphitrite*. Hand was promoted to cdr in 1867 and from 1872 to 1874 had charge of HMS *St Vincent*, a training ship for boys at Portsmouth. He was made capt in 1877 and commodore, 1886–89, when in command of the W Indies Station, with his flagship HMS *Urgent*. Mt Hand on Campbell I, just W of Bella Bella, is also named for him. W

Handfield Bay (50°21'00" 125°19'00" W of Cameleon Hbr, Sonora I, N of Campbell R). Named for John Handfield Tully, master of HMS *Cameleon* in 1863. *See* Tully I.

Hankin Cove (50°06'00" 127°14'00" E side of Kashutl Inlet, Kyuquot Sd, NW side of Vancouver I), **Hankin Island** (48°55'00" 125°22'00" Broken Group, Barkley Sd, W side of Vancouver I), **Hankin Point** (50°34'00" 127°33'00" N entrance to Rupert Inlet, S of Port Hardy, NW Vancouver I), **Hankin Point** (53°42'00" 130°24'00" SW point of Beaver Passage, McCauley I, NE of Banks I), **Hankin Rock** (49°11'00" 125°46'00" Entrance to Mosquito Hbr, W side of Fortune Channel, Clayoquot Sd, W side of Vancouver I). RN officer Philip James Hankin, born in Hertfordshire in 1836, first served on the BC coast in 1857–58 as a sub-lt on HMS *Plumper*, a survey vessel under the command of Capt George Richards. He returned, 1860–64, as 2nd lt aboard HMS *Hecate*, the *Plumper*'s replacement. In 1862, Hankin and Dr Charles Wood, the *Hecate*'s surgeon, made one of the first European explorations of N Vancouver I, crossing from Kyuquot Sd to Queen Charlotte Str (*see* Expedition Islets). Back in England in 1864, Hankin resigned from the RN and travelled to Vancouver I, where he married Isabella Gertrude Nagle (b 1846 in NZ) the following year. Gov Arthur Kennedy appointed him his secretary and then superintendent of police. It was in this latter capacity, in 1864, that he accompanied Rear Adm Joseph Denman aboard HMS *Sutlej* to Clayoquot Sd, where Denman's force burned nine First Nation villages while hunting for the Ahousaht chief responsible for destroying the trading sloop *Kingfisher* and murdering its crew. Hankin was reinstated in the RN for his conduct at Clayoquot, and although he was never again an active officer, he remained on the naval list, retiring in 1870 with the rank of cdr. He continued as a government official, serving as colonial secretary of British Honduras, 1866–68,

Sierra Leone, 1868–69, and BC, 1869–71. From 1873 to 1880 he was private secretary to the Duke of Buckingham, who was gov of Madras for much of that period. Hankin revisited Victoria as a tourist in 1919. Mt Hankin, near Port Alberni, and the Hankin Range, E of Nimpkish Lk, are also named for him. *W*

Hankin Reefs (54°33'34" 130°26'47" NW end of Tsimpsean Peninsula, N of Prince Rupert). Thomas Hankin (1843–85), born in Hertfordshire, was the younger brother of Philip Hankin (*see* Hankin Cove). He came to BC in 1858, and in about 1870, after working for the HBC and just before marrying Margaret Macaulay (c 1853–1910), he entered into a mercantile partnership with Robert Cunningham (*see* Cunningham Passage), who had briefly managed the HBC's Ft Simpson post. The pair established stores at Port Essington and Hazelton, and ran a freight-forwarding business on the Skeena R until 1877, when they separated, with Hankin keeping the Hazelton operation. He managed the Inverness Cannery on the Skeena R for Turner, Beeton & Co in 1885. Hankin Ck, which flows into the Skeena, is probably also named for him. Margaret, who was born at Victoria, a daughter of HBC employee Donald Macaulay (*see* Macaulay Point) and Margaret Snaach, a Tsimshian woman, married Hazelton Indian agent R E Loring after Hankin's death. *W*

Hanmer Island (54°04'00" 130°15'00" W of N end of Kennedy I, S of Prince Rupert), **Hanmer Point** (54°07'00" 130°04'00" SE entrance to Skeena R, SE of Prince Rupert), **Hanmer Rocks** (54°19'00" 130°48'00" In Brown Passage, W of Prince Rupert). Cdr John Graham Job Hanmer (1836–1919) and his officers made a sketch survey of the entrance to the Skeena R in 1877 aboard HMS *Daring*, a 4-gun, 660-tonne screw sloop. Their purpose was to assist the CPR in locating a suitable W coast terminus for the transcontinental railway. Hanmer, from Little Waldingfield, Suffolk, was promoted capt in 1879 and became a rear adm, retired, in 1894. Hanmer I was formerly known as White Cliff I.

Hanna Bay (54°06'00" 132°35'00" W side of Virago Sd, N end of Graham I, QCI). According to QCI historian Kathleen Dalzell, the name is derived from Kan-nah Kwoon, the Haida term for adjacent Cape Naden. Sometimes referred to as "the bay below Kan-nah," this feature was more commonly known to the Haida as Ahk-gwans (*gwans* can be translated as "rocky").

Hanna Channel (49°40'00" 126°29'00" NE of Bligh I, Nootka Sd, W side of Vancouver I), **Hanna Islet** (51°50'00" 128°01'00" Entrance to Sea Otter Inlet, SE side of Hunter I, S of Bella Bella), **Hanna Point** (50°40'00" 128°21'00" E entrance to Sea Otter Cove, NW tip of Vancouver I), **Hannah Rocks** (51°14'00" 127°59'00" W side of South Passage, Queen Charlotte Sd). Capt James

Hanna, while not as well known as later 18th-century fur traders, occupies a unique position in BC coastal history: he was the first trader to arrive, in 1785, and his visit was the first by a foreigner since that of Capt James Cook in 1778. Hanna was hired by Asia-based merchant John Cox and his partners (*see* Cox Bay) as master of the tiny, 50-tonne *Harmon*, which was renamed the *Sea Otter*. He sailed from Macao to Nootka Sd under a Portuguese flag to circumvent the trade monopolies of the British S Sea and E India companies. Despite clashing with local residents at Nootka and killing a number of them while repulsing an attack on his vessel, Hanna was successful in acquiring more than 500 sea otter furs, which brought a sufficient return in Asia for his employers to send him back to BC the following year in a larger vessel, also named *Sea Otter*. On this expedition, Hanna went N along the coast of Vancouver I and into Queen Charlotte Sd, making charts of the area and naming a number of features, including Smith Sd and Fitz Hugh Sd, which he tried on several occasions to explore but was rebuffed by stormy weather. He left the coast in Oct and arrived back in Macao in Feb 1787, carrying with him Comekela, a younger brother of the great Nuu-chah-nulth chief Maquinna and the first BC aboriginal known to have travelled to Asia. (John Meares returned Comekala safe and sound to Nootka in May 1788.) Little else is known about Hanna's life, and he is believed to have died shortly after returning from his second voyage, which had disappointing financial returns. According to Meares, "before he could engage in a third [journey], this active and able seaman was called to take that voyage from which there is no return." *W*

Hannah Island (52°21'00" 128°21'00" S of Lake I, Mathieson Channel, just NE of Milbanke Sd). Charlotte Hannah Barnes (1799–1876) was the only child of Joseph Barnes, a member of Jamaica's legislative council, and his wife Hannah. She married William Trutch, an English solicitor and landowner in the Jamaica parish of St Thomas, and had five children, moving with her family to England in 1834. In 1861, presumably after her husband's death, she followed her two engineer sons, Joseph William Trutch and John Trutch, to the colony of BC and settled at Victoria, where she is buried in the Ross Bay Cemetery. The family played significant roles in BC colonial society: Joseph Trutch (*see* Trutch I) was knighted and became BC's first lt gov; John Trutch married Zoe Musgrave, sister of BC's last gov, Anthony Musgrave; and Caroline Agnes Trutch, Charlotte's daughter, married BC's chief gold commissioner, Peter O'Reilly.

Hannah Rocks. *See* Hanna Channel.

Hansen Bay (50°44'00" 128°23'00" S of Cape Scott, NW tip of Vancouver I), **Hansen Lagoon** (50°46'00" 128°21'00" Head of Hansen Bay). Rasmus Hansen (b 1864), a Danish

H

fisherman from Seattle, anchored in this bay in 1894 and was so impressed with the extensive tidal meadows that lay just inland that he determined to try to establish a Danish agricultural colony there. In 1896, with three other prospective settlers, he succeeded in persuading the BC government to make him a land grant. The Cape Scott colony, with Hansen as president, had a population of 90 by the end of the century. Its members diked and drained considerable land, grew hay and other crops, and raised dairy cattle. But they were doomed by their remote and inaccessible location; getting produce to market was too difficult, and most of the original settlers had drifted away before WWI. Nearby Mt Hansen and Hansen Ck are also named for this N Island pioneer.

Hansen Island (49°12'30" 125°51'45" In Lemmens Inlet, Meares I, Clayoquot Sd, W side of Vancouver I). Brothers Anton (c 1878–1971) and John Hansen were Norwegian fishermen who became early settlers and long-time residents in the Tofino area. Many of their descendants still live in the district. Anton arrived in Clayoquot Sd about 1909. John was a boatbuilder and later served as mayor of Tofino, 1944–50.

Hansen Point (52°29'00" 127°52'00" S side of Roscoe Inlet, NE of Bella Bella). Believed to be named after one of the Norwegian colonists at Bella Coola in the late 1800s. There were several early Hansens in the valley, however, who also sometimes anglicized their common Scandinavian surname, spelling it Hanson. For instance, Olai Hanson, H O Hanson, Sigrid Hanson and L W Hanson were all recorded on an early list of colonists compiled by Hagen Christensen, the colony's secretary and a valley storekeeper. The first two names, in particular, are often seen spelled Hansen. H O Hanson helped set up the colony's first sawmill in 1898.

Hanson Island (50°34'00" 126°44'00" W of Harbledown I, W end of Johnstone Str). Lt James Hanson, born at London, England, served under Lt William Brougham aboard HMS *Chatham*, the armed tender that accompanied Capt George Vancouver on his historic voyage to the PNW. In 1792, Vancouver appointed him cdr of the *Daedalus*, a storeship that resupplied Vancouver at Nootka. (The ship's original cdr, Lt Richard Hergest, had been murdered in Hawaii.) Hanson took the vessel to Australia, then resupplied Vancouver's expedition again off San Francisco and accompanied it to Hawaii before returning to England, taking with him some troublemakers from *Discovery*, including the violent midshipman Thomas Pitt. He was promoted cdr in 1795 and took charge of HMS *Brazen*, a former French privateer, in 1800. That year a gale drove his ship onto the rocks in the English Channel near Brighton; Hanson and all but one of his crew members died in the disaster. His older brother John Hanson was Lord Byron's business agent, and the Byron and Hanson families were

Hanson Island, home to Paul Spong's Orca Lab, a whale research station. *Andrew Scott*

well acquainted. The people of the Kwakwaka'wakw First Nation know Hanson I as Yukusam, which can be translated as "shaped like a halibut hook." *W*

Harbledown Island (50°34'00" 126°35'00" N of W Cracroft I, W end of Johnstone Str). This 36-sq-km island, once the site of a Kwakwaka'wakw village, was named in 1865 by Lt Daniel Pender. Harbledown presumably refers to the tiny farming settlement near Canterbury that Geoffrey Chaucer called "Bobbe-up-and-doun" in the prologue to his "Manciple's Tale." One of Pender's officers may have had a personal connection to this hamlet. The remote Roman Catholic mission of St Michael's was moved to Harbledown from Ft Rupert in 1864 and supervised by Fr Leon Fouquet until 1874, when Bishop Louis D'Herbomez, citing the urgent need for more missions on the mainland, ordered it closed. George Kamano, an HBC employee of Hawaiian birth who helped found the mission, was Harbledown's first homesteader, along with his Kwakwaka'wakw wife Pauline Clahoara. A small logging and fishing community, complete with store, school and post office, existed on the N shore from the early 1900s to the 1920s. Bell & Campbell's large logging camp, later taken over by the Powell R Co, operated a little farther E, 1928–60.

Harbourmaster Point (52°04'00" 128°03'00" E side of Cooper Inlet, N side of Hunter I, S of Bella Bella). Capt James Cooper was harbourmaster of the colony of BC, based at New Westminster, when this feature was named by Lt Daniel Pender in 1866. *See* Cooper Inlet.

Harbridge Point (52°51'00" 131°45'00" N end of Talunkwan I, E of Moresby I, QCI). Named after a Vancouver man named Harbridge who owned mining claims at the E end of Talunkwan I in 1908.

Hardinge Island (50°21'00" 125°21'00" W side of Sonora I, N of Campbell R). Cdr Edward Hardinge (1830–94) served on the Pacific Station, 1861–63, in command of the *Cameleon*, an RN corvette. He was in charge of the 1863 naval expedition that hunted down a Kuper I First

Nation chief named Acheewun and his followers, who were convicted of the murders of two Gulf Is settlers and hanged (*see* Lamalchi Bay). Hardinge, promoted to capt, went on to command numerous vessels, including HMS *Juno* and *Topaze*, became a naval aide-de-camp to Queen Victoria in 1877 (the year he was made a CB) and eventually attained the rank of adm, retired, in 1890. Nearby Edward Point is also named for him. *W*

Hardwicke Island (50°26'00" 125°51'00" Between Sunderland Channel and Johnstone Str), **Hardwicke Point** (50°26'00" 125°59'00" W end of Hardwicke I). Capt George Vancouver named the island in 1792 as a compliment to Spelman Swaine, master's mate aboard HMS *Discovery* (*see* Cape Swaine). Philip Yorke, 3rd Earl of Hardwicke (1757–1834), was the MP for Cambridge, 1780–90, and as Swaine's father was a man of influence in the county, Yorke took an interest in his son and helped advance his career whenever possible. It was in this manner that many young "gentlemen" mariners, if they were fortunate enough to have a patron, ascended the ranks of the RN. Indeed, Vancouver did promote Swaine—to master of HMS *Chatham* and then to 3rd lt of the *Discovery*—but all indications are that he earned his advancement on the basis of ability, rather than as a result of who he knew. Swaine ended up as a rear adm. Philip Yorke served as lord lt of Ireland, 1801–5, lord lt of Cambridge county, 1790–1834, and high steward of Cambridge Univ, 1806. Hardwicke I, 78 sq km, was first settled by logger William Kelsey and his wife in 1911. Since 1918, members of the Bendickson family have lived there and operated a logging business. *E W*

Hardy Bay (50°44'00" 127°28'00" S side of Queen Charlotte Str, NE side of Vancouver I), **Hardy Island**

Port Hardy, about 1947. *Harbour Publishing collection*

(49°44'00" 124°12'00" Entrance to Jervis Inlet, Malaspina Str, NW of Vancouver), **Port Hardy** (50°42'00" 127°25'00" On Hardy Bay, NW of Port McNeill). Vice Adm Sir Thomas Masterman Hardy (1769–1839) was flag capt of HMS *Victory* at the Battle of Trafalgar in 1805. He was immortalized in numerous battle paintings that showed him holding the dying Adm Lord Nelson—and also by Nelson's famous deathbed request: "Kiss me, Hardy." He had earlier served as Nelson's flag capt on HMS *Vanguard*. In the War of 1812, Hardy transported Sir John Sherbrooke's army to Maine, where it captured significant territory. He later became capt of the royal yacht *Augusta* (1815–19), cdr-in-chief of the S America Station (1819–24), 1st Lord of the Admiralty (1830–34) and gov of the RN's Greenwich Hospital for sailors (1834–39). **Hardy Peak** (50°29'40" 126°01'40" Between Port Neville and Blenkinsop Bay, N side of Johnstone Str) is also named for him. Hardy I was a granite quarry in the early 1900s before being turned into a deer sanctuary, 1930–51, by a character named Tom Brazil, who looked after the property for its Seattle owner. In recent years the island has been heavily logged. The town of Port Hardy, with a population of more than 5,000, is the largest community on N Vancouver I, an important forestry and commercial fishing centre, and the terminus for northern ferries. Hardy Bay was the Puerto de Güemes of Spanish explorer Dionisio Alcalá-Galiano, named after Juan Vincente de Güemes Pacheco y Padillo, Viceroy of Mexico, 1746–55. *E W*

Hare Point (50°04'00" 124°47'00" W side of Gifford Peninsula, Desolation Sd, NW of Vancouver). Named after Cdr Richard Hare (1836–1903) of HMS *Myrmidon*, a 630-tonne gun and survey vessel that was based on the Pacific Station, at Esquimalt, in 1873. Hare, a younger son of the Earl of Listowel, had served earlier in the E Indies as lt and acting cdr of HMS *Hornet*. He was promoted capt in 1879 and, eventually, rear adm.

Harlan Point (53°09'00" 129°34'00" NW side of Campania I, Estevan Sd, S of Pitt I). Norman Harlan was senior quartermaster aboard the W coast survey vessel *William J Stewart* in the early 1940s.

Harlequin Bay (50°50'00" 127°34'00" W side of Hurst I, Gordon Channel, off N end of Vancouver I). Named in 1947 by BC land surveyor Frederick Aldous after the harlequin ducks (*Histrionicus histrionicus*) he found there.

Harling Point (48°24'00" 123°19'00" Between Gonzales Bay and McNeill Bay, Victoria). This feature was formerly known as Foul Point, as it was associated with Foul Bay, the old name for Gonzales Bay (qv), and was also sometimes referred to as Chinese Point because of the adjacent Chinese cemetery. The name Foul Bay became contentious in the 1920s, and when it was finally done away with by local residents in 1934, Foul Point

H

("a misnomer" that "has to be changed," according to regional hydrographer Henri Parizeau) went with it. The name was changed to Harling Point, in honour of Dr Fred Harling (b 1887), a dentist who came to Victoria from Bradford, England, in 1906 and lived beside the bay for 23 years. He served as an air force mechanic during WWI and studied dentistry at Portland, Oregon, earning money for school by working as a lifeguard at the Gorge in the summers. In Jan 1934, Harling died of exposure after trying to save the lives of two people off this point. According to a Songhees First Nation legend, a large boulder at the point was once a seal hunter who was turned to stone after complaining that a passing group of supernatural beings were scaring away his prey. The Songhees name for the point is Sahsima, meaning "harpoon."

Harlock Island (49°07'00" 123°10'00" Mouth of Fraser R, N of Reifel I), **Harlock Islet** (48°40'45" 123°23'52" W side of Page Passage, off NE Saanich Peninsula, just N of Sidney). Henry Edward Harlock (d 1894), who came to Canada from the US in 1884, owned land at the mouth of the Fraser R and established a salmon cannery, Harlock Packing Co, on the river's S shore, just W of Ladner, in 1887. It later became one of the numerous properties owned by Thomas Ladner and Robert Rithet of the Victoria Canning Co but was closed in 1902 after the BC Packers Assoc acquired and consolidated many of the Delta canneries. Henry's wife, Annie Jane Harlock (1860–1928), died at Vancouver. Their son, Walter Henry Harlock (1881–1962), was a marine engineer on W coast steamships.

Harmston Island (52°16'00" 128°22'00" Off SW end of Don Peninsula, NW of Bella Bella). Florence Mary Harmston (1856–1929) was born at Douglas, Isle of Man, and moved to the Comox valley with her parents, William and Florence Harmston, in 1862. She married Samuel Jackson Cliffe (1840–1908) at Cumberland about 1873 and became the mother of 10 children. The Cliffes operated the Lorne Hotel at Comox for many years. Florence is believed to have participated in the great old-timers' reunion held in Victoria in 1924 (see Adams Bay). Harmston I was adopted as a name in 1929; before that it was known as Dark I. Cliffe Rk in Hecate Str is also named for Florence, while Cliffe Glacier and Mt Harmston on Vancouver I honour the entire pioneer clan. Cliffe Point (qv) in Quatsino Sd commemorates Florence's son, Capt Thomas Cliffe.

Harness Island (49°36'00" 124°01'00" S of Bargain Bay, E side of Malaspina Str, NW of Vancouver). Named in 1945 after Arthur Creedon Harness of Victoria, a seaman and coxswain aboard the W coast survey vessel *William J Stewart*, 1935–39. In WWII he served in the Canadian merchant navy and was killed in action on Nov 23, 1941, aged 28, while 3rd officer of the US freighter *Meridian* (formerly the *Dino*, of Italian registry), which was torpedoed by a U-boat and sank in the N Atlantic, with the loss of 38 lives. His name is inscribed on the Halifax Memorial.

Haro Island (50°19'00" 125°17'00" Okisollo Channel, S of Sonora I, N of Campbell R). The historic tug *Haro* was built at Hastings Mill, Vancouver, in 1910 by master shipwright A C Macdonald. Licensed for 12 passengers, the 211-tonne, 32-m vessel towed numerous log booms through the tricky waterways at the N end of the Str of Georgia for BC Mills Timber & Trading Co, the province's largest lumber manufacturer at the time. The *Haro* had numerous owners over the years before being rebuilt at Vancouver Shipyards in 1960 with a diesel engine 20 times more powerful than its original steam model. It was renamed *Le Beau*. Presumably the tug was originally named for Haro Str (*see below*).

Cabbage Island in the right foreground, below Tumbo and Saturna islands, with Boundary Pass and Haro Strait in the distance.
Peter Vassilopoulos

Haro Strait (48°35'00" 123°19'00" Forms the BC-Washington boundary E of SE Vancouver I). Spanish naval officer Manuel Quimper, the first European to see these waters, named this strait in 1790 after his 1st officer, Gonzales López de Haro. López de Haro was no stranger to the PNW. He and Lt Estéban Martínez, in the *San Carlos* and *Princesa*, respectively, had led an expedition to Alaska in 1788 and noted increased British and Russian activity in the region. Their report strengthened Spanish resolve to occupy Nootka Sd, which Martínez and López de Haro were successful in doing in 1789. López de Haro was sent back to Mexico that July. He returned in May 1790 with Quimper in the sloop *Princesa Real* (the captured fur-trading vessel *Princess Royal*) and made a historic survey of the shores of Juan de Fuca Str. In 1792 he was again at Nootka Sd and sailed *Orcasites*—the former sloop *Adventure*, built by Capt Robert Gray at Clayoquot Sd and purchased by the Spanish for 80 sea otter pelts—back to Mexico. Other mariners of the era, including Capt George Vancouver, spelled the name Haro as Aro, Arro and Arrow. Gonzales Bay (qv), Gonzales Hill and Gonzales Point on S Vancouver I are also named for him, as is Lopez I, the most southerly of the San Juan Is. A dispute erupted between Britain and the US in 1859 over the San Juan Is and whether the boundary should run to the E of them, along Rosario Str, or to the W, along Haro Str. The disagreement led to an armed standoff—the so-called Pig War—and joint occupation of the islands before being resolved in favour of the US in 1872, when Haro Str became the border. *E*

Harriet Harbour (52°18'00" 131°13'00" S side of Skincuttle Inlet, SE end of Moresby I, QCI), **Harriet Island** (52°18'00" 131°14'00" Entrance to Harriet Hbr). Named in 1862 by mining engineer Francis Poole after the trading schooner *Harriet*, under Capt T Coffin, which resupplied him at his exploration camp on Skincuttle Inlet. Poole, who wrote with great enthusiasm about the QCI, had high praise for this site. "A more charming and more useful harbour of the same magnitude does not exist to my knowledge in the N Pacific," he claimed, "[and] has only to be known in order to be seized upon in the interests of trade and colonization." Indeed, the small mining community of Jedway, long since abandoned, was eventually located there. The Haida, however, knew the bay as Gigawai, meaning "trap," because of the violent SE squalls that afflict it. Nearby Harriet Ck is also named after the schooner *Harriet*. *D W*

Harriot Island (53°41'00" 129°44'00" In Klewnuggit Inlet, E of Grenville Channel and Pitt I). After Harriot Georgina Rowan-Hamilton (1843–1936), Marchioness of Dufferin and Ava, and wife of Lord Dufferin, Canada's third gov gen. The vice-regal pair (who at the time had the rank of earl and countess) made a cruise of the BC coast in 1876 aboard HMS *Amethyst*, during which this feature was named, as well as the nearby Countess of Dufferin Range. The marchioness received numerous awards for her charitable work, especially for her efforts to improve medical care for women in India. She also wrote several books, including one about her time in Canada, *My Canadian Journal. See* Dufferin I, as well.

Harris Island (48°25'00" 123°17'00" E of Oak Bay, E of Turkey Head and Victoria). Thomas Harris (1817–84), born in Herefordshire, was a member of Vancouver I's legislative assembly (1862), first mayor of Victoria (1862–65) and later the sheriff of Vancouver I. After working and marrying at Liverpool, he immigrated to San Francisco in 1854 and arrived at Victoria three years later, where he set up in business very successfully as a butcher and cattle dealer until going bankrupt in 1867. Harris, a man of gigantic proportions, was known as a merry host and sportsman and was president of Beacon Hill's jockey and cricket clubs. One of his first acts as mayor was to establish a "committee of nuisances" to deal with "bawdy houses, stray pigs, effluent and disagreeable stenches." Nearby

Mayor Channel is also named for him. Emily It (qv) is named for his daughter. *W*

Harrison Islands (53°38'00" 132°22'00" In Juskatla Inlet, S of Masset Inlet, Graham I, QCI), **Harrison Point** (54°00'00" 132°09'00" W entrance to Delkatla Inlet, Masset Hbr, Graham I), **Harrison Reef** (53°38'45" 132°20'30" E of Harrison Is). RN hydrographer Capt Frederick Learmonth named Harrison Point in 1907 after Charles Harrison, a troubled Anglican missionary with a drinking problem, who arrived on the QCI in 1883 with his wife, Mary Ann Hill, to take over the Old Masset church. In 1890 he resigned from the ministry and established the area's first farm on land he had bought beside Delkatla Slough. Harrison translated the Anglican prayer book into Haida and in 1895 published a Haida grammar. He also became the area's justice of the peace and a great promoter of the Anchor Investment Co, which bought part of his land in order to develop the townsite of Masset, originally to be called Graham City after the president of the affiliated Graham Steamship, Coal & Lumber Co. Officials from Graham's company, which held enormous waterfront timber leases in the QCI, named the largest of the Harrison Is after their booster in 1907, and the name eventually came to embrace the entire island group. The Harrisons returned to England in 1919, and Charles likely died about 1925, the same year his *Ancient Warriors of the N Pacific* was published. The original Haida name for Harrison I, as recorded by surveyor George M Dawson in 1878, was Has-keious. *D*

Harris Peak (50°13'24" 127°43'51" S of head of Klaskish Inlet, NW side of Vancouver I). Capt Charles Israel Harris (1867–1969), from NS, went to sea at the age of 14 and survived two shipwrecks before his 17th birthday. In 1886 he sailed to Victoria via Cape Horn in the schooner *Sapphire*, and after a few years ashore he became a member of the Victoria-based sealing fleet. He was master of several sealing vessels, including the *Mary Taylor*, *May Belle* and *E B Marvin*, as well as the *Sapphire*. Capt Harris married S America-born Rebecca Ann Cox (1872–1954) at Victoria in 1892. In 1901 he was a passenger aboard the *Islander*, which struck an iceberg near Skagway and sank, with great loss of life. The ship was reputed to have been carrying a fortune in gold and was the focus of several futile salvage efforts. Harris received a citation for valour for his actions in leading a lifeboat to safety. Harris Peak appeared on early Admiralty charts as Sharp Peak.

Harris Point (49°00'00" 125°19'00" E side of Toquart Bay, Barkley Sd, W side of Vancouver I). Civil engineer Dennis Reginald Harris (1851–1932) came to Canada in 1869 and worked as assistant surveyor for the Canada Central Rwy. He joined the CPR the following year, doing survey work on the N shore of Lk Superior and in the Hudson Bay region at first, then spent the years 1872–78 in BC,

H

surveying between Howe Sd and Lillooet, and in the Bute Inlet, Chilcotin, Fraser Canyon and Kamloops districts, among other places. In 1878 he married Martha Douglas (1854–1933), youngest daughter of BC colonial gov Sir James Douglas, at Victoria and set up a private practice there as a civil engineer, land surveyor, architect and real-estate agent. He also served as a city alderman and was Victoria's city engineer for five years. Harris received a number of Crown land grants between 1892 and 1909 in the New Westminster and Kamloops land districts and at Vancouver and Barkley Sd. After the death of Sir James in 1877, he became the surrogate head of the Douglas household and a member of Victoria's social elite. Mt Harris on the BC-Alaska border is also named for him. *See* Martha I, as well.

Harry Point (48°43'00" 123°25'00" N end of Piers I, off N tip of Saanich Peninsula, N of Victoria). After RN surgeon Henry "Harry" Piers, who served on the Pacific Station in 1857–60. *See* Piers I.

Hart Group (51°57'00" 128°06'00" Head of Kildidt Lagoon, Hunter I, S of Bella Bella), **Hart Island** (52°03'00" 128°09'00" Off NW side of Hunter I). Capt Frederick Gordon Hart (1900–1967), a graduate of the Royal Naval College of Canada, was a sub-lt aboard the destroyer HMS *Nizam* in 1918. He married Ethel Monica Davie (1901–43) at Victoria in 1925. Hart served for many years on the W coast and was in command of HMCS *Prince Robert*, the armed merchant cruiser, 1940–42, and chief of staff to the CO Pacific Command, 1943–44.

The Gitga'at First Nation village of Hartley Bay. *Peter Vassilopoulos*

Hartley Bay (53°25'00" 129°15'00" W side of Douglas Channel near S end, SW of Kitimat). The origin of the name of this Gitga'at (Kitka'ata) First Nation community is uncertain. The Gitga'at people are part of the Tsimshian cultural group and originally lived at Laxgal'tsap (Old Town) on Kitkiata Inlet, just to the N. They moved to William Duncan's "model Christian village" of Metlakatla in the 1860s and '70s, but when Duncan and many of his followers left for Alaska in 1887, a small number of Gitga'at returned to their traditional territory and established a new community at Hartley Bay, a location they knew as Txalgiu, which was closer to the transportation routes of coastal ships. In the early 2000s, Hartley Bay had a population of about 250. The village is only accessible by air or water, and its 70 buildings are connected by a series of sturdy boardwalks. On Mar 22, 2006, just after midnight, residents were called out to the wreck of the *Queen of the North*, operated by BC Ferries, which ran aground and sank off Gil I, S of Hartley Bay. The villagers rescued 99 passengers and crew members and carried them back to the village in a fleet of small fishing and recreational vessels. Two passengers died in the catastrophe.

Hartnell Point (52°36'00" 128°45'00" SW tip of Princess Royal I). Named in 1926 for George Edward Hartnell (1890–1981) of Victoria, senior accountant and purchasing officer for the federal Dept of Marine and Fisheries on the W coast. He married Mary Josephine Trainor (1895–1978) at Prince Rupert in 1921.

Hart Rock (53°21'00" 130°14'00" Off W side of Banks I, between Grief Point and Kelp Point). George Hart was a quartermaster aboard HMS *Discovery* on Capt George Vancouver's voyage of exploration. **Hart Point** (54°13'00" 133°01'00" W side of Langara I, QCI) was probably named for him as well.

Harvey Cove (50°26'00" 127°55'00" S entrance to Quatsino Sd, NW end of Vancouver I). Named in 1927 after P Harvey, a fireman aboard CGS *Restless*, 1920–21, when that vessel was involved in a survey of Quatsino Sd. Formerly known as Boat Cove.

Harvey Islands (52°31'00" 129°19'00" W of Aristazabal I, Hecate Str). 2nd Cpl William Harvey was a member of the Columbia detachment of Royal Engineers, which served in BC 1858–63. He was born at Putney, near London, and saw action as a sapper in the Crimean War. Harvey arrived in BC in Apr 1859 with the main contingent aboard the *Thames City* and probably brought his family with him. He may have been the detachment baker, as he stayed on in BC after the engineers disbanded and established the Government Bakery (1863–65) and Old Cottage Bakery (1865–70) at New Westminster. Harvey was also "refreshment steward" for the New Westminster fire dept. He received a Crown grant in the New Westminster land district in 1870 and probably died soon after, "aged about 55 years," according to an unnamed, undated New Westminster newspaper report, which described him as "in every respect a British soldier; large-hearted, brave and honest; as a citizen, he was much respected for his straightforward dealing and kindly, generous character." Flags throughout the city were lowered to half-mast "as a mark of respect for the deceased."

Harvey Point (48°42'00" 123°25'00" NE tip of Piers I, off N tip of Saanich Peninsula, N of Victoria). Named in 1965 for the Harvey family. James Harvey (1844–90), a Nanaimo merchant, came originally to BC from Scotland, was active in local politics and in 1870, at Victoria, married Agnes Dunsmuir (1849–89), second daughter of industrialist Robert Dunsmuir, BC's wealthiest man. Both James and Agnes died of typhoid. Their son James Swan Harvey (1871–1932), who was employed by insurance agents F C Davidge & Co in 1902, bought Piers I (qv) in 1909 and settled there with his wife, Mabel Agnes Gaudin (1876–1945), and family for several years before moving to Knapp I. Ownership of Piers I remained in the Harvey family until the death of Robert Oliver Dunsmuir Harvey (1901–58), son of James and Mabel, after which it was sold and subdivided into small recreational lots.

Port Harvey on West Cracroft Island. *Peter Vassilopoulos*

Harvey Point (50°32'00" 126°16'00" E entrance to Port Harvey), **Port Harvey** (50°33'00" 126°16'00" SE side of W Cracroft I, Johnstone Str). Capt Thomas Harvey (1810–68) of HMS *Havannah* served on the Pacific Station, 1855–59. He entered the RN in 1822, was promoted capt in 1848 and took charge of the southern division of the Pacific Station in 1863, aboard HMS *Leander*, with the rank of commodore. Harvey, who was the eldest son of Vice Adm Sir Thomas Harvey, became a rear adm himself in 1865. *See also* Havannah Channel. Named by RN surveyor Capt George Richards in 1860.

Harvey Rock (54°13'00" 133°02'00" Entrance to Cloak Bay, Langara I, QCI). RN officer James R Harvey assisted Capt Frederick Learmonth of HMS *Egeria* with the hydrographic survey of Port Simpson in 1906 (as a sub-lt) and the N coast of Graham I in 1907 (as a lt).

Harwood Bay (53°09'00" 129°33'00" NW side of Campania I, Estevan Sd, N of Caamaño Sd). Named in 1944 after Fred Harwood, boatswain's mate aboard the W coast survey vessel *William J Stewart* in 1943.

Harwood Island (49°52'00" 124°39'00" NE side of Str of Georgia, just W of Powell R). Capt George Vancouver named this island after "a benevolent friend and an elegant scholar." Capt John Walbran suggested that the person in question was RN surgeon Edward Harwood (d 1814), son of the classicist and biblical critic of the same name. He served aboard HMS *Providence*, 1791–94, under Capt William Bligh, when Bligh was finally able to carry out his long-delayed scheme for transplanting breadfruit plants from the S Pacific to the W Indies. Harwood was also a numismatic expert, who wrote on the subject and amassed a well-known collection of Greek and Roman coins. Vancouver, who was travelling in company with the Spanish explorers Dionisio Alcalá-Galiano and Cayetano Valdés at the time, described the shores in this area as having "a very dreary aspect, chiefly composed of rugged rocks thinly wooded with small dwarf pine trees." His survey crews went ashore at Harwood in July 1792. The Sliammon First Nation name for the island is Áhgeyksn, meaning "pointed nose," and refers to its shape. *W*

Harwood Point (49°39'00" 124°28'00" W side of Texada I, S of Gillies Bay, Str of Georgia). Named in 1945 after Commodore Henry Harwood (1881–1950), who commanded a squadron of three cruisers—HMS *Exeter*, HMNZS *Achilles* and HMS *Ajax*—at the Battle of the River Plate, where the German pocket battleship *Admiral Graf Spee* was eventually destroyed at Montevideo, Uruguay, in 1939. Harwood was knighted and promoted to rear adm for this action and served as assistant chief of naval staff until 1942, when he was named vice adm and cdr-in-chief of the Mediterranean Station. He ended WWII as an adm and cdr of the Orkneys and Shetlands.

Hastings Arm (55°31'00" 129°46'00" NW arm of Observatory Inlet, S of Stewart). Rear Adm George Fowler Hastings, CB (1814–76), was cdr-in-chief of the RN's Pacific Station, based at Esquimalt, 1866–69. His flagship was HMS *Zealous*, under Capt Richard Dawkins. Hastings established Esquimalt's RN cemetery in 1867. He saw action around the globe: in China, as cdr of HMS *Harlequin*, 1841–44; off W Africa, on HMS *Cyclops*, 1848–51; in the Mediterranean during the Crimean War with HMS *Curacoa*. He was promoted to vice adm in 1869 and served as cdr-in-chief at the Nore (on England's Thames R estuary), 1873–76. Nearby Mt Hastings is also named for him, as was Hastings townsite on Burrard Inlet, which gave its name to Hastings Mill, Vancouver's pioneer industrial establishment, and Hastings St. The Nisga'a First Nation name for Hastings Arm is K'alii Kshwan, which refers to the teeth-numbing coldness of the water that afflicted Txeemsim, grandfather of the Nisga'a, when he drank here. *W*

Hastings Island (52°38'00" 128°46'00" Entrance to Laredo Inlet, Princess Royal I). Named in 1927 for Oregon

H

Columbus Hastings (1846–1912), born in Illinois, who came to Canada in 1875. His father, Loren Hastings, crossed N America on the Oregon Trail, participated in the California gold rush and settled at Port Townsend, becoming a member of the Washington legislature. After the death of his first wife, Matilda Caroline Birch, in 1881, Oregon married Australia-born Sylvestria Theodora Smith (1846–1926) at Victoria in 1884. He was a photographer, astronomer, naturalist and spiritualist, and built one of BC's earliest telescopes and observatories. Hastings took photographs for an 1879 naval survey of First Nation coastal communities and also for anthropologist Franz Boas on Vancouver I. He eventually sold his Victoria photographic business and became collector of customs at St Michael, Alaska. *E*

Hastings Point (53°01'00" 132°15'00" N side of Inskip Channel, NW corner of Moresby I, QCI), **Hastings Reef** (54°04'00" 132°33'00" Head of Virago Sd, N side of Graham I, QCI). After RN officer George Hastings Inskip, master of HMS *Virago* on the Pacific Station, 1852–55. *See* Inskip Channel.

Haswell Bay (52°32'00" 131°36'00" E side of Moresby I, Juan Perez Sd, QCI), **Haswell Island** (52°52'00" 131°41'00" Entrance to Selwyn Inlet, S of Louise I, QCI), **Haswell Reef** (54°03'00" 132°33'00" N entrance to Alexandra Narrows, Virago Sd, Graham I, QCI). Robert Haswell (b 1768) was the first white man to set foot on the QCI, probably going ashore at Grays Cove (qv) on Anthony I, S of Moresby I, on June 11, 1789. He was likely born at Hull, Massachusetts, into a naval family and spent part of his youth in England. In 1787 he joined the first US fur-trading expedition to the PNW, serving initially as 3rd mate under Capt John Kendrick of the *Columbia Rediviva*. Disagreements with Kendrick resulted in his transferring to the *Lady Washington*, under Capt John Gray, as 2nd mate, and Haswell sailed with Gray for the rest of the voyage, returning home with him aboard *Columbia* as 1st mate. On Gray's second trip to the PNW, in 1790, Haswell also served as 1st mate. In 1792 he was put in charge of the *Adventure* (*see* Adventure Cove), a 40-tonne sloop, built by the crew of the *Columbia* at Clayoquot Sd, that was sold to the Spanish at Nootka Sd that fall. In 1801 he was master of the *Louisa*, which left Boston for the PNW and was never seen again. Haswell's valuable logs from the *Columbia* and *Adventure* were edited by historian Frederic Howay and first published in 1941. *D*

Havannah Channel (50°32'00" 126°14'00" S side of E Cracroft I, N of Johnstone Str), **Havannah Islets** (50°32'00" 126°15'00" In Havannah Channel). HMS *Havannah*, a 19-gun corvette of 874 tonnes, was assigned to the RN's Pacific Station, 1855–59, under Capt Thomas Harvey. It was launched in 1811 at Liverpool as a 36-gun frigate but was remodelled several times and enjoyed an unusually long life for a wooden ship. The *Havannah* captured numerous small French craft in 1813 and was part of an aborted attack on Baltimore the following year. It was stationed in NZ and Australia, 1848–51, and in 1858 brought a squad of 70 Royal Engineers to BC to survey the international boundary with the US from the Pacific to the colony's eastern border. Officers from the *Havannah* helped Capt George Richards survey the Johnstone Str region, and in 1860 he named many features in the area after them. The vessel spent its last decades as a boys' training ship at Cardiff, Wales, and was not broken up until 1905.

Hawk Bay (53°16'00" 129°22'00" W side of Fin I, Squally Channel, SE of Pitt I). Named by the hydrographic service in 1950 for one of the small sounding launches carried by W coast survey vessel *William J Stewart*.

Hawkesbury Island (53°36'30" 129°02'00" E side of Douglas Channel, S of Kitimat). Capt George Vancouver named this island in 1793 after Sir Charles Jenkinson (1727–1808), Baron Hawkesbury, Earl of Liverpool, describing him in his journal as "that noble and indefatigable promoter of British commerce." Jenkinson was an MP and a member of cabinet, holding a number of prominent positions over the years, including secretary to the treasury, lord of the Admiralty, master of the mint, secretary of war (1778–82) and president of the board of trade (1786–1803). He wrote several books, the best of which was said to be his *Treatise on the Coins of the Realm*. Jenkinson Point and Mt Jenkinson on Hawkesbury I are also named for him. For many years Hawkesbury, Gribbell, Maitland and Loretta islands were all thought to be one large island. *W*

Hawkins Narrows (53°25'00" 129°25'00" N end of Union Passage, SE end of Pitt I), **Hawkins Point** (52°47'00" 129°06'00" S of Surf Inlet, W side of Princess Royal I). Hazel Elizabeth Hawkins was a student draftsperson at the Victoria offices of the Canadian Hydrographic Service in 1942. In 1944, Victoria proposed that another feature in Union Passage be named Elizabeth Narrows after this young person, but Ottawa refused to approve the suggestion: "It is felt that too many names of your office staff ... have been used without reasonable discretion," a senior hydrographic service official responded.

Hawkins Rock (52°35'00" 129°10'00" Off entrance to Clifford Bay, W side of Aristazabal I). Sgt William Hawkins was a little-known member of the Columbia detachment of Royal Engineers, which served in BC 1858–63. He is believed to have returned to England when the detachment disbanded.

Hawley Rocks (53°35'00" 130°35'00" W of Rawlinson Anchorage, off NW side of Banks I). Named in 1926 after N G Hawley, who served overseas during WWI and was employed as 2nd steward aboard the W coast survey vessel *Lillooet* in 1921.

Hayden Passage (49°24'00" 126°06'00" NE of Flores I, Clayoquot Sd, W side of Vancouver I). Sidney Cuthbert Hayden (1876–1952), born at Vernon R, PEI, joined the tidal and current surveys program (then part of the federal Dept of Marine and Fisheries) in 1903 and two years later visited BC with Dr William Bell Dawson, who was in charge of the program. By 1909 he was installing tide gauges N of Vancouver I, and in 1913 made observations at Ripple Rk and elsewhere. He was then employed as senior tidal and current surveyor on the Pacific coast, 1919–28. From 1924 until his retirement in 1940 he was based at Vancouver, where as part of his duties he made an examination of the harbour currents. Hayden died at Coquitlam.

Haydon Rock (52°09'00" 131°02'00" E entrance to Houston Stewart Channel, S of Moresby I, QCI). George Inskip, master of HMS *Virago*, made a survey of Houston Stewart Channel in 1853. The ship's capt, Cdr James Prevost, named this feature after his acting 2nd master, Charles Haydon (d 1866), who retired from the RN with the rank of master.

Hayes Rock (51°07'00" 127°42'00" SE of Cape Caution, NW end of Queen Charlotte Str). Pte George Edward Hayes of Vancouver was killed in action Oct 22, 1944, aged 19, in Italy. He was serving with the Loyal Edmonton Regiment of the Royal Canadian Infantry Corps and is buried in Italy's Cesena War Cemetery. Hayes was mentioned in dispatches and also received the Silver Star, a US award for valour.

Haynes Rocks (52°27'00" 129°01'00" Off SW side of Aristazabal I). Sapper William Haynes (1835–1920), born in Kent, was a member of the Columbia detachment of Royal Engineers, which served in BC 1858–63. He arrived at Victoria in 1859 with his wife, Fanny (1840–1931, née Miller), their son and the main contingent of men aboard the *Thames City*. Haynes was a musician and the detachment bandmaster, but he is also mentioned as a gardener at the sappers' New Westminster camp. A newspaper excerpt from 1863 reveals that he was a member of the RE cricket club. He stayed on in the province after the detachment was disbanded, received a grant of land, moved to Victoria in 1864 and served as a music teacher and as bandmaster of the Victoria Volunteers until 1886. William and Fanny, married 64 years, raised a large family and at some point operated the Willows Hotel on Cadboro Bay Rd. Haynes was present at the RE reunion of 1909, when only 12 BC survivors of the original corps remained alive.

Hays Cove (54°20'00" 130°17'00" N end of Kaien I, at Prince Rupert), **Haysport** (54°10'00" 130°00'00" N side of Skeena R, SE of Prince Rupert), **Mount Hays** (54°17'02" 130°18'56" On Kaien I). Hays Cove was named in 1908 after Charles Melville Hays (1856–1912), who was gen manager, then president, of the Grand Trunk and GTP rwys, 1896–1912. Hays was born in Illinois and spent his entire career as a railway company official. It was his determination (or bullheadedness), when faced with delays and financial problems, that saw the GTP project through and linked Winnipeg, Edmonton, Prince George and Prince Rupert. His policies, on the other hand, ended up bankrupting the company and led to its nationalization. Hays drowned in the *Titanic* disaster, which occurred two years before the GTP's last spike was driven in 1914, near Ft Fraser. Haysport was established in 1910 as a station on the GTP and later became the site of a salmon cannery and cold-storage plant. The townsite was eventually abandoned. Hays Ck on Kaien I, Haysport Ck near Haysport and Melville Arm off Prince Rupert Hbr are also named for this railroad tycoon, as is the town of Melville, Sask.

Haystock Islets (48°23'00" 123°30'00" N end of Parry Bay, just SW of Albert Head, SW of Victoria). According to residents of the area, the established local name for this feature, based on its profile, is Haystack Its. The official name may be a misspelling or misinterpretation.

Hazard Point (50°30'00" 128°02'00" E side of Winter Hbr, N of Quatsino Sd, NW end of Vancouver I). Named in 1927 after Frederick J H Hazard, who acquired a Crown grant of land in the area in 1911.

Hazel Island (51°21'00" 127°31'00" N side of Boswell Inlet, E of Smith Sd and Queen Charlotte Sd), **Hazel Point** (54°07'00" 130°14'00" S side of Smith I, S of Prince Rupert). Hazel Boswell was a daughter of Que harbour engineer St George Boswell and a granddaughter of BC lt gov Sir Henri-Gustave Joly de Lotbinière. *See* Boswell Inlet. Capt John Walbran named Hazel Point in 1901 and Hazel I in 1903.

Hazel Shoal (52°37'00" 129°17'00" SE of Moore Is, W of Aristazabal I). Cpl Henry W Hazel was a member of the Columbia detachment of Royal Engineers, which served in BC 1858–63. He was a medical orderly, working under Dr John Seddall, the detachment's medical officer, and came to BC in 1859 with the main body of men aboard the *Thames City*. Hazel was ridiculed in the ship's newspaper (*The Emigrant Soldier's Gazette & Cape Horn Chronicle*) and nicknamed Matilda for his effeminate mannerisms and for leading a black cat with a blue neck ribbon around the decks. Later he was court-martialled for drunkenness and discharged from the service.

Heater Harbour (52°07'00" 131°03'00" E side of Kunghit I, QCI), **Heater Point** (50°17'00" 127°52'00" S entrance

H

to Klaskino Inlet, NW side of Vancouver I). George Heater (1861–1928) and William Heater (1865–1947) were brothers from Harbour Grace, Nfld, both master mariners, who first came to the BC coast about 1890 for the sealing. George was a very successful skipper of various Victoria-based sealing vessels, including the *Rosie Olsen*, *Ainoko* (which was charged with illegal hunting in Russian waters in 1893 but later cleared of wrongdoing), *Penelope*, *Jessie*, *Allie L Alger* and *Markland*. William acted as mate on several of his brother's ships and was then capt of the *Libbie*, *Dora Sieward* and *Arietis* in his own right. After pelagic sealing was banned in 1911, George turned to halibut fishing and later set up a herring saltery at the head of Sydney Inlet on the W coast of Vancouver I. He hired 20 young women from Scotland to work at his plant and housed them in the *Favorite*, an old converted sealing schooner, where they became quite a local attraction until the saltery was destroyed in a violent storm during the winter of 1919–20. William went into the whaling business in 1908 and served as capt of the *W Grant* for many years. Heater Point is named for George. Heater Hbr commemorates William, who spent considerable time in the QCI, operating out of nearby Rose Hbr.

Heather Islets (50°05'00" 125°02'00" Uganda Passage, W side of Cortes I, N end of Str of Georgia). Named in 1960 for Heather Maclean, oldest daughter of the islets' owners, Donald J Maclean and his wife, who planted one of the islets with various types of heather.

Heath Islet (49°29'00" 124°22'00" SW end of False Bay, Lasqueti I, Str of Georgia). John "Jack" Heath pre-empted land on the N side of Lasqueti I in 1882 and received a Crown grant in 1890; he farmed and ranched on the island for many years.

Heathorn Bay (52°50'21" 128°08'05" N end of Mathieson Channel, N of Bella Bella). Leading Stoker Arthur John Heathorn of Vancouver died in action on Sept 29, 1942, aged 21. He was serving aboard HMS *Somali*, a *Tribal*-class destroyer that was torpedoed by a U-boat while on convoy duty to Murmansk, in N Russia, and later sank while being towed to Iceland. His name is inscribed on the Halifax Memorial.

Hecate Bay (49°15'00" 125°56'00" NW of Meares I, Clayoquot Sd, W side of Vancouver I), **Hecate Channel** (49°52'00" 126°45'00" N of Nootka I, E of Esperanza Inlet, W side of Vancouver I), **Hecate Cove** (50°33'00" 127°36'00" N side of Quatsino Sd, NW Vancouver I), **Hecate Island** (51°42'00" 128°02'00" Just N of Calvert I, S of Bella Bella), **Hecate Passage** (48°25'00" 123°15'00" E of the Chain Its, E of Oak Bay and SE Vancouver I), **Hecate Rock** (54°20'00" 130°28'00" In Duncan Bay, just W of Prince Rupert), **Hecate Strait** (52°58'34" 130°38'39" Between QCI and BC mainland). HMS *Hecate*, named after an early Greek

HMS *Hecate* in Esquimalt Harbour, 1862. *BC Archives PDP05357*

goddess, was one of the main RN survey vessels to operate on the BC coast. A manoeuvrable 780-tonne paddlewheel sloop, equipped with five guns, it was launched in 1839 and saw service in the Mediterranean and off the W coast of Africa. Cdr Anthony Hoskins brought the ship out to Esquimalt in Dec 1860, and the officers of the previous survey vessel, HMS *Plumper*, including Capt George Richards, transferred to the *Hecate* in Jan 1861 and spent two full years on board—visiting, as this list of names attests, all parts of the coast. In 1861 the ship grounded E of Cape Flattery in thick fog and had to be taken to San Francisco for repairs at a drydock. Richards sailed *Hecate* back to England in Dec 1862, via Australia and S Africa, and was appointed hydrographer of the RN when he arrived in 1864. His ship was decommissioned in 1865. Hecate Lk on Nootka I and Hecate Mtn SW of Port Alberni are also named for this historic vessel, as was the community of Hecate on Nootka I, site of a cannery and sawmill in the 1920s and '30s and now abandoned. Shallow, unpredictable Hecate St, which narrows from a width of 140 km at its N entrance to 50 km at the S, is famously dangerous for mariners and the location of numerous shipwrecks. Its Haida name is Siigaay. *E W*

Heddington Point (53°08'00" 128°34'00" N entrance to Aaltanhash Inlet, E of Princess Royal I). Thomas Heddington (1774–1852) joined the RN in 1786 and served as a young midshipman aboard HMS *Chatham* on Capt George Vancouver's voyage to the PNW. He was a skilled artist, and a few of his landscape drawings survive from the voyage, along with his logbooks. Promoted lt in 1795, Heddington was at sea until 1802, then moved to a series of land-based appointments: cdr of a signal station, agent for prisoners of war and regulating capt in the impress service.

Hegan Point (54°04'00" 130°06'00" NE entrance to Telegraph Passage, mouth of the Skeena R). Sub-Lt George Vincent Hegan served on the BC coast, 1875–78, aboard HMS *Daring*, under Cdr John Hanmer. In 1877, when the CPR was searching for a W coast terminus for its transcontinental railway, the officers of the *Daring* surveyed the entrance to the Skeena R. Hegan served as flag lt to the cdr-in-chief at Malta in 1879, and in 1893, with the rank of lt cdr, he was in charge of the training brig *Kingfisher*.

Helby Island (48°51'00" 125°10'00" W side of Trevor Channel, Barkley Sd, W side of Vancouver I). Named in 1861 by Capt George Richards for Lt Cdr Alfred Prowse Hasler Helby (1828–1902), who commanded the small steam-powered gunboat *Grappler* on the BC coast, 1860–62. He brought the vessel out from England to Esquimalt and was relieved two years later by Lt Cdr Edmund Verney. Before his Pacific Station assignment, Helby had served on the Australia Station as 1st lt of HMS *Fantome*. He reached the rank of capt, retired, in 1877, then went on to serve as gov of several large British prisons, including Lewes, Coldbath Fields, Pentonville and Wandsworth. *W*

Helen Point (48°51'00" 123°21'00" NW tip of Mayne I, Gulf Is). Helen "Nelly" Holmes (1838–1914), born in Lancashire, came to Victoria in 1858. In 1860 she married HBC chief trader Joseph William McKay (1829–1900, *see* McKay Channel) and began raising a large family. Nelly Point on Princess Royal I is also named for her. In his *British Columbia Coast Names*, Capt John Walbran indicates that McKay Reach, between Princess Royal I and Gribbell I, commemorates Helen as well, but at another point in the book he seems to suggest that it is named after her husband. The area around Helen Point is a reserve and ancient village site of the Tsartlip First Nation. Archeological excavations in 1968 revealed that it was occupied more than 5,000 years ago, making it the oldest known settlement in the Gulf Is region. *W*

Helen Point (53°37'00" 129°14'00" S entrance to Kitkiata Inlet, W side of Douglas Channel, opposite Hawkesbury I, SW of Kitimat). Helen Gertrude Davies, born in PEI in 1873, was the eldest child of Sir Louis Davies, federal minister of Marine and Fisheries, 1896–1901. See Davies Bay. Capt John Walbran named this point and Gertrude Point opposite in 1898. He also named Ethel Rk in Principe Channel after Helen's sister.

Helgesen Point (48°20'00" 123°33'00" S side of Pedder Bay, S tip of Vancouver I). Hans Lars Helgesen (1831–1918), born in Norway, came to Canada in 1858 and secured a Crown grant of land in the Metchosin area in 1871. He had immigrated to N America in 1849 and joined the California gold rush. He met his wife, Irish-born Lillian Margaret Calhoun (1835–1903), at San Francisco, where she was working as a seamstress, and married her at Victoria in 1862. Hans was an adventurer at heart, and though the Helgesens became well-known pioneer settlers and farmers at Metchosin, he also joined

a number of gold-seeking ventures, fished for black cod off the QCI, salted salmon at Rivers Inlet, managed a mine in British Guiana (now Guyana) and participated in the sealing industry. From 1878 to 1886, Helgesen was MLA for Esquimalt.

Hudson's Bay Company medical officer John Sebastian Helmcken played significant roles in early BC political life. He married the eldest daughter of Gov James Douglas. *BC Archives A-01349*

Helmcken Inlet (52°46'00" 129°02'00" W side of Princess Royal I), **Helmcken Island** (50°24'00" 125°52'00" S of Hardwicke I, Johnstone Str). Dr John Sebastian Helmcken (1824–1920), born at London, was an important figure in BC's early political and social life. He came to Victoria from England in 1850 as an HBC medical officer and was first sent to Ft Rupert, where he was commissioned as a magistrate to deal with conflicts at the coal mines. Two years later he married Cecilia Douglas (1834–65), eldest daughter of Vancouver I colonial gov James Douglas. Helmcken was elected to the Island's legislative assembly in 1856 and served as speaker of both the Vancouver I and BC assemblies, 1856–71. In 1870 he was also appointed to BC's executive council. As one of three delegates sent to Ottawa to negotiate union with Canada, Helmcken demanded that a transcontinental railway be started within two years and completed within ten. He was uncertain that union—or responsible government, for that matter—was a practical option for BC, but reluctantly supported Confederation. In 1871 he turned down offers to become either the first premier or lt gov of the new province and dedicated himself instead to medicine. Helmcken resigned from the HBC in 1885 and was named founding president of the BC Medical Society. He was also president of Royal Jubilee Hospital, 1851–1910. His home in Victoria is now part of the Royal BC Museum, and his memoirs, *The Reminiscences of Doctor John Sebastian Helmcken*, were

H

published in 1975. Helmcken I was supposedly named by HBC mariner Capt Charles Dodd in 1850 while the *Beaver* was struggling against the current through Johnstone Str. Helmcken, who was also aboard, asked Dodd the name of a nearby island, and the frustrated skipper replied that it had no name but he would call it Helmcken, after the doctor, for it was, like him, "always in opposition." Helmcken Canyon, Helmcken Lk, Mt Helmcken and spectacular 137-m-high Helmcken Falls also commemorate this BC pioneer, as does Speaker Rk, E of Helmcken I. Helmcken Point on Douglas I in the Fraser R, however, is named for his wife. *E W*

Hemasila Inlet (51°32'00" 127°35'00" E side of Walbran I, Rivers Inlet). According to BC historians Helen and Philip Akrigg, when Rivers Inlet was re-surveyed in the late 1930s, a number of names were bestowed to honour the family of Methodist medical missionary George Darby, who operated a summer hospital on the inlet for many years. Hemasila was a Heiltsuk First Nation nickname given to one of the Darby children.

Heming Head (52°50'00" 131°38'25" E end of Talunkwan I, just E of Moresby I, QCI). Herbert Payne Heming (1863–1932) was born at Guelph, Ont, and came to Victoria in 1907 after spending two years in Vancouver. He married Elizabeth Aileen Domville (1870–1933). Heming had major timber and mining interests in the southern QCI and invested heavily in the development of the Hawk's Nest copper claim near Heming Head in 1909. He also owned mining properties on Portland Canal. *D*

Hemming Bay (50°24'00" 125°23'00" E side of E Thurlow I, Nodales Channel, N of Discovery Passage). Capt George Richards, in charge of Admiralty surveys on the BC coast, 1857–63, moved back to England in 1864 and was appointed the RN's chief hydrographer. In honour of the occasion, his successor in BC, Lt Daniel Pender, named a number of features in this region after hydrographic dept employees in Britain, including draftsman Pinhorn L Hemming. Hemming had never been anywhere near the PNW. Nearby Hemming Lk is also named for him.

Henderson Point (48°36'00" 123°29'00" W side of Saanich Peninsula, N of Hagan Bight, NW of Victoria). John "Russian Jack" Henderson (1831–93), born at Riga, Latvia, and his wife, Betsy Pope (1833–94), originally from England, were early settlers in the Saanich area. Jack, like so many others, had originally come to BC for the Cariboo gold rush. Betsy's parents, Abraham (1805–86) and Sarah Pope, had settled in 1874 on a homestead where Mt Newton Cottage, a heritage building built by Betsy, now stands. Jack and Betsy Henderson owned and operated the Mt Newton Hotel, 1874–93; their property included Henderson Point.

Henderson Rocks (52°10'00" 131°20'00" SE of Nagas Point, SW end of Moresby I, QCI), **Henderson Shoal** (51°24'00" 127°56'00" S of Calvert I, entrance to Fitz Hugh Sd). Lt Cdr Archibald M Henderson (1890–1955) was a long-time employee of the Fisheries Protection Branch on the BC coast. As skipper of CGS *Givenchy*, a *Battle*-class trawler and former RCN WWI minesweeper that was assigned to the fisheries dept between the wars, he responded to many emergencies in remote parts of the BC coast. Henderson also frequently assisted the hydrographic service, especially during surveys of bays and inlets along Haida Gwaii's western shorelines.

Henrietta Island (50°39'00" 126°37'00" W of Gilford I, E end of Queen Charlotte Str). After Lady Elizabeth Henrietta Kennedy, wife of Viscount Gilford and eldest daughter of Arthur Kennedy, gov of Vancouver I, 1864–66. *See* Gilford Point.

Henry Bay (49°36'00" 124°50'00" NW end of Denman I, Str of Georgia). This name, adopted in 1923, is taken from a survey made by Capt George Henry Richards and is possibly in honour of the famed RN hydrographer. *See* Richards Channel.

Henry Island (54°01'00" 130°40'00" S of Edye Passage, NW side of Porcher I, SW of Prince Rupert). After RN officer Capt William Henry Edye, who was on the BC coast in 1869. *See* Edye Passage.

Henry Point (49°38'00" 124°03'00" N entrance to Pender Hbr, Str of Georgia, NW of Vancouver). According to historian Athelstan Harvey, there are two possible sources for this name: Dr James Henry, who served on the Pacific Station as surgeon of HMS *Mutine* in 1860; or Richard P Henry, Royal Marines capt aboard HMS *Ganges*, on the Pacific Station in 1857–60.

Henry Rock (52°00'00" 128°14'00" Between SW end of Campbell I and the Prince Group, SW of Bella Bella). Named in 1944 for the passenger ship *Prince Henry* after it was transferred to the RN and converted to an armed merchant cruiser. The 109-m, 6,252-tonne steel vessel, which could load automobiles through its side doors, was built at Birkenhead, England, for the CNR in 1930 and spent its first year in the Alaska cruise trade. From 1932 to 1936 it operated in the Caribbean, then was sold to the Clarke Co of Que in 1938 and renamed the *North Star*. In 1940, when the RN took over, the *Henry* was given back its original name. It endured another conversion in 1943, to a landing ship, and took part in the Normandy invasion. After WWII it was renamed again, this time the *Empire Parkeston*, and used by Britain's ministry of transport to carry occupying troops back and forth across the English Channel. The vessel was scrapped in 1961.

Langara Fishing Lodge in Henslung Cove, 1985. *Andrew Scott*

Henslung Cove (54°11'31" 133°00'03" S side of Langara I, QCI). *Slung* is the Haida term for "bottom end of a bay," and Henslung is apparently a corruption of the Haida name for this feature. In 1919, Capt Hume Babbington operated a short-lived cannery there; later this site was the homestead for many years of Al Peevey, trapper and telephone lineman. The cove was also a popular HQ for fish camps in summer. Early charts show it as Cove Douglas, after fur trader William Douglas of the *Iphigenia Nubiana*, and Babbington Bay. *D*

Hepburn Point (53°32'00" 129°36'00" E side of Grenville Channel, at entrance to Lowe Inlet, E of Pitt I). James Hepburn (1811–69), born in Scotland, moved to Kent, England, and was trained as a lawyer. A taste for adventure and scientific pursuit led him to N America, where he became a resident of San Francisco (and a substantial property owner), and eventually to Victoria, where he lived for a number of years. Named by Lt Daniel Pender in 1868.

Herald Rock (50°43'00" 127°24'00" W side of Beaver Hbr, Daedalus Passage, NE side of Vancouver I). HMS *Herald*, an RN survey ship, was on the BC coast in 1846–47, commanded by Capt Henry Kellett. Accompanied by a small brig, HMS *Pandora*, Kellett made the earliest detailed surveys of Victoria and Esquimalt harbours, Sooke Inlet and Juan de Fuca Str. His presence in the area was partly motivated by an ongoing N American boundary dispute

between Britain and the US, which would be settled in June 1846 with the Oregon Treaty. Kellet's 454-tonne, 8-gun vessel had been launched at Kochi, India, in 1822 as the 28-gun HMS *Termagant*, but was renamed in 1824 when converted to a less heavily armed survey craft. Kellett and the *Herald* were engaged in survey work off Central America in 1848 when they were suddenly sent to the Arctic Ocean to help in the search for missing explorer Sir John Franklin. Kellett made three cruises to the Arctic in 1848–50 but found no trace of Franklin and returned to England in 1851. After a lengthy survey of the Fiji Is under Capt Henry Denham, the *Herald* was taken out of service in 1862. Herald Rk was discovered in 1903 by Cdr Cortland Simpson of the RN survey vessel *Egeria*. *W*

Herbert Head (52°58'00" 132°15'00" W entrance to Douglas Inlet, Moore Channel, NW Moresby I, QCI). Nathaniel Bland Herbert was 2nd master aboard HMS *Thetis*, on the Pacific Station, 1851–53, under Capt Augustus Kuper. He helped George Moore, master of the *Thetis*, survey the Englefield Bay region (formerly known as Gold Hbr) off NW Moresby I in 1852. Herbert was promoted to master in 1855 for his services during the Crimean War. Nearby Bland Point is also named for him.

Herbert Reefs (54°01'00" 130°14'00" Off E side of Lewis I, Arthur Passage, S of Prince Rupert). After Capt Herbert Lewis, who worked for the HBC on the BC coast for many years as a master mariner. *See* Lewis Channel.

Hergest Point (51°49'00" 128°01'00" NE entrance to Nalau Passage, SW Hunter I, S of Bella Bella). Lt Richard Hergest, a "most intimate friend" of Capt George Vancouver, was in command of the transport *Daedalus*, en route to resupply Vancouver at Nootka Sd in 1792, when he was killed by aboriginal attackers at Oahu, Hawaii. Astronomer William Gooch, coming to join HMS *Discovery*, also died in this incident. Hergest had earlier served as a midshipman aboard HMS *Adventure* on Capt James Cook's second great voyage of exploration, and was with HMS *Resolution* on Cook's third voyage (and had thus been present at Nootka Sd in 1778 with Vancouver, who also sailed on Cook's second and third voyages). The *Daedalus* kept its 1792 rendezvous at Nootka Sd, and Vancouver appointed Lt James Hanson, former 1st lt of HMS *Chatham*, as the vessel's cdr. *See also* Daedalus Point.

Heriot Bay (50°06'00" 125°13'00" E side of Quadra I, N end of Str of Georgia), **Heriot Island** (50°07'00" 125°13'00" Just N of Heriot Bay). Named in 1862 by Capt George Richards after Frederick Lewis Maitland-Heriot (1818–81), a descendant of the 6th Earl of Lauderdale. Heriot was an advocate, justice of the peace, sheriff and deputy lt of Fife, Scotland, and apparently a relative of Rear Adm Sir Thomas Maitland, cdr-in-chief of the RN's Pacific Station, 1860–62, whom Richards wished to honour. The

H

The Heriot Bay Inn was originally built in the 1890s. *Andrew Scott*

small community of Heriot Bay, which once depended on logging and fishing for survival but is now quite tourism-oriented, is the site of the historic Heriot Bay Inn and the ferry terminus for Cortes I.

Heritage Point (48°26'00" 123°15'00" SW end of Chatham Is, E of Oak Bay and Victoria). John Alexander Heritage (1865–1958) was born in the US, came to BC in 1893 and married Mary Ash Wilson (1875–1965) at Victoria in 1901. He served as an engineer aboard the *Empress of India* on the CPR's trans-Pacific line before joining the Canadian Pacific Navigation Co and the CPR's BC Coast Steamship Service in 1897. Promoted to chief engineer in 1909, he ended his career in 1931 as senior chief engineer of the *Princess* fleet. Vessels he worked on included *Charmer*, *Islander*, *Queen City*, *Amur*, *Princess Royal*, *Princess Victoria*, *Princess Charlotte*, *Princess Margaret* and *Princess Kathleen*. As Heritage wrote to regional hydrographer Henri Parizeau in 1934, he "had been passing this point of land almost every day" for 35 years.

Herman Rock (54°10'00" 129°57'00" Near the junction of the Ecstall R and Skeena R, SE of Prince Rupert). Peter Herman (1861–1906) was educated as a priest in his native Germany but joined the army instead and then became a seaman. He arrived in northern BC in 1885 to work as a logger for businessman Robert Cunningham, and in 1894 married Kate Spence at Port Essington. After also trying his hand for two years as a trapper at Lakelse Lk, Herman, backed by Simon Leiser of Victoria, built the Anglo-Alliance Cannery at Port Essington in 1898. This venture eventually went bankrupt; it was acquired about 1906 by R V Winch and Henry Doyle and renamed the Skeena R Commercial Cannery. Herman also had an interest in the Ladysmith Cannery, and he sold the Alexandria Cannery's proprietors their land. At the time of its bankruptcy, Herman's company was listed as owning a "canning plant, wharf and warehouse, 38 fishermen's houses, Herman's residence, Herman's former residence, a butcher shop, hotel building, store, real estate in Port Essington, 140

acres of land at Balmoral, a clam cannery on Dundas I, the steamer *Mamie*, two scows, three house rafts, a fish camp at a hot springs, a 60-hp boiler, a new 1903 engine, China house, other additional buildings ... the Dry Hill Mining Co, Skeena Lumber Co, a logging outfit and various sundries such as boats, nets, tools, store merchandise and hotel furnishings." Herman drowned in 1906 in a log-towing accident.

Hermit Island (49°22'00" 123°28'00" S of Keats I and Barfleur Passage, Howe Sd, NW of Vancouver). In a 1951 interview with Vancouver archivist Maj James Matthews, Isabel Sweeny (1890–1974, née Bell-Irving) claimed to have named this feature in the early 1900s, with her brother, Malcolm Bell-Irving (*see* Mickey I), while exploring the area by boat from Pasley I, the Bell-Irving family's summer domain. The island was occupied for many years by a tall, elderly hermit who lived in a driftwood shack "no bigger than a very big dog kennel" with "seal skulls all around it arranged in order." The man hunted the seals from a homemade dugout canoe, which he either sailed, or rowed standing up, facing forward and pushing on the oars. The young people befriended him and learned that he had been a clergyman in Norway but isolated himself after a sad love affair. The hermit made whatever money he needed by trapping mink and selling the pelts. His drowned body was found in the area sometime during WWI. Hermit I was bought in 1926 by Reginald Tupper, grandson of Canadian PM Sir Charles Tupper, and strata-titled by the Tupper family in 1968. Formerly known as Golby I (*see* Golby Passage), it is now home to several pretty cottages. *See also* Tupper Rk, named after Sir Charles Hibbert Tupper, Reginald's father.

Hernando Island (49°59'00" 124°55'00" NW of Savary I, NE end of Str of Georgia). Named in 1792 by Spanish explorers Dionisio Alcalá-Galiano and Cayetano Valdés in association with nearby Cortes I. Hernán Cortés (1485–1547), a Spanish *conquistador*, overthrew the Aztec empire in southern Mexico and initiated the Spanish colonization of the Americas. Hernando I, which is surrounded by beautiful beaches, was first settled and farmed in the 1880s, then railway logged in the 1910s. It was listed for sale in 1968 for $750,000. After the collapse of several resort development proposals, it was purchased and subdivided by a syndicate of wealthy owners, many of whom built spectacular summer homes there. *E*

Heron Islands (53°36'00" 130°34'00" In approach to Griffith Hbr, NW end of Banks I), **Heron Rock** (50°27'00" 128°02'00" S of Kains I, Quatsino Sd, NW end of Vancouver I). Named in 1926–27 after Arthur Heron, who was a boatswain aboard the survey vessel *Lillooet* and had been employed on the W coast by the hydrographic service since 1913. He also served as a boatswain on CGS *Restless* during the survey of Quatsino Sd, 1920–21.

Hesler Point (50°24'00" 125°09'00" N entrance to Big Bay, W side of Stuart I, mouth of Bute Inlet, N of Campbell R). This name, adopted in 1955, may be a misspelling for Hetzler, referring to an early resident family in the area. A 1927 BC directory lists Cyrus Delevan Hetzler (1872–1944) as a logger and Russell Hetzler (1898–1976) as a fisherman, both at Stuart I.

Hesquiat Harbour, west side of Vancouver Island. *Sam Beebe/Ecotrust*

Hesquiat (49°24'00" 126°28'00" E side of Hesquiat Peninsula), **Hesquiat Bar** (49°24'00" 126°26'00" Mouth of Hesquiat Hbr), **Hesquiat Harbour** (49°26'00" 126°27'00" E of Hesquiat Peninsula), **Hesquiat Peninsula** (49°24'00" 126°30'00" Just SE of Nootka Sd, W side of Vancouver I), **Hesquiat Point** (49°25'00" 126°24'00" SE entrance to Hesquiat Hbr). The Hesquiaht people are members of the Nuu-chah-nulth Tribal Council. The name, which was given to the tribe by their Nootkan neighbours, apparently refers to the sound made when a particular delicacy, herring spawn on eelgrass, is eaten. The Hesquiaht were one of the first aboriginal groups to encounter white explorers; in 1774 they traded with Juan Pérez, of the *Santiago*, who did not come ashore. In 1869 they were implicated in the notorious wreck of the US barque *John Bright*, whose surviving crew members were supposedly killed by local residents (two Hesquiaht were later convicted of murder and hanged). The early mission of Roman Catholic priest Augustin Brabant was located at the village of Hesquiat, on Hesquiat Hbr, in 1875. Hesquiat Lake and Hesquiat Point Ck are also named for this First Nation group. In 1995, much of the shoreline in the Hesquiat area was protected as part of 7,888-ha Hesquiat Peninsula Provincial Park. The remote pioneer settlement of Boat Basin, famed for the gardens created by Ada "Cougar Annie" Rae-Arthur, who arrived in 1915, is at the head of Hesquiat Hbr (*see* Rae Basin). *W*

Hevenor Inlet (53°39'00" 130°02'00" NW side of Pitt I), **Hevenor Islet** (53°38'00" 130°02'00" N side of Hevenor Inlet), **Hevenor Lagoon** (53°38'00" 129°52'00" Head of Hevenor Inlet), **Hevenor Point** (53°38'00" 130°04'00" Entrance to Hevenor Inlet). James Harvey Hevenor (1882–1964) apparently changed his surname from Heavenor because of a family dispute. After marrying Lucy Latie (1874–1944) at Vancouver in 1908, he served in WWI and lost an arm, but that did not stop his working as a logger for many years on the N coast. When a government survey team had boat trouble off Pitt I in the late 1940s, Hevenor took its members round the area in his vessel, and they named a number of features after him in appreciation. Hevenor also pre-empted land in the Kispiox R area, N of Kispiox, at the site of Hevenor Ck, in 1913. James died at Vancouver, his wife, Lucy, at Kispiox.

Hewitt Island (52°52'00" 128°30'00" N end of Hiekish Narrows and Sarah I, E of Princess Royal I), **Hewitt Rock** (52°52'00" 128°29'00" Just E of Hewitt I). Capt James Hewitt, of the schooner *Goldstream*, discovered the rock that bears his name while travelling to the QCI in 1866. He reported it to naval survey officials, and Lt Daniel Pender ensured that the hazard appeared on future Admiralty charts. Hewitt, a native of Essex, England, came to BC in 1857 aboard the *Highland Queen* and was master of several small trading vessels on the W coast, including the *Nanaimo Packet* (1867) and the steamship *Emily Harris* (1864–65).

Hewlett Bay (52°57'00" 132°20'00" S side of Moore Channel, NW side of Moresby I, QCI). William Hewlett (d 1885) was a master's assistant aboard HMS *Thetis*, on the Pacific Station, 1851–53, under Capt Augustus Kuper. He helped George Moore, master of the *Thetis*, survey the Englefield Bay region (formerly known as Gold Hbr) off NW Moresby I in 1852 and the following year was transferred to HMS *Cockatrice* off the coast of Mexico. Hewlett was promoted master in 1858 and staff cdr in 1869. He served aboard HMS *Valorous* on the S Africa (Cape) Station and was in command of the small paddle tender *Pygmy* at Portsmouth in 1875. *W*

Heynen Channel (49°10'00" 125°55'00" E of Father Charles Channel, N of Tofino, Clayoquot Sd, W side of Vancouver I). Named in 1934 for William Lambert Heynen (1856–1939), a Roman Catholic missionary at Clayoquot, 1888–92. Heynen was in Victoria in 1881 and probably taught at St Louis College, the Catholic boys' school. He was one of the first Roman Catholic priests in SE Alaska, working at Juneau and Sitka in the mid-1880s. After Clayoquot, Heynen served for several years at Nanaimo.

Hibbard Point (52°06'00" 128°26'00" S end of Houghton Is, Thompson Bay, W of Bella Bella). Named in 1944 after RCN officer James Calcutt "Stumpy" Hibbard, DSC (1908–96). Hibbard was born in Que, joined the RCNVR in 1924 and became a naval cadet two years later. At the outset of WWII he was promoted to lt cdr and had charge of the RCN destroyers *Skeena* (1940–41) and *Iroquois*

H

(1943–45). It was for his actions as a convoy escort cdr in the N Atlantic (and for helping sink a U-boat) that he was awarded the DSC and bar; he also received gallantry awards from France and Norway. In 1945, by then a capt, Hibbard was appointed deputy chief of RCN personnel. As CO of the RCN cruiser *Ontario* (1947–49), he had to deal with an "incident of mass insubordination" (i e, a mutiny) at Nanoose Hbr; the protest was aimed at his unpopular executive officer, who was transferred. In 1950, Hibbard was made commodore and chief of naval personnel at naval HQ, then served as flag officer on the Pacific coast, 1953–55, with the rank of rear adm. He retired in 1955 and died at Vancouver.

Hibben Island (52°59'00" 132°17'00" Between Moore Channel and Inskip Channel, NW side of Moresby I, QCI). Thomas Napier Hibben (1828–90) was born at Charleston, S Carolina, and came to Victoria from San Francisco in 1858. He formed a partnership with James Carswell and purchased Kierski's bookstore, then bought out his partner in 1866. On an 1864 visit to England he married Janet Parker Brown (1836–1919), born in Scotland. T N Hibben & Co was the premier bookseller and stationer in Victoria for decades and was also the local agent for Admiralty charts. Its owner became well known in the city as a businessman, landowner and pioneer. He published some of BC's earliest books, including *Dictionary of Indian Tongues* (1862), *Dictionary of the Chinook Jargon* (1871) and *Guide to the Province of British Columbia* (1877). Hibben I was formerly known as Kuper I, after Capt Augustus Kuper; its name was changed in 1905. The Haida name for this geographical feature is Gul. *D W*

Hickey Cove (51°18'00" 127°21'00" Between Naysash Bay and Adelaide Point, Naysash Inlet, N of Smith Inlet, E of Smith Sd). Capt John Walbran, of CGS *Quadra*, examined Naysash Inlet in 1903 and named this feature after William Hickey, from Ont, who owned a salmon cannery there. Hickey came to BC in 1890 and worked for seven years at Vancouver's BC Ironworks as a mechanical engineer. He had an interest in William McPherson's Dinsmore I cannery on the Fraser R, which was sold to the BC Packers Assoc in 1902. Hickey developed his Naysash Inlet cannery in partnership with Robert Kelly of Vancouver's Kelly, Douglas & Co. After selling out to Wallace Fisheries Ltd in 1911, he acquired the Kingcome Inlet cannery in 1916 and operated it until at least the early 1920s.

Hickey Islands (53°00'00" 129°31'00" E of Dewdney I, Estevan Sd, N of Caamaño Sd). Marine engineer Patrick Hickey (b 1841), from Brooklyn, NY, came to Victoria in 1861 as an employee of the HBC. His US-born wife, Emma Rebecca (1858–1924), arrived in BC in 1876.

Hickey Point (50°27'00" 126°05'00" On NE side of Vancouver I, S of Port Neville and Johnstone Str). Patrick

Joseph Hickey (c 1852–1933), born at Torbay, Nfld, came to BC in 1891 and joined the Canadian Pacific Navigation Co as a quartermaster in 1893. He was married twice, first to Catherine Francis Ryan (1858–1922), from Boston, and then, at the age of 73, to Catherine Flanagan (1869–1935), from England. Hickey became a ship's capt in 1899 and worked for many years for the CPR's BC Coast Steamship Service. He was master of the *Princess Royal* before moving to the *Princess Victoria* in 1909 and becoming a well-known skipper on the competitive Vancouver–Victoria–Seattle route. Hickey was aboard the *Victoria* in 1914 when it collided with and sank the Alaska-bound liner *Admiral Sampson* in thick fog off Point No Point. Sixteen people died. He retired in 1921.

Hicks Island (52°46'00" 129°18'00" Off NW side of Aristazabal I). The background of Thomas Benton Hicks (1831–1927) is a bit vague. He may have served with the US military, been present in the San Juan Is during the territorial dispute between Britain and the US, worked on the Whatcom Trail between Sumas and the Fraser R, and made a living as a miner. He moved to Hope about 1859, operated a mill and later raised cattle and farmed in the Agassiz area, where he became well known as a fruit farmer and served on the Kent municipal council. Hicks married Annie Spitlam (or Hathallip; d 1937), the daughter of Chief David Hathallip of the Nlaka'pamux First Nation, at Laidlaw in 1865. He is believed to have taken part in the Victoria old-timers' reunion of 1924 (*see* Adams Bay). Several other features in the region are also named for him, including Hicks Ck, Hicks Lk and Mt Hicks.

Hicks Point (54°12'00" 130°16'00" N end of Smith I, S of Prince Rupert). Robert Hicks (1828–1910), from Norfolk, England, joined the RN in 1845 but left three years later and immigrated to N America. He served in the US Navy and was a crew member on USS *Decatur* in 1854. Hicks came to Canada about 1856 and was employed as master of a number of trading vessels on the BC coast, especially in the QCI. In the late 1860s he worked in Alaska as a pilot. Hicks married Helen Burnside (1828–1905), a native of Scotland, at Victoria in 1869. In later years he was in charge of the Fraser R lightship. Hicks Point was named by Cdr John Hanmer of HMS *Daring*, who surveyed the Skeena R in 1877 after engaging Hicks as a pilot. *W*

Hiellen River (54°04'00" 131°47'00" Flows N into McIntyre Bay, N side of Graham I, QCI). Hiellen is a modification of the Haida name meaning "river by Tow Hill." A sizable Haida village was situated on the E shore of the mouth of this river, and a clam cannery also operated there, 1923–30. An early store and post office were located on the Hiellen's E bank. *D*

Higgins Island (49°30'00" 124°22'00" N side of False Bay, Lasqueti I, Str of Georgia). Hugh Harry Higgins (b 1841)

pre-empted land in this area in 1882 and received a Crown grant in 1890. He also acquired a grant of land at Boat Cove, farther E, in 1912. Higgins served as a British soldier or marine for 12 years on the San Juan Is and married a very young Mary Ann Jaffrey (1873–1947) in 1887. He is described on various census and voters lists as either a farmer or a carpenter. After separating from his wife about 1895, Higgins apparently put in a stint as keeper at nearby Sisters lighthouse, 1899–1901, but was soon back on Lasqueti, where he planted a large orchard, became a prominent member of the farmers' institute and served as the island's first road foreman. *See also* Rouse Bay.

Higgins Passage (52°28'00" 128°41'00" Between Price I and Swindle I, NW of Bella Bella). David Williams Higgins (1834–1917), born at Halifax, NS, and raised in NY, founded a newspaper in San Francisco (*The Morning Call*) before coming to BC in 1858 to join the gold rush. He had been trained as a printer, and after working as a storekeeper in Yale, he moved to Victoria in 1860 and joined Amor de Cosmos's *British Colonist*. Higgins married Mary Jane Pidwell (1846–1900) at Victoria in 1863. He was owner and editor of the *Colonist*, 1862–86 (and a supporter of BC's entry into Confederation), and used it as a launching pad into politics, serving as MLA for Esquimalt, 1886–1900, and speaker of the legislative assembly, 1890–98. His books—*The Mystic Spring and Other Tales of Western Life* (1904) and *The Passing of a Race and More Tales of Western Life* (1905)—were popular reflections of contemporary social life. Higgins also edited the *Vancouver World* newspaper, 1906–7. His Victoria mansion, Regent's Park, was built in 1885 at Fort St and St Charles; in the early 2000s it had been beautifully restored as the Amethyst Inn. **Higgins Lagoon** (52°30'00" 128°42'00" SE of Kitasu Bay, W side of Swindle I) is presumably also named for him. Pidwell Reef (qv), S of Swindle I, is named for his wife. *E*

Higgs Point (48°44'00" 123°11'00" E side of S Pender I, Gulf Is). Leonard Lewis Spalding Higgs (1867–1922) came out from England in 1886, lived for a year on Saturna I and then moved to S Pender I, where he ranched and logged. He returned to England to marry Caroline Emma Wells Batsford (1867–1956) and brought her to BC in 1892. Higgs had many family connections in the Gulf Is; his step-uncle Arthur Spalding was a S Pender pioneer, and his sisters Mabel and Winifred followed him to BC and married men they met in the area (*see* Grainger Point).

High Island (52°08'00" 131°01'00" Off NE side of Kunghit I, QCI). Named by geologist Dr George Dawson in 1878, this kelp-circled island was home to the ancient Haida village of Hlagi. Japanese prospector J Uniaka registered the Copper Coin claim there in 1913. Its actual height is about 180 m.

Hilbert Point (52°40'00" 128°47'00" NW side of Hastings I, just S of Princess Royal I). John Henry Hilbert (1844–1926) was born in Lincolnshire, England, and arrived in 1873 at Nanaimo, where other family members later joined him. His wife, Mary Jane Hilbert (1845–1913), was also born in England. Hilbert worked as a furniture dealer and undertaker, using his carpentry skills to construct caskets as well as the Wellington Methodist church and other local buildings. A model citizen, he served as a Nanaimo alderman, school and hospital trustee, board of trade member and mayor in 1890–91. He was a keen member of various fraternal organizations and acquired a good deal of property in Nanaimo. Hilbert participated in the grand old-timers' reunion held at Victoria in 1924 (*see* Adams Bay).

Hill Head (48°23'00" 123°41'00" SW side of Sooke Basin, S end of Vancouver I), **Hill Island** (50°10'00" 125°04'00" Sutil Channel, E of Burdwood Bay, Read I, N end of Str of Georgia). Hill Head was named in 1846 by Capt Henry Kellett, cdr of HMS *Herald*, after James Stephen Hill, his master and assistant survey officer. Hill served aboard the *Herald* from 1845 to 1852 and spent two of those years on the S coast of BC, charting the shores of Juan de Fuca Str. He had previously been 2nd master of HMS *Britomart* on the 1838–41 survey of the Arafura Is and NZ. During the Crimean War he did significant survey work in the Baltic. Hill was promoted to staff cdr in 1863 and died in 1867. Hill I was named by Lt Daniel Pender about 1864. *W*

Hillier Island (49°02'00" 125°19'00" W end of Pipestem Inlet, E of Toquart Bay, Barkley Sd, W side of Vancouver I). Herbert James Hillier (1873–1953) acquired a number of Crown land grants in the area between 1907 and 1912, including one that covered most of this island. He worked at first as a coal miner at Wellington and then farmed with his brother William Hillier in S Saanich's Mt Tolmie area. Herbert arrived on the W coast in the early 1900s with his US-born wife, Rosa Eberta (1876–1942), and their son, William, and became a long-time resident of Ucluelet, serving for years as a telegraph lineman and government agent.

Hill Island (54°19'00" 130°22'00" Entrance to Russell Arm, Prince Rupert Hbr). Civil engineer Arthur Edmund B Hill (1845–1921) was a member of the original 1906 survey party that laid out the GTP's new terminus at Prince Rupert. He and his brother, Albert J Hill, arrived in BC in 1880 and were hired by the CPR. They were involved with railway surveys and construction in the BC Interior and on Vancouver I, and also found employment with the Coquitlam Water Works Co. Arthur was appointed superintendent of waterworks in New Westminster in 1890. He served as a councillor in that city and worked for the BC Electric Rwy as well as for the CPR and GTP. He married Marion Robina Graham (1869–1950) at Vancouver in 1909.

H

Hill Rock (50°07'00" 123°50'00" Queens Reach, Jervis Inlet, NW of Vancouver). Named after James Hill Lawson (1840–1915), who was born at Dundee, Scotland, and came to Victoria in 1862 with his brother William Lawson. After working at the pioneer Alberni sawmill and farming on Saltspring I, James joined the HBC in 1865 and spent the next 25 years in Victoria as a clerk and assistant factor. In 1871 he married Ann Jenet MacDonald (1847–1934), who was born in England and came to Victoria with her mother in the early 1860s. Lawson's final employer was R P Rithet & Co, the Victoria-based conglomerate with interests in wholesale foods, canneries, lumber, shipping, sealing and insurance, where he became a shareholder and rose to the position of vice-president.

Hilton Point (53°49'00" 128°52'00" W side of Douglas Channel, just S of Kitimat). BC's Geographical Names Office notes that prospector John Hilton discovered and mined gold and copper on Gribbell I, S of the point, opposite Hartley Bay, around 1900. Although development work was done on the island in 1900–1905 by several US firms, no ore was ever shipped and no John Hilton is mentioned in the annual reports of the BC Ministry of Mines. A Joseph Hilton, however, was involved with the Mountain Goat, Lucy and Sarah Jane claims on Gardner Canal in 1903–4.

Hinton Island (53°21'00" 129°27'00" Between Farrant I and Pitt I). Lyman Hyde Hinton (1902–80), born at Victoria, spent many years as a provincial land surveyor at Prince Rupert. He died at Port Washington on N Pender I.

Hippa Island (53°32'00" 132°59'00" Off W side of Graham I, QCI), **Hippa Passage** (53°33'00" 132°58'00" Between Hippa I and Graham I), **Hippa Point** (53°31'00" 132°57'00" SE end of Hippa I), **Hippa Rocks** (53°34'00" 133°00'00" NW of Hippa I). Hippa I was named in 1787 by early British fur trader George Dixon of the ship *Queen Charlotte*. The fortified Haida First Nation villages reminded him of the palisaded Maori habitations he had seen in NZ, known as *pas* or *hippahs*. The Haida knew the island as Nesto (Nasduu), meaning "impregnable"; it was rich in legends and home to three ancient village sites. During WWII a small radar station was located on Hippa I, and in 1947 it was the site of a tragic shipwreck when the *Clarksdale Victory*, a US freighter heading S from Alaska, went on the rocks in a storm. Only 4 of 53 crew members survived. *D*

Hird Point (52°34'00" 128°15'00" E side of Mathieson Channel, N of Bella Bella). Named in 1948 after the 1st mate of CGS *Parry*, a small vessel used by the hydrographic service on the W coast, 1945–67, mainly for tidal and current surveys.

Hisnit Inlet (49°44'00" 126°30'00" W side of Tlupana Inlet, E of Nootka I, W side of Vancouver I), **Hisnit Islands** (50°10'00" 127°28'00" N side of Ououkinsh Inlet, NE of Checleset Bay, NW side of Vancouver I). The inlet is named after an abandoned village site, now a Nuu-chah-nulth First Nation reserve, that was located at its head and mentioned in 18th-century exploration records. According to BC historians Philip and Helen Akrigg, the word means "place of sockeye salmon." The Nootka Marble Co operated a quarry on the inlet from the early 1900s to about 1914. Hisnit Lk, near Hesquiat Hbr, derives its name from the same source.

Hjorth Bay (50°11'00" 125°08'00" W side of Read I, N end of Str of Georgia). Nils Christian Hjorth (1850–1936) was a peripatetic Norwegian seaman who jumped ship in Burrard Inlet, most likely in the 1870s, and lived at first as a fisherman. He is probably the same man who took up land in Surrey in 1885 and gave his name to Hjorth Rd, or 104 Ave (though this Surrey pioneer is sometimes referred to as Hans Christian Hjorth). He and Sven Hans Hansen operated a store for several years at Bickley Bay on E Thurlow I. (Hansen, who had a hook shaped to hold an oar in place of one hand and was known as Hans the Boatman, moved to Port Neville about 1891 and later became the first postmaster there.) Hjorth acquired a Crown land grant near Hjorth Bay in 1896 and married Alma Juliana Oberg at Vancouver in 1900. He died at Campbell R.

Hkusam Bay (50°23'00" 125°55'00" S side of Johnstone Str, NW of Campbell R). According to anthropologist Wilson Duff, Hkusam is a Coast Salish name in an area now occupied by the Kwakwaka'wakw. Randy Bouchard, an ethnographer and linguist, has translated Hkusam (or X̱'wésam) as "having fat or oil." The word refers, he suggests, to the Salmon R, which enters the ocean near Hkusam Bay, and to the former village at its mouth, once the most northerly community of the Comox (Coast Salish) people but long since abandoned by them and taken over by the Lekwiltok, the southernmost of the Kwakwaka'wakw tribal groups. The name Hkusam has been spelled many different ways over the years, including Husam, Kusam, Xusam, Koosam and Khusan. Port Kusam post office was opened in 1899 at Ruby House, a store, hotel and steamship stop built by Theodore Peterson in 1895. The post office was relocated farther up the Salmon R valley to a more populated area in 1911 and renamed Sayward. Nearby Hkusam Mtn takes its name from the same source as Hkusam Bay.

Hocking Point (49°05'00" 124°50'00" W side of Alberni Inlet, NE of Barkley Sd, S-central Vancouver I). Norman Penrose Hocking (1876–1956) was born at Swansea, Wales, and went to sea at the age of 15 on the windjammer *Templetown*. Before arriving in Canada in 1912, he had served aboard Boer War troopships and commanded vessels for the E India Co and the Burma-based Irrawaddy Flotilla Co, and in the China coastal trade. In BC he established a launch service at Deep Cove before fighting in WWI as a Royal Engineer and rising to the rank of maj. Back in Canada, Hocking joined the mercantile marine service as a skipper, then ran the Alberni mail boat out of Port Alberni for Stone Bros Ltd. He rejoined the merchant navy during WWII and was awarded the OBE for his skill and daring as a freighter capt in enemy waters in the S Pacific. After the war he lived at Victoria and operated the Mill Bay ferry for several years before retiring. Hocking Point is known locally as Rocky Point.

Hodgson Cove (53°28'00" 129°52'00" W side of Pitt I, N of Mink Trap Bay). According to BC's Geographical Names Office, this feature was named in 1944 after a hydrographic service employee who worked aboard the W coast survey vessel *William J Stewart* in 1943 as a laundress.

Hodgson Passage (54°06'00" 132°32'00" W entrance to Naden Hbr, Graham I, QCI). RN officer Oswald Tyson Hodgson was a lt aboard HMS *Egeria*, under Capt Frederick Learmonth, in 1907, when the survey vessel made a detailed examination of this area.

Hoey Narrows (53°22'00" 129°28'00" Off SE end of Pitt I, SW of Kitimat). Named in 1944 to honour Maj Charles Ferguson Hoey, VC, MC, who was killed in action Feb 17, 1944, at Arakan, Burma, aged 30. Hoey was from Duncan. He joined the British Army in 1936, trained as an officer at Sandhurst and was sent to Burma, where he received the MC in 1943 for outstanding service at Maungdaw. In 1944 he led his Lincolnshire Regiment company in attacking a heavy machine-gun position at Ngakyedauk Pass. Despite being wounded twice, he was first to reach the Japanese stronghold and, grabbing a Bren gun from a fallen man, cleared it of enemy soldiers. Hoey died of his injuries two weeks later and was awarded a posthumous VC for "his total disregard of personal safety and his grim determination to reach the objective." He is buried at Taukkyan War Cemetery in Burma; a monument to Hoey and his fellow campaigners was also unveiled at Arakan Park near Duncan in 1996. Hoey Narrows was originally to be known as Payne Narrows, after Dorothy Richardson Payne, who worked in Victoria for the Canadian Hydrographic Service, but the name was changed after complaints from Ottawa that Victoria was commemorating the local office staff too frequently and "without reasonable discretion."

Hogan Bank (52°37'00" 128°31'00" In Jane Passage, Finlayson Channel, NW of Bella Bella). Lewis Wily Hogan (1892–1948) had a machine shop, fuel float and store opposite Moses Inlet cannery in 1921, the year he married Mary Katherine Inrig (b 1898, at Metlakatla) at Vancouver. He became manager at Rivers Inlet Cannery

(1927–28), built and ran Porcher I Cannery at Humpback Bay (1928–32), then operated Saltery Bay machine shop in Rivers Inlet until 1939. In 1941 he was hired to renovate and manage the J H Todd & Sons cannery at Klemtu. Hogan built cold-storage and ice plants, modernized the canning lines, added a groundfish operation and processed herring, abalone, clams and even tuna, as well as salmon. In 1948, in bitter winter weather, he and two crew members died when the cannery tender *Louisa Todd* ran aground in Whale Channel.

Hogan Island (54°39'00" 130°25'00" N entrance to Work Channel, Tsimpsean Peninsula, N of Prince Rupert), **Hogan Point** (53°49'00" 132°08'00" N end of Kumdis I, Masset Sd, Graham I, QCI). Named for Rev William Hogan (1831–1914), a much-esteemed Anglican missionary on the BC N coast. He arrived in BC from Dublin in 1893 with his wife, Margaret Louisa Hutchinson (b 1852), and daughter. They were stationed first at Metlakatla and then for 10 years at Port Simpson. In 1909 the family went to Masset in the QCI, where Hogan spent his remaining years. He was a huge man, and his handshake was apparently much dreaded. According to QCI historian Kathleen Dalzell, Hogan was actually 21 years older than the age shown on his death certificate (62). The Church Missionary Society would not send men older than 45 to Canada, so Hogan submitted his baptismal papers, issued long after his birth, as proof of age. When he died, the Haida constructed a special bier of yellow and red cedar to carry him to his final resting place in the Masset cemetery. Hogan I was formerly known as Compton I. Father Point, N of Prince Rupert, is also named for him. *D*

Hogan Rock (52°04'00" 128°04'00" Cooper Inlet, N side of Hunter I, just S of Bella Bella). Arthur Harold Hogan (1882–1942) served with the Royal North-West Mounted Police in the Klondike region, then worked as a machinist at a Rivers Inlet cannery. A bad accident left him crippled, his legs useless. Undaunted, Hogan built a home and a machine shop and went back to his work as a machinist, only this time from a wheelchair.

Hohm Island (49°14'00" 124°50'00" Head of Alberni Inlet, NE of Barkley Sd, S-central Vancouver I). From a Nuu-chah-nulth First Nation word meaning "blue grouse." This island is also known locally as Observatory I. *See below.*

Hoik Island (49°14'00" 124°50'00" Head of Alberni Inlet, NE of Barkley Sd, S-central Vancouver I). From a Nuu-chah-nulth First Nation word meaning "willow grouse." Formerly known as Sheep I and also known locally as Deadman I. *See above.*

Hoiss Point (49°42'00" 126°33'00" SW entrance to Tlupana Inlet, Nootka Sd, W side of Vancouver I). Named after a former Nuu-chah-nulth habitation that was once

H

located nearby on the site of today's Hoiss First Nation reserve. The Hoiss Point Lodge, a floating fishing resort, operated at this location in the summer months in the early 2000s before being destroyed by fire in Nov 2006 and contaminating the region with Styrofoam debris. Hoiss Ck and Hoiss Lk are also named for this former village.

Hokonson Point (52°21'00" 127°28'00" W side of Dean Channel, NE of Bella Bella). C Hokonson is believed to have been one of the early Norwegian settlers who established a colony in the Bella Coola valley in the mid-1890s.

Holberg (50°39'00" 128°01'00" Head of Holberg Inlet), **Holberg Inlet** (50°36'00" 127°44'00" NW extension of Quatsino Sd, NW end of Vancouver I). A number of Danish settlers settled at Holberg in the early 1900s after their colonization attempt failed at Cape Scott. They named their tiny community, mostly built on floats at first, for Ludvig Holberg (1684–1754), a famous Danish historian and playwright. Holberg, born in Norway, was a professor at the Univ of Copenhagen for many years, as well as the house dramatist at Denmark's first public theatre, and is considered the founder of Danish literature. He is best known for his comedies (more than 30 in all), but also published poetry, novels and essays, and wrote extensively on philosophy and law. He was made a baron in 1747. The village of Holberg is mostly dependent on the forest industry. CFS Holberg, a radar facility, was located nearby from 1954 to 1991, and a historic trail still connects the area to Cape Scott. Holberg Inlet was formerly known as West Arm. Nearby Holberg Mtn also takes its name from this community.

Hole in the Wall (50°19'00" 125°10'00" Between Sonora I and Maurelle I, N end of Str of Georgia). The name of this channel may not be derived, as one might expect, from the appearance of its narrow, steep-walled, western entrance,

where currents can reach 12 knots (22 km/h) on the flood. According to the BC Indian Language Project, the original "hole in the wall" is a small, round indentation, about 1 m wide, in a cliff on Sonora I, submerged only at extreme high tide and known to the Homalco First Nation as Raven's Chamber Pot. The channel itself is called Sa-yei-gun, or "waist," in the Homalco (Mainland Comox) language.

Holgate Passage (52°55'00" 129°08'00" N of Webber I, Chapple Inlet, W side of Princess Royal I). This feature, originally to be known as Ursula Passage after Kathleen Ursula Chettleburgh, a junior member of the hydrographic service on the W coast in the early 1940s, was renamed Holgate Passage after officials in Ottawa complained that too many young female members of the Victoria staff were getting too many places named after them. Edwin Headley Holgate (1892–1977), born in Ont, was a widely travelled Canadian painter who was invited to join the Group of Seven in 1930, many years after it was founded. He lived mostly in Montreal and taught wood engraving there at the Ecole des Beaux Arts, 1928–34. Holgate visited the Skeena R area in 1926 with his friend A Y Jackson and Marius Barbeau, an anthropologist. He painted and sketched and later produced a series of woodcuts of Gitksan First Nation scenes. He was also an official WWII war artist. Retrospectives of his work were held by the National Gallery of Canada in 1975 and the Montreal Museum of Fine Art in 2005.

Holland Point (48°24'39" 123°22'42" Between Ogden Point and Finlayson Point, S side of Victoria). Believed to be named after George Holland, an early HBC employee, who joined the company in London, England, and came to N America in the mid-1830s as a seaman aboard the *Beaver*. In 1839 he was a schoolteacher at Ft Vancouver on the Columbia R, and four years later became postmaster at Ft Langley. Holland returned to the UK in 1848 and got his master's certificate, then sailed again to the PNW as 1st

Hole in the Wall, left of centre, at top, has currents that can reach 12 knots (22 km/h). Octopus Islands and Waiatt Bay are in the foreground. *Peter Vassilopoulos*

mate of the HBC supply ship *Norman Morison*. Apparently he was not held in high esteem by the HBC—Dr John Helmcken commented that he "was not much of a sailor or anything else"—and the company let him go in the early 1850s, after which he disappears from the historical record. Holland Point was once part of the HBC's Beckley Farm; pioneer Victoria printer and newspaper editor George Nias built a house there in 1863 that was turned into a quarantine station or "pesthouse" for smallpox victims in 1872. The point was named in 1847 by Capt Henry Kellett.

Holland Rock (54°10'14" 130°20'59" Between Greentop It and Kitson I, Chatham Sd, just SW of Prince Rupert). Swinton Colthurst Holland (1844–1922) was 3rd lt aboard HMS *Malacca*, under Capt Radulphus Oldfield, on the Pacific Station, 1866-68. He went on to have a substantial naval career, serving in the royal yacht *Victoria and Albert* in 1881-84, promoted to commodore at Hong Kong, 1896-98, and to rear adm and superintendent of Chatham dockyard, 1899-1902. He retired in 1908 with the rank of adm. His son, Vice Adm Cedric Swinton Holland, was a senior RN officer during WWII. Holland Rk lighthouse, built in 1908, burned down in 1946.

Holler Rock (52°54'00" 129°08'00" Entrance to Chapple Inlet, W side of Princess Royal I). Mining engineer Fred W Holler was superintendent of the productive gold mine at Surf Inlet on Princess Royal I from 1914 until at least the early 1920s. Holler's responsibilities were substantial, for the complex, isolated mine, owned by Belmont Canadian Mines Ltd, required extensive work before it could ship ore; a large concrete dam, 140 m wide and 14 m high, had to be constructed across the lower end of a series of lakes so that water levels could be raised and a transport route created from the head of Surf Inlet to within 1.5 km of the mine site. The dam also ensured that plenty of hydroelectric power would be available for an electric tramway connecting the mine and the lakes, and for other operations. Holler built a power station at the head of the inlet and laid out a townsite complete with hospital, store and housing for 200 workers, while at the mine he erected a crusher, concentrator, machine shops and other facilities.

Hollyburn (49°20'00" 123°09'00" N side of Burrard Inlet, just N of Vancouver). John Lawson (1869-1954) and his family were W Vancouver pioneers, settling there in 1907. Lawson, from Ont, arrived in BC in 1887 and was a railroad worker for many years. He bought land in the W Vancouver area in 1906 (parcels of which he later sold to other newcomers) and suggested the name after planting holly trees on his property, which had a stream, or "burn," running across it. He developed an early ferry service to W Vancouver, established the first school, was the area's first postmaster (1910-20) and telephone agent, and its second reeve (1913-14). Hollyburn Mtn and Hollyburn Ridge are also named after this community.

Holmes Inlet (49°27'00" 126°14'00" E side of Sydney Inlet, Clayoquot Sd, W side of Vancouver I). Col William Josiah Hartley Holmes, DSO (1871–1954), was born at St Catharines, Ont, and became a BC land surveyor in 1893. He completed a number of triangulation surveys in this district in 1913. Holmes grew up in Victoria, graduated as a civil engineer from Kingston's Royal Military College in 1891 and married Elizabeth Kew of Beamsville, Ont. He was assistant engineer during the construction of the Victoria & Sidney Rwy and was also involved in mining and railway surveys in the Kootenays in the early 1900s. Holmes served overseas in WWI as cdr of the 3rd Canadian Pioneer Corps and was in charge of the Canadian Corps Reinforcement Camp in France at the end of the war. He became aerial-photo librarian for the surveyor gen's branch before retiring in 1943. Holmes Ridge in Tweedsmuir Provincial Park is also named for him (he was in charge of camp arrangements for the gov gen's party visiting Tweedsmuir Park in 1937). Holmes Inlet was formerly known as North Bay.

Holti Point (52°11'00" 127°31'00" W side of Burke Channel, E of Bella Bella). Believed to have been named for one of the original Norwegian settlers to colonize the Bella Coola valley in 1894. This was probably J R Holte or Holt, whose name appears on several lists of colonists, and who was paid $2 a day in 1898 for working on the road through the valley. According to BC Archives, Robert Holte married Amanda Ludia Nygard at Bella Coola in 1910, while James Robert Holte died at Bella Coola in 1941, aged 80.

Holt Rock (52°16'00" 128°09'00" Off S side of Yeo I, W entrance to Return Channel, N of Bella Bella). Named in 1924 after Lt Reginald Vesey Holt (b 1884), who served on the BC coast in 1910 aboard HMCS *Rainbow*, one of two old British cruisers bought by Canada as its first naval vessels. Holt rejoined the RN, becoming capt of the heavy cruiser *Shropshire* in 1933-34, then senior naval officer on the Yangtze R in China in 1937-38. It was for his actions on the Yangtze, where he assisted in the rescue of the crew of the US gunboat *Panay*, bombed by Japanese aircraft, that he was appointed a CB, one of several honours earned in his career. During WWII, as a rear adm, Holt was RN officer in charge on the Humber estuary (1940-42) and at Newhaven (1944). He was sent to Denmark in 1945 to supervise the disarmament of a large part of the German navy. Holt retired with the rank of vice adm.

Homathko Icefield (51°07'00" 124°35'00" Between Homathko R and Chilko Lk), **Homathko River** (50°55'52" 124°51'37" Flows SW and S into head of Bute Inlet). The name of the Homalco people, which has been spelled many different ways, can be translated as "swift water." Three traditional village sites were maintained by this Northern Coast Salish group, formerly known as the Mainland

H

Comox, at the mouths of three major rivers (including the Homathko) on Bute Inlet. Most tribal members now live at Sliammon, N of Powell R, or at Campbell R. The remote, rugged valley of the 137-km Homathko R was considered as a possible railroad and wagon route into the BC Interior in the 19th century. The idea was abandoned after a crew of road builders was attacked and killed in 1864, an event that led to the so-called Chilcotin War (see Waddington Bay). Nearby Homathko Peak is named after the river. *E*

Home Bay (53°16'00" 129°05'00" NW side of Princess Royal I). Named at a very early date (about 1837) after Capt David Home, first cdr of the historic HBC steamship *Beaver* on the Pacific coast. Home had earlier been employed by the E India Co but was appointed to sail the *Beaver* to N America in 1836 and then oversee the installation of its boiler and paddlewheels. He was drowned in 1838, along with the crew of his small boat, while trying to cross the mouth of the Columbia R. *W*

Home Island (Salmon Rock) (49°23'00" 123°29'00" SW of Keats I, Howe Sd, NW of Vancouver). The source of the name Home is not really known, though two RN officers—Capt Sir James Everard Home, CB (1798–1853), and Rear Adm Sir Home Riggs Popham (see Popham I)— have both been suggested by historian Athelstan Harvey. Neither was ever on the BC coast. This speck of geography is unusual in the sense that it has *two* official names, partly because of the efforts of Maj J S Matthews, Vancouver's pioneer archivist, who urged that it be called Salmon Rk. The feature is definitely an island, however, not a rock, so this compromise was reached.

Homfray Channel (50°15'00" 124°38'00" E of E Redonda I, S of Toba Inlet, NE end of Str of Georgia). Civil engineer Robert Homfray (1824–1902), a native of Worcestershire, came to Victoria in 1859 from California, where he had been surveyor for Nevada County. He was a student of famed British engineer Isambard Brunel, whose bridge, railway and steamship projects revolutionized modern public transport. In 1861, as Alfred Waddington's surveyor, Homfray made an arduous expedition to Bute Inlet to investigate the possibility of constructing a toll road to Barkerville (see Waddington Bay). The following year he sought, without success, to become Victoria's city surveyor; later he worked on route surveys for the CPR. Homfray was something of an eccentric, erecting his own tomb in Ross Bay Cemetery years before it was required, with all the details inscribed except his date of death. In 1894 he wrote to the Victoria *Colonist*, begging to inform readers "that owing to his failing eyesight he finds himself unable to recognize his many friends, and hopes this will be held as an excuse for any involuntary oversight on his part." Nearby Homfray Ck and Homfray Lk are also named for him. *W*

Hood Point (49°25'00" 123°19'00" NE tip of Bowen I, Howe Sd, NW of Vancouver). Adm Sir Alexander Hood (1727–1814), later Viscount Bridport, was a member of a famous British naval family. He was cdr of the royal yacht *Katherine* for many years, treasurer of Greenwich Hospital and an MP, 1784–96. Capt George Richards named this feature about 1859 for Hood's role as deputy cdr, under Adm Earl Howe, in the 1794 British naval battle known as the Glorious First of June, which inspired many place names in Howe Sd. Hood's flagship in this English Channel victory was HMS *Royal George*. He served as cdr-in-chief of the Channel fleet, 1795–1800. Hood Point was the site of the Howe Sd Hotel, 1901–11; the area was purchased in 1927 as a private summer resort by a syndicate of 21 Vancouver families. *W*

Hope Bay (48°48'00" 123°16'00" E side of N Pender I, Gulf Is). Rutherford Hope (1843–1913) came to BC from Scotland in the early 1880s with his sister and brother-in-law, Helen and Lawrence Auchterlonie. They inherited and divided between them the extensive N Pender I property of Rutherford's brother, David Hope, who was killed in a hunting accident in 1882. David Hope, a true pioneer, had arrived on the island in the mid-1870s with his business partner, Noah Buckley. Rutherford was described in the 1901 BC census as an orchardist. He married Jane Reid (1856–1909), his Edinburgh sweetheart, in 1899; she came out to Victoria after her father, who had forbidden her to marry Hope, died. A few shops and a wharf are located at Hope Bay.

Hope Island (50°55'00" 127°54'00" W of Nigei I, off N tip of Vancouver I). Rear Adm Sir James Hope (1808–81) was cdr-in-chief of the RN's China Station, 1859–62, during the 2nd Anglo-Chinese (or Opium) War. He led a failed attack in 1859 on Chinese defensive positions near Tianjin while trying to deliver European ambassadors to Beijing. The following year, as part of a stronger force, he subdued Tianjin and helped an Anglo-French invasion force capture the Chinese capital. In 1863, Hope became cdr-in-chief of the N America Station, and in 1869, with the rank of vice adm, cdr-in-chief at Portsmouth. He was promoted to adm of the fleet in 1879. Hope's nephew, RN officer Edmund Verney, served on the BC coast, 1862–65. Bull Hbr on Hope I was the site of Humdaspe, the principal Nahwitti First Nation settlement after the Tlatlasikwala and Nakumgilisala tribes merged and moved from Nahwitti (qv) village at Cape Sutil. Much of Hope I is now a Kwakwaka'wakw First Nation reserve. There is a Coast Guard search and rescue station at Bull Hbr. *E W*

Hope Point (49°26'00" 123°22'00" SE end of Gambier I, Howe Sd, NW of Vancouver). Presumably after the RN's Capt William Hope (b 1766), of HMS *Bellerophon*, who took part in the 1794 English Channel victory over French forces known as the Glorious First of June. Many place names in Howe Sd were bestowed in 1860 by Capt George Richards to honour participants in this battle. Hope eventually became an adm and a knight and changed his name through marriage to Hope-Johnstone.

Hope Point (53°56'00" 133°12'00" W side of Frederick I, off NW side of Graham I, QCI). The 65-tonne brigantine *Hope* made two 19th-century fur-trading expeditions to the QCI. The tiny vessel was owned by a pair of Boston merchants, Thomas Perkins and James Magee, and was commanded by Joseph Ingraham, who had been 1st mate aboard the *Columbia Rediviva* on its historic 1787–90 visit to the PNW and subsequent circumnavigation of the globe. The *Hope*'s first journey, in 1790–91, was successful from an economic point of view. In 1792, however, on a return voyage, Ingraham apparently grew so infatuated with Haida Gwaii that he spent most of his time exploring and not enough trading. The ship's owners lost more than $40,000 on the venture. The point was named in 1907 by Capt Frederick Learmonth of HMS *Egeria* while making a survey of NW Graham I. A small radar station was established there during WWII. *D*

Hope Rocks (52°08'00" 128°32'00" In Milbanke Sd, W of Athlone I and Bella Bella). RCN officer Adrian Mitchell "Boomer" Hope, OBE (1899–1963), born at Montreal, was a cadet at the Royal Navy College of Canada in 1914. He was appointed CO of the RCN destroyer *St Laurent*, 1937–39. In 1940–41, Hope was based in Esquimalt, at shore establishment HMCS *Naden*, first as inspector of naval ordnance, then as executive officer of RCN barracks. He moved on to serve as CO of HMCS *Stadacona* (the Halifax naval depot), CO of the armed merchant cruiser *Prince Robert* (1943–44) and CO of HMCS *Somers Isles*, a training establishment in Bermuda. After WWII he became the RCN's chief of personnel and then senior Canadian liaison officer in London. Hope retired in 1951 with the rank of commodore.

Hopkins Landing (49°26'00" 123°29'00" On the W side of Howe Sd, SW of Gambier I, NW of Vancouver). George Henderson Hopkins (1853–1931), a native of Ireland, worked as a marine engineer for the British India Steam Navigation Co before becoming a partner in a Monmouthshire engineering firm. He married Isabella Ward Scott (1861–1943), from Scotland, at Cardiff in 1884. Retiring in ill health, he came to Vancouver in 1906 and bought land at this location for a summer cottage. The provincial government built a wharf there in 1908, a post office and store followed, and steamships were soon stopping at the nascent community. Hopkins and his three sons went into the towboat business, building a steam tug, the *Hopkins* (later called the *Island Rover*), on the beach in front of their home in 1910–11. Two other tugs, the *Hopkins Bros* and the *Hawser* (formerly the *Tartar*), were purchased in 1923 and 1927, respectively. At one point the

Hopkins Landing in the 1930s. Helen McCall photo. *Author's collection*

Hopkins brothers also had the W Howe Sd mail contract. Today Hopkins Landing is a residential enclave with a busy summer recreational season.

Horace Point (50°28'00" 125°46'00" SE entrance to Forward Hbr, E of Hardwicke I, N of Johnstone Str). After Lt Horace Douglas Lascelles, who served with the RN on the BC coast, 1860–65. *See* Lascelles Point.

Horda Shoals (48°50'00" 123°25'00" W of Prevost I, Gulf Is). The 1,709-tonne Norwegian steamship *Horda*, under Capt E H Svendsen, struck this hazard in 1901 while carrying a cargo of coal from Ladysmith. The feature was, in the quaint terminology of mariner and historian Capt John Walbran, "hitherto unknown."

Horn Bay (50°25'00" 125°12'00" E side of Cordero Channel, N of Sonora I and Campbell R), **Horn Point** (50°25'00" 125°14'00" Just NW of Horn Bay). Named after W H Horn, an early settler in this area, according to a note at BC's Geographical Names Office.

Hornby Island (49°31'30" 124°40'00" W side of Str of Georgia, E of Denman I). Spanish explorer José Narváez named Hornby I and Denman I the Islas de Lerena, after Spanish politician and minister Pedro Lopez de Lerena (1734–92). Hornby I received its current name from HBC officials about 1850. Rear Adm Phipps Hornby, CB (1785–1867), was cdr-in-chief on the RN's Pacific Station, 1847–51. His flagship was the 84-gun HMS *Asia*, under Capt Robert F Stopford. As a junior officer, Hornby had served aboard HMS *Victory*, Adm Lord Nelson's flagship. Promoted to capt in 1810 and made cdr of HMS *Spartan*, he supervised the surrender of Elba by French forces. He became superintendent of the hospital and victualling yard at Plymouth in 1832 and comptroller-gen of the Coast Guard in 1841–44. Hornby was appointed a lord of the Admiralty in 1852–53 and knighted in 1852. He attained the rank of adm in 1858. *See also* Mt Geoffrey, named for his son. *W*

H

Hornby Point (52°09'00" 131°07'00" NW tip of Kunghit I, QCI). William St John Sumner Hornby was present on the Pacific Station as a naval cadet aboard HMS *Portland*, 1851–52, and as a midshipman aboard HMS *Virago*, under Cdr James Prevost, 1853–55. He later served on the Australia Station with HMS *Challenger* and reached the rank of capt, retired, in 1882. Named by Cdr Prevost during his 1853 survey of Houston Stewart Channel. *W*

Hornby Rock (48°49'00" 125°18'00" SE entrance to Imperial Eagle Channel, Barkley Sd, W side of Vancouver I). After Frances Hornby Trevor, the first European woman to vist the PNW. *See* Trevor Channel. Formerly known as Danger Rk.

Horseshoe Bay scene from the 1930s. *Author's collection*

Horseshoe Bay (49°23'00" 123°16'00" E side of Howe Sd, just NW of Vancouver). This name, which is a simple description of the shape of the bay, was officially adopted in 1929 but has been noted on documents since at least 1892. The adjacent community got its start in 1909 when the PGE was being surveyed. A railway station called White Cliff City was planned for the bay; its name referred to White Cliff Point (qv), located just to the SW. Sir Charles Hibbert Tupper and Col Albert Whyte of the W Shore & Northern Land Co developed a summer resort in the area, and when the PGE began construction in 1914, Whyte persuaded the railroad to change the name of its station to Whytecliff. A post office named Whytecliff opened in 1920 and was renamed Horseshoe Bay in 1942. By the early 2000s the name Whytecliff referred to the residential area adjacent to Batchelor Cove, while the village of Horseshoe Bay is directly S of the large ferry terminal and extensive marinas. The original First Nation name for the bay was Chai-hai. *E*

Horsey Bank (54°10'00" 130°18'00" W entrance to Inverness Passage, just S of Prince Rupert). Flora McDonald (1896–1975), whose father was manager of the Inverness Cannery in the early 1900s, married Edward Noyes Horsey (1884–1964) in Prince Rupert at a very young age. She died at W Vancouver. Adjacent Flora Bank is also named for her.

Horsfall Island (52°11'00" 128°18'00" Part of the Bardswell Group, between Campbell I and Dufferin I, W of Bella Bella). Rev Thomas Horsfall (1795–1869) was the vicar of Cundall, Yorkshire, and a master at Ripon Grammar School, 1839–62. The island was named in 1902 by his grandson Capt John Walbran, author of *British Columbia Coast Names 1592–1906.*

Horswell Bluff (49°13'00" 123°56'00" N of Departure Bay, N of Nanaimo), **Horswell Channel** (49°13'00" 123°56'00" N of Newcastle I, N of Nanaimo), **Horswell Rock** (In Horswell Channel). Horswell Bluff was named in 1853 by George Inskip, master of HMS *Virago*, after a seaman of that name who assisted with surveys of Nanaimo Hbr and Departure Bay. He was a member of a boat's crew that was responsible for taking soundings. He may have distinguished himself in some way, as it was unusual for a geographic feature to be named after a lowly seaman. Only officers were so honoured for the most part.

Horton Bay (48°49'43" 123°15'02" SE side of Mayne I, Gulf Is). Coastal historian Capt John Walbran claimed that this feature was named for Robert John Horton (1834–1912), who joined the HBC as a seaman and arrived in BC in 1861. He served on the *Otter* until 1865 and was later put in charge of the HBC's fur dept at Victoria. Inconveniently, the name Horton Bay appears on an Admiralty chart published in 1861 but surveyed by Capt George Richards in 1858–60, before Robert Horton appeared on the scene. It therefore seems more likely that the bay was named in association with adjacent Curlew I (qv), after RN officer William Horton, CB (1820–83), who was cdr of HMS *Curlew*, 1856–58, and a colleague of Richards. Horton was never present in BC waters. He spent much time in the Mediterranean and Black seas before retiring with the rank of capt in or before 1870.

Hose Point (52°13'00" 128°12'00" NW entrance to Raymond Passage, just NW of Bella Bella). Rear Adm Walter Hose, CBE (1875–1965), was born on a P&O liner in the Indian Ocean. He entered the RN in 1890 and had a number of gunboat commands in Nfld and Asia before joining the RCN in 1912 as cdr of HMCS *Rainbow*. This ancient cruiser was based at Esquimalt, where Hose was also in charge of the dockyard, until 1917, at which time he transferred to Halifax and took over responsibility for E coast anti-submarine patrols. He became a commodore in 1921 and director of Canada's naval service. Hose established the successful RCNVR system in 1923 and is credited with preserving the navy during an era when Defence dept budget cuts threatened its survival. He was promoted to rear adm on his retirement in 1934. Saunders I in Lama Passage was also originally named for him but was changed in 1925. Hose Point was formerly known as Reid Point, after the manager of the Imperial Oil depot at Bella Bella in the early 1920s.

H

Hosie Islands (48°54'00" 125°02'00" In Numukamis Bay, Barkley Sd, W side of Vancouver I). John Hosie (1880–1934), a native of Edinburgh, was BC's provincial librarian and archivist, 1926–34. He came to BC in 1912 and began working for the provincial library that year, spending the period 1919–26 in charge of the legislative reference bureau. Hosie edited several works on BC history and was author of *The Arbutus Tree*, a chapbook of poetry.

Hoskins Islets (52°32'00" 131°33'00" NE of Hoskins Point), **Hoskins Point** (52°32'00" 131°34'00" E entrance to Haswell Bay, Juan Perez Sd, E of Moresby I, QCI). John Box Hoskins (1768–1824) was the ship's clerk and owners' representative (or supercargo) aboard the *Columbia Rediviva* on its second fur-trading voyage to the PNW, 1790–93. The young man was a ward of the *Columbia*'s principal investor, Joseph Barrell. The ship's first voyage had not been a financial success, and Barrell, suspecting incompetence, arranged for Hoskins to join the expedition, much to the disgust of the *Columbia*'s skipper, Capt Robert Gray. Hoskins kept an important logbook of the journey, one that was critical of Gray; it was edited by historian Frederic Howay and published in 1941. Hoskins later established a successful Boston shipping business with Colburn Barrell, Joseph's son, and eventually moved to France, where he died. *D*

Hoskyn Channel (50°11'00" 125°08'00" Between Quadra I and Read I, NE of Campbell R), **Hoskyn Point** (48°20'00" 123°36'00" N side of Becher Bay, S tip of Vancouver I), **Hoskyn Rock** (50°08'00" 125°10'00" S end of Hoskyn Channel). Staff Cdr Richard Hoskyn was appointed chief draftsman of the RN's hydrographic dept in 1864, and superintendent of charts in 1865. He had been a surveying officer for most of his career and was a particular expert on Irish waters, for which he had written a coast pilot. In 1862, as cdr of HMS *Porcupine*, he examined underwater cable routes in the vicinity of Ireland and published a treatise on deep-sea sounding. Lt Daniel Pender celebrated the 1864 appointment of Capt George Richards, formerly in charge of the BC coastal survey, as the RN's chief hydrographer by naming a number of features in the vicinity of Read I, including Hoskyn Channel, after members of the hydrographic dept. Hoskyn Point was named much earlier, in 1846, by Capt Henry Kellett, when he surveyed the S end of Vancouver I.

Hospital Bay (49°38'00" 124°02'00" N side of Pender Hbr, NW of Vancouver). St Mary's Hospital, a 12-bed facility run by the Anglican Church's Columbia Coast Mission, was established at this location in 1930. It eventually expanded to include a chapel, a staff residence and a collection of cottages for the aged but was closed in 1964 when a new St Mary's was opened in Sechelt. The original hospital building became a hotel and was still in operation in the early 2000s as the Sundowner Inn.

Hospital Point (48°56'00" 123°43'00" W entrance to Chemainus Bay, SE side of Vancouver I), **Hospital Rock** (NW end of Chemainus Bay). Chemainus Hospital was the earliest medical centre in the region, opening its doors in 1900 after a typhoid outbreak the previous year. Until 1911, when Ladysmith built a facility, it was the only hospital between Nanaimo and Victoria. Dr Herbert Rogers was the first physician to work there, retiring as medical superintendent in 1936. The hospital is the subject of one of the town's famous murals, painted by Doug Driediger. It is still a focal point for the local community.

Hosu Cove (53°39'00" 132°58'00" NE of Athlow Bay, W side of Graham I, QCI). Hosu is an adaptation of an old Haida name for Athlow Bay. It was adopted by the hydrographic service in 1946 in place of North Cove, the feature's former name, in order to avoid duplication.

Hotham Sound (49°52'00" 124°02'00" N side of Jervis Inlet, E of Powell R and NW of Vancouver). Adm William Hotham (1736–1813) won distinction as a young lt when he captured a 26-gun French privateer while in temporary charge of a smaller sloop. This and other daring actions won him the command of a frigate, HMS *Gibraltar*. In another frigate, HMS *Melampe*, he took many prizes and again won an engagement against more powerful opponents. By 1791 he was a vice adm. Three years later he was deputy cdr of the Mediterranean fleet, under Sir Samuel Hood, and then cdr-in-chief. But his stint at the top was not a success. He was "a good officer and a man of undaunted courage," according to the *Dictionary of National Biography*, and "he had done admirably in a subordinate rank, but he was wanting in the energy, force of character and decision requisite in a cdr in chief." Sir John Jervis took over the fleet in 1795. Hotham was made a baron. The Sechelt First Nation name for the sound is Smit. *W*

Hotspring Island (52°35'00" 131°26'00" Between Ramsay I and Murchison I, SE of Lyell I, QCI). This scenic spot

Enjoying the thermal pools at Hotspring Island. *Andrew Scott*

H

had a fearsome reputation for many Haida, who knew it as the Island of Fire. Mining engineer Francis Poole called it Volcanic I in 1862. Other Haida refer to it as Randll K'in Gwaayaay, or "hot-water island," and consider the place sacred: a location where the natural thermal pools can aid in physical and spiritual healing. There may have once been a village on the E side of the island. Fur trader Joseph Ingraham, investigating plumes of steam, called the area Smoke Bay in 1791. The name Hotspring I dates from George Dawson's 1878 visit. Over the years the springs became a popular destination for the region's miners and fishermen. Today tourists are the main visitors. A bathhouse has been constructed, as well as cabins for the Haida watchmen who guard the site. *D*

Hot Springs Cove (49°22'00" 126°16'00" Just W of entrance to Sydney Inlet, NW of Flores I and Tofino, Clayoquot Sd, W side of Vancouver I). The Nuu-chah-nulth First Nation name for the hot springs, which form a group of six pools near the E entrance to the cove, was Mok-seh-kla-chuck, or "smoking water," according to W coast historian George Nicholson. In 1930 a former tugboater named Ivan Clarke set up a store just N of the springs to service the salmon trollers who congregated in the cove's protected waters. He soon added a fish-buying station, fuel dock and machine shop. A post office was open 1947–73. The feature was known on charts for many years (since 1861, in fact) as Refuge Cove, but was changed in 1949 so as not to confuse it with Refuge Cove on W Redonda I. Much of the land surrounding the cove is now part of 2,667-ha Maquinna Marine Provincial Park.

Hougestol Point (50°53'00" 127°40'00" NW side of Nigei I, off N end of Vancouver I). Named in memory of Chief Motor Mechanic John Melvin Hougestol (1899–1945), of Victoria, who died while serving at HMCS *Scotian*, a naval reserve shore establishment at Halifax. He is buried in Valley View Cemetery at Camrose, Alberta.

Houghton Islands (52°07'00" 128°26'00" S entrance to Thompson Bay, W of Bella Bella). In 1944, when this feature was named, Frank Llewellyn Houghton, CBE (1897–1981), was a capt and senior RCN officer at London, England (at HMCS *Niobe*). He was born in Cornwall, England, and became a cadet at the Royal Naval College of Canada in 1913. Houghton served with the RN, 1914–23, then rejoined the RCN and took on his first command with HMCS *Festubert*, an armed trawler, in 1929. He was CO of the destroyers *Vancouver* and *Saguenay* in the 1930s, the armed merchant cruisers *Prince Robert* and *Prince Henry* during WWII, and HMCS *Warrior*, an aircraft carrier, after the war. In 1947, Houghton was appointed a commodore and assistant chief of naval staff. A year later he was promoted to vice-chief of naval staff and rear adm. He retired in 1950 and joined the International Grenfell Assoc as gen manager.

House Island (52°34'50" 131°25'25" Between Ramsay I and Murchison I, SE of Lyell I, QCI). The ancient Haida village of Ata'na, on the W side of House I, occupied one of the most attractive vantage points in the QCI. *Ata'na* was the Haida word for both village and island and refers to a particular type of dwelling; it was because of this meaning that geologist George Dawson gave the feature its English name in 1878. Ata'na is the site of one of the Haida origin or creation myths, where a supernatural being rested after the first land emerged from receding flood waters. All Raven crest Sand-Town-People trace their ancestry back to this location. *D*

Houston Stewart Channel (52°09'00" 131°07'00" Between Moresby I and Kunghit I, QCI). This important passage was called Ibbertson's Sd in 1787 by George Dixon of the *Queen Charlotte*. Two years later, Robert Gray, another fur trader, named it Barrell's Sd after Boston merchant Joseph Barrell, the main investor in the *Columbia*, Gray's vessel. An even more common description during these early days was Koyah's Str, after the region's predominant chief. It was not until an 1853 hydrographic survey that Cdr James Prevost of HMS *Virago* gave the channel its current name. William Houston Stewart (1822–1901) had been the *Virago*'s previous cdr, handing the paddlewheel sloop over to Prevost at Valparaiso, Chile, in 1852 after recapturing the southern penal colony of Punta Arenas from a group of rebels (*see also* Virago Point). Stewart, from Ayrshire, the son of an adm of the fleet, did well in the RN, becoming superintendent of Chatham, Devonport and Portsmouth dockyards before being appointed controller of the navy, 1872–81. Stewart ended his career in 1884 as a knight, an adm and cdr-in-chief at Devonport. Most of the geographical features in this channel are named after officers of the *Virago*, their friends or offspring. *W*

Houstoun Passage (48°56'00" 123°36'00" Off the N end of Saltspring I, Gulf Is). Capt Wallace Houstoun (1811–91) served on the Pacific Station aboard HMS *Trincomalee*, 1853–56, spending some of that time as part of an Anglo-French squadron that saw action during the Crimean War. In 1859 he was capt of HMS *Orion* in the Mediterranean. Houstoun was promoted to rear adm in 1865 and became an adm, retired, in 1877. His name often appears misspelled Houston.

Hovel Bay (50°40'00" 124°52'00" E side of Bute Inlet, N of Orford Bay, NE of Campbell R). Named in 1924 after John Hovel (1841–1924), a Norwegian sailor who jumped ship in BC in the 1880s. He pre-empted land and settled in this vicinity in the early 1900s and lived here in a floathome until his death, surviving as a trapper, prospector and handlogger. Hovel's rowboat was found floating on Bute Inlet in 1924, while his body was apparently discovered months later on the cliffs close to his house. It was surmised that after his boat got loose, the elderly Hovel tried to climb along the steep shorelines of the inlet to get home but didn't make it.

Howard Islet (53°16'00" 129°19'00" Off E side of Fin I, SE of Pitt I). Sgt William Ross Howard, MM, of Malakwa, W of Revelstoke, was killed in action on Jan 4, 1945, aged 22. He was a member of Princess Patricia's Canadian Light Infantry and is buried in Ravenna War Cemetery, Italy.

Howay Island (52°23'00" 131°15'00" E of Burnaby I and Moresby I, QCI), **Howay Point** (52°42'00" 128°26'00" N entrance to Watson Bay, NW end of Roderick I, N of Bella Bella). Frederic William Howay (1867–1943), born in Ont, was an eminent jurist and historian. He came to New Westminster with his family in 1874, then studied at Dalhousie Univ in Halifax. Back in BC he practised law in partnership with Robie Reid, a fellow history enthusiast. Howay served as a judge, 1907–37, and was actively involved in civic affairs. His four-volume *British Columbia from the Earliest Times to the Present*, co-authored with E O S Scholefield in 1914, and *British Columbia: The Making of a Province* (1928), were standard works on the subject for decades. He wrote and edited other books and many articles, was a member of the Historic Sites and Monuments Board of Canada, 1923–43 (and its chair for two years), and was president of the Royal Society of Canada in 1941. Howay's great collection of books and historical memorabilia, along with that of his friend Robie Reid, forms an important archive at UBC. Mt Judge Howay, NW of Stave Lk, also commemorates him. Several points on Roderick I, all named by the hydrographic service in 1948, honour BC historians. The Haida name for Howay I is Cha'odjske'la. *E*

Howe Bay (52°01'00" 131°02'00" E side of Kunghit I, QCI). Lt Richard S Howe was the capt's clerk and owners' representative (or supercargo), aboard the *Columbia Rediviva* on its first fur-trading voyage to the PNW, 1787–90. Unlike John Hoskins, his successor on the *Columbia*'s second voyage (*see* Hoskins Its), Howe was able to maintain cordial and professional relations with the expedition's leaders.

Howell Rock (52°30'00" 129°02'00" Entrance to Weeteeam Bay, W side of Aristazabal I). Cpl Robert Howell was a member of the Columbia detachment of Royal Engineers, which served in BC 1858–63. He travelled on board the *Thames City* from England with the main contingent of soldiers, arriving at Victoria in 1859. Howell stayed on in BC after the detachment disbanded, taking up the military land grant he was entitled to and purchasing additional lands at auction in partnership with Sapper James Duffy. He was listed as a labourer in New Westminster, 1876–80.

Howe Sound (49°25'00" 123°23'00" NW of Vancouver and Burrard Inlet). Capt George Vancouver named this

feature in 1794 after Adm Richard Howe (1726–99), later Earl Howe. Lord Howe, with HMS *Queen Charlotte* as his flagship, was the hero of a 1794 RN victory in the English Channel known as the Glorious First of June, in which his fleet attacked and subdued a superior French force and captured seven line-of-battle ships. British royal family members were so overjoyed at this outcome that

H

Looking north up Howe Sound. *John Lund*

Howe Sound. *Reproduced with the permission of the Canadian Hydrographic Service*

H

they went aboard Howe's vessel and presented him with a diamond-studded sword worth 3,000 guineas. Howe's rise to the rank of capt at the young age of 21 may have had something to do with the fact that his mother was related to King George II. He was treasurer of the RN, 1765–70, and, as a vice adm, cdr-in-chief of the N America Station in 1776–78, during the American Revolution. With a huge fleet he carried out the relief of Gibraltar in 1782 and then served as 1st Lord of the Admiralty, 1783–88. Howe had command of the all-important Channel fleet in 1793–95. His nickname in the RN was Black Dick. "I think we shall have a fight today," one of his seamen is notoriously supposed to have said before the famous 1794 battle, "Black Dick has been smiling." In 1859–60, Capt George Richards continued the theme begun by Vancouver and named dozens of features in Howe Sd after the officers and ships that participated at the Glorious First of June. *W*

Howse Island (52°35'00" 129°09'00" Entrance to Clifford Bay, W side of Aristazabal I). Cpl Alfred Richard Howse (1827–1909) was a member of the Columbia detachment of Royal Engineers, which served in BC 1858–63. He arrived at Victoria with his wife, Margaret Howse (1826–1883), and the main body of men aboard the *Thames City* in 1859. En route he apparently organized the Theatre Royale, an entertainment that the engineers dreamed up to while away the long voyage. Howse was a surveyor by trade and also worked with Capt Robert Parsons at the detachment's observatory, keeping meteorological records. In 1860 he was stationed at Ft Hope. Mary Moody, wife of Col Richard Moody, the detachment cdr, hoped that the Howses would return to England with her when their duties were completed. Margaret Howse was "most useful, in helping with the Washing, looking after Baby, etc, etc." Furthermore, she was "a most respectable Scotch Woman ... the only woman in the Detachment who goes regularly to Church twice every Sunday." Unfortunately for Moody, the Howses remained in BC when the engineers disbanded. Alfred received several grants of Crown land in the New Westminster land district, as well as the 60-ha military grant awarded to all those who stayed on. He was a member of the RE cricket club and manager of the New Westminster Dramatic Club (1866). The family lived in Esquimalt, 1876–80, before settling in the Vancouver area.

Hoya Passage (52°39'00" 131°42'00" Darwin Sd, between Shuttle I and Moresby I, QCI). Hoya is an adaptation of the Haida word for raven (*xhuuya*). According to historians Philip and Helen Akrigg, the actual Haida name for this feature was a term meaning "the channel behind."

Hudson Rocks (49°13'00" 123°55'00" N of Newcastle I and Nanaimo, off E side of Vancouver I). Named by the hydrographic service in 1944 in honour of those HBC officials who were stationed in this area in the very early days of European colonization. The HBC first built

a fortified trading post at Nanaimo in 1849 after the discovery of coal in the area.

Huff Rock (52°13'00" 130°58'00" E of the SE tip of Moresby I, QCI). George Albert Huff (1849–1934) was an early resident of Alberni. He was appointed the area's justice of the peace in 1890 and served as its MLA, 1895–98. Huff owned a number of steam vessels over the course of his career, including a small sternwheeler, the *Willie*, which he operated between Port Alberni and Barkley Sd for several years. In 1901 he became the local agent for the Canadian Pacific Navigation Co. Huff was also a whaling industry pioneer. He visited the S end of the QCI in 1908 on behalf of the Queen Charlotte Whaling Co, looking for a suitable whaling-station site. In 1910 he announced the purchase of land at what is now Rose Hbr (but which was originally known as Port Huff).

Hughes Passage (48°35'00" 123°17'00" Between Sidney I and D'Arcy I, Gulf Is), **Hughes Rock** (50°15'00" 127°53'00" W entrance to Klaskish Inlet, Brooks Bay, NW side of Vancouver I). William Otas Hughes (1848–1910), from Digby, NS, came to BC in 1891 with his second wife, Adeline Ophelia Hughes (1859–1942), and family. An experienced seaman, he soon found skilled work in the sealing industry and was skipper of the *Carmolite* when it was seized for illegal hunting in Russian waters in 1892. Hughes and his crew were taken to Vladivostok, then sent to Japan to make their way home to Victoria as best they could. He was also master of the sealing schooners *Mary Ellen* and *Ida Etta*. Hughes joined the Canadian Pacific Navigation Co in 1897 and was in charge of the *Willapa* for many years on Vancouver I's W coast route. He worked for the CPR after that company took over the CPN in 1901 and was the first cdr of the new steamship *Princess Royal*, built in 1907. *See below also.*

Hughes Point (53°36'00" 132°58'00" S entrance to Port Chanal, W side of Graham I, QCI). Harry Stewart Hughes (1885–1963), born at Digby, NS, was a well-known master mariner on the BC coast. He was the oldest son of William Hughes (*see above*) and lived at Brentwood Bay; in 1920 he married Margaret Gertrude Thompson (1886–1958) at Saanich. Hughes joined the CPR's BC Coast Steamship Service at 16, working along the W coast of Vancouver I in the *Tees*, *Queen City* and *Otter*, and later aboard the *Princess* ships. He served in the *Amur* as quartermaster in 1906 when his father took that vessel to earthquake-stricken San Francisco with a load of supplies and provisions. After a stint with the Pacific Whaling Co and three years on the N Atlantic as a lt with the RN in WWI, Hughes spent more than 30 years with the W coast lighthouse tender *Estevan*—first as mate and then, 1940–50, as capt. Hughes Point appeared as early as 1916 on sketch maps of the W coast of Graham I prepared by Capt Absalom Freeman.

Hull Island (50°33'00" 126°12'00" N of Boughey Bay, Havannah Channel, N of Johnstone Str). Thomas Arthur Hull (d 1905) served on the Pacific Station, 1855–59, as master of HMS *Havannah*, under Capt Thomas Harvey. He was an experienced surveyor, having learned his trade as a master's mate aboard HMS *Herald*, 1845–51, under Capt Henry Kellett. As 2nd master of HMS *Plover* he spent three years (1852–54) in the Bering Str, searching for missing Arctic explorer Sir John Franklin and making detailed magnetic observations. After his stint on the W coast, Hull was employed as a surveyor off Syria and the Ionian Is, and in the Red and Mediterranean seas. He became a naval assistant at the Admiralty hydrographic office, 1866–73, and was superintendent of charts from 1873 to 1878, retiring with the rank of cdr. Author of *Practical Nautical Surveying*, he edited several more famous works as well, including the *Sailor's Pocket Book* and *Epitome of Navigation*. Nearby Tom I is also named for him, as is, presumably, **Hull Rock** (50°31'00" 126°18'00"), just to the W, at Port Harvey. *W*

Humchitt Island (51°55'00" 127°54'00" Off SW tip of King I, Fisher Channel, SE of Bella Bella). Humchitt (or Haémzit) is the name of a hereditary chief of the Heiltsuk First Nation. Chief Humchitt's village was at Fannie Cove on Hunter I, but he and his descendants, including Moody Humchitt (1870–1949), became leaders at Bella Bella, where many people still bear this name.

Hume Rocks (52°39'00" 128°49'00" Entrance to Laredo Inlet, S end of Princess Royal I). Sapper Robert Hume was a member of the Columbia detachment of Royal Engineers, which served in BC 1858–63. He arrived at Victoria in 1859, travelling in the *Thames City* with the main body of men. Hume stayed on in BC when the contingent disbanded, taking land near Burnaby's Central Park as his military grant (awarded to sappers who chose to stay in the colony) and purchasing additional property. Early documents describe him as a miner, but after 1880 he drops from view (though an 1890 death record exists for a Robert Hume, aged 53, at Sapperton).

Humpback Bay (50°22'00" 125°41'00" At mouth of Amor De Cosmos Ck, S side of Johnstone Str, NW of Campbell R). According to BC's Geographical Names Office, this feature was named by F O Morris of Victoria after a huge shoal of humpback or pink salmon he saw in the bay in the fall of 1913.

Humpback Bay (54°05'00" 130°23'00" N side of Porcher I, S of Prince Rupert). The Porcher I Cannery was built here in 1928, just as the Great Depression got rolling, by Lewis Hogan and the Chatham Sd Fishing & Packing Co. F H Cunningham, chief inspector of fisheries for BC, 1911–21, was a major investor. It closed in 1932 and was taken over two years later by the Canadian Fishing Co for use as a summer fishing station, offering gas, provisions and repairs to the gillnet fleet until 1968, and net storage until the 1980s. The cannery buildings were in ruins by the early 2000s. A small community, usually referred to simply as Porcher I, still lingers here.

Humphreys Point (53°02'00" 129°32'00" E side of Lotbinière I, Estevan Group, SE of Banks I). Named after Caroline Watkins (1852–1926), born in Wales, who came to Canada with her family in 1862. She married Thomas Basil Humphreys (1840–90) at Victoria in 1873. He had arrived in BC from Liverpool in 1858 to search for gold but became a policeman instead at Ft Hope and Port Douglas, then a miner and auctioneer. Humphreys found his calling as a politician, joining the legislative council (1868–71) and serving as an MLA in three different ridings (Lillooet, 1871–75; Victoria District, 1875–82; and Comox, 1887–90). He was minister of Finance and Agriculture in 1876, and provincial secretary and minister of Mines, 1878–82. Caroline Humphreys moved to Seattle (where she died) about 1918 to live with a daughter but reportedly participated in the great old-timers' reunion held at Victoria in May 1924 (*see* Adams Bay). *E*

Hunter Channel (52°00'00" 128°11'00" Between Hunter I and Campbell I), **Hunter Island** (51°57'00" 128°00'00" N of Calvert I, S of Bella Bella). The 334-sq-km island is part of the traditional territory of the Heiltsuk First Nation. It was the site of an early Icelandic colony; the first settlers began to arrive about 1912 and made their living from logging and fishing. Most had left by the mid-1920s. The origin of the name is not known. More than half the island is now part of the protected, 123,000-ha Hakai Conservation Study Area, which also includes Hecate I, northern Calvert I and the smaller islands of Queens Sd. Hunter Channel was formerly known as Plumper Channel. *E*

Hunter Point (53°15'00" 132°43'00" N entrance to Cartwright Sd, SW end of Graham I, QCI). Capt George Vancouver named this feature in 1793 after his friend Dr John Hunter (1754–1809), superintendent of military hospitals at Jamaica, 1781–83, whom he met while stationed in the W Indies as a lt aboard HMS *Fame*. Hunter studied medicine at Edinburgh, and after his stint with the RN returned to the UK and settled down as a London physician. He published several medical works, including *Diseases of the Army in Jamaica* (1788), and is not to be confused with John Hunter (1728–93), a famous Scottish surgeon. The large US freighter *Kennecott* ran ashore near Hunter Point in 1923 en route from Alaska to Tacoma with a cargo of copper and salmon. The wreck was unsalvageable and remained visible for several years. Forty years later the US tug *Winquattwas* lost a valuable barge laden with construction equipment at this same dangerous spot. *D W*

H

Huntingford Point (50°07'00" 125°22'00" S side of Menzies Bay, NW of Campbell R). Cdr George Huntingford (d 1901) was present on the BC coast from 1893 to 1896, in charge of the 1,034-tonne sloop HMS *Nymphe*. He went on to serve as the superintendent of Greenwich Hospital Schools, 1897–99, and retired with the rank of capt in 1899.

Hunt Inlet (54°04'00" 130°26'00" N side of Porcher I, S of Prince Rupert), **Hunt Point** (54°06'00" 130°25'00" N extremity of Porcher I). Hunt Inlet was originally known as Jap Inlet, which suggests, in derogatory fashion, that there was once a Japanese fishing community there (*see also* Jap Point). Jap Inlet post office opened in 1926, Jap Inlet school in 1928. Many Scandinavian residents also settled in the area; some of them were instrumental in the formation of the Prince Rupert Fishermen's Co-operative. The post office name was changed to Hunts Inlet in 1943, though this was probably more due to WWII patriotism than to revulsion at a racist name. The name of the geographical feature received a slightly different spelling—Hunt Inlet—when it was changed, in association with nearby Hunt Point, in 1946. Capt George Vancouver originally bestowed the name Point Hunt but gave no hint as to its origin (it was later changed to Hunt Point). Joseph Whidbey, master of Vancouver's HMS *Discovery*, assisted by midshipman Robert Barrie, made a lengthy survey of the area, including the mouth of the Skeena R, in July 1793.

Hunt Rock (50°54'00" 127°40'00" E side of Nigei I, off N end of Vancouver I). William Hunt (1866–1949) was a son of HBC factor and Ft Rupert storekeeper Robert Hunt and his Tlingit wife, Mary Ebbets. His older brother, George Hunt, was an important interpreter and artifact collector for anthropologist Franz Boas. William fished and trapped around Rivers Inlet and worked briefly at Pine I lighthouse before becoming the third lighthouse keeper at Scarlett Point on Balaklava I in 1908. He and his wife, Annie, raised nine children on Balaklava; seven were born at the station. When he retired from the lights in 1940, at the age of 73, the citizens of Port Hardy gathered to honour him, and the mayor presented him with the Imperial Service Medal. He reported Hunt Rk as a hazard in 1917.

Hunts Inlet. *See* Hunt Inlet.

Huron Island (52°02'00" 128°21'00" Queens Sd, SW of Bella Bella). The hydrographic service, in a surge of patriotic fervour, suggested a great number of war-related place names in the early 1940s. Huron I was one of them, named in 1944 after RCN *Tribal*-class destroyer *Huron* (the island is part of the Tribal Group). The 1,748-tonne, 115-m vessel was commissioned in 1943 and had a top speed of 36 knots. It played an active role in WWII, escorting convoys on the N Russia route, battling (and defeating) German destroyer squadrons off the French coast and successfully attacking enemy convoys. The *Huron* completed several tours of duty during the Korean War, as well, before being paid off in 1963. A more modern HMCS *Huron*, an *Iroquois*-class destroyer, also served in the RCN, 1972–2005.

Hurricane Island (51°51'06" 128°11'55" Off SW Hunter I, S of Bella Bella). The single-seat Hawker Hurricane evolved in the late 1930s to become one of Britain's most successful WWII fighter aircraft. About 14,000 were built, including 1,400 produced in Canada by the Canada Car & Foundry Co. Regional hydrographer Henri Parizeau, wishing to create a patriotic aviation theme for islands in the Queens Sd area, named Hurricane I in 1944 along with several of its neighbours: Mosquito Its, Kittyhawk Group, Spitfire I, etc. The original inspiration for this idea was the nearby presence of Spider I and the fact that Anthony Fokker's first airplane, built in 1910, was named the Spin (Dutch for "spider") on account of its many bracing wires, which made it resemble a large arachnid. The fact that Shearwater RCAF seaplane base on Denny I was only 25 km away may also have influenced these names. Ironically, Spider I (qv) was charted about 1865; while the origin of its name is uncertain, it obviously had nothing to do with aircraft.

Hurtado Point (49°58'00" 124°45'00" On E side of Str of Georgia, opposite Savary I, NW of Powell R). Mariner and historian John Walbran claimed that the source of this name was Diego Hurtado de Mendoza, sent by Hernán Cortés to explore the Pacific coast of New Spain N of Mexico. Hurtado set off with two vessels in 1532, but the voyage ended with his death, either by mutiny or at the hands of California's aboriginal inhabitants. However, on a Spanish chart engraved in 1795, based on Dionisio Alcalá-Galiano's 1792 expedition, Puerto Hurtado (port, not point) appears just N of today's Hurtado Point, at the approximate location of Lund. Henry Wagner, a leading expert on PNW cartography, maintains that Puerto Hurtado was named in honour of Joaquin Hurtado, a pilot aboard the *Descubierta*, one of the ships on Alejandro Malaspina's 1789–94 round-the-world expedition. A transcription error may have resulted in the shifting of the name, as Spanish feature names were often abbreviated, and Pto (Puerto) is easily confused with Pta (Punta), especially on a poorly printed chart. The Sliammon First Nation name for the point is Xéxaxgilh, meaning "shamans"; a pair of shamans, who were also double-headed serpents, were said to live there in caves.

Hussan Bay (54°04'00" 132°34'00" W side of Virago Sd, N end of Graham I, QCI). Hussan is an adaptation of the Haida name for the bay and was applied by geologist George Mercer Dawson in 1878. Go Dang village, site of a Haida miracle legend, was located at the N end of the bay. It was here, while people were sleeping, that a seal impaled itself on a hunter's spear, thus averting almost certain starvation for a small group of Haida. *D*

Hussar Point (50°51'00" 127°39'00" SE side of Nigei I, off N end of Vancouver I). Named in association with such nearby features as Balaklava I and Cardigan Rks after Canadian-born Capt Louis Edward Nolan (1818–54) of the 15th Hussars, a key figure in the 1854 Charge of the Light Brigade. Nolan was a noted officer and author of several books, including *Cavalry: Its History and Tactics*. It was he who carried the deadly and controversial order to charge from the army cdr, Lord Raglan, to the cavalry cdr, the Earl of Lucan. Nolan was one of the first to be killed in the futile action that followed, in which British troops were decimated while attacking vastly stronger, artillery-supported enemy forces.

Hutt Island (49°25'00" 123°23'00" NW of Bowen I, Howe Sd, NW of Vancouver), **Hutt Rock** (49°24'00" 123°23'00" Just SW of Hutt I). Capt John Hutt (1746–94) commanded the 98-gun HMS *Queen*, flagship of Rear Adm Alan Gardner, in the celebrated 1794 English Channel battle known as the Glorious First of June, in which Lord Howe defeated a French fleet. Hutt, who had served on the W Indies Station in the late 1780s with Gardner and a young Lt George Vancouver, lost a leg in the action and died from his wounds afterwards, back in England. A monument to him stands in Westminster Abbey. *W*

Hutton Inlet (52°30'00" 131°34'00" W side of Juan Perez Sd, E of Moresby I, QCI), **Hutton Island** (52°31'00" 131°32'00" Entrance to Hutton Inlet), **Hutton Point** (52°32'00" 131°32'00" N entrance to Hutton Inlet). Scottish geologist and naturalist James Hutton (1726–97) is considered the father of modern geology. His *Theory of the Earth*, first published in 1788, elucidated a number of new ideas: that the planet was very much older than had been formerly surmised, that the interior of the planet was very hot, and that this internal heat transformed deposits of sedimentary rock. It took years for Hutton's revolutionary theories to be fully appreciated. Hutton Inlet was named by George M Dawson in 1878. *W*

Huxley Island (52°27'00" 131°22'00" N of Burnaby I, off SE Moresby I, QCI). Biologist Thomas Henry Huxley (1825–95) began his celebrated career as an assistant surgeon aboard HMS *Rattlesnake*, a survey vessel that made an extensive voyage to New Guinea and Australia. It was on this journey that he developed his passion for natural history, devoting himself to the study of marine invertebrates and, on his return, publishing a number of important papers. He was awarded the medal of the Royal Society in 1852 (and became the Society's president in 1883), resigned from the RN and occupied, among other posts, the chair of natural history at the Royal School of Mines, 1854–85. Huxley had a vast influence on science and education. He was Charles Darwin's great supporter, helping overcome the scientific objections and religious alarm that Darwin's theories occasioned. Huxley's own writings are extensive; his most famous work is *Evidence as to Man's Place in Nature* (1863). Huxley I was named by George M Dawson in 1878. *W*

Hvidsten Point (51°57'00" 127°45'00" E side of Burke Channel, SE of Bella Bella). John Hvidsten (1873–1922) was one of the original Norwegian colonists to settle and farm in the Bella Coola valley. He married Gea Anna Fosbak (1880–1964) at Nanaimo in 1898 and later changed the family name to Widsten. Surveyor Peter Leech wrote in an 1894 letter that he and several other settlers took their land grants "in a peculiar form, the reason being that the mountain which is very precipitous comes down close to the boundaries of their several locations."

Hyashi Cove (48°48'00" 123°18'00" N side of Otter Bay, W side of N Pender I, Gulf Is). T Hyashi (b 1853), who came to Canada from Japan in 1890, owned property here at the turn of the 19th century and cut cordwood to fuel the steam-powered canneries at the mouth of the Fraser R. He and his employees (the 1901 census lists 28 "lodgers" next to the entry for Hyashi) may have made charcoal for export as well. Hyashi's name is also seen spelled Hiashi. In the 1920s, Japanese fishermen based their fleet at Otter Bay and established a herring saltery and fish-processing plant there.

Hyde Point (52°22'00" 128°21'00" N end of Lake I, S part of Mathieson Channel, NW of Bella Bella). Named in 1929 for Julia Elizabeth Hyde, who married BC colonial politician and administrator Joseph William Trutch. *See* Lady Trutch Passage *and* Trutch I for further biographical details.

Hyphocus Island (48°56'00" 125°32'00" SW side of Ucluelet Inlet, NW of Barkley Sd, W side of Vancouver I). Hyphocus was a Nuu-chah-nulth First Nation leader, chief of the Ucluelet band at the time the British ship *Jenny* visited these waters in 1795. The island is now a peninsula, connected to Vancouver I by a causeway in the early 1960s. It is the site of Ucluelet's sewage treatment facility and is also being developed for luxury housing.

I

Ibbetson Point (54°03'00" 130°42'00" N end of William I, off NW Porcher I, SW of Prince Rupert). Named by Capt George Vancouver in 1793 after his friend John Ibbetson, who served a number of administrative roles at the Admiralty, 1755–95. In 1763 he was appointed secretary to the Board of Longitude and later also became secretary to the directors of Greenwich Seamans' Hospital. From 1783 to 1795, at which point he retired, he was 2nd secretary to the Admiralty itself. *W*

Icarus Point (49°15'00" 124°02'00" E of Blunden Point, NW of Nanaimo). Named for HMS *Icarus*, an 8-gun, 880-tonne steam-powered sloop that served on the BC coast under Cdr Ernest Fleet, 1896–98, and Cdr George Knowling, 1898–1902. One of the vessel's duties in 1896 was to search for and chart the rock that the Pacific Station flagship, HMS *Impérieuse*, struck in Sept that year in Nanoose Hbr. *Icarus*, launched in 1885 and decommissioned in 1903, was named after a character in Greek mythology who, while escaping prison on wings made of feathers and wax, flew too close to the sun. His wings disintegrated and he fell into the sea and was killed. The point was named in 1904 by Cdr John Parry of HMS *Egeria*. There is an Icarus Mtn—named for the man, not the ship—SE of Bella Coola.

Iceberg Bay (54°56'00" 129°57'30" S side of Nass Bay, NE of Prince Rupert). The name appears as Iceberg Bight on an Admiralty chart published in 1869. The Nisga'a people call this feature Ts'im Sgalt, from *ts'im*, meaning "inside," and *sgalt*, meaning "goat horn." The name refers to the shape of the bay, which the Nisga'a say was a channel during the Ice Age and achieved its present shape as the result of a meteorite explosion.

Idol Island (48°55'00" 123°36'00" S end of Houstoun Passage, W of Saltspring I, Gulf Is). This feature is presumably named because of its former use as a First Nation burial ground. Artifacts may have been left there in the early days that were interpreted by non-Native visitors as idols.

Ikeda Cove (52°18'00" 131°09'10" SE side of Moresby I, S of Skincuttle Inlet, QCI), **Ikeda Point** (52°19'00" 131°08'00" N entrance to Ikeda Cove). Japanese fisherman Arichika Ikeda (1865–1939) was the owner of Ikeda Bay Mines at Ikeda Cove, one of the earliest and most successful operations in the QCI during the pre-WWI copper-mining boom. Despite the era's prevailing racist attitudes, the popular Ikeda, with the help of 120 fellow countrymen, was shipping ore by 1906, using horses to haul tram cars of rock. He converted the ancient sternwheeler *Dawson* to a bunkhouse, built a large wharf and installed telephone lines from the minesite to Jedway, 6 km away. Ikeda sold out in 1910 to a Vancouver syndicate for $250,000 but remained a company director. During WWI a shortage of labour and ships slowed production, and by 1920 the mine had closed. Ikeda Ck is named after the cove. *D*

Ildstad Islands (50°31'00" 127°42'00" N side of Quatsino Sd, W of Drake I, NW Vancouver I). Thomas Ildstad (1867–1942) was born in Norway and immigrated to the US with his family as a child. He married Bertha Marie Brustad (1865–1964) in Minnesota and moved to BC in the early 1900s with Bertha and their seven children. In 1904, Thomas was working as a surveyor's assistant near Winter Hbr in Quatsino Sd. He and his family stayed in the area, moved to Quatsino in 1906, homesteaded and became staunch members of the local community, as did many of their descendants.

Illahie Inlet (51°39'00" 127°50'00" NE of Addenbroke I, Fitz Hugh Sd, opposite Calvert I). Illahie means "country," "land" or "earth" in Chinook jargon, the pidgin language used on the W coast by First Nation groups and early traders and settlers. Why this word was applied to the inlet is unclear. Illahee Meadows, E of Clinton, derives its name from the same source.

Imperial Eagle Channel (48°54'00" 125°12'00" Barkley Sd, W side of Vancouver I). The British fur-trading ship *Imperial Eagle*, under Capt Charles Barkley, was the first European vessel to navigate this body of water, in 1787.

The ship had formerly been owned by the E India Co and called the *Loudoun*. For its PNW venture, however, the name was changed, as the ship sailed under an Austrian flag in order to avoid the necessity of acquiring a trading licence from the E India Co. (The Austrian coat of arms features an imperial eagle, hence the new name.) The *Eagle* was a largish vessel of 360 tonnes, ship-rigged and equipped with 20 guns. At the conclusion of his visit to N America, Barkley sailed to China, then to Mauritius and Calcutta where, despite his considerable investment in the expedition, he lost control of the ship after a bitter dispute with its other backers. *See also* Barkley Sd.

Impérieuse Rock (49°16'00" 124°07'00" N of Entrance Rks, Nanoose Hbr, SE side of Vancouver I). HMS *Impérieuse*, a 7,620-tonne armoured cruiser with 14 guns, was based at Esquimalt, 1896–99, under Capt Charles Adair. It was the flagship of the Pacific Station's cdr-in-chief, Rear Adm Henry Palliser. Before BC it had been the flagship on the China Station, 1889–94. Launched in 1883 at Portsmouth dockyard, the *Impérieuse* was something of an anachronism. It was one of the last vessels designed by the RN to operate with auxiliary sail power, a concept quite ludicrous considering the weight of the ship. The Admiralty's belief in the redeeming value of sail was so engrained, however, that it took until the 20th century for the old ways to be discarded. The *Impérieuse* struck the rock named for it in 1896. It was turned into a depot ship at Portland in 1905, briefly renamed HMS *Sapphire*, became *Impérieuse* again in 1909 and was scrapped in 1914.

Imrie Island (48°42'00" 123°20'00" W side of Prevost Passage, SW of Moresby I, Gulf Is). Peter Imrie (1834–1915) and his Saanich First Nation wife, Anne (1837–1912), were Saanich pioneers. Peter came to BC from Ont in 1862 and tried his hand searching for gold in the Cariboo, Cassiar and Leech R districts. He settled at N Saanich about 1867 and resumed his original occupation of farmer. He played an active role in community affairs, helping promote the local agricultural society and serving as road foreman, school trustee and director of the Saanich Fair.

Incinerator Rock (49°04'20" 125°45'58" N end of Long Beach, SE of Tofino, W side of Vancouver I). During WWII the Canadian Army and RCAF maintained an incinerator on Long Beach adjacent to this feature. It was used to burn trash from Tofino's air base and the area's army camps. Only the concrete foundation remains. There are actually several rocks here; the largest one is an old First Nation lookout site and midden, also the location of a "surfguard" tower for Pacific Rim National Park. The name was officially adopted in 1993.

Indian Arm (49°22'00" 122°53'00" NE extension of Burrard Inlet, NE of Vancouver). This 17-km-long body of water was considered part of Burrard Inlet (qv) by its original European explorers, but was named North Arm by Capt George Richards during his surveys of 1859–60. In 1921, with the support of the Vancouver Harbour Commission, which sought a more distinctive name, Indian Arm was adopted. Indian R, at the head of the arm, was renamed at the same time, from Meslilloet R (Meslilloet is now the name of a tributary ck and a nearby mtn). Spanish cdr Dionisio

Indian Arm, looking north, with Bedwell Bay in the foreground. *Peter Vassilopoulos*

Alcalá-Galiano sent two officers, Secundino Salamanca and Juan Vernaci, to examine the feature in 1792 and later charted it as Canal de Sasamat, which he understood to be the First Nation word for either the arm or the inlet and arm combined. The area is the traditional territory of the Tsleil-Waututh First Nation, whose main reserve is on the N side of Burrard Inlet. The name of this group, which has been translated as "people of the inlet," refers to both Burrard Inlet and Indian Arm. The arm has long been a popular recreation area for Vancouver residents, and small passenger ferries served shoreline cottage communities for many years. Wigwam Inn, a 40-room lodge built at the head of the arm in 1910 and turned into a yacht club outstation in 1986, was also a major attraction. *E*

Indian Bay (49°07'00" 125°44'00" SE end of Tofino Inlet, Clayoquot Sd, W side of Vancouver I), **Indian Island** (49°07'00" 125°46'00" Just W of Indian Bay). Named for K'anuwis, a Tla-o-qui-aht First Nation reserve and former camping site on the SE end of Indian I. K'anuwis can be translated from the Nuu-chah-nulth language as "passing through" or "camping over."

Indian Channel (50°36'00" 126°38'00" N side of Harbledown I, E end of Queen Charlotte Str). May be named in connection with the Kwakwaka'wakw village at nearby Dead Point, known as Tzatsisnukomi (T'sadzisnukwame) or New Vancouver. This site was in the process of being re-established in the early 2000s by members of the Da'naxda'xw First Nation, who are an amalgamation of the Da'naxda'xw (Tenaktak) and Awaetlala people of Knight Inlet. Mound I, with its large midden deposits, and other locations along Indian Channel also have strong Kwakwaka'wakw associations.

Indian Group (50°37'00" 126°36'00" Between Crease I and Village I, E end of Queen Charlotte Str). Probably named in association with the important Kwakwaka'wakw First Nation community of Mamalilaculla (qv) on Village I. This was the main winter home of the Mamaleleqala-QweqwaSot'Enox people, with a population in the 1830s estimated at 2,000.

Indian Island (51°17'00" 127°39'00" Browning Channel, Smith Sd, N of Port Hardy). Former site of an important winter village of the Gwa'sala people, the most northerly of the Kwakwaka'wakw First Nations, located where the Nathlegalis reserve is today.

Indian Islands (50°33'00" 126°11'00" NE of Hull I, Havannah Channel, opposite E Cracroft I, N of Johnstone Str). Likely named for their proximity to the nearby Etsekin (or I'tsikan) reserve, now abandoned but once the main village site of the Ma'amtagila (or Matilpi) people, who are members of the Kwakwaka'wakw First Nation.

Indian Point (48°42'00" 123°25'00" SW tip of Piers I, off N end of Saanich Peninsula, Gulf Is). A First Nation grave was supposedly dug up here about 1914. The name was adopted in 1965.

Indian Point (49°57'00" 124°52'00" NW end of Savary I, NE end of Str of Georgia, NW of Powell R). The name predates the development of Savary I in the 1910s, and it is possible that a First Nation camp was once located at this spot. Vancouver *Province* crime reporter and Savary realtor George Ashworth claimed to have found fortifications in the area in 1910, along with human bones and artifacts. He said that a Sliammon chief had told him the point was the site of a great battle over control of the island's clam beds. Ashworth, who went on to build the Royal Savary Hotel nearby in 1928, was more promoter than reporter, however, and not to be trusted on historical matters. In 1915 the Union steamship *Capilano* sank off Indian Point—without loss of life, fortunately. The well-preserved wreck is now a favourite dive site.

Indian Reef (48°53'00" 123°38'00" N of Osborn Bay and Crofton, W side of Stuart Channel, SE side of Vancouver I). Probably named in association with the nearby Chemainus reserves on Willy I and at the mouth of the Chemainus R. The Chemainus First Nation, Cowichan First Nation and four other nations are part of the Hul'qumi'num Treaty Group, founded in 1993.

Ingraham Bay (53°49'00" 133°06'00" NW side of Graham I, QCI), **Ingraham Point** (52°14'00" 131°02'00" Near SE tip of Moresby I, QCI). Joseph Ingraham (1762–1800) was a US seaman who packed a great deal into his 38 years. During the American Revolutionary War he was captured by the British and incarcerated in a prison ship. He served as 1st mate on the historic 1787–90 voyage of the *Columbia Rediviva* to the PNW and its subsequent global circumnavigation. Then he became master of the tiny brigantine *Hope*, which made two fur-trading expeditions to the QCI in the late 19th century. Ingraham's first expedition left Boston in 1790 and arrived in the QCI in 1791. En route he discovered several previously uncharted islands in the Marquesas. He successfully disposed of a boatload of furs in China later that year, but on his second voyage, in 1792, Ingraham seems to have fallen under the spell that Haida Gwaii can cast over visitors; he spent so much time collecting plants, making maps, writing in his journal and chatting with Spanish leader Francisco de la Bodega y Quadra (who found him "an intelligent fellow of considerable talent and great experience") that he failed to attend to business. The *Hope*'s owners, Thomas Perkins and James Magee, lost $40,000 on the venture. Ingraham joined the US Navy as a lt in the late 1790s and was lost at sea. His 1790–92 journal was published in 1971. *See also* Kiokathli Inlet *and* Nesto Inlet. Frederick I in the QCI is named for his nephew, Frederick Ingraham.

Innes Passage (50°23'00" 125°10'00" Cordero Channel, between Sonora I and Gillard Is, N of Campbell R). This feature was named in 1955 after Bob and Donald Innes, two brothers who drowned in the early 1950s in a boating accident. It is believed that they attempted to cross this channel on a flood tide. The Innes family had moved its floathouse from Frederick Arm to Big Bay in 1930 and made a living for many years from logging and fishing.

Inrig Bay (51°47'00" 127°26'00" W side of Moses Inlet, N of Rivers Inlet, SW of Bella Bella). Frank Inrig (1869–1946) immigrated to BC about 1890. He married Charlotte (1870–1925), who had known him in Scotland and arrived in BC about 1896, at Kitkatla. Pioneer missionary Robert Gurd officiated at the service. Frank was a cannery man. He managed plants at Port Essington and Bella Coola early in his career but became strongly associated with Rivers Inlet, where he worked for the BC Fishing & Packing Co for many years. Eventually he went out on his own, building Goose Bay Cannery in 1926 and Moses Inlet Cannery in 1931. Frank and Charlotte's children—Mary, Jessie, Jim and Alex—were also well known in the Rivers Inlet area. Inrig Ck is named after Inrig Bay. Presumably **Inrig Point** (54°02'00" 130°05'00" E side of Telegraph Passage, near mouth of Skeena R, SE of Prince Rupert) is also named for this hard-working coastal family.

Insect Island (50°45'00" 126°37'00" Between Baker I and Eden I in the Broughton Archipelago, NE end of Queen Charlotte Str). The derivation of the name is unclear, though it appears on Admiralty charts as early as 1867, as does adjacent Fly I (now a Tsawataineuk First Nation reserve named Kukwapa). There are major middens on Insect I, suggesting extensive First Nation use. Although there is confusion about its exact location, the Kwakwaka'wakw village of Kukwapa (also spelled Xupxwapa or Xoxop'a) is believed to have been situated at the S end of Insect I, not on Fly I. Insect I is a favoured kayaking destination with a fine campsite.

Inside Passage (Between the mainland coast of BC and its offshore islands). This 1,600-km-long natural waterway, extending from Puget Sd to Skagway, Alaska, forms a mostly protected corridor that has become a coastal highway for PNW marine traffic. The Inside Passage is not an official name, however, despite its widespread acceptance. *E*

Inskip Channel (53°00'00" 132°16'00" N side of Hibben I, Kuper Inlet, NW Moresby I, QCI), **Inskip Passage** (54°35'00" 130°28'00" Entrance to Port Simpson, off NW end of Tsimpsean Peninsula, N of Prince Rupert), **Inskip Point** (54°04'00" 132°31'00" Virago Sd, N side of Graham I, QCI), **Inskip Rock** (49°12'00" 123°57'00" In Departure Bay, NW of Nanaimo). George Hastings Inskip (1823–1915) was the master of HMS *Virago*, based on the Pacific

Station, 1852–55, under Capt James Prevost. An expert surveyor, he was responsible for much hydrographic work in the QCI, on the N coast and elsewhere in BC. His journal for this period, in the possession of BC Archives, forms the basis of a 1992 book by Philip and Helen Akrigg, *HMS Virago in the Pacific 1851–55*. Inskip first became a deep-sea sailor on merchant vessels in 1839, then joined the RN as a master's assistant. He was aboard HMS *Rattlesnake* in 1846–50 (with famed biologist Thomas Henry Huxley, then a surgeon's mate) on its survey voyage to Australia. From 1871 until 1874, when he retired with the rank of capt, Inskip served at the RN hydrographic dept. George Point, SW of Victoria, is also named for him, as are Hastings Point and Hastings Reef in the QCI. The Haida knew Inskip Point as Schloot-kwoon and Hastings Reef as Tas'koo-wass Cudlay. *See below also. W*

Inskip Islands (48°27'00" 123°26'00" N of Ashe Head, Esquimalt Hbr, W of Victoria). Robert Mills Inskip (d 1900) was a naval instructor who served on the Pacific Station, 1843–47, aboard HMS *Fisgard*, under Capt John Duntze. His surveys of Esquimalt Hbr were designed to teach technical skills to junior officers. After returning to England he became a clergyman but continued in the RN and promoted an improved system for educating naval cadets that eventually resulted in the 1850s establishment of the training ship HMS *Illustrious* (superseded in 1859 by HMS *Britannia*). Inskip was appointed the vessel's chaplain and chief instructor, and was awarded a CB in 1869. He was the brother of George Hastings Inskip (*see* Inskip Channel). *W*

Insley Rock (52°15'00" 128°11'00" E of Dearth I, Seaforth Channel, NW of Bella Bella). Master mariner Asbury Insley (1829–98), born in Delaware, owned and operated numerous vessels on BC's coastal and inland waters. He was working on the Fraser R as early as 1858 and later became a skipper for the Canadian Pacific Navigation Co. Insley's career suffered a setback in 1885 when the *R P Rithet*, under his command, collided with and sank the *Enterprise*, another CPN vessel, off Cadboro Point. Two people died. An official tribunal found Insley at fault for leaving his ship in the hands of a lowly quartermaster, and his master's certificate was suspended for a year. Officers on both vessels were censured "for not making more active and determined efforts to control the excitement and assist the passengers." After reinstatement, Insley went back to the Fraser, building and running the sternwheeler *Delaware*, 1889–94. In 1898, during the Klondike gold rush, he was briefly master of the CPR's *Hamlin*, another sternwheeler, on the Stikine R. Insley Rk was formerly known as Harper Rk after Lt K Harper, a member of the RCNVR during WWI.

Inspiration Cove (48°25'00" 123°25'00" E side of Saxe Point, Esquimalt, W of Victoria). The name was adopted

I

in 1976, the year after it had been submitted to provincial authorities by Barry King, who was inspired to make a painting of this scenic feature.

Instructor Island (53°01'00" 132°19'00" Off N side of Inskip Channel, NW Moresby I, QCI). Rev William Cecil Percy Baylee was a popular chaplain and naval instructor aboard HMS *Thetis* during Capt Augustus Kuper's 1852 survey of the area. Nearby Baylee Bay, Baylee Bluff and Percy Point are also named for him.

Inverness Passage (54°11'00" 130°11'00" Between Smith I and Tsimpsean Peninsula, just S of Prince Rupert). The passage was named in 1908 after the Inverness Cannery, first in the region, built in 1876 by the N Western Commercial Co. The location chosen was originally known as Woodcock's Landing or Skeenamouth; in 1870 an inn was established there by William H Woodcock and a trading post by Robert Cunningham and Thomas Hankin (who moved to Port Essington the following year). At the time, Woodcock's Landing was the only white community on the N coast other than the HBC post at Ft Simpson; it was a stopping place for miners travelling to the Omineca gold country via the Skeena R. Historian John Walbran notes that the original Tsimshian First Nation name for the site was Willaclough, meaning "place of slides," and a number of fatal slides did indeed occur in the area. In 1880 the cannery was bought by Turner, Beeton & Co and in 1902 by J H Todd & Sons. Fires plagued the operation: 1893, 1909, 1920 and 1943 all saw serious damage done. Inverness Cannery closed in 1950, and a final fire destroyed the entire complex in 1973. Four other canneries—N Pacific (1889), Cassiar (1903), Dominion (1906) and Sunnyside (1916)—were also built on Inverness Passage. *E*

Inverness Passage at the mouth of the Skeena River. *Andrew Scott*

Ioco (49°18'00" 122°52'00" N side of Port Moody, E end of Burrard Inlet, E of Vancouver). The Imperial Oil Co began building its refinery here in 1914, and company vice-president C O Stillman dubbed the site Ioco after the initial letters of the company's name. An employee townsite was constructed in 1920, and a pipeline connected the plant to Alberta in 1953. The refinery closed down in 1995, and the site was converted to a bulk storage facility. The worker housing had mostly been eliminated by century's end. *E*

Iona Island (49°13'00" 123°12'00" Mouth of Fraser R, N of Sea I). The original name for this feature was Mole I. Then it was called McMillan I after Donald Allan McMillan (1848–1901), who settled there in 1885. McMillan gave the island its current name, which commemorates the remote spot in the Inner Hebrides where St Columba founded his influential Celtic monastery in 563. By the 21st century, BC's Iona I was home to a sewage treatment plant and a regional park and had long been joined to Sea I by a causeway. Its Halkomelem name is X'iyé'yut.

Iphigenia Point (54°11'00" 133°01'00" S side of Langara I, QCI). The 180-tonne *Iphigenia Nubiana* was one of the fur-trading ships sent from Macao to the BC coast in 1788 by an alliance known as the Merchant Proprietors. Its master was William Douglas, and it accompanied the slightly larger vessel *Felice Adventurer*, under John Meares, a principal backer of the voyage. Both ships flew Portuguese flags in order to circumvent the E India Co's monopoly on trade in the region. The *Iphigenia* wintered in Hawaii and was back on the BC coast in 1789, though it was now owned by a new consortium (which included Meares), the Associated Merchants Trading to the NW Coast of America. At Nootka Sd it was impounded and then released by the Spanish cdr Estéban Martínez, who later that year seized other vessels belonging to the Associated Merchants and took them to Mexico, precipitating the feud known as the Nootka Sd Controversy. Despite promising Martínez that he would leave the BC coast immediately, Douglas sailed N to the QCI instead and traded there very successfully before returning to Canton.

Irby Point (49°31'00" 123°18'00" S end of Anvil I, Howe Sd, NW of Vancouver). In 1794, Midshipman Frederick Paul Irby (1779–1844) of HMS *Montagu* was present at the English Channel victory known as the Glorious First of June. As capt of the frigate *Amelia* from 1807 to 1813 he gained renown for a bloody but inconclusive action against *L'Arethuse*, a French frigate. Irby was made a CB in 1831 and became a rear adm in 1837. *W*

Irish Bay (48°49'00" 123°12'00" W side of Samuel I, between Mayne I and Saturna I, Gulf Is). According to BC's Geographical Names Office, this feature recalls an Irishman named Flanigan, who had a shack on the bay.

Iron Mine Bay (48°20'00" 123°42'00" N side of Juan de Fuca Str, SE of Sooke, W of Victoria). Geologist George Mercer Dawson described the iron-ore deposits in this area in 1887 as being "near the coast and well situated for shipment." Although some primitive work was done on the ore body in the 19th century (hence the name), it was not deemed commercially viable. Nearby Iron Mine Hill is also named after these abandoned dreams.

Iroquois Island (52°02'00" 128°19'00" Queens Sd, SW of Bella Bella). The hydrographic service bestowed numerous war-related place names in 1944, including this one. HMCS *Iroquois* was a *Tribal*-class destroyer (the island is part of the Tribal Group), launched in 1941 but not really operational, due to construction and design flaws, until 1943. The ship saw convoy duty on the Gibraltar and Murmansk runs that year and was involved in numerous actions off the French coast in 1944. In 1952–54 the *Iroquois* completed three tours of duty off Korea. It was paid off in 1962 and sold for scrap in 1966. A more modern HMCS *Iroquois*, commissioned in 1972, was still in service in 2009.

The *Iroquois*, wrecked near Nanaimo in 1908. *Author's collection*

Iroquois Passage (48°41'00" 123°24'00" Off NE end of Saanich Peninsula, S of Goudge I, N of Victoria). The small steamship *Iroquois* was a frequent sight around the Gulf Is in the early 1900s and often used this channel. Built at Port Moody in 1900 and licensed for 100 passengers, the 25-m, 177-tonne vessel operated between Sidney, Nanaimo and Gulf Is ports. It had several serious accidents in its brief career, sinking off Jack Point near Nanaimo in 1908 and then capsizing N of Sidney in 1911, with the loss of 21 lives. Her skipper in this last incident, Capt Albert Sears, was charged with manslaughter as a result of the tragedy, both for setting off in bad weather with an overloaded, top-heavy ship and for deserting his command while people were still aboard; he was acquitted of the charges but his master's licence was suspended for life. After the loss of the

Iroquois, strict loading and passenger-list regulations were introduced for coastal vessels in BC.

Irvines Landing (49°38'00" 124°03'00" N entrance to Pender Hbr, Malaspina Str, NW of Vancouver). Named for Charles C Irvine, a bearded, pipe-smoking Englishman who opened a primitive store and inn at this site in the late 1880s. His original customers were loggers working up Jervis Inlet, but when tourist-bearing Union steamships began stopping at his wharf about 1891, his business expanded. Irvine sold out in the early 1900s to John and George West, though he remained as postmaster until 1903–4. In 1904, Joe Gonsalves, a Madeira Islander who had been living at Brockton Point in Vancouver, bought the operation and, together with his son-in-law Theodore Dames, built a much larger hotel. Various stores, resorts, docks, boatyards and marinas have operated at this location ever since.

The hotel and store at Irvines Landing were built in the early 1900s. The photo, dated about 1950, is by Harry Winn. *Harbour Publishing collection*

Irving Cove (49°11'00" 125°38'00" E side of Tofino Inlet, Clayoquot Sd, W side of Vancouver I), **Irving Passage** (51°19'00" 127°49'00" N entrance to Smith Sd, S of Rivers Inlet). Steamship skipper John Irving (1854–1936) was born at Portland, Oregon, and arrived in BC with his family in 1859. He married Jane Munro (1863–1950), daughter of HBC chief factor Alexander Munro, at Victoria in 1883. His father was William Irving (1816–72), an experienced steamboat man who formed several paddlewheel fleets on the Fraser R, including the Pioneer Line, the leading steamship company on the profitable New Westminster–Yale route, 1862–83. Young John took over the business on his father's death and turned Pioneer into the most prominent navigation line in BC, merging it with the HBC's marine dept in 1883 to form the Canadian Pacific Navigation Co. He managed the CPN until 1899 and remained a major shareholder until the company was sold to the CPR in 1901. Irving also took a great interest

I

in northern BC; he was MLA for Cassiar, 1894–1900, and operated steamers on the Yukon R and Atlin Lk through an independent business, the John Irving Navigation Co, which he sold to the White Pass & Yukon Route, also in 1901. He was involved, as well, in speculative mining ventures on the BC coast, including some in Clayoquot Sd, where he acquired several grants of Crown land between 1901 and 1909. After 1901, Irving travelled incessantly with his free lifetime CPR steamship pass and managed to fritter away a large fortune before he died. Mt Irving (qv), at the S end of Princess Royal I, is named for his father. *E*

Isabel Islet (54°20'00" 130°26'00" S of Metlakatla in Venn Passage, just NW of Prince Rupert). Named in 1868 by Lt Daniel Pender after Elizabeth Florence Isabel Gribbell, eldest daughter of his future brother-in-law, Rev Francis Gribbell. *See* Gribbell It.

Isabella Point (54°02'00" 132°34'00" E side of Alexandra Narrows, opposite Bain Point, Naden Hbr, Queen Charlotte Is). After Isabella Bain, wife of Archibald Bain, chief engineer aboard HMS *Virago*. *See* Bain Point.

Isabel Point (52°08'00" 128°19'00" SW side of Horsfall I, just W of Bella Bella). Capt John Walbran, of CGS *Quadra*, named this feature in 1902 after Isabella Matilda Geddes (1875–1966), the wife of Methodist medical missionary Dr Richard Whitfield Large (1873–1920). They were married at Vancouver in 1899. Dr Large established a hospital at Bella Bella in 1902 and became the first permanent physician on the central coast. He also rebuilt the Rivers Inlet summer hospital, which had burned down in 1904. In 1910 the family headed farther N, where Dr Large was appointed superintendent of the hospital at Port Simpson. Isabella Large was noted as a musical educator, establishing brass bands at Bella Bella and Port Simpson. The Port Simpson band featured a bagpipe player and performed around BC.

Isnor Islets (53°34'00" 130°33'00" S of Rawlinson Anchorage, off W side of Banks I), **Isnor Rock** (52°44'00" 129°32'00" NW of Moore Is, Caamaño Sd, off NW Aristazabal I). John Isnor, a native of NS, served on various government survey vessels in the 1920s. He was a sounder and coxswain aboard CGS *Lillooet* and also boatswain of the *Somass*.

Ivanhoe Rock (50°22'00" 125°32'00" S of E Thurlow I, Johnstone Str). This hazard was reported to the hydrographic service by Capt R E Grafton of the *Ivanhoe*,

a 165-tonne, 30-m tug built at Vancouver in 1907. In 1913 the 15-passenger vessel was owned by Kingcome Navigation Co and serviced logging camps on Kingcome Inlet. Later the *Ivanhoe* operated in the San Juan Is. Sometime after 1938, when it was refitted with a diesel engine, the tug was sold to Mexican interests.

The Ivory Island lighthouse was established in 1898. *Peter Vassilopoulos*

Ives Islet (50°30'00" 127°51'00" N side of Koprino Hbr, Quatsino Sd, NW end of Vancouver I). Edwin P J Ives secured a Crown grant of land in this vicinity in 1911.

Ivory Island (52°17'00" 128°24'00" Milbanke Sd, NW approach to Seaforth Channel). The first BC lighthouse N of Vancouver I was built at this remote spot in 1898. Few keepers stayed there very long, as the station was exposed to the open Pacific and was badly damaged by tidal waves in 1904 and 1962, and by a violent storm in 1982. It is considered an important site for providing marine weather forecasts, however, and for assisting with search-and-rescue operations, and it was still staffed in the early 2000s. The origin of the name is unclear.

Izard Point (50°08'00" 127°31'00" E entrance to Ououkinsh Inlet, Checleset Bay, NW side of Vancouver I). Lt (Engineer) Theodore Douglas Izard, of Victoria, was killed in action aboard HMCS *Athabaskan* on Apr 29, 1944, aged 26. The RCN destroyer was hit by a torpedo and sank, with the loss of 111 lives, during an engagement with four German destroyers off the coast of France. Izard's name is inscribed on the Halifax Memorial. Nearby Theodore Point is also named for him.

J

Jacinto Islands (52°56'00" 129°37'00" S end of Estevan Group, Caamaño Sd), **Jacinto Point** (54°35'00" 131°05'45" SW end of Zayas I, Dixon Entrance). After Spanish naval officer and explorer Jacinto Caamaño. *See* Caamaño Sd.

Jackobson Point (50°08'00" 127°41'00" W entrance to Nasparti Inlet, Checleset Bay, NW side of Vancouver I). Capt Victor Jackobson (b 1860) came to the BC coast from Europe in 1880. He found work with the Victoria-based sealing fleet and became skipper of several vessels including the schooner *Minnie*, named for his wife, Minnie McLean (b 1872, in Ont), whom he married at Victoria in 1888. The *Minnie* was seized by the US government in 1889 for alleged illegal hunting; more than 500 skins were confiscated. Jackobson, despite the presence of a US guard, ignored the order to proceed to Alaska and hand over his ship, and made for Victoria instead.

Jack Point (49°10'00" 123°54'00" N tip of Duke Point, Nanaimo Hbr, E side of Vancouver I). Jack Dolholt (1819–1905) lived on this point for 40 years. He was born in Norway and went to sea as a boy, arriving at NY in 1840 and San Francisco in 1849. After participating unsuccessfully in the Fraser R gold rush, Dolholt captained coal and lumber schooners in BC waters, including the *Langley* and the *Victoria Packet*, which he partly owned. He was noted for abandoning his ship one time (after "taking his tea too strong," according to historian John Walbran) in order to try to rescue his mate, who had fallen overboard. He put a small boat over the side and left his passengers to sail the vessel to Victoria, which, amazingly, they were able to do. In the early 1890s, Dolholt sold the coal rights to his land for a handsome sum to the Vancouver Coal Co. Formerly named Sharp Point by Capt George Richards in 1860 (and also known locally as Lighthouse Point), the feature was renamed by Cdr John Parry of HMS *Egeria* in 1904. The tip of Duke Point once consisted of two fingers, which were dredged and filled in the early 19th century; today the peninsula is known as Duke Point and the tip as Jack Point. *W*

Jackscrew Island (48°57'00" 123°35'00" Just NE of N end of Saltspring I, Gulf Is). A jackscrew is a screw-operated hydraulic device widely used for lifting or exerting pressure. In the aviation industry, the word refers to a long rod in the tail of an aircraft that drives the horizontal stabilizer. The island's peculiar terrain, with its miniature ridges and valleys, must have reminded someone of the threads of a jackscrew. The island was formerly used as a First Nation burial ground.

Jackson Bay (50°32'00" 125°50'00" N side of Topaze Hbr, N of Hardwicke I and Johnstone Str), **Jackson Point** (50°23'00" 125°22'00" E side of E Thurlow I, NW of Campbell R). Molesworth Greene Jackson (d 1869) was 1st lt aboard HMS *Topaze*, under Capt John Spencer, on the Pacific Station, 1859–63. He was a member of an 1863 court martial that determined the fates of 13 deserters from HMS *Cameleon*, who absconded from Nanaimo Hbr in broad daylight with one of the ship's cutters. They were captured the same evening by naval pursuers who lit a fire on Gabriola I and then hid. The deserters, confused and lost, found the seemingly abandoned fire, gathered around to cook a meal and were apprehended. The two ringleaders were later each sentenced to four years' imprisonment. Jackson was promoted cdr in 1864. Molesworth Point near Jackson Bay is also named for him, as are Greene Point and Greene Point Rapids at W Thurlow I. A small logging and fishing settlement formed at Jackson Bay in the 1910s with a store, school and boat landing; a post office operated there, 1922–56. *W*

Jackson Rock (48°45'00" 123°26'00" E side of Fulford Hbr, Saltspring I, Gulf Is). According to records at BC's Geographical Names Office, Margaret Jackson was an early teacher at Beaver Point school on Saltspring I, which was established in 1885.

Jack Tolmie Island (49°31'42" 123°57'53" SE of Turnagain I, entrance to Secret Cove, E side of Malaspina Str, NW of Vancouver). Jack Tolmie, a grandson of HBC chief factor William Fraser Tolmie (*see* Tolmie Channel) and nephew

J

of BC premier Simon Fraser Tolmie, once owned this island, according to Joseph E Henderson, a subsequent owner of the property. Henderson proposed the name in 1972, and it was adopted in 1978.

Jaffrey Rock (52°27'00" 128°49'00" Laredo Sd, W of Price I, NW of Bella Bella). No information seems to have survived about Sapper John Jaffrey, who was a member of the Columbia detachment of Royal Engineers that served in BC 1858–63.

Jagers Point (52°18'00" 127°58'00" N end of Cunningham I, Johnson Channel, NE of Bella Bella). John Frederick Jagers (1851–98), born in Germany, was a prominent master mariner with the Canadian Pacific Navigation Co, 1888–98. He arrived at Victoria in 1878 and over the course of his career had command of many well-known vessels, including the *Beaver, Barbara Boscowitz, Princess Louise, Yosemite* and *R P Rithet*. He married Rosina Helen Wagner (1863–1926) at Victoria in 1884. Jagers was capt of the *Grappler*, a former RN gunboat, sold in 1868 and converted to a coastal steamer, on its final, tragic voyage. The ship was headed N through Seymour Narrows in 1883 when its coal supply caught fire. Rudder control was lost and the vessel circled helplessly at full speed in the strong currents, flames blazing from its ports and hatches. The passengers, mainly Chinese cannery workers, panicked and swamped the few boats that the crew were able to launch. Eighty-eight lives were lost. Jagers Point was formerly known as Jenkins Point, after Cdr (Engineer) J C Jenkins of the RCN, who served in BC waters aboard HMCS *Rainbow*, 1914–17, but it was renamed in 1925.

James Bay (48°25'22" 123°22'20" E side of Inner Hbr, Victoria), **James Island** (48°36'00" 123°21'00" Between Sidney I and Saanich Peninsula, Gulf Is), **James Spit** (48°35'00" 123°20'00" Just S of James I). After BC's famed colonial gov Sir James Douglas. *See* Douglas Channel for more details. James Bay was named in 1846 by Capt Henry Kellett of HMS *Herald*, who surveyed Victoria Hbr that year. Gov Douglas later built his residence on the S shore. In 1903–4 much of the bay was filled in. A granite retaining wall was built across its entrance, and the CPR erected the Empress Hotel on the reclaimed land. The name also refers to the historic residential district in the SW corner of Victoria. The old Salishan term for James Bay was Whosaykum, or "muddy place." James I, named about 1853, was first settled in the 1870s. The 315-ha island later became a private hunting preserve and then, in 1913, site of a major explosives factory. A village on the island housed most of the plant's 800 workers until 1962; the plant itself was demolished in 1979. In the early 2000s the island was owned by Seattle's McCaw family, who listed it for sale at a mere $50 million. James always had 10 km of attractive beaches; now it also sports deluxe cottages, an airstrip and a Jack Nicklaus-designed golf course. *E*

James Bay (48°51'00" 123°24'00" NW side of Prevost I, Gulf Is). After British naval officer and boundary commissioner James Charles Prevost. *See* Prevost I. The N end of Prevost I was acquired for the Gulf Is National Park Reserve in 1995, and a park campsite was established on James Bay.

James Cone (49°41'51" 126°36'52" On Strange I, Tlupana Inlet, Nootka Sd, W side of Vancouver I). Named in 1935 after James Strange, who arrived in PNW waters in 1786 with the second fur-trading expedition to visit the BC coast. *See* Strange I. This feature is marked as Conspicuous Cone on early Admiralty charts.

James Point (53°33'00" 129°36'00" N entrance to Lowe Inlet, Grenville Channel, E of Pitt I). James Lowe (1830–79) was employed by the Bank of Dundee in Scotland before immigrating to the US in 1853 and joining his brother Thomas in San Francisco. Thomas Lowe had worked for years in the PNW for the HBC (*see* Lowe Inlet), then formed the general merchandising firm Allan, Lowe & Co in San Francisco in 1852; James became a partner in this business. In 1860 he moved to Victoria and set himself up as a commission merchant. Thomas joined him in 1862, and the flourishing firm of Lowe Bros bought out wholesaler G Vignols in 1864 and ship chandler James Southgate in 1865. Thomas retired in 1871 and moved back to Scotland in 1872, while his younger brother remained in Victoria, forming a new partnership with Thomas Stahlschmidt, which lasted until 1875. James then moved to San Francisco and lived there until he died. *W*

Sir James Douglas, governor of BC. *BC Archives A-01229*

Jamieson Point (52°34'00" 128°45'00" N entrance to Kitasu Bay, Laredo Sd, NW of Bella Bella). After Robert Jamieson (1859–1945), who was born at Dunville, Ont, and came to Victoria with his family in 1862. His Irish missionary father, also Robert Jamieson (1829–93), established the first Presbyterian church on the BC mainland, at New Westminster, and later also founded churches at Nanaimo and in the Fraser Valley. The younger Robert married Ann Mason (1860–1929) in 1883 and worked for bookseller T N Hibben & Co in Victoria before becoming a theatre and hotel manager. He took part in the old-timers' reunion held in Victoria in 1924 (*see* Adams Bay).

Jane Island (52°38'00" 128°31'00" Between Cone I and Sarah I, Finlayson Channel, NW of Bella Bella), **Jane Passage** (52°37'00" 128°31'00" Between Cone I and Jane I), **Jane Patch** (52°37'00" 128°31'00" NW end of Jane Passage), **Jane Point** (54°19'00" 129°59'00" N entrance to Davies Bay, S end of Work Channel, E of Prince Rupert). Jane Work (c 1827–80), born at Ft Colville in Washington, was the eldest daughter of HBC chief factor John Work and Josette Legacé. She was raised at fur-trading forts (Vancouver, Simpson and Victoria) and in 1850 married HBC medical officer and chief factor William Fraser Tolmie. Jane lived the next nine years at Ft Nisqually in Washington, where her husband was in charge, then settled at Victoria, where the family built a comfortable farmhouse, Cloverdale, in Saanich. The Tolmies had five daughters and seven sons, one of whom was Simon Fraser Tolmie, premier of BC, 1928–33. Mt Jane on Dowager I, NW of Bella Bella, is named for her as well. *See also* Legace Bay, Tolmie Channel *and* Work Channel. *W*

Janion Rock (52°49'00" 129°32'00" W of Rennison I, Caamaño Sd). Named after Annie Isabella Janion (1852–1920, née Rhodes), who was born at Honolulu and came to Victoria with her family about 1859. Her father, Henry H Rhodes (1824–78), served as Hawaiian consul for the colony of Vancouver I and founded an importing and auction business with Richard C Janion (1815–81) and another partner named Green. The firm, which also had a branch in Portland, Oregon, owned the Janion Hotel and built a large wharf with brick warehouses on the Victoria waterfront. In 1875, Annie married Richard William Janion (1851–88), a son of her father's business partner. He died at San Francisco. She lived on in Victoria with her five children and her sister, Emily Rhodes, and became a well-known local resident.

Janit Reef (48°50'00" 125°22'00" S of Broken Group, Barkley Sd, W side of Vancouver I). The hydrographic service decided in 1945 to honour a Russian immigrant who settled in this vicinity in the 1910s and provided surveyors with valuable information about the region's uncharted shoals and rocks. According to author R Bruce Scott, the name is probably misspelled and refers to either

John Janet (1877–1965), who married Natalie Greenthal (1880–1946) in 1911 and died at Victoria, or Julius Janet (1883–1946), who died at Port Alberni. Formerly known as Western Reef.

Janson Island (48°54'00" 125°31'00" S of entrance to Ucluelet Inlet, Barkley Sd, W side of Vancouver I). August Janson (1856–1935), who emigrated from Sweden to Canada in 1878, was a storekeeper and homesteader on the E side of Ucluelet Inlet in the early 1890s. He pre-empted the George Fraser Is about 1890. Janson died at N Vancouver.

Jap Island (51°23'00" 127°07'00" Head of Smith Inlet, SE of Rivers Inlet), **Jap Point** (54°24'00" 130°29'00" W side of Tsimpsean Peninsula, just NW of Prince Rupert). At least five geographical features in BC have shared this racist term for Japanese people. It was WWII patriotism, not sensitivity, that likely resulted in Jap Inlet on Porcher I being changed to Hunt Inlet in 1946. Jap Mtn, S of Courtenay on Vancouver I, became Nikkei Mtn in 1982 after a request by the National Assoc of Japanese Canadians. In 1976, officials of the Canadian Hydrographic Service wanted to delete Jap Point from the charts, stating that the name was "clearly derogatory." BC's representative on the Canadian Permanent Committee on Geographical Names argued against the change, however, explaining that while the expression "may be looked on by a few older-generation Japanese as derogatory," it was, in his view, merely colloquial. "From what I have been able to gather," he went on, "in talking to a younger Asiatic I know, such terms aren't considered to convey any impression of racism these days." And thus Jap Point, along with two other features—Jap I, and Jap Lk on E Thurlow I—remains in the gazetteer. While several BC place names incorporating the word "nigger" were changed in the 1960s, it was not until quite recently that other slurs were dealt with. Four instances of "Chinaman," for example, were rescinded in 1996 on the recommendation of the Vancouver Assoc of Chinese Canadians. "Squaw" was eliminated from place names in BC in 2000.

Jaques Island (48°55'00" 125°16'00" Between Jarvis I and Gibraltar I at NE side of Broken Group, Barkley Sd, W side of Vancouver I). Josiah Jaques (c 1838–1912) received a Crown grant of land at the entrance to Uchucklesit Inlet in 1884 and acquired other grants in the vicinity of Port Renfrew in 1891. He was born at Manchester and came to Victoria in 1860, participating in the Cariboo gold rush and also spending much time as a prospector on the W coast of Vancouver I. Jaques was a machinist who for many years worked as a foreman at Victoria's Albion Iron Works. A single man, he lodged at the city's Angel Hotel. This feature was originally shown as Puzzle I on an 1865 Admiralty chart and was incorrectly spelled Jacques I on pre-1945 maps.

Jay Islands (52°52'00" 129°04'00" Off W side of Racey Inlet, W side of Princess Royal I). Named for barrister George Jay (1861–1940), who was born at Norwich, England, and arrived in BC's capital city with family members in 1870. His horticulturist father, also George Jay (1830–1899), established an early Victoria nursery and seed business. Young George was admitted to the bar in 1883 and formed a law partnership with James Yates. Eventually he was appointed a Victoria magistrate. He married Emily Louisa Bowden (1864–1948) in 1885. Victoria's George Jay School, at one time the largest elementary school in BC, was named for him in 1909.

The old Foote farmhouse at Jedediah Island. *Andrew Scott*

Jedediah Island (49°30'00" 124°12'00" Sabine Channel, between Lasqueti I and Texada I, Str of Georgia). Jedediah Stevens Tucker was the eldest son of Benjamin Tucker (1762–1829), secretary to RN hero Sir John Jervis (Earl St Vincent) and later 2nd secretary to the Admiralty. Using his father's papers, Jedediah wrote a two-volume biography of Jervis in 1844. Jedediah's brother, John Jervis Tucker (1802–86), was also an RN admiral (*see* Jervis I). Jedediah I was purchased by Harry Foote in 1890 and used by his family as a retreat for 30 years. Mary and Al Palmer owned it much later, and in 1994 offered the property to the BC government at less than market value. After a major fundraising drive—and a generous contribution from the estate of local outdoorsman Dan Culver—Jedediah was acquired as a provincial marine park in 1995. The name of the 2.6-ha island, bestowed by Capt George Richard in 1860, originally appeared as Jedidiah on an 1872 Admiralty chart. Richards named nearby Tucker Bay (qv) after Benjamin Tucker. *E*

Jedway Bay (52°17'00" 131°15'00" S side of Skincuttle Inlet, SE Moresby I, QCI), **Jedway Point** (52°18'00" 131°14'00" Just NE of Jedway Bay). The name comes from the Haida word *gigawai*, meaning "entrance to a fish trap"

or "snare." Jedway Cr takes its name from the same source. Jedway Bay was the site of an important Haida village at the time of the 18th-century fur traders. In the 1910s and '20s a Japanese saltery and abalone cannery operated there. The bay was also known as Lizzie Cove and Saltery Bay. The original townsite of Jedway, located on the W side of Harriet Hbr, sprang up in the early 1900s as a service centre for the region's copper-mining boom. It had a hotel, sawmill, store, wharf, clam cannery, post office and mining recorder's office, but did not last long. In 1961 the Jedway Iron Ore Co operated an open-pit mine on the E side of the harbour and established another short-lived townsite that had all but disappeared 10 years later. *D*

Jeffrey Rock (49°29'00" 124°23'00" Entrance to False Bay, Lasqueti I, Str of Georgia). Alfred Jeffrey pre-empted land on Lasqueti I in 1889 and received a Crown grant in 1894. He was a son of William and Susan Jeffrey (the name is sometimes given as Jeffreys or Jeffries), who were among the very first white settlers on Lasqueti and who lived for a while beside Tucker Bay. Alfred homesteaded on the island, as did his brothers Robert and Abraham, and raised sheep there. There is a 1949 death record at BC Archives for Alfred Edwin Jeffrey, aged 83, at Comox.

Jelina Island (49°30'40" 124°18'20" Sabine Channel, off N end of Lasqueti I, Str of Georgia). This name is probably a misspelling of the first name of Velina Daza Lambert, the wife of Lasqueti pioneer Paul Louis Lambert (1876–1945), according to island historian Elda Copley Mason. Paul Lambert, a native of France, arrived on Lasqueti about 1919; first he bought Jervis I (qv), then the property around Lambert Lk, which is named for him. He was a miner, a telephone lineman, Lasqueti's first real-estate agent and a great island booster, full of grand but often impractical schemes, which included the raising of goats, foxes, muskrats, nutria and edible frogs. He brought Velina to Lasqueti about 1931, but she apparently returned to the eastern US after Paul's death. There is a death record for Velina Lambert (1885–1970) at Plymouth, Massachusetts. Before 1948, Jelina I was known as Ada I and misspelled on some maps as Ade I.

Jemmy Jones Island (48°27'00" 123°16'00" W side of Baynes Channel, SE of Cadboro Bay, E of Victoria). James "Jemmy" Jones (1830–82), born in Wales, was a well-known skipper on the BC coast in the 19th century, having immigrated to California in 1849 and Puget Sd in 1854. He bought or built several small schooners—the *Emily Parker*, *Wild Pigeon* and *Carolina*—all of which came to grief while trading between Puget Sd ports and Vancouver I. The *Carolina* was wrecked on the island now named for its capt. The intrepid mariner next built the *Jenny Jones*, which he converted to steam power in 1864. It was with this 29-m vessel that he performed his most celebrated escapade. Jones had been imprisoned at Victoria in 1865 for debt, and his mate, Charles Grainger, took the little steamship to the US to avoid creditors. Unfortunately, the capt had creditors everywhere and his vessel was seized anyway. Undaunted, he escaped from jail, crossed Juan de Fuca Str in a canoe and, disguised in women's clothing, boarded his ship at Olympia as a passenger. When the *Jenny Jones* tied up next night and its guardians went ashore, he hijacked it and steamed single-handedly to BC waters, where, with stealth, he was able to refuel and reprovision. Jones was then joined by the crew of a disabled sloop. He reached Mexico with his new pals, sold the vessel, was arrested and released in San Francisco, and finally returned home. Later in life he operated a schooner named *Industry*, which he swamped on the Trial Is in 1878. Jemmy Jones I became part of the Oak Bay Is Ecological Reserve in 1979. Songhees First Nation members, who gathered camas bulbs there, knew it as Bukkaynung. *E W*

Jenkinson Point (53°27'00" 129°05'00" E side of Hawkesbury I, Verney Passage, SW of Kitimat). After British politician Sir Charles Jenkinson, later Lord Hawkesbury. *See* Hawkesbury I, where Mt Jenkinson is also named for him, for more details.

Jenkins Point (52°06'00" 130°58'00" E side of Kunghit I, SE of Rainy Is, QCI). Named for Capt William H Jenkins, who was master of the cargo ship *Keeweenah*, which foundered off the entrance to Juan de Fuca Str during the great gale of Dec 1894, accompanied by the *Montserrat*, under Capt David Blackburn. Many vessels were destroyed in this storm, and wreckage was spread up and down the BC coast. Pieces from the *Keeweenah* and *Montserrat* were found in Rose Inlet in May 1895. All hands on both ships were lost.

Jenny Reef (48°55'00" 125°31'00" S of entrance to Ucluelet Inlet, N of Alpha Passage, Barkley Sd, W side of Vancouver I). The British vessel *Jenny* was on the BC coast twice in the 1790s in search of sea otter furs. For its first voyage, under James Baker, it was rigged as a schooner. Leaving Bristol in 1791, it arrived in the PNW the following year via Hawaii, where crew members took on board two young Hawaiian women. At Nootka Sd, Baker met Capt George Vancouver, who was heading for Hawaii that winter and agreed to take the girls home. Baker returned to England in Oct 1792. The 71-tonne *Jenny* was ship-rigged for its second expedition, under Capt John Adamson. It left Bristol in 1793, traded very successfully along the entire PNW coast the following summer, then sailed for China with 2,000 skins, returning to Britain in 1795. Adamson and his vessel anchored briefly at the entrance to Ucluelet Inlet in Sept 1794. The *Jenny* was owned on both of its journeys by the Bristol merchant Sidenham Teast. *See also* Adamson Rks.

Jensen Cove (50°43'00" 127°28'00" E side of Hardy Bay, NE end of Vancouver I). Probably named after Niels Peder Jensen (1865–1934), who was born in Denmark, came to Canada in 1897 and settled that year at Cape Scott with his wife, Maren (1864–1934), and their two children. Jensen Ck, a tributary of the San Josef R, is likely named for him as well. Jensen was one of the founders of the Danish agricultural colony at the cape. He was a keen dairy farmer who salvaged acres of sand dune by fencing it and planting clover, then brought in and set up a milk condensery for his wife, an expert in making butter. Their son Lars became skipper of the community boat, the *Cape Scott*, until 1910, when he was lost at sea. The colony, too far from its markets and without adequate transportation facilities, eventually failed.

Jensen Rock (49°08'00" 125°58'00" W of Wickaninnish I, E side of Father Charles Channel, Clayoquot Sd, W side of Vancouver I). Jens Peter Jensen was born in Denmark about 1865 and immigrated to Canada in 1894. He pre-empted land at Schooner Cove on Esowista Peninsula that year and received a Crown grant in 1900. Jensen was listed in the 1901 census as a carpenter. He also had a part interest, with fellow Clayoquot pioneers Filip Jacobsen and John Chesterman, in the Kallapa Mine on Meares I, which produced some copper, gold and silver ore in 1913 but was abandoned with the advent of WWI. The large drying bay on the E side of Esowista Peninsula, opposite Chesterman Beach, is known locally as Jensen's Bay.

Jepther Point (50°52'00" 127°54'00" S side of Goletas Channel, W of Shushartie Bay, N end of Vancouver I). Named after Jepther James Skinner (1868–1934), from Ont, who was an early settler at Shushartie Bay. He bought the Shushartie Trading Post in 1895 from William McGary, who had built it about 1891, and also farmed, raised livestock and did a little placer mining for gold. The post featured a store, the post office and a few sleeping rooms, and soon became a regular Union steamship stop. Skinner married Eileen Excene Godkin (1903–83) at Shushartie in 1921. He was a well-known pilot on the dangerous N coast of Vancouver I and eventually lost his life in a sudden storm on the Nahwitti Bar. Nearby Skinner Ck is also named for him.

Jeremiah Point (52°37'00" 131°41'00" Entrance to Bigsby Inlet, E side of Moresby I, QCI). After writer and geologist Dr John Jeremiah Bigsby. *See* Bigsby Inlet.

Jericho Beach (49°17'00" 123°12'00" S side of Burrard Inlet, W of False Ck, Vancouver). The name may be a corrupted form of Jerry's Cove, referring to Jeremiah Rogers (1818–79), a well-known early logger in the Vancouver area. Born in NB, he came to the PNW in the 1850s and was providing logs for Edward Stamp's pioneer sawmill at Alberni in 1860. By 1865 he was on Burrard Inlet, felling spars for sailing vessels and timber for Stamp's Hastings Mill. He cleared much of Kitsilano from his camp at Jericho Beach and is credited with being one of the first innovators to use a steam tractor to haul the area's gigantic logs to the water's edge. *E*

Jermaine Point (52°25'00" 128°17'00" E side of Dowager I, Mathieson Channel, NW of Bella Bella). Edward John Jermaine was 2nd lt aboard HMS *Scout*, under Capt John Price, and served on the BC coast, 1865–68. He was cdr of HMS *Ganges* in the late 1870s when that vessel was a training ship for boys at Falmouth. Jermaine retired with the rank of capt in 1884.

Jervis Inlet (49°45'00" 124°10'00" E of Malaspina Str, NW of Vancouver). Named in 1792 by Capt George Vancouver after RN officer Sir John Jervis (1735–1823), who at that time was a rear adm serving in the W Indies. Jervis was promoted adm in 1795 and became cdr-in-chief of the Mediterranean fleet, 1796–99. It was during this period, in 1797, that he defeated a much larger Spanish force at the Battle of Cape St Vincent, in recognition of which he was named Earl St Vincent. His devotion to naval discipline gained him a reputation, perhaps unfairly, as a tyrant. Jervis served as 1st Lord of the Admiralty, 1801–4 and cdr of the Channel fleet, 1806–7. He retired in 1811 and was named adm of the fleet in 1821 on the occasion of the coronation of King George IV. In 1792, Spanish explorer Dionisio Alcalá-Galiano named this geographic feature Bocas de Mazarredo after José María de Mazarredo y Salazar, a famous Spanish naval cdr. The inlet itself, in the traditional territory of the Sechelt First Nation, zigzags 77 km into the Coast Mtns and is the deepest fjord (at 732 m) on the BC coast. *See also* St Vincent Bay. The Sechelt First Nation name for the inlet is Lékwĕmin. *E W*

Jervis Inlet is the deepest fjord on the BC coast. *Peter Vassilopoulos*

Jervis Island (49°31'00" 124°14'00" S side of Sabine Channel, N of Lasqueti I, Str of Georgia). RN officer John Jervis Tucker (1802–86) served on the Pacific Station from 1841 to 1845 as capt of HMS *Dublin*, flagship of Rear Adm Richard Thomas. He was superintendent of Sheerness dockyard, 1854–57. Tucker retired as a vice adm in 1864

and was promoted to adm, retired, in 1869. Capt George Richards named this feature in 1860 in association with Trematon Mtn (qv) on Lasqueti I. Trematon Castle in Cornwall, which apparently resembles the mountain's profile, had a house within its ruined walls that was home to the Tucker family. Adm Tucker died there. Jervis I, Jedediah I (named after Jedediah Tucker, John's brother) and Tucker Bay (named after Benjamin Tucker, his father) are all somewhat under the shadow of this mountain. Paul Lambert (*see* Paul I) acquired Crown grants to the 94-ha island in the early 1920s and ran a goat ranch there, raising and breeding the animals and producing milk and cheese. According to Lasqueti I historian Elda Copley Mason, he sold out to a California couple for $9,000, a princely sum in the 1920s. Jervis and adjacent Bunny I, purchased for $1 million as part of the Pacific Marine Heritage Legacy, became Sabine Channel Marine Provincial Park in 2001.

Jesdal Islet (50°32'00" 127°37'00" NE of Drake I, Quatsino Sd, NW end of Vancouver I). According to BC's Geographical Names Office, Erik S Jesdal acquired a grant of Crown land in this vicinity in 1897. No record of this transaction seems to have survived, however. Formerly known as Coffin It.

Jesse Falls (53°50'00" 128°52'00" On Jesse Ck, at SW entrance to Kitimat Arm, SW of Kitimat). These conspicuous waterfalls are named after the traditional title of the chief of the Beaver clan and principal chief of the Kitamaat band. The word is pronounced *TSEE-see*. Jesse Ck and Jesse Lk take their names from the same source.

Jesse Island (49°12'00" 123°57'00" N side of Departure Bay, just N of Nanaimo). Named after a seaman named Jesse who served aboard HMS *Virago* and was a member of the boat's crew that helped sound this area in 1853. It was unusual for 19th-century seamen to have places named for them; that honour was reserved for officers and "gentlemen." George Inskip, however, master of the *Virago*, named several nearby features after his more humble helpers. In 1934, regional hydrographer Henri Parizeau tried, unsuccessfully, to have the name changed to Camas I.

Jesse Island (50°28'00" 126°02'00" W of entrance to Blenkinsop Bay, E of Port Neville, Johnstone Str). HBC cashier Robert Jesse (1839–81) was stationed for many years at Victoria. He was born in Surrey, England, and came out to BC in 1858 aboard the HBC steamship *Labouchere*. Jesse married Matilda McNeill, a daughter of pioneer HBC shipmaster William McNeill, which made him the brother-in-law of George Blenkinsop, after whom the nearby bay is named. He later left the HBC and worked as an accountant for the CPR. Jesse died at Lytton. *W*

Jessie Point (50°57'00" 126°48'00" N side of Kenneth Passage, N of Watson I and NE end of Queen Charlotte Str).

Named in association with nearby Mackenzie Sd (qv) after Jessie McKenzie (1844–82), second daughter of Kenneth McKenzie, manager of the HBC's Craigflower Farm at Victoria (there is confusion over the spelling of this surname). McKenzie and his wife and children, who arrived at Ft Victoria in 1853 aboard the *Norman Morison*, were among the very earliest colonists on Vancouver I. In 1863, Jessie married Vancouver I colonial treasurer Alexander Watson (1831–92), after whom Watson I (qv) is named. In 1871, Alexander announced in the Victoria *Colonist* that he would be living at Leith, Scotland, and managing a "large manufacturing estate," but the family must have subsequently moved to California, as both Jessie and her husband died at Oakland.

Jessop Island (52°40'00" 128°48'00" Entrance to Trahey Inlet, Laredo Sd, S end of Princess Royal I). John Jessop (1829–1901), born at Norwich, England, immigrated to Ont with his parents in 1846. He trained as a teacher under Egerton Ryerson, the influential superintendent of education for Canada West, and worked at Whitby for several years. In 1859, Jessop and several companions travelled overland to BC from Ft Garry (now Winnipeg) and joined the Cariboo gold rush. After working at Victoria and New Westminster as a journalist, he founded one of Vancouver I's earliest non-sectarian schools. Margaret Fausette (1837–97), who arrived at Victoria in 1862 in the *Tynemouth*, a famous brideship, became his wife in 1868. Jessop served as a Victoria school principal and helped write BC's first education act. From 1872 to 1878 he was BC's first superintendent of education. He eventually went on to become BC agent for the federal immigration dept. *E*

Jeune Landing on Neroutsos Inlet. *Peter Vassilopoulos*

Jeune Landing (50°26'00" 127°29'00" E side of Neroutsos Inlet, Quatsino Sd, NW Vancouver I). Frederick John Jeune (1863–1955) and Philip John Jeune (1865–1957), from Jersey in the Channel Is, were brothers who came to Victoria in the late 1880s and set up as sailmakers and

manufacturers of other canvas products. They married sisters: Frederick wed Emily Elizabeth Touet (1866–1941) in 1889; Philip wed Agnes Esther Touet (1867–1965) in 1891. The age of sail may have mostly been over by then, but tents and tarpaulins were in high demand by BC outdoorsmen, especially loggers, prospectors and surveyors, and the company flourished. Jeune Landing was one of its shipping points. Nearby Jeune Ck is also named for these pioneer businessmen. The landing later became primarily a logging settlement, site of a Western Forest Products Ltd office and a dryland timber sort.

Jewell Island (53°15'00" 131°59'00" Entrance to Skidegate Inlet, QCI). Named in 1945 after Ambrose Jewell, one of 22 passengers in the schooner *Georgianna*, wrecked in a gale in Skidegate Inlet in 1851. The vessel was stripped by a group of Haida, and the passengers and crew held for eight weeks before being ransomed by Capt Lafayette Balch of the *Demaris Cove*. See Georgianna Point *and* Balch Is for more details. Before 1945, Jewell I was known as Tree I. The local name for this feature is Indian Head I, for the shape of the cliff at the N end seen in silhouette. *D*

Jewitt Cove (49°42'00" 126°36'00" E side of Strange I, E of Nootka I, W side of Vancouver I). John Rogers Jewitt (1783–1821), born in England, sailed to the PNW in the US vessel *Boston* in 1803 as an armourer. The ship's capt, John Salter, managed to insult Chief Maquinna while trading for furs at Friendly Cove, and next day the Mowachaht leader attacked the *Boston*, killing all 27 crew members except for two, Jewitt and John Thompson, who had hidden below decks and were only found later. Maquinna recognized Jewitt's value as a skilled blacksmith and decided to keep him as a slave; Jewitt tricked the chief into believing that Thompson was his father and should also be kept alive. The two seamen remained at Nootka Sd three years until rescued by Capt Samuel Hill of the *Lydia*. They were treated well in captivity, and Jewitt acquired slaves of his own, as well as a First Nation princess, Eu-stoch-ee-exqua, as a wife. He learned a great deal about Nuu-chah-nulth First Nation culture and kept a detailed journal, which he published in 1807, after reaching Boston, the *Lydia*'s home port. Jewitt stayed in the US and married Hester Jones in 1809 but did not really achieve fame until 1815, when Richard Alsop rewrote and embellished his account and published it as *A Narrative of the Adventures and Sufferings of John R Jewitt*. Jewitt promoted his work aggressively and also performed in a play based on the book, but his moment in the sun was soon over, and he died in obscurity. His story was so unusual, though, that publishers kept returning to it, and more than 20 editions of the journal have appeared since his death. *See also* Boston Point. *E*

Jewsbury Islets (53°35'00" 130°33'00" Entrance to Griffith Hbr, off W side of Banks I), **Jewsbury Peninsula** (53°04'00"

J

129°28'00" W side of Campania I, Caamaño Sd). Arthur Jewsbury (1878–1970) was born in England and served in the Boer War, returning home in 1900 and marrying Sarah Amelia Whitehouse (1880–1949). He and his wife immigrated to Canada in the early 1900s and settled in Victoria. Jewsbury was a finishing carpenter by trade and worked on many notable Victoria buildings, including the legislature and Empress Hotel. After serving overseas in WWI he found employment with the hydrographic service as a carpenter aboard the W coast survey vessels *Lillooet* and *William J Stewart*. He retired in 1945.

Jimmy Chickens Island. *See* Mary Tod I.

Joachim Island (51°28'00" 127°44'00" S of Penrose I, N entrance to Rivers Inlet), **Joachim Point** (53°48'00" 130°38'00" W side of Goschen I, SW of Porcher I and Prince Rupert), **Joachim Rock** (53°50'00" 130°43'00" Off Cape George, W side of Porcher I), **Joachim Spit** (53°49'00" 130°39'00" Extending N from Joachim Point). After British parliamentarian and naval official George Joachim Goschen. *See* Goschen I.

Joanna Rock. *See* Joan Point *below.*

Joan Point (49°08'00" 123°49'00" W side of Dodd Narrows, SE of Nanaimo Hbr), **Joanna Rock** (52°15'00" 128°18'00" S of Don Peninsula, Seaforth Channel, NW of Bella Bella). Joan Olive White (1827–1908), a native of Scotland, married Robert Dunsmuir (1825–89) in 1847 at Kilmarnock and immigrated to N America in 1851, sailing in the tea clipper *Pekin*. After staying briefly at Ft Vancouver on the Columbia R, the Dunsmuirs travelled to Victoria in the HBC brigantine *Mary Dare* and then to Nanaimo, where Robert prospected for coal for the HBC. After his contract was up he managed coal mines at Nanaimo and, after discovering rich seams at Wellington, went into the coal business for himself in 1869, eventually becoming a mining baron, the builder of the Esquimalt & Nanaimo Rwy, MLA for Nanaimo (1882–89) and BC's wealthiest man. Joan lived at Victoria and Nanaimo for most of her life, moving into the elaborate, rusticated castle of Craigdarroch (now a Victoria museum) in 1890. Her son James Dunsmuir (*see* Dunsmuir Is) was premier of BC, 1900–1902, and lt gov, 1906–9. W

Joassa Channel (52°10'00" 128°19'00" Between Horsfall I and Dufferin I, W of Bella Bella). BC historian and mariner John Walbran named this narrow passage in 1902 after an ancient Heiltsuk First Nation village that was once located in Dundivan Inlet, near the northern entrance to Joassa Channel.

Jocelyn Hills (52°21'16" 128°39'09" SE side of Price I, NW of Bella Bella). Named by Lt Daniel Pender in 1866 after RN officer William Henry Jocelyn (1842–1910), 4th lt of HMS

Scout, who served on the Pacific Station, 1865–68, under Capt John Price and was promoted to cdr in 1877. An Irish aristocrat, he inherited the title of 6th Earl of Roden in 1897. The Jocelyn Hill located on the E side of Finlayson Arm on SE Vancouver I was named about 1900 by Cdr John Parry of HMS *Egeria* for Victoria resident Jocelyn Grant.

Joes Bay (48°55'00" 125°19'00" N side of Turtle I, Broken Group, Barkley Sd, W side of Vancouver I). The name commemorates "Salal" Joe Wilkowski, who lived at this spot on a floathouse, 1959–80. Details about his past life are sparse, but he became a well-known figure to the fishermen and local residents of Barkley Sd. Wilkowski was a hermit who originally survived by selling decorative greenery (hence his nickname) to Vancouver florists, meeting the *Lady Rose* in Peacock Channel to load and ship his products. Later he also sold clams to a shellfish-processing plant in Bamfield and worked as a maintenance man for Parks Canada. His boat was found adrift in 1980 but his body was not recovered. As a result, his death has never been officially recorded, which is probably as he would have wished it.

Joe's Bay (51°39'00" 127°45'00" N side of Fish Egg Inlet, E of Fitz Hugh Sd and Calvert I). According to records at BC's Geographical Names Office, a man named Joe Moore homesteaded in the area from 1926 until the 1960s and kept a float camp at this location. The name was adopted in 1987.

John Parker Islands (48°20'00" 123°36'00" E side of Becher Bay, S tip of Vancouver I). John Parker (1828–1917), born in Kent, England, married Mary Ann Munn (1832–1900) about 1852 and came to Victoria the following year as an HBC employee aboard the supply ship *Norman Morison*. John and Mary Ann's eldest daughter, Hannah (1853–1937, later Mrs Hannah Ball), was one of the first white children born at Ft Victoria. Parker was a master farrier and blacksmith, and after leaving the HBC he opened a livery stable on Johnson St. During the Cariboo gold rush he ran an express service between Harrison Lk and Barkerville via Seton Lk and Anderson Lk, using pack animals and stagecoaches. Parker appreciated the value of land, acquiring a 2-ha tract on Pandora Ave offered by the HBC and, in 1870, almost 500 ha at Rocky Point, E of Becher Bay, where he established a farm. The family lived for many years at Craigflower Manor and operated a butcher shop in downtown Victoria, supplied from the Rocky Point Farm. Before 1935 these islands were known as the Deadman Is.

John Passage (48°41'06" 123°23'22" Between Coal I and Goudge I, off NE Saanich Peninsula, N of Victoria), **John Rock** (48°40'56" 123°23'20" Off SE end of Goudge I). Richard John (1826–92), a native of Wales, immigrated to the US and worked in the Pennsylvania coal mines before joining the California and Fraser R gold rushes. He apparently did well enough to be able to buy 250 ha of land at N Saanich about 1869 and settle there with his wife, Ann (1823–1902, née Graer), and their family. He also bought property at Saanichton. The Johns raised cattle and grew oats for Henry Brackman's pioneer grist mill on Tsehum Hbr. They called their estate Glamorgan Farm. Several sons established themselves as farmers on the Saanich Peninsula. Victoria newspaper publisher Sam Matson owned the farm in the 1920s and kept a herd of Jersey cattle. Part of the land was expropriated for an airport in WWII; another part became Sandown harness-racing track. Glamorgan Farm still existed in the early 2000s as a 3.3-ha heritage site.

Johnson Islet (48°40'52" 123°23'45" Off NW side of Fernie I and NE end of Saanich Peninsula, N of Victoria). This feature, incorrectly spelled, was named for Conrad Johnsen (1854–1930), who pre-empted the islet in 1911 and received a Crown grant in 1913. Ownership reverted to the city of Victoria in 1928, presumably because of unpaid taxes. The next owner was Rose May Reid, in 1934, who married a local resident named Copeland. After her death, in 1962, her husband asked the BC government to rename the islet after Rose, describing Conrad Johnsen as a trapper "who only occasionally lived, as a bachelor, on the island, and who is not remembered with any local significance." BC's chief geographer turned down the request, writing that "ownership of land is not, in itself, grounds for the application of the owner's name to a geographical feature." Such a change, he wrote, "would be contrary to the principles of the Canadian Permanent Committee on Geographic Names." Nearby Rose Rk (qv) was named for her instead in 1965.

Johnson Lagoon (50°12'00" 127°39'00" W side of Nasparti Inlet, E side of Brooks Peninsula, NW side of Vancouver I). John Oswald Johnson (d 1997) was a surveyor for the hydrographic service who graduated from the Univ of Sask in 1929 and worked on the W coast of Vancouver I (1930–34), in the QCI (1935–36) and in the Str of Georgia (1939–40). He died at Seattle.

Johnson Rocks (53°34'00" 130°34'00" In Rawlinson Anchorage, off NW side of Banks I). After returning home from service overseas during WWI, a man named A Johnson found work as a sounder aboard W coast survey vessel *Lillooet* in the early 1920s.

Johnstone Point (52°53'00" 129°07'00" S entrance to Surf Inlet, W side of Princess Royal I). Andrew Johnstone (1887–1964), born in Scotland to a seafaring family, came to Vancouver with his parents in 1890. He served his marine apprenticeship from 1903 to 1906 in CGS *Kestrel*, a survey and fisheries protection vessel, then worked as a quartermaster with the Blue Funnel and Cunard lines,

returning to Vancouver in 1908 on the maiden voyage of the CPR's new *Princess Charlotte*. In 1909 he joined the Union Steamship Co as 1st mate of the *Camosun* and later also served as 1st mate of the *Venture*. After a stint overseas during WWI with the Royal Canadian Artillery, Johnstone was appointed skipper of the *Venture* and went on to become one of Union Steamship's most celebrated mariners. In 1922 he and the crew of the *Venture* rescued 238 passengers from the US ship *Queen*, which went on the rocks off the mouth of the Skeena R. In 1927, as master of the *Cardena*, he managed to dislodge the *Prince Rupert*, the CNR's crack steamer, from Ripple Rk in Seymour Narrows, where it had managed to impale itself. In fog and dangerous currents, Johnstone manoeuvred the *Cardena* alongside, made fast to the stranded vessel and, like a tug moving a liner, pulled it off its perilous perch and towed it to a safe anchorage—an astonishing feat of seamanship. Johnstone joined the BC pilotage service in 1932 and finally retired in 1954.

Johnstone Strait (50°27'00" 126°00'00" Between the NE side of Vancouver I and the Cracroft Is, Hardwicke I, Thurlow Is and the mainland). James Johnstone (1759–1823) was master (later 1st lt) of HMS *Chatham*, the armed tender that accompanied Capt George Vancouver and HMS *Discovery* to the PNW, 1791–95. It was Johnstone, while exploring with the *Chatham*'s cutter in 1792, who found this important 110-km passage connecting the Str of Georgia to Queen Charlotte Sd and the open Pacific. Dionisio Alcalá-Galiano, travelling through the strait at about the same time as Vancouver, called it Canal de la Descubierta, after one of Alejandro Malaspina's ships. Johnstone had been on the BC coast earlier, in 1787–88, as mate aboard the fur-trading vessel *Prince of Wales*, under James Colnett, and it was no doubt for this valuable experience that Vancouver found him a position on his expedition. Johnstone had, in fact, commanded the *Prince of Wales* on its return voyage from Macao to England in 1789, and he was a great friend of Archibald Menzies, naturalist and surgeon on the Vancouver voyage, who had also been the surgeon on the *Prince of Wales*. Johnstone was one of Vancouver's principal surveyors and carried out many arduous examinations of the inner coastline in small boats. He later became a capt in the RN and

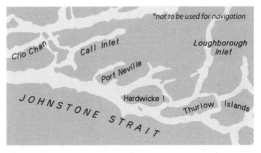

Johnstone Strait. *Reproduced with the permission of the Canadian Hydrographic Service*

Johnstone Strait, along the northeast shore of Vancouver Island, is a major route for marine traffic. *Peter Vassilopoulos*

participated in the capture of both Mauritius (in 1810, with HMS *Leopard*, flagship on the E Indies Station) and Java (in 1811, with HMS *Scipion*). He was commissioner of the RN at Bombay, 1811–17, and died at Paris. Archibald Menzies was an executor of his will. *E W*

Jones Island (52°01'00" 128°16'00" In the Admiral Group, off SW side of Campbell I, SW of Bella Bella). Named in 1944 as one of the Admiral Group for Vice Adm George Clarence "Jetty" Jones, CB (1895–1946). Born at Halifax, he was a first-term cadet at the Royal Naval College of Canada in 1911 and had his first command in the RCN destroyer *Patrician* in 1920. Jones was promoted to cdr and senior naval officer at Halifax in 1929, senior naval officer at Esquimalt in 1934 and director of naval operations and training in 1936. During WWII, as a capt, he had charge of the destroyers *Ottawa* and *Assiniboine* before being promoted to commodore and CO at Halifax (1940), then rear adm and CO Atlantic Coast (1941). Later in 1941, Jones was appointed vice-chief of naval staff. From 1944 to 1946 he was Canada's chief of naval staff, with the rank of vice adm. Besides his CB, he also received awards of honour from France, Norway and the US.

Jones Rock (50°30'00" 127°51'00" N side of Koprino Hbr, Quatsino Sd, NW end of Vancouver I). William Jeffersen Jones obtained a Crown grant of land to an island in Winter Hbr in 1908.

Jordan River (48°25'00" 124°03'00" Flows SW into Juan de Fuca Str, W of Sooke Inlet, SW end of Vancouver I).

Spanish naval officer Manuel Quimper, in the *Princesa Real* (the former British trading vessel *Princess Royal*, seized at Nootka Sd in 1789 by Estéban Martínez), explored this coastline in 1790. He called this feature Rio Hermoso in his diary, and its current name first appears on a map made by Gonzales López de Haro later in 1790. It most likely refers to Alejandro Jordán, a "presbítero" or chaplain who arrived at Nootka with Francisco Eliza in the *Concepción* and remained there for some time. A small logging community, long known as R Jordan instead of Jordan R, is located at the river's mouth; it was the site of a major hydroelectric plant from 1911 to 1971 and has become a popular surfing spot in recent years. Nearby Jordan Meadows and Jordan Ridge are named after the river. *E*

Jorey Point (54°05'00" 132°34'00" W side of Virago Sd, N side of Graham I, QCI). Mary Liscombe Jorey (d 1904) was the fiancée of George Inskip, master of HMS *Virago*, who surveyed this area in 1853. He and Mary were married in 1855. She was from a nautical family, her father, Edward Jorey, having served in the RN as a midshipman before becoming an Admiralty clerk. Inskip also named Mary Point, just to the N, after his bride-to-be. *See also* Inskip Channel. *W*

Josef Point (49°07'47" 123°42'06" E of Degnen Bay, SE end of Gabriola I, Gulf Is). Named in 1905 by Cdr John Parry of HMS *Egeria* after Spanish draftsman and mariner José Cardero. *See* Cordero Channel.

Josephine Flat (50°07'00" 125°22'00" S of Menzies Bay, just NW of Campbell R). Named in 1895 after the heroine of Gilbert and Sullivan's comic opera *HMS Pinafore*. The officers of HMS *Nymphe*, just before re-surveying Menzies Bay, had apparently seen a production of this musical at Nanaimo. So taken were they with the young actress playing the part of Josephine that they decided to honour her with a geographical name. *W*

Joseph Island (53°09'00" 130°02'00" In Hecate Str, off SW end of Banks I). This feature, formerly known as Shrub I, was renamed in 1946 because of duplication. It commemorates the famous British naturalist Joseph Banks. *See* Banks I. Nearby **Joseph Hill** (53°19'54" 129°54'05" SE side of Banks I), formerly called Bare Hill, is also named for him.

Joseph Rocks (53°49'00" 133°08'00" Off entrance to Ingraham Bay, NW side of Graham I, QCI). After US fur trader and master mariner Joseph Ingraham. *See* Ingraham Bay. Nearby Joseph Ck is also named for him.

Josette Point (53°12'00" 132°15'00" N side of Long Inlet, N of Skidegate Channel, Graham I, QCI). After Josette Legacé, a pioneer resident of colonial Victoria and the wife of senior HBC official John Work. *See* Legace Bay.

Josling Peninsula (52°57'00" 132°11'00" Between Douglas Inlet and Mitchell Inlet, Kuper Inlet, NW Moresby I, QCI), **Josling Point** (48°56'00" 123°38'00" S tip of Kuper I, Gulf Is), **Josling Point** (52°58'00" 132°13'00" N end of Josling Peninsula). John James Stephen Josling was 2nd lt aboard HMS *Thetis*, under Capt Augustus Kuper, on the Pacific Station, 1851–53. In 1857, in London, England, he married Louisa Ellen Langford, eldest daughter of Flora and Edward Langford, who had managed Colwood, one of the HBC farms established on Vancouver I by the Puget's Sd Agricultural Co. After service in England and the Mediterranean, Josling was promoted capt in 1861 and took command of HMS *Euryalus*, flagship of his former

superior officer, now Rear Adm Kuper and cdr-in-chief of the China Station. Josling was killed in 1863 during the bombardment of Kagoshima, Japan. *W*

Joyce Island (54°06'00" 130°40'00" Between Stephens I and Prescott I, Chatham Sd, SW of Prince Rupert), **Joyce Rocks** (52°20'00" 131°08'00" Entrance to Skincuttle Inlet, off SE Moresby I, QCI). Harrison Benjamin Joyce, a native of Swan I, Maine, was a master mariner with the New England Fish Co, which established a halibut fishery in Hecate Str in 1894. A fish-processing station was built on Joyce I; the halibut was packed in ice there before being sent to Vancouver, where it was forwarded to the E coast by rail. The island was named by Capt John Walbran in 1897. Capt Joyce had command of various fishing vessels, including the *Kingfisher* and the *New England*. It was aboard the latter, in 1899, that he struck a dangerous hazard off Moresby I, subsequently named the New England Rks. The nearby Gull Rks were renamed the Joyce Rks by the hydrographic service in 1945 because of an apparent duplication of features named "gull."

Juan de Fuca Strait (48°15'00" 124°00'00" Between Vancouver I and Washington state's Olympic Peninsula). The Greek master mariner Apostolos Valerianos, born at Kefalonia about 1536, worked as a pilot for Spain for 40 years and was known as Juan de Fuca. In 1596 he reportedly met an English trader named Michael Lok in Venice and told him about a voyage made four years earlier up the W coast of N America. De Fuca told Lok that the Mexican viceroy had sent him, with two small ships, to search for the Str of Anián, a hypothetical passage through N America that might provide a shortcut from Europe to China. He claimed to have entered a wide inlet between 47° and 48° N and sailed E for 20 days, finding a "very much broader Sea than was at the said entrance" extending to the NW and SE, and passing "divers Ilands in that sayling." At the mouth of the strait, he maintained, "there is on the NW coast thereof, a great Headland or Iland, with an exceeding high Pinacle, or spired Rocke,

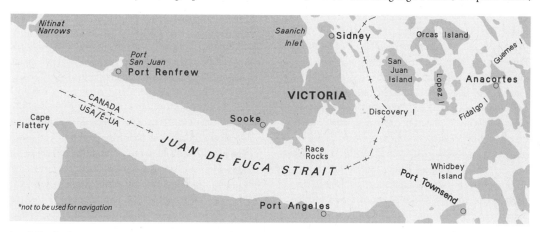

Juan de Fuca Strait. *Reproduced with the permission of the Canadian Hydrographic Service*

J

Juan Perez Sound east of Moresby Island in Haida Gwaii commemorates the first European known to have seen the BC coast. *John Alexander*

like a piller therupon." Lok tried unsuccessfully to persuade English officials to hire de Fuca, who had been promised, but did not collect, a reward for his efforts and was disillusioned with his Spanish masters. Lok's report of his meeting with the Greek pilot, which has caused much controversy over the years, was published in 1625 in a famous compilation of travel writing edited by Samuel Purchas, called *Purchas, His Pilgrims*. De Fuca's account, if fictitious, is at the very least a remarkable coincidence, as it describes the Str of Georgia, Juan de Fuca Str and Fuca Pillar off Cape Flattery fairly well. Was de Fuca the first European—by almost two centuries—to explore this part of the world? Most historians say "no" and point out that none of his assertions have ever been confirmed. In 1787, Capt Charles Barkley of the *Imperial Eagle* found an opening on the Pacific coast (completely missed by James Cook in 1778) right where de Fuca said it would be and named it after him. It is probable that the Spanish explorer Juan Pérez identified the entrance to the strait even earlier, on his northern expedition of 1774. A 1,277-ha provincial park and 47-km trail, established in 1996, now protect the BC coastline of Juan de Fuca Str. *E W*

Juan Perez Sound (52°30'00" 131°25'00" Off E side of Moresby I, QCI). Spanish naval officer Juan José Pérez Hernandez (c 1725–75) was the first European explorer known to have seen the BC coast. Born at Majorca, he came to San Blas, Mexico, in 1767 and worked on the galleons that plied between Manila and Mexico. Pérez also took part in the 1769 effort to colonize California. In 1774 he was sent by Mexican viceroy Antonio Bucareli to look into reports of Russian activity in the PNW. With Estéban Martínez as his 1st officer, Pérez sailed N in the *Santiago* and made a historic landfall off the coast of the QCI. He had peaceful contact with the Haida and named Punta Santa Margarita on NW Langara I but did not go ashore. Sailing S along the W coasts of the QCI and Vancouver I, he next approached shore at Nootka Sd, which he named Puerto

de San Lorenzo. Again he interacted with local people but did not land. Four silver spoons traded by the Spanish were shown in 1778 to a curious Capt James Cook, and Cook's comments about them were later cited by Spain as proof that its explorers had been the region's first visitors. On his 1774 expedition, Pérez bestowed BC's earliest surviving European place names: the San Christoval Range (qv) on Moresby I and Punta de San Estéban (Estevan Point, qv). On the return voyage he probably became the first European to investigate the entrance to Juan de Fuca Str (qv). His journey was a failure in the sense that he did not go far enough N to investigate the Russians. Nor did he claim any lands for Spain. Bucareli decided to mount another expedition the following year, with two vessels this time, under the overall command of Lt Bruno de Hezeta. Pérez went along as the *Santiago*'s pilot but became ill and died just before the ships arrived back at San Blas, Mexico. Perez Shoal in Juan Perez Sd is also named for him, as are the Perez Rks off Estevan Point. The sound was named in 1878 by geologist George M Dawson; it was known in the 18th century as Etches Sd, after the brothers Richard, John and William Etches, financial backers of early fur-trading expeditions to the PNW. *W*

Juan Point (53°19'00" 129°13'00" NE end of Gil I, Wright Sd, SW of Kitimat). Probably named after Juan Gil, ensign bearer on the flagship of the Spanish armada in 1588. *See* Gil I.

Juggins Bay (55°22'00" 129°47'00" W of Brooke I, Observatory Inlet, S of Stewart). Prospector Frederick Ernest Juggins filed a number of claims in the area, including the Left Over and Monarch properties near the head of the Illiance R, which empties into Alice Arm. He was active in the region from about 1908 until at least 1917; several of his interests showed promising assay values for copper and silver but never seem to have been developed. In 1918, Juggins married Elizabeth Muriel Haycock at Vancouver.

Jules Bay (50°35'00" 127°45'00" S side of Holberg Inlet, Quatsino Sd, NW Vancouver I). Probably named for Julius Rasmussen, an early mail and transportation contractor on N Vancouver I. Adopted in 1975.

July Point (50°30'00" 126°04'00" E side of Port Neville, Johnstone Str). The hydrographic service chose, in 1950, to change the name of this feature from Boulder Point, its widely duplicated former name, to July Point. It was during the month of July 1792 that two of the officers from Capt George Vancouver's HMS *Discovery*—2nd lt Peter Puget and Joseph Whidbey, the master—examined and surveyed this stretch of coastline with small boats.

Junk Ledge (53°20'00" 130°11'00" Between Wreck Point and Foul Bay, W side of Banks I). A Japanese junk may have run aground on this hazard sometime prior to 1927, when the name first appears on Admiralty charts. Small Asian junk-rigged vessels did occasionally come to grief on the W coast of N America over the years, driven by the Kuroshio ("black stream"), a warm ocean current that sweeps NE from Japan to the Aleutian Is and then along the coast of Alaska, where other currents could possibly drive damaged craft S toward California. In 1639, in an attempt to prevent its citizens from leaving the islands, the xenophobic Japanese government forbade the construction of ocean-going ships. Smaller craft were built with large square rudders, which often broke away in rough seas, leaving vessels to roll helplessly in the wave troughs until their masts worked loose. Charles Walcott Brooks, Japan's first consul in the US, compiled an 1876 list of 60 disabled junks that had drifted around the Pacific. He speculated that Asian seamen had been washing up on N American shores for millennia, influencing not only the continent's First Nation cultures and languages but also its gene pool. Later historians discredited both his list and his theories but confirmed that, in 1834, the HBC brig *Lama* had rescued three survivors (out of a crew of 14) from the *Hojun-maru*, a junk that ran aground on the Olympic Peninsula 18 months after leaving Japan. Later writers placed this wreck in the QCI—perhaps because of a mix-up over First Nation names (a major village of the Quinault people near the US wreck site appeared on old charts as Queen Hithe). Anthropologist Marius Barbeau, in the 1920s, mistakenly concluded that the wreck survivors had been taken to Fort Simpson on the N coast, the nearest HBC post to Haida Gwaii. These errors could have influenced the naming of Junk Ledge, which

likely occurred about 1926. Junk Ledge may, however, be associated instead with the nearby older names of Wreck Point and Wreck Is, which first appeared on charts in 1870.

Jupiter Island (51°45'00" 128°04'00" Planet Group, N side of Hakai Passage, S of Bella Bella). The hydrographic service named this feature in 1948, along with Mercury It and Mars It, as part of the Planet Group.

Jurassic Point (49°53'00" 127°10'00" Between Kyuquot Inlet and Esperanza Inlet, W side of Vancouver I). So named because the point is composed entirely of sedimentary rocks that are between 145 and 160 million years old and thus date from the Upper Jurassic era, when dinosaurs roamed the planet.

Juskatla (53°37'00" 132°19'00" E side of Juskatla Inlet), **Juskatla Inlet** (53°37'00" 132°25'00" S of Masset Inlet, Graham I, QCI), **Juskatla Narrows** (53°40'00" 132°21'00" Entrance to Juskatla Inlet). According to QCI historian Kathleen Dalzell, Juskatla is a modification of a Haida term meaning "inlet on the inside of Djus I" (Djus is today's Fraser I). Geologist George Dawson called the inlet Tsoo-Skatli in 1878. Many small logging outfits worked along its shores during WWI, cutting Sitka spruce for the Imperial Munitions Board. The logging camp of Juskatla was established in 1941 by Pacific Mills, a Crown Zellerbach subsidiary. It had originally been located at the village of Queen Charlotte but was moved on a series of barges to its current location in about three weeks by Parker Bonney, a former district forester at Prince Rupert. The camp, which took only the choicest spruce, used for airplane construction, was operated by Aero Timber, a Crown corporation, during WWII. After the war the Powell R Co bought Aero's assets for a scandalously low price and then merged with MacMillan Bloedel Ltd, which maintained the camp as its QCI HQ for many years. In the early 2000s, Juskatla was owned by Western Forest Products Inc. Juskatla Narrows, where ebb tides can reach 9 knots (17 km/hr), was known by the Haida as Belly-of-the-Rapids. Nearby Juskatla Mtn is named after the inlet. *D*

Justice Rock (49°46'00" 126°55'00" S of Cameron Rks, Nuchatlitz Inlet, off NW Nootka I, W side of Vancouver I). After David Cameron, chief justice of Vancouver I, 1853–65. *See* Cameron Rks. This feature was formerly known as Bare Rk and was changed to avoid duplication.

K

Kagan Bay (53°13'00" 132°12'00" N side of Skidegate Inlet, QCI). *Kagaan*, according to historians Philip and Helen Akrigg, is the Haida word for a white-footed mouse. It is also the Haida name for nearby Slatechuck Mtn. Kagan Ck is named for the Haida mouse as well.

Kaien Island (54°17'00" 130°18'00" Between Digby I and Tsimpsean Peninsula, at Prince Rupert). Kaien, a traditional Tsimshian First Nation name for the island, was adopted in 1892 when Prince Rupert Hbr (then called Tuck Inlet) was examined. According to N coast Anglican missionary William Collison, the word referred to a damp place with much fallen timber. A more widely accepted meaning, however, is "foam," especially the substance produced after a heavy rain by the Zanardi Rapids, at the S end of the island. Kaien Ck is also named for this foam, which can float on the water for a distance of several km. Kaien I was selected as the GTP terminus in 1905, and the town of Prince Rupert was laid out there. *W*

Kaiete Point (52°04'00" 127°57'00" NE end of Hunter I, SE of Bella Bella). Kaiete is the hereditary name of one of the principal chieftainships of the Heiltsuk First Nation. The chief who bore this name (also spelled Calete) in 1805 was killed while leading an attack on the US trading vessel *Atahualpa*. This incursion, which took place in a bay on the E side of Spiller Channel, was repelled, but with the deaths of 10 crew members (9 more were wounded, leaving only 4 to sail the ship) and about 40 Heiltsuk warriors.

Kains Island (50°27'00" 128°02'00" N entrance to Quatsino Sd, NW end of Vancouver I), **Kains Point** (50°28'00" 128°02'00" W entrance to Forward Inlet, N of Kains I), **Mount Kains** (50°27'36" 128°02'45" N entrance to Quatsino Sd). Que-born civil engineer Thomas Kains (1850–1901) was a draftsman for the CPR at Toronto and also did extensive survey work in Alberta and the NWT before joining BC's Dept of Lands and Works and rising to become surveyor gen of BC, 1891–98. As chief surveyor, Kains was the first to argue that if BC was to be settled in a systematic fashion, a detailed topographic survey of the entire province would be necessary. He was also an early proponent of combining triangulation with photography for surveys in mountainous country. He obtained a Crown land grant in the Quatsino area in 1892. Kains Ck and Kains Lk on N Vancouver I are also named for him. Kains I was formerly known as Entrance I; Quatsino lighthouse station, built there in 1907, was still staffed in the early 2000s.

Kains Island light tower and keeper's house, 1946. *BC Archives C-05431*

Kaisun Harbour (53°02'00" 132°28'00" N side of Englefield Bay, entrance to Inskip Channel, NW side of Moresby I, QCI). Named for Qays'un, or "Sea Lion Place," an ancient Haida village once located on the harbour. In 1840, HBC official John Work counted 18 houses and 329 people at this important outer-coast community. The village was abandoned about 1875, though the remains of house poles could still be seen in the early 2000s. A landslide destroyed part of the site in the mid-1980s. Quays'un was the birthplace of the famed blind poet and storyteller Ghandl (Walter McGregor). *D*

Kakawis (49°11'00" 125°55'00" W side of Meares I, Clayoquot Sd, W side of Vancouver I). According to regional hydrographer Henri Parizeau in 1933, Kakawis is a Tla-o-qui-aht (Clayoquot) First Nation name meaning

Prince Rupert Harbour

When great industrial projects are conceived for the BC coast, new place names are often required. The area to be developed must undergo a careful survey. Engineers and workers need to be able to refer with ease to various features of the terrain—even fairly insignificant ones. "Down by the rocks over there on the point" may not be specific enough, for instance, when it comes to setting off dynamite. Geographical names on accurate maps can provide a kind of shorthand necessary for safe, efficient communication.

And so it was that, early last century, gangs of surveyors descended on the Pacific coast just north of the Skeena River and began naming everything in sight. The western terminus of the Grand Trunk Pacific (GTP) Railway, Canada's northern transcontinental link, had finally been settled on, and it was certain that a major port and community would emerge at the chosen location. All manner of facilities had to be laid out: rail lines and stations, streets and lots, public buildings, parks, wharves and industrial sites.

Prince Rupert was selected as the terminus primarily on the strength of its harbour, which provides a sheltered, ice-free, deepwater port. The importance of the harbour outweighed the inconvenience of locating the city-to-be on Kaien Island, where it would have to be connected to the mainland by expensive bridges. Kaien, a Tsimshian First Nation word, refers to quantities of foam that accumulate on the tidal rapids at the south end of the island after a heavy rain. The name was bestowed in 1892, before the arrival of the railroad, when Samuel Parker Tuck made the first survey of the region. Tuck Inlet, where a vehicle ferry now runs from Prince Rupert to Port Simpson, extends just north of the harbour.

GTP held a contest in 1906 to name its new town. The winning entry, it decreed, must be significantly Canadian in tone, must not conflict with other names and should have no more than three syllables or 10 letters. Twelve thousand submissions were received. Unreasonably, railway officials then decided that their favourite name was Prince Rupert, which has 12 letters and commemorates the flamboyant first governor of the Hudson's Bay Company, a man who never set foot in Canada. No matter. To be fair, the grand prize of $250 was awarded not only to the Winnipeg woman who came up with Prince Rupert but also to two other entrants who suggested Port Rupert, a 10-letter name that closely resembled the one actually chosen.

Two years earlier, Fred Ritchie had made a preliminary survey of Kaien and its neighbouring islands (he later helped design Prince Rupert's sewer system), while GTP engineer James Bacon was busy choosing a site for the new town. He considered Port Simpson and Kitimat Arm but eventually settled on Kaien Island. The actual work of plotting the townsite and waterfront and starting construction was left to Bacon's assistant, Joel Pillsbury, and his crew, which included engineers William Casey and Arthur Hill. Other crew members were William Tobey, who would later become a senior railroad executive, and engineer Joseph de Stein. In 1906 a team led by federal hydrographer George Blanchard Dodge also surveyed the harbour as a prelude to preparing detailed, large-scale charts. Dodge's assistants—Philip Musgrave, Henri Parizeau and Louis Davies—would go on to respected hydrographic careers on the west coast. All these men have geographical features named for them in the area.

Some of the harbour names record the surveyors' frustrations. Delusion Bay, for instance, on the south end of Digby Island, was named by Pillsbury after he'd arrived there at high tide, decided it was a fine place to stay and set up camp. Returning several days later, at low tide, he found the bay totally dry, unapproachable in a small boat and quite useless as a campsite.

From such humble beginnings, a rich maritime heritage has emerged. Cruise ships, cargo vessels and ferries now loom over diminutive water taxis shuttling back and forth. Floatplanes take off and land. Whale-watching zodiacs, fish boats and kayaks weave about. It's only appropriate that the area's names pay tribute to the workers who transformed this northern landscape with their labour.

Kaien Island and Prince Rupert. *Courtesy Prince Rupert Economic Development Corp.*

K

"place of salmonberries." The Nuu-chah-nulth newspaper *Ha-shilth-sa*, however, translated it in 2003 as "fronted by a rock that looks like a container." From 1900 to 1971, Kakawis was the site of the Christie residential school, home to about 8,000 First Nation children over the years. The enormous Roman Catholic facility was run at first by the Benedictines and later by the Oblates of Mary Immaculate. A drug and alcohol recovery centre was built there after the school was destroyed by fire in 1983.

Kalect Island (50°54'00" 127°51'00" E side of Hope I, off N tip of Vancouver I). Chief George Kalect of Hope I was a negotiator for the Kwakwaka'wakw First Nation during the 1913–16 BC Royal Commission on Indian Affairs, also known as the McKenna-McBride Commission.

Kamai Point (48°40'44" 123°22'25" SE side of Coal I, off NE end of Saanich Peninsula, N of Victoria). Kama Kamai (c 1830-90), who pre-empted the E half of Coal I in 1873, was a native of Hawaii—otherwise known as a Kanaka. Earlier in his career he appears to have lived on San Juan I and worked there as a boatman during the Pig War, the 1860s dispute between Britain and the US over who should control the San Juan archipelago. Louis Andrew Kamai (1867–1949), Kama's son, received a Crown grant to the Coal I land in 1885 but moved to Victoria and worked there as a baker. Louis died on the Songhees First Nation reserve at Victoria. The W half of Coal I was owned by another Kanaka family, the Carneys (*see* Carney Point).

Kamano Island (50°34'00" 126°30'00" Off E end of Harbledown I, N of W end of Johnstone Str). George Kamano (c 1835–1918), of Hawaiian descent, worked for the HBC at Ft Rupert, 1854–69, and then became the first non-aboriginal person to carve a homestead out of the forests of Harbledown I (qv). Earlier he had helped build Harbledown's Roman Catholic mission of St Michael's, supervised by Fr Leon Fouquet. When the Oblates left in 1874, George and his Kwakwaka'wakw wife, Pauline Clahoara (1845-93), stayed on and raised a large family. Many of their children married local residents and remained in the region. George, whose name was also spelled Kumana, Kemana, Kaumana and Cahoomana, died at Alert Bay. Kamano I was formerly known as Coffin I, as it was once a Kwakwaka'wakw burial site.

Kamaree Point (48°40'44" 123°23'42" SW tip of Fernie I, off NE end of Saanich Peninsula, N of Victoria). Tom Kamaree, born in Hawaii about 1835, obtained a Crown grant for Fernie I and Goudge I (qv) in 1889 and farmed there for a number of years. The name was suggested in the 1960s by US oil tycoon Paul Whittier, a long-time owner of Goudge I.

Kamils Anchorage (50°01'00" 127°24'00" Between Kamils I and Spring I), **Kamils Island** (50°00'00" 127°23'00" W side of Union I, NW entrance to Kyuquot Sd, NW side of Vancouver I). Kamils I, also known locally as Mission I and Graveyard I, was a traditional burial ground and the location of a pioneer Roman Catholic mission to the Ka:'yu:'K'th (Kyuquot) people. In the 1850s it was also the site of a trading post owned by William Banfield and Peter Francis. The mission of St Marc, which eventually included a church, school and hospital, as well as outbuildings, livestock and an orchard, was established in 1880 by Fr Joseph Nicolaye and taken over in 1883 by Fr John Lemmens, who later became bishop of Victoria. The origin of the word Kamils is unknown, though it is an early name, referred to by Lemmens in his journal for 1883. It is virtually certain that Kamils was not a pioneer missionary at this location, as is sometimes suggested.

Kamin Cove (52°46'00" 128°45'00" E side of Laredo Inlet, S Princess Royal I). This name is an error, probably the result of a botched transcription. The feature is meant to commemorate US steamship tycoon Jacob Kamm (1823–1912), who was born in Switzerland and came to the US in 1831. Kamm's original trade was as a machinist and Mississippi steamboat engineer, but he went W in 1849 because of ill health and built a number of pioneer riverboats, including the *Jennie Clark*, Oregon's first sternwheeler. His companies—Oregon Steam Navigation, Union Transportation and Vancouver Transportation—were successful and Kamm became very wealthy. Over the years he built and owned dozens of well-known steamers in the US, then moved into banking and real estate. Kamm was Portland's first millionaire, and his heritage home there was for many years the city's museum. Nearby Kamin Ck is also named for him. It is not known how Kamm got changed to Kamin, but "m," written in longhand, could easily be mistaken for "in."

Kanaka Bluff (48°44'00" 123°23'00" W side of Portland I, SE of Saltspring I, Gulf Is). William Naukana (1813–1909) was one of the Hawaiian islanders (or Kanakas, a Polynesian word meaning "human beings") brought to BC in the 1830s and '40s to work for the HBC. Many of these immigrants married First Nation women and remained in BC, and small Kanaka communities were formed, especially near Vancouver and Victoria, and on Saltspring I. Naukana joined the HBC in 1845 and was employed at various posts, including Ft Langley (1848–49) and Ft Victoria (1853–56); he also lived in the San Juan Is after leaving HBC service. With his friend and son-in-law John Palua (*see* Pellow Its), he pre-empted most of Portland I in 1875, settled there with his family and farmed. Naukana eventually moved to Isabella Point on Saltspring I so his children could attend school more easily. Different renditions of his name are seen in the historical record: Nanton, Manton, Nowkin, Likameen and Lackaman. Many features in BC are named after the province's enterprising Hawaiian pioneers, including Kanaka Bar,

Kanaka Ck and Kanaka Mtn near the Fraser R and Kanaka Lk E of Salmon Arm. Kanaka Bluff was formerly known as Kanaka Point and Steep Bluff.

Kanish Bay (50°15'00" 125°20'00" NW end of Quadra I, N of Campbell R). In her book *Exploring Quadra Island*, Jeanette Taylor quotes Lekwala (or Liq'wala) speaker George Quocksister, who translates this name as "you can walk through to the other side." Lekwala is the language of the Lekwiltok (or Euclataw) people, who are closely related to neighbouring Kwakwaka'wakw First Nations and whose territory includes Quadra I.

Kankidas Point (52°18'00" 131°15'00" S side of Skincuttle Inlet, SE side of Moresby I, QCI). Kankidas was the name of an old Haida First Nation village at the head of nearby Harriet Hbr.

Kano Inlet (53°19'00" 132°39'00" S of Rennell Sd, W side of Graham I, QCI), **Kano Point** (53°19'00" 132°38'00" S side of Kano Inlet). Kano is derived from the original Haida name for the inlet. A fishing station for collecting halibut was briefly established there in 1905.

Kashutl Inlet (50°09'00" 127°18'00" Extends N from Kyuquot Sd, NW side of Vancouver I), **Kashutl River** (50°12'00" 127°18'00" Flows S into the head of Kashutl Inlet). Kashutl probably comes from the Chinook jargon word *kokshut* (also *kokshittle* or *kokshuttle*), meaning "to break" or "broken," and thus, by association, "useless" or even "destroyed." Various historians have suggested that the source of the word was the Nuu-chah-nulth First Nation term for "dead," which ultimately derived from an ancient battle or disaster. The inlet's former name was Kokshittle Arm. The current spelling was suggested by naturalist William Newcombe in 1934.

Kate Rocks (49°59'00" 127°19'00" SW of Union I, entrance to Kyuquot Sd, NW side of Vancouver I). The *Kate* was a well-known W coast sealing schooner, originally owned by pioneer sealer Capt James Warren. The vessel was active in the industry from about 1882 until at least 1897 and may have worked in BC waters as a coastal trader even earlier (several ships in the area had the word *Kate* in their names). The *Kate* was apparently visible as a wreck in Victoria's Inner Hbr until the early 1900s.

Kat Island (52°23'00" 131°22'00" Between Burnaby I and SE Moresby I, QCI). The name Kat is derived from the Haida word for deer and may also have referred to an ancient Haida village on the W side of the island.

Kawas Islets (52°38'00" 131°25'00" E of Lyell I, off E side of Moresby I, QCI). Kawas comes from the Haida word for "sea eggs" and was also the name of a subdivision of the Sta'stas Eagle crest, which lived along the N shore of

Graham I. Chief Albert Edensaw (or Idansaa), whose Haida name was Gwaayang Gwanhlin, was a prominent member of this tribal group.

Kean Point (52°33'00" 128°30'00" S end of Cone I, Finlayson Channel, NW of Bella Bella). Kean was the name of the accountant at nearby Klemtu Cannery, which operated 1927–30 and 1934–69. The plant was owned by J H Todd & Sons and was extensively upgraded and modernized by manager Lewis Hogan in 1941. This name was adopted in 1948.

Keary Rock (52°17'00" 128°38'45" Off SE side of Price I, NW of Bella Bella). Sapper James Keary (c 1826–71), a native of Ireland and a stonemason by trade, was a member of the Columbia detachment of Royal Engineers, which served in BC 1858–63. He stayed on in BC with his family and received, as did all sappers who remained, a 60-ha military land grant (believed to have been in the Mission area). Keary opened a hotel named Telegraph House, presumably located at New Westminster, where he died in an accident while hauling firewood. His son, William Holland Keary, was mayor of New Westminster for eight years.

Keats Island (49°24'00" 123°28'00" W of Bowen I, Howe Sd, NW of Vancouver). Named about 1859 by Capt George Richards for Adm Sir Richard Goodwin Keats (1757–1834), one of the RN's many heroes. He is most famous for his night attack, as capt of the 74-gun HMS *Superb*, on two 112-gun Spanish line-of-battle ships near Cape Trafalgar. In the darkness and confusion, the massive Spanish vessels *Real Carlos* and *Hermenegildo* mistakenly destroyed each other with gunfire. Keats retired from the RN in 1812. He became gov of Nfld, 1813–16, and later also gov of Greenwich naval hospital. Keats I has a small community, Eastbourne, at its E end and is a popular recreation site in summer, with numerous church camps. *E W*

Overlooking Howe Sound from Corkum's farm on Keats Island. *Andrew Scott*

Keecha Point (53°18'00" 129°49'00" SE side of Banks I). Named after the Gitxaala First Nation reserve at the mouth of nearby Keecha Ck. This important salmon stream was probably the one visited in 1787 by early fur trader James Colnett of the *Prince of Wales*. The Gitxaala (Kitkatla) people are a branch of the Tsimshian First Nation.

Keefe Island (50°20'00" 127°53'00" N of Mayday I, in Side Bay, N side of Brooks Bay, NW side of Vancouver I). Master mariner Michael Lawrence Keefe (1851–99) came to BC from Harbour Grace, Nfld, about 1887 and was skipper of various Victoria-based sealing schooners, including the *Beatrice*, *Dolphin* and *Dawn*, the latter owned by Victoria merchant and politician Thomas Earle. His wife, Agnes Keefe (b 1853), and large family joined him in Victoria in 1890. In 1892, while master of the *Rosie Olsen*, he and his vessel and crew were seized by Russian authorities and confined briefly at Petropavlovsk before being sent back to Victoria.

Keefer Bay (49°57'00" 124°47'00" N side of Savary I, NE Str of Georgia), **Keefer Rock** (49°58'00" 124°53'00" Between Savary I and Hernando I). Long-time Savary I resident Harry McMicken Keefer (1873–1964), born in Ont, came W in 1882 with his father, Hugh Forbes Keefer, a CPR contractor and member of a prominent family of engineers. Young Harry attended California Military Academy in Oakland, then worked on the Vancouver waterfront and became a marine engineer, marrying Nora Gertrude Mace in 1899. In 1910 he was part of the syndicate that bought, subdivided and aggressively developed much of Savary I. Keefer built a house there in 1913 and lived with his family on Savary the rest of his life. He was part owner of the Savary Inn, ran the island's store and served as postmaster (1915–58) and justice of the peace.

Keeha Bay (48°47'00" 125°10'00" W of Pachena Bay, SE of Barkley Sd, W side of Vancouver I), **Keeha Beach** (N side of Keeha Bay). Keeha is a modification of Kichha, the name of the Huu-ay-aht (Ohiaht) reserve at this location. Nearby Kichha Lk is also named after this reserve. The Huu-ay-aht people are members of the Nuu-chah-nulth Tribal Council, and a possible translation of this Nuu-chah-nulth word is "the other side." The spectacular crescent of Keeha Beach, a popular hiking and camping destination, is backed by large sand dunes. Keeha Bay was formerly known as Keena Bay.

Keeweenah Bay (52°06'00" 130°57'00" E side of Kunghit I, QCI). The freighter *Keeweenah*, under Capt William Jenkins, foundered off the entrance to Juan de Fuca Str during the great gale of Dec 1894. The 52-m, 2,332-tonne ship was en route from Comox to San Francisco with a full load of coal at the time, accompanied by the *Montserrat*, another coaler, under Capt David Blackburn. Many vessels were destroyed in this storm, and wreckage was spread up and down the BC coast. Pieces from the *Keeweenah* and *Montserrat* were found in Rose Inlet on the S end of Moresby I in May 1895. All hands on both ships were lost. The *Keeweenah* was built in 1891 in Michigan and was named after that state's Keweenaw Peninsula. The vessel's name is often seen spelled Keweenah or Keweenaw.

Keith Anchorage (51°39'00" 128°05'00" S side of Kwakshua Channel, N side of Calvert I, S of Bella Bella). Scottish architect John Charles Malcolm Keith (1858–1940) immigrated to California in 1887 and was living in Seattle in the early 1890s when he won an international design competition for Victoria's Christ Church Cathedral. However, when he arrived in Victoria to supervise the work, he found that the Anglican diocese had no money. The cathedral's first stone, in fact, was not laid until 1926, its twin towers only completed in 1954 and the final stained-glass window not installed until 1994. The cathedral commission may not have made Keith rich, but he profited from the publicity, settling in Victoria and becoming one of BC's most successful architects. He designed the city's First Presbyterian Church (1915; also delayed for many years), the Fisgard St police station (1920), Saanich municipal hall (1911), Calgary's Anglican Cathedral Church of the Redeemer (1904), and many commercial buildings and luxurious residences. Keith married Louisa Esther Shrapnel Barter (great-granddaughter of British artillery officer and inventor Henry Shrapnel) at Vancouver in 1908.

Keith Point (52°24'00" 128°28'00" W side of Dowager I, Finlayson Channel, NW of Bella Bella), **Keith Rock** (52°42'00" 129°26'00" NW of Moore Is, W of Aristazabal I). Anne Jane Finlayson (1856–1937) was a daughter of HBC chief factor Roderick Finlayson and granddaughter of John Work, another senior HBC official. She was born at Victoria while it was still a palisaded fort and married James Cooper Keith (1852–1914), a native of Scotland, there in 1879. In the early 1890s the Keith family moved to Vancouver, where James opened the city's first branch of the Bank of BC and later became a realtor and land developer. He was the second reeve of N Vancouver, where Keith Rd is named for him; a president of the Vancouver Board of Trade; and the owner of Passage I in the entrance to Howe Sd, which the Keith family only sold in 1959. Annie Keith took part in the great old-timers' reunion held at Victoria in 1924 (*see* Adams Bay). She died at Vancouver.

Keld Point (53°14'00" 129°22'00" S tip of Fin I, Squally Channel, N of Caamaño Sd). Thomas Keld was a boatswain aboard HMS *Discovery* on Capt George Vancouver's expedition to the PNW coast. He apparently suffered such a severe attack of dysentery at Cape Town in 1791 that his capt transferred him to a homeward-bound vessel, one of four seamen "whose constitutions seemed unequal to the service in which they had engaged." Vancouver may have been glad to get rid of Keld, as he had punished him shortly after leaving England for "drunkenness and riotous behaviour."

Kellett Point (48°23'00" 123°38'00" E side of Sooke Basin, W of Victoria, S end of Vancouver I), **Kellett Reef** (48°22'00" 123°38'00" NW of Kellett Point), **Kellett Rock** (48°32'00" 124°29'00" N side of Port San Juan, SW side of Vancouver I). Vice Adm Sir Henry Kellett (1806–75) had an important connection with the BC coast during his remarkable career. He joined the RN in 1822 and, as a lt, participated in anti-slavery campaigns and survey work in W Africa, 1826–35, aboard HMS *Eden* and *Aetna*. As a lt cdr, in charge of HMS *Starling*, he accompanied Cdr Edward Belcher, in HMS *Sulphur*, on a six-year surveying voyage around the world, 1836–42, and was promoted to capt on his return to England. In 1846–47, after PNW boundary disputes between England and the US, Kellett, in HMS *Herald*, and Lt Cdr James Wood, aboard HMS *Pandora*, made the first detailed Admiralty charts of the BC coast (#1897, #1901 and #1910, for Victoria Hbr, Esquimalt Hbr, Sooke Inlet and Port San Juan). Wood also compiled the region's first sailing directions. Partway through this commission, Kellett and his vessel were unexpectedly ordered to help search for missing explorer Sir John Franklin. He made three voyages through Bering Str in the summers of 1848–50 and is credited by Russian historians with the earliest hydrographic work done in the eastern Russian Arctic. In 1852 he took charge of HMS *Resolute* and returned to the Arctic as deputy cdr of another expedition in search of Franklin, led by his former colleague, now Capt Sir Edward Belcher. After two years of exploring, during which British knowledge of Arctic waters was greatly expanded, Belcher abandoned four of his five ships in the frozen ice and returned home, much against the advice of his senior officers, including Kellett. Indeed, the *Resolute* was found in 1855, floating free and quite seaworthy, by a US whaler; it was refitted by the US government and sent to Queen Victoria as a gift. Kellett was promoted to rear adm in 1862 and served as superintendent of Malta dockyard, 1864–67; from 1869 to 1871, as a vice adm, he was cdr-in-chief of the China Station. He published an account of the voyage of HMS *Resolute* in 1852. Henry I and Kellett Bluff in the US San Juan Is are named for him as well. *See also* Pim Head. *W*

Kellsey Point (50°22'00" 125°09'00" W side of Stuart I, mouth of Bute Inlet, NE of Campbell R). Robert Kellsey Moore (1874–1964) was a pioneer resident of the district who pre-empted land at this point in 1913 and received a Crown grant there in 1924. Moore, who was known far and wide as Mr Kellsey, was listed in the 1919 BC Directory as a fisherman and rancher. He died at Esquimalt.

Kelly Island (49°42'31" 124°12'35" W of Nelson I, E side of Malaspina Str, NW of Vancouver). Martin Kelly pre-empted the island in 1899 for use as a stone quarry and received a Crown grant for it in 1911. From 1903 to 1908 the Vancouver Granite Co based its operations there. Kelly and his business partner, a man named Murray, supervised the actual quarrying, breaking the stone out by hand and loading it on barges from an inclined tramway. Kelly I granite was particularly attractive because its vertical cracks made the stone easier to work than that on adjacent Nelson I, which also had an important early quarry. Kelly I was formerly known as Granite I; its Sechelt First Nation name is Kishálin.

Kelo Rocks (52°45'00" 131°34'00" SE of Kunga I, E of Tanu I and Moresby I, QCI). The name is adapted from the Haida word for cormorant.

Kelpie Point (51°44'00" 128°00'00" SE entrance to Hakai Passage, N end of Hecate I, S of Bella Bella). A kelpie is a shape-shifting Celtic water spirit, usually horselike in form, that is believed to haunt the rivers and lochs of Ireland and Scotland. The kelpie may appear, with preternatural noises and lights, to warn those who are about to drown, or it may cause the deaths of unfortunate victims by dragging them to deep water.

Kelsey Bay (50°24'00" 125°58'00" S side of Johnstone Str, NW of Campbell R). Charles William Kelsey (1880–1953) came to BC from Washington state in 1906 and handlogged with his brother-in-law on the central coast, eventually pre-empting land at Topaze Hbr. He and his wife, Imogene, and their three daughters became Hardwicke I's first settlers in 1911. In 1922 the family moved to the mouth of the Salmon R, on what is now Kelsey Bay, and established a store, telegraph station and post office. The three Kelsey daughters, Lillian, Anna and Evelyn, all married sons of Sayward pioneer Hans Otto Sacht. William Kelsey sold his business to Herbert Smith in 1928 but remained in the area and ran a chicken farm. He died at Campbell R. The S terminus of the Prince Rupert ferry was located at Kelsey Bay from 1966 until 1979, when it was moved N to Port Hardy. *E*

Kemano Bay (53°29'00" 128°07'00" NE end of Barrie Reach, Gardner Canal, SE of Kitimat), **Kemano Beach** (On Kemano Bay), **Kemano River** (53°29'05" 128°07'35" Flows W into Kemano Bay). Kemano was an ancient village site of the Henaaksiala (Kitlope) people, who joined Kitamaat First Nation groups to live at Kitamaat Village (now Haisla) in 1953. The Henaaksiala return to this area each year to harvest eulachon, a small fish relished for its oil. The town of Kemano, which once serviced the powerhouse that provides hydroelectricity to Alcan's smelter at Kitimat, was located 12 km upstream. Water from the Nechako R, diverted W through a series of lakes and a 16-km tunnel,

Aerial view of Kemano Bay. *Harbour Publishing collection*

drives an enormous generating station there. The townsite was abandoned in 1999 and then destroyed when Alcan decided that the mostly automated powerhouse could be operated on a fly-in basis. *E*

Kendrick Inlet (49°42'00" 126°38'00" Between Strange I and SE Nootka I, W side of Vancouver I), **Kendrick Point** (52°12'00" 131°08'00" In Rose Inlet, S end of Moresby I, QCI). John Kendrick (1740–94) was a seasoned New England skipper who commanded the first US fur-trading expedition to the PNW in 1787 aboard the *Columbia Rediviva*. He and John Gray, capt of the smaller *Lady Washington*, arrived at Nootka Sd in 1788 and spent the winter there. In July 1789, after Gray had returned from a successful trading voyage to Haida Gwaii, Kendrick sent him back to Boston with the *Columbia* while he decided to try his luck in the QCI with the *Lady Washington*. Kendrick, unfortunately, was a bullying leader and an inept trader. He managed to insult and humiliate the powerful Haida First Nation chief Koya, turning him into an implacable enemy. After selling his furs in China, Kendrick returned to the QCI in 1791 and was attacked by Koya, an assault that was rebuffed with great loss of Haida life. After this defeat the vengeful Koya became a murderous renegade, inflicting a reign of terror on the region until he was killed by John Boit and the crew of the *Union* in 1795. Later in 1791, Kendrick bought tracts of land from Chief Maquinna, in Nootka Sd, and Chief Wickaninnish, in Clayoquot Sd, complete with signed, European-style deeds. In a curious incident, his son, also John, changed his name to Juan at Nootka and joined the Spanish navy, serving faithfully as an officer and pilot for many years. Kendrick made two more trips to the BC coast in 1793–94 before being killed in Hawaii when a British ship under Capt William Brown accidentally fired a salute with a loaded cannon. Kendrick Ck on Nootka I is also named for this irascible mariner. *D E W*

Kennecott Point (53°55'00" 133°09'00" S entrance to Peril Bay, W side of Graham I, QCI). The 143-m freighter *Kennecott* was carrying 5,500 tonnes of copper ore and 40,000 cases of salmon when it ran aground at Hunter Point, S of Rennell Sd, in 1923. It was en route from Cordova, Alaska, to Tacoma at the time, travelling in heavy fog under Capt John Johnson. The crew's initial distress call gave their position as Frederick I on Peril Bay, much farther N, and it was because of this confusion, according to retired hydrographic service members, that the name Kennecott Point was adopted at this location, in 1946, instead of where the ship was actually wrecked. The crew of the *Kennecott* made it safely to land, but the vessel proved unsalvageable and remained visible on Hunter Point for many years. It had been named for the historic Alaska mining town of Kennecott, built by the Kennecott Copper Co, which, in turn, was named after nearby Kennicott Glacier (but misspelled). Robert Kennicott (1835–66) was a US naturalist who accompanied, as scientist, the 1864 Western Union Telegraph Expedition in its unsuccessful attempt to establish an overland route across Alaska. The *Kennecott* was Capt Johnson's second wreck (he had also been skipper of the ill-fated *Ohio* in 1909; *see* Ohio Rk). He became so downcast on the return voyage to Victoria that he jumped from the rescue ship and drowned. Kennecott Point appeared on early Admiralty charts as Edward Point, a name chosen by Newton Chittenden in 1884. The Haida knew the feature as Tee-kwoon, after the adjacent village of Tee (or Susk, as it was more commonly referred to by non-Haidas). *D*

Kennedy Island (54°02'00" 130°11'00" Between Arthur Passage and Telegraph Passage, entrance to Skeena R), **Kennedy Point** (53°02'00" 132°20'00" S side of Security Inlet, NW side of Moresby I, QCI). Many historians, including Capt John Walbran in his *British Columbia Place Names*, have mistakenly stated that Kennedy I is named after Arthur Kennedy, third colonial gov of Vancouver I (*see* Kennedy R). The error dates back many years. In 1866, in fact, RN surveyor Lt Daniel Pender felt confident enough in this derivation to name two features on the island, Georgy Point and Elizabeth Peak, after the gov's two daughters. Then, in 1921, an eagle-eyed civil servant noted that Kennedy I appeared on maps as far back as 1862, before Kennedy had arrived on the scene, and thus could not be named for him. Further research determined that the name most likely commemorates Dr John Frederick Kennedy (1805–59), an HBC trader and surgeon who played many important roles for the company on the N coast. He was born at Cumberland House, son of HBC chief factor Alexander Kennedy and Aggathas, a Cree woman, and educated as a physician in Scotland. Kennedy joined the company in 1829 as a surgeon aboard the brig *Isabella*, then moved to Ft Vancouver and, from 1831 to 1839, to Ft Simpson, where he was surgeon and clerk. It was Kennedy's 1832 marriage to Sudaal (Fanny), a daughter of powerful Tsimshian chief Legaic (*see* Legeak Point), that enabled the advantageous relocation of Ft Simpson from Nass Bay to the Tsimpsean Peninsula in 1834. Kennedy was part of the HBC contingent that sailed on the *Dryad* to SE Alaska in 1834 to establish a fort on the Stikine R but was rebuffed by the Russians. He was later in charge at Fort McLoughlin on Campbell I (1839–40), Ft Durham at Taku Hbr, Alaska (1840–43), Ft Stikine (1848–49) and Ft Simpson (1849–52). From 1843 to 1848 he was second-in-command at Ft Simpson, under John Work, and attained the rank of chief trader in 1847. Kennedy visited Skidegate in 1852 to investigate trading opportunities in the QCI and retired from the HBC in 1856, the year he was elected to Vancouver I's colonial legislative assembly as the member representing Nanaimo (though his family estate, named Burnbrae, was close to Victoria).

Kennedy River (49°08'00" 125°40'00" Flows into Tofino Inlet through Kennedy Lk, Clayoquot Sd, W side of Vancouver I). Arthur Edward Kennedy (1810–83) was the third gov of the colony of Vancouver I in 1864–66. He had earlier served as gov of Sierra Leone and Western Australia. He developed a hearty dislike for this outpost of Empire and its residents—a feeling reciprocated by the colonists. In 1865, Kennedy purchased Cary Castle in Victoria (built by George Hunter Cary, first attorney gen of Vancouver I) as his residence; the castle burned down in 1899, as did its successor (in 1957), but a third building on the site is still the official residence of the Crown's representative in BC (now the lt gov) and is known today as Government House. When the colonies of Vancouver I and BC were united, in 1866, Kennedy lost his job to BC gov Frederick Seymour but went on to govern in W Africa (1867–72), Hong Kong (1872–77) and Queensland (1877–83)—and to be knighted (1868). Kennedy Lk and Kennedy Range, named by members of the 1864 Vancouver I Exploring Expedition, also commemorate him, as do Arthur I and Arthur Passage near Porcher I, and Mt Kennedy near Knight Inlet. *See also* Kennedy I, which many historians have incorrectly assumed was named after Gov Kennedy. *E W*

Kenneth Passage (50°57'00" 126°49'00" N side of Watson I, W entrance to Mackenzie Sd, N of Broughton I and E end of Queen Charlotte Str), **Kenneth Point** (N tip of Watson I). Kenneth McKenzie (1846–1906) came to Victoria from Scotland in 1853 with his parents aboard the *Norman Morison*. His father, also Kenneth McKenzie, was one of the earliest colonists on Vancouver I and managed the HBC's Craigflower Farm (*see* Mackenzie Sd; there is confusion over the spelling of this surname). Young Kenneth became a clerk with the Victoria mercantile firm Henderson & Burnaby in 1862, then was appointed clerk of Esquimalt naval yard in 1866 by Rear Adm Joseph Denman, cdr-in-chief of the Pacific Station. He remained in this position until 1905, when the base was transferred by the RN to Canada, and he also farmed at Lake Hill in Saanich with other family members.

Kent Bank (51°21'00" 128°04'00" SW of Rankin Shoals, Sea Otter Group, S of Calvert I, Queen Charlotte Sd). Named in 1947 after J C Kent, who was hired in 1945 as a surveyor aboard the W coast hydrographic vessel *William J Stewart*. Kent worked in Seymour Narrows in 1945, along the Inside Passage in 1946 and in Queen Charlotte Sd and Smith Sd in 1947, then resigned that year or early in 1948.

Kent Inlet (52°43'00" 129°00'00" E side of Laredo Channel, SW side of Princess Royal I), **Kent Point** (52°19'00" 128°21'00" N entrance to Port Blackney, W side of Don Peninsula, NW of Bella Bella). James Charles Comyn Kent (1831–1922) was born at London, England, came to BC in 1862 and joined the rush for Cariboo gold. He later opened an early hardware business in Victoria, then worked as bookkeeper for the hardware firm of Edgar Marvin. In 1888 he became treasurer of the city of Victoria and held that position for 22 years. Ellen Kent (1831–1918) came to Victoria in 1864 to join her husband and was a well-known musician in the city. Kent Inlet is named for James, Kent Point for Ellen.

Ker Island (48°40'00" 123°22'00" Off Tsehum Hbr and Sidney, NE end of Saanich Peninsula, N of Victoria). Victoria's David Russell Ker (1862–1923) joined Henry Brackman (*see* Brackman I) in 1882 to form the Brackman-Ker Milling Co. Their original gristmill was located at Tsehum Hbr, but in the 1890s the partners built a much larger one on Victoria Hbr and produced flour and a variety of animal feeds. Brackman died in 1903, but under Ker the business flourished, expanding throughout BC and Canada and eventually operating dozens of warehouses, mills and elevators. Ker married Laura Agnes Heisterman (1874–1937), daughter of pioneer librarian Henry Heisterman, in 1894 and became a leading citizen of Victoria, head of the Board of Trade and the Agricultural Society. He was the son of colonial official Robert Ker (b 1825), from Scotland, who served as BC's auditor gen until Confederation and froze to death on horseback during a terrible snowstorm in 1879. Ker I was formerly known as Shell I.

Kerouard Islands (51°55'00" 131°00'00" Off the S tip of Kunghit I, QCI). Named by Jean-François de Galaup, Comte de Lapérouse, after Georgette de Kerouartz, a French aristocrat and wife of Paul-Antoine-Marie Fleuriot de Langle. Lapérouse, aboard the *Boussole*, and de Langle, on the *Astrolabe*, were sent by France in 1785 to circumnavigate the globe and search for the NW Passage. They sailed along the BC coast the following year. De Langle was later murdered in Samoa, and both vessels were wrecked in the S Pacific. Kerouartz was also the niece of the Comte d'Hector, naval cdr at Brest, the port from which the expedition sailed, and Lapérouse gave the name Cap Hector to the feature that would later be known as Cape St James. The islands were also known as the Islas de Aves and the Ladrones by Spanish explorers, and they appear on other early charts as the Proctor Is. They were designated an ecological reserve in 1979 to protect large breeding colonies of murres, auklets and puffins. They are also home to BC's largest breeding population of Steller sea lions. *D*

Ker Point (50°23'00" 127°29'00" W side of Neroutsos Inlet, SE of Quatsino Sd, N Vancouver I). Frederick I Ker was manager of the Whalen Pulp & Paper Co mill at nearby Port Alice, 1919–20.

Kersey Point (53°47'00" 128°51'00" NE end of Maitland I, N of Hawkesbury I, Douglas Channel, S of Kitimat). H Maitland Kersey (b 1861), a native of Suffolk, England, was a member of the team led by Louis Coste, chief engineer of the federal Public Works dept, that made a survey of Kitimat Hbr in 1898. Capt John Walbran of CGS *Quadra* took Coste that year to the heads of several northern inlets to examine possible railway routes to the Yukon. Kersey was managing director of the Canadian Development Co, which owned steamships and roadhouses in the Yukon during the Klondike gold rush. In his long and colourful career he also served as managing director of Canadian Pacific Ocean Services, NY agent for the White Star shipping line and director of the Allan Line. Kersey fought in the Boer War with the rank of maj, ranched in Oregon, fished in Florida, journeyed down the Nile to "darkest Africa," sailed to the Galapagos Is and Cocos Is, and became deeply involved in international yacht racing and the America's Cup. He titled his autobiography *Over the Oceans for 600,000 Miles. W*

Kestrel Rock (54°13'00" 130°23'00" S of Digby I, just SW of Prince Rupert). CGS *Kestrel* was a small federal-government steamer especially designed for fisheries protection service on the BC coast. The 282-tonne, 38-m vessel—built in 1903 at False Ck, Vancouver, by Wallace Shipyards—sported Maxim and 5-pound guns. According to a newspaper report, "strength and utility were considered in her plans rather than beauty: hence the ram nose, the solid almost pugnacious bow, and the general bulldog appearance." The writer went on to extol the ship's gear, which included "Tyzack's triple grip patent anchors, Lord Kelvin's compass and barometers, two of Ritchie's patent compasses" and "Chadburn's tell-tale self-illuminating indicators." Kestrel Rk was named in 1906 by the Geographic Board of Canada after being discovered and reported by the *Kestrel*'s cdr.

Keswar Inlet (53°38'00" 130°19'00" W side of McCauley I, N of Banks I, S of Prince Rupert), **Keswar Point** (53°38'00" 130°21'00" At entrance to Keswar Inlet). Named in 1952 after a Gitxaala (Kitkatla) First Nation reserve at this location.

Ketchen Island (50°23'00" 127°27'00" W side of Neroutsos Inlet, S of Port Alice, N Vancouver I). According to BC's Geographical Names Office, this feature was named in 1927 after civil engineer W L Ketchen, superintendent of Port Alice Pulp & Paper Mills in 1925. There is a BC Archives death record for William Laird Ketchen, aged 60, at Vancouver in 1935. He married Agnes Mary Bladon (b 1873) at Montreal in 1902.

Kettle Inlet (52°41'00" 129°14'00" W side of Aristazabal I), **Kettle Rock** (53°35'00" 130°33'00" In approach to Griffith Hbr, W side of Banks I). Named in 1926 after A M Kettle, who returned from WWI military service to become 2nd engineer aboard the W coast survey vessel *Lillooet*.

Kettle Point (49°22'00" 123°17'00" Between Larsen Bay and Batchelor Cove, E side of Howe Sd, N of Vancouver and Horseshoe Bay). This name was suggested in 1929 by the municipality of W Vancouver in honour of Capt Henry Frank Kettle (1863–1947), who, along with his wife, Mary Jane (1865–1942), was in charge of the Vancouver pilot station at Caulfeild, 1909–20. He had a long history as a deep-sea sailor and was often accompanied on his travels by Mary Jane, whom he'd married in Bermuda. Kettle was especially proud of serving on the *Cutty Sark* as 2nd mate; he claimed to have rounded Cape Horn eight times and to have been in six wrecks. He died at Caulfeild after spending the latter part of his career working for the federal Dept of Fisheries and Marine as tide-gauge keeper for the Sandhead division.

Keyarka Cove (53°36'00" 130°21'00" NE side of Banks I). Named in 1952 after a Gitxaala (Kitkatla) First Nation reserve at this location.

Keyes Point (52°21'00" 127°55'00" E side of Roscoe Inlet, NE of Bella Bella). Lt Cdr Adrian St Vincent Keyes, a retired RN submariner, briefly commanded Canada's first submarine squadron, based at Esquimalt in 1914. Two 284-tonne subs, *CC1* and *CC2*, had been hastily bought from their US manufacturer—after being rejected by Chile, their intended owner—by BC premier Richard McBride, who worried that the W coast would come under attack by German warships. Overpriced and quite ineffectual, they were brought N from Seattle, transferred to Halifax in 1917 and scrapped after the war. Keyes had served on the RN's first submarines in 1903, eventually commanding several of them, as well as on the submarine tender *Onyx*. He was working at Toronto for a railway when directed to head W and take charge of Canada's new subs. He rejoined the RN during WWI and was later awarded the DSO at Gallipoli. Before Keyes left for England, the crew of *CC1* presented him with an engraved gold watch, now in the Vancouver Maritime Museum. Nearby Mt Keyes is also named for him.

Khutze Inlet (53°06'00" 128°29'00" E of Princess Royal I), **Khutze River** (53°05'20" 128°25'26" Flows W into Khutze Inlet). Much of the inlet was logged in the 1920s, and a copper mine, connected to the head of the inlet by a tramway, was active before 1910 and again in 1925–32. Several features around the inlet are named for mining company personnel (*see* Green Spit, Meldrum Point *and* Pardoe Point). At the mouth of the river a fertile, grassy estuary provides important habitat for grizzly bears.

Khutzeymateen Inlet (54°39'00" 130°04'00" Extends SE from Steamer Passage, entrance to Portland Inlet, N of Prince Rupert), **Khutzeymateen River** (54°37'00" 129°54'00" Flows W into Khutzeymateen Inlet). The name of the inlet, adopted in 1933, is an adaptation of *K'tzim-a-deen*, a Tsimshian First Nation phrase meaning "deep valley at the end of an inlet." In 1992 a 443-sq-km portion of the Khutzeymateen R valley and estuary was named Canada's first grizzly bear sanctuary, off-limits to hunting and logging. An additional 3,850-sq-km no-hunting zone surrounds the sanctuary but is not part of the park. In the early 2000s, discussions were being held about the possibility of expanding the no-hunting zone to 8,000 sq km. *E*

Kiddie Point (49°48'00" 124°38'00" NW tip of Texada I, Str of Georgia). Thomas A Kiddie was a New Jersey metallurgist hired about 1898 by the Van Anda Copper & Gold Co to supervise the company's Texada I mining and smelting operations. He built two smelters on Texada that ran intermittently, 1899–1919. Prior to his appointment, Kiddie had been assistant manager of the Orford Copper Co of NY. BC Ministry of Mines reports from 1902–3 describe him as manager of the smelter at Ladysmith owned by Tyee Copper Co of England, which operated mines at Mt Sicker on Vancouver I. In 1905 he apparently remodelled the Crofton smelter to process copper ore from the Britannia Mine at Howe Sd. In 1906 he was listed as working in Alaska, but in 1911 was back at Texada, demonstrating a new advance in oil-fired smelter furnaces. Capt George Vancouver named this feature Point Marshall in 1792. It was changed to Cohoe Point (a name still in local use) on a 1913 Admiralty chart, and Marshall Point was transferred to a promontory on the S side of Limekiln Bay. The current name was adopted in 1945.

Kiju Point (52°14'00" 131°06'00" S side of Carpenter Bay, SE Moresby I, QCI). Kiju, chosen by the hydrographic service in 1962, is a modification of the name of the former Haida village of Kaidju, once located 6 km to the E. Kaidju, or "Songs of Victory Village," was the favourite settlement of Chief Koya, the notorious renegade (*see* Kendrick Inlet *and* Koya Bay). When naturalist and ethnologist Charles Newcombe visited the site in 1903, he reported that there were still some old lodges and pole fragments remaining.

Kilbella Bay (51°42'00" 127°21'00" At NE end of Rivers Inlet), **Kilbella River** (51°43'00" 127°21'00" Flows W and S into Kilbella Bay). Kilbella means "long river" in the Oowekyala language, which is spoken by members of the Wuikinuxv or Oweekeno First Nation (the name of the adjacent Chuckwalla R, by comparison, means "short river"). The Wuikinuxv First Nation reserve at this location, however, is spelled Kiltala. This confusion over the spelling of First Nation names may explain why the cannery (and, later, the logging camp) located on this bay at the mouth of the river was named Kildala. Built in 1906 by George Dawson and Alfred Buttimer, with Dan Groves as manager, Kildala Cannery was sold in 1925 to the Canadian Fishing Co. It ceased canning in the 1940s but was used as a gillnet camp until 1960. The Kilbella and Chuckwalla rivers are home to famous races of giant chinook salmon.

Kildala Arm (53°51'00" 128°34'00" Extends E from Kitimat Arm, S of Kitimat), **Kildala River** (53°48'00" 128°28'00" Flows NW into the head of Kildala Arm). According to historians Philip and Helen Akrigg, this name comes from the Haisla First Nation word meaning "a long way ahead." Inconsistent spelling of First Nation names resulted in a cannery located on Kilbella Bay in Rivers Inlet also being named Kildala (*see above*).

Kildidt Narrows at maximum ebb. *James and Jennifer Hamilton*

Kildidt Inlet (51°54'00" 128°06'00" Between Kildidt Lagoon and Kildidt Narrows), **Kildidt Lagoon** (51°57'00" 128°06'00" N of Kildidt Sd, in centre of Hunter I), **Kildidt Narrows** (51°53'00" 128°07'00" Entrance to Kildidt Inlet), **Kildidt Sound** (51°50'00" 128°09'00" SW end of Hunter I, S of Bella Bella). From the Heiltsuk First Nation word meaning "long inlet" or "long way inland."

Kildonan (49°00'00" 125°00'00" On NE side of Uchucklesit Inlet, NE of Barkley Sd, SW of Port Alberni, Vancouver I). Uchucklesaht Cannery, built at this location by the Alberni Packing Co in 1903, was the first cannery on the W coast

K

of Vancouver I. It was bought by the Wallace Bros Packing Co in 1909 and renamed Kildonan after a village on the Isle of Arran, the homeland in Scotland of the company's owners, Peter and John Wallace. (Kildonan itself is named after St Donan, an Irish missionary who was supposedly buried in the village.) A cold-storage component was added to the cannery in 1913, and a pilchard reduction plant in 1925. The operation was sold to BC Fishing and Packing Co in 1926 and transferred to BC Packers in 1928. At its height, Kildonan was home to 300 people. Over the years, various initiatives were undertaken to keep the cannery going, such as the canning of pilchards, herring and albacore tuna, but it closed in 1946. The rest of the plant shut down about 1960 and was destroyed by fire in 1962, all except for the manager's house, which in the early 2000s was the heart of Kildonan Cannery Lodge, a fishing and ecotourism resort. Nearby Kildonan Lk is named after the cannery.

Kilmington Point (52°52'00" 131°49'00" SW tip of Louise I, E of Moresby I, QCI). Kilmington, Somerset, was the birthplace in 1824 of famed Canadian geologist Alfred R C Selwyn. The point was named by the hydrographic service in association with Selwyn Inlet (qv), just to the S, which in turn had been named by geologist George Mercer Dawson in 1878. Kilmington Point first appeared on charts in 1927.

Kiln Bay (52°58'00" 129°09'00" N end of Chapple Inlet, W side of Princess Royal I). This name is an error and should be Kihn Bay, as it commemorates US artist Wilfred Langdon Kihn (1898–1957), who was born at Brooklyn, NY, and lived in Connecticut. A visit to a Montana Blackfoot reservation at age 19 stirred a lifelong artistic passion in Kihn for documenting First Nation cultures. He journeyed widely to accomplish this goal, and in 1924 travelled to Prince Rupert and up the Skeena R at the behest of anthropologist Marius Barbeau in order to sketch the Gitksan poles and carvings at Gitanyow, near Hazelton. Kihn was particularly well known for his magazine and book illustrations and his highly representational portraits. Kiln Bay was one of several places named for artists in 1944. The name Unity Bay, after Unity Theodora Jeffreys Baile, a junior member of the Victoria hydrographic staff, had earlier been suggested for this feature but was rejected by Ottawa officials.

Kiltuish Inlet (53°22'00" 128°29'00" Extends S from Gardner Canal, between Alan Reach and Europa Reach, S of Kitimat), **Kiltuish River** (53°19'00" 128°28'00" Flows N into Kiltuish Inlet). According to historians Philip and Helen Akrigg, this name comes from a Haisla First Nation word meaning "a long, narrow stretch of water leading outward."

Kimsquit Bay (52°50'00" 126°59'00" E side of Dean Channel, just N of the mouth of Dean R, N of Bella Coola), **Kimsquit Narrows** (52°48'00" 126°59'00" Just S of Kimsquit Bay), **Kimsquit River** (52°53'00" 127°05'00" Flows E and S into the head of Dean Channel). The name comes from a Heiltsuk First Nation word meaning "place of the canyon people" (the canyon in question being on the lower Dean R, just E of its mouth). The Kimsquit are members of the Nuxalk First Nation and once occupied several villages in this remote area, including Nut'l, the main one, located at the mouth of the Dean. Their settlements were mostly abandoned by the 1920s. Kimsquit was the site of one of the last gunboat actions on the BC coast when, in 1877, HMS *Rocket*, under Lt Cdr Charles Harris, shelled and burned Nut'l village. Several of its residents had allegedly murdered the survivors of the wreck of the *George S Wright* in Queen Charlotte Sd in 1873—though this charge was never proven. Kimsquit Cannery was constructed by Robert Draney on the E side of Dean Channel in 1901 and later (1912–24) owned by Henry Doyle and R V Winch of Northern BC Fisheries. It was purchased by BC Packers Ltd in 1928, shut down in 1935 and dismantled in 1938. On the W side of the channel, Japanese fishermen settled and set up a sawmill. Manitou Cannery was built there in 1907 by George Dawson and Alfred Buttimer, and acquired in 1925 by the Canadian Fishing Co, which closed it shortly thereafter. The Kimsquit area was at one time considered a possible western terminus for the transcontinental railroad. It has been home to many logging operations over the years and is noted worldwide for its sport fishing, especially for steelhead. The Kimsquit R was formerly known as Chatsquot R (also spelled Tsatsquot, Chedsquit and Chadsquot); this name is kept alive on the Kimsquit's N arm, now Chatsquot Ck, while Chatsquot Mtn, the highest peak in the region, towers over Kimsquit Lk. Nearby Kimsquit Peak and Kimsquit Ridge are also named for this First Nation group. *E*

Kinahan Islands (54°12'40" 130°24'19" Chatham Sd, just S of Digby I and SW of Prince Rupert). Named in 1867 by Lt Daniel Pender after Richard George Kinahan (b 1837), 1st lt of HMS *Malacca*, who served on the BC coast in 1866–68, under Capt Radulphus Oldfield, and was based at Esquimalt. He was promoted to capt in 1877, and his commands included HMS *Orontes*, *Sapphire* and *Terror*. Kinahan achieved the rank of vice adm, retired, in 1898. There are four islands in the group: W Kinahan, E Kinahan, S Kinahan and Little Kinahan. An observation post was located there in WWII, part of the defence system for Prince Rupert Harbour.

Kincolith, Kincolith River. *See* Gingolx.

Kindakun Point (53°19'00" 132°45'00" N entrance to Kano Inlet, SW side of Graham I, QCI), **Kindakun Rock** (53°19'00" 132°48'00" Off Kindakun Point). The Haida name for the point was adopted in 1897 by naturalist

Dr Charles Newcombe. It can be a dangerous spot for mariners, surrounded as it is by rocks and strong cross-currents. During WWII Kindakun Point was the site of a lonely coast-watcher station—a primitive log cabin that was still visible in the 1970s.

Pictographs at head of Kingcome Inlet. *Andrew Scott*

Kingcome Inlet (50°55'00" 126°20'00" NE of the E end of Queen Charlotte Str, W of Knight Inlet). Rear Adm John Kingcome (d 1871), with HMS *Sutlej* as his flagship, was cdr-in-chief of the RN's Pacific Station, 1862–64. Earlier in his career he had commanded the troopships *Belleisle* (1841–46) and *Simoom* (1853). Kingcome Inlet—and nearby Sutlej Channel, Belleisle Sd and Simoom Sd—were all named by surveyor Lt Daniel Pender about 1864 to honour the region's chief military officer. The *Sutlej* carried the cdr-in-chief to N Bentinck Arm in 1864 in pursuit of the killers of several white settlers, an incident associated with the so-called Chilcotin War, which was prompted by the massacre of 14 roadbuilders at the head of Bute Inlet. Kingcome went on to become a knight in 1865 and an adm, retired, in 1869. Nearby Kingcome Glacier and Kingcome Range are also named for him, as is the **Kingcome River** (50°56'00" 126°12'00" Flows S into the head of Kingcome Inlet). The fertile delta of this river was settled in 1895 by the brothers William and Ernest Halliday, who established a remote cattle ranch there (*see* Halliday I). The Charles Ck Cannery, owned by William Hickey of the Preston Packing Co, operated on Kingcome Inlet, 1914–33. A Kwakwaka'wakw First Nation village, home to the Tsawataineuk people, is located a few km up the river; known as Kingcome and also as Quaee (or Gwa'yi), it was the setting for the 1967 novel *I Heard the Owl Call My Name*, by Margaret Craven. *E W*

Kingcome Point (53°18'00" 128°54'00" Fraser Reach, NE end of Princess Royal I). Merchant mariner William Kingcome (b 1834), from Plymouth, was a nephew of Rear Adm John Kingcome, cdr-in-chief of the Pacific Station

(*see* Kingcome Inlet). He served aboard the HBC barque *Princess Royal*, under Capt John Trivett, as 2nd mate (1857–58) and 1st mate (1858–61), and was then appointed capt (1861–64) of this supply vessel, which sailed back and forth between London and Victoria. Princess Royal I was not named after the barque, however, but for the much earlier fur-trading sloop of Charles Duncan. Coast historian John Walbran speculated that Kingcome Point and nearby Trivett Point were likely applied in this vicinity (by Lt Daniel Pender, about 1866–67) because the name of the HBC vessel was the same as that of the island. *W*

King Cove (52°18'00" 128°24'00" W side of Cecilia I, Milbanke Sd). Named for Harriet Nice Holmes, who married Capt Edward Hammond King in England in 1854. The couple came to Victoria in 1859 with their children, but Edward, who published some of BC's earliest newspapers, was killed in a hunting accident in 1861 (*see* Edward King I). Harriet then married Thomas Lett Stahlschmidt (1833–88), a merchant, in 1863 and had three more children with him. Stahlschmidt was administrator of trade licences in the BC colonial government in 1866 and in 1871 represented BC at an immigration conference in Ottawa. In 1876 he moved with his family to London, where he continued to work as a merchant and also acted as BC's agent gen.

King Edward Bay (49°22'00" 123°25'00" W side of Bowen I, Howe Sd, NW of Vancouver). Named by James Frederic Malkin (1864–1950), who purchased land adjacent to this bay in 1910, the year that Edward VII died. Malkin was "a great imperialist," according to Bowen I historian Irene Howard, one of three English brothers who immigrated to Vancouver in the 1890s and founded the wholesale grocery business W H Malkin & Co. William Malkin, the middle brother, was mayor of Vancouver in 1929–30. Malkin family members built and enjoyed a number of fine summer homes on Bowen over the years and incorporated their holdings as King Edward Bay Estates. Several other features in BC are named after this member of the British royal family, including King Edward Lk in the Okanagan, and Mt King Edward and King Edward Peak in the Rockies.

King Island (52°15'00" 127°35'00" Between Dean Channel and Burke Channel, E of Bella Bella), **King Passage** (49°38'00" 126°23'00" Muchalat Inlet, S of Gore I, Nootka Sd, W side of Vancouver I). Capt George Vancouver named King's I in 1793 after a particular RN friend of his, James King (1750–84). The two had served together on Capt James Cook's third great expedition, 1776–80. King was born in Lancashire and entered the navy at age 12, not at all unusual in that era. He became acquainted with Cook off the Nfld coast and in 1776 was appointed 2nd lt on HMS *Resolution*. After Cook's death in Hawaii in 1779, he was promoted to 1st lt of the *Resolution*, and when Cdr

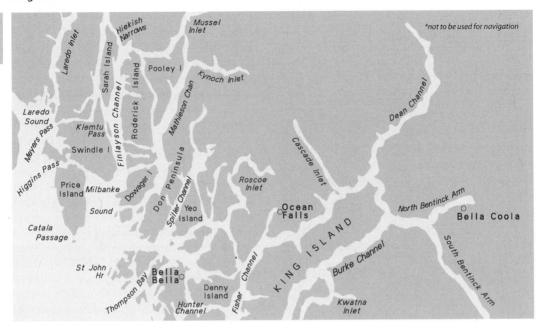

Central coast. *Reproduced with the permission of the Canadian Hydrographic Service*

Charles Clerke died later that year, he assumed command of HMS *Discovery*, the expedition's consort vessel, where Vancouver was a midshipman. King was named a capt in 1780 and the following year took HMS *Resistance* on convoy duty to the W Indies. He returned to England in ill health, however, and helped prepare the journals of Cook's third voyage for publication. He was made a fellow of the Royal Society in 1782 and died at Nice. A number of features on the BC coast (Clitheroe I, Dean Channel and Raphoe Point) are named for King's clergyman father, Rev James King. King I—mountainous, uninhabited and heavily logged—is BC's seventh largest at 824 sq km. It is home to Codville Lagoon Marine Provincial Park, named after early settler James Codville, who homesteaded in the 1890s at nearby Evans Inlet. Edward King I (qv), in Barkley Sd, was also originally named King I. *E W*

King Islets (50°10'00" 125°09'00" S end of Hoskyn Channel, between Quadra I and Read I, N end of Str of Georgia). Staff Cdr John William King (d 1882) was a naval assistant in the Admiralty hydrographic office, 1856–66. He had served on the China Station aboard HMS *Modeste* and *Wellesley* during the First Opium War, 1840–42, and was master of HMS *Vernon* at the River Plate in 1846. King compiled several editions of the *China Pilot* and *English Channel Pilot*. When Capt George Richards was appointed the RN's chief hydrographer in 1864, he turned the BC coastal survey over to his deputy, Lt Daniel Pender, and returned to the UK. Pender celebrated his boss's promotion by naming a number of geographic features in the vicinity of Read I after UK-based members of the hydrographic dept. *W*

Kingscote Point (52°05'00" 128°18'00" NW tip of Piddington I, entrance to Raymond Passage, SW of Bella Bella). Lt Cdr Robert Pringle Kingscote was born in Australia in 1884 and joined the RN, where he commanded a torpedo boat in 1906 and was listed as a lt on HMS *Drake* in 1908. He married Violet Anderton Greenwood (b 1897) in London, UK, in 1916, and they divorced in 1927. Kingscote apparently retired from the RN and immigrated to Canada before WWII but re-enlisted with the RCN. He appears in records as being temporarily in charge of Esquimalt's HMCS *Naden* barracks in 1942 and as an RN Admiralty representative on the Pacific Coast in 1944, when this feature was named.

Kingsley Point (52°07'00" 128°18'00" S end of Horsfall I, SW end of Raymond Passage, W of Bella Bella). This name was adopted in 1944 to honour Cdr Harry Kingsley (c 1900–1976), an RCN officer who spent much time on the BC coast. In the early years of WWII he was in command of HMCS *St Croix* (1940–41) and HMCS *Skeena* (1941–42). Both these destroyers came to unhappy ends later in the war (and under different cdrs): the *St Croix* was sunk by a U-boat in 1943 with the eventual loss of 146 men; the *Skeena* was wrecked off Iceland in a storm in 1944. In 1941, Kingsley and his crew rescued 34 survivors from the torpedoed Dutch merchant vessel *Tuva*.

Kingsway Rock (52°52'00" 131°40'00" Off Haswell I and SE end of Louise I, E of Moresby I, QCI). The 230-tonne, 41-m steam fishing trawler *Kingsway* was built in England in 1906 and brought to BC three years later by flamboyant German financier Alvo von Alvensleben, head of Pacific Coast Fisheries. The company built an unsuccessful fish-processing plant at Pacofi Bay (qv) on Moresby I and soon went bankrupt. The *Kingsway* was later sold to the Canadian Fishing Co as a halibut boat. In 1934 the Vancouver Tug Co renamed the vessel *La Pointe*, installed a diesel engine and ran it as a tug. *D*

Kinsman Inlet (51°56'00" 128°08'00" W side of Hunter I, E of McNaughton Group, S of Bella Bella), **Kinsman Lagoon** (51°54'40" 128°09'45" S extension of Kinsman Inlet). William Burnley Kinsman (b 1910), from Vancouver, was a coxswain on the W coast survey vessel *William J Stewart* in the 1930s. He joined the RCN in WWII and served as a lt aboard HMCS *Trentonian*, a corvette that was torpedoed by a U-boat in 1945. Kinsman was mentioned in dispatches for "conduct of the highest order" during the sinking, organizing crew members to abandon ship and picking up survivors in the ship's whaler.

Kintail Point (52°12'00" 128°11'00" NW tip of Campbell I, NE end of Raymond Passage, NW of Bella Bella). After Lt Gen Francis Humberston Mackenzie, 1st Lord Seaforth, Baron Mackenzie of Kintail. *See* Seaforth Channel.

Kiokathli Inlet (53°41'00" 132°59'00" SW side of Port Louis, W side of Graham I, QCI). A modification of the Haida name for Port Louis, with *kathli* meaning "open bay." Some early maps show this name spelled Kyokathli or Kai Qa-ti. In his *British Columbia Place Names*, Capt John Walbran claims that Kiokathli Inlet was formerly named Port Ingraham, after the early US fur trader Joseph Ingraham, but Ingraham's own journal, published in 1971, indicates that Port Ingraham was the feature now known as Nesto Inlet (qv).

Kipling Island (51°57'00" 127°54'00" Off SW end of King I, Fisher Channel, SE of Bella Bella). Charles Kipling, from London, England, joined the HBC's maritime service in 1830 as capt of the barque *Ganymede*, replacing the "intemperate" and "deranged" Capt L J Hayne, who, while returning from Ft Vancouver to England, sailed his vessel to Hobart, Tasmania, instead. (Chief factor John McLoughlin wrote that "Capt Hayne is so much addicted to Liquor I conceive it would be hazarding the safety of the Vessel to give him charge of her.") McLoughlin's opinion of Kipling was not much better. After a couple of trips with the *Ganymede* between London and the Columbia R, Kipling took the schooner *Vancouver* to northern BC in 1832 and badly damaged it running aground in Portland Canal. The chief factor blamed the accident on the skipper's incompetence. Kipling remained with the company until 1836, however, in command of the brig *Dryad*. In 1833 the *Dryad* and the *Lama* brought materials and stores from Ft Vancouver to Campbell I on the central BC coast for the building of Ft McLoughlin. In 1836, Kipling made a report to senior HBC staff about the "Sitka affair" of 1834, when Russian officials prevented the company from establishing a new post on the Stikine R.

Kipp Islet (52°29'00" 128°47'00" Off NW Price I, W entrance to Higgins Passage, Laredo Sd). Isaac Kipp (1839–1921) was born at Burford, Ont, and went to California in search of gold in 1858, followed by his brother Henry Kipp (1842–1930). The Cariboo gold rush lured them N in 1862, but they ended up in Yale, working for a cousin, Jonathan Reece, who operated a butcher shop there. Isaac also served as a police constable at Hope in the early 1860s. After helping Reece graze cattle on the Fraser Valley grasslands before moving them to Yale for slaughter, he pre-empted land in 1862 that would later become part of downtown Chilliwack. The Kipp brothers and Reece were soon running the largest farm in the region. In 1865, Isaac married Mary Ann Nelums (1839–1931), who was the first nurse and midwife in the Fraser Valley E of New Westminster and said to be the first white woman to live in the Chilliwack area. Their eldest daughter, Jenny Kipp, was the first pioneer child born there. Isaac donated land for the Chilliwack Methodist Church and became a leader in the emerging community.

Kirby Rock (49°01'00" 125°19'00" W end of Pipestem Inlet, S of Refuge I, Barkley Sd, W side of Vancouver I). R B Kirby received a Crown grant of land at the N entrance to Pipestem Inlet in 1892.

Kirkland Island (49°07'00" 123°06'00" In the estuary of the main arm of the Fraser R, between Ladner and Lulu I). Edgar Frank Kirkland (1861–1927) came to BC from Ont as a youth and married Elizabeth Watson (1864–1924) at New Westminster in 1884. He bought this island in 1902 with his brother-in-law, John Robert Watson, diking it and turning it into a dairy farm. All the milk had to be taken by boat to the mainland for sale. In 1894, before Kirkland arrived, a plant to process salmon offal had been built there in an attempt to clean up surrounding waters, which were polluted by waste from the area's numerous canneries. Kirkland I gradually merged with Rose I, immediately to the W; both were later owned by forest-industry baron H R MacMillan, who used them as private duck-shooting preserves. They were transferred to another hunting group, the Kirkland I Waterfowl Society, in the mid-1960s and eventually purchased in 1990 for $1.6 million by the Pacific Estuary Conservation Program, which transferred them to the Nature Trust of BC for protection as bird habitat. The former owners were allowed to hunt there until 2010; in return they paid for a caretaker and arranged for crops to be planted purely as bird food.

Kirshaw Islets (49°10'30" 125°47'04" Off E side of Meares I, entrance to Mosquito Hbr, Clayoquot Sd, W side of Vancouver I). This name is a misspelled tribute to William Kershaw, who received a Crown grant of land on Schooner Cove in 1894 and an additional grant in the Clayoquot area in 1914. Information on this pioneer is scanty; a William Kershaw is listed in the 1892 Victoria directory

K

as a "coal passer" on the steamship *Islander*, and there are several references to him in the Victoria *Colonist* as a "mining man" on the W coast of Vancouver I, 1898–1900. The 1903 annual report of BC's Ministry of Mines notes W Kershaw as a resident of Clayoquot and co-owner, with W H Porter, of the Poet mining claims on the Elk R. There is a 1951 death record for William Kershaw, aged 80, at Saanich. Kirshaw Its were formerly known as Double Its; the name was changed in 1934.

Kisameet Bay (51°58'00" 127°53'00" SW side of King I, E side of Fisher Channel, SE of Bella Bella), **Kisameet Islands** (In Kisameet Bay). Named in 1946, along with nearby Kisameet Lk, after an important Heiltsuk First Nation reserve and former village site at this location. In 2003 the 32-m, US-owned pocket cruise ship *Safari Spirit* ran aground in this popular but rocky anchorage and later sank. There were no injuries, though the $3-million vessel, when salvaged, was found to be a total write-off. A body of fine-grained clay on the N side of the bay has long been known to the Heiltsuk people and used for medicinal purposes. In the 1940s and '50s the deposit was partly excavated and sold as a natural pharmaceutical product and cosmetic under the trade names Absorvite and Dermavite.

Kitasu Bay (52°32'00" 128°45'00" W side of Swindle I, E side of Laredo Sd, NW of Bella Bella). Named for the Kitasoo First Nation, whose members originally lived in the region around this bay. The Kitasoo belong to the Tsimshian linguistic and cultural family. They joined together with the Xai'xais (Xixis, Haihais) people, who are members of the Heiltsuk First Nation and originally occupied the Kynoch Inlet area, to settle at Klemtu (qv) in the 1870s. The name comes from the Tsimshian word *gidestsu*, from *git-* (meaning "people of") and *disdzuu*, which refers to the large, tiered depression of a traditional dwelling place. Kitasoo is sometimes spelled Kittizoo in older documents. Nearby Kitasoo Ck, Kitasoo Lk and Kitasu Hill are also named for this First Nation group.

Kitching Point (51°05'00" 127°31'00" NE end of Slingsby Channel, NW side of Queen Charlotte Str, SE of Cape Caution). Ordinary Telegraphist Stuart Templeton Kitching, of Victoria, was killed in action on Apr 30, 1941, aged 20. He was serving aboard the RCN troopship *Nerissa*, which was torpedoed and sunk by a U-boat off the coast of Ireland while transporting Canadian troops and civilians to England. More than 200 lives were lost in the tragedy. The 5,064-tonne *Nerissa* was a Red Cross Line passenger and cargo steamer, built in 1926 for service between NY and Nfld. It was later sold to the Furness Withy Group and ran between NY, Bermuda and the W Indies. Stuart Kitching's name is inscribed on the Halifax Memorial.

Kitimat, site of an aluminum smelter, was founded in the early 1950s.
Sam Beebe/Ecotrust

Kitimat (54°03'10" 128°39'00" Head of Kitimat Arm, S of Terrace), **Kitimat Arm** (53°55'00" 128°42'00" NE extension of Douglas Channel), **Kitimat River** (54°00'00" 128°40'00" Flows S into head of Kitimat Arm). Kitamaat (or Gitamaat) is a Tsimshian name meaning "people of the snow" and refers to the First Nation inhabitants of the Kitimat R valley, which does indeed experience a heavy snowfall. According to anthropologist Jay Powell, the Kitamaat people descend from the legendary Hantlhikwilas, who paddled to this region from Rivers Inlet long ago. He dared to approach the mouth of the Kitimat R, where a monster's presence had long thwarted human settlement, and discovered that the monster was, in fact, a vast flock of gulls attracted by countless eulachon. The landing, rising and circling of the birds had been mistaken for a huge mouth opening and closing. The newcomers stayed and prospered. White missionaries and settlers arrived in the 1880s and '90s, and the GTP laid out a townsite about 1906 but then chose Prince Rupert as the western terminus for its railroad instead. The Aluminum Co of Canada selected the mouth of the river as the site for a smelter in 1950, and the modern city of Kitimat arose. It also became home to a pulp and paper mill and a methanol and ammonia plant. The Kitamaat people settled on the NE side of Kitimat Arm and were joined there about 1948 by the Henaaksiala (or Kitlope) people from Gardner Canal. Their village was called Kitamaat (or Kitimat) Mission. The Kitamaat and Henaaksiala groups are now known as the Haisla First Nation, and the official name of their community is Haisla, though it is still regularly referred to as Kitamaat (or Kitimat) Village. The nearby Kitimat Ranges are also named after this First Nation group. *E W*

Kitkatla (53°48'00" 130°26'00" On N side of Dolphin I, Browning Entrance, S of Porcher I and Prince Rupert), **Kitkatla Channel** (53°49'00" 130°28'00" Between Dolphin I and Porcher I), **Kitkatla Inlet** (53°55'00" 130°36'00" NW extension of Kitkatla Channel), **Kitkatla Islands** (53°48'00" 130°21'00" NE of Dolphin I). Kitkatla is the anglicized form of a Tsimshian term that can be translated as "people of the salt" or "those who live by the sea." The Gitxaala (or Giktxaala) First Nation, who are believed, about 1787, to have been the first members of the Tsimshian cultural group to make contact with European visitors, were often referred to in the fur-trading era as the Sebassa, after the hereditary name of a prominent chief. Kitkatla village, also known as Lach Klan, is one of the oldest continuously inhabited communities on the BC coast; its population in the early 2000s was about 450, and commercial fishing was the primary livelihood. Nearby Kitkatla Ck is named for this First Nation as well. *W*

Kitkiata Inlet (53°38'00" 129°17'00" W side of Douglas Channel, SW of Kitimat). This Tsimshian word means "people of the cane." The Gitga'at (Kitka'ata) First Nation, whose members are part of the Tsimshian cultural family, trace their origins to Damelahamid, a legendary homeland at the head of the Skeena R. When a vast flood destroyed that town, the Gitga'at moved to the Douglas Channel area on the coast, symbolically taking possession of this territory when their chief placed his ceremonial staff (or cane) in the ground—hence the name. The main Gitga'at village of Laxgal'tsap (Old Town) was located beside Kitkiata Inlet, and a large number of petroglyphs can still be seen there. The inlet's residents moved to William Duncan's "model Christian village" of Metlakatla in the 1860s and '70s, but when Duncan and his followers left for Alaska in 1887, a small number of Gitga'at returned to Douglas Channel and established a new community at Hartley Bay, a location they knew as Txalgiu, which was closer to the transportation routes of coastal ships than Laxgal'tsap. Nearby Kitkiata Ck and Kitkiata Lk are also named after this First Nation group. *W*

Kitlope Anchorage (53°15'18" 127°54'39" Head of Gardner Canal, SE of Kitimat), **Kitlope River** (53°15'00"

The Kitlope River lies at the heart of the world's largest remaining temperate rain forest. *Greg Shea*

127°52'00" Flows N into head of Gardner Canal). Kitlope (sometimes spelled Gitlope or Kitlup) is a Tsimshian name meaning "people of the rocks." The original inhabitants of the Kitlope R watershed called themselves the Henaaksiala; their descendants moved to Haisla (or Kitimat Village) about 1948 and amalgamated with the Kitamaat people to become the Haisla First Nation. The Kitlope watershed is the world's largest remaining intact temperate coastal rain forest; in a historic agreement between industrial, First Nation and government interests in 1995, almost 3,200 sq km of the valley were protected as Kitlope Heritage Conservancy. The nearby Kitlope Range and Kitlope Lk are also named for this First Nation group. *E*

Kitsault (55°28'00" 129°29'00" At SE head of Alice Arm, NE of Observatory Inlet, SE of Stewart), **Kitsault River** (55°29'00" 129°28'00" Flows S into the head of Alice Arm). Kitsault (or Gits'oohl), meaning "inside, in behind," was the name of the Nisga'a village and reserve at the head of Alice Arm and refers to the location of the site in relation to the main Nisga'a homeland in the Nass valley. *See* Alice Arm for details of the early mining history of the Kitsault R valley. In the late 1960s, interest in the region rebounded, this time for its molybdenum resources. BC Molybdenum Ltd was active on the E side of Alice Arm, 1967–72, but ceased production when the price for this metal, used mainly as a hardener in alloys, fell. In 1979, Phelps Dodge Ltd started mining again on a larger scale and built a complete town, named Kitsault, across the inlet from the mostly derelict village of Alice Arm, which had been the jumping-off point for all previous mining booms. The instant community, complete with hospital, shopping centre, theatre and indoor swimming pool, had a peak population of several hundred but was abandoned in the early 1980s when molybdenum prices plummeted again. In 2005 the townsite was sold to US entrepreneur Krishnan Suthanthiran, who spoke at that time of his desire to redevelop it as a recreational resort. Kitsault Glacier and Kitsault Lk, N of Kitsault, also derive their names from this First Nation word, which has been spelled many ways over the years, including Kitzault, Kitzaulte, Gitzault, Chigitsoult and Kitsaulte.

Kitsilano Beach (49°17'00" 123°09'00" S side of English Bay, Vancouver), **Kitsilano Point** (Just NE of Kitsilano Beach). Greer's Beach was the former name for this well-loved segment of Vancouver waterfront, which was the site of several early logging camps, 1868–86. Samuel Greer (1843–1925) settled there with his family in 1884. He claimed to own the land and was busy selling lots, much to the outrage of the CPR, which also claimed it. Railroad officials placed notices in Vancouver newspapers warning people not to buy from Greer; a furious Greer shot and wounded a deputy sheriff sent to evict him; and in 1891, chief justice Sir Mathew Baillie Begbie sent the excitable

Chief Khahtsahlano and family at Kitsilano Beach, 1907. *CVA 1376-203*

Irishman to jail, calling him a liar and a forger. From such rough-and-tumble beginnings, the neighbourhood of Kitsilano grew. The name of the beach was changed about 1905, apparently at the request of the CPR, which wished to develop a new subdivision there. Vancouver postmaster Jonathan Miller asked anthropologist Charles Hill-Tout for ideas; Hill-Tout suggested Kitsilano, after a Skxwúmish (Squamish) First Nation chief who moved to Stanley Park, just E of Prospect Point, around 1860. The chief's name was, more properly, Khahtsahlanough, meaning "man of the lakes," but Hill-Tout changed it so that it would correspond to Capilano on the opposite side of Burrard Inlet. (Many spelling variations have been noted for this name, including Quat-si-la-noq, Haatsalano, Khahtsalanough, etc.) Chief August Jack Khahtsahlano (1879–1967), who supplied important information about early Vancouver to historians and archivists, was the chief's grandson. Kitsilano Beach was dedicated as a park in 1909. The Skxwúmish First Nation name for the beach's headland was Skwayoos, meaning "face."

Kitson Island (54°11'00" 130°19'00" Off NW Smith I, Chatham Sd, S of Prince Rupert), **Kitson Islet** (Off NE side of Kitson I). Royal Marines Lt George Andrew Noble Kitson (1845–1927), from Woolwich, Kent, served on the Pacific Station in 1866–67 aboard HMS *Malacca*, under Capt Radulphus Oldfield. He retired in 1869, was appointed to the Exchequer's Office of Pleas in England and married Mary Luskey Paull at London in 1874. Lt Daniel Pender named many features in this vicinity in 1867 after the *Malacca*'s officers. Twenty-ha Kitson I is BC's northernmost marine park.

Kitson Point (53°02'00" 131°47'00" N side of Louise I, E of Moresby I, QCI). Jonathan Kitson moved to the QCI in 1905 and built one of the first homes at Queen Charlotte City about 1909. His son John attended the community's original school. The following year Jonathan obtained land on NE Moresby I and became a pioneer farmer

and rancher at Sandspit. There is a 1949 death record for Jonathan Kitson, aged 88, at N Vancouver. *D*

Kittyhawk Group (51°49'53" 128°11'09" W side of Kildidt Sd, off SW end of Hunter I, S of Bella Bella). In 1944 a number of islands in the vicinity of Queens Sd were named after WWII aircraft (*see* Hurricane I for more details). The Kittyhawk was the name given to later variations of the US-made Curtiss P-40 single-engine fighter. Almost 14,000 P-40s were built, 1938–44. The plane was rarely used in NW Europe due to its inferior performance against German fighters in high-altitude combat, but it played critical roles with Allied air forces in China, the Mediterranean, SW Asia, eastern Europe and the SW Pacific, where it was known as the Flying Tiger.

Klaquaek Channel (51°28'00" 127°41'00" Between Penrose I and Ripon I, Rivers Inlet). According to BC historians Helen and Philip Akrigg, when Rivers Inlet was re-surveyed in the late 1930s, a number of names were bestowed to honour the family of Methodist medical missionary Dr George Darby, who operated a summer hospital on the inlet for many years while based at Bella Bella. Klaquaek was a Heiltsuk First Nation nickname given to Katherine Darby, George's daughter. It was also the name of the mission's medical launch, a 9-m craft built on the inlet and sold in 1931.

Klashwun Point (54°09'00" 132°40'00" N side of Graham I, W of Virago Sd, QCI). Klashwun was the name given by the Haida First Nation to a prominent hill and landmark just W of Yatza (Ya-tze) village, also known locally as Little Mtn. Klashwun Point, originally named by George M Dawson in 1878 as Klas-kwun Point, is just N of the hill. Spanish naval officer Jacinto Caamaño named this feature Punta de Pantoja, after Juan Pantoja y Arriaga, his chief pilot, when he explored the region in 1792.

Klaskish Anchorage (50°14'00" 127°46'00" S side of Klaskish Inlet, SE of McDougal I), **Klaskish Basin** (50°15'35" 127°43'30" Head of Klaskish Inlet), **Klaskish**

Inlet (50°15'00" 127°46'00" N side of Brooks Peninsula, NW side of Vancouver I). The name may mean "ocean beach" in Kwakwala, the language of the Kwakwaka'wakw First Nation. The inlet was mistakenly shown as Port Brooks on an Admiralty chart of 1849, and this error was perpetuated by later historians. The original Port Brooks, however, was Nasparti Inlet on the S side of Brooks Peninsula, so named by early fur-trader James Colnett in 1787 (*see* Brooks Bay). The Klaskish R, which flows SW into Klaskish Inlet, takes its name from the inlet. The river valley, home to an untouched old-growth forest until 1997, has been heavily logged by Interfor; the river estuary is an ecological reserve and also a Gwat'sinuxw (Quatsino) First Nation reserve. Capt George Richards named Klaskish Inlet in 1862 while surveying the region. *W*

Klekane Inlet (53°12'30" 128°39'52" Extends N from Fraser Reach, E of Princess Royal I, just NE of Butedale, S of Kitimat), **Klekane Island** (53°10'00" 128°38'00" Just E of Work I, at junction of Fraser Reach and Graham Reach), **Klekane River** (53°14'47" 128°41'10" Flows S into Klekane Inlet). Klekane derives from the Haisla First Nation name for the inlet, T'liqana, meaning "muddy place." The inlet and river appear as place names in the 1930 gazetteer; the name for the island was adopted in 1950.

The old boardwalk at Klemtu, since dismantled. *Andrew Scott*

Klemtu (52°35'00" 128°31'00" E side of Swindle I, Finlayson Channel, NW of Bella Bella), **Klemtu Anchorage** (in Klemtu Passage), **Klemtu Passage** (Between Swindle I and Cone I), **Klemtu Point** (W side of Klemtu Passage). The fishing community of Klemtu was founded about 1875 by two First Nation groups: the Kitasoo, a Tsimshian people whose traditional territory lay around Laredo Sd, and the Xai'xais (Xixis, Haihais), who are members of the Heiltsuk First Nation and originally occupied the Kynoch Inlet area. Klemtu was chosen as a village site for its proximity to coastal shipping routes; in the early days, residents supplied fuelwood to steamers for a livelihood. Later, from 1927 to 1969, Klemtu Cannery was the main employer. Klemtu had a population of about 400 in the early 2000s and was originally called China Hat, after the unmistakable shape of neighbouring Cone I. Local people found this name repugnant, though, and it was changed

in 1902. According to BC historians Philip and Helen Akrigg, Klemtu may be a Tsimshian word meaning "to anchor" or "to tie something." Klemtu Ck enters the ocean at Klemtu. *E*

Kliktsoatli Harbour (52°09'00" 128°05'00" NW side of Denny I, at Bella Bella). This Heiltsuk First Nation name was adopted in 1925 and means "a large object inside on the water," possibly referring to a rock or island. The community here, part of Bella Bella, is also known as Shearwater.

Kloiya Bay (54°15'00" 130°12'00" S of Denise Inlet, E of Kaien I, just SE of Prince Rupert), **Kloiya River** (54°15'00" 130°11'00" Flows NW into Kloiya Bay). A Tsimshian First Nation correspondent informed BC coastal historian Capt John Walbran in 1909 that Kloiya could be translated as "a place to hide valuables." Kloiya Bay, she explained, was quite remote and off the beaten track; it provided a handy location for stowing treasured items before heading to the fishing grounds on the Skeena R. The names were spelled Cloyah and Coloyah on early charts.

Kloo Rock (52°35'00" 131°21'00" Off the N tip of Ramsay I, SE of Lyell I, E of Moresby I, QCI). This word is taken from George Mercer Dawson's Haida vocabulary, co-authored by William Fraser Tolmie and published in 1884 as *Comparative Vocabularies of the Indian Tribes of BC*. The name, which means "canoe" in the Skidegate dialect of the Haida language, was adopted by the hydrographic service in 1962.

Klue Passage (52°45'00" 131°36'00" Between Tanu I and Kunga I, E of central Moresby I, QCI), **Klue Point** (SE tip of Tanu I). Klue was the hereditary name of the town chief of Tanu, a figure of sufficient importance that this historic Eagle crest village was often simply referred to as Klue's. The name has a wealth of early spellings—Kloo, Klew, Cloo, Clew, Clough, Kliew—but is usually expressed in modern form as Xe-u or Xhyuu. It means "southeast wind" in the Haida language. Fur trader Joseph Ingraham mentions a chief of this name in 1791, as does mining engineer Francis Poole in the 1860s. The Chief Klue (c 1840–1903) known to George Mercer Dawson in 1878 had just inherited his title the year before; he was a well-known storyteller and poet as well as one of the most senior and powerful leaders in Haida Gwaii. *D*

Klunkwoi Bay (52°43'00" 131°49'00" NW side of Darwin Sd, E side of central Moresby I, QCI), **Klunkwoi Rocks** (52°44'00" 131°48'00" Entrance to Klunkwoi Bay). The name, given by George Mercer Dawson in 1878, is an adaptation of the Haida term for the bay. The town of Lockeport was built on its shores in 1908, and the area became the centre of an intense but short-lived copper-mining boom from 1908 to about 1920. *D*

K

Knapp Island (48°41'57" 123°23'58" SE of Piers I, off NE tip of Saanich Peninsula, N of Victoria). Kempster Malcolm Knapp (d 1875) was an instructor aboard HMS *America*, under Capt John Gordon, on the Pacific Station, 1845–46. He became an instructor at Portsmouth on the RN cadet training ship *Illustrious* in 1857 and moved to HMS *Britannia* in 1859 when that vessel replaced the *Illustrious*. Knapp was the *Britannia*'s chief naval instructor, 1871–75. Knapp I was named in 1858 by RN surveyor Capt George Richards. It was also known locally in the old days as Mosquito I. Joseph Quadros, a native of the Azores, pre-empted the 16-ha property (along with neighbouring Pym I) in 1889 and received a Crown grant for it the following year. Quadros had applied to become a British subject in 1881; he married a First Nation woman, Catherine Quotlunes, in 1886. Subsequent owners included legendary Hollywood film director Victor Fleming and Texas multi-millionaire Guy Waggoner, who built a luxurious home and a small but active boatyard on the island. Entrepreneur Andrew Evans and his wife, Ann, a Shinto priestess, purchased Knapp in 1995 and constructed a Shinto shrine and elaborate dojo (practice space for martial arts) there. *W*

Knarston Rock (52°43'00" 129°22'00" NE of Moore Is, off NW side of Aristazabal I). James Sinclair Knarston (1854–1923) came to BC from England in 1887 with his Scottish wife, Robina (b 1864), and daughter, Helen, and was later harbourmaster at Nanaimo. He is listed as a clerk at Nanaimo in the 1898 BC voters list and a bookkeeper in the 1901 census. Knarston Ck at Lantzville, near Nanaimo, is also named for him.

Knight Inlet (50°47'00" 125°38'00" Between Bute Inlet and Kingcome Inlet, NW of Campbell R). This major fjord, one of the longest in BC at 113 km, burrows into the heart of the Coast Mtns and is surrounded at its head by high snowfields and glaciers. It was surveyed in 1792, during Capt George Vancouver's PNW expedition, by Lt William Broughton, cdr of HMS *Chatham*. He named it after John Knight (c 1748–1831), son of a rear adm, who joined the RN at a very tender age to sail with his father. Knight was promoted to lt in 1770. He and Broughton, at that time a midshipman, both served on HMS *Falcon* in 1776 and were taken prisoner off the E coast of N America during the US War of Independence. Knight became flag capt to Lord Hood on the Mediterranean Station in 1793. During the mutiny of the Channel fleet he commanded HMS *Montagu* and later took part in the Battle of Camperdown with that vessel. He was cdr-in-chief at Gibraltar in 1805, made an adm in 1813 and knighted in 1815. On 18th-century Spanish charts, Knight Inlet was called Brazo de Vernaci, after Juan Vernaci, 1st lt of the *Mexicana* on the Dionisio Alcalá-Galiano expedition, who also explored this feature in 1792. The former logging camp at Glendale Cove, once site of a cannery (1915–50) and, since 1995, home to a resort that specializes in grizzly bear viewing, is often called Knight Inlet. A post office with that name operated there, 1919–49. *E W*

Knight Island (51°00'00" 127°32'00" One of the Southgate Group, NW side of Queen Charlotte Str, N of Port Hardy), **Knight Range** (52°46'00" 129°13'00" N end of Aristazabal I). Lt John Harry Knight (1881–1958) was an RN surveyor on the BC coast aboard HMS *Egeria*, under Cdr John F Parry, in the early 1900s and joined the Canadian Hydrographic Service in 1911. He was senior assistant to Lt Cdr Philip Musgrave on the BC coastal survey in 1913, aboard CGS *Lillooet*, and cdr of CGS *Naden* in 1914, after which he joined the RCN at Esquimalt and served briefly as cdr of HMCS *Rainbow*, the RCN's first warship, in 1917. After WWI, Knight was in charge of various Pacific survey vessels, 1920–38, including CGS *Restless*, *Somass*, *Pender* and *William J Stewart*. He developed a very extensive knowledge of the BC coast, working in Queen Charlotte Sd, Laredo Sd, Rivers Inlet, around Vancouver I and elsewhere, before retiring in 1943. Knight married Laura Rita Nisbet (1888–1978) at Oak Bay in 1925. He died at Saanich.

Knocker Islet (49°15'00" 125°56'00" N end of Hecate Bay, NW of Meares I, Clayoquot Sd, W side of Vancouver I). Malcolm D Knocker pre-empted land on Esowista Peninsula near Tofino in 1896 and received a Crown grant there in 1912.

Knox Bay, Knox Point. *See* Cape Knox.

Koeye Point (51°46'00" 127°53'00" E side of Fitz Hugh Sd, opposite Nalau I, SE of Bella Bella), **Koeye River** (Flows W into Fitz Hugh Sd just N of Koeye Point). This Heiltsuk First Nation term is believed to mean "bird sitting on the water." The 18,750-ha Koeye Conservancy, an intact old-growth rainforest watershed with some of BC's most productive salmon and grizzly bear habitat, represents an important aspect of the lands protected by the historic 2006 central coast land-use decision. The Koeye people, a branch of the Heiltsuk, formerly occupied several village sites on this river. A Heiltsuk-owned ecotourism lodge is

The *Island Roamer* sailing north in Knight Inlet. *Andrew Scott*

now located at its mouth. About 1.5 km upstream are the remains of a limestone quarry, which operated 1935–67. The nearby Koeye Range and Koeye Lk are named after the river. *E*

Koga Islet (52°25'00" 131°23'00" Off NW Burnaby I, S of Huxley I, E of S Moresby I, QCI). Named in 1962 by the hydrographic service after the Koga people, members of the Haida First Nation, who originally owned a village on Cumshewa Inlet. The Koga were unlucky, however. Historian Kathleen Dalzell tells the story of their gambling misfortune, where the entire village, after losing their homes and all their property to gamblers from Skedans, offered themselves as the stake. They lost once again, and thus became the property—slaves, effectively—of the Skedans players.

Kogangas Rock (52°37'00" 131°31'00" Entrance to Sedgwick Bay, S of Lyell I, E of Moresby I, QCI). The Kogangas people were the Sea Otter tribe of the Haida Raven crest. Their main village was near Skidegate, though they also owned other villages farther N on the E coast of Graham I. The Haida First Nation word for sea otter is *quu* (sometimes spelled koh or kou). *D*

Kohl Island (52°48'00" 128°46'00" W side of Laredo Inlet, off SW Princess Royal I). William Kohl (d 1893), of Pennsylvania Dutch heritage, was an early W coast ship owner and fur trader with extensive interests in Alaska. He came out for the California gold rush and stayed to operate steamers on the San Francisco–Sacramento run. In the 1860s, Kohl and his family lived at Victoria, but in the 1870s he bought a large property at San Mateo, California—now that city's Central Park and arboretum (Kohl's house later became the first home of San Mateo Junior College). One of his early vessels was the 160-tonne *Fideliter*, built as a steel-hulled sailing ship for a Russian firm. It was fitted with a steam engine at Victoria in 1862 and operated mainly to Portland, carrying cargo and Her Majesty's mails. In 1865 the *Fideliter* was struck by the sternwheeler *Alexandra* in one of the first sea disasters in the Victoria area. Both vessels sank but were later raised and rebuilt. Kohl was a principal of Hutchinson, Kohl & Co (later the Alaska Commercial Co), of San Francisco, which bought the assets of the Russian-American Co when Alaska was sold to the US in 1867. One of those assets was the 230-tonne *Politkofsky* (better known as the *Polly*), a Russian gunboat built at Sitka in 1863. The Victoria *Colonist* called the *Polly* "one of the most magnificent specimens of homemade marine architecture we have yet beheld. She looks as if she had been thrown together after dark by an Indian ship carpenter, with stone tools." Kohl overhauled this sidewheeler at Victoria and took it to San Francisco. The *Polly*'s whistle was brought to Seattle in 1909 and used to open the Alaska-Yukon-Pacific Exposition.

Koksilah (48°46'00" 123°41'00" On the Koksilah R, just W of its mouth), **Koksilah River** (48°45'00" 123°39'00" Flows E and N into Cowichan Bay, E side of Vancouver I). The meaning of this Halkomelem name is uncertain, and numerous interpretations have been proposed over the decades. One persistent derivation is "place of snags"; another refers to a corral of some type. The name is presumably an ancient one, however, as the Koksilah people are one of the seven tribes that make up the Cowichan (Quw'utsun') First Nation. The logging and farming community of Koksilah got its start as a station on the E&N. Nearby Koksilah Ridge is named after the river.

Kolb Island (48°40'51" 123°23'57" Just E of the NE end of Saanich Peninsula, W of Page Passage, N of Victoria). Named by local residents in 1965 after former owners of the island.

Konishi Bay (49°20'00" 123°22'00" SE end of Bowen I, Howe Sd, NW of Vancouver). Konishi was a Japanese houseboy for the Cowan family, which owned a substantial amount of land in this vicinity (*see* Point Cowan). He was the caretaker of the property and a favourite with the Cowan children. The feature was named in 1907 by family members, who rowed along the S coastline of Bowen that year and gave names to all the coves and bays.

Kon Tiki Island (50°02'00" 127°22'00" N entrance to Kyuquot Sd, just E of Walters I). This name was adopted in 1984 after being proposed by Kaare Halvorsen, the island's owner. He was apparently associated with the 1947 expedition in which Thor Heyerdahl and a crew of five men sailed a raft from S America to French Polynesia. The name of the raft was the *Kon-Tiki*, one of the ancient names of the Incan sun god Viracocha. Heyerdahl also gave the name Kon Tiki to the tiny islet off Raroia, in the Tuamotu Archipelago, where he eventually washed up after his 101-day, 7,000-km journey.

Kooh Rock (48°54'00" 125°04'00" SE side of Tsartus I, W side of Trevor Channel, NE Barkley Sd, W side of Vancouver I). Kooh is the Nuu-chah-nulth First Nation word for ice, according to *Some Account of the Tahkart Language*, an 1868 work by Rev C Knipe. Formerly known as Fog Rk.

Kooryet Bay (53°20'00" 129°54'00" Principe Channel, E side of Banks I), **Kooryet Island** (53°21'00" 129°52'00" In Kooryet Bay). The names were adopted in 1950 from the Gitxaala (Kitkatla) First Nation reserve at this location. Nearby Kooryet Ck (an important salmon stream) and Kooryet Lk (where some gold exploration work was done in the 1980s) also take their names from this reserve.

Kootenay Inlet (52°51'00" 132°11'00" NW side of Moresby I, NW of Tasu Sd, QCI), **Kootenay Point** (52°50'00"

132°16'00" Just S of Kootenay Inlet). The name is an adaptation of the traditional Haida term for the inlet and was adopted in 1946. It has no connection with the Kootenay region of SE BC. A Haida village was located at the head of Kootenay Inlet, and a trail ran from there to the head of Newcombe Inlet on Tasu Sd. The Hydah gold mine, first developed by George Chapman in 1913, was located on the inlet's NE shore. The claims, also known by the names Kootenay, Rupert and Blue Mule, were worked from time to time into the 1930s but proved unprofitable. *D*

Koprino Harbour (50°30'00" 127°51'00" N side of Quatsino Sd, NW end of Vancouver I), **Koprino River** (50°31'00" 127°51'00" Flows S into Koprino Hbr). The Koprino were a Kwakwaka'wakw First Nation and used to have their principal village in this area. They amalgamated with the Koskimo people sometime prior to George Mercer Dawson's 1878 visit and moved to Hwates (Xwatis or Quattishe), E of today's village of Quatsino. According to Dawson, the Koprino (Giopino or Gopinuxw) had formerly lived farther W, at Forward Hbr, but were driven from that area by the Gwat'sinuxw (Quatsino) First Nation many years ago. The Canadian Fishing Co built a cannery and pilchard reduction plant at Koprino Hbr in the 1920s but it was a short-lived operation.

Koskimo Bay (50°28'00" 127°53'00" SW side of Quatsino Sd, NW end of Vancouver I), **Koskimo Islands** (50°28'00" 127°51'00" E side of Koskimo Bay). According to anthropologist Wilson Duff, Koskimo means "people of Kosaa" and refers to a site on the N coast of Vancouver I, at the mouth of the Stranby R, where this group once lived. The Koskimo (known today as the Gusgimukw) are an important branch of the Kwakwaka'wakw First Nation; their traditional territories were to the S and E of Quatsino Sd and their main village was on Koskimo Bay. In 1929 they amalgamated with the Gwat'sinuxw (Quatsino) people and moved to live at Hwates (Xwatis or Quattishe), just E of the current community of Quatsino. In the 1970s they moved again, to New Quatsino, near Coal Hbr. Koskimo Ck also takes its name from this First Nation group. Wallace Fisheries Ltd built its Quatsino Cannery on Koskimo Bay in 1911 and later added a pilchard reduction plant; the operation was sold to BC Packers in 1928 and closed down in 1931.

Kostan Inlet (52°35'00" 131°42'00" S of Bigsby Inlet, SW Darwin Sd, E side of Moresby I, QCI), **Kostan Point** (52°35'00" 131°40'00" S entrance to Kostan Inlet). These names, after the Haida word for crab, were adopted by the hydrographic service in 1962.

Koutz Rock (53°41'00" 132°20'00" Just N of Richards I and Juskatla Narrows, Masset Inlet, Graham I, QCI). The name of this feature was adopted by the hydrographic service in 1953, after one of the slaves of Albert Edward

Edensaw, Haida chief of the Sta'stas Eagle crest. In the mid-1870s, Anglican missionary William Collison supposedly cured Koutz of a serious illness after local medicine men had failed to do so, thus lessening their influence over the chiefs and speeding the conversion of many Haida to Christianity. The incident is not mentioned, however, in Collison's 1915 memoir, *In the Wake of the War Canoe*.

Koya Bay (52°13'00" 131°04'00" S side of Carpenter Bay, SE end of Moresby I, QCI), **Koya Point** (52°11'00" 131°01'00" SE end of Moresby I, N of E entrance to Houston Stewart Channel). Koya (or Koyah) was the most important Haida chief in the southern QCI in the late 18th century, when the first fur traders arrived. He was family chief of all the Raven crest villages in the region. Koya was notorious for his warlike disposition, though his early dealings with George Dixon and Charles Duncan in 1787–88 and with John Gray in 1789 were amicable. Later in 1789, however, Boston capt John Kendrick seized Koya because of petty thefts aboard his vessel and mortally insulted him by cutting his hair, placing his legs in cannon barrels and threatening to fire. Kendrick returned to the QCI in 1791, and his vessel was stormed by Koya and his warriors; though almost overcome at first, the American crew managed to regain the upper hand and repel their adversaries, slaughtering a great number of them. Koya sought to avenge his disgrace and regain his princely status by attacking numerous trading ships around Moresby I until killed by John Boit and the crew of the *Union* in 1795. *D E*

Koya's Strait. *See* Houston Stewart Channel.

Krone Island (53°36'00" 130°33'00" In Griffith Hbr, off NW end of Banks I). Anton Oscar Krone (1874–1960) was a fireman aboard the W coast survey vessel *Lillooet* in the 1920s. He served overseas in WWI and on his return married Harriett Delaney (1886–1961) at Victoria in 1919. The name was adopted in 1926.

Kulleet Bay (49°01'00" 123°46'00" On Stuart Channel, just N of Ladysmith Hbr, SE side of Vancouver I). Kulleet, an anglicized form of *k̓elits'*, is a modification of the name of the original inhabitants of the area, who are members of the Chemainus First Nation and part of the Hul'qumi'num (Central Coast Salish) cultural group. The word means "sheltered area" or "protected bay" in the Island Halkomelem dialect, and the area around the bay, rich in herring and shellfish, is still a major reserve for the Chemainus people. Old versions of the name include Kulleets, Kulees and Kuleets. Before 1895 this bay appeared on Admiralty charts as Chemainus Bay, so named by Capt George Richards on his 1859 survey, after the important Hul'qumi'num winter village located there, named Shts'emines (Chemainus). Today's Chemainus Bay, farther S, was formerly known as Horseshoe Bay. It was renamed, also in 1895, because of its proximity to the logging community of Chemainus (qv), which developed in the 1860s. *W*

Kul Rocks (52°44'00" 131°36'00" Entrance to Richardson Inlet, N of Lyell I, E of Moresby I, QCI). Named by the hydrographic service in 1957 after the Haida word for mussel, as listed in George M Dawson's Haida vocabulary.

Kultah Point (50°33'00" 127°33'00" At NE entrance to Quatsino Narrows, Rupert Inlet, Quatsino Sd, N end of Vancouver I). The point was named in 1927 after a reserve at this location belonging to the Gwat'sinuxw (Quatsino) people, who are members of the Kwakwaka'wakw First Nation.

Kultus Cove (50°29'00" 127°37'00" S side of Quatsino Sd, S of Drake I, N end of Vancouver I). *Kultus* (or *cultus*) is a Chinook jargon word for "worthless" or "good for nothing." In its broadest sense it simply means "bad." (Chinook was a W coast lingua franca used by First Nation groups and early traders and settlers.) Many other BC features get their names from this word, including three creeks, two lakes, Cultus Sd and the Fraser Valley community of Cultus Lk. Kultus Cove, adopted in 1927, may be so named because it is a poor anchorage, exposed and shoal-ridden, and was frequently used as a booming ground for logs.

Kumdis Bay (53°42'00" 132°09'00" E side of Masset Inlet, Graham I, QCI), **Kumdis Island** (53°45'00" 132°10'00" At S entrance to Masset Sd), **Kumdis Slough** (53°44'00" 132°09'00" Separates E side of Kumdis I from Graham I). According to QCI historian Kathleen Dalzell, Kumdis is a modification of the island's Haida name, which means "island with long points at the mouth of the channel." It is also spelled Cumdis, Cundis and Kundis on early maps. In 1884, Newton Chittenden called it Cub I, confusing its name with that of a small island just to the W that the Haida had long used for camping and growing potatoes, and this error carried through onto some 20th-century maps. Early settler Freeman Tingley established his Pioneer Ranch at the N end of the island in 1906; in the 1930s, Kumdis was the centre of the Baxter Pole Co's logging operations. Part of Kumdis Slough dries at low tide and is known locally as the Divide. Nearby Kumdis Cr and Kumdis Lk take their names from the island. *D*

Kumeon Bay (54°42'00" 130°14'00" SE side of Steamer Passage, E of Portland Inlet, N of Prince Rupert). The Kumeon Cannery was built here in 1918 by Northern BC Fisheries Ltd to process pink and coho salmon. The operation was closed in 1921; in the mid-1920s it was leased and then purchased by the Canadian Fishing Co.

Kunakun Point (53°28'00" 132°54'00" NW entrance to Rennell Sd, W side of Graham I, QCI). The name, adopted in 1946, is an adaptation of the Haida First Nation term for

this feature. According to Haida legends, a powerful ocean spirit lived under the point.

Kunechin Islets (49°37'00" 123°48'00" Just S of Kunechin Point), **Kunechin Point** (49°38'00" 123°48'00" N entrance to Salmon Inlet, E side of Sechelt Inlet, NW of Vancouver). The Kunechin (also spelled Xénichen, Hunechin and Hunaechin) people are one of the four main groups that comprise the Sechelt First Nation. Their name has been translated as "going as far as possible," probably a reference to the location of their principal village, situated at the very head of Jervis Inlet. They had no particular connection with these geographic features, which were named in recent years by the hydrographic service. An artificial reef was created off Kunechin Point in 1992 when a decommissioned destroyer, HMCS *Chaudière*, was sunk there as a tourist attraction for sport divers. Both the point and the islets are part of Sechelt Inlets Marine Provincial Park.

Kunechin Islets in Sechelt Inlet. *Andrew Scott*

Kunga Island (52°46'00" 131°34'00" E of Tanu I and S of Louise I, E of Moresby I, QCI). The Haida First Nation name for this steep-sided, fossil-studded island was confirmed by pioneering geologist George Mercer Dawson, who visited it in July 1878 and described it as possessing "a very good section" of "dark argillites and flaggy limestones."

Kunghit Island (52°06'00" 131°05'00" SE of Moresby I, QCI). Kunghit is a modification of the ancient Haida First Nation name for the very S end of the QCI and may mean "to the south." In 1853, when Houston Stewart Channel was surveyed by the officers of HMS *Virago*, George Inskip, the ship's master, named the island after Cdr James Prevost, the ship's capt. At some point the Geographic Board of Canada became aware that one of BC's Gulf Is already commemorates Prevost, and in 1904 the old Haida name was restored to this feature. The name Kingsett I, which appears on one of Joseph Ingraham's charts from 1791–92, is thought to be an erroneous transcription of Kunghit. Many places on this island are named either for crew members of the *Columbia Rediviva*, which visited the area in 1791–92 under Capt John Gray, or for whalers associated with the station at Rose Hbr, which operated on Kunghit's N shore, 1910–43. *D*

Kunlana Point (53°58'00" 132°40'00" SW side of Naden Hbr, N end of Graham I, QCI). This name was adopted in 1948 for the ancient Raven crest village site of Kuu-lana or Kunla'na, which was located, according to ethnologist Charles Newcombe, just W of the point, on the E side of the mouth of Stanley Ck.

Kuper Inlet, Kuper Island. *See* Cape Kuper.

Kusgwai Passage (54°12'00" 133°01'00" Between Cox I and Langara I, Cloak Bay, off NW end of Graham I, QCI). Kusgwai, or Kattssequeye, was the original Haida name for Langara I. This narrow, shallow waterway was formerly known as Boat Passage, but that name was widely duplicated so the hydrographic service changed it in 1949.

Kutcous Islets (49°15'00" 126°04'30" Just SE of Kutcous Point), **Kutcous Point** (49°15'00" 126°05'00" SE tip of Flores I, Clayoquot Sd, W side of Vancouver I). Named after a reserve at this location of the Ahousaht First Nation, a member of the Nuu-chah-nulth Tribal Council. The Wild Side Heritage Trail runs past the point, and according to Stanley Sam Sr, the Ahousaht author of the trail guidebook, the name Kutcous (or Katkwuuwis) means to "cut people's heads off." It refers to a long, early 19th-century war in which the Ahousaht eventually triumphed over their neighbours, the Otsosaht First Nation, and acquired their territory on Flores I. Kutcous Point, where the Ahousaht chased down and destroyed an Otsosaht raiding party, became an important site to the victors for fishing, sealing and, especially, whaling. The name of the point was formerly spelled Cut Coast Point.

Kvarno Island (48°58'00" 125°35'00" Head of Ucluelet Inlet, near NW entrance to Barkley Sd, W side of Vancouver I). John Hartwick Kvarno (1867–1944) was born in Norway and immigrated to the US with his parents. In the early 1890s he and fellow Norwegian August Lyche (*see* Lyche I) made a trip to the W coast to look for land they could settle on and farm. While Ucluelet Inlet could hardly be described as ideal for farming, local storekeeper and trader William Spring persuaded them to stay and pre-empt property there. Kvarno did manage to farm at Ucluelet and also served as the area's provincial police constable. He married Mary Ann Lilly E Stewart (who lived to 103, dying at Victoria in 1979) at Ucluelet in 1926. Thirty-ha Kvarno I (also known locally as Staple I) was sold in the early 2000s, rezoned and readied for residential development.

Kwaikans Island (53°43'00" 132°24'00" Off NW side of Masset Inlet, Graham I, QCI). Named in 1878 by George

Mercer Dawson, who modified a Haida term meaning "big rocky island" and applied it to this feature. Around WWI it appeared on some maps as Watson I, and was known as Reject I in the 1920s (a name still in local use), as logs that were unwanted by the nearby Buckley Cove sawmill, which only cut spruce, were stored there in a cove on the island's SE side (known locally as Reject Bay). *D*

Kwakiutl Point (50°21'00" 127°59'00" S entrance to Quatsino Sd, NW end of Vancouver I). Kwakiutl, an obsolete but widely used term, was introduced by anthropologist Franz Boas in 1887 as the name for the Kwakwaka'wakw First Nation, whose members inhabit N Vancouver I and adjacent shores and speak the Kwakwala language. Many variant spellings of this name exist, especially Kwagiulth. The Kwakwaka'wakw confederacy had 28 tribes when Europeans first encountered it; by the early 2000s, due to amalgamations, extinctions and the abandonment of traditional villages, that number had shrunk to about 15. The original Kwakiutl people are the four related tribes that moved to live beside the HBC post of Ft Rupert, SE of Port Hardy, after it was built in 1849. Because white visitors and settlers interacted mainly with this group, its name became associated with all Kwakwala speakers. Kwakiutl Ck on Campbell I near Bella Bella is in the traditional territory of the Heiltsuk First Nation. The origin of the word is uncertain. *E*

Kwalate Point (50°47'00" 125°39'00" W side of Knight Inlet, opposite Glacier Bay). This Kwakwala name, adopted in 1950, means "place of the salmonberry sprouts." The fresh young sprouts of salmonberry plants were a favourite spring salad food for BC's First Nation groups. Recent geological and archeological evidence has revealed that the ancient village of Kwalate, at the mouth of nearby Kwalate Ck, home to the Da'naxda'xw people, was destroyed in the late 16th century by a tsunami caused by a gigantic avalanche on the opposite side of the inlet. Kwalate Ck is one of BC's most productive salmon streams.

Kwomais Point (49°01'00" 122°52'00" SE side of Boundary Bay, just W of White Rk, SE of Vancouver). The name was adopted in 1946 and apparently means "dog face" in the Halkomelem language, according to BC historians Philip and Helen Akrigg. This part of Surrey, known today as Ocean Park (qv), was developed in the early 1900s as a Methodist church camp and retirement community. The camp's proprietors preferred to translate the name of the point as "a place of vision." The Semiahmoo First Nation, they claimed, used the site for spiritual renewal and also for watching out for approaching enemy war canoes. Camp Kwomais, one of the oldest church camps in BC, was purchased from the United Church for $20 million by the city of Surrey in 2007. It is now a 5.6-ha park.

Kwoon Cove (52°38'00" 131°56'00" W side of Moresby I, S of Sunday Inlet, QCI). The hydrographic service adopted this name in 1964, taking it from *Comparative Vocabularies of the Indian Tribes of BC*, published in 1884 by William Fraser Tolmie and George Mercer Dawson, where *kwoon* is listed as the Haida word for whalebone.

Kwuna Point (53°13'00" 131°59'00" N entrance to Alliford Bay, SE side of Skidegate Inlet, N side of Moresby I, QCI). This feature was originally named Alliford Point, in association with Alliford Bay, by regional hydrographer Philip Musgrave in the 1910s. A much older name, applied by Capt Thomas Sinclair of the HBC, who made a sketch map of Skidegate Inlet in 1832, was Point James. Musgrave's successor, Henri Parizeau, fearing that Alliford might be confused with two other N coast points—Alfred and Alford—changed the name to Kwuna in 1945. Its meaning is not known. Ethnologist Charles Newcombe labelled this feature Ku'nt'alas on one of his maps. *D*

Kwun Point (52°46'00" 131°46'00" NW tip of Richardson I, between W end of Tanu I and Lyell I, E of Moresby I, QCI). The hydrographic service applied this name in 1957, taking it from the Haida vocabulary that appeared as an appendix to George Mercer Dawson's *Report of Progress for 1878–79*, published by the Geological Survey of Canada. It means "nose."

Kye Bay (49°43'00" 124°53'00" N side of Cape Lazo, just NE of Comox Hbr, E side of Vancouver I). Several explanations have been proposed for this name. Kye may be a word of unknown meaning from Pentlatch, the Northern Coast Salish language, now extinct, of those who used to live in this vicinity. Then again, it may be the Scottish Gaelic word for cattle, courtesy of an early settler in the area.

Kyen Point (48°57'00" 125°12'00" NW end of Imperial Eagle Channel, Barkley Sd, W side of Vancouver I). A Nuu-chah-nulth word meaning "crow," according to *Scenes and Studies of Savage Life*, an 1868 work by Gilbert Sproat, which includes a Nootkan vocabulary. *Ka'in* or *kaa'in* is a more contemporary transliteration of this word. Formerly known as Green Point.

Kynoch Inlet (52°45'00" 128°00'00" Extends E from N end of Mathieson Channel, N of Bella Bella), **Kynoch Point** (52°45'00" 128°07'00" S entrance to Kynoch Inlet). Kynoch Inlet was the original homeland of the Xai'xais (Xixis, Haihais) people, who were members of the Heiltsuk First Nation. They moved to Klemtu about 1875 and joined with the Kitasoo, a Tsimshian group whose traditional territory lay around Laredo Sd. Klemtu was chosen as a village site for its proximity to coastal shipping routes. Kynoch Inlet, noted for its waterfalls and a healthy population of grizzly bears, is a protected area, part of the 91,000-ha Fiordland Conservancy.

Kynumpt Harbour (52°12'00" 128°10'00" N end of Campbell I, S side of Seaforth Channel, just NW of Bella Bella). Lt Daniel Pender named this feature in 1867 after a Heiltsuk First Nation chief who once lived in the vicinity. The harbour was a traditional summer camp, used by the Heiltsuk for gathering berries and harvesting potatoes. HBC fur trader William Tolmie, who was stationed at nearby Fort McLoughlin from 1833 to 1836, referred to the harbour in his journal as Active's Cove. It was also known as Strom Bay for many years—and is still known locally by that name—after a family of early settlers (*see* Strom Cove). A short trail leads to Norman Morison Bay on Raymond Passage.

Aboard the *Uchuck III* in Kyuquot Sound. *Andrew Scott*

Kyuquot (50°02'00" 127°22'00" On Walters I, N of Nicolaye Channel, N entrance to Kyuquot Sd), **Kyuquot Bay** (49°59'00" 127°18'00" SW side of Union I, mouth of Kyuquot Sd), **Kyuquot Channel** (49°59'00" 127°15'00" SE of Union I), **Kyuquot Hill** (49°58'56" 127°16'41" S end of Union I), **Kyuquot Sound** (50°04'00" 127°13'00" SE of Checleset Bay, NW side of Vancouver I). Named after the Nuu-chah-nulth First Nation inhabitants of Kyuquot Sd, who originally consisted of four separate tribes, each with its own winter village, and gathered each summer at Aktis I (formerly known as Village I). Kyuquot has been translated as "different people" or "foreign people" and appears to be a name applied by Nuu-chah-nulth groups to the S. The name was written many different ways in the old days, including Caiyuquat and Cayuquet; today the preferred spelling is Ka:'yu:'K't'h. The Ka:'yu:'K't'h people amalgamated in the 1950s and '60s with the Checleset (Che:K'tles7et'h), who originally occupied territory farther NW, and moved with them in the 1970s to Houpsitas, located on Vancouver I just NE of Aktis I, close to the fishing village and commercial centre of Walters I (qv). The modern community of Kyuquot is quite spread out and generally refers to Houpsitas, Walters I and several other small inhabited islands. *E W*

L

Labouchere Channel (52°24'00" 127°14'00" Connects Dean Channel to Burke Channel, NE of King I, W of Bella Coola), **Labouchere Passage** (50°48'00" 127°03'00" N side of Queen Charlotte Str, S of Drury Inlet, N of Port McNeill), **Labouchere Point** (52°21'00" 127°11'00" NE of King I, Labouchere Channel). The paddle steamer *Labouchere* was constructed of teak and Baltic oak for the HBC at Sunderland, England, in 1858 and brought out to Victoria by Capt John Trivett the following year. Styled in the tradition of the clipper ships, the handsome 62-m, 620-tonne vessel was barque-rigged, with two funnels and 10 guns. Before running aground and then sinking in deep water N of San Francisco in 1866, the *Labouchere* made numerous trading voyages to the N Pacific coast and was commanded by a series of senior HBC capts, including John Swanson and William Mouat. During an 1862 trip to Alaska under Capt Swanson, the ship was seized briefly by Tlingit warriors at Hoonah in a dispute over the price of a sea otter skin. It was named after Henry du Pré Labouchère (1798–1869), British colonial secretary in 1855–58 and later Baron Taunton. Labouchère was a wealthy merchant and prominent Liberal politician who also served as president of the British board of trade (1839–41, 1847–52) and chief secretary for Ireland (1846–47). More than 20 years earlier, while vice-president of the board of trade, he had presided over the launch of the HBC's historic *Beaver*. W

La Croix Group (49°09'00" 126°00'00" SW of Vargas I, Clayoquot Sd, W side of Vancouver I). George Wilfrid La Croix, born in 1909 at Tisdale, Sask, joined the Canadian Hydrographic Service as a junior engineer aboard CGS *Lillooet* in 1931. He ran the tidal section, in Victoria, from 1940 to 1953, doing surveys for the RCN in the war years, including a new one of Esquimalt naval base. From 1953 to 1958 he was chief hydrographer aboard CGS *William J Stewart*. He became the first Atlantic regional hydrographer in 1959 and served as superintendent of hydrographic field requirements from 1963 until 1970, when he retired. This feature was formerly known as the Rugged Group but was renamed in 1947. Nearby Wilf Rk also commemorates La Croix.

Lacy Island (54°13'00" 133°05'00" Off W side of Langara I, N of Graham I, QCI). Although this name has been on Admiralty charts since 1853, its significance has not been recorded. The Haida know the exposed, wave-buffeted feature as Dah-ja, meaning "rock island."

Ladner harbour on the south shore of the Fraser River. *Peter Vassilopoulos*

Ladner (49°05'30" 123°04'40" On the S side of the Fraser R, just E of its mouth, S of Vancouver), **Ladner Marsh** (49°06'00" 123°04'00" Just N of Ladner), **Ladner Reach** (49°06'00" 123°05'00" Just W of Ladner Marsh). William Henry Ladner (1826–1907) and Thomas Ellis Ladner (1837–1922) were the first settlers in the area, pre-empting land about 1868 where the community of Ladner is now located. William had immigrated to Wisconsin from Cornwall, England, in 1848 to join his father and was followed three years later by Thomas. The brothers travelled to California in search of gold, then went N in 1858 to try their luck on the Fraser. They prospected, ran pack trains and built roads in the Cariboo and Big Bend districts before taking up land on the Fraser delta, marrying sisters (Mary and Edney Booth) and becoming successful farmers. William was the reeve of Ladner (formerly known as Ladner's Landing), 1880–1906, and the MLA for the area, 1886–90. Thomas became a prominent cannery man. The village of Ladner, once a burgeoning fishing port and agricultural centre, and a regular stop on the

Victoria–New Westminster steamship route, is the administrative and business hub of the district municipality of Delta. *E*

Lady Douglas Island (52°20'00" 128°26'00" S of Dowager I, W side of Don Peninsula, NW of Bella Bella). After Lady Amelia Douglas (née Connolly), wife of Vancouver I gov Sir James Douglas. Several features in this vicinity were named for members of the Douglas family. *See* Douglas I.

Lady Ellen Point (50°37'00" 127°07'00" N side of Ellenborough Peninsula, just N of Port McNeill, NE side of Vancouver I). Cdr Cortland Simpson of HMS *Egeria* was reading Sir Walter Scott's "Lady of the Lake" while re-surveying the area in the early 1900s. He named this feature after the poem's heroine, Ellen Douglas, much sought-after daughter of banished Scottish aristocrat James Douglas. Despite the attentions of rebel lord Roderick Dhu and of Scotland's King James V himself, she manages to marry her true love, the young knight Malcolm Graeme, by the end of the tale. Simpson named a feature on nearby Malcolm I after Graeme and was criticized for so doing by coastal historian Capt John Walbran (*see* Graeme Point).

Lady Islands (50°38'00" 126°25'00" S of Gilford I, entrance to Knight Inlet). After Lady Elizabeth Kennedy, wife of Viscount Gilford and eldest daughter of Arthur Kennedy, gov of Vancouver I, 1864–66. *See* Gilford Point.

Ladysmith (48°59'00" 123°49'00" W of Ladysmith Hbr), **Ladysmith Harbour** (49°00'00" 123°48'00" SE side of Vancouver I, between Duncan and Nanaimo). The town of Ladysmith was founded in 1900 by James Dunsmuir, coal baron and BC premier, as a port and residential suburb for workers at his nearby collieries. The Boer War was much in the news at the time, and Dunsmuir had just heard that the besieged S African town of Ladysmith had finally been relieved by the British Army. He named his new townsite to commemorate this accomplishment. Ladysmith, in turn, had been named in 1851 for Juana Maria de Los Dolores de León, wife of Sir Harry Smith, gov of S Africa's Cape Colony, 1847–52. The Smiths' unusual marriage occurred in 1812, during the Peninsular War, just days after 14-year-old Juana and her older sister—the last survivors of a noble Spanish family—had thrown themselves on the mercy of a group of British officers after the storming of Badajoz. BC's Ladysmith turned to logging and fishing when the coal ran out, and was the site of several sawmills. After its historic downtown was restored in the 1980s, it also became popular with recreational boaters. Ladysmith Hbr was formerly known as Oyster Hbr. *E W*

Lady Trutch Passage (52°21'00" 128°20'00" Between Lake I and the SW side of Don Peninsula, NW of Bella Bella). Julia Elizabeth Hyde (1827–95), from NY, was living in Oregon in 1855 when she met and married Joseph Trutch (1826–1904, *see* Trutch I), a British engineer. She was the sister-in-law of John Preston, Oregon's first surveyor gen, and Trutch was working at the time as Preston's assistant. The Trutches moved first to Illinois and then, in 1859, to BC, where Joseph played an influential role in colonial government, serving as chief commissioner of Lands and Works. He was named BC's first lt gov (1871–76) and, later, dominion agent for BC. Julia became Lady Trutch in 1889, when her husband was knighted. The Trutches retired to England that year, but Julia died at Victoria while she and Joseph were making a return visit to BC. Nearby Hyde Point is also named for her.

Ladysmith Harbour with Slag Point in the foreground. *Kevin Oke*

L

Lagoon Inlet (52°56'00" 131°55'00" Head of Selwyn Inlet, opposite Louise I, E side of Moresby I, QCI). This feature takes its name from the tidal lagoon located at the head of the inlet. Lagoon Bay Cannery was built in 1918 on the S shore of the inlet near the tidal rapids that give access to the lagoon. The plant was operated by the Canadian Fishing Co from 1922 until 1941, when it burned down. The inlet was often referred to incorrectly as Lagoon Bay, after the name of the cannery. *D*

Laidlaw Islands (52°38'00" 128°49'00" W of Hastings I, off SW end of Princess Royal I). James Anderson Laidlaw (b 1836), a native of Scotland, arrived in BC's Cariboo district in 1862 and later became prominent in the salmon-canning industry. He formed partnerships with such well-known businessmen as John Irving, Robert Rithet and Thomas Ladner to build and operate numerous canneries on the coast, including the Standard on the N coast, Queshela on Smith Inlet, Wannock on Rivers Inlet, and the Delta, Wellington and Harlock canneries on the Fraser R. In 1902 he and Ladner sold their Victoria Canning Co to the BC Packers Assoc.

Laing Point (52°58'45" 132°06'00" E side of Peel Inlet, Kuper Inlet, NW side of Moresby I, QCI). Scottish shipwright Robert Andrew Laing (1816–82), from St Andrews, was aboard the US schooner *Susan Sturgis*, one of several vessels that arrived in the QCI in 1852 in unsuccessful pursuit of gold. The ship moved on to the E coast of the QCI, where Chief Albert Edensaw was hired as a pilot, but during an attempt to trade with the Masset Haida, the *Sturgis* was plundered and burned and its crew imprisoned. According to some accounts, it was only because of Edensaw's negotiating skills that the crew's lives were spared; other sources claim that he helped plan the attack and shared in the loot. After Laing was released, the HBC hired him to run its Albert Head sawmill, 1853–54. He then brought his wife, Jane (1812–72), and family out to BC, established Laing Shipyards—the first facility of its kind in Victoria—and worked on most, if not all, of the early historic vessels that operated along the BC coast. *D*

Laird Rocks (53°35'34" 130°33'29" Entrance to Griffith Hbr, NW side of Banks I). Named in 1926 after S Laird, who returned from active duty in Europe in WWI to serve as 1st steward aboard the W coast survey vessel *Lillooet* in the early 1920s.

Laithwood Island (53°08'00" 129°47'00" W side of Otter Passage, between Trutch I and Banks I). The name was adopted by the hydrographic service in 1950 to remember Thomas Laithwood, a carpenter's mate aboard HMS *Discovery* on Capt George Vancouver's historic voyage of exploration to the PNW, 1791–95.

Lakken Point (50°30'00" 127°36'00" SE end of Drake I, Quatsino Sd, NW end of Vancouver I). Bernhard Christian Lakken (1860–1923) pre-empted land in the Quatsino area in 1895 and acquired a Crown grant there in 1901. His surname appears in records more frequently as Lokken; variant spellings of his first names are also found. Lokken was a farmer, prospector, school trustee and loyal member of the Scandinavian colony that settled Quatsino in the late 1890s. He died at Vancouver. The name was adopted in 1927.

Lamalchi Bay (48°56'00" 123°38'00" SW side of Kuper I, Gulf Is). A renegade Cowichan (Quw'utsun') First Nation band known as the Lamalcha occupied a village on this bay in the 19th century. Lamalchi is an anglicized version of Hwlumelhtsu or Xwlemalhtse, the Island Halkomelem name for this location, meaning "lookout place." In 1863, in one of the most sensational incidents in the history of the young colonies of BC and Vancouver I, a naval expedition was mounted against the Lamalcha, whose members were accused of murdering two white Gulf Is settlers, Frederick Marks and his married daughter Caroline Harvey, on Saturna I (*see* Murder Point). Several British warships searched for the killers, and officers in the gunboat *Forward* threatened the Lamalcha village, demanding that the suspects be given up. The residents refused, a sailor was shot dead and the gunboat then completely destroyed the village. Eighteen Lamalcha were eventually captured and taken to Victoria for a controversial trial, where four of them, including Acheewun, the chief, were found guilty and hanged. After this incident the Lamalcha amalgamated with the Penelakut First Nation and moved to the E side of Kuper I. The Lamalchi Bay site was farmed by William Conn in the 1870s and then acquired in 1880 by the New England Co, an Anglican missionary society, which built a church and school. In the 1930s a specialized cattle farm, Folded Hills, was established there by Roy and Audrey Ginn and later run by René Moeri. In its long and extremely varied history, Lamalchi Bay has also been home to a Gestalt institute and an ecological centre. It formerly appeared on charts as Village Bay but was renamed by Cdr John Parry of HMS *Egeria* during a 1905 survey. *W*

Lama Passage (52°05'00" 128°07'00" Between Denny I, Hunter I and Campbell I, S and SW of Bella Bella), **Lama Point** (54°34'00" 130°18'00" W of Worsfold Bay, Work Channel, N of Prince Rupert). The historic HBC brig *Lama* (sometimes spelled *Llama*), built in 1826 and originally owned by the Boston trading company of Bryant, Sturgis & Co, arrived in Pacific waters in 1831 under Capt William McNeill. HBC chief factor John McLoughlin, in dire need of a new trading vessel, sent Duncan Finlayson to Honolulu in 1832, where he not only purchased the 132-tonne, 23.5-m ship for $5,000 but also hired its cdr and his two mates, all of whom had useful experience on the PNW coast. The *Lama* then operated out of Ft Vancouver for five years,

Queen of the North, McLoughlin Bay, Lama Passage. *Andrew Scott*

helping to found Ft McLoughlin at Bella Bella in 1833 (hence the name Lama Passage) and transporting HBC chief trader John Work around BC's N coast in 1834–35 (hence Lama Point). In 1837 the brig was sold for $5,500 to Honolulu merchant Eliab Grimes, who employed a mariner named John Bancroft to take it to California the following year to hunt sea otters. Bancroft—an abusive, alcoholic capt—had the misfortune to be murdered by his mutinous First Nation hunters, and the remaining crew members, many of them wounded, only managed to drag themselves and their plundered vessel back to Hawaii in early 1839. **Lama Shoal** (51°00'00" 127°38'00" Between Farquhar Bank and the Storm Is, N entrance to Queen Charlotte Str) is presumably named for this ship as well. Lama Passage was formerly known as Main Passage. *W*

Lambert Channel (49°30'00" 124°42'00" Between Denman I and Hornby I, Str of Georgia). From 1857 to 1860, Cdr Lionel Lambert (b 1836) was a young RN officer on the Pacific Station, which in those days was based at Valparaiso, Chile. Until 1858 he served aboard HMS *Ganges* as flag lt to Rear Adm Robert Baynes, the station's cdr-in-chief, and had earlier held the same position with Baynes in the Baltic Sea on HMS *Resolution*, a paddle frigate. Lambert was then promoted to cdr and took charge of HMS *Vixen*, a 6-gun paddle sloop. In 1860, while taking shore leave in Lima, Peru, he disappeared. Irish politician and mercenary James Patrick Mahon, who had been travelling in the *Vixen* while trying to finance the construction of a canal across Central America, forced Peruvian authorities to investigate, and it was discovered that Lambert had been robbed and murdered while bathing in the river.

Lambert Point (54°06'00" 130°05'00" S entrance to Skeena R, E of De Horsey I, SE of Prince Rupert). Named Point Lambert by Capt George Vancouver in 1793 after "commissioner Lambert of the navy." Capt Robert Lambert (d 1810) was appointed commissioner at Jamaica in 1782, the same year that Vancouver was stationed there. He had

been promoted to capt in 1760 and was listed as retired in 1790, with a handsome pension of £250 a year. The feature is known locally as Vancouver Point.

Lancaster Reef (51°49'29" 128°09'48" W side of Kildidt Sd, S of Bella Bella). In 1944, regional hydrographer Henri Parizeau named a number of coastal features in this vicinity after WWII aircraft. The Avro Lancaster, a four-engine British heavy bomber, primarily designed for night use, became the most famous and successful bomber used in the war, flying 156,000 sorties and dropping more than 550,000 tonnes of explosives. It was known as the "Dam Buster" for its raids on Germany's Ruhr Valley. The original inspiration for Parizeau's idea was the nearby presence of Spider I and the fact that Anthony Fokker's first airplane, built in 1910, was named the Spin (Dutch for "spider") on account of its many bracing wires. Ironically, Spider I was charted about 1865, well before powered aircraft had been invented.

Lancelot Inlet (50°03'00" 124°43'00" E of Gifford Peninsula and Malaspina Inlet, N of Powell R). Several names associated with Arthurian legend were adopted in this vicinity in 1945 (Galahad Point, Grail Point, etc). Sir Lancelot, secret lover of Queen Guinevere, was one of King Arthur's knights of the Round Table, who vowed to search for the Holy Grail.

Lance's Islands. *See* Lanz I.

Lane Islet (49°09'00" 125°48'00" Dawley Passage, off SE Meares I, Clayoquot Sd, W side of Vancouver I). Gerald Eyre Lane pre-empted land on the N side of Calmus Passage in 1913 and received a Crown grant in 1919. He died at Saanich in 1966, aged 76. The name was adopted in 1934.

Lane Rock (51°55'00" 128°12'00" Cultus Sd, S of Sans Peur Passage, S of Bella Bella). In 1944, when this feature was named, Reginald John Lane, DSO, DFC (1920–2003), had the rank of wing cdr and was noted for flying the first Canadian-built Lancaster bomber across the Atlantic. The Victoria-born Lane was an experienced WWII bomber pilot, completing three tours of duty and winning a second DFC by war's end. Senior positions followed his return to Canada: CO of RCAF Station Edmonton, cdr of Air Transport Command and—with the rank of air vice-marshal—cdr of Canada's NATO-assigned 1st Air Division in Europe. His final military appointment was as deputy cdr-in-chief of NORAD, after which he was awarded the US Legion of Merit. Lane retired in 1974 as a lt gen (the air force moved to army-style ranks when Canada's armed forces were unified in 1968) and returned to Victoria with his wife, Barbara Joyce Andrews, in 1976. He was a director of the Canadian Institute for International Peace and Security, 1989–92, and was inducted into Canada's Aviation Hall of Fame in 2000.

Weathered rock formations on Langara Island. *Andrew Scott*

Langara Island (54°14'00" 133°02'00" Off NW end of Graham I, QCI), **Langara Point** (54°15'00" 133°04'00" NW end of Langara I), **Langara Rocks** (54°15'40" 133°01'29" Off N side of Langara I). Spanish cdr Jacinto Caamaño, of the *Aránzazu*, named Isla de Lángara in 1792 while surveying Dixon Entrance. Juan Francisco de Lángara y Huarte (1736–1806) was a celebrated Spanish admiral and politician, as famous for his scientific and cartographic contributions as for his naval battles. In the 1790s he served as inspector-gen and secretary of state for the Spanish navy. Spanish explorers bestowed his name on a number of coastal features in BC and Alaska, including a group of islands at the mouth of the Fraser R (probably Westham, Lulu and Sea), which José Narváez called Islas de Lángara, and Point Grey (qv), which was Dionisio Alcalá-Galiano's Punta de Lángara (hence the name of the Vancouver W-side district of Langara). Capt George Vancouver adopted the name Langara I on his 1793 chart. However, an alternative name, North I—originally given in 1787 by early British fur trader George Dixon in honour of Lord North, British PM in the 1770s—had also come into common usage, and when Cdr James Prevost of HMS *Virago* surveyed parts of the QCI in 1853, he changed Langara to North I. It remained so on Admiralty charts until about 1907, when the region was re-surveyed, this time by Capt Frederick Learmonth of HMS *Egeria*, who changed the name back to Langara. Over the years its pronunciation has shifted, with the accent now on the second syllable rather than on the first. The term North I is still in local use. The Haida know Langara I as Kiis Gwaii or Kusgwai, and it once had numerous villages. Langara Point is the W end of the headland that Juan Perez called Punta Santa Margarita in 1774—the first European sighting of the BC coast. The eastern part of this land mass is now known as St Margaret Point (qv). A lighthouse was built at Langara Point in 1913, and a radar station operated there during WWII. The Haida call Langara Rks the Sea Lion Rks; their name for the point, adjacent to a former village site, is Gwai-es-kwoon, or End-of-Island Point. There is also a Langara Lk on Langara I. *D*

Lang Bay (49°46'00" 124°21'00" E side of Malaspina Str, between Jervis Inlet and Powell R, NW of Vancouver). The three Lang brothers—Frederick, Harry and Thomas—settled in the vicinity in 1911 with their mother, Elizabeth, and stepfather, Robert Simpkins, a retired British Army officer. The bay at that time was known as Wolfsohn or Wulfsohn Bay, after Johann Wulffsohn (as his name is spelled on his 1908 marriage certificate to Florence A Maclure). He was Vancouver's German consul but had retired before WWI and died by 1917. That was the year Vancouver lawyer Robert Maitland, owner of a summer place in the vicinity, wrote with patriotic fervour to the Geographic Board of Canada to explain that local residents, upset at recent war casualties, desired a non-German name for Wolfsohn Bay. He suggested Connaught Bay, after a Canadian Army regiment from BC, or Malaspina Bay. The board secretary replied that these submissions were not considered suitable and that Maitland should write back with the names of "local lads" who had served overseas. Lang was an obvious choice as all three brothers had seen war service in Europe. The bay has been a logging centre since the late 1800s and is still an important booming and sorting ground. Cedar shakes were cut at large shingle-bolt camps; early railway- and truck-logging operations were also based there. The community of Lang Bay was completely destroyed by an out-of-control forest fire in 1922 but was soon rebuilt. Lang Ck takes its name from the bay. The Sechelt First Nation name for the bay is Kwékwenis.

Lang Cove (48°26'00" 123°25'00" E end of Constance Cove, E side of Esquimalt Hbr, just W of Victoria). RN officer Edward Wollaston Lang (d 1897) served on the Pacific Station, 1843–47, as 4th lt of HMS *Fisgard*. The *Fisgard* was one of the first vessels to anchor in Esquimalt Hbr, and Lt Cdr James Wood, who surveyed the area with HMS *Pandora* in 1846, named many features in the harbour after the *Fisgard*'s officers. Lang entered the RN in 1831 and retired as a cdr in 1870. In 1871 he reached the rank of capt, retired.

Langdale (49°26'00" 123°28'00" W side of Howe Sd, NW of Vancouver). In 1893, Robinson Henry Langdale (1835–1908) pre-empted land on the creek (also named after him) that runs into Howe Sd at this location and established a tidy homestead. He received a Crown grant in 1908. In 1955 the Black Ball Line's ferry dock was moved to this area from Gibsons, ending Langdale's agricultural seclusion. The site is now a busy BC Ferries terminal.

Langford (48°27'00" 123°30'00" Just W of Victoria), **Port Langford** (49°48'00" 126°50'00" N side of Nuchatlitz Inlet, NW side of Nootka I, W side of Vancouver I). Edward Edwards Langford (1809–95), his wife, Flora (née Phillips), and their five daughters (a son, George, was born in BC) were the first English family to immigrate to the colony of Vancouver I, in 1851. A retired army capt and gentleman farmer, Langford, from Brighton, obtained a position as bailiff of one of the four farms that the Puget's Sd Agricultural Co, an HBC subsidiary, established in the Victoria area. Langford's was the 245-ha Esquimalt Farm, which he renamed Colwood, after his former estate in Sussex. In 1855 the HBC decided to terminate its agreement with Langford, who was an incompetent manager and lived in unsustainable luxury, but gave him five years' notice. He had been named a magistrate in 1853, but when Gov James Douglas limited his authority, he became the leader of a group of disaffected settlers and a thorn in the gov's side, agitating for reform and sending numerous complaints to the colonial office in London. Langford was elected to the colony's first assembly, in 1856, but was debarred on the grounds that he lacked the necessary property qualifications. In 1861 he returned to England with his family, penniless and widely detested for his pompous, litigious nature and endless troublemaking. Nearby Langford Lk and Langford Ck are named for him, and several of Langford's daughters are also commemorated on the coast: *see* Langford Cove, Louie Bay *and* Florence Point. The Sophia Range on Nootka I is named after his fourth-oldest daughter, Sophia Elizabeth. Emma Langford, the third oldest, married John Bull, master of HMS *Plumper* (*see* Bull I). The community of Langford became a district municipality in 1992 and is the commercial centre for a cluster of suburbs just W of Victoria. *E W*

Langford Cove (52°20'00" 128°37'00" SE side of Price I, NW of Bella Bella). Mary Langford (1837–1903), born in Germany, was the second oldest of the five daughters of Flora and Edward Langford (*see* Langford). Her father was hired by the Puget's Sd Agricultural Co to establish Colwood Farm near Esquimalt Hbr, and the family arrived at Victoria from England in 1851 aboard the HBC barque *Tory*. In 1870, at London, she married Capt Herbert Lewis (1828–1905, *see* Lewis Channel), long-time HBC master mariner, and returned with him to Victoria, where she lived for the rest of her life. Mary Basin on Nootka I is also named for her.

Langley Passage (53°04'00" 129°40'00" Extends through the Estevan Group, between Caamaño Sd and Banks I). William Henry Langley (1868–1951) was born at Victoria, the son of Alfred John Langley (1820–96), a pioneer Victoria pharmacist, magistrate and member of the colonial legislative council of Vancouver I (1861–64). William married Gladys Annie Mona Baiss (1883–1978) at Victoria in 1906 and, apart from overseas service in France as a maj with the WWI Canadian Expeditionary Force, spent his entire life there, working as a barrister and solicitor. His father, Alfred, was one of three brothers from Berkshire, England, who immigrated to San Francisco in 1850 and went into the pharmacy trade. Alfred came to

Victoria in 1858 and set up shop as BC's first wholesale and retail druggist, a business that would blossom into one of the province's longest-lasting firms, eventually becoming BC Drugs Ltd—still in operation 100 years later. William Langley participated in the great old-timers' reunion held in Victoria in May 1924 (*see* Adams Bay).

Langsdorff Point (50°19'00" 127°48'00" S side of Klaskino Inlet, between Brooks Peninsula and Quatsino Sd, NW side of Vancouver I). Named for Georg Heinrich Langsdorff (1774–1852), a Prussian physician and naturalist who lived for many years in Russia and is also known by his Russian name, Grigori Ivanovitch Langsdorff. He participated in Adm Adam Krusenstern's first Russian round-the-world voyage, 1803–5, but left the expedition to visit SE Alaska and the Kodiak and Aleutian islands, returning to St Petersburg in 1808. Langsdorff became Russia's consul gen in Brazil, 1813–20, using his position to explore the region and collect examples of its flora and fauna. He mounted a Russian scientific excursion to the Amazon, 1826–29, which resulted in major collections being deposited (and lost for many years) in Russian museums, but seriously damaged his health on the journey and returned to Europe.

Langthorne Island (53°08'00" 129°32'00" Entrance to Weinberg Inlet, NW side of Campania I, between Caamaño Sd and Pitt I). William Langthorne was employed as an oiler aboard the hydrographic survey vessel *William J Stewart* in the early 1940s.

Lantzville (49°15'00" 124°04'00" Between Nanaimo and Parksville, SE side of Vancouver I). A colliery, known as Grant's Mine, was first established at this location in 1917. The townsite that grew up around the mine was named after Fraser Harry Lantz (b 1868), vice-president and, later, managing director of Nanoose Collieries Co, which worked the property in the early 1920s. Lantz was a resident of Vancouver at the turn of the century; he married Joanna Noble there in 1898. Records show that he remarried in 1905, this time to Mabel Cripps. He had been involved in the coal business for many years; in 1906 he was managing director of the Nicola Valley Coal & Coke Co. The coal at Lantzville was mostly depleted by the mid-1940s, but the village continued on as a pleasant, seaside residential community. *E*

Lanz Island (50°49'00" 128°41'00" One of the Scott Is, W of Cape Scott, off NW end of Vancouver I). David Lance (1757–1820), born in Kent, went out to Canton as a clerk for the E India Co in 1773, when only 16. He became a junior trader in 1779 and was later in charge of the Canton office. He also collaborated with other young China traders in private trading ventures. One of Lance's private efforts appears to have been the financing, along with John Cox, of Capt James Hanna's second fur-trading voyage to the PNW in 1786 (*see* Cox Bay *and* Hanna Channel). Hanna

L

gave the name Lance's Is to the archipelago off the NW tip of Vancouver I (now the Scott Is). Spanish explorers changed Lance to Lanz on their charts, and this name was later applied to the second largest (at 764 ha) of the Scott Is. David Lance, meanwhile, had made his fortune by the time ill health forced him to return to England in 1789, when he was all of 32. He married Mary Fitzhugh, sister of his trading partner William Fitzhugh (see Fitz Hugh Sd), and in 1796 built Chessel House in Hampshire, which was described by Jane Austen in a letter as "a handsome building … in a very beautiful situation." (The Austens knew the Lance family through David's clergyman brother William.) David went back to Canton in 1803 as ambassador to Cochinchina (now southern Vietnam), hoping to persuade the ruler to support British commercial interests in the region and check French expansion. He was unsuccessful in these goals but did manage to help William Kerr, the first professional plant collector in China (and a friend, as was Lance, to Sir Joseph Banks; see Banks I), to ship a cargo of rare Asian species back to the Royal Botanic Gardens at Kew. Lanz I was once home to the Yutlinuk people, who were part of the Nahwitti, a tribal branch of the Kwakwaka'wakw First Nation, but, sadly, this group succumbed to European diseases and died out in the early 1800s. Lanz was an important breeding ground for seabirds until mink were introduced about 1938 and trapped for the fur industry until the late 1960s. That was the end of the birds. Raccoons also managed to colonize the island. It is now part of Lanz & Cox Islands Provincial Park, established in 1995.

La Pérouse Bank (48°45'00" 125°55'00" SW of Barkley Sd, W of Vancouver I), **La Pérouse Reef** (54°01'00" 133°10'00" Off White Point, NW side of Graham I, QCI), **Mount La Pérouse** (53°13'39" 132°30'37" E of Cartwright Sd, SW Graham I). Jean-François de Galaup, Comte de Lapérouse (1741–1788), was a distinguished French naval officer chosen in 1785 to lead a scientific expedition intended to circumnavigate the globe and search for the NW Passage. He had joined the navy in 1756 and participated in numerous actions in the Indian Ocean, off the US coast during the American Revolutionary War, and in the W Indies, where he was on the losing side in the Battle of the Saintes. In 1782, Lapérouse (as his name is most commonly spelled) and a small squadron destroyed Ft Prince of Wales and Ft York on Hudson Bay. He commanded the *Boussole* on his great scientific journey, while Paul-Antoine-Marie Fleuriot de Langle had charge of the *Astrolabe*. They sailed S along the BC coast in 1786, naming many features in the QCI, and were the first European navigators to record the existence of the bank now named for Lapérouse off Vancouver I. In 1788, after crossing the Pacific, exploring the NE coast of Asia and visiting Australia, both vessels disappeared and were never heard from again. Not until 1827, when artifacts were found by Irish sea capt Peter Dillon, was it

discovered that the ships had been wrecked in Vanuatu (the New Hebrides). No survivors were found. Mt La Pérouse is the highest point on Graham I at 1,120 m. *D E*

Larcom Island (55°26'00" 129°44'00" At entrance to Hastings Arm, N end of Observatory Inlet, S of Stewart), **Larcom Lagoon** (55°24'00" 129°44'00" S end of Larcom I), **Larcom Point** (55°28'00" 129°44'00" N tip of Larcom I). Lt Thomas Henry Larcom (1842–77) commanded the RN gunboat *Forward* on the BC coast from 1868 until it was sold the following year. He was the second son of Maj Gen Sir Thomas Aiskew Larcom, undersecretary for Ireland, 1853–68, and was promoted to cdr in 1873. Named in 1869 by Lt Daniel Pender while doing survey work aboard the *Beaver*. *W*

Laredo Channel (52°44'00" 129°05'00" Between Princess Royal I and Aristazabal I), **Laredo Inlet** (52°48'00" 128°44'00" Extends N into Princess Royal I from Laredo Sd), **Laredo Sound** (52°29'00" 128°53'00" Between Aristazabal I and Price I, NW of Bella Bella). Spanish naval officer Jacinto Caamaño named the Canal de Laredo in 1792 while heading S in the frigate *Aránzazu* after surveying Dixon Entrance. His chart indicates that the canal included Squally Channel and Campania Sd, as well as Laredo Channel. Capt George Vancouver adopted the term but applied it only to the southern section of this series of waterways. It is presumed that the name refers to the ancient port of Laredo on the N coast of Spain, known for its Aug festival of flowers and for its carnival ritual, in which a giant sardine is paraded through town and then burned on the beach.

Large Bedford Island. *See* Pim Head.

Larsen Point (52°06'00" 131°00'00" S of High I, Balcom Inlet, E side of Kunghit I, QCI). Norwegian whaling capt Louis Larsen was master of a number of different vessels for the Consolidated Whaling Corp and Western Whaling Co from the 1930s to the '50s. Two of the ships he was known to have skippered were the *Brown* and the *James Carruthers*.

Larso Bay (52°10'00" 126°51'00" E side of S Bentinck Arm, just S of Bella Coola). According to records at BC's Geographical Names Office, V Larso was an early settler in the Bella Coola valley. Larso Bay was the site of a logging camp, long since abandoned, and known locally as Camp Two Bay. A ruined wharf was still visible in the early 2000s. Nearby is one of the world's largest western red cedar trees, 5 m across and more than 1,500 years old.

Lascelles Point (51°05'00" 127°39'00" SE of Buccleuch Point and Cape Caution, N entrance to Queen Charlotte Str). Horace Douglas Lascelles (1835–69), a British nobleman and RN officer, arrived on the Pacific Station in

1860 as 1st lt of HMS *Topaze*. As cdr of HMS *Forward*, a gunboat assigned to patrol the BC S coast and maintain law and order, he was involved in several military actions between 1861 and 1865, including an intensive search for the murderers of Gulf Is settlers Frederick Marks and Caroline Harvey (*see* Murder Point). It was Lascelles, with the *Forward*, who destroyed the village on Lamalchi Bay in Apr 1863 in retaliation for the shooting death of one of his sailors. When criticized in the press for lack of resolve in dealing with the Lamalcha, he became incensed and permitted crew members to kidnap and scare the offending journalist, Charles Allen. Allen sued and Lascelles had to pay him damages. The young aristocrat was wealthy, however, and the incident did him little harm. He was a prominent member of Victoria's social elite and an enthusiastic rider and racer of horses. He invested in real estate with former ship capt James Southgate and established Nanaimo's Harewood coal mine (named for his father, Henry Lascelles, the 3rd Earl of Harewood), where industrialist Robert Dunsmuir got his start. Lascelles returned to England in 1865 and resigned from the RN the next year with the rank of cdr. He came back to Victoria in 1868 and died of a sudden illness shortly thereafter at Esquimalt. In 1865, RN surveyor Daniel Pender named a number of features around Forward Hbr after Lascelles (Douglas Bay, Horace Point, Mt Lascelles) and his sisters (*see* Blanche Point, Cust Point, Louisa Point *and* Maud Point). Pender also named Thynne Peninsula (qv) after his mother, Lady Louisa Thynne; Mt Egremont after his brother, Egremont William Lascelles; Mt Harewood after his father, Henry Lascelles, the 3rd earl; and the Wharncliffe Range after his sister, Lady Susan Charlotte Lascelles, who became Countess of Wharncliffe after marrying Edward Montagu-Stuart-Wortley-Mackenzie, 1st Earl of Wharncliffe. *W*

Laskeek Bay (52°49'00" 131°35'00" SE of Louise I, off E side of Moresby I, QCI). Named by geologist George Mercer Dawson in 1878 after an old Tsimshian First Nation term meaning "of the Eagle clan" and referring to the prominent Eagle crest village of Tanu on nearby Tanu I. Tanu is sometimes described in early accounts of the region as Laskeek village. *W*

Lasqueti Island (49°29'00" 124°16'00" W of the S end of Texada I, Str of Georgia). Spanish explorer José Narváez, in the *Santa Saturnina*, was the first European to see Lasqueti I, in July 1791. He named it Isla Texada, after senior naval officer Felix de Tejada. This name appears on the chart drawn by Juan Pantoja, the pilot aboard the *San Carlos*, the other vessel in the 1791 expedition. (Narváez originally gave the name San Felix to today's Texada I.) Francisco Eliza, the overall expedition cdr, shifted the names around on his official chart, changing San Felix to Texada I (qv) and giving Lasqueti its current name, after Juan Maria Lasqueti, also a prominent Spanish naval officer. Lasqueti is believed to

Lasqueti Island in the central Strait of Georgia. *Peter Vassilopoulos*

have been part of an expedition that surveyed the Brazilian coast in the late 1770s. Lasqueti I was first settled in the 1860s. Over the years, residents raised sheep, operated a cannery, logged and fished for their livelihoods—though recently tourism and marijuana production have become important as well. Lasqueti is the least developed of the major islands in the Str of Georgia and is served only by a private passenger ferry. *E W*

Latch Islet (52°27'00" 127°47'00" Near head of Roscoe Inlet, NE of Bella Bella), **Latch Point** (E of Latch It). These two features were named in 1957 for the way they appear to fit together.

Latona Passage (49°31'00" 123°27'00" Between Woolridge I and the NW side of Gambier I, Howe Sd, NW of Vancouver). After HMS *Latona*, a 38-gun frigate that participated, under Capt Edward Thornbrough, in the 1794 English Channel naval battle known as the Glorious First of June. The *Latona* was stationed so as to repeat the signals of Adm Lord Howe, the cdr-in-chief, but later plunged into the thick of the fight to assist the line-of-battle ships. In 1859–60, Capt George Richards named dozens of features in Howe Sd after the officers and ships that participated in the British victory. Built in 1781 at Limehouse, the *Latona* later served in the W Indies, 1806–11, and in 1813 was converted to a hospital ship. Camp Latona, on the N side of Gambier, was established by BC's Catholic churches in 1959 but sold to The Firs, a Washington-based evangelical group, four decades later, after camp enrollments had severely declined.

Latta Island (51°59'00" 128°13'00" N end of the McNaughton Group, W of Hunter I, S of Bella Bella). After Canadian WWII commander Lt Gen Andrew George Latta McNaughton. *See* McNaughton Group.

Lauder Island (53°29'00" 132°46'00" Off N side of Seal Inlet, W side of Graham I, QCI), **Lauder Point** (54°07'00" 133°06'00" N of Sadler Point, NW end of Graham I).

L

Dr William Lauder was the surgeon aboard the *Queen Charlotte*, under Capt George Dixon, and spent the years 1786–87 in the PNW on one of the earliest British fur-trading voyages to the region.

Laundy Rock (52°48'00" 129°23'00" SW of Rennison I, off NW end of Aristazabal I). Named for Ellen Cridge (1867–1952), daughter of Victoria's pioneer Anglican clergyman Edward Cridge (*see* Cridge Banks). She was born at Victoria and married Thomas Herbert Laundy (1865–1957) there in 1891. Laundy, from Scotland and recently widowed, worked at first as a clerk with the Bank of BC. He later became a minister in the Reformed Episcopal Church, which his father-in-law had established in Victoria in 1874 after breaking with the Anglican Church and its Victoria-based bishop, George Hills, over theological differences. The Laundy family took part in the grand old-timers' reunion held at Victoria in 1924 (*see* Adams Bay).

Laura Point (48°52'00" 123°18'00" N of Miners Bay, NW side of Mayne I, Gulf Is). From 1858 to 1860, RN hydrographer Capt George Richards named several points in this vicinity after prominent local women of the day. Georgina Point (qv), for instance, commemorates the wife of a senior RN officer on the Pacific Station. Helen Point (qv) is named for the spouse of an HBC chief trader. Edith Point (qv) recalls a niece of Sir James Douglas. Laura Point was also probably intended to honour a well-known resident of early Victoria, but the individual who inspired this name is, unfortunately, no longer known.

Laurel Point (48°25'28" 123°22'34" S side of Inner Hbr, Victoria Hbr, Victoria). Victoria pioneer James Anderson, son of HBC explorer Alexander Caulfield Anderson, recalled that the "laurels" at this former First Nation burial ground were really arbutus trees. The feature's local name in the late 1800s was Sehl's Point, as it was here that Jacob Sehl constructed his pioneer furniture factory in 1885. Next door to this large brick structure he erected a spectacular Queen Anne-style mansion for his family, but both buildings were destroyed by fire in 1894 (*see* Sehl Rk).

Laurier Cove (54°24'00" 130°15'00" E side of Tuck Inlet, just N of Prince Rupert). Lawyer and journalist Sir Wilfrid Laurier (1841–1919) was Canada's seventh PM, 1896–1911, and the most important politician of his era. The country's first francophone leader was a dedicated Liberal, famed both for his personal charisma and his passionate belief in national unity. This feature was probably named in either 1906, when Tuck Inlet was surveyed, or 1910, when Laurier visited the newly minted city of Prince Rupert. Many places in BC are named after this famous Canadian, including Laurier Glacier and Mt Sir Wilfrid Laurier in the Rockies, and Laurier Pass and Mt Laurier in the Peace R district.

Laverock Point (53°31'00" 130°29'00" W of Kingkown Inlet, W side of Banks I). The *Laverock* was a homemade, 5-m sailboat in which Anglican missionary John Antle, accompanied only by his nine-year-old son Victor, made an 800-km journey along the BC coast in 1904 to explore the feasibility of establishing a seagoing mission. Over the next 70 years, Antle's Columbia Coast Mission built many boats, churches and hospitals on the coast in an effort to meet the spiritual and medical requirements of its far-flung residents. One of the mission's later vessels, the *Rendezvous*, was rechristened the *Laverock II* in 1956. The name of the point was adopted in 1952 in association with the nearby Antle Is (qv).

Lawn Hill (53°24'44" 131°55'32" E side of Graham I, N of Skidegate, QCI), **Lawn Point** (53°26'00" 131°55'00" Just N of Lawn Hill). Lawn Point and Lawn Ck both take their names from 130-m-high Lawn Hill, as did the small agricultural community of Lawn Hill, which grew up nearby around a post office, store and hotel. The E Coast Farmers' Institute established an experimental farm in the area. The settlement was active in the 1910s and '20s but was later abandoned. The hill was apparently known in earlier days as Lone Hill and Long Hill, and Lawn is probably a modification of one of these names. *D E*

Law Point (49°09'09" 123°41'52" N side of Silva Bay, E end of Gabriola I, Gulf Is). Alexander Law, a native of Scotland, came to Gabriola I in 1907 with his son Robert and purchased land at the E end of the island from John and Louisa Silva. Robert Brown Law (1873–1939) married Ruby Margaret Stenhouse (1884–1963) at Vancouver in 1911, and they both lived on Gabriola for the rest of their lives, raising four children and taking active roles in community affairs. Robert was a school trustee for many years. Some historians consider Law Point to be the Punta de Gaviola of Spanish naval officer José Narváez, who in 1791, in the *Santa Saturnina*, became the first European to explore the Str of Georgia.

Lawson Harbour (54°01'00" 130°15'00" N end of Lewis I, Arthur Passage, NE side of Porcher I, S of Prince Rupert). A small fishing and logging community flourished at this location after WWI, with a school and a population that peaked at around 40 people. The well-known Swedish boatbuilder Emil Rosang constructed trollers and halibut boats in the harbour in the 1920s and '30s, working mostly with hand-sawn red and yellow cedar. He also repaired numerous Prince Rupert vessels at his yard. The settlement was later abandoned, though its remains could still be seen in the early 2000s. The origin of the name Lawson is not known with certainty.

Lawyer Islands (54°07'00" 130°20'00" Between Marcus Passage and Malacca Passage, S of Prince Rupert). Named during Lt Daniel Pender's Admiralty survey of 1867 or

1869 in association with nearby Bribery It and Client Reefs. The significance of the names is not recorded.

Laxgalts'ap (55°01'50" 129°34'30" N side of lower Nass R, E of Nass Bay). Laxgalts'ap—a Nisga'a First Nation community known for many years as Greenville—was one of 34 official names adopted in 2000 as part of the Nisga'a Treaty. It can be interpreted as "a dwelling place located on the site of an ancient village." The original settlement here, called Gitxat'in, was destroyed long ago by fire. The modern community was spelled Lachkaltsap in the 1930 gazetteer, but the name was changed in 1950 to Greenville, after Rev Alfred Eli Green (1851–1914), who served there as a Methodist missionary, 1877–90. A native of Northamptonshire, Green taught at New Westminster and Nanaimo before marrying Elizabeth Jane Gilbert (1857–1936), from Cornwall, at Victoria in 1878. He was a close associate of Thomas Crosby and, like Crosby, caused controversy by backing First Nation land claims on the N coast. In 1890, Green moved to Vancouver and established a number of churches in the Lower Mainland, including Fairview Methodist, where he and his wife were members. He was appointed federal inspector of Indian schools in BC in the early 1900s. Greenville Ck, a tributary of the Nass R, is also named for him. Laxgalts'ap is a popular spot for catching and processing eulachon. It was only connected to the rest of the Nass valley by road in 1985. *E*

Lax Kw'alaams, formerly known as Port Simpson. *Andrew Scott*

Lax Kw'alaams (54°33'24" 130°26'01" S shore of Port Simpson, NW end of Tsimpsean Peninsula, N of Prince Rupert). This Tsimshian First Nation term meaning "place of wild roses" was the original name given to the settlement that sprang up in 1834 beside Ft Simpson, an important HBC trading post on the N coast of BC. The name was a difficult one for Europeans to spell, and many variations have been recorded, including Laxtgu'alaams, Lach Goo Alams, Lochgwaahlamsh and Larhkwaralamps. The community was known for most of its life as Port Simpson, which is also the name of the body of water it faces; *see* Port Simpson for more detail and a brief history. In 1986

the Geographical Names Office agreed to the Tsimshian band council's request that "the village of Port Simpson be changed to its original Indian name of Lax Kw'alaams"; the post office name was changed the following year. *See also* Rose I.

Lay Point (52°13'00" 128°10'00" N end of Campbell I, just N of Bella Bella). Named for RN officer J R Lay, who was a lt aboard HMS *Egeria*. He served under Capt Morris Smyth, 1899–1900, and Cdr Cortland Simpson, 1900–1902. The vessel was involved with survey work in Johnstone Str, 1900–1901. Formerly known as Shelf Point.

Lazo. *See* Cape Lazo.

Leach Islet (48°50'00" 125°14'00" Near SE entrance to Imperial Eagle Channel, Barkley Sd, W side of Vancouver I). 2nd Cpl Peter John Leech (c 1828–99), as the name is more commonly spelled, was part of the Columbia detachment of Royal Engineers, which served in BC 1858–63. Born at Dublin, he joined the force during the Crimean War, trained as a surveyor and served with the international commission that determined Turkey's boundaries. In BC he was the detachment astronomer and apparently spent much time at the small observatory established at the unit's New Westminster HQ. Leech stayed on after the sappers disbanded and was chosen deputy leader of the 1864 Vancouver I Exploring Expedition, an early effort to map the interior of the island. This group discovered gold on a tributary of the Sooke R, later named the Leech R, and in the ensuing excitement a short-lived mining camp named Leechtown sprang up. In 1873, Peter Leech married Mary Macdonald (1837–92), who had come to Victoria in 1862 in the brideship *Tynemouth*. He worked on several remote surveying projects in BC's Nass and Stikine districts, including the Collins Overland Telegraph line that was abandoned when cables were successfully laid across the Atlantic. He became an HBC employee, 1868–83, eventually taking charge of the company's Esquimalt trading post, and was later named Victoria's city surveyor, 1884–92. In 1894, at the age of 70, he was appointed to accompany a colony of Norwegian settlers to the Bella Coola valley, lay out their homesites and build a road. The colonists found his work most unsatisfactory and described him as "extremely feeble ... certainly not the kind of man to send into a heavily wooded country full of brush and windfall." The government was also displeased and recalled him the following year. Leach It was named by Capt George Richards in 1865. It is not known if Leech I N of Kuper I is also named for this pioneer. *E W*

Leading Hill (49°51'33" 127°00'52" W side of entrance to Port Eliza, Esperanza Inlet, NW side of Vancouver I), **Leading Hill** (50°55'47" 127°23'39" Between Blunden Hbr and Shelter Bay, N side of Queen Charlotte Str), **Leading Island** (51°41'00" 128°07'00" Choked Passage, between

L

Calvert I and Starfish I, S of Bella Bella), **Leading Islet** (50°41'00" 126°40'00" Dusky Cove, W side of Bonwick I, E end of Queen Charlotte Str), **Leading Peak** (49°32'20" 123°18'16" Anvil I, Howe Sd, NW of Vancouver), **Leading Peak** (54°30'21" 130°22'56" Tsimpsean Peninsula, between Lax Kw'alaams and Georgetown Mills, N of Prince Rupert), **Leading Point** (53°11'00" 129°06'00" E side of Whale Channel, S of River Bight, NW end of Princess Royal I), **Leading Point** (54°59'00" 129°50'00" S entrance to Nass R, just E of Nass Bay), **Leading Shoal** (54°28'00" 130°27'00" Entrance to Big Bay, Tsimpsean Peninsula, N of Prince Rupert). In navigation and position fixing, a leading line is formed by a pair of markers and used to "lead" vessels or indicate safe passage through potentially dangerous waters. While the markers are generally artificial, prominent geographical features, such as the ones listed above, are sometimes employed instead. Leading Peak on Anvil I, for instance, was named by Capt George Vancouver in 1792 because an imaginary line drawn between this mountain and Passage I at the entrance to Howe Sd could be used to stay safely W of the hazardous sand banks and mud flats that form off Lulu I and the mouth of the Fraser R.

Leadman Passage (52°44'00" 129°25'00" W of Anderson Is, W of N end of Aristazabal I). Hydrographer Heamen Lawrence Leadman (1887–1967) began his career in 1913, on Lk Superior. Over the years he conducted dozens of surveys—in NS, Gulf of St Lawrence, Magdalen Is, Great Slave Lk, Nfld and elsewhere. He was officer in charge of CGS *Bayfield* (1929–31), CGS *Cartier* (1932–39) and CGS *Acadia* (1947–48). During WWII he did military work for the Hughes Owens Co in Ottawa. From 1944 until 1952, when he retired, he oversaw ship requirements for the hydrographic service, drawing up plans for new launches, making inspections and supervising conversion work. He also wrote the Mackenzie R pilot. The passage was named in 1926 to honour Leadman's only work stint on the BC coast, which occurred in 1923 when he was in charge of the houseboat *Somass*.

Learmonth Bank (54°28'00" 133°05'00" W end of Dixon Entrance, N of Langara I), **Learmonth Island** (53°41'00" 132°27'00" Off SW side of Masset Inlet, E of Wathus I, Graham I, QCI), **Mount Learmonth** (52°41'35" 128°37'41" SE end of Princess Royal I). Capt Frederick Charles Learmonth (1866–1941) of the RN conducted regular surveys of the BC N coast with HMS *Egeria*, 1906–9, operating primarily in the QCI, Dixon Entrance, Hecate Str and Port Simpson areas. He was later promoted to adm and knighted, and served as chief Admiralty hydrographer, 1919–24.

Leavitt Lagoon (53°21'00" 129°38'00" Head of Port Stephens, SW side of Pitt I). Flight Lt Robert Frederick Leavitt, from Regina, joined the RAF in 1939 and was attached to the photographic reconnaissance unit of Bomber Command. In 1941, while undertaking a mission along the coast of Norway, his plane was hit by anti-aircraft fire and Leavitt suffered a head injury. Despite a damaged engine and the loss of all instruments, he managed to complete his reconnaissance and return to base, a feat for which he was awarded the DFC. He returned to duty after two months' leave in Canada but was lost over the Atlantic when the aircraft he was travelling in disappeared on Sept 21, 1941. Leavitt was 25 years old. He is commemorated on the Air Forces Memorial at Runnymede, England.

Lee Bay (49°38'16" 124°03'55" NW of Irvines Landing, Sechelt Peninsula, NW of Vancouver). Members of the Lie family came to N America from the Trondheim area of Norway in the 1880s and made their way to Victoria, eventually settling at Whonnock on the Fraser R with a group of other Norwegian immigrants. Ole Andreas Olsen Lie (1867–1947) farmed at Whonnock, spent time in the Yukon with his brothers during the Klondike gold rush and also worked as a fisherman, visiting Pender Hbr about 1907. He married Frida Louisa Johansson (1878–1963) at Whonnock in 1896 and at some point changed the spelling of his surname to Lee. Ole, Frida and their children moved to Pender Hbr in 1917 and settled on Lee Bay, where they homesteaded and fished. Lee descendants still live in the region.

Leeke Islets (49°13'00" 126°03'00" N side of Brabant Channel, NW of Vargas I, Clayoquot Sd, W side of Vancouver I). According to BC's Geographical Names Office, C C Leeke pre-empted land at the S end of Wickaninnish Bay in 1900. No trace of this settler seems to have lingered in other official records. Formerly known as the Twin Its.

Leeson Point (50°32'00" 127°37'00" At W entrance to Bergh Cove, N of Drake I, Quatsino Sd, NW Vancouver I), **Leeson Rock** (In Bergh Cove). Jobe "Joseph" Lee Leeson (c 1842–1915) was one of the first pre-emptors of land in the Quatsino Sd area, in 1891. Originally from Northamptonshire, and trained as a miller, he immigrated to Canada with his wife, Anna (1841–1918), and son Ben in 1886 and lived in the Cariboo and at New Westminster for several years. After settling at Winter Hbr, Jobe opened the J L Leeson & Son Trading Post, which catered to whalers and local First Nation residents, and also built a crab and clam cannery. He subdivided his property and tried to develop a community called Queenstown by selling lots as far afield as Chicago and London, England. At the 1893 Chicago World's Fair, Leeson interested a man named Christian Nordstrom in the Quatsino Sd region, and the following year Nordstrom and a group of Scandinavian colonists formed the settlement of Quatsino. Benjamin William Leeson (1866–1948), born at Coventry, held a variety of jobs in the Quatsino area: postmaster, mining recorder, provincial constable and customs officer. He began taking photographs in the late 1880s and compiled a valuable historic record of pioneer and First Nation life on N Vancouver I. His fiancée, Evelyn May Hawkins (1877–1971), came out from England and married him in 1912. The couple lived at Quatsino until 1936 and then moved to Vancouver. Leeson Rk commemorates Jobe, while the point was named after Ben. Leeson Ck and Leeson Lk, just W of Winter Hbr, are named for the family as well. *See also* Winter Hbr, which was formerly known for many years as Leeson Hbr.

Legace Bay (54°31'00" 130°14'00" E side of Work Channel, N of Prince Rupert), **Legace Point** (52°28'00" 128°25'00" SW end of Susan I, Finlayson Channel, NW of Bella Bella). Josette Legacé (c 1809–96) was born near Kettle Falls, Washington, daughter of a French-Canadian fur trapper and a Spokane Native American woman. She became the wife of HBC officer John Work in 1825, accompanying him on his trading expeditions in the western US and joining him in 1836 at Ft Simpson, where he was in charge until 1846. During that period, Work visited the QCI and, in 1840, made the first census of Haida Gwaii, noting also the numbers of houses and memorial poles. In 1849 the Work family moved to Ft Victoria, where John, now a chief factor and senior HBC official, purchased a large property and built a mansion, called Hillside. He was later a member of colonial Vancouver I's legislative council, 1853–61. Josette successfully made the transition to upper-class chatelaine and was known in Victoria for her hospitality and kindness. She outlived her husband by 35 years. Six of her daughters married either HBC officers or other prominent early residents of BC's capital city. Josette Legacé often appears in the historical record as Suzette, and Suzette Bay near Legace Point is also named for her, as is Josette Point in the QCI. It is uncertain, though, whether Suzette is an alternative personal name or an error for Josette. *See also* Work Channel.

Legace Island (53°13'00" 132°12'00" Kagan Bay, Skidegate Inlet, QCI). Named for Peter Legacé, who accompanied HBC chief factor John Work to the QCI from Port Simpson in 1850 to investigate rumours that gold had been discovered in Mitchell Inlet. He may have been a relative of Josette Legacé, Work's wife (*see above*). RN surveyor Lt Daniel Pender gave this feature the name Triangle I in 1866, but the hydrographic service changed it in 1947.

Legeak Point (53°49'00" 128°43'00" E side of Amos Passage, N end of Douglas Channel, S of Kitimat). This traditional First Nation name for a line of dominant Tsimshian Eagle clan chiefs is more commonly spelled Legaic, though many variations are recorded, including Legaik, Ligeex and Legex. The word comes originally from the Heiltsuk language and means "chief of the mountains." The first Legaic was born in the Kitimat area but lived at

his mother's village of Metlakatla, where he was able to control much of the regional fur trade in the late 1700s. The second Legaic moved his tribe to Ft Simpson in 1834 after marrying his daughter Sudaal to the HBC's Dr John Kennedy (*see* Kennedy I), thereby establishing himself as a key middleman between the white traders and surrounding First Nation tribes and building an economic empire that brought great prestige to the Eagle clan. Anglican missionary William Duncan converted the third chief, Paul Legaic, to Christianity in 1863 and took advantage of his trading influence to wrestle business away from the HBC. Paul Legaic is believed to have died at Port Simpson about 1869. Subsequent chiefs took the name Legaic until the 1930s but no longer played such a pivotal role in NW coastal life.

Leggeat Point (53°17'00" 129°30'00" Entrance to Tuwartz Inlet, SE end of Pitt I). This feature was named in 1944 after Matthew Leggeat (1900–1965), a seaman and quartermaster aboard the W coast survey vessel *William J Stewart* in the early 1940s.

Leighton Island (52°20'00" 128°20'00" Entrance to Lambard Inlet, W side of Don Peninsula, NW of Bella Bella). Margaret Leighton (1849–1944), born in Moray, Scotland, immigrated with her family to Nevada and California, where her father had mining and steamship interests, and then, in 1863, to Victoria, where she attended Angela College. While visiting her uncle Thomas Buie, a magistrate and store owner at Lytton, she met Robert Burns McMicking (1843–1915), at that time the telegraph agent at Quesnel, and they were married at Lytton in 1869. Robert would later go on to establish and manage some of BC's earliest telephone and electric companies (*see* McMicking Inlet). Margaret moved to Victoria with her husband in 1870 and became a well-known resident of that city, founding the Victoria Literary Society, engaging in much charitable work and attending the 1924 old-timers' reunion (*see* Adams Bay). She was the sister of James Leighton (*see below*). McMicking Inlet and McMicking Point are also named for her.

Leighton Point (53°04'00" 129°07'00" W side of Barnard Hbr, S end of Whale Channel, NW side of Princess Royal I). James Buie Leighton (1851–1945) was the younger brother of Margaret Leighton (*see above*). He was also born in Moray, Scotland, and came with his family to the US in the early 1850s and to Victoria in Sept 1863. In the 1870s he moved to Savona, where he ranched, ran a ferry and had a contract to transport mail. Leighton married Savona native Jane Elizabeth Uren (1861–1938) at Clinton in 1882. Both he and his wife died at Kamloops. Nearby Leighton Lk, constructed for irrigation purposes and now well known for its rainbow trout, is named for the Leighton family as well.

Leiner River (49°55'00" 126°39'00" Flows SW into NE end of Tahsis Inlet, W side of Vancouver I), **Mount Leiner** (49°57'44" 126°34'31" Just NE of Tahsis Inlet). Carl Leiner (1883–1923) pre-empted land at the mouth of the river in 1912 and received a Crown grant in 1919.

Lelu Island (54°12'00" 130°17'00" Between Smith I and Ridley I, S of Prince Rupert). The name means "wolf" in the W coast Chinook jargon used by early traders, settlers and First Nation groups. According to BC historian Capt John Walbran, the island and surrounding area were once overrun by these animals. Lelu (often spelled lelou or leloo) presumably comes from the French word for wolf, *le loup.*

Lemmens Inlet (49°12'00" 125°52'00" S side of Meares I, just NW of Tofino, Clayoquot Sd, W side of Vancouver I). John Nicholas Lemmens (1850–97) was a Roman Catholic priest from Holland who served as a missionary at Kyuquot in 1883–85, Barkley Sd in 1885–86 and Clayoquot in 1886–88. He was educated and ordained at Louvain College, Belgium, and came to Victoria in 1876, working first as pastor of St Peter's, Nanaimo, 1876–83. He represented the diocese of Victoria at an important plenary council in Baltimore in 1884. In 1888 he was appointed bishop of Victoria and became deeply involved in the construction of the new Roman Catholic cathedral, St Andrew's, which he dedicated in 1892. Lemmens died in Guatemala of a fever while raising funds for St Andrew's. The inlet was marked on charts as Disappointment Inlet until 1934 and is still known by that name locally.

Lempriere Bank (52°23'00" 129°02'00" Laredo Sd, S of Aristazabal I). Lt Arthur Reid Lempriere was an officer in the Columbia detachment of Royal Engineers that served in BC 1858–63. He studied engineering at the Royal Military Academy, Woolwich, becoming a 2nd lt in 1853, and spent much of the Crimean War at Heligoland, an island and former British colony off the German coast, used as a British military depot during the Russian conflict. Lempriere was a friend of British artist John Millais and served as the model for his famous 1852 painting *The Huguenot.* He arrived at Esquimalt in 1859 with the main body of sappers and kept an important journal of his 14-month stay in the colony, during which time he served as the commissary officer, acquired land and also worked as a photographer and architect, designing New Westminster's Holy Trinity Church as well as other structures. In May 1859, Col Richard Moody, his CO, sent him to explore and cut potential trails between Ft Hope and Boston Bar. In Aug, Lempriere was put in charge of a squad of sappers and sent to the San Juan Is, where a territorial dispute with the US over ownership of the archipelago threatened to escalate into violence. He was promoted to capt and spent time in early 1860 working on the Cariboo wagon road N of Ft Yale, but was transferred back to England that June. Lempriere married three times

and had a long career with the RE, retiring in 1882 with the rank of maj gen. Lempriere Ck, Mt Lempriere and Lempriere railway station on the CNR line—all located near the junction of the Albreda and N Thompson rivers—are also named for him. A Japanese internment camp, served 1942–45 by the Lempriere post office, was located near the station during WWII.

Lenfesty Point (48°30'00" 123°33'00" N of Sawluctus I, W side of Finlayson Arm, just NW of Victoria). Named for William Nicholas Lenfesty (1873–1951), who acquired a Crown grant of land in this vicinity in 1911. He and partner Charles Pichon were early gunsmiths in Victoria. Their store also sold fishing tackle, "cutlery," and "all kinds of sporting goods."

Lennard Island lighthouse station in 1982. *Jim Ryan*

Lennard Island (49°07'00" 125°55'00" SW end of Templar Channel, just S of Tofino, Clayoquot Sd, W side of Vancouver I). Named in 1861 by RN surveyor George Richards after one of BC's earliest tourists: Charles Edward Barrett-Lennard (1835–74). He was a British cavalry lt and the grandson of Sir Thomas Barrett-Lennard, an eccentric baronet who was in the habit of dressing so shabbily that the police mistakenly detained him as a vagabond. Charles and his friend Capt Napoleon Fitzstubbs came out to BC in 1860 on the *Athelstan,* with Barrett-Lennard's 18-tonne cutter, the *Templar,* as deck cargo. The pair unloaded this small yacht at Victoria, sailed it round Vancouver I and then sold it to Robert Burnaby and William Henderson, prominent Victoria businessmen. Barrett-Lennard returned to England and published an account of their cruise, *Travels in British Columbia, with the Narrative of a Yacht Voyage Round Vancouver's Island,* in 1862. The book was reprinted in 1973. *See also* Stubbs I (Clayoquot Sd) *and* Templar Channel. A powerful lighthouse was built on the island in 1904 with well-known local resident Frank Garrard as the first keeper. *W*

Lenz Islet (52°12'00" 128°29'00" Off W side of Athlone I, Milbanke Sd, W of Bella Bella). Caroline Lenz (1855–1935) was born at Milwaukee, where her father, Jacob Lenz (1819–99), owned a brewery. In 1871 she married her cousin Simon Leiser (1851–1917), who had emigrated from Germany in 1868 to become her father's apprentice—and eventual partner. The Leisers determined to seek out new opportunities in the PNW and in 1873 moved to Victoria, where Simon opened a coffee and spice shop. He then went to the remote Cassiar gold district and built a toll trail, complete with trading posts, from the Stikine R to the gold diggings. He returned to Victoria in 1880 and—with the help of his father-in-law and his brother Gustav, who had followed him W—established a successful wholesale grocery business, Simon Leiser & Co, which had branches around BC and became a major supplier for the Klondike gold rush. Leiser also went into the sealing trade and was soon one of Victoria's leading businessmen and civic benefactors, serving two terms as president of the board of trade. This, however, did not prevent an angry Victoria mob from vandalizing his store, as well as other businesses with Germanic names, following the sinking of the *Lusitania* in 1915. The Leisers were prominent members of the city's Jewish community, and Caroline was an accomplished pianist. Their home, on St Charles St, was designed by Samuel Maclure and is a heritage site today. Kelly, Douglas & Co bought Simon's business after his death in Vancouver of a sudden stroke. Simon's brother Gustav married Caroline's sister Sophia. He and his brother-in-law Moses Lenz formed the Victoria wholesale dry goods firm Lenz & Leiser.

Leonard Point (50°36'00" 126°56'00" N side of Cormorant I, off NE end of Vancouver I, just E of Port McNeill), **Leonard Rock** (50°36'00" 126°58'00" Just W of Cormorant I). Named by Capt George Richards, of the RN survey vessel *Plumper*, after Frederick Lewis Leonard, a surgeon aboard HMS *Alert*. He served on the Pacific Station 1858–61, under Cdr William Pearse.

Leonide Point (53°12'00" 132°08'00" W side of Renner Passage opposite Maude I, W of Skidegate Inlet, QCI). Lt Daniel Pender named this feature Nose Point in 1866, but the hydrographic service changed it in 1945 because of duplication elsewhere. The *Leonide* was the sloop that mining engineer Francis Poole chartered in 1863 to take him from Victoria, where he had been briefing officers of the Queen Charlotte Mining Co on his progress, to the QCI. He had originally come to Haida Gwaii the year before to search for copper along the shores of Skincuttle Inlet. In 1863 he inadvertently brought the dread disease smallpox back with him to the Burnaby I area. Later in the 1860s the *Leonide* is recorded carrying a cargo of lumber from Sewell Moody's Burrard Inlet mill to S America. *D*

Leopold Islands (52°59'00" 132°10'00" Kuper Inlet, E of Hibben I, NW Moresby I, QCI). After Adm Sir Augustus Leopold Kuper, who, as an RN capt, surveyed this area in 1852 with HMS *Thetis* and named the feature after himself. *See* Cape Kuper.

Leroy Bay (51°16'00" 127°40'00" S side of Browning Channel, Smith Sd, N of Port Hardy), **Leroy Island** (In Leroy Bay), **Leroy Rock** (S side of Browning Channel). Named after the Leroy Bay Cannery, which was built in 1929 by Kingcome Packers Ltd. The plant burned down in 1937 and was not rebuilt, though the site was later used as a seasonal camp by Nelson Bros Fisheries Ltd. According to BC's Geographical Names Office, the name was especially requested by BC land surveyor Noel Humphrys on behalf of cannery owner J J Stump. Nearby Leroy Lk gets its name from the same source. Leroy I was known earlier as Surf I and Murray I.

Lerwick Point (53°51'00" 130°00'00" N entrance to Kumealon Inlet, Grenville Channel, SE of Prince Rupert). Lerwick, the largest town on Scotland's Shetland Is (and the northernmost town in the UK), was the birthplace of Robert Alexander Hunter (1866–1949), who joined the Canadian Pacific Navigation Co as a quartermaster in 1889. In 1896 he married Emma Eliza Ann Robson (b 1873) at Mayne I. In later years, Hunter became a capt with the BC Coast Steamship Service, a branch of the CPR, which took over the CPN fleet in 1901, and served as master of the *Charmer*, *Princess Adelaide*, *Princess Charlotte*, *Princess Victoria* and other vessels. He was in charge in 1918 when the *Princess Adelaide* struck a rock in Active Pass, off Mayne I, in the fog. The accident ripped a 13-m gash in the ship's side that cost $200,000 to repair; Hunter had his licence suspended for six months for not being on the bridge at the time. CPR officials had so much confidence in their employee, however, that they kept him on full salary during the suspension and even sent him to Britain for a holiday. He resumed command of the CPR's vessels on his return to duty.

Leslie Point (52°57'00" 132°13'00" W side of Douglas Inlet, S of Hibben I, NW Moresby I, QCI). After Dr Archibald Leslie Archer, assistant surgeon aboard HMS *Thetis* in 1852. *See* Archer Point.

Levesque Bay (50°39'00" 126°22'00" S side of Gilford I, W of Stormy Bluff, at entrance to Knight Inlet). Middy Levesque began logging at Scott Cove on Gilford I about 1918, in partnership with Art McIntyre and Fidel Laviolette. According to author and local resident Bill Proctor, the trio constructed a sawmill near Loose Lk on Gilford I and used the lumber to build a dam at the lake and a flume from the lake to the beach. When the water level rose sufficiently, the dam gates were opened and all . the logs that had been stored in the lake were guided to

L

salt water by the flume. After about 10 years, Levesque and his partners moved on and were replaced by the employees of Triangle Logging, who used trucks and were able to operate more efficiently.

Levy Point (53°05'00" 129°12'00" NE end of Ashdown I, Whale Channel, between Gil I and Princess Royal I). Henry Emanuel Levy (1843–1929), born at Wellington, NZ, also lived in Australia, California and England before arriving at Esquimalt, by himself, in the steamer *Panama* in 1859. Only 16 years old, he lied about his age and managed to get a job as a policeman and a position with the Tiger Engine Co fire brigade. Levy was a born entrepreneur and was soon successful enough to bring his mother and siblings out to Victoria from England. With their help his empire flourished. The Levys had real-estate and business interests in both Victoria and Seattle, including a soda-water factory, fish-processing plant, salmon saltery and hop yard. Henry married Eva Rostein (1862–1946) of Seattle in 1882. After the great 1889 fire in that city destroyed many of his properties, he spent most of his time in Victoria. He was probably best known for one of his oldest enterprises: the Arcade Oyster Saloon (later known as Levy's), which he and his brother Joseph established in 1865. The restaurant was famed for its gourmet seafood and also for Cocky, its pet cockatoo. Henry participated in the Victoria old-timers' reunion of 1924 (*see* Adams Bay).

Lewall Inlet (51°46'00" 128°05'00" E side of Stirling I, W end of Hakai Passage, S of Bella Bella). Bernard Cecil "Bunny" Lewall (1895–1994) was commissioned a BC land surveyor in 1923 and practised for more than 40 years. He came to BC with his family in 1908 and settled first at Walhachin near Kamloops Lk, then at Ashcroft. Seriously wounded during WWI at the 2nd Battle of the Somme, he was able to resume survey work in BC after the war and joined the firm of Underhill & Underhill. He married Ellen McKenzie (1903–85). Lewall was employed on the central BC coast in the 1920s, when this inlet was named for him. He later worked in the US (on the General Electric building in New Jersey), the UK and Argentina, returning to BC in 1947 and specializing in railroad surveys for the PGE and CNR. Lewall was chief construction engineer on the PGE line from Prince George to Ft St John.

Lewis Bay (48°41'00" 123°23'00" W side of Coal I, just E of N end of Saanich Peninsula, N of Victoria). Capt Frederick E Lewis (1887–1963), a native of Tarrytown, NY, came to Canada from California in 1939 and purchased Coal I, where he built a luxurious estate. He was active in marine and yachting circles and took a keen interest in search-and-rescue work. Nearby Cap Rks are also named for him, and Stranger Passage (qv) is named after one of his yachts.

Lewis Channel (50°11'00" 124°56'00" Between Cortes I and W Redonda I, N end of Str of Georgia), **Lewis Cove** (50°49'00" 127°03'00" N side of Labouchere Passage, S of Drury Inlet, N of Port McNeill), **Lewis Island** (54°00'00" 130°14'00" Between Porcher I and Kennedy I, S of Prince Rupert), **Lewis Point** (50°33'00" 126°51'00" W entrance to Beaver Cove, W end of Johnstone Str, NE side of Vancouver I), **Lewis Reef** (48°25'00" 123°17'00" NW of Chain Its, W of Oak Bay, off SE tip of Vancouver I), **Lewis Rocks** (50°49'00" 127°03'00" S of Lewis Cove). Herbert George Lewis (1828–1905) was a long-serving master mariner and officer in the marine dept of the HBC on the BC coast. He was born in Hertfordshire and first went to sea with the E India Co, joining the HBC in 1846 as 3rd mate of the *Cowlitz* and arriving at Victoria the following year. After a stint on the N coast at Ft Simpson, he returned to England and served on the HBC barque *Tory* as 2nd mate, 1850–52, sailing to Victoria and back via China. From 1853 onwards, Lewis worked mostly in BC, as 1st mate of the *Otter* and then as cdr of the *Beaver*, *Otter*, *Labouchere*, *Princess Louise* and *Enterprise*. Because of his experience in inland waters, he was often called upon to act as a pilot for RN vessels on the PNW coast. In 1870, at London, England, he married Mary Langford (1837–1903), daughter of pioneer Vancouver I settler and HBC farm bailiff Edward Langford. After retiring from the HBC in 1883, Lewis was appointed BC agent of the federal Dept of Marine and Fisheries, 1886–92, then worked as an independent shipping master at Victoria. Herbert Reefs off Lewis I are also named for him, while Langford Cove (qv) recalls his wife. Lewis Channel was the Canal de Separacion of Spanish explorer Dionisio Alcalá-Galiano; this was where his ships, the *Sutil* and *Mexicana*, parted ways with those of Capt George Vancouver. *W*

Licka Point (50°34'00" 126°41'00" E end of Hanson I, W end of Johnstone Str, off NE side of Vancouver I). This name was adopted in 1974 after a request by the colleagues of Capt Otto Licka (1909–74), a well-known master mariner with the Alaska Ferry System and a seafarer in PNW coastal waters for 45 years. A resident of Washington state, he spent most of his career in the towboat business and with the Alaska Steamship Co but became a pilot on the Seattle–Alaska ferry run in 1968 and made more than 200 trips in that capacity.

Liddell Rocks (52°38'00" 129°30'00" SW of Moore Is, Hecate Str, W of Aristazabal I). Lance Cpl Robert Liddell, about whom virtually nothing is known, was a member of the Columbia detachment of the Royal Engineers, which served in BC 1858–63. The feature was named in 1927.

Lighthouse Bay (49°01'00" 123°35'00" Between Race Point and Virago Point, Porlier Pass, NW end of Galiano I, Gulf Is). A pair of light towers were erected on Race and Virago points in 1902 as range markers to guide ships through the dangerous waters of Porlier Pass. With its rocks, reefs and swirling, 10-knot (18.5-km/h) currents, the pass had long been recognized as unsafe and was the site of numerous wrecks. By the late 1800s, though, steam vessels bound from Vancouver for Ladysmith's coal-loading facilities were risking this shortcut on a regular basis. Pressure grew on the federal government to provide navigation aids before a major mishap occurred. Francis "Sticks" Allison became the first keeper and tended both lights from a residence on Lighthouse Bay until 1942. Fatal accidents continued to take place in the pass, however, including the loss of the tugs *Peggy McNeil* in 1923 and *Point Grey* in 1949. The original tower on Virago Point was still standing in the early 2000s, though the Race Point tower was demolished in 1996 and replaced with a beacon. Both lights are now automated.

Lihou Island (53°00'00" 132°25'00" Englefield Bay, NW side of Moresby I, QCI). Norman Reginald W Lihou (1880–1963), from England or the Channel Is, was a member of A E Wright's provincial survey party in this area in 1924. According to BC's Geographical Names Office, he also served as the cook on a 1920 forest survey on the N shore of Hardwicke I, where Lihou Lk is named for him. In 1932 he married Mary Elizabeth Vines (1889–1940) at N Vancouver. QCI historian Kathleen Dalzell tells of a legend associated with the Haida community once located on Lihou I. This village was known as Throwing-Grease-Around, as it was wealthy enough to be offhand in its use of eulachon oil, a valuable condiment. The inhabitants were attacked by people from nearby Kaisun, and the four who survived were transformed into large stones that made loud, eerie sounds when they banged against each other in stormy weather. *D*

Lillie Point (52°18'00" 128°22'00" NE side of Cecilia I, off SW end of Don Peninsula, NW of Bella Bella). After Elizabeth "Lillie" Reid, youngest daughter of pioneer HBC master mariner James Murray Reid. *See* Reid Passage. Mt Lillie on Knight Inlet is also named for her.

Lillooet Passage (51°59'00" 128°15'00" N of Simonds Group, Queens Sd, SW of Bella Bella). Named for the Canadian government vessel *Lillooet*, built by BC Marine Rwys Co (also known as Bullen's shipyard) in Esquimalt and launched in 1908. The 50-m, 493-tonne *Lillooet* was the mainstay of the Canadian Hydrographic Service on the Pacific coast until 1932 and saw regular use as a survey ship under hydrographers Philip Musgrave and Henri Parizeau, and skippers Frederick Griffith and J J Moore. In 1932 the vessel was sold to the Pacific Salvage Co of Victoria and rebuilt as the *Salvage Chieftain*. In the mid-1950s, by which time its name had been restored to *Lillooet*, it was still in operation, employed as a towboat in the coastal barge trade. The Lillooet (Lil'wat) people, based at Mt Currie on the Lillooet R NE of Whistler, are part of the St'at'imx First Nation. Their name may mean "wild onion."

Lima Point (54°14'00" 130°23'00" S end of Digby I, just SW of Prince Rupert). Frederick Lima (d 1897) was a paymaster aboard HMS *Malacca*, under Capt Radulphus Oldfield. He served on the Pacific Station in 1866–67 and retired from the RN in 1883 with the rank of chief paymaster. Lt Daniel Pender surveyed this area in 1867 with the ancient *Beaver*, hired from the HBC, and named a number of features after the *Malacca* and its crew. Prince Rupert Hbr was formerly known as Lima Hbr.

Lime Bay (48°26'00" 123°23'00" N side of Inner Hbr, Victoria Hbr, SE end of Vancouver I). Site of a kiln and primitive loading facility built in colonial times to provide growing Victoria with lime, an essential material used in the early days to make mortar and whitewash and improve acidic soils. The bay once was much larger, extending almost to the E&N tracks, but was gradually filled in between 1935 and the late 1950s.

Limekiln Bay (49°47'00" 124°38'00" NW end of Texada I, Str of Georgia). Texada I's rich limestone deposits have been exploited since the 1880s. In the early days the mineral was heated in simple stone or brick kilns directly on the island's shores in order to produce lime, which has a great number of industrial uses, especially in the production of plaster, cement, fertilizer and pulp and paper. Several lime kilns were erected on this bay in the early 1900s and taken over by the Pacific Lime Co in 1910; brick ruins can still be seen, along with large piles of slag. In the early 2000s, the quarries at the N end of Texada continued to be BC's largest suppliers of limestone.

Limekiln Cove (48°27'00" 123°27'00" NE side of Esquimalt Hbr, just W of Victoria). For many years this body of water, located at the end of Helmcken Rd, was known as Helmcken Cove (after early HBC medical officer and politician John Helmcken, who owned but never lived on the surrounding land), and it appears as such in the 1966 gazetteer. An alternative name, dating from at least the 1880s, was Limekiln Cove, and this latter name inadvertently appeared on a chart in 1974. The hydrographic service discovered that local residents preferred Limekiln to the gazetted name, so instead of correcting the chart, the service rescinded the name Helmcken Cove in 1982 and made Limekiln official. Several lime kilns in the area, including ones on the old Colwood and Craigflower HBC farms, date back to colonial times, and limestone was intensively quarried and burned around Esquimalt Hbr in the early 1900s—at Atkins Rd in Langford, Rosebank in Colwood and Parson's Bridge in View Royal. According to Capital Regional District records, remains of an old kiln were found during blasting operations at the corner of Helmcken Rd and the Old Island Hwy, only two blocks from the cove. A limestone quarry at this location may have been leased by Craigflower Farm, and the kiln operated by John

L

Greig (see Greig I), who is believed to have also been in charge of another Craigflower kiln in the early 1850s. A plaque beside Limekiln Cove states that this was where "the gallant sailing ships from the old world stopped to replenish their supply of fresh water."

Lime Point (52°47'00" 128°20'00" NE side of Griffin Passage, between Roderick I and Pooley I, N of Bella Bella). The records at BC's Geographical Names Office sometimes offer intriguing but frustratingly inconclusive hints about the origins of certain names. This feature, for instance, is said to commemorate an "incident with a bucket of lime while surveying." No other information is given. The name was adopted in 1949.

Lina Island (53°14'00" 132°07'00" W of Bearskin Bay, W of Skidegate Inlet, QCI), **Lina Narrows** (53°14'00" 132°08'00" Between Lina I and Graham I). The name is an adaptation of the Haida word for the First Nation fort that once occupied one of the Balch Is, just off the SE side of Lina I. There were a number of important Haida habitations on Lina over the years, including Lina village, Gaodjaos ("Drum Village") and Gasins ("Gambling Sticks"), where significant petroglyphs are located. About a dozen white settlers developed homesteads on the island in the early 1900s. RN surveyor Lt Daniel Pender named Lina I in 1866.

Lindbergh Island was named after famed aviator Charles Lindbergh.

Lindbergh Island (49°31'00" 124°17'00" Scottie Bay, N side of Lasqueti I, Str of Georgia). In 1927, after Charles Augustus Lindbergh (1902–74) made his historic solo, non-stop trans-Atlantic flight, Lasqueti I resident and US native Paul Lambert requested—through his MP, Alan Neill—that this feature be named for the world's newest hero. An exchange of correspondence followed that, while amusing, also neatly reflects various official attitudes to the naming process. Regional hydrographer

Henri Parizeau wrote that "the island itself is such an unimportant feature, with regard to navigation, that under ordinary circumstances [it] would not have been named.... You will please note that I am not taking responsibility for naming this island." BC's chief geographer, George Aitken, then picked up the ball. "It is a very small marine feature," he responded, "to carry a name so world-renowned as Lindbergh. If Mr Lambert insists upon this naming, it is suggested that a more prominent geographical feature can be selected ... to perpetuate the admiration of BC and Canada for the courage displayed by Col Lindbergh in his crossing of the Atlantic." Robert Douglas, secretary of the Geographic Board of Canada, had the final word: "I have to say that the Board has always avoided approving the names of US citizens for Canadian geographical features. However, the present island is so small that in the opinion of the Board its name is immaterial, and whatever name is satisfactory to Mr Lambert ... and to yourself will be acceptable."

Lindgren Point (50°32'00" 127°35'00" S of Hecate Cove, Quatsino Sd, NW Vancouver I). Gust Lindgren (c 1848–1915) supposedly pre-empted land in this area in the late 1890s, but no trace of his application appears in the records, nor does he seem to have received a Crown grant.

Lindsay Bay (53°09'00" 129°33'00" NW side of Campania I, NE end of Estevan Sd, S of Pitt I). This name was adopted in 1944 to recognize Norman Lindsay (1894–1948), who piloted one of the survey launches carried aboard the government hydrographic vessel *William J Stewart* in the early 1940s.

Lindsay Rocks (52°34'00" 129°15'00" W of entrance to Clifford Bay, W side of Aristazabal I). Sgt James Lindsay (1829–90) was a member of the Columbia detachment of the Royal Engineers, which served in BC 1858–63. He was born at Fife, Scotland, joined the Royal Artillery at the age of 18 and served for many years at Gibraltar. Lindsay's sister was also with him in BC, married to a fellow sapper, Cpl John McKenney. Sgt Lindsay was a bit of a tippler, apparently, and gained the nickname Whispering Jimmy for his loquacious behaviour while under the influence. He spent much time travelling the new Cariboo Wagon Rd as it slowly made its way to the BC Interior—supervising roadbuilding contracts, escorting gold-laden stagecoaches and transporting prisoners. He is reported to have made the 600-km journey from Williams Ck to Yale by horse and sternwheeler in a mere 30 hours. Lindsay retired from the army when the detachment disbanded, received the long service and good-conduct medal and stayed in BC, taking up land at Maple Ridge with his sister and brother-in-law. He later became a policeman in the gold district, eventually rising to the position of chief constable of the Cariboo. James Lindsay died at Barkerville.

Linn Rock (52°16'15" 128°43'35" W of S tip of Price I, NW of Bella Bella). Sapper John Linn (1821–76) came to BC with the Columbia detachment of the Royal Engineers, which served in the colony 1858–63. He was born at Edinburgh and joined the British Army in 1846. His first N American posting was at Halifax, in 1848. Linn, a mason by trade, married Mary Robertson (d 1907) in NS in 1857 and returned to England that year, shortly before embarking once again with his bride in the *Thames City* for BC. The first of the Linns' six children was born en route to Esquimalt, where the vessel arrived in 1859. When the detachment disbanded, Linn chose to remain in the colony and took his free military land grant on the N shore of Burrard Inlet, where he built a cottage beside a stream that began appearing in local records as Linn's Ck as early as 1878. (Before that it was known as Fred's Ck, presumably after early settler Frederick Howson, or as Kwa-hul-cha by First Nation residents.) The Linn children went to school at Moodyville. For some reason, Linn was frequently misspelled Lynn, and it was this latter version of the name that stuck, not only for Lynn Ck but also for all the other names that were later derived from it: Lynn Lk, Lynn Peaks, Lynn Valley (a residential suburb that developed in the early 1900s), Lynn Canyon and Lynnmour (situated between Lynn Ck and the Seymour R).

Linthlop Islet (50°30'00" 127°51'00" E side of Koprino Hbr, Quatsino Sd, NW Vancouver I). Howard Douglas Linthlop (c 1877–1961), from Halifax, secured Crown grants of land in this vicinity in 1909 and 1912, and was described in the 1908 BC voters list as a prospector at Quatsino. He married Eilleen Gladys Bentley at Vancouver in 1918, and the Linthlops' daughter, Hilda, was born at Courtenay the following year. Howard died at Vancouver.

Lion Island (49°10'00" 123°00'00" Off the W tip of Annacis I, Gravesend Reach, lower Fraser R). In 1884, early entrepreneur Alexander Ewen built a large cannery here, traces of which can still be seen. He became a major player in the BC cannery trade and served as president of the BC Packers Assoc, 1901–7. The name of the island may refer to the Lion brand of sockeye salmon produced at this plant. A group of Japanese fishing families, led by Jinsaburo Oikawa, colonized Lion I (and adjacent Don I) in 1902. These immigrants produced salted salmon, salmon roe, soy sauce and sake, and worked at nearby canneries, but the islands were slowly abandoned after Oikawa returned to Japan in 1917. They are now owned by Metro Vancouver and reserved for future park use. *E*

Lion Islets (48°54'00" 123°20'00" N of Whaler Bay, SE side of Galiano I, Gulf Is). The feature was named by local resident A Gayzer for its shape, which strongly resembles a crouching lion when viewed from a particular angle. This unusual fact was brought to the attention of readers of *Maclean's* in 1939, though the photo, which ran in the magazine's "Scrapbook" section, clearly showed a lion with no tail. The correspondent apologized for this absence and speculated that perhaps the creature was a Manx lion.

Lions Bay (49°27'00" 123°14'00" E side of Howe Sd, NW of Vancouver). A cluster of summer cottages here, served by a flag stop on the PGE railway line, was named after the nearby twin peaks known as The Lions. The iconic mountains overlook downtown Vancouver and were named about 1890 by BC Supreme Court judge John Hamilton Gray for their resemblance to couchant lions. They were called Chee-Chee ("The Twins") by the Skxwúmish (Squamish) people and have had a variety of colloquial names over the years, including The Sisters, Sheba's Breasts, Sheba Peaks and Twin Peaks. Lionsview, a district of N Vancouver, is also named for them, as is the Lions Gate Bridge. The village of Lions Bay grew into a permanent community with the opening of the Sea to Sky Hwy in 1958 and was incorporated in 1971.

Lions Gate. *See* First Narrows.

Lippy Point (50°28'00" 128°06'00" W entrance to Grant Bay, SW of Winter Hbr, Quatsino Sd, NW side of Vancouver I). Thomas Sargent Lippy and William Grant received Crown grants of land in this area in 1904–5. Many years after abandoning his property, Lippy apparently returned to Quatsino Sd, as a grant was issued to him in the same vicinity in 1928. Lippy Ck, E of Neroutsos Inlet, is presumably named for him as well.

Liska Islet (50°43'00" 126°43'00" SW of Crib I, Sunday Hbr, E end of Queen Charlotte Str). Named in 1952 for Able Seaman Vincent Liska, who drowned off N Korea Dec 4, 1950, aged 28. He was on night patrol with HMCS *Cayuga* at the time and was lost overboard while the destroyer was engaging a shore battery. A native of the Czech Republic, he had lived at Victoria with his wife, Carol, and at Natal in the E Kootenays before WWII. He also served on the BC coast in 1944 as a crewman with the survey vessel *William J Stewart*. Liska is believed to be the only BC resident to die in the Korean War who has a place named for him in his home province. He is commemorated on the Korean War Memorial at the Military Museums in Calgary. Liska It was formerly known as Scrub I.

Little Church Island. *See* Church I.

Little Cridge Island. *See* Cridge I.

Little D'Arcy Island. *See* D'Arcy I.

Little Espinosa Inlet. *See* Espinosa Inlet.

Little Genn Island. *See* Genn Is.

L

Littlejohn Point (53°19'00" 129°43'00" N entrance to Port Stephens, SW side of Pitt I). Named in 1944 for G Littlejohn, chief steward aboard the W coast survey vessel *William J Stewart* in the early 1940s. The feature was formerly known as Bluff Point.

Little Kinahan Island. *See* Kinahan Is.

Little Popham Island. *See* Popham I.

Little Shell Island (48°40'00" 123°22'00" One of the Little Group, S of Coal I, E of N end of Saanich Peninsula, N of Victoria). This island and neighbouring Ker I, which was formerly known as Shell I, were named for the large deposits of shell on the beaches. When Shell I was renamed, the hydrographic service saw no reason to also change Little Shell I, as it was part of the Little Group and its name was still appropriately descriptive.

Lizzie Rocks (52°20'00" 128°22'15" S of Lake I, at S end of Perceval Narrows, off SW side of Don Peninsula, NW of Bella Bella). Elizabeth Wilhelmina "Lizzie" Fisher (1849–1932) was born at Liverpool and came to Esquimalt with her family in 1863 on the *Strathallan*. Her father, William Fisher (1811–91), the scion of a wealthy shipping family, served as MLA for Esquimalt, 1875–78. In 1869 she married lawyer and politician Charles Edward Pooley (1845–1912; *see* Pooley I, which is a little N of Lizzie Rks). The Pooleys lived at first at New Westminster but soon built a fine residence, Fernhill, in Esquimalt and played prominent roles in the social life of early Victoria.

Loap Point (52°43'00" 129°01'00" N entrance to Kent Inlet, SW side of Princess Royal I). Loap is the Tsimshian First Nation word for stone or rock, according to the 1884 *Comparative Vocabularies of the Indian Tribes of BC*, by William F Tolmie and George M Dawson. Formerly known as Philip Point, after John Maison Philip, a member of the W coast hydrographic survey staff in the early 1940s, but renamed in 1944.

Lochalsh Bay (52°32'00" 128°21'00" N side of Jackson Passage, between Roderick I and Susan I, N of Bella Bella). Named, in association with nearby Roderick I and Finlayson Channel (qv), after the birthplace of fur trader Roderick Finlayson, who played an important role with the HBC in the early development of Victoria. The Kyle of Lochalsh (a modification of the Gaelic for "strait of the foaming lake") is located on the NW coast of Scotland, 100 km W of Inverness, near the Skye Bridge, built in 1995 to connect the Isle of Skye to the mainland. It is the terminus of a scenic single-track railway line. Lochalsh Bay is the site of an aquaculture operation.

Lock Bay (49°11'00" 123°49'00" NE side of Gabriola I, Gulf Is). Nick Doe of the Gabriola Historical & Museum Society has suggested that this name, applied in 1859 by RN surveyor Capt George Richards, might have been intended to honour Michael Lock or Lok (c 1532–c 1621), a 16th-century English mercer, trader and adventurer. It was Lok who initially publicized Greek pilot Juan de Fuca's claims to have discovered the Str of Anián, a hypothetical passage through N America that supposedly provided a shortcut from Europe to China (*see* Juan de Fuca Str for a more detailed outline of this controversy). Richard Mayne, who served as 1st lt to Capt Richards, 1857–61, and who dedicated his 1862 book, *Four Years in BC and Vancouver I*, to his cdr, devotes much space in his first chapter to Lok and de Fuca and was obviously fascinated by the story. It is possible that the bay was named at his urging. Lok travelled widely in Europe, seeking markets for his family's business and becoming obsessed with travel literature and maps. He translated early travel documents into English, served as an important source for historian Richard Hakluyt and backed the Baffin I explorations of Martin Frobisher, an investment that bankrupted him.

Locke Island (52°16'00" 128°16'00" S entrance to Spiller Channel, NW of Bella Bella), **Lockeport** (52°43'00" 131°50'00" W side of Klunkwoi Bay, E side of Moresby I, QCI), **Locke Shoal** (52°50'00" 131°53'00" Head of Pacofi Bay, N of Lockeport). Capt Louis P Locke (1852–1918), a native of NS, had the tragic distinction of presiding over the PNW's worst maritime disaster—the sinking of the *Princess Sophia*. Before coming to BC with his English wife, Emily, and five children about 1892, Locke had worked for the Red Star Line, which ran between Antwerp, NY and Philadelphia. He was a respected master mariner with the CPR's BC Coast Steamship Service for many years and served as skipper of the *Princess Beatrice* and *Amur* on the QCI route between 1907 and 1912. The islands at that time were undergoing a mining boom, and Locke took great interest in such speculative activities as the buying and selling of mining claims. In 1908, when a community of prospectors sprang up beside Klunkwoi Bay, residents did not seem able to decide on a name for their new settlement. The capt suggested Lockeport, after his NS hometown, which had been established by his ancestors. After the copper ran out about 1918, a cannery was built at Lockeport, but that also shut down in the 1930s and the place turned into a ghost town. Louis Locke, meanwhile, moved on as a ship's master to the *Princess Sophia*, on the run between Skagway and Vancouver. At 3 AM on Oct 24, 1918, in a violent snowstorm, the vessel ran aground on Vanderbilt Reef in Alaska's Lynn Canal. At first the 75-m, 2,104-tonne *Sophia* seemed in no immediate danger, and Locke kept the passengers on board rather than try to disembark them in such rough weather. The following day, though, the gale increased in force, and the ship was driven across the reef and foundered. In all, 343 lives were lost; only a dog survived the wreck. Locke I was named in 1925. It was formerly known as Creak I and also as Shenton

I, after Cdr John Thomas Shenton (1862–1953), a retired RN officer who enlisted with the RCN during WWI and in 1916 investigated the wreck of the *Carelmapu* off the W coast of Vancouver I. Tofino residents had complained that the crew of the Clayoquot lifeboat were derelict in their response to this tragedy, in which 18 people perished. Shenton died at Nanaimo. *D E*

Lock Island (53°29'00" 129°55'00" S entrance to Ala Passage, W side of Pitt I). Named in 1944 for J Lock, the storeskeeper aboard the W coast survey vessel *William J Stewart* in the early 1940s.

Logan Bay (49°07'53" 123°41'58" SE end of Gabriola I, Gulf Is). Kingsley "King" S Logan (1903–56) and his wife, Annie (1904–85), moved to this location from Richmond, BC, in the early 1940s and built the first house on the bay. King was born at Winnipeg and arrived at Vancouver with his family about 1913. Annie, from Manitoba, moved with her family to Sask in 1908. The Logans were married in Sask in 1925 and came the same year to Steveston, where King taught English and art. On Gabriola he was a fisherman and owned a gillnetter named *Alobe II* (an acronym made up of A for Annie, and LO and BE for their daughters Lois and Betty). Annie Logan was well known for her musical abilities and community piano-playing, and all the family members were actively involved in the Gabriola community. The name of the bay was adopted in 1992.

Logan Inlet (52°47'00" 131°44'00" E side of Moresby I, S of Selwyn Inlet, QCI). Sir William Edmund Logan (1798–1875) was the founder and first director of the Geological Survey of Canada. He was born at Montreal, educated at Edinburgh and worked for his uncle, a London businessman, for 20 years. In 1831 his uncle sent him to manage a copper mine and smelter in Wales; Logan made detailed geological maps of the surrounding coal fields and developed theories about coal formation that are still mainly valid. In 1842 he applied for and won the new job of provincial geologist for Canada, and the following year set up the first office of the geological survey. For more than a quarter of a century he supervised the production of books and maps that detailed the country's mineral resources, especially on the N shores of the Great Lks, where rich beds of copper, nickel, uranium and iron were revealed. Logan engaged in extensive fieldwork in the Canadian wilderness, which in the mid-1800s required great strength and endurance. He died and is buried in Wales. Logan Inlet was named in 1878 by George M Dawson, who would become director of the geological survey in 1895. *W*

Logan Rock (53°02'30" 129°28'00" Off S end of Jewsbury Peninsula, W side of Campania I, N of Caamaño Sd). Named in 1944 for Horace Logan (1913–79), a coxswain aboard the W coast hydrographic survey vessel *William J Stewart* in the early 1940s.

Logarithm Point (53°33'00" 129°57'00" NW entrance to Ala Passage, off W side of Pitt I). A 1921 coast triangulation party under Alfred Wright, a surveyor with the BC Lands Service, applied a number of surveying-related place names to this region. Other associated names, including this one, were added by the hydrographic service in the early 1950s. A logarithm, which represents the power to which a fixed base must be raised to produce a given number, can be used to simplify a complex mathematical calculation. *See also* Azimuth I, Cosine Bay, Sine I *and* Tangent I.

Lohbrunner Island (52°29'00" 128°44'00" Off N side of Price I, Higgins Passage, NW of Bella Bella). According to records at BC's Geographical Names Office, the feature was named in 1947 for "Mr Lohbrunner, who made a report to this office on the drying bank westward of the island, Oct 1946." This cryptic note almost certainly refers to Maxmillan Edmund Lohbrunner (1887–1973), an eccentric Victoria resident who had been to sea in the early 1900s aboard the sealing schooners *Diana* and *Enterprise*. He was born at NY and came to BC as a child. After sealing ended in 1911, Lohbrunner roamed the N coast, fishing, trapping, buying furs and exploring. In 1947 he purchased at public auction, for $300, the *Green*, one of the PNW's last remaining whaling ships. He told the *Colonist* newspaper that he was going to fix it up for use in his business, the Deepsea Fish Co. Instead, he moored it at the foot of Herald St, along with a sailboat named *Mel* and a raft laden with junk, and lived aboard for 20 years—much to the chagrin of Victoria's tourism dept. The *Green* became a notorious eyesore, but its owner slyly evaded many appeals and attempts to have him move on. There was a certain amount of public sympathy. As Larry Slaght, marine agent for the Dept of Transport, commented in a 1967 interview: "The trouble is he's married to that thing. To take it away would be like burning down his house." The vessel eventually sank; only the mast and harpoon gun remained above water. These were blasted off with explosives and ended up at the Maritime Museum of BC in Victoria. Maxie's brother Edmund Lohbrunner (1904–85) was a prominent Victoria nurseryman and world-renowned expert on alpine plants, which he travelled widely to collect.

Loken Point (52°18'00" 127°34'00" N side of King I, NE of Bella Bella). Ole John Loken (1866–1961) or Lokken, as the surname is more usually spelled, was a member of the original group of Norwegian settlers that colonized the Bella Coola area in the mid-1890s. He travelled to the Yukon to try his luck in the Klondike gold rush, then returned to the Bella Coola valley, fished for a living and married Inga Sofie Sylvester (1881–1947) there in 1906. In 1905, with four partners, Lokken established a sawmill and lumber business on a tributary of the Salloomt R that remained in operation until 1936. He died at Coquitlam, but his descendants still live in the Bella Coola area.

L

Lombard Point (52°29'00" 128°56'00" SE side of Aristazabal I), **Lombard Rocks** (52°44'00" 129°26'00" W of Leadman Passage, NW side of Aristazabal I). Charles Amand Lombard (1846–1938) was born at Paris and came to Victoria in 1858 with his Chilean stepfather, who went into business as a coffee merchant, and his mother, Louise L'Hôtelier (who had been an opera singer in France; *see* Balagny Passage). Lombard ran a music store in Victoria and became well known as a local actor, musician and singer, and also as a supporter of the arts.

London Slough, located between Reifel and Westham islands in the municipality of Delta. *Peter Vassilopoulos*

London Slough (49°06'00" 123°10'00" Between Reifel I and Westham I, mouth of the Fraser R). Named for George William London (1869–1942), who came to BC from Ont with his parents about 1879. His father, Richard London (1844–1930), established a farm on Westham I that George eventually took over and operated with his son, George Ernest London. He married Jeannie Dalziel (1877–1956) at Ladner in 1897. His uncles Charles and William Henry London were early farmers on Lulu I. They built a store and temperance hotel at the foot of No 2 Rd, where a community known as London's Landing soon sprang up, complete with post office, church, school and government wharf. A steamship stopped there each day on its route between Ladner and New Westminster to pick up farm products and passengers. The name London Slough was adopted in 1947 and then withdrawn, as aerial photographs showed that it no longer existed. Later photos revealed that the feature had reformed, and the name was reinstated.

Lone Rock Point (49°21'00" 122°55'00" W side of Indian Arm, NE of Deep Cove and Vancouver). The original name of this feature, adopted in 1948, was Lone Rk, but an extensive landfill project ended up connecting the rock to the mainland, necessitating a change of name in 1979 to Lone Rk Point.

Longbeak Point (49°37'00" 124°50'00" N tip of Denman I, Str of Georgia). RN surveyor Capt George Richards named this feature Beak Point on one of his early coastal surveys, and the N end of Denman is shaped surprisingly like a seabird's elongated head and bill. It was renamed Longbeak Point in 1923, presumably because the name Beak Point was duplicated elsewhere.

Loquillilla Cove (50°52'00" 127°45'00" S side of Nigei I, Goletas Channel, off N end of Vancouver I). A long-abandoned Nahwitti First Nation village was once located on this cove. According to BC historians Helen and Philip Akrigg, the name is a Kwakwala word that may mean "to fish for halibut."

Loran Passage (51°15'00" 127°49'00" Between Table I and Egg I, at entrance to Smith Sd, NW of Port Hardy). LORAN, an acronym for long-range navigation, is a government-operated radio navigation system that uses multiple land-based, low-frequency radio transmitters to determine the location and speed of a receiver. It was invented during WWII by US banker and physicist Alfred Lee Loomis, who also played an instrumental role in the development of radar. By the early 2000s, LORAN-C, a version of the system still in use at that time, was rapidly being made obsolete by GPS, a global navigation-satellite system. The names of both Loran Passage and nearby Radar Passage were adopted in 1948, when these technologies were still fairly new.

Lord Bight (54°14'00" 133°05'00" Off W side of Langara I, extreme NW end of QCI). This feature was apparently named in 1907 by Capt Frederick Learmonth of the RN survey vessel *Egeria* after a seaman who helped crew one of the ship's sounding launches.

Lord Island (49°47'00" 126°51'00" Mary Basin, Nuchatlitz Inlet, W side of Nootka I, off W side of Vancouver I), **Lord Waterfall** (49°53'00" 126°46'00" E side of Zeballos Inlet, N of Nootka I). Seattle native William Ross Lord (1866–1945) was an experienced cannery man on the W coast of BC. His father, Donald Ross Lord, a carpenter and building contractor, had helped build the first salmon cannery on the Columbia R about 1866. Early in his career, William worked as a steamship engineer, both in Washington state and on the Fraser R. By 1890, the year he married Mary Whiteside (1866–1954), from Ont, at Eburne, he was managing the Garry Point Cannery at Steveston, which was sold the following year to Henry Bell-Irving's Anglo-BC Packing Co. Lord went on to manage other Anglo-BC canneries, including the Britannia at Steveston and the British American and N Pacific on the Skeena R. He later established a salmon saltery on Nootka I near Friendly Cove, and in 1916 joined with the Everett Packing Co to build a cannery and pilchard-reduction plant there, owned by Everett subsidiary Nootka Packing Co, which Lord managed until 1926. Both William and Mary Lord died at Vancouver.

Lord Point (48°51'00" 123°19'00" N of Village Bay, NW side of Mayne I, Gulf Is). From 1928 to 1946, John William Clifford Lord (d 1951) was the postmaster at New Westminster, where he had married Jessie Duncan Symington in 1907. The Lords owned recreational property on Mayne I at this location and lived there permanently after Clifford retired.

Lorenz Point (50°10'00" 127°38'00" E side of Nasparti Inlet, between Kyuquot Sd and Quatsino Sd, NW side of Vancouver I). Ernest Louis A Lorenz (1864–1911), from Germany, went to sea at the age of 15 and arrived in the PNW on a barque named *Sovereign of the Seas*. He settled first at Nanaimo, then joined the sealing schooner *Juanita* in 1891 and was later master of the schooners *Theresa* and *Mascott*. In 1899, at Vancouver, he married Emily Wood (1876–1949), who had arrived in Canada from England in 1888. Lorenz appears to have abandoned his seafaring ways after marriage; he is listed in the 1901 census and 1902 Victoria directory as a clerk at the Hotel Victoria.

Loretta Channel (53°44'51" 128°53'48" Between Loretta I and Maitland I, at junction of Devastation Channel and Douglas Channel, S of Kitimat), **Loretta Island** (53°44'32" 128°51'47" E side of Loretta Channel). Loretta Gobeil was married to Joseph E Gobeil of Canada's Dept of Public Works (*see* Gobeil Bay). Loretta I, long considered part of Hawkesbury I, was probably named by Capt John Walbran of the lighthouse tender and survey vessel *Quadra* in 1898. That was the year Walbran took Gobeil and Louis Coste, the dept's chief engineer, on a W coast tour of inspection. According to former UBC anthropologist Jay Powell, Loretta I was used by the Haisla people as a refuge when caught by the frequent gales that blow down Kitimat Arm. Their name for the feature is Ademgwa'linuxw, meaning "having sandhill cranes," while Loretta Channel is known as Sawiksewa, meaning "to go through it."

Lorne Islet (52°17'00" 128°06'00" E side of Return Channel, between Yeo I and Chatfield I, just N of Bella Bella). The 48-m, 260-tonne *Lorne* was one of the best-known, most powerful steam tugs ever to work the BC coast. Built in 1889 for industrialist James Dunsmuir at Victoria's Laing Shipyards, it was designed to tow the large sailing vessels that found it difficult to enter and leave Juan de Fuca Str in adverse weather. After Dunsmuir sold the *Lorne* in 1903, it towed rail barges and giant Davis rafts of bundled logs for several different owners. It was noted for salvage work, but also had its share of accidents; in 1930, for instance, the log barge *Pacific Gatherer*, towed by the *Lorne*, managed to destroy the central span of the Second Narrows bridge and interrupt rail service to N Vancouver for four years. The old tug was retired in 1936 and broken up the following year. It was named after John Douglas Sutherland Campbell (1845–1914), the Marquess of Lorne, who married Princess Louise, a daughter of Queen Victoria, and served as Canada's gov gen, 1878–83. Lorne founded the Royal Society of Canada and the Royal Canadian Academy of Arts. He and his wife made a lengthy visit to the BC coast in 1882. *See also* Louise I.

Lost Islands (52°48'00" 131°29'00" NE of Kunga I, off E side of Moresby I, QCI). Regional hydrographer Henri Parizeau gave this name to these islands in 1923 because, up until that time, they had not appeared on any chart. They were also known in the early days as the Seal Is.

Lost Lagoon (49°18'00" 123°08'00" Just W of Coal Hbr, downtown Vancouver). This 17-ha feature was originally part of Coal Hbr but was turned into an artificial lake when the Stanley Park causeway was constructed in 1916. The name comes from a poem, "The Lost Lagoon," by writer and performer Pauline Johnson (1861–1913), who left a fuller description of the naming in her 1911 book, *Legends of Vancouver*. She wrote that she had always resented the "jarring, unattractive" name of Coal Hbr. "When I first plied paddle across the gunwale of a light little canoe, and idled about its margin, I named the sheltered little cove the Lost Lagoon. This was just to please my own fancy, for, as that perfect summer month drifted on, the ever-restless tides left the harbour devoid of water at my favourite canoeing hour, and my pet idling-place was lost for many days—hence my fancy to call it the Lost Lagoon." Piped-in salt water was replaced by fresh in 1929 and the lake stocked with trout. Boating and fishing were popular pastimes until banned to protect wildlife in 1938. In 1936 the fountain was added, not without controversy, to celebrate Vancouver's 50th anniversary. *E*

Lotbinière Island (53°01'38" 129°34'21" SE island in the Estevan Group, W side of Estevan Sd, SE of Banks I). Sir Henri-Gustave Joly de Lotbinière (1829–1908) was lt gov of BC from 1900 to 1906. This French-born lawyer and politician served a succession of Liberal governments in Lower Canada (1861–67), Que (1867–85) and Canada (1867–74, 1896–1900). He was premier of Que, 1878–79, and controller and minister of Inland Revenue under Wilfrid Laurier, 1896–1900, in which role he was noted for opposing political patronage. Laurier appointed him lt gov of BC at a time of administrative instability, when the legislature was composed of quarrelling factions rather than organized parties. As an experienced outsider, Joly de Lotbinière was able to exert considerable control over an unruly assembly, refusing to accept one premier's resignation, dismissing a scandal-ridden cabinet and choosing Richard McBride as premier in 1903. The island was formerly known as East I but was renamed in 1950. *E*

Loudoun Channel (48°56'00" 125°23'00" W side of Barkley Sd, W side of Vancouver I). The *Loudoun* was the former name of the *Imperial Eagle*, the ship that early fur trader Charles Barkley brought to the W coast of

Loughborough Inlet

Vancouver I in 1787. The 360-tonne, 20-gun vessel was originally owned by the E India Co, and Barkley, a former E India Co capt, took command of it in 1786 for its voyage to the PNW. Because it was sailing under an Austrian flag in order to evade the E India Co's trading monopoly, its name was changed. *See also* Barkley Sd *and* Imperial Eagle Channel. Loudoun is an area in SW Scotland and the name of a former village there.

Loughborough Inlet, just east of Knight Inlet. *Greg Shea*

Loughborough Inlet (50°31'00" 125°32'00" N of Johnstone Str and W Thurlow I, between Knight Inlet and Bute Inlet). Named by Capt George Vancouver in 1792 after Alexander Wedderburn, 1st Baron Loughborough (1733–1805). A Scottish lawyer and friend of the powerful Earl of Bute, Wedderburn was called to the English bar in 1757 and engaged the noted actors Thomas Sheridan and Charles Macklin to give him elocution lessons. He served as solicitor gen (1771–78), attorney gen (1778–80), chief justice of common pleas (1780–93), lord high steward (1793–95) and lord chancellor (1793–1801). Loughborough left politics in 1801 and was made the Earl of Rosslyn. This feature was named Brazo de Salamanca, after Lt Secundino Salamanca of the *Sutil*, by the Spanish explorer Dionisio Alcalá-Galiano. In the early 1920s, Loughborough Inlet was the site of one of BC's first major truck-logging operations, run by Northern Pacific Logging Co using cabless White vehicles with solid rubber tires. *W*

Louie Bay (49°44'00" 126°56'00" S side of Nuchatlitz Inlet, NW side of Nootka I, W side of Vancouver I). Louisa Ellen Langford (1832–88) was the eldest daughter of Flora and Edward Langford (*see* Langford), who came out from England in 1851 with their five children to establish Colwood Farm for the HBC. In 1857, back in London, she married Capt John Josling (*see* Josling Peninsula) of the RN, whom she had met while he was serving on the Pacific Station in 1851–53 as 2nd lt of HMS *Thetis*. He was killed in 1863 at the bombardment of Kagoshima, Japan, while commanding HMS *Eurylus*. Louisa died in Pakistan, at Murree in the Punjab. Louie Bay was formerly known

as Louie Ck ("creek" being an old Admiralty term for a shallow, drying inlet).

Louisa Cove (52°11'00" 128°29'00" W side of St John Hbr, W side of Athlone I, W of Bella Bella). After Louisa Townsend, who came to Victoria in 1862 aboard the brideship *Tynemouth* and married architect Edward Mallandaine. *See* Mallandaine Point.

Louisa Point (50°28'00" 125°46'00" N entrance to Forward Hbr, E of Hardwicke I, N of Johnstone Str). Lady Louisa Isabella Lascelles (1830–1918) was a sister of Lt Horace Lascelles, who was in command of the RN gunboat *Forward* on the BC coast, 1861–65 (*see* Lascelles Point). She married Charles Henry Mills (1830–98), 1st Baron Hillingdon, a banker and Conservative MP. Horace Lascelles was also a British aristocrat, a son of the Earl of Harewood, and many features in the vicinity of Forward Hbr were named after his family, including four points that commemorate his sisters.

Louise Island (52°59'00" 131°47'00" E side of Moresby I, QCI), **Louise Narrows** (52°57'00" 131°54'00" Between Louise I and Moresby I). Princess Louise Caroline Alberta (1848–1939), fourth daughter of Queen Victoria, married John Douglas Sutherland Campbell (1845–1914), Marquess of Lorne, in 1871 and accompanied him to Canada in 1878 when he was appointed gov gen. The vice-regal couple made a lengthy, busy visit to Victoria in 1882, much to the delight of civic authorities, who erected faux-Gothic arches and other pseudo-structures, which the eminent BC historian Margaret Ormsby described as "hideous monstrosities," in their honour. Victoria residents, wrote Ormsby, got quite used to seeing Louise "strolling down Government St, or examining needlework at a church bazaar, or even buying cakes in a bake-shop." While she may have enjoyed Victoria, the homesick Louise, a talented painter and sculptor, heartily disliked Ottawa and was happy to return to England in 1883. Though her relationship with her husband became strained over the years, she was devastated by his death from pneumonia and spent her final decades as something of a recluse. Louise I, the third-largest island in the Queen Charlotte archipelago, was named by geologist George Mercer Dawson in 1878 to commemorate the princess's arrival in Canada. Lk Louise and the province of Alberta are also named for her. Louise Narrows formerly dried at low tide but was dredged in 1967 so that loggers could travel between Lagoon Inlet and Cumshewa Inlet. *See also* Lorne It. *W*

Louis Islands (52°43'00" 129°05'00" Off Channel Point, E side of Aristazabal I). Louis Ramsbotham Davies (1879–1964) had a 40-year career as a hydrographer on the BC coast. He was born in Ont and transferred to Prince Rupert in 1907 after a year on the Lk Superior survey and a year in

Ottawa. He worked on nearly every part of the coast—the mouth of the Skeena R, Hecate Str and Dixon Entrance, Milbanke Sd and the W coast inlets of Vancouver I—and was hydrographer in charge of several vessels, including the *Naden, Somass* and *Armentières*. His last field season was in 1937; after that date he served as assistant to the supervising hydrographer at Victoria and, from 1940 to 1947, as supervisor of chart production and distribution. The nearby Ramsbotham Is are also named for him. His father (Cdr Robert Watts Davies of the RN) and uncle (Sir Louis Davies, minister of Marine and Fisheries, 1896–1901) have places named after them on the BC coast as well (*see* Davies Bay *and* Watts Narrows).

Louis Point (53°41'00" 133°02'00" SW entrance to Port Louis), **Louis Rocks** (53°42'00" 133°02'00" NW of Louis Point), **Port Louis** (53°42'00" 132°58'00" W side of Graham I, W of Masset Inlet, QCI). The protected harbour of Port Louis was named in 1791 by Capt Prosper Chanal, after Lt Louis Marchand of the French trading and exploration vessel *La Solide*. Louis' brother, Etienne Marchand, was the leader of the expedition, which made a circumnavigation of the world, 1790–92. Louis and Chanal, in a longboat, surveyed the NW coast of Graham I from Parry Passage to Hippa I. Louis Point was known to the Haida people as Twoo-ts Chigoas, according to QCI historian Kathleen Dalzell, while Port Louis was called Kio-kathli. *See also* Chanal Point *and* Marchand Point. *D*

Louis Point (53°49'00" 128°46'00" S tip of Coste I, Kitimat Arm, near entrance to Kildala Arm, S of Kitimat). After Louis Coste, chief engineer of the federal Dept of Public Works in the 1890s and early 1900s. *See* Coste I.

Louscoone Inlet (52°11'00" 131°14'00" S end of Moresby I, QCI), **Louscoone Point** (52°07'00" 131°14'00" SW entrance to Louscoone Inlet). The name of the inlet was bestowed in 1853 by Admiralty surveyors and is probably an attempt to transliterate the Haida name for this feature. QCI ethnologist Charles Newcombe gave the name Lgadjukun to Louscoone Point in 1897. Detailed charts of the inlet (formerly known as Louscoone Hbr) were not made until 1935, when Henri Parizeau of the Canadian Hydrographic Service surveyed the area.

Lovekin Rock (49°04'05" 125°45'20" N end of Long Beach, SE of Tofino, W side of Vancouver I). Named for businessman and philanthropist Arthur Charles Lovekin (1862–1949), who was born in Ont and died at Victoria but lived most of his life in California, moving there in the 1880s and working as a surveyor and in the gold-processing and funeral industries. He was involved for a number of years with sugar manufacturing in Hawaii, and met his wife, Helen Stevens (1866–1954), there. The Lovekin family moved back to California in the early 1900s and settled at Riverside, where Arthur had an orange plantation. He also grew cotton in the Blythe area. He took a keen interest in conservation, leading efforts to preserve much of Mt San Jacinto, near Palm Springs, as a state park, and donating land to Riverside Community College. The Lovekins bought property near Tofino about 1927 and built a luxurious summer retreat overlooking Long Beach. The family apparently gave tracts of land for the military hospital that was built in the area, along with an airport, in 1942–43, and for the construction of the road between Tofino and Ucluelet. Parks Canada purchased Lovekin's remaining holdings from his son in 1974 and removed the buildings the following year.

Lowe Inlet (53°33'00" 129°35'00" Extends E from Grenville Channel, opposite Pitt I). Thomas Lowe (1824–1912), a native of Scotland, joined the HBC in 1841 and travelled on the *Vancouver* to Hawaii, then on the *Cowlitz* to Sitka, where he arrived in 1842. From Sitka he was sent to Ft Durham on Alaska's Taku Hbr as Dr John Kennedy's second-in-command until that post was closed in 1843, at which time he sailed S and helped build the new fort at Victoria. Later in 1843, Lowe accompanied James Douglas to Ft Vancouver on the Columbia and was based there until 1850, during which time he travelled overland twice to York Factory on Hudson Bay, carrying "accounts and despatches." When gold was discovered in California, he left the HBC and went first to Oregon City and then to San Francisco, where he formed trading companies with other ex-HBC employees and his brother James Lowe (*see* James Point). Thomas moved to Victoria in 1862 and, with James, who had settled there in 1860, established the firm of Lowe Bros, which bought out wholesaler G Vignols in 1864 and ship chandler James Southgate in 1865. He retired in 1871 and returned to Scotland. The inlet was named for Thomas in 1844 by Capt Charles Dodd of the HBC steamer *Beaver*. Mt Lowe, near the head of Knight Inlet, was probably also named for him in about 1865, by RN surveyor Capt George Richards. The Lowe Inlet Cannery, built by Robert Cunningham and John Rood and later owned by BC Packers, operated from 1890 to 1930 and was torn down in 1937. The Tsimshian people know the inlet as Kmodo, and its head, where the Kumowday R drains Lowe Lk and flows over scenic 7-m-high Verney Falls, is an important First Nation fishing site and Kitkatla reserve. The area, popular with boaters, was protected as a provincial marine park in 1993. *E W*

Lowrie Bay (50°42'00" 128°22'00" S of Hansen Bay, N of Cape Russell, NW end of Vancouver I). This feature commemorates the master of the *Captain Cook*, whose name is now accepted by most historians to have been Henry Laurie, not Lowrie. Laurie was accompanied on his 1786 voyage—the second-earliest fur-trading venture to the BC coast after James Hanna's daring effort of 1785—by Capt John Guise, aboard the tiny *Experiment*, and E India Co factor James Strange, who was in overall command

L

of the expedition. Bombay merchant David Scott had provided the financing. The adventurers sailed to Nootka Sd from India via Java, then travelled N to Queen Charlotte Sd and Alaska before returning to Asia. Their journey was of great significance historically, but the financial returns were poor, much to the disappointment of their backers.

Luard Shoal (52°24'00" 128°53'00" Laredo Channel, SE of Aristazabal I). Capt Henry Reynolds Luard (1828–70) was an officer with the Columbia detachment of Royal Engineers, which served in BC 1858–63. He was born at Warwick, England, into a landowning family with an ancestral home in Lincolnshire and sugar plantations in the W Indies, and attended the Royal Military Academy at Woolwich, 1845–47. For the next three years he was posted to the Royal School of Military Engineering at Chatham, then went back to Woolwich in 1850–53 and to the W Indies in 1853–56. In 1858, after volunteering for foreign service in BC, he took command of the main contingent of sappers and their families and embarked on the *Thames City*, eventually arriving at Esquimalt the following Apr. Luard's responsibilities included the camp at Sapperton and troops quartered there, the routine maintenance of law and order, and contracts with civilians for roadbuilding and supplies. He pre-empted land, which he later sold, in the Similkameen district. The dashing capt, who played the flute and was "a good-hearted, considerate man," according to his fellow soldiers, attracted the affections of Caroline Mary Leggatt (c 1844–1914) of Victoria, and the pair were married there in 1863. (Caroline's widowed mother, Fanny, later married Thomas Lett Wood, a Cambridge-educated lawyer who served as attorney gen of Vancouver I and solicitor gen of colonial BC before becoming chief justice of Bermuda, 1871–77.) Gov James Douglas had a high opinion of Luard, whom he considered to have "intelligence, method, order and gentlemanly character," and wished to offer him the job of chief commissioner of Lands and Works when the sappers disbanded. However, Col Richard Moody, the detachment CO and previous holder of this position, refused to allow Luard to remain behind in BC. Back home in England, Luard was posted to Portsmouth, 1864–66, and then to Ireland, where he died of a sudden illness.

Lucan Islands (50°50'00" 127°38'00" W side of Balaklava I, Browning Passage, off N end of Vancouver I). After British officer George Charles Bingham, 3rd Earl of Lucan (1800–88), who was cavalry cdr during the Crimean War and became famous for his role in the 1854 Charge of the Light Brigade. In this action the light cavalry, under the command of the Earl of Cardigan, Lucan's brother-in-law, made a disastrous attack on a strong Russian artillery position and was decimated. There was much confusion over the transmittal of orders, and after the debacle Lord Raglan, the overall army cdr, blamed the defeat on Lucan and censured him in dispatches. Lucan was recalled to England but made a staunch defence of his actions, escaped blame and went on to achieve the rank of field marshal. He never again saw battlefield duty, however. In 1863–64, RN surveyor Lt Daniel Pender named several features in this vicinity after the people and places associated with this military catastrophe. *W*

Lucy Island (54°11'00" 132°59'00" In Parry Passage, between Langara I and NW end of Graham I, QCI). This wooded landform received a number of different names on early fur-trading charts. Naice I was an adaptation of its Haida name. Hippa I and Middle I were applied by Joseph Ingraham in 1791–92. Spanish explorer Jacinto Caamaño designated it Isla de Navarro in 1792. The island received its current name in 1853 during an Admiralty survey by Capt James Prevost and Master George Inskip of HMS *Virago*, but the identity of Lucy is not known. *D*

Lucy Islands (54°18'00" 130°37'00" In Chatham Sd, SE of Melville I, W of Prince Rupert). Lucy McNeill (1834–1914) was the second daughter of HBC chief factor and master mariner William McNeill and his first wife, Mathilda, a Kaigani Haida chief. In 1856 she married Hamilton Moffatt (1832–94, *see* Moffat Is), who was in charge of various HBC trading posts, including Ft Rupert and Ft Simpson on the coast, and also worked for the federal Dept of Indian Affairs, 1873–93, based at Victoria, mostly as assistant to superintendent Israel Powell. Lucy was a "miraculously unfettered Victorian female," according to BC memoirist Helen Meilleur. "She was so adaptable that she could occupy the VIP cabin aboard the *Labouchere* on the trip N and then set off in a canoe for weeks of weather-exposed travel to Indian villages, her back braced against a bale of blankets. Lucy makes the balancing of two heritages look as effortless as riding on a teeter-totter." A lighthouse station was built on the E island in 1907, one of two marking the entrance to the port of Prince Rupert. It was automated in the 1980s. The islands were named by Capt George Richards of HMS *Hecate* about 1862.

Luke Island (52°06'00" 127°52'00" Entrance to Evans Inlet, Fisher Channel, E of Bella Bella), **Luke Passage** (52°06'00" 127°51'00" Between Matthew I and King I, entrance to Evans Inlet). Named after one of the four evangelists who wrote the gospel accounts in the New Testament. Luke is claimed to also be the author of the *Acts of the Apostles* and may have been a physician born at Antioch. Lt Daniel Pender named several nearby features after the evangelists about 1866, probably in association with Port John (which does not commemorate a biblical figure, however, being named by Capt George Vancouver after his friend the Rev John Fisher). On the other side of the province, Luke Ck in the Kootenays was also named after Luke the Evangelist, by Fr Leon Fouquet.

Lulu Island (49°10'00" 123°06'00" Mouth of the Fraser R, S of Vancouver). Several attempts have been made over the years to clarify the origin of this name. An early BC yearbook claimed that it honoured a Hawaiian or Kanaka employee of the HBC. A pioneer settler account suggested it was an adaptation of the Chinook jargon word *lolo*, meaning "to carry," and referred to an early portage route. The most widely accepted explanation, however, is that it was named in 1862 by Col Richard Moody, CO of a detachment of Royal Engineers serving in BC, after Lulu Sweet, a young member of the first theatrical troupe ever to perform at New Westminster. According to historian John Walbran, "her conduct, acting and graceful manners gave great satisfaction, and were appreciated to such an extent by her friends and patrons that the island was named after her." Lulu I was important for farming for many years and was also the site of numerous salmon canneries, but is now largely occupied by the city of Richmond. *E W*

A view of Lund from the 1910s. *Author's collection*

Lund (49°58'00" 124°46'00" NW of Powell R, E of Campbell R, NE side of Str of Georgia). Named by Charles and Frederick Thulin, who logged and pre-empted land at this location in 1890, after their ancient Swedish hometown. The original Lund was founded around AD 1000 and, with its early 12th-century cathedral, became an important Christian centre. Lund's 17th-century university is Sweden's largest. The name comes from the Old Norse *lundr*, meaning "forest." The Thulin brothers went on to establish and develop the present-day city of Campbell R (*see* Thulin Passage). Lund is now the northern terminus of Hwy 101 and the site of a historic hotel; most residents earn their livelihoods from fishing, logging and tourism. Nearby Lund Lk takes its name from the community. *E*

Lupsi Cupsi Point (49°15'00" 124°49'00" N end of Alberni Inlet, S central Vancouver I). A Nuu-chah-nulth village named Lupsi-Kupsi, noted for its fine sand beach and rich beds of camas and wild onion bulbs, once occupied the area where the paper mill now sits. Nearby Lupsi Cupsi Ck also takes its name from this former First Nation community.

Luxana Bay (52°03'00" 131°03'00" E side of Kunghit I, QCI). This feature was named by Capt Charles Duncan of the *Princess Royal*, an early British fur trader on the BC coast. Duncan was part of James Colnett's 1786–88 expedition to the PNW, financed by Richard Etches and the King George's Sd Co. In 1788 he sailed through Dixon Entrance and Hecate Str, thus proving the insularity of the QCI, which had been suspected by earlier European visitors. His chart of the area named this bay Lux Aena, which supposedly means "handsome women" in the Haida tongue. A 1791 Spanish chart shows the bay as Puerto de Buenas Mugeres ("Hbr of Good Women").

Luxmoore Island (52°59'00" 132°21'00" Off W side of Hibben I, Englefield Bay, NW Moresby I, QCI). Benjamin Luxmoore (or Luxmore) was an RN clerk aboard HMS *Thetis* and served on the Pacific Station, 1851–53. Before that he was off the W coast of Africa with HMS *Centaur*. He was promoted to paymaster in 1856 on HMS *Atalanta*. This feature was known as Hole I by the local Haida people, as it has a natural rock arch. It received its current name from Capt Augustus Kuper, who made a survey of the area in 1852. *D*

Lyall Harbour (48°48'00" 123°12'00" W side of Saturna I, Gulf Is), **Lyall Point** (48°58'00" 125°19'00" E side of David Channel, N of Broken Group, Barkley Sd, W side of Vancouver I). Dr David Lyall (1817–95) served in BC, 1857–61, as the surgeon aboard HMS *Plumper*, survey vessel of Capt George Richards, and as a member of the N American Boundary Commission, which he accompanied as a botanist. He had a most unusual career. Born in Scotland and educated at Aberdeen, Lyall managed to make a journey to Greenland as surgeon on a whaling vessel before joining the RN in 1839. Perhaps because of this Arctic experience, he was assigned later that year to the Antarctic expedition of Sir James Ross as assistant surgeon and naturalist on HMS *Terror*. Along with famed botanist Joseph Hooker, who was aboard HMS *Erebus*, he spent three years exploring the region and forming a collection of 1,500 plant species. The Lyall Is off Victoria Land are named for him, as are a gastropod and several plants. In 1847 he was chosen to accompany Capt John Stokes, who had sailed with Darwin on the *Beagle*, as surgeon and naturalist of HMS *Acheron* on a survey of the NZ coast, where Lyall made another important botanical collection and wrote papers on unusual NZ bird species such as the kakapo. His next adventure, in 1852, was to the Arctic. He joined HMS *Assistance* as surgeon and naturalist and was part of Sir Edward Belcher's failed expedition in search of Sir John Franklin. After service in the Crimean War he joined the *Plumper* briefly in PNW waters before being transferred to the boundary commission. Again he amassed an abundance of plant specimens. On his return to the UK he was allowed to remain on an RN salary while residing at Kew Botanical Gardens in order to arrange

L

and write up his collections. Lyall was elected a fellow of the Linnean Society in 1862 and was married in 1866. He spent the rest of his career in England, part of the time as surgeon at Pembroke dockyard, then retired in 1873 with the rank of deputy inspector-gen of hospitals and fleets. A number of other geographic features in BC are also named for him: Mt Lyall on the BC-Alberta border, Mt David and Lyall Ck on Saturna I, David I and David Channel in Barkley Sd. The Hul'qumi'num (Coast Salish) name for Lyall Hbr is Tl'uqayum, meaning "calm waters."

Lyche Island (48°57'00" 125°33'00" Ucluelet Inlet, NW side of Barkley Sd, W side of Vancouver I). August Herman Lyche (1864–1939), who was born at Dramman, Norway, came to Ucluelet in the early 1890s with fellow settler John Kvarno (*see* Kvarno I) and was induced to stay by trader William Spring. He received a Crown grant of land there in 1907. Lyche married Alice Greenwood Lee (1871–1928) at Victoria in 1890 and died at Port Alberni. This feature was known for many years as Channel I and first appeared with that name on an 1863 Admiralty chart. It was changed to Lyche I in 1934 in order to avoid duplication.

Lyell Island shoreline, Haida Gwaii. *John Alexander*

Lyell Bay (52°39'00" 131°39'00" E side of Darwin Sd, W side of Lyell I), **Lyell Island** (52°40'00" 131°30'00" Off the E side of central Moresby I, QCI), **Lyell Point** (52°42'00" 131°43'00" Westernmost extremity of Lyell I). Sir Charles Lyell (1797–1875), born in Scotland and educated at Oxford, worked as a lawyer before dedicating himself to the study of geology. He wrote numerous books—including *Principles of Geology*, *The Antiquity of Man* and two travel volumes based on his visits to Canada and the US in the 1840s—and had a powerful influence on Charles Darwin. Lyell was famed as a popularizer of uniformitarianism, which held that geological transformation was the result of minute changes accumulated over enormous periods of time. He won the Royal Society's Copley Medal and

the Geological Society's Wollaston Medal, and many geographical features are named for him around the world, as well as craters on Mars and the moon. Lyell Ck, Lyell Icefield and Mt Lyell near the BC-Alberta boundary N of Golden also commemorate this eminent scientist. Lyell I, which has been heavily logged and once had a large forestry camp on its N shore, was the focal point for the numerous environmental protests that eventually resulted in the 1987 protection of the S Moresby region as Gwaii Haanas National Park Reserve. More than 75 Haida elders and activists were arrested there in 1985 for blocking loggers' access. The island was named by George Mercer Dawson in 1878; its Haida name is Tllga Kun Gwaayaay. Lyell Bay was named False Bay by Dawson that same year but was changed to its present form in 1952 to avoid duplication. *D W*

Lyman Point (52°05'37" 130°56'14" NE side of Kunghit I, QCI). Sir Lyman Poore Duff (1865–1955) was chief justice of Canada, 1933–44. Born and educated in Ont, he moved to Victoria in 1894 and established a busy legal practice. Duff was named to the BC Supreme Court in 1904 and to the Supreme Court of Canada in 1906, where he sat for more than 37 years. He was chairman of the Royal Commission on Transportation, which inquired into railroad problems in 1931–32. Duff's 1940 court decision upholding the authority of the federal government to abolish appeals to the British privy council had the effect of establishing a fully self-regulating court system in Canada. Lyman Point was designated East Point by George Mercer Dawson in 1878 but was renamed in 1945 to avoid duplication.

Lynn Creek, Lynnmour, Lynn Valley. *See* Linn Rk.

Lyons Cove (49°30'20" 123°54'30" On Halfmoon Bay, W of Sechelt and NW of Vancouver). This feature commemorates Frank Alexander Lyons (1894–1980), from Ireland, and Eva Lyons, long-time residents of Halfmoon Bay. They came to the area about 1940 to work for Redrooffs Resort; Frank managed the rental cottages and Eva looked after the dining room. The name was adopted in 1988 after being submitted by the Sunshine Coast Regional District, with a petition of support from local residents.

Lyons Point (50°27'00" 127°31'00" E side of Neroutsos Inlet, Quatsino Sd, NW Vancouver I). Ormond Oscar Lyons (1892–1957), originally from NS, was the doctor at Port Alice in the 1920s. He married Anita Merle Elderkin (1891–1958), also from NS, and died at Vancouver. The feature was formerly known as Lyons It.

M

Maast Island (54°00'00" 132°10'00" Masset Hbr, N side of Graham I, QCI). According to a local story recorded by QCI historian Kathleen Dalzell, a man named Massetta, an officer on an early trading vessel, died while visiting the area and was buried on the island, which the Haida named after him. Massetta was difficult to pronounce, however, and became corrupted to Masheet or Mah-sh-t. Geologist George Mercer Dawson used the spelling Maast in 1878 and speculated that the nearby village of Masset (qv) must derive its name from the island, which was also known in pioneer days as Massett I and Goat I (because livestock were often left there to graze). It was called Goose I by US fur trader Samuel Crowell when he chose it in 1791 as the site for building a small sloop—the fourth European-style vessel constructed in the PNW and the first in the QCI. He had brought the necessary materials out from Boston on his ship, the *Hancock*. Crowell and his men were attacked by a group of Haida when the new tender was ready for launching but still managed to finish it and sail off. *D*

Mabbott Island (50°28'00" 127°54'00" SW of Koskimo Is, S side of Quatsino Sd, NW end of Vancouver I). Named in 1927 after a man named Mabbott, who was the caretaker of the Quatsino Cannery in the early 1920s. The cannery was built on Koskimo Bay in 1911 by Wallace Fisheries Ltd; later a pilchard reduction plant was added. BC Packers bought the operation in 1928 and closed it down three years later.

Mabbs Islet (53°01'00" 131°56'00" NE entrance to Carmichael Passage, NW side of Louise I, E of Moresby I, QCI). Named in 1926 for Capt Edward Mabbs (1880–1942), master for many years of the GTP (later CNR) steamship *Prince John* on its regular runs to the QCI. He married Barbara Violet Leicester at Vancouver in 1918 and died in the Skeena district.

Mabens Beach (48°45'00" 125°08'00" S of Pachena Bay, SE of Barkley Sd, W side of Vancouver I). William (1867–1952) and Charlotte M Maben (1884–1963, née Marshall) were pioneer homesteaders on Pachena Bay in the 1920s

and later moved closer to Bamfield. Their original home, called Cedar Cottage, was then occupied by William's brother, John Maben (1880–1969), and his wife Mamie and family, who moved there from British Malaya. A third brother, James (1883–1951), and his wife Elizabeth (1885–1965, née Stevenson) and their daughter were the home's final occupants. There is no sign today of this pioneer outpost except a little rockwork along the stream that runs through the property.

Macaulay Point (48°25'00" 123°25'00" Between Esquimalt Hbr and Victoria Hbr, SE end of Vancouver I). Donald Macaulay (c 1805–68) was the bailiff or manager of Viewfield, one of four farms established around Esquimalt Hbr in 1850 by the Puget's Sd Agricultural Co, an HBC subsidiary. He was born in the Hebrides and came to Sask with the HBC in 1832, then overland to the PNW in 1834, working at first on the brig *Lama* under Capt William McNeill. From 1837 to 1850 Macaulay was posted to Ft Simpson on BC's N coast as a "middleman" and interpreter. In 1857, when Viewfield was merged with neighbouring Constance Cove Farm and placed under Thomas Skinner's management, Macaulay was again sent N to Ft Simpson. His final employment, until his accidental drowning in Esquimalt Hbr, was as keeper of the HBC's powder magazine at Esquimalt. Viewfield Farm, about 250 ha in size, included Macaulay Point, which had been labelled Sailor Point on Capt Henry Kellett's 1847 chart of the area but was changed about 1851. A Songhees First Nation reef-net site named Mukwuks was located just off the point. *W*

MacDonald Bay (53°12'00" 129°20'00" W side of Gil I, Squally Channel, SE of Pitt I). Sgt Albert Ernest MacDonald, MM, from Victoria, was killed in action on Feb 6, 1945, aged 25. He was a member of the Canadian Scottish Regiment, Royal Canadian Infantry Corps, and is buried at Holten Canadian War Cemetery in the Netherlands.

Macdonald Island (50°11'00" 123°48'00" Princess Louisa Inlet, N end of Jervis Inlet, NE of Powell R). This name

M

was adopted in 1979 after a request by the Princess Louisa International Society, which wished to commemorate James Frederick Macdonald (1889–1978), who was instrumental in preserving part of Princess Louisa Inlet (qv) as a park. "Mac," as he was familiarly known, was born at Seattle into a family that owned a successful wholesale grocery business. He first came to the inlet in 1919. Then in 1927 he bought land beside Chatterbox Falls and built a fine cabin there, where he entertained visiting boaters until the home burned down in 1941. For many summers thereafter he moored a floathouse beside his property instead. In 1953, concerned that the scenic inlet would fall into private hands, he gave his land in trust to a yachtsmen's association, and in 1965 it became a provincial marine park. The island, which was purchased for the park in 1972, was formerly known as Hamilton I, after a man who had a very different vision for the inlet. Thomas Hamilton (1894–1969), developer of the variable pitch propeller and an aviation industry pioneer, was, like Mac, also rich and American. He bought the island and much surrounding land in 1940–41, then spent lavishly to build the Malibu Club, a large, luxurious, chalet-style lodge at the inlet's entrance that catered, briefly, to millionaires and movie stars before closing down in 1950 (*see* Malibu It).

Macdonald Island (52°58'00" 129°41'00" W of Dewdney I, Estevan Group, S of Banks I, Hecate Str). Josephine Macdonald (1858–1945) was born at San Francisco and came to the gold-rush town of Port Douglas at the head of Harrison Lk with her parents in 1860. In 1880 she married Fraser York (1858–1942), whose family had arrived at Nanaimo from England in 1854 and who was born at Yale, where his father had built a boarding house. Fraser York was purportedly the first white child to be born on the BC mainland. The young couple moved to a farm on Sumas Prairie, where York's parents had settled in 1865. York later spent 23 years as the customs officer at the Whatcom Rd border crossing. In the mid-1920s, regional hydrographer Henri Parizeau named many features on the remote northern coast after participants in the Victoria old-timers' reunion of 1924 (*see* Adams Bay). Josephine, who died at Huntingdon in the Fraser Valley, and Fraser, who died at Port Coquitlam, are both believed to have attended this get-together.

Macdonald Point (50°41'00" 125°44'00" W entrance to Glendale Cove, S side of Knight Inlet). William John Macdonald (1832–1916), a native of Scotland, came to the PNW on the barque *Tory* as an HBC employee in 1851. A militia capt, he accompanied Gov James Douglas and a large naval force in pursuit of a Cowichan First Nation chief named Tathlasut, who was captured, tried and hanged in front of his tribe in 1856 for shooting a white settler. Macdonald married Catherine Balfour Reid (1833–1914), second daughter of HBC master mariner James Murray Reid, and retired from the HBC in 1858. He

played significant roles in Vancouver I's colonial life: gold commissioner, collector of customs, Sooke representative on the legislative assembly (1860–63). In 1868, as a member of BC's legislative council, he helped ensure the removal of the capital from New Westminster to Victoria. Macdonald became a prominent Victoria merchant and property investor, and the city's third mayor, 1866–67. He was also mayor at the time of Confederation, when he was named one of BC's three federal senators, a position he held from 1871 to 1915. In 1876 he built an ornate, turreted stone villa named Armadale, after the home of the Macdonald clan on the Isle of Skye; set in 11 ha of parkland on Ogden Point, it was one of Victoria's finest residences. A number of features near Knight Inlet were named after Macdonald and his extended family by William Blakeney, who served under Lt Daniel Pender as assistant surveying officer aboard the *Beaver*, 1863–65, and also married one of James Reid's daughters. *W*

Mace Point (49°57'00" 124°46'00" NE tip of Savary I, NE end of Str of Georgia). William Arthur Mace (1879–1975) was born in NB but moved with his family to Vancouver, where he married Laura Josephine Ibbotsen (1886–1969) in 1907 and worked as a farmhand and a carpenter. He and his family arrived on Savary I in 1913 to build a hotel for his brother-in-law, Savary developer Harry Keefer, and decided to settle there. Over the years, Mace constructed many of Savary's cottages, and his descendants became well established on the island. The point was formerly known as Green Point after Savary's first white settler, John Green (1817–93), who built a trading post nearby in 1886 and was murdered, along with his partner Thomas Taylor, in the course of a bloody robbery by Hugh Linn. Linn was the son of the former Royal Engineer who gave his name to Lynn Ck in N Vancouver. He was eventually tracked down and captured on Shaw I in Washington state, then tried at Victoria, found guilty and hanged for the crime in 1894.

Machta Point (50°00'00" 127°09'00" N entrance to Cachalot Inlet, Kyuquot Sd, NW side of Vancouver I).

Cachalot, located near Machta Point, was one of BC's most productive whaling stations. It operated from 1907 to 1924. *BC Archives C-06076*

Named after a reserve of the Ka:'yu:'K't'h (Kyuquot) First Nation near this site. The remains of the Cachalot whaling station and pilchard reduction plant were still visible in the early 2000s less than 1 km from Machta Point.

Mackenzie Anchorage (48°51'00" 125°11'00" Between Diana I and Helby I, Deer Group, Barkley Sd, W side of Vancouver I). HMCS *Mackenzie* was a destroyer escort built in Montreal and launched in 1961. The 110-m, 2,380-tonne vessel spent most of its career on the BC coast, based at Esquimalt and engaged in a number of training exercises with other Pacific Ocean navies, visiting India in 1964, the Far E in 1965, Australia and NZ in 1970, Japan in 1986 and Central America in 1988. Its crew made front-page news in 1973 when they boarded and seized the drug-running vessel *Marysville*. The *Mackenzie* used this anchorage on several occasions, including in 1970 on the eighth anniversary of its commissioning. The name was adopted in 1971. The ship was decommissioned in 1993 and sunk as an artificial reef off Gooch I near Sidney in 1995.

Mackenzie Bay (53°13'00" 132°05'00" N side of Maude I, W end of Skidegate Inlet, QCI), **Mackenzie Cove** (53°02'00" 132°21'00" N side of Security Inlet, NW side of Moresby I), **Mackenzie Island** (53°41'00" 132°59'00" Entrance to Kiokathli Inlet, Port Louis, W side of Graham I), **Mackenzie Passage** (53°19'00" 132°25'00" Head of Shields Bay, Rennell Sd, SW side of Graham I). John David Mackenzie (1888–1922), born at Baddeck, NS, conducted an important examination of Graham I in 1913–14 for the Geological Survey of Canada. He named a number of creeks and lakes, especially in the Yakoun valley, and wrote a book, *Geology of Graham Island*, published in 1916. Macdonald, who was educated at MIT and Cornell, also undertook a geological survey of BC's Flathead district and published a report for Canada's Dept of Mines, mostly concerning the availability of coal. His surname is often spelled with a capital "K," and his personal name is sometimes given as James. He died at Que.

MacKenzie Beach (49°08'00" 125°54'00" E side of Templar Channel, just S of Tofino, W side of Vancouver I). This well-established local name was adopted in 1975 to honour Bob and Doris MacKenzie. They ran a resort here in the 1960s and '70s and owned a large piece of property, which was subdivided about 1970 and developed for additional tourism facilities. Previously known as Garrard's Beach (*see* Garrard Group).

MacKenzie Cove (49°28'00" 123°22'25" Centre Bay, S side of Gambier I, Howe Sd, NW of Vancouver). Alexander (1870–1949) and Eunice MacKenzie bought 20 ha of waterfront here in 1925 and built a large summer house, which was destroyed by fire about 1940. After WWII, family members built six individual homes

around the cove. By 1990, when MacKenzie Cove was adopted as a local name, three of Alexander's sons were still living there, and the other cottages were owned by various relatives.

Mackenzie Sound (50°55'00" 126°42'00" N of Broughton I and E end of Queen Charlotte Str, W and N of Kingcome Inlet). Kenneth McKenzie (1811–74) was an early immigrant to Vancouver I and bailiff of Craigflower Farm. (Most historians agree that the surname should be spelled McKenzie; Kenneth himself spelled it both ways.) He was born at Edinburgh, son of a surgeon, attended college there, married Agnes Russell in 1841 and had a large family. McKenzie supervised his father's heavily encumbered estate until it was sold in 1851, then agreed to manage one of the properties owned by the Puget's Sd Agricultural Co, a subsidiary of the HBC. He arrived at Ft Victoria in 1853 on the *Norman Morison* with a party of 73 persons, including labourers, blacksmiths, carpenters and a schoolteacher, and moved to the Craigflower lands between Esquimalt Hbr and the Gorge Waters, where he built a fine manor house (which still stands) and many other structures, cleared land, planted fields, milled grain and lumber, and operated a lime kiln and brickworks. Gov James Douglas appointed him a magistrate and, in 1854, made him superintendent of all four HBC farms. In the late 1850s McKenzie developed a thriving trade selling meat, vegetables and, especially, bread to the RN, which by then was using Esquimalt Hbr on a regular basis. The amounts produced were quite impressive: Craigflower could supply more than 400 kg of meat and 180 kg of vegetables per day—and 4,500 kg of biscuit on 24 hours' notice. The demand for bread took all of the farm's own wheat and forced McKenzie to import grain from as far away as Oregon. Victoria's bakers complained bitterly. Despite Craigflower's productivity, it never turned more than a modest profit, and the HBC was unhappy with McKenzie's confused account-keeping. His farm contract was terminated and in 1866 he moved to the Lake Hill district of S Saanich, where he had bought land. Jessie Point (qv) is named after his daughter, Kenneth Passage (qv) and Kenneth Point for his son. *W*

Macktush Bay (49°07'00" 124°49'00" W side of Alberni Inlet, near Sproat Narrows, NE of Barkley Sd, Vancouver I). According to Nuu-chah-nulth artist and writer George Clutesi, who was a member of the Port Alberni-based Tseshaht First Nation, this name means "burned across." Macktush Ck, which has the same meaning, enters the inlet just S of the bay.

MacLeod Shoal (52°07'00" 131°12'00" Entrance to Louscoone Inlet, S end of Moresby I, QCI). William MacLeod was 1st mate of the *King George*, under Capt Nathaniel Portlock, which made an early fur-trading expedition to the PNW, accompanied by the smaller *Queen*

M

Charlotte, under Capt George Dixon. The two vessels, sent to N America in 1785 by the British trading consortium known as the King George's Sd Co, briefly visited the W coast of the QCI in 1786 before overwintering in Hawaii. The following year, Dixon and the *Queen Charlotte* came back to Haida Gwaii for a longer and very successful session of trading and exploration, while Portlock, MacLeod and the *King George* traded on the Alaska coast. MacLeod is mentioned in Dixon and Portlock's 1789 publication, *A Voyage around the World.* D

Macneill Point (52°58'00" 132°11'00" E entrance to Mitchell Inlet, Kuper Inlet, NW Moresby I, QCI). This feature, despite the spelling discrepancy, is presumed to be named for HBC chief factor William Henry McNeill. In 1851, when the HBC became aware that there was gold on the QCI, Gov James Douglas sent the *Una*, under Capt Willie Mitchell, to the discovery site with a party of miners. McNeill went along as supervisor. The miners clashed with a group of Haida, who had expected to barter for the ore, and withdrew with about $75,000 worth of gold. On the journey back to Victoria, the *Una* was wrecked in Neah Bay, on the SW side of Juan de Fuca Str, then pillaged and burned by Makah First Nation warriors. The crew and the miners managed to escape aboard the US schooner *Susan Sturgis*, which happened to sail by. The gold, however, sank to the bottom of the bay. The QCI strike turned out to be of minor consequence. *See* McNeill Bay for a more detailed biography.

Macnicol Point (51°15'00" 127°46'00" Alexandra Passage, Smith Sd, NW of Port Hardy). Robert Macnicol (1888–1961), from Victoria, was executive secretary of the BC Command of the Royal Canadian Legion, 1927–47. He served overseas during WWI as regimental quartermaster-sgt with the Western Scots and was wounded at the Somme. Macnicol became involved with veterans' organizations after the war and was president of a Victoria Legion branch. In 1936–37 he was a member of the Veterans' Assistance Commission. During WWII he organized the Canadian Legion War Services in BC, then went to England as CLWS overseas manager before returning to Ottawa as executive assistant to the CLWS gen manager. From 1949 to 1956, Macnicol was BC representative to the Legion's Dominion Council, and in 1957 he became president of the BC Command. He died at Saanich. The point was named in 1945.

Macoah Passage (48°58'00" 125°23'00" W side of Barkley Sd, NE of Ucluelet, W side of Vancouver I). Macoah (also Mahcoah, Ma-co-ha), located on the passage, was the principal winter village of the Toquaht First Nation, whose members today belong to the Nuu-chah-nulth Tribal Council. Indeed, this feature appeared on official charts as Village Passage until 1934. Macoah is a very ancient occupation site and plays a significant role in Toquaht mythology and oral traditions. The name means "house on the point," according to archeologist Alan McMillan. Although abandoned by the 1920s, the Macoah reserve continued to be important to the Toquaht people, and in the mid-1980s a small population moved back to re-establish a community there, which in the early 2000s consisted of about a dozen homes, a store and a health services centre.

The public moorage floats at Madeira Park. *Brian Lee*

Madeira Park (49°37'00" 124°01'00" SE side of Pender Hbr, E side of Malaspina Str, NW of Vancouver). Named after his homeland by early Pender Hbr settler Joe Gonsalves (1857–1939), who in 1904 bought the hotel and store at Irvine's Landing that Charles Irvine had originally developed. Together with his son-in-law, a Russian seaman named Theodore Dames, "Portuguese Joe," as he was known, built a much larger hotel and saloon at the landing and became a well-regarded resident of the area. He had originally come to BC from Madeira I in 1874 to run a store that his uncle, Gregorio Fernandez, established at Gastown. Gonsalves married Susan Harris or Harry (1866–1938), of the Skxwúmish (Squamish) First Nation, at Vancouver in the early 1880s and was an important member of the long-lasting community at Brockton Point, maintaining his property there until the city of Vancouver forced residents to move in 1931. Madeira Park, just E of Irvine's Landing, is now the commercial centre of Pender Hbr, home to a shopping mall, marina and several resorts.

Madge Island (50°03'00" 124°43'00" Isabel Bay, W side of Lancelot Inlet, E of Malaspina Peninsula, NW of Powell R). Madge Wolfenden (1893–1992) was born at Victoria, the youngest daughter of Richard Wolfenden, who was a cpl in the Columbia detachment of Royal Engineers that served in BC 1858–63. She grew up in the James Bay area and attended Victoria High School and Victoria College, which at that time was affiliated with McGill Univ. Trained as a librarian, Madge worked for the provincial archives from 1914 to 1953, serving as assistant archivist, 1934–53, and acting provincial archivist, 1942–45. She contributed numerous articles to the *BC Historical Quarterly*, which she helped publish, and to other journals. After retiring in 1953 she married James H Hamilton, a former consul to Costa Rica and founder of the Vancouver Merchants' Exchange, a marine trade association. Her father, Richard Wolfenden (1836–1911), who married twice and had 12 children, was in charge of the Royal Engineers' printing press at Sapperton. He remained in BC when the detachment disbanded and became superintendent of the government printing office, 1863–1911, first at New Westminster and later at Victoria. Wolfenden was also an officer in the local militia, retiring with the rank of lt col. Madge I was formerly known as Mary I.

Madigan Point (52°11'00" 127°54'00" SE end of Cunningham I, E of Bella Bella). Engineer Benjamin Madigan (1838–1920) immigrated to the US from Ireland as a young man and learned his trade at the Delamater Iron Works in NY. After working on steamships on the Cuba route, Madigan and his NY-born wife Margaret Francis (1838–96) moved to San Francisco and then to Victoria in 1862, where Ben found employment on the *Diana* and the *Thames*. He went on to become chief engineer on a number of historic BC vessels, including the *Isabel, Otter, Sir James Douglas, Maude, Cariboo Fly, Beaver, Alexander, Sardonyx* and *Barbara Boscowitz*. As part owner for several years of the *Beaver*, he made numerous mechanical improvements to that pioneer sidewheeler, replacing engines and boilers. Both Ben and Margaret died at Victoria. Madigan Point was known until 1925 as Pilcher Point, after Lt H B Pilcher, who served on HMCS *Rainbow* and was also in command of Esquimalt's naval dockyard in the early days of WWI.

Madrona Bay (48°51'27" 123°29'00" In Ganges Hbr, Saltspring I, Gulf Is), **Madrona Island** (50°36'00" 126°38'00" SE of Crease I, Carey Group, N of Harbledown I, E end of Queen Charlotte Str), **Madrona Point** (49°19'00" 124°14'00" NW side of Northwest Bay, at Parksville, E side of Vancouver I). Named for the arbutus, Canada's only native broadleaf evergreen and one of the iconic trees of the southern BC coast. Fr Juan Crespi, chronicler of a Spanish expedition to Monterey Bay in California, gave the name *madroño* to this species in 1769 because of its resemblance to the Mediterranean *madroño* or strawberry tree. Today it is commonly known in the US as the madrona or madrone. Archibald Menzies, naturalist on Capt George Vancouver's voyage to the PNW, made the first botanical description in 1792. In his honour, the tree was given the scientific name *Arbutus menziesii*. Madrona I and Madrona Point originally appeared on charts as Arbutus I and Arbutus Point but were changed in the 1940s to avoid duplication.

Magee Channel (51°29'00" 127°39'00" Between Walbran I and Ripon I, Rivers Inlet). According to BC historians Helen and Philip Akrigg, this feature was named after Irene Magee, a young nurse working at Dr George Darby's Rivers Inlet hospital at the time a new coastal survey was being conducted in the late 1930s. The name was adopted in 1947.

Magicienne Point (50°55'00" 127°48'00" SE end of Vansittart I, Bate Passage, off N end of Vancouver I). HMS *Magicienne* was posted to the Baltic Sea during the Crimean War, where it was commanded by Capt Nicholas Vansittart, after whom Vansittart I (qv) is named. The 16-gun, 2,086-tonne paddle frigate, launched in 1849, also saw service in the Mediterranean, E Indies and China before being decommissioned in 1866. This feature, formerly known as Nose Point, was renamed in association with Vansittart I.

Magin Islets (50°52'00" 126°38'00" N of Stackhouse I, entrance to Kingcome Inlet, N of E end of Queen Charlotte Str). Probably named after Capt Thomas Magin (d 1873), who came to BC in 1859 in charge of a company of approximately 165 Royal Marines sent from China to preserve law and order in the young colony. The contingent was put under the overall command of Col Richard Moody, CO of the Columbia detachment of Royal Engineers, which arrived around the same time. The marines were mostly employed in garrison, guard and training duties; about half of them (though not Magin) were sent to San Juan I in 1860 and remained there as part of a joint US-British military occupation of the area until a boundary dispute was settled in 1872. Magin was promoted to maj in 1868 and lt col in 1869; he retired in 1872. According to historian John Walbran, Lt Daniel Pender named Mt Magin, N of Loughborough Inlet, after the capt while surveying the area in 1864–65. In 1864, Pender also named Sutlej Channel (qv), just W of the Magin Its, after HMS *Sutlej*, flagship of Rear Adm Joseph Denman, cdr-in-chief of the Pacific Station, which Capt Magin is known to have served aboard in the mid-1860s. Presumably **Magin Saddle** (50°53'00" 127°49'00" Nigei I, off N Vancouver I) is named for him as well.

Magneson Point (52°46'00" 132°02'00" S side of Tasu Sd, W side of Moresby I, QCI). Louis Magneson (1862–95), from Norway, was master of the Victoria sealing schooner *Walter A Earle* (formerly called the *Sylvia Handy*), which was lost with all 32 hands during a severe gale on Apr 14, 1895, off Cape St Elias in the Gulf of Alaska. The vessel was hunting seals with two other schooners, the *Libby* and *Favorite*, at the time, and those vessels were barely able to ride out the storm. It was afterwards discovered that the probable cause of the disaster was the loss of the *Earle*'s rudder. The same gale also caused the destruction of another sealing schooner, the *C G White*, which was wrecked on a reef. Eleven crew members perished.

Mahatta River (50°28'00" 127°48'00" S side of Quatsino Sd, NW Vancouver I). Mahatta is a Kwakwala name meaning "having sockeye salmon," and the Koskimo First Nation once had a summer village here. A remote forestry camp was established just E of the mouth of the Mahatta in the 1950s by Alaska Pine & Cellulose Co (which later became Rayonier Canada Ltd). About 300 people were working at the site by 1967. The camp, which had its own post office, was dismantled in the late 1980s when a road finally connected the area to Port Alice. A yard and log dump, owned in the early 2000s by Western Forest Products Inc, is still maintained at this location.

Mahk Rock (48°57'00" 125°13'00" E end of Sechart Channel, S of Alma Russell Is, Barkley Sd, W side of Vancouver I). *Mahk*, or *ma'ak*, is a Nuu-chah-nulth First Nation word meaning "grey whale." Formerly known as North Rk.

Mahope Point (50°06'00" 127°34'00" W of Bunsby Is, Checleset Bay, NW of Kyuquot Sd, NW side of Vancouver I). This feature is named after a former Nuu-chah-nulth fishing station and summer camping site located at the mouth of a river that enters Checleset Bay near the point. The area is now a reserve belonging to the Ka:'yu:'K't'h/ Che:K'tles7et'h' (Kyuquot/Checleset) First Nation. The name was adopted in 1947.

Mainguy Island (48°54'00" 123°41'00" Mouth of the Chemainus R, SE of Chemainus, SE side of Vancouver I). Daniel Wishart Mainguy (1842–1906) was a native of Guernsey and came to Victoria, around Cape Horn, on the *Strathallan* in 1863. He was one of the first settlers in the Chemainus district, pre-empting several pieces of land, including this island, in the mid-1860s. Mainguy returned to Europe in 1876–78, then came back to Vancouver I and, in 1884, married Mary Elizabeth Fry (1856–1943) at Victoria. She had arrived in BC from Ont in 1865. The Mainguys lived on and farmed their island, which today is uninhabited but at one time was connected to Vancouver I by a bridge. In about 1890 they built a larger home on the S bank of the Chemainus R at Westholme. Daniel worked on the construction of the CPR and in 1884 became the provincial police constable for the Chemainus area. He was renowned for his sense of humour. In *Water over the Wheel*, local historian William Olsen describes an incident where Mainguy confiscated a cargo of black market liquor and sent the smugglers in custody to Victoria. When his superiors asked how he'd got rid of the illicit hooch, the constable supposedly replied by telegram: "Am destroying contraband as fast as my health will permit." Mainguy Rk in Hakai Passage is named for Daniel's youngest son (*see below*).

Mainguy Rock (51°41'56" 128°06'27" S side of Hakai Passage, S of Stirling I, S of Bella Bella). Vice Adm Edmond

Rollo Mainguy, OBE (1901–79), was the youngest son of Daniel Mainguy (*see* Mainguy I). He was born at Victoria, where he married Maraquita Francis Cynthia Nichol (1906–81) in 1927, then made his home base at Duncan. The Mainguys later divorced, and Edmond married Elspeth Lucas (1914–89) in 1956. He was a cadet at the Royal Naval College of Canada at Halifax, where he witnessed the Halifax explosion of 1917. After special training in England, he was appointed signals officer at HMCS *Naden*, then became western cdr of the RCNVR. Mainguy was executive officer of HMCS *Vancouver* in 1930 and CO in 1936; during WWII he was CO of the destroyers *Assiniboine* and *Ottawa* before commanding destroyer squadrons at Halifax and Nfld. He is credited with the first Canadian kill of an enemy submarine. In 1942 he was named chief of naval personnel and, in 1944, cdr of the RCN cruiser *Uganda*. After the war he received a series of rapid promotions to vice adm and served as CO Pacific Coast, CO Atlantic Coast and chief of naval staff. His 1949 investigation of mutinous behaviour aboard RCN ships, the Mainguy Report, recommended reforms in naval disipline and organization. After retirement from the RCN in 1956, Mainguy took charge of the Ont Mental Health Assoc and the Great Lakes Shipping Corp, then retired again in 1965 and settled at Qualicum Beach. He died at Nanaimo. His son Daniel Nicholas Mainguy was also an RCN vice adm and vice-chief of the defence staff, 1983–85. Mainguy Rk appeared on early Admiralty charts as East Rk but was renamed in 1944.

Maitland Island (53°43'49" 128°57'07" Douglas Channel, N of Hawkesbury I, S of Kitimat). After H Maitland Kersey, who helped make an early survey of Kitimat harbour in 1898. *See* Kersey Point.

Makai Point (53°40'30" 132°21'00" W entrance to Juskatla Inlet, S of Masset Inlet, Graham I, QCI). Makai was a Tlingit First Nation chief who had been captured and adopted by the Haida at Masset. He was known for his violent temper—especially while drinking and gambling. In his 1916 memoir *In the Wake of the War Canoe*, Anglican missionary William Collison describes how he was able to convert Makai to Christianity in the 1870s after successfully treating him for a burst blood vessel. The reformation of such an intractable individual left a deep and favourable impression on the Haida, according to Collison. Named by the hydrographic service in 1953.

Malacca Passage (54°06'00" 130°21'00" Between Porcher I and the Lawyer Is, S of Prince Rupert). HMS *Malacca*, a 13-gun, 1,595-tonne steam corvette named after a small state on the Malaysian Peninsula, served on the Pacific Station, 1866–68, under Capt Radulphus Oldfield. It was built in Burma in 1853 and then sailed to England to have engines installed before seeing service in the Mediterranean. After an uneventful three years based at Esquimalt, the *Malacca* grounded on Brotchie Ledge outside Victoria Hbr and was temporarily repaired and sent back to England. It was sold to Japan as a naval training ship about 1870 and renamed the *Tsukuba*, after a famous, double-peaked Japanese mountain. The corvette was broken up in 1906. Lt Daniel Pender named many features in the Prince Rupert area after the *Malacca*'s officers while surveying the area in 1867. **Malacca Patch** (48°26'00" 123°25'00" N side of Constance Cove, Esquimalt Hbr, just W of Victoria) is also presumably named after this vessel. *W*

Malahat (48°32'53" 123°33'55" Just N of Malahat Ridge), **Malahat Ridge** (48°36'12" 123°35'27" W side of Squally Reach, Saanich Inlet, NW of Victoria). Various meanings have been advanced for this First Nation name, including "place to get bait" and "infested with caterpillars." The summit of the ridge, known as Yaas or Yos, is a sacred place to local Salish people. According to BC historians Helen and Philip Akrigg, it was home to such a legendary rainmaker that all one had to do was point to the high ground and the skies would open. The ridge was once a notable impediment to travellers on S Vancouver I; today it is crossed by 16-km Malahat Drive, a hwy route famous for its panoramas. In fact, the old post office name for the community of Malahat was Scenic View. Nearby Malahat Ck takes its name from the ridge, which appears as the Beddingfield Range on an 1865 Admiralty chart. *E*

Malaspina Inlet (50°03'00" 124°47'00" Between Malaspina and Gifford peninsulas, just S of Desolation Sd), **Malaspina Peninsula** (50°01'00" 124°46'00" On NE side of Str of Georgia, NW of Powell R), **Malaspina Point**

A portrait of explorer Alejandro Malaspina in the uniform of a brigadier of the Spanish navy, 1795. *Museo Naval, Madrid*

(49°12'00" 123°52'00" NW end of Gabriola I, Gulf Is), **Malaspina Strait** (49°40'00" 124°15'00" Between Texada I and the BC mainland). Alejandro Malaspina (1754–1810), born at Mulazzo in Italy, was an officer in the Spanish navy and one of his era's great explorers. He had gained a broad naval experience by 1786, when he was chosen to lead a commercial circumnavigation of the world for the Royal Philippines Co in the frigate *Astrea*, which he successfully concluded in 1788. The following year he recruited a group of celebrated scientists and officers to make an official Spanish scientific expedition to the Pacific, which lasted until 1794. In 1791, upon reaching Acapulco with his custom-built vessels *Descubierta* and *Atrevida*, he received orders to proceed N and search for the mythical passage across N America known as the Str of Anián. Leaving some of his crew in Mexico, Malaspina spent that summer off Alaska, then visited Nootka Sd on his return journey. Back in Mexico he took over another Spanish expedition that had been organized to explore Juan de Fuca Str, putting his own officers, Dionisio Alcalá-Galiano and Cayetano Valdés, in command of the two ships and sending them on what would turn out to be a history-making journey. Malaspina continued on his way that Dec, visiting the Philippines, NZ, Australia, Tonga, Chile and the Falkland Is. On his return to Spain he got into trouble for criticizing government colonial policy, was imprisoned and, in 1803, deported to Italy. His vast scientific collections and detailed charts and logs were confiscated and stored away, and his great voyage almost forgotten until 1885, when his journals were finally published. Malaspina Inlet was named by Alcalá-Galiano and Valdés in 1792. Malaspina Point was formerly known as Miles Point. Capt George Vancouver referred to Malaspina Str as the Canal del Nuestra Signora del Rosario, this being a version of the name that Francisco Eliza gave to the entire Str of Georgia in 1791. Capt George Richards of HMS *Plumper* named it Malaspina Str in 1859. Malaspina Lk and Malaspina Peak near Tahsis Inlet also commemorate this intrepid Spanish navigator, as do Malaspina Glacier in Alaska and a settlement in Chubut province, Argentina. *E W*

Malcolm Island (50°39'00" 126°59'00" Off NE side of Vancouver I, opposite Port McNeill), **Malcolm Point** (50°40'00" 127°06'00" NW side of Malcolm I, S of Numas I). Named in 1846 by Cdr George Gordon of HMS *Cormorant* for Adm Sir Pulteney Malcolm (1768–1838). Malcolm served on several RN stations before being promoted to capt in 1794 and was flag capt to Rear Adm Peter Rainier on HMS *Suffolk* and *Victorious* before commanding HMS *Renown* and then HMS *Donegal* in the Mediterranean. Malcolm arrived too late for the Battle of Trafalgar, though he provided valuable assistance afterwards to the disabled ships and prizes. He played an important role in the 1806 Battle of St Domingo in the W Indies and was named capt of the Channel fleet in 1812 aboard HMS *Royal Oak*. In 1816–17, now with the

Waterfront scene from Sointula on Malcolm Island. *Kevin Oke*

rank of rear adm, he was appointed cdr-in-chief of the St Helena Station, where he had responsibility for a famous prisoner, Napoleon Bonaparte. As a vice adm, Malcolm was cdr-in-chief of the Mediterranean fleet, 1828–31 and 1833–34. His final promotion, to adm, retired, came in 1837. Malcolm I (83 sq km) is well known for its Finnish heritage, the result of an ambitious turn-of-the-century colonization attempt at the village of Sointula (qv) by a group of socialist-minded utopians. *E W*

Malcolm Passage (53°11'00" 128°40'00" E end of Fraser Reach, N of Work I, off NE side of Princess Royal I). Billy Malcolm (1909–66), manager of the Canadian Fishing Co's Butedale cannery on Princess Royal I, 1945–60, became a household name on the BC coast. He began his career in 1928 with BC Packers as the storekeeper at the San Mateo cannery in Barkley Sd, then worked as a company salesman until joining Canfisco. Malcolm was an ex-alcoholic and staunch AA supporter who provided employment and a supportive atmosphere at Butedale for other recovering alcoholics. He also managed Canfisco's modern Oceanside cannery at Prince Rupert for a short period. He died at Butedale.

Malibu Islet (50°10'00" 123°51'00" Just S of Malibu Rapids), **Malibu Rapids** (SW end of Princess Louisa Inlet, Queens Reach, Jervis Inlet). Seattle-born Thomas Hamilton (1894–1969), developer of the variable pitch propeller and an aviation industry pioneer, fell in love with Princess Louisa Inlet in 1938 while cruising the BC coast aboard his sumptuous pleasure craft, the *Malibu*. The vessel was built at Seattle in 1928 for Merritt and Rhoda Adamson, who were connected with the 5,300-ha Malibu Ranch NW of LA: Merritt, a lawyer, had been ranch superintendent before marrying Rhoda Rindge, the owner's daughter, and becoming a wealthy dairyman. (The name Malibu comes from Humaliwo, a Chumash First Nation village located at the mouth of what is now Malibu Ck, and has been translated as "where the mountains meet the sea," "where the surf is loud" and "place on the cliff.")

Hamilton bought much land around Princess Louisa in 1940–41 and spent lavishly to build the Malibu Club, a large, luxurious, chalet-style lodge at the inlet's entrance that catered, briefly, to millionaires and movie stars (including Bing Crosby, Bob Hope, Barbara Stanwyck, William Holden, Conrad Hilton) before closing down in 1950. In 1954 the resort was purchased as a Christian camp by Young Life. The 38-m *Malibu Princess*, built at Vancouver in 1966 to ferry 2,500 campers a year to their summer retreat, was still in use in 2008.

Mallandaine Point (52°54'00" 129°08'00" N entrance to Surf Inlet, W side of Princess Royal I). Named for Louisa Townsend (1831–1925), born at London, England, who came out to Vancouver I in 1862 aboard the brideship *Tynemouth* with her younger sister Charlotte. She worked as a governess before marrying Victoria architect Edward Mallandaine (1827–1905) in 1866 and raising five children. Louisa Cove on Athlone I is also named for her, while Townsend Point (qv) is named for her sister. Her husband, Edward, had an eventful life. He was born at Singapore, where his father, Maj John Mallandaine, was a senior colonial and E India Co official; lived in France; studied architecture in England; and went to Australia in search of gold in 1852. Back in London he married and was widowed, then left to try his luck in the Fraser R goldfields. He opened an unsuccessful private school at Victoria, became a municipal tax collector, worked as a surveyor, dabbled in art, published Victoria's first city directory in 1860 (plus an important provincial directory in 1887) and managed to participate in short-lived gold rushes to the Leech R and Cassiar districts. Mallandaine's career as an architect never really flourished, though he did build several Victoria-area warehouses and schools; his St Luke's Church in Saanich still stands. Mallandaine Pass and Mallandaine Ck in the E Kootenays are probably named for Louisa and Edward's eldest son, also Edward Mallandaine (1867–1949). He was an architect and adventurer as well as a pony express rider, CPR land agent,

Malibu Rapids, entrance to Princess Louisa Inlet, with the Young Life summer camp on the left. *Peter Vassilopoulos*

surveyor, coroner, magistrate, lt col with the Canadian Forestry Corps in WWI, co-founder and three-time reeve of the town of Creston. It is 18-year-old Eddie Mallandaine who is peering around the side of Donald Smith's top hat as the white-bearded CPR financier drives home the last spike at Craigellachie in the famous 1885 photograph. *E*

Mallory Islands (52°12'55" 128°15'40" In Dundivan Inlet, N end of Horsfall I, W of Bella Bella). Robert Roy Mallory (1920–79) was born at Vancouver and raised in the QCI at Port Clements. He served overseas with the Canadian Army, 1942–45, joined the federal Dept of Fisheries in Jan 1946 and married Freda Claire Hall. Mallory served with fisheries in the QCI until 1956 and was then assigned to Bella Bella. In 1959 he was transferred to Prince Rupert and was serving as the dept's northern marine superintendent at the time of his death. The name was submitted by Capt Stewart C Hills of Prince Rupert and adopted in 1988.

Malone Point (50°33'00" 126°13'00" SE side of E Cracroft I, Havannah Channel, N of Johnstone Str). Royal Marines Lt Anthony Malone served aboard HMS *Havannah*, under Capt Thomas Harvey, on the Pacific Station, 1855–59. He left the service as a maj in 1877 and was promoted to lt col, retired, in 1879. Nearby Mt Anthony on E Cracroft I is also named for him.

Maltby Islets (49°14'00" 125°46'00" N end of Fortune Channel, NE of Meares I, Clayoquot Sd, W side of Vancouver I). George Albert Maltby (1867–1963), from Derbyshire, came to the Clayoquot area in 1892 and pre-empted land on Schooner Cove, where he received a Crown grant in 1898. He later acquired Crown land on Cox Bay, planting an orchard and vegetable garden there and raising cattle. Maltby sold produce to sealers and traders and, later, to the residents of Tofino and Clayoquot. A carpenter by trade, he worked on local building projects, conducted the first census of the area and served for a time as a justice of the peace. He moved to Tofino in the 1950s and then to Victoria, where he died. The Maltby Its were identified as the Ripple Its on early Admiralty charts, but the name was changed in 1934.

Mamalilaculla (50°37'10" 126°34'30" W end of Village I, E end of Queen Charlotte Str). The Mamaleleqala-QweqwaSot'Enox people are a branch of the Kwakwaka' wakw First Nation and traditionally had their main winter community on Village I. BC historians Helen and Philip Akrigg give "seems to be swimming" as one possible translation of the tribal name, which has had many different spellings over the years. The village itself is called Memqumlis (Memkumlis, 'Mimkwamlis), which means "islands in front," according to anthropologist Franz Boas. It was once a sizable place, with a population estimated at 2,000 in the 1830s. That number had shrunk to 90 by 1911. In 1921 the Cranmer family held a famous potlatch

here, resulting in numerous arrests and the confiscation of traditional regalia. A school and tuberculosis sanatorium were established on the island in 1920 and operated by Anglican missionary Kathleen O'Brien until 1945. The village site, with its beautiful setting and atmospheric ruins, was abandoned in the 1960s but has seen a resurgence of visitors in recent years. *E*

Remains of an old First Nation lodge at Mamalilaculla. *Andrew Scott*

Mamie Rock (51°19'00" 127°35'00" E of Central I, Smith Sd, N of Port Hardy). The tiny 55-tonne steamer *Mamie*, built at New Westminster in 1887, hit this rock in 1897, under Capt Henry Smith, while carrying a load of fresh salmon from Quascilla Bay to Rivers Inlet. Named by Capt John Walbran of the Dept of Marine and Fisheries, who examined the rock in 1903.

Mamin Bay (53°37'00" 132°19'00" E side of Juskatla Inlet, S of Masset Inlet, Graham I, QCI), **Mamin Islets** (53°38'00" 132°19'00" At entrance to Mamin Bay), **Mamin River** (53°37'00" 132°19'00" Flows N into Mamin Bay). Mamin is an adaptation of the river's Haida name, applied by geologist George Mercer Dawson in 1878, and the bay and islets are named after the river. The Mamin valley is one of the richest red cedar areas in the QCI and produced many of the finest Haida war canoes. One of these giants, partly shaped and then abandoned for some reason, can still be seen in the vicinity, just SE of the bay. The First Nation reserve at the mouth of the river is a former Eagle village site. (Note that all Haida belong to one of two primary social divisions: Eagle or Raven.) The forestry camp of Juskatla, QCI HQ of MacMillan Bloedel Ltd for many years and owned in the early 2000s by Western Forest Products Inc, is adjacent to the reserve. *D*

Mamquam Blind Channel (49°41'00" 123°09'00" Near mouth of Squamish R, N end of Howe Sd, N of Vancouver). This Skxwúmish (Squamish) First Nation word may be onomatopoeic—formed from a sound associated with what is named. Traditional sources suggest that it imitates or echoes the murmur of the smooth-running lower

M

stretches of the Mamquam R, which joins the Squamish R near the head of Howe Sd. Nearby Mamquam Icefield, Mamquam Lk and Mamquam Mtn are all named after the river.

Mandarte Island (48°38'00" 123°17'00" E of Sidney I and Saanich Peninsula, Gulf Is, N of Victoria). This name is a misspelling, as it honours Joseph Marie Mandart (1818–93), a Breton priest from Vannes, France, who established Our Lady of the Assumption, the first Roman Catholic church in the Saanich area, about 1869. After training at Louvain College, Belgium, he came to BC in 1863 and lived initially at Victoria, learning English and preparing for missionary work. Mandart was sent to the Cowichan area in 1864 and then established the first permanent mission to the First Nations of the Saanich Peninsula the following year—an undertaking he was associated with for three decades. In 1866 he was named vicar gen of the diocese of Vancouver I. Mandart spent six months at Sitka in 1868, helping that community establish a Roman Catholic parish, and in 1877–78 he accompanied Bishop Charles Seghers to Ft Kennicott, Alaska, where the two were involved with missionary work in the surrounding district. Fr Joseph is buried in the cemetery at Our Lady of the Assumption church. Mandarte I was formerly known as Bare I and Ridge I; it is a First Nation reserve and the largest seabird breeding colony in the southern Str of Georgia, supporting thousands of auklets, puffins, cormorants and guillemots. *E*

Man Island (53°08'00" 129°46'00" W end of Otter Passage, between Banks I and Trutch I). This feature was formerly known as Cone I but was renamed in 1950 after Stephen Man, an able seaman aboard HMS *Discovery* on Capt George Vancouver's historic 1791-95 voyage of exploration to the PNW.

Mannion Bay (49°23'00" 123°20'00" E side of Bowen I, entrance to Howe Sd, just NW of Vancouver). Joseph Mannion (1839–1918), from Ireland, came to BC in 1862 in search of gold but found work instead with the Collins Overland Telegraph Co. He helped build Burrard Inlet's Hastings Mill in 1875 and soon owned the Granville Hotel in Gastown and Gladstone Hotel on the trail to New Westminster. He married Sabina Grant in 1881. Mannion was a founding alderman of the city of Vancouver but moved with his family in 1888 to Bowen I, where he operated a brickyard on this bay with Vancouver businessman David Oppenheimer. About 1900 he sold his home to John Cates, who turned it into the Monaco Hotel and then developed the Mannion property into an elaborate resort for city daytrippers, complete with campground, Japanese tea garden, dance pavilion and general store. This successful enterprise he sold in 1920 to the Union Steamship Co, which expanded it and ran it for another 30 years. Mannion lived in Vancouver after leaving Bowen and later moved to the BC Interior for health reasons. On the earliest (1860) Admiralty charts this bay was labelled Deep Cove. Its name was changed to Lodge Cove (after a newly renovated Union Steamship hotel) in the 1930s and Deep Bay in 1949. Mannion Bay was adopted in 1979. Mannion Ck on Gambier I is also named for this hotelier, who bought land there in 1884 but sold it shortly afterwards. *E*

Mannion Bay on Bowen Island was once the site of a popular Union Steamship resort for Vancouver daytrippers. *Peter Vassilopoulos*

Manor Point (48°20'00" 123°33'00" S side of Pedder Bay, NW of Fossil Point, S end of Vancouver I, SW of Victoria). According to a notation at BC's Geographical Names Office, the point was named in 1934 after Manor Farm, "one of the original farms of this district."

Mansell Point (52°39'00" 128°48'00" S tip of Jessop I, off S end of Princess Royal I). Frances Parker (1840–1931) was born at London, England, and came to Victoria about 1862. She married Henry Mansell (1833–1910), another British immigrant, who arrived in 1865 and set himself up as a shoe and bootmaker. The Mansells became well established in the city and operated a family-run retail store on Government St for many years. Frances is believed to have taken part in the grand old-timers' reunion held at Victoria in 1924 (*see* Adams Bay).

Mansons Landing on Cortes Island. *Andrew Scott*

Manson Bay (50°04'00" 124°58'42" W side of Cortes I, N end of Str of Georgia), **Manson Passage** (49°57'00" 124°53'00" Between Hernando I and Savary I, S of Cortes I), **Mansons Landing** (50°04'00" 124°59'00" SW side of Cortes I). Named after Michael Manson (1857–1932), one of four brothers who immigrated to Canada from the Shetland Is. He arrived in BC about 1876, started his career as a merchant at Nanaimo and then eloped with Jane Renwick (1862–1939), the unhappy daughter of his tyrannical business partner. The couple married at Victoria in 1878 and had 13 children, many of whom died in a diphtheria outbreak. The Mansons were the first white settlers on Cortes I, establishing a trading post in 1887 beside the sandspit at Mansons Landing, a feature long known to First Nation residents as Clytosin and now part of Mansons Landing Provincial Marine Park. Michael, his younger brother John (1869–1957) and friend George Leask all pre-empted land in the area in the 1880s, and John remained on Cortes until his death. Michael was Cortes I's first postmaster and also a justice of the peace; he investigated several sensational crimes in the district, including the murders of Jack O'Connor, in 1893, and Chris Benson, in 1894, on Read I. After leaving Cortes

in the late 1890s to become superintendent at James Dunsmuir's Wellington Colliery Co at Comox, Michael served as Conservative MLA for the Comox riding, 1909–16. He then farmed on Hernando I before returning to politics as MLA for the Mackenzie riding, 1924–32. Michael Manson died at Bella Coola. *W*

Manson Point (52°10'00" 128°00'00" N side of Denny I, Gunboat Passage, just E of Bella Bella). Donald Manson (1796–1880), born at Caithness, Scotland, had a long career with the HBC, joining in 1817 and taking part in several expeditions across the western prairies in the early 1820s. He was transferred to the W coast in 1825, serving at Ft Vancouver, Ft Langley (which he helped build) and Ft George before taking charge at Ft Simpson on the N coast, 1831–34. He married Félicité Lucier (d 1867) in 1828. Manson constructed Ft McLoughlin near Bella Bella (hence the naming of Manson Point) and remained there until 1838, then took over Ft Kamloops in 1841 and Ft Stikine in 1843. From 1844 to 1857 he was based at Ft St James and had control over New Caledonia, a vast district in BC's northern Interior. Manson apparently gained such a reputation as a bully that his promotion to chief factor was denied. He retired from the HBC in 1857, moved to Oregon and farmed beside the Willamette R. His biographer, Harriet Munnick, described him as "tough, obstinate, a little grim, honest, humourless and a titan for work." Several features in northern BC are also named for him, including Manson Arm, Manson Lks, Manson R and the community of Manson Ck. Manson Ridge, SE of Hope, commemorates his participation in the early fur brigades from New Caledonia, which had to cross the Coast Mtns over nearly impassable trails to Ft Yale and Ft Hope in the late 1840s, after the Columbia R route to Ft Vancouver was closed due to First Nation conflict. Manson Point was formerly known as Reef Point.

Manzanita Cove (54°45'35" 130°26'30" E side of Wales I, Portland Inlet, near BC-Alaska boundary). This cove does not commemorate the hairy manzanita (*Arctostaphylos columbiana*), a spreading evergreen shrub that only grows S of Campbell R, over 600 km away. Instead, the name refers to a US lighthouse tender called the *Manzanita*— as do a number of other geographical names on or beside Revillagigedo I in SE Alaska: Manzanita Bay, Manzanita Ck, Manzanita I and Manzanita Lk. The 47-m vessel was built for the US government in 1879 at Baltimore and came to the PNW, where it was mostly employed on Puget Sd, in 1886. In 1901 the *Manzanita* was sent N to help support efforts to establish the international boundary between Canada and Alaska—hence the suite of names. It sank in Puget Sd in 1905 after colliding with the barge *Columbia*, then was sold and rebuilt as the tug *Daniel Kern*. Another US lighthouse tender with the same name was built in 1908; it also served in Puget Sd.

Maple Bay (49°44'32" 124°37'57" N of Favada Point, NW side of Texada I, Str of Georgia). A huge maple tree stood on the shore of the bay and was used as a landmark by fishermen for many years. According to Texada I historian Bill Thompson, a large still was operated at this location by a local landowner. The well-established name was adopted in 1989.

Maple Bay (55°25'20" 130°00'40" E side of Portland Canal, W of Anyox, BC-Alaska border), **Maple Point** (55°25'30" 130°00'50" N side of Maple Bay). Only the small, scraggly Douglas maple (*Acer glabrum*) grows this far N. The Outsider Mine was established here about 1905 by the Brown Alaska Smelting Co of Seattle, which built aerial tramways and a substantial wharf in order to load and ship a rich copper-gold ore to its short-lived smelter at Hadley on Prince of Wales I in Alaska until 1908. The Granby Consolidated Mining, Smelting and Power Co, which had a major mine at nearby Anyox, took the property over in 1916 and shipped large quantities of ore to its Anyox smelter from 1924 to 1928. The remote workers' community at Maple Bay was substantial enough in the mid-1920s to require a post office. The ruins of the mine and wharf were still visible in the early 2000s.

Mapleguard Point (49°28'00" 124°44'00" E side of Deep Bay, NW of Bowser, E side of Vancouver I). This geographical feature was formerly known as Maple Point, but the name was changed to avoid duplication in 1923. Its rich covering of maples contrasted strongly with the prevailing conifers and made a useful landmark for avoiding offshore shoals. The 2004 edition of *Sailing Directions*, however, notes that "few maple trees remain."

Maquinna Point (49°35'00" 126°40'00" S tip of Nootka I, off W side of Vancouver I). Maquinna is the hereditary name of the principal Mowachaht (Nuu-chah-nulth) chieftain at Nootka Sd, on the W coast of Vancouver I. The Maquinna that this feature is named after was born about 1760 and held power when the first European fur traders and explorers arrived in the PNW in the late 18th century. Considered an astute diplomat as well as a capable warrior and leader, he managed to control much of the fur business in the region and made Nootka Sd the focal point for trading activities. Maquinna had extensive interactions with all the main Spanish, British and US visitors to the region. The feature appears on early Spanish charts as Punta de Macuina. *E W*

Mara Rock (48°53'00" 125°29'00" SW entrance to Loudoun Channel, Barkley Sd, W side of Vancouver I). John Andrew Mara (1840–1920) pre-empted and sold many pieces of land over the course of his adventurous life, including the northernmost of the Stopper Is, NE of Mara Rk in Barkley Sd, for which he received a Crown grant in 1892. He lived at Victoria 1900–20 but is primarily known for the long business and political career he enjoyed in the Kamloops and Shuswap areas. Mara was born at Toronto and travelled across Canada with the Overlanders of 1862 in search of Cariboo gold. After settling at Kamloops he worked at first as a packer, then as a miller and merchant, then as the owner of a fleet of steamboats on the Thompson R and Shuswap Lk. He was said to have precipitated the murderous 1879 rampage of the McLean gang in the Nicola valley by seducing Annie McLean, sister to three of the gang's members, and fathering her child. In 1882, at Victoria, he married Alice Telfer Barnard (1858–1906), daughter of Francis Barnard, the famous gold-rush stagecoach and express operator. Mara acquired important ranchlands near Enderby and Sicamous, and helped establish both the Shuswap & Okanagan Rwy and the Columbia & Kootenay Steam Navigation Co. He was a strong supporter of Confederation and served as MLA for the Kootenay and Yale ridings, 1871–86, speaker of the legislature, 1883–86, and Conservative MP for Yale, 1887–96. In the BC Interior, Mara Ck, Mara Hill, Mara Lk, Mara Meadows, Mt Mara, Mara Point and the village of Mara all commemorate him. Mara Rk was formerly known as Black Rk. The name was adopted in 1934. *E*

Marble Bay. *See* Varney Bay.

Marchand Point (53°34'00" 132°59'00" NW entrance to Hippa Passage, W side of Graham I, QCI), **Marchand Reef** (54°11'00" 133°01'00" Off S side of Parry Passage, between Langara I and Graham I). Named after Capt

Early Spanish drawing of Maquinna, the Mowachaht chief at Nootka Sound during the early fur-trade era. *BC Archives A-02678*

Etienne Marchand (1755–93), cdr of the French ship *La Solide*, which visited the QCI in 1791 on its voyage around the world. He was born in the W Indies, at Grenada, and became interested in the PNW after meeting fur trader Nathanial Portlock at St Helena in 1789. The 275-tonne vessel, built by the wealthy House of Baux in Marseilles to search out scientific and commercial opportunities, first visited Alaska, then anchored in Cloak Bay off Langara I for several weeks and made the earliest charts of Parry Passage. Deputy cdr Prosper Chanal, accompanied by Lt Louis Marchand, the capt's brother, also surveyed the NW coast of Graham I by longboat as far S as Hippa I. Marchand then sailed to Nootka Sd, Hawaii, Macao, Mauritius and back to France. He later died on the island of Réunion. The journals of Marchand, Chanal and ship's surgeon Claude Roblet were published in several volumes at Paris, 1798–1800, translated into English in 1801 and reprinted in 1970. Edited by Charles Fleurieu, these works contain important early descriptions of Tlingit and Haida culture. *D*

Marchant Rock (53°05'00" 129°48'00" Off W side of Truth I, S of Banks I, Hecate Str). George Marchant (c 1843–1925), from Cornwall, came to BC in 1867 and was employed as a seaman on the historic sidewheel steamer *Beaver*, 1867–70, while it was leased to the RN for survey work. Marchant apparently noticed this dangerous rock while the crew of the *Beaver* were taking a meal break in 1869, and was responsible for having it investigated and charted. The *Beaver*'s cdr, Lt Daniel Pender, named it for him that same year. Marchant served aboard the *Beaver* several times; he was mate, 1876–77, and capt on that vessel's unfortunate final journey in 1888, when it was wrecked in Vancouver Hbr at Prospect Point. He was also master of several other small ships in PNW waters, including the *Muriel*, *Rainbow*, *Alexander* and the infamous *Union*, which consisted of a threshing-machine engine mounted on a scow. Chains drove a pair of sidepaddles on this novel craft, which had no reverse gear and had to be coasted to a stop with the help of a pole. The *Union* ended its days working for N Vancouver's Moodyville Mill. Marchant's final humiliation came in 1902, when the new steam tug *Superior* was swamped while towing a boom of logs in Burrard Inlet under his command. The newspapers could not resist pointing out that Marchant had now managed to wreck BC's oldest and newest vessels. *W*

Marco Island (52°31'00" 131°30'00" E entrance to Hutton Inlet, Juan Perez Sd, E side of Moresby I, QCI), **Marco Rock** (Just E of Marco I). James Marco (1880–1909) was superintendent of the Ikeda Bay copper mine at Ikeda Cove (qv) on SE Moresby I. He died at the minesite in 1909, apparently after breathing poisonous fumes while investigating some unexploded dynamite. The names were adopted by the hydrographic service in 1962. *D*

Marcus Passage (54°06'00" 130°14'00" S and W of Smith I, mouth of Skeena R, S of Prince Rupert). After CPR engineer and surveyor Marcus Smith. Mt Marcus, N of Bute Inlet, is also named for him. *See* Smith I.

Margaret Bay (48°30'00" 123°18'00" W of Gordon Head, Saanich, N of Victoria). This feature appears on old maps as St Margaret Bay, but the name was changed to Margaret Bay in 1954. One source claims that it was named for Cecilia Margaret Finlayson (1870–1955, later Cecilia Cotton), who supposedly granted a public access to the bay via what is now Balmacarra Rd. HBC chief factor Roderick Finlayson, her father, owned a large piece of property adjacent to Gordon Head. Another explanation for the origin of the name holds that it was bestowed by BC politician Dr John Ash, who took a group of friends to the bay that included Charles and Rebecca Jane Pollock of Cedar Hill Farm and their young daughter Margaret. In a fit of whimsy, Ash is said to have made a present of the name to the little girl, then later used his influence to ensure that it stuck.

Margaret Bay (51°20'00" 127°30'00" E end of Smith Sd, N of Port Hardy). Fisherman John Iverson (1887–1967) bought land on this bay in 1916 in order to comply with a rule that restricted fishing to local homesteaders. His property was purchased later that year by Robert Chambers of Western Packers Ltd, who built a sockeye salmon cannery there that was taken over in 1923 by the Canadian Fishing Co. It operated until 1945, then remained open as a gillnet camp until 1957. Only traces of the cannery were still visible in the early 2000s. Iverson went on to fish for the BC Packers cannery on nearby Boswell Inlet and then worked as a fish buyer at Bute Inlet and elsewhere. The origin of the name is uncertain.

Marina Island (50°04'00" 125°03'00" Off SW side of Cortes I, N end of Str of Georgia), **Marina Reef** (50°02'00" 125°03'00" S of Marina I). The island was named in 1792 by the Spanish explorers Dionisio Alcalá-Galiano and Cayetano Valdés, in association with nearby Cortes I. Hernán Cortés, Spanish conquistador, acquired Doña Marina (also known as La Malinche or Malintzin) as an Aztec slave and made her his mistress and interpreter. She supposedly bore him a son and played a powerful role in her people's defeat, acting as an advisor to Cortes and an intermediary between vanquishers and vanquished. Marina remains an icon of both victimization and treachery in her country's culture to this day and serves as a conflicted symbolic mother figure to the people of colonial Mexico. RN surveyors changed Marina I to Mary I in 1849, then changed it back again in 1906. (Mary I continued in use as a local name, though, for many years.) Marina Reef was formerly known as Boulder Reef. A Sliammon First Nation village—Shet-kay-jeh (Shítká'ji), which means "to tie a rope around a tree"—occupied the

M

N end of Marina in the 19th century. A settler community formed in the early 1900s on the E side of the island, where a post office called Chamadaska operated, 1910–23. This word may be an adaptation of an old First Nation name meaning "the island that stretches," referring to the drying reefs at either end. *W*

Mariners Rest (49°28'00" 123°28'00" W of Gambier I, Thornbrough Channel, Howe Sd, NW of Vancouver). This rock has become a popular spot for scattering the ashes of deceased sailors and seafarers. The name was adopted in 1979.

Marion Rock (52°17'00" 131°06'00" SE entrance to Collison Bay, SE side of Moresby I, QCI). After nurse Marion M Goodwin, who married Anglican missionary William Collison and became the first white woman to live on the QCI. *See* Goodwin Point *and* Collison Bay.

Marion Rock (54°13'00" 130°25'00" NW of the Kinahan Is, just SW of Prince Rupert). In 1906, after it was decided that the GTP would have its terminus at what would soon become the city of Prince Rupert, hydrographer George Blanchard Dodge made a marine survey of the area. He named this feature after his mother.

Markale Passage (50°04'00" 127°12'00" Between Moketas I and Hohoae I, Kyuquot Sd, NW side of Vancouver I), **Markale Peninsula** (50°04'00" 127°10'00" SW end of Fair Hbr, S entrance to Tahsish Inlet, Kyuquot Sd), **Markale Point** (50°04'00" 127°11'00" W side of Markale Peninsula). The isthmus leading to Markale Peninsula was the site of Maxqet, one of the Ka:'yu:'K't'h (Kyuquot) First Nation's four winter villages. In 1928 the Anglo-BC Packing Co built the Caledonia cannery just S of the village site, along with a pilchard reduction plant. It only operated for a short time, and the wharf was in ruins by 1947. An aquaculture operation was located in the vicinity in the early 2000s.

Mark Bay (49°10'54" 123°56'00" S end of Newcastle I, N side of Nanaimo Hbr, E side of Vancouver I). After Mark Bate, first mayor of Nanaimo (*see* Bate Point for a more detailed biography). Mt Mark on Vancouver I is also named for him. Mark Bay was known locally for many years as Echo Bay.

Mark Bluff (53°33'00" 129°35'00" N side of Lowe Inlet, E of Grenville Channel, opposite Pitt I). After Capt Mark Pike, a Victoria-based sealer and master mariner who was originally from Nfld. *See* Pike Point.

Markland Point (53°51'00" 128°49'00" SW side of Kitimat Arm, N end of Douglas Channel, S of Kitimat). Olive Neata Markland (b 1879), a student at the Univ of Toronto, worked for several years in the early 1900s as a teacher and assistant at the Methodist mission at Kitamaat village

(known today as Haisla). She married Blanchard Perley Steeves at Nelson in 1914.

Markle Inlet (53°36'00" 129°56'00" N of Markle Passage), **Markle Island** (53°34'00" 129°59'00" N side of Markle Passage), **Markle Passage** (53°34'00" 129°58'00" N and E of Sine I, N of Anger I, W side of Pitt I). Markle was the name of the engineer on the *Ala*, the vessel used in a coast triangulation survey of this region in 1921 by Alfred E Wright of the BC Lands Service.

Mark Rock (52°07'20" 127°50'45" In Port John, SW side of King I, E of Bella Bella). After one of the four evangelists who wrote the gospel accounts in the New Testament. St Mark is claimed to also have been the first pope of Alexandria and founder of Christianity in Africa. He supposedly died at Alexandria in the 1st century AD. Lt Daniel Pender named several nearby features after the evangelists about 1866, probably in association with Port John (which does not commemorate a biblical figure, however, being named by Capt George Vancouver after his friend the Rev John Fisher).

Marktosis (49°17'00" 126°03'00" On McNeil Peninsula, SE side of Flores I, Clayoquot Sd, W side of Vancouver I). This site, on the E side of Matilda Inlet, is the main residential village of the Ahousaht First Nation, which is part of the Nuu-chah-nulth Tribal Council. The commercial settlement of Ahousat (qv) is located on the W side of the inlet, though the name Ahousat is often used to refer to the combined community. In the early 1800s the Ahousahts prevailed over their traditional enemies, the Otsosahts, and took control of their territory, which included Marktosis, supposedly an ancient Otsosaht burial place. Ahousaht elder Stanley Sam defined the name in 1997 as an anglicization of *maaktusiis*, which means "moving from one side to another." This translation accords with earlier ones such as "camp on either side of the bay" and "landing place on either side." Nuu-chah-nulth author George Clutesi suggested "village of the peninsula." Pioneer missionary Augustin Brabant offered a different interpretation, however, believing that the name was probably derived from Nuu-chah-nulth words for "bury" and "coffin."

Marlborough Heights (49°56'33" 123°54'15" Above Vancouver Bay, E side of Prince of Wales Reach, Jervis Inlet, NW of Vancouver). Probably named in association with nearby Mt Spencer, which commemorates Capt John Spencer, who served on the Pacific Station, 1859–63 (*see* Spencer Ledge). Spencer was the grandson of the 3rd Duke of Marlborough and the great-great-grandson of British statesman John Churchill, 1st Duke of Marlborough (1650–1722) and one of Europe's most famous and successful generals.

Richard Marpole, railway executive and engineer, developed the wealthy Vancouver suburb of Shaughnessy. *BC Archives D-01223*

Marpole (49°12'00" 123°08'00" N side of the N Arm of the Fraser R, S part of city of Vancouver). This Vancouver neighbourhood is named for railway engineer Richard Marpole (1850–1920), a native of Wales, who came to Canada to work for the Northern Rwy of Canada and joined the CPR in the 1880s. He supervised railway construction in the Algoma, Nipissing and Lk Superior regions before becoming the company's western superintendent, 1897–1907, and then vice-president of the E&N. Marpole oversaw the development of Shaughnessy as an upmarket residential suburb, buying the first home there himself in 1909. Marpole Lk and Mt Marpole in Yoho National Park are also named for him. The Marpole neighbourhood was once an important First Nation habitation, and vast middens were excavated there in the 1940s and '50s, producing a treasure trove of stone tools, carvings and copper ornaments. The area became the site of an early store, opened by Harry Eburne in the 1870s, and a Methodist church; sawmills soon sprang up, and railway and bridge connections made Marpole a crossroads. In the early 2000s it was a district of modest apartment buildings. *E*

Marrack Island (53°58'00" 130°09'00" Part of the Gibson Group, between Pitt I and Kennedy I, S of Prince Rupert). RN surveyor Lt Daniel Pender named this feature in 1868 after William Marrack, who was serving on the Pacific Station at the time as a midshipman on HMS *Pylades*, under Capt Cecil Buckley. Marrack was promoted to capt in 1888 and later commanded HMS *Calypso*, 1891–95, while it was part of the RN's training squadron. He became a rear adm in 1902. *W*

Marr Island (49°43'17" 124°10'40" Blind Bay, S entrance to Jervis Inlet, NW of Vancouver). This name was adopted in 1990 for Petty Officer Telegraphist David Marr of the RCN, who was killed in action June 25, 1940, aged 30, while serving aboard HMCS *Fraser*. The destroyer sank off the coast of France, with the loss of 45 lives, after a tragic collision with HMS *Calcutta* while attempting to rescue refugees. Marr was a resident of the Vancouver area before the war and enlisted at HMCS *Naden* in Esquimalt. He is commemorated on the Halifax Memorial.

Marsden Islands (50°44'00" 126°40'00" Between Mars I and Eden I, part of the Broughton Archipelago, NE end of Queen Charlotte Str). Marsden is an amalgam of the names of the two islands on either side, Mars and Eden.

Marshall Inlet (52°28'15" 131°29'00" SW of Werner Bay, off Juan Perez Sd, E side of Moresby I, QCI). Chemist T Rhymer Marshall was sent to the QCI in 1902 by the BC Mining Bureau to investigate the presence of coal. He was guided by William Robertson, who first discovered coal in the Yakoun valley, but was apparently more impressed by the quality of the deposits he saw than by their commercial quantity. Dr Marshall was originally from Glasgow and had been a professor at the Univ of Edinburgh and Univ College, Cardiff. Named by the hydrographic service in 1962 and known locally by fishermen for many years as North Werner Bay. *D*

Marshall Island (52°06'00" 130°58'00" Keeweenah Bay, E side of Kunghit I, QCI). The hydrographic service adopted this name in 1962 in association with nearby Prevost Point. Cdr James Prevost had been carrying out a survey of Houston Stewart Channel in HMS *Virago* in 1853 when he was relieved by Cdr Edward Marshall (d 1862), who completed the job and then took the *Virago* to Russia, where it was part of the Anglo-French squadron that attacked Petropavlovsk in 1854 during the Crimean War. Marshall was promoted to capt in 1857.

Marshall Point (49°47'00" 124°38'00" S end of Limekiln Bay, NW end of Texada I, Str of Georgia). Capt George Vancouver gave this name to the "NW point" of Texada I (today's Kiddie Point) in 1792 but provided no hint as to whom Marshall might be. Historian Edmond Meany has suggested that Vancouver may possibly have been honouring William Marshall (1745–1818), an agriculturist and author of books on the rural economy of England. In 1785 Marshall published a work on N American trees and shrubs that could very likely have been part of the *Discovery*'s library. Vancouver's Point Marshall was changed to Cohoe Point in 1913 and to Kiddie Point (qv) in 1924. In 1952 the hydrographic service resurrected the older name and applied it to this feature, 2 km S of Kiddie Point.

M

Marshall Reef (52°04'00" 128°29'00" W of the McMullin Group, S of Athlone I, Queens Sd, W of Bella Bella). RCNR lt cdr Jack Ernest Montague Marshall (1884–1964) worked on CPR Empress ships before WWII. He served as chief examination officer at the Esquimalt naval base, 1940–44, and also took on the job of extended defence officer at HMCS *Givenchy* in 1944, the year this feature was named by the hydrographic service. *Givenchy* was the shore establishment at Esquimalt that administered auxiliary vessels and the dockyard. Marshall received the RCNR officer's decoration in 1944.

Marsh Bay (50°55'00" 127°21'00" N side of Stuart Point, N side of Queen Charlotte Str, opposite Port Hardy). Capt Robert George Marsh, from Vancouver, was killed in action Oct 24, 1944, at the age of 30. He was serving with the Royal Welsh Fusiliers of the Royal Canadian Infantry Corps and is buried at Uden War Cemetery in the Netherlands.

Mars Islet (51°45'00" 128°04'00" Planet Group, N side of Hakai Passage, S of Bella Bella). Named by the hydrographic service in 1948, along with Jupiter I and Mercury It, as individual members of the Planet Group.

Martha Island (52°20'00" 128°22'00" Between Lady Douglas I and Lake I, Milbanke Sd). Martha Douglas (1854–1933) was the youngest daughter of Sir James Douglas, BC's colonial gov, and Lady Amelia Douglas. She was born and raised in Victoria, then travelled with her sister Agnes Bushby to England, where she attended Landsdowne House school near Wimbledon, 1872–74. Martha married civil engineer Dennis Reginald Harris (1851–1932) in a splendid society wedding at Victoria in 1878, the year after the death of Sir James. She and her husband were part of the Victoria elite, living with Lady Douglas in the family home until Amelia died in 1890, then moving to Eastdon Hall on Burdett Ave. Martha was well known for her creative abilities, especially in lacemaking, spinning and weaving. She took a genuine interest in her First Nation heritage, collecting aboriginal basketry and maintaining friendships with local Songhees families. Her 1901 book, *History and Folklore of the Cowichan Indians*— illustrated by Margaret "Daisy" Maclure, wife of famed architect Samuel Maclure, and reprinted in 2004—was the first collection of First Nation stories commercially published in BC. *See also* Harris Point.

Martin Cove (49°37'18" 124°03'40" W side of Francis Peninsula, Pender Hbr, Malaspina Str, NW of Vancouver), **Martin Island** (49°38'00" 124°04'00" Entrance to Pender Hbr). Martin I appears on an Admiralty chart dating from 1863 and is thus an old name. Former BC assistant archivist Madge Wolfenden has suggested that the name possibly honours RN officer Cornwallis Wykeham-Martin (1833–1903), who apparently served on the Pacific Station

as a lt aboard HMS *Alert* in 1859. In 1855 he was involved in the Crimean War attack on the Finnish fortress of Sveaborg (Suomenlinna) as cdr of the gunboat *Bullfrog*.

Martini Island (54°15'00" 130°25'00" Off SW side of Digby I, just SW of Prince Rupert). Named after Friedrich von Martini (1822–97), a Swiss armourer, who also designed lacemaking machines and internal combustion engines. Martini developed a breech-loading, lever-actuated firing mechanism that was combined with a barrel designed by Scotsman Alexander Henry to produce one of the British Army's most successful rifles, in use from 1871 to about 1900. It was the first breech-loading service rifle to employ a metallic cartridge. Other standard-issue British Army rifles also used Martini actions. The company he founded went on to produce automobiles and machines for folding and binding books. It merged with Grapha Maschinenfabrik Hans Müller AG in 1969 and is today known as Muller Martini, a leading manufacturer of web presses and book-making equipment.

Martin Islands (50°06'00" 124°49'00" Desolation Sd, NE end of Str of Georgia). These geographical features were named by Admiralty surveyors about 1861 in association with nearby Mink I and Otter I, all after fur-bearing animals. The spelling should thus be Marten, not Martin. In 1945 the name was changed to the Tory Is, after the chartered HBC supply barque *Tory*, which sailed from England to Victoria around Cape Horn and back via China in 1850–52. It was changed back to the Martin Is about 1962, after local residents lobbied to have the old name reinstated. *See also* Twin Is.

Martin Point (53°43'00" 132°11'00" S end of Kumdis I, E side of Masset Inlet, Graham I, QCI). This former Haida village site was named after pioneer Graham I merchant James Martin. According to QCI historian Kathleen Dalzell, he arrived in the islands in 1908 and lived there all his life, establishing a general store at Masset, then opening branches at Nadu, Sewall and Port Clements.

Martin River (52°21'00" 127°43'00" Flows S into Cousins Inlet, just W of Ocean Falls, NE of Bella Bella). Archie B Martin (d 1945), from Bellingham, Washington, became gen manager of the Ocean Falls Co in 1912 and stayed on in that position when the pulp and paper mill at Ocean Falls was taken over in 1915 by Pacific Mills Ltd (owned by Crown Willamette Co of Portland, later Crown Zellerbach Corp). He was executive vice-president of Crown Zellerbach at the time of his death. Martin Lk, which is drained by the Martin R, is also named for him.

Martin Rock (50°19'00" 127°53'00" SW of Mayday I, Side Bay, just S of Quatsino Sd, NW end of Vancouver I). Capt Martin (his first name has unfortunately been lost) was an early skipper in the Victoria-based, W coast sealing industry.

He arrived in 1892 from Halifax, bringing with him the schooner *Arietes* and making the trip, via Cape Horn, in 128 days. (There were several master mariners named Martin in the seal trade, including Daniel J Martin, born 1872, of the *Saucy Lass*, and Patrick J Martin, 1866–1940, of the *Agnes McDonald*, both from Nfld. Thomas Martin, born about 1864, served as mate on the *Lillian May*.)

Marvinas Bay (49°40'00" 126°37'00" E side of Nootka I, N end of Cook Channel, Nootka Sd, W side of Vancouver I). According to coastal historian Capt John Walbran, Marvinas is a corruption of Mawina or Moweena, the Nuu-chah-nulth term for the bay. The name was adopted by early Spanish and British visitors to Nootka Sd, including Capt James Cook. Pioneer Roman Catholic missionary Augustin Brabant suggested that the name could be translated as "a village on the way or along the channel." The bay was often used by fur traders and naval vessels as a larger and better-protected alternative to Friendly Cove. RN cdr William Broughton refitted the sloop *Providence* there in 1796, and it was at Marvinas Bay that the US vessel *Boston* was captured by Mowachaht chief Maquinna in 1803 and most of its crew massacred. *W*

Marvin Islands (52°32'00" 128°45'00" Head of Kitasu Bay, W side of Swindle I, NW of Bella Bella). Edward Benjamin Marvin (1830–1911), born at Halifax, came to Victoria in 1859 and founded the ship chandlery firm of E B Marvin & Co on Wharf St. A sailmaker by trade, he had first headed to California to participate in the gold rush and lived in San Francisco 1852–57. He then sought gold in Australia and BC, arriving in the PNW in 1858. After setting up his chandlery, Marvin served as a city councillor in the 1870s and, in partnership with Capt John G Cox, became deeply involved in the Victoria-based sealing industry. The schooner *E B Marvin* was named for him, and he and Cox owned the *Triumph*, *Annie E Paint*, *Vera*, *Carlotta G Cox* and *Sapphire*, as well. At the age of 70, Marvin married Minerva Taber Adams (1836–1917, née Woodman), a widow and native of Windsor, NS, at Victoria. She and her family were also early immigrants to BC. Her son, Frank Woodman Adams (1856–1920), became a business partner of Marvin and later managed the company. The Marvins moved to LA in 1911 and both died there. Edward Marvin is not to be confused with US consul and Victoria hardware and machinery merchant Edgar Marvin (1824–91), a partner in the firm of Marvin & Tilton, which also had a store on Wharf St.

Mary Anne Point (48°52'00" 123°19'00" SE end of Galiano I, Gulf Is). RN hydrographer Capt George Richards named Georgina Point (qv), Helen Point (qv) and Edith Point (qv) in this area in 1858–60 after prominent local women of the day. Mary Anne Point also probably honoured a well-known resident of early Victoria, but the source of the name is no longer known. The point cannot have

been named after former local residents Mary Matthews and her sister Anne Grubb, as has been claimed, because they did not live there until at least the 1880s, and this name appeared on Admiralty chart 2689 in 1859. *See also* Matthews Point.

Mary Basin (49°47'00" 126°51'00" Near the head of Nuchatlitz Inlet, NW side of Nootka I, W side of Vancouver I). After Mary Langford, daughter of early Vancouver I settler Edward Langford. *See* Langford Cove.

Mary Island. *See* Marina I.

Mary Point (50°03'00" 124°53'00" SE tip of Cortes I, NE end of Str of Georgia). In June 1792, Capt George Vancouver named the two features that bookend the entrance to Desolation Sd after two of his sisters: Mary, born in 1753, and Sarah, born in 1752 (*see also* Sarah Point). Vancouver was the youngest of six siblings. While quite a bit of information has been uncovered about his twin brothers Charles (1756–1811) and John (1756–1829), very little is known about his three sisters, the eldest of whom, Bridget, was born in 1751. John Vancouver helped George write *A Voyage of Discovery to the N Pacific Ocean and Round the World* and prepared the first edition for publication after his brother's death. Mary Point was renamed Turn Point by Capt George Richards in 1860 (the name appears on his 1864 chart), then changed back to Mary Point by the hydrographic service in 1945.

Mary Point (54°03'00" 132°34'00" W side of N entrance to Alexandra Narrows, Virago Sd, N side of Graham I, QCI). After Mary Liscombe Jorey, who married RN officer George Inskip. *See* Jorey Point.

Mary Tod Island (48°26'00" 123°18'00" Just N of Turkey Head, Oak Bay, just E of Victoria). Fur trader John Tod (*see* Tod Inlet) settled at Oak Bay in 1851 upon his retirement from the HBC. His large property was opposite and just N of Mary Tod I, which he named after his favourite daughter about 1856. Mary Tod (1843–1912) was born at Ft Thompson, later known as Kamloops, and moved with her family to Ft Nisqually on Puget Sd before arriving at Ft Victoria in 1849. Her mother, Sophia Lolo, is believed to have been the eldest daughter of long-time HBC employee Jean-Baptiste Lolo (*see* Mt Lolo). In 1864, at Victoria, Mary married John Sylvester Bowker (c 1822–98), a US resident who had previously farmed on the San Juan Is. Bowker and Mary's younger brother, John Tod Jr, raised sheep on S Pender I, commuting from Oak Bay by sailboat. Mary Tod died at LA, where she had started spending the winters when she grew older. The island was shown on 1861 and 1864 Admiralty charts as Todd I and Mary Todd I. It was known locally for many years as Jimmy Chickens I, after a fisherman, clam digger and notorious drinker who lived there with his spouse Jenny. This jovial eccentric, who was

M

unhappily "possessed by Demon Rum," according to a newspaper report, was perhaps better known to Victoria's policemen than any other resident of the area, having spent so much time in their company. Chickens was well liked except when stealing fowl (hence his name) or when he and Jenny caroused on their island late into the night, disturbing the wealthy owners of nearby waterfront properties. Jimmy was particularly noted for his poor sense of time; he once brought the alarmed proprietor of Oak Bay's Mt Baker Hotel to the door at 4 am in response to his frantic knocking, only to ask if he had a match. This gentleman, John Virtue, eventually bought Mary Tod I and donated it to Oak Bay municipality in 1929 on the condition that nothing should ever be built there. Both Jimmy, who died in 1901, and Jenny were buried on Mary Tod I. Songhees First Nation members know it as Kohweechella, meaning "where there are many fish."

Maskelyne Island (54°38'00" 130°27'00" S entrance to Work Channel, S side of Portland Inlet, N of Prince Rupert), **Maskelyne Point** (54°39'00" 130°27'00" N end of Maskelyne I). Maskelyne Point was named in 1793 by Capt George Vancouver after Nevil Maskelyne (1732–1811), a British mathematician and astronomer. He was a clergyman as well as a scientist, and became a fellow of the Royal Society in 1758. In 1761, Maskelyne was sent to St Helena to observe the transit of Venus; during the voyage he discovered a method of determining longitude by observing the position of the moon. Two years later he went to Barbados as chaplain of HMS *Louisa* to pursue further longitudinal studies. Maskelyne was appointed Astronomer Royal in 1765 and held that office until he died. He was responsible for publishing the *Nautical Almanac*, an annual set of calculations for lunar distances, used by navigators to find longitude at sea. *W*

Maskill Point (53°11'00" 128°39'00" W entrance to Klekane Inlet, Princess Royal Channel, opposite Butedale on Princess Royal I). Charles Maskill was an able seaman and later quartermaster's mate aboard HMS *Chatham*, under Lt William Broughton, on Capt George Vancouver's 1791–95 expedition to the PNW.

Mason Rock (52°28'00" 129°20'00" S of Harvey I, W of Aristazabal I, Hecate Str). T Mason Johnston, from Ottawa, was the son of Alexander Johnston, deputy minister of the federal Dept of Marine and Fisheries, 1910–33 (*see* Mt Johnston). This feature was named in 1927, when Mason was a youngster, by regional hydrographer Henri Parizeau, who also named nearby Frances Rk and Steele Rk after Mason's mother.

Masset (54°01'00" 132°06'00" E side of Masset Hbr), **Masset Harbour** (54°03'00" 132°13'00" N entrance to Masset Sd), **Masset Inlet** (53°43'00" 132°20'00" S end of Masset Sd), **Masset Sound** (53°55'00" 132°07'00" N end of

Haida village of Old Masset, about 1915. *Author's collection*

Graham I, QCI). The important Haida First Nation village of Masset, the largest community in the QCI, takes its name from nearby Maast I (qv). The origin of the word Maast is uncertain, though it may be a corruption of the name of an early European trader who died in the area. The village applied for a post office in the early 1900s, but when its application was allowed to lapse, a non-Haida settlement that had grown up 2 km to the SE, originally known as Graham City, pirated the name Masset for its post office instead. The original Haida community is now called Old Masset or, simply, Haida. It consists of three ancient village sites: Uttewas, meaning "white slope" and probably referring to a small hill nearby; Edjao, just SE of the hill; and Ka-yung, farther SE still. When smallpox decimated their ranks, the Haida abandoned dozens of villages and congregated in just two: Masset and Skidegate. The HBC had a trading post at Masset for many years, and an Anglican mission was established in 1876. Commercial fishing has been an important source of jobs in the 20th century. A Canadian Forces Base just E of Masset acts as a signal-monitoring station for Canada's national intelligence agency. Masset Sd was known as Hancock's R in the early fur-trading days, after the vessel of Capt Samuel Crowell of Boston. *D E W*

Masterman Islands (50°45'00" 127°25'00" E of entrance to Hardy Bay, E of Duval I, just E of Port Hardy, NE side of Vancouver I). Capt George Richards named these islands about 1862 in association with Hardy Bay (qv), which had been named earlier, in 1850, after Vice Adm Sir Thomas Masterman Hardy, who had been flag capt to Lord Nelson at Trafalgar. Masterman was the maiden name of Hardy's mother, Nanny. *W*

Matchlee Bay (49°37'00" 126°04'00" SE end of Muchalat Inlet, S of Gold R, W side of Vancouver I). Named after the First Nation reserve at the head of this bay near the mouth of the Burman R. The word is believed to be a variant of *muchalee*, which is the original Nuu-chah-nulth name for the Gold R valley, according to author George Nicholson.

The Muchalaht people, who belong to the Nuu-chah-nulth cultural group, are "those who live beside the Muchalee R." Muchalat Inlet (qv) is named for them. The Mowachaht ("people of the deer"), who occupied the more westerly portions of Nootka Sd, were traditional enemies of the Muchalaht, who lived farther E, and many battles were fought over the rich sockeye salmon resources of Gold R. The Muchalaht were reduced in number by the endless attacks and retreated inland but eventually intermarried with their enemies; today the two groups are allied and live at the same village site. Nicholson has suggested that the names of the tribes are both derived from the same linguistic source. Nearby Matchlee Ck and Matchlee Mtn are named after Matchlee Bay.

Mathers Point (53°40'00" 130°05'00" N of Hevenor Inlet, Pitt I). RCAF flight lt James Wilson Mathers, DFC, was killed in action Sept 28, 1944. He was born at Weyburn, Sask, but became a resident of Vancouver, where he enlisted. Mathers was a member of No 162 Squadron, based in the Mediterranean for much of the war, where he carried out numerous secret—and extremely dangerous—low-level flights with Wellington medium bombers to determine the position of enemy radar and radio units and then jam them. He is buried at Khayat Beach War Cemetery in Israel.

Matheson Inlet (52°27'00" 131°28'00" S of Werner Bay, E side of Moresby I, QCI). J Matheson was a mining speculator in the Lockeport area in the early 1900s. He and his partner, D Bowser, apparently owned the Surprise copper claim on Klunkwoi Bay in 1908, adjacent to the better-known Last Chance group of properties. The inlet was known locally by fishermen for many years as South Werner Bay. *D*

Mathews Rock (54°12'00" 130°16'00" Off S side of Lelu I, Inverness Passage, just S of Prince Rupert). Named by the hydrographic service in 1927 after Edward J Mathews, who secured a number of Crown grants of land in the vicinity of Lelu I 1905–07.

Matilda Inlet (49°17'00" 126°04'00" SE side of Flores I, Clayoquot Sd, W side of Vancouver I). Capt George Richards, with the RN survey ship *Hecate*, named this feature Matilda Ck in 1862, "creek" being an old term for a small cove or inlet that dries at low tide. The *Matilda* was a trading schooner that operated on the BC coast in the 1860s; in 1864, for instance, it took a large shipment of lumber to Victoria from the Burrard Inlet sawmill. Matilda Inlet was the scene of a massacre in 1864 when a party from the nearby First Nation village of Ahousat attacked the sloop *Kingfisher* and killed its crew. The vessel was then pillaged and burnt. This incident naturally outraged the colonial government, which sent HMS *Sutlej* and *Devastation*, under Rear Adm Joseph Denman, to the area to apprehend and punish the murderers. The ships destroyed nine villages and dozens of canoes while searching for the culprits, killing at least 15 people, and brought several prisoners to Victoria, where they were charged but then acquitted on the bizarre ground that the testimony of First Nation witnesses was inadmissable because they could not be sworn to tell the truth, having no belief in Christian values or the Bible. The leader of the Ahousaht pirates, Chief Chapchah, and most of his followers were never captured. *W*

Matlahaw Point (49°23'00" 126°29'00" SE end of Hesquiat Peninsula, between Nootka Sd and Clayoquot Sd, W side of Vancouver I). Chief Matlahaw (d 1876) of the Hesquiat First Nation was presented with a silver medal by the Canadian government for organizing rescue parties and saving the crew of the US barque *Edwin*, which ran onto the reefs off Hesquiat Hbr in Dec 1874. He also received a cash award from US authorities. Five years earlier, two local residents had been hanged for murdering the crew of the *John Bright*, wrecked at the same location, and the medal and cash were a way of encouraging the Hesquiats' new, improved behaviour. In 1875, Chief Matlahaw fell from grace, however, when he contracted smallpox and, in torment, shot Fr Augustin Brabant, pioneer W coast Roman Catholic missionary, in the hand and shoulder. Brabant survived his wounds and, on returning to Hesquiat, founded a First Nation police force. Matlahaw was never charged with a crime and died soon after. This feature was formerly known as Boulder Point but was changed in 1934 to avoid duplication.

Matlset Narrows (49°14'00" 125°48'00" Off NE side of Meares I, Clayoquot Sd, W side of Vancouver I). Matlset, or Maalhsit, was a former Tla-o-qui-aht (Clayoquot) First Nation village once situated on the narrows. The name, which was adopted in 1947, means "cold water." The narrows was formerly known as Race Narrows.

Matthew Island (52°07'00" 127°51'00" In entrance to Evans Inlet, E side of Fisher Channel, W side of King I, E of Bella Bella), **Matthew Passage** (52°06'00" 127°51'00" Between Matthew I and King I). After one of the four evangelists who wrote the gospel accounts in the New Testament. St Matthew was also one of the 12 apostles. Tradition holds that he was a tax collector. RN surveyor Lt Daniel Pender named several features in this vicinity after the evangelists about 1866, probably in association with nearby Port John (which does not commemorate a biblical figure, however, being named by Capt George Vancouver after his friend the Rev John Fisher).

Matthews Island (50°29'00" 128°02'00" W side of Forward Inlet, S of Winter Hbr, Quatsino Sd, NW end of Vancouver I). Named in 1927 after Louis C Matthews, who was a resident on this island in 1918.

M

Matthews Point (48°52'00" 123°20'00" W of Mary Anne Point, S side of Galiano I, Gulf Is). Named by Cdr John Parry of HMS *Egeria* in 1905 for the Matthews family—Mark Reginald Matthews, his wife Mary (née Grubb), their three children and Mary's sister Anne Grubb—who are believed to have lived on nearby Mary Anne Point in the late 19th century.

Matute Island (49°42'00" 126°38'00" In Kendrick Inlet, E side of Nootka I, W side of Vancouver I). The hydrographic service named this feature in 1934 after Spanish naval officer Juan Matute, who served at the Mexican port of San Blas and is believed to have made at least one voyage to Nootka Sd in the late 18th century (probably in 1790) as cdr of the storeship *Aránzazu*.

Maude Bay (48°52'00" 123°17'00" NE side of Mayne I, Gulf Is), **Maude Island** (49°16'00" 124°05'00" Just N of Lantzville, off entrance to Nanoose Hbr, NW of Nanaimo, E side of Vancouver I). Midshipman Eustace Downman Maude (1848–1930) served on the Pacific Station, 1865–68, aboard HMS *Scout*, under Capt John Price. His father, Sir George Maude, was a Crown equerry or member of the British royal household. Eustace joined the RN in 1861 and was promoted to lt in 1871 after being wounded in action against Malay pirates. He served aboard the royal yacht *Victoria and Albert*, 1876–78, and was present, on HMS *Temeraire*, at the 1882 attack on Alexandria. After retiring in 1885 with the rank of cdr, and marrying Amy Williams (1860–1946), Maude and his wife headed to N America, where they lived in Oregon before coming to BC in 1896 with their children and putting down roots on Mayne I. Eustace served as a justice of the peace and owned the Point Comfort Hotel, which he soon turned into a private residence and allowed to collapse into a genteel disarray while the family hosted elegant dinner parties and musical soirees. Maude was fondly remembered by his peers for attempting, at the age of 77, to single-handedly sail his yawl *Half-Moon* to England via the Panama Canal. He injured himself off the California coast and had to be towed part of the way home. **Maude Islet** (50°51'00" 126°44'00" N side of Broughton I, entrance to Greenway Sd, N of E end of Queen Charlotte Str) and **Maud Island** (50°37'00" 126°36'00" Between Crease I and Village I, E end of Queen Charlotte Str) may also both be named after this pioneer. Maud I appeared on an 1867 Admiralty chart as Indian I; it is not known how the name lost its "e." *W*

Maude Channel (53°13'00" 132°06'00" Between Lina I and Maude I), **Maude Island** (53°12'00" 132°05'00" W end of Skidegate Inlet, between Graham I and Moresby I, QCI). Heavily logged Maude I, the largest island in Skidegate Inlet, was named by Lt Daniel Pender during an 1866 survey. The origin of the name is not known. In 1945, to avoid confusion with Maude I off Nanoose Hbr (*see above*), the hydrographic service suggested changing the

name to Recovery I, after the brig *Recovery*, which served the HBC, 1852–61, as a coastal trading vessel, guard ship at Nanaimo and customs vessel off the mouth of the Fraser R during the gold rush. Strangely, the Geographic Board of Canada turned down the request, and Maude remained unchanged. The Haida people know the island as Ha'ina. There are two former village sites: Hotao, or Xo'tao; and Haina, or Xa'ina ("Sunshine Town"). Haina is a very old habitation spot that was abandoned and then reoccupied in the 1850s as the residents of outlying W coast Haida villages, their numbers greatly reduced by smallpox and tuberculosis, decided to live together at one location. Haina then became known as New Gold Hbr. It was again abandoned in the 1890s as its inhabitants joined with other southern Haida to form one central village at Skidegate. *D*

Maud Point (50°29'00" 125°45'00" N side of Forward Hbr, E of Hardwicke I, N of Johnstone Str). Lady Maud Caroline Lascelles (1846–1938) was a sister of Lt Hon Horace Lascelles, who was in command of the RN gunboat *Forward* on the BC coast, 1861–65 (*see* Lascelles Point). She married Lord George Francis Hamilton (1845–1927), son of the Duke of Abercorn, a long-time Conservative MP who served as 1st Lord of the Admiralty, 1885–92, and secretary of state for India, 1895–1903. Lascelles was also a British aristocrat, a son of the Earl of Harewood, and many features in the vicinity of Forward Hbr were named after his family, including four points that commemorate his sisters.

Maud Rock (51°27'00" 127°38'00" S of Ripon I, Rivers Inlet). According to BC historians Helen and Philip Akrigg, Maud was the name of a young nurse working at Dr George Darby's Rivers Inlet hospital at the time a new coastal survey was being conducted in the late 1930s.

Maurelle Island (50°17'00" 125°09'00" Off NE side of Quadra I, N of Campbell R). Maurelle I, Sonora I and Quadra I were all considered by early explorers to be part of one large feature, originally known as Valdes (or Valdez) I, and did not receive their current names until 1903; Maurelle was known for some time as Middle Valdes I. Spanish naval officer Francisco Antonio Maurelle (1754–1820) was deputy cdr to Francisco Bodega y Quadra on two epic explorations of the BC and Alaska coasts in 1775 and 1779 that went farther N than any previous Spanish expeditions. He was born in Galicia, in NW Spain, and is believed to have originally spelled his name Mourelle. After apprenticing as a pilot at age 14, he transferred in the 1770s to Mexico, where he was based at San Blas. On the 1775 expedition, Bodega and Maurelle, on the *Sonora*, sailed almost to Cape Fairweather in Alaska after becoming separated off the BC coast from their companion vessel, the *Santiago*, under Lt Bruno de Hezeta. In 1779 they sailed on the *Favorita*, accompanied by Ignacio de Arteaga on the *Princesca*, and reached Cook

Maurelle Island upper left, Settlers Group at centre. *Peter Vassilopoulos*

Inlet at the W end of the Gulf of Alaska in their search for the NW Passage. Maurelle prepared important charts and sailing directions from these voyages that were used by subsequent explorers, including Capt George Vancouver, and also published a book describing early Spanish voyages in the PNW. In 1780 he sailed the *Princesca* from San Blas to Manila and returned via Tonga and Tuvalu, making several new discoveries in the S Pacific. Maurelle served in Europe in the Napoleonic Wars and was promoted to the rank of adm in 1818. Maurelle I, 54 sq km in size, was mostly logged before WWI and has few inhabitants. *E W*

Maurus Channel (49°12'00" 125°56'00" Between Meares I and Vargas I, just N of Tofino, Clayoquot Sd, W side of Vancouver I). Benedictine priest Maurus Snyder (b 1865), a native of Switzerland, was ordained in 1890. He was part of the original group of Benedictines who founded Mt Angel Abbey in Oregon, and he served as a professor at Mt Angel College, 1890–1900. For the next decade, Fr Maurus worked as principal of the Christie residential school at Kakawis on Meares I. He oversaw the expansion of the school, adding two wings in 1904 and installing hot-water heating, electric light plants and a steam laundry. In 1912, Snyder returned to Mt Angel Abbey as treasurer, becoming prior in 1914, publications editor in 1921 and chaplain to Portland's Sisters of Mercy in 1927. Maurus Channel was known until 1934 as Deception Channel.

Maycock Rock (50°20'00" 125°20'00" Off S entrance to Cameleon Hbr, Sonora I, N of Campbell R). James D Maycock was a midshipman aboard HMS *Sutlej*, the flagship of Rear Adm John Kingcome, and served on the Pacific Station in 1863–64. He was assigned temporarily to HMS *Cameleon* in 1863. He later served on HMS *Hibernia*, the flagship of Rear Adm Henry Kellett, superintendent of the Malta dockyard. *W*

Mayes Point (50°17'00" 125°04'00" N tip of Read I, N end of Str of Georgia). In the 1860s, Lt Daniel Pender named many geographic features in this area after naval officers who served under Capt George Richards, hydrographer of the RN 1864–74. (Richards had been Pender's predecessor as the primary RN surveyor on the BC coast.) William Mayes (d 1904) worked under several chief hydrographers, including Richards, as he spent 20 years in this dept of the Admiralty, retiring in 1885 as superintendent of compasses with the rank of staff capt. *W*

Maynard Cove (48°27'00" 123°16'00" Between Cadboro Point and Ten Mile Point, Saanich, NE of Victoria). Named in 1934 after Joseph Maynard (1840–1929), who was one of the first homesteaders in the Cadboro Bay area. Born in England, he immigrated to Canada in 1873 and is listed in the 1881 census as a railway labourer and the 1882 Victoria directory as an expressman. In 1886, at Victoria, Joseph married Catherine Taylor (1841–1920), who had come out from Scotland earlier that year. The couple established a poultry farm on their Cadboro Bay property. Joseph's better-known older brother was the photographer and shoemaker Richard Maynard (1832–1907), whose wife, Hannah Maynard (1834–1918), operated Victoria's first photographic studio. Maynard Cove appears as Boat Cove on an 1861 Admiralty chart; it is well known locally as Smuggler's Cove.

Maynard Head (49°42'00" 124°12'00" N entrance to Billings Bay, W end of Nelson I, Malaspina Str, NW of Vancouver). Lorne Edward Maynard (1892–1972), from Ont, lived for many years in N Dakota, Oregon and Alberta (where he married his first wife, Jennie May Fyke, and had three children, all of whom died young). He served overseas during WWI. Maynard arrived at Vancouver in 1928 and obtained a veteran's land grant at Billings Bay. He also acquired a small boat, the *Therma*, that was chartered to take the provincial boiler inspector around the S coast and, later, to transport children to and from the one-room school at Ballet Bay. Maynard was also postmaster at Billings Bay, 1949–63. He and his second wife, Carol Moe (1907–1997), were married in 1937, raised another family on the bay, then sold their property and moved to Pender Hbr in 1966.

Mayne Bay (48°59'00" 125°19'00" E of David Channel, SE of Toquart Bay, Barkley Sd, W side of Vancouver I), **Mayne Island** (48°50'42" 123°16'51" E of Saltspring I, Gulf Is), **Mayne Passage** (50°24'14" 125°29'44" Between W Thurlow I and E Thurlow I, N of Johnstone Str, NW of Campbell R), **Mayne Point** (50°23'00" 125°33'00" W end of E Thurlow I). Richard Charles Mayne (1835–92), son of long-serving London police chief Sir Richard Mayne, was educated at Eton and entered the RN in 1847. He served in the Crimea before being promoted to lt in 1856 and posted to the Pacific Station, 1857–61. Mayne assisted Capt George Richards (who named all these features except Mayne Point) aboard the survey vessels *Plumper* and *Hecate* and also made several overland journeys to report

The south end of Mayne Island at left with Horton Bay in the foreground and Bennett Bay in the distance. *Kevin Oke*

on the practicability of building roads from the head of Jervis Inlet to the Cariboo goldfields and from Nanaimo to Alberni Inlet. In 1861 he returned to England and the following year published a useful book on his PNW experiences, *Four Years in British Columbia and Vancouver Island*. As a capt, Mayne commanded HMS *Eclipse*, 1862–66, during which time he was wounded while fighting Maoris in NZ and afterwards awarded a CB. He had the important job of surveying the Strs of Magellan, 1866–69, with HMS *Nassau* and ended his career as cdr of HMS *Invincible* in the Mediterranean. Mayne was promoted to rear adm, retired, in 1879 and was the Conservative MP for Pembroke and Haverfordwest, 1886–92. Richard Rk in Barkley Sd is also named after him. The 23 sq km of Mayne I were settled in the 1860s, and it had a permanent population of about 1,000 in the early 2000s, augmented in summer by tourists. Early homesteaders raised sheep and orchards, and many Japanese Canadians, originally hired to cut cordwood for the Fraser R canneries, arrived after 1890. Mayne Passage was the Canal de Olavide of Spanish explorer Dionisio Alcalá-Galiano, named after Martin de Olavide, one of Alejandro Malaspina's officers on the *Atrevida*. E W

Mayor Channel (48°25'00" 123°17'00" Between Oak Bay and Great Chain I, off SE Vancouver I). After Thomas Harris, first mayor of Victoria. *See* Harris I.

May Point (50°29'00" 127°51'00" NW tip of the Koskimo Is, Quatsino Sd, NW end of Vancouver I). Named in 1927 for William Delchante May, who acquired Crown grants of land in this vicinity in 1886 and 1911. This may be the same William May, born about 1831 in England, who is listed in the 1891 census as a farmer on the N end of Vancouver I. His wife Susan, born about 1834, and 11-year-old daughter Toddle were also recorded.

Mazarredo Islands (54°05'00" 132°33'00" W side of Virago Sd, N side of Graham I, QCI). This group of islands was named in 1907 by Capt Frederick Learmonth of HMS *Egeria* while re-surveying Virago Sd. An early Spanish name for the sound, bestowed in 1792 by explorer Jacinto Caamaño, had been Puerto Mazarredo, and this name was adopted as Port Maseredo by Capt George Vancouver. Dionisio Alcalá-Galiano, who charted much of the southern BC coast in 1792, travelling part of the way with Vancouver, gave the name Bocas de Mazarredo to Jervis Inlet. Isla de Mazarredo was an old Spanish name for Nootka I, bestowed either by Estéban Martínez in 1789 or by Alejandro Malaspina in 1791. All these names commemorate José María de Mazarredo y Salazar (1745–1812), a famous Spanish naval cdr of the time, who later became a politician and director gen of the navy.

McAllister Islet (50°28'00" 127°59'00" N side of Quatsino Sd, NW of Gillam Is, NW end of Vancouver I). John McAllister secured several Crown grants of land in this area between 1888 and 1892. The feature appears as Bare Islet on early Admiralty charts but was changed in 1927 to avoid duplication.

McAlmond Point (52°49'00" 132°04'00" W side of Newcombe Inlet, Tasu Sd, W side of Moresby I, QCI). Capt Elijah H McAlmond (1827–1913), from Belfast, Maine, came to the W coast of N America about 1850 and worked on sailing vessels out of San Francisco. He settled at Dungeness, Washington, and left the sea for a period, then built the schooner *Rebecca* in 1861 and operated it in Puget Sd and off Alaska until 1865. It was McAlmond and the *Rebecca* that first brought mining engineer Francis Poole to the QCI's Skincuttle Inlet region in 1862 to look for copper. After serving as a pilot for the next decade or so, McAlmond built the schooner *Champion* at Port Townsend in 1880 and hunted seals off Cape Flattery with his son Henry McAlmond (b 1861) of Port Angeles, also a seafaring man. Henry first worked on the *Champion*, then skippered a pilot boat named the *Ariel*, a cargo steamer named the *Puritan* and several sealing schooners. After retiring, he purchased a prune orchard at Port Williams near Dungeness.

McArthur Point (52°18'00" 128°06'00" S side of Yeo I, Return Channel, N of Bella Bella). According to records at BC's Geographical Names Office, the point was named in 1925 for J McArthur, dock agent for the CNR Steamship Co at Victoria in the early 1920s. This is probably James McArthur (1881–1956), who is listed in the 1901 census as a clerk working for the Canadian Pacific Navigation Co. His father, also James McArthur (1845–97), was a marine engineer with CPN and the Pioneer Line for many years. James Sr and Andrew Gray brought two traction engines out from Scotland in the early 1870s for use on the Cariboo Rd, but these proved unsuccessful. James Sr later worked as an engineer at the Moodyville sawmill and at one time owned an interest in the historic paddle steamer *Beaver*.

McBey Islets (49°07'00" 125°49'00" In Tsapee Narrows, Browning Passage, SE of Tofino, Clayoquot Sd). Nellie Georgina Stewart (1883–1922) was born in the Shetland Is and acquired her love of the natural world from her father, a headmaster and botanist. She and her husband, Thomas Pert McBey (1875–1934), immigrated to BC and lived at Cameron Lk, where Nellie continued to pursue her interests as a naturalist, searching out and raising a variety of native plants. In 1920 she discovered the first Canadian examples of California myrtle (*Myrica californica*) on these islets, which were owned at the time by John Wilson Thompson of Tofino. Early Admiralty charts show them as the Dinner Its, but the name was changed in 1934 by regional hydrographer Henri Parizeau.

McBride Bay (49°51'00" 126°43'00" NE side of Nootka I, W side of Vancouver I). Named in 1926 by C L Roberts, who surveyed the bay for Arthur D McBride of Vancouver. McBride was involved with the construction of the Hecate cannery and pilchard reduction plant, built at the W entrance to the bay by the Gosse Packing Co and later owned by BC Packers. Hecate operated 1926–31, then closed and reopened from 1936 to the late 1940s, processing herring after the pilchards disappeared. The plant was demolished in 1954, though some remains were still visible in the early 2000s. A large sawmill owned by a British company, Nootka Wood Products Ltd, operated on the bay in the late 1930s.

McBride Bay (50°43'00" 125°26'00" Head of Loughborough Inlet, between Knight Inlet and Bute Inlet). Dr Alexander McBride (d 1898) was assistant surgeon on HMS *Bacchante*, flagship of Rear Adm Sir Thomas Maitland, cdr-in-chief on the Pacific Station, 1861–62. He was promoted to surgeon in 1865 and fleet surgeon, retired, in 1876. Named by Capt George Richards of the RN survey vessel *Hecate* about 1862.

McBride Bay (51°18'00" 127°32'00" N side of Greaves I, Smith Inlet, N of Port Hardy). This local name for the bay was adopted by Capt John Walbran in 1903 while making a preliminary survey of Smith Inlet with CGS *Quadra*. Frederick J McBride (1852–1904), from NB, was logging here for the Takush Saw Mill Co in 1897.

McCall Bank (49°20'00" 123°39'00" W of Howe Sd, Str of Georgia). Albert Arthur McCall (1877–1947), a fisherman and boatbuilder who grew up at Gibsons Landing and had a small boatyard in N Vancouver, first reported this bank. He was the elder son of Gibsons pioneer Arthur Simpson McCall (1851–1935), who came to BC from Ont and worked at first as a drayman, hauling shingle bolts and other materials with his horse and wagon, later becoming a realtor and justice of the peace for the Gibsons area. Albert married Hattie Gibson, daughter of Gibsons Landing founder George Gibson, in 1900. He owned a

salmon troller named the *Klickitat*, named for the sound made by its engine, and also built two small boats at N Vancouver, the *Ootsa* and the *Service*, which he used for towing logs. He died at W Vancouver. McCall Bank, a rich fishing ground, was discovered in the 2000s to be home to a number of glass sponge reefs—agglomerations of aquatic animals that attach themselves to the floor of the ocean and form massive but easily damaged structures 20 m high and dozens of square km in extent.

McCall Island (49°09'00" 125°43'00" W side of Tofino Inlet, NE of Warne I, Clayoquot Sd, W side of Vancouver I). Named in 1934 for Robert McCall, who pre-empted land on Esowista Peninsula SE of Tofino in 1912 and received a Crown grant there in 1914.

McCarthy Island (48°27'00" 123°27'00" W side of Esquimalt Hbr, E of Thetis Cove, W of Victoria). Lt Henry Hotham McCarthy (d 1903) was a Royal Marines officer aboard HMS *Fisgard*, under Capt John Duntze, on the Pacific Station, 1843–47. He was promoted to maj in 1864. Named by Lt Cdr James Wood of the survey vessel *Pandora* in 1847.

McCaw Peninsula (49°11'00" 125°40'00" Between Tofino Inlet and Tranquil Inlet, Clayoquot Sd, W side of Vancouver I). Robert Daniel McCaw (1884–1941), from Welland, received his professional training in Ont and was commissioned as a Dominion land surveyor in 1909. He headed W and worked in Alberta and BC, becoming a partner in the firm Wheeler, Campbell & McCaw and marrying Ethel McConnell. In 1912–13, McCaw laid out roads on the W coast of Vancouver I and also made an early photo-topographical survey for a road between Banff and Windermere. Photo-topography became his specialty. He worked on the W coast of Vancouver I in 1935–36 and 1939–41, determining the route for the road between Alberni and Tofino-Ucluelet, and in the Findlay R area 1937–38. He was also active in the Cariboo and Kamloops districts and provided background information for many BC place names over the years. McCaw had to ascend numerous peaks to take survey readings. He became a keen mountaineer and chairman of the Victoria branch of the Alpine Club of Canada, 1916–22. He was also on the board of the BC Land Surveyors corporation for several years and president in 1934.

McClinton Bay (53°39'00" 132°35'00" W side of Masset Inlet, Graham I, QCI). QCI historian Kathleen Dalzell uncovered the following information about S R MacClinton, whose name was adopted—and apparently misspelled—for this feature in 1907. A civil engineer from Vancouver, he had located timber claims around Masset Inlet for the Graham Steamship, Coal & Lumber Co and then toured the area with company officials. By 1909 he was managing director of the Moresby I Development and

M

Prospecting Co, which held timber rights and mineral claims on Moresby I. McClinton Ck, site of a fish hatchery in the 1920s and '30s, runs into the bay, which was named Tin-in-ow-a by geologist George M Dawson in 1878. *D*

McClusky Bay (51°38'00" 127°47'00" N side of Fish Egg Inlet, E of Fitz Hugh Sd and Calvert I). This locally used name was submitted in 1985 by the staff of Sidney's Institute of Ocean Sciences, a research facility operated by Fisheries and Oceans Canada. According to the IOS submission, McClusky was "a local tough guy" who gillnetted the creek that entered the head of the bay. The name was adopted in 1987.

McColl Rock (52°36'00" 129°18'00" SE of Moore Is, W of Aristazabal I, Hecate Str). Sgt William McColl (1819–65) was a member of the Columbia detachment of Royal Engineers, which served in BC from 1858 to 1863. He arrived at Esquimalt in Oct 1858 on *La Plata* with the party of men led by Capt Robert Parsons. McColl's wife, Ann Baseley (1832–1913), and four children came out on the *Marcella* in 1860. That was the year McColl and a squad of engineers marked out a route from Ft Hope over the Coast Mtns to Princeton on the Similkameen R. Edgar Dewdney and Walter Moberly later obtained the contract to build this trail. In 1861, McColl and his men surveyed the site of the Alexandra Bridge, the first bridge over the Fraser R, built in 1863 by Joseph Trutch. McColl acquired several pieces of land in BC, and he and his family stayed on when the detachment disbanded. He set up for business as a surveyor in 1863 with his friend and fellow sapper George Turner, and was laying out First Nation reserves for Gov James Douglas in 1864—but was reduced to collecting tolls on the Alexandra Bridge in 1865, the year he died at Yale. Three years later his widow married Turner (*see* Turner Rk). McColl Ck, a tributary of the Tulameen R, is also named for him.

McConnachie Shoal (52°50'00" 131°57'00" In Pacofi Bay, E side of Moresby I, SW of Louise I, QCI). Named by the hydrographic service in 1947 after the manager of the Pacofi fish plant. This troubled project was built in 1909 by the Pacific Coast Fisheries Co to freeze fresh fish and produce fish oil and fertilizer but was plagued by poor weather and financial problems. McConnachie, whose first name is unknown, was in charge there in 1910–11.

McCoy Cove (53°02'30" 131°39'34" N side of Cumshewa Inlet, NE Moresby I, QCI), **McCoy Rocks** (53°35'00" 130°35'00" Off Griffiths Hbr, W of N end of Banks I, Hecate Str). Named in the 1920s by the hydrographic service after W H McCoy, from Liverpool, who worked as a fireman on board the Canadian government survey vessel *Lillooet* after serving overseas during WWI. McCoy Cove was formerly known as McKay's Hbr after a post was established there in the early 1870s by trader and sealer

Capt Hugh McKay. In the 18th century it was also referred to as Berry Cove and Hope Cove by early fur-trading visitors. *D*

McCreight Point (53°12'30" 129°30'00" S end of Pitt I). John Foster McCreight (1827–1913) was the first premier of BC. He was born in Ireland and practised law in Australia before immigrating to BC in 1860. In 1871 he was one of 25 members elected to BC's first provincial legislature and was appointed premier and attorney gen by Lt Gov Joseph Trutch. He resigned in 1872 with a reputation as a difficult, unlikeable man who was opposed to democracy and responsible government. Colonial jurist Henry Crease found him "bad tempered ... extremely credulous ... excessively obstinate" and "utterly ignorant of politics." No one, however, ever questioned his integrity or self-discipline. McCreight left politics in 1875 and served on the BC Supreme Court, 1880–97, before retiring to England. Presumably **McCreight Island** (53°42'00" 132°27'00" Off N side of Masset Inlet, Graham I, QCI) and **McCreight Rock** (53°42'00" 132°28'00" N of McCreight I), which were named in 1910 by hydrographer Lt Cdr Philip Musgrave, also commemorate him, as does McCreight Lk NW of Campbell R. *E*

John Foster McCreight, BC's first premier. *BC Archives A-01449*

McCroskie Islands (52°16'00" 127°55'00" W side of Johnson Channel, off E side of Cunningham I, NE of Bella Bella). This name, applied by the hydrographic service in 1925, is a spelling error, as these islands honour coastal pioneer Edward McCoskrie (1852–1925). He was born at Liverpool and went to sea at the age of 14, immigrating to Canada in the early 1870s and marrying Achsah M Tork (1852–92) at Port Dover, Ont. McCoskrie came to Victoria with his family and worked as a skipper for the Canadian Pacific Navigation Co and also in the salvage business with the steamer *Mascotte*. He retired to Galiano

I in 1894 with his second wife, Emma Gibbson (1857–99), but after her death and that of their infant son Harry, he married a third time, to Alice Jane (1864–1949), and headed N, working at Nass Hbr and Skagway, running a sawmill at Hartley Bay, 1905–10, and serving as a timber inspector. In 1912 he was appointed harbourmaster at Prince Rupert, where the flute-playing capt and his wife kept a small steam launch called the *Nora*. McCoskrie's descendants (the name is also seen misspelled McCoskie) had a long association with Galiano I. Edward's architect father, also Edward (1821–93), followed his son to Victoria and set up a flourishing practice there. The McCroskie Is were formerly known as the Knox Is, and also as the Nixon Is, after Cdr Edward Atcherley Eckersall Nixon, retired RN officer and commandant of the Royal Naval College of Canada, 1911–22.

McCulloch Rock (54°35'00" 131°12'00" E end of Dixon Entrance, W of Zayas I, NW of Prince Rupert). William McCulloch (1827–1906) was born in Ireland and went to sea at the tender age of 12. He arrived in BC from London as mate of the barque *Nanette*, which was wrecked on Race Rks in 1860. Remaining on the W coast, he served as a master of local trading schooners, including the *North Star*, which he took to San Francisco during the US Civil War and was fired on while entering the harbour there after being mistaken for an enemy ship. In 1864, at Victoria, he married Sarah Taylor Marsdon (1833–1916), who came out from England in 1863 on the brideship *Robert Lowe*. McCulloch was in charge of the *Fidelater* when it was struck by the *Alexander* at Victoria in 1865, remaining at the wheel after the collision and single-handedly managing to beach the stricken vessel. He became a Victoria-based pilot, 1868–74, then worked for the marine dept of the HBC and its successor, the Canadian Pacific Navigation Co, from 1874 to 1892, at which time he retired. McCulloch also had a short stint with the People's Navigation Co as capt of the *Amelia*. He discovered this rock in 1875 while taking the HBC's *Otter* from Masset to Port Simpson. *W*

McCurdy Point (48°34'00" 123°31'00" W side of Squally Reach, Saanich Inlet, NW of Victoria). Named in 1934 after inventor and entrepreneur Arthur William McCurdy (1856–1923), who built a summer home on Malahat Dr overlooking Saanich Inlet. Born at Truro, NS, he moved to Baddeck, where he edited the local newspaper, worked for Alexander Graham Bell and created, among other innovations, an automated, portable, film-developing system that he sold to George Eastman of Kodak. McCurdy came to Victoria about 1902 with his second wife, Hattie Mace. He helped bring the Dominion Astrophysical observatory to Saanich, served as the first president of the Canadian Club of Victoria and ran as a Liberal candidate for Esquimalt in the 1916 provincial election, losing by only two votes. McCurdy was also president in the early

1900s of the Nootka Marble Co, which owned a quarry at Nootka Sd. He moved to Washington, DC, in 1921. His son, John Alexander Douglas McCurdy (1886–1961), was a renowned Canadian aviator, who in 1909 made Canada's first aircraft flight with the *Silver Dart* and much later in life served as lt gov of NS.

McCutcheon Point (53°42'00" 130°06'00" N entrance to Newcombe Hbr, NW side of Pitt I). Flight Lt Elvet Baxter McCutcheon of the RCAF was killed in action on Jan 16, 1945. He was born in Sask but made his home at Vancouver, where he enlisted. A pilot with No 420 Squadron, he was awarded the DFC for completing a bombing run over the German port of Wilhelmshaven despite his Halifax aircraft being extensively damaged in a collision. McCutcheon is buried at Hanover War Cemetery in Germany.

McDougal Island (50°14'00" 127°47'00" Klaskish Inlet, N side of Brooks Peninsula, NW side of Vancouver I). Donald A McDougal was a wireless operator and survey assistant on the BC coast aboard CGS *William J Stewart* in the 1930s. Named by regional hydrographer Henri Parizeau, along with the nearby Donald Its, in 1946. McDougal I was formerly known as Shelter I.

McEchran Cove (52°42'00" 131°49'00" S side of Klunkwoi Bay, E side of Moresby I, QCI). According to QCI historian Kathleen Dalzell, this feature was named after Hugh McEchran, a prospector who was very active in the Lockeport and Jedway areas of Moresby I in the early years of the 20th century. The name may be a misspelling for McEachern or McEacheran, however, as these are the names he is listed under in BC's annual mining reports, 1907–26. McEchran staked the Last Chance group of copper claims, located at the head of this cove, with his partners Irving Wintermute and James Jones in 1907. He was also active in the Huston Inlet area farther S, where he supervised development work on the Hope claims, which he owned, and on J S McMillan's Thunder Mtn properties.

McGee Point (52°48'00" 131°44'00" S side of Talunkwan I, off E side of Moresby I, QCI). Named by the hydrographic service in 1957 after H O McGee, who had an interest, together with Herbert Heming (*see* Heming Head), in the copper properties at the E end of Talunkwan I. It was McGee, apparently, who supervised the actual development work on these claims in the early 1900s.

McGowen Rocks (52°38'00" 129°26'00" SW of the Moore Is, off W side of Aristazabal I, Hecate Str). Lance Cpl John McGowan (as his name is more commonly spelled) was a member of the Columbia detachment of the Royal Engineers, which served in BC from 1858 to 1863. He came out from England on the *Thames City* with the main body of men and arrived at Esquimalt in 1859. McGowan remained in BC after the detachment disbanded and

M

married Mary Watt at New Westminster in Nov 1863. Little else is known about him.

McGown Point (52°13'00" 128°15'00" N end of Horsfall I, Seaforth Channel, just NW of Bella Bella). James McGown (1863–1926), a native of Glasgow, married Jessie Meiklejohn Hoey (1864–1956) in 1888 and found work with the Canadian Pacific Line, settling at Vancouver in the early 1890s. In 1894 he was 3rd engineer on the *Empress of India*. He rose in the ranks of the company to become superintendent engineer with Canadian Pacific Ocean Services Ltd, a firm formed in 1915 when the Allan steamship line was merged with other CPR marine services. CPOS became Canadian Pacific Steamships Ltd in 1921. McGown's surname is sometimes seen spelled McGowan. McGown Point was formerly known as Witty Point, after RCN artificer engineer J T Witty, but was changed in 1925.

McGrath Island (55°26'00" 129°45'00" W of Larcom I, S end of Hastings Arm, N end of Observatory Inlet, S of Stewart). Joseph McGrath was co-owner in the early 1900s of the Lucky Seven and Little Joe lead-zinc claims on Glacier Ck in the Bear R district at the N end of Portland Canal near Stewart. He also staked four claims in the Red Wing copper group in the same vicinity in 1909. There is a death record for Joseph McGrath, aged 77, at Vancouver in 1943. The name was adopted in 1970.

McGrath Point (50°05'00" 127°11'00" E side of Moketas I, Kyuquot Sd, NW side of Vancouver I). Capt Luke McGrath (b 1861), from Halifax, commenced his seafaring career on the schooner *Revere* from the fishing port of Gloucester. He came to Victoria in 1890 and served as the skipper of several sealing schooners in the early days of the industry, including the *Penelope* and *Florence M Smith*.

McGregor Bank (52°25'00" 128°32'00" Milbanke Sd, S entrance to Finlayson Channel, NW of Bella Bella). Named for Mary McGregor (b about 1820), who with her husband John (b about 1810) and three children came to BC from Ayrshire in 1849 on the HBC barque *Harpooner*. The McGregors were part of a group of Scottish colliers hired to work at the HBC's Ft Rupert mines. In 1850, in response to the primitive living conditions and poor equipment, McGregor and his relative Andrew Muir went on what was likely BC's first strike. Ft Rupert manager George Blenkinsop had them arrested and jailed, an action he was later criticized for by senior HBC officials. The McGregor family left Ft Rupert for California but then moved to Nanaimo when the coal mines were developed there in 1852. Their daughter Margaret is believed to be the first white girl born at Nanaimo, in 1854.

McGregor Point (54°41'00" 130°05'00" In Khutzeymateen Inlet, N of Prince Rupert). One possible source for this name is Andy McGregor, who was the first foreman of the Skidegate Oil Co's dogfish-liver plant on the QCI. Established in 1879 at Skidegate Landing, the refinery produced a high grade of lubricating oil for a number of years. A second, more likely possibility is that the feature is named after George McGregor (1863–1947), a Victoria tugboat operator and major shareholder in the Boscowitz Steamship Co, who joined the Union Steamship Co as its Victoria agent when Union bought out Boscowitz in 1911. McGregor, who had notoriously poor eyesight yet loved to operate all manner of vehicles and vessels, stayed with Union for more than 25 years. The promontory was formerly known as Long Point.

McHarg Bank (53°17'00" 130°30'00" Off W side of Banks I, Hecate Str). Lt Col William Hart-McHarg (1870–1915) was born in Ireland and lived in Belgium before coming to Canada in 1885. He trained as a lawyer, practising in Rossland and, later, in Vancouver, and was also a militia officer and marksman. McHarg served overseas in the Boer War and in WWI, where he was killed on a reconnaissance mission in Belgium during the 2nd Battle of Ypres while commanding the 7th Infantry Battalion (1st BC Regiment). Mt McHarg on the BC-Alberta border is also named for him, while nearby Mt Worthington is named after Lt Col Donald Worthington, the WWII cdr of the BC Regiment, who was killed in action in 1944. Vancouver's first Georgia Viaduct, built 1913–15, was originally called the Hart-McHarg Bridge.

McInnes Island lighthouse station. *James and Jennifer Hamilton*

McInnes Island (52°15'45" 128°43'20" Off SW side of Price I, Hecate Str, NW of Bella Bella). Thomas Robert McInnes (1840–1904) was born on Cape Breton I and educated at Harvard and Chicago's Rush Medical College. He settled with his family in Ont but moved to BC in 1874 and established a medical practice at New Westminster, where he became involved in politics, serving as mayor, 1877–78, and MP, 1878–81. He was also superintendent of what in the old days was known as the BC lunatic asylum. In 1881 he was appointed to the senate, and from 1897 to

1900 he served as a controversial BC lt gov. Dr McInnes used his authority to dismiss and appoint several premiers in a turbulent political era, alienating both the public and the legislature, and was then himself removed from office by PM Wilfrid Laurier—the only BC lt gov to suffer this fate. He ran for election again as an MP in 1903 but was soundly defeated and died a year later. McInnes I was formerly known as Outer I but was renamed in 1927 to avoid duplication. A manned lighthouse station was built there in 1921. *E*

McIntosh Bay (50°52'00" 126°31'00" N side of Simoom Sd, N of Gilford I and E end of Queen Charlotte Str). RCAF flying officer John David McIntosh, from Simoom Sd, was killed in action on Feb 15, 1944, aged 21. He was a member of No 550 (RAF) Squadron, which flew Lancaster heavy bombers during WWII, and is buried at the Berlin 1939–1945 War Cemetery.

McIntosh Point (53°45'00" 133°01'00" E entrance to Otard Bay, W side of Graham I, QCI). Named in 1946 by the hydrographic service after J W McIntosh (b 1864) from NS, a police chief at New Westminster, 1905–10. He moved to the QCI with his wife Margret (b 1868, also from NS) and family and became active in land speculation and promotional schemes in the pre-WWI years. In 1910 he was chairman of the short-lived Masset Inlet Settlers' Assoc. McIntosh was also involved with plans to drill for oil at the former Haida village of Tian on the W side of Graham I and dig for coal at Skonun Point on Graham's N coast. Neither scheme came to anything. *D*

McIntosh Rock (54°18'00" 130°22'00" In Prince Rupert Hbr, E of Digby I). Named by hydrographer Lt Cdr Philip Musgrave in 1907 after Robert Leck McIntosh (1865–1945), postmaster at Prince Rupert, 1907–21. He came to the N BC coast in 1901 to work for cannery man Peter Herman at Port Essington and was postmaster there in 1906. While McIntosh is frequently mentioned as Prince Rupert's first postmaster, dept records indicate that he was actually the second, after W G Russell, who served for five months in 1906–7. A well-known photo shows McIntosh standing outside a large white tent, which functioned as the new city's first post office. He had many other business and property interests in Prince Rupert and Terrace, and McIntosh and his wife were also prominent supporters of the local Anglican church.

McIntyre Bay (54°05'00" 132°00'00" N side of Graham I, QCI). John McIntyre was an 18th-century Macao merchant who was involved with early fur-trading activities on the PNW coast. The bay was named in 1789 by Capt William Douglas of the *Iphigenia Nubiana*, who knew McIntyre, as did Boston-based trader John Ingraham, who became his friend while at the same time realizing that "the pleasantries and friendliness shown to me were for ulterior

purposes only." McIntyre was associated with the Canton-based merchants James Cox and Daniel Beale, who in turn were involved with most of the trading consortia that sent expeditions in the late 1780s from Asia to the PNW in order to acquire sea otter furs. *D*

McIntyre Point (48°46'35" 123°14'35" NW of Razor Point, SE side of N Pender I, Gulf Is). This name was adopted in 2000 for RCNVR leading cook Thomas James McIntyre, from Victoria and Pender I, who was killed in action Apr 16, 1945, aged 32, while serving aboard HMCS *Esquimalt*. The minesweeper was on routine patrol when it was torpedoed by a U-boat and sank off Halifax Hbr within sight of shore. McIntyre survived the explosion only to die of exposure in the N Atlantic's frigid waters—as was the case with many of the 44 crew members who perished. He is buried at Esquimalt's Veterans Cemetery.

McKay Bay. *See* Cape McKay.

McKay Channel (49°10'00" 123°55'00" Off S end of Protection I, Nanaimo Hbr), **McKay Point** (49°11'55" 123°55'25" NE side of Newcastle I, just N of Nanaimo), **McKay Reach** (53°19'00" 129°00'00" Between N end of Princess Royal I and Gribbell I, S of Kitimat). Joseph William McKay (1829–1900) was a valued and long-serving HBC official in the PNW. He was born at the fur-trading post of Rupert's House on the W shore of Hudson Bay and came to Ft Vancouver on the Columbia R in 1844. Transferred to Vancouver I in 1846, he rose to the position of second-in-command at Ft Victoria and was much relied upon by chief factor James Douglas, who sent him on missions to the Comox and Cowichan valleys and to San Juan I. According to coast historian John Walbran, a First Nation visitor to Ft Victoria, having his rifle repaired by the blacksmith, commented that black rocks like those used in the forge could easily be found at Nanaimo. McKay induced the visitor, with a reward, to return the next year with samples and was then sent by Douglas in 1852 to establish a coal mine at Nanaimo. He also erected the community's first buildings and constructed the historic bastion. In 1854, Douglas dispatched McKay to Ft Simpson on the N coast, where the proximity of Russian Alaska and the unfolding events of the Crimean War required an HBC representative with great tact and judgment. In 1856 he was elected to Vancouver I's first legislative assembly, serving until 1859. McKay married Helen Holmes (*see* Helen Point) at Victoria in 1860, was promoted to chief trader and went on to oversee several HBC posts in the BC Interior. He resigned from the company in 1879 and dedicated himself to his personal business interests, which were extensive. Later in life he worked as a cannery manager, Indian agent and BC's assistant superintendent of Indian Affairs. McKay Point was named by HBC officials in 1853 while surveying Nanaimo Hbr. McKay Reach, also named by HBC officers, was adopted by RN surveyor Lt

Daniel Pender in 1866. Anthropologist Jay Powell reports that Haisla First Nation members know McKay Reach as T'lat'lasaxsiwa, meaning "to go through to open water." McKay Peak on Vancouver I also honours Joseph McKay, whose name, confusingly, is often seen spelled MacKay, Mackay and Mckay. *E W*

McKay Island (49°19'00" 126°03'00" E of Flores I, Clayoquot Sd, W side of Vancouver I). Ellen McKay was a Presbyterian teacher with the Women's Missionary Society who first came to Flores I in 1900 with Rev John Russell. Russell established a mission at Ahousat in 1895 and later built a day school there as well. McKay, who also served at the Ucluelet mission, worked with First Nation children on the W coast of BC for 17 years. Formerly known as Cone I but changed in 1934 to avoid duplication.

McKay Passage (49°37'00" 126°37'00" E of SE end of Nootka I, W side of Vancouver I). Named after John McKay, surgeon's mate on the *Experiment*, which was part of James Strange's fur-trading expedition from Asia to the PNW in 1785–86. McKay—whose name is more commonly spelled Mackay—was a native of Ireland who had acquired a little medical training and joined the E India Co as a soldier. He volunteered to stay with Chief Maquinna and the Mowachaht people for several months, to study their language and customs, and was left at Nootka Sd with ample provisions. He was no ethnographer, however. He survived quite well at first but then committed a major cultural indiscretion, stepping over the cradle of Maquinna's child, and was virtually banished from the tribe. Strange and his ships never returned, and McKay spent the next year in considerable discomfort, living in rags, frequently ill and always hungry. He was able to make no record of his stay and was rescued in 1787 by Capt Charles Barkley of the *Imperial Eagle*, but not before helping Barkley trade with Maquinna and obtain a large quantity of sea otter furs. McKay returned to the Orient on the *Eagle* and then made his way to India, where he was interviewed in 1788 by a former shipmate, Alexander Walker, who wrote an account of the Strange expedition.

McKay Range (53°44'00" 132°30'00" NW of Masset Inlet, Graham I, QCI). John W McKay was a timber cruiser from Seattle who had been asked by the *American Lumberman*, a leading Chicago-based trade periodical, to evaluate the QCI timber holdings of the Graham Steamship, Coal & Lumber Co. He travelled with Graham officials to Masset Inlet in 1907, and the magazine devoted an entire issue to the company's plans to develop a lumber industry in the area. Those proposals came to nought, however, perhaps because of depressed economic conditions, though the Graham company held on to its QCI properties for many years. *D*

McKay Reef (49°07'00" 125°58'00" E side of Father Charles Channel, SW of Wickaninnish I, Clayoquot Sd, W side of Vancouver I). Capt Hugh McKay (1824–82), originally a cooper from Sutherland in Scotland, was a familiar name on the W coast of Vancouver I in the colonial era. He came to Victoria about 1852 and settled at Sooke, where he went into business with William Spring, making barrels and putting up salted fish. He and Spring purchased a series of modest sailing vessels, including the *Ino*, *Morning Star*, *Surprise*, *Alert*, *Favorite* and *North Star*, and pursued trading opportunities from Washington to Alaska. They also opened a number of small trading posts. Starting in the mid-1860s, McKay and Spring pioneered the Victoria-based sealing industry, becoming two of its most successful practitioners. McKay went into business for himself about 1870, buying the sealing schooner *Onward* at San Francisco and then purchasing the *Alfred Adams* and the *Juanita*. McKay Reef was named in 1862 by Capt George Richards of the RN survey vessel *Hecate*, in association with nearby Surprise Reef. *W*

McKechnie Point (52°58'00" 129°08'00" N end of Chapple Inlet, W side of Princess Royal I). Dr Robert Edward McKechnie, CBE (1861–1944), was born at Brockville, Ont, and educated at Charlottetown and McGill Univ. He moved to BC in 1891 and set up a medical practice at Nanaimo, serving as president of the BC College of Physicians and Surgeons in 1897, 1906 and 1910. McKechnie was elected Nanaimo MLA in 1898 and served as a cabinet minister without portfolio, 1898–1900. He was the first president, in 1900, of the BC Medical Assoc. In 1904 he moved his practice to Vancouver. McKechnie was president of the Canadian Medical Assoc in 1914 and 1920, and chancellor of UBC, 1918–44. He received many awards over the course of his long career. A proposal to name this feature Kathleen Point, after Kathleen Chettleburgh, a junior member of the hydrographic staff, was rejected by Ottawa officials in 1944 on the grounds that too many BC staff member names had "been used without reasonable discretion."

McKenney Islands (52°39'00" 129°29'00" W of Moore Is, off W side of Aristazabal I, Hecate Str). Cpl John McKenney (1830–97) was a member of the Columbia detachment of Royal Engineers, which served in BC 1858–63. He was an Irishman whose love of liquor apparently caused him to appear eight times in the regimental defaulters' book and be court-martialled twice. McKenney came out with his wife, who was the sister of fellow sapper James Lindsay, and stayed on when the detachment disbanded. He and Lindsay took up free grants of land, offered to all those sappers who wished to remain in the colony, in the Maple Ridge area, where they farmed. McKenney, whose name often appears spelled McKenny, became a prominent member of the community, serving as a founding councillor when Maple Ridge was incorporated as a municipality in 1874, as reeve in 1879 and as municipal treasurer in 1887.

McKenzie Bight (48°33'00" 123°30'00" SE side of Saanich Inlet, NW of Victoria). Named in 1934 after Alexander Murray McKenzie (1852–1935), a native of Pictou, NS, who worked in the coal mines on Newcastle I near Nanaimo. He first came to Saanich in 1873 but then joined the gold rush to the Cassiar district and afterwards worked on survey parties for the CPR, seeking routes through the Rocky Mtns. He bought land in Saanich and married Helen Thomson (b 1863) at Victoria in 1880. She also was a local pioneer, one of 15 children born to William and Margaret (née Dyer) Thomson, the second white family to settle in central Saanich and founders of a successful farm known as Bannockburn. While he is listed in some records as a farmer and hotelkeeper, McKenzie did not actively farm his property but worked as a builder, logger and surveyor all over BC, retiring in 1924 and settling down on his homestead. He and Helen had eight children, and many of their descendants still live in the region.

McKenzie Cove (50°54'00" 126°35'00" N side of Kingcome Inlet, N of E end of Queen Charlotte Str). William George McKenzie (1899–1949) disappeared from his gillnetter, the *Billy Mac*, near this spot in 1949 and was presumed drowned. He was born at Kenora, Ont, came to Michel, BC, with his parents when he was two and went to school at Nanaimo, Merritt and Vancouver. McKenzie worked at pulp mills on Vancouver I and at a Sidney kelp plant before becoming a fisherman and popular resident of Minstrel I for 23 years. He joined the RCN's Fishermen Reserve Service during WWII. Local fishers erected a white marble cross in McKenzie's memory on the shoreline close to where he went missing.

McKenzie Shoal (53°13'00" 130°15'00" Off W side of Banks I, Hecate Str). Named in 1950 for George Charles McKenzie (1776–1828), from Edinburgh, a midshipman aboard HMS *Discovery* on Capt George Vancouver's expedition to the BC coast, 1791–95. He was only 16 when he joined up and seems to have been demoted to able seaman for part of the trip, but he was returned to his former rank in 1792. McKenzie was one of several crew members on the voyage who kept a journal, which still exists. He went on to a successful career in the RN, being promoted to capt in 1808 and seeing action aboard HMS *Wolf* off Cuba in 1805, with HMS *Cruiser* in 1808 in the Baltic and with HMS *Creole* in 1814, when he and the capt of HMS *Euryalus* fought two French frigates to a draw in the Cape Verde Is.

McKernan Rock (52°18'00" 127°57'00" In Johnson Channel, N of Beaumont I, just NE of Bella Bella). Named in 1981 after Capt V McKernan, who was in command of the CNR steamship *Prince Albert* in the early 1920s.

McKiel Rock (50°04'00" 127°36'00" SW of Bunsby I, Checleset Bay, NW side of Vancouver I). Records at BC's Geographical Names Office suggest that this feature commemorates John McKiel (or McKeil), a member of the crew of the sealing schooner *Maggie Mac*, which was lost off the NW coast of Vancouver I in 1892 with all hands. The ship sailed from Victoria in Jan and the last word from it was in a letter, dated at Clayoquot in Mar, from Capt John Dodd. In 1893, residents of Quatsino Sd recovered pieces of the vessel in a small cove S of Cape Scott, and it was presumed that the schooner had come to grief somewhere near the Scott Is. No traces of the 23 men on board were ever found. Another possible source for the name is Robert Esdale McKiel (1857–1908), a master mariner in the Victoria-based sealing trade. He was born in NS and went to sea early, as was the custom, at the age of 14. He came to BC in 1886 and took command of the sealing schooner *Mary Taylor*, in which he narrowly escaped from an overzealous US revenue cutter during a territorial dispute. Over the next few years he skippered the *Western Slope*, *Beatrice*, *E B Marvin*, *Maud S*, *Carrie C W*, *Dora Sieward* and *Annie E Paint* in the Bering Sea and off the coast of Japan. McKiel was appointed pilot for the Clayoquot area in 1906. It is not known if the two men were related.

McLean Cove (49°58'00" 127°14'00" Just E of Rugged Point, entrance to Kyuquot Channel, Kyuquot Sd, NW side of Vancouver I). Named by the hydrographic service in 1950 after 15-year-old Bruce McLean, who drowned off this coast in 1948 when the mission boat *Messenger II* was wrecked in a violent storm. He was the son of missionary doctor Herman Alexander McLean (1896–1975) and his wife Marion Hester (1902–87, née Card). Herman McLean studied medicine at Univ of Manitoba and worked at Bella Coola for several years before attending Bible school in Alberta. In 1937, Rev Percy Wills of the Shantymen's Christian Assoc persuaded him to make a medical tour of Vancouver I's W coast, and the two men decided to establish the Nootka Mission General Hospital on the N shore of Esperanza Inlet. McLean and his family spent 35 years at the hospital, which closed in 1973, a year after Herman and Marion retired to Victoria. *E*

McLean Fraser Point (52°13'00" 131°25'00" W of Flamingo Inlet, SW side of Moresby I, QCI). Named in 1946 after Dr Charles McLean Fraser (1872–1946), head of the zoology dept at UBC, 1920–40, and director of the Pacific Coast Biological Station near Nanaimo for 12 years. He started his career as an Ont high-school science teacher, then did graduate work at the Univ of Toronto and Univ of Iowa. Fraser spent the summer of 1935 on board the hydrographic survey vessel *William J Stewart*, collecting marine and intertidal specimens along the coastline, and apparently began his studies at this location. He is best known for his work on hydroids—small predatory animals that are related to jellyfish and corals. *D*

M

McLean Island (50°02'00" 127°25'00" N of Spring I, N entrance to Kyuquot Sd, NW end of Vancouver I), **McLean Point** (50°01'00" 127°25'00" S end of McLean I). Brothers Daniel (b 1851) and Alexander McLean (1858–1914), from Sydney, Cape Breton, were legendary skippers in the early W coast sealing industry. Daniel sailed out of NY on deepwater ships and came to the PNW about 1880. He prospected and placer-mined on the BC and Alaska coasts from his tiny sloop, the *Flyaway*. Alex arrived on the Pacific coast in 1881 as 2nd officer on the clipper ship *Santa Clara*. Settling at Victoria, he worked aboard the *Sir James Douglas*, *Beaver* and other local vessels. In 1883 the brothers decided to go seal hunting, which they did at first with the San Francisco schooner *City of San Diego*. In subsequent years, Daniel became Victoria's most successful sealer, securing substantial harvests with the *Mary Ellen*, *Triumph* and *Edward E Webster*, and setting a record in 1886 by bringing back 4,268 skins. Alex, who worked for several years in partnership with William Spring, was almost as prolific and operated the *Favorite*, *Rose Sparks*, *Bonanza* and other schooners. One of his vessels, the *J Hamilton Lewis*, was seized by a Russian warship in 1891. McLean and his crew were imprisoned for four months for supposedly hunting in Russian territorial waters, then released and sent to Korea. The brothers were easily identified in their waterfront haunts; they grew huge matching handlebar moustaches that measured more than 50 cm from tip to tip. According to journalist Peter Murray in *The Vagabond Fleet*, Alex's could be tied behind his neck. A rumour spread that Alex was the model for Wolf Larsen in Jack London's epic 1904 novel *Sea Wolf*; both London and McLean denied this at the time, though the story is still in circulation. Alex suffered an accidental death by drowning in Vancouver's False Ck. *E*

McLean Shoal (53°02'00" 131°41'00" Off N side of Cumshewa Inlet, NE Moresby I, QCI). Named in 1926 for Capt Neil McLean, master of the CNR steamships *Prince John* and *Prince Charles*, both of which served the QCI on a regular basis. He was a veteran skipper with the company, having joined in 1910 when it was the coastal steamship service of the GTP and known as the Prince Line. McLean was capt of the *Prince George*, one of the company's flagships, on its final journey in 1945. The vessel ran aground in heavy fog near Ketchikan, and a fuel tank caught fire and exploded, killing a crewman in the engine room. McLean was able to beach the *George* and get all the passengers and remaining crew off, then stayed aboard while the ship was towed to a safe place. A rescue tug had to nudge its bow right up to the rail of the burning hulk (later deemed a complete loss), so that McLean could step onto its deck. It turned out that he had never learned how to swim.

McLellan Island (53°03'00" 131°45'00" Off N side of Cumshewa Inlet, NE Moresby I, QCI), **McLellan Point** (53°09'00" 132°17'00" S side of E Narrows, Skidegate Channel, between Graham I and Moresby I). John McLellan (1875–1951), from London, Ont, worked as an assayer at Rossland and Port Simpson, 1900–1906. He then acquired the land at Mitchell Inlet (also known as Gold Hbr) where the HBC found gold and precipitated BC's short-lived first gold rush in 1851–52. McLellan and his partner, Frederick Bourne, discovered another small, rich vein of gold near the original HBC workings and had a three-stamp mill in place by 1910, which operated until 1933. The pair also developed an unsuccessful mine N of Skidegate, the South Easter. In 1921, McLellan married Queen Charlotte City teacher Lesley Barraclough and built a fine home on the E end of Lina I in Skidegate Inlet. *D*

McLeod Bay (50°28'00" 125°59'00" N side of W end of Sunderland Channel, opposite Sayward, N of Johnstone Str). After John Alexander McLeod, who went upcoast about 1892 and worked in various logging camps, including at the Moodyville Sawmill Co's Jackson Bay operation, where he was employed as a bucker. He pre-empted land on McLeod Bay and lived there for many years, fishing, trapping and growing a large garden as well as logging, and received a Crown grant for his property in the early 1920s. McLeod moved to Port Neville when he became ill. He died in 1929.

McLeod Island (49°15'37" 125°52'10" In Cypress Bay, Clayoquot Sd, W side of Vancouver I). Ewen McLeod (the surname is also often spelled MacLeod), from the Isle of Raasay in Scotland, was a Glasgow policeman before immigrating to Canada in 1903. After a stint on a sealing schooner he settled at Clayoquot and became the region's provincial police constable. He married Mabel, a US resident who visited the area, in 1910. His brothers Murdo and Alex McLeod joined him in 1910–12, as did his cousin Jack. (John McLeod, unrelated but from the same part of Scotland, also came to Clayoquot Sd about this time.) Alex and Murdo served overseas during WWI. Murdo returned to Clayoquot in 1919, married Julia, John McLeod's sister, and worked as a fisheries officer. Alex came back in 1925 with his wife Catherine and five kids and served as coxswain of the Tofino lifeboat for 21 years. Ewen and Mabel eventually moved to Lytton, where he worked as the local Indian agent. Many McLeod descendants still live in the Clayoquot region. McLeod I was named by hydrographer G E Richardson in 1986, according to BC's Geographical Names Office, "after a long-time resident of the area," though it's not certain which McLeod Richardson had in mind.

McLoughlin Bay (52°08'00" 128°09'00" E side of Campbell I, just S of Bella Bella), **McLoughlin Point** (48°25'00" 123°24'00" W entrance to Victoria Hbr, SE end of Vancouver I). Physician and fur trader John McLoughlin (1784–1857) was born in Que and joined the NWC in

Trader and administrator John McLoughlin. *BC Archives A-01638*

McLoughlin Bay, was abandoned in 1843, and no trace of it remains; McLoughlin Ck and McLoughlin Lk, both on Campbell I, are named after the fort. Port Simpson (the body of water, not the community) was known for many years as McLoughlin's Hbr. McLoughlin Point was named by HBC officials about 1845 and adopted by Capt Henry Kellet when he made the first survey of Victoria Hbr in 1846–47 with HMS *Herald. E W*

McMicking Inlet (53°04'00" 129°28'00" E of Jewsbury Peninsula, W side of Campania I, N of Caamaño Sd), **McMicking Island** (54°04'00" 130°18'00" Off NE side of Porcher I, S of Prince Rupert), **McMicking Point** (48°25'00" 123°18'00" Just E of McNeill Bay, SE end of Vancouver I). The inlet and point are named for Margaret Leighton, who married Robert Burns McMicking (1843–1915) in 1869 at Lytton. *See* Leighton I for further biographical details. McMicking I is named after her husband Robert, who was born in Welland County, Ont, and travelled from Winnipeg to Quesnel in 1862 with the Overlanders, led by his brother Thomas McMicking. (Thomas became town clerk and deputy sheriff at New Westminster but drowned in the Fraser R in 1866 in a futile attempt to save his son William.) Robert worked in a New Westminster grocery store, then joined the Collins Overland Telegraph Co. At the time of his marriage he was in charge of the telegraph office at Quesnel, but the following year the McMickings moved to Victoria, where Robert managed the Western Union office. A skilled mechanic and electrician as well as an effective manager, McMicking was responsible for bringing the first telephones to BC and for founding Victoria's first electric company and street-lighting system. He was provincial superintendent of telegraphs, a Victoria alderman and school trustee and, later, president of the Victoria and Esquimalt Telephone Co. McMicking I was formerly known as Elizabeth I but the name was changed in 1927. *E*

McMullen Point (50°15'00" 125°24'00" Discovery Passage, S of Elk Bay, W of Quadra I, NW of Campbell R). Maj James Edward Temple McMullen, from Vancouver, was killed in action Oct 6, 1943, aged 31, during the Allied invasion of Italy. An officer with the Seaforth Highlanders, he had worked as a lawyer before enlisting in the Canadian Army. McMullen is buried at the Moro R Canadian War Cemetery in Italy.

McMullin Group (52°03'00" 128°25'00" S of the Bardswell Group, Queens Sd, SW of Bella Bella). Lt Col John Hugh McMullin (1869–1943), a British Army officer born at Madras, India, and educated in England, was the respected commissioner of the BC provincial police, 1923–39. He came to Canada in 1893 and settled in the Okanagan, then joined the force in 1901 after serving in the Boer War. McMullin rose in rank to inspector and was responsible for the Vancouver I region, but resigned in 1910 to become

1803, working mainly at Ft William on Lk Superior and becoming a partner in the company in 1814. He emerged as leader of those NWC partners wishing to merge with the HBC, and when that coalition was negotiated in 1821, he was appointed chief factor of the Rainy Lk district in SW Ont. In 1825, HBC gov George Simpson, impressed with McLoughlin's managerial capabilities, named him superintendent of the vast Columbia district W of the Rockies, based at Ft George (Astoria), a position he would hold for the next 20 years. Fearing US expansion in the region, the company quickly built Ft Vancouver on the N shore of the Columbia R and Ft Langley on the Fraser R. McLoughlin established farms, a flour mill and a sawmill to reduce dependence on imports, and he acquired the *Cadboro* (and later the *Beaver*) to extend coastal trade. In the early 1830s, McLoughlin constructed a chain of trading posts in the PNW: Ft Nass (renamed Ft Simpson) in 1831, Ft McLoughlin (near Bella Bella) and Ft Nisqually in 1833. In 1839 the HBC agreed to supply agricultural products from the Columbia district to the Russian American Co. In the 1840s, disagreements arose between Simpson and McLoughlin: the former wanted to conduct coastal trading from ships, oppose incoming settlers and establish Ft Victoria in case the British lost control of the Oregon Territory; the latter preferred land posts, co-operation with settlers and maintaining the regional HQ at Ft Vancouver. Things fell apart after McLoughlin's son was murdered at Ft Stikine in 1842. Simpson considered it "justifiable homicide," while the chief factor mounted a vindictive campaign against his superior to clear his son's name. He left the HBC in 1846 and retired to Oregon City, where he owned land and ran various businesses, and became known as "the father of Oregon." Ft McLoughlin, built on

government agent at Prince Rupert. He served overseas in WWI and accepted the position of BC's chief police officer just after a new Police and Prisons Regulations Act had been adopted, on condition that he would have to endure no political interference and the reforms outlined in the new act would be implemented immediately. McMullin supervised an expansion and modernization of the force and saw it through the demanding 1930s, a decade of unprecedented labour unrest and unemployment. He died at Oak Bay. The McMullin Group was formerly known as the Broken Group, but its name was changed in 1944 to avoid duplication.

McMurray Point (53°51'00" 130°00'00" S entrance to Kumealon Inlet, Grenville Channel, SE of Prince Rupert). Robert William McMurray (1885–1969), from Ardrossan, Scotland, joined the CPR's trans-Atlantic steamship service in 1910. During WWI he served in the RN as a lt cdr. In 1925 he brought both the *Princess Kathleen* and *Princess Marguerite* out to Victoria from the Clyde shipyards, where they were built, and later that year he was named marine superintendent of the CPR's BC Coast Steamship Service. McMurray became gen manager of the BC service in 1934 and in 1945 moved to Montreal as managing director of Canadian Pacific Steamship Lines. He retired to Victoria in 1951.

McNab Creek (49°34'00" 123°23'00" Flows S into Thornbrough Channel, N of Gambier I, Howe Sd, NW of Vancouver). John McNab and John George Robertson, both Westham I farmers and both originally from Ottawa, disappeared under suspicious circumstances in this vicinity while on a trapping and fishing expedition in 1886. In Nov of that year, more than seven months after the pair had left their homes, a search party found their camp at the mouth of this creek. Extraordinarily, their Chinese servant, Lun, was still there. He reported that McNab and Robertson had gone out in their small sloop about three weeks after setting up camp and disappeared. Not knowing what to do—and terrified of the local First Nation people—he had waited for them all this time. No trace of the men or the boat was found. Lun was held on suspicion of foul play but apparently was not prosecuted. The mystery was never solved.

McNaughton Group (51°56'00" 128°14'00" W side of Hunter I, Queens Sd, S of Bella Bella), **McNaughton Point** (49°33'00" 124°00'00" E side of Malaspina Str, S of Bargain Bay, NW of Sechelt). Gen Andrew George Latta McNaughton, CB, DSO (1887–1966), commanded the Canadian Army overseas, 1939–43. He was born at Moosomin, Sask, and studied engineering at McGill Univ, entering the militia and serving overseas in WWI as an artillery cdr. After rising rapidly through the professional army ranks to chief of general staff, 1929–35, he began a modernization drive for Canada's armed forces. He was

president of the National Research Council, 1935–39. During WWII, McNaughton, who was determined to keep the Canadian forces in one formation and had approved Canada's participation in the ill-fated Dieppe raid, fell from political favour and resigned in 1943. He served as minister of National Defence, 1944–45, and was a prominent public figure for many years after: president of the Atomic Energy Control Board, permanent delegate to the UN, chairman of the Canadian section of the International Joint Commission and Permanent Joint Board on Defence. Latta I at the N end of the McNaughton Group is also named for him.

McNeill Bay (48°24'43" 123°18'48" S of Oak Bay, SE tip of Vancouver I). William Henry McNeill (1801–75) was born at Boston and became a master mariner by age 22. In 1824 he commanded the brig *Convoy* on a voyage to Hawaii and the QCI, and for several years he traded between Boston and S America, W Africa and Hawaii. In 1832, while he was trading for furs in the PNW for Boston merchants Bryant, Sturgis & Co, his vessel, the *Lama*, was acquired by the HBC. McNeill and his two mates had the kind of local experience that HBC chief factor John McLoughlin was looking for; he offered them jobs, and they accepted. McNeill continued to command the *Lama*—rescuing three Japanese seamen in 1834 from their First Nation captors after their junk had wrecked off Cape Flattery—then transferred to the *Beaver*. In 1837 he located the harbour on the S end of Vancouver I that would soon become the site of Ft Victoria. He was promoted to chief trader in 1839 and put in charge of Ft Stikine (1845), Ft George (1848), Ft Rupert (which he established in 1849) and Ft Simpson (1851–59, 1861–63). It was McNeill who was sent to the gold discovery site at Mitchell Inlet in the QCI to oversee the initial, unsuccessful extraction of ore in 1851. He was made a chief factor in 1856 and retired in 1863 to an 80-ha estate in Oak Bay, located on the body of water that bears his name. Even his retirement was active. He was appointed to the BC pilot board in 1868 and ran the steamship *Enterprise* between Victoria and New Westminster, 1872–74. McNeill had a large family by his two First Nation wives, Mathilda (d 1850), a Kaigani Haida chief, and Martha (1826–83), a high-ranking Nisga'a; his descendants contributed in many ways to the life of early Victoria. The N Vancouver I community of Port McNeill (qv) is also named for him, as is Macneill Point (qv) in the QCI. McNeill Bay is often referred to locally by its unofficial name of Shoal Bay. A Songhees First Nation village named Chikawich was once located beside the bay; the name means "big hips" and referred to the placement of the houses along the shoreline. *E W*

McNeill Point (53°03'00" 129°13'00" S end of Ashdown I, NE end of Campania Sd, NW of Princess Royal I). Named by the hydrographic service in 1926 after Donald Henry McNeill (1854–1928), the eldest grandson of Capt William

McNeill (*see* McNeill Bay), who was born at the McNeill home on the family's namesake bay. He worked as a government guide in the 1880s, searching out agricultural land and leading groups of potential immigrants to various parts of Vancouver I, especially in the Nitinat and San Juan river valleys, and also determining routes for telegraph lines. He was listed in the 1901 census as a gardener. McNeill took part in the grand old-timers' reunion held at Victoria in 1924 (*see* Adams Bay).

McNeil Peninsula (49°17'00" 126°04'00" SE end of Flores I, Clayoquot Sd, W side of Vancouver I). Named in 1934 for Jean McNeil (1867–1917), from Ont, who was a missionary with the Presbyterian Women's Missionary Society. She came to Flores I in 1900 as an assistant to Rev John Russell, who established a Presbyterian mission at Ahousat in 1895 and built a day school there also. McNeil married Presbyterian missionary John Ross (*see* Ross Passage) at Alberni in 1909 and continued to work at Ahousat as a teacher and matron. She died at Ucluelet.

McNiffe Rock (50°31'00" 127°36'00" E of Drake I, Quatsino Sd, NW Vancouver I). The hydrographic service named this feature in 1927 after William McNiffe (1828–91), who received Crown grants of land in the vicinity in 1884. He was a native of Sligo, Ireland, and a very early immigrant to Victoria, arriving in 1858. In 1865 he married Annie Jane Irvine (1843–96), another Victoria pioneer, who had come there from the Orkney Is with her family in 1862. McNiffe was a hotelier and saloon keeper, operating the Grotto in Trounce Alley. Nearby McNiffe Ck is also named for him.

McNutt Point (52°56'00" 132°12'00" E side of Douglas Inlet, Kuper Inlet, NW side of Moresby I, QCI). Named after the 2nd mate of the HBC brigantine *Una*, which was sent twice in 1851 to nearby Mitchell Inlet, where gold had recently been discovered. After the second visit, during which the HBC's miners managed to extract $75,000 worth of gold before being chased off by a group of hostile Haida, who had expected to barter for the ore, the *Una* was wrecked on an uncharted reef in Neah Bay on its way home to Victoria. The vessel was pillaged and burnt by members of the Makah First Nation, though the crew and miners were rescued by the US schooner *Susan Sturgis*. The gold ore, of course, is still at the bottom of Neah Bay.

McPhail Point (48°36'00" 123°31'00" W side of Saanich Inlet, NW of Brentwood Bay and Victoria). Angus McPhail (1809–84), a Gaelic-speaking HBC employee from Lewis in the Outer Hebrides, came to Canada in 1837, sailing from the Orkney Is to York Factory on the *Prince Rupert* and then travelling overland to Ft Langley, where he worked from 1838 to 1846. He married a First Nation woman there, who died giving birth to his first child, Anne. From 1846 to 1855 he was a dairyman at Ft Victoria, where he married his second wife, Angele (d

about 1863), in 1851. McPhail may also have worked at Ft Simpson. He was the first non-Native settler in central Saanich, moving there with his wife and daughter in 1855. He appears on the voters list of 1859 as Aeneas McPhail, and his homestead, located SW of Mt Newton, was known as Bay Farm. His second daughter, Marie, was born in 1859; both daughters settled in the district. McPhail seems to have sold part of his land in 1860 to Peter Lind, and the rest in 1862 to Alphonse Verdier, his son-in-law, who had married 16-year-old Anne earlier that year; the properties were acquired by farmer James Hagan about 1872.

McPhee Point (52°52'00" 129°08'00" S of Racey Inlet, W side of Princess Royal I). J D McPhee worked for the Union Steamship Co as mate on various vessels pre-WWI. After returning from overseas duty, where he served with Tobin's Tigers, the 29th (Vancouver) Battalion of the Canadian Expeditionary Force, and was wounded in action, he became master of the *Chilcoot*. In 1927 he was appointed the first master of the *Chilliwack*.

McPherson Point (54°15'00" 132°59'00" NE side of Langara I, off NW end of Graham I, QCI). Named in 1907 after the carpenter of HMS *Egeria*, a prodigious axeman. The vessel was doing survey work in the area at that time, under Capt Frederick Learmonth. According to QCI historian Kathleen Dalzell, the Haida called the rocky, precipitous promontory Ta-Kwoon, meaning "mussel point." Two small villages once perched on either side: Ta ("Mussel Town") to the S and Ah Dongas ("Village around the Point") to the N. It's possible that McPherson Ck and McPherson Lk at the N end of the Don Peninsula, N of Bella Bella, are named for the same person, as Capt Learmonth and HMS *Egeria* were also surveying in those waters in 1909.

McQuarrie Islets (49°54'00" 127°13'00" S end of Barrier Is, just S of Kyuquot Sd, off NW side of Vancouver I). This name was adopted in 1946 for H N McQuarrie, who, according to the records of the Canadian Hydrographic Assoc, participated in surveys of the W coast of Vancouver I (1930–36) and Rivers Inlet (1937) aboard CGS *Lillooet* and CGS *William J Stewart*. He resigned from the service in 1938. These records probably refer to Hector Neil McQuarrie (1906–82), who was born at Lanark, Scotland, and came to Canada with his family in 1913. His shipwright father Charles McQuarrie (1875–1948) worked at Burrard Drydock in N Vancouver.

McRae Cove (49°45'00" 124°17'00" W side of Scotch Fir Point, N entrance to Jervis Inlet, SE of Powell R), **McRae Islet** (Just SW of McRae Cove). Farquhar "Fred" McRae (1864–1924) was born in Ont and lived in the US for several years (his first name is also seen spelled Farquar). He came to the BC coast in the late 1880s, pre-empting land at the entrance to Jervis Inlet and receiving several

Crown grants in the early 1900s. McRae's intention was to farm, but first he had to log, initially with oxen, then with horses, and finally with a tractor and steam donkey. He built a house on the cove about 1910 and married in 1913. His sister joined the household, and the McRaes became pioneer settlers in the region, eventually creating a substantial farm, threshing their own grains and raising sheep, poultry (including turkeys) and other products for the Vancouver market.

Meade Bay (50°42'00" 126°35'00" W side of Gilford I, E side of Retreat Passage, NE end of Queen Charlotte Str). After RN officer Richard James Meade, Viscount Gilford, who served on the Pacific Station, 1862–64. *See* Gilford Bay. Formerly known as Camp Bay.

Meade Point (52°30'00" 129°01'00" E side of Weeteeam Bay, SW side of Aristazabal I). Lance Cpl John Meade was a member of the Columbia detachment of Royal Engineers, which served in BC 1858–63. He came to the PNW on the *Thames City* with the main contingent of men, and he good-humouredly participated in the ship's theatrical performances, playing an "oyster girl," a carabineer, Mrs Wiffles and Mariette in various productions. Very little is known, however, of his career in BC—or if he even stayed in BC when the detachment disbanded. Meade applied in 1861 to pre-empt land in what is now the W End of Vancouver but allowed his claim to lapse.

Meares Bluff (48°52'00" 125°17'00" E side of Effingham I, Broken Group, Barkley Sd, W side of Vancouver I), **Meares Island** (49°11'00" 125°50'00" Just N of Tofino, Clayoquot Sd, W side of Vancouver I), **Meares Point** (54°11'00" 133°01'00" NW side of Graham I, facing Parry Passage, QCI), **Meares Spit** (49°10'00" 125°55'00" Extends SW from Schindler Point, W side of Meares I). John Meares (c 1756–1809) joined the RN in 1771, became a lt in 1778 and resigned in 1783 to enter the merchant service. We next catch sight of him in Calcutta where, with the Bengal Fur Co, a trading syndicate in which he may have had a part interest, he organized one of the first fur-trading expeditions to the PNW, in 1786. The company's two vessels—the *Nootka*, commanded by Meares, and the smaller *Sea Otter*, under William Tipping—explored the Alaska coast, where Meares was forced to overwinter, losing 23 crewmen to scurvy and other diseases, until rescued by George Dixon in the *Queen Charlotte*. The *Sea Otter* was never heard of again. Meares returned to Asia and formed a new alliance, the Merchant Proprietors, with both Canton and Bengal partners, and outfitted a second expedition; the *Felice Adventurer*, which he commanded, and the *Iphigenia Nubiana*, under William Douglas, set off from Macao in 1788 under a Portuguese flag in order to circumvent the E India Co's monopoly on trade in the region. Meares spent that summer on the W coast of Vancouver I, where he claimed to have bought land

This John Meares portrait was engraved by Charles Bestland about 1790 from a painting by Sir William Beechey. *BC Archives PDP05179*

at Friendly Cove (which Chief Maquinna later denied); he also erected a storehouse there and built a 40-tonne schooner, the *North West America*—the first non-Native vessel constructed on the BC coast. After returning in the fall to Macao, Meares merged his consortium with that of his principal competitor, British merchant Richard Cadman Etches, and formed the Associated Merchants of London and India Trading to the NW Coast of America, which sent James Colnett, with the *Argonaut* and *Princess Royal*, to Nootka Sd in 1789. It was there that Spanish naval officer Estéban Martínez impounded several Associated Merchants vessels, on the grounds that they were violating Spain's control of the region, and took them and their crews to Mexico. On hearing this news, Meares sailed from China to London and, by exaggerating the extent of the "Nootka Sd crisis," persuaded the British cabinet to defend its rights in the Pacific—and get an indemnity for Meares and his partners—by threatening military action against Spain. Meares published *Voyages Made in the Years 1788 and 1789, from China to the N W Coast* in 1790. The book overstated his accomplishments and belittled his fellow explorers. He developed a reputation as a manipulator and a liar—a man of "notorious falsity," according to Boston trader Robert Haswell—and had disappeared into obscurity by the mid-1790s. Meares Ck just E of Tofino is also named for him. Meares Bluff, formerly known as Bold Bluff, was renamed to avoid duplication in 1934. Meares I (85 sq km) was the site of major protests against MacMillan Bloedel logging plans in the 1980s. *E W*

Meay Islet (51°40'00" 128°05'00" S of Rattenbury I, Kwakshua Channel, between Hecate I and Calvert I, S of

Bella Bella). Named in 1945 after Thomas Meay, master of the 327-tonne HBC barque *Pruth*, which sailed from London to Victoria in 1861.

Meiss Passage (52°45'00" 129°18'00" N entrance to Borrowman Bay, off NW side of Aristazabal I). This name was adopted in 1926 after Alexander Meiss (1864–1928), who was born at Victoria and, in 1896, became a saloon and hotelkeeper and general trader at Horsefly in the Cariboo district. He married Matilda Clara Gaspard (1870–1942) of Dog Ck in 1898. Meiss constructed the new, three-storey City Hotel at Horsefly in 1904. He was a member of the village's first school board and acquired its first automobile, a McLaughlin. In 1912 he and two partners built a toll bridge over the Horsefly R. Matilda Meiss was the community's postmaster, 1916–23. Alexander is believed to have taken part in the great Victoria old-timers' reunion of 1924 (*see* Adams Bay). He died at his adopted hometown of Horsefly. Meiss Ck and Meiss Lk near Horsefly are presumably named for him as well.

Meldrum Point (53°06'00" 128°31'00" N side of Khutze Inlet, SE of Butedale and E of Princess Royal I). Prospector Charles William Meldrum (1862–1932), from St Lin, Que, discovered the Western Copper ore body E of the head of Khutze Inlet in the early 1900s and staked a number of claims there in 1908. The claims were seriously investigated in the late 1920s by the Detroit Mining Co, which built an aerial tramway from the minesite to the valley bottom and a railway out to salt water, but the stock market crash of 1929 put an end to development of the property and the mine never went into production. Meldrum died at Vancouver.

Mellersh Point (50°47'00" 124°57'00" W side of Bute Inlet, S of Bear Bay). Capt George Richards of the survey vessel HMS *Hecate* named this feature in 1862 after Capt Arthur Mellersh (1812–94), an RN officer who was a friend and correspondent of Charles Darwin but had never been to the PNW. He served aboard HMS *Beagle*, 1825–36, as midshipman and then mate and was thus a shipmate of Darwin, who was the *Beagle*'s naturalist in 1831–36 when the vessel surveyed the coasts of S America and circumnavigated the world. Mellersh enjoyed a varied career in the RN, spending time in the Caribbean and off the coast of Syria, and suppressing piracy in the S China Sea. He commanded HMS *Rattler* in the 1852 Burma campaign and HMS *Forte*, flagship of Rear Adm Richard Warren, on the S America Station (during which commission he offered to find fossils for Darwin and bring them back to England). He retired in 1864 and was appointed an adm, retired, in 1884. Nearby Mellersh Ck is named after the point.

Melville Arm (54°20'00" 130°20'00" N side of Prince Rupert Hbr). After Charles Melville Hays, president and

gen manager of the GTP. *See* Hays Cove. Formerly known as Douglas Arm.

Melville Island (54°22'50" 130°44'50" One of the Dundas Is, W Chatham Sd, NW of Prince Rupert). After Henry Dundas, Viscount Melville and Baron Dunira, RN treasurer 1783–1801. *See* Dundas I.

Archibald Menzies, physician and botanist, accompanied George Vancouver on his survey of the BC coast. *BC Archives PDP05374*

Menzies Bay (50°07'00" 125°23'00" W side of Discovery Passage, N of Campbell R), **Menzies Point** (52°19'00" 127°02'00" W side of S Bentinck Arm near its entrance, W of Bella Coola), **Mount Menzies** (50°13'50" 125°29'49" NW of Menzies Bay, E Vancouver I). Archibald Menzies (1754–1842) was a physician and a trained botanist, born in Scotland, who worked as a gardener before attending Univ of Edinburgh, 1771–80. After joining the RN as an assistant surgeon in 1782, he served in the W Indies and was later posted to Halifax. He collected botanical specimens in NS and sent seeds to Sir Joseph Banks at the Royal Botanic Gardens at Kew, then studied at Sir Joseph's famous library on his return to England in 1786. Banks obtained two good jobs for Menzies: surgeon (1786–89) on the merchant vessel *Prince of Wales*, which fur trader James Colnett took to the BC coast, 1787–88; and naturalist (1791–95) on HMS *Discovery* for Capt George Vancouver's historic PNW voyage. Menzies also took over the duties of surgeon on the *Discovery* after A P Cranstoun, the original doctor, became ill. He quarrelled with Vancouver over the care of his specimens, which were kept in a small greenhouse on the quarterdeck, and other matters, and was nearly court-martialled. After leaving the RN in 1802, he practised medicine in London and became an expert on mosses and ferns. Menzies was also a skilled botanical artist. He published little but is

M

noted for introducing the monkey puzzle tree from Chile to England and for gathering at least 400 species new to science on his journeys. The arbutus (*Arbutus menziesii*) and the Douglas fir (*Pseudotsuga menziesii*) are named for him, as are a number of N American, Hawaiian, NZ and Australian tree and plant species, including types of beech, spirea, campion, delphinium, saxifrage, bottlebrush, banksia and currant. Vancouver named Menzies Bay and Menzies Point in 1792. Menzies Ck is named after Menzies Bay, which it flows into. *E W*

Mercer Point (53°09'00" 132°31'00" W entrance to Dawson Inlet, NW side of Skidegate Channel, Graham I, QCI). After geologist George Mercer Dawson, who explored the QCI in 1878. *See* Dawson Cove.

Mercury Islet (51°45'00" 128°04'00" Part of the Planet Group, N side of Hakai Passage, S of Bella Bella). Named by the hydrographic service in 1948, along with Jupiter I and Mars It, as individual members of the Planet Group.

Merilia Passage (52°23'00" 128°29'00" Between Dowager I and the Gaudin Is, Milbanke Sd, NW of Bella Bella). Isabella Merilia (1807–85)—whose surname has also been identified as Melville or, more commonly, Mainville—entered into marriage in 1822 with HBC clerk Charles Ross (c 1794–1844, *see* Ross Bay). She grew up at the fur-trading post of Lac La Pluie (Rainy Lk), Ont, daughter of a European father and an Ojibway mother. Isabella accompanied Ross to more than a dozen different HBC posts between 1822 and 1844 (the longest posting he had was 1824–30 at Ft Babine) and bore him numerous children. She had a church wedding in 1838 at Ft Vancouver, where her surviving children were baptized. Ross, who was promoted to chief trader in 1843 and spent the last two years of his life in charge of building Ft Victoria, described Isabella in a letter to his sister: "I have as yet said nothing about my wife; whence you will probably infer that I am rather ashamed of her—in this, however, you would be wrong. She is not, indeed, exactly fitted to shine at the head of a nobleman's table, but she suits the sphere [in which] she has to move much better than any such toy—in short, she is a native of the country, and as to beauty quite as comely as her husband!" The Ross family had acquired a large plot of land on Victoria's S shore, and after her husband's premature death, probably from appendicitis, Isabella farmed there with her wayward offspring, who were in constant trouble with the law. She was BC's first registered female landowner and named her property Fowl Bay Farm, which was probably an erroneous reference to adjacent Foul Bay (*see* Gonzales Bay). Isabella married again, in 1860, to Lucius O'Brien, but this union was short-lived and unhappy; Lucius is referred to in different accounts as a fortune hunter, swindler and bigamist. Several of her sons died young and two were jailed and then banished from the colony for robbery. Her estate was carved up and sold to pay her bills; part of it later formed the heart of Ross Bay Cemetery. Isabella was maintained in old age by her daughter Flora and lived in a cottage on the convent grounds of the Sisters of St Ann. Merilia Passage was formerly known as Alexander Passage or Alexandra Passage.

While waiting for favourable tides, mariners have long carved the names of their boats on signs at Mermaid Bay. *Alan Haig-Brown*

Mermaid Bay (50°24'00" 125°12'00" S side of Dent I, Cordero Channel, off NE Sonora I, N of Campbell R). Named in 1955 for the tugboat *Mermaid*, which used to anchor in this bay. This historic 28-m steam sidewheeler was built in Victoria in the mid-1880s for Burrard Inlet's Hastings Sawmill Co. Capt E C Bridgeman was an early skipper. It later saw service in the Nanaimo area, working for the coal companies. Small craft and tugs towing log booms often use the bay as an emergency moorage when they cannot make it through the entire sequence of tidal rapids in this vicinity and are forced to wait until the next slack tide.

Mermaid Cove (49°46'45" 124°11'30" W of Saltery Bay, N side of Jervis Inlet near its mouth, E of Powell R). A 3-m-tall bronze mermaid was placed here in 20 m of water as an attraction for divers in 1989. Known as the Emerald Princess, Canada's first underwater statue was created by Saltspring I sculptor Simon Morris. A second, identical 270-kg casting was installed on Sunset Reef at Grand Cayman in the W Indies in 2000. The name was adopted in 1990.

Merritt Lagoon (51°56'25" 128°02'20" E of Kildidt Lagoon, Hunter I, S of Bella Bella), **Mount Merritt** (51°58'58" 128°02'28" NE of Kildidt Lagoon). Lt Col Charles Cecil Ingersoll Merritt, VC (1908–2000), was born at Vancouver and educated at Royal Military College, Kingston, Ont. In private life he was a lawyer. He was awarded the VC—the second received by a Canadian soldier during WWII—for gallantry and leadership while commanding the S Saskatchewan Regiment during the disastrous 1942 raid on Dieppe. Merritt was taken prisoner in this action and spent the remainder of the war at various camps, including Colditz. After hostilities ended, he was elected Conservative MP for Vancouver Burrard, 1945–49, then returned to his law practice. He also served as CO of the Seaforth Highlanders, 1951–54. Mt Merritt was named in 1944, Merritt Lagoon in 1992. *E*

Approaching Merry Island lighthouse, Halfmoon Bay. *Andrew Scott*

Merry Island (49°28'00" 123°55'00" Between Thormanby Is and SW side of Sechelt Peninsula, S entrance to Welcome Passage, Str of Georgia). A wealthy but unpopular Glasgow MP and industrialist named James C Merry (1805–77) was the owner of the racehorse Thormanby, winner of the Epsom Derby in 1860. At its height, his family coal-mining business operated 23 collieries, three ironworks and employed 4,500 men. A heavy gambler, Merry had a number of successful racehorses trained at the Russley Park stables in Lambourn, Wiltshire. RN capt George Richards and his officers, aboard survey vessel *Plumper*, applied many horse-racing names to this area in 1860 after hearing news of that year's Derby. One can only presume that he and some of his men had laid winning wagers on the race. The Sechelt First Nation name for the channel is Chichxwalish and for the island is Népshílin. *W*

Mesachie Nose (52°20'35" 127°09'45" N side of Burke Channel, S entrance to Labouchere Channel, W of Bella Coola). *Mesachie* means "wicked" or "bad" in Chinook jargon, the pidgin language used on the W coast by First Nation groups and early traders and settlers. When a SW wind is blowing, the Nose is apparently a bad place to be,

as an unpleasant backwash can form off its precipitous cliff. Alexander Mackenzie took a compass bearing off this headland on his historic overland journey of 1793. Formerly known as Masachiti Point and Mesachie Head. Mesachie Lk, the logging community on the S shore of Cowichan Lk, derives its name from the same source.

Mesher Rock (52°44'00" 129°18'00" Entrance to Borrowman Bay, off NW side of Aristazabal I). Named in 1926 for Isabella Muir (1870–1940), who was born at Sooke, the daughter of Robert Muir, who came to BC in 1849 with his father and brothers to work at the Ft Rupert coal diggings (*see* Muir Cove). She married general merchant Frederick James Mesher (1870–1945), from England, at Victoria in 1894, but the two soon divorced, and Mesher wed Sophia Mateo in 1896. He was a son of George C Mesher (1830–1912), an important contractor, who constructed many commercial and apartment buildings in Victoria. Isabella is believed to have taken part in the Victoria old-timers' reunion of 1924 (*see* Adams Bay).

Metcalf Islands (50°17'00" 125°22'00" W end of Okisollo Channel, between Quadra I and Sonora I, NW of Campbell R). Lance Cpl William Henry Metcalf, VC, MM (1894–1968), was born in Maine but fought in WWI as a member of the 16th (Canadian Scottish) Battalion of the Canadian Expeditionary Force. He was awarded his VC for an action at Arras, France, in 1918 when, under intense fire, he led a tank to destroy an enemy machine-gun strongpoint, eliminating a crucial impediment to the advance of the battalion. Metcalf returned to Maine after the war and worked there as an auto mechanic. He is buried at Bayside Cemetery, Eastport, Maine. His VC was donated to the Canadian Scottish Regiment Museum at Victoria in the late 1990s. The Metcalf Is were named in 1924.

Metchosin (48°23'00" 123°32'00" SW of Victoria, between Parry Bay and Royal Roads). A number of possible meanings have been offered for this Salishan First Nation word, including "smelling of fish oil" or "place of fish oil"—derivations that may be related to the beaching of a dead whale in the area. HBC chief factor James Douglas mentioned the name after visiting the area in 1842. Once agricultural and still semi-rural, Metchosin is now a residential suburb of Victoria and a district municipality. Metchosin Ck and Metchosin Mtn are named after the district. *E*

Metford Island (54°15'00" 130°22'00" Off entrance to Delusion Bay, S side of Digby I, SW of Prince Rupert). William Ellis Metford (1824–99) was a British engineer who designed a type of rifling used on the standard Lee-Metford and Martini-Metford service rifles of the late 1800s. He lived in India briefly in the 1850s but worked

M

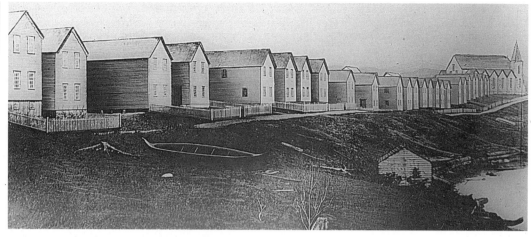

The "model" village of Metlakatla in the 1870s. *Harbour Publishing collection*

mostly in England, creating bullets and shells that were noted for their accuracy; many of his prototypes were adopted by the British armed forces. The names of several small-arms designers were applied to features in this vicinity in the early 1900s.

Metlakatla (54°20'00" 130°26'00" NW side of Venn Passage facing Digby I, just W of Prince Rupert), **Metlakatla Bay** (54°19'00" 130°28'00" NW side of Digby I). The name of this famous village and mission site is an adaptation of the Tsimshian word for the area, Metla-kah-thla, which has been translated as "a passage between two bodies of salt water." Metlakatla was an important Tsimshian First Nation settlement before its residents moved to Ft Simpson in the early 1830s. They returned in 1862, led by Anglican lay missionary William Duncan (*see* Duncan Bay), both to escape the plague of smallpox that swept the coast that year and to establish a "model Christian village," which operated successfully until 1887, when Duncan, in conflict with his Anglican bishop, led his flock N to Annette I in SE Alaska. In its time, Metlakatla was a well-known showplace with European-style homes, a fire hall, school, tannery, cooperage, sawmill, cannery, newspaper and the largest church in NW America. Its population was about 1,200. A fire destroyed many of the buildings, including the great church, in 1901. In the early 2000s the community had only about 120 residents. Many spelling variations are found for this name on old charts, including Metlah Catlah, Metla-kathla, Methlakahtla and Metla Catla. The current form seems to have became standard about 1890. *E W*

Mexicana Point (50°55'00" 127°59'00" W end of Hope I, off N tip of Vancouver I). The *Mexicana* was a tiny, 14-m-long schooner commanded by Spanish naval officer Cayetano Valdés on a historic 1792 exploration of the BC coast and circumnavigation of Vancouver I. Valdes accompanied Dionisio Alcalá-Galiano, cdr of the *Sutil*, on this voyage, part of which was spent travelling with

Capt George Vancouver and his two ships. Valdés and Alcalá-Galiano left San Blas, Mexico, in Mar, repaired the *Mexicana*'s broken mast at Nootka Sd in May, sailed up Juan de Fuca Str in June and returned to Nootka at the end of Aug. Mexicana Point was named by the explorers as they passed W out of Goletas Channel and realized they were back in the Pacific Ocean. **Mexicana Hill** (49°03'09" 123°38'22" E of Blackberry Point, Valdes I, Gulf Is), named by Capt George Richards about 1859 in association with Valdes I, also commemorates this vessel. The *Mexicana* returned to the PNW in 1793 under Juan Martínez y Zayas and explored the Washington coast and Columbia R. *W*

Meyer Island (53°14'00" 132°11'00" Kagan Bay, off S side of Graham I, Skidegate Inlet, QCI). William Meyer (1850–1915) was born in Germany and worked as a seaman around the world, arriving at Victoria in 1875. He married Henrietta Marcella Moore (1857–1935), the daughter of well-known riverboat owner Capt William Moore, at Victoria in 1876. As master of the barque *Estells*, Meyer transported Victoria's first cargo of water pipe. He went into business with his father-in-law and brought the *Sardonyx* out to Victoria from Liverpool in 1882. When Moore retired, Meyer joined the Canadian Pacific Navigation Co as a skipper. He had command of many pioneer PNW steamers, including the *Otter*, *Princess Louise*, *Western Slope*, *Maude*, *Grappler* and *Islander*, but was primarily associated with the *Danube*, which he had charge of in 1891 when it struck a rock (soon named Danube Rk) just SW of Meyer I. He was also cdr of the *Danube* in 1893, when it was held at Portland for allegedly bringing in 633 illegal Asian immigrants. The Meyers retired to California and both died there. Meyer I was formerly known as Reef I but the name was changed in 1945 to avoid duplication. *D*

Meynell Point (50°37'00" 126°55'00" S side of Malcolm I, SE end of Queen Charlotte Str, off NE side of Vancouver I). This feature was named by the Geographic Board of Canada in 1906, in association with Malcolm I. Capt

Henry Meynell (c 1789–1865), who entered the RN in 1803, was flag capt on HMS *Newcastle* to Rear Adm Sir Pulteney Malcolm in 1816. Malcolm at that time was cdr-in-chief of the St Helena Station and responsible for a famous prisoner of war: Napoleon Bonaparte. Meynell became a gentleman usher to George IV and William IV, and master of the household to Queen Victoria. He was an MP, 1826–47, and achieved the rank of adm, retired, in 1862. *W*

Miall Islet (52°31'00" 128°17'00" E entrance to Jackson Passage, between Susan I and Roderick I, Mathieson Channel, N of Bella Bella), **Miall Point** (52°30'00" 128°16'00" SE end of Susan I). Edwin Rose Miall was an RN paymaster aboard HMS *Scout*, under Capt John Price, on the Pacific Station, 1865–68. He became a chief paymaster, retired, in 1883. Miall Point was named by surveyor Lt Daniel Pender in 1866.

Miami Islet (49°02'00" 123°42'00" Stuart Channel, N of Thetis I, Gulf Is). The steamship *Miami*, 100 m in length and 2,740 tonnes, struck a submerged reef near this location and sank in Jan 1900. It was built at Sunderland, UK, in 1891 and owned by the Pacific Coast Steamship Co. The vessel, under Capt Wallace Langley, had just picked up more than 4,000 tonnes of coal in Ladysmith Hbr from the Dunsmuir collieries and was on its way to San Francisco. All the crew members were saved, but the loss was valued at the time at $300,000. The wreck, which can be visited by scuba divers, was sold at auction to a Seattle company for $4,000 and later stripped of anything valuable.

Michael Bank (53°03'00" 129°31'00" E of Prior I, Estevan Group, Estevan Sd, SE of Banks I). Named in 1949 after Jules Leonard Michael (1851–1911), a native of Camberwell, England, who came to Victoria in the 1860s and married Ruth E Ferguson (b 1862), also from England, at Nanaimo in 1880. One record suggests that Michael first arrived in BC as a very young member of the crew of HMS *Sparrowhawk* in 1865. He is listed in various records as a miner and general labourer at Nanaimo in the early 1880s, and thereafter as a farmer in the Cedar area S of Nanaimo.

Michelsen Point (50°35'00" 127°42'00" S side of Holberg Inlet, S of Straggling Is, Quatsino Sd, NW Vancouver I). Named in 1970 after Hans Theodore Michelsen (1875–1956, sometimes spelled Michelson), who received a Crown grant of land between Holberg and San Josef Bay in 1912. He died at Nanaimo. This feature was formerly known as Mickelsen Point.

Michigan Creek (48°43'00" 125°04'00" Flows S into Pacific Ocean, E of Pachena Point, SW Vancouver I). The 514-tonne coastal steamer *Michigan*, under Capt Graves, was wrecked at the mouth of this creek in Jan 1893. The strongly built, 48-m vessel was constructed in 1888 at Skamokawa, Washington, and normally ran between Puget Sd and San Francisco. In 1890 it caught fire at sea but managed to reach Astoria, where the flames were extinguished by the local fire dept. In 1893 the *Michigan* was carrying a full cargo of general merchandise when it met its end. The crew of 21 and four passengers escaped in the ship's boats, though one crewman wandered off and died of exposure after the accident. Several US tugs and the revenue cutter *Oliver Wolcott* came to the vessel's aid, but it was fatally damaged. Ironically, the Victoria salvage vessel *Mascotte*, which saved most of the cargo, was itself wrecked at this same spot later in the year. The *Michigan*'s boiler and part of its shaft and propeller could still be seen on the reef in the early 2000s.

Mickey Island (49°22'00" 123°27'00" Off NE side of Pasley I, entrance to Howe Sd, NW of Vancouver). Malcolm "Mickey" McBean Bell-Irving (1892–1950) was one of 10 children of prominent Vancouver cannery owner Henry Ogle Bell-Irving, who acquired nearby Pasley I as a family retreat in 1909. Mickey fought in WWI, serving as a pilot in the Royal Flying Corps, where he was awarded the DSO and MC and seriously wounded in action. (His five brothers also distinguished themselves, collectively winning two DSOs, an OBE, two DSCs, four MCs and a Croix de guerre; Alan Duncan Bell-Irving was one of Canada's first air aces.) Henry Bell-Irving purchased the island, known at the time as White I, in 1915 and presented it to Mickey after he received the DSO. His injuries prevented him from working after the war; he married Nora Jones in 1921 and lived at Victoria for many years. On Mickey's death, his ashes were strewn over the island. Its name was changed to Weyburn I (after HMCS *Weyburn*, lost in WWII; *see* Weyburn Rk) in the 1940s, in association with Golby I, the old name for Hermit I (qv), which had been named after the *Weyburn*'s cdr, Thomas Golby (*see* Golby Passage). The current name of Mickey I was finally adopted in 1951.

Middle Arm (49°11'00" 123°09'00" Between Sea I and Lulu I, mouth of the Fraser R). This branch of the river was also known, until the 1960s at least, as Moray or Morey Channel, after Sgt Jonathan Morey of the Royal Engineers, and was so marked on many charts. There were attempts to officially adopt this name in place of Middle Arm, but in the interests of air safety (the channel is a major landmark for pilots landing at the airport) and because of the long history of the admittedly undistinguished name, Middle Arm was confirmed in 1959. Another former name for this feature is S Fork of the N Arm of the Fraser, which is technically a more accurate description. Morey Channel (qv) now refers to one specific section of Middle Arm.

Middleton Point (51°47'00" 128°00'00" E side of Nalau I, Fitz Hugh Sd, S of Bella Bella). Early PNW fur trader Charles Duncan, capt of the *Princess Royal* in 1788, gave

M

the name Sir Charles Middleton's Sd to the body of water now known as Fitz Hugh Sd. The hydrographic service called this feature Middleton Point in 1945 in order to keep that earlier reference alive. Sir Charles Middleton (1726–1813) was a rear adm, comptroller of the RN and Tory MP in 1788. He was later appointed 1st Lord of the Admiralty (in 1805) and an adm of the red, and given the title of Baron Barham. In addition to his RN service, Middleton also played a key behind-the-scenes role in the abolition of the slave trade, helping reformers gather evidence against slavery and providing support for the abolitionist movement.

Mike Inlet (52°32'00" 131°47'00" W side of Moresby I, N of Gowgaia Bay, QCI). Named about 1912 by Capt Absalom Freeman of the Canadian Fishing Co after Mike Scott, one of his skippers. Scott operated the halibut trawler *New England* for a number of years.

Mikuni Point (48°49'00" 123°12'00" NW side of Saturna I, Gulf Is). Named in 1969 for Kisuki or Kisuke Mikuni (c 1860–1910), a Japanese farmer and entrepreneur who lived on Saturna and Tumbo islands in the 1890s. He had been persuaded to come to Canada from Yokohama in 1884 by a Victoria merchant named Charles Gabriel, who made buying trips to Japan to supply his store, the Japanese Bazaar, which sold Asian specialty goods. Gabriel also acted as Japan's consul at Victoria. Mikuni worked as a clerk for Gabriel and became his assistant in the Tumbo I Coal Co, formed in 1889 to exploit the small coal seams that had earlier been discovered on both Saturna and Tumbo. By 1893, 21 men, mainly from Japan, were working on Tumbo, and a 60-m shaft had been sunk. The mine was abandoned, however, after water seeped in and a boiler exploded, killing the contractor and an engineer. Mikuni started farming at Winter Cove on Saturna but sold out in 1896 to Gilbert Ainslie and moved to Vancouver and, finally, New Westminster. He became involved in numerous ventures, including newspaper publishing, logging, quarrying stone and gravel for Vancouver's CPR dock and operating a rice mill. After his death his widow, Sanoko Mikuni, ran a dry goods store at New Westminster for many years.

Milbanke Sound (52°19'00" 128°33'00" Between Price I and Athlone I, W of Bella Bella.) Named in 1788 by pioneer fur trader and mariner Charles Duncan, who was on the BC coast that year as master of the *Princess Royal*, part of an expedition sent to the PNW from London in 1786 by Richard Etches and the King George's Sd Co, under the command of James Colnett. Duncan made a number of small sketch charts of various locations on the coast, including Milbanke Sd, that were afterwards published by Alexander Dalrymple, hydrographer of the British E India Co (and later the first hydrographer of the British Admiralty). Capt George Vancouver had copies of Duncan's charts on his 1791–95 voyage to the PNW and retained Duncan's name for the sound. Adm Sir Mark Milbanke (1724–1805) was a prominent RN officer, capt of HMS *Guernsey, Barfleur, Princess Royal* and *Namur*, and cdr-in-chief and gov of Nfld, 1789–92. As settlement in Nfld was officially discouraged at the time, he sent back potential immigrants and demolished buildings but still managed to protect the valuable fishery. Milbanke ended his career as cdr-in-chief at Portsmouth, 1799–1803. Cape Mark off the SW end of Athlone I is also named for him. *W*

Miles Island (52°04'00" 128°19'00" S of Stryker I, Raymond Passage, Queens Sd, W of Bella Bella). RCN officer George Ralph Miles, OBE (1902–51), from Halifax, was a cadet at the Royal Naval College of Canada in 1916 and a midshipman by 1919. In 1934, as a lt, he was appointed assistant director of naval reserves. His first command was the destroyer *Saguenay* (1939–41). In 1942–43, as a cdr, he was in charge of various Halifax shore establishments, then became the first CO of the new destroyer *Athabaskan* in 1943. Further promotions followed: chief of staff to CO Atlantic Coast (1944); chief of naval personnel and member of the Naval Board of Canada (1946); CO of the aircraft carrier *Magnificent* and senior naval officer afloat (1948–49); officer-in-charge, Montreal area, and aide-de-camp to the gov gen (1949); and commodore-in-command, RCN Esquimalt Barracks (1950). The name was adopted in 1944.

Miles Point (51°04'00" 126°51'00" S side of Seymour Inlet, N of Queen Charlotte Str). After Lt Henry Towry Miles Cooper of the Royal Marines, who served in BC 1859–66. *See* Cooper Reach.

Milhus Rock (48°59'00" 125°09'00" Vernon Bay, N of Imperial Eagle Channel, Barkley Sd, W side of Vancouver I). Supposedly an adaptation of a Nuu-chah-nulth First Nation word meaning "flat ground." Formerly known as Edward Rk but changed in 1934.

Millar Bay (53°35'00" 130°33'00" S of entrance to Norway Inlet, W side of Banks I). Named in 1926 after William Millar, who returned from overseas service during WWI to become the 3rd engineer aboard the W coast survey vessel *Lillooet* in the early 1920s.

Millar Channel (49°19'00" 126°04'00" E of Flores I, Clayoquot Sd, W side of Vancouver I). Named in 1934 after Rev J L Millar, Presbyterian missionary and principal of the Ahousat residential school. The boarding school replaced the older day school in 1904–5, and Rev J C Butchart was its first principal. Millar took over the operation about 1906–9, and his wife also worked there as assistant teacher. In 1910 he was transferred to Manitoba as principal of the Portage la Prairie residential school. Millar was back at Ahousat in 1918 and continued as principal until 1928, seeing the school through the 1925 merger of Methodist and Presbyterian churches that formed the United Church.

Mill Bay (48°39'00" 123°33'00" NW side of Saanich Inlet, NW of Victoria). A US immigrant named Henry S Sheppard operated the first sawmill at this site, applying to lease the land in 1860. In those days it was the only mill between Nanaimo and Esquimalt. The stream that flows E into the bay and once powered the mill was originally known as Mill Ck, but the name was changed before 1924 to Shawnigan Ck, after the lake it drains. The sawmill was taken over about 1863 by William Sayward, from Maine, and he soon became the largest lumber merchant on Vancouver I. In 1865 his products were being shipped to San Francisco. By the early 2000s, Mill Bay had turned into a small waterfront community, home to Brentwood College, and was the terminus of a ferry across Saanich Inlet to Brentwood Bay. Mill Bay was labelled Mill Ck Bay on an early 1859 map of the district. *E*

Mill Bay (54°59'00" 129°54'00" N side of Nass Bay, W of the mouth of the Nass R, NE of Prince Rupert). Henry Croasdaile (*see* Croasdaile I) built a plant here in 1877 for processing eulachon, a small, oily fish much treasured by First Nation groups, who render it into a food condiment known as "grease." The following year he built a sawmill, the earliest in the area, and in 1879 the first salmon cannery on Nass Bay. The plant was sold in 1889 and rebuilt by the BC Canning Co, then sold again in 1893 to the Federation Brand Salmon Co. Henry Doyle's Kincolith Packing Co acquired it in 1908. Doyle added a cold-storage facility and can-making machinery, and turned Mill Bay into one of the most modern, productive canneries in BC. It changed hands twice more—to Northern BC Fisheries Ltd and the BC Fishing & Packing Co—before shutting down in 1937. Mill Bay remained open as a fishing camp for another 22 years.

Miller Bay (54°16'00" 130°16'00" SE side of Kaien I, Prince Rupert). Named after Martin Miller, who came to BC from Switzerland and worked as a sawyer at the Big Bay Lumber Co sawmill at Georgetown Mills. He moved to Prince Rupert and ran a shingle mill on this bay for many years until the late 1930s. During WWII, an RCAF hospital was built there to care for the casualties that were expected from the Aleutian Is campaign, but the facility was not needed and did not open until after the war, when it was transferred to the federal Dept of Indian Affairs and operated as a First Nation TB sanatorium. It was known as the Miller Bay Hospital, but the bay itself was called Hospital Cove for a period of time before being officially renamed Miller Bay. The hospital buildings were used as a fish hatchery in the 1980s but were eventually abandoned.

Millerd Point (50°15'52" 124°57'30" N side of Redonda Bay, NW side of W Redonda I, Deer Passage, NE of Campbell R). Named in 2006 after RCAF flight sgt William Francis Millerd, from Vancouver, in association with the Millerd family's cannery operation at Redonda Bay in the 1930s and '40s. William Millerd was serving as a radio operator and gunner with No 408 (RAF) Squadron when he was killed in action on May 16, 1942, aged 24. He was flying his 11th mission, laying mines off the coast of Denmark and attacking German ships, when his Hampden bomber was shot down. He is buried at Aarhus West Cemetery in Denmark. Millerd Ck, which flows W into Knight Inlet near Glendale Cove, is named for William's father, Francis Millerd (1884–1976), who came to Vancouver from Ireland in 1908. He married Annie Ellen Frances Findon (1885–1970), from England, the following year. Francis worked in the fishing industry and was a partner in Gosse-Millerd Packing Co Ltd, the second-largest cannery operator in BC, 1913–23. He then purchased the Somerville Canning Co, which had a floating cannery, and from 1929 to 1935 was a partner in Queen Charlotte Fisheries Ltd and Millerd Packing

Mill Bay, west side of Saanich Inlet. *Kevin Oke*

The Casualties of War

Most geographical features on BC's long coastline are named for older folks. This is as it should be; it normally takes years to build up the kind of reputation that might prompt a government department to name a mountain or island after you. It is the long-serving, by default, who get the recognition—the ones with the impressive resumés, the lists of achievements, the networks of friends. The rewards go to those who put in the time.

In 2006, Millerd Point was named after WWII war hero William Francis Millerd from Vancouver. *Courtesy Millerd family*

There are exceptions to this trend, however. In one category of BC place names scarcely any nominee is over 25. The reason is simple—and sad; these are the places named for the casualties of war. Since the early 1950s more than 1,000 British Columbians have been commemorated this way on the province's maps and charts. War fatalities are, in fact, one of the few sources of new names that BC's Geographical Names Office will consider.

The practice began after World War II, when aerial surveying really came into its own. The legendary Gerry Andrews—teacher, engineer, forester, surveyor, writer and artist—had been the first to introduce aerial photography in BC, in 1931. During the war, Andrews served in air photo intelligence and learned the latest photogrammetric techniques, which he used to help chart Normandy's beaches for the invasion of 1944. In peacetime, naturally, as BC's chief air survey engineer, he applied the latest science to the mapping of the province's hinterlands, work that he continued from 1951 to 1968 in his roles of surveyor general and provincial boundary commissioner.

Andrews, who died in 2005 at the age of 101, was able to hire numerous ex-RCAF flyers to work on the post-war surveys. He bought used military cameras, and the province purchased a pair of Avro Anson aircraft to provide solid camera platforms. The demand for maps increased, especially from the mining, forestry, oil and power industries. And hundreds of place names were needed to make sense of the new maps. Commemorating a few of the more than 3,700 men and women from BC who had died in action in World War II alone seemed at the time like an obvious solution.

At first it was fairly easy to track down family members and ask to use a name. Rarely was permission refused; people were honoured—thrilled, even—that next of kin might be remembered this way. But as the years went by it became more difficult to locate the relatives of war casualties. And the demand for names declined as mapping became more complete. At some point the government decided that the names of the war dead would only be used at the express request of their families. The procedure was made more ceremonial. Beginning in 1989, the previous year's commemorations were recognized each Remembrance Day with a press release and a message from the relevant provincial minister.

Eventually, even this formality fell by the wayside. In 1997, for instance, 14 geographical features were named for those who died in the two world wars. In 1998 that number had fallen to nine, and the following year it was down to three. Cook Point on the north side of Nelson Island, at the entrance to Jervis Inlet, was one of the names granted in 1999. It recalled the sacrifice of Flying Officer Ray James Cook of Victoria, who was 21 when his plane crashed near Bezancourt, France, on January 28, 1944.

The names of war fatalities continue to be applied to BC's geographical features, though it can take much time and community consultation to find an appropriate site, which may not actually be associated with the deceased person. After all, most war fatalities hail from urban areas in southern BC, which are all "named out." One of the most recent names to be adopted is Millerd Point on the north side of Redonda Bay, northeast of Campbell River. It keeps alive the memory of 24-year-old Flight Sergeant William Francis Millerd, from Vancouver, a wireless operator and air gunner with the RAF's 408 Squadron, whose Hampden aircraft was shot down on May 16, 1942, while attacking a German warship. He is buried at Aarhus West Cemetery in Denmark. Millerd's family used to operate a cannery at Redonda Bay, so the location is fortuitous. The name was adopted on Remembrance Day, 2006.

Co Ltd. In 1936 he founded Francis Millerd and Co Ltd, which ran canneries at W Vancouver, Redonda Bay and Prince Rupert, and operated a fleet of fishing boats. After he retired, his sons took over management of the company, which wound up in 1978.

Miller Islet (49°47'00" 123°57'00" S end of Prince of Wales Reach, N of Egmont Point, Jervis Inlet, NW of Vancouver). This feature, formerly known as One Tree I, was renamed in 1945, presumably in association with nearby Captain I (qv), which was named in 1860 after HMS *Captain*, the vessel from which Commodore Horatio Nelson flew his pennant at the 1797 Battle of Cape St Vincent (setting in motion his fabled career). Capt Ralph Willett Miller (1762–99) was cdr of the *Captain* at the time. He was born at NY and had a short but action-packed naval career, fighting in the W Indies, Mediterranean and off N America. Miller also served with Nelson aboard HMS *Theseus* and participated with distinction at the Battle of the Nile. He was killed by an accidental explosion on the *Theseus*.

Miller Point (54°15'00" 130°23'00" E entrance to Delusion Bay, S end of Digby I, just SW of Prince Rupert). Jack A Miller was a levelman—a survey team member who operates a surveyor's level—for the GTP and a draftsman on the first surveys of Prince Rupert Hbr, done in the early 1900s when the area was chosen as a railway terminus and townsite.

Miller Reef (48°50'00" 125°20'00" W end of Imperial Eagle Channel, Barkley Sd, W side of Vancouver I). Named after William Miller, 2nd officer on the *Imperial Eagle*, the fur-trading vessel that Capt Charles Barkley sailed from London to the PNW and then to China and India, 1786–88. Miller was killed on the Washington coast in 1787 in an altercation with local Quileute First Nation inhabitants. The *Eagle* had anchored near the mouth of the Hoh R while Barkley sent two boats ashore to get water. The smaller boat, with Miller, purser John Beale and four seamen, explored up the river and was not seen again. Next day, when a heavily armed party was sent out to search for the missing men, only their bloodied clothes were found. Barkley named the site of this calamity the Destruction R; the name was later transferred to a nearby offshore island, location of an 1888 lighthouse.

Mill Point (48°40'22" 123°24'56" W side of Tsehum Hbr, S entrance to Blue Heron Basin, NE end of Saanich Peninsula, N of Victoria). Henry Brackman (*see* Brackman I) built a small gristmill at this location in 1878. Four years later, David Russell Ker (*see* Ker I) joined him as a partner. The Brackman-Ker Milling Co went on to build a larger mill at Victoria and become one of Canada's most successful producers of flours and animal feeds.

Mill Stream (48°27'20" 123°27'30" Flows SE then NE into the head of Esquimalt Hbr, just NW of Victoria). In 1848 the HBC built the first sawmill in BC on this creek, about 500 m above the present Parson's Bridge. Lumber was shipped from the sawmill to Ft Langley and California in 1849 and later also to Hawaii. In 1850 the first flour or gristmill was built just below the sawmill. Mill Stream was not a very satisfactory source of power, however, as it was often too low in summer and sometimes too high in the spring: a freshet in 1855, for instance, washed out the waterwheel and damaged both mills, which were rebuilt but soon seem to have been abandoned as more productive sites were developed at Sooke, Nanaimo and Mill Bay (qv). The waterway was marked Rowe Stream on Joseph Pemberton's 1855 map of SE Vancouver I. Mill Hill, just W of the head of Esquimalt Hbr, also takes its name from these early installations, while the rural residential community of Millstream is located near the waterway's upper reaches.

Milne Island (52°37'00" 128°46'00" NE side of Laredo Sd, S of Princess Royal I). George Lawson Milne (1850–1933) was a long-serving Victoria physician who was born in Morayshire, Scotland, and immigrated to Ont in 1856 with his parents. He came out to the W coast in 1880, where he married Ellen "Nellie" Catherine Kinsman (1865–1941) at Victoria in 1882. Milne served as Victoria's medical health officer, 1885–92, and as the medical immigration officer for the port of Victoria, 1903–24. He also played active roles with the BC Medical Council, Royal Jubilee Hospital, Victoria school board and BC Liberal Assoc, and was elected MLA for Victoria City, 1890–94. His brother, Alexander Roland Milne (1838–1904), was collector of customs at Victoria for many years. The island was named in 1926, two years after Dr Milne retired.

Milnes Landing (48°23'00" 123°42'00" E side of the mouth of Sooke R, Sooke Hbr, S end of Vancouver I). Named in 1934 after Edward Milne (1857–1943), who had worked in Hong Kong for a Scottish sugar-refining company before coming to Montreal in 1883. There he married his fiancée, Janet Kerr (1858–1934), and the couple travelled to Victoria before buying land and farming at Sooke. They were joined by other family members, and the extended Milne clan played a major role in the development of the Sooke district, opening a general store in 1893, establishing a dairy farm, building a steamship landing and operating a horse-drawn freight service to Victoria. Edward was postmaster at Milnes Landing, 1895–1940, retiring at age 83.

Milthorp Point (51°14'00" 127°47'00" N of Hoop Bay, between Cape Caution and Smith Sd, NW of Port Hardy). RCNR lt Patrick Reginald Fairburn Milthorp, from Victoria, was killed in action on Feb 10, 1942, aged 32. He was serving aboard HMCS *Spikenard*, a *Flower*-class corvette commanded by Lt Cdr Hubert Shadforth, which was torpedoed in the mid-Atlantic while on convoy duty.

M

There were only eight survivors out of a crew of 65. Lt Milthorp had worked as an RCMP officer before enlisting. He is commemorated on the Halifax Memorial. Milthorp Point was named in 1956.

Miners Bay on northwest side of Mayne Island. *Kevin Oke*

Miners Bay (48°51'00" 123°18'00" NW side of Mayne I, Active Pass, Gulf Is), **Miners Channel** (48°38'00" 123°17'00" E of Sidney I, N of Victoria). These features were named in 1859 by Capt George Richards of the survey vessel *Plumper*, after the great stream of would-be miners that surged from Victoria to the Fraser R during the 1858–59 gold rush. Many of these hopeful souls, who crossed the Str of Georgia in anything that would float, including dinghies, canoes and rafts, travelled via Miners Channel and paused at Miners Bay, which became a popular halfway camping spot on the journey.

Minette Bay (54°01'13" 128°37'41" Head of Kitimat Arm, just S of Kitimat). According to historian John Walbran, the bay was named in 1898 by Louis Coste, chief engineer of Canada's Dept of Public Works, after his wife. As capt of CGS *Quadra*, Walbran had taken Coste and his party to examine the heads of several coastal inlets that year as possible termini for a proposed railway to the Yukon. However, a 1924 report of the Geographic Board of Canada states that the feature is named after one of the seven children of Joseph-Israel Tarte, who was Canada's minister of Public Works, 1896–1902. The fact that Minette is often a nickname confuses the issue. The old First Nation village site on this bay, today a Haisla reserve, was known as Zagwis or Jugwees. Minette Bay Ck flows NW into the head of the bay.

Mink Island (50°06'00" 124°46'00" Desolation Sd, NE end of Str of Georgia, NW of Powell R). Named by Admiralty surveyors about 1861 in association with nearby Otter I and Martin Is after local fur-bearing animals (though Martin should really be Marten). In 1945, because another Mink I existed only 60 km away in Cordero Channel, regional hydrographer Henri Parizeau changed the name

to Repulse I, after HMS *Repulse*, the Pacific Station flagship, 1872–77. The island's owner, Eustace "Rui" Shearman of Vancouver, had bought Mink I at a tax sale about 1930 after its previous owner, a fur farmer, had gone broke. When Shearman saw a revised chart of the area in 1961, he complained to the Geographic Board of Canada that "a man named Parizeau" had, "on some whim," changed the names of many places in the locality. "Can you tell me," he asked, "what steps I can take to apply for the restoration of the original name?" When BC's chief geographer learned that the name Mink I was still in widespread local use, he hinted to Shearman that a petition signed by local residents might change official minds. In 1962, after the property owner had obtained the signatures of nearly everyone living at nearby Refuge Cove, Squirrel Cove and Lund, the name Mink I was restored. "No one with whom I was in contact," Shearman commented, "was in favour of the name Repulse Island."

Minnis Bay (53°20'00" 129°27'00" S side of Hinton I, between Farrant I and Pitt I). RCAF pilot officer Harvey B Minnis, from Victoria, was killed in action on Apr 27, 1943. He was part of No 115 (RAF) Squadron, which flew medium and heavy bombers (Vickers Wellingtons and Avro Lancasters), mainly on night sorties over Germany's industrial Ruhr region. Minnis was awarded the DFC for completing a number of missions "with courage and determination" over "many of the enemy's most heavily defended targets including Hamburg, Duisburg, Berlin and Essen." He is buried at Reichswald Forest War Cemetery in Germany. Minnis Bay was named in 1950.

Minstrel Island at the entrance to Knight Inlet. *Andrew Scott*

Minstrel Island (50°37'00" 126°19'00" E of Turnour I, junction of Clio Channel and Chatham Channel, entrance to Knight Inlet). Named, along with nearby Bones Bay, Negro Rk and Sambo Point, after a troupe of amateur performers aboard HMS *Amethyst*, which carried Lord Dufferin, the gov gen, and Lady Dufferin on a cruise to Metlakatla in 1876. These entertainers put on minstrel shows, based on black cultural stereotypes, and presumably such a show was staged in the vicinity for the vice-regal couple. The island was first settled in the early 1900s and became the site of a general store and hotel in 1907. A small community sprang up to provide services to the region's very active logging and fishing industries. The Minstrel I Hotel was at one time reputed to sell more beer than any other pub in BC and developed a fairly notorious reputation for rowdiness.

Miracle Beach (49°51'00" 125°06'00" N of Courtenay, S of the mouth of the Oyster R, E side of Vancouver I). According to a local First Nation myth, a supernatural spirit appeared to inhabitants of this area in the guise of a starving stranger. After it was fed and befriended, the being revealed its true nature to its hosts and granted them wealth and prosperity, while at the same time warning them that pride in their good fortune would lead to their downfall. Proud they became, of course, and were attacked and brought low by their enemies. Once again the spirit came to save them. This time, wanting to emphasize its message, the divine being worked a great miracle, turning a princess from the tribe into Mitlenatch I. A different explanation for the name holds that when a major fire swept through the district about 1900, this area was "miraculously" spared. The beach and uplands, once owned by Theed Pearce, a noted naturalist and former mayor of Courtenay, were purchased from Frank Pottage in 1950 and made into a provincial park. Later additions have expanded the park's size to 135 ha.

Miskatla Inlet (53°49'00" 128°56'00" Extends N from Gilttoyees Inlet, NW side of Douglas Channel, S of Kitimat). Miskatla or Mesgatli (Misgatlee) is the Haisla First Nation name for Foch Lagoon. According to former UBC anthropologist Jay Powell, the name was somehow mistakenly applied in the 1920s to this inlet, which the Haisla people know as Kiyasa.

Mission Group (50°00'00" 127°24'00" W of Union I, N entrance to Kyuquot Sd, NW side of Vancouver I). This archipelago consists of Aktis I (formerly Village I), Kamils I (formerly Mission I), Spring I and some smaller islands and islets. Pioneer Roman Catholic missionary Augustin Brabant first visited the main Ka:ʼyu:ʼK'tʼh (Kyuquot) First Nation village on Aktis I in 1874 and erected a large cross on Kamils I. In 1879 he returned and arranged with village leaders for St Marc's mission to be established on Kamils I by priest Peter Nicolaye the following year. Fr John Lemmens took over in 1883. A church, school, hospital and outbuildings were eventually constructed. In the early 1900s the mission was transferred to Aktis I, where a series of churches was built. Kyuquot village members moved in the 1970s to nearby Houpsitas on Vancouver I. In the early 2000s, Kamils I was uninhabited and used mainly as a burial ground.

Mission Island. *See* Kamils Anchorage.

Mission Point (49°26'00" 123°43'00" S end of Trail Bay, just SE of Sechelt, Str of Georgia, NW of Vancouver). The name of this point, which is on the Tsawcome reserve of the Sechelt First Nation, presumably refers to the Roman Catholic mission established at nearby Sechelt by Fr Paul Durieu in 1862, at the height of one of the BC coast's worst smallpox epidemics. Out of the thousands of Sechelt people who had inhabited the area earlier in the century, only 167 remained at the Sechelt mission by 1876. A series of landmark churches (most of which later burned down) were built at Sechelt, culminating in 1907 with the beautiful Our Lady of Lourdes.

Mission Point (54°20'00" 130°26'00" N side of Venn Passage, Metlakatla Bay, just W of Prince Rupert), **Mission Mountain** (54°22'17" 130°22'42" NE of Metlakatla). These features are presumably named after the famous Anglican mission at Metlakatla (qv), where William Duncan established a "model Christian village" in 1862. *See* Duncan I for more information.

Mist Bluff (50°33'00" 126°16'00" E side of W Cracroft I), **Mist Islets** (50°33'00" 126°16'00" Port Harvey, E side of W Cracroft I, N of Johnstone Str), **Mist Rock** (50°25'00" 127°30'00" E side of Neroutsos Inlet, Quatsino Sd, NW Vancouver I). RN officer Henry Wentworth Mist (1833–95) was 2nd lt aboard HMS *Havannah* on the Pacific Station, 1855–58. He was born at Fulham and entered the RN in 1847. After his promotion to cdr in 1863, Mist returned to the PNW in charge of HMS *Sparrowhawk*, 1868–72. He investigated the 1869 wreck of the US barque *John Bright* near Estevan Point and the alleged massacre of the survivors by local Hesquiaht First Nation members. After two suspects were later convicted of murder, Mist returned to Hesquiat village with the police and a portable gallows, and arranged for the culprits to be hanged in front of the assembled tribe. That same year, Frederick Seymour, gov of the colony of BC, died of a sudden illness on Mist's gunboat at Bella Coola after settling a feud on the N coast between members of the Tsimshian and Nisgaʼa First Nations. W

Mitchell Bay (50°38'00" 126°51'00" SE side of Malcolm I, E end of Queen Charlotte Str), **Mitchell Inlet** (52°57'00" 132°10'00" Between Douglas Inlet and Mudge Inlet, Kuper Inlet, NW side of Moresby I, QCI). William Mitchell (1802–76), of the HBC's marine service, first came to the Pacific coast in 1837. He was a native of Aberdeen, Scotland, and served as 1st mate of various HBC vessels from 1837 to 1850, including the *Sumatra*, *Vancouver*, *Cadboro*, *Beaver* and *Columbia*. In 1851, Mitchell was rated a master mariner and commanded the *Una* and *Recovery* until 1859, when he was placed in charge of Ft Rupert. As skipper of the *Una* he participated in BC's

M

earliest gold rush, travelling to the QCI in the spring of 1851 with John Work to investigate the reported presence of gold at Mitchell Inlet. He returned that fall with chief trader William McNeill and a party of miners and became involved in an ugly scuffle with the Haida at the inlet over the removal of gold ore. After leaving the QCI with about $75,000 worth of ore, the *Una* ran aground in Neah Bay and was destroyed by members of the Makah First Nation. The crew and the miners were rescued by the US schooner *Susan Sturgis*, but the gold was lost. Mitchell returned to the QCI yet again, in 1852, with the *Recovery* and a heavy guard, but found that the discovery site had only a small pocket of gold. He retired from HBC service about 1863 and spent the rest of his days at Victoria. Mitchell was familiarly known as "Willie," and Willie I NW of Mitchell Inlet is named for him as well. The inlet is also widely but unofficially known as Gold Hbr. *D W*

Mitchell Cove (49°28'00" 123°22'00" W side of Port Graves, Gambier I, Howe Sd, NW of Vancouver). This name was adopted in 1985 for William Gandy Mitchell (1856–1940), who emigrated from NZ to Canada about 1880 and made his home on Gambier I's West Bay. He later moved to Port Graves, to a property located beside this cove. The Mitchells are one of the oldest families on Gambier, five generations having lived there. William's son Joe Mitchell (1892–1985) was the first white child born on the island.

Mitchell Cove (53°22'00" 129°28'00" Payne Channel, SE end of Pitt I). Named in 1950 for RCAF flight lt Charles George Mitchell (b 1912), who was killed in action on Mar 8, 1945. He was born at Lloydminster, Alberta, educated at Vermilion School of Agriculture and later lived at Victoria. Mitchell served with No 35 (RAF) Squadron, which flew Halifax and Lancaster bombers over Germany and Italy, and was awarded the DFC for displaying "the utmost fortitude, courage and devotion to duty" while completing more than 40 operational sorties. He is buried at Hamburg Cemetery in Germany.

Mitchell Island (49°12'09" 123°05'31" N Arm of the Fraser R, Richmond, between Lulu I and Vancouver). This feature, today an industrial zone reached from Vancouver's Knight St bridge, was formerly three islands: Mitchell, Twigg and Eburne. Alexander Mitchell (1847–1931), from Que, acquired his property in the early 1880s (his Crown grant is dated 1885) and farmed there for 50 years. Married three times and widowed twice, he raised a large family and served several terms as a Richmond and S Vancouver councillor and school board secretary. The neighbouring island was owned from 1889 to 1936 by John James Connolly Twigg, who bought it from James Bell, the original 1880 Crown grantee (Twigg I was known earlier as Mason's I and Bell's I). Sand dredged from shipping channels was used to join the three properties in

1937, and the name Twigg Island was cancelled in 1951. Twelve years passed before Western Canada Steel Ltd, which owned Twigg I at that time and operated a steel mill there, realized that the name had been eliminated, and the company objected to the change, claiming that it affected "countless legal documents" and "property descriptions," and caused "great confusion" and "hardship." By then, however, it was too late to change the name back. A low-level vehicle bridge, in use until 1974, was built in 1893 from Vancouver's Fraser St, via Mitchell I, to Lulu I (it was partly washed away in the great Fraser R flood of 1894). A private railway bridge connected the steel mill to Vancouver in 1958. Both these structures have since been mostly removed.

Mitchell Point (50°37'00" 125°33'00" W side of Loughborough Inlet, N of Heydon Bay, NW of Campbell R). John Frederick Mitchell (1831–1915) was assistant surgeon aboard HMS *Bacchante* and served on the Pacific Station in 1861–62. He joined the RN in 1856 and rose to the rank of fleet surgeon, retired, in 1878. Mitchell died at London, England.

Mitlenatch Island seabird sanctuary. *Peter Vassilopoulos*

Mitlenatch Island (49°57'00" 125°00'00" N end of the Str of Georgia, just SE of Campbell R). The word is a corruption of a Sliammon First Nation name, Métl'nech, meaning "calm at the end" or "calm back end," which probably refers to sheltered areas at either end of the island. Mitlenatch is an important nature reserve and the largest seabird colony in the N Str of Georgia, home to significant breeding populations of gulls, cormorants, guillemots, auklets and oystercatchers. While the 155-ha island—known to naturalists as "the Galapagos of Georgia Str"—is a provincial nature park, most of it is closed to the public; only a short trail is accessible to visitors. *E*

MK Bay (53°59'00" 128°39'00" E side of Kitimat Arm, N of Wathl Ck, just SE of Kitimat). This name, adopted in 1987, is an abbreviation for Morrison-Knudsen, the large US corporation that built the transmission lines from the massive power-generating station at Kemano to the aluminum smelter at Kitimat, 75 km N, in the mid-1950s. The Boise-based company used this bay as a base during the construction process. Morrison-Knudsen was involved in some of N America's largest construction projects, including the Hoover Dam, San Francisco Bay Bridge, Trans-Alaska Pipeline and Kennedy Space Center. In 1996 it was acquired by Washington Group International, which in turn became a division of San Francisco's URS Corp in 2007.

Mocino Point (50°18'00" 127°50'00") N entrance to Klaskino Inlet, Brooks Bay, just SE of Quatsino Sd, NW side of Vancouver I). After Spanish scientist José Mariano Mociño, an early visitor to Nootka Sd, whose surname is more commonly spelled Moziño. *See* Mozino Point.

Modeets Islands (53°36'00" 132°28'00") In Juskatla Inlet, S of Masset Inlet, Graham I, QCI). According to writer and adventurer Newton Chittenden, Modeets was an important and influential Haida shaman. Chittenden met the "medicine man" in 1884 at the Maude I village of New Gold Hbr and was shown his collection of charms, wands and rattles, some of which the visitor purchased. The shaman's hair, never cut or combed since he entered the profession, was tied up in a knot on the back of his head and reminded Chittenden of "a large hornet's nest." Modeets, wrote Chittenden, "put on a portion of his fantastic regalia, and executed a medicine dance. The doctor than dressed me in his wildest and most barbaric costume, when *by special request* I imitated his performance, in a manner which 'brought down the house.'" Named by the hydrographic service in 1953.

Moffatt Islands (54°27'00" 130°44'00") E of the Dundas Is, NW of Prince Rupert). Hamilton Moffatt (1832–94) joined the HBC in London in 1849 and came out to Victoria as an apprentice clerk aboard the barque *Cowlitz*, arriving in 1850. Coastal historian John Walbran states that he was born on the Isle of Wight and educated in Ireland; his HBC service record lists his home parish as Stromness in the Orkney Is. Moffatt married Lucy McNeill (1834–1914), second daughter of HBC chief factor William McNeill (*see* McNeill Bay), at Victoria in 1856. He was posted to Ft Rupert on northern Vancouver I, 1851–59, during which time he made a very early journey across Vancouver I, from the Nimpkish R to Nootka Sd and return, in 1852. Moffatt was posted to Ft Simpson, 1859–62, then became chief trader at Ft Rupert until 1864, Ft Simpson 1864–66, Ft Kamloops 1866–69, Ft Babine 1869–70 and Ft St James 1870–72. He worked for the federal Dept of Indian Affairs, 1873–93, based at Victoria, mostly as assistant to superintendent Israel Powell. The nearby Lucy Is (qv) are named after his wife. *W*

Mohun Shoal (52°15'00" 128°30'00") NW of the Bardswell Group, Milbanke Sd, NW of Bella Bella). Emmaline Jane

Tod (1835–1928) was the daughter of HBC fur trader John Tod (*see* Tod Inlet) through his marriage to Eliza Waugh (c 1807–57). She was born at Ft Alexander on Lk Winnipeg. Her mother was committed to a psychiatric institution in Britain after suffering a breakdown, and Emmaline (often written Emmeline) was raised by relatives in Montreal. In 1856 she joined her father at Ft Victoria but soon married William Henry Newton (1833–1875), who had arrived in BC in 1851 as an assistant to Edward Langford, manager of Colwood, one of the Victoria-area farms established by the Puget's Sd Agricultural Co. (Her wedding ring is said to have been forged by an HBC blacksmith from a US $2.50 gold piece.) Newton later worked as an HBC clerk, and Emmaline moved with him to Ft Langley, where he was in charge, 1859–64. After his death (from "congestion of the brain"), Emmaline married Edward Mohun (1838–1912), a British land surveyor and civil engineer, in 1878 and lived at Victoria. John Tod had a poor opinion of his daughter, writing that "her ardent and dominant spirit, joined to selfish ambition, will never allow her to rest satisfied with anything less than the lion's share of this world's goods." Nearby Emmaline Bank is also named after her. Mohun Ck and Mohun Lk on Vancouver I are probably named for her husband, who did survey work in the area. He came to Victoria in 1863, worked for the CPR in the early 1870s, searching for railway routes through the Rocky Mtns, and was later employed by BC's Dept of Lands and Works.

Molesworth Point (50°31'00" 125°48'00") N side of Topaze Hbr, E of Jackson Bay, N of Hardwicke I and Johnstone Str). After RN officer Molesworth Greene Jackson, 1st lt of HMS *Topaze*, who served on the Pacific Station, 1859–63. *See* Jackson Bay.

Mollison Point (53°17'00" 129°29'00") Entrance to Tuwartz Inlet, S end of Pitt I). Named in 1944 after Charles Mollison, who worked aboard the W coast survey vessel *William J Stewart* in the early 1940s and whose occupation is listed at the BC Geographical Names Office as "driver."

Monarch Head (48°46'00" 123°06'00") E of Bruce Bight, S side of Saturna I, Gulf Is). Named by RN surveyor Capt George Richards about 1858 after HMS *Monarch*, which served on the Pacific Station, 1854–57, as the flagship of Rear Adm Henry Bruce. The 84-gun, 2,073-tonne line-of-battle sailing ship was built at Chatham in 1832 and modelled on the French vessel *Canopus*. While in PNW waters it was under the command of Capt George Patey. The *Monarch* was decommissioned in 1866.

Monckton Inlet (53°19'00" 129°38'00") W side of Pitt I), **Monckton Point** (53°19'00" 129°39'00") N side of Monckton Inlet). Philip Marmaduke Monckton (1892–1965) was commissioned as a BC land surveyor in 1913 and worked extensively in coastal and northern BC for the provincial Dept of Lands. He was born and raised in S Africa and educated in England, coming to BC with his parents in 1908. After serving overseas during WWI as a capt in the Royal Welsh Fusiliers, Monckton participated in Alfred Wright's 1921 survey of the W coast of Pitt I aboard the *Ala*. He also made an ambitious winter surveying expedition from Telegraph Ck to Atlin in 1930. Mt Monckton (1,183 m), S of the Liard R near Lower Post, is named for him, as he was the first occupant of the triangulation station there while conducting surveys on the BC-Yukon-NWT boundary in 1939. During WWII he performed surveying and engineering duties for the RCAF in BC and Que. Monckton owned mineral claims on Vancouver I in the Zeballos R drainage, where Monckton Ck also commemorates him. He retired in 1957. Both Philip and his wife Lavender (1895–1987) died at Vancouver.

Money Maker Reef (48°50'37" 123°27'25" Entrance to Ganges Hbr, Saltspring I, Gulf Is), **Money Makers Rock** (48°51'24" 123°29'54" Head of Ganges Hbr). Named in 1982, after the fact that boat owners damage their vessels regularly at these sites, keeping local repair yards in the money.

Monk Bay (52°40'00" 128°52'00" Head of Laredo Sd, S end of Princess Royal I). Minnie Young (1865–1943) was born at London, England, and came to Victoria with her parents in 1870. She married Edward John Monk (1865–1941) at Victoria in 1887. He was a teamster, also from England, who arrived in Canada in 1873. The Monks participated in the Victoria old-timers' reunion of 1924 (*see* Adams Bay). Monk Bay was named in 1927.

Monkey Beach (53°27'31" 128°56'24" Just N of Riordan Point, E side of Boxer Reach, between Princess Royal I and Hawkesbury I, SW of Kitimat). This established local name was adopted in 2007. Haisla First Nation cultural narratives identify the area as home to the sasquatch (known to the Haisla as *bekwis* or *b'gwus*). According to anthropologist Jay Powell, a consultant to the Haisla, the tidal flats, highly valued for shellfish gathering, are called Awamusdis, while the camping zone at the N end of the beach is called Q'waq'waksiyas. This Kitamaat region provides the title—and the setting—for Haisla author Eden Robinson's highly praised 2000 novel *Monkey Beach*.

Monks Islet (49°14'00" 126°01'00" W end of Calmus Passage, N of Vargas I, Clayoquot Sd, W side of Vancouver I). Named in 1934 for Harold Monks (1893–1974), who came to Clayoquot Sd from England in 1914, lured by letters he had exchanged with a distant relative, and pre-empted land on the NW side of Vargas I. He built a shack, worked on the corduroy road across the island and also found employment on the seine boats belonging to the Clayoquot Sd Canning Co. Monks went overseas in the latter years of WWI, serving as a gunner and signaller with Canadian forces in France and Belgium. Even though he received a Crown grant for his Vargas property when he returned in 1919, he chose instead to live at Tofino and continued to work for the cannery, eventually becoming skipper of the seiner *Kennfalls*. Monks married teacher Catherine Hacking in 1934, and the couple took over the Imperial Oil agency at Tofino. Harold also worked at the lifeboat station, while Katie was a driving force behind the establishment of a new Tofino hospital. The family homesite at Grice Point is known locally as Monks Bluff.

Montagu Channel (49°32'00" 123°16'00" E side of Howe Sd, between Anvil I and the mainland, N of Vancouver), **Montagu Point** (50°38'00" 126°12'00" S side of Knight Inlet, opposite Gilford I). The 74-gun HMS *Montagu*, built at Chatham in 1779, was part of the English Channel fleet under Adm Lord Howe that defeated the French in the 1794 battle known as the Glorious First of June. Its cdr, who was killed in the action, was Capt James Montagu (1752–94), who had apparently requested this ship because it had been named after one of his ancestors. He had previously served on the N America station and had then commanded the frigates *Medea*, in the English Channel, and *Juno*, in the E Indies. Montagu Channel was named about 1859 by RN surveyor Capt George Richards after both the ship and the man. Montagu Point, however, commemorates the ship only, as it was named in association with Knight Inlet (qv). Capt John Knight commanded the *Montagu* in 1797 during the mutiny of the Channel fleet, in which his vessel was commandeered by its seamen and the ship's surgeon tarred and feathered. Knight later played a notable role with the *Montagu* at the Battle of Camperdown. Montagu Point was formerly known as Long Point but was renamed to avoid duplication in 1949. *W*

The busy Galiano Island anchorage of Montague Harbour. *John Lund*

Montague Harbour (48°53'00" 123°24'00" SW side of Galiano I, Gulf Is). This name appears on an 1860 chart surveyed by Capt George Richards and likely refers to an RN officer or vessel. There have been a large number of ships with the name *Montagu* or *Montague* in the RN, however, and dozens of officers, including several admirals and other distinguished figures (*see* Montagu Channel). The specific source of the name is uncertain. A 97-ha area around the harbour became BC's first provincial marine park in 1959. It is still one of the province's most popular boating destinations. The site, with its white shell beach and numerous middens, has a history of First Nation occupation that dates back more than 3,000 years. This feature was apparently also known in the old days as Stockade Hbr.

Montgomery Point (50°28'00" 128°01'00" E entrance to Forward Inlet, N side of Quatsino Sd, NW end of Vancouver I). Named in 1927 after Robert Elinton Montgomery, who acquired a Crown grant of land in the vicinity in 1908. This shadowy figure came to Quatsino in 1902, according to local historian Gwen Hansen, and bought land at Bergh Cove. He built a large home and lived there alone for a short time, then rented the house out and moved to Victoria. In 1907 the Victoria *Colonist* reported that a Col R E Montgomery—"a capitalist interested in several properties ... accompanied by a party of visitors from Texas"—was travelling the W coast of Vancouver I on the *Tees* and "visiting the Sydney Inlet mines." In 1908, R E Montgomery of Ft Worth, Texas, was said to be interested in Ben Leeson's clam cannery at Winter Hbr. Montgomery was also rumoured to be a former poker partner and confederate of the notorious US Civil War outlaw William Quantrill, whom some suspect of living in the Quatsino Sd area in the early 1900s under the name John Sharp. In 1929, Montgomery (or his estate, as he appears to have died in the mid-1920s) donated land for the new Quatsino school. Montgomery Ck flows into Forward Inlet near Montgomery Point.

Montserrat Bay (52°06'00" 130°59'00" SW of the Rainy Is, off NE side of Kunghit I, QCI). The ore carrier *Montserrat*, under Capt David Blackburn, foundered off the entrance to Juan de Fuca Str during the great gale of Dec 1894 while attempting to assist the coal freighter *Keeweenah*. The stoutly built, 68-m vessel, constructed in England in 1881 for the California copper trade, had been chartered by Blackburn as a coal freighter. Many vessels were destroyed in this storm, and wreckage was spread up and down the BC coast. Pieces from the *Keeweenah* and *Montserrat* were found in Rose Inlet at the S end of Moresby I in May 1895. All hands on both ships were lost. Blackburn had a reputation for overloading his vessels and for taking weather-related risks that other capts would not consider. *D*

Moody Banks (52°23'00" 128°55'00" Laredo Sd, SE of Aristazabal I, NW of Bella Bella), **Port Moody** (49°18'00" 122°52'00" SE extension of Burrard Inlet, E of Vancouver). Col Richard Clement Moody (1813–87) was cdr of the Columbia detachment of Royal Engineers, which served in BC 1858–63. He was born in Barbados and joined the engineers in 1830 after graduating from the Royal Military Academy at Woolwich. After serving in Ireland and the W Indies, he went to the Falkland Is, where he was lt gov and then gov, 1841–49. In 1858, Moody arrived at Victoria with a contingent of men to take up appointments as lt gov of BC and chief commissioner of lands and works. His wife, Mary Susannah (née Hawks), and four children accompanied him. He visited Ft Langley, travelled to Yale to suppress a miners' uprising and chose New Westminster as the new colony's first capital. His mandate was to maintain law and order, lay out townsites, build roads and bridges, and report on the colony's resources, and he set about these tasks in a slow, often impractical manner that irritated Gov James Douglas, who considered Moody's plans extravagant for a colony "not yet disassociated from the primeval forest." Moody purchased much land in BC and turned one piece of property near New Westminster into a model farm named Mayfield. In 1863, however, along with his offficers (but unlike the majority of his men), he chose to return to England. In 1866, newly promoted to maj gen, he retired to Lyme Regis. Capt George Richards of the survey vessel *Plumper* named Port Moody (the body of water) in 1860. The land adjacent was chosen by the Canadian government as the original terminus of the CPR, and the first train from Montreal arrived there in 1886. The CPR then shifted the end of its track to Vancouver, which slowed growth considerably at Port Moody. A sawmill and an oil refinery were the main industries at first, and while the city developed primarily as a residential suburb of Vancouver, it still has an active port and several important industrial facilities. *E W*

Moody Point (53°32'00" 128°59'00" N end of Ursula Channel, N of Princess Royal I, S of Kitimat). Named about 1875 by members of a CPR land survey team searching for a suitable terminus for the transcontinental railroad. Sub-Lt Thomas B Moody served aboard HMS *Boxer*, under Lt Cdr William Collins, 1871–75. The RN gun vessel conducted a marine survey of N coast inlets for the same purpose while it was stationed on the BC coast. According to former UBC anthropologist Jay Powell, the area in the vicinity of the point is known by Haisla First Nation members as Owagewa.

Moodyville. *See* N Vancouver.

Moolock Cove (53°27'00" 129°49'00" Head of Mink Trap Bay, W side of Pitt I). Named in 1944 after HMCS *Moolock* (*FY 16*), one of six naval patrol boats built at Victoria about 1941 for BC's Fishermen Reserve Service fleet in WWII. The 26-m vessel was dispatched to Estevan Point in 1942 to investigate the alleged shelling of the lighthouse station there by a Japanese submarine. Lt Donald Peck was in command for several years and apparently towed the *Pender*, a houseboat used by the hydrographic service,

The Royal Engineers

Some of BC's most under-appreciated pioneers were the Royal Engineers, who came from England in 1858 and '59 at the chaotic height of the Fraser River gold rush. These "sappers," as they were called, were skilled tradesmen: carpenters, bricklayers, surveyors, stonemasons, blacksmiths, printers—the cream of the British Army, in fact. They kept the peace; surveyed townsites; constructed roads, bridges and public buildings; and marked the boundary between BC and the United States along the 49th parallel. In 1863, when their main detachment was disbanded, the majority of the men chose to stay in the province and take up free 60-hectare grants of land. They were exactly the kind of settlers that BC needed at the time: industrious, cheerful, useful and willing to endure primitive conditions. Many have coastal places named for them.

Engineer Thomas Argyle served as lighthouse keeper at Race Rocks in the 1870s and '80s and supposedly found a sunken treasure there while diving for seafood in the area's dangerous waters. An islet in nearby Becher Bay is named after him. *BC Archives F-04749*

A few names are well known. Port Moody, for instance, recalls the leader of the engineers, Col Richard Moody, the first lieutenant-governor of the colony of British Columbia. Sapperton, a New Westminster suburb, was the original site of their main camp. Sapper John Linn settled at the mouth of a North Vancouver creek; his name, misspelled Lynn, is now attached to numerous North Shore features. Cpl Peter Leech discovered gold on southern Vancouver Island and had a once-thriving mining community, Leechtown, named for him. The unfortunate Cpl James Duffy, who froze to death on the trail between Harrison Lake and Lillooet, is commemorated by the Duffey Lake route over the Coast Mountains. The surname of another Royal Engineer was made famous by one of his offspring; sapper John Maclure's son Samuel, the first white child born at New Westminster, became one of the province's pre-eminent architects. But most of the engineers have long been forgotten.

About 225 of these unsung heroes served here, many accompanied by their families. They were, by all accounts, an outstanding body of men. The sappers defused a potential armed uprising by American miners near Yale. They built much of the Cariboo Wagon Road—a route now followed by the Trans-Canada Highway—blasting it out of the sheer walls of the Fraser Canyon. Their cultural contributions were numerous. The sappers' band, with many talented musicians, played at all sorts of functions. Royal Engineers built the BC mainland's first church and first theatre, designed its first school, established a government printing office and an early weather observatory (run by Peter Leech), sketched the colony's coat of arms and its postage stamps, and inaugurated its first building society, social club, hospital and library.

It was the rank and file who remained in the province. The better-paid officers, whose career expectations would be dashed if they stayed, went home in 1863. But men like Thomas Argyle, the detachment armourer, could expect to better their lot in BC. Argyle took a grant of land at Metchosin, near Victoria, sired a large family and spent 20 years as lighthouse keeper at Race Rocks. Richard Bridgman, William Deas and James Ellard ended up running hotels and roadhouses. A few fell on hard times: Crimean War veteran Jock McMurphy, with more medals than anyone in his detachment, had to work as a labourer and government clerk. Seventeen former sappers served as police constables. One was John Jane, who later became a well-established storekeeper near Kamloops and a justice of the peace. Jane, William McColl, George Turner, John Maclure and others set themselves up as surveyors. Some sappers, like Lewis Bonson, turned to farming. Even Daniel Alman, who disgraced the detachment by deserting, left his name on a landscape feature.

Of the 130 or more engineers known to have stayed in the province after 1863, only 25 were still alive in 1900, and only 12 made it to a 1909 luncheon held in their honour by William Keary, mayor of New Westminster and son of former sapper James Keary (killed in an accident in 1871). Thomas Argyle died in 1919, aged 80. Philip Jackman, last of the sappers, died in 1927. He helped lay out the streets of New Westminster, lost a toe working on the Dewdney Trail, crushed his hand building another trail, worked as a policeman, storekeeper, surveyor and fisheries warden, was reeve of Langley for three years and had 21 grandchildren. A provincial park and railway station in the Rocky Mountains are named for him.

from this cove in 1943. The *Moolock* was sold in 1946, converted to a fishing seiner and renamed the *Western Girl*. In Chinook jargon, the pidgin language used on the W coast by First Nation groups and early traders and settlers, *moolock* (or *moolack*) was the word for elk.

Moore Channel (52°57'00" 132°16'00" S of Hibben I, Kuper Inlet, NW side of Moresby I, QCI). George Moore (d 1890) was the master of HMS *Thetis*, under Capt Augustus Kuper, and served on the Pacific Station, 1851–53. He made a survey of this channel in 1852, the year the *Thetis* was sent to the region. Gold had recently been discovered at nearby Mitchell Inlet, and Vancouver I gov James Douglas wanted a local naval presence to ensure British control of the area (which was known, unofficially, as Gold Hbr at the time). Moore reached the rank of cdr, retired, in 1870. Moore Hill on Thetis I in the Gulf Is is also named for him. *W*

Moore Head (52°09'00" 131°03'00" S side of E entrance to Houston Stewart Channel, N side of Kunghit I, QCI). Named in 1853 by Cdr James Prevost of HMS *Virago*, after his 2nd lt, Lewis James Moore, who assisted with the survey that year of Houston Stewart Channel. Moore commanded the paddle sloop *Argus* during the 1862 bombardment of Kagoshima, Japan, and was promoted to capt in 1863. In 1868, while capt of HMS *Eclipse*, he was reprimanded "for suffering the ship to ground off Heligoland ... to the hazard of the same ship." From 1869 to 1873 he was capt of HMS *Barrosa* and part of Rear Adm Geoffrey Hornby's flying squadron, which visited Pacific ports (including Esquimalt) in 1869–70. A mineral claim was registered at Moore Head in 1913 by J Uniaka, who did some development work on the property, then later abandoned it.

Moore Islands (52°40'00" 129°25'00" Off NW side of Aristazabal I, Hecate Str). Capt J J Moore worked for the Canadian Hydrographic Service from 1915 until at least 1944 (though he served in the RCN for several years during WWI). He was sailing master aboard the survey vessels *Lillooet* (1922–32) and *William J Stewart* (1932–44). The establishment of a Fishermen Reserve Service on the BC coast during WWII is said to have been his original idea. The Moore Is were named for him in 1926.

Moore Point (54°15'00" 130°25'00" SW side of Digby I, just W of Prince Rupert). Named in 1907 after John Wheeler Moore (1866–1946), a native of N Carolina and locating engineer for the GTP at the time this area was first surveyed in the early 1900s. He was known for building railroads through mountains and highways through swamps. Much of his N Carolina hwy work was constructed on pilings, which gave a "wavy ride" when they settled but were still in use a century later. Moore was also noted for his financial instability. "On one day he would be driving a Rolls Royce," according to his nephew

John R Moore, "and on the next he would be bankrupt again." Moore and his wife Elizabeth (*see* Elizabeth Point) lived in a "tent-house" on Prince Rupert's Centre St, 1906–8, after which Moore, who had resigned from the GTP in 1907, returned to N Carolina. The Prince Rupert *Empire* reported that Elizabeth was "the first lady to make her home in Prince Rupert."

Moore Rock (50°54'00" 127°17'00" S of Bradley Lagoon, Blunden Hbr, N side of Queen Charlotte Str, NE of Port Hardy). F Moore was an able seaman aboard the RN survey vessel *Egeria*, which served on the BC coast 1898–1910. The name was adopted in 1917.

Moos Islet (49°58'00" 127°19'00" One of the Barrier Is, SW of Union I, Kyuquot Sd, NW side of Vancouver I). Capt Nils Moos (b 1851) was born in Denmark and became a seaman as a boy, then immigrated to the PNW about 1869 and worked initially on the *Surprise*, one of the first sealers at Victoria. His personal name can also be found spelled Nels, Niels and Neils. He spent 20 years on the sealing schooners, serving as master or mate of the *Alert*, *Favorite*, *Dolphin*, *Thornton*, *Kate* and *Onward* before becoming skipper of the Victoria pilot boat. There is an 1883 marriage record at Victoria for Neils Moos and Johana Thornberg.

Mooyah Bay (49°38'00" 126°27'00" SW side of Muchalat Inlet, SE of Anderson Point, Nootka Sd, W side of Vancouver I). Named in 1934 after the Nuu-chah-nulth First Nation reserve at the head of the bay, once the site of a winter village of the Muchalaht people. A large logging camp has been located on the bay for many years. The Mooyah R enters the ocean here.

Morehouse Bay (52°16'00" 128°06'00" W side of Chatfield I, N of Bella Bella), **Morehouse Rock** (52°46'00" 129°06'00" Off NE side of Aristazabal I, Laredo Channel). Capt Walter Scott Morehouse (1872–1934), born in NS, learned to sail on the E coast before coming to Victoria and working in the sealing industry. He joined the Boscowitz Steamship Co and became skipper of the *Venture*. When Union Steamship bought out Boscowitz in 1911, he came over to the new company but soon transferred to the recently established GTP Coast Steamship Co (later Canadian National Steamships), where he was master of the *Prince John*, *Prince Albert* and, eventually, the *Prince George*, one of the GTP flagships. Morehouse (whose name is often seen misspelled Moorhouse) was capt of the *Prince John* in 1920 when it was hit in a blinding snowstorm by the *Prince Albert*, under Capt H L Robertson, near Skidegate Inlet. Between them, the skippers managed to beach the *John* in shallow water, where it was later salvaged. All aboard were saved. A court of inquiry held both capts blameless and commended them for their calm handling of the accident. A former president of the Canadian Merchant Service

Moresby Island

Guild, Morehouse was appointed a pilot at Vancouver in 1924. He died of a heart attack at Fraser Mills while waiting to guide a British freighter down the Fraser R at daybreak. Presumably **Morehouse Passage** (51°51'00" 127°53'00" S entrance to Namu Hbr, E side of Fitz Hugh Sd, SE of Bella Bella) is named for him as well.

Moresby Island (48°43'00" 123°19'00" W side of Swanson Channel, SE of Saltspring I, Gulf Is), **Moresby Island** (52°25'00" 131°30'00" S of Graham I, QCI), **Moresby Passage** (48°43'00" 123°21'00" W of Moresby I, Gulf Is). Rear Adm Fairfax Moresby (1786–1877) was cdr-in-chief of the Pacific Station, 1850–53, with HMS *Portland* as his flagship. He entered the RN in 1799 and was promoted to capt in 1814. Moresby spent a number of years on the African coast, in command of the frigate *Menai*, doing survey work and vigorously suppressing the slave trade. He was made a rear adm in 1849, knighted in 1855 and achieved the highest rank in the RN, adm of the fleet, in 1870. The northern Moresby—BC's third-largest island (2,787 sq km) after Vancouver I and Graham I—was

Looking out at Moresby Island in the Gulf Islands. *Kevin Oke*

not to be used for navigation

Moresby Island, Queen Charlotte Islands. *Reproduced with the permission of the Canadian Hydrographic Service*

named in 1853 by Cdr James Prevost of HMS *Virago*, who happened to be Moresby's son-in-law. This island became the focal point of a bitter conservation battle from 1974 until 1987, when it was largely protected as Gwaii Haanas National Park Reserve, co-managed by the Haida people. The other two features were named in 1858, when Moresby was a vice adm, by surveyor Capt George Richards. The southern Moresby I (6.5 sq km), settled since 1863, supported a dairy farm in the 1910s; its owners have included a German nobleman, BC lt gov Thomas Paterson, and a retired merchant from China named Horatio Robertson. This eccentric built a fancy home on Moresby and was known for mistreating his Chinese employees, who were sometimes seen pulling him through the streets of Victoria in a rickshaw. Mt Moresby, the highest point on the larger Moresby I (1,148 m), is also named for the adm, as is Point Fairfax in the Gulf Is, which may, in addition, be named after his eldest son, Lt Fairfax Moresby (*see* Fairfax I). A campsite and boat launch at the head of Gillatt Arm, Cumshewa Inlet—once the site of a Rayonier logging camp, since moved S to Sewell Inlet—is known as Moresby Camp. *E W*

Moresby Islets (52°58'00" 132°21'00" W of Hibben I, Englefield Bay, NW side of Moresby I, QCI). John Moresby (d 1922) was the third son of Adm Sir Fairfax Moresby (*see* Moresby I). He also served on the Pacific Station, as a gunnery lt aboard HMS *Thetis*, 1851–53, under Capt Augustus Kuper. Moresby spent time on the China Station, participating in the 1863 bombardment of Simonoseki, Japan, as cdr of HMS *Argus*. In 1873, by now capt of HMS *Basilisk*, he was the first to explore and chart the Port Moresby area of Papua New Guinea, which is named for his father. Moresby was promoted to rear adm in 1881 and adm, retired, in 1893. He was appointed the naval assessor to the British board of trade in 1890. Nearby Moresby Lk is also named for him; apparently he climbed the hillside at the head of Mitchell Inlet in 1852, accompanied by midshipman Nowell Salmon, and explored the area by foot. Named by Capt Kuper in 1852. *W*

Morey Channel (49°10'50" 123°08'44" Between Lulu I and the SE side of Sea I, Middle Arm, mouth of the Fraser R), **Morey Rock** (52°25'00" 129°19'00" S of the Harvey Is, W of Aristazabal I). Sgt Jonathan Morey (1824–84) was a member of the Columbia detachment of Royal Engineers, which served in BC 1858–63. He and his pregnant wife travelled to the PNW on the *Thames City* with their children and the main contingent of men; Frances Morey (1821–1901, née Cobbs) gave birth to a daughter on the long journey to Esquimalt. The family stayed in BC when the detachment was disbanded, and Morey became a colonial police constable. In 1871 he was appointed New Westminster's first policeman and filled this position until 1878, after which he may have moved to Hope, where he apparently did "contracting." He died at New Westminster.

His son, Henry Morey (1862–1936), ran a book and stationery business at New Westminster and was a well-known local choirmaster and organist. Morey Channel is the section of the Middle Arm (qv) that runs between what used to be Dinsmore I (now filled in and part of Sea I) and Lulu I. The vestiges of Dinsmore I—named for John Dinsmore (1847–1924), who homesteaded there in 1885, and formerly known as Brough's I, after John Brough, the first settler (in 1869)—are approximately between the Dinsmore Bridge and Burkeville.

Morfee Island (49°13'00" 125°57'00" Off NE side of Vargas I, N of Tofino, Clayoquot Sd, W side of Vancouver I). In 1930, RCAF flight lt Arthur Laurence "Laurie" Morfee (d 1986) undertook the first W coast air photo missions for the Canadian Hydrographic Service. He was stationed at the Jericho seaplane base on several occasions (1925–26, 1928–29, 1932) in his early career. Morfee, born at London, England, went on to become a distinguished senior officer. In WWII he commanded several vital training facilities, then served as air officer commanding Nfld and cdr-in-chief of the Eastern Air Command. He was awarded the CBE, CB and US Legion of Merit, and retired to NS in 1948 with the rank of air vice-marshal. Morfee Ck, Morfee Lks and Mt Morfee near Williston Lk are also named for him. Morfee I was named by regional hydrographer Henri Parizeau in 1934.

Morgan Point (53°57'00" 133°08'00" NE entrance to Peril Bay, W side of Graham I, QCI). Named in 1907 by Capt Frederick Learmonth of HMS *Egeria* while making a survey of the N and W coasts of Graham I. Morgan was a seaman who fell down a cliff while on duty and suffered a painful injury.

Morgan Rock (52°43'00" 131°48'00" Off Klunkwoi Bay, Darwin Sd, off E side of Moresby I, QCI). Elbert Monfort Morgan (b 1861 in Ohio) and his sons, Henry and Harry, came to the QCI in 1907 from Nelson. They prospected in the Jedway area, then moved N and found signs of copper just W of Klunkwoi Bay. The Morgans settled at the new town of Lockeport and bought a recently opened general store, which Elbert's married daughter Noralee operated with her husband, Ernie Marshall. Elbert and his two sons continued prospecting and trying, unsuccessfully, to develop a profitable mine. The family stayed in the vicinity until 1912, with Elbert bringing a new bride, Sarah Fenelon, to Lockeport that year. The Morgans were associated with many of the area's major mineral claims, including the Apex, Montana and Copper Belle. Their store was later sold to another well-known but unrelated Morgan: William Morgan. According to QCI historian Kathleen Dalzell, William was somewhat casual as a storekeeper. His prices were based not on costs but on guesses or whims, though he nevertheless managed somehow to survive. It is not certain which Morgan this feature is named after. *D*

Morgan Shoal (50°47'00" 127°15'00" NW of Malcolm I, E of Hardy Bay, Queen Charlotte Str). Private Lawrence Herwood Morgan, of the Royal Canadian Army Service Corps, was killed in action on Apr 1, 1945, aged 20. A native of Princeton, BC, he is buried at Groesbeek Canadian War Cemetery in the Netherlands. The name was adopted in 1951.

Moriarty Point (50°16'00" 125°25'00" W side of Discovery Passage, S of Elk Bay, E side of Vancouver I). William Moriarty (1832–86) was 1st lt aboard the RN survey ship *Plumper* and served on the Pacific Station, under Capt George Richards, 1857–61. HMS *Hecate*, a larger, better survey vessel, was brought out to the PNW for Richards in 1861, under Cdr Anthony Hoskins. When Hoskins returned to England with the *Plumper*, Moriarty went back as well. In 1860 he had married Mary Annie Reid (d 1873), a daughter of Victoria resident and former HBC master mariner James Murray Reid (*see* Reid I). Moriarty was promoted to cdr in 1866, reached the rank of capt, retired, in 1881 and died in Ireland. This feature was formerly known as Otter Point, after the HBC steamship *Otter*, but was renamed by Richards after his former deputy in 1864. Moriarty Ck, Moriarty Lk and Mt Moriarty, all W of Nanaimo, are also named for him.

Morison Passage (52°44'00" 129°19'00" Entrance to Borrowman Bay, NW side of Aristazabal I). Named in 1926 for Charles Frederic Morison (1844–1933), who was born at London, England, and arrived at New Westminster in 1862. He worked at first on the Cariboo Rd and at the Moodyville sawmill, and in 1866 was employed by the Collins Overland Telegraph Co. Morison then became a merchant and trader and was later an HBC clerk at Port Simpson, where he helped establish the Georgetown sawmill on nearby Big Bay and married Odille Dubois (1856–1933), a local resident, in 1872. Odille, half Tsimshian, half French Canadian, was also a well-known figure on the N coast—a linguist, nurse, ethnographer and noted singer. She and Charles assisted anthropologist Franz Boas gather Tsimshian artifacts for Chicago's Field Museum, and Odille translated many Tsimshian legends into English (some of which were published under her name) as well as Anglican texts into Tsimshian. The Morisons lost three of their children to a diphtheria epidemic in 1879. They also lived at Hazelton and Port Essington, where Charles worked as a manager for Robert Cunningham's numerous business interests, before settling permanently at Metlakatla.

Morpheus Island (49°09'00" 125°53'00" NE entrance to Browning Passage, just E of Tofino, Clayoquot Sd, W side of Vancouver I). This island served as Tofino's first cemetery, 1900–1950, and before that it may have been a Tla-o-qui-aht First Nation burial ground. Many of Tofino's early settlers were buried there until a graveyard was selected

closer to Tofino in the late 1940s. The name Morpheus was apparently chosen during a 1914 survey of the area to avoid duplication with the numerous other Burial, Cemetery or Graveyard islands on the BC coast. The local people, incidentally, refer to this feature as Cemetery I. Morpheus, of course, is the Greek god of dreams.

Morris Bay (52°21'00" 128°26'00" NW side of Lady Douglas I, Milbanke Sd, NW of Bella Bella). Named in 1929 after Victoria trader and businessman Morris Moss. *See* Moss Passage.

Morrison Point (53°40'00" 130°06'00" E side of McCauley I, Petrel Channel, opposite NW Pitt I). RCAF flight lt Roy Gordon Morrison, born at Victoria in 1914 but a resident of Vancouver, was killed in action on July 14, 1943. Only three months earlier he had been awarded the DFC for acts of heroism aboard a damaged Halifax heavy bomber while attacking Stettin, Germany (now Szczecin, Poland), with No 35 (RAF) Squadron. The plane, its rudder jammed and navigation equipment destroyed, had caught fire, but its determined crew members were able to regain control and, with Morrison's skills as a navigator, fly it back to England. A member of RCAF No 405 Squadron at the time of his death, he is buried at Jonkerbos War Cemetery in the Netherlands. Morrison Point was named in 1950.

Morris Rocks (50°18'00" 127°52'00" NW of Heater Point, Klaskino Inlet, SE of Quatsino Sd, NW side of Vancouver I). John Morris (b 1847), a native of Wales, first set off to sea at the age of 19. He immigrated to Victoria and joined the pelagic sealing fleet, working first as master of the *Black Diamond* (in 1881) and later serving as capt of the *Onward* and *Alfred Adams*. He also worked out of Seattle on the schooner *Seventy-Six*.

Morrow Island (50°43'00" 126°41'00" E end of Sunday Hbr, S of Eden I, Broughton Archipelago, NE end of Queen Charlotte Str). RCNVR lt David James Morrow, from Vancouver, was killed in action on Nov 24, 1944, aged 28, while serving aboard HMCS *Shawinigan*. This *Flower*-class corvette worked mainly as an escort on N Atlantic convoy runs, 1941–44. It was torpedoed by a U-boat while on anti-submarine patrol off S Nfld and sank with the loss of all 91 crew members. Morrow is commemorated on the Halifax Memorial. The island was named in 1957.

Morrow Island (51°37'40" 127°45'45" N side of Fish Egg Inlet, between Rivers Inlet and Fitz Hugh Sd). Named in 1992 for RCAF flying officer Hugh Francis Morrow, who was killed in action on June 17, 1944, aged 22, on a bombing raid over the Netherlands. Born and raised in Vancouver, Morrow was serving with RCAF No 432 Squadron, which operated Handley Page Halifax Mk III heavy bombers for most of 1944. He is buried at Gorssel General Cemetery in the Netherlands.

Morse Basin (54°17'15" 130°14'30" E side of Kaien I, Prince Rupert), **Mount Morse** (54°23'03" 130°18'20" Tsimpsean Peninsula, W of Tuck Inlet, N of Prince Rupert). Frank Watrous Morse was vice-president and gen manager of the GTP during the period that the railway line was constructed from Winnipeg to Edmonton and across northern BC to Prince Rupert. He eventually resigned from the company, to be replaced by Edson Chamberlain, who became GTP president in 1912. Morse Basin was named in 1909, Mt Morse in 1908. Prince Rupert's Morse Ck is also named for him, as is the town of Watrous, Sask.

Mortimer Spit (48°46'00" 123°15'00" NW end of S Pender I, Gulf Is). This name was adopted in 1969 after John Mortimer (1842–1921), from Scotland, who came to Canada in 1878 with his English wife, Nanny Opil (1841–1904). He was a stonecutter by trade and settled in Victoria, where he operated a stone yard and "marble works" from the early 1880s, initially with a partner named Reid. One of his quarries was near the isthmus between N and S Pender Is, which in those days were still connected (another quarry, for marble, was on Nootka Sd). Mortimer cut many of the historic gravestones for Victoria's pioneer residents, including that of Gov James Douglas. His son, Arthur John Mortimer (1878–1926), later joined him in the business.

Moser Point (49°09'03" 125°57'40" SE point of Vargas I, Clayoquot Sd, W side of Vancouver I). Charles Moser (b 1874) was a Benedictine missionary, better known on the W coast of Vancouver I as Fr Charles. He was born in Switzerland and ordained in 1898, then came out to Mt Angel Abbey near Portland, Oregon, which sent a number of Benedictine priests to BC. His first appointment was in 1900 to the First Nation mission at Opitsat in Clayoquot Sd. In 1910 Fr Charles took over Augustin Brabant's pioneer mission at Hesquiat. He was principal of the Christie residential school at Kakawis, 1919–22, and was in charge of all northern W coast Roman Catholic missions from 1919 to 1930. Moser was recalled to Mt Angel in 1930 and made sub-prior. In 1966, at the age of 92, he was chaplain at St Mary's Hospital in Astoria. His *Reminiscences of the West Coast of Vancouver Island* were published in 1926, along with work by fellow missionaries Brabant, John Lemmens and Peter Nicolaye. Nearby Father Charles Channel and Father Charles Rk are also named for him.

Moses Point (48°41'00" 123°29'00" N entrance to Deep Cove, NW end of Saanich Peninsula, NW of Sidney and Victoria). Named after Daniel David Moses (1832–1910), born in Wales, who immigrated to Pennsylvania and moved to California in 1855. Daniel and his brother Evan walked to Idaho and back in search of gold, then moved to the Cariboo. Daniel settled at Victoria in 1863 and was an early farmer in N Saanich, marrying Mary Barton (1827–1901), from England. At one point the

Moses farm apparently included this point of land as well as much of the shoreline of Deep Cove. The 1901 census lists the recently bereaved Moses living in Victoria. His son Christopher Moses (1870–1947) was running the N Saanich farm at that time. The family later sold much of its property to the BC Electric Railway Co as the northern terminus for its Saanich line. Moses Point was formerly known as James Point but was changed in 1934.

Mosley Point (53°28'24" 129°29'10" SE side of Grenville Channel, opposite Red Bluff Ck, SE of Lowe Inlet, SW of Kitimat). After Capt Clifford Claude Mosley Sainty of the CPR's BC Coast Steamship Service. *See* Sainty Point.

Mosquito Islets (51°50'04" 128°09'50" Off SW Hunter I, W side of Kildidt Sd, S of Bella Bella). While most of BC's numerous mosquito-related place names celebrate a certain annoying insect, this feature is an exception. It was named in 1945 by regional hydrographer Henri Parizeau, in association with nearby Spider I. Despite the fact that Spider I had been named about 1865 by the British Admiralty and obviously had nothing to do with planes, Parizeau wished to create an aviation theme for islands in the Queens Sd area; the fact that Anthony Fokker's first aircraft was called (and resembled) the Spider gave him an excuse. The de Havilland Mosquito was a twin-engine British fighter-bomber that was also used for reconnaissance and other purposes during WWII. Almost 8,000 Mosquitoes were produced up until 1950, and the fast, versatile plane was universally admired. Other related names in the vicinity include Hurricane I, Spitfire I and the Kittyhawk Group.

Moss Passage (52°21'00" 128°25'00" Between Lady Douglas I and Dowager I, E side of Milbanke Sd, NW of Bella Bella). Morris "Fitz" Moss (1841–96), born at London into a wealthy Jewish family and educated at London Univ College, was an early and somewhat unusual immigrant to BC. After moving to San Francisco and working for the fur dealers Liebes & Co, he was sent as the firm's agent to Victoria in 1862, where he invested privately in a trading schooner and also speculated heavily in sealing and mining ventures. Elegant and cultured, Moss was well regarded at Victoria, and in 1883 he married 25-year-old Hattie Bornstein (1858–1911), daughter of a leading city fur trader. Moss turned out to be an impractical businessman, however; several of his schemes came to naught, and he was accused by wealthy entrepreneur Alfred Waddington of profiteering and dealing in stolen goods. Gov James Douglas liked him, though, appointing him a justice of the peace and government agent on the NW coast. In 1892 Moss disappeared, and it was feared that he had been murdered. As it turned out, he was merely attempting to evade his debtors and his family and was later found hiding out at Denver, where he died. One of his sealing schooners, the *Black Diamond*, was seized in the Bering

M

Sea by US officials in 1889 for supposed illegal hunting. When the seizure itself was deemed illegal in 1897 and compensation paid, nobody was present to represent Moss's estate; some money eventually went to the vessel's First Nation crew members. Moss Passage was named by Lt Daniel Pender of the *Beaver* about 1867. Nearby Morris Bay also commemorates this eccentric pioneer. *W*

Mouat Bay (49°38'00" 124°27'00" W side of Texada I, Str of Georgia), **Mouat Channel** (48°25'00" 123°17'00" N of Gonzales Point, W of Great Chain I, E of Oak Bay and Victoria), **Mouat Islands** (49°38'00" 124°28'00" Just W of Mouat Bay), **Mouat Point** (48°47'00" 123°19'00" W side of N Pender I, Gulf Is), **Mouat Reef** (48°24'32" 123°17'50" Between Gonzales Point and Trial Is, S of Oak Bay), **Mouat Rock** (50°49'22" 127°34'25" NW of Duncan I, Goletas Channel, off N end of Vancouver I). William Alexander Mouat (1821–71) was a master mariner and trader for the HBC on the BC coast for many years. Born at London, he initially came out to the PNW in 1845 as 2nd mate of the brigantine *Mary Dare*. Except for a stint in 1848 as a pilot on the Columbia R bar, he remained with the *Dare* until 1853, rising to capt and trading between Ft Vancouver and Hawaii before taking the ship back to England. Mouat returned to the W coast in 1855 with his wife Mary Ann (*see below*) and commanded various HBC steamships, including the *Enterprise* and *Otter*. He was master of the *Labouchere* in 1866 when it sank near San Francisco. Mouat was then posted to Kamloops Lk, where he was skipper of the steamship *Martin*; after that he took charge of the Ft Rupert trading post. Mouat died in Knight Inlet while on a canoe journey to Vancouver I. Mouat Ck on Texada I is named after Mouat Bay. *W*

Mouat Cove (52°17'00" 128°19'00" W side of Berry Inlet, Don Peninsula, N of Bella Bella). Named after Mary Ann Mouat (1826–96), who came to Victoria in 1855 aboard the HBC ship *Marquis of Bute*, accompanied by her husband, Capt William Alexander Mouat (*see above*), who had already spent eight years in the PNW. She was also from London and developed a reputation in the colony as an excellent pianist and a lover of music. Mary Mouat was a true Victoria pioneer: her two eldest children were born within the palisades of the old HBC fort.

Mould Rock (52°16'53" 128°45'00" W of S end of Price I, NW of Bella Bella). Sapper Charles A Mould was a member of the Columbia detachment of Royal Engineers, which served in BC 1858–63. He travelled to the W coast with his wife on board the *Thames City* with the main contingent of men, arriving in 1859. Mrs Mould was apparently unable to conform to the restrictions of military life. In Apr 1860, Col Richard Moody, cdr of the detachment, wrote, "In consequence of the repeated acts of misconduct of Mrs Mould ... I have been obliged at last, after many warnings, to order her to be struck off

the Strength of the Detachment for Rations and Quarters." She left the Sapperton camp and travelled to the Harrison R, where her husband was working. The pair then seem to have deserted with another sapper, James Gillies (or Gillis). "There is but little doubt that [they have] gone over into American Territory," Moody wrote later that month.

Moulds Bay (50°08'00" 125°11'00" E of Open Bay, E side of Quadra I, N of Campbell R). Named in 1981 for the Mould family, which lived in this vicinity in the 1940s. John Allen Mould (1907–85) is buried at the Quadra I Cemetery. He married Jessie Margaret Munro (1915–96), from Ont, at Powell R in 1939. They lived on Cortes I also, and moved to Campbell R in 1948.

Mount Arrowsmith (49°13'26" 124°35'41" S of Cameron Lk, between Parksville and Port Alberni, Vancouver I). Aaron Arrowsmith (1750–1823) and his nephew John A Arrowsmith (1780–1873) were distinguished British geographers and map-makers from Durham. Aaron moved to London to work for the engraver John Cary and became famous for his 1790 map of the world and his detailed maps of N America (1796) and Scotland (1807). John joined his uncle in 1810 and developed the family business, publishing an important new map of N America in 1821 and *London Atlas* in 1834. He followed these with a series of detailed and immaculate maps of Australia, Africa, India and elsewhere, receiving in 1863 the gold medal of the Royal Geographical Society, which he had helped found. Arrowsmith maps and charts were so highly regarded for their accuracy and thoroughness that the name became synonymous with cartographic excellence. The 1,817-m mountain was named about 1853; nearby Arrowsmith Lk also commemorates this map-making family. The First Nation name for the mountain is Kulth-ka-choolth, meaning "jagged face."

Mount Artaban (49°28'03" 123°20'26" SE side of Gambier I, Howe Sd, NW of Vancouver). This 614-m mountain was named by Rev A T F Holmes, of Lulu I, after the

Mount Artaban, to the right of centre, looms over Port Graves and southeast Gambier Island. *Peter Vassilopoulos*

Anglican Church's Camp Artaban, located nearby at the head of Port Graves. The name was adopted in 1929. Camp Artaban, in turn, is named after the protagonist of Henry van Dyke's book *The Story of the Other Wise Man*, a popular Christmas tale published in 1896. Van Dyke was a Princeton literature professor and clergyman who also served as US ambassador to the Netherlands during the WWI era.

Mount Brodie. *See* Brodie I.

Mount Bury (50°26'25" 127°54'51" S entrance to Quatsino Sd, NW side of Vancouver I). Sir George Bury (1866–1958) was born at Montreal and went to work for the CPR as a junior clerk in 1881. He was in charge of sleeping and dining cars at age 21, divisional superintendent by 24, then rose to western gen manager and, by 1912, vice-president. The Connaught and Spiral tunnels through the Selkirks and Rockies were built under his supervision. In 1917, at the request of the British government, he travelled to Russia to study that country's railway system and report on its revolution. Bury was knighted in 1917 for his services as wartime commissioner of railways and became president of the historic Dominion Atlantic Railway, a CPR subsidiary. He soon retired to Vancouver and ministered to his business interests, which included mines in the Quatsino Sd area and the Whalen Pulp & Paper Co mill at Port Alice. Mt Bury, formerly known as Gap Mtn, was renamed in 1927 by regional hydrographer Henri Parizeau. It is not to be confused with Bury Peak near Nootka Sd, which was likely named in association with Mt Albemarle after England's famous Keppel family (Earl of Albemarle and Viscount Bury were two of that family's traditional titles).

Mount Cardin (53°01'05" 129°05'12" S side of Barnard Hbr, NW side of Princess Royal I). Canadian politician Pierre Joseph Arthur Cardin (1879–1946) was born at Sorel, Que. He trained as a lawyer and was elected Liberal MP for the riding of Richelieu, 1911–46. Cardin served in the cabinets of PM Mackenzie King as minister of Marine and Fisheries, 1924–30, minister of Public Works, 1935–42, and minister of Transport, 1940–42. Mt Cardin (960 m) was named by the hydrographic service in 1926.

Mount Carl (52°55'21" 131°42'26" SE side of Louise I, off NE Moresby I, QCI). Zoologist G Clifford Carl (1908–70) was the third director of the BC Provincial Museum, 1940–69. In 1970 he was briefly curator of the provincial government's maritime biology division. He was born at Vancouver and earned degrees at UBC and Univ of Toronto. Carl had a special interest in the province's amphibians and reptiles, though he also wrote about marine life, freshwater fish and invasive, introduced species. He was author or co-author of several dozen

books and booklets and also wrote numerous articles on the natural history of BC. He lectured extensively during his career, making museum tours of the US in 1953, 1957, 1959 and 1960; in 1946 he visited Alaska's Pribilof Is as a guest of the US Fish and Wildlife Service. Mt Carl (938 m) was named by the hydrographic service in 1948.

Mount Colnett. *See* Colnett Point.

Mount David. *See* Lyall Hbr.

Mount Davies. *See* Davie Bay.

Mount de la Touche (52°42'07" 132°02'10" SE of entrance to Tasu Sd, W side of Moresby I, QCI). This conspicuous 1,123-m peak, visible from all points of approach at sea, was named in 1786 by Jean-François de Galaup, Comte de Lapérouse, while sailing S along the W coast of the QCI on his never-finished circumnavigation of the globe. He also gave the name Baie de la Touche to the present Englefield Bay. It is not known precisely who de la Touche was. He may have been Lapérouse's 1st lt aboard the *Boussole*. Most historians, however, believe that the French navigator intended to honour Louis-René Levassor de Latouche-Tréville (1745–1804), who, as a capt, had joined Lapérouse in 1781 in a successful attack on an English convoy near NS. Latouche-Tréville later became a French adm and a hero of the American Revolutionary and Napoleonic wars. He was one of the few French adms to engage Lord Nelson and come away victorious. He commanded French fleets in the W Indies and Mediterranean in the early 1800s and was about to play a key role in Napoleon's planned invasion of England when he died of a sudden illness aboard his ship, the *Bucentaure*. The Haida First Nation name for the mountain is Qanra Cayaa.

Mount Dick (49°30'19" 124°09'38" S end of Texada I, Str of Georgia). The origin of this name is not known. The suggestion that it commemorates long-serving BC mines inspector Archibald Dick (1842–1915), who was born in Scotland and came to Nanaimo in 1866, cannot be correct, as Mt Dick (347 m) appears on an Admiralty chart published in 1865 and was presumably named by the RN's Capt George Richards, who surveyed the area in 1860 aboard HMS *Plumper*.

Mount Emmons (53°22'07" 132°42'47" Behind Cone Head at S entrance to Rennell Sd, SW side of Graham I, QCI). C D Emmons (b 1864) was a well-regarded veteran QCI prospector who had also done some ambitious exploration work in Alaska. He was born in Michigan and graduated from the American Institute of Mining and Metallurgical Engineering. Emmons came W to Oregon and then, in 1889, to Alaska, where he got a job as deputy collector of customs for the Bering Sea area, based at Unalaska. In 1897 he became the first white explorer to

M

reach the headwaters of the Tanana R, and in 1899 he travelled over the ice from Skagway to Ft Selkirk in the Yukon and on to the headwaters of the White R. Emmons came to the QCI in 1904 and worked there for about 40 years, prospecting and surveying extensively, especially on Graham I. Mt Emmons (535 m) was named in 1946. *D*

Mount Gardner. *See* Gardner Canal.

Mount Geoffrey (49°30'55" 124°41'35" E side of Hornby I, W side of Str of Georgia). The 332-m high point of Hornby I was named in 1860 by Capt George Richards after Geoffrey Thomas Phipps Hornby (1825–95), capt of HMS *Tribune* on the Pacific Station in 1859–60. Hornby brought a company of Royal Marines to BC from China to maintain order during Britain's dispute with the US over the San Juan Is. The restraint of senior RN officers, including Hornby, did much to calm tempers during this minor altercation, allowing a diplomatic solution to be achieved at a later date. Hornby had been in BC waters earlier in his career, as flag lt to his father, Rear Adm Phipps Hornby (*see* Hornby I), who was cdr-in-chief of the Pacific Station, 1847–51, with HMS *Asia* as his flagship. The young Hornby was promoted cdr while in BC, then made a rapid ascent through the RN hierarchy, eventually outdoing his father by attaining, in 1888, the rank of adm of the fleet. Like his father, he was knighted (in 1878); he also served as a lord of the Admiralty (1874–77). Hornby was cdr-in-chief of the Mediterranean Station (1877–80), president of the Royal Naval College (1881), cdr-in-chief at Portsmouth (1885) and chief naval aide-de-camp to Queen Victoria (1886). *W*

Mount Gowlland. *See* Gowlland Hbr.

Mount Hulke (53°16'09" 129°32'23" W side of Tuwartz Inlet, S end of Pitt I). RCAF squadron leader Cecil Walter Lloyd Hulke, from Victoria, was killed in action Oct 3, 1943, aged 36. He was the son of Brig Gen W B Hulke, DSO, and was serving at the time in N Africa with No 243 (RAF) Wing. Hulke is commemorated on the Alamein Memorial at the El Alamein War Cemetery in Egypt.

Mount Irving (52°45'58" 128°53'58" S side of Henderson Lk, S end of Princess Royal I). Capt William Irving (1816–72) was born at Annan, Scotland, and went to sea at a young age. He learned the steamboat trade in NB and Oregon, finding financial success on the Willamette and Columbia rivers before arriving at Victoria in the late 1850s. With his partner, Capt Alexander Murray, he established a paddlewheel fleet on the Fraser R and Harrison Lk, then bought Murray out, sold the company in 1862 and formed the Pioneer Line, which became the leading transportation outfit on the profitable New Westminster–Yale route, 1862–83. Irving's firms had a number of historic paddlewheelers constructed in Victoria, including the *Governor Douglas*

(the first sternwheeler built in colonial BC, in 1858), *Colonel Moody* (1859), *Reliance* (1862) and *Onward* (1865). His son John Irving (*see* Irving Cove) took over the family firm on his father's death and, in 1883, merged it with the HBC's marine dept to form the Canadian Pacific Navigation Co, the most prominent steamship line in BC. William Irving's New Westminster home, built in 1864, is now a museum. Mt Irving (783 m) was named in 1926 by regional hydrographer Henri Parizeau. *E*

Mount Johnston (52°36'23" 129°04'20" E of Clifford Bay, Aristazabal I). The highest point on Aristazabal I, at 331 m, was named in 1927 by regional hydrographer Henri Parizeau after Alexander Johnston (1867–1951), deputy minister of Marine and Fisheries in the federal government, 1910–33. Johnston was a former publisher of the *Sydney Record*, Cape Breton MLA (1897–1900) and MP (1900–1908). He served as Canadian delegate to several international conferences on life-saving at sea and telegraphy, and he was instrumental in helping his friend Guglielmo Marconi establish the first radio station in Canada, at Table Head, NS. Frances Rk and Steele Rk off Aristazabal I are named for his wife, and Mason Rk for his son.

Mount Kains. *See* Kains I.

Mount Kermode (52°57'25" 131°51'29" W side of Louise I, off NE Moresby I, QCI). Naturalist Francis Kermode (1874–1946) was the second director of the BC Provincial Museum, succeeding John Fanin in 1904 and serving until 1940. He was born at Liverpool, England, came to Victoria with his parents in 1883 and joined the museum at a young age in 1890. Kermode married Margaret A Fowler (1879–1936) at Vancouver in 1900. He made numerous expeditions—to the W coast of Vancouver I; to the N coast, Okanagan and Atlin regions; and to the QCI with Dr Charles F Newcombe in 1895—to gather specimens for the museum's natural history, geology and ethnology collections. In 1905, at the annual meeting of the NY Zoological Society, what was believed to be a new species of white bear was named for him. Northern BC's *Ursus americanus kermodei* was later discovered to be a rare genetic variant of the grizzly bear; today, the protected animal is better known as the "spirit bear" and was made BC's official mammal in 2006. Mt Kermode was named in 1925; at 1,080 m, it is the highest point on Louise I.

Mount Lolo (50°09'00" 125°21'00" W side of Quadra I, E of Seymour Narrows, N of Campbell R). Jean-Baptiste Lolo (1798–1868) was a Metis, probably of Iroquois and French-Canadian parentage. He joined the fur trade as an interpreter and by 1822 was working at Ft St James. At Ft Fraser he acquired the nickname St Paul as a result of his great admiration for this biblical figure. From 1828 he was based at Ft Thompson (later Kamloops), where he became a vital intermediary between the HBC and the interior Salish First Nation tribes and was accorded the honorary title of chief. John Tod, chief trader at the fort, 1842–49, married Lolo's daughter Sophia. Lolo Ck, Lolo Lk, Mt Lolo, Paul Ck, Paul Lk and Paul Peak, all in the Kamloops area, are named for him as well. *See also* Tod Inlet *and* Mary Tod I.

Mount McGrath (54°09'28" 130°15'29" W side of Smith I, S of Prince Rupert). William Edmund McGrath was master of HMS *Malacca*, under Capt Radulphus Oldfield, on the Pacific Station, 1866–67. He retired with the rank of navigating lt in 1870. Named by RN surveyor Daniel Pender in 1867.

Mount Morse. *See* Morse Basin.

Mount Newton (48°36'45" 123°26'39" John Dean Provincial Park, N Saanich, Saanich Peninsula, NW of Victoria). The origin of this name is not certain. It first appears on an 1855 map by HBC surveyor Joseph Pemberton (later surveyor gen of the colony of Vancouver I). It is known that, in 1854, Pemberton had a draftsman named Newton as an assistant. He "is not so well qualified to be of service in outside work," Pemberton wrote in a letter to the HBC in London, "but his artistic talents and his diligence in applying them render him a decided acquisition." Other historians have claimed William Henry Newton (1833–1875) as the source of the name. He arrived in BC in 1851 as assistant to Edward Langford, manager of Colwood, one of the Victoria-area farms established by the Puget's Sd Agricultural Co. Newton later worked as an HBC clerk, married Emmaline Tod (daughter of HBC fur trader John Tod) and moved to Ft Langley, where he was in charge, 1859–64. The 305-m feature's traditional Wsanec (Saanich) First Nation name is Láu'wel'new, meaning "place of escape."

Mount Oldfield (54°18'12" 130°17'10" NE side of Kaien I, just S of Prince Rupert). RN officer Radulphus Bryce Oldfield, CB (1827–77), served on the Pacific Station, 1866–67, as capt of HMS *Malacca*. In 1847 he had sailed with Capt Henry Keppel in HMS *Maeander* and participated in the campaign by the first Rajah of Sarawak, Sir James Brooke, to suppress piracy in the Borneo region. During the Crimean War he was a lt aboard HMS *Bellerophon* and HMS *London* until promoted to cdr for his gallant actions on shore during the siege of the Black Sea port of Sevastopol. Lt Daniel Pender, of the hired survey vessel *Beaver*, named a number of features in the vicinity after the officers of the *Malacca* in 1867.

Mount Ozzard (48°58'00" 125°29'00" E of Ucluelet Inlet, NW side of Barkley Sd, W side of Vancouver I). James William Ozzard (d 1902) was secretary to Rear Adm Sir Thomas Maitland, cdr-in-chief on the Pacific Station,

1860–62, with his flag on HMS *Bacchante*. Ozzard had the rank of paymaster in 1845 and was promoted to chief paymaster in 1872. The 766-m prominence, known as Chuumata to the Nuu-chah-nulth people, was named by Capt George Richards of the survey vessel *Hecate* in 1861. It has a Coast Guard radar and communications station at the summit.

Henri Dalpe Parizeau. *Courtesy Canadian Hydrographic Service, Pacific Region*

Mount Parizeau (52°46'11" 129°14'02" N end of Aristazabal I), **Parizeau Point** (54°17'00" 130°22'00" E side of Digby I, S end of Prince Rupert Hbr). As the federal government's regional hydrographer on the Pacific coast, 1920–46, Henri Dalpe Parizeau (1877–1954) may have named more BC coastal features in his lifetime than any other person. He was born at Montreal, educated as an engineer at McGill Univ and worked first for the Montreal Hbr Commission. In 1901 he joined the federal Dept of Public Works as assistant resident engineer for Ont's Thousand Is district, then was transferred to the hydrographic survey in 1904. Parizeau first came to the W coast in 1906 to help George Dodge survey Prince Rupert Hbr after it was chosen as the GTP terminus. He remained in BC until 1909 as 1st assistant to Lt Cdr Philip Musgrave, his predecessor as regional hydrographer, then supervised surveys in Hudson Bay and the Great Lakes. During his long career as officer-in-charge at Victoria, Parizeau investigated nearly every part of the BC coast, at first with CGS *Lillooet* and then with the *William J Stewart*. A special interest in toponymy (the study of place names) and regional history convinced him that the province's geographical names should reflect its heritage—and the efforts of its early settlers, in particular. He also felt a need to eliminate the "unnecessary and dangerous duplication" of names, which could make coastal navigation confusing

M

and, in a pre-GPS era, could easily misdirect rescue craft in emergencies. As a result, Parizeau spent much time researching relevant regional names and was responsible for applying hundreds of them to coastal features. A certain lack of diplomacy, however, when dealing with new names sometimes brought him into conflict with local residents—and with the Geographic Board of Canada, which held that old, long-established names should not be arbitrarily or capriciously changed. Despite losing a few toponymic battles over the years, Parizeau did ensure that BC pioneers received widespread recognition on coastal charts. In 1946, the year he retired, he was awarded an MBE for his work on secret naval projects in WWII. In 1967 a new ocean survey vessel, CGS *Parizeau*, was launched, equipped with the latest research gear, and went on to a long career in Canada and the US. The conspicuous, 291-m dome of Mt Parizeau, easily visible in all directions, was named in 1946. Many nearby features commemorate fellow officers of the hydrographic survey.

Mount Parke (48°50'24" 123°17'49" Just E of Village Bay, Mayne I, Gulf Is). RN surveyor Capt George Richards named this feature in 1858 after Lt John Grubb Parke (1827–1900), a topographical engineer, who was chief astronomer and surveyor for the US on the N American Boundary Commission, 1857–61. He was born in Pennsylvania and entered the Corps of Engineers after graduating from the US Military Academy in 1849. Before joining the boundary commission he produced an important 1851 map of New Mexico and was involved in surveying US railroad routes and territorial boundary lines. During the US Civil War, Parke was appointed a brig gen of volunteers and took over command of the IX Corps, seeing action in a number of important battles. He served as chief of staff of the Army of the Ohio and acting cdr of the Army of the Potomac and ended the war as a maj gen. He served in peacetime as a col with the Chief of Engineers office at Washington, in charge of river and harbour work, and ended his career as superintendent of the US Military Academy, 1887–89. At 271 m, Mt Parke is the highest point on Mayne I.

Mount Parry (52°52'52" 128°45'32" W side of Laredo Inlet, S of Mellis Inlet, Princess Royal I). This 1,052-m peak was named for RN officer John Franklin Parry (1863–1926), who had two commissions on the BC coast as cdr of the RN survey vessel *Egeria*, in 1903–6 and 1908–10. The grandson of Arctic explorer Rear Adm Sir William Parry (*see* Parry Bay), he entered the RN in 1877 and was promoted to cdr in 1899 while on survey duty off Australia with HMS *Dart*. During his time on HMS *Egeria*, Parry made detailed surveys of NW Vancouver I, Active Pass and the Str of Georgia, and around Porcher I, Chatham Sd and Dixon Entrance. He became a capt in 1905 and a rear adm in 1916. In 1910 he was named assistant hydrographer of the RN, and from 1914 to 1919 he was chief hydrographer,

a position his famous grandfather had held in 1823–29. In 1920, as Sir John Parry, he served as the first presiding director of the International Hydrographic Bureau. He was promoted to adm, retired, in 1925.

Mount Paxton (50°05'48" 127°27'56" SE side of Malkscope Inlet, just NW of Kyuquot Sd, NW side of Vancouver I). Henry Paxton (1856–1941), from England, first arrived in Victoria about 1880 and, as an experienced seaman, had no trouble landing a job with a sealing schooner. In 1886, as skipper of the *Black Diamond*, owned by Morris Gutman, he was warned out of the Bering Sea by US officials and later put in a claim for lost prospective income because of "molestation." Harry, as he was known, was capt of the 23-tonne *Wanderer*, which he partly owned, for many years. He brought in good catches most years, except in 1889, when he had to return to Victoria after his First Nation crew—having heard that American warships were seizing sealers—refused to continue, and in 1894, when his vessel was seized.

Mount Plowden (50°58'14" 126°27'18" Near E entrance to Wakeman Sd, Kingcome Inlet, NE of Port McNeill), **Plowden Bay** (49°32'00" 123°28'00" W side of Howe Sd, N of Woolridge I, NW of Vancouver). After Henry Claude Plowden (1867–1943), who pre-empted land beside the bay and received a Crown grant in 1917. A landing at his property became a Union Steamship port of call. Plowden Bay was later the site of a logging camp.

Mount St Patrick (50°40'39" 128°19'37" N side of San Josef Bay, NW tip of Vancouver I). Capt James Hanna, the first fur trader to reach the PNW, in 1785, returned the following year and made a chart of NW Vancouver I, on which he gave the name St Patrick's Bay to what is now San Josef Bay. Mt St Patrick (422 m) was named in 1947 to honour this historic reference. Nearby St Patrick Ck also owes its name to Hanna's early map.

Mount Shepherd (49°32'05" 124°11'15" S end of Texada I, Str of Georgia). In Aug 1792, when Henry Shepherd was trading for sea otter furs on the N BC coast with the brig *Venus*, he met Capt George Vancouver near Calvert I and was able to tell him that his storeship, the *Daedalus*, had arrived at Nootka Sd. The Spanish naval officer Francisco Bodega y Quadra was waiting for him there as well, to discuss the terms of the Nootka Convention, under which Spain would relinquish control of the PNW region. Shepherd had arrived on the W coast that June, travelling with the *Halcyon*, under Capt Charles Barkley. He returned to China, via the Hawaiian Is, at the end of the trading season. Mt Shepherd (884 m) on Texada first appears on an Admiralty chart in 1868. Another Mt Shepherd, in the vicinity of Sooke on Vancouver I, is found on an earlier chart (1865), but that feature was renamed Mt Manuel Quimper in 1939.

Mount Stephens (50°58'15" 126°39'46" NW of Kingcome Inlet, N of E end of Queen Charlotte Str), **Mount Stephens** (54°07'39" 130°40'15" S end of Stephens I), **Port Stephens** (53°20'00" 129°39'00" W side of Pitt I, N of Monckton Inlet), **Stephens Island** (54°10'00" 130°46'00" Off NW Porcher I, SW of Prince Rupert), **Stephens Narrows** (In Port Stephens), **Stephens Passage** (54°08'00" 130°38'00" Between Stephens I and Prescott I). Mt Stephens near Kingcome Inlet (1,727 m) and Stephens I were named by Capt George Vancouver—in 1792 and 1793, respectively—after Sir Philip Stephens (1725–1809), who began his career as a clerk in the RN and later became secretary to Rear Adm George Anson. He served as secretary to the Admiralty, 1763–95, and as a lord commissioner of the Admiralty, 1795–1806. He was an MP, 1759–1806, as well. Philip Point N of Broughton I is also named for him, as are Philip Cone on Stephens I and Philip I just to the W. Port Stephens is a very early coastal name, bestowed by British fur trader Charles Duncan, who visited the harbour in 1788 in the sloop *Princess Royal*. James Colnett of the *Prince of Wales*, whom Duncan had accompanied to the PNW in 1786, dedicated an account of his travels to Stephens. It was, he wrote, "the only mark of gratitude I had the power of shewing him for the services he wished to render me." Stephens Passage was formerly known as Canoe Passage. Stephens I is shown as Skiakl I on at least one early chart. Mt Stephens on Stephens I has a height of 425 m. *W*

Mount Tomlinson (55°02'02" 129°56'29" N of Nass Bay and Gingolx, E of Observatory Inlet, NE of Prince Rupert), **Tomlinson Point** (50°54'00" 127°15'00" E entrance to Blunden Hbr, N side of Queen Charlotte Str, NE of Port Hardy). Robert Tomlinson (1842–1913) was an Irish missionary who received medical training at Trinity College before joining the Church Missionary Society. He came out to Metlakatla in 1867, and later that year, with Rev Robert Doolan, he established an Anglican mission at Gingolx (formerly Kincolith) on Nass Bay, where he remained until 1879. He went to Victoria by canoe in 1868, where he married Alice Woods (1851–1933, *see* Alice Arm), a BC civil servant's daughter; then he was paddled back to Gingolx with his bride, a round trip of about 2,000 km. In 1879 he established a mission in the Kispiox valley, then worked at Metlakatla (1883–87), where he was a supporter and confidant of William Duncan. When Duncan was forced out of Metlakatla in 1887 and went to Alaska, Tomlinson resigned from the missionary society and founded a non-sectarian mission, Meanskinisht, at Cedarvale on the Skeena R. He rejoined Duncan at New Metlakatla on Annette I from 1908 to 1912. His son, Robert Jr, also worked on the N coast as a missionary. The 1,032-m mountain was named by RN surveyor Lt Daniel Pender in 1868. *E W*

Mount Tuam (48°43'37" 123°29'05" SW end of Saltspring I, Gulf Is). This name is an adaptation of the Cowichan (Quw'utsun') First Nation word *chuan*, which can be translated as "facing the sea." It first appears on an Admiralty chart published in 1861. Variant spellings are often seen, including Chuan, Tsuam, Tuan and Tchuan. Chuan was the name given to the entire island on a map accompanying Gov James Douglas's 1854 "Report of a Canoe Expedition along the East Coast of Vancouver Island." Sheep were raised on the slopes of the 632-m mountain in the late 1800s; a century later it was home to a Tibetan Buddhism centre. *See also* Saltspring I.

Mount Tzouhalem overlooking Genoa Bay. *Kevin Oke*

Mount Tzouhalem (48°46'42" 123°36'52" Just E of Duncan, SE Vancouver I). Named after one of the most feared of the Cowichan war chiefs, who led an attack on Ft Victoria in 1844. The dispute arose over the fort's cattle, which roamed freely over First Nation territory. When Tzouhalem killed some cows, the HBC insisted that he pay for them, and when he refused, the company forbade him access to the fort and would not trade with him or his men. Tzouhalem and his angry followers then stormed the fort's palisade but were easily rebuffed by HBC trader Roderick Finlayson, whose demonstration of the power of cannon fire was so convincing that the First Nation leader decided to settle his debts and leave the cattle alone. Tzouhalem's casual and unpredictable brutality, especially applied to the husbands of women he desired, so alienated his tribe that he was banished and went to live in a cave on this 483-m mountain. He was eventually killed on Kuper I in 1854 while trying to add to his harem of 14 wives. There are, as one might expect, many spelling variants of this name. Tzohailim Hill appears on the 1855 SW Vancouver I map of surveyor Joseph Pemberton; Tzohailin Hill on an 1864 Admiralty chart. The former official spelling of Tzuhalem was changed in 2000 to the present form, which is preferred by the Cowichan (Quw'utsun') First Nation. Nearby Tzouhalem Ck is also named for this historical figure, as is a mostly residential settlement on the eastern outskirts of Duncan.

M

Mount Verney (52°11'12" 128°02'01" S end of Cunningham I, just NE of Bella Bella), **Verney Passage** (53°30'19" 129°04'23" Between Gribbell I and SE side of Hawkesbury I, SW of Kitimat). Lt Cdr Edmund Hope Verney (1838–1910) commanded the RN gunboat *Grappler* on the BC coast, 1862–65. He was a British aristocrat, son of baronet Sir Harry Verney, grandson of Adm Sir George Hope and nephew of Adm Sir James Hope (*see* Hope I). Verney's Vancouver I letters, edited by Allan Pritchard and published in a scholarly edition in 1996, provide much insight into this officer's complex character as well as the social life of the colony. While critical of the colonial administration—he found Gov James Douglas "pompous and ridiculous," for instance, and considered Chief Justice David Cameron an "inane booby"—Verney still took a far more active interest in local affairs than the average RN officer posted to Esquimalt. Influenced by his abolitionist father, he espoused progressive causes, becoming a charter member of Victoria's first female immigration committee, which housed, fed, found jobs for and otherwise assisted new arrivals. He also served as a Vancouver I magistrate and commissioner of the Colonial Lighthouse Board, and in 1864 founded the Victoria branch of the Mechanics' Institute, which promoted adult education. As cdr of the *Grappler*, he participated in the 1863 Lamalcha incident, in which members of a renegade First Nation band from Kuper I were pursued, captured and punished for the murders of two white Gulf Is settlers (*see* Murder Point). Back in England, where he was promoted capt in 1877, Verney's views got him into trouble; in 1879 the Admiralty expressed "severe displeasure" when he attended a Portsmouth anti-flogging rally. He retired from the RN in 1884 and served six years as the Liberal MP for N Buckinghamshire. Then his life took a bizarre turn. He was expelled from parliament and his name struck from the navy list in 1891 after he was found guilty of "procuring a girl under the age of 21, Miss Nellie Maud Baskett, for an immoral purpose." A year in prison, though, did not prevent Verney from succeeding his father as 3rd baronet in 1894. Edmund Passage at the entrance to Rivers Inlet is also named for him. Mt Verney was formerly known as Verney Cone. Another Mt Verney, on the N side of Queen Charlotte Str, is named for his father, Sir Harry Verney (*see* Calvert Point). Verney Passage was named by Lt Daniel Pender in 1864. According to anthropologist Jay Powell, Haisla First Nation members know the S end of the passage as Qamu'ya. *W*

Mount Warburton Pike (48°46'28" 123°10'18" S side of Saturna I, Gulf Is). Wealthy English sportsman, explorer and author Warburton Mayer Pike (1861–1915) was educated at Rugby School and Oxford, and came to BC in 1884, intent on satisfying his keen desire to hunt big game. He bought property at Oak Bay and on Mayne and Saturna islands, and operated a 600-ha sheep ranch and significant sandstone quarry on Saturna (*see* Taylor Point).

Mount Warburton Pike on Saturna Island. *Kevin Oke*

Pike was a great traveller, employing managers to run his various businesses. Before coming to BC he had traversed Iceland and been a cowboy in Wyoming and a miner in California. After BC he spent much time in Alaska and the N, writing *The Barren Grounds of Northern Canada* in 1892 and *Through the Sub-Arctic Forest* in 1896. He also became involved in mining and railroad schemes in the Cassiar gold district, where a cairn was erected in his honour at the N end of Dease Lk. In 1912, Pike bought the S half of Discovery I, just E of Victoria, and built a house there, then returned to England to enlist for WWI. Rejected on account of his age and poor health, he became deeply depressed and committed suicide. The mountain, at 497 m, is the highest point of Saturna I. *E*

Mouse Islets (50°05'00" 125°14'00" Gowlland Hbr, W side of Quadra I, just NE of Campbell R). Cdr Cortland Simpson of the RN survey vessel *Egeria* named a number of features in the vicinity after animals in 1900.

Moutcha Bay (49°47'00" 126°27'00" E side of head of Tlupana Inlet, Nootka Sd, W side of Vancouver I). Named after the Mowachaht/Muchalaht First Nation reserve at the head of this bay. At the time of first European contact, this was the site of a Nuu-chah-nulth winter village (often spelled Mooacha), said to be home to Tlupana, a Mowachaht chief second in importance only to Maquinna. Capt George Vancouver, accompanied by Spanish official José Manuel de Álava, visited this place in 1794 but spelled its name Mooetchee (and its chief's name Clewpaneloo). According to pioneer Roman Catholic missionary Augustin Brabant, Moutcha was famous for its herds of deer. He suggested that the name was derived from *mooach* or *mowach*, the Nuu-chah-nulth word for deer. Author Laurie Jones gives Mowatca as an alternative spelling for Moutcha and translates the word as "place where the deer come to drink." Both writers indicate that the name of the Mowachaht, "people of the deer," comes from Moutcha. *See* Mowitch Point.

Mowitch Point (54°10'00" 130°01'00" N side of the Skeena R, NW of Port Essington, SE of Prince Rupert). *Mowich* or *mowitch* is the word for deer or "venison" in Chinook jargon, the pidgin language used on the W coast by First Nation groups and early traders and settlers. The word was probably adapted from the Nuu-chah-nulth language (*see* Moutcha Bay); the Mowachaht, for instance, one of the Nuu-chah-nulth First Nations, are "people of the deer." There are dozens of Mowich or Mowitch place names in the PNW, including half a dozen in BC. The name of this feature dates back to at least 1888, when it appeared on an official plan of the region.

Mozino Point (49°51'00" 126°41'00" NE end of Tahsis Narrows, W of Tahsis Inlet, W side of Vancouver I). José Mariano Moziño (1757–1820) made the first detailed scientific survey of the native inhabitants and flora and fauna of BC. Born in Mexico and educated at the Tridentino Seminary, he graduated in philosophy in 1778 and then took a degree in medicine. He was a participant in the Royal Scientific Expedition to New Spain, an ambitious project organized by Spanish botanist Martín Sessé that sent experts to all corners of New Spain—and beyond. Moziño, along with botanist José Maldonado and artist Atanasio Echeverria, accompanied Francisco Bodega y Quadra to Nootka Sd in 1792 and stayed there more than four months. He wrote a frank account of his time at Nootka, describing not only the customs of the aboriginal people but also the sometimes brutal treatment of them by the Spanish, especially regarding the sexual use of slaves and spread of syphilis. He also compiled the first Spanish/Nuu-chah-nulth dictionary and catalogued the local plants and animals. Moziño worked for Sessé in Mexico, Guatemala and the W Indies, then travelled with him to Madrid in 1803. When Napoleon named his brother Joseph Bonaparte king of Spain, Moziño was appointed director of the Royal Museum of Natural History and professor of zoology at the Royal Academy of Medicine. Unfortunately, when the French withdrew from Spain in 1813, at the end of the Peninsular War, he was arrested as a traitor and had to flee to France. He returned to Spain in 1817. Moziño's original papers were lost, but, luckily, copies were made of some of his manuscripts and drawings. A version of his *Noticias de Nutka* turned up in 1880, was published in 1913 and finally translated into English in 1970. He also wrote *Flora de Guatemala*; the resplendent quetzal (*Pharomachrus mocinno*), Guatemala's national bird, is named for him. The scientist's surname is sometimes spelled Mociño; Mocino Point on Brooks Bay also commemorates him.

Muchalat Inlet (49°39'00" 126°14'00" Extends E from the E side of Nootka Sd, W side of Vancouver I). Named after the Muchalaht people, who are a branch of the Nuu-chah-nulth cultural group. The Muchalaht are "those who live beside the Muchalee R"; Muchalee is believed to be

the original Nuu-chah-nulth name for the Gold R valley. The Mowachaht, or "people of the deer," who occupied the more westerly portions of Nootka Sd, were traditional enemies of the Muchalaht, and many battles were fought over Gold R's rich sockeye salmon resources. The Muchalaht were reduced in number by the endless attacks and retreated inland, but they eventually intermarried with their enemies and moved to Yuquot on Nootka I. The two tribes, now allied, moved in 1968 to Ahaminaquus, where the Gold R joins the sea and the main Muchalaht village had once been situated. By then the region was the site of intense logging activity; the Tahsis Co had its main camp at the mouth of the Gold R by 1955, and the E Asiatic Co built a pulp mill there in 1965. In 1996, tired of pollution, noise and truck traffic, the Mowachaht/Muchalaht moved again, to Ts'xanah, just N of the village of Gold R. The inlet was once known as Muchalat Arm and, even earlier, as Guaquina Arm (*see* Guaquina Point). Spanish visitors to Nootka Sd in the 18th century called it Fondo de Guicananish and Brazo de Guaquinaniz—names that probably refer to famed Nuu-chah-nulth chief Wickaninnish. Muchalat Lk and Muchalat R are also named for the Muchalaht First Nation. *E W*

Aerial view of Mud Bay, southeast of Vancouver. *Peter Vassilopoulos*

Mud Bay (49°05'00" 122°53'00" NE extension of Boundary Bay, SE of Vancouver). There are seven places officially called Mud Bay in BC, plus 20 or more other place names with the words "mud," "muddy" or "mudflat" in them. This one, named for the oozing tidal flats at the mouths of the Serpentine and Nicomekl rivers, is of very early origin, as a post office called Mud Bay was proposed for the adjacent farming district in 1876 (it finally opened in 1881). A record at BC's Geographical Names Office suggests that the bay may have been named—probably with a hearty round of curses—at the time road construction began in the area, which was first settled in the 1860s. The Semiahmoo Wagon Road, from New Westminster via Mud Bay to the US border, was built in 1873–74 and partly based on earlier trails. The bay was once enormously rich in small native Olympia oysters. *E*

M

Mudge Inlet (52°58'00" 132°08'00" Between Mitchell Inlet and Peel Inlet, Kuper Inlet, NW side of Moresby I, QCI). Henry Colton Mudge (1829–73) was a marine lt aboard HMS *Thetis*, under Capt Augustus Kuper, and served on the Pacific Station, 1850–53. In 1852 the *Thetis* was sent to NW Moresby I to conduct a survey of the area and maintain a naval presence after the recent discovery of gold in the vicinity. Nearby Colton It and Colton Point are also named for him. He was the grandson of Adm Zachary Mudge, after whom Cape Mudge (qv) is named. *W*

Mudge Island, southeast of Nanaimo. *Kevin Oke*

Mudge Island (49°08'00" 123°47'00" Part of the De Courcy Group, just S of Gabriola I, Gulf Is). Named about 1859 by Capt George Richards for William Tertius Fitzwilliam Mudge (1831–63), a lt aboard HMS *Pylades*, under Capt Michael de Courcy. He served on the Pacific Station, 1859–60. Mudge drowned in the wreck of HMS *Orpheus* on the Manaku bar in NZ. He was a great-nephew of Adm Zachary Mudge, who sailed with Capt George Vancouver as a lt and for whom Cape Mudge (qv) is named. Mudge I was first settled by David Roberts in 1881. He and his wife, Mary Martin, raised a family there and were well known locally for their "mammoth" apples (625 grams each, with a diameter of 35 cm) and "monster" Queen Anne cherries. Up until the mid-1970s, when the island was extensively subdivided, it had only a handful of residents; in the early 2000s there were about 60 full-timers and a population of more than 200 in summer. According to the Gabriola Historical & Museum Society, Mudge was labelled Portland I on an unpublished chart used in the 1850s by HMS *Virago*. *W*

Mugford Island (49°11'30" 125°40'40" In Tranquil Inlet, a branch of Tofino Inlet, Clayoquot Sd, W side of Vancouver I). This name was adopted in 1986 for RCNR able seaman Robert Burns Mugford, from Sooke, who died in action on Aug 17, 1941, aged 32. He was serving at the time on HMCS *Allaverdy*, a patrol vessel that was part of the Fishermen Reserve Service on the BC coast. He is buried in the cemetery at Knox Presbyterian Church, Sooke.

Muir Cove (52°17'38" 128°39'30" SE side of Price I, NW of Bella Bella), **Muir Point** (48°21'21" 123°44'59" On N side of Juan de Fuca Str, just NW of entrance to Sooke Hbr, at SW end of Vancouver I). John Muir (1799–1883), his wife Anne (1802–75, née Miller) and their four sons came to BC from Ayrshire in 1849 on the HBC barque *Harpooner*, part of a related group of Scottish colliers hired to work at the HBC's Ft Rupert mines. In 1850, in a dispute over working conditions, many of the miners, including John's son Andrew Muir, went on what was probably BC's first strike. Ft Rupert manager George Blenkinsop had them arrested and jailed, an action he was later criticized for by senior HBC officials. The following year, after his contract expired, John Muir moved to Sooke and farmed, later returning to oversee the HBC coal operations at Nanaimo, 1852–54. In 1853 he purchased the Sooke estate of Capt Walter Grant, the first independent settler on Vancouver I, and settled there permanently in 1854, calling his property Woodside and building the colony's first steam sawmill and also a flour mill. Muir was a magistrate and a member of Vancouver I's initial elected colonial assembly, 1856–59 (he was one of only 43 residents who qualified as voters by owning a requisite 8 ha of land). He and his sons established a lumber yard at Victoria in 1860. Supplied by their sawmill, it remained in operation for more than 30 years. Andrew Muir was Vancouver I's first sheriff, 1857–59. Muir Cove is believed to be named for Anne Muir, while Muir Point was named for the family in general. Muir Ck and Mt Muir in the Sooke area also honour these noteworthy pioneer immigrants. *E*

Muir Rocks (50°23'00" 127°28'00" W side of Neroutsos Inlet, E of Quatsino Sd, NW end of Vancouver I). Named in 1927 after the accountant at Whalen Pulp & Paper Co, Port Alice, in the early 1920s.

Mumford Cove (55°22'00" 129°44'00" W side of Brooke I, S of Larcom I, Observatory Inlet, S of Stewart). The name was adopted in 1970 after William Franklin Mumford, who pre-empted land in this area in 1912.

Munroe Rock (48°35'00" 123°18'00" SE end of Sidney Channel, between Sidney I and James I, Gulf Is). Hugh Munroe (b about 1851), from Ont, was an early settler and landowner on James I. He is listed in the 1891 BC census as a house builder and contractor residing at Nanaimo.

Munro Island (52°26'00" 129°00'00" S of Aristazabal I). Named in 1927 after Alexander Munro (1824–1911), the last HBC chief factor in Victoria. He was a native of Tain, Scotland, and came to Victoria in 1857. His wife, Jane Urquhart (1825–1914), and children joined him a year later. Munro entered HBC service as a clerk in 1861 and was promoted to factor in 1872 and chief factor two years later. He and Jane had a large family; his daughter Jane married steamship magnate John Irving, while Elizabeth married wealthy merchant and politician Robert Rithet; his son Arbuthnot died in the sinking of the *Iroquois*. At the time of his retirement in 1890, Munro was the senior chief factor in the HBC's western district. He is buried at Ross Bay Cemetery.

Munro Shoal (52°36'00" 129°31'00" NW end of Wright Passage, W of Aristazabal I). Named in 1928 for Cpl Andrew Munro (or Munroe), who was a member of the Columbia detachment of Royal Engineers, which served in BC 1858–63. He deserted from the detachment's HQ at Sapperton sometime prior to June 1861, and nothing else is known about him.

Munsie Point (52°14'00" 128°10'00" SW side of Chatfield I, Seaforth Channel, just N of Bella Bella), **Munsie Rocks** (49°58'00" 127°18'00" SW of S end of Union I, entrance to Kyuquot Sd, NW side of Vancouver I). William McGillivray Munsie (1849–1906) began his career as a master mariner and ship owner in the early days of the W coast sealing trade. He was born at Pictou, NS, and came to Victoria about 1878 with his wife, Catherine (1848–1923, née Dunn), and children. Munsie started sealing with the *Carolina* (once owned by missionary William Duncan) in 1880 and soon acquired other schooners, including the *Viva*, *Mary Taylor*, *Pathfinder*, *May Belle*, *Arietas*, *Otto* and *City of San Diego*, several of which he operated in partnership with Victoria grocer Frederick Carne. He incorporated six of his vessels as the Victoria Sealing & Trading Co, 1895–1903. Eventually Munsie bought Carne out and joined forces with Victoria businessman Simon Leiser, becoming involved in lumbering (the Shawnigan Lk Lumber Co), mining, real estate and fishing, as well as sealing. In 1903 he sent his newest schooner, the *Florence M Munsie* (named after his youngest daughter), from Halifax to the Falkland and S Shetland Is in search of seals; two years later it was wrecked, without loss of life, off Cape Horn en route to Victoria. Munsie Point was known before 1925 as Hanson Point, after RN lt Francis Beversham Hanson, who served in the RCN during WWI.

Murcheson Cove (48°53'21" 123°20'05" SE side of Galiano I, Gulf Is). Findlay Murcheson (1827–1910) was born in Scotland and came to Canada in 1851. His wife, Mary (1830–1909), joined him in 1854. The Murchesons arrived on Galiano in 1882 and homesteaded on Whaler Bay. Findlay, who became a road foreman, fire warden and school trustee on the island, received a Crown grant for his property in 1903. The cove was originally called Murchison Cove in 1969, but the name was changed in 1996 to reflect the correct spelling of the family surname.

Murchison Island (52°36'00" 131°23'00" SE of Lyell I, E of Moresby I, QCI). Sir Roderick Imprey Murchison (1792–1871) was born in Scotland and first pursued a career in the British Army, seeing action in Spain in 1809 before

resigning six years later and getting married. He devoted himself to the study of geology, becoming president of both the Geological Society of London and the Royal Geographical Society, which he helped found in 1830. His great work, *The Silurian System*, was published in 1839. It describes an order of succession for certain British rock formations, based on distinctive organic remains and fossil types, and helped thinkers of the era conceive of a geological time scale. Murchison carried out surveys in Russia, 1840–45; he was able to successfully predict that gold would be discovered in Australia by noting similarities between that continent's mountains and the Urals. He was knighted in 1846, appointed director-gen of the Geological Survey of Britain in 1855 and also made director of the Royal School of Mines and the Museum of Practical Geology. At least 15 features commemorate him on this planet, and a crater on the moon is named for him as well. Murchison I, which was named by geologist George Mercer Dawson in 1878, has several ancient village sites. The Haida knew it as Da'a, according to naturalist Dr Charles Newcombe. Mt Murchison, just W of Squamish, also honours this eminent scientist. *D W*

Murder Point (48°46'00" 123°09'00" S side of Saturna I, Gulf Is). It was here, in Apr 1863, that Frederick Marks and his young married daughter Caroline Harvey were slain by members of the Lamalcha band, a renegade Cowichan First Nation group from Kuper I. Marks and Harvey were in the process of moving from Waldron I in the San Juans to settle on Mayne I. Separated in a sudden squall from a second vessel carrying the rest of the family, they were forced to seek shelter on Saturna. Their bodies were never recovered; searchers found only a smashed boat, campfire remains and the family's two dogs. The murders were one of the most sensational events to have occurred in the young colonies of BC and Vancouver I, and British warships rushed to find the perpetrators. Several First Nation villages were fired on before 18 Lamalcha were captured on Galiano I and charged with these murders and with the death of a seaman on HMS *Forward*, shot while the gunboat was bombarding a Lamalcha village. Local newspapers described the Victoria trial as a blatant miscarriage of justice: the defendants had no counsel and understood little about the proceedings; interpreters were either biased or non-existent; hearsay evidence was accepted; and confessions were coerced. Four of the prisoners were found guilty and afterwards hanged.

Muriel Rocks (52°25'00" 129°18'00" SE of Conroy I, off SW side of Aristazabal I). Muriel Mary Wells (1904–85, née Church) was a guest aboard the government survey vessel *Lillooet* about 1927. Her husband, John Wells (1890–1975), whom she'd recently married in Victoria, was the ship's 1st officer. Muriel was apparently the first person to notice water breaking over these dangerous hazards and bring them to the surveyors' attention. They were later named for her and marked on the region's hydrographic charts. Wells Rks, farther N, are named for her husband. John and Muriel Wells were long-time residents of Victoria.

Murphy Range (53°00'00" 129°11'00" N of Surf Inlet, W side of Princess Royal I). Denis Murphy (1870–1947), son of a Cariboo gold miner and roadhouse operator, became the first native-born judge on the Supreme Court of BC in 1909. He was called to the bar in 1895 and elected MLA for Yale, 1900–1902, serving also as provincial secretary. As a commissioner and judge, Murphy investigated, among other issues, illegal Chinese immigration (1910), a S Wellington coal mine disaster that resulted in 19 deaths (1915), allegations of corrupt practices in a Vancouver by-election (1916), reports of bribery in the attorney gen dept by liquor interests (1927) and the regulation of chiropractors (1931). After his first wife died at a young age, Murphy married Helen Maud Cameron (1878–1969) in Ont. He sat for 26 years on the board of governors of UBC and took part in the old-timers' reunion held at Victoria in May 1924 (*see* Adams Bay).

Murray Anchorage (53°01'00" 129°39'00" NW side of Dewdney I, Estevan Group, SE of Banks I), **Murray Rock** (52°29'00" 129°02'00" Approach to Weeteeam Bay, SW side of Aristazabal I). Lance Cpl John Murray (1833–1905) was a member of the Columbia detachment of Royal Engineers, which served in BC 1858–63. A cobbler by trade, he travelled to BC with the main contingent of men on the *Thames City*, accompanied by his wife, Jane Fuller (1824–96), and at least one child. His son John was born on the long voyage. Murray stayed on in BC after the contingent disbanded and lived at first in New Westminster, working as a shoemaker and boatbuilder. He was also secretary of the Hyack fire dept and active in the local militia (in 1866 he was listed as a sgt in the Seymour Artillery Co). In 1883, after a stint in Victoria, where Murray was keeper of the Berens I lighthouse, he moved his wife and seven children to Port Moody, where he had received a military land grant in 1870 (grants were given to all Columbia sappers who chose to remain in the colony). He built a hotel, the Rocky Point, and subdivided and sold much of his land, which forms the core of today's city. John Murray Jr (1859–1942), who established a butcher shop at Port Moody and was also a police constable and game warden, helped lay out the townsite and name its streets. Known as "Mr Port Moody," he married Clara Winnifred Dominy (1864–1950) in 1897 and served as an alderman when the community incorporated as a city in 1913. John Murray Jr was later a councillor for Burnaby, 1914–18 and 1924–25. Murray Rk is named for the father, Murray Anchorage for the son.

Murray Point (50°40'00" 125°44'00" E side of Glendale Cove, S side of Knight Inlet). After HBC master mariner Capt James Murray Reid, who came to BC in 1852. See Reid I.

Murray Shoals (52°01'00" 128°18'00" W of the Admiral Group, Queens Sd, SW of Bella Bella). Rear Adm Leonard Warren Murray, CB, CBE (1896–1971), was born in NS and became a first-term cadet at the Royal Naval College of Canada in 1911. He was promoted to lt cdr in 1925 and attended Royal Naval Staff College in 1927, taking over as senior naval officer at Esquimalt, 1929–31. Murray was cdr of the destroyer *Saguenay*, 1932–34, then senior naval office at Halifax. At the beginning of WWII he was promoted capt and named director of naval operations and training, then deputy chief of naval staff. He served as cdr of the destroyer *Assiniboine*, 1940–41, before being named flag officer for Nfld. As a rear adm he was CO Atlantic Coast in 1942 and cdr-in-chief Canadian NW Atlantic in 1943. Murray was the only Canadian to command a naval theatre of war in WWII. When the Halifax riots, a two-day orgy of looting and mayhem, erupted on VE Day, naval authorities were blamed for preparing inadequately, and Murray, as senior officer, became the scapegoat, resigning from the RCN in 1946 and moving with his wife, Jean, to England, where he embarked on a second career as a lawyer and municipal politician. The Murray Shoals were named in 1944, presumably in association with the nearby Admiral Group.

Musclow Islet (48°41'02" 123°23'51" W side of Iroquois Passage, between Goudge I and NE end of Saanich Peninsula, N of Victoria). This name was adopted in 1965 on the recommendation of local residents after a fisherman named Clarence Ludwig Musclow (1895–1989), who lived on the islet for a number of years in a shack with a small wharf. He was born in Ont and married Susan Young Dickson, from Scotland, at Vancouver in 1920. Musclow died at Nanaimo and is buried in the Gabriola I Cemetery.

Musgrave Peaks (53°05'27" 129°39'14" On Trutch I, part of the Estevan Group, between Banks I and Aristazabal I). Lt Cdr Philip Cranston Musgrave (1866–1920) was in charge of hydrographic surveys on Canada's Pacific coast, 1908–19, based aboard CGS *Lillooet*. Originally an RN officer, he became a civilian assistant to hydrographer Capt William Tooker on the Nfld survey, 1902–6. In 1907, under George Blanchard Dodge, he conducted the shore survey at Prince Rupert when it was chosen as the GTP terminus. Musgrave died unexpectedly at Esquimalt. Cranston I off Pitt I is also named for him. The higher of the two Musgrave Peaks, which were formerly known as the Musgrave Range, has an elevation of 293 m. One summit was once home to a radio communications facility with conspicuous microwave antennas; the other sported a triangulation station for surveying.

Musgrave Point (48°45'00" 123°33'00" W side of Saltspring I, SW of Bruce Peak, Gulf Is), **Musgrave Rock** (48°44'00" 123°33'00" Just SE of Musgrave Point). Edward Musgrave bought the 2,800-ha S Saltspring I landholdings of the Pimsbury brothers in 1885. The four brothers, from England, had settled on the SW coast of Saltspring in 1874 and raised sheep on the western slopes of Bruce Peak and Mt Tuam. Musgrave only stayed on the island for seven years, selling out to Clive and Edward Trench, but he gave his name to several features, including Musgrave Landing. This isolated settlement, cut off from the rest of the island until 1924, consisted mostly of employees of the enormous sheep ranch, which ran more than 1,000 head and could produce nearly two tonnes of wool at a shearing. The island's entire SW massif, now given the four separate names of Mt Sullivan, Bruce Peak, Hope Hill and Mt Tuam, was once known locally as Musgrave Mtn. The authors and adventurers Miles and Beryl Smeeton farmed at Musgrave, 1946–55. *E*

Mushroom Point (49°55'00" 127°13'00" S of the mouth of Kapoose Ck, E of Grassy I, SE of Kyuquot Sd, NW side of Vancouver I). This name was adopted in 1950 after the peculiar outline or shape of this feature, which resembles a mushroom.

Musqueam (49°14'00" 123°13'00" At the mouth of the Fraser R, N of Sea I, SW side of Vancouver). This important Coast Salish site, now a First Nation reserve, was the main village of the X'muzk'i'um (Musqueam) people, who occupied the mouth of the Fraser and the area now known as Vancouver at the time of first contact with European explorers. It was here, after descending the river that bears his name, that Simon Fraser met such a hostile reception that he decided to turn back and explore no further. X'muzk'i'um (or XwMuthkwium) is an adaptation of the Halkomelem word *masqui* (or *muxqui*), "an edible grass that grows in the river." Much of the Musqueam reserve is leased as housing and a golf course. In 2007, BC agreed to transfer about 90 ha of land, including the University Golf Course and Bridgeport Casino lands, to the X'muzk'i'um First Nation. *E*

Mussel Bay (52°55'00" 128°02'00" NE end of Mussel Inlet), **Mussel Inlet** (52°54'00" 128°07'00" NE extension of Sheep Passage, E of Princess Royal I), **Mussel River** (Flows SW into the head of Mussel Inlet). Mussel Inlet was named by Capt George Vancouver in 1793. It was here, at Poison Cove, that a number of his crew members became ill after eating tainted mussels for breakfast. Seaman John Carter (*see* Carter Bay) died shortly thereafter, probably from paralytic shellfish poisoning. Mussel Inlet acquired

its current spelling in the 1874 edition of the Admiralty chart for the region; it was misspelled Muscle Inlet on earlier editions.

Muster Rock (52°16'20" 128°23'17" Between Ivory I and Watch I, S entrance to Perrin Anchorage, Seaforth Channel, NW of Bella Bella). Named, but misspelled, for Lucy Sophia Musters (1844–75), the wife of retired British Army officer William Chaworth Musters. The Musters were among the first settlers at Comox in 1862 and brought with them the district's first team of horses for ploughing. Lucy and her grey pony Kangaroo became familiar and well-loved sights in the Comox valley. When she fell ill, two settlers paddled to Nanaimo, a 14-hour trip, for assistance, but no doctor was available and the medicines they returned with were, ultimately, of little use. William and his four older children returned to England after Lucy's death, leaving the two-week-old baby, also Lucy Sophia, with a sympathetic family in Victoria, the Warners (*see* Warner Rk). In 1901, at Victoria, young Lucy married Arthur William Currie, who went on to become the first Canadian cdr of the Canadian Expeditionary Force in WWI and a hero of Vimy Ridge. When Arthur was knighted in 1917, she became Lady Currie.

Myrmidon Point (50°04'00" 124°48'00" NE tip of Malaspina Peninsula, NE end of Str of Georgia). The steam-powered gunboat HMS *Myrmidon*, built at Chatham in 1867, was posted to Esquimalt in 1873. The 795-tonne, four-gun vessel responded to the wreck of the USS *Saranac* (*see* Saranac I) on Ripple Rk and was also used for surveying. It was paid off at Hong Kong in 1889, decommissioned and sold. The Myrmidons of Greek mythology were skilled warriors who accompanied Achilles to Troy. The word, somewhat unfairly, has come to mean an unquestioning follower or servant.

Myrtle Point (49°47'00" 124°27'00" E side of Malaspina Str, between Albion Point and Grief Point, SE of Powell R), **Myrtle Rocks** (49°47'00" 124°28'00" Just NW of Myrtle Point). According to a report in the *Powell R News*, the point was named after Myrtle McCormick, whose family was among the first settlers and loggers in the vicinity in the late 1800s. Bloedel, Stewart & Welch had a large railway logging operation here from 1911 to the mid-1920s. By the early 2000s the area had been transformed into a residential community, regional park and golf course. Nearby Myrtle Ck is named after the point.

N

Nab Patch (51°18'00" 127°37'00" N entrance to Takush Hbr, Smith Sd, N of Port Hardy). Named after Birkby Nab in Yorkshire, hereditary homestead of the Greaves family, who were ancestors of Anne Walbran, wife of BC mariner and author Capt John Walbran. Walbran named nearby Birkby Point after this farm in 1903.

Naden Harbour, Naden River. *See* Cape Naden.

Naden Islets (54°23'00" 130°16'00" W side of Tuck Inlet, S of Tuck Narrows, just N of Prince Rupert). George Ratcliffe Naden (1865–1953) was born at Derby, England, and moved to Ont in 1883. There he married Margaret Hogarth Dunn (1867–1920) of Owen Sd. The Nadens came to BC in 1891. They lived first at Greenwood, where George was an alderman, 1899–1901, mayor, 1901–6, and president of the board of trade, 1902–4. In 1907 he became the Liberal MLA for Greenwood and served in the legislature until 1909. The family then moved to Prince Rupert, where George's career unfolded in a familiar fashion: alderman, 1910–13, and president of the board of trade, 1913–15. In 1915 he was appointed deputy minister of Lands and moved to Victoria. The Nadens are buried at the Ross Bay Cemetery.

Nagas Point (52°11'00" 131°22'00" W entrance to Flamingo Inlet, SW end of Moresby I, QCI), **Nagas Rocks** (Just SE of Nagas Point). Nagas was the name of a Raven crest village located just inside the point. QCI historian Kathleen Dalzell relates that the inhabitants of the village, known as the Slave People after a derogatory comment by the wife of a chief, met their fate after they treacherously murdered a group of visitors from Masset. The Massets planned and executed a colossal retribution, killing every man in the village and taking away all the healthy women and children as slaves. Nagas Point was formerly known as Post Point. *D*

Nahmint Bay (49°04'00" 124°52'00" W side of Alberni Inlet, at mouth of Nahmint R, S of Port Alberni, Vancouver I). This bay is named for the Nahmintaht people, whose main village was apparently located on the Nahmint R, which was once home to a famous run of large and much-fought-over spring salmon. The Nahmintaht were wiped out by another First Nation group, the Hitatso'ath, who took over the rich fishery at Nahmint Bay and later amalgamated with several other local tribes to form the Ucluelet First Nation. The Ucluelets occupied the Nahmint area seasonally until the late 1800s and still have a reserve at the mouth of the Nahmint R, called Kleykleyhous. Prospector Frank Gerrard and his family settled on the bay in 1894 and investigated the area's copper deposits but were not able to develop them. Extensive railway logging occurred later, and a successful sport-fishing lodge operated until 1974, by which time the salmon run had become severely depleted. Nahmint Lk, Nahmint Mtn and the Nahmint R all take their names from the original Nahmintaht First Nation. *E*

Nahwitti Bar (50°53'00" 128°00'00" S of W end of Hope I, W Goletas Channel, off N end of Vancouver I), **Nahwitti Point** (50°54'00" 127°59'00" SW side of Hope I). The name refers both to a fortified former village site, located on Cape Sutil, and to the Nahwitti First Nation, whose traditional territory was the very N end of Vancouver I and the islands offshore. More than a dozen different variations of the name can be found in early documents, especially Nawitty and Newitty. The Nahwitti are actually an amalgamation of three groups—the Tlatlasikwala, Nakumgilisala and Yutlinuk—all of whom spoke the same dialect of Kwakwala, the language of the Kwakwaka'wakw people. After the Yutlinuk, who lived on the Scott Is, died out in the early 1800s, the Tlatlasikwala and Nakumgilisala joined together at Nahwitti in the 1850s before establishing their principal village at Humdaspe on Hope I. Spanish explorer Dionisio Alcalá-Galiano noted the settlement on Cape Sutil in 1792. The Nahwitti were subject to two of the RN's earliest punitive actions in BC after refusing to surrender the suspected murderers of three British deserters. An armed party from HMS *Daedalus* burned a camp (on Nigei I, possibly) in 1850, and another naval force, from HMS *Daphne*, attacked and destroyed a

Nahwitti village in 1851. (This may have been the Cape Sutil site or else Humdaspe at Bull Hbr; reports conflict. *See also* Daedalus Passage, Daphne Point *and* Deserters Group.) Most Nahwitti members now live at Alert Bay or near Quatsino Sd. Nahwitti Cone, Nahwitti Lk, Nahwitti Mtn and Nahwitti R are also named for this First Nation. The Nahwitti Bar is a shallow subterranean ridge or sill formed by a glacial moraine; turbulent tide rips and overfalls develop there under certain conditions, and the area can be notoriously dangerous for small craft.

Nakons Islet (52°26'00" 131°21'00" SE of Huxley I, off NW side of Burnaby I, E of S Moresby I, QCI). The Nakons (or Nikons) were a subgroup of the Haida Eagle crest known as the Yadus, or Great House People. Nestecanna, a famous Skidegate chief who was once captured and enslaved by his enemies on the BC mainland, was a member of this clan. He was freed by ransom and managed to overcome the deep shame associated with such treatment by becoming wealthy and holding extravagant potlatches. Named by the hydrographic service in 1962. *D*

Nakwakto Rapids (51°06'00" 127°30'00" At junction of Slingsby Channel and Schooner Channel, entrance to Seymour Inlet, NW side of Queen Charlotte Str, N of Port Hardy). This area is part of the traditional territory of the Nakwakto (Nak'waxda'xw, Nakoaktok) people, who are members of the Kwakwaka'wakw First Nation. Their main village, Ba'as (Pahas), was located at Blunden Hbr, to the SE. The Nakwakto produced some notable artists, including Hiamas, or Willie Seaweed, whose carved poles can still be seen at Alert Bay. The tribe moved to Port Hardy in the early 1960s when the federal government threatened to cut off funding if they remained in their isolated location. The Nakwakto Rapids are the fastest on the BC coast (and one of the fastest in the world), reaching 15 knots (27 km/h) on a strong ebb tide and causing Turret Rk (qv) in the middle of the rapids to tremble. The duration of slack water is only about six minutes. The rapids were named by RN surveyor Lt Daniel Pender on the *Beaver* in 1865. *W*

Namu (51°52'00" 127°52'00" On Namu Hbr), **Namu Harbour** (51°52'00" 127°53'00" NE side of Fitz Hugh Sd, just S of SW entrance to Burke Channel, SE of Bella Bella), **Namu Range** (51°51'00" 127°47'00" SE of Namu Hbr). Namu is a Heiltsuk First Nation word meaning "place of high winds," referring especially to the SE blasts that sweep over the 914-m Namu Range and give nearby Whirlwind Bay its name. Archeological excavations have revealed that Namu was used by aboriginal people as a habitation site, at least seasonally, for 11,000 years or more and is thus one of the longest continually occupied places in Canada. In 1893, Robert Draney built a cannery at this spot and added a sawmill in 1911. The cannery was rebuilt and changed hands several times, eventually becoming one of the largest and most efficient fish-processing complexes on the BC

coast. BC Packers Ltd was the owner by 1928 and added a reduction plant, a cold-storage component and a modern ship-repair yard. Fire destroyed the facility in 1961 but it was rebuilt, and the cannery operated until 1970, the cold storage until 1988. BC Packers sold the site in 1991, and subsequent owners have fought a losing battle to maintain marine services and preserve Namu's buildings, with the hope of establishing some kind of tourism or heritage attraction. Namu Lk and Namu R derive their names from the community and harbour. *E*

The steamship *Maude* taking on coal at Nanaimo in 1875 with the landmark bastion in the background. *BC Archives F-05229*

Nanaimo (49°10'00" 123°56'00" SE side of Vancouver I), **Nanaimo Harbour** (49°10'00" 123°54'00" Just E of Nanaimo). This important BC coastal city takes its name from the area's Island Halkomelem First Nation inhabitants, the Snuneymuxw, who still occupy the region. Many different spellings for this name are found in early documents, including Sna Ney Mous, Sne-ny-mo and Snanaimuq. The Snuneymuxw were a confederacy of five extended families whose winter villages—Solachwan, Tewahlchin, Ishihan, Anuweenis and Kwalsiarwahl— were located in the general area. The exact meaning of the name is uncertain, but it seems to refer to a shared locale; "meeting place" or "people of many names" are two common translations. Explorer José Narváez, the first European to see this harbour, in July 1791, called it Boca de Winthuysen, after Spanish naval officer Francisco Xavier de Winthuysen, and this name was still in use by HBC officials in the early 1850s, after which Nanaimo (or Nanymo) Bay was preferred. A trading post was built here by the HBC in 1849, after coal deposits were discovered nearby, and the settlement that soon grew up around it was originally called Colvile Town, after HBC governor Andrew Colvile (*see* Colvile I). Coal was the city's main reason for existence until WWII, when the seams ran out and Nanaimo diversified to become a regional business and manufacturing centre. Incorporated in 1874, it is the second-largest community on Vancouver I. Nanaimo Lks and the Nanaimo R (known by First Nation groups as Quamquamqua, or "strong, strong water") are also named for the Snuneymuxw. The harbour was first surveyed in 1853 by George Inskip, master of HMS *Virago*, then again by Capt George Richards in 1860 and Cdr Morris Smyth in 1899. *E W*

Nanakwa Shoal (53°50'00" 128°50'00" W of Coste I, Douglas Channel, S of Kitimat). Named in 1953 after the Kitimat area's first newspaper, called *Na-na-kwa* ("Dawn on the Pacific Coast") and published four times a year (1893–1906) by Rev George Raley on the Kitamaat Mission's primitive printing press. This monthly bulletin or newsletter carried mission tracts and appeals mixed in with local news.

Nanat Islet (48°53'00" 125°05'00" E side of Trevor Channel, S of Tzartus I, Barkley Sd, W side of Vancouver I). Nanat was the head chief of the Huu-ay-aht (Ohiaht) First Nation in 1817, when Capt Camille de Roquefeuil visited SE Barkley Sd with the *Bordelais*. Roquefeuil circumnavigated the globe in 1816–19 on a trading voyage, attempting to find new markets for France. He anchored in Grappler Inlet, to which he gave the name Port Desire. Roquefeuil, who in 1823 published an account of his voyage that gives a useful European view of early First Nation life on the BC coast, noted that Nanat was arrogant and treated his subordinate chiefs harshly, often taking away and keeping the presents that the Europeans had given them. Nanat It, named in 1934, was formerly known as Mark It.

Nangwai Islands (52°24'00" 131°37'00" Off N entrance to Gowgaia Bay, SW side of Moresby I, QCI), **Nangwai Rock** (52°24'00" 131°36'00" Just SE of Nangwai Is). US fur trader Joseph Ingraham explored this area in 1791 and named the southernmost island after Ebenezer Dorr, the supercargo or owner's representative aboard the *Hope*, Ingraham's vessel. The passage between the islands he named Port Perkins after the *Hope*'s co-owner, Boston importer Thomas Perkins, whose specialty was trade with China. Neither name stuck. The Haida people know the islands as Nangwai, and the hydrographic service decided to adopt that name for them in 1949 and for the nearby rock in 1962.

Nankivell Islands (50°54'00" 127°18'00" N side of Queen Charlotte Str, just SW of Blunden Hbr, NE of Port Hardy), **Nankivell Point** (49°17'00" 124°08'00" NW of Wallis Point, N of Nanoose Hbr, SE side of Vancouver I), **Nankivell Point** (54°08'00" 132°48'00" Near mouth of the Jalun R, W of Virago Sd, N side of Graham I, QCI). Lt John Howard Nankivell (b 1882) served aboard the survey vessel *Egeria* in the early 1900s. Before that he was on the battleship *Jupiter*. It appears that Nankivell liked what he saw of the BC coast and later immigrated to Victoria, where he may have had relatives. There is a death record for him at Victoria, dated 1959. The two southern features were named by Cdr John Parry of HMS *Egeria* in 1904,

the QCI point by Capt Frederick Learmonth in 1907. Nankivell was involved with surveys of Nanoose Hbr, Active Pass, Moresby Passage, Gabriola Passage, Port Simpson and Browning Entrance.

Nanoose Bay on southeast Vancouver Island. *Peter Vassilopoulos*

Nanoose Bay (49°16'00" 124°12'00" Head of Nanoose Hbr), **Nanoose Harbour** (49°16'00" 124°10'00" NW of Nanaimo, SE side of Vancouver I), **Nanoose Hill** (49°16'29" 124°09'36" NE side of Nanoose Hbr). Nanoose Bay refers to the community, Nanoose Hbr to the body of water. The word is a corruption of the name of the original Island Halkomelem inhabitants of the region, the Snaw Naw As, who have a reserve on the harbour. This Lantzville-based First Nation is related to the Snuneymuxw of the Nanaimo region; its members were frequently known as the Nonooas in earlier times. BC historians Helen and Philip Akrigg give two possible translations for the name: "a collection of families at one place" or "pushing inward" (referring to the shape of Nanoose Hbr). White agricultural settlement began in the area in the 1880s; several small communities and a large sawmill sprang up. The harbour is HQ for a controversial Canadian Forces base used by the US Navy to test torpedoes and other naval weaponry in the nearby Str of Georgia. In 1999, after a series of protests and attempts by the province to prevent nuclear-powered vessels entering the region, the federal government expropriated 217 sq km of ocean floor and signed a long-term agreement allowing the US to continue testing. Nanoose Ck and Nanoose Hill (formerly known as Notch Hill) also derive their names from the Snaw Naw As people, as does Nonooa Rk in Nanoose Hbr. *E W*

Napier Island (51°19'00" 127°34'00" Entrance to Boswell Inlet, Smith Sd, S of Rivers Inlet). After early Victoria meteorologist Frank Napier Denison. *See* Denison I.

Napier Point (52°08'00" 128°08'00" E side of Campbell I, just S of Bella Bella). Named by Lt Daniel Pender about 1867 after Archibald Napier, the HBC officer in charge of the trading post and general store at Bella Bella, 1867–71, and later at Bella Coola. HBC records state that he committed suicide in 1875 "by taking strychnine." Archibald Point on the opposite side of the channel is also named for him.

Nares Hills (52°42'37" 128°46'44" Between head of Trahey Inlet and Laredo Inlet, Princess Royal I), **Nares Islets** (54°28'00" 130°52'00" Hudson Bay Passage, between Dundas I and Baron I, NW of Prince Rupert), **Nares Point** (49°12'10" 123°55'30" N end of Newcastle I, just E of Nanaimo), **Nares Rock** (48°59'00" 123°45'00" Entrance to Ladysmith Hbr, W side of Stuart Channel, SE of Nanaimo), **Nares Rock** (49°38'00" 124°04'00" NE of Pearson I, entrance to Pender Hbr, SE Malaspina Str, NW of Vancouver). Two brothers—Lt George Edward Nares and Cdr John Dodd Nares—served on the BC coast aboard the RN survey vessel *Egeria*, though not at the same time. Both were sons of a famous father, Adm Sir George Strong Nares (1831–1915), who in the 1870s led a remarkable oceanographic expedition aboard HMS *Challenger* and conducted extensive exploratory and survey work in the Arctic and Magellan Str. Lt George Nares (1873–1905) was with HMS *Dart* on the Australian Station, where he married Catharine "Minnah" Walch (1877–1940), from Tasmania, in 1901. He served aboard HMS *Egeria* in 1903–4. John Nares (1877–1957) spent eight years on the Australian Station with HMS *Penguin*, 1894–1902, before joining HMS *Research* and later serving in BC with the *Egeria*, 1907–10. He briefly became the *Egeria*'s last cdr in 1910 before the vessel was sold. John Nares, in fact, made the final Admiralty survey in BC, of Malaspina Str in 1910, as all hydrographic work after the sale of the *Egeria* was taken over by the Canadian government. Nares commanded the survey vessel *Fantome* off Australia and Tasmania, 1911–13, then worked at the Admiralty hydrographic dept for most of WWI, though at the end of the war he took part in naval operations off Palestine as cdr of HMS *Enterprise*, winning the DSO. After WWI he returned to surveying—in the Red Sea, Strs of Malacca, Mediterranean and off W Africa—becoming assistant hydrographer of the RN and rising in rank to vice adm, retired. He was also a director of the International Hydrographic Bureau. While it is fairly certain that Nares Hills and Nares Rk at Pender Hbr are named for John, and Nares Point for George Edward, it is unclear which members of this illustrious naval family the remaining features commemorate. Nares Point was formerly known as Boulder Point, named on an 1853 HBC survey, but was renamed by Cdr John Parry in 1903.

Narrow Island. *See* Wallace I.

Narvaez Bay (48°46'00" 123°06'00" E end of Saturna I, NW of Monarch Head, Gulf Is), **Narvaez Island** (49°38'00" 126°35'00" One of the Spanish Pilot Group, SW of Bligh I, Nootka Sd, W side of Vancouver I). Spanish naval officer José Maria Narváez (1768–1840), born at Cadiz, Spain, was sent out to Havana in 1784 and spent three years working in the Caribbean before being assigned to San Blas naval base in Mexico. He accompanied Estéban Martínez and Gonzales López de Haro on their 1788 expedition to Alaska and was also present the following summer at Nootka Sd when Martínez seized several British vessels and instigated the Nootka Sd "crisis." Narváez explored the entrance to Juan de Fuca Str in 1789 with one of these ships, the *North West America* (renamed the *Santa Gertrudis la Magna*), and then sailed another captured vessel, the *Princess Royal* (the Spanish *Princesa Real*), back to San Blas. In 1791, as cdr of the *Santa Saturnina*, he became the first European to see the Str of Georgia, which the Spanish named the Canal de Nuestra Senora del Rosario. He was under the command of Francisco Eliza, in the *San Carlos*, on this voyage but did most of the surveying, taking his vessel as far N as Comox and later preparing one of the most significant early charts of the BC coast. Narváez remained with the Spanish navy until Mexican independence in 1821, doing survey work and helping to put down various rebellions against Spanish rule. After joining the Mexican navy in 1821 and being elected Guadalajara's provincial deputy, he served as cdr at San Blas, 1822–27, and continued to work as a surveyor, producing important maps of Mexico's coastlines and northern boundaries. He died at Guadalajara. Narvaez Bay, formerly known as Deep Cove, was named in 1946, Narvaez I in 1934. *E W*

Narwhal Reef (53°03'46" 129°35'02" Entrance to Devlin Bay, W side of Estevan Sd, between Prior I and Trutch I, SE of Banks I). The Canadian Coast Guard buoy tender *Narwhal* "discovered" this previously uncharted reef with near-disastrous results in May 1981. H E Adams, the *Narwhal*'s cdr, reported that "the ship came very close to running aground that day. Good luck and a sharp lookout sure helped to avoid an embarrassing situation and a lot of paperwork." The 81-m vessel's home port was Dartmouth, NS, and with its limited icebreaking capabilities, it had spent much time in the 1970s doing survey work in Hudson Bay. Based at Victoria on temporary duty for 31 months, the tender serviced aids to navigation around Vancouver I and in the Prince Rupert area and took part in search and rescue incidents. "The *Narwhal* crew made many friends along the BC coast," according to Adams. "We spread Eastern hospitality from Victoria to Prince Rupert. Some of my crew married beautiful BC girls." Built in 1963, the ship was sold in 2000 to Florida businessman Arnie Gemino, completely refurbished as a $30-million expedition yacht (with a pirate-themed decor) and renamed the *Bart Roberts*. Narwhal Reef was surveyed in detail in 1985 and named in 1988.

Nash Point (52°41'00" 128°34'00" SE side of Princess Royal I, just N of Alexander Inlet). Sub-lt Robert Arthur Nash of the RCN was killed in action Apr 29, 1944, aged 22, while serving aboard HMCS *Athabaskan*. The

N

Tribal-class destroyer was torpedoed and sunk in the English Channel, with the loss of 129 lives, while engaging four German *E*-class destroyers and numerous torpedo boats in company with HMCS *Haida*. Nash was posthumously mentioned in dispatches "for gallant and distinguished service." He is buried at Plouescat Communal Cemetery in France.

Nasoga Gulf (54°52'00" 130°06'00" E side of Portland Inlet, between Nass Bay and Khutzeymateen Inlet, N of Prince Rupert). The meaning of the name, which first appears on an Admiralty chart in 1868, is uncertain, though the Nisga'a people know this feature as Ts'im Sgaawa'a. *Ts'im* can be translated as "inside or within something" and *sgaawa'a* as "preventing someone from doing something." The name refers to a legend involving Txeemsim, the grandfather of the Nisga'a people, hurling a rock toward the mouth of the Nass R and creating the isthmus at the head of the gulf that connects the Myler Peninsula to the mainland, thus cutting off a route to the much-contested eulachon fishing grounds for enemy groups. The gulf is mislabelled on some early maps as Nasoka Bay or Nosoka Gulf.

Nasparti Inlet (50°08'00" 127°40'00" W of Ououkinsh Inlet, Checleset Bay, SE of Brooks Peninsula, NW side of Vancouver I). Named by Capt George Richards of HMS *Hecate* in 1862 after the First Nation inhabitants of the area, who also appear on early maps and in documents as the Nespod, Nasparte, Naspatte, Naspahtee and Nasparto. This geographic feature was the original Port Brooks (*see* Brooks Bay), named by early fur trader James Colnett in 1787. It was in this inlet, according to historian John Walbran, that the trader Robert Gray was attacked in 1792 and "obliged to kill" a number of his aggressors. The Nasparti, however, later complained to the Spanish at Nootka Sd that it was they who had been attacked, and that Gray had taken by force all their sea otter furs, which they had refused to sell at the prices offered. Gray named the inlet Bulfinch's Sd after Dr Thomas Bulfinch, a well-known physician in Boston at that time, and spent considerable time there with the *Columbia Rediviva* in 1791–92. *W*

Nass Bay (54°58'00" 129°54'00" Mouth of the Nass R), **Nass Harbour** (54°56'00" 129°56'00" SW side of Nass Bay), **Nass Point** (55°01'00" 130°00'00" E entrance to Observatory Inlet, N entrance to Nass Bay), **Nass River** (54°58'37" 129°53'22" Flows S and W from the Skeena Mtns into Nass Bay and Portland Inlet, NE of Prince Rupert). The name Nass (or Naas) comes from a Tlingit First Nation word meaning "food basket" and refers especially to the great abundance of eulachon and salmon found on the lower river. The Nisga'a people, who occupy the lower Nass valley, know the river as Lisims, meaning "murky." Suspended glacial sediments are responsible for much of the murkiness. The grandfather of the Nisga'a

people, Txeemsim, created the river by walking from its headwaters at Magoonhl Lisims (Nass Lk) to the ocean. Capt George Vancouver was the first European to visit the area, in 1793. The aboriginal people he encountered, who told him the river was named Ewen Nass (*ewen* meaning "great" or "powerful"), were probably Tlingit. The name Nass R was in use by HBC officials by 1828; Ft Simpson, established on Nass Bay in 1831 (but moved farther S, to Port Simpson, in 1834), was originally called Ft Nass. Nass Bay was a centre for salmon canning, 1879–1942. The cannery at Nass Hbr—often referred to as McLellan's Cannery, after James A McLellan, its founder—operated from 1887 to 1928 and was home to the region's first post office. Six other canneries were located on the bay: Arrandale, Port Nelson, Pacific Northern, Cascade, Mill Bay and Croasdaile. The Nass Ranges, between the Skeena R and Nass R, and Nass Camp, a small, non-aboriginal settlement in the Nass valley, are named after the river. On a primitive early map of the region, the Nass is shown flowing into the head of Alice Arm and is named Simpson's R. *E W*

Navvy Jack Point (49°20'00" 123°10'00" N side of Burrard Inlet, just W of First Narrows, W Vancouver). "Navvy Jack" was the nickname of pioneer W Vancouver settler John Thomas, who was born in Wales about 1832, immigrated to N America as a young man and made his way to BC for the Cariboo gold rush. He ran freight in the Interior, then moved to Burrard Inlet in 1866 and operated a ferry. He found success with a gravel operation at the mouth of the Capilano R and supplied materials to building sites around the inlet with his 5-tonne sloop ("navvy" is British slang for a construction labourer). Thomas bought a half-interest in Gastown's Granville Hotel and married Rowia, a Skxwúmish (Squamish) First Nation woman and granddaughter of Chief Capilano. They were the first settlers at W Vancouver, building a home there in 1873 (which still stands—the oldest continuously occupied residence in the Lower Mainland—though much altered and no longer on its original site) on a homestead that covered much of today's Ambleside. Later in life, after serving on N Vancouver's first municipal council, Thomas succumbed again to the lure of gold and died at Barkerville about 1900. The term "navvy jack," meaning a mix of sand and gravel used for making concrete, has entered the language locally and is widely employed by building supply companies. The point was formerly known as Newcastle Point and also, until 1949, as Reardon Point, after Capt Joseph Robert Reardon (1862–1907), one-time 1st officer of the *Empress of China* and an early Vancouver pilot. *E*

Naylor Bay (48°51'00" 123°19'00" NW end of Mayne I, Gulf Is). Emma Collinson (1873–1954) grew up on Mayne I, the daughter of William Collinson, the island's first storekeeper and postmaster (*see* Collinson Point),

Nisga'a First Nation Names

In 50 or 100 years, the place names in the BC gazetteer will need extensive revision. This won't be because of global warming—though that phenomenon may well cause hundreds of changes, with islands becoming islets, islets reduced to rocks, and rocks turned into shoals—but will be a result of First Nation treaties. One aspect of most treaty negotiations involves the restoration of traditional names as "official" names. Upcoming treaties will likely each contain a section specifying names to be changed, and as each agreement is implemented, charts and maps will need to be updated.

For instance, when the Nisga'a First Nation treaty was ratified on May 11, 2000, 34 Nisga'a place names became official designations. Some of the names were new, applied to geographical features that had either English or totally erroneous "Indian" official names. Other names simply made minor improvements to existing terminology.

The Nisga'a homeland is on either side of the lower Nass River in northern BC. The Nisga'a people are like the salmon, moving between fresh and salt water; their largest village can be found safely inland, some 40 kilometres from the mouth of the Nass, but they also rely on the ocean for food and livelihoods. There are villages on Nass Bay and at the entrance to the river, and many important cultural and historic sites are located farther away, on Portland Canal and Portland and Observatory inlets.

The main Nisga'a community of New Aiyansh is reached by road from Terrace via the Nisga'a Highway, which runs north along Ksi Sii Aks (formerly the Tseax River) and Lava Lake. It's a spectacular region to visit, site of Canada's most recent volcanic event, which happened about 250 years ago. A huge outpouring of lava flowed from the main crater, which can be reached on foot by taking a fairly arduous guided tour, to the Nass River, which was actually constricted and reconfigured by the molten basalt.

Recently built roads and bridges now allow vehicular travel to the other Nisga'a villages. In the old days, Gitwinksihlkw (which used to be called Canyon City) could only be approached by boat or by crossing a daunting pedestrian suspension bridge over the racing river. The name can be translated as "people of the salamander's habitat," though salamanders have disappeared from the area since the upsurge of volcanic activity. Farther west, you can visit Laxgalts'ap (formerly Greenville), near the river mouth, and Gingolx (formerly Kincolith), on Nass Bay, both accessible for many decades only by boat or floatplane.

The name Laxgalts'ap (pronounced *lach-ALL dzap*) means "dwelling place situated on an earlier dwelling place" and recognizes the fact that a village originally located here was destroyed by fire. Gingolx (pronounced *gin GOLch*) is a gorgeous spot, perched beside Nass Bay and surrounded by soaring mountains. A neat grid of streets is dominated by a historic missionary church and a modern, red-roofed community centre. The name is usually translated as "place of scalps" and refers to an ancient battle between Nisga'a and Haida. Nearby First Nations often raided the Nass Bay area for its incredibly rich resources of eulachon, a small fish from which a much-loved oil and food condiment is made.

Fishery Bay, where the river widens at its mouth, was the heart of the eulachon harvest, which today is in serious decline. Under the terms of the Nisga'a treaty, this long-standing name changes to Ts'im K'ol'hl Da'oots'ip, which means "behind the fortress." A huge rock on the bay provided protection for the Nisga'a during times of war. Farther afield, near the entrance to Alice Arm, is Xts'init (pronounced *sti NIT*), which means "across to" and may refer to an isthmus that connects Perry Peninsula to the mainland. Farthest away are X'uji (*OOD zi*), on Portland Canal, which used to be the Georgie reserve, and Sgamagunt, "the flat part of the river," just south of Stewart.

The new Nisga'a names are described in a nifty feature on the website of the BC Geographical Names Office (*www.ilmb.gov.bc.ca/bcnames*). Click on "What's New" at the right side of the screen, and then on "Nisga'a Treaty names." Two detailed maps locate all the sites, and the names can be clicked for further information. Each name has its own web page, complete with a pronunciation guide and an audio accompaniment. Some pages even have miniature slide shows of historic and contemporary images.

Gingolx on Nass Bay. *Andrew Scott*

N

who turned his Miners Bay home into a boarding house in 1895. She went to school in Victoria, where, in 1906, she married William Brooke Glassy Naylor (b 1865), whose father, also William Brooke Naylor, was sheriff of Vancouver I, 1860–66. The younger William was listed as a miner in the 1901 BC census. Emma and her husband expanded her father's boarding house after his death and named it Grandview Lodge; in the early 2000s it was still operating as the Springwater Lodge, BC's oldest continuously functioning inn. The attractions at Grandview Lodge, apparently, were the fishing and the food. Emma played a major role with both, as she was one of the area's leading rowboat guides as well as a fabulous cook. The name was adopted in 1969 at the request of the Gulf Is Branch of the BC Historical Assoc.

Naysash Bay (51°19'00" 127°21'00" N of Hickey Cove, Naysash Inlet), **Naysash Inlet** (51°20'00" 127°16'00" N side of Smith Inlet, N of Port Hardy). BC mariner and author John Walbran, who commanded the Canadian government lighthouse tender *Quadra* on the BC coast, 1891–1903, made a preliminary survey of Smith Inlet in 1903. He recommended to the Geographic Board of Canada that the First Nation name for the "gloomy," narrow, unnavigable inlet be made official, and so it came to pass. *W*

Naze, The. *See* The Naze.

Nealon Point (52°18'00" 128°03'00" N side of Chatfield I, E end of Return Channel, N of Bella Bella). Named in 1925 for Francis David Nealon (1881–1944), from Ont, who was the dock agent for Canadian National Steamships at Vancouver in the early 1920s.

Neavold Point (52°16'00" 127°39'00" N side of Dean Channel, just S of Ocean Falls, NE of Bella Bella). Neavold is a misspelling of the name of an early settler in the Bella Coola valley, Andrew O Nesvold (1863–1933). His name does not appear on the list of original Norwegian colonists who arrived in the valley in 1894, but by 1905 he is noted as one of five partners in the Salloomt R sawmill and lumber business that operated in the valley until 1936. Nesvold was seriously injured in an accident at the mill when a large pulley broke apart and hit him, breaking both of his legs and leaving him unfit for any kind of heavy work. He died at Bella Coola. The point was named by the hydrographic service in 1953.

Nedden Island (53°02'00" 131°57'00" N end of Carmichael Passage, Cumshewa Inlet, NE side of Moresby I, QCI), **Nedden Rock** (52°17'00" 128°07'00" Entrance to Morehouse Bay, W side of Chatfield I, N of Bella Bella). Named in 1926 for Capt Henry Emil Nedden (1877–1952), who was master of the *Prince Rupert*, once the pride of the GTP's W coast steamship fleet. Earlier in his career he navigated in QCI waters as skipper of the *Prince John*. He was also one of the few master mariners to command the CNR's *Prince Robert* in BC. The *Robert*, along with its sister ships the *Prince Henry* and *Prince David*, proved unsuitable for W coast service and had to be moved to the Atlantic. In 1935, however, Nedden was chosen to guide the luxurious vessel on four 11-day cruises to Alaska.

Needham Point (50°23'00" 125°36'00" E entrance to Knox Bay, S side of W Thurlow I, Johnstone Str). After RN officer Henry Needham Knox, who served on the Pacific Station in the early 1850s. *See* Cape Knox.

Negro Rock (50°35'00" 126°22'00" SW of Minstrel I, Clio Channel, N of W Cracroft I and Johnstone Str). Named, along with nearby Bones Bay, Minstrel I and Sambo Point, after a troupe of amateur performers aboard HMS *Amethyst*, which carried Lord Dufferin, the gov gen, and Lady Dufferin on a cruise to Metlakatla in 1876. These entertainers put on minstrel shows, based on black cultural stereotypes, and a performance of this type was presumably staged in the vicinity for the vice-regal couple. While the federal government moved in 1966 to change a number of place names that incorporated the word "nigger," it was not until quite recently that other racial slurs were abolished. Four instances of "Chinaman," for example, were rescinded in 1996 on the recommendation of the Vancouver Assoc of Chinese Canadians. "Squaw" was eliminated from place names in BC in 2000. Two features with "Jap" in the name have been replaced, though three remain. "Negro," however, could still be found in the early 2000s in three BC geographical names. Besides Negro Rk, Negro Ck and Negro Lk in the E Kootenays continued to exist. They were changed from their former names of Nigger Ck and Nigger Lk back in the 1960s. No one, it seems, is anxious to change them again.

Neilson Island (49°09'00" 125°53'00" N entrance to Browning Passage, NE of Tofino, Clayoquot Sd, W side of Vancouver I). Named after Charles Neilson, a landowner in the vicinity. The feature's local name is Bond I.

Nelles Island (52°01'00" 128°16'00" Part of the Admiral Group, Queens Sd, SW of Bella Bella). Adm Percy Walker Nelles, CB (1892–1951), was Canada's senior naval officer during WWII. Born at Brantford, Ont, he started his career in 1908 as a cadet on a fisheries protection vessel. He became a lt in 1914 and served as flag lt to the director of naval services in 1917. Nelles was sent to Britain's Royal Naval College in 1925, and for the next four years, with the rank of cdr, he was CO Pacific Coast, at Esquimalt. His first commands were the RN cruiser *Dragon*, in 1930, and HMCS *Saguenay*, a destroyer, in 1932. The following year Nelles was promoted to capt and attended Imperial Defence College in the UK before being named assistant chief of naval staff and then chief of naval staff in 1934.

He remained in this position throughout most of WWII, rising to the rank of vice adm. In 1944 he went to London as head of the Canadian Naval Mission Overseas and retired in 1945. Nelles oversaw the expansion of the RCN from a few hundred men in 1934 to a wartime peak of more than 45,000.

Nelly Point (53°17'00" 129°06'00" NW side of Princess Royal I). After Helen "Nelly" McKay, wife of HBC fur trader and businessman Joseph McKay. *See* Helen Point *and* McKay Channel.

Nels Bight (50°47'00" 128°21'00" E of Cape Scott, NW end of Vancouver I). Early local settler Nels (or Nils) C Nissen is believed to have been the namesake for this feature—and for nearby Nissen Bight as well. Little seems to be known about him.

Nelson Island, at left, and Agamemnon Channel, looking northeast into the Jervis Inlet region. *Peter Vassilopoulos*

Nelson Island (49°42'00" 124°08'00" Entrance to Jervis Inlet, Malaspina Str, SE of Powell R), **Nelson Rock** (49°39'00" 124°07'00" Just S of Nelson I). Nelson I was named after Adm Lord Nelson (1758–1805) by RN surveyor George Richards about 1860. Horatio Nelson was the RN's greatest hero, dying aboard his flagship, HMS *Victory*, at the Battle of Trafalgar. He played significant roles, either as cdr-in-chief or as a subordinate cdr, in several of Britain's most famous sea victories, including the battles of Cape St Vincent (1797), the Nile (1798) and Copenhagen (1801), after which he was created a viscount. Noted for his inspirational leadership and sometimes unorthodox tactics, Nelson became an almost legendary figure in British military history. Mt Nelson and Nelson Ridge W of Port Neville also commemorate him, as does Mt Nelson W of Windermere Lk in the Kootenays. This latter feature (3,283 m) was named in 1807 by explorer David Thompson, who heard of the victory at Trafalgar and Nelson's death after his historic crossing of the Rocky Mtns via Howse Pass. Another Mt Nelson, E of Mabel Lk in the Shuswap district, honours Nels Peter Nelson, born in Sweden in 1841 and supposedly a direct descendant of

Horatio. Nels Nelson was pressed into the RN but jumped ship at Vancouver in 1891 and settled in the Okanagan. Capt Richards named a number of features around the mouth of Jervis Inlet in association with the celebrated adm. *E W*

Nelson Point (52°53'00" 131°40'00" SE side of Louise I, E of Moresby I, QCI). Named in 1957 for Pete Nelson (d 1908), who staked a number of claims in the Sewell Inlet area in 1907–8 in partnership with Capt James Johnstone, owner of the sloop *Pride of the Islands*. He was killed by a falling branch while building a cabin. *D*

Nepean Sound (53°11'00" 129°40'00" N of Caamaño Sd, separating Banks I, Pitt I, Trutch I and Campania I), **Nepean Rock** (53°13'00" 129°37'00" Off SW end of Pitt I, Nepean Sd). Nepean Sd was named in 1788 by fur trader and mariner Capt Charles Duncan of the *Princess Royal* and adopted by Capt George Vancouver in 1793. British MP Sir Evan Nepean (c 1751–1822) succeeded Sir Philip Stephens as secretary to the Admiralty in 1795. Earlier in his career he had served as an RN clerk and purser and was later appointed undersecretary of state for the home and war depts, 1782–95. After his stint as Admiralty secretary, he became chief secretary for Ireland, 1804–5, commissioner of the Admiralty and gov of Bombay, 1812–19. He was made a member of the privy council in 1804. Nepean Rk, formerly known as Brodie Rk, was named in 1950. The city of Nepean, Ont, is also named for him, as are several locations in Australia and India.

Neptune Bank (49°18'00" 123°03'00" E of Second Narrows, Vancouver Hbr). This bank, which has several shoals of less than 12 m, lies just off Neptune Bulk Terminals, N America's largest bulk-loading terminal, located on the N shore of Vancouver Hbr. A navigational marker placed there in 1970 became so well known locally as the Neptune Bank buoy that this name was officially adopted by the Geographic Board of Canada in 1975. The terminals ship mostly coal, potash, fertilizer, canola oil and agricultural products.

Neroutsos Inlet (50°24'00" 127°31'00" SE of Quatsino Sd, NW Vancouver I). Master mariner Cyril Demetrius Neroutsos (1868–1954) was born in England and went to sea at the age of 14, sailing on clipper ships and circumnavigating the globe several times before he was 18. As a young merchant marine officer he sailed to Australia, S America and the E Indies, then joined the British India Steam Navigation Co for eight years. In 1894 he was working for Forward Bros of London, running vessels to Morocco, Madeira and the Canary Is. Neroutsos arrived in the PNW in 1898 aboard the *Garonne* and was employed in Seattle during the Klondike years as port capt for the Frank Waterhouse Co. He moved to Victoria in 1901 with his wife, Ada Sarah (1871–1952), and family to work for

N

the Canadian Pacific Navigation Co, which was soon to become the CPR's BC Coast Steamship Service. That Aug he was 1st officer on the *Islander* when the veteran steamship struck a reef or iceberg off Douglas I, Alaska, and sank in 16 minutes. Capt Hamilton Foote and 41 other crew members and passengers lost their lives in this W coast disaster. In 1911, Neroutsos was named marine superintendent of the CPR's coast service, then assistant manager and finally, from 1928 until he retired in 1934, gen manager.

Nesbitt Rock (53°26'00" 129°53'00" Entrance to Mink Trap Bay, W side of Pitt I). John Arthur Nesbitt (1916–67) was a wireless operator and radio technician aboard CGS *William J Stewart*, 1937–40. In 1939 he was sent to Seattle and Oakland to learn the latest techniques of radio acoustic ranging, an early non-visual navigation system. Nesbitt died at Vancouver. Formerly known as Greentop Rk but renamed in 1944.

Nesook Bay (49°46'00" 126°25'00" E side of Tlupana Inlet, NE of Nootka Sd, W side of Vancouver I). Nesook was the name of a Mowachaht First Nation habitation site, now abandoned, at the head of this bay. In the early 2000s the bay was home to aquaculture operations; Western Forest Products Ltd also had a dryland log-sorting and barge-loading operation there. A Nuu-chah-nulth reserve is located on the bay, though its name is spelled Nesuk. The Nesook R flows W to join the Tlupana R just E of Nesook Bay.

Ness Islands (53°52'00" 130°34'00" In Kitkatla Inlet, Porcher I, SW of Prince Rupert), **Ness Rock** (52°51'00" 129°44'00" SW end of Aranzazu Banks, Caamaño Sd, NW of Aristazabal I). The Ness brothers, of Norwegian heritage, were fishermen and boatbuilders in the Porcher I area. Andrew Cornelius Ness (1888–1965) pre-empted the middle (and largest) of the Ness Is in 1922 and received a Crown grant in 1927. He married Louise A Beniteau at Prince Rupert in 1924. George Ness married Hannah Scott there in 1926. The brothers built fishing vessels in the region in the 1920s and '30s, including the 14-tonne halibut boat *Inez H* (1920) and the 12-m seiner *C N* (1928). Andrew's boat, the *Celtic No 1*, was built at the Wahl family shipyard at Dodge Cove on Digby I in 1936. A note at BC's Geographical Names Office says that Ness Rk was named in 1926 after two fisherman brothers who "gave us the only reliable information to locate this rock."

Nesto Inlet (53°34'00" 132°55'00" NE of Hippa I, W side of Graham I, QCI). Nesto (Nasto, Nestow) was the original Haida First Nation name for nearby Hippa I. The word means "impregnable," and the island was once home to three ancient fortified habitation sites. Nesto Inlet was called Skaloo by the Haida and was widely referred to by 19th-century mariners as Skaloo Inlet before the hydrographic service changed the name to Nesto. In the early 1790s, officers of the US fur-trading vessel *Hope* named the inlet Port Ingraham, after their capt, Joseph Ingraham. Coastal historian John Walbran incorrectly identifies Kiokathli Inlet (qv), farther N, as the former Port Ingraham, but Ingraham's own journal, first published in 1971, leaves no doubt that this name referred to the feature known today as Nesto Inlet. *See also* Ingraham Bay. *D*

Netherby Point (52°55'00" 128°30'00" S entrance to Green Inlet, Graham Reach, opposite E side of Princess Royal I). Named in association with Graham Reach after Netherby Hall, ancestral home of British statesman Sir James Graham (*see* Graham I). The hall, located near Longtown, Cumbria, not far from the Scottish border, is on the once-great Netherby estate, the remains of which were still owned by the Graham family in the early 2000s.

Nettle Island (48°56'00" 125°15'00" N end of the Broken Group, Barkley Sd, W side of Vancouver I). This feature was marked as Little I on the preliminary manuscript chart for Barkley Sd prepared by Capt George Richards, of the RN survey vessel *Hecate*, in 1861. On the published edition of the chart, however, which appeared in 1865, the name had been changed to Nettle I. Could this have been the result of a misreading of Little? Part of the island is a reserve and former habitation site of the Sheshaht First Nation, a member of the Nuu-chah-nulth Tribal Council.

Nevay Island (52°12'00" 128°09'00" Entrance to Ormidale Hbr, N side of Campbell I, just N of Bella Bella). The Scottish poet John Nevay (1792–1870) was born and educated at Forfar, N of Dundee in the council area of Angus. He worked as a handloom weaver but gained a minor reputation for his lyric verse, published in half a dozen small volumes over the course of his life. Named by RN surveyor Lt Daniel Pender about 1867.

Neville Point (50°29'00" 126°05'00" W entrance to Port Neville), **Port Neville** (50°30'00" 126°00'00" Off N side of Johnstone Str, between Cracroft Is and Hardwicke I). Port Neville was examined by Lt Peter Puget and Joseph Whidbey, master of HMS *Discovery*, in 1792. Capt George Vancouver named it and pronounced it "very snug and commodious," though the source of the name is not certain. Coastal historian John Walbran suggested Lt John Neville, a Royal Marines officer who was killed aboard HMS *Queen Charlotte*, Adm Lord Howe's flagship in the Battle of the Glorious First of June. But that battle was in 1794 and the port named in 1792, so he seems an unlikely candidate. The politician Richard Aldworth Neville, 2nd Baron Braybrooke (1750–1825), is another possibility. He was a fellow of the Society of Antiquaries and held the offices of vice adm and lord lt of Essex and provost marshal of Jamaica, but, again, these appointments all occurred well after Vancouver had left on his voyage to the Pacific. PNW cartography expert Henry Wagner proposed John

Port Neville, on the north side of Johnstone Strait. *Peter Vassilopoulos*

Neville of the *Mariner* but provided no further details. An RN vice adm named Neville commanded a squadron of vessels in the Caribbean in 1697 and died there of disease, along with many of his men. Hundreds of Nevilles appear in British peerage catalogues. A tiny community named Port Neville sprang up at the mouth of the inlet, site of a steamship landing and an early store established by Hans Hansen in 1891. Later, when railway logging became important in the area, a sawmill was built. Port Neville was formerly known as Port Neville Inlet. It was the Brazo de Cardenas of Spanish explorer Dionisio Alcalá-Galiano, possibly named after Pedro Cárdenas, a Spanish naval officer who was part of a 1776–77 expedition to Brazil. *E W*

Newberry Cove (52°28'00" 131°27'00" S of Werner Bay, Juan Perez Sd, SE side of Moresby I, QCI), **Newberry Point** (52°28'00" 131°26'00" E side of Newberry Cove). Maj Newberry was the owner of QCI mining claims at Harriet Hbr, Lockeport, Tasu Sd and Mitchell Inlet in 1908. Named by the hydrographic service in 1962.

New Brighton (49°27'02" 123°26'16" SW side of Gambier I, Howe Sd, NW of Vancouver). Named about 1910 by Thomas Austin (1855–1946), the first settler in this area, after the seaside resort of Brighton, England. Austin, apparently a native of Newcastle-under-Lyme, arrived in BC in 1892 and lived on Gambier from 1901 to 1945, then moved to Vancouver, where he died. New Brighton post office opened in 1919, and a small rural community grew up, complete with a tiny general store. In the early 2000s a BC Ferries water taxi connected New Brighton to nearby Langdale on the Sunshine Coast.

Newby Island (52°14'00" 128°08'00" Off SW side of Chatfield I, Seaforth Channel, just N of Bella Bella). John Newby (1849–1926), a Victoria master mariner and pilot, came to Canada from England in 1880 and was joined in 1886 by his wife, Millicent (1849–1908), and their young daughter. In the early 1880s he was capt of the barque *Tiger*, carrying lumber between Victoria and China. In

1883 the Japanese Medal of the Red Ribbon was presented to Newby for saving the lives of 12 Japanese seamen. He had picked the men up off the coast of Asia in a dismasted hulk and brought them on the *Tiger* to BC, where it was learned that they had been drifting for four months before being rescued. Newby I was formerly known as Withers I, after RCN paymaster Lt Arthur Leslie Withers (1882–1961), and before that as Tree I.

Newcastle Island (49°11'00" 123°56'00" N side of Nanaimo Hbr, off E side of Vancouver I), **Newcastle Island Passage** (49°11'00" 123°57'00" W of Newcastle I). HBC officials realized in the early 1850s that coal was abundant in the Nanaimo region. They named this island, which had clear evidence of coal seams, after the ancient British coal city of Newcastle upon Tyne. The name appears on the first map of the area, made by surveyor Joseph Pemberton in 1852. Coal mining took place there, 1853–83. Quarries also operated from 1870 to 1932, producing sandstone (used in the Nanaimo post office and the US Mint at San Francisco) and grinding stones for the pulp industry. A Japanese herring saltery and shipyard were established on Newcastle as well. In 1930 the CPR bought the 3.4-sq-km island and turned it into a resort, complete with dance pavilion, wading pool, tea house, playing fields and floating hotel. The city of Nanaimo acquired the property in 1955, and it became a provincial marine park in 1961. Newcastle I Passage was shown as Exit Passage on Pemberton's 1852 map and identified the preferred route used by sailing vessels departing Nanaimo Hbr. *E W*

Newcastle Island Passage off Nanaimo. *John Lund*

Newcombe Bay (53°13'00" 132°03'00" NE side of Maude I, Skidegate Inlet, QCI), **Newcombe Channel** (48°55'00" 125°29'00" W side of Barkley Sd, W side of Vancouver I), **Newcombe Inlet** (52°50'00" 132°04'00" N part of Tasu Sd, NW side of Moresby I, QCI), **Newcombe Peak** (53°01'13" 131°59'18" S side of head of Cumshewa Inlet, NE Moresby I). Dr Charles Frederic Newcombe (1851–1924), from Newcastle upon Tyne, immigrated to Oregon in 1884 with his wife, Marion Arnold (1858–91), and their five children and then moved to Victoria in 1889. He became BC's first psychiatrist, but he was also a keen naturalist and ethnologist, and much of his time seems to have been taken up botanizing, collecting and exploring, especially in the QCI, where he made a number of useful early sketch surveys and maps. He was hired by museums (including Chicago's Field Museum) to acquire totem poles and other First Nation artifacts, and he later made substantial ethnological contributions to the BC Provincial Museum. Newcombe was also an early collector of paintings by Emily Carr. The bare, rocky pinnacle of Newcombe Peak (1,050 m) is a useful landmark for mariners. *D E*

Newcombe Harbour (53°42'50" 130°05'20" E side of Petrel Channel, NW end of Pitt I), **Newcomb Rocks** (50°30'00" 127°40'00" W side of Drake I, Quatsino Sd, NW end of Vancouver I). Capt James Alfred Holmes Newcomb (1859–1934), born in NB, was a fisheries protection officer on the BC coast, 1903–23. His name is often misspelled Newcombe. He came to Vancouver in 1888 with his wife, Jane Broadfoot Duff (1864–1952), a native of the Isle of Man, and worked for the Union Steamship Co for 12 years, commanding, among other vessels, the *Cutch* on its Nanaimo and Skagway runs. He was master of the *Cutch* in 1900 when it struck a reef S of Juneau and was abandoned. Newcomb was later capt of various federal patrol ships in the fisheries protection service, especially CGS *Kestrel* and *Malaspina*. He was responsible for apprehending, sometimes at gunpoint, US fishboats poaching in BC waters and was often appointed a magistrate in remote districts. During WWI he served as examiner of ship's papers at Esquimalt. Newcomb was a former president of the Vancouver Pioneers Assoc. Captain Cove and Captain Point on Pitt I are also named for him.

Newcomb Point (49°38'00" 123°41'00" S side of Salmon Inlet, E of Sechelt Inlet, NW of Vancouver). Named in 1950 after a logging family that operated in this vicinity and on the N side of the inlet in the 1930s and '40s. The correct spelling of their surname, apparently, was Newcombe. According to Sunshine Coast historians Betty Keller and Rosella Leslie, the Newcombes ran a typical gyppo outfit that practised high-lead logging close to salt water and used wood-burning steam donkey engines. They sold out to John Bosch Logging Ltd in 1947.

New England Rocks (52°20'00" 131°09'00" Entrance to Skincuttle Inlet, SE side of Moresby I, QCI). Named after the halibut vessel *New England*, which struck these hitherto unknown rocks in 1899 while under the command of Capt Harrison Joyce. The 216-tonne, 37-m ship was custom-built in New Jersey in 1897 for the Boston-based New England Fishing Co, which bought the Canadian Fishing Co in 1906 and developed it into one of the largest salmon canners on the BC coast. The innovative design of the *New England*, which was a mothership carrying dories to do the

actual fishing, was inspired by the Atlantic coast halibut fishery. The vessel, later commanded by Capt Absalom Freeman, survived its encounter with the rocks and was still in service in the 1920s. *D W*

Newton Cove (49°53'00" 126°56'00" SW side of Espinosa Inlet, N side of Esperanza Inlet, W side of Vancouver I). The Newton brothers, from Britain, settled on the NW coast of Nootka I with their families in the 1910s. Stanley Newton (1881–1951) built the first home, in 1914, and Gordon Newton (1888–1941), who married Adelaide Blakemore at Alberni in 1914, joined him shortly thereafter. The brothers developed their property with beautiful gardens and trails, acquired Crown grants in 1924 and 1930, and ran a store and post office there, 1919–42. The post office was named Centre I but was not actually *on* Centre I, which is located in Esperanza Sd opposite the Newton lands. Herman McLean, the missionary doctor at Esperanza, built a summer retreat on the cove. Gordon Newton is buried at this peaceful spot, as is his father, William Broderick Newton (1849–1922). Newton Hill, on the NW end of Nootka I (formerly known as Christmas Hill), was named after the brothers in 1946. It is likely that **Newton Entrance** (50°19'00" 127°56'00" Approach to Klaskino Inlet, SE of Quatsino Sd, NW side of Vancouver I), named in 1946, also commemorates this pioneer family.

Newton Point (53°08'00" 132°30'00" E entrance to Dawson Inlet, NW side of Skidegate Channel, SW side of Graham I, QCI). After adventurer and travel writer Newton Chittenden. *See* Chittenden Point.

Nicholas Islands (50°56'00" 127°48'00" N of Vansittart I, Shadwell Passage, off N end of Vancouver I). After Capt Nicholas Vansittart, an RN officer active in the 1840s and '50s. *See* Vansittart I.

Nicholas Shoal (53°14'00" 130°20'00" S of N Danger Rks, W of Banks I, Hecate Str). John Nicholas (c 1771–1805) joined HMS *Chatham*, the tender to Capt George Vancouver's HMS *Discovery*, as a midshipman in 1791. He was promoted lt on Vancouver's return to England and made a capt in 1801. Nicholas was cdr of HMS *Eurydice* in 1804 and escorted a convoy of fur-laden ships across the Atlantic from Canada that year. He fell ill and died after returning from the Mediterranean with the *Eurydice* the following year.

Nichol Island (53°04'00" 129°43'00" Off SW side of Trutch I, Estevan Group, SE of Banks I). Walter Cameron Nichol (1866–1928) was lt gov of BC, 1920–26. He was born in Ont and became a successful journalist at the Hamilton *Spectator* in the 1880s, then moved to Toronto in 1887 and started the original *Saturday Night* magazine, which lasted only one issue. Ten years later, he and his wife travelled to the Kootenays and then to Victoria, where he landed a job editing the weekly *Province* newspaper. In 1898, Nichol moved with the paper to Vancouver, where it went daily, and he managed to buy a controlling interest in it in 1901. Under his ownership the *Province* strongly supported the federal Conservatives and, as a reward, PM Sir Robert Borden appointed him lt gov, the only journalist to serve in this office. Nichol sold the paper to the Southam family in 1926 and retired to Victoria. *E*

Nicholls Island (50°50'00" 126°36'00" Off NE side of Broughton I, Penphrase Passage, just S of Kingcome Inlet). It has been suggested that this feature was named after William Nicholl, the surgeon aboard HMS *Chatham*, who accompanied Capt George Vancouver's expedition to the PNW. There is no evidence of this, however, either at the time of the voyage or later, and a note at BC's Geographical Names Office states that it is unlikely that Capt Vancouver would have named an island this small.

Nicholson Cove (49°03'00" 123°45'00" NW of Yellow Point, SW of Nanaimo, SE side of Vancouver I). According to K A Morley, who proposed this name in 1984, Christian F Nicholson (1875–1959) purchased 80 ha of land surrounding the cove in 1907.

Nicholson Island (52°19'00" 127°56'00" NE of Cunningham I, entrance to Roscoe Inlet, NE of Bella Bella). Named in 1925 for Capt Charles H Nicholson (d 1959), who was appointed gen superintendent of GTP shipping operations in 1910. He continued to manage GTP's steamships on the BC coast after they came under the control of the CNR.

Nicolaye Channel (50°00'00" 127°20'00" Between Union I and the Mission Group, off N entrance to Kyuquot Sd, NW side of Vancouver I). Roman Catholic priest Peter Joseph Nicolaye (b 1850), from the Limburg region of the Netherlands, was educated at Louvain College, Belgium, and arrived at Victoria in 1876. He was a pioneer missionary on the W coast of Vancouver I, serving at Hesquiat, 1876–78, at St Leo's (the Barkley Sd mission to the Huu-ay-aht or Ohiaht First Nation on Numukamis Bay), 1878–80, and at Kyuquot, 1880–90. Nicolaye became vicar gen of the diocese of Victoria about 1890 but was dismissed from that office in 1903 by Bishop Bertrand Orth for continued opposition to his superiors' decisions. In 1908, Nicolaye managed to engineer Orth's removal from office and return to Europe under the shadow of a sexual misconduct scandal.

Nicomekl River (49°04'00" 122°52'00" Flows SW into Mud Bay, E of Boundary Bay, SE of Vancouver). An HBC party, led by chief trader James McMillan, paddled up this 25-km-long stream in 1824 while exploring the lower Fraser Valley. The expedition left the Nicomekl at its head, followed a portage route to the Salmon R and descended the Salmon to the Fraser R. Three years later, McMillan established Ft Langley just N of the mouth of the Salmon (the trading post would later be rebuilt farther E). The Coast Salish people had long used the Nicomekl as a means of reaching the central valley from Boundary Bay, and the name may refer to a First Nation group that once lived at the mouth of the river. The origin of the name is uncertain, however; some writers have claimed that it is a cognate of Nicomen, the Halkomelem name for an island in the Fraser farther E, which is believed to mean "flat part." A settlement named Nicomekl formed about 20 km upstream in the 1890s around Maj Robert Hornby's School of Farming, which attracted young Englishmen to come and learn about Canadian farming methods. The Nicomekl R, which used to flood regularly, once supported a rich salmon fishery. The mud flats at its mouth were a productive oyster habitat until the 1960s, by which time they were badly polluted. For years the river served as a transport corridor for beaver pelts, salted salmon, farm produce and lumber. Today it is heavily controlled and diked—a "drainage ditch," as one newspaper reporter described it in 1975. *E*

Nigei Island (50°53'00" 127°45'00" In Queen Charlotte Str, just E of N tip of Vancouver I). Capt George Vancouver named this feature Galiano I on his 1798 chart, in honour of Spanish explorer Dionisio Alcalá-Galiano, who sailed through Goletas Channel in 1792. It was changed to Nigei I (pronounced *NEE-gee*), the hereditary name of the principal chief of the Nahwitti First Nation, in 1900 in order to avoid duplication with Galiano I in the Gulf Is. BC historians Helen and Philip Akrigg point out that *nigei* can also be translated as "mountain" in the Kwakwala language spoken in this region. A small fishing and boatbuilding community occupied Cascade Hbr on the N side of the 62-sq-km island in the 1930s and early '40s. *E W*

Nile Point (49°46'00" 123°59'00" NE end of Nelson I, Jervis Inlet, NW of Vancouver). Named by the hydrographic service in 1945 in association with Nelson I to commemorate Horatio Nelson's victory in the 1798 Battle of the Nile. Nelson was a rear adm at the time, in command of a squadron of 14 vessels with HMS *Vanguard* as his flagship. He attacked a French fleet of 15 ships at night at Aboukir Bay, Egypt, and by managing to slip some of his vessels around the end of the French line, he was able to fire on his opponents from both sides and achieve a decisive victory. All but four of the French ships were captured or destroyed, and the British took 3,000 prisoners. French losses may have been as high as 1,700 men against Britain's 218.

Nimmo Bay (50°57'00" 126°43'00" N side of Mackenzie Sd, N of Broughton I, NE of Port McNeill), **Nimmo Islet** (50°56'00" 126°41'00" Just SW of entrance to Nimmo

N

Bay), **Nimmo Point** (Just E of Nimmo It). Nimmo Bay was named in 1865 by Lt Daniel Pender while surveying Mackenzie Sd. Nimmo It and Nimmo Point were adopted by the hydrographic service in 1958. The origin of the name is not known. Nimmo Bay Resort, one of the world's most luxurious fly-fishing and adventure lodges—where clients are chauffeured to their daily activities by helicopter—was founded near here by Craig Murray in 1980.

Nimpkish Bank (50°34'00" 126°57'00" At the mouth of the Nimpkish R, Broughton Str, E of Port McNeill), **Nimpkish River** (50°34'00" 126°59'00" Flows NW into Broughton Str through Nimpkish Lk, NE Vancouver I). The 'Namgis or Nimpkish people, whose traditional territory coincides largely with the boundaries of the Nimpkish R watershed, are a branch of the Kwakwaka'wakw First Nation. Capt George Vancouver visited their principal village, Xwalkw, located at the mouth of the river, in 1792 and called it Cheslakee's after the paramount chief at that time. In 1880 the 'Namgis moved to Cormorant I, where their community, adjacent to Alert Bay, is today called 'Yalis. The traditional name of the Nimpkish R, Gwa'ni, honours a 'Namgis creation myth, in which Kaniki'lakw, the Transformer, changes his father-in-law, Gwa'nalalis, into a salmon-rich river so that he can provide food for his descendants forever. 'Namgis has been translated as "those who are one when they come together." *E W*

Ninstints Point (52°08'00" 131°12'00" E entrance to Louscoone Inlet, S end of Moresby I, QCI). Ninstints is an adaptation of the hereditary name of the town chief at Skun'gwaii, or Red Cod Island Town, the celebrated Haida First Nation village and UNESCO World Heritage Site on nearby Anthony I. Skun'gwaii was often referred to as Ninstints by early fur traders, and the two names have become somewhat synonymous. Many variations of this word exist, including Nan Stins, Ninstens and Nungstins; it can be translated as "he who is two." Although there were many chiefs named Ninstints, the most notable one reached the height of his fame between about 1866 and the early 1880s, after which the village was abandoned. Ninstints became so prodigiously wealthy through his control of the fur trade that he was able to host 10 extravagant potlatches, a feat that only one other Haida, the great Edensaw, could accomplish. *D E*

Nissen Bight (50°48'00" 128°18'00" E of Cape Scott, NW end of Vancouver I). Early local settler Nels (or Nils) C Nissen is believed to have been the namesake for this feature and for nearby Nels Bight as well. Little seems to be known about him, unfortunately.

Nitinat Bar (48°40'06" 124°51'00" Across the entrance to Nitinat Narrows), **Nitinat Lake** (48°45'00" 124°45'00" SW side of Vancouver I), **Nitinat Narrows** (48°40'00" 124°51'00" Between Nitinat Lk and the Pacific),

Nitinat River (48°49'17" 124°40'55" Flows SW through Nitinat Lk into the Pacific, SE of Barkley Sd). Named for the Ditidaht First Nation, whose traditional territory centres on Nitinat Lk. Nitinat or Nittinaht is an older spelling of Ditidaht, which has been translated as "people from a place in the forest." The Ditidaht, who have political and cultural links to the larger Nuu-chah-nulth confederacy, are not members of the Nuu-chah-nulth Tribal Council and speak a different, though related, language. Their principal village was originally located at Whyac, at the mouth of the narrows. The Ditidaht then moved slightly SE to Clo-oose. Since the 1960s they have lived at a reserve close to the N end of the lake. A number of other nearby geographic features are also named for this group, including Nitinat Cone, Nitinat Falls and Nitinat Hill. Shallow Nitinat Bar is a dangerous impediment to navigation when tide and weather conditions are adverse. *E W*

Looking into the entrance to Nitinat Narrows and Nitinat Lake on the west side of Vancouver Island. *James and Jennifer Hamilton*

Nixon Island, Nixon Rock (50°16'00" 125°22'00" N side of Kanish Bay, NW Quadra I, E of Discovery Passage, NW of Campbell R). Paymaster Cdr Francis Robert Woodcock Nixon, from Victoria, was killed in action Apr 30, 1941, aged 37. He was aboard the *Nerissa*, a former Red Cross Line passenger and cargo steamer that was owned by the Bermuda & W Indies Steamship Co and saw service during the war as an RCN troopship. En route from Halifax to England it was torpedoed by a U-boat off the coast of Ireland and sank in four minutes with the loss of 209 lives. Nixon is commemorated on the Halifax Memorial.

Noble Islets (50°49'00" 127°35'00" S of Hurst I, E end of Goletas Channel, off N end of Vancouver I, NW of Port Hardy). Edward Rothwell Noble (d 1877) arrived on the BC coast in 1863 as a midshipman aboard HMS *Sutlej*, the flagship of Rear Adm John Kingcome. He served temporarily on the *Beaver*, the historic HBC paddle steamer that was hired by the RN as a survey vessel, under Lt Daniel Pender. Noble was promoted to lt in 1870 and retired in 1876. The islets were named by Lt Pender in 1864.

Noble Lagoon (52°32'00" 129°02'00" Head of Weeteeam Bay, SW side of Aristazabal I). Lance Cpl John Noble was a member of the Columbia detachment of Royal Engineers, which served in BC 1858–63. Little is known about him other than that he apparently left BC or died before 1907. The hydrographic service originally assumed that there were two separate lagoons here. The second one was named for Bugler Daniel Harris, also a Columbia detachment member, who is believed to have deserted prior to June 1861. Upon closer examination it was determined that there was only one lagoon, but with two entrances, and Harris Lagoon was deleted in 1952.

Nodales Channel (50°24'00" 125°20'00" Between E Thurlow I and Sonora I, N of Campbell R). Spanish explorers Dionisio Alcalá-Galiano and Cayetano Valdés anchored at the N entrance to this passage in July 1792. Secundino Salamanca, 1st lt of the *Sutil*, was sent ahead to Loughborough Inlet with the ship's boat. En route he investigated Cordero Channel and Phillips Arm, which Alcalá-Galiano called Canal de Engaño, after the Spanish word for deception or hoax (Phillips Arm is a dead end). Nodales Channel, while apparently not examined, was named Canal de los Nodales by the expedition leaders. According to PNW cartographic expert Henry Wagner, there is "no doubt" that this name refers to the brothers Bartolomé García (c 1574–1622) and Gonzalo García de Nodal (c 1578–1622), who made a significant 1618–19 exploration of Magellan Str and Cape Horn. Among their achievements were the first circumnavigation of Tierra del Fuego and the discovery of the Diego Ramirez Is. The Nodales sailed into Drake Passage (the farthest S that humans would reach for 150 years) and made detailed charts of the entire region, much to the benefit of future Spanish colonization efforts. Bartolomé was a capt of the Spanish armada and Gonzalo an envoy to Chile. The brothers would probably have gone on to fame and fortune had they lived longer, but both were drowned in 1622 in a fierce hurricane that wrecked the armada on the Florida Keys. Bartolomé was cdr of the treasure-laden *Atocha*, which, despite much searching, lay undiscovered for 363 years until found in 1985 by US wreck hunter Mel Fisher. Thurston Bay was a maintenance facility and operations centre for the BC Forest Service's marine dept, 1914–41, and home to a number of loggers and other settlers in the 1920s and '30s. A school was established, and Nodales post office operated from 1925 to 1941. Today the area is a provincial marine park.

Noel Bay (49°03'00" 123°36'00" E side of Valdes I, Gulf Is). James Gordon Noel (1923–85), a manager at forestry giant MacMillan Bloedel Ltd and superintendent of the Duke Point sawmill in Nanaimo for several years, had a summer home on this part of Valdes I. The name was proposed in 1985 by Dr J Crosby Johnston, who was head of Calgary General Hospital before retiring to BC, and adopted in 1986. The feature is known locally as Oyster Bay.

Nolan Point (50°50'00" 127°37'00" S end of Balaklava I, NE end of Goletas Channel, off N end of Vancouver I, NW of Port Hardy). In 1863–64, RN surveyor Lt Daniel Pender named Balaklava I and several other features in the vicinity after people and places associated with the 1854 Charge of the Light Brigade in the Crimean War. In 1903, Cdr Cortland Simpson of HMS *Egeria*, on re-surveying the area, added this name, after Capt Louis Edward Nolan of the 15th Hussars, the Canadian officer who carried the order from Lord Raglan, army cdr-in-chief, to the Earl of Lucan, cdr of the cavalry, and then to the Earl of Cardigan, who led the fatal charge against the Russian artillery, which resulted in heavy British losses. Capt Nolan was also killed in the action. *W*

Nomad Islet (52°24'45" 131°24'30" S of Wanderer I, between Burnaby I and S Moresby I, QCI). Named by the hydrographic service in 1962, presumably in association with Wanderer I (qv), which was named much earlier by geologist George M Dawson after his sailing schooner.

Nonooa Rock (49°16'00" 124°06'00" Entrance to Nanoose Hbr, S of Wallis Point, SE side of Vancouver I, NW of Nanaimo). Nonooa or Nonooas is an old version of the word Nanoose, which in turn is a corruption of the name of the original Island Halkomelem inhabitants of the region, the Snaw Naw As, who have a reserve on Nanoose Hbr. *See* Nanoose Bay. The rock was named by the hydrographic service in 1944.

Noon Breakfast Point (49°16'00" 123°16'00" Just SE of Point Grey, western tip of city of Vancouver). The feature was named in 1981 to recognize the efforts of one of the boat crews dispatched by Capt George Vancouver in 1792 while HMS *Discovery* was anchored at Birch Bay. This expedition, under the command of Lt Peter Puget, followed the coast past today's Blaine and White Rock, then around Boundary Bay to the E side of Point Roberts, where the crew stopped for lunch. Afterwards, the men rowed N steadily for 10 and a half hours across the tidal flats that mark the mouths of the Fraser R. That night, unable to find space to set up a tent or make a proper cooking fire, they slept uncomfortably in their boat and early in the morning rowed again, against the current, to this bluff, which Puget called in his journal "Noon Breakfast Point," where they were finally able to rest and eat. The name was suggested by J E Roberts of Victoria, who wished to honour Vancouver's crew members for the hardships they regularly endured while manning small open boats on many long survey expeditions.

Nootka Cone (49°37'11" 126°39'14" SE end of Nootka I), **Nootka Island** (49°45'00" 126°45'00" NW of Nootka Sd), **Nootka Sound** (49°36'00" 126°34'00" W side of Vancouver I, NW of Clayoquot Sd). The important coastal name Nootka, which arose from a confused incident in

N

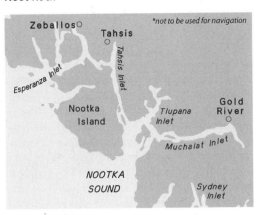

Nootka Sound. *Reproduced with the permission of the Canadian Hydrographic Service*

Looking south along the shore of Nootka Island. *Peter A. Robson*

the 1770s, is representative of the origins of many so-called First Nation names, which are, in fact, often clumsy misinterpretations, by early white visitors, of aboriginal words. Capt James Cook was the first European to visit Nootka Sd, in 1778. He initially called it King George's Sd but later changed this to Nootka Sd under the impression that Nootka was the First Nation name. It is not known precisely how this misapprehension came about. Pioneer missionary Augustin Brabant was one of the first to suggest that the Nuu-chah-nulth word *nootka-a*, meaning "go around," is what local residents were replying when Cook attempted—with a great deal of body language, no doubt—to find out the name of the place. They may have been directing him to an anchorage or safe passage, or simply responding to his gestures. And thus the historic site of the first serious cultural exchanges in the PNW between Europeans and Americans—a place made additionally famous by the conflict soon to ensue between British and Spanish colonizers—received its name as the result of a blunder. The Nuu-chah-nulth inhabitants of the region were for almost two centuries known officially as the Nootka. The Spanish claim to the PNW was based on the fact that Juan Perez, in 1774, had probably been the first to see (but not land at) Nootka Sd, which he named Puerto de San Lorenzo. Later Spanish explorers altered the

name to Puerto de San Lorenzo de Nuca (also Noca, Nutka and Nutca). Nootka I they named Isla de Mazarredo, after noted Spanish adm José María de Mazarredo y Salazar. Spain's attempts to exert control over the region were abandoned in 1795. The main summer village of Chief Maquinna and the Mowachaht (a branch of the Nuu-chah-nulth), located at Friendly Cove on the SE end of Nootka I, was called Yuquot (qv), meaning "windy place." A cannery, pilchard reduction plant and boat-repair facility named Nootka (site of a sport-fishing lodge in the early 2000s) were located just N of Yuquot, 1917–50. A post office called Nootka also operated in the area, 1909–55. *E W*

Noot Rock (50°30'00" 127°40'00" E of Brockton I, Buchholz Channel, Quatsino Sd, NW end of Vancouver I). John "Jack" Roach Noot (1878–1928) married Hannah Elizabeth "Bessie" Wall (b 1881) at Victoria in 1903 and settled on the S shore of Quatsino Sd, near Klootchlimmis Ck, in 1907. He had come in 1882 with his family to Victoria, where his father, George Noot, worked as a customs clerk. In 1912, the year their son George Edmond (d 1972 at Port Hardy) was born, Jack and Bessie received a Crown grant for their land. Bessie taught at Quatsino school, 1908–9, and Jack was hired as the region's first forest service ranger in 1919. In 1922, when Jack was transferred, the family left Quatsino and moved to Alert Bay.

Noot Shoal (53°07'00" 130°06'00" SW of SW end of Banks I). Named after John Noot (b about 1762), a native of Newton Bushel, Devon, who was a bosun's mate aboard HMS *Discovery* on Capt George Vancouver's 1791–95 expedition to the PNW.

No Point. *See* Point No Point.

Nordstrom Cove (50°29'00" 127°55'00" N side of Quatsino Sd, W of Koprino Hbr, NW end of Vancouver I). Two family groups by the name of Nordstrom were among the original founders of the Scandinavian colony of Quatsino. Christian Nordstrom (1847–1918), a native of Sweden who had immigrated to N Dakota, was the colony's main organizer. He had attended the 1893 Chicago Exposition and met Jobe Leeson there, one of Quatsino Sd's first settlers, who was trying to develop a community at Winter Hbr, where he owned land. Leeson encouraged Nordstrom to visit BC, which he did. He liked what he saw, put a group of settlers together and, along with his teenaged son George, moved to Quatsino in Nov 1894 and carved a homestead out of the wilderness. Also part of that founding group were Charles Frederick Nordstrom (b 1839), another Swedish widower, and his three children. It is not known if the two Nordstrom families were related. Both received Crown grants in 1901 for their 1895 land pre-emptions. Nordstrom Cove, formerly known as Boat Cove, was named in 1927. Nearby Nordstrom Ck takes its name from the cove.

Norgar Islet (50°30'00" 127°39'00" S of Drake I, Buchholz Channel, Quatsino Sd, NW end of Vancouver I). Thomas (or Thor) Gunderson Norgar (1861–1920), from Norway, joined the Scandinavian colony at Quatsino in 1895. He brought a stock of goods with him and opened the community's first general store. A post office and government wharf were soon built beside the store. Norgar received a Crown grant for his land in 1901 but later moved to Clayoquot Sd, where he also pre-empted land and received several Crown grants. Norgar It was formerly known as Single It. Norgar Lk, N of Clayoquot Sd, is presumably named for him as well.

Norman Island (50°55'00" 127°56'00" In Bull Hbr, S side of Hope I, off N end of Vancouver I). After Norman Godkin, an early pioneer in the region. *See* Godkin Point. Formerly known as Indian I.

Norman Morison Bay (52°12'00" 128°12'00" NW side of Campbell I, just NW of Bella Bella). The *Norman Morison* (often misspelled Morrison) was an early HBC supply ship that made annual journeys between England and Victoria, 1849–53, under Capt David Wishart and brought some of Vancouver I's first colonists to the W coast. The 36-m, 512-tonne vessel, built of teak in Burma in 1846 and rigged as a barque, was acquired by the HBC in 1848. It first arrived at Ft Victoria in Mar 1850, after a typical five-month journey around Cape Horn, with 80 immigrants, including the HBC's new medical officer, Dr John Helmcken. George Holland served as mate on that voyage. A number of other noted residents (all with coastal features named for them) came on later trips, including Jane Cheeseman, James Deans, Henry Ella, Kenneth McKenzie, John Parker and Thomas Skinner. The deserters famously murdered near Ft Rupert in 1850 (*see* Deserters Group) were from the *Morison*. The ship was sold after returning from its third voyage in 1853 and later sailed from London to India for the firm of Teighe & Co. According to *Lloyd's Register of Shipping*, it disappeared in 1865 or 1866 en route from Australia to India.

Norman Point (49°29'00" 124°40'00" S point of Hornby I, Str of Georgia). RN officer Francis Martin Norman served on the Pacific Station, 1859–60, as 3rd lt of HMS *Tribune*, under Capt Geoffrey Hornby. He is listed as a cdr, retired, in 1863. Named by Capt George Richards of HMS *Plumper* in 1860.

Normansell Islands (52°33'00" 129°10'00" SW of Clifford Bay, off SW Aristazabal I). Cpl James Normansell (1830–84), from Birmingham, England, was a member of the Columbia detachment of Royal Engineers, which served in BC 1858–63. He was the detachment's senior cpl and was charged in BC with the supervision of roadbuilding gangs, both civilian and military. Col Richard Moody, the contingent's CO, requested—and received—extra payment for him from Gov James Douglas for the "very heavy pecuniary responsibilities" he was saddled with. Normansell remained in the colony after the engineers disbanded, received a military land grant and also purchased additional land in the New Westminster land district with fellow sapper Peter Leech. In 1865, during a gold rush in the Kootenays, he was appointed police constable at Wild Horse Ck, and for the next decade he held various colonial and provincial government positions in the Kootenay area, including chief constable, postmaster and collector of customs. In the early 1880s he may have participated in the Cassiar gold rush in northwestern BC. Normansell died at Victoria.

Norris Rocks (49°29'00" 124°39'00" S of Hornby I, Str of Georgia). John Thomas Hammond Norris served on the Pacific Station, 1859–60, as master of HMS *Tribune*, under Capt Geoffrey Hornby. He was promoted to staff cdr in 1863 and his name appears on the retired list in 1870. Named by Capt George Richards of HMS *Plumper* in 1860.

North Arm (49°12'00" 123°05'00" Mouth of the Fraser R, separating Sea I and Lulu I from Vancouver and Burnaby). The section of the Fraser R N of Sea I was known, until at least the 1920s, as the N Fork of the N Arm. The S Fork of the N Arm (today known as Middle Arm, qv) ran between Sea I and Lulu I. While this terminology, technically speaking, is correct, entrenched local usage led the hydrographic service, in the 1930s, to change the official description of the N Arm, extending it from New Westminster to the jetty W of Iona I. The older "N Fork" designation became obsolete. According to *Sailing Directions*, the N Arm is known locally as The Ditch.

North Bentinck Arm. *See* Bentinck Narrows.

North Broughton Island. *See* Broughton Archipelago.

North Island. *See* Langara I *and* St Margaret Point.

Northness Point (53°46'00" 129°54'00" E side of Grenville Channel, between Baker Inlet and Kxngeal Inlet, SE of Prince Rupert). Named after the Shetland Is home of Capt N W Thompson of the CPR's BC Coast Steamship Service. He first joined the service in 1912 and worked mainly aboard the *Tees* along the W coast of Vancouver I. His initial master's appointment was on the *Princess Maquinna* in 1923. From that date until 1944, when he retired, Thompson commanded vessels on all the major routes of the steamship service.

North Pender Island (48°47'00" 123°17'00" One of the main Gulf Is). Named after RN hydrographer Daniel Pender; *see* Pender Canal for biographical details. N and S Pender islands were once connected by a narrow neck (called Indian Portage), and the combined land mass was

N

known as Pender I. A canal was cut in 1903 (though a reconnecting bridge was not built until 1955). N Pender, which at 27 sq km is much larger than S Pender, has always been more populous. The first settlers, Noah Buckley and David Hope, arrived in the 1870s. Hope died in 1882, and Buckley sold his land about the same time to Oliver Grimmer, who in turn sold it to his brother Washington. The Grimmer family and later homesteaders turned N Pender into a flourishing farming settlement. Small fish-processing plants were established in the 1920s. Communities eventually grew up at Hope Bay, Port Browning and Port Washington. By the early 2000s, several large residential subdivisions had been developed on N Pender, and the island had become a popular recreational destination with a population of 2,000. Its Sencoťen (Coast Salish) name is S'dáyes, meaning "wind drying." *E*

The North Vancouver waterfront, about 1910. *Author's collection*

North Pender Island in the Gulf Islands. *Kevin Oke*

North Race Rock. *See* Race Passage.

North Thormanby Island. *See* Thormanby Is.

Northumberland Channel (49°09'00" 123°51'00" Between Gabriola I and E side of Vancouver I, just E of Nanaimo). HBC officials named this channel in 1852 for Algernon Percy, 4th Duke of Northumberland (1792–1865), after the discovery of coal at Nanaimo. The English county of Northumberland was so famous for its coal that its name had become synonymous with coal manufacturing and wealth. Percy was an RN adm and 1st Lord of the Admiralty at the time this feature was named. He was a Conservative MP and president of the Royal Institution of GB and the Royal National Lifeboat Institution. Nearby Duke Point and Percy Anchorage are also named for him. *W*

North Vancouver (49°19'00" 123°04'00" N side of Burrard Inlet, just N of Vancouver). Named after Capt George Vancouver (*see* Vancouver for a brief biography). N Vancouver is in the traditional territory of the X'muzk'i'um (Musqueam) and Skxwúmish (Squamish) First Nations.

The community got its start in the early 1860s when the Pioneer sawmill was established. Sewell Moody purchased the mill in 1865 and greatly expanded it, and the settlement became known as Moodyville. The District of N Vancouver was incorporated in 1891 and at first covered the entire N Shore, from Deep Cove to Horseshoe Bay; the City of N Vancouver incorporated separately in 1907, and the District of W Vancouver in 1912. Shipbuilding was once an important industry in N Vancouver, though in recent years the district has developed as a residential suburb of Vancouver, with a commercial centre on Lonsdale Ave. *E*

Norway Island (48°59'00" 123°37'00" Trincomali Channel, E of Kuper I, Gulf Is). Horatio Fillis Norway served on the Pacific Station, 1853–56, as master aboard HMS *Trincomalee*, under Capt Wallace Houstoun. He was promoted to staff cdr in 1863. Capt George Richards named this feature Indian I in 1859, but Cdr John Parry of HMS *Egeria*, seeking something more distinctive, changed it to Norway I while re-surveying the area in 1905. One hundred years later this 12-ha private paradise, complete with three homes, a protected dock, pool, spa, boathouse, tennis court, fruit orchard, workshop and power plant, changed hands for $4 million.

Nowell Bank (50°45'00" 126°51'00" Nowell Channel, NW of Holford Its), **Nowell Channel** (50°42'56" 126°49'25" SW side of Broughton I, NE end of Queen Charlotte Str, E of Port Hardy). After RN officer Nowell Salmon, who served on the Pacific Station, 1851–53. *See* Salmon Channel.

Nubble Point (53°51'00" 130°34'00" N side of Goschen I, S of Porcher I and Prince Rupert). Named in association with Nubble Mtn, which rises S of the point on Goschen I. The word "nubble" is a diminutive of "nub" and means "a small knob or lump," according to the Oxford dictionary.

Nuchatlitz Inlet (49°46'00" 126°56'00" W side of Nootka I, off W side of Vancouver I), **Nuchatlitz Reef** (49°46'00" 126°59'00" In entrance to Nuchatlitz Inlet). Named after the First Nation inhabitants of the region, the Nuchatlaht, a member group of the Nuu-chah-nulth Tribal Council. The name has been translated as "people of a sheltered bay" and "people from a place with a mountain behind the village." The Nuchatlaht traditionally occupied several villages on the NW side of Nootka I but moved in the late 1980s to Oclucje, a site at the head of Espinosa Inlet, in order to be connected by road to Zeballos and the rest of Vancouver I. Nuchatlitz Inlet was originally named Ensenada de Ferrer by Dionisio Alcalá-Galiano and Cayetano Valdés in 1792 (*see* Ferrer Point). Nuchatlitz Ck is named after the inlet.

Nucleus Reef (51°34'30" 127°48'24" SE of Blair I, E side of Fitz Hugh Sd). The *Nucleus* was a tug or survey launch used, together with the Canadian Hydrographic Service barge *Pender*, on a 1984 survey of this area's numerous rocks, reefs and shoals. The name was suggested by the regional superintendent of Fisheries & Oceans Canada and adopted in 1991.

Numukamis Bay (48°55'00" 125°02'00" E side of Trevor Channel, opposite Tzartus I, Barkley Sd, W side of Vancouver I). Numukamis (Numuqumyis), at one time the main winter village of the Huu-ay-aht people, was located on this bay at the mouth of the Sarita R. The Huu-ay-aht (or Ohiaht) still have a large reserve at this location, and a number of families were living there in the early 2000s. The band, which belongs to the Nuu-chah-nulth Tribal Council, also owns an oyster-culture operation in the vicinity. According to BC historians Helen and Philip Akrigg, the name means "something private" or "personally owned." St Leo's, an early Roman Catholic mission, was founded here about 1878 by pioneer missionary Augustin Brabant. Joseph Nicolaye (1878–80) and Louis Eussen (1880) later served at St Leo's.

Nutcracker Bay (50°19'00" 125°17'00" S side of Sonora I, N side of Okisollo Channel, N of Campbell R). The bay is the site of a TimberWest Forest Corp log-booming operation. The name was adopted in 1982, when Crown Zellerbach Canada Ltd was the forestry company that owned the booming grounds. According to a CZ source, the feature was named after a forest worker was involved in a donkey-engine accident at this location that injured a "delicate part of his anatomy."

Nyggard Point (52°09'00" 127°34'00" SE side of King I, E of Bella Bella). This name is a misspelling of Nygaard. Jakob J Nygaard (1845–1904) was one of the original Norwegian pioneers who settled the Bella Coola valley in 1894. Like many of the colonists, he had earlier immigrated to Minnesota, where he worked as a tailor, but he was unhappy with life on the American prairie. Despite his unlikely trade, he adapted well to the wilderness and carved out a large homestead. Some of Nygaard's many descendants still live in the area. Named by the hydrographic service in 1957.

Nymphe Cove (50°08'00" 125°22'00" W side of Discovery Passage, N entrance to Menzies Bay, N of Campbell R). Named after HMS *Nymphe*, an 8-gun sloop of war that was based at Esquimalt, 1893–96, under Capt George Huntingford. The gunboat was sent to Seymour Narrows in 1895, where crew members recorded tidal observations. At the same time, Lt Bertram Chambers, who named this feature, re-surveyed Menzies Bay. The 1,034-tonne, 60-m steamship, launched at Portsmouth dockyard in 1888, was renamed *Wildfire* in 1906 and became a training vessel at Sheerness. After seeing action in WWI and being badly damaged off the Belgian coast, the sloop underwent two more name changes, to *Gannet* in 1916 and *Pembroke* in 1917. It served as an accommodation ship on the R Medway in Kent before being sold in 1920 and broken up the following year at Milford Haven. The *Nymphe*'s figurehead has been restored for display at Chatham Historic Dockyard. *W*

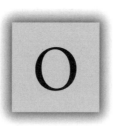

O

Oak Bay, just east of Victoria. *Peter Vassilopoulos*

Oak Bay (48°26'00" 123°18'00" Off SE tip of Vancouver I, just E of Victoria and district municipality of Oak Bay). Named after the great profusion of Garry oaks (*Quercus garryana*) that flourish in this region. Retired HBC officer John Tod was the first white settler in what is now the district municipality of Oak Bay, establishing Willows Farm in 1850. His home, built in 1851, is the oldest continuously occupied dwelling W of Ont. The Oak Bay area was agricultural until the 1890s, with summer cottages on the waterfront, and then developed as one of Canada's most affluent suburbs, with a wealth of architecturally significant homes. The name Oak Bay first appears on the 1847 chart of RN surveyor Capt Henry Kellett. An even older name, from HBC chief factor John McLoughlin's 1830s map, is Bone Bay. *E*

Oaks Bluff (48°45'00" 123°16'00" W side of N Pender I, Gulf Is). The extreme S end of N Pender I was fenced off about 1900 to raise sheep, and this 250-ha range was known as The Oaks. The name, of course, came from the abundant Garry oaks (*Quercus garryana*) in the area.

Until 1911, when the property was sold, the Hamilton and Brackett families conducted what they called "sheep runs" there, driving the half-wild animals into corrals at Wallace Point for shearing and for separating out the marketable lambs. A substantial picnic lunch was always part of this Pender I tradition.

Oaks Point (49°30'00" 124°00'00" NE point of N Thormanby I, S end of Malaspina Str, NW of Sechelt and Vancouver). Capt George Richards and his officers, aboard the RN survey vessel *Plumper*, apparently enjoyed the occasional flutter. They gave the area many horse-racing names in 1860 after hearing happy news of that year's Epsom Derby. The Oaks, for three-year-old fillies, was another long-established race held annually at the Epsom Downs racecourse. It was founded in 1779 by the Earl of Derby and named after the house at which the earl and his guests were staying. *W*

Observatory Hill (48°31'12" 123°25'07" Between Elk Lk and Prospect Lk, southern Saanich Peninsula, just N of Victoria). The Dominion Astrophysical Observatory was constructed on this 230-m hill in 1917. The feature had long been known as Saanich Hill, and later as Little Saanich Mtn, but the new name was adopted in 1924 after a submission by observatory director John Plaskett. The observatory's 1.8-m telescope was, for a short time, the largest in the world. The site is also home to a 1.2-m scope, which is equipped for spectroscopy, and an interpretive centre for visitors.

Observatory Inlet (55°15'00" 129°49'00" N extension of Portland Inlet, N of Prince Rupert). Capt George Vancouver named this body of water in 1793 because he stopped here to check the accuracy of his chronometers and to measure longitude and latitude. HMS *Discovery* and *Chatham* spent almost a month at Salmon Cove on the W side of the inlet, the site of Vancouver's "observatory," in July and Aug, during a period of fine weather, and Joseph Whidbey, master of the *Discovery*, made many astronomical observations and calculations. Vancouver himself led a longboat expedition to survey the channels and islands to the NW, in what is now Alaska. It was on this trip that the boats were attacked by Tlingit warriors, and two of Vancouver's men were wounded, including sailmaker's mate Roderick Betton, who was severely injured. Betton I, Escape Point and Traitors Cove in Behm Canal all commemorate this event. *E W*

Ocayu Island (49°08'20" 125°45'25" NW of Warne I, E of Tofino, Clayoquot Sd, W side of Vancouver I). A logging company purchased this previously unnamed island in the late 1970s, dubbed it Fantasy I and proceeded to clearcut it, much to the dismay of local townsfolk. The name Fantasy was considered "inappropriate" and "in poor taste," according to a note at BC's Geographical Names Office, and in the late 1980s, after the property had been sold, an alternative name was sought. The new owner and Tofino-area residents agreed that Ocayu, a Nuu-chah-nulth First Nation word meaning "towards" or "coming together," was acceptable, and the replacement name was adopted in 1992.

Ocean Falls (52°21'00" 127°42'00" Head of Cousins Inlet, toward W end of Dean Channel, NE of Bella Bella). A powerful waterfall here, by which Link Lk emptied into Cousins Inlet, not only provided the pulp and paper town of Ocean Falls with a name but also with an essential source of electricity. The lake was dammed in the early 1900s, a sawmill went into operation in 1909, and a pulp and paper mill was established in 1912. At its peak this remote community—famed for being the wettest inhabited place in Canada, with an average annual rainfall of 4,386 mm—had a population of over 4,000. Several companies owned the mill over the years until Crown Zellerbach Canada closed it down in 1973. A provincial government effort to revive it fizzled, and by 1980 most residents had left. In the early 2000s about 40 people lived in the vast, decaying townsite. *E*

Ocean Park (49°02'00" 122°52'00" E side of Boundary Bay, in Surrey, SE of Vancouver). The name was chosen by Methodist minister William Pascoe Goard (1862–1937) and may have originally been suggested by municipal official and realtor Henry Thrift. Goard purchased property at this location in the early 1900s for a church retirement community and waterfront retreat; the land was later held by the Ocean Park Syndicate, a group of Lower Mainland Methodists. The Great Northern Rwy built a station there, and the district became a residential suburb of Surrey. Camp Kwomais, one of the oldest summer church camps in BC, was established about 1910. In 2007 the city of Surrey purchased it from the United Church for $20 million; it is now a 5.6-ha park. The site was labelled North Bluff on early Admiralty charts, in association with South Bluff, located between Drayton Hbr and Birch Bay S of the US border. *E*

Octopus Islands (50°17'00" 125°13'00" Off NE side of Quadra I, in Okisollo Channel, N of Campbell R). According to a note at BC's Geographical Names Office, the name is likely descriptive of the islands' shape. The two largest islands are privately owned, but the smaller islands and two sections of adjacent Quadra I comprise a 760-ha provincial marine park, established in 1974. A portage trail leads from Waiatt Bay to the W side of Quadra I.

Octopus Point (48°48'00" 123°34'00" W side of Sansum Narrows, opposite Burgoyne Bay on Saltspring I, SE side of Vancouver I). The origin of the current name is uncertain, but prior to 1946 the feature was known officially as Burial Point, a name bestowed by RN hydrographer Capt George Richards in 1858. In the 1861 edition of the chart for the area, the feature appears as Grave Point, an unfortunate error as there is another Grave Point just 6 km to the NW. Future editions corrected the mistake, but the name was later changed by the hydrographic services to Octopus Point to avoid confusion.

Ocean Falls, with Cousins Inlet in the distance. *Andrew Scott*

O

Odegaard Rocks (52°09'00" 127°31'00" W of Mapalaklenk Point and Kwatna Inlet, S side of Burke Channel, E of Bella Bella). Hans Odegaard (1865–1949) was one of the original Norwegian settlers to colonize the Bella Coola valley, pre-empting land there in 1894 and receiving a Crown grant in 1901. He married 23-year-old Sirianna Gorden at Bella Coola in 1904. Sirianna died at Ocean Falls in 1919, Hans at Bella Coola; several of their descendants continue to live in the region.

Odin Cove (52°12'00" 128°11'00" E of N entrance to Raymond Passage, Seaforth Channel, just NW of Bella Bella). Named in 1925 after Capt George Francis Odin (1837–1910), who was born at NY and came W in 1858. He worked first on Puget Sd aboard the schooner *Sea Foam* but soon arrived in BC, where he developed a reputation as one of the most skilful and fiercely competitive of the pioneer riverboat skippers. Odin worked on the Stikine R in the mid-1870s as capt of the *Gem, Gertrude* and *Alaskan*. In the early days of CPR construction he was on the Fraser with the *Gertrude, Western Slope, Cassiar, Glenora* (which he co-owned), *Gladys* and *Delaware*. He went back N in 1889 to advise the HBC on the Skeena R's navigation potential. The company had the sternwheeler *Caledonia* built at New Westminster in 1891, and Odin took it upstream to Hazelton—a feat that had hitherto been considered impossible. George's son, Frank Odin (1863–99), then took over the Skeena operation. He was born at Point Roberts and began steamboating on the Fraser R at age 14. He was master of the *Royal City* before he turned 21 and worked for many years for John Irving's Pioneer Line and Canadian Pacific Navigation Co as a Fraser R pilot. Frank was also an early steamboat skipper on the Columbia and Kootenay rivers, and he earned the nickname "Nighthawk" for his uncanny ability to navigate in dark and foggy weather. Odin Cove was formerly known as Grouse Cove.

Odlum Island (51°41'00" 128°07'00" W of Adams Hbr, SW Hakai Passage, S of Bella Bella), **Odlum Point** (51°42'00" 128°07'00" NE end of Odlum I). Maj Gen Victor Wentworth Odlum, CB, CMG, DSO (1880–1971), was born at Cobourg, Ont, and spent three years in Japan, where his father worked, before arriving at Victoria in 1889. He fought in S Africa in the Boer War and served with acclaim in WWI, where he commanded the BC Regiment and helped pioneer the first Allied trench raids, an effective guerilla technique later copied by the Germans. Before the war, Odlum had worked as a newspaper reporter and then as a bond and insurance broker. He married Eugenia Tressa Rogerson at Victoria in 1904. In the 1920s he edited the *Vancouver World* and then became owner of the *Daily Star*, which he used to aggressively promote his anti-alcohol, anti-union, anti-Chinese views. He was an MLA for Vancouver, 1924–28, and a director of the CBC in the 1930s. At the outset of WWII, Odlum commanded the 2nd Canadian Division, but he was appointed high commissioner to Australia, 1941–42, and the country's first ambassador to China, 1943–46. After WWII he was ambassador to Turkey, 1947–52. Mt Odlum on the BC-Alberta border was named for him in 1917, Odlum I in 1944. A CPR station W of Hope, originally called Petain after French gen and WWI hero Henri Philippe Pétain, was renamed Odlum in 1940 after Pétain collaborated with Germany at the beginning of WWII. *E*

Ogden Channel (53°52'00" 130°18'00" Between Porcher I and Pitt I, S of Prince Rupert), **Ogden Point** (48°24'54" 123°23'12" E entrance to Victoria Hbr, SE end of Vancouver I). Peter Skene Ogden (1790–1854) was an important HBC official in western N America in the early 19th century. Born at Quebec City and educated at Montreal, he joined the NWC in 1810 and became a fur trader in Sask and at Spokane House, where he was in charge at the time of the company's merger with the HBC (and where he married Julia Rivet, of the Spokane tribe). He stayed on with the HBC and led a series of arduous forays (known as the Snake R expeditions) into Nevada, California, Idaho and Utah, where Ogden is named for him, in search of furs. He established Ft Simpson on the N BC coast in 1831, then was promoted to chief factor in charge of the New Caledonia district, 1835–44, with his HQ at Ft St James. In 1846, after the resignation of John McLoughlin, Ogden moved to Ft Vancouver and served as one of three administrators (with John Work and James Douglas) in charge of the Columbia district. He died at Oregon City. Ogden Channel and Ogden Point are old names, bestowed by HBC officers in 1837 and 1843, respectively. Peter Point and Skene Cove on Ogden Channel are also named for him. *E W*

Ogilvie Island (53°41'00" 132°59'00" Just S of the entrance to Port Louis, W side of Graham I, QCI). Named by John Mackenzie during (or just after) his 1913–14 geological survey of Graham I after fellow surveyor William Ogilvie (1846–1912), who worked in NW Canada from 1875 to 1898. Ogilvie surveyed the Pelly R district in 1887 (with George Mercer Dawson) and the Alaska–Yukon boundary at the Yukon R in 1887–88. He undertook extensive field surveys (1893–95) in NW BC, where 2,347-m Mt Ogilvie is named for him, and aided in making the maps used in 1903 to determine the present Alaska-BC boundary. In 1896 he surveyed the Klondike goldfields and the townsite of Dawson City. Ogilvie was commissioner of the Yukon, 1898–1901, and elected a fellow of the Royal Geographical Society in recognition of his pioneering northern work. A mountain range N of Dawson City was named in his honour in 1966. His book *Early Days in the Yukon* was published in 1913.

Ohala Islets (53°39'00" 132°23'00" In Juskatla Inlet, S of Masset Inlet, Graham I, QCI). Named by the hydrographic service in 1953 after Ohala (or Oahla), a slave girl owned by Steilta, head chief of the Masset Eagle crest. In his 1915 memoir *In the Wake of the War Canoe*, Anglican missionary William Collison tells the story of a conflict over the ownership of certain slaves that arose between Steilta and a Kaigani chief named Kinneelawash-Haung. After Steilta's death, Collison apparently managed to negotiate a settlement between the chief's heirs and Kinneelawash-Haung that not only avoided open warfare but also transferred Ohala, who had suffered great abuse from Steilta, to the Kaigani chief, who owned a slave wishing to marry Ohala.

Ohiat Islet (48°51'00" 125°11'00" E side of Imperial Eagle Channel, S of Satellite Passage, Barkley Sd, W side of Vancouver I). The Ohiat (or Ohiaht) First Nation, which is known today as the Huu-ay-aht, occupies as its traditional territory the SE side of Barkley Sd. It is a member group of the Nuu-chah-nulth Tribal Council, and the name has been translated as "the people who recovered." The Huu-ay-aht were the first aboriginal people to meet Capt Charles Barkley and other early European fur traders and explorers who entered Barkley Sd. Their main community, just S of Bamfield on Pachena Bay, is called Anacla. Ohiat It was formerly known as Ragged Islet.

Ohio Rock (52°49'00" 128°27'00" Off E side of Sarah I, N end of Finlayson Channel, N of Bella Bella). The *Ohio* hit this hazard in 1909 and sank in nearby Carter Bay, with the loss of four lives. It was en route from Seattle to Nome, Alaska, under Capt John Johnson, when it struck the uncharted rock after midnight and filled rapidly with water. Johnson just managed to ground the vessel in Carter Bay and get most of the 135 passengers and crew off before it sank. The 110-m, 2,816-tonne *Ohio*, built in 1873, had criss-crossed the Atlantic, between NY, Philadelphia and Antwerp, for 25 years before it became obsolete and was transferred to the Alaska run, where it changed owners several times and was reaching the end of its career. Though its engines and propeller were salvaged, the old vessel was never refloated, and part of the hull could still be seen above water in Carter Bay in the early 2000s. Capt Johnson later presided over the wreck of the *Kennecott* (*see* Kennecott Point). This second failure was too much for him, and after being rescued he jumped into the ocean and drowned.

Ohlsen Point (50°32'00" 127°34'00" W entrance to Quatsino Narrows, Quatsino Sd, NW end of Vancouver I). Henry Albrecht Ohlsen (1867–1944) was told that he had TB and should move to a dry climate. Instead, in 1904 he perversely migrated from Iowa to the mouth of the San Josef R at the NW end of Vancouver I with his wife, Emma, their daughter and his mother. In 1908 he opened a general store and post office there, which became the centre of a small, mostly Scandinavian community that flourished in the pre-WWI era and attracted several settlers from the failed Danish colony at Cape Scott. Henry and Emma

received Crown grants for their land in 1911–12, and Henry ran the San Josef post office until his death in 1944, at which point it closed. Ohlsen Point was formerly known as Turn Point.

Okime Island (50°02'00" 127°21'00" Entrance to McKay Cove, just N of entrance to Kyuquot Sd, NW side of Vancouver I). The name may possibly be derived from a Nuu-chah-nulth word meaning "sunny." In the early 2000s, the island was the site of the Kyuquot Health Centre, a remote outpost nursing clinic.

Okisollo Channel, north of Quadra Island. *Peter Vassilopoulos*

Okisollo Channel (50°17'00" 125°12'00" N and NE sides of Quadra I, N of Campbell R). Okisollo is an adaptation of a Kwakwala or Lekwala word meaning "channel" or "passageway." When Capt George Vancouver travelled through this region in 1792, it was occupied by the Coast Salish tribes of the Island Comox. In the early 1800s, however, the Lekwiltok First Nation took control of Quadra I and the surrounding area and forced the Island Comox farther S. The Lekwiltok are part of the Kwakwaka'wakw cultural alliance, and their language, Lekwala, is related to Kwakwala. Place names in the vicinity changed over the years to reflect this altered ownership. Okisollo has appeared on old charts as Okis Hollow Channel. The nearby **Okis Islands** (50°19'00" 125°16'00") are possibly an abbreviation of this name.

Oland Islet (52°13'00" 128°10'00" Off N side of Campbell I, Seaforth Channel, just N of Bella Bella). John Eric Wodehouse Oland, DSC (1895–1948), from NS, entered Royal Naval College at Halifax in 1911 as a cadet and was promoted to lt in 1917. He married Denise Victoria Harris, a granddaughter of Sir James Douglas, in 1919 at Victoria (*see* Denise Inlet). Oland was cdr of HMCS *Patrician*, 1922–24, before being transferred to the Esquimalt shore establishment of HMCS *Naden*. During WWII he served as naval officer-in-charge at St John, NB (HMCS *Captor*), and retired in 1945 with the rank of cdr. He was awarded his DSC in WWI for rescuing a number of seamen after

O

the accidental collision of two RN destroyers off Scotland. Oland It was named in 1924. Before that it was known as McLeod It, after veteran NS master mariner John McLeod (b 1856), who worked in the sealing trade and was then employed for many years by the CPR's BC Coast Steamship Service. Another old name for this feature was Whitestone It.

Oldham Rock (52°26'00" 128°58'00" S of Aristazabal I). Named for Sapper William Oldham, a member of the Columbia detachment of Royal Engineers, which served in BC 1858–63. He was a printer and worked with the primitive lithographic press, the first in BC, that the engineers brought with them to Sapperton. Little else is known about him other than the fact that he wanted to purchase the press and its related equipment when the detachment disbanded in 1863.

O'Leary Islets (50°06'00" 127°39'00" Entrance to Nasparti Inlet, Checleset Bay, just SE of Brooks Peninsula, NW side of Vancouver I). Capt William O'Leary (1853–1926), from NS, was a skipper with the Victoria-based sealing fleet. His wife, Alice McKenna (c 1860–1929), was from Cape Breton. He brought the schooner *Pathfinder* out from the E coast to Victoria in 1885 for owner William Munsie, and the following year he took it offshore so that federal officials could determine the potential for a black cod fishery W of Vancouver I. In 1887, Munsie had a banner year with the *Pathfinder*; O'Leary, hunting in contested waters, managed to evade US revenue cutters and return to Victoria with 2,811 skins worth $20,000. One of his hunters, Joe Dupont, took 57 seals in a single day. O'Leary brought another schooner, the *Ocean Belle*, out from NS in 1889, this time for the trading firm of Hall & Goepel. In 1893, with the *Geneva*, he again came home with more than 2,000 skins. In later years he worked for the Dunsmuir collieries on the steamship *Pilot* and then served as a whaling skipper with the *St Lawrence* and the *Orion*. The O'Leary Its were formerly known as The Haystacks.

Ole's Cove (49°32'23" 123°58'40" W side of Sechelt Peninsula, S of Pender Hbr, Str of Georgia). Ole Elmholdt, born at Oslo, Norway, in 1910, served as a steward in the Norwegian merchant marine during WWII, then immigrated to Canada in 1948. He worked for the Black Ball Line, running the food concession on the Horseshoe Bay–Langdale ferry and then on the Earls Cove ferry across Jervis Inlet. In 1952, Elmholdt bought land at this location, built a dining room and some cabins, and opened a resort by the name of Ole's Cove. Over the next decade or so, that name also became attached to the adjacent body of water and was adopted as an official name in 1992. In 1969, Elmholdt sold his resort and it was renamed Lord Jim's. It changed hands again about 2005, was extensively refurbished and is, at the time of writing, known as Rockwater Secret Cove Resort.

Olive Point (51°20'00" 127°32'00" S entrance to Boswell Inlet, NE end of Smith Sd, N of Port Hardy). Olive Boswell was a daughter of Que harbour engineer St George Boswell and a granddaughter of BC lt gov Sir Henri-Gustave Joly de Lotbinière (see Boswell Inlet). Capt John Walbran noted that the name, which he bestowed in 1903, was "also suggested by the noticeable light-green colour of the arbutus trees on the point." W

Oliver Cove (52°18'44" 128°21'10" E side of Port Blackney, SW end of Don Peninsula, NW of Bella Bella). Susan Jane Oliver (1822–1903), from Suffolk, married Rout Harvey (1827–1905), from Bury St Edmonds, and came to Victoria from England with her husband and family in 1861. A daughter, Annie Harvey (1861–1940), was born on the voyage. Rout originally worked in the wholesale dept of J H Turner & Co, a dry goods specialist. This business evolved into a major importing, wholesaling and merchandising operation under the name of Turner, Beeton & Co; it also manufactured clothing and owned one of Victoria's largest wharves. Harvey evolved along with it, eventually becoming gen manager. From about 1880 until 1906 the family lived at Stoneyhurst, a palatial Rockland Ave home on 3 ha of land. The area around Oliver Cove, which was formerly known as East Bay, was designated a 74-ha provincial marine park in 1992.

Oliver Islet (53°02'00" 131°56'00" At head of Cumshewa Inlet, off NE side of Moresby I, QCI), **Oliver Point** (53°12'00" 131°59'00" S side of Alliford Bay, N end of Moresby I), **Oliver Rock** (52°17'00" 131°03'00" N of Rankine Is, off SE Moresby I). William Oliver (1848–1937), from Scotland, was a well-known Methodist missionary at Sandspit. He apprenticed as a carpenter in the shipyards of the Clyde and then sailed the seven seas. While ashore at Victoria, he became so drunk (a common occurrence for Oliver at the time) that his ship left without him. He worked in area shipyards and was helped out of his alcoholism by pioneer preacher Ebenezer Robson. In gratitude, Oliver devoted himself to church work, building the *Glad Tidings* for famed N coast missionary Thomas Crosby in 1884 and working on the vessel as engineer and then as skipper until it was wrecked in 1903. He fell in love with the QCI and settled at Sandspit, purchasing the dogfish oil plant at Skidegate Landing as an investment and continuing his work as a missionary and boatbuilder. The *Udal*, *Thomas Crosby III* and *Melvin Swartout* were some of the vessels he constructed. Oliver Point, also known in the early days as Fossil Point, was named by the hydrographic service in the early 1910s; Oliver It was named in 1926. Mt Oliver (800 m) on the W side of Moresby I commemorates him as well. D E

Oliver's Landing (49°35'00" 123°13'15" E side of Howe Sd, S of Squamish, N of Vancouver). This name was adopted in 1999 after a submission by United Properties, a developer building a large, self-contained, waterfront community at this site that includes homes, a marina and a golf course. The project was taken over in 2002 by Caleb Chan's Burrard International Holdings Inc. The landing is located at the mouth of Furry Ck and was named in association with it after Oliver Furry, a trapper and prospector who had a cabin on McNab Ck and staked the claims in 1897 that eventually became the Britannia Mine. Furry and his partner W A Clark sold a 50 percent interest in the Britannia group of claims to Leopold Boscowitz, who used false documents to cheat the unschooled and ailing Furry out of part of his share. After Furry's death at Essondale in 1905, his brother, Ira Furry, took legal action to restore the family's interest in the mine.

Olsen Island (49°30'00" 124°22'00" NW entrance to False Bay, Lasqueti I, Str of Georgia). Andrew Olsen pre-empted land in this vicinity in 1891 and received a Crown grant in 1896. He was apparently one of several Lasqueti settlers to sell his property to John Stapleton Grey Pemberton, an Englishman and absentee landlord who assembled a large estate on the NW part of the island. This holding, later known as the Lasqueti Land Co, was farmed and used to raise sheep and eventually logged and subdivided.

Ontario Point (51°50'00" 127°53'00" E side of Fitz Hugh Sd, between Kiwash Cove and Warrior Cove, just S of Namu, SE of Bella Bella). Named in 1946 after HMCS *Ontario*, a *Minotaur*-class light cruiser originally built for the RN as HMS *Minotaur* but transferred to the RCN in 1944. The 169-m, 10,095-tonne vessel, constructed at Belfast, N Ireland, arrived too late to see active service during WWII but did assist with post-war operations at Hong Kong, Manila and Japan. The *Ontario* served as an RCN training vessel until 1958 and was broken up at Osaka, Japan, in 1961.

Onward Point (53°14'00" 131°55'00" S side of Skidegate Inlet, NE end of Moresby I, QCI). The hydrographic service named this feature in 1946 after the pioneer schooner *Onward*, which the Cowgitz Coal Mining Co chartered in 1865 at Victoria to bring supplies to its workers at the Cowgitz Mine, located farther W. RN surveyor Lt Daniel Pender originally named this spot Welcome Point in 1866; it was also known locally as Mission Point. There were several other, later vessels named *Onward* on the BC coast, including a sealing schooner and a Fraser R sternwheeler. Racoon Point (qv) in Kyuquot Sd was formerly known as Onward Point.

Oona Point (53°57'00" 130°14'00" Just E of the community of Oona R), **Oona River** (53°57'00" 130°15'00" E side of Porcher I, S of Prince Rupert). *Oona* is the Tsimshian word for the skunk cabbage, a plant that does well in this area. A small, mostly Scandinavian, logging, trapping and fishing settlement formed here in the early 1900s, shortly

after nearby Prince Rupert had been chosen as the GTP terminus. A modest sawmill was constructed in the village in 1921, initially owned by Julius Hadland, and later by John Group. Box lumber and heavier timbers were produced for the canneries; local cedar was cut for boatbuilding. Group and several other artisans established boatyards, and as many as 130 fishing boats were constructed and launched before 1980. By the early 2000s, Oona R, with about 30 permanent residents, was the largest surviving community on Porcher I. *E*

Openit Peninsula (49°22'00" 126°16'00" SW entrance to Sydney Inlet, opposite Flores I, NW of Clayoquot Sd, W side of Vancouver I). Named for the Ahousaht First Nation reserve on the E side of the peninsula. According to BC historians Helen and Philip Akrigg, *openit* is a Nuu-chah-nulth word meaning "place of calm waters."

Opitsat on Meares Island was rebuilt after being destroyed in 1792 by fur trader Robert Gray, captain of the *Columbia*. *Elsie Hulsizer*

Opitsat (49°10'00" 125°55'00" SW end of Meares I, N of Tofino, Clayoquot Sd, W side of Vancouver I). Opitsat (or Opitsaht) is the main community of the Tla-o-qui-aht First Nation, a member group of the Nuu-chah-nulth Tribal Council. In the early 2000s the village had a population of about 200. The name was translated as "island that the moon lands on" (in the Nuu-chah-nulth newspaper *Ha-shilth-sa*) and as "place having an island in front" (by BC historians Helen and Philip Akrigg). In 1792, in one of the more infamous acts committed by an early fur trader on the BC coast, Capt Robert Gray of the *Columbia*, hearing that the Tla-o-qui-aht were planning an attack, burned Opitsat to the ground. John Boit, his 5th mate, was "grieved to think Capt Gray shou'd let his passions go so far. This Village ... contained upwards of 200 Houses ... [and] ev'ry door you enter'd was in resemblance to an human and Beasts head, the passage being through the mouth.... This fine Village, the Work of Ages, was in a short time totally destroy'd."

O'Reilly Beach (48°50'00" 123°24'00" Head of James Bay, Prevost I, Gulf Is). John O'Reilly was an early landowner

O

on Prevost I. The beach is now part of the Gulf Is National Park Reserve. The name was submitted by the Gulf Is Branch of the BC Historical Assoc in the late 1960s.

Orford Bay (50°36'00" 124°52'00" E side of Bute Inlet, NE of Clipper Point, NE of Campbell R). This bay was once home to a Homalco First Nation winter village named Pí'pknech, which has been translated, mysteriously, as "white a little bit on the back end." It is now the site of a Homalco reserve, a large salmon hatchery and, in late summer and fall, an increasingly popular grizzly bear viewing area. There is also a logging camp and booming ground nearby; 600 men lived and worked here in the 1920s when the bay was the HQ for Trafford Bernard's extensive railway logging operation. The bay is named after the Orford R, which runs into it. The river, which was known before 1922 as the Salmon R, is probably named for George Walpole, the 3rd Earl of Orford (1730–91). Orford was lord lt of Norfolk, 1757–91, and "a much respected friend" of Capt George Vancouver, who named a headland in Oregon (known today as Cape Blanco) after him in 1792. The nearby town of Port Orford, Oregon, keeps Vancouver's historic reference alive.

Oriflamme Passage (54°35'00" 130°40'00" Between Green I and Connis Rks, Chatham Sd, NW of Prince Rupert). Named for the US paddle steamer *Oriflamme*, which was built in 1864 at Brooklyn, NY, as a gunboat for the US Navy but never commissioned, as the end of the Civil War reduced the need for warships. The 70-m, 1,179-tonne vessel was sold and worked briefly on the China coast before being bought in 1866 by Benjamin Holladay's Oregon Steamship Co and run between San Francisco and Portland. Holladay was a transport tycoon who owned railroads and steamships in Oregon and was known as the "Stagecoach King." He was famous for his lavish lifestyle and often used the *Oriflamme* as a private yacht for parties and special events. It was sold for scrap and dismantled in 1879. *W*

Orion Point (52°07'00" 131°01'00" N entrance to Heater Hbr, NE side of Kunghit I, QCI). The 29-m *Orion* was built in 1904 at Christiana, Norway, for Sprott Balcom's Pacific Whaling Co and was the first steam whaler on the BC coast. Designed to be used from a shore station, it was based periodically at nearby Rose Hbr. The *Orion* had a long life in BC waters, seeing service off the W coast of Vancouver I in the 1910s and operating out of Kyuquot Sd and Naden Hbr for William Schupp's Victoria Whaling Co (later the Consolidated Whaling Corp Ltd) in the 1920s). It was sold about 1930 and converted to a private yacht, then was renamed the *Pluvius* and ended its days as a Vancouver Hbr fireboat in the 1930s and '40s.

Orlebar Point (49°12'00" 123°49'00" N tip of Gabriola I, Gulf Is). Formerly known as Berry Point (and still known locally by that name) but renamed by the hydrographic service in 1945 after Lt Cdr Vere Bernard Orlebar, who commanded the RN gunboat *Rocket* on the Pacific Station, 1879–82. He had earlier served as a lt on HMS *Chanticleer*. This feature is the Punta de Casatilli of Spanish explorer and naval officer José Narváez, named in 1791 after Spanish nobleman Francisco Javier Everardo Tilly, cdr of a naval fleet that attacked Portuguese forces and territories in S America in 1777.

Orlomah Beach (49°22'00" 122°53'00" W side of Indian Arm, NE of Vancouver). Vancouver realtor and insurance agent John Joseph Banfield (1855–1934) acquired this waterfront property prior to WWI. Orlomah is a composite word made from the names of his three children—Orson ("Or"), Lois ("lo") and Mae ("ma")—and his wife Harriet ("h"). After his death the land was sold and became Camp Jubilee, owned today by an alliance of labour unions. Orson Banfield (1897–1983) joined his father in the realty and insurance business and was a Vancouver alderman in the 1960s. Both men were key volunteers in helping the Vancouver General Hospital expand; the Banfield Pavilion is named in the family's honour. Orlomah Beach was originally a port of call for Harbour Navigation vessels, and the company mistakenly listed the stop in its timetable as Orlohma. This misspelling appeared on charts for a number of years until Orson complained.

Ormidale Harbour (52°12'00" 128°08'00" N side of Campbell I, just N of Bella Bella). Lt Daniel Pender named this feature about 1867 after Robert Macfarlane, Lord Ormidale (1802–80), a Scottish judge. He was sheriff of Renfrewshire, 1853–62, and a judge of the court of session, Scotland's supreme civil court, 1862–74. *W*

Ormiston Point (53°34'00" 129°39'00" W side of Grenville Channel, NW of Lowe Inlet, E side of Pitt I). Master mariner Silas Charles Herbert Ormiston (1874–1925) was born on Cape Breton I. In 1902 he married Clara May Morash (1874–1950), also from NS, and moved to Victoria, where he joined the CPR's BC Coast Steamship Service as a quartermaster in 1905. Ormiston was appointed master of the *Otter* in 1912 and later commanded both the *Princess Royal* and the *Princess Mary*. He retired in 1924 and died at Victoria, where he is buried at Ross Bay Cemetery. Ormiston Point was formerly known as Mountain Point. Nearby Silas Point is also named for him.

Ormond Point (53°44'00" 129°50'00" W entrance to Kxngeal Inlet, Grenville Channel, opposite Pitt I). After Capt Thomas Ormond Griffin of the CPR's BC Coast Steamship Service. *See* Griffin I.

Orveas Bay (48°22'00" 123°52'00" SW side of Vancouver I, between Sooke Bay and Sheringham Point). According to the PNW cartography expert Henry Wagner, Spanish naval officer Manuel Quimper gave the name Ensenada de Orbea to a feature at or near this location in 1790, while making the first survey of Juan de Fuca Str—though the name does not appear on the important 1790 charts prepared by Gonzales López de Haro, Quimper's 1st officer. On Francisco Eliza's chart of 1791, however, the name Ensenada de Orveas is present and seems to refer to Sooke Bay. The origin of the name is unknown. Orveas Ck takes its name from the bay.

Orwig Islets (54°08'00" 130°03'00" S of Veitch Point, mouth of the Skeena R, SE of Prince Rupert). Torsten Matheas Orwig (1849–1924), from Norway, received a Crown grant of land in this vicinity in 1912. He came to Port Essington with his family in the late 1890s and was one of the first full-time boatbuilders on the N BC coast. Sometime during WWI he moved to Prince Rupert and established a boatyard at Seal Cove. Ed Wahl, later to become the N coast's principal boatbuilder, with yards at Dodge Cove and Prince Rupert, took over Orwig's facilities in the early 1920s. Torsten died at Prince Rupert; his wife Beret Kristina Orwig (1852–1939) died at Vancouver.

Osborn Bay (48°52'00" 123°38'00" W side of Stuart Channel, just N of Crofton, SE side of Vancouver I). Named in 1859 by Capt George Richards of the survey ship *Plumper* after well-known RN officer Sherard Osborn, CB (1822–75). Osborn entered the navy as a lowly sailor and served as a gunner's mate aboard HMS *Collingwood* while that vessel was Rear Adm Sir George Seymour's flagship on the Pacific Station, 1843–46. He was promoted to lt on the *Collingwood* and then to cdr in 1852 for his work searching for Sir John Franklin in the Arctic Ocean. Osborn was back in the Arctic in 1852–54, still searching for Franklin, as cdr of HMS *Pioneer*, one of the vessels that Sir Edward Belcher, the expedition's cdr-in-chief, ordered abandoned in the ice, much against Osborn's wishes. He was made capt and awarded the CB for his distinguished work during the Crimean War, where he took part in the capture of several Russian ports and was senior officer in the Sea of Azov. Osborn later saw action off China, participating in the 1859 attack on Canton and repressing piracy during the Taiping Rebellion, 1862–64. He became a rear adm in 1873 and a member of the RN's Arctic committee, 1874–75. Osborn was also an author (*Last Voyage and Fate of Sir John Franklin* and *Arctic Exploration*) and a businessman, with interests in railways, telegraph construction and cable laying. Nearby Sherard Point is named for him. *W*

Osland (54°08'00" 130°10'00" E side of Smith I, at mouth of the Skeena R, just S of Prince Rupert). This once-thriving fishing community is now mostly abandoned, though a few homes are still occupied on a seasonal basis. Osland was founded about 1912–13 by Icelandic Canadians from Winnipeg, Gimli, Selkirk, Lundar and Steep Rk in Manitoba. The population peaked in the 1920s at around 80 people. Besides fishing, the villagers also worked at nearby canneries. A Japanese family, the Sakamotos, established a boatyard in the 1930s and early '40s, and several other boatbuilders also operated at Osland, which had three public docks, a school, post office and general store. Most inhabitants had moved to Prince Rupert by the early 1950s. The name may be a N American adaptation of *åsland*, from the Old Norse; a possible translation is "land on a ridge or hill." Nearby De Horsey Passage is known locally as Osland Passage.

Osment Inlet (52°32'00" 128°42'00" Head of Kitasu Bay, SW side of Swindle I, NW of Bella Bella). Quartermaster-Sgt David Shorthose Osment (b 1830) was a member of the Columbia detachment of Royal Engineers, which served in BC 1858–63. Born at London, he learned carpentry from his father and joined the sappers in 1852. Osment participated in the Siege of Sevastopol during the Crimean War and was promoted to sgt in 1857. He travelled to BC aboard the *Thames City* with his very pregnant wife, Agnes, and their daughter Agnes Elizabeth. Mrs Osment gave birth to Fanny Marina shortly after the ship left England, one of nine children born on the voyage. While in BC, in addition to his quartermaster duties, Osment was a keen member of the detachment cricket and drama clubs. When the engineers disbanded, he returned to England with his family, which by then included five children, and spent more than seven years at Gibraltar, where Agnes bore two more children and David was promoted to sgt maj. He was discharged in 1875, and the family moved to St Vincent in the W Indies.

Oswald Bay (53°02'00" 129°39'00" Between Dewdney I and Barnard I, W side of the Estevan Group, SE of Banks I), **Oswald Point** (52°51'00" 129°21'00" NW tip of Rennison I, off NW end of Aristazabal I). After Oswald Rennison Parker, who worked on the BC coast for the hydrographic service before becoming dockmaster at the Esquimalt drydock. *See* Parker Passage. Apparently he surveyed the W coast of Estevan Is in 1923 from a base camp on Oswald Bay. Before 1946, Oswald Point was known as Cliff Point.

Otard Bay (53°46'00" 133°00'00" N of Port Louis, W side of Graham I, QCI). Otard Bay and Otard Ck, which flows W into the head of the bay, were named after a close but unidentified friend of Capt Prosper Chanal, deputy cdr of the French trading vessel *La Solide*, who explored this area by longboat in 1791. *La Solide*, under Capt Etienne Marchand, anchored for several weeks at Cloak Bay in the QCI while circumnavigating the world in search of knowledge and profit. QCI historian Kathleen Dalzell reports that Otard Bay is probably the Stowe Hbr of explorer Newton Chittenden. The Haida people, who used a trail from Naden Hbr to the mouth of Otard Ck, knew the bay as Tou-kathli: *tou* meaning "the place of food" or "mussels," and *kathli* meaning "an open bay or slough." *D*

The steamship *Otter* at Bella Bella in 1880. *BC Archives A-00106*

Otter Anchorage (54°31'00" 130°27'00" W side of Tsimpsean Peninsula, SE of Finlayson I, N of Prince Rupert), **Otter Channel** (53°12'00" 129°32'00" Eastern extension of Nepean Sd, between Campania I and Pitt I), **Otter Cove** (50°19'00" 125°27'00" NW side of Discovery Passage, NW of Campbell R), **Otter Passage** (53°08'00" 129°45'00" Between Banks I and Trutch I), **Otter Shoal** (53°24'00" 129°17'00" In Coghlan Anchorage, W of Promise I, S of Hartley Bay, N of Wright Sd). These names all honour the historic *Otter*, the second steamer in the PNW and the first to be driven by a propeller instead of a paddlewheel. The 37-m, 264-tonne, barque-rigged vessel was built for the HBC in London in 1852 and arrived at Victoria the following year. It worked in all corners of the BC coast—conveying HBC officials on company business, carrying passengers and freight, and towing slower, sail-powered vessels—and soon became a familiar sight, especially in northern waters, as famous in its own way as the *Beaver*. The *Otter* was commanded by a series of distinguished mariners, including William Mouat, John Swanson and Herbert Lewis, and is reputed to have sparked off the Fraser R gold rush by conveying some of the precious metal to San Francisco in 1857 for deposit at the mint. It also laboured on the Stikine R during the 1862 Stikine and 1874 Cassiar gold rushes, and it carried men and supplies to the head of Bute Inlet in the misguided 1862 roadbuilding effort that resulted in the Chilcotin War. In 1880 the *Otter* hit a rock near Bella Bella and sank but was raised, repaired and soon sent back to work. In 1883, when the HBC marine dept merged with John Irving's Pioneer Line, it became part of the Canadian Pacific Navigation Co fleet. It was converted to a coal barge in 1886 and burned for its metal in 1890. A decade later the CPN built another *Otter*, which became part of the CPR's coastal fleet until sold in 1931. It was destroyed by fire at Malkscope Inlet in 1937. *E W*

Otter Bay (48°48'00" 123°18'00" W side of N Pender I, SE of James Point, Gulf Is), **Otter Island** (50°07'28" 124°43'56" E side of Desolation Sd, NE of Mink I, NW of Powell R). These geographical features commemorate the animal, not

the boat (*see* Otter Anchorage). Otter Bay is the site of N Pender I's ferry terminal; its Hul'qumi'num (Coast Salish) name is Sqə'utl'um, meaning "place of otters." Otter I was named by Admiralty surveyors about 1861 in association with nearby Mink I and the Martin Is (which should have been spelled Marten), all after fur-bearing mammals.

Otter Point (48°21'00" 123°49'00" N side of Juan de Fuca Str, E of Orveas Bay, SW end of Vancouver I). RN surveying officer Henry Charles Otter (1807–76) was never on the BC coast but gained a reputation (and a promotion) for his Baltic surveys while in command of HMS *Alban* during the Crimean War. As capt of HMS *Firefly*, he also destroyed several enemy vessels in the Gulf of Bothnia during the Russian conflict. Otter helped land the western end of the transatlantic telegraph cable at Trinity Bay, Nfld, in 1858 and was widely admired for his detailed surveys of the rugged W coast of Scotland. He was named a CB in 1867 and achieved the rank of rear adm, retired, in 1870. This feature was originally named Otter Head in 1846 by Capt Henry Kellett of HMS *Herald*.

Ovesen Point (52°25'00" 127°14'00" NE end of King I, Labouchere Channel, W of Bella Coola). Andreas Kristian Ovesen (1859–1934) was one of the Norwegian settlers who colonized the Bella Coola valley in the late 1890s. He received a Crown grant for his land in 1901. Mrs Ovesen was the community midwife and nurse in the early days.

Owen Bay. *Peter Vassilopoulos*

Owen Bay (50°19'12" 125°13'32" S side of Sonora I, N of Campbell R). In the mid-1860s, Lt Daniel Pender named many features in this area after RN officers who worked in the British hydrographic office under Capt George Richards. Because Evans Bay (qv), Frederick Arm, Frederic Point and Owen Point all commemorate Capt Sir Frederick John Owen Evans, hydrographer of the RN, 1874–84, many writers have concluded that Owen Bay is also named for him. But there is no evidence that this is so. According to the Geographic Board of Canada, the

O

bay commemorates William Gaskell Owen (1850–1903), who served as 1st officer on the *Sir James Douglas* and the *Quadra*, lighthouse tenders on the Pacific coast, until 1902. He was born at Liverpool, came to Canada in 1862 and lived at Victoria, where he married Louisa James (1859–1923) in 1884. It is strange, however, that William Owen is not mentioned in *British Columbia Coast Names 1592–1906*, the classic reference work by John Walbran, who was capt of CGS *Quadra* for most of the period that Owen was mate. The community of Owen Bay formed in the 1920s around the homestead of Logan Schibler, with a school, dock, store, post office and sawmill. By the 1960s it had mostly dispersed. According to many boaters, the bay is haunted. *E*

Owen Island (Just S of Owen Point), **Owen Point** (48°33'00" 124°30'00" W entrance to Port San Juan, SW side of Vancouver I). Named in 1846 by Capt Henry Kellett of HMS *Herald* after the prominent RN surveying officer William Fitzwilliam Owen (1774–1857), whom Kellett had served with earlier. Owen explored the Maldive Is in 1806 as cdr of HMS *Seaflower*, and after being imprisoned by the French at Mauritius in 1808–10, he surveyed Canada's Great Lks, 1815–16, and the coast of Africa, 1821–31. In 1833 he published *A Narrative of Voyages to Explore the Shores of Africa*. Owen was engaged in survey work on the E coast of N America in the 1840s as cdr of HMS *Columbia*. He was promoted to rear adm in 1847 and vice adm in 1854. *W*

Owen Point (50°27'00" 125°19'00" N of junction of Nodales Channel and Cordero Channel, N of Campbell R). After Capt Sir Frederick John Owen Evans, hydrographer of the RN, 1874–84. *See* Evans Bay.

Owikeno Point (51°42'00" 127°27'00" At junction of Hardy Inlet and Moses Inlet, N side of Rivers Inlet). Named after Oweekeno (also known as Katit), the principal village of the Oweekeno First Nation. This settlement, with a population of about 60, is located just E of the mouth of the Wannock R, which connects nearby Owikeno Lk to Rivers Inlet. According to BC historians Helen and Philip

Akrigg, there are several possible meanings for the name, including "portage makers" or "those who carry on the back," and "right-minded people" or "people talking right." The spelling can vary wildly: Wikeno, Owekano, O-wee-kay-no, Awikenox, Weekeemoch, etc. The Oweekeno people speak Oowekyala, a northern Wakashan language, and are closely related to the Heiltsuk First Nation of Bella Bella. Their numbers were much reduced in the mid-1800s through epidemics and inter-tribal warfare. Rivers Inlet Cannery, built at the mouth of the Wannock in 1882 and sometimes known as Oweekayno cannery, was the first in the region. *E W*

Owl Island (48°49'35" 123°23'55" Off W end of Prevost I, Gulf Is). This locally established name, descriptive of the shape of the island, was submitted by James Stuart, harbourmaster at Ganges, in 1988, at the time of the Canadian Hydrographic Service's revisory survey of the Gulf Is. The name was adopted later that year.

Oyster Bay (49°54'00" 125°10'00" E side of Vancouver I, between Courtenay and Campbell R). The SE coast of Vancouver I is BC's richest oyster-growing region. In fact, Baynes Sd, just S of Oyster Bay, accounts for about 40 percent of the province's oyster production. The Pacific or Japanese oyster (*Crassostrea gigas*), introduced from Asia in the early 1900s, is the dominant commercial species; two other introduced species and the native Olympia oyster are also found in the PNW. In the early 2000s, BC was producing about 6,000 tonnes of oysters annually, with a wholesale value of approximately $20 million. The Oyster R, popular with fly fishers, flows E into the Str of Georgia here, and a number of beach resorts, parks and marinas can be found near the mouth of the river. *E*

Oyster Bay (51°38'00" 127°41'00" N side of Fish Egg Inlet, E of Fitz Hugh Sd and Calvert I, SE of Bella Bella). This bay, which is known locally as Oyster Lagoon, is claimed to be the most northerly habitat for oysters on the BC coast.

Oyster Harbour. *See* Ladysmith Hbr *and* Page Point.

P

The Pachena Point lighthouse station was built in 1908. This aerial photo was taken in 1981. *Jim Ryan*

Pachena Bay (48°47'00" 125°08'00" Just E of Cape Beale, SE of Barkley Sd, W side of Vancouver I), **Pachena Beach** (48°47'00" 125°07'00" Head of Pachena Bay), **Pachena Point** (48°43'00" 125°06'00" S side of Pachena Bay), **Pachena River** (48°48'00" 125°08'00" Flows SW into Pachena Bay). Pachena Bay is the site of Anacla, the main community of the Huu-ay-aht (Ohiaht) First Nation. Anacla is also the Huu-ay-aht name for Pachena Bay. Pachena, meaning "foamy" or "sea foam on rocks," actually refers to the former village site of P'aachiida, on Port San Juan to the SE. Early surveyors mistakenly applied the name to this bay instead. P'aachiida was once the main village of the Pacheenaht (or Pacheedaht) First Nation, whose traditional territory lies between Sheringham Point and Bonilla Point, though most tribal members live today at Port Renfrew. Both the Huu-ay-aht and Pacheenaht have cultural links to the larger Nuu-chah-nulth confederacy (as does their mutual neighbour, the Ditidaht), but only the Huu-ay-aht belong to the Nuu-chah-nulth Tribal Council. Pachena Point originally appeared on charts as Beghadoss Point, after a vessel wrecked in the vicinity in

1879. This ship, a British barque bound from Shanghai to Moodyville under a Capt Williams, was driven onto a reef in heavy fog. Its name appeared in most newspaper reports as *Becherdass-Ambiadass*, though other spellings have been noted as well. A lighthouse was built on the point in 1908. Nearby Pachena Cone also appears on early Admiralty charts of the area; Pachena Lk was named later. The Pachena R was identified as the Cache R on the map made by John Buttle's 1864 Vancouver I Exploring Expedition. *E*

Pacofi Bay (52°50'00" 131°52'00" Off Selwyn Inlet, W of Talunkwan I, E side of Moresby I, QCI). This name is an abbreviation for Pacific Coast Fisheries Ltd, a company headed by the flamboyant Alvo von Alvensleben, a Prussian nobleman, financier and alleged spy who was interned in the US during WWI. He built a fish-processing and reduction plant on the bay in 1909 that soon went out of business. A salmon saltery operated at the site, 1927–36, using the old buildings, and BC Packers built a new cannery there in 1938 that ran until 1949. During construction of the cannery, workers discovered underground concrete structures of unknown function; rumours swirled that Alvensleben had intended his plant to be a submarine base. The cannery fell into ruin after use as a logging camp. In the mid-1990s a luxurious but unsuccessful fishing lodge was built on the bay; it was listed for sale in the early 2000s. Pacofi Ck takes its name from the bay. *D*

Paddon Point (48°50'00" 123°15'00" E side of Mayne I, Gulf Is). Named after George Locke Paddon (1878–1930), one of the seven sons of Canon William Francis Locke Paddon (1844–1922), who first visited BC in 1885. Canon Paddon was looking for a place to settle where his delicate health would not be endangered, and Victoria fit the bill. He emigrated from Ireland in 1889 along with his wife, Kathleen Rebecca Robinson (1852–1945), their nine children and a tutor. In 1896, after working as chaplain for the Jubilee Hospital and at the Victoria jail, he became the Anglican clergyman for the Gulf Is. The canon arranged for St Mary Magdalene Church to be built on Mayne I in 1897, and he provided services there twice a month, commuting from Victoria until 1904 and then settling on the island. George Paddon married Mabel Hilda Gaugh (1878–1954) on Mayne I in 1910. He died at Chilliwack, Mabel at N Vancouver. The name was suggested in 1968 by the Gulf Is Branch of the BC Historical Assoc.

Page Island (48°56'00" 125°23'00" In Loudoun Channel, SE of Forbes I, Barkley Sd, W side of Vancouver I). C M Page received a Crown land grant in Barkley Sd, on the N side of Useless Inlet, in 1892. The feature was formerly known as Round I.

Page Lagoon (49°13'00" 123°57'00" SE end of Hammond Bay, just N of Nanaimo, SE side of Vancouver I). This geographic feature, more commonly called Page's Lagoon, was the site of an important if short-lived whaling station. Built in 1907 by Victoria's Pacific Whaling Co, it employed more than 125 men and managed to wipe out the entire humpback population of the Str of Georgia in three months. The facility then turned dogfish into fertilizer for four years before being dismantled and moved to the QCI. Humpbacks were not seen again in the strait until 1976. The lagoon was named for local landowner Louis Page. In 1917, Joseph E Piper bought Page's 57-ha property and attempted to raise sheep, but they were eaten by cougars. Piper and his two sons then rented out their land for recreational cabin use, and the lagoon turned into a popular vacation spot. A sawmill also operated in the vicinity. By the time developer Deane Finlayson acquired the land around the lagoon in the mid-1950s, it had become known locally as Piper's Lagoon. Finlayson subdivided most of it and attempted, unsuccessfully, to build a marina and resort on the rest. In 1983 the remaining land became an 8-ha regional park, officially known as Piper's Lagoon Park. Page Lagoon, also an official name, still appears on hydrographic charts.

Page Passage (48°40'50" 123°23'50" Separates Johnson It and Fernie I from Kolb It and Kamaree It, off NE end of Saanich Peninsula, N of Sidney). William Page (1839–98), who received a Crown grant for land at N Saanich in 1876, was one of the area's earliest settlers. He married Emma (b about 1833), a First Nation woman, farmed and raised a family. Apparently Page had come out to Victoria as an HBC employee and worked at first as a shepherd and sheep shearer.

Page Point (49°01'00" 123°49'00" E side of Ladysmith Hbr, SE of Nanaimo, SE side of Vancouver I). Fisherman and farmer David Page (1836–1918), from England, pre-empted land on Ladysmith Hbr in the 1870s and received a Crown grant in 1885. His holdings were rich in native oysters (Oyster Hbr was the old name for Ladysmith Hbr), and Page became one of BC's first cultivators and harvesters of the tasty bivalve. In the early 2000s his property, formerly the site of a yachting lodge, was home to the Page Point Inn and Marina.

Paige Point (53°11'00" 129°32'00" NW point of Campania I, Nepean Sd, S of Pitt I). Named in 1949 after Staff Sgt Herbert Melvin Paige of the Royal Canadian Ordnance Corps, aged 26, who was killed in action Jan 11, 1944, during the fighting at Ortona and the Moro R in Italy. He was originally from Edmonton. Paige is buried at the Moro R Canadian War Cemetery.

Paisley Point (53°45'00" 129°02'00" SW entrance to Drumlummon Bay, Douglas Channel, SW of Kitimat). Paisley is a town in Scotland, now part of Greater Glasgow, where the Canadian government lighthouse tender *Quadra* was built in 1891 by the engineering and shipbuilding firm Fleming & Ferguson. The company operated from 1886 to 1969, manufacturing steam engines and a variety of specialized vessels, including dredgers, floating cranes, small warships, coasters and harbour craft. The town of Paisley was once famous for its weaving industry; the Paisley pattern, still popular for shawls and ties, originated there. Paisley Point was named in 1898 by BC coastal historian John T Walbran, who was capt of the *Quadra* at the time.

Palliser Rock (49°37'00" 124°50'00" N of Denman I, Str of Georgia). Rear Adm Henry St Ledger Bury Palliser (d 1907) was cdr-in-chief on the RN's Pacific Station, based at Esquimalt, 1896–99. His flagship was the cruiser *Imperieuse*, under Capt Charles Adair. Palliser entered the RN in 1852 and saw service as a junior officer in the Crimean War. He was promoted to capt in 1878, commodore at Hong Kong in 1891, rear adm in 1893 and reached the rank of adm, retired, in 1904. He had famous relatives: Capt Frederick Marryat, early practitioner of the sea novel and author of *Mr Midshipman Easy*, was an uncle, and Capt John Palliser, who travelled the Canadian West in 1857–59 as leader of the British N American Exploring Expedition, was a cousin. Rear Adm Palliser was deeply intrigued by a legend claiming that treasure was buried on Cocos I off Costa Rica. He paid the island one visit in his flagship in 1897 and another, after he retired in 1899, on his private vessel, the *Lytton*, but found no gold. A third venture, in 1905, had to be abandoned when Palliser and a partner, the fabulously wealthy William Wentworth-FitzWilliam, 7th Earl FitzWilliam, found that a competitor had acquired from the Costa Rican government the sole right to hunt treasure on the island. If riches were ever found there, the fact was not advertised. Cocos I is now a national park. *W*

Palmer Anchorage (52°37'00" 128°45'00" S end of Thistle Passage, SW end of Princess Royal I). Lt Henry Spencer Palmer (1838–93) was a member of the Columbia

P

detachment of Royal Engineers, which served in BC 1858–63. The son of a British Army officer, he was born at Bangalore, India, and educated at Bath and the Royal Military Academy at Woolwich. He came to BC with the main contingent of men in the *Thames City* and was a major contributor to the ship's journal, *The Emigrant Soldiers' Gazette and Cape Horn Chronicle*, writing editorials and articles on natural history. Palmer surveyed trails from Harrison R to Lillooet and from Ft Hope to Ft Colville on the Columbia R, supervised road construction and in 1862 was sent to seek an alternate route to the goldfields from Bella Coola to Ft Alexandria (Palmer Lk and Mt Palmer in the Chilcotin–Cariboo honour this expedition). In 1863, just before returning to England after the detachment disbanded, he married Mary Jane Pearson Wright (1847–1934), daughter of Rev Henry Wright, BC's first Anglican archdeacon. After several years in southern England, Palmer made a geographical and historical survey of the Sinai Peninsula, 1868–69. In 1874, by now a maj, he went to NZ as head of the observation party for the transit of Venus. He spent 1875–78 in Barbados and 1878–83 in Hong Kong and Japan before returning to serve in England. Palmer was back in Asia in 1885, in charge of building the Yokohama waterworks, and although he retired from the Royal Engineers in 1887 with the rank of maj gen, he remained in Japan and supervised the construction of Yokohama Hbr until his premature death from typhoid fever. Another geographic feature in BC named after this intrepid figure is Palmer Pond, which he mentioned in his journal, while travelling the HBC Brigade Trail in 1859, as a "pretty little lake." Presumably Palmer Ck, which flows into Chilcotin Lk, and the Palmer Range, E of Barkerville, also commemorate him.

Pamphlet Cove (50°31'00" 127°39'00" N side of Drake I, Quatsino Sd, NW end of Vancouver I). Thomas Pamphlet (1836–1916), from Essex, began his career in 1849 on the brig *Eston Nab*. After serving in the RN in the Crimean War, he came to Victoria in 1856 aboard the barque *Agnes Garland*. He had a deep acquaintance with some of BC's earliest sailing vessels, commanding the *Ino* in 1857 and buying the *Violet*, built on Pachena Bay by pioneer traders Peter Francis and William Banfield, the following year. During the Fraser R gold rush, "Capt Tom," as he was widely known, carried passengers and freight to Ft Langley. He acted as a pilot and interpreter when HMS *Satellite* went to Barkley Sd in 1859 to investigate the pillaging of the US brig *Swiss Boy* (*see* Swiss Boy Island). Pamphlet spent 1860–66 as skipper of the *Meg Merrilies*, carrying lumber for BC's first export sawmill at Alberni, then served as a pilot at Victoria for the next decade. He later had charge of several historic vessels, including the *Beaver*, *Sir James Douglas*, *Enterprise* and *Emma*, and apparently even had time to pre-empt land at Quatsino Sd in 1884. His wife, Elizabeth (1834–1907), was born at Ft Simpson. Pamphlet Cove was formerly known as

Quiet Cove. Tom Point in the Gulf Is is also named for him. *W*

Pam Rock (49°29'00" 123°18'00" In Queen Charlotte Channel, E of Brigade Bay on Gambier I, Howe Sd, NW of Vancouver). Named for the Union Steamship Co's *Lady Pam*, which frequented these waters. This 46-m, 277-tonne vessel was built at Glasgow in 1893 as a private yacht called the *Santa Maria*. It was acquired in 1914 by the All Red Line, which operated a scheduled run between Vancouver and Powell R and made charter trips to the company's waterfront resort at Selma Park, just S of Sechelt. Union Steamship bought the All Red Line in 1917 and renamed the *Santa Maria* the *Chilco*. In 1935 it was completely remodelled and named the *Lady Pam*. It ended its days as a hulk and became part of the breakwater at Oyster Bay in 1945. Pam Rk was formerly known as White Rk.

Pandora Head (50°54'00" 126°53'00" W entrance to Grappler Sd, W of Kinnaird I, N side of E Queen Charlotte Str, N of Port McNeill), **Pandora Hill** (48°25'30" 123°13'41" E end of Discovery I, off Oak Bay and SE end of Vancouver I). Pandora Hill (38 m) was named in 1847 by Lt Cdr James Wood, after his survey vessel *Pandora*, which was employed in making the first Admiralty charts of the BC coast, 1846–48. The 3-gun, 289-tonne brig, which was launched in 1833, left England in 1845 as tender to the larger HMS *Herald*, under Capt Henry Kellett. The two ships charted the S coast of Vancouver I, including Victoria and Esquimalt harbours and Sooke Inlet, until Kellett was sent to the Arctic to join the search for explorer Sir John Franklin. The *Pandora* conducted survey work off Australia, 1850–56, and then served as a Coast Guard vessel until it was decommissioned in 1862. Pandora Peak on the N side of Port San Juan commemorates the fact that the vessel also surveyed this area in 1847. Pandora Head was named by Lt Daniel Pender in 1865. *W*

Pan Rock (52°30'00" 127°52'00" Roscoe Inlet, W of Quartcha Bay, NE of Bella Bella). Named by the hydrographic service in 1957 "for its general appearance."

Panther Point (48°56'00" 123°32'00" S tip of Wallace I, Trincomali Channel, off NE side of Saltspring I, Gulf Is). The US clipper ship *Panther* drifted onto a reef off this point in Jan 1874 and became a total loss. The 60-m, 1,160-tonne vessel, under Capt John Balch, was being towed by the *Goliath* from Nanaimo with a load of coal when a blinding snowstorm forced the tug to cast it off. The *Colonist* newspaper reported that the sidewheel steamer *Cyrus Walker* spent 19 days trying to float the ill-fated *Panther* before it was abandoned. The clipper, built near Boston in 1854, had been operated out of San Francisco by the historic firm of Pope & Talbot since 1868. Panther Point was named in 1905 by Cdr John Parry of HMS *Egeria*.

Pantoja Islands (49°36'00" 126°34'00" Part of the Spanish Pilot Group, SW of Bligh I, Nootka Sd, W side of Vancouver I). Juan Pantoja y Arriaga was a Spanish naval officer who served on the Pacific coast in the late 18th century. He first sailed off BC in 1779 as 2nd pilot of the *Princesa*, under Ignacio de Arteaga. On this early expedition, Arteaga was accompanied by Juan Francisco de la Bodega y Quadra in the *Favorita* and spent much time exploring SE Alaska, Prince William Sd and Cook Inlet. Pantoja surveyed the S coast of California in 1782 with Estéban Martínez; his journal of this voyage has been translated and published, and his map of San Diego Hbr was used decades later to fix the W end of the US-Mexico boundary. In 1791 he was 1st pilot of the *San Carlos*, under Francisco Eliza, and one of the first Europeans to see and explore the Str of Georgia. The following year he sailed as 1st pilot of the *Aránzazu* with Jacinto Caamaño, who surveyed Dixon Entrance while searching for the fictitious Str of Fonte and named Punta de Pantoja, now Klashwun Point, on Graham I after his officer. The Arriaga Is in Hecate Str are also named for him. The Pantoja Is were once known as the Centre Is.

Pardoe Point (53°06'00" 128°27'00" S shore of Khutze Inlet, E of Princess Royal I). Named in 1929 after Edward "Ted" Pardoe Wilson, construction engineer at that time for the Western Copper Mine, located about 8 km up the Khutze valley and connected to the head of Khutze Inlet by a tramway. The property was active prior to 1910, and again, under several different owners, between 1925 and 1932. *See also* Green Spit.

Paril River (53°29'18" 128°45'57" Flows N into Ochwe Bay, S side of Gardner Canal, S of Kitimat). The Haisla First Nation knows this feature as Oswilh, according to anthropologist Jay Powell. A log sort and booming ground, operated in the early 2000s by Triumph Timber Ltd, is located near the mouth of the river.

Parizeau Point. *See* Mt Parizeau.

Parker Bay (48°21'00" 123°32'00" SW end of Parry Bay, SW of Metchosin, near S tip of Vancouver I). This feature is presumably named after John and Mary Parker, pioneer settlers in the district. John (1827–1917), from Kent, England, a farrier and blacksmith, married Mary Ann Munn (1832–1900) about 1852. They arrived at Victoria in 1853, on the third voyage of the HBC supply ship *Norman Morison*. John worked at the Albert Head sawmill, operated a livery stable and mail transport service, participated in the Cariboo gold rush and drove a stagecoach for an express company. In 1859 he bought 500 ha of land from the HBC at Rocky Point and farmed. Later, with his sons, he opened a butcher shop in Victoria, which he supplied from his farm. Many of John and Mary's children and grandchildren were early settlers of the Colwood-Metchosin region.

Parker Island (48°53'00" 123°25'00" E side of Trincomali Channel, W of S end of Galiano I, Gulf Is). Lt George Ferdinand Hastings Parker of the RN served on the Pacific Station, 1857–60, at first in HMS *Ganges*, flagship of Rear Adm Robert Baynes, and then in HMS *Scout*, under Capt John Price. He entered the RN in 1848, and before coming to the Pacific was appointed to HMS *Duke of Wellington*, the RN's finest battleship. Parker retired with the rank of capt in 1882. The 162-ha island was named by Capt George Richards of HMS *Plumper* in 1859. It was acquired in 1913 by horticulturist Percy T James, who cleared several hectares and started the James Bros Seed Co, a very successful mail-order flower and vegetable seed business that flourished until about 1945. The company soon outgrew Parker I, however, selling it for $4,500 in 1917 and moving to nearby Saltspring I. In 1923 a NY purchaser got the island for a mere $2,300 and held on to it for more than 50 years, but it was eventually subdivided into 37 lots and is now home to a number of million-dollar waterfront retreats. *W*

Parker Island, just off Galiano Island. *Andrew Scott*

Parker Passage (52°48'00" 129°21'00" Between Rennison I and the Anderson Is, off NW end of Aristazabal I), Parker Point (53°42'00" 132°29'00" N side of Masset Inlet, just SW of Buckley Bay, Graham I, QCI). Oswald Rennison Parker (1885–1941) served as a junior hydrographer on the BC coast, 1911–14 and 1919–24, working mostly on surveys of Hecate Str and Queen Charlotte Sd. During WWI he was an RN officer attached to the Admiralty's hydrographic office. Later he became dockmaster at the Esquimalt graving dock. The point was named to recognize the role that Parker played in the pre-WWI surveys of Masset Inlet and Port Louis. The passage was named in 1926. Oswald Bay (qv), Oswald Point and Rennison I also honour him. Parker married Edith Mary Lawson (1875–1948), daughter of pioneer Victoria merchant James Hill Lawson, at Victoria in 1914.

Parker Rocks (53°35'00" 130°34'00" Approach to Griffin Hbr, NW end of Banks I, Hecate Str). Named for A Parker,

P

who worked as a coal trimmer aboard the government survey vessel *Lillooet* in the early 1920s after returning from overseas service during WWI. (A trimmer made sure that coal was spread evenly in the ship's holds, usually using just a shovel.)

Parkin Islets (54°38'00" 130°28'00" SW of Maskelyne I, S entrance to Portland Inlet, off N tip of Tsimpsean Peninsula, N of Prince Rupert), **Parkin Point** (48°44'00" 123°19'00" NE tip of Moresby I, SE of Saltspring I, Gulf Is). George Henry Parkin (1828–1902), from Cornwall, was 3rd lt aboard HMS *Portland*, flagship of Rear Adm Fairfax Moresby, on the Pacific Station, 1850–53. He entered the RN in 1840 and served in the Mediterranean and at NZ before being promoted to capt in 1866. Parkin commanded HMS *Crocodile*, 1870–73, HMS *Triumph* in 1877, and the hospital and receiving ship *Victor Emmanuel* in Africa and Hong Kong. He was also capt of the steam reserve at Portsmouth and superintendent of Pembroke dockyard, and achieved the rank of vice adm, retired, in 1888. The point was named by RN surveyor Capt George Richards in 1858, the islets by George Inskip, master of HMS *Virago*, during the 1853 survey of Port Simpson.

Parkins Rock. *See* Cape Parkins.

Park Island (52°26'00" 131°24'00" W of Huxley I, off SE Moresby I, QCI). C H Park owned numerous mining claims at Jedway, just to the S, during the copper-mining boom of 1906-9. The Eagle Tree property on Harriet Hbr was a special interest of his, and in 1908 he bought the Surprise claim in Huston Inlet. Named in 1962 by the hydrographic service. *D*

Parksville (49°19'00" 124°19'00" On Parksville Bay), **Parksville Bay** (49°20'00" 124°19'00" Between Northwest Bay and Qualicum Beach, E side of Vancouver I). Nelson P Parks (1824–1910), his wife, Elizabeth (c 1836–1913), and his sons, George and James, all from the US, acquired property in this area in 1884 and farmed. Nelson was appointed the area's first postmaster, 1886–91; in the 1901 census his occupation is listed as shoemaker. He and his wife appear to have migrated farther N in the early 1900s; Nelson died at Union Bay, Elizabeth at Cumberland. George and James moved away from the area also, and both died at Kamloops. The community of Parksville was a stop on the Nanaimo–Port Alberni wagon road until the arrival of the E&N in 1910. It developed rapidly as a commercial centre for logging and agriculture and as a popular retirement and summer recreation spot. In the early 2000s it had a population of about 10,000. *E*

Parlane Islet (53°36'00" 130°35'00" N approach to Griffith Hbr, off NW end of Banks I, Hecate Str). Peter Strachan Parlane (1888–1968) returned from overseas service in WWI and worked on the BC coast for the Canadian

Hydrographic Service. He served as coxswain of one of CGS *Lillooet*'s launches in the early 1920s. Parlane married Dorothy Jane Horton (1890–1981) at Victoria in 1922. He died at Saanich, his wife at Prince George. The original name adopted for this site, in 1926, was Parlane Point, but more detailed surveys showed that the point was actually on a small island, so the name was changed in 1952.

Parminter Point (48°54'00" 123°36'00" W of St Mary Lake, W side of Saltspring I, Gulf Is). Rev Henry Parminter (d 1899) was the chaplain aboard HMS *Ganges*, the flagship of Rear Adm Robert Baynes, cdr-in-chief on the RN's Pacific Station, 1857-60. He was first appointed a chaplain in the RN in 1850 and served on the N America and W Indies stations, 1852–56, with HMS *Vestal*. Parminter appears to have published a pamphlet called *The Power and Speed of Steam Vessels* (1878). The point was named in 1905 by Cdr John Parry of HMS *Egeria* while re-surveying adjacent waters.

Parry Bay (48°22'00" 123°31'00" Between Albert Head and William Head, off Metchosin, SW of Victoria, S end of Vancouver I), **Parry Passage** (54°11'00" 133°01'00" Between Langara I and NW end of Graham I, QCI). Rear Adm Sir William Edward Parry (1790–1855) was a noted RN officer, Arctic explorer, author and hydrographer. As cdr of the brig *Alexander*, he accompanied John Ross on his 1818 search for a NW passage. The following year he was chosen to lead an Arctic expedition as cdr of HMS *Hecla*; on this voyage he became the first European ship capt to safely overwinter in the high Arctic and the first to reach 110° W, at Melville I. Parry led a third northern expedition, 1821–23, that spent two winters in the ice and explored Foxe Basin and Melville Peninsula. A fourth voyage, in 1824–25, to Lancaster Sd and Prince Regent Inlet, was less successful as ice conditions were overly severe and the support vessel, HMS *Fury*, was lost. Parry's last Arctic expedition, an attempt to reach the N Pole over the ice, got as far as 82°45', the farthest point N attained at that time. He served as hydrographer of the RN, 1823–29, then resigned to manage the Australian Agricultural Co's operations in New S Wales, 1829–34. Back in England, in poor health, he held several civil and naval appointments, supervising victualling yards and hospitals, the home packet service and the RN's conversion to steam power. He died in Germany seeking medical treatment. William Head on Parry Bay is also named for him, as are numerous other geographical features, including Parry Sd in Ont, Parry Crater on the moon and Parry Channel in the Arctic. His grandson, Adm Sir John Franklin Parry (*see* Mt Parry), spent time on the BC coast and, like his famous forebear, served as hydrographer of the RN. Parry Bay was named the Rada de Solano by Spanish explorer Manuel Quimper in 1790—no doubt after naval leader and explorer José Solano y Bote, the Marquess of Socorro. Parry Passage also had other, earlier names, including Cox's Passage (given by

William Douglas), Cunneyah's Strs (by Joseph Ingraham) and Puerto de Floridablanca (by Jacinto Caamaño). Parry Bay was named in 1846 by Capt Henry Kellett of HMS *Herald*, Parry Passage in 1853 by Cdr James Prevost of HMS *Virago*. Both were friends of Sir Edward Parry. *W*

Parry Island (54°06'00" 130°39'00" W of Prescott I, off N end of Porcher I, SW of Prince Rupert). George E Parry pre-empted this island in 1909 and received a Crown grant in 1917. The island was surveyed and named in 1910 by BC land surveyor Hugh Youdall, who did much work in the early 1900s along the line of the GTP and also laid out the townsite of Hazelton.

Parry Patch (52°41'00" 128°32'00" In Tolmie Channel, off NE end of Swindle I and SE end of Princess Royal I). Named for CGS *Parry*, a 27-m, 99-tonne diesel vessel that saw duty with the Canadian Hydrographic Service from 1947 to 1967 on all parts of the BC coast. With its crew of 13 and survey staff of four, it conducted hydrographic, tide and current surveys and also assisted in the 1958 demolition of Ripple Rk. The *Parry* was originally built in 1941–42 as HMCS *Talapus*, a patrol vessel for BC's WWII Fishermen Reserve Service, then converted to hydrographic use after the war. It was renamed to honour Sir John Franklin Parry (*see* Mt Parry), who served two commissions as an Admiralty surveyor on the BC coast as capt of HMS *Egeria* and later became hydrographer of the RN, 1914–19. According to a reference in Carol Popp's *Gumboot Navy*, the *Parry* was later owned by Cloverleaf Shipping.

Parry Point (54°05'00" 130°09'00" S end of De Horsey I, entrance to Skeena R, SE of Prince Rupert). Rev William Warner Parry (d 1901) was a chaplain and instructor on HMS *Malacca*, under Capt Radulphus Oldfield, and served on the Pacific Station in 1866–68. He was later chaplain on HMS *Defense* (1869) and HMS *Iron Duke* (1878). The point was named by hydrographer Lt Daniel Pender about 1867.

Parsons Anchorage (52°31'00" 128°44'00" Head of Kitasu Bay, W side of Swindle I, NW of Bella Bella). Capt Robert Mann Parsons (1829–97) was a member of the Columbia detachment of Royal Engineers, which served in BC 1858–63. Like all RE officers, he was a graduate of the Royal Military Academy at Woolwich. Parsons was the only man in the contingent who did not volunteer to go to BC; instead, as an expert surveyor and highly skilled map-maker, he was assigned to the detachment from his previous posting in Ireland to command its survey unit. He and his party of 20 sappers were the first to arrive in BC, in Oct 1858, travelling via Panama and San Francisco, and spent their time in BC laying out settlements, drafting and printing maps, and inspecting road works. Parsons, who never married, returned to England in 1863 and worked at Chatham, then became superintendent of the ordnance survey office at Southampton in 1869. He retired from the army in 1879 with the rank of maj gen. Parsons Channel, Robert Point and Mann Point—all features on or adjacent to Barnston I in the Fraser R near Surrey—are believed to be named for him as well.

Parsons Point (48°21'00" 123°44'00" W entrance to Sooke Inlet, W of Victoria, S end of Vancouver I), **Parsons Spit** (W of Parsons Point). William Forster Parsons was 2nd master aboard the RN survey vessel *Herald*, under Capt Henry Kellett, who in 1846–47 made some of BC's earliest Admiralty charts along the S coast of Vancouver I. Kellett named these features in 1846. Parsons retired with the rank of staff cdr in 1872.

Partington Point (49°32'00" 124°13'00" SW side of Texada I on Sabine Channel, Str of Georgia). Named after Richard William Partington, who lost his life in Milbanke Sd in Jan 1925. He was born at Manchester and first came to BC aboard a CPR vessel, probably the *Princess Adelaide*, as a deck officer about 1910. After returning to England and commanding RN minesweepers during WWI, he moved permanently to Vancouver, where he married Marjorie Annie Milton (1895–1958) in 1923 and worked as a skipper with the W Vancouver ferries. In 1925, while in charge of the *Haysport No 2* and carrying 67 tonnes of blasting powder and caps to Alaska for mining work, he is believed to have struck Vancouver Rk and blown up. The name was adopted in 1964 after a request by members of the Partington family.

Pasley Island (49°22'00" 123°27'00" W of Collingwood Channel and Bowen I, Howe Sd, NW of Vancouver). Adm Sir Thomas Pasley (1734–1808) played a distinguished role in the English Channel battle known as the Glorious First of June. In 1860, Capt George Richards of the survey vessel *Plumper* named many features in Howe Sd after participants in this 1794 naval victory over the French. Pasley entered the RN in 1751, was promoted to post capt in 1771 and served in both the W and E Indies. After the Glorious First of June he was appointed cdr-in-chief at the Nore and at Plymouth. Pasley I was a traditional whaling base for First Nation groups and was also used by the crew of the Lipsett Whaling Co in the late 1860s. Several fishermen lived there with their families in the 1870s; official land pre-emptions on the island started in the late 1880s. The first non-Native birth in the Howe Sd area, that of Josephine Silvey in 1872, took place on Pasley. The island was purchased in 1909 by Henry Ogle Bell-Irving, who had made a fortune in BC's salmon-canning industry; he turned Pasley into a summer camp for the Bell-Irving clan. In 1950 Henry Pybus Bell-Irving, grandson of Henry Ogle and a former BC lt gov, formed a syndicate to buy the island from fellow Bell-Irving family members for $25,000. It is now owned corporately by a group of shareholder families. *W*

P

Pasley Passage (50°52'00" 126°39'00" N side of Stackhouse I, entrance to Kingcome Inlet, NE of Port McNeill), **Pasley Rock** (50°52'00" 126°40'00" In Pasley Passage). Russell Graves Sabine Pasley (1838–84) was flag lt to Rear Adm John Kingcome, cdr-in-chief on the Pacific Station, 1862–64, with HMS *Sutlej* as his flagship. Russell Pasley, a great-grandson of Adm Sir Thomas Pasley (*see* Pasley I), was promoted to capt in 1871 and commanded several warships, including HMS *Niobe* and *Simoom*. The passage was named by Lt Daniel Pender, RN hydrographer, in 1864. W

Passage Island with West Vancouver in the distance. *Peter Vassilopoulos*

Passage Island (49°20'36" 123°18'20" S end of Queen Charlotte Channel, E entrance to Howe Sd, just NW of Vancouver). The Skxwúmish (Squamish) First Nation name for this 13-ha island is Smismus-sulch, meaning "the waves go over it all the time," according to Howe Sound historian Doreen Armitage. The feature's current name was bestowed in 1792 by Capt George Vancouver for its position in the passage between Bowen I and the mainland. Vancouver noted that "Passage and Anvil islands in one" provided an ideal line for staying safely W of the mud flats at the mouth of the Fraser R. The island was considered as a site for a lighthouse in the 1870s, but Point Atkinson was chosen instead. Land developer and former N Vancouver reeve James Keith bought Passage in 1893, and it stayed in the Keith family until 1959, with a hermit named Jack Thompson living there in the 1930s and '40s. In 1965, realtor Phil Matty purchased the property for $65,000 and subdivided it into 61 waterfront lots, about half of which had been built on by the early 2000s. W

Pat Bay. *See* Patricia Bay.

Paterson Point (48°27'00" 123°27'00" W side of Esquimalt Hbr, SE end of Vancouver I). George Yates Paterson (d 1889) served on the Pacific Station in 1843–47 as 3rd lt aboard HMS *Fisgard*, under Capt John Duntze. He was promoted to cdr in 1860. When Lt Cdr James Wood, of HMS *Pandora*, surveyed Esquimalt Hbr in 1847, he named many features after the officers of the *Fisgard*, which was one of the first RN vessels to anchor there.

Patey Rock (48°42'00" 123°31'00" In Satellite Channel at mouth of Saanich Inlet, S of Saltspring I, NW of Victoria). RN officer George Edwin Patey (d 1862) served on the Pacific Station, 1854–57, as capt of HMS *Monarch*, the 84-gun flagship of Rear Adm Henry Bruce. He had been appointed a lt in 1840 and a capt in 1851; after his Pacific posting he had several commands in the Mediterranean and with the British Coast Guard. Patey was a well-known RN name; a later George Edwin Patey (1859–1935)— this one an adm and a knight—was cdr-in-chief of the Australian fleet during and after WWI. Patey Rk was named in 1858 by Capt George Richards of the RN survey vessel *Plumper*.

Patricia Bay (48°39'00" 123°27'00" E side of Saanich Inlet, N of Victoria). Named after Princess Patricia of Connaught (1886–1974), a daughter of Prince Arthur, Duke of Connaught, and a granddaughter of Queen Victoria. She came to Canada with her parents when the duke served as the country's 10th gov gen, 1911–16. Attractive and outgoing, the princess became very popular with Canadians, and in 1918 she was named col-in-chief of the Princess Patricia's Canadian Light Infantry, an appointment she held until her death. She relinquished her royal titles when she married Alexander Ramsay, an RN officer and a commoner, in 1919 and became plain old Lady Patricia, but still remained a prominent member of the royal family. Ramsay ended up an adm, lord of the Admiralty, knight and chief of naval air services. Patricia Bay (or Pat Bay as it is frequently referred to today) was long known as Union Bay but was renamed sometime after 1912, probably because of the princess's visit to Victoria that year, when her father laid the cornerstone of the Provincial (Connaught) Library. The short-lived Fraser Valley farming community of Patricia was also named for her in the 1910s. An aerodrome and seaplane station, established beside Patricia Bay in 1939, developed

Patricia Bay, home to the Canadian Hydrographic Service. *Peter Vassilopoulos*

after the war into Victoria International Airport. The bay is the site of the Institute of Ocean Sciences, operated by Fisheries and Oceans Canada, and home to the W coast HQ of the Canadian Hydrographic Service.

Patrician Cove (50°43'30" 127°25'00" NW side of Beaver Hbr, just E of Port Hardy, NE end of Vancouver I). Named about 1983 after the motor yacht *Patrician*, which had burned and sunk there the previous year. Jon Bowman and Ann Kenyon of Seattle, the owners of the 26-m, 177-tonne fibreglass vessel, had anchored in the cove on their way home from a two-month cruise in BC and Alaska. The engine room somehow caught fire in the middle of the night, and the boat had to be abandoned. No one was injured. The cove is known locally as Hook Ass Bay, supposedly after an incident in which a fish hook accidentally got caught on someone's backside.

Patrick Point (50°06'00" 123°48'00" SW end of Queens Reach, Jervis Inlet, NW of Vancouver). This feature honours Prince Arthur William Patrick Albert, Duke of Connaught and Strathearn (1850–1942), third son of Queen Victoria. He had a long career in the British Army and was appointed a field marshal in 1902, cdr-in-chief in Ireland, 1900–1904, inspector-gen of the forces, 1904–7, and Canada's 10th gov gen, 1911–16. He married Princess Luise Margarete of Prussia in 1879. Named by Capt George Richards of HMS *Plumper* about 1860 in association with nearby Mt Wellington and Mt Arthur, which commemorate Arthur Wellesley, the renowned Duke of Wellington, who was Prince Arthur's godfather. *W*

Patrol Island (48°42'00" 123°25'00" Off N end of Saanich Peninsula and SW side of Piers I, N of Victoria). Formerly known as Spit I but renamed in 1933. Adjacent Piers I (qv) had been expropriated by federal authorities in 1932 for use as a special prison camp for Doukhobor inmates. Prison guards apparently used this tiny island as a station for patrolling the camp.

Pattinson Group (51°52'00" 128°07'00" S of Kildidt Narrows, Kildidt Sd, off S side of Hunter I, S of Bella Bella). Several features in BC, including Pattinson Lk in the Kamloops area and Pattinson Peak near Williston Lk, commemorate BC land surveyor Hugh Pattinson (1892–1953), who worked for the BC government for many years and conducted a 1929 PGE resources survey in the Williston Lk area. It is not known, however, if regional hydrographer Henri Parizeau, who named this group of islands in 1944, intended to honour the same person.

Pattullo Point (54°24'50" 130°17'39" W side of Tuck Inlet at head of Prince Rupert Hbr). Regional hydrographer Henri Parizeau named this feature in 1927, when Thomas Dufferin "Duff" Pattullo (1873–1956) was still a BC cabinet minister. He would go on to become premier,

1933–41. Born in Ont, Pattullo worked at first as a banker and journalist, then moved to Dawson City in 1897 as secretary to the Yukon's first commissioner. He later was assistant gold commissioner. Pattullo got into politics in 1904 as a Dawson City alderman, then moved to Prince Rupert in 1908, where he was elected city councillor, mayor and, finally, from 1916 to 1945, MLA. He was immediately appointed minister of Lands. Pattullo was chosen leader of the provincial Liberal party in 1930. As premier he was a social reformer who eased BC through the Depression years with a package of measures aimed to assist the poor and unemployed. Mt Pattullo, NE of Stewart, is also named for him, as is the Pattullo Bridge across the Fraser R at New Westminster. The Pattullo Glaciers and Pattullo Range in Tweedsmuir Provincial Park were named in association with the visit to BC of Gov Gen John Buchan, Baron Tweedsmuir, in 1937. Pattullo, as premier, had issued the invitation to visit and accompanied the vice-regal tour. *E*

Paul Island (49°30'00" 124°13'00" NE of Lasqueti I, Sabine Channel, Str of Georgia). Paul Louis Lambert (1876–1945), from France, came to Lasqueti I after WWI and acquired Crown grants to nearby Jervis I (qv) in 1922 and 1924. He had hoped to build a sanatorium for sick children on his property, but ended up establishing the Jervis I Goat Ranch instead, where he raised and bred goats and produced goat milk and cheese. Later he bought land on Lasqueti around Lambert Lk, which is named for him. His wife, Velina Daza Lambert, arrived on Lasqueti about 1931. Paul was a miner, telephone lineman, Lasqueti's first real-estate agent and an island "booster," whose numerous, often impractical, schemes included the raising of foxes, nutria, muskrats and edible frogs, as well as the aforementioned goats. An attempt to have a small island off Lasqueti named for this pioneer initially failed, as the hydrographic service felt there were already enough features called Lambert in BC, so Paul was chosen as a compromise. There is also a Jelina I (qv) not far away, likely named (but misspelled) for his wife.

Pay Bay (52°59'00" 132°19'00" W side of Hibben I, off NW Moresby I, QCI). This body of water was named Rocky Bay when originally surveyed in 1852 by Capt Augustus Kuper of HMS *Thetis*. It was renamed much later by the hydrographic service to avoid duplication. The name Pay Bay refers to the fact that two of the small islands in the bight, Luxmoore and Rogers (qv), commemorate RN paymasters who were aboard *Thetis* at the time of the 1852 survey.

Payne Bay (48°52'00" 123°23'00" W side of Galiano I, Gulf Is). Flight Sgt Humphrey Owen Blake Payne, who enlisted in the RCAF at Vancouver but was from Galiano I, was killed in action Feb 14, 1943. He was a member of No 406 (Lynx) Squadron, the first Canadian night-fighter

P

unit, which was initially based in Northumberland and equipped with Blenheim and Beaufighter aircraft. Payne is buried at Brookwood Military Cemetery near London, UK.

Payne Channel (53°20'00" 129°28'00" Between Hinton I and SE side of Pitt I, N of Squally Channel). Dorothy Richardson Payne became a clerical assistant in the Victoria office of the hydrographic service in 1940. In 1944 it was proposed that another feature, a narrows SW of Kitimat, also be named for her, but this became Hoey Narrows after objections from hydrographic HQ in Ottawa. Staff there wanted to see "not more than one feature named after any one person." A senior civil servant noted that "too many names of your office staff ... have been used without reasonable discretion."

Payne Point (48°48'00" 123°13'00" W side of Saturna I, Gulf Is). This point is believed to be named after Gerald Fitzroy Payne (1870–1952), a wealthy young Englishman who followed his older brother Charles out to BC in 1886. Charles had bought property in the Gulf Is and at Oak Bay, and built a house on Saturna I with his friend Warburton Pike. The two men also had a nice little steam launch, the *Saturna*, built at a boatyard in Victoria. Charles returned to England but Gerald stayed on and over the years acquired more than 350 ha of land on Saturna; additional Payne brothers and sisters joined him there. In 1897–98 he and a group of Gulf Is compatriots made several journeys to the Stikine region and joined the Klondike gold rush. In 1899, Gerald married Elizabeth Clara Finnerty (1877–1958), a nurse from San Francisco. He built a small sawmill and farmed on Saturna until 1935, then sold up and moved to Sidney, where he died. *See also* Digby Point.

Pearce Point (54°03'00" 130°33'00" W entrance to Refuge Bay, NW side of Porcher I, SW of Prince Rupert). Joseph Whidbey, master of HMS *Discovery* under Capt George Vancouver, made a long journey with the ship's boats in 1793 to examine the region around the mouth of the Skeena R and southern Chatham Sd. Vancouver named this feature Point Pearce but provided no further explanation in his journal about the origin of the name. NZ historian and James Cook expert John Robson has speculated that he may have been referring to William Pearce, chief clerk at the Admiralty in the 1790s.

Pearl Rocks (51°22'00" 128°00'00" At NE end of the Sea Otter Group, S of Calvert I, Queen Charlotte Sd). These rocks were one of the first features on the BC coast to be named by an 18th-century fur trader. Capt James Hanna of the *Sea Otter*, who made the first trading voyage to the PNW in 1785, returned the following year and ventured N of Vancouver I into Queen Charlotte Sd. He bestowed a handful of place names on the region, several of which are still in use today. Two of his charts survive, as do fragments

of his journal. According to the journal of Archibald Menzies, Capt George Vancouver's naturalist, Hanna's original name for this feature was Peril Rks, a statement that has been corroborated by such distinguished historians as Henry R Wagner and W Kaye Lamb. In Vancouver's published narrative and chart, the name was mysteriously changed to Pearl, an obvious corruption.

Pearse Canal (54°56'00" 130°20'00" Forms the BC-Alaska boundary, on the NW side of Wales I and Pearse I), **Pearse Canal Island** (54°47'00" 130°36'00" At SW entrance to Pearse Canal), **Pearse Island** (54°52'00" 130°20'00" W side of Portland Inlet, N of Prince Rupert). Pearse I was named in 1868 by RN hydrographer Lt Daniel Pender after a US artillery capt in command at Ft Tongass, an early military and customs post on nearby Tongass I, 1868–70. Evidence provided by the National Archives and Records Service, Washington, DC, suggests that Pender misspelled the capt's surname and actually had in mind Capt Charles H Peirce. The US government originally claimed Pearse I, but it was awarded to Canada in 1903 under the final settlement of the Alaska Boundary Tribunal. *W*

Pearse Islands (50°35'00" 126°52'00" Off W entrance to Johnstone Str, between Malcolm I and NE Vancouver I), **Pearse Passage** (50°35'00" 126°53'00" Between Cormorant I and the Pearse Is), **Pearse Peninsula** (50°47'00" 126°33'00" SE end of Broughton I, Fife Sd, off NE end of Queen Charlotte Str), **Pearse Reefs** (50°36'00" 126°51'00" N of Pearse Is). Cdr William Alfred Rumbulow Pearse (d 1890), of HMS *Alert*, served on the Pacific Station, 1858–61, during which time he and his crew did survey work in the QCI. He entered the RN in 1832, was promoted to capt in 1862 and achieved the rank of rear adm, retired, in 1878. The Pearse Is were named about 1860 by Capt George Richards of HMS *Plumper*. Pearse Passage, formerly known as Race Pass, was renamed in 1949 by the hydrographic service to avoid duplication with similar names.

Pearse Point (52°45'00" 129°18'00" NW side of Aristazabal I). Named for Mary Charlotte Roper (1869–1943), who was born at Lac la Hache and died at Oak Bay. She married Ernest Theodore W Pearse (1860–1915) in the Kamloops district in 1885. Ernest, from England, came to Victoria as a young man to join his uncle, Benjamin W Pearse, Vancouver I's surveyor gen and a member of the colony's executive and legislative councils. After Confederation, Benjamin became BC's chief commissioner of Lands and Works and surveyor gen, then resigned to become the senior BC official for the federal Dept of Public Works. Ernest served as a police constable and, later, government agent, at Kamloops. Mary and Ernest's Rhodes scholar son, 2nd Lt Walter Josiah Pearse of the Royal Horse Artillery, was killed at Vimy Ridge on Apr 9, 1917, aged 26, and is buried at Ecoivres Military Cemetery, Mont-St

P

Eloi, France. Mary is believed to have participated in the grand old-timers' reunion held at Victoria in May 1924 (*see* Adams Bay).

Pearson Island (49°38'00" 124°05'00" E side of Malaspina Str, W of Pender Hbr, NW of Vancouver). This feature, which appears on Admiralty charts as early as 1863, is possibly named for astronomer William Pearson (1767–1847), co-founder in 1820 of Britain's Royal Astronomical Society. Born at Whitbeck, Cumberland, "he early manifested a love for mechanism, and contrived and executed various machines for exhibiting and explaining astronomical phenomena," according to Charles Weld in *A History of the Royal Society*. In 1817, Pearson was appointed rector of S Kilworth, where he built an observatory and employed a full-time assistant, whom he trained in astronomical matters. He published his two-volume *Introduction to Practical Astronomy* in 1824 and 1829.

Pearson Point (55°27'00" 129°30'00" NW side of Alice Arm, NE of Observatory Inlet, SE of Stewart). Ole Pearson, from Sweden, and his three partners (Ernest Carlson, Karl Eik and Ole Evindsen) staked the original Dolly Varden claims near the head of Alice Arm in 1910. The site of the discovery—and the name that he was supposed to give to it—apparently came to Pearson in a dream. In 1915 the four prospectors sold out to US investors, who built a narrow-gauge railway and the famous Dolly Varden Mine, which only operated 1919–21 and was ultimately unsuccessful, despite being rich in silver. Pearson also staked two claims in the Red Point Group in the same region about 1916. Each of the partners received $10,000 in the Dolly Varden deal; Pearson took his share, went back to his native country and bought a farm.

Peatt Islets (52°59'00" 129°36'00" In Gillen Hbr, S end of Dewdney I, part of the Estevan Group, N of Caamaño Sd). Edith Green (1858–1935) and Arthur Henry Peatt (1852–1916) were early Vancouver I pioneers, both arriving in the colony as children about 1860. They married at Victoria in 1883. Arthur's father, also named Arthur, took up land at Colwood in 1862 and farmed. After his death in 1891, Arthur Jr and his brother Alfred inherited the estate. Arthur Jr was the district road superintendent for 22 years and also a partner in the McQuade ship chandlery business. The islets were named in 1926 for Edith, who was a driving force behind the Colwood Women's Institute and a prominent fundraiser for a number of civic construction projects. She is believed to have taken part in the great old-timers' reunion held in Victoria in May 1924 (*see* Adams Bay). Peatt Ck on nearby Princess Royal I was named for Arthur Peatt Jr in 1928.

Peck Island (50°14'00" 125°09'00" Part of the Settlers Group, SE end of Okisollo Channel, S of Maurelle I, NE of

Campbell R), **Peck Reef** (48°42'00" 123°24'00" Off E side of Piers I and N end of Saanich Peninsula, NW of Victoria). Lt Col Cyrus Wesley Peck, VC, DSO (1871–1956), was born in NB and came to New Westminster in 1887 with his family. He took military training and volunteered for the Boer War but was not accepted. After some time in the Klondike, he lived in Prince Rupert for a number of years, where he became involved in the salmon-canning business (he was a co-owner of the Cassiar cannery, built on the Skeena R in 1903) and married Kate Elizabeth Chapman in 1914. Peck went overseas that year with the Canadian Scottish Regiment. He won his VC in Sept 1918 at Cagnicourt, France, when, under intense enemy machine-gun fire, he personally scouted the terrain to be covered, directed tanks and led his infantry battalion to its objective. Pierre Berton called him "one of the most belligerent battalion cdrs in the Corps—a bulky, black-browed British Columbian with an enormous walrus moustache who believed senior officers should not hang back in battle." In 1917, despite being away from Canada, he was elected a Unionist MP for Skeena but was defeated in 1921. Peck was a Conservative MLA representing the Gulf Islands, 1924–33, and was then appointed to the Canadian Pension Commission, holding that post until 1941. He died at Sidney. Peck Lk in the Skeena area, and Cyrus Rks and Wesley I off Quadra I, are also named for him, as was the *Cy Peck*, a ferry with a long history in the Gulf Is (formerly the CPR's *Island Princess* and, before that, the *Daily* of Puget Sd).

Peck Shoal (53°28'00" 129°56'00" Off S side of Anger I, Principe Channel, between Banks I and Pitt I). Named in 1944 after Lt Donald Peck, a member of BC's Fishermen Reserve Service in WWII. Peck was skipper of HMCS *Moolock* (*FY 16*), one of six patrol boats built in BC for the FRS, and towed the Canadian Hydrographic Service houseboat *Pender* in this area on several occasions in 1943. He also had command of several other FRS vessels, including HMCS *Ekholi*, *Spray*, *BC Lady* and *Merry Chase*. On *Merry Chase*, he was one of the first to respond to the 1941 shelling of Estevan Point lighthouse, supposedly by a Japanese submarine—the only instance of an enemy attack on the BC coast during WWII. Later that year, Peck was appointed a special recruiting officer at HMCS *Burrard* in Vancouver.

Peculiar Point (49°51'00" 127°06'00" N entrance to Esperanza Inlet, NW of Catala I, W side of Vancouver I). The original name for this feature, suggested by Juri (George) Alexander Jeletzky, a renowned research scientist working in the area for the Geological Survey of Canada, was Funny Point. This name was not considered acceptable by the hydrographic service, so it was changed in 1950 to Peculiar Point. The rocks at this location apparently have an unusual form and were created by especially complicated tectonic forces. Jeletzky's work with fossil molluscs helped

P

accurately date events that took place during the Upper Jurassic and Lower Cretaceous periods.

Pedder Bay (48°20'00" 123°33'00" S side of William Head, S tip of Vancouver I). This body of water was named in 1846 by Capt Henry Kellett of HMS *Herald*, probably after a friend, William Pedder, who was stationed in Hong Kong when Kellett was there in 1840–42 with HMS *Starling*. Pedder, a former RN officer, served as 1st lt aboard the E India Co's *Nemesis* and was appointed Hong Kong's first harbourmaster and marine magistrate in the early 1840s. Pedder Wharf was the colony's main landing place until the 1890s, and Pedder St continues to be a major thoroughfare in the core of Hong Kong's Central District. In BC, Pedder Ck is named for the bay. When Spanish naval officer Manuel Quimper made the first European exploration of Juan de Fuca Str in 1790 with the *Princesa Real*, he called this feature Rada de Eliza, after his superior officer Francisco Eliza. *W*

Peel Inlet (52°59'00" 132°06'00" SE extension of Kuper Inlet, NW Moresby I, QCI), **Peel Island** (50°44'00" 127°24'00" NW of Deer I, Beaver Hbr, just E of Port Hardy, NE end of Vancouver I), **Peel Point** (52°59'40" 132°09'10" S entrance to Peel Inlet). Francis Peel (d 1873) was 3rd lt aboard HMS *Thetis*, under Capt Augustus Kuper, and served on the Pacific Station, 1850–53. In 1857 he was cdr of HMS *Buzzard* off the E coast of S America. Peel was promoted to capt, retired, in 1872. Peel Point was named by officers of *Thetis* during an 1852 survey of the area; Peel Inlet, known to the Haida people as Naawe, may have been named at the same time. Peel I first appears on a chart of Beaver Hbr made in 1851 by Lt George Mansell of HMS *Daphne*. The previous year it had been marked as Wellesley I on a survey sketch made by William Dillon, master of HMS *Daedalus*, after George Wellesley, capt of that vessel.

Peile Point (48°51'00" 123°24'00" N tip of Prevost I, E of Saltspring I, Gulf Is). Named after Mountford Stephen Lovick Peile (1824–85), who served as 1st lt of HMS *Satellite*, under Capt James Prevost, on the Pacific Station, 1857–60. He was later appointed to HMS *Royal Adelaide*, flagship of the port adm at Devonport. As cdr of HMS *Espoir*, off the W coast of Africa, 1864–67, he was senior officer of the RN's Bight of Benin division. Peile was promoted to capt in 1867 and commanded HMS *Simoom* until retirement in 1875. Peile Point was named by Capt George Richards of HMS *Plumper* in 1859.

Pelham Islands (53°49'00" 130°23'00" In Kitkatla Channel, W of Gilbert I, S of Porcher I and Prince Rupert). Samuel Pelham, a Tsimshian lay preacher and evangelist, was the first Anglican missionary to the Kitkatla First Nation, about 1880. He had been a hereditary chief before William Duncan, the famed Anglican missionary at Metlakatla,

converted him in the early 1860s. He also worked as a preacher at Metlakatla, serving on the village council there and acting as 1st mate and capt of Duncan's mission schooner, the *Carolina*. However, when Duncan broke with Bishop William Ridley and moved to Alaska with most of his followers in 1887, Pelham stayed behind and supported Ridley. Named by the hydrographic service in 1952.

Pelican Cove (52°21'00" 131°15'30" SE side of Burnaby I, off SE Moresby I, QCI), **Pelican Point** (52°21'00" 131°15'00" S entrance to Pelican Cove). Named by the hydrographic service in 1962 after Dr Charles Newcombe's 5.5-m open sloop *Pelican*, which the ethnologist used to explore the QCI in 1897. Pelican Point is one of many fossil-rich sites in the region. Pelican Cove was where pioneer mining engineer Francis Poole set up his main camp, 1862–64. *See also* Newcombe Bay *and* Poole Inlet. *D*

Pellow Islets (48°44'00" 123°21'00" Off E side of Portland I, N of Sidney and Saanich Peninsula). According to Tom Koppel, author of *Kanaka: The Untold Story of Hawaiian Pioneers in BC and the PNW*, this name refers to John Palua (c 1818–1907, also known as Johnny Pallow, Pellow, Palau or Polua). He was a Kanaka, or Hawaiian Islander, who came to BC about 1859 to work for the HBC and then lived on San Juan I in the 1860s. He married Sophie, the daughter of his friend and colleague William Naukana (*see* Kanaka Bluff). The two men pre-empted most of Portland I in 1875, settling there with their families and developing a large farm. They eventually received Crown grants to the entire island (in 1887 and 1890).

Pelly Island (48°26'00" 123°23'00" Victoria Hbr, SE end of Vancouver I), **Pelly Point** (49°06'00" 123°11'00" NW tip of Reifel I, S entrance to the S Arm of the Fraser R, opposite Steveston). Sir John Henry Pelly (1777–1852), son of an E India Co master mariner, was appointed an HBC director in 1806 and became gov in 1822, overseeing the company's affairs after its merger with the NWC and until 1852. Pelly authorized a number of expeditions—by Peter Warren Dease, Thomas Simpson and John Rae—to explore Arctic Canada, and many places in the N are named for him. He also served as a director and, eventually, as gov (1841–42) of the Bank of England. In 1838, Pelly and George Simpson, gov of Rupert's Land, travelled to Russia and negotiated a deal with the Russian American Fur Co; in exchange for fresh produce from its PNW farms and an annual rent of 2,000 sea otter furs, the HBC would be granted trading rights in the Alaska panhandle. Pelly Point was named by Capt Aemilius Simpson of the HBC schooner *Cadboro* in 1827. Pelly I, site of an early light, was named about 1844 by HBC officials at Ft Victoria and adopted by Capt Henry Kellett when he surveyed Victoria Hbr in 1846. Mt Pelly in the Similkameen district is supposedly named after Sir Henry's grandson, Richard Stuart Pelly (1846–1928), a land surveyor with the provincial government. *W*

Pelorus Point (48°43'00" 123°17'00" E end of Moresby I, SE of Saltspring I, Gulf Is). A pelorus is a surveying instrument similar to a compass, used to take bearings on distant objects. The word is said to derive from the name of Hannibal's pilot, who was killed when Hannibal thought—erroneously, as it turned out—that his guide was misleading him; in remorse, the Carthaginian cdr is supposed to have named Cape Peloro, at the NE tip of Sicily, after the murdered man. The entire story is apocryphal. Pelorus Peak, in the Homathko Snowfield, was named because it was a compass bearing point for the 1957 Homathko Expedition party. The exact circumstances of the 1934 naming of Pelorus Point are, unfortunately, not known.

Pemberton Bay (52°57'00" 129°35'00" S end of Dewdney I, Estevan Group, NW of Aristazabal I), **Pemberton Point** (50°47'00" 126°38'00" S side of Broughton I, Fife Sd, off NE end of Queen Charlotte Str, NE of Port McNeill). Joseph Despard Pemberton (1821–93), from Ireland, was surveyor gen of the colony of Vancouver I, 1859–64, and a member of its first legislative assembly, 1856–59. He was educated at Dublin's Trinity College and worked as a railroad engineer before joining the HBC and arriving at Victoria in 1851. Pemberton laid out a townsite at Victoria, divided the surrounding areas into lots, established prices, surveyed the E coast of Vancouver I, led two expeditions to the W coast, built roads and bridges, and designed the colony's first school and church. He was, as Gov James Douglas wrote, "a fortunate selection," and his land policies had a strong influence on the region's evolving character. When surveys were needed on the BC mainland during the Fraser R gold rush, Pemberton laid out townsites at Ft Yale, Ft Hope, Port Douglas and Derby, near Ft Langley. He oversaw settlement in the Gulf Is and N to the Comox area, and was the architect of the 1860 pre-emption law, which allowed homesteaders to occupy unsurveyed land. He played an important political role in early BC, being appointed to Vancouver I's executive and legislative councils in 1864 and twice elected to the legislative council established when BC and Vancouver I became a single colony in 1866. Pemberton bought a large estate in SE Victoria and Oak Bay, which he named Gonzales, and he married Theresa Jane Grautoff at London, England, in 1864. The noted artist Sophia Theresa Pemberton was one of their six children. He retired in 1868 and devoted himself to family and business interests, founding an engineering, surveying and real-estate firm, Pemberton & Son, that still existed in the early 2000s in the form of Pemberton Holmes Ltd, a Victoria real-estate company. Vancouver's Pemberton Securities Inc, acquired by RBC Dominion Securities Inc in 1989, was another offshoot of Pemberton & Son. The farming community of Pemberton, N of Vancouver—once a stop on the trail to the goldfields—is also named after this pioneer figure, as are many nearby features, including Pemberton Ck, Pemberton Pass, Pemberton Meadows, Pemberton Portage and Pemberton Valley. *E W*

Pender Canal (48°46'00" 123°15'00" Between N Pender I and S Pender I, Gulf Is), **Pender Harbour** (49°38'00" 124°04'00" SE side of Malaspina Str, between Sechelt and Powell R, NW of Vancouver), **Pender Point** (50°29'00" 127°35'00" W entrance to Neroutsos Inlet, SE arm of

Aerial view of Pender Harbour, with Madeira Park at lower right. *Peter Vassilopoulos*

P

Quatsino Sd, NW end of Vancouver I). As one of the main hydrographic surveyors to work on BC's coast, Lt Daniel Pender (d 1891) was responsible for naming hundreds of geographic features. He served in HMS *Porcupine*, an RN survey vessel, off the W coast of Scotland in the mid-1850s, then arrived in the PNW in 1857 as 2nd master of HMS *Plumper*, under Capt George Richards. In 1861, by now a master (or navigating lt), he moved to HMS *Hecate*, which replaced the *Plumper* as the coast's main survey ship. When Richards and the *Hecate* were recalled in 1862, the RN hired the historic HBC paddle steamer *Beaver* and put Pender in command; for the next seven years he carried on the hydrographic work with, as historian John Walbran pointed out, "the greatest zeal." He was promoted to staff cdr in 1869, the same year he married Amy Maria Gribbell, the sister of Victoria clergyman Frank Gribbell, at Esquimalt. The Penders returned to England in 1871, and Daniel was appointed to the Admiralty hydrographic office, becoming the RN's assistant hydrographer in 1879. He reached the rank of capt, retired, in 1884. Daniel Point, Mt Daniel and Pender Hill, all in the Pender Hbr vicinity, are also named for him, as are Pender Lk on N Pender I, Mt Pender on Campania I and, presumably, **Pender Rock** (54°31'00" 130°27'00" S end of Cunningham Passage, off NW Tsimpsean Peninsula, N of Prince Rupert). Pender Canal, an artificial feature, was dug in 1903 for the convenience of politician and steamship owner Thomas Paterson; two major archeological middens were revealed in the process. The area's Hul'qumi'num (Coast Salish) name is Tl'e'ulthw, meaning "permanent houses." Pender Hbr was named by Capt George Richards in 1860; it was once the site of Kálpilín, a large Sechelt First Nation winter village. Today the harbour is home to several small, scenic, retirement and recreational communities. *E W*

Pender Island, Pender Islands. These are not official geographic names. *See* N Pender I *and* S Pender I for brief community histories; *see* Pender Canal for a short biography of Daniel Pender, for whom Pender I was named by Capt George Richards in 1859. The main post office, located on N Pender I, has for many years been called Pender I (singular)—and that name is still in widespread use. As a geographic term, however, it is obsolete, as it refers to a time prior to 1903 when today's N and S Pender islands were one feature, connected by a narrow isthmus known as "the Portage." According to PNW cartography expert Henry Wagner, the original Spanish name for Pender I was Isla de Zayas (or Sayas), given in 1791 by Juan Pantoja y Arriaga, a naval officer on the *San Carlos* and one of the first Europeans to see the Gulf Is. He probably named it after Juan Martínez y Zayas, also a Spanish officer who sailed on the BC coast (*see* Zayas I). Francisco Eliza, cdr of the *San Carlos*, is believed to have changed the name to Isla San Eusebio.

Pendrell Sound (50°15'00" 124°43'00" Nearly bisects E Redonda I, N of Desolation Sd, NE of Campbell R). It has been speculated that railroad promoter Alfred Penderell Waddington (*see* Waddington Bay) is the source of this name, but the suggestion is completely unproven. Water temperatures in the sound are the warmest on the BC coast in summer, the result of a lack of current, tidal exchange and wind, and can reach 26°C. This mildness allows oysters to breed and produce spat or seed on a regular basis, a rare phenomenon in BC waters. In 1950 the sound was made a reserve to protect Pacific oyster breeding stocks, and commercial growers still collect spat there despite recent improvements in hatchery-produced seed.

Penelakut Spit (48°59'00" 123°38'00" NE side of Kuper I, NW of Saltspring I, Gulf Is). The Penelakut First Nation, part of the Coast Salish confederacy known today as the Hul'qumi'num, were famous for their skills as sea-lion hunters. They traditionally occupied village sites on Kuper I and Galiano I and at the mouth of the Chemainus R, with their main winter settlement—the largest First Nation community in the Gulf Is—at Penelakut Spit. The village's traditional Hul'qumi'num name was Penálaxeth', meaning "log buried on the beach"—a reference perhaps to sand partly covering houses built close to the ocean. Indian land commissioner Gilbert Sproat visited Penelakut in 1877 and described its appearance as "one long house, 3 or 400 yards in length, but in reality ... divided into 15 large compartments." The sand point was formerly named White Spit by Capt George Richards in 1859 but was renamed in 1905 by Cdr John Parry of HMS *Egeria*. W

Penelope Point (51°48'00" 127°23'00" E side of Moses Inlet, N of Nelson Narrows, Rivers Inlet, SE of Bella Bella). British aristocrat Penelope Atkins (d 1795) married George Pitt, the 1st Baron Rivers (1722–1803), after whom Capt George Vancouver named Rivers Inlet (qv). She was the daughter of Sir Henry Atkins, 4th baronet of Clapham in Surrey. The point was named by the hydrographic service in 1947, in association with Rivers Inlet.

Penn Harbour (52°58'00" 128°57'00" E side of Surf Inlet, W side of Princess Royal I). Named in 1926 after Fred H Penn, gen manager of the large gold mine located on Princess Royal I and owned by Belmont Surf Inlet Mines Ltd. Penn was originally the mill superintendent from 1917, when the mine opened, until 1921, when he was promoted to mine superintendent. The Surf Inlet Mine was a complex operation with several extraction sites. After the ore was crushed and concentrated, it travelled via electric tramway and then by barge along a series of lakes to a loading facility and townsite at the head of the inlet. The lakes were modified with a large dam to create an efficient transport route. The mine was closed in 1926 but opened again in 1934 and functioned until 1942. Penn Hbr was formerly known as Eagle Hbr and Hole-in-the-Wall.

Penn Islands (50°11'00" 125°01'00" In Sutil Channel, E of Read I, NE of Campbell R). In 1864, Capt George Richards, who had played an important role surveying the BC coast since 1857, was named the RN's chief hydrographer. In honour of this occasion, Lt Daniel Pender, who had assisted Richards and since taken over the BC survey, named a number of features in the vicinity after officers working in the Admiralty's hydrographic office in London. Staff Cdr James Penn (d 1882) served as a naval hydrographic assistant for many years and retired in 1870.

Penrose Bay (50°01'00" 124°44'00" E side of Malaspina Peninsula, S of Coode Peninsula, Okeover Inlet, E of Campbell R). After Capt Trevenen Penrose Coode of the RN, who served on the Pacific Station, 1864–66, as cdr of HMS *Sutlej*. *See* Coode I *and below*.

Penrose Island (51°30'00" 127°43'00" N entrance to Rivers Inlet, SE side of Fitz Hugh Sd). BC coastal historian Capt John Walbran mentions that this feature was named in 1865 by Lt Daniel Pender, of the hired survey vessel *Beaver*, "after a friend of his named Penrose who was visiting the coast at that date." RN officer Trevenen Penrose Coode (*see* Coode I *and above*) was serving on the BC coast in 1865, but it is not known if he was the Penrose in question. A large portion of Penrose I, together with some smaller islands, was named a 2,013-ha provincial marine park in 1982.

Pepin Point (54°24'00" 130°15'00" E side of Tuck Narrows, Prince Rupert Hbr). George Pepin was a draftsman for the GTP and a member of one of the early survey crews that mapped Prince Rupert Hbr and the surrounding areas in the early 1900s before the new railroad terminus was constructed.

Percival Cove (48°48'45" 123°19'04" In Grimmer Bay, W side of N Pender I, Gulf Is). Spencer Percival (1864–1945) and his wife, Annie Mary Lowe (1860–1934), immigrated to Canada from England about 1895 and lived at first in Manitoba. They moved to BC around 1903 and settled on N Pender I, buying the home and acreage of pioneer Washington Grimmer. The Percivals planted a large orchard and called their property Sunny Side Ranch. In 1910, Spencer built the first general store at Port Washington; he served as postmaster, 1912–13 and 1914–21. He also donated the land for St Peter's Anglican church at Port Washington in 1914. Annie was a talented musician and artist who organized island concerts and other entertainments. The Percivals later subdivided their land, and Spencer became a well-known breeder of white Wyandotte chickens. The name for the cove was submitted by the Gulf Is Branch of the BC Historical Assoc in the late 1960s.

Percy Anchorage (49°08'15" 123°47'10" Between Gabriola I and Mudge I, E of Nanaimo, off SE Vancouver

I). Algernon Percy was the 4th Duke of Northumberland and also served as 1st Lord of the Admiralty. *See* Northumberland Channel for more information. Capt George Richards of HMS *Plumper* named this feature in association with the channel in 1860. Percy is a Norman name, taken from the village of Percy in the NW French dept of Manche. Norman chieftain William de Percy, who accompanied William the Conqueror to England in 1066, was the 1st Baron Percy. *W*

Percy Point (53°02'00" 132°21'00" E entrance to Security Inlet, NW Moresby I, QCI). Rev William Cecil Percy Baylee was a popular RN chaplain and naval instructor aboard HMS *Thetis* during Capt Augustus Kuper's 1852 survey of this area. Nearby Baylee Bay, Baylee Bluff and Instructor I are also named for him.

Perez Rocks (49°25'00" 126°36'00" NW of Estevan Point, SE of Nootka Sd, W side of Vancouver I), **Perez Shoal** (52°33'00" 131°34'00" NE of Hoskins Point, Juan Perez Sd, E of Moresby I, QCI). After 18th-century Spanish naval officer and explorer Juan Pérez. *See* Juan Perez Sd.

Pering Islets (50°38'00" 126°38'00" Between Crease I and Midsummer I, E end of Queen Charlotte Str, NE of Port McNeill), **Pering Point** (52°38'00" 128°30'00" SE tip of Sarah I, Finlayson Channel, NW of Bella Bella). After Sir Henry Pering Pellew Crease, attorney gen of the colonies of Vancouver I and BC. *See* Crease I. The Pering Its were formerly known as the Bush Is but were renamed by the hydrographic service in 1954, in association with Crease I, in order to avoid duplication.

Perley Island (50°36'09" 126°19'05" Entrance to Lagoon Cove, off N side of E Cracroft I, SW side of Knight Inlet, E of Port McNeill). This feature was named about 1982 to commemorate Perley Sherdahl, a resident of the Minstrel I area since 1929. He was born in Alberta and lived in California before coming to the central coast. Sherdahl was a logger who, with his wife, Jean, raised a family on a floathouse that he moored for many years in Lagoon Cove. The Sherdahls bought the Minstrel I Hotel about 1960. According to sailor and guidebook author John Chappell, the purchase occurred after Perley was refused a drink at the notoriously rowdy hotel one night when things were really roaring. He went straight to Vancouver, bought the establishment, came back and fired the manager. Sherdahl was lost at sea, somewhere near Viscount I in Knight Inlet, on Aug 6, 1977, after heading off in an open boat to inspect some logging equipment. The name was submitted by David Sedgley, proprietor of Cracroft Marine Service, Lagoon Cove, in 1981.

Perpendicular Bluff (49°46'00" 126°27'15" NE side of Tlupana Inlet, Nootka Sd, W side of Vancouver I). In 1934, regional hydrographer Henri Parizeau wished to

P

rename this feature Martinez Bluff, after Spanish naval officer Estéban Martínez, who commanded the Spanish outpost in Nootka Sd in 1789. He seized several British vessels and sent them to Mexico, along with their imprisoned crews, nearly precipitating war between Spain and England. Parizeau felt that this new name, besides being more distinctive, would also commemorate the "bluff" made by Martínez in impounding the ships. The Geographic Board of Canada denied his request, however, deciding "that Perpendicular Bluff is a good descriptive name which makes the feature readily identifiable in the area."

Perrin Anchorage (52°17′00″ 128°23′00″ Between Ivory I and Watch I, off SW end of Don Peninsula, Seaforth Channel, NW of Bella Bella). Anglican clergyman William Willcox Perrin (1848–1934) was the second bishop of BC, succeeding George Hills, who resigned in 1892. Perrin grew up at Bristol, was ordained in 1871 and had been vicar of St Luke's, Southampton, for 12 years before coming to BC. His sister Edith Perrin (d 1909) accompanied him to Victoria and became well known as a reformer and feminist, helping improve laws to protect women and children. When her brother decided to marry in 1904, at the age of 56, Edith returned to England. William followed in 1911 after he was appointed bishop of Willesden, London, a position he held until 1929. The anchorage was named in 1898 by John Walbran, cdr of the lighthouse tender *Quadra*. Perrin, he wrote to his superior in Ottawa, "was with me in the surveying boat and was most useful in taking down for me all my angles with the accompanying soundings and positions." W

Peter Bay (52°05′00″ 128°16′00″ N side of Piddington I, off SW side of Campbell I, SW of Bella Bella). After Midshipman Peter Grosvenor Piddington, a native of Victoria, who died when the British battleship *Royal Oak* was sunk at Scapa Flow in 1939. *See* Piddington I.

Peter Cove (48°44′00″ 123°14′00″ S end of N Pender I, Gulf Is). Named in 1859 by Capt George Richards, of the RN survey vessel *Plumper*, after Assistant Surgeon Peter William Wallace, who was in charge of the Esquimalt naval hospital, 1857–65. *See* Wallace Point. During the Prohibition era, the cove became a favoured spot for smugglers to transfer liquor to small, fast US boats for the run across the border. Several incidents of hijacking apparently occurred at this site.

Peter Point (53°53′00″ 130°18′00″ SE side of Porcher I, Ogden Channel, S of Prince Rupert). Named in association with Ogden Channel (qv) after fur trader and senior HBC official Peter Skene Ogden.

Peters Narrows (53°22′00″ 129°27′00″ In Union Passage, between NW end of Farrant I and SE end of Pitt I). Capt

Frederick Thornton Peters, VC, DSO, DSC (1889–1943), from Nelson, was one of Canada's most highly decorated military men—and has been referred to as "the bravest Canadian of them all." The son of Frederick Peters, a former premier and attorney gen of PEI who later moved to BC, he was born at Charlottetown, educated at Victoria and Nelson, and attended naval college in England. Peters won his DSO and DSC in WWI, then served in the merchant marine in the 1920s and '30s. He was awarded the VC in WWII for a "suicide charge" he made in 1942 as cdr of HMS *Walney*, a former Coast Guard cutter, in a courageous effort to cut the defensive boom across the harbour at Oran during Allied landings on the N African coast. In the face of point-blank fire from enemy shore batteries and warships, the *Walney* led a landing force through the boom and reached the jetty, disabled and ablaze, before sinking. Peters was the only survivor of 17 men on the vessel's bridge. He was taken prisoner, but when Oran was later captured he was released and carried through the streets in a victory parade. Peters also received a bar to his DSC in WWII, plus the US DSC. Tragically, he died on Nov 11, 1943, in an accidental aircraft crash en route to the VC presentation ceremonies in London. He is commemorated on the Naval Memorial at Portsmouth, England. Mt Peters, NW of Nelson, is also named for him. It had originally been suggested that this geographic feature be named Elizabeth Narrows, after Hazel Elizabeth Hawkins, a student draftsperson at the Victoria hydrographic office in the early 1940s, but Ottawa refused to sanction the proposal. Hawkins Narrows at the N end of Union Passage had already been named for this young woman.

Peterson Islet (50°23′00″ 125°54′00″ S side of Race Passage, SW of Helmcken I, Johnstone Str, just E of Kelsey Bay). Presumably named for Theodore Peterson (c 1859–1936), a native of Denmark, who came to BC as the cook on a sailing vessel, took up land at nearby Hkusam Bay in 1895 and married a Lekwiltok First Nation woman. He and a partner, Edward Wilson, built the Ruby House—a combined store, post office, hotel and saloon—and the bay became a steamship stop for that part of the coast. The post office, called Port Kusam, was open from 1899 to 1911. In 1925, Frederick Kohse and his wife purchased Ruby House and turned it into their family home. Peterson moved to Vancouver and bought a confectionary business. Peterson It was formerly known as Hkusam It.

Petrel Channel (53°41′00″ 130°07′00″ Between NW Pitt I and McCauley I), **Petrel Islets** (53°43′00″ 130°08′00″ In Petrel Channel, W of Newcombe Hbr), **Petrel Point** (53°34′00″ 130°00′00″ SE entrance to Petrel Channel), **Petrel Rock** (54°14′00″ 130°25′00″ N of Kinahan Is, S of Digby I, just SW of Prince Rupert), **Petrel Shoal** (51°17′00″ 127°37′00″ Takush Hbr, Smith Sd, N of Port Hardy). While it is likely that all these features derive their names from a ship rather than a bird, there is some confusion over which ship that might be. According to records at BC's Geographical Names Office, Petrel Rk was named in 1907 by regional hydrographer Lt Cdr Philip Musgrave "after a Canadian fisheries patrol vessel." This would suggest CGS *Petrel*, built at Owen Sd, Ont, in 1892 and used on the Great Lks until 1905, then on the Atlantic coast until 1923, when it was sold. The 174-tonne, 36-m vessel was equipped with three machine guns and served in WWI but was never in BC waters. Another, smaller government vessel named *Petrel* was built in BC in 1906, at the Victoria Machinery Depot, for the Dept of Public Works. This 122-tonne, 27-m tug was later sold and had a lengthy career as a towboat on the Pacific coast. Owned after WWII by the Canadian Western Lumber Co and then by Coastal Towing Ltd, it met a tragic fate, sinking in a storm off Cape Mudge en route to Quadra I in Dec 1952. All seven crew members, including Capt Donald Horie, were lost. Then there was HMS *Peterel*, an 11-gun RN screw sloop that served on the Pacific Station, 1872–76, under Cdr Cecil Stanley and Cdr William Cookson. This ship, often spelled *Petrel*, was involved in the 1873 search for survivors of the *George S Wright*, wrecked near Cape Caution en route from Alaska to Nanaimo. It was later a lightship off the coast of Ireland and a coal depot. The name Petrel Channel was adopted in 1933; Petrel Its and Petrel Point were named by the hydrographic service in 1950, in association with the channel. A petrel, of course, is a fast-flying pelagic seabird about the size of a gull, usually only seen far from shore.

Philip Inlet (51°34'00" 127°46'00" Between Fish Egg Inlet and Addenbroke Point, off SE Fitz Hugh Sd, opposite Calvert I), **Philip Narrows** (52°42'00" 129°00'00" Kent Inlet, off Laredo Channel, SW side of Princess Royal I). John Maison Philip was a member of the W coast hydrographic staff in the 1940s and served mainly aboard CGS *William J Stewart*. He was involved in a survey of Fitz Hugh Sd in 1942 and also participated in hydrographic work in Prince Rupert, Vancouver and Esquimalt harbours; Seymour Narrows; the Str of Georgia; and the W coast of Vancouver I. Philip was employed by the BC Forest Service as well. Loap Point, near Philip Narrows, was formerly known as Philip Point but was renamed in 1944.

Philip Island (54°09'00" 130°49'00" Off W side of Stephens I, SW of Prince Rupert), **Philip Point** (50°52'00" 126°39'00" NE entrance to Sutlej Channel, N of Broughton I, NE of Port McNeill). After Sir Philip Stephens, long-time secretary to the Admiralty in the late 18th century. *See* Mt Stephens for more information. Philip Cone on Stephens I is also named for him. Philip I has had a number of names over the years. First it was known as China I. That was changed to Parry I in 1947, after RN officer John Parry of the survey vessel *Egeria*, and then to Philip I in 1951.

Philips Cove (54°19'00" 130°23'00" W of Russell Arm, N side of Prince Rupert Hbr), **Philips Point** (54°16'00" 130°22'00" E side of Digby I, Prince Rupert Hbr). From 1896 to 1910, Henry Philips was private secretary to Charles Melville Hays, gen manager, then president, of the GTP. He later became assistant secretary of the CNR. Philips and Hays made a brief visit to BC's N coast in 1904, shortly before Prince Rupert was confirmed as the GTP's western terminus. These features were named in 1907, while Prince Rupert Hbr was being prepared for its expected role as a great port.

Phillimore Point (48°52'00" 123°23'00" W side of Galiano I, SE of Parker I, Gulf Is). Lt Henry Bouchier Phillimore (1833–96) served on the Pacific Station, 1858–60, aboard HMS *Ganges*, flagship of Rear Adm Robert Baynes. He was promoted to capt in 1864 and commanded several warships, including HMS *Sphinx* and *Belleisle*. Phillimore was appointed a rear adm and was made a CB in 1880. He retired as an adm in 1892. Named by RN surveyor Capt George Richards of HMS *Plumper* in 1859.

Phillips Arm, north of Cordero Channel. *Peter Vassilopoulos*

Phillips Arm (50°31'00" 125°24'00" N of Cordero Channel, between Loughborough Inlet and Bute Inlet, N of Campbell R). For a small, out-of-the-way inlet, Phillips Arm has seen a fair amount of bustle over the years. It was once a rich fishing area, home to the Kwiakah people, a Kwakwala-speaking First Nation whose name means "to club." Then, in the mid-1890s, came the prospectors, who turned the inlet into a hotbed of activity second only to Texada I in the region. Dozens of claims were staked along the shoreline and beside the Phillips R, which flows SW through Phillips Lk into the head of the arm. Several gold mines were established, the largest of which was the Doratha Morton, on Fanny Bay, which processed ore on-site with cyanide to extract the precious metal. A large forestry camp was located on the inlet in the 1970s, with a post office that operated 1973–82. In the early 1990s some innovative dirigible logging was done in the vicinity. A decade later, aquaculture operations were flourishing on the arm. But nobody, unfortunately, seems to know who Phillips was. *E*

Philliskirk Hill (53°16'06" 130°02'20" E of Grief Point, on the SW side of Banks I). George Philliskirk (b about 1768) was a boatswain's mate on HMS *Discovery* when Capt George Vancouver left on his voyage of discovery to the PNW in 1791. He was promoted boatswain of HMS *Chatham* after several ill crew members were sent home in 1792 on the storeship *Daedalus*.

Phipps Point (49°32'00" 124°43'00" W side of Hornby I, Str of Georgia). After RN officer Geoffrey Thomas Phipps Hornby, who served on the Pacific Station, 1859–60, as capt of HMS *Tribune. See* Mt Geoffrey.

Picture Island (52°10'00" 127°56'00" Between Cunningham I and Denny I, Gunboat Passage, E of Bella Bella). Named, somewhat feebly, "after its picturesque appearance," according to Geographical Names Office records.

Piddell Bay (50°21'00" 125°18'00" Cameleon Hbr, W side of Sonora I, N of Campbell R). Alfred Henry Piddell was the secretary's clerk aboard HMS *Sutlej,* flagship of Rear Adm John Kingcome, cdr-in-chief on the Pacific Station, 1862–64. While in BC waters he served temporarily in HMS *Cameleon* in 1863. He had the RN rank of assistant paymaster and was appointed in that capacity to HMS *Prince Consort,* on the Mediterranean Station in 1865–67. Lt Daniel Pender, with the hired RN survey vessel *Beaver,* named many features in this area in 1863 after the *Cameleon*'s officers.

Piddington Island (52°05'00" 128°16'00" Off SW side of Campbell I, SW of Bella Bella). Midshipman Peter Grosvenor Piddington of the RN, a native of Victoria, died in action, aged 20, when the British battleship *Royal Oak* was torpedoed and sunk by a U-boat at Scapa Flow in the Orkney Is in 1939. Nearby Peter Bay is also named for him. The *Royal Oak* was an obsolete WWI vessel, and its sinking had little effect on the course of the war, but the tragically heavy loss of life—833 men—so early in the conflict was demoralizing, as was the realization that German submarines could strike with effect at such a major and well-defended naval base, and one so close to home. Piddington is commemorated on the Naval Memorial at Portsmouth, England.

Pidwell Reef (52°26'00" 128°34'00" N end of Milbanke Sd, off S side of Swindle I, NW of Bella Bella). Named after Mary Jane Pidwell (1846–1900), who was born in PEI and travelled with her family overland to California and thence to Victoria, arriving about 1859. Her father, John Trevasso Pidwell (1811–67), from Cornwall, became an influential Victoria merchant before his accidental death at Esquimalt; he represented Saltspring I on Vancouver I's colonial legislative assembly, 1863–64 and 1865–66. Her mother, Elizabeth (1817–83, née Davison), died at San Francisco. A brother, C J Pidwell, was an early furniture dealer in Victoria. In 1863, Mary married David Williams Higgins (1834–1917), owner and editor of Victoria's *Colonist* newspaper, 1862–86. According to a contemporary report, "the 20 bachelors in the *Colonist* office, after brushing away a slight regret at the loneliness of bachelordom, heartily drank a bumper" at the wedding. Higgins was also MLA for Esquimalt, 1886–1900, speaker of the BC legislature, 1890–98, and a popular author (*see* Higgins Passage). Mary was an active suffragette and sat on committees to assist female immigrants and improve medical and hospital care for women. Formerly known as Sandstone Reef.

Pier Point (53°12'00" 132°15'00" In Anchor Cove, Kagan Bay, S side of Graham I, QCI). The enormous (215-m) wharf that served the Cowgitz Mine was located here. The Cowgitz was an early QCI coal operation that ran sporadically between 1864 and 1872 but suffered endless problems. Despite the fact that the coal was ultimately insufficient in quality and quantity, a 2-km-long tramway was built from the mine to the pier, and several buildings—bunkhouses, offices and a mess hall—constructed beside it. *D*

Piers Island (48°42'00" 123°25'00" Off NE end of Saanich Peninsula, N of Victoria). Henry Piers (1818–1901) was the surgeon aboard HMS *Satellite,* under Capt James Prevost, and served on the Pacific Station, 1857–60. He had earlier been in the Indian Ocean on anti-slavery patrol with HMS *Cleopatra,* 1844–47, and in the Arctic as surgeon on Capt Robert McClure's HMS *Investigator.* This famous vessel had to be abandoned in the ice at Banks I in 1853 after proving the existence of the NW Passage. McClure and his crew were discovered by Lt Bedford Pim and taken by sledge to Capt Henry Kellett's HMS *Resolute* off Melville I. After another winter in the Arctic, *Resolute* was also forsaken, along with several other frozen-in vessels under the overall command of Capt Sir Edward Belcher. The expedition's members, whose original purpose had been to search for Sir John Franklin, then returned home. (*See* Belcher Point, Kellett Point *and* Pim Head for more information.) Piers became staff surgeon at Chatham dockyard in 1870 and a deputy inspector-gen of hospitals and fleets in 1873. Harry Point on Piers I is also named for him. The 97-ha island was originally settled by Wilhelm Schmidt, who received a Crown grant for it in 1880. In 1901 it was bought by Edward Clive Phillipps-Wolley, noted author, sportsman, investor, diplomat, lawyer, army officer and imperialist (*see* Clive I). Piers I was expropriated by the federal government in 1932 as a prison camp for 570 Doukhobor men and women convicted of an unusual form of civil disobedience: public nudity. This form of punishment was found unworkable, however, and the prisoners were mostly released by 1935.

Piers is now subdivided into about 130 waterfront lots, with the central portion reserved as parkland. According to BC historians Helen and Philip Akrigg, the Wsanec (Saanich) First Nation people knew it as Crow I because of the many crows that roost there. *E W*

Pigot Islets (48°53'00" 125°24'00" In the Broken Group, E of Loudoun Channel, Barkley Sd, W side of Vancouver I). Robert Pigot, born about 1775 at Dulwich, S London, was a 16-year-old midshipman when he joined HMS *Discovery*, under Capt George Vancouver, for a historic four-year expedition to the PNW. He spent the whole journey on the *Discovery* and kept a journal that still exists, but he seems to have been demoted to able seaman for part of the voyage. He was appointed a lt in 1796. In 1805, aboard HMS *Cambrian*, he helped capture the French schooner *Matilda* off Florida. Pigot was ordered to take this vessel up the nearby St Mary's R, where he captured two more ships in a daring manoeuvre, despite being under heavy fire, and returned to the relative safety of the ocean. He was badly wounded in the process, however, and although it appears he was promoted to cdr as a result of this action, nothing more is known about him, suggesting that his injuries ended his naval career.

Pike Island (54°19'00" 130°27'00" In Metlakatla Bay, just W of Prince Rupert). Cdr John William Pike (d 1894) served on the Pacific Station, 1862–64, as capt of the paddle sloop *Devastation*. Before coming to the PNW he had been cdr of HMS *Banshee* in the Mediterranean, HMS *Antelope* off W Africa and HMS *Vigilant* in the English Channel. Pike made a concerted effort to stem the illegal trade in liquor on the BC coast, confiscating cargoes and seizing vessels at Hornby I, Ft Rupert and in northern BC. The *Devastation* was sent to the mouth of the Stikine R in 1862 to protect miners from First Nation attacks during a short-lived gold rush. Pike also took part in two important local naval actions. In 1863 he was involved in the pursuit of the Lamalcha, a renegade Cowichan First Nation band accused of the murder of two white settlers in the Gulf Is (*see* Lamalchi Bay*)*. The following year the *Devastation* went to Clayoquot Sd to investigate the pillaging of the sloop *Kingfisher* and murder of its crew by an Ahousaht First Nation group. In a follow-up assault on the Ahousaht, the RN destroyed nine villages and killed at least 15 people. Pike returned to England as inspecting cdr of the Coast Guard, 1865–67, and was promoted to capt in 1868 and rear adm, retired, in 1885. He was a fellow of the Royal Geographical Society. Pike Ck, which flows into Devastation Channel S of Kitimat Arm, is also named for him. The Pike Ck watershed, according to anthropologist Jay Powell, is known to the Haisla First Nation as Xaisabisc Wiwaa, with *wiwaa* meaning "many creeks." *W*

Pike Point (53°33'25" 129°34'45" S side of Nettle Basin, Lowe Inlet, E side of Grenville Channel, E of Pitt I). Mark

Pike (1861–1944), from Nfld, was a master mariner who moved to BC in 1890 with his wife, Lillie (1863–1924), and became a skipper in the Victoria sealing trade. In the mid-1890s he worked for William Munsie as capt of the *City of San Diego*, taking 1,043 seal skins in 1893 and 1,554 in 1894, most of them off the coast of Japan. Pike Point was formerly known as David Point but was renamed in 1946. Nearby Mark Bluff is also named for this pioneer.

Pillar Bay (54°09'00" 132°55'00" N side of Graham I, just E of Parry Passage, QCI), **Pillar Rock** (54°09'00" 132°53'00" E end of Pillar Bay). Geologist George Mercer Dawson named Pillar Rk, a 29-m-high pinnacle of conglomerate and sandstone, topped with trees and salal, in 1878. Dawson gave its Haida name as Hla-tad-zo-woh. The bay is named after the rock. *D*

Pilling Rock (50°24'00" 127°59'00" SW of Harvey Cove, S entrance to Quatsino Sd, NW end of Vancouver I). Alfred Edward Pilling (1864–1951), a master stonemason from Norfolk, England, came to Quatsino with his wife, Theresa, and two children around 1904. He homesteaded and prospected and received a Crown grant for land in the area in 1911, but the family moved to the drier climate of Kamloops about 1913 when Mrs Pilling became ill. The Pillings' son Richard and his wife, Sally, returned to Quatsino in the mid-1920s and raised a family there.

Pillsbury Cove (54°20'00" 130°23'00" N side of Prince Rupert Hbr, E of Venn Passage), **Pillsbury Point** (54°18'00" 130°21'00" NW side of Kaien I, at Prince Rupert). Joel Horace Pillsbury (1874–1958), assistant harbour and townsite engineer for the GTP at Prince Rupert, was responsible for the original surveys of the area and for many of the harbour's geographical names. He was born at Kansas City, Missouri, raised in Massachusetts, graduated from MIT in 1896 and married Amelia Florence Hall (1877–1941). Early in his career he designed coastal fortifications on the US E coast. Pillsbury and his team of engineers and carpenters arrived on Kaien I in May 1906 and proceeded to clear rights of way, lay out streets, and build a dock, office and sleeping quarters. He later superintended the construction of the Prince Rupert drydock and shipyard, and after WWI became manager of the Pacific Stevedoring Co, served two terms as a Prince Rupert city councillor and was active on the board of trade. Pillsbury moved to Vancouver in 1934 when he was appointed a commissioner of the Workmen's Compensation Board. He retired in 1945 and died at Richmond. The point was named by federal hydrographer G Blanchard Dodge in 1906. It was formerly known to ship captains as Omega Point, as it was the last promontory to round before reaching the safety of the harbour. The cove was named in 1908.

Pilot Bay. *See* Descanso Bay.

P

Pimbury Point (49°11'00" 123°57'00" S end of Departure Bay, at Nanaimo, SE side of Vancouver I). Edwin Pimbury (1835–1909) was a pioneer merchant at Nanaimo. A native of Gloucestershire, he came to Canada via Australia in 1856 with his brother Augustus, then gravitated to BC about 1861 for the Cariboo gold rush. Two other brothers joined them in Canada. After residing at Victoria and Cobble Hill, the four bachelors established a large sheep ranch on S Saltspring I in 1874, selling out to Edward Musgrave in 1885. Edwin was elected MLA for Cowichan, 1875–82. He eventually settled at Nanaimo, established himself as a pharmacist and acquired considerable property holdings. He died at Duncan. The point, named in 1904 by Cdr John Parry of HMS *Egeria* on his re-survey of Departure Bay, became the site that year of a coal-mining operation. *W*

Pim Head (48°22'00" 123°39'00" S side of Sooke Basin, S end of Vancouver I). This feature was probably named after Rear Adm Bedford Clapperton Trevelyan Pim (1826–86), one of the RN's most extraordinary officers. He was a midshipman on HMS *Herald* during Capt Henry Kellett's 1846 survey of S Vancouver I. The nearby Bedford Is (qv) are also named for him, and both names appear on Kellett's 1848 chart of the area. In 1848–49, Pim joined Capt Thomas Moore and HMS *Plover* in the search for Arctic explorer Sir John Franklin, who had not been heard from for four years. One of Pim's duties was to travel by land from Kotzebue Sd to Norton Sd in W Alaska, questioning the Inuit about Franklin's possible whereabouts. In 1851–52 he was sent to St Petersburg in Russia in an unsuccessful attempt to gain support for a search for Franklin in Siberia. Pim became part of Sir Edward Belcher's five-vessel Arctic expedition of 1852, sailing with Capt Kellett again, this time in HMS *Resolute*. Belcher was looking for Franklin, of course, but also for Robert McClure of HMS *Investigator*, who had gone missing in the western Arctic. After the discovery of a note from McClure on Melville I, Pim, with two other men, made a daring, 28-day sledge journey in Mar 1853 to Banks I, where the *Investigator* was frozen in, and led 63 survivors back to the *Resolute*. After another winter in the ice, Belcher controversially abandoned four of his ships and returned home. Lt Pim went on to commands in the Baltic, during the Crimean War, and off China, sustaining wounds on both commissions. In 1859, by now a cdr, he surveyed a route for a proposed canal across Nicaragua, then indiscreetly invested in this scheme while on the W Indies Station with HMS *Gorgon*. The Admiralty criticized him for this conflict of interest, so he retired, acquired a law degree and established a practice that specialized in Admiralty cases. Pim made three more journeys to Nicaragua and was elected Conservative MP for Gravesend, 1874–80. He was named to the Royal Geographical Society and the Institute of Civil Engineers, wrote at least eight books and eventually reached the rank of rear adm, retired, in 1885. A window and plaque in the church of the Seamen's Institute at Bristol commemorate him, as does Pim I off Ellesmere I in Canada's high Arctic. *W*

Pinder Rock (48°55'00" 125°23'00" Loudoun Channel, W of Peacock Channel, Barkley Sd, W side of Vancouver I). Civil engineer William George Pinder (1850–1936) pre-empted land on the W side of Barkley Sd in 1892. He had arrived in Victoria from England in 1871 and joined a CPR survey crew laying out the railroad along the Thompson R between the Fraser R and Shuswap Lk. Pinder had connections: Joseph Trutch, BC's first lt gov, was his uncle. From 1873 to 1876 he worked in the Thompson and Coquihalla regions and in the Kimsquit R area, then became assistant engineer for the CPR on the Thompson section of line. After marrying Annie Marie Henrietta Devereux (b 1856) in 1877 at Victoria, he played a major role in the construction of the E&N, especially the railway's southern portion between Victoria and the Malahat. Pinder was involved in finalizing survey work along the BC-Washington boundary in the early 1900s, and he also worked for the Dunsmuir Collieries for many years, helping shift their operations from the Nanaimo area to the Comox valley. He eventually went into general practice, doing survey work at Kitselas Canyon, Ft Simpson, Work Channel, Portland Canal, Graham I and in BC's northern Interior. Pinder Ck and Pinder Peak near Nimpkish Lk are named for him as well. Pinder Rk was formerly known as Shag Rk (shag is another name for cormorant).

Pine Island (50°59'00" 127°43'00" N of Nigei I, W entrance to Queen Charlotte Str, NW of Port Hardy). About 40 BC landscape features have the word "pine" in their names, so this one is hardly remarkable. It is a remarkable site, however—the location of one of BC's most isolated and exposed lighthouse stations, built in 1907. The station was completely destroyed in 1967 by a fierce storm with 185 km/h winds. Keepers Rex and Elizabeth Brown and their two daughters managed to escape with their lives and left the island soon after for Victoria. The station was rebuilt on higher ground. Many historians believe that Pine I, named by Capt George Richards of HMS *Hecate* in 1860, was the mysterious Alleviation I of Capt George Vancouver, mentioned in his journal but not marked on his chart. Author John Walbran claimed that Redfern I (qv) was a more likely candidate.

Pinkerton Islands (48°57'00" 125°17'00" N of the Broken Group, SE of Lyall Point, Barkley Sd, W side of Vancouver I). James H Pinkerton pre-empted land on Sechart Channel in 1891. As soon as he had received a Crown grant to his property, in 1895, he sold part or all of it to James Crawford Anderson, a local prospector and speculator. Anderson, in turn, sold the land to Sprott Balcom and William Grant, of the Pacific Whaling Co. They built BC's first modern whaling station there, Sechart, which operated 1905–17. The Pinkerton Is were formerly known as the Hundred Is.

Pinnace Channel (50°02'00" 127°11'00" E side of Hohoae I, Kyuquot Sd, NW side of Vancouver I), **Pinnace Rock** (48°54'00" 125°16'00" Part of the Broken Group, W side of Imperial Eagle Channel, Barkley Sd, W side of Vancouver I). A pinnace is a small boat that can be carried aboard a larger vessel (especially a warship) and used as a tender or for other purposes. In the age of sail the pinnace was usually schooner-rigged and also equipped with multiple sets of oars. The exact circumstances that led to the naming of these two features are not known, however.

Piper Point (49°33'00" 123°48'00" SW side of Sechelt Inlet, NW of Vancouver). After Private James Cleland Richardson, VC (1895–1916), who was a piper with the Seaforth Highlanders. He came to Vancouver from Scotland in 1913 and worked at a False Ck factory while the rest of his family moved to Chilliwack, where his father had been named chief of police. Richardson then went overseas with the 16th Scottish Battalion of the Canadian Expeditionary Force. He won his VC on Oct 8, 1916, at the Battle of the Somme, when he rallied his company at Regina Trench, playing the pipes under intense enemy fire while his fellow soldiers cut their way through a thicket of barbed wire and managed to capture their objective. Later the same day, after realizing he had left his bagpipes behind, he was killed trying to retrieve them. James is commemorated at Adanac Military Cemetery, Miraumont, France. In the Sechelt Inlet area, nearby Richardson Lk and Mt Richardson are also named for him. Piper Point was formerly known as Little Rocky Point but was renamed in 1945.

Pipestem Inlet (49°02'00" 125°15'00" E of Toquart Bay, W of Effingham Inlet, Barkley Sd, W side of Vancouver I). The inlet, which appears on the 1861 chart of Capt George Richards, was probably named for its shape: it narrows down to form a "mouthpiece" of sorts at the E end, while the stem opens up into the "bowl" of Toquart Bay to the W. The waters of Pipestem Inlet get quite warm in summer, making this one of the few places in BC where oyster spat or seed can be commercially produced and collected. In 1925, HMCS *Armentières*, a patrol boat and minesweeper, sank in the inlet and was later raised after striking Armentières Rk (qv). A pilchard-reduction plant was briefly located at the W end of Pipestem in the 1930s.

Pirates Cove (49°05'55" 123°43'40" SE side of De Courcy I, just S of Gabriola I, Gulf Is). This feature, formerly known as Gospel Cove or The Haven, was the site of the main colony of Brother XII, a former British mariner whose real name was Edward Arthur Wilson (1878–1934). He and his followers, many of whom were from the US and quite wealthy, built a home beside the cove and developed an old farm in the island's interior in the late 1920s and early '30s. His cult, called the Aquarian Foundation, had thousands of supporters and also owned property on Vancouver I

Pirates Cove on De Courcy Island. *John Lund*

at nearby Cedar-by-the-Sea and on Gabriola and Ruxton islands. The name Pirates Cove probably refers to some of Brother XII's activities and behaviour in the area, which could be seen as piratical. He had, for instance, a number of crude fortifications built around the cove, and intruders were warned off with rifle fire. He was reputed to keep his considerable fortune in the form of gold and to store it in glass jars on De Courcy. Some people believe it is still there, and many holes have been dug in the vicinity—unsuccessfully, so far. A 31-ha area around the cove became a provincial marine park in 1966.

Pitt Island (53°30'00" 129°47'00" Between Banks I and McCauley I and the BC mainland, S of Prince Rupert), **Pitt Point** (53°53'00" 130°06'00" NE end of Pitt I). In 1792, Joseph Whidbey, master of HMS *Discovery*, made a long exploratory journey with the ship's boats from Nepean Sd via Grenville Channel to Chatham Sd and back. Upon his return, Capt George Vancouver gave the name Pitt's Archipelago to the group of islands that now includes Pitt, McCauley, Porcher and their smaller outliers. Years later, when more detailed surveys were done, the name Pitt was reserved for the archipelago's main island—the fifth largest in BC at 1,373 sq km. Vancouver was honouring William Pitt the younger (1759–1806), who was Britain's PM at the time of his voyage. He had become PM in 1783, at the astonishing age of 24, and remained in that office, with a three-year hiatus, until his death. He was also the son of a PM (William Pitt the elder). In the sense that he consolidated his powers in order to supervise and co-ordinate the various government depts, the younger Pitt was the first modern British PM. He rehabilitated Britain's finances after the US War of Independence, improving the tax system, issuing banknotes and controlling the national debt. However, he failed to realize his goals of reforming parliament and abolishing the slave trade. Many other features in BC are named for him, including the Pitt R, Pitt Lk, Pitt Marsh, Mt Pitt on Pitt I, Mt Pitt near the headwaters of the Pitt R, and the community of Pitt Meadows. *E W*

Pitt Shoal. *See* Chatham Sd.

P

Pivot Mountain (54°00'56" 132°59'52" E side of Beresford Bay, NW end of Graham I, QCI). This prominent, 586-m peak is somewhat isolated and thus easily identified by mariners. It was named before WWI during a survey of the region for oil and coal, though the origin of the name is unknown. It is apparently known as Sqat-telagans to the Haida people. *D*

Planet Group (51°45'00" 128°04'00" S of Underhill I and Hunter I, N side of Hakai Passage, S of Bella Bella). Named in 1948 by the hydrographic service for its individual component islands: Mercury, Mars and Jupiter.

Plover Point (49°12'00" 125°46'00" E side of Meares I, E of Wood Its, Clayoquot Sd, W side of Vancouver I), **Plover Reefs** (49°11'00" 126°05'00" S side of Brabant Channel, W of Blunden I, Clayoquot Sd). The Plover Reefs were named by Capt George Richards of HMS *Hecate* in 1861, after HMS *Plover*, a vessel he knew well. The 215-tonne brig, formerly the *Bentinck*, had been purchased by the RN as a survey cutter in 1842. It was stationed in the E Indies in 1842–46, under Cdr Richard Collinson, at the same time Richards was there as a lt on HMS *Sulphur*. The *Plover* also spent considerable time in the Arctic, 1848–54, assisting in the search for Sir John Franklin. Richards was also involved in this endeavour, 1852–54, as 1st officer of HMS *Assistance*, commanded by Capt Edward Belcher. The *Plover* passed five winters in the Arctic altogether, under Cdr Thomas Moore and Cdr Rochfort Maguire, serving mostly as a storeship on the W coast of Alaska; it was restocked each year by a vessel sent N from the Pacific Station. The ship was condemned and sold at San Francisco in 1854. *W*

Plowden Bay. *See* Mt Plowden.

Plumper Bay (48°26'40" 123°25'55" E side of Esquimalt Hbr, just W of Victoria), **Plumper Bay** (50°09'40" 125°20'30" W side of Quadra I, NE of Seymour Narrows), **Plumper Cove** (49°24'00" 123°28'00" W side of Keats I, Howe Sd, NW of Vancouver), **Plumper Harbour** (49°42'00" 126°38'00" E side of Nootka I, W of Strange I, Nootka Sd, W side of Vancouver I), **Plumper Hill** (50°28'25" 128°00'19" E entrance to Forward Inlet, Quatsino Sd, NW end of Vancouver I), **Plumper Islands** (50°35'00" 126°47'00" Between Hanson I and Pearse Is, Weynton Passage, W end of Johnstone Str), **Plumper Passage** (48°25'00" 123°15'00" W of Discovery I, E of Virtue Rk, off SE tip of Vancouver I), **Plumper Point** (50°10'00" 125°21'00" SW side of Plumper Bay, Quadra I), **Plumper Sound** (48°46'00" 123°13'00" Bounded by Mayne I, Saturna I, N Pender I and S Pender I; Gulf Is). HMS *Plumper* was one of the main hydrographic vessels on the BC coast, serving there 1857–61 under Capt George Richards. With the exception of Plumper Hill and Plumper Point, all these features were named by

A painting by Edward Bedwell, 2nd master of HMS *Plumper*, shows the ship aground at Discovery Island. *BC Archives A-00238*

Richards, who obviously felt affection for his 591-tonne, 43-m vessel, despite its inadequate size and advancing age. A barque-rigged steam sloop equipped with eight guns, it was launched at Portsmouth in 1848 and employed in the W Indies and off S America and W Africa before coming to the PNW. The *Plumper* was replaced after more than three years of work in BC, and Richards and his survey officers—Lt Richard Mayne and masters Edward Bedwell and Daniel Pender—continued their efforts on the larger HMS *Hecate*. In Jan 1861, Cdr Anthony Hoskins took the *Plumper* back to the UK, where it was sold in 1865. It is unusual to have two coastal features with identical names, but Plumper Bay on Quadra I, according to a 1944 record at BC's Geographical Names Office, was "so well established, and the feature so much in use as a shelter, that the name ... should be retained, even as a duplication." Plumper Reach on the Fraser R is also named for this vessel. Active Pass in the Gulf Is was known locally for many years as Plumper Pass, and the post office on Mayne I operated under that name, 1880–1900. Hunter Channel, N of Hunter I, was formerly Plumper Channel, and Schloss I in Quatsino Sd was known as Plumper I. The name Plumper Hill, for a feature called Brown Hill and Burnt Hill in earlier days, was adopted in 1927 (the ship did survey duty in Quatsino Sd in 1860); Plumper Point, originally North Point, was renamed by the hydrographic service in 1944 in association with Plumper Bay. The word "plumper" is curious. Five RN warships have had this name, the first one launched in 1794. In the 18th century a plumper was a heavy or sudden blow or shot, but the word has since gone out of use. *W*

Poca Cove (49°25'00" 123°19'00" N side of Cates Bay, NE end of Bowen I, Howe Sd, NW of Vancouver). Poca is the Spanish word for "small."

Pocahontas Bay (49°44'00" 124°26'00" NE side of Texada I, Str of Georgia), **Pocahontas Point** (48°59'01" 124°54'50" N side of lower Alberni Inlet, E of entrance to Uchucklesit

Inlet, W side of Vancouver I). Pocahontas Point is named after the first merchant ship to arrive at the head of Alberni Inlet, in 1861, to take on a cargo of lumber from BC's first export sawmill. Edward Stamp had established this pioneer, steam-driven facility—known as the Anderson Mill after the English family who financed it—the previous year, and over the next half-decade it cut the region's enormous Douglas firs and sent them to China, Australia, Hawaii, S America and Great Britain. The *Pocahontas*, under Capt Cyrus Sears, was from Boston, but Stamp chartered it at San Francisco to carry a load of spars to England. The longest spar, intended as a flagpole, was 55 m in length—60 cm at the butt and 28 cm at the tip—and had to be shortened slightly before it would fit on board. It is not known if Pocahontas Bay also commemorates this vessel, but the Texada I name is an old one, appearing on a 1908 mining survey and in the 1899 annual report of BC's Ministry of Mines. The bay is famous as the site of a major still built in 1929, one of the largest on the Pacific coast during the Prohibition era. It was said to be capable of producing 2,000 litres of 192-proof grain alcohol a week, much of which went to the US, and operated for about a year before the police shut it down. Mt Pocahontas on Texada I, topped by a radio tower, was named in 1924 after Pocahontas Bay but appears on maps as early as 1912.

Pocket Inlet (52°36'00" 131°53'00" SE of Tasu Sd, W side of Moresby I, QCI). Explorer Newton Chittenden named this feature Grand View Inlet in 1884, calling it "one of the securest retreats for small boats ever seen." Early fishermen called it God's Pocket, supposedly because the inlet's entrance points extended far enough N and S to completely protect the inner harbour and reminded them of a pocket flap. Capt Absalom Freeman named it Pocket Hbr on his 1912 map, and this later became Pocket Inlet. The Haida First Nation name for the inlet is Raw Radagaas. *D*

Pocock Island (52°48'00" 128°45'00" W side of Laredo Inlet, S side of Princess Royal I). The name was adopted by the hydrographic service in 1928 after W R T Pocock, a resident of Victoria in the 1880s and '90s. Mt Pocock, on the W side of Douglas Channel, was apparently named after Sub-Lt Charles Ashwell Boteler Pocock (1829–99) of the RN, who was stationed at Esquimalt about 1850 and whose daughter Lena Ashwell became a well-known British actress.

Poett Nook (48°53'00" 125°03'00" S side of Numukamis Bay, NE side of Barkley Sd, W side of Vancouver I). Dr Joseph Henry Poett was a British physician who immigrated to San Francisco and established a practice there in 1849, after living for many years at Santiago, Chile. He became a large landowner in the San Mateo area. Poett visited Victoria in 1860–61 and took a great interest in potential deposits of copper at Barkley Sd. Capt George

Richards of the survey ship *Hecate* named this feature after him in 1861, as well as nearby Poett Heights, a range of hills. Poett Ck, which flows into Poett Nook, was named in 2005.

Point Ash (48°21'00" 123°34'00" W end of Pedder Bay, S tip of Vancouver I). Dr John Ash (1821–86), a pioneer Victoria physician, came to Victoria from England in 1862 and acquired large parcels of property in this area in 1863. His plan to build a dock in Pedder Bay and connect the bay by canal to Matheson Lk did not come to fruition, though he did construct an expensive stone dam on the lake. Ash was married twice: to Dorothy Agar (1823–74) and Adelaide de Veulle. He was a sponsor of Robert Brown's 1864 Vancouver I Exploration Expedition and was elected to Vancouver I's colonial legislative assembly, 1865–66, as a representative for Esquimalt. After Confederation, Ash was elected an MLA, 1872–82, and served as provincial secretary (1872–76) and BC's first minister of Mines (1874–76). In his *Reminiscences*, fellow doctor John Helmcken had this to say: "Ash was a clever, well read man with a good memory; of remarkable physique and structure—very broad shoulders and of bulldog style, very pleasant to his friends but of hasty and quarrelsome temper—hated to be contradicted—his opinion being final." Mt Ash and Ash R on S Vancouver I are also named for him.

Point Atkinson lighthouse. *Peter Vassilopoulos*

Point Atkinson (49°20'00" 123°16'00" N entrance point to Burrard Inlet, at Vancouver). Named by Capt George Vancouver for a "particular friend" of his—probably Thomas Atkinson (1767–1836), who was a follower of Adm Lord Nelson and served as master of HMS *Victory* during the Battle of Trafalgar. Atkinson had earlier taken part in several other notable actions, including at Cape St Vincent, Tenerife, the Nile, Acre and Copenhagen. Later he became master attendant at the Halifax dockyard in NS and ended his career as senior master attendant of Portsmouth dockyard. Vancouver examined this area personally in June 1792 with HMS *Discovery*'s boats,

P

accompanied by Lt Peter Puget. A lighthouse went into operation here in 1875; the present structure, now a national historic site, was built in 1912 and automated in 1994. Edwin and Ann Woodward were the first keepers, but it was Walter and Jane Erwin (*see* Erwin Point) who were most closely associated with the station. They were there for 30 years, between 1880 and 1910. The station's foghorn, known as "Old Wahoo," fell silent in 1996.

Point Cowan (49°20'00" 123°22'00" SE end of Bowen I, Howe Sd, NW of Vancouver). George Henry Cowan (1858–1935) was an Ont lawyer who moved to Vancouver in 1893 to practise law and politics. He was the city's solicitor, 1907–10, served as a Conservative MP, 1908–11, and wrote an anti-Asian pamphlet that helped increase the head tax paid by Chinese immigrants. Between 1899 and 1917 he and his wife, Josephine (1869–1960, née Downie), bought more than 400 ha of land at the S end of Bowen I, rented out cottages to friends and established a farm at Seymour Bay, where a dock was built and Union steamers stopped until about 1950 (the landing was listed as Cowans Point on the steamship timetable). Point Cowan post office operated 1911–35. *E*

Point Cumming (53°19'00" 129°07'00" SW end of Gribbell I, S of entrance to Douglas Channel). Capt George Vancouver named this feature without explanation in 1793. There was an able seaman called John Cummings aboard HMS *Discovery*, but it is unlikely that he was the source, as Vancouver normally reserved the honour of a place name for RN officers or European notables. Only seamen who died on the voyage or were severely wounded had places named after them. NZ historian John Robson claims that this feature commemorates Alexander Cumming (c 1732–1814), a celebrated Scottish clock and chronometer maker who lived in London and supplied the RN. Cumming, a founding member of the Royal Society of Scotland, was also a mathematician, author and inventor, and took out the first British patent for a "water-closet," in 1775. Cumming Point (qv) on Drury Inlet is named for a different person.

Point Ellice (48°26'00" 123°22'00" NW point of Upper Hbr, Victoria Hbr, SE end of Vancouver I). Edward "Bear" Ellice (1783–1863) was a powerful London merchant-banker and a director of the HBC. He became involved in the fur trade, in which his wealthy father had business interests, in the early 1800s, travelling frequently between London and Canada, where he also owned considerable property. Ellice played a leading role in the merger of the NWC and HBC in 1821. He entered politics in England, serving as MP for Coventry (1818–26 and 1830–63), treasury secretary (1830–32) and war secretary (1832–34). His son, also Edward Ellice, became a member of the 1857 British parliamentary committee appointed to investigate the HBC's affairs and then deputy gov of the HBC, 1858–63. The point was named by Ft Victoria's

HBC officers and adopted by Capt Henry Kellett on his 1846 survey of Victoria Hbr. Point Ellice House, now a beautifully restored historic site, was built there in 1861 and purchased by colonial gold commissioner Peter O'Reilly and his wife, Caroline, in 1867. The 1896 collapse of nearby Point Ellice Bridge was Canada's worst transit accident, causing 55 deaths. *E W*

Pointer Island (52°03'49" 127°56'55" W side of Fisher Channel, off NE end of Hunter I, SE of Bella Bella). A lighthouse station was built here in 1899 to mark the S entrance to Lama Passage. It was operated for many years by members of the Codville family (*see* Codville Hill). The original building was demolished and replaced with more modern facilities in 1949, but the station was eventually deemed obsolete and replaced by an automated light. It was dismantled in 1989. The origin of the name Pointer is not known.

Point Fairfax (48°42'00" 123°18'00" S point of Moresby I, Gulf Is). After Rear Adm Fairfax Moresby of the RN, cdr-in-chief of the Pacific Station, 1850–53. *See* Moresby I. The point may also be named after Lt Fairfax Moresby, the admiral's son (*see* Fairfax I).

Point George (50°29'00" 126°01'00" W entrance to Blenkinsop Bay, Johnstone Str). After early HBC employee George Blenkinsop, who worked at Ft Rupert in the 1850s. *See* Blenkinsop Bay.

Point Grey (49°16'00" 123°16'00" S entrance to Burrard Inlet, Vancouver), **Point Grey Beach** (49°17'00" 123°14'00" S side of Burrard Inlet, W of English Bay). Capt George Vancouver named Grey Point in 1792 after his friend Capt George Grey (1767–1828). The son of an earl, Grey entered the RN in 1781 and was soon promoted post capt. He was appointed capt of HMS *Victory*, flagship of Adm Sir John Jervis, in 1796 and was present at the Battle of Cape St Vincent. Grey remained flag capt when Jervis took command of the Channel fleet and in 1801 became capt of the royal yacht *Amelia*. He later served as commissioner of the Sheerness and Portsmouth dockyards and was created a baronet in 1814. Point Grey was the Punta de Lángara of Spanish explorer Dionisio Alcalá-Galiano, named for senior naval officer Juan Francisco de Lángara (*see* Langara I), and it was near here that Galiano and Cayetano Valdés, with the *Sutil* and *Mexicana*, had a friendly encounter with Vancouver and William Broughton of HMS *Discovery* and *Chatham*. The residential district of Langara (or Langarra, as the post office, open 1914–22, was spelled), adjacent to Point Grey, keeps alive the old Spanish name. The Point Grey area, now home to UBC and some luxurious suburbs, was formerly a government reserve. It was part of the municipality of S Vancouver, established in 1892, then became the separate municipality of Point Grey from 1908 until 1929, when it united with Vancouver. *W*

Point No Point (48°23'30" 123°59'10" Between Sooke and Jordan R, S end of Vancouver I). Point No Point first appears on a map of Vancouver I in 1897. Its official name—adopted in 1957—is Point No Point (Glacier Point). On the 1900 edition of Admiralty chart #1911 it appears as Glacier Point (Point No Point) instead. It is not known how the unusual, double-barrelled moniker arose. The more familiar name supposedly refers to the feature's ambiguous or deceptive appearance when viewed from certain angles. "It's a promontory that's a point from one side, not the other," writes Vancouver I poet Jane Munro, who uses the name as a metaphor for uncertainty in her 2006 book *Point No Point*. A rustic resort, still flourishing in the 2000s, was established there in 1952 by retired nurse Evelyn Packham. Another Point No Point, at Vancouver, just SE of Point Grey, was rescinded as an official name in 1979 (though it still often appears on maps). An early source suggested that this second feature was so called "because it is not much of a point." Point No Point in Washington state received its name because it appears less of a promontory at close range than it does from a distance.

Point North. *See* Langara I *and* St Margaret Point.

Point Roberts. *See* Roberts Bank.

Poise Island (49°30'00" 123°45'00" In Porpoise Bay, S end of Sechelt Inlet, NW of Vancouver). The hydrographic service chose this name, a contraction of the word "porpoise," in 1945. The feature was known locally in the 1920s as Cook's I, after Thomas John Cook, early Sechelt settler and the area's first justice of the peace, who owned it in 1912. Sechelt historian Helen Dawe, who was Cook's granddaughter, considered the new name most regrettable and referred to Poise as a "cutesy" abbreviation. It was also known as Skeleton I and Deadman's I in the early days, as it had been a Sechelt First Nation burial ground until the mid-1870s; the Sechelt people know the island as Smémkw'áli.

Poison Cove (52°54'00" 128°02'00" Head of Mussel Inlet, E of Sheep Passage and Princess Royal I). Named in 1793 by Capt George Vancouver. It was here that seaman John Carter and other crew members ate tainted mussels for breakfast while surveying Mussel Inlet in two small boats. Several men became ill, and Carter died a few hours later, undoubtedly from paralytic shellfish poisoning. He was buried at Carter Bay (qv). The other sick crewmen drank warm seawater as an emetic and recovered. Poison Cove Ck flows NW into Poison Cove.

Polkinghorne Islands (50°48'00" 126°56'00" Just W of Broughton I, NE side of Queen Charlotte Str, NE of Port McNeill). RN officer Charles James Polkinghorne was master of HMS *Fantome*, a brig on the Australia Station, 1850–56. He was appointed cdr of HMS *Cumberland*, guardship at Sheerness dockyard, in 1864, then served in HMS *Achilles* before becoming a capt and harbourmaster at Portsmouth dockyard in 1874. Polkinghorne retired in 1879. Lt Daniel Pender of the *Beaver* named this feature about 1865, along with nearby Brig Rk and Fantome Point. It was unusual for Pender to name coastal features after RN personnel who hadn't actually served in BC, so Polkinghorne may have been a friend or former shipmate of his. *W*

Pollard Cove (48°46'00" 123°16'00" E side of N Pender I, Gulf Is). Elijah Pollard (1875–1963) came to S Pender I from England in 1894 and with a partner, Arthur Stanford, made a near-disastrous prospecting trip to Bella Coola, where the intrepid duo were forced to eat their packhorse. He and Stanford both took up land on S Pender in 1895 and farmed. Pollard became foreman of road construction on the island and was active in public affairs. He married Elizabeth Green at Victoria in 1897 and later moved to N Pender, where he and his wife built a home on Browning Hbr that they named The Maples. Pollard was elected a school trustee in 1913. The name of the cove was adopted in 1969 after being recommended by the Gulf Is Branch of the BC Historical Assoc. Richardson Bluff on S Pender I was formerly known as Pollard Bluff, after the same family.

Poole Inlet (52°22'00" 131°18'00" SE side of Burnaby I, off SE Moresby I, QCI), **Poole Point** (52°22'00" 131°15'00" SE tip of Burnaby I). Mining engineer Francis Poole, hired by the Queen Charlotte Mining Co of Victoria, searched for copper in the vicinity of Poole and Skincuttle inlets, 1862–64. He arrived aboard the schooner *Rebecca* and first set up camp on Skincuttle I, later moving to Pelican Point on Burnaby I. Poole named many features in the vicinity, including Burnaby I and Skincuttle I. His venture was unsuccessful, betrayed by unspectacular results and mutinous employees, but he fell in love with the QCI and wrote an 1872 book (republished in 1972) that described the islands as "a picture of loveliness," where "the very atmosphere seems laden with the perfume of its vegetation." Geologist George M Dawson commented that Poole's book was "chiefly remarkable for the exaggerated character of the accounts it contains," while George Woodcock noted its "insufferably bombastic style." Poole believed that he had unwittingly helped spread the dread disease smallpox on the coast by introducing it to the Bella Bella and Bella Coola regions on an earlier mining expedition. Poole Inlet was named by regional hydrographer Henri Parizeau in 1935. Nearby Francis Bay also commemorates this pioneer prospector, as does Mt Poole on NE Moresby I. *D*

Pooley Island (52°43'00" 128°14'00" Between Mathieson Channel and Griffin Passage, NW of Don Peninsula, N of Bella Bella), **Pooley Point** (52°41'00" 128°12'00" E side of Pooley I). Charles Edward Pooley (1845–1912),

P

from England, arrived in Victoria in 1862 and joined the Cariboo gold rush before working as a colonial civil servant in New Westminster. He studied law under Chief Justice Matthew Begbie and was appointed deputy registrar and then registrar of the Supreme Court of BC, 1866–79. Pooley married Elizabeth Wilhelmina Fisher (1849–1932, see Lizzie Rks) at Victoria in 1869 and was admitted to the bar in 1877. He set up a law practice in Victoria with future BC premier Alexander Davie and went into politics, serving as Esquimalt MLA, 1882–1906, speaker of the legislature, 1887–89 and 1902–6, and president of the executive council, 1889–95. The Pooleys built Fernhill, one of Esquimalt's finest residences, and became key members of Victoria's social elite, growing wealthy as Charles tended to the legal and business interests of the Dunsmuir family. His epitaph at Ross Bay Cemetery, which we can only hope he did not write himself, reads, "A Just Man Made Perfect." Charles Head and Counsel Point on Pooley I are also named for him. A son, Robert Henry Pooley (1878–1954), who followed his father as Esquimalt MLA, 1912–37, became attorney gen in 1928–33; Pooley Ck, which flows into Dease R, is named for him. A daughter, Annie Bickerton Pooley (1875–1962), married Adm Sir Victor Stanley, son of the 16th Earl of Derby, in 1896. Pooley I was formerly known as James I but was renamed in 1946.

Poor Mans Rock (49°26'00" 124°10'00" Off SW end of Lasqueti I, Str of Georgia). *Poor Man's Rock* is a novel written in 1920 by Pender Hbr author Bertrand Sinclair (1881–1972). The rock in the title is a real one, and its name was made official in 1981. Kelp and currents keep fish boats away from the rock's rich salmon resources, which allowed hand trollers to earn a living in the old days. "Only a poor man trolled in a rowboat," Sinclair wrote. The rock "had given many men a chance." *Poor Man's Rock* may be a melodrama, where the grey-eyed daughter of a villainous cannery owner falls in love with a fearless young hero, but it still manages to examine the monopolistic cannery industry in a fairly astute manner. Sinclair, whose real name was William, was originally from Scotland. He became a cowboy in Montana and a novelist in San Francisco and Vancouver before moving to Pender Hbr, where he also worked full-time for a few years as a commercial fisherman. Several of his 15 novels (he also wrote hundreds of short stories) were made into silent films. *Poor Man's Rock* is believed to have sold more than 80,000 copies—a number to swoon over today. *See* Sinclair Bank.

Pope Rocks (49°02'00" 125°20'00" In Toquart Bay, NW side of Barkley Sd, W side of Vancouver I). Frederick Samuel Pope (b 1864), from England, pre-empted land NW of Toquart Bay in 1892. He was listed that same year in the Victoria directory as a clerk at Victoria's Albion Iron Works. Frederick married Elizabeth S Stafford at Victoria in 1893, and the Pope family may have moved later to S California. Formerly known as Black Patch Rks.

Popham Island (49°22'00" 123°29'00" SE side of Barfleur Passage, W of Bowen I, Howe Sd, NW of Vancouver). This feature was named by Capt George Richards in 1860, the same year that he named many other places in Howe Sd after participants in the great 1794 British naval victory known as the Glorious First of June. Most historians assume that the island commemorates Home Riggs Popham (1762–1820), a British naval officer from this era. This assumption has been reinforced by the fact that a Home I is located not far away. At the time of the Glorious First of June, however, Popham was serving under the Duke of York in Flanders as superintendent of inland navigation. His career was a checkered one, marked by much litigation over commercial dealings and an Admiralty court martial for his unauthorized attempt to promote a rebellion at Buenos Aires. He did a great deal of useful survey work, though, and was the author in 1803 of *Coast Signals*, a manual used by the RN for many years. Popham seems to have been forgiven for his transgressions, as he was promoted to rear adm in 1814 and knighted the year after. The island is a private nature refuge, owned in recent years by money manager Rudy North, and home since 1983 to the Murray A Newman Field Station, a research facility operated by the Vancouver Aquarium. Adjacent Little Popham I was named in 1951.

Porcher Inlet (53°57'00" 130°27'00" Extends into centre of Porcher I from E side of Kitkatla Inlet), **Porcher Island** (53°58'00" 130°25'00" SW of mouth of Skeena R, S of Prince Rupert), **Porcher Narrows** (53°53'00" 130°28'00" S end of Porcher Inlet), **Porcher Peninsula** (53°54'00" 130°42'00" SW extension of Porcher I). Cdr Edwin Augustus Porcher (d 1878) of HMS *Sparrowhawk* served on the Pacific Station 1865–68, during which time he investigated instances of unrest on the Nass R that threatened the Anglican mission at Kincolith (Gingolx). He entered the RN in 1837 and served as mate on HMS *Fly* during an important survey expedition to Australia, 1842–46. After joining HMS *Hibernia* in 1857 for a special assignment in the Middle East, Porcher co-authored an account of archeological discovery at Cyrene. He was also a talented artist; many of his watercolours are held by BC Archives and the National Library of Australia. Porcher was promoted to capt in 1868, retired in 1872 and then travelled about Europe until he died in Germany. Edwin Point and Porcher Ck on Porcher I also commemorate him. The 531-sq-km island was named by Lt Daniel Pender of the survey vessel *Beaver* about 1867. It is the traditional territory of the Kitkatla First Nation, but attracted a number of settlers after Prince Rupert developed. Several small communities were founded, including Oona R, which still survives, and a short-lived salmon cannery and dogfish oilery were established. *E W*

Porlier Pass (49°01'00" 123°35'00" SE of Nanaimo, between Galiano I and Valdes I, Gulf Is). Boca de Porlier

Porlier Pass, looking southwest. *Peter Vassilopoulos*

was named by Spanish naval officer José Maria Narváez on his historic 1791 examination of the Str of Georgia—the first by a European explorer. Antonio Porlier y Sopranis, Marquis of Bajamar, was Spain's minister of justice at the time of Narváez's voyage. The name, misspelled on charts as Portier Pass for many years, was corrected by the Geographic Board of Canada in 1905. Numerous vessels have come to grief in this rock-infested but much-used channel, where currents of up to 10 knots (18.5 km/h) occur on spring tides, and impressive overfalls and whirlpools are generated. Several rocks in the pass are named for vessels that "discovered" them: *see* Romulus Reef *and* Virago Point. The 59-m sidewheel steamer *Del Norte* hit the reefs S of Canoe Its in 1868 and sank while trying to back out of the passage in thick fog. The tug *Peggy McNeil* met its end there in 1923, with the loss of five crew members. A sixth survived only by climbing onto a bell buoy and then swimming to one of the tug's scows. Another tug, the *Point Grey*, hit Virago Rk in 1949 and was visible as a wreck for years before being washed into deeper waters. The pass is known locally as Cowichan Gap. *E W*

Portage Cove (50°05'00" 124°44'00" NE end of Gifford Peninsula, SE side of Desolation Sd, NW of Powell R). The Sliammon First Nation name for the flat isthmus at the head of this cove is Kígíyin, meaning "short crossing from one bay to another." It was once a popular portage route for canoes, as it eliminated a much longer paddle around Gifford Peninsula. In recent years, however, the isthmus, which is not part of Desolation Sd Marine Provincial Park, has been turned into a productive orchard and garden by its private owners, and portage attempts are not looked on with favour.

Portage Inlet (48°27'40" 123°25'10" NW of Gorge Waters, head of Victoria Hbr, just W of Victoria). This name was identified on Joseph Pemberton's 1855 map of SE Vancouver I and on early Admiralty charts from the 1860s. An ancient First Nation trail led between the head

of Portage Inlet and Thetis Cove on Esquimalt Hbr, across what is now Portage Regional Park in the municipality of View Royal. In the 19th century, RN crews heading to Victoria from the Esquimalt base would sometimes portage small boats across this piece of land if they wanted to avoid rough outside waters.

Port Alberni. *See* Alberni Inlet.

Port Alexander (50°51'00" 127°40'00" SE end of Nigei I, off NE Vancouver I). After RN officer Alexander Fraser Boxer. *See* Boxer Point. The feature was formerly known as Alexander Hbr.

Port Alice (50°23'00" 127°27'00" E side of Neroutsos Inlet, Quatsino Sd, NW end of Vancouver I). The Whalen Pulp & Paper Co built a pulp mill at this location in 1917 and named the townsite after Alice Whalen (1851–1922, née Broad). Alice was the mother of the entreprenurial Whalen brothers, from Port Arthur, Ont, who developed a short-lived pulp-mill empire in BC. James Whalen (1868–1929) was the driving force behind the company, though his brothers William, John and George were also involved. In 1917 the Whalens took over pulp mills at Woodfibre and Swanson Bay, as well as at Port Alice, but went into receivership in 1923. BC Pulp & Paper Co was formed in 1925 to take over and expand the Whalen mills. Port Alice, the only pulp mill on Vancouver I until 1945, was sold to the Koerner family's Alaska Pine & Cellulose Ltd (later Rayonier Canada Inc), in 1951. A new townsite, located 4 km from the mill, became BC's first "instant" municipality in 1965. The mill was owned by Western Forest Products Inc in the early 2000s and closed in 2004, then was sold to Neucel Specialty Cellulose Ltd in 2006 and reopened. *E*

Bird's-eye view of the Port Alice pulp mill, 1949. *Courtesy Tim Woodland*

Port Blackney. *See* Blackney Channel.

Port Brooks. *See* Brooks Bay, Klaskish Anchorage *and* Nasparti Inlet.

P

Port Browning. *See* Browning Channel.

Port Canaveral. *See* Canaveral Passage.

Port Chanal. *See* Chanal Point.

Port Clements (53°41'00" 132°11'00" E side of Masset Inlet, Graham I, QCI). The land at this location was pre-empted in 1908 by Elias James Tingley (1881–1964), who was trying to establish a townsite on Masset Inlet. At first he called his development Queenstown, a name suggested by James Martin, who had agreed to establish a general store at the new community and who hailed from Queenstown, Ireland (now known as Cobh). Tingley's application for a post office by that name was denied, however, and in 1913 he chose Port Clements instead, after Herbert Sylvester Clements (1865–1939), the region's MP. Clements returned the favour by arranging for the area's government wharf to be built at Tingley's townsite. Clements, a native of Ont, was a Conservative politician, broker, farmer and real-estate agent. He was originally sent to parliament from Ont, representing Kent West in 1904–8. After his defeat in the 1908 election, he moved to BC and was elected from the Comox-Atlin riding, 1911–17, and from Comox-Alberni, 1917–21. Port Clements, with a population of about 500 (half what it was in the early 1900s), survives as a logging and sawmilling centre, though tourism has become more important in recent years. Many residents work at nearby Juskatla. The village has a fine museum of local QCI history. *D E*

Porteau Cove (49°33'00" 123°14'00" E side of Howe Sd, S of Furry Ck, NW of Vancouver). This feature appears as Schooner Hbr on a 1908 mining survey map. The name Porteau—a contraction of *porte d'eau*, or "water gate" in French—was apparently suggested by a certain Mr Newberry, the accountant at the Deeks Sand & Gravel Co, which operated a quarry at the site in the early 1900s. John Frederick Deeks, owner of the gravel pit, was also postmaster of Porteau post office, open 1912–28. The PGE reserved land for a station at Porteau before 1914, but the line was not built through this area until 1955. A summer resort, with daily Union steamship service, was developed for Vancouver visitors. It was known at first as Porteau Landing but had its name changed, by petition, to Glen Eden in 1953. A 50-ha provincial marine park was established at the cove in 1981, with an artificial reef of five sunken ships offshore for scuba divers. The present name was officially restored in 1983. *E*

Port Edward (54°13'00" 130°17'00" NW of the mouth of the Skeena R, just S of Prince Rupert). This northern fishing village and Prince Rupert satellite community got its start about 1905, when land was staked by speculators hoping that it, and not Prince Rupert, would be designated the terminus of the GTP. A townsite was laid out in 1908

Port Edward, just south of Prince Rupert. *Peter Vassilopoulos*

and named after King Edward VII (1841–1910), the British monarch from 1901 to 1910. Port Edward developed as a fish-processing centre after losing the railway to its neighbour; several early canneries were located in the area, including the N Pacific, constructed in 1889 and now restored as a museum. The Port Edward Cannery was built right in the village in 1913 but did not open until 1918. It ran until 1931 and was later converted to a reduction plant that turned fish offal from all the Skeena R canneries into fertilizer. Nelson Bros Fisheries Ltd (later BC Packers Ltd) also operated a large cannery at Port Edward, 1943–81. In WWII the US Army built a major camp at Port Edward to supply its forces moving to and from Alaska through Prince Rupert. The army also built roads to connect the isolated village to the wider world. *E*

Port Eliza. *See* Eliza Passage.

Port Elizabeth (50°40'00" 126°28'00" S side of Gilford I, Knight Inlet, E of Port McNeill). After Lady Elizabeth Kennedy, wife of Viscount Gilford and eldest daughter of Arthur Kennedy, gov of Vancouver I, 1864–66. *See* Gilford Point. Named by Lt Daniel Pender about 1867.

Porter Bight (48°50'00" 123°21'30" NE side of Prevost I, E of Saltspring I, Gulf Is). Named in 2000 for Flight Lt John Edward Porter, from Victoria, who died in action over France on Aug 25, 1944, aged 22. He had completed 25 successful missions before being shot down while piloting a Lancaster heavy bomber with No 101 (RAF) Squadron. Two gunners survived the crash, but the other crew members, including Porter, are buried in the village cemetery at Boult-aux-Bois, Ardennes, Frances.

Porter Island (52°57'00" 129°34'00" E entrance to Pemberton Bay, S side of Dewdney I, Caamaño Sd), **Porter Reef** (52°16'00" 128°19'00" Entrance to Berry Inlet, Seaforth Channel, S end of Don Peninsula, NW of Bella Bella). James Porter (1822–1905) came to Victoria from England with his wife and two children in 1853, aboard the HBC supply ship *Norman Morison*. He was employed by the Puget's Sd Agricultural Co, an HBC subsidiary, as a farm labourer on Constance Cove Farm in Esquimalt. Porter I is probably named for his son, also James Porter (1851–1926), who was born in Kent and came to Victoria with his parents. James Jr worked for the provincial government and likely attended the old-timers' reunion of 1924 (*see* Adams Bay). Porter Reef, formerly known as Midge Reef, is believed to be named for Mary Ann Porter (1853–1935), a sister of James Jr, who was born shortly after the family arrived at Victoria. She married three times, to Thomas Craigie (d 1882), John Blackmore (in 1885) and William Cooper (in 1908), and died at Victoria, as did her brother and parents.

Port Essington in the early 1900s. *Author's collection*

Port Essington (54°09'00" 129°58'00" W side of mouth of the Ecstall R, S side of mouth of the Skeena R, SE of Prince Rupert). Capt George Vancouver gave the name Port Essington to the mouth of the Skeena, not realizing that it was the estuary of a major river. Later, the name became associated solely with the pioneer community founded on the S side of the river mouth by trader Robert Cunningham in 1871. (It seems strange that Vancouver failed to recognize the Fraser, Skeena and Nass as major rivers, dismissing their shallow channels and thickly vegetated mud flats as insignificant. From eye level, however, the mouths and lower reaches of the great rivers gave little hint of their upstream grandeur.) Vancouver was honouring his friend William Essington (1753–1816), who joined the RN at a young age, was a capt by 30, rose to vice adm on the strength of his performance as third-in-command at the 1808 Battle of Copenhagen and gained a knighthood in 1816. A Port Essington on the N coast of Australia is also named for him. In 1795, on his way home from the PNW, Vancouver met Essington and HMS *Sceptre* near St Helena and accompanied them back to England together with a convoy of E India Co vessels. Port Essington, accessible only by water, became the main stopping place on the lower Skeena, home to six salmon canneries, a sawmill, hotels, stores, brothels and a peak population of 2,000. From this terminus, flat-bottomed

sternwheelers churned up the Skeena to Hazelton. The town went into a long decline after Prince Rupert was born, and fire destroyed what remained in the 1960s. Spokshute Mtn, just SE of Port Essington, keeps alive the Tsimshian First Nation name for this site, which can be translated as "autumn camp ground" and refers to the annual visit to the area by local tribes for the rich salmon fishery. *E W*

Port Graves (49°28'00" 123°21'00" S side of Gambier I, E of Centre Bay, Howe Sd, NW of Vancouver). In 1859–60, Capt George Richards named many features in Howe Sd after participants in the Glorious First of June, a 1794 British naval victory over the French. Vice Adm Thomas Graves (1726–1802) was second-in-command of the Channel fleet, under Lord Howe, at that battle and was rewarded by being named Baron Graves of Gravesend. He had the unfortunate experience, as a rear adm, of being in charge of a doomed squadron of warships and a large merchant convoy bound from Jamaica to England in 1782. The ships were struck by a catastrophic cyclone, which destroyed more than 100 vessels and killed 3,000 men. Graves managed to escape the disaster in a merchant brig, though his flagship, HMS *Ramillies*, was lost, as was the 110-gun *Ville de Paris*, a prize of war and supposedly the finest and most expensive ship of that era. Port Graves is known locally as Long Bay. The Skxwúmish (Squamish) people call it Charl-kunch, or "deep bay." *W*

Port Guichon (49°05'00" 123°06'00" S side of mouth of the Fraser R, SW of Ladner). This agricultural settlement was named after Laurent Guichon (1836–1902), from the Savoy region of France, who took part in the Cariboo gold rush and then ranched in the Nicola valley with his brothers. He and his wife, Peronne (1854–1922, née Rey), took up farmland in Delta in the early 1880s. Laurent, who was also involved in the hotel business in New Westminster, built a store, wharf and hotel on his property and later subdivided some land for a townsite. Port Guichon was the terminus of a Great Northern Rwy branch line from Cloverdale, 1903–31; a rail and passenger ferry operated from the port to Sidney, connecting with the GNR's Vancouver I line. A number of Croatian immigrants, mostly Catholic fishing families, settled at Port Guichon.

Port Hardy. *See* Hardy Bay.

Port Harvey. *See* Harvey Point.

Port Huff. *See* Huff Rk *and* Rose Hbr.

Port Ingraham. *See* Ingraham Bay, Kiokathli Inlet *and* Nesto Inlet.

Port John (52°07'00" 127°50'00" N side of Evans Inlet, W side of King I, E of Bella Bella). After Rev John Fisher, Bishop of Salisbury, 1807–25. *See* Fisher Channel.

P

Portland Bay (52°47'00" 132°11'00" Between Tasu Sd and Kootenay Inlet, W side of Moresby I, QCI), **Portland Island** (48°44'00" 123°22'00" SE of Saltspring I, NE of Saanich Peninsula, Gulf Is). HMS *Portland* was the flagship of Rear Adm Fairfax Moresby, cdr-in-chief of the Pacific Station, 1850–53. The 52-gun, 1,339-tonne wooden sailing vessel was launched in 1822, served in the Mediterranean, 1834–38, and was decommissioned in 1862. Portland Bay was named in association with nearby Chads Point; Capt Henry Chads was the cdr of the *Portland* while it was in BC waters. Portland I, which was named in 1858 by Capt George Richards of HMS *Plumper*, in association with nearby Moresby I, was first settled by Hawaiian Islanders who had formerly worked for the HBC, including William Naukana and John Palua (*see* Kanaka Bluff). From 1927 to 1933 it was owned by Maj Gen Frank "One-Arm" Sutton, a soldier of fortune who helped Manchurian warlord Chang Tso-lin gain control over half of China. He planned to turn the 194-ha property into a luxurious resort with the best pheasant shooting in the British Empire, but fortunately for the pheasants, he went bankrupt. In 1958, when Princess Margaret was visiting BC, Premier W A C Bennett gave her the island; the Geographic Board of Canada briefly contemplated changing the name to Princess Margaret I but then thought better of it. The idea was that she would donate it back to the province as a park, but four years passed before anything was done, by which time outdoors club members were writing Her Highness embarrassing letters. Today, however, this Gulf Is jewel is forever protected as Princess Margaret Provincial Marine Park. The island's Sencoťen (Coast Salish) name is Sxecoten, meaning "dry mouth." *E*

Portland Canal (55°15'00" 130°00'00" Northern extension of Portland Inlet along the BC-Alaska boundary to Stewart), **Portland Inlet** (54°44'00" 130°24'00" NE of Chatham Sd, N of Prince Rupert). Capt George Vancouver named the canal in July 1793 after William Henry Cavendish Bentinck, 3rd Duke of Portland (1738–1809). He was a figurehead PM of Britain, briefly in 1783 and again in 1807–9, and occupied several other cabinet positions during his career, including home secretary (1794–1801) and lord president of the council (1801–5). Bentinck was also chancellor of Oxford Univ (1792–1809), president of London's Foundling Hospital (1793–1809) and lord lt of Nottinghamshire (1795–1809). Vancouver originally gave the name Brown Inlet to what is now Portland Inlet, after Capt William Brown of the trading vessel *Butterworth*, who had provided him with valuable information about the region (*see* Brown Passage). The Geographic Board of Canada, however, changed the name to Portland Inlet in 1924. Vancouver explored Portland Canal personally, using HMS *Discovery*'s yawl and launch, and was accompanied by the sloop *Prince Leboo*, one of Capt Brown's tenders. In 1903 the Alaska Boundary Tribunal determined that Portland Canal would form

part of the southern boundary between BC and Alaska. Portland Ck is named after Portland Canal, into which it flows. The Nisga'a people know the entire Portland Inlet/Portland Canal body of water as K'alii Xk'alaan (with *k'alaan* meaning "at the back of"). *E W*

Port Langford. *See* Langford.

Portlock Point (48°50'00" 123°21'00" E side of Prevost I, Swanson Channel, W of Mayne I, Gulf Is). Nathaniel Portlock (1749–1817), a native of Virginia, was an early fur trader on the Pacific coast. He joined the RN in 1771 and served as a master's mate aboard HMS *Discovery* on Capt James Cook's third voyage, 1776–80, during which many crew members acquired sea otter furs at Nootka Sd and sold them for great profit in China. Because of his PNW experience, Portlock, by then an RN lt, was chosen in 1785 to lead one of the first British trading expeditions to the W coast of N America, organized by Richard Cadman Etches and the King George's Sd Co. Portlock, in the *King George*, and George Dixon (who had been the armourer on HMS *Discovery* while Portlock was master's mate), with the smaller *Queen Charlotte*, made a successful journey, trading off Alaska in 1786–87 and returning to England in 1788. The two men published *A Voyage Round the World*, a narrative of their expedition, in 1789. Portlock later commanded HMS *Assistant* and in 1791 accompanied Capt William Bligh to the Pacific to help him carry breadfruit plants to the W Indies. In 1799 he captured a Dutch vessel with HMS *Arrow* and was promoted to capt. A lighthouse station at Portlock Point, constructed in

The light at Portlock Point, Prevost Island. *Andrew Scott*

1896, exploded and burned in 1964, killing keeper James Heanski. The light was later automated. *E W*

Port Louis. *See* Louis Point.

Port McNeill (50°35'00" 127°06'00" S side of Broughton Str, S of Malcolm I, NE side of Vancouver I). The logging community of Port McNeill sprang up in 1937 and soon became the service centre for a large surrounding area. It had a population of about 3,000 in the early 2000s and was the terminus for ferries running to Alert Bay on Cormorant I and Sointula on Malcolm I. It is named after the adjacent body of water, also known as Port McNeill, which in turn was named by HBC officials for Capt William McNeill, who established Ft Rupert near Port Hardy in 1849. The port was surveyed by Capt George Richards of HMS *Plumper* in 1860. *See* McNeill Bay for a more detailed biography of chief factor William McNeill. *E*

The pulp and paper mill at Port Mellon. *Andrew Scott*

Port Mellon (49°31'00" 123°29'00" W side of Thornbrough Channel, W side of Howe Sd, NW of Vancouver). Henry Augustus Mellon (1840–1916) was a former RN officer who came to Canada from England and worked as a master mariner for the Allan Line and Dominion Steamship Co. In 1886 he and his wife, Susanna Gertrude Clarke (c 1844–1926), moved to Vancouver, where he found employment as a marine surveyor and insurance agent, and as an examiner of masters and mates. He was eventually named a police magistrate and became vice-president of the British Canadian Wood Pulp & Paper Co, which built a mill on Howe Sd in 1907–9. Susanna Mellon was a major fundraiser for the arts in early Vancouver. Henry Mellon apparently chose the location for the pulp operation, and the site was named after him. The mill changed hands over the years and was taken over in 1951 by Canadian Forest Products Ltd. After Oji Paper Co of Japan became a joint owner in 1988, the mill was modernized and expanded, operating under the name Howe Sound Pulp & Paper Co. A small townsite for workers and their families was only accessible by water until 1953, when a road was built to

Gibsons, where most employees live today. Before Port Mellon mill was constructed, a resort named Seaside—a popular summer destination for boat trips from Vancouver—was located here. *E*

Port Montgomery. *See* Tasu Head.

Port Moody. *See* Moody Banks.

Port Neville. *See* Neville Point.

Port Renfrew (48°33'00" 124°25'00" SE side of Port San Juan, SW side of Vancouver I). The San Juan valley was settled by Europeans in the late 1880s and early 1890s, after the provincial government promised to build a road there from Sooke. A small community on Port San Juan (qv), originally known as San Juan, was apparently so often confused with San Juan I to the E that it was renamed Port Renfrew in 1895, possibly after the Prince of Wales (the future King Edward VII), one of whose titles was Baron Renfrew. Many homesteaders moved away, however, when the promised road did not materialize (it was finally built in 1958). Another round of construction occurred about 1900, when a wharf, store, hotel and sawmill were built at Port Renfrew in expectation that an iron mine would be established in the area. This hope was also dashed. Logging finally put the village on the map in the early 1900s; railway operations brought the timber to tidewater, where it was towed to Victoria mills. Today Port Renfrew, population about 400, is a starting point for the W Coast and Juan de Fuca marine trails. *E*

Port Renfrew in Port San Juan. *Peter Vassilopoulos*

Port San Juan (48°33'00" 124°27'00" SW side of Vancouver I, NW side of Juan de Fuca Str), **San Juan Point** (48°32'00" 124°27'00" E entrance to Port San Juan). In 1789, Spanish explorer José Maria Narváez was sent from Nootka Sd by Estéban Martínez to make a brief examination of the entrance to Juan de Fuca Str. He apparently visited Port San Juan on the feast day of John the Baptist (June 24). The following year, when Manuel Quimper made the first

P

European exploration of Juan de Fuca Str, he named this bay Puerto de San Juan ó de Narváez (Port San Juan *or* Port Narváez) after his fellow officer. The early fur traders knew it as Poverty Bay. Capt George Vancouver adopted the name Port San Juan on his chart, which is probably why it still exists today. The San Juan R and San Juan Ridge are named after the port, which was surveyed in 1847 by Lt Cdr James Wood of HMS *Pandora*. The San Juan Is in Washington state were named by Francisco Eliza in 1791, probably also after John the Baptist (San Juan Bautista). In 1859 a dispute erupted between Britain and the US over this archipelago. Should the international boundary run to the E, along Rosario Str, or to the W, along Haro Str? The disagreement led to an armed standoff—the so-called Pig War—and joint occupation of the islands before being resolved in favour of the US in 1872, when Haro Str became the border. *W*

Port Simpson (54°35'00" 130°25'00" NW side of Tsimpsean Peninsula, N of Prince Rupert). The name refers both to a body of water and to a Tsimshian First Nation community. The marine feature was long known as McLoughlin's Hbr, after senior HBC official John McLoughlin (*see* McLoughlin Bay), by whose authority the historic trading post of Ft Simpson was moved to this location in 1834. The harbour of Port Simpson first appears on an 1856 Admiralty chart prepared from George Inskip's 1853 survey, made while HMS *Virago* was being repaired on the beach beside the fort. Ft Simpson was named after Lt Aemilius Simpson (1792–1831) of the RN; it was originally erected on Nass Bay in 1831 and called Ft Nass. Simpson, from Scotland, was a hydrographer and a relative of George Simpson, the HBC gov for N America (his stepmother was George's aunt). In 1826, George offered his cousin a job as a surveyor; Aemilius took three years' leave from the RN and the two men travelled together to Upper Ft Garry (now Winnipeg), where survey work was required on the US boundary. Later that year Aemilius went overland to Ft Vancouver and charted the lower N shore of the Columbia R. In 1827, with the *Cadboro*, he made the first survey of the lower Fraser R and helped establish Ft Langley. Despite being an unpopular disciplinarian, Simpson was highly regarded by both McLoughlin and Gov Simpson and in 1829 was appointed superintendent of the HBC's marine dept. He was also made a chief trader. After selecting the site for Ft Nass and helping Peter Ogden with its construction, Simpson became ill and died there in 1831. The post was renamed in his honour. Its location was found to be unsatisfactory, and in 1834 it was moved S, along with its founder's remains. The rebuilt fort on McLoughlin's Hbr was a great success in its early days, producing large volumes of furs. About 2,000 members of the Tsimshian First Nation moved there in the 1840s and named their settlement Lax Kw'alaams (qv), or "place of wild roses." Famed Anglican missionary William Duncan got his start at the fort in 1857, and

Thomas Crosby, a Methodist, made it his base in 1874. The name of the community was changed to Port Simpson in the 1880s (in 1986 it changed again, to Lax Kw'alaams). In the early 1900s, nearby Prince Rupert became the regional centre, relegating Port Simpson to backwater status. HBC influence waned; the trading post burned down in 1914 and only a store operated from 1934 to 1954. By the 21st century there were few signs that this quiet Tsimshian community of 1,200 was once the most important outpost of the British Empire on the N Pacific coast. *E W*

Port Stephens. *See* Mt Stephens.

Port Washington (48°49'00" 123°19'00" W side of N Pender I, Gulf Is). After N Pender I pioneer Washington Grimmer. *See* Grimmer Bay.

Potts Bay (50°39'01" 126°37'16" NE side of Midsummer I, entrance to Knight Inlet, NE of Port McNeill). Named in 1959 for Flying Officer James Murray Clarke Potts, from Alert Bay, who was shot down over Burma on Jan 3, 1945, aged 24, while serving with No 215 (RAF) Squadron. His name is inscribed on the Singapore Memorial at Singapore's Kranji War Cemetery. The squadron, based at Calcutta, India, 1942–45, carried out bombing operations using Vickers Wellington and Consolidated Liberator aircraft. Nearby Potts Lagoon was named after his father (*see below*).

Potts Lagoon (50°33'17" 126°25'51" N side of W Cracroft I, Johnstone Str, E of Port McNeill). Murray Clarke Potts (1877–1954), from Ont, took courses in practical science at the Univ of Toronto, moved W and became a law student at Victoria in 1901. He married Catherine Louise Thompson (d 1948). In 1908, however, in a complete change of direction, he pre-empted land on the S side of this lagoon and fashioned a farm there, complete with cattle and a horse for ploughing. Potts received a Crown grant for his land in 1913 and acquired another grant, in the Nanaimo area, in 1921. In 1946 he moved from Cracroft to Alert Bay, where he became the Indian agent. Potts died at Vancouver. Nearby Potts Bay is named for his son (*see above*).

Potts Point (49°27'43" 123°21'51" W side of Port Graves, S side of Gambier I, Howe Sd, NW of Vancouver). Named in 1945 after Maj Gen Arthur E Potts (1891–1983), who was born in Northumberland, England, and educated at Univ of Edinburgh before doing graduate work at Cornell Univ. He entered WWI as a private, served in France, was wounded twice and emerged a lt. Potts became a prof of agriculture at the Univ of Sask (head of the dairy dept) and developed an officer training corps there, serving also as a militia col. In WWII, as a lt col, he took the Saskatoon Light Infantry overseas, and in 1941, by then a brigadier, he led the 2nd Canadian Infantry Brigade in Operation

Gauntlet, a successful raid that destroyed rich coal mines on the Norwegian island of Spitsbergen that German forces had intended to use. Potts was promoted to maj gen in 1943 and commanded the 6th Infantry Division, based at Victoria, and then Military District #2 in Toronto. After the war he served as a district administrator with the Dept of Veterans Affairs, retiring in 1955. Potts Point was formerly known as Boulder Point.

Poverty Bay. *See* Port San Juan.

Powell Hill (49°54'00" 124°32'54" N side of Powell R), **Powell River** (49°51'00" 124°32'00" E side of Str of Georgia, NW of entrance to Jervis Inlet, SE of Campbell R). Dr Israel Wood Powell (1836–1915), from Ont, was educated at McGill Univ in Montreal and first practised medicine at Port Dover. He moved to NZ and then, in 1862, to Victoria, where he worked as a surgeon and married Jane Branks in 1865. Powell was a leading Freemason in BC and a prominent public figure: member of Vancouver I's colonial legislative assembly, 1863–66, and chairman of the board of education, 1867–69. A staunch supporter of Confederation, he was offered the post of BC's first lt gov but chose to be superintendent of Indian Affairs instead, a position he held from 1872 to 1889. Powell took a non-confrontational approach to First Nation issues, supporting claims to land and justice but promoting assimilation and opposing potlatch ceremonies. He became a major collector of aboriginal artifacts and an astute and wealthy investor in land, especially in downtown Vancouver. Later in life, Powell was appointed the first president of the Medical Council of BC and the first chancellor of UBC. Powell R and Powell Lk were named in 1880 by Lt Cdr Vere Orlebar of HMS *Rocket*. The community of Powell R, located where the river enters the Str of Georgia, formed around one of BC's first pulp and paper mills, built in 1910–12 by the Brooks, Scanlon & O'Brien Co. This mill,

later owned by the Macmillan, Bloedel & Powell R Co, was at one time the world's largest, with 2,000 employees. The Powell R townsite, a well-preserved classic company town, was preserved as an official heritage area in 1995. The district of Powell R, established in 1955, also includes the former villages of Wildwood Heights and Cranberry Lk, as well as the commercial and residential centre of Westview. *E*

Powell Island (53°41'00" 132°22'00" S side of Masset Inlet, Graham I, QCI). William H Powell (1884–1948) was one of the hydrographers taking part in a survey of this area conducted in 1910 by Lt Cdr Philip Musgrave of the Canadian Hydrographic Service. Powell also participated in a survey of Dixon Entrance that year but then resigned at the end of the season. He was born in NS and graduated from McGill Univ with an engineering degree in 1909. Powell served as Vancouver's chief surveyor for many years and was engineer for the Greater Vancouver Water District, 1928–48. He also taught at UBC. In 1934 he received the Gzowski Gold Medal, awarded by the Engineering Institute of Canada for outstanding achievement.

Power Squadron Reef (49°11'10" 123°55'00" N of Protection I, E of Newcastle I, just NE of Nanaimo). This name was adopted in 1988 after being submitted by officers of the Nanaimo Power Squadron, who wished to commemorate the 20 years their organization had conducted courses in the region on boating skills and marine safety.

Powrivco Bay (52°41'00" 131°33'00" N side of Lyell I, off E side of Moresby I, QCI), **Powrivco Point** (52°42'20" 131°35'30" S side of Atli Inlet, Lyell I). Powrivco was the telegraph code name for the Powell R Co, which was a major purchaser of logs in the region, especially from the T A Kelley logging camp, located at the SW end of Atli

Early view of the Powell River paper mill. *Author's collection*

P

Inlet (*see* Takelley Cove). The company was founded in 1909 by the three US owners of the Brooks, Scanlon & O'Brien Co. They built a pulp and paper mill at Powell R and later established logging operations at Kingcome Inlet and in the QCI. After WWII the Powell R Co expanded by acquiring logging companies and sawmills, and was soon one of the world's largest producers of newsprint. In 1960 it merged with another major BC forestry company to become the Macmillan, Bloedel & Powell R Co. Powrivco Bay first appears on maps of the region in 1927. The point was named by the hydrographic service in 1957, in association with the bay. *E*

Prager Islands (53°46'00" 130°31'00" Between Goschen I and Dolphin I, Browning Entrance, S of Porcher I and Prince Rupert). Named after Dr A E Prager, an Anglican medical missionary stationed at Metlakatla and Kitkatla in the mid-1880s.

Preedy Harbour (48°59'00" 123°41'00" Off SW side of Thetis I, NW of Saltspring I, Gulf Is). Lt George William Preedy (1817–94) served in HMS *Constance*, under Capt Richard Courtenay, on the Pacific Station, 1846–49. He entered the RN in 1828 and was promoted to capt in 1855. Preedy was made a CB in 1858, when he was capt of HMS *Agamemnon*, after helping lay the first trans-Atlantic telegraph cable, which only worked for a couple of weeks. He was capt of HMS *Liffey*, 1858–62, in the English Channel, Mediterranean and W Indies, and also of HMS *Cumberland* at Sheerness dockyard. Preedy ended his career as flag capt to Adm William Martin, cdr-in-chief at Devonport, aboard HMS *Royal Adelaide*. He retired from the RN in 1870 and eventually rose to the rank of vice adm, retired, in 1879. The harbour was named by the Admiralty hydrographic office in 1853.

Preston Island (49°23'00" 123°28'00" S of Keats I, entrance to Howe Sd, NW of Vancouver), **Preston Point** (50°51'00" 126°51'00" N side of Tracey Hbr, N Broughton I, NE of Port McNeill). Named after Samuel Preston, who pre-empted land at Vancouver's Kitsilano Beach in 1873. According to records collected by Vancouver archivist Maj J S Matthews, Preston was a brother-in-law and employee of Jeremiah Rogers, the pioneer logger who cleared much of Kitsilano from his camp at Jericho Beach. Samuel's brother Robert was supposedly the camp foreman. In 1882, Preston sold his land to Samuel Greer, but unfortunately for the purchaser, the property turned out to be part of a 2,500-ha grant given to the CPR by the province of BC. The CPR didn't recognize Greer's title (Preston had never acquired a Crown grant) and sent Sheriff Thomas Armstrong to evict him. Greer shot the sheriff, and Justice Matthew Begbie sent him to jail. He contested the loss of the property for many years, but without success. Preston I was formerly known as Round I but was renamed in 1945. Its owner, Richard G Bates of Vancouver, tried in vain to change its

name to Bates I in 1973, after his relative, Sir Percy Bates, a former chairman of Cunard Steamships Ltd.

West side of Prevost Island, Gulf Islands. *Kevin Oke*

Prevost Island (48°50'00" 123°23'00" E of Ganges Hbr and Saltspring I, W of Mayne I, Gulf Is), **Prevost Passage** (48°42'00" 123°19'00" E of N Saanich Peninsula, S of Moresby I, Gulf Is), **Prevost Point** (52°06'20" 130°56'50" E side of Kunghit I, QCI). RN officer James Charles Prevost (1810–91) served two commissions on the Pacific Station: 1850–54 and 1857–60. He entered the navy in 1823 and was promoted to cdr in 1845. From 1850 to 1852 he was assigned to HMS *Portland*, flagship of station cdr-in-chief Rear Adm Fairfax Moresby, who was also Prevost's father-in-law. (He had married 22-year-old Ellen Mary Moresby in 1842.) Prevost took command of the paddle sloop *Virago* at Valparaiso in 1852 and was sent to the QCI to maintain order after the plundering of the US schooner *Susan Sturgis*. With the assistance of George Inskip, the *Virago*'s master, he spent much time in 1853 doing survey work along the NW coast of Graham I, in Houston Stewart Channel and near Ft Simpson. A religious man, Prevost was appalled by the wretched conditions that prevailed at First Nation camps around HBC posts, especially Ft Simpson. Back in England he persuaded the Church Missionary Society to send a representative to the N BC coast, and William Duncan, who would later gain fame for his Anglican mission at Metlakatla, travelled to Victoria in 1856 aboard Prevost's new command, HMS *Satellite*. During this second stint in BC, Prevost, now a capt, was also chief British envoy on the international commission set up to survey the US-Canada border, but he was unable to resolve the San Juan Is boundary squabble, which nearly escalated into an armed conflict. Later he appeared as a witness when the dispute went to arbitration under the auspices of Emperor Wilhelm I of Germany. Prevost ended his career as superintendent of the Gibraltar naval base, 1864–69, and reached the rank of adm, retired, in 1880. Several other geographic features in BC are named for him, including Prevost Hill in Saanich, Mt Prevost NW of Duncan, Charles Is in the QCI, and James Bay and Charles Rks at Prevost I. Prevost Hill, Prevost I and Prevost Passage were named by Capt Henry Richards of HMS *Plumper* in 1858–59. The island's Sencoťen (Coast Salish) name is Wáwen, meaning "place of seal hunting," while the Huľqumi'num people know it as Hwu'eshwum, or "place of seals." Kunghit I in the QCI was formerly called Prevost I but was renamed by the Geographic Board of Canada in 1904. *E W*

Price Bay (48°27'00" 123°27'00" N end of Esquimalt Hbr, SE end of Vancouver I). This name, adopted in 1966, commemorates Henry (1837–1909) and Richard Price (1839–1921), who bought the Six Mile House at nearby Parson's Bridge about 1894 and turned it into a hotel. The Six Mile was one of BC's oldest pubs, established by William Parson in 1856. The Price brothers came out to Canada from Ireland—Henry in 1862 and Richard in 1866—and joined the Cariboo gold rush, then farmed in the Colwood area. Richard married Hannah Maria Birkenhead at Victoria in 1896.

Price Island (52°24'00" 128°42'00" Between Laredo Sd and Milbanke Sd, NW of Bella Bella). Capt John Adolphus Pope Price (d 1874) served on the Pacific Station, 1865–68, as capt of HMS *Scout*. He entered the RN in 1829, was present at the 1840 siege of Acre and participated in the Crimean War as 1st lt of HMS *Nile*. In 1869, Price was appointed commodore and senior officer at Hong Kong, with his pennant on HMS *Princess Charlotte*. He retired from the RN in 1870. Named by Lt Daniel Pender, Admiralty hydrographer on the BC coast, in 1866. Chalk I in Barkley Sd, formerly known as Price I, was probably named for him as well. *W*

Pride Rock (52°39'00" 128°51'00" N end of Laredo Sd, off S side of Princess Royal I). Sapper Charles Pride (1837–97) was a member of the Columbia detachment of Royal Engineers, which served in BC 1858–63. He apparently chose to stay on in BC after the unit was disbanded, but little is known of his later life. He was listed as being an inmate of the New Westminster insane asylum in 1896.

Priestland Cove (49°31'00" 123°55'00" In Halfmoon Bay, Str of Georgia, NW of Sechelt and Vancouver). Charles Priestland, a plasterer by trade, pre-empted land on this cove in 1892 and settled there with his English wife, Clara (1858–1933). A wharf was built, steamships stopped, and from 1904 to 1931, Clara ran the local post office, which was originally called Welcome Pass but renamed Halfmoon Bay in 1914. She was also in charge of the telegraph office. Charles died in the late 1890s and Clara remarried, to John Lyell, also from England, who worked as a fisherman and trapper. Lyell became the prime suspect in the 1922 murder of a young logger named Rob Rainey. He disappeared and is thought to have fled to Australia.

Prince Group (52°00'00" 128°15'00" Off SW end of Campbell I, Queens Sd, SW of Bella Bella). Named in 1944 after the ships of the Prince Line, owned by CN Steamships. In the 1910s, when the Prince Line was still a GTP operation, it included such vessels as the *Prince Albert* and *Prince John*, as well as the much larger and finer *Prince George* and *Prince Rupert*. The Prince Group, however, refers only to the three luxurious steamships built for CN in the UK in 1930 and converted in 1939 to armed merchant cruisers for the RN: the *Prince David*, *Prince Henry* and *Prince Robert*. For more information on these individual vessels *see* David Ledge, Henry Rk *and* Robert I, all located in the vicinity of the Prince Group. *E*

Prince Leboo Island (54°27'00" 130°59'00" SW of Dundas I, Dixon Entrance, NW of Prince Rupert). The *Prince Leboo* (also spelled *Le Boo* and *Lee Boo*) was a small, 50-tonne sloop present on the BC coast in 1792–94. It was commanded by a mariner named Sharp and was part of a fur-trading expedition led by Capt William Brown of the *Butterworth* (*see* Brown Passage). Brown and his vessels encountered Capt George Vancouver in Chatham Sd in 1793 and led HMS *Discovery* and *Chatham* to safe anchorage at the N end of Stephens I. Brown provided Vancouver with valuable information about the area and sent the *Prince Leboo* to guide him on his explorations of Portland Canal and Observatory Inlet.

Prince of Wales Range (50°19'23" 125°47'04" S of Johnstone Str, E of Sayward, NW of Campbell R), **Prince of Wales Reach** (49°54'00" 123°55'00" Jervis Inlet, E of Powell R, NW of Vancouver). These features were named for King Edward VII (1841–1910) while he was the Prince of Wales. Albert Edward Saxe-Coburg-Gotha held this title, traditionally given to the heir apparent to the British throne, longer than anyone in British history: 59 years (though Prince Charles would surpass this in 2011). He became king in 1901, on the death of his mother, Queen Victoria. Prince of Wales Reach was named by Capt George Richards of HMS *Plumper* about 1860.

Prince Rupert (54°19'00" 130°19'00" NW side of Kaien I, just N of the mouth of the Skeena R), **Prince Rupert Harbour** (54°20'00" 130°18'00" Off W and NW sides of Kaien I). Kaien I was chosen as the terminus for the GTP in the early 1900s, and land clearing and construction began in 1906. Several informal names emerged for the new community: Baconville, after GTP harbour engineer James Bacon, for the dockside area where the GTP offices were erected; Knoxville, after miner John Knox, for one residential district; and Vickersville, after police chief John Vickers, for another. The GTP decided to hold a public contest to name the future city and offered a prize of $250 for the winner. About 12,000 entries were received, and the name Prince Rupert, submitted by Eleanor Macdonald of Winnipeg, was chosen. But there was a problem; the

Water taxis in Prince Rupert Harbour. *Andrew Scott*

rules stipulated that entries should not contain more than ten letters. Prince Rupert has 12. So GTP officials, to appear fair, also awarded $250 to two other entrants who had submitted a name that closely resembled Prince Rupert but actually complied with the rules: Port Rupert. Both versions commemorated the flamboyant Prince Rupert of the Rhine (1619–82), who was created Duke of Cumberland by his uncle, Britain's King Charles I, and who also held the title of Duke of Bavaria. A successful soldier in an unsuccessful cause, he commanded the Royalist cavalry in the English Civil War at the tender age of 23 but was banished from Britain by parliament in 1646. Rupert spent his exile as a Caribbean buccaneer, then returned after the Restoration to become England's naval cdr, a talented artist and inventor, and the first gov of the HBC. The huge Hudson Bay watershed, originally granted to the HBC as a trading monopoly, was named Rupert's Land in his honour. Prince Rupert Hbr was formerly known as Lima Hbr, while Tuck Inlet, which today refers only to the waters NE of Prince Rupert Hbr, was considered at one time to extend to Digby I. In 1907, though, D'Arcy Tate of the GTP's legal dept informed Canada's minister of the Interior that his company "[desired] to discontinue the use of the names Lima Hbr and Tuck's Inlet, and to substitute therefor Prince Rupert Hbr." The GTP's desire was speedily fulfilled, in 1908. Prince Rupert, of course, grew into an important port—albeit more slowly than most people anticipated—and today sends grain and coal to Asia as well as serving as a commerical fishing centre and a ferry and cruise ship terminus. The HBC post of Ft Rupert on NE Vancouver I was also named after the dashing prince, as is nearby Rupert Inlet (qv). *E W*

Princesa Channel (49°43'00" 126°38'00" E of Nootka I, N of Strange I, Nootka Sd, W side of Vancouver I). The Spanish naval frigate *Princesa* (often spelled *Princesca*) was built at San Blas, Mexico, in 1777 and participated in a number of historic voyages on the Pacific coast of N America. Ignacio de Arteaga took the vessel to Alaska in 1779, accompanied by Juan Francisco de la Bodega y Quadra in the *Favorita*, in an attempt to discover the NW

Passage before Capt James Cook should find it. In the early 1780s the *Princesa* was used to supply Monterey and San Diego from Mexico, often with Estéban José Martínez in command. The vessel sailed to Alaska again in 1788, this time commanded by Martínez (with the *San Carlos*, under Gonzales López de Haro, as consort), to investigate the extent of Russian activity in the PNW. Spanish authorities were alarmed at what they discovered, and Martínez and López de Haro were sent N again from Feb to Dec 1789, with the same vessels, to establish a Spanish base at Nootka Sd. The *Princesa* returned to Nootka in 1790, under Jacinto Caamaño, and in 1792, under Salvador Fidalgo, and spent the winter of 1792–93 there, guarding the Spanish outpost. In 1794, Fidalgo and the *Princesa* took José Manuel de Álava, who became the Spanish commissioner for the Nootka Sd treaty after Quadra died, to Nootka to continue negotiations with Capt George Vancouver. Princesa Channel was formerly known as Boat Channel.

Princess Alice Island (52°08'00" 128°26'00" S of Athlone I, Bardswell Group, Queens Sd, W of Bella Bella). Princess Alice, Countess of Athlone (1883–1981), was a granddaughter of Queen Victoria; her father was Prince Leopold, the queen's youngest son. She married Sir Alexander Cambridge, Earl of Athlone (*see* Athlone I), who was named gov gen of Canada, 1940–46, and had earlier served as gov gen of S Africa, 1924–31. The princess was a strong supporter of the war effort while she lived in Canada and revisited the country several times after her husband's tour of duty was finished. She was named the first chancellor of the Univ of the W Indies, in 1950. At her death she was the last surviving grandchild of Queen Victoria and the longest-lived member of the British royal family (a record since broken by Queen Elizabeth the Queen Mother and by Princess Alice, Duchess of Gloucester).

Princess Bay (48°43'00" 123°22'00" SE end of Portland I, NE of Saanich Peninsula, Gulf Is). This name was adopted in 1978 in association with Princess Margaret Marine Park, which comprises the whole of Portland I. The park was named in 1967 after the sister of Queen Elizabeth II, who visited BC in 1958 (*see* Portland Bay for more information). Princess Bay was formerly known as Princess Margaret Bay and Tortoise Bay.

Princess Louisa Inlet (50°11'00" 123°48'00" E side of Queens Reach, N end of Jervis Inlet, NW of Vancouver). Capt George Richards of HMS *Plumper* named many features around Jervis Inlet in 1860 after Queen Victoria and the members of her immediate family. It is not exactly certain whether he had Princess Louise (1848–1939), the queen's fourth daughter, in mind as this inlet's namesake, or Princess Mary Louise Victoria, Duchess of Kent (1786–1861), the queen's mother. For a brief biography of Princess Louise—whose husband, the Marquess of Lorne, became gov gen of Canada—*see* Louise I. Queen Victoria's mother was a German widow who married Prince Edward, the fourth son of King George III. The future queen was their only child. The inlet, now a provincial marine park, is a BC scenic icon, surrounded by steep mountain slopes and draped with waterfalls. Its Sechelt First Nation name is Swíwelát, which has been translated as "facing the rising sun." *See* Macdonald I *and* Malibu It for more details. *E*

Princess Royal Channel (53°10'00" 128°40'00" Between Princess Royal I and the mainland coast), **Princess Royal Island** (52°55'00" 128°50'00" Between Pitt I and Swindle I, E of Caamaño Sd and Aristazabal I), **Princess Royal Point** (49°45'00" 126°27'00" SW of Nesook Bay, W side of Tlupana Inlet, Nootka Sd, W side of Vancouver I). The *Princess Royal*, a small sloop of about 60 tonnes—presumably named after Princess Charlotte, the eldest daughter of King George III—had an extraordinary career on the BC coast. It left England in 1786, under Charles Duncan, accompanying the larger *Prince of Wales*, under James Colnett, on a fur-trading expedition to the PNW, financed by Richard Etches and the King George's Sd Co. After spending the summer of 1787 on the BC coast and the winter in Hawaii, the vessels returned to BC in 1788 and separated, with Duncan trading along the N coast opposite the QCI. He named the entire archipelago between Pitt I and Princess Royal I after his ship. Capt George Vancouver, in 1793, honoured Duncan and his vessel by applying the name Princess Royal to one specific island. Colnett and Duncan sold their furs in China in 1788, and Duncan sailed the *Prince of Wales* back to England. Colnett then took the *Argonaut* to BC in 1789, accompanied again by the *Princess Royal*, this time under the command of Thomas Hudson. Both ships were seized at Nootka Sd by Spanish naval officer Estéban Martínez and taken, along with their crews, to Mexico, thus precipitating the sabre-rattling episode known as the Nootka Crisis. In 1790, by which time Spain had agreed to return the *Princess Royal* to its rightful owners, Spanish naval officer Manuel Quimper sailed the vessel (now renamed the *Princesa Real*) back to Nootka Sd; Francisco Eliza, Spanish cdr at Nootka, then sent it to make the first European exploration of Juan de Fuca Str. In 1791, Quimper finally returned the sloop to the British at Macau, but it was in such poor shape that the Spanish had to offer a cash payment instead. The hulk was damaged by a hurricane soon after and sold for salvage. Princess Royal I, at 2,274 sq km, is the fourth-largest island in BC and has been the site of a salmon cannery (Butedale), a gold mine (Surf Inlet) and enough clearcut logging to concern biologists studying the region's population of rare white Kermode bears. Princess Royal Channel was named in association with the island by the hydrographic service in 1926; Princess Royal Point was adopted as a name in 1935. *E W*

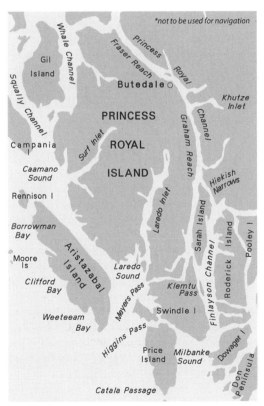

not to be used for navigation

Whale Channel · Gil Island · Squally Channel · Fraser Reach · Princess Royal Reach · Butedale · Khutze Inlet · Campania I · Surf Inlet · PRINCESS ROYAL ISLAND · Graham Reach · Channel · Caamano Sound · Rennison I · Laredo Inlet · Hiekish Narrows · Borrowman Bay · Sarah Island · Pooley I · Moore Is · Aristazabal Island · Laredo Sound · Roderick Island · Finlayson Channel · Clifford Bay · Klemtu Pass · Meyers Pass · Swindle I · Weeteeam Bay · Higgins Pass · Price Island · Milbanke Sound · Dowager · Don Peninsula · Catala Passage

Princess Royal Island. *Reproduced with the permission of the Canadian Hydrographic Service*

Kermode bear, Princess Royal Island. *Greg Shea*

Princess Royal Reach (50°02'00" 123°52'00" Between Queens Reach and Prince of Wales Reach, Jervis Inlet, NW of Vancouver). Named about 1860 by Capt George Richards of HMS *Plumper* after Princess Victoria (1840–1901), the eldest child of Queen Victoria and Prince Albert. In 1858 she married Prince Frederick of Prussia (1831–88) and later became the empress of Germany and queen of Prussia. Princess Royal is a title traditionally (though not automatically) granted to the eldest daughter of the king and queen of England.

Principe Channel (53°29'00" 129°59'00" E of Banks I, W of Pitt I and McCauley I), **Principe Islets** (53°15'00"

P

129°38'00" SE end of Principe Channel, off SW Pitt I). Spanish naval officer Jacinto Caamaño and the *Aránzazu* were assigned in 1792 to explore the BC N coast on either side of Dixon Entrance and search for the fictitious Str of Fonte (supposedly a navigable sea passage across N America). Caamaño sailed S between Banks I (which he called Isla de la Calamidad, or Calamity I) and McCauley and Pitt islands (which he thought were one and called Isla Enriquez, after famed Spanish naval official Juan Antonio Enriquez) and named this passage Canal del Principe (Spanish for "prince"). The name survived because Capt George Vancouver, who had a copy of Caamaño's chart, adopted it in 1793. PNW cartography expert Henry Wagner has suggested that Carlos, Prince of Asturias (1748–1819), is the *principe* in question. He became King Charles IV of Spain, 1788–1808, then abdicated in favour of Napoleon.

Pringle Rock (50°08'00" 124°44'00" SW of Melville I, NE side of Desolation Sd, NW of Powell R). Rev George Charles Fraser Pringle (1873–1949) was in charge of the Presbyterian Loggers' Mission on the BC coast, 1920–25, and then superintendent of BC coastal missions for the United Church. He was born in Ont and went to the Yukon, 1899–1910, where he was ordained. He ministered to miners in the region around Dawson City. After serving in WWI he was chaplain on the Canadian hospital ship *Araguaya* before coming W to work as a missionary. Pringle was based at Van Anda on Texada I and responsible for a vast area extending as far N as Knight Inlet. He travelled to all the logging camps, First Nation villages, canneries and other settlements by boat, at first in the derelict launch known as the *Mina W* and then in his 12-m mission boat *Sky Pilot*. He wrote several books about the coast mission and the Yukon, including *Tillicums of the Trail*, *Adventures in Service* and *In Great Waters*.

Prior Island (53°03'00" 129°36'00" Between Trutch I and Lotbinière I, Estevan Group, SE of Banks I), **Prior Passage** (52°27'00" 128°59'00" Between S tip of Aristazabal I and Munro I, Laredo Sd, NW of Bella Bella). Edward Gawler Prior (1853–1920), from Yorkshire, came to BC in 1873 as a mining engineer and worked as assistant manager of a Nanaimo coal company. He served as BC's inspector of mines in the late 1870s, then went into the hardware and machinery business, and also became a politician, winning election as a Victoria MLA, 1886–88 and 1901–3, and as Victoria's MP, 1888–1901 (except for a brief period when he was made Dominion controller of inland revenue). Prior's 1900 victory as an MP was declared void due to election irregularities, and he was named BC's minister of Mines instead, becoming premier in 1902–3 before being dismissed by the lt gov for awarding a major government contract to his own company. He ran for MP again in 1904 but was defeated. Prior remained active in business and in the militia, and, despite the scandal of his premiership, was

appointed lt gov of BC for 1919–20, dying in office. Prior Passage was named by the hydrographic service in 1927 and Prior I in 1950. Prior Lk N of Victoria, and Prior Peak in the Kootenays are also named for him. *E*

Procter Rocks (52°51'00" 131°45'00" Off S side of Selwyn Inlet, E side of Moresby I, QCI). Named after Thomas Gregg Procter (1862–1913), a real-estate promoter from Nelson who travelled to the E side of Moresby I in the early 1900s to try his mining luck. Like many others, he did not stay long. He was from England and had been a midshipman in the RNR as a youngster. Procter came to Nelson about 1890 and was soon manager of the Kootenay Valley Co, which speculated in land in the region. In 1891 he built a lodge on the W arm of Kootenay Lk, known as Procter's Landing, then sold it in 1903 to Gilbert Snow, who turned it into the well-known Outlet Hotel. Some CPR workers settled nearby, and a sawmill opened in 1906, followed by a jam factory. Procter became the village's first postmaster, 1906–8, but retired to Oak Bay, where he died.

The historic steamship *Beaver* aground at Prospect Point. *VPL 798*

Prospect Point (49°19'00" 123°08'00" S side of First Narrows, Burrard Inlet, Vancouver). The point, obviously named for its fine view of the N Shore mountains, was the site of an early lighthouse marking the SW entrance to Vancouver Hbr. The light was constructed in 1888 and kept by John Grove until 1926, when it was automated. In 1910 a signal station was built on the cliff above the lighthouse, near where the restaurant is today; it regulated all shipping activity through First Narrows until 1939, when the Lions Gate Bridge was built. In the 19th century this Stanley Park site was known as Observation Point. The shoreline directly below became the final resting place of the PNW's first steamship, the *Beaver*, which was run onto the rocks in 1888 by an inebriated crew and remained there for years.

Protection Island (49°10'44" 123°55'12" SE of Newcastle I, Nanaimo Hbr, off SE side of Vancouver I). This feature was first named Douglas I, after Vancouver I gov James

Douglas, by the officers of the HBC. In 1853 it became Protection I—a name descriptive of the island's position, which shelters the harbour of Nanaimo. Coal mining ocurred there from the 1880s to the 1930s, and a quarry provided sandstone for the Nanaimo courthouse. Today it is a residential suburb of Nanaimo, but one that can only be reached by water.

Providence Rock (52°08'45" 128°33'00" Milbanke Sd, SW of Athlone I, off Cape Mark, W of Bella Bella). Named in 1948 for Sister Mary Providence (Mary Ellen Tucker, 1837–1904), who arrived at Victoria in 1859 to become superior of the Sisters of St Ann. The first members of this community of nuns had come out the year before and established a school. Sister (later Mother) Providence supervised the activities of her order in western Canada for more than 20 years, and though she rarely left the convent, she had a far-reaching influence. An orphanage and a hospital were opened in Victoria, and convents and schools in New Westminster, Kamloops, Vancouver, Nanaimo, Duncan and Mission. In Nora Lugrin's *Pioneer Women of Vancouver I*, Sister Providence is described as "the greatest woman of the time in BC." Providence Rk was known before 1948 as Discovery Rk.

Prowse Point (49°29'00" 124°21'00" S side of False Bay, Lasqueti I, Str of Georgia). Richard Prowse, a former cpl in the Royal Marines, pre-empted land on Lasqueti I in 1879 and 1884, receiving Crown grants in 1884 and 1889. He had moved to the island prior to 1875, making him one of its very first European settlers. It is believed that, during his stay there, he prospected for gold and was involved in early mining ventures. Prowse, whose name is sometimes spelled Prouse, may later have moved to the Nanaimo area and worked as a road foreman.

Prussian Island. *See* Allies I.

Pruth Bay (51°39'00" 128°07'00" W end of Kwakshua Channel, NW end of Calvert I, S of Bella Bella). The *Pruth* was a 327-tonne HBC barque and supply ship that sailed, under master Thomas Meay, from London to Victoria in 1861. A record also exists of the *Pruth* sailing from London to NZ in 1858. The vessel was named for a river in Russia. In the 2000s, Pruth Bay was the site of a luxurious fishing lodge called The Cliffs at Hakai Beach.

Puffin Cove (52°30'00" 131°44'00" NW of Gowgaia Bay, W side of Moresby I, QCI). Named in 1963 by former US Navy officer Neil Carey (b 1922) and Betty Lowman Carey (b 1914), a resourceful US couple who moved to the QCI in 1964. The Careys had originally visited the islands in 1955 in their 6-m Grand Banks dory, the *Thunderbird*. They settled first at Sandspit but soon built a cabin and second home at Puffin Cove, transporting most of their construction materials and possessions in a converted

8-m lifeboat, the *Skylark*. The Careys both wrote books about the Pacific coast. Neil is the author of *A Guide to the Queen Charlotte Islands* (1975) and *Puffin Cove* (1982). Betty's *Bijaboji* (2004) recounts her daring journey by dugout canoe from Puget Sd to Alaska in 1937. The QCI are an important breeding ground for tufted puffins— brightly coloured seabirds with large parrot-like bills. Another geographic feature named for this iconic species is **Puffin Islet** (48°54'00" 125°23'00" Broken Group, E side of Loudoun Channel, Barkley Sd, W side of Vancouver I), marked on an 1861 Admiralty chart by RN hydrographer George Richards.

Puget Bluff (50°09'00" 125°21'00" W side of Quadra I, Seymour Narrows, NW of Campbell R), **Puget Cove** (48°26'00" 123°15'00" E side of Chatham I, SW side of Haro Str, just E of Oak Bay and Victoria). Peter Puget (1765– 1822) was 2nd lt aboard HMS *Discovery* at the beginning of Capt George Vancouver's historic voyage of exploration to the PNW. He joined the RN as a capt's servant in 1778 and met Vancouver in 1783 when assigned to HMS *Europa* in the W Indies. Puget was appointed 1st lt of the *Discovery* in 1792, when Zachary Mudge was sent back to England with dispatches, and cdr of HMS *Chatham*, the *Discovery*'s tender, at the end of that year, when Lt William Broughton also went home with official documents. In 1797, just before he was promoted to post capt, he married Hannah Elrington (1779-1849), and the following year he assisted Vancouver with the text and charts from his PNW voyage. Puget had a number of commands in the RN, including HMS *Goliath*, in which he played an important role at the 1807 2nd Battle of Copenhagen. He went on to appointments as commissioner of the navy at Flushing (1809) and at Madras, India (1810–18), where he was responsible for the upkeep and provisioning of all RN vessels in the region. In 1815, Puget was made a CB and in 1821 became a rear adm. The main feature named after this officer, of course, is Puget Sd in Washington state, which he explored with the ship's boats in 1792. Puget Bluff was formerly known as North Bluff, Puget Cove as Refuge Cove. *W*

Pullen Island (52°03'00" 128°17'00" Off SW side of Campbell I, just SW of Bella Bella). Named in 1944 by regional hydrographer Henri Parizeau after RCN officer Hugh Francis Pullen (1905–83). He was born at Toronto and lived mostly at Halifax, attending the Royal Naval College of Canada as a cadet in 1920. Pullen was a noted destroyer cdr in WWII and was CO at one time or another of HMCS *St Francis*, *Ottawa* and *St Laurent*. He also served as superintendent of the naval armament depot at Halifax and as executive officer of the cruiser *Uganda*. After the war, Pullen was promoted to capt and appointed director of naval reserves (1945–47), CO of the destroyer *Nootka* (1947–48) and CO of the cruiser *Ontario* (1949– 51). He became commodore in 1951, and rear adm and

P

chief of naval personnel in 1953. His final posts, before his 1960 retirement, were senior officer Pacific (1955–57) and maritime cdr Atlantic (1957–60). Pullen would go on to play important roles in the formation and operation of maritime museums on both the E and W coasts of Canada. Pullen I was formerly known as Cliff I.

Pulteney Point (50°38'00" 127°09'00" SW end of Malcolm I, off NE side of Vancouver I, opposite Port McNeill). After Adm Sir Pulteney Malcolm of the RN. *See* Malcolm I. In the early 1900s, Cdr Cortland Simpson of HMS *Egeria* renamed this feature Graeme Point (qv), but the Geographic Board of Canada changed it back to Pulteney Point shortly thereafter, following a complaint by author and mariner John Walbran. A lighthouse was erected on the point in 1905 and staffed until 1913 by Austin Makela, one of the leaders of the utopian Finnish colony of Sointula. The colony was established on Malcolm I in 1901 but collapsed the same year the light station was built. *W*

Pulton Bay (50°18'00" 125°16'00" N end of Quadra I, Okisollo Channel, N of Campbell R), **Pulton Point** (50°18'00" 125°17'00" W side of Pulton Bay). A note at BC's Geographical Names Office suggests that Pulton Bay was named in 1902 by Lt Col William Anderson, Canada's superintendent of lighthouses and chief engineer of the Dept of Marine and Fisheries, after a "lumberman using Okisollo Channel."

Purcell Rock (52°39'25" 127°01'10" NE of Skowquiltz Bay, N side of Dean Channel, NW of Bella Coola). Supposedly named after a gold miner who prospected in this area in 1899—probably Michael E Purcell (1857–1925), from Wales, who had a long career as a mining engineer working mainly in Rossland.

Purfleet Point (49°10'00" 122°59'00" W tip of Annacis I, lower Fraser R). This feature appears on an Admiralty chart from 1859–60 and is presumably named for Purfleet, Essex, a village on the Thames R, SE of London. In the 18th century, after a serious explosion at the Woolwich Garrison, the British government stored gunpowder at this site and stationed a garrison there to protect it. Five partly buried magazines, each with walls more than 1 m thick, were surrounded by moats and additional walls. Only one is preserved today, part of the Purfleet Garrison Heritage and Military Centre.

Purvis Point (49°08'00" 123°49'00" W end of Mudge I, S of Gabriola I, Gulf Is). Lt John Child Purvis (1832–1904) served on the Pacific Station, 1859–61, aboard HMS *Pylades*, under Capt Michael de Courcy. He came from an old naval family and entered the RN in 1845, winning promotion to lt in 1854 and cdr in 1865. He was back on

the Pacific Station for a second stint in 1866–69, under Capt Richard Powell, in HMS *Topaze*. In 1868 he helped erect a monument to Alexander Selkirk, the castaway who served as a model for Daniel Defoe's *Robinson Crusoe*, on remote Juan Fernández Is off Chile (*see* Topaze Hbr). Purvis became a capt in 1872 and worked his way up the retired list to vice adm, in 1894. Named in 1905 by Cdr John Parry of HMS *Egeria*, who was doing survey work in the area (and had originally planned to call the feature Zachariah Point, perhaps assuming, incorrectly, that Mudge I was named after Capt George Vancouver's 1st lt Zachary Mudge). *W*

Pylades Channel (49°06'00" 123°42'00" Between Valdes I and the De Courcy Group, S of Gabriola I, Gulf Is), **Pylades Island** (49°04'00" 123°41'00" Southernmost island in the De Courcy Group). These features were named by Capt George Richards of HMS *Plumper* about 1859, after the RN screw corvette *Pylades*, 21 guns and 1,160 tonnes. The vessel was built at Sheerness dockyard in 1854 and spent the Crimean War in the Baltic, then served two commissions on the Pacific Station: 1859–61, under Capt Michael de Courcy, and 1868–70, under Capt Cecil Buckley. The death in Apr 1859 of John Jeffries, paymaster of the *Pylades*, resulted in one of Victoria's first naval funerals. The ship also spent much time in the W Indies before being sold and broken up in 1875. Pylades is a figure from Greek mythology, son of King Strophius of Phocis and a close friend of Orestes. *W*

Pym Island (48°42'00" 123°23'00" W side of Shute Passage, N of Coal I, off NE end of Saanich Peninsula, N of Victoria). Named about 1858 by coastal surveyor Capt George Richards after Sub-Lt Frederick Whiteford Pym, who had been one of his junior officers on the Arctic exploration vessel *Assistance*, 1852–54. Richards was part of a squadron, under the overall command of Sir Edward Belcher, sent to search for the missing Sir John Franklin. Several of Belcher's vessels, including HMS *Assistance*, were abandoned during the search, much against the wishes of their cdrs. Frederick Pym is not to be confused with Bedford Pim, another RN officer who was also in the Arctic at the same time (in HMS *Resolute*, under Capt Henry Kellett; *see* Pim Head). Pym went on to become lt cdr of the gunboat *Skylark* during the Crimean War. Pym I was known in the 19th century as Quadros I, after Joseph Quadros from the Azores, who received a Crown grant for it and neighbouring Knapp I in 1890. Quadros paid $1 an acre for his land, so Pym I cost him $5. By 2008 the 2-ha property had appreciated somewhat in value; with a luxurious home, indoor pool, four guest cottages, caretaker's residence, tennis court, extensive dock and manicured grounds, it was for sale for just under $10 million. *W*

Q

Qlawdzeet Anchorage (54°13'00" 130°46'00" N end of Stephens I, Brown Passage, W of Prince Rupert). According to Odille Morison, the N coast linguist (*see* Morison Passage) who assisted anthropologist Franz Boas, Qlawdzeet is the original Tsimshian name for this feature and can be translated as "clam bay." More literally, the word means "place of the hissing noise"; *zeet* is onomatopoeic and represents the sound made when a great number of clams eject water through their siphons. This is the safe anchorage that Capt William Brown of the *Butterworth* led Capt George Vancouver and his vessels to in 1793 (*see* Brown Passage). **W**

CGS *Quadra* **at Victoria.** *BC Archives B-09770*

Quadra Hill (48°56'04" 123°28'11" NW of Montague Hbr, Galiano I, Gulf Is), **Quadra Island** (50°12'00" 125°15'00" E of Discovery Passage, NW end of Str of Georgia), **Quadra Saddle** (49°46'00" 126°26'00" E of Tlupana Inlet, Nootka Sd, W side of Vancouver I). After Spanish naval officer and explorer Juan Francisco de la Bodega y Quadra. *See* Bodega Anchorage for biographical details. Quadra I, Sonora I and Maurelle I were all originally thought to be one large land mass, which was known as Valdes (or Valdez) I after Spanish naval officer Cayetano Valdés, who explored this region with Dionisio Alcalá-Galiano in 1792. When it was realized, in the 1870s, that there were three islands, they

were called the Valdes Is or Valdes group. It was not until 1903 that the islands received individual names. Today, 276-sq-km Quadra I has a ferry connection, more than 2,000 inhabitants and an economy that revolves around logging, fishing, aquaculture and tourism. There are two commercial centres, at Heriot Bay and Quathiaski Cove. *See below also.* **E W**

Quadra Rocks (52°09'00" 131°06'00" In Houston Stewart Channel, S of Moresby I, QCI). After CGS *Quadra*, a federal lighthouse and fisheries tender on the BC coast, which struck these rocks in May 1892 en route to the Bering Sea to observe the sealing trade. Capt James Gaudin was in command at the time; he was able to beach the ship nearby and make temporary repairs while one of his officers took a small boat to Port Simpson to request assistance. The 53-m, 1,474-tonne patrol vessel was built at Paisley, Scotland, in 1891 and brought out to Esquimalt by Capt John Walbran, who would command it for much of its early career (and who later wrote the classic reference book *British Columbia Coast Names*). The *Quadra* visited nearly every part of the BC coast and twice carried Canada's govs gen on official cruises: the Earl of Aberdeen in 1896, and the Earl of Minto and Lady Minto in 1901. In 1917 the vessel collided in thick fog with the CPR's *Charmer* in Nanaimo Hbr. Deemed too badly damaged to repair, it was sold to the Britannia Mining & Smelting Co, converted to a bulk carrier and used to transport copper ore from Howe Sd to a Tacoma smelter. Next the *Quadra* was acquired by the Canadian-Mexican Shipping Co. It made several successful voyages between Vancouver and the US as a rum-runner before being caught off California in 1924 with more than $1 million worth of liquor and sold for scrap at San Francisco for $1,625. The ship was, of course, named for 18th-century Spanish naval officer Juan Francisco de la Bodega y Quadra (*see* Bodega Anchorage *and also* Quadra Hill). **D**

Quadros Point (48°42'05" 123°23'42" NE tip of Knapp I, off NE end of Saanich Peninsula, N of Victoria). Joseph Quadros, a native of the Azores, pre-empted Knapp I and neighbouring Pym I in 1889 and received a Crown grant for them the following year. He had applied to become a British subject in 1881 and married Catherine Quotlunes, his First Nation wife, in 1886. The point was named by the hydrographic service in 1962. Pym I (qv) was formerly known as Quadros I. *See also* Knapp I.

Quait Bay (49°17'00" 125°51'00" NE side of Cypress Bay, N of Meares I, Clayoquot Sd, W side of Vancouver I). This Nuu-chah-nulth First Nation word means "calm," according to regional hydrographer Henri Parizeau, who changed the name of the feature from Calm Ck in 1933. (A creek, in early Admiralty terminology, referred to a small marine inlet, often one that was dry at low tide.) The bay was the site of a shingle and sawmill in the 1920s and '30s, operated by John Darville, from Washington state, and his sons. The Darvilles also built boats there, many powered by auto engines converted to marine use. Eighty years later, Quait Bay was home to the luxurious floating Clayoquot Wilderness Resort, which has since moved its base to the head of Bedwell Sd.

Qualicum Bay (49°24'00" 124°38'00" Between Nanaimo and Courtenay, E side of Vancouver I), **Qualicum Beach** (49°21'00" 124°27'00" SE of Qualicum Bay), **Qualicum River** (49°24'00" 124°37'00" Flows E and N into Str of Georgia, just SE of Qualicum Bay). The name is an adaptation of a Pentlatch First Nation word for chum salmon (sometimes also spelled Quall-e-hum or Quallchum in early accounts of the region). The Pentlatch people—a Northern Coast Salish group occupying traditional territory on the E coast of Vancouver I and on Denman and Hornby islands—were decimated in the 19th century by disease and inter-tribal warfare. Their language became extinct by 1940 and lingers on only in a few place names such as Qualicum. The town of Qualicum Beach got its start as an agricultural settlement around the mouth of the Little Qualicum R in the 1880s. It developed as a resort area and in the early 2000s had the highest proportion of senior citizens of any community in BC: 35% of the population is over 65. *E*

Quarantine Cove (48°21'00" 123°32'00" S end of Parry Bay, W of William Head, S end of Vancouver I). Presumably named in association with nearby William Head, which was a quarantine station, 1894–1958, where passengers on suspect deep-sea vessels were inspected for infectious diseases (usually smallpox) before arrival at Victoria and Vancouver. In 1959 the site was turned into a minimum security prison. Nearby Quarantine Lk is probably also named after the William Head facility.

Quarry Bay (48°34'00" 123°31'00" Between Sheppard Point and McCurdy Point, W side of Saanich Inlet, NW of Victoria). The Bamberton cement plant and limestone quarries were established just N of here in 1912 by the Portland Cement Construction Co. The operation was shut down in 1916, when home building slowed because of WWI. In 1919 the company merged with the BC Cement Co, founded in 1904 by Robert Butchart on the E side of Saanich Inlet. Quarry Lk, just E of Tod Inlet, was named for the original BC Cement operation, and the Butchart Gardens got their start when Jennie Butchart, Robert's wife, decided to beautify the worked-out quarries near her Tod Inlet mansion. Butchart closed his original cement works in 1921 and expanded operations at Bamberton, bringing in limestone from quarries at Texada I and Cobble Hill. By the 1950s Bamberton was one of the largest cement producers in the PNW. The plant closed in 1981, and the company village was abandoned. In the 1990s an unsuccessful attempt was made to develop the Bamberton property as an enormous residential complex.

Quarry Bay (49°40'00" 124°08'00" S side of Nelson I, Malaspina Str, SE of Powell R). Nelson I granite, highly regarded for its density and weight, has been quarried since the 1880s, with the first large-scale operations taking place next to this bay in 1894, when BC stone was chosen for the huge US Navy drydock at Bremerton, Washington. The next year, Quarry Bay granite was used for the foundations of the new legislature at Victoria and for the seawall around that city's inner harbour. The 150-ha quarry site, owned by the Vancouver Granite Co, was closed down in 1903 when operations shifted to nearby Kelly I, S of Blind Bay. The original workings were reopened in 1908, leased to a Seattle company, then taken over again by Vancouver Granite, which for the next two decades supplied stone for Esquimalt's new drydock and for dozens of buildings at Vancouver, including the courthouse, and at UBC. The Nelson I quarries, which also gave their name to nearby Quarry Lk, operated sporadically in the 1940s and closed in 1949.

Quarry Point (52°54'00" 128°31'00" W side of Graham Reach, N of Sarah I, E side of Princess Royal I). Named by the hydrographic service in 1949 after two quarries that operated near this spot in the 1910s and supplied limestone to BC's first pulp mill at nearby Swanson Bay. Calcium compounds from limestone are used in the kraft pulping process to recover and recycle the sodium compounds that "cook" the wood chips and break them down.

Quascilla Bay (51°17'00" 127°22'00" S side of Smith Inlet, N of Port Hardy). Named in 1890 by Capt John Walbran after the former First Nation inhabitants of the area, who are part of the larger Kwakwaka'wakw cultural confederacy and known today as the Gwa'sala. (This word, which has been translated as "northern people," has had many spellings over the years, including Goasila, Kwasila and Quoasi'la.) The Gwa'sala once had a fortified village at this site, called Wyclese or Waitlas, which was estimated by Peter Puget and Joseph Whidbey of HMS *Discovery* to have a population of about 250 in 1792. Its inhabitants tried hard to persuade the British naval officers to visit, making "signs too unequivocal to be misunderstood, that the female part of their society would be very happy in the pleasure of their company." The "civil offers" were declined, however, the British "having no leisure to comply with these repeated solicitations." The ruins of the settlement, according to Walbran, were still visible in the early 1900s, after the tribe had moved to Takush Hbr. The Gwa'sala later joined their neighbours from Seymour Inlet, the Nak'waxda'xw, at Blunden Hbr and then were forced by federal authorities to move to Tsulquate, a suburb of Port Hardy, in 1964. *W*

The community of Quatsino on Quatsino Sound. *Andrew Scott*

Quathiaski Cove on Quadra Island. *Peter Vassilopoulos*

Quathiaski Cove (50°03'00" 125°13'00" SW side of Quadra I, Discovery Passage, just NE of Campbell R). This may be a Northern Coast Salish word meaning "island in the mouth," referring to Grouse I, located at the entrance to the cove. Other translations are also recorded, including "place on N side of the point." Pidcock Bros built a salmon cannery on the cove in 1904, and the village that grew up around it was the largest in the area until the mid-1920s, when Campbell R emerged as the regional centre. The cannery changed hands several times and in 1938 was sold by its long-time owner, the Quathiaski Canning Co, to BC Packers. It was destroyed by fire in 1941 and not rebuilt. Quathiaski Cove continues to be one of the hubs of Quadra I, along with Heriot Bay, and was linked by ferry to Campbell R in 1960. *E*

Quatsino (50°32'00" 127°39'00" N side of Quatsino Sd), **Quatsino Narrows** (50°33'00" 127°34'00" Connects Quatsino Sd to Holberg Inlet), **Quatsino Sound** (50°30'00" 127°35'00" N of Brooks Bay, NW end of Vancouver I). Quatsino is an anglicized version of the name of the Gwat'sinuxw people, one of several Kwakwaka'wakw First Nations that once occupied this remote region. The word has been translated as "people of the N country," "downstream people" and "people who live on the other side." The traditional territory of the Gwat'sinuxw was

on the N side of the sound, near the entrance. The other main surviving nation in this region is the Gusgimukw, or Koskimo. The two groups settled at Hwates (Quattishe), just E of the non-Native community of Quatsino, then moved in the early 1970s to New Quatsino near Coal Hbr. A boatload of Scandinavian immigrants settled on the sound in the mid-1890s; their colony, called Scandia, developed into today's isolated village of Quatsino. The sound, which appears as Quatsinough Hbr on an 1849 Admiralty chart, was charted by RN surveyor George Richards in 1860–62. Fishing and logging provide most jobs in the area, though whaling and copper mining have also been important. *E W*

Queen Charlotte Channel (49°22'00" 123°18'00" E of Bowen I, SE Howe Sd, just NW of Vancouver). Capt George Richards named many features in Howe Sd in 1859–60 after the officers and vessels that participated in the 1794 English Channel battle known as the Glorious First of June. HMS *Queen Charlotte*, a 104-gun line-of-battle ship built at Chatham in 1790, was Adm Lord Howe's flagship in this famous engagement with the French fleet, in which seven French vessels were captured or destroyed. The *Queen Charlotte* was serving off Italy in 1800 as the flagship of Mediterranean fleet cdr-in-chief Adm Lord Keith when it accidentally caught fire and then exploded, causing the deaths of 673 crewmen. *W*

Queen Charlotte Islands (53°00'00" 132°00'00" Separated from northern BC mainland by Hecate Str and Dixon Entrance). This offshore archipelago, the traditional home of the Haida First Nation, is the largest on the BC coast—9,596 sq km in area. It consists of hundreds of islands, including Graham and Moresby, the largest in BC after Vancouver I. Spanish naval officer Juan Pérez was the first European to sight the QCI, in 1774, but did not land. The name was applied in 1787 by early British fur trader George Dixon after his vessel, the *Queen Charlotte*, which, in turn, commemorated the wife of England's King George III. Dixon and Nathaniel Portlock, of the *King George*, spent 1786–87 in the PNW, sponsored by the King George's Sd Co of London. Dixon was the first European to trade extensively with the Haida. He sailed the length of the W coast of the QCI in 1787, then rounded Cape St James and cruised partway up the E side of the archipelago. The French explorer Lapérouse, in the area in 1786, had suspected the insularity of the QCI; Dixon was sure of it. Neither made a circumnavigation, however, nor did Charles Duncan, in the *Princess Royal*, the following year, though he sailed farther N in Hecate Str. The US fur trader Robert Gray, in 1789, called the archipelago Washington's I. The Haida people know their homeland as Haida Gwaii ("islands of the people"), and this name is becoming increasingly popular. As BC premier Gordon Campbell said in 2007, "I hear people talk far more about Haida Gwaii today than the QCI." An older Haida name is Xaadala Gwayee (Xhaaydla Gwaayaay), meaning "islands on the boundary between worlds"—the worlds being those of forest, sea and sky. Another name in popular usage is "Galapagos of the North," referring to the unique ecology of the QCI, which partly escaped recent glaciation. The village of **Queen Charlotte** (53°15'15" 132°05'00" N side of Skidegate Channel, S side of Graham I), which is often referred to locally as Queen Charlotte City, takes its name from the QCI, as do the Queen Charlotte Mtns. *D E W*

Queen Charlotte Sound (51°30'00" 128°30'00" Between QCI and Vancouver I), **Queen Charlotte Strait** (50°45'00" 127°15'00" Between NE Vancouver I and BC mainland). Named after Queen Charlotte (1744–1818), the wife of King George III of England. She was born the Duchess Sophia Charlotte of Mecklenburg-Strelitz, married the British king in 1761 and gave birth to 15 children. The marriage was, by all accounts, a happy one, at least until George became permanently insane about 1811. Charlotte was a well-educated supporter of the arts; Johann Christian Bach was her music teacher, and Mozart dedicated work to her. She was also a keen amateur botanist who helped develop what are now the Royal Botanic Gardens at Kew. English fur trader James Strange named Queen Charlotte's Sd in 1786, during a trip along Goletas Channel with small boats from the *Captain Cook* and *Experiment*, the two vessels in his expedition. However, according to PNW cartography expert Henry Wagner, it was not the sound that Strange named but what we know today as Queen Charlotte Str. Capt George Vancouver also applied the name Queen Charlotte Sd to today's strait on his 1798 chart. He wrote in his journal that a certain Mr S Wedgborough of the *Experiment* was first to use the name, but Wagner claims that this was a mistake on Vancouver's part. US fur trader Joseph Ingraham, capt of the brig *Hope*, gave the name Pintard's Sd to Queen Charlotte Str. In 1920 the hydrographic service found it necessary to distinguish between the inner channel and the open waters beyond, and decided that a line drawn between Cape Sutil on Vancouver I and Cape Caution on the mainland would serve to divide strait from sound. *E W*

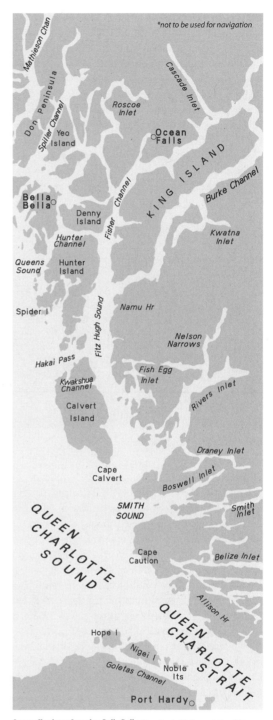

Queen Charlotte Sound to Bella Bella. *Reproduced with the permission of the Canadian Hydrographic Service*

Queen Island (53°42'00" 132°57'00" In entrance to Port Louis, W side of Graham I, QCI). This feature was named by Port Clements townsite promoter Eli Tingley in 1911, on the invitation of regional hydrographer Lt Cdr Philip Musgrave. Tingley chose to honour his 9-m boat, designed in classic Columbia R gillnetter style and named the *Queen*. He had brought the vessel to Masset Inlet in 1908

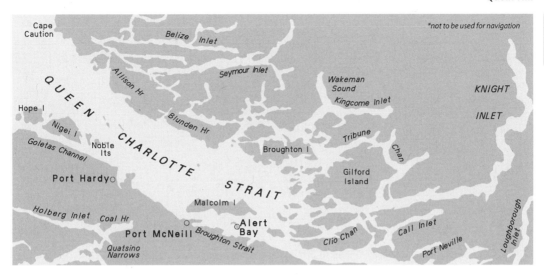

not to be used for navigation

Queen Charlotte Strait and Knight Inlet. *Reproduced with the permission of the Canadian Hydrographic Service*

on board the CPR steamship *Amur* and sailed it across Hecate Str on many occasions. Tingley later added a small engine and a cabin and sold the *Queen* to his real-estate rival, Charlie Adam. **D**

Queen Point (53°19'14" 127°56'31" Between Whidbey Reach and Egeria Reach, Gardner Canal, SE of Kitimat). Named in 1907 by Capt Frederick Learmonth of HMS *Egeria* after the 98-gun RN vessel *Queen*, flagship in 1793 of Rear Adm Alan Gardner, whose career is commemorated by many features in Gardner Canal (qv). HMS *Queen*, launched on the Thames in 1769, participated in the 2nd Battle of Ushant in 1781 and was badly damaged in the 1794 battle known as the Glorious First of June, where the ship's cdr, Capt John Hutt, was killed. The *Queen* was cut down to two decks and 74 guns in 1811 and then finally broken up in 1821.

Queens Reach (50°10'00" 123°53'00" N end of Jervis Inlet, NE of Powell R, NW of Vancouver). RN hydrographer Capt George Richards named this feature about 1860 after Queen Victoria (1819–1901), who succeeded to the British throne in 1837. Many other geographical sites around the inlet were named by Richards after other members of the queen's family.

Quequitz Reefs (53°33'00" 133°01'00" W of Hippa I, off W side of Graham I, QCI). The name is adapted from an old Haida reference indicating that sea otters were common here. The feature has also been spelled Qogi'ts.

Quineex Reef (50°06'00" 127°45'00" In approach to Nasparti Inlet, Checleset Bay, NW of Kyuquot Sd, NW side of Vancouver I). Named after a Ka:'yu:'K't'h/Che:K'tles7et'h' (Kyuquot/Checleset) First Nation reserve located on the SW side of Brooks Peninsula. Its former name, West Reef, was changed by the hydrographic service in 1946.

Quinn Rock (50°27'00" 128°15'00" NW of Cape Parkins, SE of Lippy Point, NW of Quatsino Sd, off NW end of Vancouver I). This feature was probably named after James Quinn, the keeper at the Quatsino lighthouse station on Kains I for several years in the early 1920s. He was a former sailor who was already 70 years old when he took up the position.

Quisitis Point (48°59'00" 125°40'00" SE of Wickaninnish Bay, NW of Barkley Sd, W side of Vancouver I). The hydrographic service named this point in 1934 after the nearby Ucluelet First Nation reserve of Quisitis or Kwisitis. The word can be translated from the Nuu-chah-nulth language as "other side of the beach."

Quoin Hill (51°28'58" 127°43'36" On Penrose I, entrance to Rivers Inlet, N of Cape Caution), **Quoin Island** (50°53'00" 127°51'00" In Bate Passage, between Hope I and Nigei I, off N end of Vancouver I). These names are descriptive of the features' shapes. A quoin generally refers to a wedge of some sort and has a number of technical meanings. Quoins can be stones forming the corner of a wall; they can secure type in a chase or forme, prevent casks from rolling, and be used to raise or lower a heavy gun.

Rabbit Island (49°29'00" 124°11'00" SW end of Sabine Channel, between Texada I and Lasqueti I, Str of Georgia). This well-established local name, which refers to the 14-ha island's shape, was adopted by the hydrographic service in 1983. US sailor and businessman Henry Wheeler owned Rabbit I in the 1990s and equipped it with a lodge, four cabins, a bathhouse, a desalination plant and equipment to produce solar and wind power. In 2002 he donated the property to southern California's Orange Coast College, which operated a field station there for summer classes in island ecology, biology, kayaking and photography. Six years later it was purchased for $2.2 million by a trio of Alberta veterinarians as a refuge for traumatized dogs.

Raby Islet (52°11'00" 128°28'00" Entrance to St John Hbr, W side of Athlone I, W of Bella Bella), **Raby Rock** (52°44'00" 129°18'00" Entrance to Borrowman Bay, off NW side of Aristazabal I). William Raby (1834–1900), from Cambridge, was a Victoria pioneer, arriving in BC about 1855, probably on the same boat that brought HBC chaplain Edward Cridge and his wife, Mary. Cridge appointed Raby sexton and verger of BC's first Anglican church in 1856. He married Mary Ann Herbert (1827–65) that year in Victoria. Raby was a jack of all trades: watchman, carpenter, cobbler, painter, butcher, storekeeper and "assistant to missionaries." In a Victoria *Colonist* article, written many years later, he is quoted saying, "[I was] a jobbin' all round the country, getting my hands in more trades in a week than I had fingers and toes." After his wife's death, Raby appears to have fallen on hard times. He spent several years as a shepherd in Saanich—where his daughter, Mary Ann (1857–1942), was taken in and raised by the William Thomson family— and was listed as a barber in the 1881 BC census. About a decade later, indigent and ill, he became a resident of Victoria's Home for the Aged and Infirm. In 1872, at the Thomsons' Bannockburn Farm, Mary Ann Raby married William Richardson (1846–1917), who had jumped ship from the *Helvetia* at Victoria in 1863 and found work on the Thomson farm. The Richardsons worked for various farmers in the district before acquiring their own land in

S Saanich and raising a family of 14 children. Raby It is named after Mary Ann, Raby Rk after her father William.

Race Rocks lighthouse viewed from the sea. *Jim Ryan*

Race Passage (48°18'00" 123°32'00" Off S end of Vancouver I, N of Race Rks), **Race Rocks** (S of Race Passage, SE of Christopher Point). Nine-knot (17-km/h) tidal currents or "races" form in this area, especially where flows are channelled around the Race Rks. Dangerous rips and overfalls can form in Race Passage when strong winds oppose the tide. The rocks were named about 1842 by HBC officials at newly established Ft Victoria, and the name was adopted in 1846 by Capt Henry Kellett of HMS *Herald*, who wrote that "this dangerous group is appropriately named, for the tide makes a perfect race around it." North Race Rk was formerly known as Nanette Rk, after the 350-tonne barque *Nanette*, one of more than 35 ships to have been wrecked in the vicinity. The *Nanette* met its fate only a few days before BC's second lighthouse became operational on Great Race Rk in 1860. Other vessels that foundered nearby, often with heavy loss of life, include the *Rosedale* (*see* Rosedale Rk), *Idaho, Rosamond, Eemdyk* (*see* Eemdyk Passage), *Hope, Tyee* and *Sechelt.* The historic lighthouse, built of cut and numbered stones brought round Cape Horn from Scotland, was automated in 1996. Thomas Argyle (*see* Argyle It) was its keeper for many years. The rocks are an ecological reserve, home to a variety of seabirds and marine life; Lester B Pearson United World College of the Pacific maintains a research station there. **Race Passage** (50°23'00" 125°52'00" S of Helmcken I and Hardwicke I, Johnstone Str), **Race Point** (49°01'00" 123°35'00" NW tip of Galiano I, S side of Porlier Pass, Gulf Is) and **Race Point** (50°07'00" 125°20'00" E of Menzies Bay, W side of Discovery Passage, NW of Campbell R) are very likely tide-related names also, as severe tidal flows are experienced at all three locations. *E W*

Racey Inlet (52°52'00" 129°04'00" E of entrance to Surf Inlet, W side of Princess Royal I). Percy Wise Racey was a US mining engineer who was active in mine development and management in BC for more than 30 years. He married Olga Mabel Watson at Summerland in 1915. Racey was engineer at the Surf Inlet gold mine in 1921 and mine superintendent in 1922–23. Before arriving at Princess Royal I, he supervised mining work in the Alice Arm and Stewart areas. By 1929 he is listed as gen manager of the Oregon Copper Co and is also involved with the Sally property near Greenwood. Racey then became superintendent of the Belmont Mine at Tonopah, Nevada, and the Argonaut Mine at Jackson, California. In 1934 he was a consulting engineer for the Windpass Gold Mining Co, which had an operation near Kamloops. P W Racey & Associates of Seattle had an interest in a Khutze R property on the BC coast, 1939–41. Racey Inlet was named in 1926 and was known before that as the South Arm of Surf Inlet.

Racoon Point (49°59'00" 127°18'00" W side of Union I, Kyuquot Sd, NW side of Vancouver I). This feature was formerly known as Onward Point, after a well-known sealing schooner based in Victoria in the 1880s and first owned by Hugh McKay and William Spring. In 1947 the hydrographic service changed the name in order to commemorate HMS *Racoon*, a British warship that played a minor role in PNW history during the War of 1812. John Jacob Astor and the Pacific Fur Co had established an early trading post at the mouth of the Columbia R that stood in the way of the NWC, a British enterprise. During the war, the NWC and the RN joined forces, with the intention of capturing the fort, and the *Racoon* was sent out to Oregon along with the *Isaac Todd*, an armed NWC vessel. In 1813, however, a group of local Nor'westers pre-empted the use of force by negotiating a buyout of Astor's facilities on the Columbia. When the *Racoon* arrived on the scene, its officers were upset to find that no fighting—and thus no prize money—would be involved. The ship's cdr, William

Black, had to satisfy himself with a symbolic gesture of conquest: changing the name of the trading post from Ft Astoria to Ft George. The *Racoon*, launched in 1808, was decommissioned in 1838 after service in S America, the E and W Indies, St Helena, off W Africa and as a convict hospital ship at Portsmouth.

Radar Beaches (49°04'00" 125°50'00" Below Radar Hill), **Radar Hill** (49°05'03" 125°50'29" Just SE of Tofino, in Pacific Rim National Park, W side of Vancouver I). A long-range radar station, part of the Pinetree Line, an early-warning defence against incoming missiles, was built on the hill in the early 1950s and closed down in 1958. The buildings were dismantled by 1971. Several years later, Transport Canada installed a VOR (VHF omni-directional radio range) facility there. In 1998 a Korean War memorial was located on the hill. Radar Beaches and Radar Hill both became well-established local names and were adopted by the hydrographic service in 1975.

Radar Passage (51°18'00" 127°49'00" Between Brown I and Cluster Reefs, entrance to Smith Sd, NW of Port Hardy). Named in 1948 for the innovative technology of radar, which was still fairly new at that date. Radar uses electromagnetic waves to identify the range, altitude, direction and speed of moving or fixed objects. The term, coined in 1941, is an acronym for "radio detection and ranging" but has since entered the language as a standard word. WWII greatly spurred the development of radar systems, which are widely used today by meteorologists, air traffic controllers, police and the military. *See also* nearby Loran Passage, named at the same time.

Rae Basin (49°28'20" 126°24'15" Head of Hesquiat Hbr, NW of Tofino, W side of Vancouver I). Ada Annie Jordan (1888–1985), from Sacramento, married Willie Francis John Rae-Arthur (1873–1936) at Vancouver in 1909 and moved to this remote part of Clayoquot Sd in 1915. She remained there for 70 years and became legendary, not only for her extraordinary garden but also for her endurance and feisty personality. A crack shot and scourge of large, marauding mammals, she became known as "Cougar Annie," outliving four husbands, raising eight children (three more died as infants) and creating a mail-order nursery garden business that shipped plants and seeds across Canada. Annie's garden is maintained by the non-profit Boat Basin Foundation, and her life is commemorated in author Margaret Horsfield's *Cougar Annie's Garden.* A post office, known as Boat Basin, was located at the site from 1936 to 1982 (and run by Annie out of her home for most of that period). The cove at the head of Hesquiat Hbr was also called Boat Basin until 1934, when its name was changed by the hydrographic service to Rae Basin. Nearby Rae Lk is also named for this pioneer W coast family. *E*

R

Rafael Cone (49°16'55" 126°11'11" S end of Flores I, NW of Tofino, Clayoquot Sd, W side of Vancouver I), **Rafael Point** (49°17'00" 126°14'00" W side of Flores I). The names Bahia de San Rafael and Puerto de San Rafael appear on several early Spanish maps just S of Nootka Sd and may have originally been applied by José Narváez in 1789. They probably refer to Sydney Inlet. Capt George Vancouver transferred the name to his chart at the present location of Rafael Point, and the "St" or "San" was presumably dropped over the years. The Punta de Machado of explorer Gonzales López de Haro may also have been Rafael Point. The archangel Rafael (Raphael) is usually associated with healing; the name is Hebrew for "God heals."

Raglan Point (50°52'00" 127°38'00" N end of Balaklava I, Gordon Channel, NW of Port Hardy). Part of a suite of names given in 1863–64 by Lt Daniel Pender to commemorate the famous Charge of the Light Brigade during the Crimean War. Gen FitzRoy James Henry Somerset, 1st Baron Raglan (1788–1855), was the British Army cdr in the Crimea in 1854. He had spent most of his career as military secretary to the Duke of Wellington and was as much a diplomat as a soldier. The futile charge of the Earl of Cardigan's light cavalry, and its decimation by the Russian artillery, may have partly been caused by Raglan's unclear orders. Raglan blamed the debacle on his senior cavalry cdr, the Earl of Lucan, and was later promoted to field marshal. *W*

Rainbow Channel (49°14'00" 123°53'00" N of Newcastle I, between Snake I and Hudson Rks, entrance to Nanaimo Hbr, SE side of Vancouver I), **Rainbow Island** (52°10'00" 128°04'00" W end of Gunboat Passage, just E of Bella Bella). HMCS *Rainbow* and *Niobe* were Canada's first warships, presented to the nation by Britain in 1910. Both were obsolete cruisers that had seen limited service before their transfer to N America and were used mostly for training by their new owner. The 3,265-tonne, 96-m *Rainbow* was launched in 1891 and based at Hong Kong and in the Mediterranean before being decommissioned by the Admiralty. It was stationed at Esquimalt, 1910–20, and was sent to Vancouver in 1914 to force the *Komagata Maru*, a vessel filled with hopeful Sikh immigrants, to return to India. During WWI the *Rainbow* patrolled the Pacific coast but saw no action. After the war it was used as the depot ship at Esquimalt and then sold for scrap in 1920. Rainbow Channel, formerly known as Middle Channel, was named in 1944. Rainbow I used to appear on charts as Deer I; its current name was adopted in 1925. Rainbow Mtn, N of Bute Inlet, was also named for this vessel after being climbed in 1985 by an RCN mountaineering party.

Raley Point (53°54'59" 128°41'27" N entrance to Clio Bay, E side of Kitimat Arm, S of Kitamaat Village). Named in 1898 by Capt John Walbran of CGS *Quadra* after George Henry Raley (1864–1958), who was born in Yorkshire and immigrated to Ont in 1882 to farm. He became a Methodist minister instead and married Maude Giles, daughter of a Brockville physician, in 1890. He and his wife moved to BC in 1893, where Raley served as a Kitimat missionary, 1893–1904, and was then appointed superintendent of all Methodist missions on the BC coast N of Alert Bay. In 1906 he transferred to Port Simpson and in 1914 moved to the Fraser Valley, where he worked as principal of the Coqualeetza residential school until 1934 and then retired to Vancouver. He was a great accumulator of First Nation artifacts, and his collection, mostly assembled at Kitimat and Port Simpson, is now housed at UBC's Museum of Anthropology, the Vancouver Museum and the Royal Ont Museum. Raley was a relatively progressive and very well-liked administrator and one of the few to address economic issues, arguing for the formation of a guild to market and sell First Nation arts and crafts. Nearby Raley Ck is also named for him. *W*

Ralph Grey Point (48°49'00" 123°11'00" S end of Samuel I, off NW Saturna I, Gulf Is). Ralph Geoffrey Grey (1861–1943) came to BC with an Irish friend, George Rutherford, and bought 170-ha Samuel I, located between Mayne I and Saturna I, in 1889. Rutherford returned home and Grey became the sole owner of the property, receiving a Crown grant in 1905. He was supposedly a distant—and very much poorer—relative of the Earl Grey who was gov gen of Canada in 1904–11. Ralph farmed Samuel I and took an active part in Gulf Is community affairs. In 1900 he married Winifred Grace Spalding Higgs (1871–1951), who had come to BC in 1896 to visit her brother, Leonard Higgs, on Saturna. Winifred's sister Mabel later married Martin Grainger (*see* Grainger Point). The Grey family moved to Esquimalt in 1910 and also lived at Vancouver. The name was suggested by the Gulf Is Branch of the BC Historical Assoc and adopted in 1969.

Ralph Islands (53°43'00" 130°25'00" Off W side of McCauley I, Browning Entrance, N of Banks I). Named by the hydrographic service in 1947 in association with nearby Spicer I (qv). RN officer Napoleon Ralph Spicer served on the Pacific Station, 1865–68.

Ralston Islands (53°28'00" 129°58'00" S of Anger I, Principe Channel, between Banks I and Pitt I). Named in 1943 for the 2nd cook of the W coast government survey vessel *William J Stewart*.

Ram Bluff (52°27'00" 127°14'00" NE entrance to Labouchere Channel, opposite NE King I, W of Bella Coola). A descriptive name suggested by the appearance of the feature and applied by the hydrographic service in 1957.

Ramillies Channel (49°31'00" 123°20'00" Between Gambier I and Anvil I, Howe Sd, NW of Vancouver). HMS

Ramillies, a 74-gun ship of the line under Capt Henry Harvey, took part in the 1794 British naval victory known as the Glorious First of June. During the battle, Harvey helped his brother, Capt John Harvey of HMS *Brunswick*, destroy the French vessel *Vengeur*. In 1859–60, RN surveyor George Richards named many features in Howe Sd after the participants in this famous English Channel engagement. The *Ramillies*, built at Rotherhithe in 1785, also served in the Baltic and the W Indies before being converted to a hospital ship in 1831 and broken up in 1850.

Ramsay Island (52°34'00" 131°24'00" E side of Moresby I, SE of Lyell I, Queen Charlotte Is), **Ramsay Passage** (52°34'00" 131°25'00" NW of Ramsay I), **Ramsay Point** (52°33'30" 131°26'00" W side of Ramsay I), **Ramsay Rocks** (52°34'00" 131°27'00" W of Ramsay I). Sir Andrew Crombie Ramsay (1814–91) was an eminent Scottish geologist. He joined the British Geological Survey in 1841, became its director gen in 1872 and was knighted in 1881. Ramsay also served as a professor of geology at Univ College, London, and lectured at the Royal School of Mines. In 1862 he was elected a fellow of the Royal Society and president of the Geological Society of London. He wrote many books, including the *Physical Geology and Geography of Great Britain*, which first appeared in 1863 as a series of "six lectures delivered to working men" and was expanded in later editions. Ramsay I was named in 1878 by Dr George M Dawson of the Geological Survey of Canada; its Haida name is Xiina Gwaayaay. The other features were named much later by the hydrographic service. Andrew Pt and Crombie Pt also commemorate him.

Ramsbotham Islands (52°42'00" 129°03'00" Laredo Channel, between Aristazabal I and Princess Royal I). Louis Ramsbotham Davies worked as a hydrographer on the BC coast from 1907 to 1947. *See* Louis Is for a more detailed biography. Formerly known as the Channel Is.

Ramsden Point (54°59'00" 130°06'00" S end of peninsula between Portland Canal and Observatory Inlet, N of Prince Rupert). Named by Capt George Vancouver in 1793 after Jesse Ramsden (1735–1800), a scientific and astronomical instrument maker who supplied several of the nautical devices used on Vancouver's voyage. He was born in Yorkshire but learned his trade in London and developed a great reputation for his mechanisms. Vancouver held him in high regard. Ramsden's particular area of expertise was in upgrading sextants, theodolites, heliostats and the like so that finer and more accurate measurements could be made. He developed an advanced "dividing engine" for marking graduations on measuring instruments, and made improvements in eyepieces. Ramsden was elected to the Royal Society in 1786 and received its highest award, the Copley Medal, in 1795 for his technical contributions to the field of surveying. *W*

Random Point (53°13'00" 132°15'00" N entrance to Anchor Cove, Kagan Bay, S side of Graham I, QCI). The sloop *Random* brought George Robinson, superintendent of the Cowgitz coal-mining operation, from New Westminster to the QCI in 1865, along with a party of miners. Capt Hallett of the *Random* made a survey of the area, and a certain amount of development work was done, but the venture was found unfeasible and more or less abandoned by 1872. Random Point was named by the hydrographic service in 1945; before that it was known as North Point.

Rankin Cove (49°10'00" 125°43'00" W side of Tofino Inlet, Clayoquot Sd, W side of Vancouver I), **Rankin Rocks** (49°11'00" 125°42'00" Just E of Rankin Cove, entrance to Tranquil Inlet). John S Rankin pre-empted land N of Florencia Bay, SE of Tofino, in 1900. MacMillan Bloedel Ltd later built a logging camp at Rankin Cove with sorting and loading facilities. Rankin Ck flows S into Rankin Cove. The Rankin Rks were formerly known as the Yellow Rks.

Rankine Islands (52°15'00" 131°03'00" N entrance to Carpenter Bay, off SE end of Moresby I, QCI). Geologist George M Dawson named these islands in 1878 after his younger brother Rankine Dawson (1863–1913), who acted as his assistant on his 1878 exploration of the QCI. George described the 15-year-old Rankine as "a singularly reticent travelling companion" whom he hoped to "improve" during the summer. Rankine graduated from McGill Medical School in 1882 and worked as a medical officer for the CPR and as a surgeon on P&O liners before marrying Gloranna Coats in 1896 and settling in London, England. He was prone his entire life to bouts of depression, and after he moved his family from London to Montreal and back, Gloranna left him and his health declined. He died in a London nursing home. Rankine edited *Fifty Years of Work in Canada*, the 1901 autobiography of Sir John William Dawson, his famous father, who was a geologist, paleontologist, author and principal of McGill Univ.

Rankin Shoals (51°22'00" 128°03'00" W of Pearl Rks, Sea Otter Group, off S side of Calvert I, Queen Charlotte Sd). The hydrographic service named this feature in 1947 after D A Rankin, a surveyor who worked aboard the W coast hydrographic vessel *William J Stewart*, 1941–47. He participated in surveys of the Str of Georgia, the Inside Passage, and Vancouver and Esquimalt harbours.

Rant Point (49°16'00" 125°50'00" SW entrance to Bedwell Sd, Clayoquot Sd, W side of Vancouver I). Geraldine Muriel Rant (1890–1963) pre-empted Welcome I in nearby Cypress Bay in 1912 and received a Crown grant for the property in 1917. She had accompanied her large family to BC from England in 1894. Parents Annie and William John Rant (1851–1930) settled at Colwood and farmed, though William, a former British Army capt who had seen

R

action in S Africa and India, also held a number of posts as a provincial civil servant. Rant Point was formerly known as Turn Point.

Raphoe Point (52°43'00" 126°58'00" W side of Dean Channel, NW of Bella Coola). Capt George Vancouver named Raphoe Point in 1793 in association with King I (qv) and "Dean's Canal" (Dean Channel), after Rev James King (d 1795), dean at the old episcopal city of Raphoe, Ireland. The dean was the father of Capt James King, a great friend of Vancouver's, with whom he had sailed on Capt James Cook's third expedition, 1776–80. Another Raphoe Point was mistakenly named nearby on an early Admiralty chart—on the N side of King I, opposite the entrance to Cousins Inlet—but was changed to Rattenbury Point in 1926.

Raspberry Bluff (54°11'00" 129°56'00" E of the mouth of the Ecstall R, S side of the Skeena R, just SE of Prince Rupert), **Raspberry Cove** (52°10'00" 131°05'00" N side of Houston Stewart Channel, S end of Moresby I, QCI), **Raspberry Islands** (54°11'00" 129°57'00" At the mouth of the Ecstall R). Almost a dozen members of the raspberry clan (genus *Rubus*) grow on the BC coast, but it was probably the salmonberry (*Rubus spectabilis*) that early explorers had in mind when bestowing these names. The Raspberry Is were named by Capt George Vancouver in 1793. Joseph Whidbey, master of HMS *Discovery*, had reported an abundance of berries there while examining the Skeena R with the ship's boats. The islands marked the easternmost extent of his journey, as he and Midshipman Robert Barrie decided that it was pointless to go any farther in the shallow waters, which were strewn with rocks and sandbars, and subject to dangerous currents. Raspberry Cove was named in 1853 by the officers of HMS *Virago*, which stopped there to take on water. Raspberry is a popular place name in BC; four creeks, a lake, a pass, a harbour (on Williston Lk) and a Doukhobor community in the W Kootenays all commemorate this marvellous edible fruit. *D W*

Rassier Point (49°11'00" 125°56'00" E tip of Vargas I, NW of Tofino, Clayoquot Sd, W side of Vancouver I). Victor Rassier (1887–1964), a native of Little Falls, Minnesota, was ordained a Roman Catholic Benedictine priest in 1915. After studying in Italy he was sent to Mt Angel Abbey in Oregon, where he taught at Mt Angel College, becoming rector there from 1917 to 1925 and then working at the abbey press, 1925–29. Fr Victor was transferred to W Coast mission work and served as principal of Christie residential school at Kakawis in Clayoquot Sd, 1929–35. In need of a rest after these exertions, he went to France to study Gregorian chant at Solesmes Abbey and elsewhere. On his return to Mt Angel, he was appointed choirmaster. To celebrate the centenary of the first Catholic mass conducted in Oregon, Fr Victor directed a special choir

of 1,000 children at Portland in 1939. He was pastor at St Mary's by the Sea, Rockaway, Oregon, 1947–61, then returned to Mt Angel Abbey, where he is buried.

Rathtrevor Beach (49°19'00" 124°16'00" Just S of Parksville, NW of Nanaimo, E side of Vancouver I). Gold prospector William H Rath (1830–1904), a native of Ireland, came to this area about 1886 and bought land from the E&N in 1895. He and his wife, Elizabeth, built a log cabin and barn and created the Wildrose Farm. William was appointed the district's justice of the peace. After his death, Elizabeth and her children continued to run the farm and eventually established a successful campground on the property. The Irish name "trevor" was apparently added to the family name in order to give the camping business a more lyrical sound. The area was acquired as a popular provincial park in 1967, and the Rath's heritage farm fields have been preserved as part of the site.

Architect Francis Rattenbury designed BC's legislature and the Empress Hotel, among other buildings. *BC Archives F-02163*

Rattenbury Island (51°41'48" 128°04'50" Off W side of Hecate I, S side of Hakai Pass, S of Bella Bella). The name was adopted by the hydrographic service in 1945 to commemorate architect Francis Mawson Rattenbury (1867–1935). He was born at Leeds and trained in England, immigrating to BC in 1892. A fine draftsman, he soon became the province's pre-eminent architect, winning a competition for Victoria's new legislature in 1893. Rattenbury went on to design many other important buildings, including the Empress Hotel, Hotel Vancouver, the original Lk Louise Hotel (since burned and rebuilt), the Vancouver Courthouse, Victoria's Crystal Gardens and the Pacific cable station at Bamfield. He served at various times as chief architect for the CPR and for the Bank of Montreal. His work was not particularly original but brought a new level of worldly grandeur and craftsmanship to large civic projects that perfectly matched the province's growing aspirations. Rattenbury married Florence Eleanor Nunn (1870–1929) at Victoria in 1898 and lived at Oak Bay, where he designed several mansions and was elected to council. His own home, Iechinihl at 1701 Beach Dr, still stands. In the early 1920s the architect caused a scandal by openly carrying on an affair with the much younger Alma Clarke Pakenham (1896–1935), a talented and twice-married musician and writer. After an acrimonious divorce, Francis and Alma married in 1925, but social ostracism ruined his career and drove the couple to England. Francis was killed in his Bournemouth home by the family chauffeur, who had become his wife's lover. Alma and her paramour were charged with murder, and a sensational trial followed. The chauffeur was convicted and served seven years. Charges against Alma were dropped, but she committed suicide a few days later. *E*

Rattenbury Point (52°14'46" 127°45'57" W side of King I, opposite entrance to Cousins Inlet, W of Bella Coola). John Eustace Rattenbury (1883–1974) married Annie Phyllis May Davies (1886–1966) at Vancouver in 1914 and moved two years later to Ocean Falls, where he worked for the Pacific Mills Co, possibly as a draftsman. He also served as the area's tide-gauge attendant for the hydrographic service in the early 1920s. Around 1945 he transferred to Powell R and worked at the pulp and paper mill there. Rattenbury died at Vancouver. The feature formerly appeared on early charts as Raphoe Point, but this was a cartographic error; the name had mistakenly been applied to two locations on Dean Channel. The incorrect Raphoe Point was renamed Rattenbury Point in 1926.

Raven Bay (49°44'00" 124°30'00" SE of Van Anda, E side of Texada I, Str of Georgia), **Raven Cove** (52°15'00" 128°09'00" W side of Chatfield I, just N of Bella Bella), **Raven Island** (52°42'00" 131°49'00" Klunkwoi Bay, E side of Moresby I, QCI). The common raven (*Corvus corax*) was the most important creature in PNW First Nation culture: transformer, cultural hero, trickster, creator of the world. It was the embodiment of supernatural power. Greedy, dishonest, lustful and high-spirited, Raven was the ultimate practical joker. It is not surprising that this bird should be the source of a number of BC place names, as well as appearing frequently in First Nation art. Raven creeks (three) and lakes (four) abound in the province, and Mt Raven reigns over the junction of the Craig and Iskut rivers, E of the Stikine R in the Cassiar district.

Rawlinson Anchorage (53°35'00" 130°33'00" S of Griffith Hbr, W side of Banks I). After returning from overseas service in WWI, George Rawlinson joined the Canadian

Hydrographic Service and worked as a launch driver aboard the W coast survey vessel *Lillooet* in the early 1920s. In the autumn of 1920, while caught in a storm, Rawlinson and his launch took refuge in this anchorage. Junior hydrographer Oswald Parker, who was present at the time and in charge of the launch, named the feature after his driver.

Ray Island (51°02'00" 127°31'00" S of Roy It, W entrance to Allison Hbr, NW side of Queen Charlotte Str, N of Port Hardy). The origin of the name is not known, but it is curious that this feature was named on the same day—Jan 24, 1946—as neighbouring Roy It.

Raymond Passage (52°10'00" 128°16'00" Between Horsfall I and Campbell I, just W of Bella Bella). The feature was named in 1834 by officials at the HBC post of Ft McLoughlin, just S of today's Bella Bella. Raymond was the capt of a US trading vessel that managed to reach the fort by way of this channel. The name was changed to Hecate Channel, but in 1903 the Geographic Board of Canada decided that, to avoid duplication, it should be changed back to its original form.

Raynor Group (50°53'00" 127°14'00" N side of Queen Charlotte Str, S of Bradley Lagoon), **Raynor Point** (51°09'00" 127°44'00" Just SE of Cape Caution, Queen Charlotte Sd). After RN surveying officer Edward Raynor Blunden, who served on the BC coast in the early 1860s. *See* Blunden Bay.

Ray Point (50°34'00" 126°11'00" N entrance to Call Inlet, E of the Cracroft Is, S of Knight Inlet). Henry Johns Ray (d 1903) was assistant paymaster aboard HMS *Havannah*, under Capt Thomas Harvey, on the Pacific Station, 1855–59. He returned to the BC coast in 1885–88 with HMS *Triumph*, the flagship of Rear Adm Michael Culme and, later, Rear Adm Algernon Heneage. Ray was promoted to the rank of fleet paymaster in 1886 and retired in 1889. Capt George Richards named a number of features in this area in 1860 after the officers of the *Havannah*, who assisted him with his survey.

Ray Rock (50°06'00" 124°44'00" E side of Desolation Sd, E of Mink I, NE end of Str of Georgia). Formerly known as Grey I but renamed in 1945 by the hydrographic service after RN officer Edward Hood Lingard Ray of the corvette *Tenedos*, who was stationed at Esquimalt in 1873 but became ill and had to be invalided back to England. As a midshipman aboard HMS *Royalist* in 1846, Ray had been singled out for the "gallant" role he played in a successful engagement against pirates off the Borneo coast. He later served in the W Indies and the Mediterranean, and was cdr of HMS *Implacable*, a training ship for boys at Devonport, from 1864 to 1866.

R

Raza Island (50°18'00" 125°00'00" Between Maurelle I and W Redonda I, NE of Campbell R), **Raza Passage** (50°20'00" 125°00'00" NW of Raza I, between Calm Channel and Pryce Channel), **Raza Point** (50°18'00" 125°02'00" W tip of Raza I). The originator of this Spanish name, which appears on an 1860 chart by Capt George Richards, is not known with certainty. The feature was labelled Isla Pineda on the map prepared from Dionisio Alcalá-Galiano's 1792 survey—probably after Lt Col Antonio Pineda, the chief naturalist on Alejandro Malaspina's 1789–94 expedition. In modern Spanish, *raza*, a noun, can mean "race" or "breed," "cleft in a horse's hoof," "woven stripe in fabric," "ray of light," or "fissure." The adjective *raso* or *rasa* means "flat," "clear" or "open." But according to PNW cartography expert Henry Wagner, in the 18th century *isla raza* "was a rather common name for a level island or perhaps one which had no vegetation on it." The problem with this explanation, however, is that BC's Raza I is far from flat; indeed, it is a heavily forested cone that towers rapidly to 878 m. So the name remains somewhat of a mystery.

Read Island (50°14'00" 125°05'00" Between Quadra I and Cortes I, N end of Str of Georgia), **Read Point** (50°08'00" 125°09'00" SW tip of Read I). Capt William Viner Read was a naval assistant at the Admiralty's hydrographic HQ in England. In 1864, when Capt George Richards was promoted to the position of hydrographer of the navy, Lt Daniel Pender named Read I and a number of other features in the vicinity after subordinate officers in the hydrographic dept. Pender was Richards's successor as chief RN surveyor on the BC coast. Viner Point and Mt William on Read I are also named after Read, as are a number of features on Gilford I: Mt Read, Viner Lk and Viner Sd. Read I, home to a handful of loggers, ranchers and resort operators, had a peak population of about 100 in the late 1920s and early '30s. There are two tiny communities: Surge Narrows on the NW side and Read I on the SE. *E*

Reay Island (48°41'00" 123°20'00" W side of Prevost Pass, E of Coal I and N end of Saanich Peninsula). William Reay (1820–90) and his brother Charles Henry Reay (1821–99) came out from England in 1854 and joined the gold rush before settling down and farming in the N Saanich area. According to the BC government *Gazette*, they received land grants in 1871. Through pre-emption and purchase they eventually owned about 450 ha of land, stretching from today's airport area to Bazan Bay, where Reay Ck is also named for them. William was the first magistrate in N Saanich and ran unsuccessfully for the BC legislature in 1875. According to local lore, the Reay brothers were shipwrecked when they first arrived at Esquimalt, and after struggling to shore in a canoe, they swore that they would never venture on the ocean again. Reay I is part of the Gulf Is National Park Reserve.

Reba Point (52°09'00" 128°20'00" E side of Potts I, S end of Joassa Channel, N end of Queens Sd, W of Bella Bella). Capt John Walbran of CGS *Quadra* named this feature in 1902 after Anna Rebecca Kissack, from Paisley, Ont, who was the first nurse at the Methodist hospital established that year at Bella Bella by Dr Richard Large. In 1903 she married Dr William Benjamin Laurence Donald (1874–1928), of Port Hope, Ont, and moved to the Peace R district of northern Alberta, where she raised three children and William worked as an Indian agent and physician for the North-West Mounted Police. Walbran and the *Quadra* were making a survey of nearby Joassa Channel at the time.

Rebecca Point (52°23'00" 131°17'00" E side of Burnaby I, off SE Moresby I, QCI), **Rebecca Spit** (50°06'00"

Rebecca Spit on Quadra Island, Drew Harbour behind. *Peter Vassilopoulos*

125°11'00" SE side of Quadra I, E of Drew Hbr, NW end of Str of Georgia). The 32-tonne *Rebecca* was the vessel that first brought mining engineer Francis Poole to the QCI's Skincuttle Inlet area in 1862 in search of copper. The point was named by the hydrographic service in 1962, exactly a century later. Capt Elijah McAlmond of Dungeness, Washington, was the *Rebecca*'s skipper. He built the small trading schooner in 1861 and operated it on Puget Sd and off BC and Alaska until 1865, when he sold it at San Francisco. Rebecca Spit was named by Lt Daniel Pender about 1864. *W*

Reception Point (49°28'00" 123°53'00" SW end of Sechelt Peninsula, S of Halfmoon Bay, NW of Vancouver). This feature was formerly known as Welcome Point, named in association with nearby Welcome Passage. The hydrographic service changed the name in 1944 in order "to avoid duplication and retain identity."

Recovery Point (52°59'00" 132°10'00" W entrance to Mudge Inlet, Kuper Inlet, NW side of Moresby I, QCI). In 1852 the HBC brig *Recovery* was sent to nearby Mitchell Inlet, where gold had recently been discovered. The previous year the *Una*, under Capt Willie Mitchell, had made two voyages to the discovery site. On the second trip, despite an ugly conflict with the Haida, Mitchell had managed to leave with about $75,000 worth of ore, but it was lost on the journey home when the *Una* ran aground in Neah Bay and was then destroyed by members of the Makah First Nation. On the 1852 expedition, Mitchell took a strongly armed party with him aboard the *Recovery*, but was able to avoid violent interactions with the Haida. The gold, however, turned out to be only a small strike and was soon depleted. The *Recovery* was built in the US about 1849 as the *Orbit*. It arrived at Esquimalt in 1851, badly damaged by a winter storm, and was purchased, refitted and renamed by the HBC, which used it to trade on the BC coast for a decade, then sold it in 1861. The brig made several trips to Hawaii, carried coal to San Francisco, and served as a guard vessel at Nanaimo and a customs ship at the entrance to the Fraser R during the gold rush in 1858–59. *D*

Redfern Island (50°54'00" 127°35'00" W of the Walker Group, Queen Charlotte Str, off NE end of Vancouver I). Dr Thomas Redfern was assistant surgeon aboard the 16-gun HMS *Scylla*, under Capt Frederick Herbert, on the Pacific Station in 1870. He served a second commission on the BC coast in 1874 as surgeon of the gunboat *Rocket*, under Lt Cdr Charles Harris, but died suddenly in 1877 at Victoria's naval hospital of heart disease and was buried at the naval cemetery in Esquimalt. Historian and mariner John Walbran claimed that this feature was Capt George Vancouver's Alleviation I, named in 1792 but not retained or marked on his published chart. James Johnstone, master of HMS *Chatham*, travelling in the ship's cutter,

had finally obtained a clear view of the Pacific Ocean from this spot, thus proving the insularity of Vancouver I and "alleviating" Vancouver's concern about reaching open water. Alleviation Rk, just NW of Redfern I, keeps this vanished historical name alive. Other historians believe that Pine I (qv) was Alleviation I. Redfern I was named in 1870 by Lt Daniel Pender.

Redfern Point (53°04'00" 129°11'00" E side of Casanave Passage, Campania Sd, W side of Princess Royal I). Charles Edward Redfern (1839–1929), from London, England, immigrated to Victoria in 1862 aboard the *Tynemouth* and set up as a jeweller and watchmaker. He married Eliza Arden Robinson (1852–1906), also from England, at Victoria in 1877 and raised a large family. Redfern was an active local politician; he served as a James Bay alderman and was elected mayor of Victoria in 1883, 1897, 1898 and 1899. He took part in the city's grand old-timers' reunion, held in 1924 (*see* Adams Bay). Eliza Redfern was an early social reformer in Victoria, a tireless worker for the Children's Aid Society and other charitable organizations.

Redford Point (52°05'00" 128°14'00" W side of Campbell I, opposite Piddington I, SW of Bella Bella). Lt Cdr W Redford worked for the federal fisheries patrol service on the BC coast. He was a member of the RCNR for many years, joining in 1923. In 1939–40 he served as capt of the *Malaspina*, a former fisheries and Dept of Transport ship that was reactivated during WWII as a patrol and training vessel. Later in the war, Redford had command of several minesweepers, including HMCS *Wasaga*. The point was named by the hydrographic service in 1944.

Redonda Bay (50°15'00" 124°57'00" NW side of W Redonda I), **Redonda Islands** (50°13'00" 124°50'00" NE of Cortes I, entrance to Toba Inlet, NE of Campbell R). Thinking that E Redonda and W Redonda islands were one large circular feature, Spanish navigators Dionisio Alcalá-Galiano and Cayetano Valdés named them Isla Redonda in 1792, after their shape (*redondo* or *redonda* means "round" in Spanish). Redonda Is, however, is not an official name; *see* E Redonda I *and* W Redonda I for more detailed individual entries. Redonda Bay on W Redonda, formerly known as Deceit Bay, takes its name from the island. Francis Millerd (*see* Millerd Point) established a salmon cannery on the bay in the mid-1930s; it operated until 1942 and then again 1946–48. The cannery's steam power was provided by the boilers from the *Transfer*, an old CPR Fraser R paddle steamer. A small but vigorous community formed around the plant, with a store, school, post office and steamship landing. Redonda Bay also became a centre for local logging activity, home to a shingle mill. Later a minimum-security prison camp operated there. The place was mostly abandoned by the 1980s, and only a few pilings remain today. The Klahoose First Nation name for the bay is Téxém'aajim, meaning "red cedar place." *E*

R

Reed Point (49°17'00" 122°52'00" S side of Port Moody, just E of Vancouver). This name was adopted shortly after the death of Cdr Archibald Heurtley "Cappy" Reed (1873–1965), harbourmaster with the Vancouver Harbour Board for many years and a pilot with the BC Pilotage Authority. A native of Durham, England, he apprenticed in the wool clipper *Invercargill* at the age of 15 and was 2nd mate of the clipper *Langstone* by the time he was 20. Reed first came to Vancouver in 1896 as a junior officer aboard the Canadian-Australian Line's *Warrimoo*. In 1899 he joined the RNR and served during the Boxer Rebellion in HMS *Terrible* and *Argonaut*. Three years later he was working for the CPR on the Pacific *Empress* ships and commanded the *Tartar* on its final voyage to the Orient. Reed was appointed Vancouver's first harbourmaster and port warden in 1911, a position he held, with breaks for war service, for more than three decades. In WWI he had charge of the decoy or Q-ship HMS *Underwing*—an armed merchant vessel disguised to look like an easy target and lure U-boats to the surface where they could be destroyed. In WWII he was RCN officer in charge at Prince Rupert. A fitness fanatic and accomplished watercolour painter, Reed also found time later in life to act as commissioner of BC's Sea Scouts association. Reed Point is now the site of one of the largest marinas in BC.

Refuge Cove and its historic store. *Peter Vassilopoulos*

Refuge Cove (50°07'00" 124°51'00" SW side of W Redonda I, E of Campbell R, NE end of Str of Georgia), **Refuge Lagoon** (50°08'00" 124°50'00" Just NE of Refuge Cove). While the name of this placid anchorage, which appeared on Admiralty charts as early as 1860, is self-explanatory, the community here has been through some intriguing changes. A logging and fur-farming settlement sprang up in the 1910s, with a school, store, post office and community hall, where dances were held on Saturday nights. In the early 1970s a group of families and individuals agreed to run the cove's commercial facilities, which by then included a fuel dock and liquor store, as a co-operative venture. Boat rentals and a café soon appeared. Today the

cove—known to the Klahoose First Nation as Th̓elhtn—is as much a refuge for kayakers in need of cappuccinos as it is a place of shelter. It is one of several spots on BC's turbulent coast with the name "refuge." **Refuge Island** (54°07'00" 132°18'00" E of Wiah Point, between Virago Sd and Masset Hbr, N side of Graham I, QCI), for instance, provides a sanctuary from Dixon Entrance storms, while another **Refuge Island** (49°02'00" 125°19'00" Entrance to Pipestem Inlet, E of Toquart Bay, W side of Vancouver I) offers protection from the open waters of Barkley Sd. **Refuge Bay** (54°03'00" 130°32'00" NW side of Porcher I, SW of Prince Rupert) was the site of a small settlement and landing from the 1910s to the 1930s. The Surf Point and Edye Pass gold mines were located nearby. *E*

Reid Island (49°00'00" 123°37'00" Between Thetis I and the N end of Galiano I, Gulf Is). James Murray Reid (1802–68), from the Orkney Is, worked for the HBC's marine dept for many years, serving as mate on the supply vessels that travelled between Britain and Hudson Bay. He came to the BC coast in 1852 in command of the brigantine *Vancouver*. In 1854 the *Vancouver* grounded on Rose Spit in the QCI in a storm, and Reid had to send a boat to Port Simpson for help. The crew and some of the stores were removed, and then the vessel and its main cargo of rum were set afire to prevent their falling into the hands of the Haida, who were aggressively claiming rights to the wreck. This incident brought an end to Capt Reid's employment with the HBC, though he went on to become a successful businessman in Victoria. Murray Point in Knight Inlet is also named for him. Several of his daughters married notable figures, including Senator William Macdonald (*see* Macdonald Point) and RN officers William Moriarty (*see* Moriarty Point) and William Blakeney (*see below*). Part of Reid I was pre-empted in 1881 by Portuguese homesteader Joseph Silvey; 10 years later his son Domingo Silvey applied for the rest. Three generations of Silveys lived on the island as loggers and fishermen, building a school there and permitting two Japanese families to construct herring salteries on the SW side. After Domingo's death in 1941, 92-ha Reid I was divided among family members and gradually sold off, the last piece going in 1974. It is now home to more than 30 recreational properties. A small Silvey family cemetery still bears testament to this pioneer clan of Portuguese immigrants. *W*

Reid Passage (52°18'00" 128°22'00" Between Blair Inlet and Mathieson Channel, off SW end of Don Peninsula, NW of Bella Bella). Named after Elizabeth "Lillie" Reid (d 1873), youngest daughter of HBC master mariner James Murray Reid of Victoria (*see above*). She married RN officer William Blakeney, who served on the BC coast as assistant surveying officer aboard the hired HBC vessel *Beaver* and then returned to England, where he was chief paymaster to the hydrographic office (under Capt George Richards). Elizabeth died at a young age in Surrey,

England. Nearby Lillie Point is also named for her, as is Mt Lillie on Knight Inlet. *See* Blackney Channel.

Reid Point (52°47'00" 132°01'00" S side of Tasu Sd, W side of Moresby I, QCI). RCN officer Howard Emerson Reid (1897–1962) came to the QCI in 1935 and made an examination of potential W coast anchorages and harbours for the Dept of National Defence. He was born in Que, attended the Royal Naval College of Canada and then went on to a celebrated career in the RCN. Reid served as a junior officer with various vessels during WWI and had his first command on HMCS *Festubert*, a *Battle*-class trawler, in 1923. Later he was CO of HMCS *Patriot* (1923–25), HMS *Sepoy* (1929), HMCS *Skeena* (1936–37) and HMCS *Fraser* (1937–38). Reid also held numerous administrative posts, including cdr-in-chief Halifax (1933), RCN director of operations and training (1934) and CO Atlantic coast (1939). He was promoted to commodore and deputy chief of naval staff in 1940, then CO Nfld in 1942. As a rear adm he was the naval representative to the Canada-US joint board of defence, 1943–46, and ended his career as a vice adm and chief of naval staff, 1946–47. Reid was made a CB in 1944 and was also awarded the US Legion of Merit and French Légion d'honneur. He retired from the RCN in 1948 and died at Victoria.

The Fraser estuary bird sanctuary of Reifel Island. *Peter Vassilopoulos*

Reifel Island (49°06'00" 123°11'00" Mouth of the Fraser R, between Westham I and Lulu I). Named for George Conrad Reifel (1893–1973), a Vancouver brewer and distiller, who acquired the island in 1926. His father, Henry Reifel (1869–1945), had established an early Vancouver brewery on Brewery Ck in Mt Pleasant, which later expanded to become Vancouver Breweries (purchased by Carling O'Keefe). The Reifel family acquired great wealth during Prohibition and developed a number of downtown Vancouver properties, including the Commodore Ballroom and the Vogue and Studio theatres on Granville St. George Conrad's son, George Henry Reifel (1922–92), farmed Reifel I, growing sugar beets during

WWII, then donated part of the island to the Crown in 1973 as a migratory bird sanctuary, operated today by the BC Waterfowl Society. More land on Reifel and adjacent Westham I was purchased over the years, and the George C Reifel refuge now comprises about 3.5 sq km of foreshore. Reifel I was formerly known as McNab I (*see* McNab Ck) and Smoky Tom I, after early residents. It has silted in and become joined to Westham I in several places. *E*

Rennell Sound on southwest Graham Island. *Andrew Scott*

Rennell Reef (53°23'00" 132°45'00" Entrance to Rennell Sd), **Rennell Sound** (53°24'00" 132°44'00" SW side of Graham I, QCI). Rennell Sd was named by British fur trader George Dixon, who, as capt of the *Queen Charlotte*, was one of the leaders of an early expedition to the PNW in 1786–87. The name, which appears on a map of NW America published in 1789 in Dixon's *Voyage Round the World*, commemorates James Rennell (1742–1830), an English geographer, historian and pioneer oceanographer. He joined the RN as a midshipman at age 14 and learned the basics of marine surveying, then worked for the E India Co for a number of years, becoming surveyor gen of the Bengal region. After being attacked and severely wounded on the Bhutan frontier, Rennell retired to London and devoted the next 53 years to geographical research. He prepared important maps of India and wrote *Currents of the Atlantic Ocean*, the first work of its kind, which was published posthumously in 1832 and remained a standard reference text for the next century. French explorer Lapérouse named Rennell Sd the Baie de Clonard in 1786, after one of his officers; the Haida knew it as Chalo-kathli. Its shoreline was not accurately charted until 1935–36, when hydrographer Henri Parizeau completed a detailed survey. *D*

Renner Point (53°02'00" 131°53'00" N tip of Louise I, off NE Moresby I, QCI). QCI pioneer Joseph Renner ranched and farmed at the W end of Maud I in Skidegate Inlet. He was born in Switzerland and had pre-empted land on Graham I at Lawn Hill in 1909, but left it to search

R

elsewhere for work. In 1914 he married Lena Hubley, the widow of a former Lawn Hill neighbour, and the couple moved to Maud I, where Joseph had received a Crown grant in 1911. The Renners were famed for their homespun hospitality until Lena died of burns received from a domestic accident. The point was named by the hydrographic service in 1926. The waterway separating Maud I and Leonide Point to the W is known locally as Renner Pass. *D*

Rennison Island (52°50'00" 129°20'00" Just W of the N end of Aristazabal I). After Victoria hydrographer, WWI naval officer and dockmaster Oswald Rennison Parker. *See* Parker Passage.

Repulse Point (49°29'00" 124°44'00" SW side of Denman I, Baynes Sd, W side of Str of Georgia). Named after HMS *Repulse*—the 11th ship in the RN to bear that name—a 28,654-tonne, 242-m battlecruiser that was launched in 1916 and saw limited action in WWI. It was sunk, along with the battleship *Prince of Wales*, off Singapore in Dec 1941 by Japanese torpedo bombers. Casualties were heavy: 513 on the *Repulse* and 327 on the *Prince of Wales*. The loss of these two vessels was a major Allied disaster, demonstrating the vulnerability of even the largest warships to aerial attack and signalling the demise of the battleship as the dominant naval force. The *Repulse* visited Vancouver and Victoria in 1924 with HMS *Hood* and the Special Service Squadron, under Vice Adm Sir Frederick Field.

Repulse Rock (48°33'00" 123°32'00" E side of Finlayson Arm, SW of Elbow Point, off SW side of Saanich Peninsula). HMS *Repulse*—the ninth ship of that name in the RN—was the Pacific Station flagship in 1872–77 and a frequent sight at Esquimalt. This 5,614-tonne vessel was the last wooden battleship built for the RN. The hull was laid down in 1861, but work then ceased until 1866, when conversion to an ironclad took place. The *Repulse*, while reputed to have the best accommodations in the fleet, was something of an anachronism: its armour was so heavy that it could only carry a single row of guns on either side of the main deck, even though it had originally been designed with two gun decks. There was thick steel plating along the waterline, but the wood of the upper bow and stern areas remained exposed to avoid top-heaviness. The ship was assigned to the Pacific because that was thought to be the place it was least likely to see action. The *Repulse* could make 12.5 knots under steam and 10.5 under sail and is believed to have covered more distance under sail than almost any other ironclad. It became the guard ship at Hull, 1881–85, and was scrapped in 1889. Repulse Rk was labelled Beacon Rk on the 1855 map that Joseph Pemberton prepared for the HBC, and on an 1871 Admiralty chart; the name was changed by the hydrographic service in 1934 to avoid duplication. Local fishermen know it as the White Lady—a reference to the

navigation aid located there. Mink I (qv) in Desolation Sd was renamed Repulse I after this vessel in 1945, but the change was reversed after local residents complained.

Rescue Bay (52°31'00" 128°17'00" SE entrance to Jackson Passage, Susan I, Mathieson Channel, N of Bella Bella). Records at BC's Geographical Names Office suggest that the incident referred to by this name, while admirable, was not exactly front-page news. A pet spaniel that had jumped from a Klemtu-bound fish packer was retrieved here on a dark night by the crew of the W coast hydrographic vessel *Parry*. Nearby Spaniel Point also takes its name from this event.

Reservation Point (54°25'00" 130°06'00" N entrance to Quottoon Inlet, Work Channel, just NE of Prince Rupert). Named by the hydrographic service in 1965 in association with Nishanocknawnak First Nation reserve, a traditional Tsimshian site, which is located on the point. Nishanocknawnak is one of numerous reserves in the region used by the residents of nearby Lax Kw'alaams (Port Simpson).

Reserve Point (48°51'00" 123°19'00" Between Miner Bay and Naylor Bay, W side of Mayne I, Gulf Is). This feature is located at the E edge of the Mayne I First Nation reserve, a traditional territory of the Tsartlip First Nation, which is based at Brentwood Bay on the Saanich Peninsula.

Resolution Cove (49°36'00" 126°31'00" E side of Clerke Peninsula, S end of Bligh I, entrance to Nootka Sd, W side of Vancouver I). HMS *Resolution*, the larger of Capt James Cook's two expedition vessels, was repaired here in 1778 during the explorer's month-long stay on the BC coast. Cook named the site Ship Cove. The 419-tonne, 12-gun sloop was built at Whitby in N Yorkshire in 1770 as the N Sea collier *Marquis of Granby* and was purchased by the Admiralty a year later. The vessel was rebuilt to accommodate naturalist Joseph Banks and his entourage, but the changes were found to affect its seaworthiness and were reversed. Banks then refused to accompany the expedition and was replaced by Johann and George Forster. Cook commanded this ship on both the second (1772–75) and third (1776–80) of his great voyages, calling it "the fittest for service of any I have seen." When he arrived at Nootka Sd, both his vessels were in urgent need of refits after being buffeted by near-continuous Pacific gales. Masts and yards were replaced using timber from local forests. After its return to England in 1780, the *Resolution* was converted to a transport and sailed to the E Indies, where it was captured by the French, sent to Manila and never seen again. Various reports have circulated concerning the fate of this famous vessel (that it foundered, was recaptured by the British or ended up as a coal hulk at Rio de Janeiro), but none have ever been confirmed. *W*

A watercolour by John Webber showing Captain James Cook's Resolution and Discovery at Nootka Sound in 1778. *Harbour Publishing collection*

Restless Bight (50°22'15" 127°58'11" N side of Kwakiutl Point, at entrance to Quatsino Sd, NW end of Vancouver I), **Restless Mountain** (50°20'08" 127°56'19" N side of Brooks Bay, between Quatsino Sd and Kyuquot Sd), **Restless Rock** (52°15'00" 128°10'00" S entrance to Return Channel, S of Yeo I, N of Bella Bella). The *Restless* was a 64-tonne, 22-m steam tug, built at New Westminster in 1906 for the federal Dept of Marine and Fisheries and, later, the RCN. It was used as a survey vessel by the Canadian Hydrographic Service, 1920–23, especially in Quatsino Sd. Cdr John Knight was in charge, assisted by Louis Davies and engineer T Salmon. In 1921 the *Restless* took part in a survey of Ripple Rk in Seymour Narrows; in 1922 it worked in Johnstone Str and Gunboat Passage, and in 1923 in Victoria and Esquimalt harbours. The tug was laid up in 1924 and sold in 1927. Restless Bight was formerly known as Open Bay and Grant Bay.

Restoration Bay (52°07'00" 127°38'00" E side of Burke Channel, SW of Kwatna Inlet, E of Bella Bella). Named by Capt George Vancouver after he and his crew celebrated May 29, 1793—Restoration Day—at this location. This was the date in 1660 that King Charles II entered London and was restored to the throne that his father, Charles I, had lost (along with his head) during the English Civil War. While Restoration Day was a statutory public holiday in Vancouver's time, its importance gradually waned and its official status was abolished in 1859. The day (also known as Oak Apple Day or Royal Oak Day, in honour of the oak tree in which Charles II hid while escaping from the Roundhead army in 1651) is still recognized with events at several places in England. The *Discovery* and *Chatham* anchored at the bay for two weeks in May and June 1793 while making repairs, taking astronomical observations, brewing spruce beer and trading with the local inhabitants. As was usual with these layovers, the ships' boats were used to survey the surrounding region. Restoration Point on Puget Sd in Washington state had been named by Vancouver on May 29, 1792, also to commemorate Restoration Day. *W*

Retreat Passage (50°42'00" 126°36'00" Between Bonwick I and Gilford I, E end of Queen Charlotte Str, W of Knight Inlet). Retreat Passage appears on the 1867 edition of an Admiralty chart based on 1860 and 1865 surveys by Capt George Richards and Lt Daniel Pender, respectively. According to a note at BC's Geographical Names Office, the name may refer to a raid on the Kwikwasut'inux (Kwakwaka'wakw) village of Gwa'yasdams on Gilford I by Nuxalk First Nation warriors in the late 1850s.

Reverie Passage (53°28'42" 130°25'52" Between the Antle Is and the Shadforth Is, Kingkown Inlet, NW side of Banks I). The *Reverie* was a 12-m yawl belonging to Rev John Antle, the Anglican missionary who established the Columbia Coast Mission on the BC coast in 1904. In 1938, two years after retiring, Antle went to England to pick up the *Reverie*, for which he had traded a piece of land at Maple Bay. The vessel was apparently built in 1934 on a tea plantation in Assam, in India's hill country, then taken 1,300 km by rail to the coast. Next it went to England by freighter before finally being launched in the Thames. At the age of 73, Antle sailed it across the Atlantic and through the Panama Canal to BC, a journey that took him two years. He lived aboard the *Reverie* at Vancouver but then set off again, this time to the W Indies, when he was 83. Bad weather and poor health brought an end to this voyage at San Francisco, however. The feature was named in association with nearby Antle Is (qv).

Reynard Point (48°43'50" 123°19'49" NW tip of Moresby I, SW of N Pender I, Gulf Is). This feature is probably named after members of the Reynard family, who were early pioneers on the Saanich Peninsula. Anglican minister James Reynard (1829–75), from Yorkshire, served at Barkerville during the gold rush in the late 1860s and built St Saviour's church there, which still stands. A former Methodist, he was ordained as a priest at Victoria in 1868 and served as curate of Christ Church Cathedral. At Barkerville, Reynard suffered the indifference and open ridicule of the miners when he tried to establish a church

R

and ended up building much of it single-handedly, with great financial difficulty. When his health deteriorated he moved, with his family, first to St Paul's at Nanaimo in 1871 and then to Saanich in 1874, where he became rector of St Stephen's Church at Mt Newton. His son Arthur Tallis Reynard (1870–1943) farmed at Saanichton. The point is shown in error on a 1935 chart as Reef Point.

Reynolds Point (49°06'00" 123°48'00" N entrance to Boat Hbr, SE of Cedar, SE side of Vancouver I). S H Reynolds, managing director of South Wellington Coal Mines Ltd of Victoria in 1909, is a possible source for this name. The company (soon to be reorganized as Pacific Coast Coal Mines Ltd) opened a new mine that year, the Fiddick Colliery, 6 km SE of Nanaimo, and built a loading facility at Boat Hbr. According to the BC mining ministry's annual report, the waterfront construction, which was connected to the minesite by rail, resulted in a "wharf where ships of deepest draught can be loaded promptly." The Fiddick was a large operation, employing 347 men in 1910 and producing 156,000 tonnes of coal.

Rhodes Island (49°16'00" 125°55'00" W side of Cypress Bay, N of Meares I, Clayoquot Sd, W side of Vancouver I). Henry Harrison Rhodes (1840–1915), originally from Seattle, pre-empted land on Clayoquot Sd S of Cypress Bay in the early 1900s. A prospector, he was quoted in the Victoria *Colonist* about the excellent potential that existed for gold mining around Clayoquot Sd. Rhodes died at Tofino. Formerly known as False I.

Rhodes Point (54°13'00" 133°02'00" S side of Fury Bay, W side of Langara I, off NW Graham I, QCI). Named in 1907 by Capt Frederick Learmonth of the RN survey vessel *Egeria* after one of the ship's stokers. Seaman Rhodes helped crew a sounding boat during a reconnaissance of this area.

Richard Point (49°16'00" 124°07'00" N side of Nanoose Hbr, NW of Nanaimo, E side of Vancouver I). After Richard P Wallis, a major landowner in this district in the early 1900s. *See* Wallis Point.

Richard Rock (48°59'00" 125°20'00" In David Channel, E of Stopper Is, Barkley Sd, W side of Vancouver I). After Lt Richard Mayne, who served as an RN survey assistant on the BC coast, 1857–61. Named by Capt George Richards in 1861. *See* Mayne Bay.

Richards Channel (50°57'00" 127°27'00" N of Ripple Passage, NE of Walker Group, off NW side of Queen Charlotte Str). Capt George Henry Richards (1819–96) was the most important early marine surveyor on the BC coast. When one considers his immense contribution— and the large number of place names he bestowed—it is surprising that so few features honour him. He was from

Cornwall and joined the RN in 1832, serving at first in the W Indies and then, under Sir Edward Belcher, in the Pacific, where he trained as a surveyor. In the 1840s he worked on surveys of the Falkland Is and NZ. Richards was deputy cdr of HMS *Assistance* from 1852 to 1854 on Belcher's controversial Arctic search for Sir John Franklin, during which a number of British warships were abandoned in the ice. He made several arduous sledge journeys on this assignment, covering more than 3,000 km in all, and was promoted to capt on his return to England. In 1856, as cdr of HMS *Plumper*, he was sent to Esquimalt to assist Capt James Prevost, the chief British envoy to the US-Canada boundary commission. As Britain's second commissioner, Richards made a detailed survey of the waters between Vancouver I and the US mainland in 1858. In 1859 he helped provide a military presence during the gold rush and also completed surveys of the Fraser R and the E coast of Vancouver I. Provided with a bigger vessel, HMS *Hecate*, in 1860, he went on to chart much of the southern BC coast before taking the *Hecate* back to England in Dec 1862, leaving Lt Daniel Pender in charge of the remaining hydrographic work. During his time in BC, Richards drew a great number of very accurate charts and wrote the first two editions of the *Vancouver I Pilot*. He was appointed hydrographer of the RN in 1864 and a rear adm in 1870; after retirement in 1874 he was knighted, made a fellow of the Royal Society and rose to the rank of adm, retired. Richards also had a significant 20-year post-naval career as head of the Telegraph Construction & Maintenance Co, which laid more than 120,000 km of underwater cable under his direction. Richards Channel was formerly known as North Channel; it was renamed in 1948 by Maj William Firth, BC's chief geographer. Mt Richards on Vancouver I commemorates this significant historical figure (as does Richards St in downtown Vancouver), and Henry Bay on Denman I may be named for him as well. *E W*

Richards Island (48°27'00" 123°26'00" Thetis Cove, E side of Esquimalt Hbr, SE end of Vancouver I). Lt Fleetwood John Richards was a Royal Marines officer aboard HMS *Fisgard*, under Capt John Duntze, on the Pacific Station, 1843–47. He went on to a significant career in the marines, reaching the rank of maj gen in the light infantry in the mid-1880s.

Richardson Bay (48°50'00" 123°21'00" SE side of Prevost I, W of Mayne I, Gulf Is). John Richardson (b 1859) was the first keeper at Portlock Point lighthouse on Prevost I, which was built in 1895–96. He and his wife, Sarah Jane (1862–1931), had come out to Canada from England in 1890; their daughter Viola was born on Prevost in 1901. The Richardsons, who, according to BC lighthouse chronicler Donald Graham, had standing orders to wind up a spring-loaded fog bell so that it rang every 15 seconds in dirty weather, left the station in 1905. The name was submitted by the Gulf Is Branch of the BC Historical Assoc and adopted in 1969.

Richardson Bluff (48°45'00" 123°14'00" W side of S Pender I, Gulf Is). Gerald Francis Richardson (1873–1932) was a pioneer settler on S Pender I, coming out to BC in the 1890s and forming a business partnership with his friend Charles Long. The pair attempted, unsuccessfully, to drive a flock of sheep to the Klondike in 1898. Richardson built a home on S Pender in 1912 and farmed on his property after serving in France in WWI. Greenburn Lk, once part of his estate, was named after his home in England. Much of his land is now part of the Gulf Is National Park Reserve. The bluff—another name submitted by the Gulf Is Branch of the BC Historical Assoc and adopted in 1969—was formerly called Pollard Bluff (*see* Pollard Cove).

Richardson Cove (49°27'00" 124°16'00" S side of Lasqueti I, Str of Georgia). Thomas Richardson (1868–1937), a native of Scotland, came to BC and married Janet Agnes McNeil (1867–1958), also from Scotland, at Nanaimo in 1895. They lived on the S coast of Lasqueti in the late 1890s, and Tom worked as a shepherd for an early sheep-raising venture on the island. Nearby Graveyard Bay is named after the grave of their daughter Maggie, who died on Lasqueti in 1899, aged two. The Richardsons left for Nanaimo in the early 1900s.

Richardson Head (53°21'00" 132°30'00" S side of Rennell Sd, SW side of Graham I, QCI), **Richardson Inlet** (52°44'00" 131°39'00" Between Lyell I and Tanu I, off E side of Moresby I, QCI), **Richardson Island** (52°45'00" 131°45'00" NW of Lyell I, at head of Richardson Inlet), **Richardson Passage** (52°43'00" 131°43'00" Between Richardsun I and Lyell I), **Richardson Point** (52°35'00" 131°35'00" S tip of Lyell I, NW side of Juan Perez Sd). James Richardson (1810–83) came to Canada from Scotland as a young man and farmed at Beauharnois, Que. He became interested in geology and made such an impression on Sir William Logan, founder of the Geological Survey of Canada, that Logan invited him, in 1846, to become a survey assistant. He remained with the survey until his death, making early use of photography in field work in Que and Ont in the 1850s and later conducting a major survey of NW Canada. In 1872–73 he reported on Vancouver I's coal-mining prospects and also compiled a report on the old Cowgitz coal mine on Skidegate Inlet. Operations there had ceased recently, after ongoing problems, but the mine's owners continued to hope that the property could be made profitable. In this, however, they were deluded. In 1874, Richardson travelled in the sloop *Triumph* to northern BC, where he undertook surveys in Gardner Inlet for the CPR. Richardson Inlet was named by fellow geologist George Mercer Dawson in 1878, Richardson Head by the hydrographic service in 1948 and Richardson Passage by the service in 1962. The W end of the passage is known locally as Richardson Narrows. Richardson I was

formerly called Little Lyell I. A Richardson Point on the S side of Gardner Canal, named for the geologist by CPR officials in 1874, has since been rescinded as an official name. Several fossils also commemorate this hard-working, self-taught scientist. *D W*

Richardson Range (52°41'00" 128°54'00" E of Kent Inlet, SW Princess Royal I). George Richardson (1826–1922) was born in Kent, England, and immigrated, along with 79 others, to Victoria in 1850 on board the HBC supply vessel *Norman Morison*. The HBC's new medical officer, Dr John Helmcken, was a shipmate on the same voyage. By 1920, Helmcken and Richardson were the only two survivors of the journey still alive. Richardson, who probably first worked as a farm labourer, went on to become a hotelkeeper in Victoria. He built the Victoria Hotel (renamed the Windsor in 1890), one of BC's first brick buildings, in 1858, the same year his soon-to-be wife, Mary Ann (c 1838–1911), arrived in the city from England. The structure, now a gift shop, was still standing in the early 2000s, covered in mock-Tudor siding, at 901 Government St. The hotel was damaged—and Richardson badly singed—by an explosion in 1876 when the proprietor went in search of a gas leak with a candle. Gas mains had recently been installed, and people were not yet familiar with the dangers.

Richards Point (55°17'00" 129°49'00" W side of Observatory Inlet, S of Stewart). After Capt Richard Dawkins, who was stationed on the RN's Pacific Station, 1866–69. *See* Dawkins Point.

Richards Shoal (52°42'00" 129°23'00" NE of the Moore Is, off NW Aristazabal I, Hecate Str). Francis Gilbert Richards (c 1854–1925), born at Dodgeville, Wisconsin, came to BC with family members in 1862. His father, also Francis Gilbert Richards (1821–96), a native of Cornwall, had immigrated to Wisconsin in 1847 and then headed W to California in search of gold. Gold also lured him to the Fraser R and the Cariboo. He finally settled at New Westminster and became chief of the volunteer fire dept. His son moved to Victoria, where he married Elizabeth Davey (1852–1923), also from the US, in 1879 and worked as a realtor and hotelkeeper. Richards Jr ran unsuccessfully in both the 1890 and 1894 provincial elections, then was appointed Victoria's sheriff in 1902. After retiring in 1923, he participated in the Victoria old-timers' reunion of 1924 (*see* Adams Bay).

Richard III Bank (54°01'00" 132°34'00" In Alexander Narrows, S of Virago Sd, N side of Graham I, QCI). Named in 1907 by Capt Frederick Learmonth of HMS *Egeria* during a re-survey of Naden Hbr. The *Richard III* was an old ship that had been converted to an ore carrier and used to haul coal from Alaska. In Dec 1906 it grounded on the rocks of Virago Sd; the following winter it was towed by

R

Haida salvagers into Naden Hbr and beached near Bain Point, just SW of the bank. The Haida people know this feature as Ow'way-stah, a name associated with Ow'way, the Haida word for Naden Hbr, which can be translated as "many sandbanks." *D*

Many of the dykes that surround Richmond and protect it from flooding have walking paths. *Peter Vassilopoulos*

Richmond (49°10'00" 123°07'00" Lulu I and Sea I, just S of Vancouver), **Richmond Island** (49°12'00" 123°09'00" Off NW Sea I in N Arm of Fraser R). Wildly varying explanations have been offered over the years for the origin of the municipal name. Richmond appears in local newspapers from 1862, thus disqualifying claims that it was named after the English home of early settler William Ferris or the Yorkshire birthplace of Mary Boyd, wife of the first reeve; both of these worthies arrived in the area after that date. It now seems fairly certain that the name derives from the Richmond (or Richmond View) Farm, established on Sea I in 1861 by Hugh McRoberts (1816–83). A native of Ireland, he had followed the lure of gold to Australia, California and Yale before settling at the mouth of the Fraser R. He also helped build historic trails from Yale to Boston Bar and from New Westminster to Point Grey. BC historians Helen and Philip Akrigg suggest that one of his daughters named the farm after a beloved spot in Australia. McRoberts eventually sold his farm (which had grown to include part of Lulu I) and established a dairy in New Westminster. His nephews Samuel and Fitzgerald McCleery were early settlers in S Vancouver. The municipality of Richmond, comprising Sea I, most of Lulu I, and 12 smaller islands, was incorporated in 1879. Farming and salmon canning were the traditional industries (at one point Richmond had 49 canneries). Bridges connected the municipality to Vancouver by 1889; a railway followed in 1902; and Vancouver's main airport opened on Sea I in 1931. Richmond has seen a huge population increase, especially among Asian immigrants, since 1980, with vast residential suburbs and shopping malls taking over the farmland. It reincorporated as a city

in 1990 and had a population of over 150,000 in the early 2000s. Richmond I, though part of Richmond, is now attached to Vancouver's shoreline by a short causeway; named after the municipality, it is largely paved and used for lumber storage by a forestry company. *E*

Ridley Island (54°13'00" 130°19'00" S of Kaien I, just S of Prince Rupert). William Ridley (1836–1911) became the first bishop of the Anglican diocese of Caledonia, formed when the original diocese of BC was divided in three in 1879. He was born in England and worked as a carpenter before training as a missionary. After serving in India, and also as vicar of St Paul's in Huddersfield, UK, he immigrated to BC with his wife, Jane, to take up his new position. Ridley established his see at Metlakatla and immediately ran into conflict with the resident missionary, William Duncan (*see* Duncan I), who opposed him at every turn. The feud between the two men verged on violence, and in 1887, Duncan led more than 800 First Nation followers to SE Alaska to establish a new community. Ridley stayed at Metlakatla for almost 20 years and increased the number of missions in his diocese, travelling to remote villages in his small boat, the *Evangeline*. He translated religious documents into First Nation languages and published a number of books about his experiences. Formerly known as Flat I and N Porpoise I, Ridley I was named, on the suggestion of Capt John Walbran of CGS *Quadra*, by the Geographic Board of Canada in 1905, when the island was surveyed. Ridley, recently retired, returned to England that same year. Nearby Bishop I is also named for him. The cathedral and see of the diocese of Caledonia were moved to Prince Rupert in 1907. *E W*

Ridout Islets (49°09'00" 125°43'00" W side of Tofino Inlet, W of mouth of Kennedy R, Clayoquot Sd, W side of Vancouver I). Named after James Ridout (b 1872), who pre-empted land on Esowista Peninsula in 1896. He was listed as a reporter and a US native in the 1901 BC census.

Riley Cove (49°24'00" 126°13'00" NW end of Flores I, NW of Tofino, Clayoquot Sd, W side of Vancouver I). Riley Cove, which appears as Rileys Cove on some early maps, is supposedly named after Clayoquot pioneer and former RN seaman Reece Riley (1847–1918), who arrived in the district in 1898, did some prospecting, and established a boat-repair facility and marine ways in the area. In Wrigley's *BC Directory* for 1918 he is listed as a Tofino resident: "boatman, lightkeeper, boats for hire." Pioneer logger William Gibson, who had large timber holdings in Sydney Inlet, had a forestry camp at Riley Cove in 1917; a pilchard-reduction plant operated there in the 1920s. Riley Ck and Riley Lk drain into the cove.

Ring Point (53°13'00" 129°36'00" S end of Principe Channel, SW end of Pitt I). David Babington Ring, a lawyer and a native of Dublin, was in his mid-50s when he immigrated to Victoria about 1859. He became a prominent figure in the Vancouver I colony, acting as attorney gen in 1863 during the temporary absence of George Hunter Cary, whose mental health was deteriorating, and serving as the first president of the Law Society of BC, 1869–74. He was elected to Vancouver I's legislative assembly, 1861–63, as the member from Nanaimo, during which time he introduced a controversial bill to protect deserted wives. Later he was the Nanaimo representative on the BC legislative council—and an outspoken opponent of Confederation. Ring was an experienced attorney, the author in the 1840s of several legal texts, but he was also temperamental and eccentric, known for political feuding and for arguing with judges. Ring Point was formerly known as Wolf Point but was renamed by the hydrographic service in 1945.

Riordan Point (53°27'00" 128°55'00" N entrance to Bishop Bay, Boxer Reach, opposite E side of Gribbell I, N of Princess Royal I). Thomas Travers Riordan was the surgeon aboard HMS *Boxer*, 1871–75, while that gun vessel was stationed on the BC coast. He was promoted to staff surgeon in 1878. A number of features in this vicinity were named about 1875 by members of a CPR land-survey team searching for a suitable terminus for the transcontinental railroad. The *Boxer*, under Lt Cdr William Collins, had conducted a marine survey of N coast inlets for the same purpose.

Ripon Island (51°28'00" 127°39'00" S of Walbran I, N entrance to Rivers Inlet), **Ripon Point** (51°19'00" 127°32'00" N entrance to Smith Inlet, E of Smith Sd, N of Port Hardy). Capt John Walbran, coastal historian and cdr of the lighthouse tender *Quadra*, named the point in 1903 after his birthplace, the small cathedral city of Ripon in N Yorkshire. Walbran attended historic Ripon Grammar School, where his grandfather, Rev Thomas Horsfall, was a master for many years. *W*

Ripple Rock (50°08'00" 125°21'00" In Seymour Narrows, Discovery Passage, between Vancouver I and Quadra I). This impediment to shipping was named by Capt George Richards in 1860. The rock's twin peaks were a mere 2.7 m and 7 m, respectively, below the surface, and the strong tides that surged around them created the namesake "ripple." Despite its 16-knot (30-km/h) currents, Seymour Narrows is a major navigation channel, and the rock soon became the site of numerous tragedies: over the years more than 100 vessels managed to strike it, and at least 114 people have lost their lives at the site. The USS *Saranac*, a paddle steamer, hit the obstacle and foundered in 1875; the RN corvette *Satellite* grounded there in 1884; and the CNR steamship *Prince Rupert*, travelling in thick fog, was almost wrecked in 1927. A 19th-century scheme to cross Seymour Narrows called for a piling on Ripple Rk to support a railway bridge; wiser heads later determined

that the hazard should be demolished. Two attempts were made in the 1940s, but nine workers died in an accident and work was abandoned. Another effort in the mid-1950s saw a tunnel drilled out to the rock from Maud I and filled with 1,237 tonnes of explosives. On Apr 5, 1958, one of the world's largest non-nuclear peacetime blasts was successfully set off—watched by thousands of Canadians on CBC television. Ripple Rk's two heads now have 13.7 m and 15.2 m of water over them. *E*

Ripple Rock explosion, April 5, 1958. *MCR Photo by R E Olsen*

Rip Point (48°53'00" 123°19'00" SE side of Galiano I, Gulf Is). Named for the tide rips that often occur on Fairway Bank, the shoal located midway between Rip Point and Georgina Point.

Rippon Point (53°55'00" 130°12'00" N end of Pitt I, S of Prince Rupert). Capt Thomas Rippon (1883–1939), a native of Nottingham, UK, joined the CPR's BC Coast Steamship Service as a seaman in 1905 and was soon appointed an officer. His first command, in 1916, was the *Princess Beatrice*. After that date he served as a master, mostly on the CPR's triangle run between Vancouver, Victoria and Seattle, and was appointed the service's marine superintendent in 1934. Rippon married Norma Rose Cavin at Vancouver in 1917. In 1922 he was capt of the *Princess Royal* when it rammed and sank the PGE steam tug *Clinton*, bound from Squamish with a rail barge in tow, at Vancouver Hbr's First Narrows. When fire broke out at the CPR's Vancouver terminal in 1938, it was Rippon's quick action that saved the *Princess Charlotte*; the steamer was tied to the pier but he quickly mustered a skeleton crew and managed to cast the vessel off and move it to safety. Rippon Point, formerly known as Hill Point, was named by the hydrographic service in 1945.

Ritchie Island (54°20'00" 130°25'00" Venn Passage, N of Digby I, just W of Prince Rupert), **Ritchie Point** (54°20'00" 130°17'00" N end of Kaien I, Prince Rupert). In 1904–5, as part of the preparations for the coming of the GTP's transcontinental railway, Joseph Frederick Ritchie (1863–1939) made a survey of Kaien I and the

R

surrounding islands and waterways. Born and educated at Aylmer, Que, he became accredited as both a Dominion and a BC land surveyor, then worked at Lethbridge as a surveyor and realtor in the early 1890s and married Jane Adams at Rossland in 1896. Ritchie and his family settled at Prince Rupert, where he collaborated with A R Barrow on the townsite's subdivision survey in 1908–9 and made many additional surveys in later years along the Skeena R and on the N coast. Ritchie I was formerly known as Marten I. *W*

Rithet Island (52°13'00" 128°08'00" Off NE side of Campbell I, just N of Bella Bella). Robert Paterson Rithet (1844–1919) came to BC in 1862 to join the gold rush. Two years later he settled at Victoria, where he would transform himself into one of the province's wealthiest merchants. He was born in Scotland and trained as a clerk at Liverpool. At Victoria, in 1871, he established a wholesale grocery business with San Francisco entrepreneur J Andrew Welch. In 1875 he married Elizabeth Jane Hannah Munro (1853–1952), daughter of Alexander Munro, the HBC's senior official in western Canada. R P Rithet & Co soon expanded into shipping, salmon canning, insurance, lumber, sugar and sealing. Rithet was president of the Victoria board of trade and the main force behind the British Pacific Rwy Co. He had large farms at Royal Oak and Delta, offices in California and Hawaii, and his Victoria Wharf & Warehouse Co constructed Victoria's outer wharf. Steamship magnate John Irving, Rithet's brother-in-law, named his finest Fraser R sternwheeler the *R P Rithet* in 1882 to honour his soon-to-be business partner in the Canadian Pacific Navigation Co. Rithet was also a politician: mayor of Victoria, 1885–86, and MLA for Victoria, 1894–98. Rithet Ck and Rithets Bog in Greater Victoria are named for him as well. Rithet I was formerly known as Grassy I and Holme I—after Cdr Hugh Edward Holme, who served as CO of HMCS *Niobe* during WWI. *E*

River Jordan. *See* Jordan R.

Rivers Inlet (51°28'00" 127°35'00" N of Port Hardy and Smith Sd). Capt George Vancouver named this feature in 1792 after George Pitt, 1st Baron Rivers of Strathfieldsaye (1721–1803). Pitt was a Tory MP for many years, an ambassador to Sardinia and Spain, and a lord lt of Hampshire and Dorset. Mt Rivers, N of Cape Caution, is also named for him. His wife, Penelope Atkins, was a celebrated beauty, whom author Horace Walpole praised as "all loveliness within and without" while describing Pitt as "her brutal half-mad husband." Penelope Point on nearby Moses Inlet is named for her. Vancouver's subordinates Lt Peter Puget and Joseph Whidbey, master of HMS *Discovery*, explored the inlet by boat while the expedition's ships lay at anchor in Safety Cove on Calvert I. A relative of George Pitt, the notorious Thomas Pitt, later Lord Camelford (*see* Grenville Channel), was a "gentleman" seaman on HMS *Discovery*. Vancouver had this troublemaker flogged and sent home in disgrace, an action that so inflamed the young Pitt that he later challenged his former capt to a duel and attacked him on a London street. Rivers Inlet became famous for its salmon production and was home to 17 canneries between 1882 and the 1950s. It also had a hospital, 1897–1950. Today the inlet is closed to commercial fishing but home to several luxurious floating sport-fishing lodges. Logging is also important in the area. The main community is Dawsons Landing (qv). Rivers Inlet Cannery, the first to be built in the region, was located at the head of the inlet near the mouth of the Wannock R; a post office named Rivers Inlet operated there, 1890–1942. *E W*

Rix Island (53°31'00" 128°44'00" In Alan Reach, Gardner Canal, S of Kitimat). George Alexander Rix (1865–1945), from Ont, taught at Barrie before graduating from Univ of Toronto in 1893 and being ordained an Anglican clergyman. He served at various Ont churches and as dean of Wycliffe College, 1894–1913, then moved with his family to Prince Rupert, where he was appointed canon of St Andrew's Cathedral and, later, archdeacon of Prince Rupert. After Bishop Frederick Du Vernet's death in 1924, Rix became administrator of the diocese of Caledonia for four years before his consecration as the third bishop of Caledonia, a position he held until his death. His wife, Sadie (1876–1945, née Gillespie), died less than three months before him. Rix was a masterful fundraiser, managing to replace the Prince Rupert Coast Mission's aging vessel and build a bishop's residence. Rix I was formerly known as Channel I but was renamed by the hydrographic service in 1946 in order to avoid duplication.

Robb Bluff (49°40'00" 124°57'00" N side of Comox Hbr, E side of Vancouver I), **Robb Point** (52°16'00" 128°24'00" SW end of Surf It, off Ivory I, at SW end of Don Peninsula, NW of Bella Bella). Isabella Robb (1816–88), trained as a nurse, came to Vancouver I in 1862 as the matron for the Columbia Emigration Society aboard the brideship *Tynemouth*. She was accompanied by her Aberdeenshire husband, James Robb (1818–89), and their three children. The Robbs went that same year to Comox, where Isabella became the first white woman settler in the Comox valley. James and his son William pre-empted 113 ha of waterfront in what is now downtown Comox and developed successful farms; the Victoria *Colonist* reported in 1869 that James had grown a turnip weighing 42 pounds (19 kg). Comox's town wharf was built adjacent to their land in 1874, and James was appointed the district registrar of lands. Robb Bluff, known earlier as River Bluff, was renamed by the hydrographic service in 1945. Robb Point was formerly called Surf Point.

Roberson Islets (52°19'00" 127°58'00" Return Channel, off S end of Florence Peninsula, NE of Bella Bella), **Roberson Point** (54°19'00" 130°24'00" N side of Venn Passage, N of Digby I, just W of Prince Rupert). Harold Langhorne Roberson (1877–1932), from England, worked on tugboats for the GTP during Prince Rupert's early days. In 1908 he and his wife, Marian Lingen Burton (1878–1952), also from England, were the first couple to be married in the city's new Anglican church. They returned to the UK during WWI; she drove ambulances and he worked on decoy or Q-ships—armed merchant vessels disguised to look like easy targets to lure U-boats to the surface, where they could be destroyed. Back in Prince Rupert after the war, Harold, known to all as "Skipper," rose through the ranks of the GTP and CNR to become master of the *Prince Rupert*. The Robersons moved to Victoria in the 1920s, and Harold worked for the pilot service. He died at Sooke. The Roberson Its were named in 1924 to honour the steamship route to Ocean Falls that Skipper pioneered by way of Return Channel and Johnson Channel. Roberson Point was named in 1911.

Robert Arm (51°25'00" 127°28'00" E of Fishhook Bay, SW extension of Draney Inlet, just E of entrance to Rivers Inlet, N of Port Hardy). After cannery owner and operator Robert Draney. *See* Draney Inlet. Formerly known as the W Arm of Draney Inlet.

Robert Island (51°59'00" 128°15'00" S end of the Prince Group, off SW side of Campbell I, SW of Bella Bella). The *Prince Robert* was one of three luxurious CNR passenger ships built in the UK for use on the BC coast. They went into service in 1930 but soon proved too expensive to operate and too unwieldy in BC's intricate waterways. The 111-m, 6,334-tonne *Prince Robert* ran on a few Alaska and W Indies cruises in the 1930s but was otherwise laid up at Vancouver. During WWII, converted to an armed merchant cruiser, it searched for enemy shipping in the Pacific, undertook convoy duties in the Atlantic and Mediterranean, and also served in NZ, the Aleutians and Hong Kong. After the war the *Prince Robert* was purchased by Charlton Steam Shipping, a Greek company, and renamed the *Charlton Sovereign*. It was sold again in 1951, to the Italian firm Fratelli Grimaldi, and underwent an extensive rebuild. This time around, as the *Luciana*, it was put to work as a W Indies cruise ship. The vessel was broken up in 1962. Robert I was named by the hydrographic service in 1944.

Robert Island (53°53'00" 130°40'00" W of Gurd I, Kitkatla Inlet, SW of Porcher I and Prince Rupert). After Rev Robert Winter Gurd, missionary to the Tsimshian First Nation at Kitkatla. *See* Gurd Inlet.

Roberts Bank (49°03'42" 123°10'39" E side of Str of Georgia, between mouth of the Fraser R's S Arm and Tsawwassen). This feature, which first appeared on an Admiralty chart in 1853, was sketched by Aemilius Simpson aboard the HBC schooner *Cadboro* in 1827. It was named in association with Point Roberts, S of Tsawwassen, which lies in US territory and is thus not a BC geographical feature. Capt George Vancouver, who examined this portion of coastline personally with Lt Peter Puget in HMS *Discovery*'s yawl, named Point Roberts in 1792 after his friend and fellow RN officer Henry Roberts (1757–96). Roberts, from Sussex, had sailed with Vancouver on Capt James Cook's second and third expeditions (he was a midshipman on the second voyage, a master's mate on the third—both times aboard HMS *Resolution*). An artist and draftsman, he prepared the charts that appeared in the official published account of Cook's three journeys. Roberts was present in Hawaii at Cook's death and tried gallantly to prevent the fatal attack on his cdr by Hawaiian islanders. He was selected to command the 1790 expedition to the PNW with HMS *Discovery*; Vancouver was originally to have been his deputy. However, the voyage was postponed and Roberts, by then a cdr, reassigned. Vancouver was appointed to the

R

Roberts Bank and Deltaport. *Courtesy Port Metro Vancouver*

top job instead. Roberts was promoted to capt in 1794 and died of yellow fever in the W Indies while cdr of the frigate *Undaunted*. His portrait, by Thomas Gainsborough, hangs at Floors Castle, near Kelso in Scotland. A deep-water "superport" was built to load coal at Roberts Bank in 1970 and expanded in 1983; Deltaport, a large container-loading facility, was added to the complex in 1997. *E W*

Roberts Bay (48°40'00" 123°24'00" E side of N Saanich Peninsula, just N of Sidney, N of Victoria), **Roberts Point** (48°40'00" 123°23'00" Just E of Roberts Bay). After Samuel Roberts (1835–1908), who bought 125 ha of land on Roberts Bay from Richard John in the early 1870s and established the Beaufort Farm. He had immigrated to Canada from Wales in 1862 and joined the Cariboo gold rush, where pioneer flour-mill operator Henry Brackman was one of his partners. Brackman later bought 33 ha of his N Saanich property. In 1871, at Victoria, Roberts married 16-year-old Agnes Gough (1856–1919), one of the first white children born at Nanaimo, and started a large family; Roberts descendants lived in the district for many generations. Roberts Point was proposed as a name by Gulf Is MLA Alex McDonald in 1934; the feature was known before that as Pleasant Point.

Roberts Creek (49°25'00" 123°39'00" NW of Gower Point, E side of Str of Georgia, NW of Vancouver). Thomas William Roberts (1867–1959), from England, pre-empted land at the mouth of the creek in 1889 and received a Crown grant for the property in 1898. His parents, Thomas and Charlotte Roberts, came out from England and homesteaded there until about 1897, then migrated to Vancouver. Thomas's brother John Francis

"Frank" Roberts, recently widowed, brought his family to Roberts Ck in 1900 and took over the homestead. It was Frank's son Louis Harry Roberts (1884–1979) who had the greatest impact on the growing rural community; he built boats and houses and ran a sawmill, store and post office until the 1920s, when he moved to Merry I and then to Nelson I. Agriculture, logging and recreation have been important to "The Creek" ever since. Roberts Ck was home to several communes in the 1960s and retains a vibrant countercultural atmosphere. The area's Sechelt First Nation name is Xwésám. *E*

Robertson Banks (54°07'00" 130°05'00" Mouth of the Skeena R, E of De Horsey I and Smith I, SE of Prince Rupert). Named in 1909 after Andrew Stuart Robertson (1865–1940), from Que, an accountant and one of the early owners of the Claxton Cannery and sawmill, located in this area. He married Rosina Hawkins (1866–1947), also from Que, at Vancouver in 1892. Robertson sold the cannery complex to John Wallace of the Wallace Bros Packing Co in 1900.

Robertson Island (53°15'00" 132°05'00" Bearskin Bay, Skidegate Inlet, off S end of Graham I, QCI), **Robertson Rock** (52°57'00" 129°35'00" Head of Pemberton Bay, S side of Dewdney I, N entrance to Caamaño Sd). William Archibald Robertson (1832–1926), a native of Perthshire, Scotland, came to eastern Canada with his family when he was two years old. He went to the US, served as an officer during the US Civil War, lived for a while in California and arrived at Victoria in 1865, where he set up as a blacksmith and wagon maker, and married Martha Matilda Mayne (1849–92) in 1869. Robertson was also a politician: Victoria MLA in 1874–75, city alderman and school trustee for a number of years, and unsuccessful candidate for MP in 1887. He prospected widely on Vancouver I, finding silver and coal on the Koksilah R and staking, in the mid-1880s, along with ex-sealer Jimmy Shields, a large coal field in the QCI's Yakoun R valley, which was never developed. According to QCI historian Kathleen Dalzell, he named Robertson I, which is the site of a number of middens, and owned it at one time. Another source suggests that regional hydrographer Lt Cdr Philip Musgrave applied the name in the 1910s. It appears on maps from about 1919. The barge *Black Wolfe* was wrecked on the island in 1929. *D*

Robinson Island (50°54'00" 127°17'00" Blunden Hbr, S of Bradley Lagoon, N side of Queen Charlotte Str, NE of Port Hardy). RN officer George Robinson served on the RN survey vessel *Actaeon* off the coast of China and also worked on a survey of the coast of Nfld, 1864–71. He was promoted to staff cdr in 1873 and spent 1873–76 in the UK at the Admiralty hydrographic office. While Robinson was never on the BC coast, this feature was named by Lt Daniel Pender in 1863 at the request of William Blakeney, his paymaster and surveying assistant aboard the hired HBC vessel *Beaver*. Blakeney had served with Robinson on the China Station.

Robinson Point (53°42'00" 130°07'00" Petrel Channel, E side of McCauley I, opposite Newcombe Hbr on Pitt I). Named after Flight Lt Edward La Page Robinson, DFC, from Vancouver, who was killed in action Oct 2, 1943, aged 33, when his Lockheed Ventura light bomber crashed. He flew more than 110 sorties with RCAF No 145 Squadron, and attacked and sank the German submarine *U-658* in 1942 when the vessel was surfacing in the Atlantic NE of St John's. He is buried at the Gander War Cemetery in Nfld.

Robins Point (52°09'00" 128°04'00" E entrance to Kliktsoatli Hbr, N side of Denny I, just E of Bella Bella). Samuel Matthew Robins (b 1834), from Cornwall, came to BC in 1863 and worked for the Vancouver Coal Mining & Land Co, where he rose to become superintendent from 1884 to the early 1900s. The company took over the Nanaimo collieries—and a large portion of surrounding land—from the HBC in 1862. It laid out and sold building lots for a townsite at Nanaimo and established a number of recreational facilities. In 1889 the firm was reorganized and changed its name to the New Vancouver Coal Mining & Land Co; in 1903 it was sold to the Western Fuel Co of San Francisco. Robins was also appointed a justice of the peace for Nanaimo, where a street and park commemorate him. Robins Point, formerly known as Noble Point, was named in 1925.

Robson Bight (50°29'00" 126°35'00" SW end of Johnstone Str, SE of Telegraph Cove, NW of Campbell R), **Robson Point** (50°29'00" 125°45'00" N side of Forward Hbr, E of Hardwicke I, NW of Campbell R), **Robson Rock** (50°26'00" 128°01'00" N entrance to Quatsino Sd, E of Kains I, NW end of Vancouver I). Lt Cdr Charles Rufus Robson, from Yorkshire, had command of the gunboat *Forward* from 1859 until his untimely death at Esquimalt from a riding accident in 1861. Although young, he had already seen a fair amount of action by the time he arrived on the W coast, having served at the bombardment of Sveaborg during the Crimean War and been assigned to take a damaged US vessel, whose officers had all died from yellow fever, from Africa to Philadelphia. In BC, he and the crew of HMS *Forward* rescued everyone aboard the US brig *Consort*, which was wrecked in San Josef Bay in 1860. In 1860–61, Robson and his gunboat were involved in several punitive actions against Lekwiltok and Haida First Nation warriors in the Cape Mudge region. Robson's funeral, attended by more than 1,500 people according to the *Colonist* newspaper, was the largest ever held in Victoria to that date. Robson Bight was protected as an ecological reserve in 1981 (and later named for Michael Bigg, a highly regarded whale researcher) because killer whales congregate in its rocky shallows and engage in an unusual body-rubbing behaviour. The traditional Kwakwaka'wakw First Nation name for the site is Usaq, which can be translated as "grey-haired" and refers to burned or dead trees that once marked the area. Named about 1861 by Capt George Richards of HMS *Hecate*, Robson Bight became part of Lower Tsitika R Provincial Park in 2001. Robson Point was formerly known as Mills Point, Robson Rk as N Danger Rk. *E W*

Robson Channel (48°50'00" 123°14'00" Between Curlew I and SE end of Mayne I, Gulf Is). This name was one of many submitted in 1969 by the Gulf Is Branch of the BC Historical Assoc. Frederick James Robson (1847–1937), from Pimlico, London, came to BC on the brideship *Robert Lowe* in 1863. He pre-empted land on Lulu I and then joined the Cariboo gold rush. After abandoning the prospector's life, he bought a canoe and explored the Gulf Is, deciding to settle instead at Horton Bay on Mayne I in 1871. Robson and John Ackholm, a Swedish sailor, established a farm called Glenwood on Mayne and then went into business with Tom Collinson, another Gulf Is pioneer. Robson's brother William and his family later joined him from NZ and opened a hotel and store at Miners Bay. Glenwood Farm thrived for many years and was known for its chickens and dairy and beef cattle. After Frederick's death, the business was operated by two of his nephews.

Robson Cove (50°30'00" 127°52'00" N side of Koprino Hbr, Quatsino Sd, NW end of Vancouver I). Named after John Robson, who received Crown grants for land in this vicinity in 1879 and 1884. Formerly known as North Cove. An individual named John Robson (*see* Annacis I) later became premier of BC, but it seems doubtful that this could be the same person.

R

Robson Island. *See* Annacis I.

Roche Cove (48°22'00" 123°38'00" E side of Sooke Basin, S end of Vancouver I, W of Victoria), **Roche Point** (49°18'00" 122°57'00" W entrance to Indian Arm, N side of Burrard Inlet, N Vancouver). Richard Roche served two commissions on the Pacific Station; he was a midshipman on HMS *Herald* in 1846–47, under Capt Henry Kellett, and 3rd lt on HMS *Satellite*, 1857–60, under Capt James Prevost. He sailed with Kellett from 1852 to 1854 also, as a mate on HMS *Resolute*, during the search for Sir John Franklin in the Arctic. Roche covered about 1,300 km on various sledge journeys while in the N and spent a total of 78 days away from his ship. He was promoted to cdr in 1864, served in the Mediterranean, 1873–75, and reached the rank of capt, retired, in 1879. Roche Cove was named by Kellett in 1846, Roche Point by Prevost. Roche Hbr off San Juan I in Washington state was also named for this officer, by Capt George Richards of HMS *Plumper* in 1858. At that time San Juan I was considered by the RN and the HBC to be part of British territory. *W*

Rochester Island (52°19'00" 127°59'00" In Return Channel, between Florence Peninsula and Cunningham I, NE of Bella Bella). John Young Rochester (1852–1942), from Burnstown, Ont, married Jennie Cerena Bryson (1858–1934), from Que, in 1881 and travelled out to western Canada. He worked as superintendent of the Yukon Telegraph Line, then moved to BC around the turn of the century. In the 1920s he became marine superintendent of the CNR's barge and ferry service, a company subsidiary that was mainly concerned with transporting railway cars between Vancouver I and the mainland, and also with providing auto and railcar service on Okanagan Lk. He and his wife retired to N Vancouver.

Rocket Shoal (48°59'00" 123°38'00" In Clam Bay, between NE Kuper I and SE Thetis I, Gulf Is). The RN gunboat *Rocket* served two commissions on the BC coast: 1874–79, under Lt Cdr Charles Harris, and 1879–82, under Lt Cdr Vere Orlebar. The 48-m, 530-tonne steam vessel, launched in 1868 and armed with four guns, took Indian Affairs superintendent Dr Israel Powell on coastal tours of inspection in 1879 and 1881. In 1877 the *Rocket* engaged in one of the last naval actions against a BC First Nation group when it shelled and destroyed the remote Nuxalk village of Nut'l at the mouth of the Dean R. The inhabitants were suspected of murdering the survivors from the *George S Wright*, wrecked in Queen Charlotte Sd in 1873, but the charges against them were never proven. Rocket Shoal was named by the RN hydrographic dept in 1880. HMS *Rocket* was decommissioned and sold in 1888. *W*

Rockfish Harbour (52°53'00" 131°48'00" S side of Louise I, off NE side of Moresby I, QCI). Named by George M Dawson of the Geological Survey of Canada in 1878.

According to his journal of July 13, 1878, he "found the fishing very good and caught about three dozen good-sized 'rock cod' of at least four species. Very gaily coloured and ... first-rate eating."

Fort Rodd, overlooking Fisgard light. *James and Jennifer Hamilton*

Rodd Point (48°26'00" 123°27'00" W side of Esquimalt Hbr near entrance, just W of Victoria). John Rashleigh Rodd (1816–92) was 1st lt of HMS *Fisgard*, under Capt John Duntze, and served on the Pacific Station in 1843–47, during which time the *Fisgard* was one of the first RN vessels to anchor in Esquimalt Hbr. Lt Cdr James Wood of HMS *Pandora*, who surveyed the hbr in 1847, named many of its features after the *Fisgard*'s officers. Rodd entered the RN in 1830, commanded the hospital ship *Belleisle* in the E Indies in the late 1850s and was promoted to capt in 1862. He retired in 1866 and reached the exalted rank of adm, retired, in 1888. Rodd Hill, where a set of coastal defences was built, 1895–1900, is also named for him. The top of the hill was removed to install one of the fort's gun batteries. Ft Rodd Hill remained operational until 1956, by which time it had become obsolete, and is today a national historic park. *E*

Roderick Cove (52°41'00" 128°21'00" Head of Watson Inlet, NW end of Roderick I), **Roderick Island** (52°38'00" 128°22'00" E side of Finlayson Channel, NW of Bella Bella), **Roderick Island** (53°15'00" 132°05'00" In Bearskin Bay, Skidegate Inlet, QCI). After Roderick Finlayson, HBC official and businessman at Victoria. *See* Finlayson Arm. Roderick Lk at the head of Watson Inlet is also named for him. Roderick I and nearby Finlayson Channel were both named by Lt Daniel Pender about 1866; Pender is also believed to have named the Roderick I in the QCI.

Roe Islet (48°48'00" 123°19'00" In Otter Bay, W side of N Pender I, Gulf Is). Robert Roe (1854–1939) immigrated to Canada from Glasgow with his wife and sons in 1896 and worked as an engineer on CPR coastal steamers. He then pre-empted land on N Pender I and farmed. In 1907 the

Roes bought additional property on N Pender that they eventually turned into a popular summer resort named Roesland, which operated until 1994. According to an early brochure, "Ladies summering without their men folk need have no worries about heavy luggage. Everything is made as convenient as possible." The resort advertised evening bonfires: "far into the night songs are sung and tales are told—with no mosquitoes to mar the pleasure." Fifteen-ha Roesland was purchased in 1998 from its latest owners, the Davidson family, for $2.6 million and added to the Gulf Is National Park Reserve. The area around Roe Lk on N Pender I, also named for these pioneer settlers, became part of the reserve too; it was acquired from a German syndicate for $3.25 million. The name Roe It was submitted by the Gulf Is Branch of the BC Historical Assoc in 1969.

Rogers Island (52°59'00" 132°20'00" Off W side of Hibben I, Englefield Bay, NW side of Moresby I, QCI). William Rogers was a clerk and assistant paymaster aboard HMS *Thetis*, under Capt Augustus Kuper, and served on the Pacific Station, 1851–53. In 1855 he was appointed clerk to the secretary of Vice Adm Sir George Seymour, aboard HMS *Victory* at Portsmouth. The island was named by Capt Kuper in 1852, while the *Thetis* surveyed Kuper Inlet and maintained the peace during the short-lived excitement of the QCI gold rush.

Rogerson Rock (52°29'00" 129°05'00" Off SW side of Aristazabal I, Hecate Str). Sgt William Rogerson was a member of the Columbia detachment of Royal Engineers, which served in BC 1858–63. He and his wife came to BC with the main contingent of men, travelling aboard the *Thames City* and arriving in 1859. They returned to England when the detachment disbanded in 1863.

Rogers Point (53°41'00" 129°45'00" S entrance to Klewnuggit Inlet, Grenville Channel, S of Prince Rupert). This feature was labelled Camp Point on Admiralty charts as early as 1872. It was renamed in 1946 by regional hydrographer Henri Parizeau in honour of Capt Oliver Hazard Perry Rogers (1873–1958) of the CPR's BC Coast Steamship Service. Rogers was born in Maine, part of an extended seafaring family, and came to BC in the early 1890s to live with a widowed aunt. William Rogers (1830–1908), an uncle, was the first member of this clan to settle in BC, where he became a Fraser R paddleboat capt and manager and part owner of the Mainland & Nanaimo Steam Navigation Co. The *Robert Dunsmuir* and the *City of Nanaimo* were the firm's two main vessels. The Rogers family produced a number of master mariners, including Perry, who worked at first on Fraser R sternwheelers and tugs, and then on the freighter *Lapwing* before joining the BCCSS in 1908. He was appointed a capt in 1917, served as skipper of the *Charmer*, *Otter* and many of the *Princess* ships, and helped found the Canadian Merchant Service

Guild. Perry Rogers retired in 1938 and died at New Westminster, where the Rogers family home at 107 Park Row has been restored as a heritage building.

Rolston Island (50°01'00" 127°22'00" S of McKay Cove, entrance to Kyuquot Sd, NW side of Vancouver I). Charles Merle Rolston (1873–1947), from Ont, was the Vancouver regional manager for Imperial Oil in 1928, the year the company established a fuel station on this island for the community of Kyuquot. George Aitken, BC representative to the Geographic Board of Canada, wrote to regional hydrographer Henri Parizeau that "the Imperial Oil Co is most anxious to have a euphonious name, and suggested either Imperial or Rolston.... Imperial is too glorious a word to place upon so small a feature, so, believing you would concur, we selected Rolston as the more suitable." Rolston, who married Annie Maud Smith (1873–1953) at Vancouver in 1905, is often credited with the creation of the first gas station in Canada, at the SW corner of Smythe St and Cambie St in Vancouver about 1907. He built a concrete pillar and attached a gravity-fed kitchen water tank on top of it. A length of garden hose was used to fill up waiting automobiles. Rolston spent 40 years with Imperial, retiring in 1934, and was instrumental in getting the Imperial Oil refinery built at Ioco in 1914–15. Rolston I was known before 1928 as Scrub I.

Romulus Reef (49°01'00" 123°35'00" W side of Porlier Pass, between Galiano I and Valdes I, Gulf Is). This feature was originally known as Romulus Rk, after the 1,562-tonne German freighter *Romulus*, under Capt Wilhelm Berndt, which struck it in 1893 while heading for the open ocean with a load of coal from Nanaimo. The ship made it to Esquimalt Hbr where it was beached, partly unloaded and then repaired at the graving dock. The hitherto-unknown hazard was named by Capt John Walbran of CGS *Quadra*, who examined and charted it later that year. About 1972 the rock was reduced by blasting in order to improve navigational safety; there are now depths of 7.3 m over it. The name was changed to Romulus Reef in 1987.

Rondeault Point (49°26'52" 126°25'56" E side of Hesquiat Hbr, between Nootka Sd and Clayoquot Sd, W side of Vancouver I). Named by regional hydrographer Henri Parizeau in 1934 after Rev Pierre Rondeault (1824–1900), a Roman Catholic missionary from Que who was ordained at Montreal in 1857 and came to Victoria the following year. He assisted Rev Augustin Brabant with the construction of the church at Hesquiat in 1875 but otherwise spent his entire career in the Cowichan district, where he operated a First Nation mission and also farmed. Rondeault is best known for his work on the so-called Butter Church near Duncan. This historic structure, which still stands but is partly derelict and no longer used, was built of local sandstone in 1870, the work paid for through the sale of butter produced on Rondeault's farm. Rondeault

R

Point was formerly known as East Entrance Point but was changed to avoid duplication.

Rooney Bay (53°16'00" 131°59'00" SE end of Graham I, QCI), **Rooney Point** (54°01'00" 132°10'00" NW side of Masset Sd, Graham I). Matthew Rooney, an Irish adventurer who arrived in San Francisco in 1851 from Australia, was capt of the ill-fated US schooner *Susan Sturgis*, which sailed to the QCI in 1852 in response to rumours of gold. When Rooney and his crew found no signs of gold in the Mitchell Inlet area, they headed to the E coast of the QCI and travelled N to Skidegate, prospecting and trading. At Skidegate, Chief Edensaw (or Edenshaw) came aboard to pilot the *Sturgis* along the N shore of Graham I, where the vessel was hijacked, pillaged and burned by the Masset Haida. At this point, contemporary accounts diverge: some say that Edensaw saved the lives of the crew by persuading the Massets to exchange them for ransom; others claim he helped plan the attack and shared in the loot. After gaining his freedom, Rooney apparently returned to San Francisco, spent the late 1850s in Taiwan as cdr of a Jardine Matheson opium-receiving ship and was last heard from off the coast of Africa, where he was twice taken prisoner by indigenous tribes. Rooney Bay was formerly known as Village Bay but was renamed by the hydrographic service in 1945. Capt Frederick Learmonth of the RN survey vessel *Egeria* named Rooney Point in 1907, in association with nearby (misspelled) Sturgess Bay. *D*

Roquefeuil Bay (48°52'00" 125°07'00" E side of Trevor Channel, NE of Bamfield Inlet, Barkley Sd, W side of Vancouver I). Lt Camille de Roquefeuil (1781–1831), in command of the French vessel *Bordelais*, circled the globe in 1816–19 on a trading voyage, attempting to find new markets for France. The vessel spent two weeks in Barkley Sd, mostly in Grappler Inlet, in Sept 1817, then wintered in California and returned to the Alaska and BC coasts the following year, passing time in Haida Gwaii and with Chief Maquinna at Nootka Sd. Roquefeuil's account of his voyage, published in 1823, provides a detailed European view of early First Nation life on the BC coast. This feature was formerly known as Kelp Bay.

Rosedale Rock (48°18'00" 123°32'00" N side of Juan de Fuca Str, SE of Race Rks, off S tip of Vancouver I). The British merchant vessel *Rosedale* ran aground on this hazard in 1862, en route from London, England, to Victoria. The ship floated free but was damaged and had to be beached at Ross Bay in Victoria. There the cargo was unloaded and the *Rosedale*, assisted by a number of local vessels, was towed to Esquimalt. The owners of these helpful craft later engaged in a round of lawsuits over salvage rights, which were eventually settled in favour of the *Thames*, an old steamer belonging to the Alberni Saw Mill Co. Several other ships were wrecked on the rock in

later years, including the *Nicholas Biddle* (1867) and the *Idaho* (1889). It was finally marked with a buoy in 1900. *W*

Rose Harbour, once a thriving whaling station. *John Alexander*

Rose Harbour (52°09'00" 131°05'00" N side of Kunghit I, off S end of Moresby I, QCI), **Rose Inlet** (52°11'00" 131°09'00" N of Houston Stewart Channel, S end of Moresby I), **Rose Point** (54°11'00" 131°39'00" Extreme NE tip of Graham I, QCI), **Rose Spit** (54°12'00" 131°38'00" Northern extension of Rose Point). George Rose (1744–1818) was a British politician and writer who served briefly in the RN before joining the civil service. An MP from 1784 to 1818 and close friend of PM William Pitt, he held a number of political offices, including secretary to the treasury (1782–1801), clerk of the parliaments (1788–1818), vice-president of the board of trade (1804–6, 1807–12), paymaster of the forces (1804–6) and treasurer of the navy (1807–18). Rose was involved in the development of foreign trade and took a keen interest in the early British fur-trading expeditions to the PNW. The name Rose Hbr was originally given in 1787 to today's Rose Inlet by James Johnstone, who later sailed with Capt George Vancouver but was at that time mate aboard James Colnett's fur-trading vessel *Prince of Wales*. The Rose Hbr on contemporary charts was known for many years as Port Huff, after George Huff of Port Alberni, who was sent to the area to select a site for a whaling station. The facility built at Port Huff by the Pacific Whaling Co in 1910 was called Rose Hbr, which caused confusion, and eventually the old names were changed to their current forms. Rose Hbr turned into one of the most productive whaling stations on the BC coast, operating until 1943. Its equipment was moved to Coal Hbr on Vancouver I in 1948 and the site abandoned. By the early 2000s, few remains were visible; a guest house at the harbour catered instead to tourists visiting Gwaii Haanas National Park Reserve. Rose Point was named in 1788 by Capt William Douglas of the brig *Iphigenia Nubiana*, another early fur trader. At certain stages of the tide, dangerous overfalls form off Rose Spit, where the waters of Dixon Entrance meet those of Hecate Str. Many ships have been wrecked there over the years, including two historic HBC vessels named *Vancouver*, which came to grief in 1834 and 1854. Rose Point was called Cape Lookout by Robert Gray of the *Columbia* in 1791; Joseph Ingraham of the *Hope* chose Sandy Point and Masset Spit on his 1792 chart. Jacinto Caamaño of the *Aránzazu* gave it the name Punta Invisible, also in 1792, as the point is dangerously obscure in poor weather, and Capt George Vancouver adopted this term. The Haida know Rose Point as Nai and Rose Spit as Nai-kun, or "the long nose of Nai." Nai-kun ("Point Town") village was located on the E side of Rose Point. Rose Spit became a provincial ecological reserve in 1970. *D E W*

Rose Island (54°33'00" 130°26'00" At Lax Kw'alaams, NW side of the Tsimpsean Peninsula, N of Prince Rupert). The Tsimshian First Nation name for the old community of Port Simpson (qv) is Lax Kw'alaams (qv) or "place of wild roses." Part of the community is located on Rose I, which is connected to the mainland by a bridge and causeway. In 1981, at the Port Simpson Band Council's request, the BC government changed the name Village I, which dated back to at least 1907, to Rose I, which has a closer association with the traditional Tsimshian community name.

Rosenfeld Rock (48°48'10" 123°02'15" NE of East Point, off E end of Saturna I, Gulf Is). Named after the US ship *John Rosenfeld*, under Capt James Baker, which ran aground on this obstacle in 1886 while being towed from Nanaimo, laden with coal, by the tug *Tacoma*. The tug, commanded by Capt Cameron, drew far less water than the larger vessel and passed safely over the rock, but the 2,057-tonne *Rosenfeld* could not. The two-year-old ship, built in Maine and on its way to San Francisco, was a total wreck. Both vessels were supposedly more than 2 km off course at the time of the accident. The ancient paddle steamer *Beaver* was quickly chartered to take a cargo of coal off the doomed craft. *W*

Rose Rock (48°40'55" 123°23'50" N end of Page Passage, E of Canoe Bay, off NE end of Saanich Peninsula, N of Victoria). Named after Rose May Copeland (1895–1962, née Reid), who purchased nearby Johnson It (qv) in 1934 and lived there for many years, owning the property until her death. She was a pioneer in the area and a well-known and respected member of the community. An attempt to have Johnson It renamed for her was denied by the BC government in 1964, and this name was adopted instead the following year after being submitted by local residents.

Ross Bay (48°24'28" 123°20'38" E of Clover Point, S side of Victoria). Named for members of the Ross family, who owned a 60-ha waterfront estate here in Victoria's colonial days. Charles Ross (c 1794–1844), from Kincraig, Scotland, joined the HBC in 1818 and worked as a clerk at remote trading posts across the Canadian

NW. In 1822 at Lac La Pluie (Rainy Lake), Ont, he wed Isabella Merilia (1807–85), whose surname also appears as Melville or Mainville (*see* Merilia Passage). Ross was promoted to clerk in charge at Connolly Lk in 1830–31 and also held that position at Ft Vermilion, Cumberland House, Kootenay, Fraser Lk and Ft McLoughlin between 1833 and 1843. He became a chief trader for the last two years of his life and supervised construction of the new HBC post at Ft Victoria, then died prematurely, probably from appendicitis. Isabella, who was BC's first registered female landowner, called her property Fowl Bay Farm and homesteaded there with several sons, but the land was soon carved up and sold to pay various debts. A second marriage was short-lived. Several of her sons died young, while two others were jailed and then banished from Vancouver I for robbery. Part of the estate ended up as today's historic Ross Bay Cemetery. According to the Songhees First Nation website, the Salishan name for the Ross Bay area is Wholaylch, meaning "pussy willows."

Ross Island (52°10'00" 131°07'00" At entrance to Rose Inlet, S end of Moresby I, QCI). Dr William Ross was assistant surgeon aboard HMS *Virago*, under Cdr James Prevost, and served on the Pacific Station, 1852–55. During this period the *Virago* was sent to the QCI to maintain order after the plundering of the US schooner *Susan Sturgis*; it also spent much time doing survey work along the NW coast of Graham I, in Houston Stewart Channel and near Ft Simpson. Ross was promoted to staff surgeon in 1868 and became a deputy inspector-gen of hospitals and fleets, retired, in 1881. Named by Cdr Prevost in 1853.

Ross Islets (53°40'00" 132°24'00" N of Yestalton Bay, Masset Inlet, Graham I, QCI). C C Ross was one of the hydrographers taking part in a survey of Masset Inlet, conducted in 1910 by Lt Cdr Philip Musgrave of the Canadian Hydrographic Service. Ross also participated in a survey of Dixon Entrance that year but then resigned at the end of the season.

Ross Passage (49°20'00" 126°03'00" E of Flores I, NE of McKay I, Clayoquot Sd, W side of Vancouver I). Named for John Telford Ross (1868–1964), a Presbyterian missionary and teacher who came to Diana I in Barkley Sd in 1905. He was appointed principal of Ahousat's large First Nation residential school about 1910–16, after which he taught at Ucluelet. Ross was married several times, including to fellow missionary Jean McNeil (*see* McNeil Peninsula) at Alberni in 1909 and to Louisa Perkins at Victoria in 1918. He died at Qualicum. According to *Hidden from History: The Canadian Holocaust*, Ross served as the local magistrate at Ahousat and "personally arrested dozens of Indians for potlatching, dancing and other native practices made illegal by federal laws."

R

Rouse Bay (49°28'00" 124°11'00" SE end of Lasqueti I, S side of Bull Passage, Str of Georgia). William Fredrick Rouse (1854–1932), a former smelter worker at Nanaimo, and his wife, Margaret, were early settlers on Lasqueti I. In the mid-1890s William married again, to Mary Ann Higgins (1873–1947, née Jaffrey), the former wife of another Lasqueti pioneer, Hugh Harry Higgins (*see* Higgins I; Lasqueti historian Elda Copley Mason says that the two couples exchanged spouses). William and Mary Ann moved to Earls Cove in 1909, and three years later they hooked their small tugboat, the *May*, to a floathouse they had built and towed their large family to the Francis Peninsula in Pender Hbr. There William made a living as a beachcomber while Mary Ann Rouse became a well-known midwife.

Routh Islet (49°43'15" 124°10'55" In Blind Bay, S entrance to Jervis Inlet, E side of Str of Georgia). Named in 1990 to honour Motor Mechanic John Meredith Routh of the RCNVR, from Vancouver, who died on Feb 14, 1945, aged 28, at Ostend, Belgium, during a disastrous harbour fire that destroyed five of the eight vessels in the 29th Canadian Motor Torpedo Boat Flotilla and killed 63 of the flotilla's seamen. His name is inscribed on the Halifax Memorial. John's brother, Cpl Patrick Albert Darnley Routh, is also commemorated by a BC place name: Mt Routh, N of Germansen Landing in the Cassiar district. He was killed in action at Monte Cassino, Italy, on May 23, 1944, aged 24, while a member of the Princess Patricia's Canadian Light Infantry. Patrick Routh is buried at the Cassino War Cemetery, Italy.

Rowley Reefs (50°24'00" 127°58'00" S of Gillam I, entrance to Quatsino Sd, NW end of Vancouver I). Rev James Farmer Rowley received a Crown grant of land on Quatsino Sd in 1911. Formerly known as South Reefs.

Roy (50°31'00" 125°32'00" S of Statham Point, SE side of Loughborough Inlet, N of Johnstone Str, NW of Campbell R). "I gave the name on spur of the moment when getting PO established. Reminiscent of 'Rob Roy,' my highland forbear." So wrote Dugald McGregor, postmaster at the tiny mining and logging settlement of Roy, to Canada's chief geographer, James White, in 1905. That year White had circulated a request for place name information to each post office in Canada. The Roy post office opened in 1896 and closed in 1943. The original name of Scottish outlaw Rob Roy was Robert Roy MacGregor. *E*

Royal Cove (48°44'00" 123°22'00" N end of Portland I, SE of Saltspring I, Gulf Is). In 1978, when a name for this feature was required by BC's parks branch, Royal Cove was suggested. This somewhat uninspired selection was meant to associate the cove with HMS *Portland*, after which Portland I (qv) is named, because the vessel was part of the Royal Navy.

Royal Point (48°25'10" 123°24'50" SE of Saxe Point at Esquimalt, SE end of Vancouver I), **Royal Roads** (48°25'00" 123°27'00" Between Albert Head and Esquimalt Hbr, W of Victoria). The first European to explore this part of the BC coast was Spanish naval officer Manuel Quimper, in 1790. He gave the name Rada de Valdés y Bazan—after Antonio Valdés y Bazan, the Spanish minister of marine—to the feature now known as Royal Roads. Capt Henry Kellett of HMS *Herald*, who surveyed the area in 1846, labelled it Royal Bay in association with the new settlement of Ft Victoria, named after Queen Victoria, and nearby Albert Head, named after Prince Albert, the queen's consort. An 1873 Admiralty chart located Royal Bay close to the W shore and referred to the centre of the bay as Esquimalt Roadstead. A roadstead ("road" for short) is an anchorage that is less enclosed and secure than a harbour, and as more and more vessels began to wait in Royal Bay before entering Esquimalt or Victoria harbours, the name Royal Roads came into common usage. In 1910 it officially replaced Royal Bay. Hatley Park, the former estate of coal baron James Dunsmuir, located to the W of Royal Roads, became the site of Royal Roads Military College, 1942–94, and then reopened as Royal Roads Univ in 1996. Royal Roads Peak, NE of Bute Inlet, was climbed (and named) by a naval mountaineering party in 1985 to honour the 75th anniversary of the RCN. In 1989, when Esquimalt land developers tried to give the name Point Royal to an officially unnamed geographic feature just SE of Saxe Point, a hornet's nest of controversy was stirred up. Local residents, some of whom knew the feature as Plaskett Point, objected to the change, fearing an invasion of condominiums and restrictions in public access. They were overruled by the municipality of Esquimalt, and the name Royal Point, a variation on the original suggestion, was adopted in 1990. Low-density development prevailed, however, and luxurious single-family homes soon lined the point's shores.

Roy Island (53°19'00" 129°36'00" In Monckton Inlet, W side of Pitt I). Named in 1944 after long-serving Pacific coast hydrographer Roy Ettershank. *See* Ettershank Is.

Roy Islet (51°02'00" 127°31'00" N of Ray I, W entrance to Allison Hbr, NW side of Queen Charlotte Str, N of Port Hardy). The origin of the name is not known, but it is curious that this feature was named on the same day—Jan 24, 1946—as neighbouring Ray I.

Royston (49°39'00" 124°57'00" S side of Comox Hbr, E side of Vancouver I). William Roy (b 1840), from Scotland via NS, worked as a miner in the collieries at Cumberland in the late 1880s. He and his wife, Christiana (b 1838), also ran a boarding house there. The family bought land on Comox Hbr in 1890 and farmed. In 1910, with realtor and developer Frederick Warren, Roy laid out a townsite on his property and called it Royston, partly because of

Royston breakwater is constructed from old hulks. *Rob Morris*

and *Beaver* (and partly owning the latter for a number of years), then joined the Canadian Pacific Navigation Co in 1883. Rudlin worked mostly on the CPN's Vancouver–Victoria route with the *Charmer* and *Islander*, becoming one of the most prominent steamboat men on the coast. When the company was taken over by the CPR in 1901, he continued on as a senior capt with the new owners until his sudden death. *W*

Rudolf Bay (52°25'00" 128°45'00" W side of Price I, E side of Laredo Sd, NW of Bella Bella). Mary Martha Amelia Rudolf (née Laumeister) was born at San Francisco in 1853 and came to Victoria with her parents, Frank and Agnes Laumeister, in 1858. She married Henry Rudolph (1827–79), from Germany, a pioneer jeweller and watchmaker in Victoria. (Frank Laumeister became a well-known merchant and freight operator during the Cariboo and Cassiar gold rushes. His name will forever be associated with a famous but completely unsuccessful attempt to introduce camels to BC and use them to haul freight on the Douglas and Cariboo roads.)

Rum Island (48°40'00" 123°17'00" Just E of Gooch I, E of N end of Saanich Peninsula, Gulf Is). This tiny 4.7-ha island, which lies only about 1 km from the Canada-US boundary, supposedly served as a staging point for liquor smugglers crossing the border to Stuart I in Washington state during the Prohibition era. Renee Maccaud Nelson bequeathed the property to the BC government in 1978 and specified that it be called Isle-de-Lis for the wild lilies that bloom there in spring. Isle-de-Lis Marine Park was transferred in the early 2000s to the Gulf Is National Park Reserve. The island's Sencoťen (Coast Salish) name is Xelexátem, meaning "crossways."

Rungé Island (53°26'00" 129°51'00" S side of Mink Trap Bay, Principe Channel, off W side of Pitt I). Named in 1944 by the hydrographic service after Patricia Rungé, a stewardess aboard the W coast government survey ship *William J Stewart* in 1942–43. She married W O Williams, a hydrographer who worked on surveys of Fitz Hugh Sd, Prince Rupert and Vancouver harbours, the Str of Georgia and Seymour Narrows from 1942 to 1945 and then resigned from the service.

his surname and partly because Warren was a native of Royston in Hertfordshire, England. Nearby Roy Ck is also believed to be named after Will Roy. The Comox Logging & Rwy Co hauled its timber to Royston for many years and boomed logs there before towing them to the mills. A breakwater of derelict ships, which once provided protection for the booming grounds, is still visible just offshore. *E*

Rudge Rock (52°13'00" 128°05'00" S entrance to Troup Passage, between Cunningham I and Chatfield I, just N of Bella Bella). This feature was formerly known as Lifton Rk, after the RCNVR's Lt George Henry Lifton of Victoria, and then as Dot Rk. It was renamed by the hydrographic service in 1924 after George Oscar Rudge (1854–1934), who was born in NB, where his father had a stonecutting business. George went to San Francisco in 1875, then to New Westminster, and then to Seattle for three years, where he set up a marble-cutting yard that was destroyed by fire. Back in BC he settled at Victoria and again established himself as a marble and stone cutter. He was joined by other family members, including his older brother Henry. George later moved to Port Simpson, where he married Sarah Julia L Alexander (1876–1953) in 1899. He served as the lighthouse keeper at nearby Birnie I, 1905–17, and also operated a hotel and general store at Port Simpson. Rudge moved back to Victoria with his wife in the 1920s.

Rudlin Bay (48°25'00" 123°14'00" S side of Discovery I, just E of Oak Bay and Victoria). George Rudlin (c 1834–1903), born in Essex, got his first job at age 12 on a fishing boat. He served in the RN during the Crimean War and immigrated to BC in 1856. In 1862, with a partner named Jay, he proceeded to log Discovery I, just E of Victoria, and then acquired the schooner *Discovery* (formerly the *Circus*) at Victoria the following year. Rudlin married Sophia Hill (1830–1914) at Victoria in 1868 and became an active trader on the BC coast with the *Discovery* and with the *Black Diamond*, which he used mainly to transport coal from Nanaimo to Victoria. He moved over to steam vessels, commanding the *Emma*, *Grappler*

Rupert Inlet (50°35'00" 127°30'00" NE arm of Quatsino Sd, NW Vancouver I). The inlet, formerly known as Rupert Arm, was named after Ft Rupert, the HBC trading post established not far away on Beaver Hbr on the NE coast of Vancouver I. Chief trader William McNeill supervised the building of the fort in 1849, after coal had been found in the region, and served as its first manager, with George Blenkinsop as his assistant. A number of Kwagiulth people (members of the Kwakwaka'wakw First Nation) settled beside the post in a community now known as T'sakis. Better deposits of coal were soon found

R

near Nanaimo, but Ft Rupert continued as a significant base for the HBC until 1883, when it was sold to its factor, Robert Hunt. The trading post burned down in 1889, and today a crumbling chimney is all that remains of this historic structure. Ft Rupert itself was named after Prince Rupert of the Rhine (1619–82), the first gov of the HBC (*see* Prince Rupert for biographical details). Rupert Inlet appears on the 1860 chart of Capt George Richards. The controversial Island Copper Mine operated on its N shore, 1971–95, and dumped millions of tonnes of mine tailings into the ocean. *E W*

Rushbrook Passage (54°36'00" 130°27'00" Between the Tsimpsean Peninsula and Birnie I, N of Prince Rupert). Named in 1927 after Anglican clergyman Walter Field Rushbrook (1868–1951), first superintendent of the Prince Rupert Coast Mission, 1911–28, and skipper of the mission boat *Northern Cross*. Rushbrook came to BC's N coast in 1903 and served as a minister at Port Essington. He conducted the first church service at Prince Rupert, in a tent, in Nov 1906. In 1909, supplied with a small gas launch, he began visiting Skeena R communities, and in 1911 he was put in charge of a regular coast mission that made monthly visits to many of the settlements along the N coast. When his health declined, Rushbrook, by now a canon, moved to St Peter's, Prince Rupert, as minister and was appointed diocesan historian in 1938. The channel, formerly known as Choked Passage, is "encumbered with drying reefs and below-water rocks," according to *Sailing Directions*.

Russell Arm (54°19'00" 130°21'00" N side of Prince Rupert Hbr, opposite Prince Rupert), **Russell Point** (Entrance to Russell Arm). E G Russell (d 1907) was the aggressive western agent for the GTP at the time the railway company was negotiating with the BC government and the federal Dept of Indian Affairs for land in the Prince Rupert area. The GTP, of course, located its Pacific terminus on Kaien I, site of the present-day city of Prince Rupert. During the complex discussions, an apparent rift developed between the company and Russell, who regularly seemed to overstep his mandate and authority. His advice was ignored and his subsequent fall from corporate grace is believed to have caused him to commit suicide.

Russell Banks (52°41'00" 129°20'00" E of Moore Is, Beauchemin Channel, off NW Aristazabal I). Thomas Russell (1836–1912) was born at Haddington, Scotland, and immigrated to Victoria in 1852–53. He came out in the HBC supply ship *Norman Morison* with his brother-in-law Kenneth McKenzie, who had been appointed bailiff, or manager, of the HBC's Craigflower Farm. Russell worked at first on the Craigflower estate and then taught at historic Craigflower school. His wife, Sarah Russell (1838–1905), came to Victoria from England in 1858. Thomas went into the grocery business, then became a Victoria

city employee, serving as water commissioner in 1876, as city assessor and collector, and as city treasurer. He died at Nanaimo.

Russell Channel (49°14'00" 126°06'00" S of Flores I, Clayoquot Sd, W side of Vancouver I). John W Russell (b 1866), from Ont, was a Presbyterian missionary who, in 1895, established a mission at Ahousat on Flores I in Clayoquot Sd, later building a church and a small day-school there. He had originally come to the W coast, accompanied by his wife, Adeline (b 1866), and their four children, to teach at Ucluelet. Russell is believed to have resigned his position about 1903 due to poor health. After his departure, the day school was expanded into a large residential school.

Russell Island (48°45'00" 123°24'00" Entrance to Fulford Hbr, off SE side of Saltspring I, Gulf Is). The origin of this name is not definitively known, though it may commemorate British PM Lord John Russell. RN surveyor Capt George Richards named Cape Russell (qv) on NW Vancouver I after the politician about 1862, and Russell I first appears on Admiralty charts around the same time. The 13-ha island has extensive middens from First Nation use. Its original non-Native settler was William Haumea, a Kanaka or Hawaiian Islander, who had come to Saltspring about 1873 with his First Nation wife and his daughter, both named Mary. After pre-empting land SW of Beaver Point, he acquired Russell I, settled there in 1886 and grew fruit and vegetables. Maria Mahoi (1855–1936), born on the Saanich Peninsula, inherited the property from Haumea and may have been his daughter. She and her second husband, George Fisher (1865–1948), moved to Russell in 1902 and developed a remarkably self-sufficient homestead, part of which can still be discerned. Both George and Maria spent the rest of their lives on the island. It was sold about 1960 to the Rohrer family of Long Beach, California, for use as a summer retreat. In 1997, for $1.8 million, it became part of the Gulf Is National Park Reserve. The island's Hul'qumi'num (Coast Salish) name is Ts'umeqwus, meaning "sasquatch."

Russell Reef (48°49'00" 123°10'00" Off N side of Saturna I, Gulf Is). This name was submitted in 1968 by the Gulf Is Branch of the BC Historical Assoc for "a pioneer settler on Saturna I." None of the early pre-emption or settlement records, however, show a Russell on Saturna.

Ruth Island (49°16'55" 124°06'40" NE of Nanoose Hbr, SW of Winchelsea I, off E side of Vancouver I). Named in 1905 by Cdr John Parry of HMS *Egeria* in association with nearby Maude I, which commemorates former RN officer Eustace Maude, who later settled on Mayne I (*see* Maude Bay). Ruth Katinka Maude (1886–1914) was his eldest daughter. She came to N America from England with her family and grew up on Mayne I, where her father was a magistrate and owned a hotel. In 1907 she married Harold Digby Payne (1872–1954), another Mayne I pioneer, and had four children with him but died at a young age. Payne remarried (to Jessie Ryle) and moved to Oak Bay and, later, to N Saanich.

Rutley Islands (48°58'00" 125°10'00" S of entrance to Effingham Inlet, Barkley Sd, W side of Vancouver I). John Irwin A Rutley (b 1903), originally from Ont, grew up in Sask and graduated from the Univ of Sask as a civil engineer in 1930. He joined the Canadian Hydrographic Service that year and participated in dozens of surveys between 1930 and 1948, visiting almost every part of the BC coast. Rutley married Florence Hamilton at N Vancouver in 1931. He was appointed regional chart superintendent in 1949 and served in that position until he retired in 1968. The feature was named in 1933; before that it was known as the Twin Is.

Ruxton Island (49°05'00" 123°42'00" Part of the De Courcy Group, W of Valdes I, Gulf Is), **Ruxton Passage** (49°05'00" 123°43'00" Between Ruxton I and De Courcy I). Lt William Fitzherbert Ruxton (1830–95) served on the Pacific Station, 1859–61, aboard HMS *Pylades*, under Capt Michael de Courcy. He was promoted to capt in 1865 and ended his career with the exalted rank of adm, retired. Named by Capt George Richards of HMS *Plumper* in 1860. Ruxton and De Courcy islands were purchased about 1929 for $10,000 from the family of Nanaimo pioneer William Flewett (*see* Flewett Point) by the Aquarian Foundation. Cult leader Edward Wilson, better known as Brother XII, apparently used Ruxton I as a place of banishment for out-of-favour disciples. It was sold, along with neighbouring Pylades I, for about $5,000 in the late 1940s. Around 1966 it was sold again, without Pylades this time, for almost $70,000 to a Nanaimo realtor and subdivided into 200 lots, most of which, thankfully, were still undeveloped in the early 2000s.

Ryan Point (54°22'00" 130°29'00" N entrance to Duncan Bay, SW side of Tsimpsean Peninsula, just NW of Prince Rupert). Named in 1862 by William Duncan, the well-known Anglican missionary at Metlakatla, after Rt Rev William Vincent Ryan (1816–88), principal of London's Highbury College, where Duncan received his Church Missionary Society training. Ryan was born in Ireland, educated at Oxford, ordained in 1841 and served at the Liverpool Collegiate Institute before coming to Highbury in 1850. From 1854 to 1867 he was the first Anglican bishop of Mauritius. Ryan had "pronounced evangelical views" and "notable powers of organization," according to BC coastal historian Capt John Walbran. *W*

Rylatt Rock (52°27'00" 129°05'00" W of Prior Passage, off SW Aristazabal I, Hecate Str). Sgt Robert M Rylatt was a member of the Columbia detachment of Royal Engineers, which served in BC 1858–63. He was born at Lincoln and apprenticed as a stonemason, joining the engineers and serving in Turkey and Russia during the Crimean War. Shortly after the war he married Fanny Morrison and travelled to BC in 1859 aboard the *Euphrates*, in charge of a cargo of stores and provisions and a small contingent of men. At the engineers' HQ in New Westminster, Rylatt served as commissary, responsible for the detachment's food supplies. He also took an active part in the Theatre Royal, the RE drama club, playing a number of female roles. His performance as the Hon Frederick Fitz-Fudge in *The Artful Dodge* "was so well played," according to the *British Columbian*, "that it gives cause for regret that so good an actor should be forced by the exigencies of the Company to assume women's parts." Rylatt and his wife stayed on in BC when the detachment disbanded. He and fellow engineer Alfred Hawkins formed a partnership as masons and bricklayers, and Rylatt received a military grant of land on Barnston I. In 1871 he joined the CPR survey in BC and spent two years in eastern BC, working under Walter Moberly, the chief surveyor, during which time his wife died (in 1872). Rylatt moved away to Washington state and eventually remarried, about 1879. His remarkable memoir of his surveying adventures (1871–73), stored away in a leather-bound journal by his family for more than 100 years and illustrated with coloured drawings, was published by the Univ of Utah in 1991.

S

Marinas on northeast side of Saanich Peninsula. *Kevin Oke*

Saanich (48°33'00" 123°22'00" On Saanich Peninsula), **Saanich Inlet** (48°37'00" 123°30'00" W of Saanich Peninsula), **Saanich Peninsula** (48°32'00" 123°25'00" SE end of Vancouver I, just N of Victoria), **Saanichton** (48°36'00" 123°25'00" On Saanich Peninsula, W of Saanichton Bay), **Saanichton Bay** (48°36'00" 123°23'00" E side of Saanich Peninsula). There is some uncertainty over the origin of the word *Saanich*, which designates the local First Nation people, who today call themselves the Wsanec and comprise four separate bands: the Pauquachin, Tsartlip, Tsawout and Tseycum. According to David Elliott, author of *Saltwater People*, a resource book used in local Native studies programs, the word means

"elevated" or "emerging" and refers to the appearance of Mt Newton (Láu'wel'new to the Wsanec) when viewed from offshore to the E. Thus the Wsanec are the "emerging" people. The rolling Saanich Peninsula, which includes the municipalities of Highlands, Saanich, Central Saanich and N Saanich, has much valuable agricultural land and was settled and farmed in the 1860s. Saanichton, formerly served by both a railway and an interurban tramline, developed as an early agricultural centre. Today the peninsula is home to Victoria's airport, a major ferry terminal and some of the province's most luxurious homes and suburbs. Saanichton Bay was once known locally as Siwash Bay. *E*

Saavedra Islands (49°37'00" 126°37'00" E of the S end of Nootka I, Nootka Sd, W side of Vancouver I). Spanish naval officer Ramon Antonio Saavedra y Giraldes (or Guiralda) was sent to Nootka Sd with the *San Carlos* in 1791. He brought news to Francisco Eliza, the Spanish cdr at Nootka, of the signing of the Nootka Sd Convention, which granted Britain free access to the PNW and restored all British property previously confiscated. Eliza left Saavedra in charge at Nootka while he and José Narváez went off on a historic exploration of the Str of Georgia. That summer, Saavedra entertained Alejandro Malaspina, who was en route from Alaska to Mexico, for two weeks, then sailed the *San Carlos* back to San Blas, Mexico. He was sent N again in 1793 and put in charge of the Nootka establishment until Mar 1795, at which time he dismantled the fort and returned to Mexico. Eliza (or Juan Pantoja) named the entrance to Clayoquot Sd for him in 1791 (Las Bocas de Saavedra). Capt George Vancouver adopted this name but it is no longer in use. Mt Saavedra in the Clayoquot region also commemorates him.

Sabine Channel (49°30'00" 124°11'00" Between Texada I and Lasqueti I, Str of Georgia). Gen Sir Edward Sabine (1788–1883) was an Irish scientist, explorer, soldier and ornithologist who became a leading expert on terrestrial magnetism. After a brief career in the Royal Artillery, he accompanied several famous expeditions as astronomer, including the first Arctic voyage of John Ross in 1818 and William Parry's 1819–20 search for the NW Passage. Sabine was also noted for contributions to geodesy, oceanography, glaciology, vulcanology, meteorology and various aspects of scientific measurement. He was president of the Royal Society, 1861–71. The channel was named by Capt George Richards in 1861. Mt Sabine in the Kootenays also commemorates him. The Sechelt First Nation name for the channel is Chichxwalish. *W*

Sabiston Island (52°13'00" 128°06'00" S entrance to Troup Passage, Seaforth Channel, just N of Bella Bella). This feature was formerly known as Haddon I, after Oak Bay resident and RCN paymaster Lt Gerald Philip Haddon (1885–1926), and then as Gray I. It was renamed in 1924 by the hydrographic service after John Flett Sabiston (1828–1902), a seaman and native of the Orkney Is, who came to Victoria in 1850 as a labourer on the HBC supply ship *Norman Morison*. He found work on the HBC's *Beaver*, married Jane (1832–1921), who was born in Alaska of Russian heritage, and soon rose to the rank of sailing master. The HBC transferred him to Nanaimo, where he was a manager at the collieries, continuing in that position after the mines had been taken over by the Vancouver Coal Mining and Land Co. In 1867 he went back to sea as a pilot and plied that trade off BC and Alaska for the next 30 years. He was appointed Nanaimo's first harbourmaster in 1875. His son, also John Sabiston (1853–98), worked as a Nanaimo-based mariner and pilot as well and was skipper of the *Wanderer* on George M Dawson's QCI explorations in 1878.

Sac Bay on Moresby Island. *Andrew Scott*

Sac Bay (52°32'00" 131°40'00" Off S side of De la Beche Inlet, E side of Moresby I, QCI). This 1962 name, bestowed by officials of the hydrographic service, is descriptive of the feature's shape.

Sadler Island (53°30'00" 132°54'00" SW side of Skelu Bay, just NW of Rennell Sd, W side of Graham I, QCI), **Sadler Point** (54°06'00" 133°06'00" N entrance to Sialun Bay, NW

side of Graham I). John Sadler was the carpenter aboard the *Queen Charlotte*, under Capt George Dixon, on one of the earliest British fur-trading expeditions to the PNW, 1785–88. Dixon and his crew were the first Europeans to trade extensively with the Haida, sailing the full length of the W coast of the archipelago in 1787 and partway up the E side. Dixon was one of the first Europeans to become convinced that the land of the Haida was, indeed, a group of islands and well separated from the mainland. The point was named by Capt Frederick Learmonth of HMS *Egeria*, who re-surveyed the area in 1907; the Haida know it as Shlickalkwoon, or "seal bank point."

Safety Cove (51°32'00" 127°55'00" E side of Calvert I, Fitz Hugh Sd, NW of entrance to Rivers Inlet), **Safety Mountain** (51°32'40" 127°56'55" Overlooking Safety Cove, E side of Calvert I), **Safety Point** (N entrance to Safety Cove). There are a number of coastal features in BC with the words "safe" or "safety" in them. Most, obviously, denote a secure passage or anchorage for vessels. Safety Cove is the oldest and most historic of these names and was designated Port Safety by British fur trader Charles Duncan of the *Princess Royal*, who stayed there briefly in 1788. Capt George Vancouver, after sailing W through Johnstone and Queen Charlotte straits in 1792—and running both his vessels aground—renamed the feature Safety Cove. He anchored there that Aug, checked his ships for damage, took on wood and water, and explored the mainland coast between Smith Sd and Burke Channel with the ships' boats. Then, after hearing from the trading vessel *Venus* that Spanish officials were waiting to negotiate with him, he headed S to Nootka Sd. Safety Cove was settled briefly in the 1910s and was later a base for floating logging camps. Its First Nation name, Oatsoalis, was adopted for the creek that flows E into the head of the cove.

Sagen Islet (51°55'00" 127°53'00" Off SW end of King I, Burke Channel, SE of Bella Bella). Severin Sagen (1885–1942) was a pioneer settler in the central coast region. He died on Hunter I.

Sager Islands (52°54'00" 129°09'00" Entrance to Chapple Inlet, W side of Princess Royal I). William Sager (1887–1953) was the first doctor at the Belmont Surf Inlet Mines on Princess Royal. In 1918 his wife, Esther Mary "Hettie" (1887–1961, née Duckers), became the mother of the first child born at the mines (*see* Duckers Is). Sager emigrated from England to Canada in 1909, was ordained as a Methodist minister at Montreal and studied medicine at Queen's Univ in Kingston, Ont. He married Hettie at Rhode I in 1914 and took a job at the Methodist hospital in Hazelton, BC, in 1916. Sager had arranged to become a medical missionary in China, but at the last minute Hettie balked at the prospect and the family went to Surf Inlet instead, 1917–20. He was appointed superintendent at Port Simpson General Hospital, 1920–26, replacing Dr R W

S

Large, who had died suddenly. The Sagers then moved to the Lower Mainland so their children could attend school there. William practised medicine at Port Coquitlam, became Burnaby's public health officer, 1931–43, and also worked as a doctor at Wallace shipyards and Pender Hbr. In 1945 he and Hettie moved to Crescent Beach, where the family had spent many happy summers, with the intention of retiring, but William opened a practice in White Rk instead and became district coroner and acting medical officer for Surrey in 1950. The Sager Is were formerly known as the S Surf Is.

Sage Rock (52°57'00" 129°35'00" Entrance to Pemberton Bay, S side of Dewdney I, Estevan Group, NW side of Caamaño Sd). Named for Enoch Sage (1858–1945), one of the first white children to be born at Nanaimo. His parents, Jesse and Mary Ann Sage, arrived in BC in 1854 on the HBC's *Princess Royal*, part of a shipload of immigrants brought out from England to work at Nanaimo's coal mines. Enoch was listed as a baker at Nanaimo in the 1881 census, a coachman in 1891 and a "teamster, hackdriver and drayman" in 1901. In 1890, at Nanaimo, he married Ida May Sullivan (1873–1956), who had immigrated to Canada from the US with her parents in 1876. Enoch died at Essondale, Ida at Coquitlam. It is believed that they took part in the Victoria old-timers' reunion of May 1924 (*see* Adams Bay).

Sager Rock (54°39'00" 130°27'00" Off Maskelyne Point, N of the Tsimpsean Peninsula, just N of Port Simpson). Beatrice Sager (1896–1970), from Blackburn, England, was a VAD (Voluntary Aid Detachment) member during WWI at Whalley Hospital in Lancashire. She immigrated to Canada in 1925 and trained as a nurse at Vancouver and at Port Simpson General Hospital, where her brother Dr William Sager was superintendent (*see* Sager Is). Beatrice married Eulise Worthington Dowd (1894–1980) at Port Coquitlam in 1930. She died at White Rk, Eulise at Kelowna.

St Ines Island (48°58'00" 125°22'00" W of David Channel, SW of the Stopper Is, Barkley Sd, W side of Vancouver I). This feature appears as plain Ines I on the manuscript chart prepared by Capt George Richards of HMS *Hecate* in 1861. By the time the chart was published in 1865, however, the name had been changed to St Ines. The derivation is unknown. St Ines is generally considered to be the same person as St Agnes, who suffered a martyr's death in 301 for refusing to marry the son of a Roman prefect. She is the patron saint of chastity, girls, engaged couples, rape victims, virgins and gardeners.

St James Island. *See* Cape St James.

St John Point (49°31'00" 124°35'00" E tip of Hornby I, Str of Georgia). Lt Frederick Edward Molyneux St John (1838–1904), from Newcastle, served on the Pacific Station, 1859–60, aboard HMS *Tribune*, under Capt Geoffrey Hornby. He was one of a troop of Royal Marines brought from China to BC to maintain order during Britain's dispute with the US over the San Juan Is. The feature was named by Capt George Richards of HMS *Plumper* in 1860. After leaving the service, St John came back to Canada with his wife, Katherine (d 1903, née Ranoe), in 1868 and joined the *Toronto Globe*. He accompanied the Red River Expedition, sent W in 1870 to quell the Riel uprising, as a special correspondent and also travelled with Lord and Lady Dufferin when the gov gen and his wife visited BC in 1876 (about which St John wrote a book, *A Sea of Mountains*). His career included stints as clerk of the Manitoba legislature and secretary of its Protestant board of education, sheriff and Indian commissioner in the NWT, emigration agent and London secretary for the CPR, head of the CPR's advertising agency, and editor of both the *Winnipeg Standard* and the *Manitoba Free Press*. He was also a playwright. According to Beatrice Freeman of the Gulf Is Branch of the BC Historical Assoc, **St John Point** (48°49'00" 123°14'00") on the S tip of Mayne I is also named for him. It seems unlikely, however, that the hydrographic service would name two points after the same person, especially when the features are quite close to one another.

St Margaret Point (54°15'00" 133°02'00" N side of Langara I, off NW Graham I, QCI). On July 19, 1774, the day before St Margaret's Day, Spanish naval officer and explorer Juan Pérez became the first European to sight the BC coast. He named his historic landfall—off the NW tip of Langara I (qv) in the QCI—Punta Santa Margarita, and although he had peaceful contact with the Haida there, he did not go ashore. In 1793, Capt George Vancouver named the headland Point North, in association with North I, as Langara I was commonly referred to in the early days. Point North was also known for many years as Cape North. When the Langara lighthouse was built at the cape in 1913, the hydrographic service decided to apply two names to the large land mass. The most westerly point became Langara Point, and the eastern end of the headland was called St Margaret Point, to keep alive the famous name given by Pérez. The historical existence of St Margaret the Virgin, or Margaret of Antioch, is doubtful, but her cult became widespread in Europe. She is considered the patron saint of pregnancy. *D*

St Vincent Bay (49°49'00" 124°05'00" N side of Jervis Inlet, W of the mouth of Hotham Sd, E of Powell R). British naval cdr Sir John Jervis was created Baron Jervis of Meaford and Earl St Vincent in 1797 after his major victory over a larger Spanish fleet at the Battle of Cape St Vincent earlier that year. *See* Jervis Inlet for a more detailed biography. The bay was named by Capt George Richards about 1860. Presumably **St Vincent Bight** (50°27'00" 126°09'00" S side of Johnstone Str, NW of Campbell R and just SW of Port Neville) and nearby Mt St Vincent are named for him as well. Cape St Vincent, in Portugal, is the southwesternmost point in Europe. It is named after St Vincent of Saragossa, the patron saint of Lisbon. *W*

Sainty Point (53°22'20" 129°18'51" SE entrance to Grenville Channel, just W of Hartley Bay, SW of Kitimat). Capt Clifford Claude Mosley Sainty (1874–1956), a native of Colchester, England, came out to Victoria with his wife, Isabelle (1875–1958, née Wilson), and joined the CPR's BC Coast Steamship Service as a 2nd officer in 1909. His first appointment as a master was on the *Princess Ena* in 1912. A good proportion of his early service was on the Alaska run, and he was in command in 1927 when the *Princess Charlotte* hit Vichnefski Reef in thick fog. The vessel was towed into Wrangell, Alaska, where it became the object of a bitter salvage dispute. Sainty retired in 1938. The name was adopted by the hydrographic service in 1946. Nearby Mosley Point also commemorates him.

Salal Island (52°20'00" 128°28'00" Off W side of Lady Douglas I, head of Milbanke Sd, NW of Bella Bella), **Salal Point** (52°21'00" 128°28'00" N end of Salal I). The omnipresent coastal shrub *Gaultheria shallon*, which can form thickets so dense they're almost impenetrable, is a member of the heather family. Its juicy berries, either fresh or dried into cakes, were an important food for First Nation groups. In 1828, botanist David Douglas introduced salal to English gardeners as an ornamental species. *E*

Salamanca Point (48°54'00" 123°21'00" E side of Galiano I, N of Whaler Bay, Gulf Is). Spanish naval officer Secundino Salamanca was 1st lt of the *Sutil*, under Dionisio Alcalá-Galiano, during the 1792 circumnavigation of Vancouver I made by that vessel, in company with the *Mexicana*, under Cayetano Valdés. Salamanca and his counterpart aboard the *Mexicana*, Juan Vernaci, also led trips in the small ships' boats in order to examine and survey the many inlets and side channels in the region. Alcalá-Galiano named Loughborough Inlet after Salamanca. The point was named by Cdr John Parry of HMS *Egeria* in 1905, when Active Pass was re-surveyed.

Salient Point (53°28'00" 128°23'00" N side of Europa Reach, Gardner Canal, SE of Kitimat). This feature was originally named Bold Point but was changed by the hydrographic service in 1952 to avoid duplication. Salient, meaning "important" or "notable," might be considered a synonym for "bold." The word can also mean "pointing or projecting outward," however, as in an angle or part of a fortification. A creek and two mountains in BC have this name as well.

Salisbury Cone (52°09'00" 127°50'00" NE of Salisbury Point, King I), **Salisbury Point** (52°07'00" 127°51'00"

W side of King I, N side of Evans Inlet, E of Bella Bella). Named in association with Rev John Fisher, a "much respected friend" of Capt George Vancouver (*see* Fisher Channel). Fisher was appointed bishop of Exeter, 1803–7, and bishop of Salisbury, 1807–25.

Salish Sea (49°30'00" 124°00'00" Includes Str of Georgia, Juan de Fuca Str and Puget Sd). In 1990, Bert Webber, a US marine sciences professor, proposed a unified name for the bodies of water—Str of Georgia (qv), Juan de Fuca Str (qv) and Puget Sd—straddling the Canada-US border on the Pacific coast. His suggestion, Salish Sea, was turned down brusquely at the time by Washington state and BC governments. The idea refused to disappear, however, and was raised again on a broader scale in 2008 by First Nation leaders; it soon gained support from scientists, politicians, mariners, resource professionals and the media. In 2009, when this book went to press, Salish Sea was far from being officially adopted, though both governments had recently announced that they were open to discussing and considering the new name. The Salish people, who live around the shores of the Salish Sea (and inland as far as Idaho), are those who speak one of the Salishan family of First Nation languages.

Sallas Rocks (48°35'00" 123°17'00" S of Sidney I, W side of Haro Str, Gulf Is). Sallas, a First Nation name for Sidney I (qv), was adopted by HBC officials about 1850 and used by early settlers for many years—even after Capt George Richards of HMS *Plumper* officially changed the island's name to Sidney in 1859. The original meaning of the word seems to have been lost. Sallas Rks, formerly known as Dot Rks, were renamed by the hydrographic service in 1934 in order to keep alive the older aboriginal word.

Sallie Point (50°43'00" 125°44'00" N side of Knight Inlet, NW of Duncan Bight, N of Glendale Cove). William Blakeney, assistant surveying officer under Lt Daniel Pender aboard the *Beaver* in 1865, named a group of geographical features in this vicinity in association with his brother-in-law, William Macdonald. Macdonald would become a prominent BC businessman and politician (*see* Macdonald Point). Sallie was his favourite horse.

Salmon Channel (50°43'00" 126°49'00" Between George Passage and Nowell Channel, W of Bonwick I, E end of Queen Charlotte Str). RN officer Nowell Salmon (1835–1912) entered the RN in 1847 and served as a midshipman aboard HMS *Thetis*, under Capt Augustus Kuper, on the Pacific Station, 1851–53. In 1852, while the *Thetis* was stationed in the QCI to preserve the peace after the recent discovery of gold, Salmon and Lt John Moresby explored the area around Mitchell Inlet on foot. Salmon served in the Baltic in the Crimean War, and in India in 1857, where he was awarded the VC for exceptional bravery during the relief of Lucknow. He was knighted in 1887 and went on

S

to reach the RN's highest rank, adm of the fleet, in 1899. He was also cdr-in-chief at Portsmouth during the grand review held in honour of Queen Victoria's diamond jubilee in 1897. Salmon Channel was named by Lt Daniel Pender in the *Beaver* about 1866. Nearby Nowell Bank and Nowell Channel are named for him as well. *W*

Salmon Cove (55°16'00" 129°50'00" W side of Observatory Inlet, N of Nass Bay, NE of Prince Rupert). Named in 1793 by Capt George Vancouver "from the abundance of that kind of fish that were there taken." Crew members put a seine net across the mouth of a creek entering the cove and packed away thousands of spawning fish for future use. The *Discovery* and *Chatham* spent more than three weeks anchored at this spot in July and Aug 1793, while Vancouver and his officers made extensive surveys of the southern Alaska panhandle and Nass Bay areas in the ships' boats. He also set up an observatory in the cove where, because of the fine weather, Joseph Whidbey was able to correct the ships' positions and confirm the rates of their chronometers. The Nisga'a First Nation name for this site is Gwinmilit, where *milit* means "steelhead."

Salmon Islands (50°28'00" 127°48'00" S side of Quatsino Sd, NW end of Vancouver I). T Salmon was engineer in charge of the W coast survey vessel *Restless*, 1920–24, under Cdr John Knight. He participated in the survey of Quatsino Sd made by the hydrographic service in 1920–21.

Salter Point (49°41'00" 126°35'00" SE tip of Strange I, Nootka Sd, W side of Vancouver I). Capt John Salter, a mariner with much experience in the E Indies trade, was master of the ill-fated US vessel *Boston*, which was attacked and later destroyed by members of the Nuu-chah-nulth First Nation at Nootka Sd in 1803. Salter, who had insulted Maquinna, the Nuu-chah-nulth chief, was massacred with all his crew except two, John Jewitt and John Thompson, who were held captive for nearly three years until rescued by Capt Samuel Hill of the brig *Lydia*. Jewitt's narrative of his captivity, *The Adventures and Sufferings of John R Jewitt*, became a bestseller. *See also* Jewitt Cove.

Saltery Bay (49°47'00" 124°10'00" N of Nelson I, N side of Jervis Inlet, SE of Powell R), **Saltery Bay** (49°52'00" 126°49'00" N end of Nootka I, Esperanza Inlet, W side of Vancouver I). Salteries were primitive packing plants that used salt to preserve fish—usually salmon or herring. The HBC preserved salmon this way at Ft Langley and Ft Simpson, both for local use and for export; the fish were cleaned and trimmed, then split lengthwise and packed in large barrels between layers of salt. Numerous independent salteries were established on the BC coast over the years, often by Japanese operators, who prepared their fish especially for the Japanese market, and several were later turned into canneries. As canneries proliferated, salteries declined. Saltery Bay on Jervis Inlet is today the site of a provincial park and a BC Ferries terminus. *E*

Saltspring Island (48°45'00" 123°29'00" Largest of the Gulf Is, E of Duncan off SE side of Vancouver I). The Saanich First Nation people knew this place as Cuan, a name that can be translated as "each end" and refers to the high ground at the N and S ends of the island. The Cowichan (Quw'utsun') people called it Klaathem, meaning "salt." To complicate matters, the Cowichan also gave the name Chuan, meaning "facing the sea," to a mountain on the

Fulford valley on Saltspring Island, with Mount Maxwell to the right. *Kevin Oke*

S end of the island, known today as Mt Tuam (qv). On a map accompanying an 1854 report, Gov James Douglas named the entire island Chuan. The following year, on a map of SE Vancouver I produced for the HBC by surveyor Joseph Pemberton, it is labelled Saltspring I. This latter name was bestowed by HBC officials, who were interested in extracting salt from numerous briny springs located at the N end of the island. In 1859, Capt George Richards changed the name to Admiral I, after Rear Adm Robert Baynes, who was cdr-in-chief of the Pacific Station, 1857–60 (*see* Baynes Sd). The Geographic Board of Canada, however, recognizing that Saltspring continued to be in widespread favour and use, changed the name back in 1905. An alternative, unofficial form of the name—Salt Spring Island—has numerous diehard supporters, especially on the island itself, which has seen dramatic population growth in recent years and been transformed from an agricultural backwater to a trendy retirement and recreational destination. *E W*

Salubrious Bay (50°02'00" 124°44'00" S end of Gifford Peninsula, S of Desolation Sd, NW of Powell R). This name apparently got its start when a government climate chart referred to the area as "salubrious." The word stuck, became locally established and was submitted as an official name by local resident G B Goudriaan in 1981. "Salubrious" means "conducive or favourable to good health."

Salvesen Island (53°36'00" 133°00'00" Off S side of Athlow Bay, off W side of Graham I, QCI), **Salvesen Point** (53°35'00" 133°00'00" S entrance to Athlow Bay). Sigvart Salvesen (1878–1957), from Norway, worked in this region for the Canadian Fishing Co, under Capt Absalom Freeman, 1907–11. He had been a seaman from an early age and is reported to have rounded Cape Horn 13 times before arriving in Vancouver on the clipper ship *Laura*. Salvesen worked as a high-liner with the halibut fleet and as 2nd mate on coastal passenger ships. He towed Davis rafts (great bundles of logs woven together with cables) from the QCI to the mainland as skipper of such well-known tugs as the *J R Morgan*, *Lorne* and *Sudbury I*. His Haida nickname apparently meant "he who can smell weather." Capt Freeman, who named the point in 1912, originally used the spelling Selvesen, and this form of the word was adopted on charts by the hydrographic service (in 1933 for the point and 1946 for the island). It was changed to Salvesen in 2000 after family members confirmed that the earlier version was incorrect.

Sambo Point (50°35'00" 126°21'00" N side of W Cracroft I, E entrance to Bones Bay, N of Johnstone Str). Named, along with nearby Minstrel I, Negro Rk and Bones Bay, after a troupe of amateur performers aboard HMS *Amethyst*, which carried Lord Dufferin, the gov gen, and Lady Dufferin on a cruise to Metlakatla in 1876. These entertainers put on minstrel shows, based on black cultural stereotypes, in which "Mr Bones" and "Sambo" were stock characters. Presumably, such a show was staged in the vicinity for the vice-regal couple.

Samuel Island (48°49'00" 123°13'00" Between Saturna I and Mayne I, Gulf Is). After RN surgeon Samuel Campbell, on the BC coast 1857–62. *See* Campbell Bay. The 132-ha island was pre-empted in the 1890s by Ralph Grey and George Rutherford. Grey soon became the sole owner, receiving a Crown grant for the property in 1905. He farmed there and, in 1900, married Winifred Higgs, who had come out from England in 1896 to visit her brother Leonard Higgs on Saturna I. Her sister Mabel Higgs also lived on Samuel I and later married Martin Grainger (*see* Grainger Point), an author and BC's chief forester, 1916–20. The Greys left the island in 1910, and it was eventually sold as a recreational property to a series of wealthy owners, including A J T Taylor, the engineer who developed British Properties in W Vancouver and built the Lions Gate Bridge. He constructed a luxurious six-bedroom mansion there, complete with hand-carved gargoyles on the roof beams, as well as a smaller lodge. Grocery baron Garfield Weston also owned the island for several years in the late 1940s.

Samuel Rock (52°15'00" 131°07'00" N side of Carpenter Bay, SE end of Moresby I, QCI). After US fur trader Samuel Crowell, who visited the QCI in the early 1790s with the brig *Hancock*. *See* Crowell Point.

San Carlos Point (49°41'00" 126°31'00" N tip of Bligh I, Nootka Sd, W side of Vancouver I). The 16-gun, 175-tonne Spanish naval supply ship *San Carlos* was present at many pivotal events in the early exploration of the Pacific coast. It was built in 1767 on the Santiago R, near the newly established naval shipyard and port of San Blas in Mexico. In 1775, under Manuel Manrique and, later, Juan Manuel de Ayala, it was sent to chart San Francisco Bay. In 1788, Gonzales López de Haro took the vessel N to Alaska, accompanying Estéban Martínez in the *Princesa*, to report on Russian activity on the Pacific coast. The following year López de Haro and the *San Carlos* were at Nootka Sd, helping Martínez establish the Spanish base there, and in 1790 the ship was back at Nootka, this time under the command of Salvador Fidalgo, who made a long expedition with it to Prince William Sd in Alaska later that year. The ship's next cdr was Ramon Antonio Saavedra, who sailed it back to Nootka Sd in 1791. From there, Francisco Eliza, the cdr at Nootka, took it into Clayoquot Sd and then up Juan de Fuca Str, along with José Narváez in the *Santa Saturnina*, on the first European exploration of the Str of Georgia (though it was Narváez who did most of the exploring). The *San Carlos* was back at Nootka in 1793–95, under Saavedra, who dismantled the Spanish base under the terms of the Nootka Sd Convention. Carlos I E of Gabriola I is also named after this vessel.

San Christoval Range (52°37'00" 131°50'00" On the central part of Moresby I, QCI). These mountains, which rise to 1,068 m, have the oldest surviving European or "western" name in BC—Sierra de San Cristóbal—given on account of their height by Spanish naval officer and explorer Juan Pérez on July 23, 1774. Four days earlier, Perez, in the *Santiago*, had made a historic landfall off Langara I, becoming the first European to lay eyes on BC. He gave the name Punta Santa Margarita to Langara's NW tip, but that headland is now known as Langara Point. (St Margaret Point, qv, farther E, was named much later by the hydrographic service in order to keep Perez's historic name alive.) San Cristóbal is St Christopher, the patron saint of travellers, who was legendary for his size and fearsome appearance.

Sandford Island (48°52'00" 125°10'00" E side of Imperial Eagle Channel, SW of Fleming I, Barkley Sd, W side of Vancouver I). After surveyor and engineer Sir Sandford Fleming. *See* Fleming Bay. Besides his many other achievements, Fleming was a great supporter of a trans-Pacific telegraph cable from Canada to Australia and NZ, which was completed in 1902. Apparently the cable, which had its Canadian terminus at Bamfield, ran just past the S end of this island. Formerly known as Hill I.

Sand Heads light, at the mouth of the shifting main channel of the Fraser River. *Peter Vassilopoulos*

Sand Heads (49°06'00" 123°18'00" Just W of the mouth of the Fraser R, Str of Georgia). This spot, which identifies the northern entrance to the main channel of the Fraser R, has been marked over the years by a series of light towers and vessels. Entering the Fraser, with its ever-shifting sandbars, has always been a nightmare for mariners. Gold seekers were demanding a lightship at the river mouth as early as 1859, but it was not until 1865 that colonial authorities purchased a New Westminster vessel, renamed it the *South Sand Heads* and anchored it offshore, where for 14 years it indicated a safe route upstream. In 1879, despite concerns that a stationary beacon would soon be made obsolete by the Fraser's tortuous, changing channels, a unique lighthouse, North Sand Heads, was built of braced iron piles twisted deep into the silt, topped with an eight-sided wooden tower. By 1905 this odd structure was more than a km off the main channel and had to be complemented with a lightship, an ancient Coast Guard cutter named the *Mermaid*, built in 1853. The *Mermaid*'s replacement, the *Sand Heads No 16* (a former pilot boat named the *Thomas F Bayard*), lasted until 1957. By 1960 a stone jetty had been built out to Sand Heads from Steveston, and the Dept of Transport felt comfortable enough to erect another fixed light there, which was still standing in the 2000s. The name is often also seen spelled Sandheads.

Sandilands Island (53°10'00" 132°06'00" S of W end of Maude I, Skidegate Inlet, between Graham I and Moresby I, QCI). Evelyn Montague Sandilands (1863–1939), a former insurance agent, was appointed a gold commissioner and magistrate for the QCI in 1908, with his office at Jedway. He was transferred to Queen Charlotte City in 1912 and given the additional duties of government agent and superintendent of roads. His wife, Malinda Sutherland (1878–1979), whom he married at Vancouver in 1913, did not like the QCI, and the couple soon moved to the BC Interior. Sandilands was listed as a mining recorder at Windermere in 1918. He died at Kaslo. Sandilands I, originally called South I by George M Dawson in 1878, was renamed by the hydrographic service in 1917. Sandilands Peak in the W Kootenay district is also named for him. *D*

Sandpiper Beach (49°30'00" 124°38'00" SE side of Hornby I, Str of Georgia). This name was adopted in 1976 after a subdivision of "summer or retirement properties" was developed in the area by the Nanaimo Realty Co. Two creeks and a lake in BC are also named for this family of dainty shorebirds.

Sandspit (53°15'00" 131°49'00" NE end of Moresby I, QCI), **Sandspit Point** (51°41'00" 128°07'00" NW side of Calvert I, Hakai Pass, S of Bella Bella). Sandspits are common geographical features on the BC coast. These narrow, low-lying tongues of sand and shingle, which can project into the sea or partway across an inlet, are formed by "longshore drift," where sedimentary material is driven along a coastline by oblique wave action, then deposited at an angle to the shore by backwash or a countercurrent. The QCI community of Sandspit was first settled in the early 1900s and got an economic boost in the 1940s when the Crown Zellerbach logging company established a base there. An RCAF airstrip built at Sandspit in 1943 is now the QCI's main airport. The tip of the spit is called Spit Point and was known to the Haida as Kil'kun; Kil village ("Sand Spit Point Town") lay just SE. A dangerous bar extends N of the spit for a distance of more than 10 km. *D E*

Sandstone Islands (53°12'00" 132°14'00" Entrance to Long Inlet, S end of Graham I, Skidegate Inlet, QCI),

Sandstone Point (49°52'00" 127°10'00" Between Esperanza Inlet and Kyuquot Inlet, NW side of Vancouver I), **Sandstone Rocks** (48°55'00" 123°37'00" E side of Stuart Channel, S of Tent I, W of N end of Saltspring I, Gulf Is). Sandstone is a porous sedimentary rock composed of sand grains, usually bound together by silica or calcium carbonate. This type of stone weathers easily and—in the Gulf Is region, especially—can become eroded and sculpted by wind and waves into fantastic curved formations or "galleries." The Sandstone Is were named by RN surveyor Daniel Pender (originally as Sand Stone Is). There are also three Sandstone creeks and a Sandstone Lk elsewhere in BC.

Sandy Cove (49°20'00" 123°14'00" Just E of Point Atkinson, near N entrance to Burrard Inlet, W Vancouver). This feature was officially designated Ettershank Cove in 1929, after pioneer Burrard Inlet pilot Capt William Ettershank (*see* Ettershank Point), but that name was rescinded in 1949 in favour of Sandy Cove, which had become well established locally. The bay is sandy at its high-water edge but is really a large mud flat when the tide is out. The feature was also known locally as Sherman Cove, after nearby Sherman post office, established in 1926 and named for Vancouver city councillor Alfred Henry Sherman, who owned and subdivided land here before moving in the 1920s to California, where he died.

Sangster Island (49°26'00" 124°12'00" S of Lasqueti I, Str of Georgia). James Sangster (c 1812–58), a native of Port Glasgow, Scotland, joined the HBC's marine dept in 1827 as an apprentice aboard the *Eagle*. From 1832 until the late 1840s he was mostly based at Ft Vancouver. Sangster served on many of the HBC's early sailing vessels, including the *Vancouver*, *Cowlitz* and *Lama*, and worked his way up the ranks until he was given his first command, the historic paddle steamer *Beaver*, in 1839. He was later capt of the *Cadboro* and the *Una*. About 1851 he retired from the HBC and was appointed Victoria's pilot, harbourmaster and collector of customs. Sangster died, apparently by his own hand, at Esquimalt. The island, which appears on charts in 1860, was named by HBC officials about 1850; in 1973, still unlogged, it was listed for sale at $100,000.

Sangster Point (52°59'00" 132°11'00" E tip of Hibben I, Kuper Inlet, NW side of Moresby I, QCI). Lt James Sangster was a Royal Marines officer who served on the Pacific Station aboard HMS *Thetis*, under Capt Augustus Kuper, 1851–53. Kuper named this feature in 1852 while the *Thetis* was in the QCI maintaining the peace after a short-lived gold rush.

San Josef Bay (50°39'00" 128°19'00" At the NW end of Vancouver I, W of the head of Holberg Inlet). The name initially appears on the 1793 chart of Spanish naval officer Dionisio Alcalá-Galiano. Capt James Hanna, who made the first fur-trading visit to the PNW in 1785, called it St Patrick's Bay on his second trip, in 1786. On his chart, Hanna also labelled the river that flows into San Josef Bay—known today as the San Josef R—as the Parry R. James Strange, another British fur trader who visited the area in 1786, named this feature Scott's Bay, after his friend and patron David Scott (who is commemorated by nearby Cape Scott and the Scott Is). In 1860 the RN gunboat *Forward* made a daring rescue of the crew and passengers of the US brig *Consort* in San Josef Bay. A pioneer settlement formed there in the early 1900s, centred around Henry Ohlsen's store, and included many members from the failed Danish colony at Cape Scott. Most residents had left, however, by WWI. The RCAF base at the foot of nearby Mt Hansen, which served for many years as home to those who manned the radar facilities on Mt Brandes, was also known as San Josef. St Joseph was the husband of Mary, mother of Jesus, and is the patron saint of workers. San Josef Mtn, E of Frederick Arm and N of Campbell R, is named after the *San Josef*, a Spanish ship of the line captured by Horatio Nelson at the Battle of Cape St Vincent in 1797. *E W*

San Juan Islands, **San Juan Point**. *See* Port San Juan.

San Mateo Bay (48°56'00" 124°59'00" At SE entrance to Alberni Inlet, Barkley Sd, W side of Vancouver I). This name was adopted from Spanish charts by Capt George Richards about 1860 but it is not known how or by whom it was originally applied. San Mateo is Matthew the Evangelist, one of the 12 apostles of Jesus and the patron saint of accountants. A cannery was built on the bay in 1918 by the Gosse-Millerd Packing Co, and pilchard reduction equipment was added later. The plant was acquired by BC Packers in 1928, closed that year and abandoned in 1936. The bay was the site of aquaculture operations in the early 2000s.

San Miguel Islands (49°35'00" 126°37'00" E of Yuquot Point, off SE Nootka I, Nootka Sd, W side of Vancouver I). Estéban Martínez, Spanish cdr at Nootka in 1789, gave the name San Miguel to the fortifications that he immediately began to build on the islands bordering the S side of Friendly Cove. His journal for May 15 reads: "Observing that the best situation for the defense of this port is the point to the NE which forms the entrance, I gave orders to begin to place an embankment on the hill located on this point, where ten cannon could be mounted." A 1791 Spanish map of Friendly Cove (published in 1802) shows a bastion on the most northeasterly of the San Miguels. Martínez may also have built a gun emplacement on San Rafael I (qv), the largest island in the group. However, Archibald Menzies, the botanist and doctor on Capt George Vancouver's voyage, who visited the cove in Aug 1792, describes the fort, "if it might be called such," as "no other than two guns mounted on a small platform on the outer point of the cove, with a flag staff on which the

S

Spanish colours were hoisted and a small guard mounted to give the appearance of a place of defence." San Miguel, or St Michael, was an archangel and is the patron saint of the warrior.

San Rafael Island (49°35'00" 126°37'00" One of the San Miguel Is, off SE Nootka I, Nootka Sd, W side of Vancouver I). This island is today the site of the Nootka lighthouse station, which began operating in 1911. It may have been fortified by the Spanish occupants of Friendly Cove in the early 1790s, as was the neighbouring island to the NE (*see* San Miguel Is). Presumably it was named by them as well. St Raphael, the patron saint of healing, was an archangel like St Michael. The Spanish also referred to this geographical feature as Isla de los Cerdos, or Hog Island.

San Simon Point (48°26'00" 124°06'00" NW of mouth of the Jordan R, N side of Juan de Fuca Str). Named by Spanish naval officer Manuel Quimper during his 1790 survey of Juan de Fuca Str. St Simon, the patron saint of curriers, sawyers and tanners, was one of the 12 apostles of Jesus.

Sans Peur Passage (51°56'00" 128°12'00" W side of Hunter I, S of Bella Bella). The 64-m motor yacht *Sans Peur*, built in England in 1933, was the private vessel of the 5th Duke of Sutherland, the immensely rich Sir George Granville Sutherland-Leveson-Gower. The duke was hunting bear on the BC coast while on a voyage around the world when war broke out in 1939, and the yacht was immediately transferred to the RCN, which used it as a training ship and also to conduct anti-submarine patrols on the W coast. *Sans peur* is French for "without fear." It is the motto of the Clan Sutherland and appears on its coat of arms and crest. The 3rd duke also had a yacht with this name. The channel, marked as Choked Passage on an 1867 Admiralty chart, was renamed by the hydrographic service in 1944.

Sansum Island (52°57'00" 132°09'00" Mitchell Inlet, Kuper Inlet, NW side of Moresby I, QCI), **Sansum Narrows** (48°48'00" 123°34'00" Between W side of Saltspring I and E side of Vancouver I), **Sansum Point** (48°47'00" 123°33'00" W side of Sansum Narrows, S of Octopus Point). RN officer Arthur Sansum was 1st lt aboard HMS *Thetis*, under Capt Augustus Kuper, and served on the Pacific Station, 1851–53. He died suddenly of a stroke at Guaymas, Mexico, in 1853 and is buried there. Sansum I was named by Capt Kuper about 1852, Sansum Narrows by Capt George Richards in 1858.

Santa Cruz de Nuca Mountain (49°40'55" 126°40'31" SE side of Nootka I, Nootka Sd, W side of Vancouver I). Puerto de la Santa Cruz was the original name given by the Spanish to Friendly Cove. (Santa Cruz de Nuca also appears on Spanish charts from this era.) PNW cartography expert Henry Wagner suggests that it was

probably bestowed by Estéban Martínez, the Spanish cdr at Nootka, in 1789, because he arrived there that year on May 5, just after the traditional Holy Cross feast day of May 3. In order to keep this historic name alive, regional hydrographer Henri Parizeau adopted it in 1935 for the highest summit (915 m) on Nootka I.

Santa Gertrudis Cove (49°36'00" 126°37'00" SE side of Nootka I, Nootka Sd, W side of Vancouver I). After the historic vessel *Santa Gertrudis la Magna*, built by British fur trader John Meares at Friendly Cove in 1788 as the *North West America*. This 40-tonne schooner was the first non-Native vessel constructed on the BC coast. After being launched in Sept, it was sailed to Hawaii by Robert Funter, 2nd mate of the *Felice Adventurer* under John Meares, and brought back by Funter to the BC coast the following year. In June 1789 it was one of the vessels seized by Estéban Martínez, Spanish cdr at Nootka, who refitted it and renamed it for Gertrude the Great, a 13th-century German Benedictine and mystic. (It is not to be confused with the Spanish frigate *Santa Gertrudis* that Francisco Bodega y Quadra took to Nootka in 1792.) Later in 1789, José Narváez was sent with the schooner to explore the coast of Vancouver I from Nootka Sd to the entrance of Juan de Fuca Str. The pilot José Verdia then took the *Gertrudis* to Mexico in Oct. According to author Jim McDowell, it was dismantled at San Blas; Francisco Eliza brought the pieces back to Nootka Sd the following year and used them to build the *Santa Saturnina* (*see below*). The name of the cove was adopted by the Geographic Board of Canada in 1930.

Santa Saturnina Point (49°46'00" 126°26'00" E side of Tlupana Inlet, S of Nesook Bay, Nootka Sd, W side of Vancouver I), **Saturnina Island** (49°08'41" 123°40'40" One of the Flat Top Is, off E end of Gabriola I, Gulf Is). The small schooner *Santa Saturnina*, the second European vessel built in the PNW, was brought in pieces to Nootka Sd by Francisco Eliza and assembled there in 1790. Most of those pieces are believed by historians to have likely come from the *Santa Gertrudis la Magna* (*see above*). Launched in Nov and equipped with seven guns, the *Saturnina* was named after German martyr St Saturnina, patron saint of farmers and wine merchants. In 1791, under José Narváez, it participated in a historic exploration of the Str of Georgia, led by Eliza in the *San Carlos*. The *Saturnina*, however, being smaller and drawing less water, did much of the work, sailing around Texada and Lasqueti islands and sighting Desolation Sd and Nanaimo Hbr. Narváez commemorated his vessel by giving the name Punta de Santa Saturnina to the SE point of Saturna I (*see* Saturna Beach). That Aug the pilot Juan Carrasco took the *Saturnina* back to San Blas, Mexico. The vessel returned briefly to Nootka the following year with instructions for Salvador Fidalgo, who was in command there the winter of 1792–93.

Santiago Mountain (49°48'08" 126°36'28" E side of Tahsis Inlet, above mouth of the Tsowwin R, opposite Nootka I, W side of Vancouver I). The 25-m, 205-tonne *Santiago*, built at San Blas, Mexico, about 1773, was the vessel commanded by Spanish naval officer and explorer Juan Pérez when he became the first European to sight the BC coast, in 1774 (*see* Juan Perez Sd). Pérez, who did not go ashore, made his initial landfall off Langara I in the QCI, then later anchored off Nootka Sd and Estevan Point. In 1775 the *Santiago* went N again, this time under the command of Bruno de Hezeta and accompanied by the schooner *Sonora*. Pérez was Hezeta's deputy aboard the *Santiago*. The ships were separated and Hezeta only reached Vancouver I, but on his way back S he explored the mouth of the Columbia R, the first European to see this landmark. (In the meantime, the *Sonora*, under Francisco Bodega y Quadra, went farther N than any Spanish explorer had been before, to the approximate latitude of Glacier Bay in Alaska.) Santiago Ck, named after the mountain, flows into Tahsis Inlet.

Sapir Point (50°15'00" 127°48'00" N entrance to Klaskish Inlet, Brooks Bay, NW side of Vancouver I). Named to honour influential anthropologist and linguist Edward Sapir (1884–1939), who spent much time studying the languages and cultures of First Nation groups on the BC coast. He was born in Poland and educated in the US, where he became a student of Franz Boas. Between 1910 and 1925 he organized and ran the Canadian national museum's anthropological division, where he wrote a seminal book, *Language*, and important works on Nuu-chah-nulth and other PNW languages. Sapir taught at the Univ of Chicago, 1925–31, before becoming head of the anthropology dept at Yale Univ.

Sarah Head (52°53'00" 128°30'00" N end of Sarah I), **Sarah Island** (52°46'00" 128°30'00" Off SE side of Princess Royal I, E of Tolmie Channel, NW of Bella Bella), **Sarah Passage** (52°38'00" 128°31'00" S of Sarah I, N of Jane I), **Sarah Point** (54°33'00" 130°27'00" E side of Finlayson I, S entrance to Port Simpson, NW of Prince Rupert). After BC pioneer Sarah Work, daughter of HBC chief factor John Work and wife of chief factor Roderick Finlayson. *See* Work Bay. Sarah I was named by Lt Daniel Pender of the hired survey vessel *Beaver* in 1867. Sarah Ck and Sarah Lk NE of Prince Rupert also commemorate her, as does Mt Sarah on Swindle I.

Sarah Point (50°04'00" 124°50'00" NW tip of Malaspina Peninsula, NE end of Str of Georgia). Named in June 1792 by Capt George Vancouver after his sister Sarah (b 1752). He also named Mary Point (qv), at the SE tip of Cortes I, at the same time after another sister. The two points bracket the entrance to Desolation Sd. While a fair amount has been uncovered about Vancouver's twin brothers, Charles and John, virtually nothing is known about his three

sisters (Bridget, the eldest, was born in 1751). Author and historian John Walbran suggests that Sarah Point may also commemorate Vancouver's grandmother, who died in 1769. *W*

Saranac Island (49°15'00" 125°54'00" NW of Meares I, Clayoquot Sd, W side of Vancouver I). The 10-gun US warship *Saranac*, named after a river in NY state, was launched in 1848 at the Portsmouth navy yard in Maine. The 1,950-tonne, 66-m paddle sloop served in S America and the Mediterranean before being transferred to the Pacific coast in 1857 for use as a patrol vessel. It was en route from San Francisco to Sitka in 1875, under Capt W W Green, to pick up First Nation artifacts for Philadelphia's 1876 Centennial International Exposition, when it struck Ripple Rk in Seymour Narrows doing about 14 knots (26 km/h). The vessel immediately began to founder, but the crew managed to get it close to Vancouver I before it sank, and all hands reached shore. HMS *Myrmidon* and the HBC ship *Otter* responded to the scene of the disaster and brought the survivors to Victoria. *W*

Saratoga Beach (49°51'00" 125°06'00" S of mouth of the Oyster R, between Campbell R and Courtenay, E side of Vancouver I). Named after a resort and trailer park at this location. According to Don and Marj Thexton, the resort's proprietors in the 1970s, it was named by a Mr Clarkson, one of the owners of this property in the 1930s, after Saratoga, a city in California's Santa Clara valley. Another source suggests that the resort was named after the spa and horse-racing town of Saratoga Springs in NY.

Sardonyx Point (52°16'00" 127°56'00" W side of Johnson Channel, on Cunningham I, NE of Bella Bella). The coastal steamship *Sardonyx* was built in the UK in 1869 and purchased by a Victoria business syndicate in 1882. The 52-m, 509-tonne vessel ran between Victoria and San Francisco for a few months but was found to be too expensive to operate. In 1884 it took a cargo to China and was chartered by a Mexican company the following year. In 1887 the Canadian Pacific Navigation Co acquired the steamer and operated it to northern BC and also to Portland, but in 1890, en route to Skidegate from Port Simpson under Capt W J Smith, it struck a reef off the E coast of the QCI and was totally wrecked. The crew and passengers rowed lifeboats to Skidegate, and the *Barbara Boscowitz* then took them safely to Victoria. Sardonyx is a semi-precious mineral—a type of quartz with bands of colour, usually red, brown and white. Sardonyx Point was formerly known as Peard Pt, after F Peard, the coxswain on a sounding launch during a 1922 hydrographic survey of the area, but was renamed in 1925.

Sargeant Bay (49°28'00" 123°51'00" S end of Sechelt Peninsula, W of Trail Bay, Str of Georgia, NW of Vancouver). This name is a spelling error, as the bay

S

commemorates Frederick Sargent, who pre-empted land here in 1887 and received a Crown grant for his homestead in 1892. The area around the bay was logged, and a steam-powered sawmill located by the shore. In the 1920s and '30s a small resort was established on the bay; subsequent owners made unsuccessful attempts to develop a marina and condominium complex. A 57-ha waterfront and upland area was protected as Sargeant Bay Provincial Park in 1990, largely through the efforts of the Sargeant Bay Society; an 83-ha portion around Triangle Lk was added to the park at a later date. Formerly known as Nor-West Bay and then, strangely, as Southeast Bay, this geographical feature was given its current name by regional hydrographer Henri Parizeau in 1925. The Sechelt First Nation people know it as K'wéxwmínem, after a medicinal plant that grows there.

Sargeaunt Passage (50°41'00" 126°11'00" Between Viscount I and the mainland, off SE Gilford I, NW side of Knight Inlet). RN officer Frederic Anthony Sargeaunt (1840–98) served on the Pacific Station, 1868–71, as 1st lt of HMS *Charybdis*, under Capt Algernon Lyons. He was promoted to cdr in 1871 and stationed at Folkestone with the Coast Guard, then served as cdr of the *Clyde*, an RNVR drill ship based at Aberdeen. Sargeant reached the rank of capt in 1886. Named by Lt Daniel Pender of the *Beaver* in 1868. *W*

Sargison Bank (48°55'00" 125°26'00" S of Forbes I, W side of Barkley Sd, W side of Vancouver I). According to Barkley Sd historian R Bruce Scott, A G Sargison pre-empted land on the N side of Barkley Sd in 1893. Government records, however, show that A G Sargison received a Crown grant for land in the Metchosin district in 1883. The first Sargisons—George Andrew (1827–1900), from Yorkshire, and his wife, Margaret (1830–1905, née Barnard)—arrived at Victoria from San Francisco in 1873, having lived in Montreal and Toronto in the 1840s and '50s. An accountant and notary public, George served as Victoria's chief census officer in 1891 and played a prominent role in city temperance organizations. One of the couple's 10 children was Albert George Sargison (1862–1929), also an accountant. He was born in Quebec and married Fanny Adele Eugenie Jackson (1862–1930), from London, UK, at Victoria in 1884. Albert became co-owner (with editor W H Ellis) of the Victoria *Colonist*, 1886–1892, then sold the newspaper to James Dunsmuir. He also served as a Victoria city councillor in 1910.

Sargison Reef (52°12'00" 131°21'00" In Flamingo Inlet, S of Sperm Bay, S end of Moresby I, QCI). Named by the hydrographic service in 1963 after Capt G Sargison, who was master of the whaling vessel *Green*, based at Rose Hbr, in 1929. George Stanley Sargison (b 1896) was the son of Victoria accountant and newspaper owner Albert Sargison (*see above*).

Sarita Bay (48°53'00" 125°02'00" S side of Numukamis Bay, E side of Barkley Sd, W side of Vancouver I). While the origin of this name is not really known, it appears (in the form of Sarita Valley) on Admiralty charts as early as 1861. In Spanish, *Sarita* is a diminutive for *Sara*, and it is just possible that the feature was named by Spanish naval officer José Narváez, who explored and surveyed Barkley Sd in 1789. The nearby Sarita R, site of a dryland log sort in the early 2000s, was probably the first feature to be named, followed by the bay, Sarita Lk and Sarita Falls. The Huu-ay-aht (Ohiaht) First Nation had a winter village on the bay, and an early Roman Catholic mission, St Leo's, was established there in the late 1870s, followed by a pilchard reduction plant in the 1920s and '30s, and a large Bloedel, Stewart & Welch logging camp in the 1940s and '50s. *E*

Sartine Island (50°49'00" 128°54'00" One of the Scott Is, W of Cape Scott, off the NW tip of Vancouver I). In 1786 the French explorer Jean-François de Galaup, Comte de Lapérouse, visited the PNW and gave to today's Scott Is, off the NW end of Vancouver I, the name Îles Sartine. Sartine I, formerly known as W Haycock I, was renamed by the hydrographic service to keep this small slice of history alive. Lapérouse disappeared in 1788, somewhere in the S Pacific, with his ships the *Boussole* and *Astrolabe*. Forty years passed before it was discovered that all hands had been lost when the vessels were wrecked in the New Hebrides. Antoine de Sartine, Comte d'Alby (1729–1801), was born at Barcelona and for many years served as one of the chief administrators of Paris (lt gen of police). He was also secretary of state for the navy, 1774–1780. Treeless 28-ha Sartine I was named an ecological reserve in 1971 in order to protect colonies of breeding seabirds.

Sasamat Lake (49°19'00" 122°53'00" E of Bedwell Bay, Indian Arm, Burrard Inlet, E of Vancouver). When the old name for this feature, Deer Lk, had to be changed in 1948 because of its proximity to Deer Lk in Burnaby, Maj J S Matthews, Vancouver's city archivist, suggested Sasamat Lk. The name appears on a chart by Spanish explorer Dionisio Alcalá-Galiano, who explored Burrard Inlet in 1792 and sent two officers, Secundino Salamanca and Juan Vernaci, to examine Indian Arm. Alcalá-Galiano named the arm Canal de Sasamat, which he understood to be the local First Nation word for either the arm or for the inlet and arm combined. Sasamat may also have been a First Nation name for an ancient village site at the mouth of the Seymour R. Another old name for Sasamat Lk was Windermere Lk.

Satellite Channel (48°43'00" 123°26'00" S side of Saltspring I, Gulf Is), **Satellite Passage** (48°52'00" 125°11'00" E of Imperial Eagle Channel, N of Helby I, Barkley Sd, W side of Vancouver I), **Satellite Reef** (49°10'00" 123°56'00" Nanaimo Hbr, E side of Vancouver I). HMS *Satellite*, a 21-gun steam corvette of 1,326 tonnes, was present on the Pacific Station, 1857–60, under Capt James Prevost, and in 1869 as well, under Capt William Edye. It was launched at Devonport dockyard in 1855 and saw service in S America and China before being broken up in 1879. Capt Prevost was a major supporter of missionary work and brought William Duncan, who would later gain fame for his Anglican mission at Metlakatla, out with him to BC in 1857. During the 1858 gold rush, the *Satellite* acted as a guardship, checking miners' licences at the mouth of the Fraser R. In 1859 it investigated the plundering of the *Swiss Boy*, a US brig that had been stripped of everything valuable by local First Nation warriors while beached for repairs in Barkley Sd. Prevost was able to bring the perpetrators (who viewed their activities as salvage rather than pillage) peacefully to Victoria, where they were charged with robbery but released. A different HMS *Satellite*, an 8-gun corvette, also served in BC waters, under Capt Charles Theobald, 1883–86, and under Cdr Albert Allen, 1894–97. Capt George Richards named Satellite Channel in 1859 and Satellite Passage in 1861. *See also* Prevost I. *W*

Saturna Island's Winter Cove is a popular anchorage. *Peter Vassilopoulos*

Saturna Beach (48°47'00" 123°12'00" In Breezy Bay, W side of Saturna I), **Saturna Island** (48°47'00" 123°09'00" SE of Saltspring I, S end of Str of Georgia, Gulf Is), **Saturna Point** (48°48'00" 123°12'00" W side of Saturna I). Saturna I was named after the Spanish naval schooner *Santa Saturnina*, the second European vessel built in the PNW, which was in turn named after St Saturnina, a German martyr (*see* Santa Saturnina Point for more information on this historic vessel). In 1791 the *Saturnina*, under José Narváez, and the *San Carlos*, commanded by Francisco Eliza, made the first European exploration of the Str of Georgia. At some point during this voyage, Narváez named the S tip of the easternmost Gulf island after his ship: Punta de Santa Saturnina. The island itself soon (by 1862 at the latest) became known as Saturna, a corrupted form of Saturnina. The most remote of the main Gulf Is, Saturna developed slowly after settlement began in the 1870s. Even today it has few tourism facilities. Much of

the island is protected as part of the Gulf Is National Park Reserve. Its Sencoťen (Coast Salish) name is Tekteksen, meaning "long nose." *E W*

Saturnina Island. *See* Santa Saturnina Point *and also* Saturna Beach.

Saumarez Bluff (49°52'41" 123°54'13" W side of Prince of Wales Reach, SW of Vancouver Bay, Jervis Inlet, NW of Vancouver). Adm James Saumarez, 1st Baron de Saumarez (1757–1836), was one of the heroes of the RN. He was born on Guernsey, joined the navy as a young midshipman and was promoted to lt at the age of 19 for his bravery in action. Saumarez distinguished himself in the battles of Groix, Cape St Vincent and the Nile, and found himself a rear adm at the age of 44. The 1801 Battle of Algeciras Bay, in which Saumarez's squadron trounced a much larger French and Spanish fleet, cemented his fame. He was named an adm in 1814 and raised to the peerage in 1831. Nearby Saumarez Lk is also named for him. *W*

Saunders Island (52°10'00" 128°06'00" S of Dryad Point, N end of Lama Passage, near Bella Bella), **Saunders Point** (52°36'00" 128°36'00" N side of Meyers Passage, SE end of Princess Royal I). Frank Taunton Saunders (1866–1937) was born in India, where his father was a capt in the E India Co and then a maj gen in the Indian Army. He became a seaman and jumped ship in 1894 at Vancouver, where he met and married Frances Oliver (1869–1961), from Ont, and joined the Union Steamship Co. In 1905 he was appointed capt of the *Camosun* on its initial run to northern BC. (In 1906 the *Camosun*, under Saunders, was the first passenger vessel to call at the new town of Prince Rupert.) Later he worked as a skipper for the GTP, then joined the pilotage service and by 1924 was the Prince Rupert agent for the Dept of Marine and Fisheries. Saunders I was formerly known as Narrows I and then as Hose I, after Rear Adm Walter Hose (*see* Hose Point), but was renamed by the hydrographic dept in 1925.

Savary Island (49°56'00" 124°49'00" W of Malaspina Peninsula, NE end of Str of Georgia, NW of Powell R). This 450-ha wooded sandbar was named Savary's I by Capt George Vancouver in 1792, but no one has been able to discover who Savary was. Vancouver found the Malaspina Str shoreline "very dreary," but Savary I and its neighbours "presented a scene more pleasing and fertile." Lt Peter Puget and Joseph Whidbey, master of HMS *Discovery*, spent a night on Savary while surveying the region with two of the ship's boats; Archibald Menzies, the expedition's doctor and naturalist, described their campsite as "a delightful plain with a fine smooth beach ... that rendered the situation both desirable and pleasant and such as they of late seldom enjoyed." In 1910 the island was subdivided by a real-estate syndicate into hundreds of tiny lots and marketed as a "South Sea island paradise." A hotel

Aerial view of Savary Island looking south. *Photex Studio Inc, Vancouver*

and wharf were built, and Savary became very popular with Vancouver holidaymakers. This is still the case today, and the island's many visitors and seasonal residents are putting a heavy strain on its limited infrastructure and water resources. Sliammon First Nation members know Savary as Áyhus, or "double-headed serpent," a reference to the island's shape. According to legend, the Transformer changed this creature into the island as it was trying to return to its cave on Hurtado Point. *E*

Sawluctus Island (48°30'00" 123°33'00" Near the head of Finlayson Arm, S end of Saanich Inlet, just W of Victoria). Sawluctus is the Saanich First Nation name for the Goldstream R, which flows into the head of Finlayson Arm and means "fishing area tucked inside the arm." Sawluctus I was adopted as a name by the hydrographic service in 1934. Before that it was known as Dinner I—a name that appears as early as 1861 in the *Vancouver I Pilot*. The island is also known locally as Goldstream I.

Saw Reef (52°27'00" 131°17'00" Off N side of Burnaby I, off SE side of Moresby I, QCI). Named in 1878 by George M Dawson of the Geological Survey of Canada for its jagged appearance.

Saxe Point (48°25'00" 123°25'00" NW of Macaulay Point, between Victoria Hbr and Esquimalt Hbr, SE end of Vancouver I). After Prince Albert of Saxe-Coburg and Gotha, husband of Queen Victoria. Saxe-Coburg and Saxe-Gotha were two Saxon duchies in the present-day German states of Bavaria and Thuringia. Lt Cdr James Wood of HMS *Pandora* originally gave the name Cape Saxe to this feature in 1847, in association with nearby Gotha Point and Coburg Peninsula. Albert Head, just to the SW, had already been named the year before by Capt Henry Kellett of HMS *Herald*.

Saycuritay Cove (53°13'00" 129°33'00" SW end of Pitt I, facing Otter Channel). David G Leen, of Duncan, anchored overnight in this cove in 1977. It was late in the season, and when he and his friends heard a *sécurité* warning on the marine radio, they feared that a dangerous SE gale might be forecast. To their relief, the message merely concerned a floating stump many km away. Someone suggested that the unnamed cove might be called Sécurité or Saycuritay (his friends were from Seattle and "not completely familiar" with French pronunciation), and Leen proposed this name to the BC government the following year. There are three marine distress calls: *mayday*, for grave danger; *pan-pan*, for emergencies that are not life threatening; and *sécurité*, for navigational and meteorological warnings.

Sayward (50°23'00" 125°58'00" SW side of Salmon Bay, Johnstone Str, NW of Campbell R). William Parsons Sayward (1818–1905) was a pioneer BC lumberman and well-known Victoria entrepreneur. He was born in Maine and trained as a carpenter, living in Florida and California before arriving at Victoria in 1858 and opening a lumber yard. In the early 1860s he married Ann Chambers (1824–70) and bought Henry Sheppard's historic sawmill at Mill Bay on Saanich Inlet. Sayward's business flourished, and by 1865 he was shipping lumber as far away as San Francisco. He built a larger mill on Victoria Hbr in 1878 and also owned a sawmill in Washington state, a fleet of ships and barges, a great deal of property, extensive timber leases on Vancouver I and elsewhere, and interests in electricity, water, pulp and paper, mining, cattle and sealing companies. Sayward sold his Victoria mill in 1892 and retired in 1896, moving to California, where he died. The logging community of Sayward, which William Sayward is not known to have ever actually visited, was originally known as Salmon R. Its name was changed in 1911. *See also* Hkusam Bay. *E*

Scarf Island (50°09'00" 127°40'00" Entrance to Nasparti Inlet, Checleset Bay, NW side of Vancouver I). Named after Oscar Scarf (1864–1949), born at Victoria, who entered the sealing trade as a hunter aboard the *Pathfinder* in 1887. He later became capt and part owner of the *Enterprise* and is listed in the 1901 BC census as mate of the towboat *Pilot*. In 1907, the year he married Martha Elizabeth Harris, Scarf towed the largest log boom ever seen to that time from Port San Juan into Victoria Hbr; it contained over 300,000 m of spruce and measured almost half a km in length. Scarf post office, W of Sooke near Otter Point, was named after him; Oscar served as postmaster there from 1911 to 1915. Scarf I was formerly known as Hat I. **Scarf Reef** (50°18'00" 127°59'00" SW of Lawn Point, Brooks Bay, NW end of Vancouver I) may be named for him as well.

Scarlett Point (50°52'00" 127°37'00" N side of Balaklava I, Gordon Channel, SW side of Queen Charlotte Str, NW of Port Hardy). This feature was named by Capt George Richards in 1864 in association with Balaklava I. James Yorke Scarlett (1799–1871), cdr of the 5th Dragoon Guards, was a British Army brigadier who led a daring and successful heavy cavalry charge against a superior Russian force at the 1854 Battle of Balaklava during the Crimean War. He was knighted and later went on to become a gen and adjutant-gen of the army. Balaklava I and several other places at the N end of Vancouver I had been named earlier by Lt Daniel Pender to honour the futile Charge of the Light Brigade. A lighthouse established on the point in 1905 was manned from 1908 to 1940 by William Hunt and his family (*see* Hunt Rk). Hunt was the son of HBC factor and Ft Rupert storekeeper Robert Hunt. *W*

Scarrow Reef (48°56'00" 123°31'00" In Retreat Cove, W side of Galiano I, Gulf Is). For the last 20 years of his life, Dr Hartford G Scarrow (1911–86) was a permanent resident of the small community at Retreat Cove. Members of the N Galiano Community Assoc, who proposed this name in 1986 after Scarrow's death, wrote in their submission that "we have recently had a loss in our community of a very fine gentleman who gave much to us and, in fact, was responsible for a great number of things happening on Galiano I, particularly in the '60s and '70s.... This reef, which is exposed at low tide, but covered at high tide, has been the cause of a number of accidents to boats sailing in this area.... It presently is unnamed on the charts and we felt that if it was named it would be more noticeable to navigators and perhaps be less of a hazard to boaters."

Schindler Point (49°11'00" 125°56'00" SW tip of Meares I, Clayoquot Sd, W side of Vancouver I). Joseph Schindler (1882–1969), born in Oregon, entered the Roman Catholic Benedictine order in 1902 and was ordained as a priest in 1908. He became a missionary at Clayoquot, 1910–16, and was appointed principal of the Christie residential school at Kakawis, 1916–19. Recalled to Mt Angel Abbey in Oregon, Schindler served as administrator of the abbey farm, but he returned to the W coast of Vancouver I in 1932 and resumed mission work at Hesquiat. At the time of his death he was senior monk at Westminster Abbey in Mission and the oldest member of the Benedictine Federation of the Americas.

Schloss Island (50°30'00" 127°51'00" In Koprino Hbr, Quatsino Sd, NW end of Vancouver I). Benjamin Schloss received a Crown grant for this island and adjacent areas in 1892. The feature is also known as Plumper I.

Schmidt Point (48°42'00" 123°24'00" E end of Piers I, off N tip of Saanich Peninsula, N of Victoria). Named in 1965 by the hydrographic service after Wilhelm Schmidt, who obtained Piers I (qv) by Crown grant in 1880 and homesteaded there with his family. Wilhelm Point on Piers I is also named for him. Schmidt transferred ownership of the property to his wife, Amie, in 1886, and she sold it to John Bethune in 1897 for $1,510.

Schofield Point (52°33'00" 128°26'00" S side of W entrance to Jackson Passage, NW end of Susan I,

Finlayson Channel, NW of Bella Bella). This is a spelling error for Scholefield, as the point honours BC historian Ethelbert Olaf Stuart Scholefield (1875–1919), co-author with Frederic Howay in 1914 of the four-volume *British Columbia from the Earliest Times to the Present*. He grew up in New Westminster and Esquimalt and worked at the provincial library under R Edward Gosnell, the first provincial librarian, eventually replacing him as librarian in 1898 and as provincial archivist in 1910. Scholefield and Gosnell co-authored *A History of British Columbia* for the BC Historical Assoc in 1913. The point was named by the hydrographic service in 1948 in association with a group of features on nearby Roderick I, including Howay Point, that commemorate prominent BC historians.

Schooner Cove (49°17'00" 124°08'00" N of Nanoose Hbr, S of Nankivell Point, SE side of Vancouver I), **Schooner Reef** (49°16'00" 124°07'00" Just N of Schooner Cove). Richard Nixon Rk was the name originally submitted for Schooner Reef by a group of boat owners from nearby Schooner Cove, where a large marina, complete with restaurant and hotel, is located. This suggestion was rejected, as the Geographical Names Board of Canada will not consider the names of non-Canadians "unless the person to be commemorated has had a significant association with the feature or the surrounding area, and the application is in the public interest." The board determined, however, that Schooner Reef was a name in local use, and this was adopted instead in 1979. (Before the Geographic Board of Canada was established in 1897 to standardize naming procedures and policies across the country, the above rule obviously did not apply, and hundreds of BC features were named after "foreigners." The original board changed its own name several times—to the Canadian Board on Geographic Names in 1948, the Canadian Permanent Committee on Geographical Names in 1961, and the Geographical Names Board of Canada in 2000).

Schram Rocks (52°43'00" 129°29'00" NW of Moore Is, entrance to Caamaño Sd, Hecate Str). Mary Caroline Schram (1829–1921) was born at London, Ont, of United Empire Loyalist stock and married Capt Lewis Nunn Agassiz (1827–80, *see* Agassiz Banks), a retired British Army officer. She came to BC with four children in 1862 to join her gold-seeking husband. The family lived at Hope and Yale before settling in the eastern Fraser Valley in 1867 on a farm they named Ferney Coombe. The community that grew up around their home is now known as Agassiz. *See also* Goodfellow Point.

Schreiber Point (54°21'00" 130°17'00" N side of Prince Rupert Hbr). Sir Collingwood Schreiber (1831–1918), an engineer and civil servant, was born in England and immigrated with his family to Canada in 1852. He became chief engineer of all federal government railway operations in 1873 and replaced Sandford Fleming as the

S

CPR's chief engineer in 1880. In 1892 he was appointed deputy minister of Railways and Canals, a position he held until 1905, when he was named consulting engineer for the GTP. Schreiber kept working into his 80s and was knighted in 1916. Sir Charles Tupper claimed that he'd never met an individual "with so great a love of, or capacity for, work." Schreiber Canyon and Schreiber Ck near the Stikine R are also named for him.

Schubert Point (52°19'00" 128°21'00" SW side of Don Peninsula, opposite N end of Cecilia I, NW of Bella Bella). Named after Catherine O'Hare (1835–1918), a native of Ireland and the first European woman to come overland to BC from eastern Canada. She arrived in the US with her family in 1850 and married a German immigrant, Francis Augustus Schubert (1825–1908), in 1856. The Schuberts moved to Minnesota and then, in 1860, to Ft Garry (now Winnipeg), where they ran an inn and store. In 1862 the family headed W to the Cariboo goldfields with a party of Overlanders. Catherine reached Ft Kamloops just in time to give birth to her fourth child—believed to be the first white girl in the district. The family settled first at Lillooet, where Augustus farmed and prospected and Catherine ran a school, then moved to Armstrong in 1883. This feature appeared on Admiralty charts as Rain Point as early as 1872 but was renamed by Henri Parizeau of the hydrographic service in 1929. *E*

Scoones Point (48°52'08" 123°18'37" SE end of Galiano I, Gulf Is). British seaman Alexander Edward Scoones (1876–1952) bought 2.5 ha of land at Mary Ann Point from the Burrill brothers in 1897 and settled down there for several years before returning to England to complete an engineering course. He then went to Brazil, and it was nearly two decades before he returned to Galiano, with his brother Paul Scoones (1875–1961), a retired mathematics teacher from Eton. A year later, Edith Isabell Olliff (1891–1963), a singer, came out as well, to be Alec's bride. The Scoones family contributed a great deal to the early social and cultural life of Galiano. The name was suggested by the Gulf Is Branch of the BC Historical Assoc about 1968.

Scotch Fir Point (49°44'00" 124°16'00" N entrance to Jervis Inlet, Malaspina Str, SE of Powell R). Capt George Vancouver named this point in June 1792 because it was home to "the first Scotch firs we had yet seen." Scotch fir is an old name for the Scots pine (*Pinus sylvestris*), a tree that grows only in Europe and northern Asia. Vancouver may have been referring to the shore pine (*Pinus contorta*), though why he had not seen this species before is a mystery, as it is a common sight on the BC coast.

Scott Channel, **Scott Islands**. *See* Cape Scott.

Scott Point (48°50'00" 123°25'00" E side of Saltspring I, W entrance to Long Hbr, Gulf Is). Horticulturist William

Ernest Scott (1866–1934) was born in Yorkshire and immigrated to NZ in 1883, then lived in the W Indies. He arrived in BC in the early 1890s with his three brothers, Frank, Geoff and Harold, and settled on Saltspring, where he developed a 285-ha ranch known as Fruitvale, noted in the early 1900s for its orchards and dairy cattle. William Scott married Ella Clark Innes (1868–1950) in 1893. He was appointed a justice of the peace for the area, became a member of the provincial board of horticulture and served as BC's deputy minister of Agriculture, 1910–16. Scott Point, once part of Fruitvale Farm, was named by Cdr John Parry of HMS *Egeria* while re-surveying Ganges Hbr in 1905. *W*

Scottys Point (50°24'55" 125°54'20" SW side of Hardwicke I, Johnstone Str, NW of Campbell R). This long-established local name was adopted by BC's Geographical Names Office in 1995 after John "Scotty" Sumpton, who owned property in this vicinity in the WWI era.

Scouler Entrance (50°18'18" 127°50'02" Entrance to Klaskino Inlet, Brooks Bay, N of Brooks Peninsula, NW side of Vancouver I). John Scouler (1804–71), a Scottish naturalist and physician, studied medicine at the Univ of Glasgow and became a student of botanist William Hooker. He was hired by the HBC as surgeon on the *William and Ann* in 1824 and sailed with David Douglas, another naturalist (who would spend much time in the PNW and after whom the Douglas fir is named), to the Columbia R, stopping along the way at Madeira, Brazil, the Juan Fernández Is and the Galápagos. He and Douglas were the first naturalists to explore the Oregon country, and Scouler also visited the S BC coast and QCI in 1825 and wrote an early treatise on the ethnography of the region. His *Journal of a Voyage to NW America* was reprinted in the *Oregon Historical Quarterly* in 1905. Scouler also made a collecting voyage as a ship's surgeon to S Africa and the Indian Ocean. Although he practised medicine at Glasgow (and co-founded the *Glasgow Medical Journal*), his deeper interests led him to professorships of natural history at Anderson's Univ (later the Univ of Strathclyde) and of mineralogy at the Royal Society, Dublin. He also promoted the study of paleontology in Scotland and Ireland, prepared a geological exhibition, contributed to a range of scientific journals and was a noted linguist and classical scholar. A number of plant and fossil species are named for him. Scouler Entrance was originally marked False Entrance on Admiralty charts as early as 1865 but was changed by the hydrographic service in 1946.

Scroggs Rocks (48°25'00" 123°26'00" Entrance to Esquimalt Hbr, SE end of Vancouver I). Edward Scroggs was a mate on the RN survey vessel *Herald*, under Capt Henry Kellett, and helped make the earliest detailed charts of Victoria and Esquimalt harbours, Sooke Inlet and Juan de Fuca Str in 1846–47. He was promoted to lt in 1847. *W*

Scudder Point (52°27'00" 131°14'00" NE tip of Burnaby I, off SE side of Moresby I, QCI). Geologist George M Dawson named this feature in 1878. According to QCI historian Kathleen Dalzell, the word is an adaptation of the Haida name for the point, Skwaay Kun, which, in turn, was probably taken from the Haida word for Burnaby I, Skwaay Kungwa'i. A Haida village named Skwaay was once located just N of the point. *D*

Scylla Rock (50°55'00" 127°36'00" N of Redfern I in Gordon Channel, W entrance to Queen Charlotte Str, N of Port Hardy). HMS *Scylla*, a wooden steam corvette of 1,331 tonnes and 21 guns, was launched in 1856 and served in the Mediterranean and China. In 1869, under Capt Frederick Herbert, the 60-m vessel joined Commodore Geoffrey Hornby's flying squadron and helped "show the flag" in S America, S Africa, Australia, NZ and Japan before arriving at Esquimalt in 1870. There it joined the Pacific squadron for a year and relieved HMS *Charybdis*. Ironically, Scylla and Charybdis were the two sea monsters in Greek mythology that guarded the Str of Messina. There are also Scylla and Charybdis mountains in the Kootenays. HMS *Scylla* was decommissioned in 1882.

Sea Bird Point (48°25'00" 123°13'00" SE end of Discovery I, off Oak Bay and SE tip of Vancouver I). The 410-tonne US sidewheeler *Sea Bird* was built at NY in 1850, taken around Cape Horn to California and then, in 1857, transferred to Puget Sd, where its owners had secured a US mail contract. Under Capt Francis Conner, it became the second steamship to go up the Fraser R to Ft Hope during the 1858 gold rush. On its return journey it ran aground E of Agassiz on what is now known as Sea Bird I and was stuck there for several months. In Sept 1858, on a second journey between Victoria and the Fraser, the 69-m vessel caught fire and was beached on Discovery I, where it burned to the waterline. Two passengers died. The ship's engines were later salvaged and used on the *John T Wright*. *W*

Seabrook Point (53°01'00" 129°12'00" S entrance to Casanave Passage, Campania Sd, W side of Princess Royal I). Roads Seabrook (c 1836–1921), born at London, Ont, married Louise Annette Holloway (1841–1911), from London, England, and migrated in the early 1860s to New Westminster, where he worked as a shipping agent. The family moved to Victoria about 1868, and Roads (which is an anglicized form of a Dutch name) became a successful businessman, vice-president of R P Rithet & Co and a founder of the Victoria Sealing Co. His son, Bagster Roads Seabrook (1865–1950; Bagster was a family surname on his mother's side), was born at New Westminster and became general manager of Victoria's Albion Iron Works at age 30. Better known as an inventor, Bagster introduced the first automobile to Victoria (a steam model, in 1903) before moving to Toronto, NY, LA and Seattle, where he worked

as a consulting engineer. His many profitable inventions included a bicycle brake, a rock crusher, a railway axle, a type of phonograph and, in 1926, a *Business Manual on Handling Computations*.

Seafire Island (51°52'00" 128°08'00" E side of Kildidt Sd, off S side of Hunter I, S of Bella Bella). In 1944–45, regional hydrographer Henri Parizeau named a number of features in the Queens Sd area after WWII aircraft. The Seafire was a naval version of the very successful British single-seat fighter, the Supermarine Spitfire. With its folding wings and arrestor hook, the Seafire was especially adapted for operating from aircraft carriers. Many different models were produced; the first ones went into service in 1942 and some later designs were still in use during the Korean War. Seafire I was formerly known as Passage I.

Seaforth Channel (52°14'00" 128°18'00" E of Milbanke Sd, N of the Bardswell Group and Campbell I). Named by HBC officials in the 1840s for Lt Gen Francis Humberston Mackenzie, 1st Lord Seaforth, Baron Mackenzie of Kintail (1754–1815). He was MP for the county of Ross, 1784–90 and 1794–96, and lord lt of Ross, 1794–1815. Seaforth was appointed gov of Barbados, 1800–1806, and also served as a colonial official in British Guiana (Guyana). He raised the army battalion known as the Seaforth Highlanders, a regiment of which is based in Vancouver. Kintail Point on Campbell I is also named for him. *W*

Sea Island (49°11'00" 123°10'00" Mouth of the Fraser R, NW of Lulu I). This island, now completely diked, was once so flat and marshy it was hard to tell what was ocean and what was land—hence the name, applied by Capt George Richards in 1859. A different explanation holds that, of all the Fraser estuary's main islands, this one is nearest the sea. It was also known in the early days as McRoberts I, after Hugh McRoberts, the first white settler on the island, in 1861, who established one of BC's earliest and largest farms there (*see* Richmond for a more detailed biography). A community named Eburne (qv) grew up on the NE part of the island around an early hotel and cannery. The Vancouver International Airport opened on Sea I in 1931; when it expanded in the 1960s, most of the remaining farms disappeared. The Halkomelem First Nation name for the island is Sq'sazun, though the meaning of the word is not known. *E*

Sea Lion Rock (50°23'00" 125°09'00" W of Whirlpool Point, Yuculta Rapids, off W side of Stuart I, N of Campbell R). A number of vessels named *Sea Lion* have graced PNW waters over the decades. This feature commemorates a historic tug that went aground and sank here in 1930 but was later salvaged. The name was suggested by local residents in 1955. The 198-tonne, 35-m towboat, built at Vancouver for independent owner Capt George French in 1905, was the only tug in BC to boast a piano in its wood-

The steam tug *Sea Lion* entering Vancouver Harbour in 1933.
Harbour Publishing collection

panelled cabin and a melodious 13-note whistle that could run up and down an entire musical scale. The *Sea Lion* played a role in the drama of the *Komagata Maru*, the Japanese vessel denied the right to disembark its S Asian passengers at Vancouver Hbr in 1914; 160 police and immigration officers stormed the steamer from the tug but were rebuffed when migrants pelted them with coal. The *Sea Lion* was purchased in 1916 by the Young & Gore Tug Boat Co of Vancouver (later Island Tug & Barge Ltd) and given a $200,000 rebuild in 1957, when its steam engine was replaced with an 800-hp diesel. It later became a private yacht, an oceanographic research vessel, a floating eco-adventure lodge and a dilapidated loggers' bunkhouse. The tug was overhauled in 2001 and moored at the Vancouver Maritime Museum until sold privately in 2008. Another *Sea Lion*, based in Puget Sd, attended the stricken steamship *Clallam* in Juan de Fuca Str in 1904 in one of the PNW's worst marine tragedies (54 people died); this tug sank off Race Rks in 1909 after being struck by the *Oceania Vance*. There was also a well-known Victoria sealing schooner of the 19th century called *Sea Lion*, and an old former lightship that bounced around Vancouver docks in the early 1980s in such a state of disrepair that it was eventually banished.

Sea Otter Cove (50°41'00" 128°21'00" NW of San Josef Bay, NW end of Vancouver I), **Sea Otter Group** (51°20'00" 128°08'00" S of Calvert I, entrance to Smith Sd, Queen Charlotte Sd), **Sea Otter Inlet** (51°50'00" 128°03'00" SE side of Hunter I, S of Bella Bella). The first traders to arrive in the PNW were searching almost exclusively for the lustrous skins of the sea otter, so it is no surprise that three of their vessels were named *Sea Otter*. The publication of Capt James Cook's journals in 1784–85 had alerted Asian merchants to the possibility that great profits could be made selling sea otter furs in China. Capt James Hanna, in the tiny, 50-tonne *Harmon*, renamed the *Sea Otter*, was first off the mark, in 1785. His journey was funded by John Cox and partners, and Hanna sailed to Nootka Sd from Macao (*see* Hanna Channel). He returned the following year in a larger, 110-tonne ship, also named *Sea Otter*.

A third *Sea Otter*, under William Tipping, sailed to the Alaska coast in 1786 and was never seen again. These place names all commemorate the vessel used by Hanna on his second voyage. Hanna himself gave the name Duncan's Hbr to what is today known as Sea Otter Cove; John Meares called it Sea Otter Hbr on his 1790 chart; James Strange, another early trader, referred to it as Oxenford Bay. Sea Otter Inlet was formerly known as Sea Otter Ck and Crab Hbr. The Sea Otter Group was named about 1865 by Lt Daniel Pender of the *Beaver*. W

Sea Pigeon Island (52°17'00" 131°17'00" Entrance to Huston Inlet, S side of Skincuttle Inlet, off SE side of Moresby I, QCI). Geologist George M Dawson named this feature in 1878 after the pigeon guillemot (*Cepphus columba*), a small black and white seabird that is abundant in the QCI.

Seapool Rocks (48°49'00" 125°12'00" SW end of Trevor Channel, Barkley Sd, W side of Vancouver I). Named in 1933 after the British freighter *Seapool*, which struck these rocks in the fall of 1928. This 4,121-tonne vessel, built in 1913, also struck an iceberg off Nfld in 1921 but made it safely to St John's Hbr. It was renamed the *Pilcot* in 1936 and then sold to an Estonian shipping company in 1939. As the *Vapper* it was torpedoed and sunk by a U-boat in 1940. Formerly known as the Channel Rks.

Sechart Channel (48°56'00" 125°15'00" N of Broken Group, Barkley Sd, W side of Vancouver I). After the Tseshaht First Nation, whose members are part of the Nuu-chah-nulth Tribal Council and whose traditional territory was in Barkley Sd. The name Tseshaht refers to the smell of whale bones and is a reminder that the Tseshaht people were once skilled whalers. About two centuries ago they expanded their territory up Alberni Inlet to include the rich salmon resources of the Somass R. Today the main Tseshaht community is located at Port Alberni. Other common spellings of the name include Sheshaht and Seshart. The whaling station of Sechart was

Sea Otter Cove on northwest Vancouver Island. *James and Jennifer Hamilton*

established on Sechart Channel by the Pacific Whaling Co in 1905 and closed down in 1917. The station buildings housed a pilchard packing plant in the 1930s. *E*

Sechelt's first hotel, built in 1899. *Author's collection*

Sechelt (49°28'00" 123°46'00" S end of Sechelt Peninsula, head of Sechelt Inlet), **Sechelt Inlet** (49°36'00" 123°48'00" S of Jervis Inlet, E of Sechelt Peninsula, NW of Vancouver), **Sechelt Islets** (In Sechelt Rapids), **Sechelt Peninsula** (49°40'00" 123°55'00" S of Jervis Inlet, W of Sechelt Inlet), **Sechelt Rapids** (49°44'00" 123°53'00" At mouth of Sechelt Inlet). The Sechelt First Nation now spells its name Shíshálh, after its language, Sháshíshálem, which is a branch of Salishan. Many variants of the name have been recorded over the years, including Seashelth, Seshal and Sicatl. The Sechelt people were the first aboriginal group in Canada to achieve self-government, in 1986. They live today mostly at Ch'átlich in the Sechelt Indian Government District, where Paul Durieu established a Roman Catholic Oblate mission in 1868; a large church and residential school were later erected. The non-Native community of Sechelt, which got its start in the 1890s with Herbert Whitaker's development of a hotel and store, is adjacent to Ch'átlich. Nearby Sechelt Ck and Sechelt Lk are also named after this First Nation group. Sechelt Inlet (or Álhtúlich in Sháshíshálem) is the site of several small provincial marine parks. The Sechelt Rapids in Skookumchuck Narrows can reach peak speeds of 14 knots (26 km/h). *E*

Second Beach (49°18'00" 123°09'00" E side of English Bay, W of Lost Lagoon, Vancouver). In 1858, Second Beach served as a campground for miners en route to the Fraser R gold rush. Later, it became a favourite spot for social and family outings for local residents. The name refers to the fact that as one moves N along the shoreline away from the W End, this is the second main beach encountered. Its First Nation name was Stait-wouk, which could apparently be translated as "white clay." A bathhouse was constructed there in 1912, and a "draw and fill" seawater pool built in 1932. During the summer, water was held behind large gates at high tide and allowed to warm up for a few days for swimming; once a week at low tide the pool was emptied and the process repeated. In 1995 the old pool was replaced with a new heated facility.

Second Narrows (49°18'00" 123°02'00" Burrard Inlet, S of mouth of Seymour R, Vancouver). This constriction, formed where the deltas of Lynn Ck and Seymour R extend into the inlet, was named by RN surveyor Capt George Richards about 1859–60 (as was First Narrows). Several proposals were made to bridge the site in the 1910s, but nothing was constructed until 1925, when the N Shore municipalities formed the Burrard Inlet Tunnel & Bridge Co and a combined road/rail crossing was completed. It was wrecked by a barge in 1930 and closed for four years. A new six-lane road bridge was built in 1956–60 and renamed the Ironworkers Memorial Second Narrows Crossing in 1994 to honour 18 workers killed in 1958 when it partly collapsed. The old span was converted to railway-only use in 1963 and replaced by the CNR with a new train crossing in 1969. *E*

Ironworkers Memorial Second Narrows Crossing. *Peter Vassilopoulos*

Second Point (49°57'00" 124°49'00" N side of Savary I, Str of Georgia). Denotes the second point W of the government wharf. Adopted quite recently, in 1983, as a well-established name, along with First Point.

Secord Rock (50°25'00" 125°13'00" Cordero Channel, NW of Horn Point, off NE side of Sonora I, N of Campbell R). Probably named after Anderson Secord, who homesteaded at Amor Point on Bute Inlet in 1898 and moved to Stuart I in 1907. A note at BC's Geographical Names Office states that he operated a "mercantile boat" for many years, serving tugboatmen and fishermen. He also appears as a fisherman himself in directories and on voters lists. Adopted by the hydrographic service in 1955.

Secretary (Donaldson) Island (48°20'00" 123°42'00" Off Iron Mine Bay, just SE of entrance to Sooke Inlet, S end of Vancouver I). This unusual double-barrelled designation results from the uncharacteristic persistence

S

of a supposedly obsolete name. Secretary I was originally adopted by Capt Henry Kellett, who made an RN survey of this area in 1847, and may have been named as such even earlier, by HBC official James Douglas, though its derivation is not known. In 1859, Capt George Richards gave the same name to a different feature, off Saltspring I, and these Secretary Is (*see below*) became more widely known than the island in Juan de Fuca Str. In 1911, to avoid confusion, the original Secretary I was changed to Donaldson I, after Alexander Dawson Donaldson (1839–1909). He had come to Wisconsin from Scotland as a young man and was then lured to BC, as were so many others, by the Cariboo gold rush. He married Amanda Woolsey (1854–1930) at Victoria in 1879 and had numerous occupations: freightman on the Cariboo Rd, carpenter, wide-ranging prospector for gold and marble, and Hastings Mill employee. The Donaldsons settled at Victoria and about 1901 bought Robert Weir's Silver Spray Farm at E Sooke. In 1981 the Canadian Hydrographic Service sought to change Donaldson I back to Secretary I as local mariners were still, after the passage of 70 years, using the old name. BC's representative to the Canadian Permanent Committee on Geographical Names, D F Pearson, acknowledged that "Donaldson seems not to have taken hold" and that it was "pretty evident that Secretary should be rejuvenated." He was concerned, though, that there would be confusion if the name was reversed suddenly. Despite the fact that Pearson was "normally reluctant to support double naming," a compromise—Secretary (Donaldson) I—was reached. A notation at the Geographical Names Office, written in 1982, reads: "Donaldson to be dropped after about 10 years." In 2009, though, the double name was still very much alive.

Secretary Islands (48°58'00" 123°35'00" In Trincomali Channel, off N end of Saltspring I, Gulf Is). Named in 1859 by Capt George Richards because of the islands' proximity to Southey Point on Saltspring I. James Southey was secretary to Rear Adm Robert Baynes, cdr-in-chief on the RN's Pacific Station, 1857–60. *See* Southey Point for a more detailed biography.

Secretary Point (50°57'00" 127°54'00" N side of Hope I, NE of Bull Hbr, off N end of Vancouver I). After paymaster James Ashby, who was secretary to a number of senior RN officers. Named by Capt George Richards, the RN's chief hydrographer, in 1864 in association with nearby Ashby Point (qv).

Secret Cove (49°32'00" 123°57'00" W side of Sechelt Peninsula, NW of Halfmoon Bay, NW of Vancouver). The entrance to this sheltered cove is hidden behind Turnagain I. Several marinas are located there, as well as a range of other tourism facilities. The Sechelt First Nation name for the cove is Stl'ítl'kwu.

Secret Island (48°49'00" 123°23'00" Off SW side of Prevost I, E of Saltspring I, Gulf Is). This feature, known unofficially as Iskit I, was transferred in 1939 from its owner, Max Enke, who was languishing in a German prisoner-of-war camp in Belgium (*see* Enke Point), to the custodian of enemy property. It was acquired in 1944 by Fulford Hbr merchant and postmaster Fred Cudmore and sold 10 years later to David Conover of Wallace I, a resort owner and confidant of Marilyn Monroe (*see* Conover Cove). Conover, who logged the island, requested the name Secret (his second and third choices were Enchanted I and Paradise I), and it was adopted by the hydrographic service in 1955. The island was later subdivided into 38 lots and developed as recreational property.

Seddall Shoals (52°27'00" 128°48'00" Off NW side of Price I, Laredo Sd, NW of Bella Bella). Staff Assistant Surgeon John Vernon Seddall (1831–70) was a member of the Columbia detachment of Royal Engineers, which served in BC 1858–63. He was born at Malta, where his father was a wine merchant and mason, and trained as a doctor at Edinburgh. Seddall joined the British Army in 1854 and was present during the Crimean War at the siege and fall of Sevastopol. He transferred to the Royal Engineers in 1858 and arrived in BC the following year on the *Thames City* with the main contingent of men. As well as attending to the detachment's medical needs, Seddall also served the community at large (and without charge) as a coroner and general physician. He was well liked, apparently—a musician, an amateur naturalist and a thoroughly sociable young man—and in 1863 he became engaged to a Miss Leggatt at Victoria, though for some reason they did not marry. Seddall returned to England in 1863, along with most of the other officers, and was promoted to surgeon in 1867, the year he married Ellen Golding at Rochester. He died while posted to S Africa. A CNR station was also named for him on the Thompson R NE of Lytton.

Sedgwick Bay (52°38'00" 131°34'00" S side of Lyell I, off E side of Moresby I, QCI), **Sedgwick Point** (52°36'00"

Secret Cove on the Sunshine Coast. *Peter Vassilopoulos*

131°33'00" W entrance to Sedgwick Bay). Adam Sedgwick (1785–1873), born in Yorkshire, was a professor of geology at Cambridge Univ, 1818–70, and president of the Geological Society, 1829–31. He spent much time studying rock stratification in N Wales and elsewhere in Europe, often with famed geologist Roderick Murchison, and came up with a system for classifying the rocks of the Cambrian and Devonian era (which he and Murchison named). Despite his influence as a geologist, Sedgwick, who was also an Anglican clergyman, steadfastly resisted the theory of evolution. The bay was named by geologist George M Dawson in 1878, the point by the hydrographic service in 1962. Mt Sedgwick, NW of Howe Sd, is also named for him, in association with nearby Mt Roderick and Mt Murchison. *D W*

Seegay Islets (53°37'00" 132°25'00" In Juskatla Inlet, S of Masset Inlet, Graham I, QCI). Named by the hydrographic service in 1953 after Haida chief Seegay, a Raven crest leader who, on his deathbed in 1876, requested the presence of Anglican missionary William Collison at Masset. The great decline of the Haida population due to smallpox and TB had caused Seegay to reconsider his religious beliefs, and the openness of Chief Seegay to Collison's presence in the QCI enabled the British clergyman to establish the first mission to the Haida later that year at Masset.

Sehl Rock (52°44'00" 129°17'00" Borrowman Bay, off NW side of Aristazabal I). Victoria-born Francis Joseph Sehl (1871–1958) worked in the city as a bookkeeper and was later appointed provincial tax collector. His father, also Frank Sehl (1831–90), a native of Germany, came to Victoria about 1870 and was for many years the proprietor of the Teutonia Saloon. His uncle Jacob Sehl (1833–1904) was an even earlier immigrant to Victoria, arriving in 1858. In 1885 Jacob built a spectacular mansion and Victoria's first furniture factory on Laurel Point (qv), which was originally known as Sehl's Point. He also operated a large, two-storey retail furniture store on Government St. Frank J Sehl worked as a clerk at the Victoria post office in the 1880s and '90s and is listed in the 1902 Victoria directory as an accountant with the CPR Telegraph Co. He married Elizabeth Kezia Styles (1873–1963), another BC-born pioneer, in 1895. The Sehls took part in the Victoria old-timers' reunion of May 1924 (*see* Adams Bay).

Sekani Island (53°03'00" 129°37'00" In Gillespie Channel, between Prior I and Trutch I, Estevan Group, SE of Banks I), **Sekani Reef** (53°03'00" 129°36'00" Just E of Sekani I). Sekani I was named in 1941 after the RCAF supply vessel *Sekani*, which often operated in conjunction with the ships of the hydrographic service. The 26-m *Sekani*, launched in 1940 as RCAF *Siwash* (the name was quickly changed when its derogatory nature was pointed out), was used especially to supply remote radar and radio posts on the BC coast during WWII. Air force personnel, most of

whom were unused to ocean travel, knew it as the "Sick Annie." The Sekani are an Athabaskan First Nation and live in the northern Interior of BC. Other features named for them in the province include Sekani Bay on Carp Lk and Sekani Lk SW of McLeod Lk. *See also* Gillespie Channel.

Selby Cove (48°50'00" 123°24'00" W side of Prevost I, E of Saltspring I, Gulf Is), **Selby Point** (48°51'00" 123°24'00" Just N of Selby Cove). Lt William Derenzy Donaldson Selby (d 1892) served on the Pacific Station, 1857–60, aboard HMS *Ganges*, the flagship of Rear Adm Robert Baynes. He was promoted to cdr in 1865 and capt, retired, in 1880. Named by Cdr John Parry of HMS *Egeria* while re-surveying Ganges Hbr in 1905.

Selkirk Water (48°26'19" 123°22'52" Part of Victoria Hbr, between Bay St bridge and Gorge Waters, Victoria). Thomas Douglas, 5th Earl of Selkirk (1771–1820), was a Scottish philanthropist who sponsored immigrant colonies in Canada. He was extremely wealthy, which was fortunate, as he needed to become a controlling shareholder of the HBC before he could establish his most famous agricultural experiment, the Red River Colony, in 1812. The settlement was never particularly successful and caused early outbreaks of violence with local Métis residents and the rival NWC. In 1818, Selkirk returned to England, bankrupt and in declining health, and later died in France. Selkirk Water was named by HBC officials and adopted by Capt Henry Kellett in 1846 while surveying Victoria Hbr. The Selkirk Mtns in the Kootenays, Mt Selkirk in the Rockies and Selkirk Bay on McNaughton Lk are also named for him, as are a number of places in Manitoba. *W*

1920s view of Selma Park resort. *Author's collection*

Selma Park (49°28'00" 123°44'00" E side of Trail Bay, just SE of Sechelt, Str of Georgia, NW of Vancouver). This coastal resort was developed in 1914 by the All Red Line and named after one of the company's vessels, the *Selma*, acquired in 1911 and used as a cargo and passenger ship between Vancouver and Powell R. The 43-m, 234-tonne *Selma* was built at Glasgow in 1881 as the *Santa Cecilia*,

S

the private pleasure craft of Sir Henry Paget, 4th Marquess of Anglesey. Stories abound of mad parties and excessive behaviour aboard the yacht; Prince Albert Edward, the future King Edward VII, was a guest, as was actress Lillie Langtry. The Union Steamship Co bought All Red's assets in 1917, and the *Selma*, renamed the *Chasina*, operated on Howe Sd and Sunshine Coast routes for six years, then was sold and became a rum-runner until 1928. In 1931, en route to Macao from Hong Kong, the vessel and its crew of 11 disappeared and were never seen again. Union Steamship Co developed Selma Park, adding cottages and a dance hall, then sold the property in 1944. The resort operated as Totem Lodge until it burned down in 1952. The Sechelt First Nation name for Selma Park is Xéláxan. *E*

Sels Islet (52˚25'00" 131˚25'00" Entrance to Skaat Hbr, W of Burnaby I, off SE side of Moresby I, QCI). Named by the hydrographic service in 1962 after a Raven crest tribe of the Kunghit Haida First Nation. The Sels were also known as the "Slave People," after a dismissive comment made by the wife of a rival chief, but later grew powerful. According to early 20th-century linguist John Swanton, the name meant "food-steamers" and was applied contemptuously to Haida families of low social rank.

Selvesen Island, **Selvesen Point**. *See* Salvesen I.

Selwyn Inlet (52˚52'00" 131˚46'00" Between S end of Louise I and E side of Moresby I, QCI), **Selwyn Point** (52˚51'00" 131˚50'00" W side of Selwyn Inlet), **Selwyn Rocks** (52˚54'00" 131˚52'00" Near head of Selwyn Inlet). Noted geologist Alfred Richard Cecil Selwyn (1824–1902),

born in the UK and educated in Switzerland, joined the Geological Survey of GB as an assistant geologist in 1845. In 1852 he married his cousin, Matilda Charlotte Selwyn (d 1882), and immigrated to Australia, where he became director of the Geological Survey of Victoria, sat on many boards and commissions, and assessed the coal and gold reserves of Tasmania and S Australia. Selwyn came to Canada in 1869 as the second director of the geological survey and oversaw its expansion into a modern, transcontinental institution. He travelled extensively, making several visits to BC. In 1871 he came to see how the Geological Survey of Canada could assist with the building of the Pacific railway; in 1875, accompanied by botanist John Macoun, he examined a Peace R route for a railroad; and in 1884 he led a field trip of British scientists to the province. After retirement in 1895, Selwyn served as president of the Royal Society of Canada and moved to Vancouver, where he died. The inlet was named in 1878 by George M Dawson, who succeeded Selwyn as director of the GSC; the point and rocks were named by the hydrographic service in 1957. Nearby Alfred Point and Cecil Cove also commemorate Selwyn, as do Mt Selwyn in the Kootenays, the Selwyn Range in the Cariboo Mtns and the Selwyn Mtns on the Yukon-NWT border. Kilmington Point is named for his birthplace in Somerset.

Semiahmoo Bay (49˚01'00" 122˚50'00" On the BC-Washington border, SE of Boundary Bay and Vancouver, S of White Rk). The Semiahmoo people are a Coast Salish group closely related to the Lummi and Samish First Nations who live S of the international border. They once occupied a larger area that included the shores of Mud

Semiahmoo Bay and Drayton Harbour viewed from the tip of Semiahmoo Spit in Washington state. *Peter Vassilopoulos*

and Boundary bays and extended to the S side of Birch Bay in US territory. The word is often reported to mean "half moon"—presumably a reference to the curve of the shoreline—but this translation is dubious. The main Semiahmoo First Nation community today is located at the mouth of the Campbell R. The bay was the site of an early sawmill; a pioneer trail to the US border from New Westminster was known as the Semiahmoo Trail. Many variations of the name are recorded, including Semiamo, Semiamu and Semiahoo.

Senanus Island (48°36'00" 123°29'00" In Saanich Inlet, W of Hagan Bight, NW of Victoria). Senanus is an old name that appears in the first *Vancouver I Pilot* prepared by Capt George Richards in 1861. According to historians Helen and Philip Akrigg, it is a Saanich (Sencoṯen) word meaning "chest" or "torso." Apparently it was also the name of a well-known chief of the Tsartlip First Nation. Senamis is a variant spelling on some old maps. The island is a reserve and ancient burial ground for the Tsartlip people, who are part of the larger Wsanec (Saanich) group of First Nations.

Seppings Island (48°51'00" 125°12'00" E side of Imperial Eagle Channel, SW of Diana I, Barkley Sd, W side of Vancouver I). Robert Seppings (1767–1840), born in Norfolk and apprenticed as a shipwright at a young age, was a noted British naval architect who came up with a number of advances in the design and construction of warships. He invented "Seppings blocks," which greatly reduced the time and labour needed for inspecting the lower hulls of vessels in drydock. In 1813 he was appointed surveyor of the RN, and the following year he was knighted. HMS *Cockatrice*, tender to the flagships on the Pacific Station in 1848–57, was designed by Seppings in 1832. The island was named by Capt George Richards of HMS *Hecate* in 1861.

September Morn Beach (49°22'00" 123°20'00" E side of Bowen I, Howe Sd, NW of Vancouver). According to members of the Dorman family, who owned this property, the name is derived from a famous nude painting, *Matinée de septembre*, by French artist Paul Émile Chabas. The image, which shows a woman standing in shallow water preparing to swim or bathe, was shown without controversy in Paris in 1912. When exhibited in Chicago, however, the mayor of the city charged the gallery owner with indecency but lost the ensuing court case. The scandal greatly increased the notoriety of the artwork, of course, and lithographed copies of the painting circulated for years. It was obviously known to the Dorman family, whose younger members—the boys at one time and the girls at another—used to swim nude at this beach along with their friends.

Septimus Point (52°06'00" 127°50'00" S side of Evans Inlet, NW of Sagar Lk, King I, E of Bella Bella). After RN surgeon Septimus Evans, who served on the BC coast, 1868–70. *See* Evans Inlet.

Sere Rock (52°44'00" 129°17'00" In Turtish Hbr, Borrowman Bay, NW side of Aristazabal I). Francis Sere (1858–1933), born at Sacramento, California, came to Victoria with his family in 1859. His father, John Bernard Sere (1827–1914), a native of France, had worked in S and Central America in the 1840s and then joined the California and Fraser R gold rushes. In California he married Anne Catherine Paris (1820–1902), also from France. The Seres eventually settled in Victoria, where John, with a partner, ran the Hotel de France on Government St and, later, Richmond House in the Mt Tolmie area, where he also established an orchard business and feed store that his son eventually took over. Frank married Anna Seraphina Kerg (c 1866–1924), from Ohio, late in life, in 1918 at Oak Bay. Frank Sere is believed to have taken part in the Victoria old-timers' reunion of May 1924 (*see* Adams Bay).

Setsup Bluff (49°00'00" 125°00'42" W side of Uchucklesit Inlet, off SW side of Alberni Inlet, NE of Barkley Sd, W side of Vancouver I). *Setsup* (or *saʔsup*) is the Nuu-chah-nulth First Nation name for the king or chinook salmon. This feature is also known locally as Steep Bluff.

Settlers Group (50°14'00" 125°08'00" N end of Hoskyn Channel, S of Maurelle I, NE of Campbell R). According to a note at BC's Geographical Names Office, this tiny archipelago was named by the hydrographic service in 1924 after several settlers who had located in the area.

Sewell Inlet (52°53'00" 131°56'00" W side of Selwyn Inlet, E side of Moresby I, opposite Louise I, QCI), **Sewell Point** (52°54'00" 131°53'42" N entrance to Sewell Inlet). Sewell Inlet first appears on Admiralty charts in 1907, but the origin of the name seems to have been lost. Early newspapers referred to the site as Jewell Inlet. A government trail was cut to the head of the inlet in 1908, and several prospectors built cabins in the area during the pre-WWI QCI mining boom. Rayonier Ltd moved its Moresby logging camp, formerly at the head of Cumshewa Inlet, to this site in 1969, and logging roads connected Sewell Inlet to Newcombe Inlet on Tasu Sd on the W coast of Moresby I. Western Forest Products Ltd, which bought Rayonier in 1980, continued to operate a large camp at Sewell Inlet until 2005, when the company's harvesting areas in the region were taken over by BC Timber Sales. At its height the community boasted a store, school, post office, pub and bowling alley. Sewell Point was named by the hydrographic service in 1957. Sewell Inlet Ck, obviously, also gets its name from the inlet. *D*

Sewell Islet (53°26'00" 129°52'00" Entrance to Mink Trap Bay, W side of Pitt I). Company Sgt Maj Travers Fenn

Sewell, from Victoria, was serving with the Westminster Regiment (Motor) of the Royal Canadian Infantry Corps in N Africa when he died from wounds, aged 33, on Apr 12, 1943. He is buried at Bone War Cemetery, Annaba, Algeria. This feature was formerly known as Canoe It.

Seymour Bay (49°21'00" 123°21'00" E side of Bowen I, NE of Cowan Point, Howe Sd, NW of Vancouver). Named after Alexander George Richard Augustus Seymour (d 1922), a cultured, well-educated bachelor who pre-empted land here in 1890, planted a garden and orchard, and lived as a recluse. "Agra," as he was nicknamed from his initials, had the misfortune, according to Bowen I historian Irene Howard, to fall in love with a member of the nobility while working in England as a tutor. They could not marry, of course, and thus the only other option, short of suicide, was for Seymour to become a hermit. In 1907, shortly after receiving his Crown grant, he sold his property to George Cowan, after whom Point Cowan (qv) is named.

Seymour Inlet (51°04'00" 127°10'00" S of Belize Inlet, N of Queen Charlotte Str, N of Port Hardy), **Seymour River** (49°18'07" 123°01'28" Flows S into Burrard Inlet, N Vancouver), **Seymour River** (51°12'00" 126°40'00" Flows S into Seymour Inlet). Frederick Seymour (1820–69) was born at Belfast and spent 20 years in Britain's colonial service, starting as assistant colonial secretary of Van Diemen's Land (Tasmania) and becoming lt gov of British Honduras in 1862. After returning to England to recuperate from a tropical illness, he was offered the governorship of BC, which he accepted, arriving at Victoria in 1864. Although the mainland colony that Seymour inherited from recently knighted Sir James Douglas was beset with financial difficulties, he continued to build roads to BC's goldfields, incurring large but necessary debts. The so-called Chilcotin War, in which a number of people were killed after Tsilhqot'in First Nation members prevented the building of a private road from Bute Inlet to the BC Interior, required his immediate attention. Seymour returned to England in 1865 and married Florence Maria Stapleton (d 1902), and the following year he presided over the union of Vancouver I and BC and became gov of the new combined colony. His lack of decisiveness, however, resulted in Victoria becoming the capital instead of New Westminster, as Seymour had intended. He showed a similar disinclination to become involved in the other burning issues of the day: legislative reform and the

Seymour Inlet. *Reproduced with the permission of the Canadian Hydrographic Service*

question of Confederation. Seymour suffered from poor health in the late 1860s, exacerbated, many historians believe, by acute alcoholism, and he died at Bella Coola while on his way home from talks with N coast First Nation leaders. He is buried at the old naval cemetery in Esquimalt. Many other features are also named for him in BC, including Seymour Lk N of Vancouver; Seymour Heights and Mt Seymour on Vancouver's N Shore; Seymour Arm, Seymour R, Seymour Range and Seymour Pass N of Shushwap Lk; Mt Seymour on Quadra I; Mt Seymour in the QCI; and Frederick Bay and Frederick Sd near Seymour Inlet. Stapleton Point (qv) in Mathieson Channel is named for his wife. *E W*

Seymour Narrows, looking north. *Peter Vassilopoulos*

Seymour Narrows (50°09'00" 125°21'00" Discovery Passage, N of Menzies Bay, NW of Campbell R). Rear Adm Sir George Francis Seymour (1787–1870) was cdr-in-chief on the Pacific Station, 1844–48, with HMS *Collingwood* as his flagship. At that time the station was based at Valparaiso, Chile. An aristocrat and son of a vice adm, Seymour rose rapidly through the RN ranks and saw considerable action, being seriously wounded at the Battle of St Domingo. He was promoted to capt in 1806, appointed master of the robes to King William IV, 1830–37, knighted in 1831, made a rear adm in 1841 and served as a lord of the Admiralty, 1841–44. After his stint on the Pacific Station, Seymour went on to be cdr-in-chief on the N America and W Indies stations, 1851–53, and cdr-in-chief at Portsmouth, 1856–59. He reached the RN's highest rank, adm of the fleet, in 1866. In 1846, Seymour Narrows was mentioned in official correspondence as "Sir George Seymour's Narrows." It is a dangerous body of water, with currents that can reach 16 knots (30 km/h). In the days when Ripple Rk (qv) lay just below its surface in the centre of the channel, many large vessels came to grief there. Capt George Vancouver called it "one of the vilest stretches of water in the world." Ripple Rk was reduced in height in 1958 in one of the world's largest non-nuclear explosions. Seymour Hill on S Vancouver I is also named after Sir George, while Georgina Point (qv) and Georgina Shoals are named after his wife, Georgina Mary Berkeley. *E W*

Shadforth Islands (53°29'20" 130°24'30" In Kingkown Inlet, NW side of Banks I). Named after Victoria resident and master mariner Percival Shadforth (1878–1946), who was born and raised in Durham, England, and went to sea at 16. He had his master's papers by age 26, then immigrated to Canada, working at first for New Westminster steamship entrepreneur Capt E J Fader and then for the Consolidated Whaling Co of Victoria, as capt of the whaling tender *Grey*. Shadforth married Evelyn Annie Blenkinsop (1878–1949), also from Durham, at Vancouver in 1911 and returned to Britain during WWI to serve on minesweepers. Back in Victoria after the war he worked on coastal steamships and became a well-known member of the BC Pilotage Assoc, an organization he later helped bring under government control. Shadforth Ck N of Prince George is named after his brother, Lt Cdr Hubert G Shadforth, who was killed in action while in command of HMCS *Spikenard*, a corvette torpedoed and sunk in the N Atlantic by a U-boat on Feb 10, 1942. Hubert had come to Victoria in 1905; he also served in the RN in WWI and worked as a pilot and for the CPR.

Shadwell Passage (50°55'00" 127°49'00" Between Hope I and Vansittart I, off N end of Vancouver I). RN officer Charles Frederick Alexander Shadwell (1814–86) was an expert on nautical astronomy and wrote several standard texts on the subject. He was a capt in 1864 when Capt George Richards, the RN's chief hydrographer, named this feature after him, and he had seen action at the bombardment of Acre in 1840, in the 2nd Anglo-Burmese War of 1852–53 and during the 2nd Opium War of 1856–60. He was elected a fellow of the Royal Society in 1861. Shadwell was promoted to rear adm in 1869 and served as cdr-in-chief on the China Station, 1871–74, during which period he was knighted. He was appointed president of the Royal Naval College at Greenwich, 1878–81, and reached the rank of adm, retired, in 1879. The US warship *Suwanee* was completely wrecked on a rock in this passage in 1868 (*see* Suwanee Rk). **W**

Shaffer Point (51°04'00" 127°07'00" N side of Seymour Inlet, N of Queen Charlotte Str, NE of Port Hardy). Chief Motor Mechanic Thomas Winfield Shaffer of the RCNR died in an accident at Steveston on Feb 5, 1941, aged 47. He was born in Montana and lived at Victoria before moving to Steveston. Shaffer, who married Ellen Jones at Vancouver in 1925, was a mining engineer and also well known on the W coast as a master mechanic on fishing vessels. He is buried at Burnaby (Ocean View) Burial Park.

Shaft Point (49°11'00" 123°57'00" W side of Newcastle I, Nanaimo Hbr, SE side of Vancouver I). Newcastle I is riddled with old coal-mining shafts. The HBC realized in the early 1850s that the entire Nanaimo region was rich in coal, and mining took place on the island from 1853 to 1883.

Shag Islet (49°14'00" 126°03'00" N side of Brabant Channel, E of Bartlett I, Clayoquot Sd, W side of Vancouver I), **Shag Rock** (54°09'00" 132°39'00" E of Klashwun Point, off N side of Graham I, QCI). Shags and cormorants are largish seabirds, members of the Phalacrocoracidae family. The word "shag" means "a mass of hair," and the name originally referred to crested cormorants, specifically *Phalacrocorax aristotelis*, the common shag, found in Europe, SW Asia and N Africa. Three species of cormorants inhabit the BC coast, of which two—the double-crested (*Phalacrocorax auritus*) and pelagic (*Phalacrocorax pelagicus*)—sport head tufts in breeding season and could perhaps be considered shags. Shag Rk, known by the Haida as Y'ah, was named by geologist George Mercer Dawson in 1878. A number of manganese mineral claims were filed in the vicinity in the 1950s and '60s. *D*

Shah Point (49°02'00" 123°36'00" SE side of Valdes I, Gulf Is, SE of Nanaimo). HMS *Shah* was stationed in Esquimalt, 1876–78, under Capt Frederick Bedford, as the flagship of Rear Adm Algernon de Horsey, cdr-in-chief of the Pacific Station. It later served in S Africa during the Anglo-Zulu War. The 5,670-tonne, 26-gun steam frigate was designed by Sir Edward Reed and built at Portsmouth in 1873. It was originally to be named *Blonde* but was rechristened after the visit of the Shah of Persia. The *Shah* was converted to a coal-storage hulk in 1904, sold in 1919 and wrecked at Bermuda in 1926. Shah Point, formerly known as Bare Point, was renamed by regional hydrographer Henri Parizeau in 1946.

Shakes Islands (53°48'00" 130°29'00" Between Goschen I and Dolphin I, S of Porcher I and Prince Rupert). Shakes is an anglicized version of the hereditary name of one of the main chiefs of the Kitkatla First Nation; many other spellings of the name are found, including Saiks, Seeks, Sheuksh and Syacks. These islands commemorate Chief William Ewart Gladstone Shakes (d 1901), a widely respected 19th-century leader on the N coast, who adopted his personal names when he was baptized. According to BC historian Capt John Walbran, Shakes sent Queen Victoria a potlatch present of $100 and received in return two valuable rugs and a large, steel-framed engraving of Her Britannic Majesty. Nearby Chief Point, Ewart I and Gladstone Is are also named for this charismatic figure. **W**

Shakespeare Banks (52°50'00" 129°25'00" W of Rennison I, off NW Aristazabal I, SW entrance to Caamaño Sd, Hecate Str). Noah Shakespeare (1839–1921) immigrated to Victoria from England in 1863 on the *Robert Lowe*, one of the "brideships" that brought unmarried young women to BC to serve as domestic servants. After toiling for a Nanaimo coal company for a year, he was able to bring out his wife, Eliza Jane (1838–1923, née Pearson), and son. The family moved to Victoria, where Noah set himself up as a photographer and Eliza Jane opened a "fancy

S

shop." He later also worked as a realtor, tax collector and manufacturer's agent. After running unsuccessfully as an MLA in 1875, Shakespeare was elected a city councillor in 1878, 1880 and 1881. In 1882 he was the mayor of Victoria. As president of the Workingmen's Protective Assoc, which lobbied for restrictions on Chinese immigration, he rode a wave of anti-Chinese sentiment to Ottawa, defeating former premier Amor de Cosmos in 1882 to become the city's Conservative MP. He was a main instigator of the Chinese Immigration Act, which created the much-hated head tax, but resigned as MP in 1887 to take the job of Victoria postmaster, a position he held until 1914.

Shannon Bay (53°39'00" 132°30'00" SW side of Masset Inlet, Graham I, QCI). Charles M Shannon (b 1853) was vice-president of the Graham Steamship, Coal & Lumber Co, which was formed about 1906 and held substantial timber and coal leases and vast amounts of waterfront on Masset and Juskatla inlets in the 1910s and '20s. He was born in Kentucky and had been a prospector, reporter and newspaper owner before going into politics. Shannon served three terms as a senator in the New Mexico legislature, became a member of the Democratic National Committee and collector of internal revenue under President Grover Cleveland, and later had major interests in several mining companies. He accompanied officials of the Graham company to Masset Inlet in 1907, and the bay was named for him at that time. Large-scale logging began at Shannon Bay in the early 1920s, and a cannery was built there in 1926 by the Gosse Packing Co. BC Packers took it over in 1928, closed the plant in 1931 and reopened it 1936–40. The bay was then used by a series of forestry companies as a booming ground. Newton Chittenden named it Zoos Inlet in 1884, after its plentiful jellyfish. *D*

Shannon Rock (52°56'00" 129°34'00" Entrance to Pemberton Bay, S side of Dewdney I, Estevan Group, NW side of Caamaño Sd). William Shannon (1843–1928) was born at Sligo, Ireland, and immigrated to Ont with his parents in 1849. He and his brother Thomas sought their fortunes in the wider world and eventually arrived in BC, via S America, Mexico and California, about 1863 for the Cariboo gold rush. Will owned and sold land on Lulu and Sea islands and in the S Vancouver area, hauled freight with oxen on the Cariboo Rd, became an early storekeeper in the Okanagan valley and bought and sold more land in Chilliwack and Surrey. Tom and younger brother Joseph settled and farmed in the Surrey district they named Clover Valley. Will married Eliza McIndoo in Ont in 1886 and moved back to Vancouver, entered the real-estate business and became a successful entrepreneur. Shannon Falls on Shannon Ck in Howe Sd (formerly known as Fairy Falls) is believed to have been named in association with a brickworks he owned at that location—one of his many commercial interests (he also developed a hop-growing enterprise in the Squamish valley in the 1890s).

Shapland Cove (50°29'00" 127°48'00" N side of Quatsino Sd, just E of Koprino Hbr, NW end of Vancouver I). Master mariner George Shapland (1839–1921) pre-empted land on this cove in 1912 and acquired a Crown grant for his property in 1919. He also received Crown grants in the New Westminster land district in 1906 and 1907. Shapland is believed to have immigrated to BC with his second wife sometime after 1892, when his first wife, Ellen (née Harrison), died in England. He apparently also built a house in Vancouver in 1913. The name of the cove was adopted in 1968 after a request from the Geological Survey of Canada.

Sharbau Island (51°25'00" 127°42'00" S entrance to Rivers Inlet, N of Port Hardy). Named by Lt Daniel Pender of the *Beaver* in 1865 after Henry Sharbau (1822–1904), a draftsman at the RN hydrographic dept in England at the time that Capt George Richards, who had been Pender's predecessor as the chief marine surveyor on the BC coast, was head of the dept. Sharbau was born in Germany but came to Scotland as a young man and worked for the ordnance survey and the Admiralty in the Hebrides and western lochs. He was appointed an assistant at hydrographic HQ, 1865–74, then served as a surveyor and draftsman in Japan and England before joining the Royal Geographic Society as chief draftsman in 1881. Sharbau's work was noted for its painstaking detail; his map of Tibet, first published in 1894, was considered an especially important contribution to cartography.

Sharp Bay (53°10'00" 129°33'00" NW end of Campania I, S side of Otter Channel, opposite S end of Pitt I). Sgt Charles John Sharp of the Royal Canadian Corps of Signals was killed in action Dec 19, 1941, aged 26, during the fall of Hong Kong. He was from Vancouver and had been mentioned in dispatches for gallantry. Sharp is buried at the Stanley Military Cemetery on Hong Kong I.

Sharp Island (49°11'00" 125°52'00" E side of Lemmens Inlet, Meares I, Clayoquot Sd, W side of Vancouver I). Named after William Sharp (1902–87), a former chairman or mayor of the Tofino village council, 1958–61, who died at Tofino. The name was adopted in 1986 on the recommendation of G E Richardson of the hydrographic service. Sharp Ck, on Meares I just opposite Sharp I, was named for him in 1959.

Sharp Passage (50°51'00" 126°38'00" Between Stackhouse I and N side of Broughton I, Sutlej Channel, entrance to Kingcome Inlet, NE of Port McNeill). William Henry Sharp was the master aboard HMS *Sutlej*, under Capt Matthew Connolly, on the Pacific Station in 1865–66. *Sutlej* was the flagship of the station's cdr-in-chief, Rear Adm John Kingcome. Sharp ended his RN career as a staff capt at Devonport dockyard in 1882.

The boaters' haven of Shawl Bay. *Peter Vassilopoulos*

Shawl Bay (50°51'00" 126°34'00" Between Gregory I and Wishart Peninsula, SE entrance to Kingcome Inlet, NE of Port McNeill). This protected anchorage has been popular with sailors and fishermen for years. There are a number of floathouses in the bay, and a floating marina with laundry and shower facilities. Regular floatplane and water-taxi services are available to Port McNeill and elsewhere. Alf Didriksen and his family operated a logging camp there for several decades, while Edna and Al Brown developed a resort and a small store. The origin of the name, however, is not known.

Shearer Point (52°47'00" 132°04'00" W entrance to Newcombe Inlet, Tasu Sd, W side of Moresby I, QCI), **Shearer Rock** (52°47'00" 132°03'00" Just SE of Shearer Point). The point was originally named after RCAF officer William R Shearer, who came to the QCI in 1935 on a special mission for the Dept of National Defence. Shearer retired from the armed forces in 1963 as a squadron leader and cdr of RCAF Station Pagwa, an Ont radar facility. Shearer Rk was named by the hydrographic service in 1962, in association with the point.

Shears Islands (49°00'00" 125°19'00" N end of David Channel, S of Toquart Bay, Barkley Sd, W side of Vancouver I). Walter Shears (1853–1918) received a Crown grant of land on the W side of Toquart Bay in 1892. An early immigrant to Victoria from England, he worked as a clerk for J H Turner's wholesale business and married Anne Pickstone (b 1854), also from England, at Victoria in 1874. In the 1880s, under the name Shears & Partridge, he was a dry goods merchant, and by the 1890s he had become a customs appraiser for the federal government and paymaster to the BC Brigade of Garrison Artillery. He also served as a Victoria city councillor in 1882–83. The Shears Is were formerly known as the Sisters Is.

Shearwater Island (52°09'00" 128°05'00" In Kliksoatli Hbr, N side of Denny I, just E of Bella Bella), **Shearwater Point** (53°28'00" 128°36'00" N side of Gardner Canal, Alan Reach, S of Kitimat). HMS *Shearwater* was launched in 1900 at England's Sheerness dockyard and spent most of its working life based at Esquimalt as part of the Pacific Station. The RN phased out its Pacific squadron at the start of WWI, and the 63-m, 889-tonne vessel was transferred to the RCN in 1914, along with its sister ship, the *Algerine*, and recommissioned as HMCS *Shearwater*. Two of the sloop's eight guns were removed and used in a shore battery that defended Seymour Narrows. The *Shearwater* served as a tender to two submarines, *CC-1* and *CC-2*, which the BC government, in a fit of nerves, acquired from the US in 1914 (they had originally been built for the Chilean navy but the deal fell through). In 1917 the tender escorted its charges through the Panama Canal to Halifax and spent the rest of the war as a support vessel on the Atlantic coast. It was sold in 1919 and renamed the *Vedas*. The name Shearwater was later assigned to a naval air base in Halifax, but it also became associated with the non-Native part of Bella Bella located on Denny I, site of an RCAF flying-boat station in WWII and, later, a shipyard and resort operated by Shearwater Marine Ltd. Shearwater Point was named in 1907 by Capt Frederick Learmonth of HMS *Egeria* while surveying Gardner Canal. The hydrographic service named Shearwater I, formerly known as Harbour I, in 1924. Both names ultimately honour a family of pelagic seabirds, whose members often visit the BC coast. Shearwaters are smaller relatives of the albatross; they spend most of their lives at sea and migrate great distances to breeding colonies in the southern hemisphere. It is not known if **Shearwater Passage** (49°53'00" 124°43'00" Between Harwood I and Savary I, NW of Powell R) is named after the bird or the ship. *E*

HMCS *Shearwater* in 1914, together with the two submarines, *CC-1* and *CC-2*, that the BC government purchased from the US at the beginning of WWI. *BC Archives A-07062*

Sheldens Bay (53°09'00" 131°45'00" S of Copper Bay, NW side of Moresby I, QCI). Sandspit-area pioneers Capt

S

Charles Richard Sheldon (1859–1915) and his wife built a cabin at this site and homesteaded in the early 1900s. They received a Crown grant for their land in 1913. The geographical name is a spelling error.

Sheldon Islet (53°41'00" 130°25'00" NW of Baird Point, off NW McCauley I, Browning Entrance, S of Prince Rupert). Rev Alfred Harold C Sheldon (1853–88) was appointed the resident Anglican missionary at Port Essington in 1884. He had trained as a doctor in England, then came to BC and ministered for several years in the mining camps of the Omineca gold district. In 1888, while returning from Port Simpson by canoe, Sheldon, Elizabeth Cunningham (the Haida wife of Port Essington entrepreneur Robert Cunningham; *see* Cunningham Passage) and two First Nation paddlers were drowned in the Skeena R when their frail craft overturned in rough water.

Shepherd Point (53°24'00" 128°55'00" E side of Gribbell I, Ursula Channel, S of Kitimat). Cpl Reginald Alastair Shepherd, MM, from Victoria, was killed in action Apr 5, 1945, aged 31. He was a member of the N Shore (NB) Regiment of the Royal Canadian Infantry Corps and is buried at Holten Canadian War Cemetery in the Netherlands. This name appeared on charts for many years as Shephard, after being misspelled on the original Dept of National Defence casualty lists for WWII. It was not corrected until 1973.

Sheppard Point (48°34'00" 123°31'00" W side of Saanich Inlet, S of Bamberton, NW of Victoria). Named after Henry S Sheppard, who came to the Saanich district from the US about 1860 and built one of BC's earliest sawmills, at Mill Bay, just N of this location. At the time, it was the only mill between Nanaimo and Esquimalt. William Sayward purchased it about 1863 and greatly expanded the operation, eventually becoming the largest lumber merchant on Vancouver I. This feature was formerly known as Turn Point.

Sherard Point (48°52'00" 123°37'00" SE end of Osborn Bay, W side of Stuart Channel, near Crofton, SE side of Vancouver I). After author, Arctic explorer and RN officer Sherard Osborn. *See* Osborn Bay.

Sherberg Island (50°32'00" 127°38'00" N of Drake I, Quatsino Sd, NW end of Vancouver I). Ole Anderson Sherberg (1859–1931), from Norway, was a pioneer storekeeper and telegraph operator at Quatsino. He was a widower, and his original name, which he later changed, was Skjarberg. Ole and his sons Henry and Oliver were members of a group of Scandinavian colonists who came to settle on Quatsino Sd in 1894. He became a school trustee in 1899, opened his store in 1902 and sold out to Gus Moerman in 1912. Like most of the other settlers, Sherberg was a keen prospector, staking a number of

claims and working for several years at the Yreka copper mine on nearby Neroutsos Inlet in the early 1900s. The island was named by the hydrographic service in 1926.

Sheringham Point (48°23'00" 123°55'00" W side of Orveas Bay, N side of Juan de Fuca Str, SW end of Vancouver I). Named in 1846 by Capt Henry Kellett of HMS *Herald*, who made an early survey of this region, after a compatriot of his, fellow RN surveyor William Louis Sheringham (d 1873). He entered the navy in 1808, was a cdr at the time Kellett was in this area, and eventually attained the rank of vice adm, retired, in 1871. Sheringham assisted Sir Francis Beaufort with his reorganization of the Admiralty's hydrographic dept in the 1830s and was in charge of a number of surveys in subsequent years, including several on the coasts of Wales and Cornwall, but appears never to have visited BC waters. Sheringham Point was named Punta de San Eusebio by Spanish naval officer Manuel Quimper in 1790. A lighthouse was built on the point in 1912 and automated in 1989. *W*

Sherman. *See* Sandy Cove.

Sherman Islet (53°33'00" 130°07'20" In Principe Channel, off S end of McCauley I, opposite E side of Banks I). Flying Officer Lawrence Sherman, from Vancouver, was killed in action on June 13, 1944, aged 24. He was a member of No 162 (Bomber Reconnaissance) Squadron and was awarded the DFC for attacking and sinking a U-boat with his Canso aircraft while under heavy fire. A day later he himself was shot down by another sub. Sherman is commemorated on England's Runnymede Memorial.

Shields Bay (53°21'00" 132°29'00" Head of Rennell Sd, SW side of Graham I, QCI), **Shields Island** (53°20'00" 132°27'00" In Shields Bay), **Shields Rock** (53°20'00" 132°28'00" Just N of Shields I). The bay and island were named in 1885 by veteran prospector William Robertson for James Shields, a US-born former sealer who had accompanied him to the QCI that year and helped stake out a large coalfield in the Yakoun R valley. Their plan, which attracted numerous speculators over the years but was never realized, was to ship coal out to Shields Bay by rail. To further this goal, Jimmy Shields staked out a townsite on the bay for a proposed loading facility. Nearby Shields Ck is named for him as well. The following year he acquired land E of Queen Charlotte City that he also hoped to develop. Shields I was called Edward I by Newton Chittenden in 1884 and Cross I by Capt Holmes Newcomb of the Fisheries Protection Branch in the early 1920s. Shields Bay was also known locally as Yakoun Bay. Shields Rk was named much later by the hydrographic service, in association with the bay and island. *D*

Shields Point (49°33'00" 124°40'00" N side of Hornby I, W side of Str of Georgia). A number of individuals named

Shields reserved land on Hornby I in the late 1800s. James Shields was a very early pre-emptor, in 1873, while the application of F W Shields is dated 1887. Theo N Shields received a Crown grant for his property in 1891. This feature, which is also known locally as Grassy Point, is named after F W Shields.

Ship Cove. *See* Resolution Cove.

Ship Point (48°25'27" 123°22'16" E side of Inner Hbr, Victoria Hbr, Victoria). This very old name in the heart of Victoria, a few metres away from the original location of Ft Victoria, appears on early charts of the harbour but seems to have largely disappeared by the 1870s, when wharves began to proliferate in the vicinity. In 1974, after a long occupancy by Ocean Cement, the site was acquired by the city and improved with a seawall. A local realtor suggested it be called Churchill Point, but city archivist Ainslie Helmcken convinced the mayor and council that the historic name of Ship Point should be readopted. Today, mid-sized commercial vessels dock there, and a night market and other special events are held in the area.

Shoal Bay on Thurlow Island. *John Alexander*

Shoal Bay (50°27'00" 125°22'00" NE end of E Thurlow I, Cordero Channel, N of Campbell R). The name of this feature has an obvious origin, as the waters at the head of the bay become shallow quite rapidly. A historic logging and mining community was located at this site, beginning in the 1880s. A hotel, store and post office (simply named Thurlow) made Shoal Bay a supply centre and a regular stopping place for steamships. Peter and Rose MacDonald's Thurlow Hotel, a coastal landmark, burned down in 1919. A new facility, the Shoal Bay Lodge, was built in the 1960s but met the same fate as its predecessor in 2000. Several cottages, a pub and café, bathhouse and laundry building have been rebuilt but were listed for sale in 2008. *E*

Shoal Point (49°12'00" 122°55'00" NE tip of Annacis I, lower Fraser R, just E of Lulu I). The NE part of Annacis I (qv) was formerly separate, and known as Robson I, after its early owner John Robson, who later became a

premier of BC. The original Shoal Point was located at the NE end of Robson I and appears as such on Admiralty charts dating back to 1859. When Annacis was developed as an industrial park in 1954, the channel between the two islands was filled in and the combined land mass artificially extended to the NE, obliterating Shoal Point. In 1957 the hydrographic service agreed to reapply the name to the NE tip of the new, altered Annacis I.

Shotbolt Bay (51°39'00" 127°21'00" S side of Rivers Inlet near its head, opposite Kilbella Bay, N of Port Hardy), **Shotbolt Point** (52°44'00" 129°07'00" NE side of Aristazabal I, W side of Laredo Channel). Thomas Shotbolt (1842–1922), a native of Lincolnshire who arrived in BC via Panama in 1862, was a pioneer pharmacist at Victoria and operated a drugstore on Johnson St. He married Lavinia Palmiter (1854–1945), also from England, at Victoria in 1875. Shotbolt was an early investor in BC's cannery and forestry sectors. He bought land on this bay in 1879, apparently as a site for Robert Draney's Rivers Inlet Cannery, the first in the region. In 1882, however, Draney unloaded the lumber and other materials for the cannery, in the dark, at the mouth of the Wannock R, 5 km from the proposed site. He decided to build there instead of at Shotbolt Bay. In 1889, Shotbolt became one of the founding directors of the BC Paper Manufacturing Co, which produced the province's first paper at Alberni. He was an active Freemason, the inaugural president of the BC Pharmaceutical Assoc and a vigorous promoter of street lighting and an electric streetcar system for Victoria. According to Capt John Walbran, the name Shotbolt Bay was adopted by the RN's hydrographic dept in 1890, the year Walbran made a sketch survey of Rivers Inlet. Shotbolt Ck, which flows N into the bay, also commemorates the entrepreneurial druggist. Gonzales Hill in Victoria, at the foot of which Shotbolt built Hollywood, a substantial home, on a 4-ha estate, was known locally in the early days as Shotbolts Hill.

Shushartie Bay (50°51'00" 127°52'00" S side of Goletas Channel, opposite W end of Nigei I, N end of Vancouver I). The name is an adaptation of a Kwakwala word meaning "place to find cockles" and may have been adopted by HBC officials as early as 1838. The bay was a well-known refuge for fur-trading vessels and was also used by early US whalers, who buried several shipmates in the area in 1844. It was first surveyed in 1850 by William Dillon, master of HMS *Daedalus*, and named Port Shucartie. William McGary's trading post, built about 1891, was taken over in 1895 by Jepther Skinner, who operated a store, post office and primitive hotel there—in later years with his wife, Eileen—until his death by drowning in 1934. A small salmon cannery also operated at this location, 1914–28. Shushartie was a port of call for Union steamships until the 1940s, but its buildings are now long abandoned. The nearby features of Shushartie

Lk, Shushartie Mtn, Shushartie R and Shushartie Saddle are all named after the bay. *E W*

Shute Passage (48°43'00" 123°23'00" SW of Portland I, NE of Piers I and Coal I, NE of the N end of Saanich Peninsula, N of Victoria), **Shute Reef** (48°43'00" 123°26'00" NW of Piers I, Satellite Channel, off N end of Saanich Peninsula). Capt James Shute of the Royal Marines served on the Pacific Station, 1859–63, aboard HMS *Topaze*, under Capt John Spencer. He was promoted to maj in 1872. These features were named by Capt George Richards of HMS *Plumper* about 1860. Mt Shute, N of Topaze Hbr, also commemorates him.

Shuttle Island (52°40'00" 131°42'00" In Darwin Sd, between E side of Moresby I and Lyell I, QCI), **Shuttle Passage** (Between Shuttle I and Lyell I), **Shuttle Reef** (52°42'00" 131°44'00" Just N of Shuttle I). Geologist George Mercer Dawson named Shuttle I in 1878 because its shape and position in Darwin Sd reminded him of a shuttle on a loom. The passage and reef were named much later, in association with the island, by the hydrographic service—the reef in 1922 and the passage in 1957. Several gold claims have been staked on Shuttle I over the years. It was also the site of a logging camp for "aeroplane" spruce during WWI. *D*

Shuttleworth Bight (50°51'00" 128°08'00" NE of Cape Scott, W of Cape Sutil, N end of Vancouver I). Henry Shuttleworth (1870–1941), from England, built a homestead on the bight, at the mouth of the Stranby R, in 1905. Three years later he married Marie Christensen (d 1938), sister of the area's first settler, Soren Christensen. Harry, as he was usually known, planted fruit trees and raised cattle; he was appointed the area's road foreman, postmaster (of Stranby post office) and justice of the peace. His brother Robert and his family arrived in the area in 1911, and a small group of other settlers gradually formed a modest community. A school opened. Many people left during WWI, however, and by the 1920s only a hardy few remained. Henry and Marie both died at Alert Bay.

Sibell Bay (48°59'00" 123°47'00" NE side of Ladysmith Hbr, SE side of Vancouver I). Cdr John Parry, in charge of the RN survey vessel *Egeria*, named this feature in 1904 after Sibell Brandon, the sister of one of his lts, Vivian Brandon. Lt Brandon and Lt George Nares were responsible that year for the re-survey of Ladysmith Hbr.

Sidney (48°39'00" 123°24'00" NE end of Saanich Peninsula, N of Victoria), **Sidney Channel** (48°37'00" 123°20'00" Between Sidney I and James I), **Sidney Island** (48°37'00" 123°18'00" Off E side of Saanich Peninsula), **Sidney Spit** (48°39'00" 123°20'00" N tip of Sidney I). The town of Sidney is named after Sidney I, which was originally known by its ancient First Nation name, Sallas (*see* Sallas Rks; an

alternative First Nation name for the island, from the Coast Salish Sencoťen dialect, is Wyomecen, meaning "land of caution"). The meaning of the word Sallas has been lost, unfortunately, but it remained in use for many years, even after Capt George Richards of HMS *Plumper* renamed the island for his surveyor colleague Frederick William Sidney in 1859. Sidney, who entered the RN in 1833, just months after Richards, was a junior officer on an expedition up the Niger R in Africa in 1842. He participated in surveys of the Azores (on HMS *Styx*), S America (on HMS *Cyclops*) and Australia (on HMS *Pelorus*) and retired in 1869 with the rank of capt. The HBC tried to colonize 900-ha Sidney I, offering land for sale in 1860 for "six shillings an acre" but finding few buyers. It was later owned by a group of Victoria businessmen and used as a hunting preserve. The Sidney Tile & Brick Co established a brickworks there in the early 1900s. The lagoon and spit at the N end are important wildlife areas and were protected as a provincial marine park (now part of the Gulf Is National Park Reserve) in 1981. The rest of the island, with the exception of some small conservation zones, was subdivided as recreational property. In summer a passenger ferry connects the park to Sidney, a community of 11,000 and the business centre of the Saanich Peninsula. After the townsite was settled and logged in the 1880s, a railway to Victoria was built and agriculture, brick-making and sawmilling all became important. Sidney is a recreational and retirement spot today, conveniently close to the BC Ferries terminus at Swartz Bay. The town's location was known to Saanich First Nation members as Tseteenus, meaning "sticking out." *E W*

Sidney Spit at the north tip of Sidney Island. *Kevin Oke*

Sidney Bay (50°31'00" 125°36'00" W side of Loughborough Inlet, just N of Beaver Inlet, NW of Campbell R). Sidney Thomas Franklyn (1851–83) was born in England and arrived at Victoria on the HBC barque *Princess Royal* with his mother and siblings in 1860. His father, William Hales Franklyn, had come to BC the previous year as stipendiary magistrate and government agent for Nanaimo but in 1867 was appointed chief civil commissioner for the Seychelles, a British protectorate in the Indian Ocean. Sidney remained in BC and became a mariner. He was the pilot on the coastal freighter *Grappler* on its fatal voyage through Seymour Narrows to the N coast canneries in 1883. The vessel caught fire, and 88 passengers and crew, including Franklyn, lost their lives. Mt Franklyn near Cowichan Lk and the Franklyn Range near Sidney Bay are named for William Franklyn. Mt Harold, NW of Sidney Bay, is named for Harold Franklyn (1850–88), Sidney's elder brother, who also stayed in BC after his father was promoted, working for the Canadian Pacific Navigation Co and then as mate of the *Cariboo Fly* before his premature death from heart disease. *W*

Sieward Hill (50°21'06" 127°52'03" W side of Keith R, head of Side Bay, Brooks Bay, NW side of Vancouver I). Henry Ferdinand Sieward (b 1853), a native of Germany, learned his trade as a seaman in England. He came to NS in 1880 and Victoria about 1886, where he worked for the trading company Hall, Goepel & Co. Sieward was sent back to NS in 1888 to purchase the schooner *Araunah* for the sealing industry and was the vessel's skipper when it was confiscated by Russian authorities off the Kamchatka Peninsula; he and his crew eventually made their way back to Victoria via Siberia and Japan. In 1889 he made a successful sealing expedition in the *Walter L Rich*. Again he was sent to NS to bring sealing schooners (*Ocean Belle* and *Geneva*) W by way of Cape Horn. Sieward went into business for himself in 1891, purchasing a new schooner in NS, which he named the *Dora Sieward* after his daughter. Later he also acquired the *Mascotte*. Sieward Hill was named in 1937 by regional hydrographer Henri Parizeau.

Silas Point (53°42'00" 129°45'00" N entrance to Klewnuggit Inlet, E side of Grenville Channel, opposite Pitt I). After Capt Silas Ormiston, a master mariner for the CPR on the BC coast. *See* Ormiston Point.

Silva Bay (49°09'00" 123°42'00" E end of Gabriola I, Gulf Is). John Silva (c 1837–1929), a native of Portugal, came to Victoria in 1854 as a seaman and jumped ship there. He ran a fruit and vegetable store in the city for a few years and married Marelee Holowaat (c 1858–1926), a young Lyackson First Nation woman from Valdes I, who was working for a Victoria family and went by the name of Louisa. In 1873 the Silva family moved to a land pre-emption at Village Bay on Mayne I, then moved again, after the drowning deaths of two of their children, to the E end of Gabriola I in 1883. John and Louisa homesteaded, and John fished from his boat, the *Corliss Queen*, which he constructed at Silva Bay.

Silvester Bay (51°09'00" 127°45'00" NW side of Queen Charlotte Str, SE of Cape Caution, NW of Port Hardy). Victualling Petty Officer Charles Victor Silvester, of Victoria, died on Nov 24, 1941, while serving aboard HMCS *Columbia*. He is buried at Fossvogur Cemetery in Reykjavik, Iceland.

Simonds Group (51°57'00" 128°17'00" W of McNaughton Group, Queens Sd, SW of Bella Bella). Named in 1944 by the hydrographic service for Lt Gen Guy Granville Simonds, CB, CBE, DSO (1903–74), a Canadian military leader in WWII. He was born in England and immigrated with his family to Victoria in 1912. Simonds graduated from Kingston's Royal Military College in 1921 and went to Europe in 1939, where he rose rapidly through the ranks during WWII. In 1943, as a maj gen, he was cdr of the 1st Canadian Infantry Division in Italy; the following year, promoted to lt gen, he led the 2nd Canadian Corps in the invasion of NW Europe and conquest of Germany. Simonds was a favourite of 8th Army cdr Gen Bernard Montgomery, who considered him the most effective of the Canadian generals. After the war he served as chief instructor at Britain's Imperial Defence College, 1946–49, commandant of Canada's National Defence College, 1949–51, and chief of the general staff, 1951–55. Granville Is and Guy I, both located nearby, also commemorate him.

Simoom Sound (50°51'00" 126°30'00" E and N of Wishart Peninsula, between Tribune Channel and Kingcome Inlet, NE of Port McNeill). In 1864, RN marine surveyor Lt Daniel Pender named a number of features in this area in association with Rear Adm John Kingcome, who was cdr-in-chief of the Pacific Station at that time (*see* Kingcome Inlet). HMS *Simoom*, named after a hot, dust-laden wind characteristic of the Arabian desert, was one of Kingcome's early commands. It had been designed as a 20-gun frigate but was reduced during construction to an 8-gun troopship. The 2,650-tonne, steam-powered vessel was

Silva Bay at the east end of Gabriola Island. *Kevin Oke*

Simoom Sound. *Peter Vassilopoulos*

launched in 1849 and saw service in Australia, China and the Mediterranean before being decommissioned in 1887. Kingcome commanded it in 1853, when he was a capt. As a troopship, the *Simoom* apparently had a galley that could prepare meals for 1,000 men and distill more than 400 litres of fresh water from salt water per hour. It was never on the BC coast, however. Capt George Vancouver anchored in this sound with HMS *Discovery* and *Chatham* for a week in the summer of 1792 while exploring the surrounding area with the ships' boats. Simoom Sd was home to a floating logging camp in the early 1900s; a post office opened in 1912 in John Dunseith's general store. This office was moved to the W side of Gilford I in 1936 and to nearby Echo Bay in 1973 but, confusingly, retained its Simoom Sd name. *E*

Simpson Point (48°21'00" 123°43'00" E side of Sooke Inlet, opposite Whiffin Spit, S end of Vancouver I). This is an old name, adopted from the 1846 survey by Capt Henry Kellett, but its derivation is uncertain. The feature is known locally as Donaldson Point, after Alexander Donaldson, a former local resident. *See also* Secretary (Donaldson) I.

Simpson Rock (50°59'00" 127°31'00" Part of the Southgate Group, N of the Walker group, NW side of Queen Charlotte Str, N of Port Hardy). Cdr Cortland Herbert Simpson was in charge of the RN survey vessel *Egeria* on the BC coast, 1900–1903. After leaving BC he was promoted to capt and transferred to the Australia Station, where he commanded the survey ship *Penguin*. (His father was also an RN officer named Cortland Herbert Simpson.) The rock was named by Cdr John Parry, who took over from Simpson aboard the *Egeria*.

Sims Islet (49°43'25" 124°11'10" In Blind Bay, S entrance to Jervis Inlet, SE of Powell R). Named in 1990 for Ordinary Coder John Richard Sims, from Vancouver, who died on Aug 12, 1944, aged 19, while serving with the RCNVR at HMCS *Bytown*, a naval shore establishment in Ottawa. He is buried at Vancouver's Mountain View Cemetery.

Sinclair Bank (49°42'00" 124°17'00" W of Nelson I, Malaspina Str, SE of Powell R). William Brown "Bertrand" Sinclair (1881–1972) was a writer and fisherman who immigrated to Ont from England with his mother in 1889. Infatuated by cowboy culture, he left home at a young age and travelled to the US, where he eventually married Bertha Bower, also a writer. She modelled the protagonist of her novel *Chip of the Flying U* on Sinclair. He divorced, remarried, became a well-known author of westerns and moved to BC in about 1912. His later novels, including *The Inverted Pyramid* and *Poor Man's Rock*, are set in BC, in the coastal milieux of the fisherman and logger. In 1932, despite his considerable success, Sinclair became a commercial salmon troller, more or less giving up the occupation of writing. He settled for many years at Pender Hbr. *See also* Poor Mans Rk. *E*

Sine Island (53°34'00" 129°58'00" N of Anger I, off W side of Pitt I), **Sine Point** (NE end of Sine I). These features were named by a coast triangulation party under A E Wright, a surveyor with the BC Lands Service, in 1921. A sine is a mathematical ratio between the sides of a right-angled triangle and is used in surveying to measure gradients and distances. Other nearby features (Azimuth I, Logarithm Point, Cosine Bay, Cosine I, Cosine Point, Tangent I, Tangent Point) are also named after surveying terms.

Sinnett Islets (52°32'00" 129°20'00" SE of the Gander Group, off W side of Aristazabal I, Hecate Str). 2nd Cpl Charles Sinnett was a member of the Columbia detachment of Royal Engineers, which served in BC 1858–63. In 1859 he was part of a squad of sappers, under Lt Arthur Lempriere, sent to explore and cut potential trails between Ft Hope and Boston Bar. Sinnett produced a fine map of this region, which accompanied Lempriere's report. Sinnett Ck in the Tulameen area is also named for him and commemorates the fact that he surveyed the mule road to the Similkameen area in 1860–61.

Sir Edmund Bay (50°49'00" 126°36'00" NE side of Broughton I, Penphrase Passage, NE of Port McNeill), **Sir Edmund Head** (50°49'00" 126°35'00" E end of Broughton I). The headland was named about 1864 by RN surveyor Lt Daniel Pender of the *Beaver* after Sir Edmund Walker Head (1805–68), gov of the HBC from 1863 to 1868. A distinguished scholar and author as well as a prominent civil servant, Head was appointed lt gov of NB in 1848 and helped prepare the colony for representative government. In 1854 he became gov gen of British N America, serving until 1861.

Sivart Island (52°32'00" 131°35'00" Entrance to Haswell Bay, Juan Perez Sd, off E side of Moresby I, QCI), **Sivart Rock** (52°32'00" 131°36'00" Just SW of Sivart I). Miels R Sivart (1843–1915), a native of the Netherlands, and his US-born wife, Annie, operated a general store at Jedway in the early mining days from 1907 to 1912. Their son-in-law, Clayton Bourne, ran the Jedway sawmill, and their daughter, Bertha Gertrude Bourne, gave birth to Jedway's first baby, in 1908. Sivart died at New Westminster. *D*

Siwash Bay (50°40'00" 125°47'00" S side of Knight Inlet, W of Glendale Cove), **Siwash Cove** (49°16'00" 126°11'00" S side of Flores I, Clayoquot Sd, W side of Vancouver I), **Siwash Rock** (49°19'00" 123°09'00" N side of English Bay, just SW of First Narrows, Burrard Inlet, Vancouver), **Siwash Rock** (50°21'00" 125°28'00" S of Turn I, E end of Johnstone Str, off S side of E Thurlow I, NW of Campbell R). *Siwash* was the word for a Native or aboriginal person in the Chinook jargon used on the W coast by First Nation groups and early traders and settlers. The word was derived from the French *sauvage*, which, despite its similarity to the English word "savage," simply means "wild" or "untamed." It was originally a neutral term, synonymous with "local," but as racist attitudes persisted and grew over the years, the word became derogatory, a sign of contempt. While many other racist place names have been changed in BC, Siwash survives. In addition to the coastal names listed above, there are four Siwash creeks and three Siwash lakes in the province, plus Siwash I in the Pitt R, Siwash Point on Okanagan Lk, Siwash Mtn SW of Nelson and Siwash Rk Mtn NW of Vernon. Siwash Rk in Stanley Park was called Nine Pin Rk on early Admiralty charts, after the bowling game. The Halkomelem First Nation name for this feature is S'i'lix, while the Squamish people know it as Sl'kheylish, or "he who is standing up" (and the name of the rock may, in fact, actually be a distortion of this phrase). According to a Squamish legend with many variations, the 15-m pinnacle was once a man named Skalsh, an honest, unselfish tribal member, who was found ritually cleansing himself at this location by Q'uas the Transformer, a supernatural being, who turned Skalsh to stone as an example of how Q'uas wanted people to live. A searchlight was placed on top of the rock during WWII. Its sheer slopes were home for several months in 1966 to Russell, a mountain goat who managed to escape from Stanley Park Zoo.

Siwiti Rock (50°54'00" 127°16'00" E of Robinson I, Blunden Hbr, N side of Queen Charlotte Str, NE of Port Hardy). This feature was named by Cdr John Parry of HMS *Egeria* in 1903 while re-surveying Blunden Hbr. Siwiti was the principal chief of the Nak'waxda'xw (Nakwakto) First Nation at that time. Their main village, Ba'as, was located at Blunden Hbr. The Nak'waxda'xw moved to Port Hardy in the early 1960s.

Skaat Harbour (52°24'00" 131°26'00" W side of Burnaby Str, SE side of Moresby I, QCI). Geologist George Mercer Dawson applied this name, a modification of a Haida First Nation word meaning "good hunting place," to the harbour in 1878. *Skaat* is also the Haida word for falcon.

Skaga Island (52°41'00" 131°23'00" E of Lyell I and Moresby I, Hecate Str, QCI), **Skaga Point** (54°00'00" 132°08'00" NE side of Masset Sd, just S of Masset, N end of Graham I, QCI). Skaga is an adaptation of the Haida First Nation word for a shaman or medicine man. Because of its patchy tree coverage, geologist George Mercer Dawson gave the name Tuft I to this feature in 1878. In 1957, for unknown reasons, the hydrographic service changed the name to Skaga and applied Tuft to a nearby cluster of islets, one of which also sports a few scrubby trees.

Skaiakos Point (49°36'00" 123°49'00" W side of Sechelt Inlet, SW of mouth of Salmon Inlet, NW of Vancouver). The name refers to one of the subgroups of the Sechelt (Shíshálh) First Nation. Several versions of this word have been recorded, including Sqaiaqos and Klay-ah-kwohss, but the spelling Xíxus is preferred today. The Xíxus people traditionally occupied the coastal area between Lang Bay and Roberts Ck, with their main villages at Kálpilín (Pender Hbr) and Ch'átlich (Sechelt).

Skaloo Inlet. *See* Nesto Inlet.

Skedans Bay, Louise Island, Haida Gwaii. *Andrew Scott*

Skedans Bay (52°57'00" 131°38'00" E side of Louise I, off NE Moresby I, QCI), **Skedans Islands** (52°57'00" 131°34'00" E of Skedans Point, Hecate Str), **Skedans Point** (52°58'00" 131°36'00" E tip of Louise I, N entrance to Skedans Bay). Skedans is a corruption of Gida'nsta, the hereditary name of the head chief of this important Haida Gwaii settlement. The word means "from his daughter," which is a respectful title children use when addressing a high-ranking personage. The village itself, a Raven crest site located at Skedans Point, was named K'uuna (Koona, Q'una) or Huadji-lanas, meaning "grizzly bear town." HBC official John Work recorded 738 residents and 30 lodges there about 1840, but when geologist George Dawson visited in 1878 (and first adopted the name Skedans Bay), only 16 houses were habitable. The site was abandoned in 1888–90 when villagers moved to Haina on Maude I; in 1893, everyone went to Skidegate. Emily Carr made a

S

painting visit to Skedans in 1907, and several decaying memorial and mortuary poles still adorned this beautiful spot in the early 2000s. Skedans Point was shown as Summer Point on the 1791 map of US fur trader Joseph Ingraham. The Skedans Is first appeared on an HBC map in 1852, labelled Skedance Is. Skedans Ck, which drains into the bay, is named for the village. *D*

Skedin Islet (50°30'00" 127°50'00" N side of Koprino Hbr, Quatsino Sd, NW end of Vancouver I). August E Skedin (b 1863), a native of Sweden, was one of the original settlers who founded the Scandinavian colony of Quatsino in late 1894. He homesteaded there and received a Crown grant of land in 1901. Skedin had immigrated to BC with his wife, Erika (b 1866), and three daughters in the early 1890s; in 1896 the couple celebrated the new-world birth of their first son by naming him Vancouver. August, who was one of the colony's initial school trustees, sold most of his property to Alfred Pilling in 1911. Skedin It was formerly known as Cone It.

Skeena Banks (54°12'00" 129°55'00" In the Skeena R, E of the mouth of the Ecstall R), **Skeena River** (54°01'00" 130°07'00" Flows SW into Chatham Sd just S of Prince Rupert). The name of the river is an adaptation of the Tsimshian First Nation phrase *k'shian*, which can be translated as "water of the clouds." Joseph Whidbey, master of HMS *Discovery*, explored the mouth of the Skeena in 1793 with two of the ship's boats and reported to Capt George Vancouver that the river that flowed into the ocean there was insignificant—full of rocks,

mud flats and gigantic uprooted trees, and generally not worth investigating. "Thus," points out BC historian John Walbran, "the Skeena was overlooked much in the same way as the Fraser, from ignorance as to what the entrance of a large river would be like when deploying into the sea." Fur trader Charles Duncan of the *Princess Royal* gave the name Ayton's R to the Skeena in 1788; Simpson's R and Babine R were other early names. It did not appear on maps as the Skeena until much later and was not surveyed until the 1900s. Today, of course, the 621-km-long Skeena is known to be the second-largest river totally within BC, and its valley has become a major transportation corridor. Several inland features are also named in association with the river, including the Skeena Mtns in northern BC and Skeena Crossing near Hazelton. *E W*

Skegness (48°27'00" 123°17'00" SW entrance to Cadboro Bay, just N of Oak Bay, SE end of Vancouver I). This point is named for the English town of Skegness, which was originally a small port and fishing village located on the E coast of Lincolnshire. The arrival of a railroad in 1875, however, combined with the area's fine beaches, resulted in the site becoming a well-known resort—home to the first Butlin's holiday camp, built in 1936. The BC feature appears on local maps as early as 1913.

Skene Cove (53°51'00" 130°21'00" N of Sparrowhawk Point, SW side of Ogden Channel, SE side of Porcher I, S of Prince Rupert). After Peter Skene Ogden, an important HBC official in western N America in the early 19th century. *See* Ogden Channel.

The Skeena River, at 621 km, is the second-largest river totally within BC. *Sam Beebe/Ecotrust*

Skerry Bay (49°30'00" 124°14'00" W of Boho I, N side of Lasqueti I, Sabine Channel, Str of Georgia). *Skerry* is a Scottish Gaelic word for a reef or small rocky island. The term is still used around the Scottish coast and also in Nfld; it comes from the Old Norse *sker*, meaning a low reef in the sea. BC's Skerry Bay, a well-established local name, was adopted in 1981.

Early view of the Haida village of Skidegate. *Author's collection*

Skidegate (53°16'00" 131°59'25" SE side of Graham I, at NE entrance to Skidegate Inlet), **Skidegate Channel** (53°09'00" 132°20'00" Between S side of Graham I and N side of Moresby I, western extension of Skidegate Inlet, QCI), **Skidegate Inlet** (53°14'00" 132°00'00" Between SE Graham I and NE Moresby I, eastern extension of Skidegate Channel), **Skidegate Landing** (53°14'50" 132°00'30" Just SW of the community of Skidegate). Skidegate is a hereditary name of the head chief of this important Haida community. The word is usually translated as "red paint stone"—a reference to a type of rock found on the inlet that the Haida ground up and used as paint—but ethnographer John Swanton gave its meaning as "son of the chiton." A legend related by QCI historian Kathleen Dalzell explains the word as a corruption of the name for an exceedingly scarce sea-flower, much desired by a Haida maiden. Her suitor searched so long and hard for this rarity that he was nicknamed after the flower, but he eventually found an example and won the girl's favour. Later, after becoming chief, he adopted the name and handed it down to his successors. An early European name for the inlet was Trollope's R, given by fur trader Charles Duncan of the *Princess Royal* in 1788. Robert Gray of the *Columbia Rediviva* called it Hatches Sd, after Cromwell Hatch, one of his vessel's owners. US skipper Joseph Ingraham showed the inlet on his 1791 map as Skit-i-kiss Bay (he also gave the name Great Sd to the W entrance to Skidegate Channel). Its Haida name is Xanaa Qaahlii. In the 1850s the central portion of the channel was known as Swanson Labyrinth. Many spelling variations are recorded for Skidegate, including Skettegats, Skittagets, Skit-ei-get, Skitekat, Sge'dagits, etc.

The names for the inlet and channel were finally adopted in their current form on Admiralty charts by Lt Daniel Pender of the *Beaver* in 1866. Skidegate Landing refers to the area around the ferry terminus, formerly known as the Oil Works after Haida Gwaii's first industry, a dogfish oil plant, built in 1876. The adjacent bay had two unofficial names: Sterling Bay, after William Sterling, the refinery's co-owner, and Skidegate Hbr. Two townsite proposals—Graham City, at the landing, and Queen Charlotte City, farther W—competed for settlers; only Queen Charlotte City survived. The Haida reserve of Skidegate has been home to four different settlements over the centuries. The Eagle crest community of Hlgaiu ("place of stones"), once lined with dozens of memorial and mortuary poles, was the direct ancestor of today's village. Skidegate was known as Skidegate Mission for many years, but in 1992 the band council and United Church officials requested that "mission" be dropped. In 2007 a magnificent new museum, the Haida Heritage Centre at Kaay Llnagaay, was opened just S of the village. *D E W*

Skincuttle Inlet (52°20'00" 131°13'00" SE side of Moresby I, S of Burnaby I, QCI), **Skincuttle Island** (52°21'00" 131°14'00" In Skincuttle Inlet, SW of the Copper Is). The name is a bastardization of the Haida term for the island, said by historians Helen and Philip Akrigg to be a compound of words meaning "seagull" and "to scoop." This approximation of the name was originally applied about 1862 by early QCI mining engineer Francis Poole. Poole also attempted to mimic the Haida name for the inlet, coming up with Sockalee Hbr (for Suu Kaalhi, meaning "lake inlet"). In 1878, geologist George M Dawson gave the name Skincuttle to the inlet, and Sockalee was deleted. The US fur trader Joseph Ingraham had called the inlet Port Ucah in 1791 after an important chief in the region (also known as Ugah) who visited Robert Gray on the *Columbia Rediviva*, as well. *D*

Skinner Bluff (48°46'00" 123°36'00" N side of Cowichan Bay, W side of Genoa Bay, SE Vancouver I), **Skinner Islands** (53°06'00" 129°18'00" In Squally Channel, off SW Gil I, SE of Pitt I), **Skinner Point** (48°45'00" 123°36'00" Just S of Skinner Bluff), **Skinner Rock** (52°18'00" 128°30'00" In Milbanke Sd, W of Cecilia I, NW of Bella Bella). Thomas James Skinner (1812–89) was working for the E India Co in London when he accepted a job on Vancouver I as the bailiff or manager of one of the farms established by the Puget's Sd Agricultural Co, a subsidiary of the HBC. He and his wife, Mary Lowdham Skinner (1816–96, née Goode), arrived at Victoria in 1853 aboard the *Norman Morison* with their five children. A sixth child, Constance, was one of the first white girls born at Ft Victoria. Skinner's farm, known as Oaklands and located on Constance Cove, was a success, and Thomas became a leading citizen in the colony, winning election to Vancouver I's first legislative assembly as the representative for Esquimalt, 1855–59.

S

In 1864 he and his family moved to the Maple Bay area of the Cowichan Valley and established their own farm; Thomas acted as the region's justice of the peace and was a councillor and warden of N Cowichan district. Skinner Bluff and Skinner Point were named for him by Capt George Richards of HMS *Plumper* about 1859; Skinner Cove in Esquimalt Hbr also commemorated him before it was eliminated by the huge Dominion drydock that opened in 1927. The Skinner Is, formerly known as the Windy Is, are named for Mary Skinner (1851–1942), one of the family's five daughters, who never married and remained on the family farm with her bachelor brother, Ernest Meeson Skinner (1847–1918). Skinner Rk, formerly known as Bare Rk, is named for Mary Lowdham Skinner. Constance Lindsay Skinner, who moved to the US and enjoyed a prolific career as a novelist, playwright, poet and journalist, was a granddaughter of Thomas and Mary. *E W*

Skittagetan Lagoon (52°33'00" 131°39'00" NW of Hoskins Point, at N approach to De la Beche Inlet, E side of Moresby I, QCI). Named by the hydrographic service in 1962 for a First Nation language classification that encompassed the dialects of Haida. The word was adapted from Skittagets, a variation of Skidegate (qv), the hereditary name of an important Haida head chief. In the 1830s, linguist Albert Gallatin, who served 13 years as US treasury secretary, applied this name to the linguistic group that included those who spoke Haida. This use of the term was later also adopted by the famous geologist, anthropologist and explorer John Wesley Powell.

Surfing the standing wave at Skookumchuck Narrows. *Brian Lee*

Skookumchuck Narrows (49°44'00" 123°53'00" N end of Sechelt Inlet, SE side of Jervis Inlet, NW of

Vancouver), **Skookum Island** (49°44'00" 123°53'00" Just S of Skookumchuck Narrows). *Skookum* meant "strong" (or "big") in the Chinook jargon used on the W coast by First Nation groups and early traders and settlers. *Chuck* was the term for water. Of all the words in Chinook's disappearing vocabulary, these two, perhaps, have had the greatest staying power and are still in frequent use. They appear in numerous place names around BC: Skookum Ck, Skookum Gulch, Skookum Lk, Skookumchuck Ck, Skookumchuck Mtn, Skookumchuck Rapids (in the Shuswap R) and the two communities of Skookumchuck, one on the Lillooet R and the other on the Kootenay R. Skookum I was formerly known as Boulder I but was renamed by the hydrographic service in 1945, in association with nearby Skookumchuck Narrows. The Sechelt Rapids in the narrows can reach peak flows of 14 knots (26 km/h). The Sechelt First Nation name for the narrows is Stl'íkwu. *E*

Skudas Point (52°44'00" 131°41'00" NW end of Lyell I, Richardson Inlet, off E side of Moresby I, QCI). Named in 1957 by the hydrographic service after the Haida First Nation village of Skudas, which was located just E of the point. This settlement, whose name translates as "too late town," was an Eagle crest site led by a brother of Klue, the town chief at Tanu. It was already in ruins when visited by geologist George Mercer Dawson in 1878. *D*

Skwakadanee Point (53°28'00" 132°50'00" NW entrance to Seal Inlet, W side of Graham I, QCI). According to QCI historian Kathleen Dalzell, the word is an adaptation of the feature's Haida First Nation name, which can be translated as "point of heavy seas."

Sky Pilot Rock (50°08'00" 124°43'00" E end of Desolation Sd, NE end of Str of Georgia, E of Campbell R). Named by the hydrographic service in 1958 after the mission boat of Rev George Pringle, who was in charge of the Presbyterian Loggers' Mission on the BC coast, 1920–25, and then supervised coastal missions for the United Church. He travelled to logging camps, First Nation villages, canneries and other settlements throughout the region, first in a launch named the *Mina W* and then in the 12-m *Sky Pilot*. A creek and mountain SE of Squamish are also named Sky Pilot, but it is not known for certain whether they commemorate Pringle's vessel. *See also* Pringle Rk.

Sladden Island (53°36'00" 130°34'00" In approach to Griffin Hbr, W side of Banks I). Nelson George Sladden (1881–1969) worked as an oiler aboard the W coast federal survey vessel *Lillooet* in 1921 after returning from overseas service in WWI. He died at Victoria.

Slag Point (49°00'00" 123°48'00" W side of Ladysmith Hbr, SE of Nanaimo, SE side of Vancouver I). An alternative name for this feature in the early 1900s was

Slack Point, because the land there had been partly created out of coal slack, deposited in the vicinity when Ladysmith was an important port for the Dunsmuir collieries. "Slack," or "sleck," refers to the dust and fine screenings from a coal mine; it is undesirable as fuel as it normally contains a good deal of slate and dirt. "Slag" is more properly a byproduct of smelting and usually consists of the silicates and other unwanted dross left over after the metal has been extracted. Smelting never took place at Ladysmith, and slag has no real connection with coal mining, but the word might have been confused with slack and thus resulted in this name.

Slater Rocks (51°01'00" 127°32'00" Entrance to Allison Hbr, NW side of Queen Charlotte Str, N of Port Hardy). Arthur Slater (1876–1955), a native of the Shetland Is, served with the BC Coast Steamship Service for 40 years. He was listed as a deckhand on the *Princess Louise* in the 1901 BC census and rose in the ranks to become master of that vessel and also of the *Princess Joan* and other CPR steamships. Slater retired from the BCCSS in 1941 and died at Victoria.

Slingsby Channel (51°05'00" 127°34'00" N side of Bramham I, NW side of Queen Charlotte Str, N of Port Hardy), **Slingsby Point** (51°05'00" 127°38'00" NW side of Fox Is, Slingsby Channel), **Slingsby Rock** (51°05'00" 127°32'00" In Treadwell Bay, Slingsby Channel). Lt Daniel Pender of the *Beaver* named the channel in 1865 after Sir Charles Slingsby (1824–69), a Yorkshire nobleman who was killed crossing the river Ure while hunting with his foxhounds. The reason for this choice of name is not known. *W*

Sloman Island (49°10'00" 125°53'00" Entrance to Lemmens Inlet, Meares I, Clayoquot Sd, W side of Vancouver I). James Sloman (1863–1944), from England, immigrated with his wife, Clara (1867–1944), to the US, where their son Harold (1897–1957) was born. The family arrived in BC in 1900. James, who had worked as a policeman, soldier, sheriff and railwayman, was listed as an engineer in the 1901 BC census but soon moved to Clayoquot Sd, where he was employed by Thomas Stockham and Walter Dawley, early traders and hotelkeepers in the region. Their first store was located on Stockham I, opposite the Tla-o-qui-aht (Clayoquot) First Nation village of Opitsat and just W of Sloman I, and they went on to open two branch operations and take over the larger store on Stubbs I (Clayoquot). Sloman became manager at the trading posts at Nootka (1901–5) and Ahousat (briefly in 1903). In 1907 he formed a partnership with John McKenna and went into business for himself, buying Sing Lee's early store in Tofino and operating it until 1927. Slomans still live in the area. Sloman I is called Knocker I by local residents. The Tla-o-qui-aht people know it as Tchimiktsets and once maintained a seasonal village or campsite there in order to harvest clams on the extensive adjacent tidal flats.

Sluggett Point (48°35'00" 123°28'00" Brentwood Bay, W side of Saanich Peninsula, NW of Victoria). John (1829–1909) and Fanny Sluggett (1833–1904, née Downs), both from Devon, England, immigrated to Ont in 1855. They had seven children there, and John became a successful farmer at Elderslie. He came to BC in 1875—lured, apparently, by glowing reports of the Pacific coast—and bought about 300 ha of land beside Brentwood Bay (qv). The rest of the family travelled W the following year. John and his grown sons established another thriving farm, and in 1892 they opened a post office, named Sluggett, for the district, which John served as postmaster until 1908. Brentwood Bay was originally known as Sluggett Bay, but when the BC Electric Rwy's Saanich line was built through the area in 1913, the interurban station was named Brentwood, after the English hometown of the BCER's chairman. Sluggett post office was renamed Brentwood Bay in the 1920s, and Sluggett Bay soon followed. The original Brentwood College, which burned down in 1947 and was later rebuilt at Mill Bay, was first erected in 1923 on land donated by the Sluggett clan.

Small Inlet (50°16'00" 125°17'00" Head of Kanish Bay, NW end of Quadra I, N of Campbell R). Squadron Leader Norville Everett Small, DFC, AFC, from Vancouver, died in action Jan 7, 1943, aged 33. He was born at Allandale, Ont, and joined the RCAF in 1928, but spent much of the 1930s in commercial aviation. During WWII, Small served as a senior instructor and ferry pilot, transporting aircraft to the UK. He was credited with several successful attacks on U-boats and was the first member of Eastern Air Command to sink a submarine. Small was killed when his Canso flying boat accidentally crashed. He is buried at Gander War Cemetery in Nfld.

Smithe Point (52°20'00" 131°19'00" S tip of Burnaby I, off SE side of Moresby I, QCI). William Smithe (1842–87) was BC's premier and chief commissioner of Lands and Works in 1884, the year that Newton Chittenden was engaged to explore and report on the resources of the QCI for the provincial government. Smithe, an Englishman, came to BC in 1862 and established a farm near Cowichan Lk. He became a community leader and ran successfully as an MLA in the first legislature formed after the province joined Confederation in 1871. In 1876 he was named minister of Finance and Agriculture, and two years later took over the leadership of the opposition. Smithe was premier 1883–87, and had he not died prematurely in office, he probably would have enjoyed a brilliant political career. He managed to settle a number of bitter disputes between Vancouver I and the mainland, and between BC and Canada, while premier. He also passed some notable anti-Chinese legislation, however, and was responsible for severely limiting the size of First Nation reserves while favouring white settlers. This feature was named by the hydrographic service in 1962. *E*

Smithers Island (52°46'00" 129°04'00" Entrance to Helmcken Inlet, E side of Laredo Channel, SW side of Princess Royal I). Frederick Ramon Smithers (1923–2006) was a student draftsman in the Victoria office of the Canadian Hydrographic Service when this feature was named in 1944. He was born at Vancouver and grew up in W Vancouver, joining the CHS as a cartographer in 1940. He also worked for Boeing Aircraft in Vancouver during WWII. Smithers learned his trade under regional hydrographers Henri Parizeau, Walter Willis and Robert Young, assisting survey parties at sea as well as doing mapping work on dry land. He worked for the CHS for 38 years and served as regional chart superintendent from 1973 until he retired in 1978.

Smith Inlet (51°19'00" 127°25'00" Eastern extension of Smith Sd), **Smith Sound** (51°18'00" 127°40'00" Between Rivers Inlet and Queen Charlotte Str, SE side of Queen Charlotte Sd). Fur trader James Hanna gave the name Smith's Inlet to what is now Smith Sd in 1786, during his second expedition to the PNW. It is therefore one of the oldest European place names on the BC coast. Hanna, in fact, was the first European explorer to visit this area, though his attempts to enter Fitz Hugh Sd (which he also named) were defeated by rough weather. It is not known conclusively who Smith was, though PNW cartography expert Henry Wagner has suggested the famed British botanist Sir James Edward Smith (1759–1828). The other names that Hanna bestowed in the PNW, however, mostly honoured British merchants in Asia, colleagues of his employers. Smith, a friend of Joseph Banks, bought the collection of Swedish natural historian Carolus Linnaeus and founded the Linnean Society at London. He wrote extensively about botany and, to a lesser extent, entomology, and his books include the four-volume *English Flora* and the profusely illustrated, 36-volume *English Botany*. Smith Inlet is the traditional territory of the Gwa'sala people, who form the most northerly branch of the Kwakwaka'wakw First Nation. The inlet was an important sockeye salmon producer, especially in the 1920s, and the site of four canneries. *E*

Smith Island (54°09'00" 130°14'00" Just W of mouth of the Skeena R, S of Prince Rupert). British civil engineer Marcus Smith (1815–1904) had worked in England, Wales and S Africa before coming to Canada to join the staff of the Intercolonial Rwy. In 1872 he was appointed chief resident assistant in BC to Sandford Fleming, the CPR's chief engineer, in charge of surveying potential routes through the mountains to the coast. He came to favour a northern line for the railroad, through Pine Pass, along Bute Inlet and down Vancouver I to Victoria. Fleming, needless to say, preferred another route. Smith, notorious for his bristly, cantankerous personality, later oversaw the construction of the railway between Port Moody and just S of Yale. From 1886 to 1892 he served as a consulting

engineer to the federal government. He died at Ottawa. Smith I, formerly known as McGrath I, was named by CPR survey officials about 1880, five years after the eminent engineer had travelled through the area on the HBC steamer *Otter*, en route from Port Essington to Metlakatla. Nearby Marcus Passage is also named for Smith, as is Mt Marcus N of Bute Inlet. His son Arthur Gordon Smith (1865–1944), a lawyer, became a civil servant in BC, holding a number of senior positions, including that of deputy attorney gen. *W*

Smith Point (53°15'00" 132°03'00" N side of Bearskin Bay, Skidegate Inlet, SE side of Graham I, QCI). Salvation Army officer Thomas N Smith was raised in eastern Canada and sent to work in Alaska during the Klondike era. His girlfriend, Jessie Randall, joined him, and the pair were married at Wrangell before moving to Port Simpson to take charge of the Salvation Army corps there. The Smiths and their two sons arrived in the QCI in 1910. They lived at Sandspit and then at Queen Charlotte City, homesteading and taking on a variety of jobs. Tom even worked on the survey vessel *Lillooet* for several months as an oiler, which is probably why this feature was named for him. In 1924 the family moved away from the QCI so their older children could go to high school. *D*

Smith Rock (50°48'00" 126°25'00" SW side of Tribune Channel, off NW Gilford I, NE of Port McNeill). Ordinary Seaman William Roy Smith, an RCNVR member from Vancouver, was killed in action Nov 24, 1944, aged 19, while serving aboard HMCS *Shawinigan*. The corvette was on patrol duty in Cabot Str when it was torpedoed and sunk by a U-boat. All 91 crew members died. Smith is commemorated on the Halifax Memorial.

Smokehouse Bay (48°34'00" 123°29'00" SW of Willis Point, SE side of Saanich Inlet, NW of Victoria). Former landowner Samuel Whittaker, who lived on the bay for three decades (*see* Whittaker Point), smoked fish there. The bay was apparently also known at one time as Whittaker Bay. The local name for the beach is Ricky's Roost, after another former property owner in the area, a man named Rickerson, whose beach parties were well regarded.

Smuggler Cove (49°31'00" 123°58'00" W side of Sechelt Peninsula, NW of Halfmoon Bay, Welcome Passage, NW of Vancouver). An interpretive sign at this picturesque little provincial marine park claims that the notorious Larry Kelly, famed for smuggling Chinese immigrants to the US, used this hideaway to load his human cargoes. Kelly attached chains and iron weights to his clients, who paid $100 each for this indignity, and threatened to toss them overboard at the first sign of trouble. Or so the story goes. In truth, it is far more likely that the cove got its name from the liquor trade, which really *was* a profitable business during the US Prohibition era—when a 50-cent

Smuggler Cove on Sechelt Peninsula. *Peter Vassilopoulos*

bottle in Vancouver might be worth $12 in Seattle. And if you were making the liquor yourself, and thus paying no taxes, the cost dropped even further. The largest illegal distillery on the BC coast, which produced thousands of litres of bootleg liquor a month until discovered and shut down by the RCMP, was at Pocahontas Bay on Texada Island. Smuggler Cove, with its narrow, hard-to-detect entrance and secluded bays, was the apparent staging area for this substantial enterprise. There is also a Smugglers Cove on Bowen I and one in Barkley Sd. Their histories, however, are unknown.

Smugglers Nook (48°44'00" 123°14'00" SE end of N Pender I, Gulf Is). The Gulf Is that bordered Boundary Pass, especially Saturna and the Penders, were often used by smugglers. The traffic was mostly N to S, and the contraband consisted at first of wool, from the area's flourishing sheep ranches, and opium, brought into Victoria on liners and other large vessels from Asia. These goods would be traded for groceries, which were generally cheaper in the US, and cash. Chinese labourers were also smuggled across Boundary Pass to circumvent restrictive US immigration laws. During the US Prohibition era (1920–33), liquor smuggling in the area became a big business, and violence was not uncommon. Secluded coves such as Smugglers Nook were favoured as rendezvous and stash points, where booze could be transferred from larger boats to small "runners," which took it across the border.

Smyth Head (48°19'00" 123°36'00" E side of Becher Bay, SE of Fraser I, S tip of Vancouver I). Capt William Henry Smyth (1788–1865) was a well-known RN surveying officer, astronomer and writer on scientific topics. He entered the service of the E India Co as a youth, joined the RN in 1805 and saw action off China, India and Australia. Smyth began survey work, as a lt, in the Mediterranean and completed charting Sicily with HMS *Aid* in 1817. As cdr of HMS *Adventure*, he conducted a number of significant Mediterranean surveys between 1821 and 1824 and was promoted to capt. Smyth spent the rest of his

life in literary and scientific pursuits, establishing a large private observatory at Bedford, England, from which he studied deep sky objects. He published several books on astronomy, including a survey of double stars and nebulae (known as the *Bedford Catalogue*) that became a standard reference for many years, and was elected president of the Royal Astronomical Society. Smyth, who reached the rank of adm, retired, in 1863, also wrote, edited and translated works about history and travel, including *The Sailor's Word-Book*. Smyth Head was named by Capt Henry Kellett of HMS *Herald* on his 1846 survey of the S Vancouver I region. *W*

Smyth Passage (54°05'00" 132°31'00" Between Alexandra Narrows and Virago Sd, N side of Graham I, QCI). Named in 1907 by Capt Frederick Learmonth of HMS *Egeria* after one of his officers, Lt Sydney Keith Smyth. Smyth, who assisted Learmonth with a re-survey of the Virago Sd area that year, went on to attain the rank of capt and commanded the light cruiser *Enterprise* and armed merchant cruiser *Scotstoun* in WWII. He was the son of an earlier cdr of the *Egeria* on the BC coast; Capt Morris Henry Smyth (1853–1940) had brought the survey vessel out to BC from England in 1898 to continue the work left off by Cdr Daniel Pender in 1871. He served as its cdr until relieved in 1900 and eventually became a vice adm. It is probable that **Smyth Island** (53°40'00" 132°28'00" SW side of Masset Inlet, Graham I) is also named after either Lt Smyth or his father.

Snake Island (49°13'00" 123°53'00" Between Rainbow Channel and Fairway Channel, NW of Gabriola I, Gulf Is). Cdr John Parry of HMS *Egeria* named this feature while re-surveying the Nanaimo area in 1904. Its previous name, given by Admiralty hydrographers about 1860, was Lighthouse I. There is a light beacon on Snake I, but the lighthouse for Nanaimo Hbr, established in 1875, was built on nearby Entrance I instead. Snake I, which is narrow and elongated, and thus vaguely snake-like, is also apparently home to large numbers of garter snakes. Two RCN vessels, the *Saskatchewan* and the *Cape Breton*, were sunk off Snake I in 1997 and 2001, respectively, to create artificial reefs for divers.

Snass Islands (53°53'00" 130°32'00" Near entrance to Porcher Inlet, S side of Porcher I, S of Prince Rupert), **Snass Point** (53°54'00" 130°33'00" Just W of Snass Is, opposite Gurd I). *Snass* was the word for rain or wet in the Chinook jargon used on the W coast by First Nation groups and early traders and settlers. BC, appropriately, is also home to a Snass Ck, Snass Lk and Snass Mtn.

Sneath Islands (53°32'00" 130°32'00" SE of Solander Point, off NW end of Banks I). George Sneath was a lay preacher and missionary to the Haida, 1879–1882. He had originally been sent from England by the Church Missionary Society

S

to its E African mission, but his health broke down and he was forced to return. He was posted instead to Metlakatla on the N BC coast and then replaced William Collison as the Anglican missionary at Masset. In 1882, Sneath left BC to join a Presbyterian mission in Washington state, but he died that year when he accidentally choked on a powdered medicine.

Snider Islet (54°16'00" 130°26'00" Off W side of Digby I, Chatham Sd, just W of Prince Rupert), **Snider Rock** (54°15'00" 130°26'00" Just S of Snider It). Named after Jacob Snider (1811–66), a US inventor from Georgia who patented a method for converting muzzle-loading rifles into breech-loading models. The Snider-Enfield rifle was widely used by British forces throughout the Empire in the 1860s and '70s. Snider died in Britain in poverty while trying to receive the government compensation he had been promised. The hydrographic service, for reasons unknown, named several features in this vicinity after the inventors of rifles.

Snowden Island (49°02'00" 125°20'00" Toquart Bay, N side of Barkley Sd, W side of Vancouver I). Northing Pinckney Snowden (c 1859–1904) acquired a Crown land grant NW of Toquart Bay in 1892. This was presumably for investment purposes, as he seems an unlikely homesteader. Six years earlier, for instance, in 1886, he had married Emily Ellen Dunsmuir (1864–1944), a daughter of industrialist Robert Dunsmuir, BC's wealthiest man. Ashnola, a palatial Jacobean mansion on Gorge Rd (later called Sissinghurst and now Gorge Rd Hospital), was built as a wedding present for the fortunate couple. Snowden, who was listed in the 1891 BC census as a real-estate agent, died in England. Emily remarried later that same year, at Victoria, and went with her wealthy new husband, Henry Randall Burroughes (b 1863) of Burlingham Hall, Norfolk, to live in England. Snowden I was formerly known as Image I but was renamed by the hydrographic service in 1934. N P Snowden is also listed as receiving a Crown grant in the Sayward land district in 1892, and there is a Snowdon Ck (sic) N of Campbell R.

Snug Cove (49°23'00" 123°20'00" E side of Bowen I, S of Mannion Bay, Howe Sd, NW of Vancouver). This name, obviously descriptive of a cozy anchorage, was originally applied by Admiralty surveyor Capt George Richards in 1860. Capt Jack Cates established his Terminal Resort there in the early 1900s and then sold out in 1920 to the Union Steamship Co, which greatly expanded and developed the estate as a holiday destination for picnickers and vacationers. The resort's steamship wharf was located on Snug Cove, along with a store, a number of rental cottages and extensive picnicking grounds, while a hotel and tennis courts were on adjacent Mannion Bay (then called Deep Cove); in between were more picnic areas, a dance bowl and a tea room. Union general manager Harold Brown

Snug Cove on Bowen Island. *John Lund*

suggested in 1929 that Snug Cove be renamed Wharf Cove, and the hydrographic service adopted this change in 1937. Islanders raised such a fuss, however, that the original name was reinstated in 1949. Today the cove is the site of a marina and Bowen I's BC Ferries terminus.

Soames Point (49°25'00" 123°29'00" W side of Howe Sd, NE of Gibsons, NW of Vancouver). George Soames (1832–1914), from England, was the first settler at this location, in 1888. He and his wife, Mary Ellen (1849–1926), also from England, and their children homesteaded there and received a Crown grant in 1890. A younger brother, William Soames, settled on the adjacent property and received his Crown grant in 1907. George, who was listed as a rancher in the 1901 BC census, loaded scows with gravel from his beach and had them shipped to Vancouver for road construction. Nearby Soames Ck and Soames Hill are also named for him.

Soar Point (54°11'00" 130°16'00" N entrance to Inverness Passage, N end of Smith I, S of Prince Rupert), **Soar Rock** (52°31'00" 129°02'00" In Weeteeam Bay, SW side of Aristazabal I). Lance Cpl Henry Soar (1832–89) was a member of the Columbia detachment of the Royal Engineers, which served in BC 1858–63. He remained in BC after the detachment disbanded, received a military land grant and worked as a saddler and harness maker in Victoria, 1876–87. Henry Soar also received a Crown grant for land in the Inverness Passage vicinity in 1871. He was a good musician apparently, a member of the Victoria Volunteers band, led by fellow Royal Engineer William Haynes, which welcomed the first transcontinental train at Port Moody in 1886. Soar was secretary of Victoria's volunteer fire dept for many years. Soar Point was formerly known as Tree Point. Both features were named about 1926.

Sobry Island (50°01'00" 127°23'00" N of Kamils I, N side of Kyuquot Sd, NW side of Vancouver I). Named in 1947 after Rev Emile Sobry (1861–1943), a Roman Catholic missionary who was in charge of the mission and day school at Kyuquot, 1897–1911. From 1911 to 1920 he was the teacher and missionary at Yuquot in Nootka Sd. Sobry died at Victoria.

Sockeye Point (49°41'00" 123°50'00" S entrance to Narrows Inlet, E side of Sechelt Inlet, NW of Vancouver). The origins of this First Nation word are difficult to pin down, as many different Salishan languages and dialects have a word for this treasured species of salmon (*Oncorhynchus nerka*). The term probably comes from the Halkomelem language spoken by the central Coast Salish people of the Lower Mainland and S Vancouver I and may refer to "the fish of fish," or "finest species of salmon." Recorded spelling variations include *soukai*, *sukkai*, *sthéqi* and *tsésqey*. The word *scaqay* for sockeye is found in the Twana and Puget Salish languages farther S, while the Sechelt (Shíshálh) people, just to the N, use the word *stsékay*. Sockeye Peak, N of Knight Inlet, is so named because it is "a big lens of salmon-coloured rock, fish-shaped too," according to mountaineer Don Munday. BC also has two creeks and a railway station named Sockeye.

Early postcard view of the Finnish village of Sointula on Malcolm Island. *Harbour Publishing collection*

Sointula (50°38'00" 127°01'00" S side of Malcolm I, E side of Rough Bay, Broughton Str, SE Queen Charlotte Str). A group of Finnish settlers, led by journalist Matti Kurikka, formed a socialist utopian colony here in 1901 and received Malcolm I as a land grant from the provincial government. They named their settlement Sointula, which is the Finnish word for harmony. About 2,000 people joined (and left) the commune before it disintegrated in 1905. About half the original colonists, however, remained on the island and pre-empted land. They built homesteads, farmed, logged and developed a very active commercial fishery. The community of Sointula today, while no longer utopian, still has a distinctly Finnish atmosphere and a flourishing population of about 700. It is connected by ferry to Port McNeill. *E*

Solander Island (50°07'00" 127°56'00" Off NW end of Brooks Peninsula, NW side of Vancouver I), **Solander Point** (53°33'00" 130°33'00" NW of Kingkown Inlet, NW side of Banks I). Daniel Carlsson Solander (1733–82)

Solander Island off Brooks Peninsula. *Peter A. Robson*

was a Swedish botanist and student of Carolus Linnaeus who came to England in 1760 and worked at the British Museum as an assistant librarian. He accompanied naturalist Joseph Banks on Capt James Cook's first voyage of discovery, 1768–71, on HMS *Endeavour* and made an important collection of Australian plants. After returning to England, Solander worked for Banks as a secretary and librarian, and travelled with his employer to Iceland and the Faroe and Orkney islands in 1772. The following year he was appointed keeper of printed books and keeper of the natural history dept at the British Museum. Many plant species are named in his honour, as are the Solander Is off NZ. BC's Solander I, which is an 8-ha ecological reserve and important breeding site for seabirds, was originally named Solander Rk in 1860 by Capt George Richards of the survey vessel *Plumper*. Early fur trader George Dixon called this feature Split Rk in 1786. *W*

Solide Islands (53°42'00" 132°59'00" In the approach to Port Louis, W side of Graham I, QCI), **Solide Passage** (54°11'00" 132°59'00" Between Langara I and Lucy I, off NW end of Graham I). *La Solide*, a well-equipped, 275-tonne vessel built by the wealthy House of Baux in Marseilles, made a voyage around the world in 1790–92, under Capt Etienne Marchand, in search of scientific knowledge and commercial opportunity. It anchored at Cloak Bay for several weeks in 1791, and its officers made the earliest charts of the NW coast of Graham I. The passage was named by Capt Frederick Learmonth of HMS *Egeria* during a 1907 hydrographic survey. *See also* Chanal Point *and* Marchand Point. *D*

Somass River (49°14'47" 124°49'12" Flows SE and S into the head of Alberni Inlet, central Vancouver I). This Nuu-chah-nulth name is usually translated as "flowing down"—a reference to the river's current. In 2003 the Nuu-chah-nulth newspaper *Ha-Shilth-Sa* gave the translation "washing" for *somass* or *tsu-ma-uss*. The natural resources of the river and its estuary have long been of vital importance to such Nuu-chah-nulth groups as the Opetchesaht and Tseshaht First Nations. The name appears on an Admiralty chart published in 1863. *E*

Sombrio Point (48°29'00" 124°17'00" SE of Port San Juan, N side of Juan de Fuca Str, SW end of Vancouver I). Named by the hydrographic service in 1934 after the Sombrio R, which enters Juan de Fuca Str just NW of this point. The Rio Sombrio, or "shady river" in Spanish, was in turn named by one of the early Spanish naval officers in the area—either Manuel Quimper, who made the first European survey of Juan de Fuca Str in 1790 with the *Princesa Real* (the captured British fur-trading vessel *Princess Royal*), or José Narváez, who explored the entrance to the strait the year before. Prior to 1934 this feature was apparently known as Mondofía Point, after Estéban Mondofía, 1st pilot of the *Princesa Real*. Mondofía, who understood Russian, also made two voyages to Alaska: with Estéban Martínez in 1788 and Salvador Fidalgo in 1790. (PNW cartography expert Henry Wagner locates the original Punta de Mondofía, named by Narváez in 1789, at the W entrance to Hesquiat Hbr.)

Somerville Bay (54°47'00" 130°13'00" N side of Somerville I), **Somerville Island** (54°44'00" 130°17'00" Between Steamer Passage and Portland Inlet, NW end of Khutzeymateen Inlet, N of Prince Rupert). Lt Daniel Pender, while surveying in the area in 1868 with the *Beaver*, named the island after Mary Somerville, the mother of the Cunningham brothers, Robert and John, who became prominent residents of the N coast. Mary, from the N of England, married George Cunningham, a native of Ireland. Her older son, Robert (*see* Cunningham Passage), came to Metlakatla as a missionary in 1862 but ended up as a successful merchant and entrepreneur at Port Essington. John, the younger brother, operated a store at Metlakatla until 1901 and then opened a new store and the Queen's Hotel at Port Essington.

Songhees Point (48°26'00" 123°22'00" N side of Inner Hbr, Victoria Hbr, SE end of Vancouver I). The Songhees people, a Northern Straits First Nation, live at the S end of Vancouver I in the Victoria area. They and the Kosapsom or Esquimalt people are jointly known as the Lekwammen or Lekwungen. Many versions of the name have been recorded, including Songish, Songhies and Songees. Several Songhees villages were located in the central Victoria area before Ft Victoria was built in 1843: at James Bay, near Beacon Hill and where the legislative buildings stand today. Many tribe members congregated around the fort at first but then moved across the harbour to a site in Victoria West known for years as Old Songhees Village. In 1911 they were persuaded by Victoria's white settlers to move to their current reserve near View Royal. According to the Songhees First Nation website, the name derives from the Stsanges people, who lived at Stsangal, a small bay on the N side of Albert Head. BC historians Helen

and Philip Akrigg have speculated that Songhees may be an adaptation of a word meaning "people gathered from scattered places." Songhees Point appears on Capt Henry Kellett's Admiralty chart published in 1847. *E W*

Sonora Island (50°22'00" 125°15'00" N of Quadra I and Campbell R, SE of E Thurlow I), **Sonora Point** (50°26'00" 125°19'00" NW end of Sonora I). Sonora I, Maurelle I and Quadra I were all considered by early explorers to be part of one large feature, originally known as Valdes (or Valdez) I, and did not receive their current names until 1903. When it was realized, in the 1870s, that there were three islands, they were called the Valdes Is or Valdes Group. Sonora I was named after the Spanish naval vessel *Sonora*, which made a historic voyage along the PNW coast under the command of Francisco de la Bodega y Quadra (*see* Bodega Anchorage). The *Sonora* was a tiny schooner, only 11 m in length, with a crew of 14, built at San Blas, Mexico, about 1767. It accompanied the larger *Santiago*, under Bruno de Hezeta, in 1775 to investigate Russian activity in Alaska. The ships were separated and Hezeta only reached Vancouver I, but Quadra and the *Sonora* went farther N than any Spanish expedition had been before, to the approximate latitude of Glacier Bay in Alaska. The 145-sq-km island, bound on three sides by some of the fiercest tidal rapids in BC, has seen little settlement but plenty of logging over the years. Owen Bay (qv) on the SE shore and Thurston Bay (qv) on the W side were the only settlements; Owen Bay, with a store, school and sawmill, was active from the 1920s to the '60s, while Thurston Bay, now a provincial marine park, was HQ for the BC Forest Service's marine dept, 1911–41. *E W*

Sooke (48°22'30" 123°43'30" W side of Sooke Hbr, S end of Vancouver I, SW of Victoria), **Sooke Basin** (48°22'45" 123°39'30" E of Sooke Hbr), **Sooke Bay** (48°22'00" 123°46'00" W side of Sooke Hbr), **Sooke Harbour** (48°22'00" 123°43'00" Between Sooke Inlet and Sooke Basin), **Sooke Inlet** (48°21'00" 123°43'00" Entrance to Sooke Hbr), **Sooke River** (48°23'00" 123°42'00" Flows S into Sooke Hbr). The inlet was named in 1846 after the region's First Nation inhabitants by Capt Henry Kellett of HMS *Herald*, who made an early survey of the S end of Vancouver I. The name of the Sooke people was originally pronounced *soak* and was spelled Soke or Soake by the area's pioneers; many other spellings have also been recorded, including Sàòk, Sock, Sok and Tsohke. The preferred form today is T'sou-ke. The word supposedly derives from the name of a stickleback fish that was found at the mouth of the Sooke R. Spanish naval officer Manuel Quimper, who was the first European to explore the area, in 1790, called the inlet Puerto de Revillagigedo, after Juan Vicente de Güemes Padilla Horcasitas y Aguayo, 2nd Count of Revillagigedo and viceroy of New Spain, 1789–94. Sooke Lk and the Sooke Hills are named after the river. Sooke was one of the first areas in BC to be settled

Sooke Harbour on south end of Vancouver Island. *Peter Vassilopoulos*

by Europeans, in 1849. It was the site of the province's earliest steam-powered sawmill. By 2009 the municipality of Sooke had a population of about 12,000 people. *E W*

Sophia Islands (50°32'00" 126°38'00" S of W end of W Cracroft I, Johnstone Str). After Sophia Cracroft, niece of Sir John Franklin. *See* Cracroft Inlet.

Soquel Bank (48°41'00" 125°15'00" W of Pachena Point, S of Barkley Sd, off W side of Vancouver I). Named after the four-masted US schooner *Soquel*, under Capt Charles Henningsen, which was wrecked on nearby Seabird Rks in Jan 1909, en route from Peru to Port Townsend. The Bamfield lifeboat station was notified, but its motorized vessel had been badly damaged just two weeks previously; instead, an oar-powered boat had to be brought to the scene on the steamship *Leebro*. William Gillen and the lifeboat crew managed, at great risk, to pluck the crew of the schooner from a reef, but the capt's wife and child, tragically, had been killed earlier when a broken mast fell on them. The CPR steamer *Tees* and US revenue cutter *Manning* also assisted in the rescue. The 60-m, 700-tonne *Soquel*, built at San Francisco in 1902, was a total loss.

Sorenson Point (50°34'00" 127°34'00" NW entrance to Quatsino Narrows, Holberg Inlet, NW Vancouver I). According to BC's Geographical Names Office, the point was named for Valdemar Axel Sorenson, who pre-empted land at the mouth of the San Josef R in 1903 and received a Crown grant there in 1913 (his name is spelled Sorensen on the land office documents). Two other Scandinavian pioneers named Sorenson were active in Quatsino Sd, however; both were from Norway. Gunder Sorenson (1864–1921), one of the original colonists in the Bella Coola valley in 1894, joined Quatsino's Scandinavian community several years later. Tobias ("Tom") Sorenson (1869–1946) came to Quatsino in 1898 from Minnesota. They both settled on Hecate Cove. Gunder farmed, served as a school trustee and was a keen prospector, co-owner of numerous claims in the region. Tobias was the provincial

police constable for Quatsino. He sold part of his property in 1912 and moved back to the US, but returned to live and work at the Benson Lk Coast Copper Mine, E of Port Alice. In 1935, Tobias, his wife, Garnette, and their seven children established a homestead opposite Port Alice, on the W side of Neroutsos Inlet, and raised pigs. Nearby Sorenson Ck is named after the family. Sorenson Point was formerly known as Phillip Point.

Soulsby Cove (52°24'00" 131°33'00" S side of Gowgaia Bay, W side of Moresby I, QCI), **Soulsby Point** (52°01'00" 128°11'00" SE side of Campbell I, S of Bella Bella). Cdr Henry Wickens Stephens Soulsby (1896–1971) was born at Toronto but raised in England. He returned to Canada in 1912, graduated from the Royal Canadian Naval College and spent WWI as a junior officer on RN destroyers. In 1920 he and Gladys Emily Cunningham (1895–1987), from Halifax, were married in England. In the early 1920s, Soulsby worked for the RN as a hydrographer off the E coast of Britain and at Bermuda before being recalled to the RCN for service at Halifax, Ottawa and Esquimalt. On the W coast he had command of several minesweepers, including HMCS *Armentières*, in which he covered more than 65,000 km, patrolling and surveying. He was based at Esquimalt in WWII as assistant to the naval officer in charge and cdr of the dockyard. He was also sent to the Aleutian Is as naval observer during the recapture of Kiska. Soulsby retired in 1944 and devoted himself to wood carving and watercolour painting, two skills he excelled at. Soulsby Point was named by the hydrographic service in 1935 after the *Armentières* and its cdr anchored there on a special mission for the Dept of National Defence. Nearby Commander Point is also named for him. A WWII RCAF outpost was built near Soulsby Cove to watch for Japanese warships. The men who staffed the cabin had an excellent camping holiday during the war but never saw anything worth reporting. *D*

South Bedford Island. *See* Pim Head.

South Bentinck Arm. *See* Bentinck Narrows.

Southey Bay (48°56'00" 123°36'00" N end of Saltspring I, Gulf Is), **Southey Island** (49°17'00" 124°06'00" NE of Nanoose Hbr and Wallis Point, NW of Nanaimo, off E side of Vancouver I), **Southey Point** (48°57'00" 123°36'00" N tip of Saltspring I). James Lowther Southey (d 1882) was secretary to Rear Adm Robert Baynes, who was cdr-in-chief on the Pacific Station, 1857–60, with HMS *Ganges* as his flagship. Southey reached the rank of chief paymaster in 1881. The island and point were named in 1859 by Capt George Richards of the RN survey vessel *Plumper*. The Secretary Is off Southey Point also commemorate him.

Southgate Group (51°00'00" 127°32'00" S of Bramham I, NW side of Queen Charlotte Str, N of Port Hardy),

S

Southgate Island (51°01'00" 127°32'00" Part of the Southgate Group), **Southgate River** (50°53'11" 124°47'16" Flows SW and W into Waddington Hbr, head of Bute Inlet). James Johnson Southgate (d 1894) was a British master mariner who came, via San Francisco, to Victoria in 1858 and set himself up in business as a chandler and general merchant. He had success supplying goods to the RN, built two of Victoria's earliest commercial brick buildings and became a prominent citizen. Southgate was Saltspring district's elected representative to the Vancouver I legislative assembly, 1860–63, and also served as the representative from Esquimalt, 1864–65. RN officer and nobleman Douglas Lascelles was his partner in a number of real-estate investments. In 1865 he sold his firm, J J Southgate & Co, to the Lowe brothers (*see* Lowe Inlet) and retired to England, though he returned to BC on a number of occasions, sometimes for prolonged periods. The Southgate R was named in 1862 by Capt George Richards of the RN survey ship *Hecate*, the Southgate Group by Lt Daniel Pender of the *Beaver* in 1864. Southgate Glacier and Southgate Peak take their names from the nearby river. *W*

South Kinahan Island. *See* Kinahan Is.

South Pender Island showing Bedwell Harbour and the marina at Poets Cove Resort. *Kevin Oke*

South Pender Island (48°45'00" 123°13'00" One of the main Gulf Is). Named after RN hydrographer Daniel Pender; *see* Pender Canal for biographical details. N and S Pender islands were once connected by a narrow neck (called Indian Portage), and the combined land mass was known as Pender I. A canal was cut in 1903 (though a reconnecting bridge was not built until 1955). S Pender, which at 9 sq km is much smaller than N Pender, has always been less populous. In 1863, in the days before settlement, it was the site of a notorious murder when two men, camped at Bedwell Hbr while on a hunting trip, were shot in their tent. One died. Three Cowichan (Quw'utsun') First Nation men were later hanged for the crime. The island developed later than its neighbours because all the useful land was at first owned by one man, former HBC official John Tod, who acquired 450 ha of property there in the 1860s. His son John Tod and son-in-law John Bowker raised sheep on S Pender but lived at Oak Bay. The Tod lands were sold to James Alexander in 1879, and 330 ha passed to Arthur Spalding in 1886; Spaldings have lived on the Penders ever since. By 2009 much of quiet, rural S Pender was part of the Gulf Is National Park Reserve, while a luxurious resort named Poets Cove dominated Bedwell Hbr. *E*

South Thormanby Island. *See* Thormanby Is.

Spakels Point (54°43'00" 130°13'00" E side of Somerville I, Steamer Passage, near NW end of Khutzeymateen Inlet, N of Prince Rupert). According to William Flewin, a pioneer resident of Port Simpson, this name is a Tsimshian First Nation word meaning "to eat mussels." At one time, apparently, a number of Tsimshian people died from eating tainted mussels gathered at this location, which is the site of a Tsimshian reserve.

Spaniel Point (52°31'00" 128°16'00" SE entrance to Jackson Passage, Susan I, Mathieson Channel, N of Bella Bella). Named for a small dog that jumped from a Klemtu-bound fish packer in the middle of the night and was gallantly rescued by the crew of the hydrographic survey vessel *Parry*. Nearby Rescue Bay also takes its name from this event.

Map from the 1792 expedition of Spanish explorer Dionisio Alcalá-Galiano. *From Relacíon/Historical Atlas of BC*

Spanish Bank (49°17'00" 123°13'00" SW side of Burrard Inlet at Vancouver, just W of English Bay). This is where Capt George Vancouver, much to his surprise, encountered the Spanish naval vessels *Sutil* and *Mexicana*, under Dionisio Alcalá-Galiano and Cayetano Valdés, in June 1792. Vancouver was returning from a long surveying expedition to Jervis Inlet in HMS *Discovery*'s launch and yawl, his own vessels being anchored farther S, at Birch Bay. The Spanish officers had also been sent to survey the PNW coast. They gave Vancouver a warm welcome, exchanged information, fed him "a very hearty breakfast" and, several days later, travelled N with him along the mainland coast. Spanish Bank was so designated by Capt George Richards of the RN survey vessel *Plumper* in 1859. It is known locally as Spanish Banks. The name English Bay also pays tribute to this historic meeting.

Spanish Pilot Group (49°38'00" 126°35'00" SW of Bligh I, Nootka Sd, W side of Vancouver I). A pilot was an NCO rank in the 18th-century Spanish navy that roughly corresponded with the RN rank of master. Pilots were often highly trained and more than capable of running a ship and handling navigation and survey duties. Various pilots accompanied the early Spanish expeditions to the PNW, and regional hydrographer Henri Parizeau proposed, in 1934, to commemorate six of them—Juan Carrasco, José Narváez, Juan Pantoja, Secundino Salamanca, José Verdia and Juan Vernaci—with this group of islands. Parizeau also suggested many other new names for the Nootka Sd region, causing a controversy in his dept, as some of his superiors and the local MP did not want to see wholesale changes. As a result, only four of the individual names were approved, along with the archipelago or group name. Salamanca and Carrasco were rejected, and two original names, Clotchman I and Spouter I, left unaltered. Salamanca is honoured elsewhere on the coast (*see* Salamanca Point), but Carrasco, who sailed with both Manuel Quimper in 1790 and José Narváez in 1791 on their historic surveys of Juan de Fuca and Georgia straits—and who was the first European to explore the entrance to Puget Sd—remains uncommemorated. *See also* Narvaez Bay, Pantoja Is, Verdia I and Vernaci I.

Sparrowhawk Point (53°49'00" 130°20'00" SE side of Porcher I, Ogden Channel, S of Prince Rupert), **Sparrowhawk Rock** (54°31'00" 130°28'00" Off S end of Finlayson I, Chatham Sd, SW of Port Simpson, NW of Prince Rupert). HMS *Sparrowhawk*, a steam-powered gunboat launched in 1856, saw service on the China Station before being based on the BC coast, 1865–68 under Cdr Edwin Porcher, and 1868–72 under Cdr Henry Mist. The 613-tonne, 4-gun vessel struck the rock named for it in 1866 but survived the collision. The ship's officers were called to defuse an escalating feud between members of the Tsimshian and Nisga'a First Nations in 1868 and 1869. After Frederick Seymour, gov of the colony of BC,

had more or less settled the dispute and was returning to Victoria on the *Sparrowhawk*, he died of a sudden illness aboard ship at Bella Coola. Cdr Mist also investigated the 1869 wreck of the US barque *John Bright* near Estevan Point and the alleged massacre of the survivors by local Hesquiaht First Nation residents (*see* Hesquiat *and* Mist Bluff). The *Sparrowhawk* was sold in 1872 to an Oregon company for $20,000, with Sewell Moody buying its engines for $5,000 for his Moodyville sawmil. In its new role as a cargo vessel, the *Sparrowhawk* made several voyages to China with lumber but was eventually lost in a storm off the China coast. *W*

Speaker Rock (50°24'00" 125°51'00" E of Helmcken I, Johnstone Str). After Dr John Sebastian Helmcken, who was speaker of Vancouver I's legislative assembly at the time the rock was named, by Lt Daniel Pender, in 1863. *See* Helmcken Inlet.

Spearer Point (53°12'00" 130°01'00" SW side of Banks I, between Grief Point and Terror Point). Thomas Spearer (born c 1764), from Liverpool, was a quartermaster aboard HMS *Discovery* on Capt George Vancouver's historic expedition to the PNW, 1791–95.

Spencer Bank (52°46'00" 129°38'00" SW of Rennison I and NW end of Aristazabal I, entrance to Caamaño Sd). Pioneer Victoria merchant David Spencer (1837–1920) immigrated to Victoria from Wales in 1863 and became a bookseller, then entered the dry goods business. He was a staunch Methodist—a temperance activist and lay preacher. In 1873 he established a dept store, David Spencer Ltd, on Government St and became very successful, expanding to Nanaimo in 1890 and Vancouver in 1906. David Spencer stores, known for their imported British goods, also sprang up in smaller BC towns. The retail chain was operated by Spencer's sons after his death and sold to Eaton's in 1948. *E*

Spencer Cove (50°30'04" 127°52'34" N side of Koprino Hbr, Quatsino Sd, NW end of Vancouver I). Stephen Allen Spencer (1829–1911) received a Crown grant for land in this vicinity in 1884. He was born in Connecticut but came W about 1858 and sought gold in the Cariboo before settling at Victoria, where he operated a photographic studio (Oregon Hastings was his partner for several years). He also took many of the earliest photographs in the QCI and Barkerville. Spencer moved to Alert Bay in the early 1880s, opened a general store and, with Thomas Earle, established the Alert Bay Canning Co. He later bought Earle out and managed the cannery until 1902, when he sold to BC Packers and retired to Victoria. When he was almost 60, Spencer married a much younger Annie Hunt (1856–1924) from Ft Rupert; together they raised five sons. Spencer Cove was formerly known as Duck Cove but was renamed by regional hydrographer Henri Parizeau in 1927.

Spencer Ledge (48°25'00" 123°16'00" Between Hecate Passage and the Chain Its, E of Oak Bay, off SE tip of Vancouver I). This feature, named in 1862 by Capt George Richards, probably commemorates RN officer John Wellbore Sunderland Spencer (1816–88) of HMS *Topaze*, who served on the Pacific Station, 1859–63, as commodore of the station's southern division. A grandson of the 3rd Duke of Marlborough, he entered the RN in 1829, was promoted to capt in 1854 and reached the rank of vice adm, retired, in 1874. Spencer was also an aide-de-camp to Queen Victoria. Richards, an RN surveyor, named a number of features after Spencer and his illustrious family in the early 1860s, including Mt Spencer in Topaze Hbr, and Mt Spencer, Marlborough Heights and Mt Churchill in Jervis Inlet (Spencer's father, Francis, was Baron Churchill). Nearby Sunderland Channel and Wellbore Channel are named for him as well. *See also* Topaze Hbr.

Sperm Bay (52°13'00" 131°21'00" E side of Flamingo Inlet, SW end of Moresby I, QCI). This local name, adopted by the hydrographic service in 1946, was given by whaling capts working out of nearby Rose Hbr, who brought many sperm whales to the station located there. The bay is considered a good anchorage for small boats. Sperm whales, which appear off the PNW coast in summer, especially W of the QCI, are a large, toothed species. They dive to great depths of a km or more and feed mainly on squid. Very fine oils and a waxy spermaceti were extracted from their huge heads and used for lubrication, candles, medicines, lipsticks and face creams. More than 5,000 were killed off BC between 1905 and 1966.

Spicer Island (53°46'00" 130°22'00" Between Schooner Passage and Beaver Passage, Browning Entrance, S of Porcher I and Prince Rupert), **Spicer Point** (53°46'00" 130°19'00" E tip of Spicer I). RN officer Napoleon Alexander Ralph Spicer served on the Pacific Station, 1865–68, as 2nd lt of HMS *Sparrowhawk*, under Cdr Edwin Porcher. He retired in 1871. Named by RN surveyor Capt George Richards about 1860. The nearby Ralph Is also commemorate him.

Spider Anchorage (51°50'00" 128°13'00" Off SW end of Hunter I, Queens Sd, S of Bella Bella), **Spider Channel** (51°51'00" 128°14'00" Between Spider I and Spitfire I), **Spider Island** (51°51'01" 128°15'10" Off SW end of Hunter I). In 1944, regional hydrographer Henri Parizeau gave a number of islands in the Queens Sd area WWII warplane names (*see* Hurricane I, Mosquito Its, Kittyhawk Group, Spitfire I, etc). The original inspiration for this idea, apparently, was the presence of Spider I and the fact that Anthony Fokker's first airplane, built in 1910, was named the Spin (Dutch for "spider") on account of its many bracing wires, which made it resemble a large arachnid. Spider I, however, appears on Admiralty charts from the mid-1860s, and though the name's significance is not recorded, it certainly had nothing to do with aircraft. A wooden roadway, the remains of which were still visible in 2008, was built across the island in WWII to a large radar station at Breadner Point, now in ruins. Spider Anchorage was named in association with the island by the hydrographic service in 1944.

Spiller Channel (52°21'00" 128°11'00" Between Yeo I and Don Peninsula, N of Bella Bella), **Spiller Inlet** (52°33'00" 128°06'00" Head of Spiller Channel), **Spiller Passage** (50°43'00" 126°41'00" N of Arrow Passage, W of Mars I, NE end of Queen Charlotte Str), **Spiller Range** (54°02'00" 130°21'00" NE Porcher I, S of Prince Rupert). Cpl Richard Spiller of the Royal Marines served on the paddle steamer *Beaver*, 1863–70, under Lt Daniel Pender, while it was hired from the HBC and used by the RN as a survey vessel. Normally only officers were commemorated on RN charts, but Spiller was the loyal and long-serving personal attendant of Lt Pender, who named these features—and also Spiller R on Porcher I—after him between 1865 and 1867. Spiller Channel is believed to have been where the US trading vessel *Atahualpa* was attacked by Chief Kaiete and a group of Heiltsuk warriors in 1805. The vessel managed to escape, but only after most of its crew members had been killed or wounded.

Spilsbury Point (50°00'00" 124°56'00" NW tip of Hernando I, S of Cortes I, E of Campbell R, N end of Str of Georgia). Ashton Wilmot Spilsbury (1872–1960) came to BC from England in the late 1880s and bought his older brother's homestead at Whonnock on the Fraser R, which he turned into a dairy farm. He married Alice Maud Blizard, from London, UK, at Vancouver in 1897. In 1914 the Spilsbury family moved to Savary I, where Ashton and Alice had spent their honeymoon, and for the next decade lived in a large tent. They finally built a home on Savary, and Ashton logged, built roads and worked for the island's resort hotels. The Spilsburys relocated to N Vancouver in the mid-1940s. Their son Jim (Ashton James Spilsbury, 1905–2003) became a well-known BC entrepreneur and author, a pioneer in early coastal airline and radio-communication businesses. Spilsbury Point was formerly known as Tongue Point and also as Raines Spit, after an early settler on Hernando I who had a home at this location in the late 1800s; it received its current name in 1945. *E*

Spípiyus Point (49°40'30" 123°51'50" W side of Sechelt Inlet, opposite Narrows Inlet, NW of Vancouver). *Spípiyus* is the Sechelt First Nation word for marbled murrelet, an endangered seabird that feeds in adjacent waters and nests at high altitudes in the old-growth trees of the Sechelt Peninsula. The names of Spípiyus Point and nearby Spípiyus Peak in the Caren Range were adopted in 1997 on the recommendation of Sechelt First Nation elder Gilbert Joe and the Friends of Caren, a conservation organization.

Spipiyus Provincial Park, 2,979 sq km, was established in 1999 to protect the 2,000-year-old yellow cedars of the Caren Range, believed to be some of the oldest trees in Canada, as well as the nesting habitat of the murrelet.

Spitfire Channel (51°52'00" 128°12'00" N and E of Hurricane I, SW of Hunter I, S of Bella Bella), **Spitfire Island** (51°51'00" 128°13'00" Between Spider I and Hurricane I, off SW Hunter I). The Spitfire was the most successful British fighter aircraft of WWII and gained immortal fame during the Battle of Britain. Built by Supermarine Aviation Works Ltd, a subsidiary of Vickers-Armstrongs Ltd, it was fast, manoeuvrable, well armed and much loved by pilots. Its design evolved in the 1930s, and the plane began mass-production in 1938; by 1948 more than 20,000 had been turned out, in 24 different variants or "marks." The last flight of a Spitfire in RAF service took place in 1957. The island was formerly known as Ruth I but was renamed in 1944, the year that regional hydrographer Henri Parizeau, in a burst of patriotic fervour, named a number of features in the Queens Sd area after WWII aircraft. *See also* Hurricane I, Mosquito Its, Kittyhawk Group, etc.

Spouter Island (49°37'00" 126°33'00" Part of the Spanish Pilot Group, SW of Bligh I, Nootka Sd, W side of Vancouver I). In 1934, regional hydrographer Henri Parizeau attempted to change this name to Salamanca I, after the Spanish pilot Secundino Salamanca, 2nd officer of the *Sutil*, employed in the exploration of the E coast of Vancouver I and the adjacent mainland in 1792 (*see* Salamanca Point). Parizeau was on a name-changing binge in Nootka Sd at the time, and there was bureaucratic resistance to some of his proposals, including this one (*see* Spanish Pilot Group). The old name of Spouter, which appears on an Admiralty chart dated 1866, based on an 1862 survey by Capt George Richards, was kept. The significance of the name is not known, but Spouter was certainly not a Spanish pilot.

Spratt Bay (49°45'00" 124°31'00" NE side of Texada I, SE of Sturt Bay, Malaspina Str). This name appears as Spratt's Bay in annual reports of BC's Ministry of Mines as early as 1896 but was not officially adopted until 1950. It most likely honours Charles Joseph V Spratt (1873–1941), who owned the nearby Raven group of claims in 1897 with partners Edward Blewett, William Blewett and J Wilson. The following year their claims were listed as the property of the Spratt Copper & Gold Co. The son of pioneer industrialist Joseph Spratt (1834–88), Charles was born and died at Victoria; in 1894 he married Sacramento native Marguerite Ethel Deuel (1873–1946). His father, who came to California from England in 1853 in pursuit of gold, established Victoria's Albion Iron Works in the early 1860s with John Kriemler. It was the largest foundry and machinery manufacturer in the PNW and was later

owned by William Irving, then by Robert Dunsmuir and R P Rithet. In 1951 Spratt Bay became the site of a loading facility for a nearby limestone operation, owned since 1959 by the Imperial Limestone Co. The feature's local name is Butterfly Bay because of its proximity to Butterfly Point.

Spratt Point (52°12'00" 128°10'00" E side of Kynumpt Hbr, N end of Campbell I, N of Bella Bella). This feature is probably named after Capt Charles Spratt, a pioneer BC mariner who operated the tug *Czar*, which was built in Victoria in 1896 for Vancouver's Hastings Mill. Spratt later owned the sternwheeler *Strathcona*, which he ran on Howe Sd and the E coast of Vancouver I. Spratt Point was formerly known as Berry Point and also as Barber Point, after Lt Cdr R A Barber of the RCNR, who served aboard HMCS *Rainbow* and *Stadacona* during WWI; it received its current name in 1924.

Spring Cove (48°56'00" 125°32'00" W side of Ucluelet Inlet near its entrance, NW side of Barkley Sd, W side of Vancouver I), **Spring Island** (50°00'00" 127°25'00" W of Union I, NW entrance to Kyuquot Sd, NW side of Vancouver I). William Spring (1831–84), a well-known BC sealing capt and trader, established a store on this cove in 1869. He was born in Russia, where his Scottish civil engineer father was working for a railway company, and went to sea at a young age, arriving at Victoria from Hawaii in 1853 on the schooner *Honolulu Packet*. Spring went into business with Hugh McKay, a cooper, making barrels and putting up salted fish. The pair purchased a series of modest sailing vessels, including the *Ino*, *Morning Star*, *Surprise*, *Alert*, *Favourite* and *North Star*, and pursued trading opportunities from Washington to Alaska. They also opened a number of small trading posts on the W coast of Vancouver I and were joined in 1864 by another partner, Peter Francis, who later ran the Ucluelet store. Beginning in the mid-1860s, McKay and Spring pioneered the Victoria-based sealing industry, becoming two of its most successful practitioners. After William's death, his son Charles Spring (1860–1938), who had been born at New Westminster and grew up in the trading business, took over his father's sealing enterprise. It was Charles who suggested the name of the cove, in 1912. It was later the site of a federal government lifeboat station.

Springer Point (50°18'00" 125°13'00" S side of Sonora I, S of Owen Bay, Okisollo Channel, N of Campbell R). Benjamin Springer (1841–98), a native of Ont, was the sawmill manager at Moodyville, 1882–90. He had come to BC about 1863 for the Cariboo gold rush and first worked at the mill in 1872 as a tallyman, then as bookkeeper. He and his US-born wife, Fanny Mary (1853–1905, née Nias), who was one of Vancouver's first schoolteachers, were married at New Westminster in 1874. (It is often said that Springer married the sister of Jonathan Miller, pioneer Vancouver policeman and postmaster. Indeed, the two

S

men were brothers-in-law and close friends, but it was Miller's marriage to Springer's sister, Margaret, that was the cause of the connection.) Later the Springers moved into Invermere, or the Big House, a fancy colonnaded residence at the Moodyville mill site, originally built for co-owner Hugh Nelson. Benjamin added a tennis court and croquet lawn. He resigned as mill manager in 1890 and set up a general commission and insurance business in Vancouver, where he became a major property owner, building such early brick structures as the Masonic Temple on W Cordova St and the Leland block on Hastings St. He was a board of trade member, justice of the peace, school trustee and commissioner of pilots, and had many mining interests. A Springer daughter, Mabel Ellen, whose married name was Boultbee (1876–1953), became a well-known journalist and social maven, editing the *Vancouver Sun*'s women's pages for many years. She was not the first white child born on Burrard Inlet as is sometimes claimed; Henry Alexander, son of Hastings sawmill manager Richard Alexander, preceded her in 1873, and there may well have been others.

Sproat Bay (48°54'00" 125°05'00" SE side of Tzartus I, W side of Barkley Sd, W side of Vancouver I), **Sproat Narrows** (49°07'00" 124°49'00" In Alberni Inlet, at mouth of the Franklin R). Gilbert Malcolm Sproat (1834–1913), from Scotland, came to Vancouver I in 1860 as the representative of the British financial backer of BC's first export sawmill, built by Edward Stamp at Alberni. Sproat succeeded Stamp as the mill's manager in 1863, was named a justice of the peace and developed commercial interests in Victoria. After returning to England in the mid-1860s, he published a book about the province, *Scenes and Studies of Savage Life*, and was appointed BC's first agent gen, 1871–75. Sproat came back to BC the following year to work as an Indian reserve commissioner but resigned in 1880 after criticizing the reserve process, particularly the lack of aboriginal consultation and disregard for human rights. He was named a gold commissioner and magistrate in the Kootenays instead, 1885–90, then left the civil service to become a real-estate promoter. Sproat retired to Victoria in 1898. He evidently had trouble getting people to spell and pronounce his name correctly. "I say nothing against Brussels sprouts, which I love to eat," he wrote to the provincial archivist in 1908, "but tell your typist that I was christened with an 'a' and not a 'u.'" Sproat Bay appears on an Admiralty chart surveyed by Capt George Richards in 1861 and published in 1865. Sproat Narrows, originally known as First Narrows, was renamed by the hydrographic service in 1945. Sproat Lk and Sproat R on Vancouver I and Mt Sproat in the W Kootenays are also named for him. *E W*

Spurn Head (48°27'00" 123°17'00" S side of Cadboro Bay, just N of Oak Bay and Victoria). This feature, which appears on a T N Hibben & Co map of Victoria dated

1913, is named for a narrow sandspit on the E coast of Yorkshire, England, at the mouth of the Humber estuary—the site of a lifeboat station and obsolete lighthouse. Several promontories around Cadboro Bay are named after famous British coastal landmarks.

Squamish Harbour, head of Howe Sound. *Peter Vassilopoulos*

Squamish (49°45'00" 123°08'00" Head of Howe Sd, N of Vancouver), **Squamish Harbour** (49°39'00" 123°14'00" Head of Howe Sd), **Squamish River** (49°41'07" 123°10'50" Flows S into the head of Howe Sd). The town and harbour are named after the river, which is in turn named for the First Nation people who have traditionally occupied this region and today call themselves the Skxwúmish. The river appeared as Squawmisht on an 1863 Admiralty chart, and many other obsolete spellings have been recorded, including Chomes, Whoomis, Skqo'mic and Squohamish. The name has been translated as "people of the sacred water" (older interpretations usually give "strong wind" as the meaning). The Squamish area was first settled by Europeans in the late 1880s, and a small logging and agricultural community gradually formed. About 1909 the owners of the Howe Sd & Northern Rwy, after secretly buying up large tracts of land, announced that Squamish would henceforth be known as Newport. Several years of townsite promotion and property speculation ensued; even the post office name was changed from Squamish to Newport Beach, 1912–14. When the BC government took over the railway in 1912 and turned it into the PGE, a competition was held for schoolchildren to suggest a new name for the terminus and growing village. Out of the 2,000 entries received, PGE vice-president D'Arcy Tate chose Squamish, and in 1914 the old name was reinstated; the $500 prize was split between 28 winners. Squamish today is a district municipality with a population of 14,000. Forestry remains the dominant industry. *E*

Squire Point (50°35'00" 126°09'00" NE of Hull I, S side of Call Inlet, between Knight Inlet and Johnstone Str). Edmund Joseph Squire was 3rd lt aboard HMS *Havannah*, under Capt Thomas Harvey, on the Pacific Station, 1855–

S

59. The feature was named by Capt George Richards of the RN survey vessel *Plumper* in 1860.

Squirrel Cove on Cortes Island. *Peter Vassilopoulos*

Squirrel Cove (50°08'00" 124°55'00" E side of Cortes I, E of Campbell R, opposite Desolation Sd). Members of the Klahoose First Nation, encouraged by Roman Catholic Oblate missionaries who provided money to build a church, moved to a reserve at this location in 1896. Before then their winter village sites had been at Brem Bay in Toba Inlet and at the head of Toba. A non-Native community first formed across from the Squirrel Cove reserve about 1914, when a man named Ewart opened a store in a tent. The Klahoose name for the cove is Tu'kw (or Tork). Its meaning is not known.

Squitty Bay (49°27'00" 124°10'00" E end of Lasqueti I, central Str of Georgia). According to island historian Elda Copley Mason, the name is supposedly a contraction of the word Lasqueti.

Stackhouse Island (50°51'00" 126°39'00" W of Gregory I, Sutlej Channel, off N side of Broughton I, NE of Port McNeill). Lt Thomas Stackhouse served on HMS *Sutlej* on the Pacific Station, 1863–64. He entered the RN in 1844, retired as a cdr in 1870 and reached the rank of capt, retired, in 1878. The *Sutlej* was the flagship of station cdr-in-chief Rear Adm John Kingcome.

Stag Island (50°05'00" 125°13'00" Gowlland Hbr, W side of Quadra I, just NE of Campbell R). Cdr Cortland Simpson of the RN survey vessel *Egeria* named a number of features in the vicinity after animals in 1900.

Staines Island (48°27'07" 123°17'00" E side of Cadboro Bay, N of Oak Bay and Victoria), **Staines Point** (48°23'40" 123°18'17" S tip of Trial Is, S of McNeill Bay and Oak Bay municipality, off SE end of Vancouver I). Robert John Staines (1820–1854) was born in England and educated at Cambridge Univ. He taught in Ireland and France, and in 1846 married Emma Frances Tahourdin, also a

well-educated teacher. In 1848, Staines was ordained an Anglican clergyman and hired by the HBC as Ft Victoria's schoolmaster and chaplain. He arrived in the colony the following year on the barque *Columbia* with his wife and her young nephew. He soon grew disenchanted with the HBC's colonial rule, joining a faction of settlers who did "everything in their power," according to Gov James Douglas, "to slander the HBC, and to produce impressions unfavourable to [its] character and government." Suspected of writing scathing anonymous letters to the colonial office in London and to US newspapers, Staines was fired as schoolmaster by the HBC. The disaffected colonists raised funds to send him to England with petitions protesting the appointment of David Cameron, the gov's brother-in-law, as chief justice of the Supreme Court. In 1854, Staines departed on the *Duchess of San Lorenzo*, but that vessel capsized in Juan de Fuca Str and all aboard perished. Emma and her nephew returned to England in 1855. Regional hydrographer Henri Parizeau named both features in 1934: Staines I, formerly known as Ellen I, is named for Emma Staines; Staines Point, formerly known as Ripple Point, is named for her husband.

Staki Bay (52°15'00" 131°22'00" Head of Flamingo Inlet, SW end of Moresby I, QCI), **Staki Point** (52°14'00" 131°21'00" SE entrance to Staki Bay). The bay was named by the hydrographic service in 1946 after Sta'ki, the ancient Haida First Nation word for Flamingo Inlet. Staki Point was named in 1963, in association with the bay.

Stalkungi Cove (52°46'00" 131°45'00" W end of Tanu I, off E side of Moresby I, QCI), **Stalkungi Point** (W tip of Tanu I). Stalkungi is an adaptation of the Haida First Nation word for moccasin. The names of both features were adopted by the hydrographic service in 1957.

Stamp Narrows (49°11'00" 124°49'00" Alberni Inlet at the mouth of Cous Ck, Vancouver I W of Nanaimo), **Stamp Point** (49°13'00" 124°50'00" W side of Alberni Inlet, entrance to Port Alberni). Edward Stamp (1814–72), an English ship's capt who came to Puget Sd in 1857 to take on a load of lumber, saw a land of economic opportunities. He returned the following year and established a general store at Victoria, then went back to England to raise funds for a sawmill at Alberni. This operation, known as the Anderson Mill after its British investors, was BC's first serious lumber exporter, and Stamp managed it from 1861 to 1863. He moved briefly to Port Neville, where his employees cut spars, before settling on Burrard Inlet in 1867 and constructing the famous Hastings Mill, around which the city of Vancouver would eventually form. Stamp fell out with his investors in 1869 and went into the fish-curing business at New Westminster. He was also the Esquimalt member for the Vancouver I legislative assembly, 1865–66, and Lillooet's representative to the BC legislative council, 1867–68. The province's first industrialist died suddenly

S

of a heart attack while in London raising funds to build a cannery. Stamp Narrows was formerly known as Second Narrows. Stamp Point was adopted from Lt Cdr Philip Musgrave's 1912–13 chart of Port Alberni and the Somass R. Stamp Falls and the Stamp R on Vancouver I are also named for this pioneering entrepreneur. *E W*

Staniforth Bank (53°35'00" 128°49'00" S end of Devastation Channel, entrance to Gardner Canal, S of Kitimat), **Staniforth Point** (53°34'00" 128°49'00" Near W entrance to Gardner Canal). The point was named by Joseph Whidbey, master of HMS *Discovery*, possibly after John Staniforth, a ship owner at Hull, England, and Tory MP, 1802–18. Whidbey was in charge of a long surveying expedition in this region—from Douglas Channel and Gardner Canal to Chatham Sd—with the *Discovery*'s boats in 1793. He was accompanied on this epic journey by Midshipman Robert Barrie.

Vancouver Harbour from Stanley Park. *John Lund*

Stanley Park (49°18'00" 123°08'30" At Vancouver, Burrard Inlet, S entrance to Vancouver Hbr). This 4-sq-km urban oasis, site of the early Squamish First Nation village of Khwaykhway, was named a government military reserve by Col Richard Moody of the Royal Engineers in 1860. It was leased to the city of Vancouver as a park in 1887 and officially opened the following year, named by Sir Donald Smith, the railroad financier and former HBC gov, after Sir Frederick Arthur Stanley, 1st Baron Stanley of Preston (1841–1908), gov gen of Canada from 1888 to 1893. The son of Sir Edward Smith-Stanley, a three-time British PM, he was also a successful politician in his own right: an MP, 1865–86; British war secretary, 1878–80; colonial secretary, 1885–86; and board of trade president, 1886–88. In 1893 he became the 16th Earl of Derby. It was Lord Stanley who, in 1892, donated a trophy for Canada's top amateur hockey club: the Stanley Cup. The area covered by the park and downtown Vancouver was named Coal Peninsula in 1860 by Capt George Richards of HMS *Plumper*. His chief engineer, Francis Brockton, had discovered this useful mineral there the year before. *E*

Stansung Islets (52°44'00" 131°36'00" Off N side of Lyell I, Richardson Inlet, E of Moresby I, QCI). Stansung is a modification of the Haida First Nation word meaning "four." The hydrographic service chose this name in 1957 because there are four islets in the group.

Stapledon Island (54°12'00" 130°17'00" E side of Lelu I, just S of Prince Rupert). Named in 1907 after Bartholomew Stapledon (1847–1914), a pioneer in the N coast salmon cannery trade and manager of the Inverness Cannery in the 1890s. A native of Chatham, NB, he came to Victoria from Que about 1883 with his Que-born wife, Jane (c 1846–1921, née Skillen), and their family. The Stapledons also lived at Port Essington before retiring to Victoria, where Bartholomew died. Stapledon Ck, which flows into the Skeena R at Tyee railway station, is also named for him. Stapledon received a Crown grant of land at that location in 1892.

Stapleton Point (52°21'00" 128°22'00" W side of Lake I, Mathieson Channel, NW of Bella Bella). Florence Maria Stapleton (d 1902), daughter of Sir Francis Stapleton, a baronet, married Frederick Seymour in England in 1866 and came back with him to the distant colony of BC, where he was gov (*see* Seymour Inlet). Seymour died on the job in 1869, and Florence returned home. Formerly known as Hunger Point.

Stark Islet (55°25'00" 129°45'00" W of Larcom I, Observatory Inlet, S of Stewart). After prospector and mining engineer John Edmund Stark (1860–1930), who was very active in this region through the first three decades of the 1900s. Stark's parents were Louis and Sylvia Stark, perhaps the best known of the free blacks who came to BC from California in 1859 and formed a black community on Saltspring I, where John was born. He staked claims in the Stewart and Portland Canal areas in the early 1900s, on the Telkwa and Morice rivers and, in 1907, at the head of Alice Arm. Stark became strongly associated with Alice Arm and the Illiance R for the next 20 years and liked to claim that he was the first "white man" to settle permanently in the vicinity. He died at Anyox. Nearby Stark Ck, which flows W into the Kitsault R, is also named for him.

Stark Point (53°37'00" 130°03'00" Near S entrance to Hevenor Inlet, W side of Pitt I). Flight Lt George Douglas Stark, DFC, from Vancouver, was killed in action Aug 2, 1944, aged 21. He was a member of No 425 Squadron, which flew night missions over Germany in 1944 with Handley Page Halifax bombers. Stark had flown more than 30 sorties at the time of his death, including ones against Berlin, Essen, Stuttgart and Frankfurt. He is buried at Stonefall Cemetery in Harrogate, Yorkshire, England.

Starling Point (49°24'00" 126°14'00" NW tip of Flores I, Clayoquot Sd, W side of Vancouver I). Named by the hydrographic service in 1945 after HMS *Starling*, the tender that accompanied HMS *Sulphur*, under Cdr Edward Belcher, on his surveying expedition to the W coasts of N and S America and subsequent circumnavigation of the world, 1836–42. The *Starling*, under Lt Cdr Henry Kellett, was a 4-gun cutter, a tiny schooner of only 98 tonnes, launched in 1829 and sold in 1844. Both vessels were at Nootka Sd in 1837 taking astronomical observations. Both cdrs would go on to have famous careers in the RN (*see* Belcher Point *and* Kellett Point).

Statham Point (50°31'00" 125°32'00" E side of Loughborough Inlet, N of W Thurlow I and Johnstone Str, NW of Campbell R). A notation at BC's Geographical Names Office states that this feature was probably named after the hamlet of Statham, in Cheshire, England, which could have been the birthplace of one of the naval officers involved in the Admiralty surveys of the region in 1860–62 (by Capt George Richards) or 1863–69 (by Lt Daniel Pender). Capt Richards had with him as officers Richard Mayne, John Bull, Daniel Pender, Edward Bedwell, John Gowlland, George Browning and Edward Blunden. Lt Pender's officers were William Blakeney, George Brodie, Browning and Blunden. All are familiar names on the BC coast.

Staunton Shoal (51°18'00" 127°48'00" N of Table I, entrance to Smith Sd, NW of Port Hardy). After Sub-Lt George Staunton Brodie, an RN officer who served on the BC coast, 1865–70. *See* Brodie I. Formerly known as George Rk.

Steele Reefs (50°18'00" 127°53'00" Entrance to Klaskino Inlet, Brooks Bay, NW side of Vancouver I). Capt John Steele (1858–1900) was born on PEI and came to BC to join the sealing fleet as master of the schooner *Penelope* in 1888. He later also served as capt of the *Winifred*, *Theresa* and *Ainoko*. In 1892 he retired from sealing to join the crew of the *Barbara Boscowitz* as mate and pilot. Steele was mentioned in the Victoria *Colonist* newspaper in 1896 as capt of the Canadian Pacific Navigation Co's *Rainbow* and is believed to have ended his career as a wharfinger at Victoria.

Steele Rock (52°28'00" 129°22'00" SE of Conroy I, off W side of Aristazabal I, Hecate Str). Frances Steele became the wife of Alexander Johnston, deputy minister of Marine and Fisheries in the federal government, 1910–33, and a former Cape Breton newspaper publisher, MLA and MP (*see* Mt Johnston). Nearby Frances Rk is also named for her, while Mason Rk (qv) is named for her son.

Steel Point (53°49'00" 128°42'00" E side of Amos Passage, E of Kitimat Arm, S of Kitimat). Named (but incorrectly spelled) by the hydrographic service in 1952 for prospector and miner James L Steele (b 1867), a native of PEI, who was active in the Kitimat region, 1900–1910. In company with his partner John Dunn, he staked numerous copper, gold and silver claims in the area, including the Golden Crown, Paragon, Peerless and Porcupine properties. In 1903–5 he was listed in the annual reports for BC's Ministry of Mines as the mining sub-recorder for the Kitimat district.

Steilta Islets (53°38'00" 132°24'00" In Juskatla Inlet, S of Masset Inlet, Graham I, QCI). Steilta (also Stilta, Stelta or Stultah) was a famous Haida Eagle crest chief at Masset. He converted to Christianity just before his death in 1876 and was supposedly the first Haida chief to be interred rather than placed in a mortuary box and then lodged in a mortuary house or cave. Steilta may have been involved in the pillage and burning of the US schooner *Susan Sturgis* in 1852; his Masset house had an unusual carved eagle over the doorway, said to have been taken from the sternboard of that plundered vessel.

Stenhouse Shoal (54°20'00" 130°56'00" W entrance to Brown Passage, SW of Melville I, W of Prince Rupert). Alexander A Stenhouse was a pioneer businessman and resident of Victoria. In 1861, according to coastal historian Capt John Walbran, he was a sheriff's officer "in charge of various vessels which had been infringing the customs and excise laws." Sadly, an 1869 report in the Victoria *Colonist* stated that he was "in a destitute state in San Francisco ... having entirely lost his sight from ophthalmic disease." The name appeared on charts as early as 1863.

Stephens Island, Stephens Narrows, Stephens Passage. *See* Mt Stephens.

Stephenson Point (50°08'00" 125°22'00" E side of Menzies Bay, SW of Seymour Narrows, just NW of Campbell R). Rear Adm Henry Frederick Stephenson, CB (1842–1919), was cdr-in-chief on the Pacific Station, 1893–96. He entered the RN in 1855, served in the Crimean War as a junior officer, was promoted to lt in 1861 and commanded the gunboat *Heron* on Lk Ontario during the Fenian raids in 1866. As a capt he took part, with HMS *Discovery*, in the British Arctic Expedition of 1875–76, accompanying Capt George Nares in HMS *Alert* on a failed attempt to reach the N Pole. During this journey, Cdr Albert Markham, second-in-command of the *Alert*, took a sledge party to 83°20'26" N, the highest latitude reached at that time. Stephenson was promoted to rear adm in 1890. The cruiser *Royal Arthur*, under Capt Frederick Trench, was his flagship during his sojourn at Esquimalt. He was knighted in 1897 and served as cdr-in-chief of the Channel squadron, 1897–98. Stephenson reached the rank of adm in 1901 and became principal naval aide-de-camp to King Edward VII from 1902 to 1904. *W*

S

Stevens Island (51°00'00" 127°32'00" One of the Southgate Group, NW side of Queen Charlotte Str, N of Port Hardy). Named by Cdr John Parry of HMS *Egeria* after John Stevens, the vessel's boatswain, who participated in a resurvey of this area in 1903.

Stevenson Cove (52°34'00" 131°39'00" W entrance to Darwin Sd, E side of Moresby I, QCI). Stevenson, whose personal name is unrecorded, was a prospector at nearby Lockeport during the short-lived QCI copper-mining frenzy of the early 1900s. With his partner, Sullivan, he staked the Tiger claim near Anna Inlet and operated an open-cut mine there in 1907–8. The feature was named by the hydrographic service in 1962.

Fish boats and cannery workers at Steveston in the 1960s.
Harbour Publishing collection

Steveston (49°08'00" 123°11'00" SW end of Lulu I, mouth of the Fraser R, Richmond, S of Vancouver), **Steveston Bar** (49°07'00" 123°11'00" Just SE of Steveston), **Steveston Bend** (49°08'00" 123°14'00" Mouth of the Fraser R, W of Garry Point), **Steveston Island** (49°07'00" 123°10'00" Just SE of Steveston). Manoah Steves (1828–97), a native of NB, arrived in BC in 1877 and was joined by his wife, Martha (1830–1920), and six children the following year. The family had left NB in 1868 and farmed in Ont and Maryland, US, before moving W. Manoah bought 160 ha on SW Lulu I, grew a variety of crops and built up a flourishing dairy farm. His eldest son, William Herbert Steves (1860–99), developed a townsite called Steves on family land in 1889 as a market and supply centre for the area's farmers and the many canneries that lined the banks of the Fraser at this location. The name of the village soon became Steveston, and Steves family descendants have been active in the region ever since. At its pre-WWI peak, Steveston also supported a thriving boatbuilding industry and hoped to rival Vancouver in influence. Its promoters called it Salmonopolis. Steveston today has retained much of its heritage character and is a popular tourist destination,

home to the Gulf of Georgia Cannery, a national historic site. Steveston Bar and Steveston I are different parts of the same feature, which has changed shape and size over the years. The bar, to the W, is submerged at low tide; the island, which is wooded, is to the E. Originally, in 1936, the entire body of land was known as Steveston Bar; in 1947, however, the two separate names were introduced. Steveston I has sometimes been referred to as Shady I. Steveston Bend is the sharp turn to the S that the river's outgoing main channel makes just W of Steveston. *E*

Stewardson Inlet (49°26'00" 126°18'00" Extends SW from Sydney Inlet, N of Hot Springs Cove, W side of Clayoquot Sd, W side of Vancouver I). Alan Eden Stewardson (1906–76) graduated from UBC and joined the Canadian Hydrographic Service as a junior hydrographer in 1929. He was involved in surveys of the W coast of Vancouver I (1930–36), Rivers Inlet (1937) and the Str of Georgia (1939–40) before retiring in 1941 due to ill health. He died at New Westminster. The inlet, formerly known as West Arm, was named for him in 1933 by regional hydrographer Henri Parizeau. A logging camp with booming and barge-loading facilities was established near the head of the inlet in the early 1970s. A post office named Stewardson Inlet operated at the camp, 1974–78.

Early street scene from Stewart's commercial district. *Author's collection*

Stewart (55°56'00" 129°59'00" Head of Portland Canal, on BC-Alaska boundary, N of Prince Rupert). Two prospector brothers from Victoria, Robert M and John W Stewart, settled at this location in 1902, just before a copper, gold and silver boom swept the area. They established the Stewart Land Co in 1906, laid out a townsite and had interests in several of the area's mines. Robert became the community's first postmaster, 1905–9, and also the region's justice of the peace. Stewart, with BC's northernmost ice-free harbour, boasted a population of 4,000 or more in its pre-WWI heyday and had a local railroad with 20 km of track. It experienced a number of booms and busts over the years, benefiting between the 1920s and the 1940s from the productive Premier and Big Missouri gold mines, and later from the giant Granduc copper operation. As mining activity dwindled, however, the town declined to its present backwater status, where prospectors mingle with tourists, recreationists and filmmakers who come to take advantage of Stewart's authentic "ghost town" atmosphere and spectacular mountain scenery. *E*

Stewart Bay (53°41'00" 132°10'00" E side of Masset Inlet, at Port Clements, Graham I, QCI). This feature was named in 1907 by Eli Tingley, who founded the townsite of Port Clements, after his friend Allan Stewart. QCI historian Kathleen Dalzell tells the story of how Stewart, who was helping Tingley search for land, accidentally cut his foot with an axe while setting up camp at this location. The gash was a serious one, and Stewart's companions had to hike nearly 15 km in order to find a boat in which they could transport him to safety and have his wound properly attended. As they set off with the injured man, Tingley declared that their campsite would be known in the future as Stewart Bay. *D*

Stewart Passage (53°26'00" 130°25'00" Between Surge Rks and NW side of Banks I). Named for the federal survey vessel *William J Stewart*, built on Georgian Bay, at Collingwood, Ont, in 1932 and designed for hydrographic work. It spent 43 years as the Pacific flagship of the Canadian Hydrographic Service. The 72-m, 1,175-tonne steamship had a large chart room beneath the bridge, which surveyors used as a seagoing office, and fairly comfortable officers' quarters, though crew members lived in more cramped conditions. A seamen's union agent described the *Stewart* in 1946 as "one of the slums of the sea," with bunks that "were worse than those at Oakalla," a prison in Burnaby. The vessel was also a poor sea boat, with a "stomach-wrenching corkscrew motion" in a quartering sea, according to Sandy Sandilands, the

ship's hydrographer-in-charge in the late 1960s. It was named for William James Stewart (1863–1925), Canada's first chief hydrographer. He spent only a brief time on the W coast, conducting a Burrard Inlet survey in 1891, but did extensive mapping work on the Great Lks, Lk Winnipeg and the St Lawrence R. More importantly, he developed and administered a national hydrographic service, planned for its future expansion and served as Canadian representative on international commissions concerned with boundaries, water management, transport and communications. During WWII the *Stewart* was equipped with a 12-pound gun and twin Oerlikons and carried out hush-hush missions for the RCN that included locating safe anchorages and putting defence booms in place. In 1944 the vessel had its only serious accident, hitting notorious Ripple Rk in Seymour Narrows. The hull was badly damaged but the crew managed to beach the ship in nearby Plumper Bay before it sank. After major repairs the *Stewart* continued in federal service until 1975, when it was retired and sat at a Victoria dock for five years. Then Bob Wright of Oak Bay Marina purchased it and sprang for a $2-million facelift that turned the elderly vessel into a luxurious floating hotel and restaurant named the *Canadian Princess*. It was towed to Ucluelet where it remained in the early 2000s, the heart of a well-known Oak Bay Marine Group fishing resort.

Stewart Point (50°35'00" 127°35'00" E entrance to Coal Hbr, Holberg Inlet, NW end of Vancouver I). John Robertson Stewart received a very early Crown grant in the Quatsino district, dated 1872. He and his partner, W R Meldrum, were wholesale merchants at Victoria, with premises on Wharf St, and had been interested in the harbour adjacent to this point for 10 years. They had hoped, with the help of a British investor, to develop what was thought in the early days to be a valuable coal deposit

Federal hydrographic vessel *William J Stewart*, which spent 43 years surveying the BC coast. *BC Archives B-06186*

S

there. Stewart died in 1873 on a trip to his homeland in Scotland and thus never had to suffer the indignity of learning that the coal seams on his property were small and of poor quality. *See also* Coal Hbr.

Stikine River (56°39'00" 131°50'00" Flows SW across northern BC and the BC-Alaska boundary to enter the sea near Wrangell, Alaska). The name of BC's fourth-longest river, at 589 km, is a Tlingit First Nation word that simply means "the river," in the sense of "the definitive or great river." Although European explorers have known it by that name since the end of the 18th century, the alternative names St Francis R and Pelly's R are also found in early documents. The word Stikine has numerous spelling variants; Stikeen, Stickeen, Stachine, Stah-keena, Stahkin, Stickienes and Sucheen have all been recorded. The river served as a transportation route to a number of northern gold rushes in the late 1800s; sternwheeled paddle steamers operated on its lower reaches for almost a century. The Stikine Territory, N of the river to the 62nd parallel and E to the 125th meridian, was established by Britain in 1862 in order to secure its potential gold wealth; unfortunately, this initiative brought into being the Alaska Panhandle, as the territory did not include the coast. The Stikine Territory was added to the colony of BC in 1863. The Stikine Plateau, where the river's source is located, and the Stikine Ranges in N-central BC are named after the river. *E*

The Stikine River estuary. *Sam Beebe/Ecotrust*

Stilique Bay (53°37'00" 132°23'00" S side of Juskatla Inlet, S of Masset Inlet, Graham I, QCI). The name is an adaptation of the Haida First Nation word for a river otter. *D*

Stillwater Bay (49°46'00" 124°19'00" Between Lang Bay and Frolander Bay, E side of Malaspina Str, SE of Powell R). This feature is believed to have been named by US lumberman John O'Brien after the old Minnesota town on the Wisconsin border (now a suburb of Minneapolis) where he had formerly lived. O'Brien acquired tracts of timber S of Powell R in 1900 and merged his O'Brien Logging Co in 1908 with the BC timber holdings of the Brooks-Scanlon Lumber Co, also from Minnesota (and one of the largest timber businesses in the US). The new firm that resulted, the Brooks, Scanlon & O'Brien Lumber Co, then founded the Powell River Co, which later became part of MacMillan Bloedel Ltd and the Weyerhaeuser Co. In 1909, Brooks, Scanlon & O'Brien established a major railway-logging camp at Stillwater Bay, with employee accommodations and a large repair facility. The camp, which was not converted to truck logging until 1955, has been owned since 2002 by Olympic Forest Products and is still used as a dryland log sort. The bay was formerly known as Scow Bay, because scows were used to bring logging locomotives to the site for repair from other parts of the coast. *E*

Stockham Island (49°10'15" 125°54'00" In Heynen Channel, between Tofino and Opitsat, Clayoquot Sd, W side of Vancouver I). Thomas Stockham (1859–1933) came to Canada from England in 1879 and worked at various trades, first arriving on the W coast of Vancouver I with a party of timber surveyors. In 1891 he and a partner, Walter Dawley (*see* Dawley Passage), built a store from salvaged shipwreck lumber on Stockham I opposite the Tla-o-qui-aht (Clayoquot) First Nation village of Opitsat on Meares I. The pair opened trading posts at Nootka in 1894 and Ahousat in 1896, and added a hotel to their Stockham I operation in 1898. They then took over and expanded the pioneer store and hotel on nearby Stubbs I in 1902. Stockham married Agnes Mary McKenna at Victoria in 1903 and underwent an acrimonious breakup with Dawley the following year. He later purchased two sealing schooners, the *Ella G* and the *Thomas F Bayard*, and made a huge claim for compensation when the sealing industry was shut down in 1911 (eventually receiving less than 5 percent of what he had demanded).

Stone Island (49°10'00" 125°54'00" Just NE of Tofino, entrance to Lemmens Inlet, Clayoquot Sd, W side of Vancouver I). Methodist missionary William John Stone (1864–1944) and his wife, Christina (1870–1950), both from Ont, came with their children to Clo-oose on the W coast of Vancouver I in 1894 and established a mission there. The family moved to Clayoquot in 1902. Stone was later (about 1910) head of the Clayoquot Liberal Assoc. Both he and his wife died at Victoria.

Stone Point (51°37'00" 127°30'00" S side of Rivers Inlet). Named after Cpl A W Stone, a resident of the Rivers Inlet area for many years. His son Francis Stone worked as manager of the Goose Bay Cannery. This feature was formerly known as Christopher Point but was renamed by the hydrographic service in 1942. It is also known locally as Long Point.

Stopford Bay (50°49'00" 126°40'00" N side of Broughton I, NE of Port McNeill), **Stopford Point** (50°03'00" 124°44'00" SE side of Gifford Peninsula, Lancelot Inlet, NW of Powell R). Lt Robert Edward Stopford (1841–68) served on the Pacific Station in the early 1860s. In 1864, while an officer on HMS *Sutlej*, he was promoted to senior lt of HMS *Devastation* after that vessel's cdr had been invalided home. Both the *Sutlej*, which was the flagship of the station's cdr-in-chief, Rear Adm Joseph Denman, and the *Devastation* went to Clayoquot Sd in 1864 to investigate the murders of the crew of the trading sloop *Kingfisher*. They ended up shelling and burning nine First Nation villages in pursuit of Chapchah, the Ahousaht chief involved in the piracy. Stopford was drowned in Asia while commanding a gunboat, HMS *Starling* (Starling Point is named for an earlier RN vessel). Robert Hills and Mt Stopford on N Broughton I are also named for him. *W*

Stopford Point (55°12'00" 130°05'00" Between Dickens Point and Dent Bluff, E side of Portland Canal, N of Prince Rupert). Lt Robert Wilbraham Stopford (1844–1911) served on the Pacific Station, 1866–69, aboard HMS *Zealous*, the flagship of the station's cdr-in-chief, Rear Adm George Hastings. He was also in BC in 1869–70 as 1st lt of HMS *Chanticleer*, under Capt William Bridges. Stopford was promoted to capt in 1885 and spent 1892–95 as capt of Britain's Royal Naval College. He came from an old naval family; both his father and grandfather were noted adms. He himself achieved the rank of vice adm in 1904. The point was named by RN surveyor Daniel Pender, of the hired vessel *Beaver*, in 1869. *W*

Stork Rock (54°25'29" 130°18'00" Head of Tuck Inlet, just N of Prince Rupert). Named after Alfred Stork (1871–1945), from Bolton, Ont, a Prince Rupert hardware dealer and the city's first mayor, elected in 1910. Before coming to the N coast in 1908 he had lived at Fernie, where he also served as mayor (in 1904). Stork was an active figure in the city's social circles and also CO of its first military organization, the Earl Grey's Own Rifles. He served as Liberal MP for the Skeena, 1921–26, but retired shortly after losing the 1926 election and returned to eastern Canada.

Storm Bay (49°40'00" 123°49'00" E side of Sechelt Inlet, S of the mouth of Narrows Inlet, NW of Vancouver). Storm Bay is presumably named for the fact that it provides good shelter for small craft in stormy weather; in fact, it is probably the most protected anchorage in Sechelt Inlet. A Vancouver company, Sechelt Brick & Tile, started a brickworks there in 1907, but the clay was poor and the plant soon closed. The bay has been home since the late 1960s to a vibrant summer community of experimental artists, most of whom have been associated at one time or another with the Western Front, a well-known Vancouver artists' co-operative.

Storm Rock (51°39'25" 127°49'30" Illahie Inlet, E side of Fitz Hugh Sd, opposite NE end of Calvert I, SE of Bella Bella). The name was submitted in June 1985 by the staff of the Institute of Ocean Sciences at Sidney, BC, after the survey launch *Storm*, which suffered considerable damage on this rock while working in Illahie Inlet.

Story Point (52°09'00" 128°08'00" NW end of Denny I, E side of Lama Passage, just S of Bella Bella). Vice Adm William Oswald Story, CBE (1859–1938), a retired RN officer, returned to active service in WWI for the RCN. He was born in Ireland, saw action as a young man in the E Indies and Egypt, and had his first command with the N Sea fisheries service. After promotion to capt in 1901 he became CO of the cruisers *Narcissus*, *Grafton* and *Cumberland* and the battleships *Canopus* and *London*. He married Olave Janet Baldwin, a native of NZ, in 1892. Story was promoted to rear adm in 1911 after serving with the Coast Guard, then retired from the RN the following year and immigrated to Guelph, Ont. When war broke out in 1914, he was named superintendent of Esquimalt dockyard, promoted to vice adm in 1917 and appointed superintendent of Halifax dockyard. He became a CBE in 1920. After the war, Adm Story retired again but remained active as honorary supervisor of the Navy League of Canada. He died at Montreal. Story Point was formerly known as Grave Point and then as Gould Point, after Capt Isaac Gould, who was Story's predecessor at Esquimalt dockyard (*see* Gould Rk). The feature received its current name in 1924.

Stradiotti Reef (49°55'00" 124°49'00" S of Savary I, Str of Georgia). Named by the hydrographic service in 1945 for Henry Felix Stradiotti, from Vancouver, whose body was recovered near this spot after his 19-m fish packer, the *Carolina Marie*, foundered in a gale on Dec 27, 1944. He was 27 years old, a former schoolteacher and graduate of UBC, where he had been a rugby star. The bodies of the three other crew members were never found and the tragic incident was never satisfactorily explained: the boat, suspected to have hit Mystery Reef, was not holed, the abundant life-saving gear never used, the throttle left wide open, the stove lit and the radio telegraph turned off. The boat's papers were later found to be missing.

Strait of Georgia. *See* Georgia, Str of.

Strange Island (49°42'00" 126°37'00" S end of Tahsis Inlet, E of Kendrick Inlet, Nootka Sd, W side of Vancouver I), **Strange Rock** (50°44'00" 128°25'00" S of Guise Bay, SW of Cape Scott, NW end of Vancouver I). James Charles

S

Stuart Strange (1753–1840), a Madras-based employee of the E India Co, led the second fur-trading expedition to the PNW, in 1786. He was born at London, the son of well-known Scottish engraver Sir Robert Strange and brother of Sir Thomas Andrew Strange, who served as chief justice of NS and Madras. With the support of Bombay merchant David Scott and the approval of the E India Co, he set off from Bombay in Dec 1785 with two well-equipped ships, the *Captain Cook*, under Capt Henry Laurie, and the *Experiment*, under Capt John Guise. Strange visited Nootka Sd, the Cape Scott area and the Alaska coast, but the voyage was a financial disaster and he was unable to interest backers in a second trip. Two valuable journals were kept by expedition members, however: one by Strange, who named Cape Scott and Queen Charlotte Sd, and one by Alexander Walker, who was in charge of a squad of soldiers assigned to build a shore depot if circumstances permitted (they didn't). Strange left the E India Co in 1795, returned to England and became an MP for Sussex. He married Anne Dundas, widowed daughter of influential politician Henry Dundas (*see* Dundas I), in 1798 but was back in India in 1804 in need of money. Strange was able to retire in 1815 and move to Scotland. James Cone on Strange I is named for him as well; the island is also known locally as Narrow I. Strange Rk was formerly called Black Rk.

Stranger Passage (48°41'49" 123°23'34" Between Knapp I and Pym I, just NE of Swartz Bay and Saanich Peninsula, N of Victoria). Named by the hydrographic service in 1965 after Capt Frederick Lewis's luxurious 34-m yacht *Stranger*. Lewis had come to BC from California in 1939 and purchased nearby Coal I, where he built a fine estate (*see* Lewis Bay). *Stranger*, the eighth (and last) yacht of that name owned by Lewis, used this passage regularly and was, in fact, the only large vessel to do so. Yacht number seven, built at Seattle in 1938 by Lake Union Drydock & Machine Works, was, at 41 m, supposedly the largest private yacht constructed in the US since the 1929 stock market crash.

Strathdang Kwun (53°40'00" 132°13'00" W entrance to Yakoun Bay, SE side of Masset Inlet, Graham I, QCI). This point was named by geologist George Mercer Dawson in 1878 after Sahldungkun, the Haida First Nation village formerly located there. According to QCI historian Kathleen Dalzell, the feature may have been known by the Haida as Yah-koon, or "straight point," and thus have been the original source of the name Yakoun, now applied to the nearby river, bay and lake. Dalzell also explains that early settlers called the point Cooper Johnny, with *cooper* being an adaptation of a Haida word meaning "strong" or "outstanding." This name became modified even further, to Copen Johnny Point, or simply Johnny Point—names that are still in occasional local use. The point is now a Masset First Nation reserve called Satunquin. *D*

Strawberry Island (49°09'00" 125°54'00" Just N of Tofino, Duffin Passage, Clayoquot Sd, W side of Vancouver I). Tofino residents used to go over to the island to pick wild strawberries, hence the name, which was submitted by hydrographer G E Richardson in 1986. An alternative local name was Leich I, a misspelled reference, apparently, to Ed Leach, a Tofino fisheries officer who was murdered in 1927. He was living on nearby Arnet I but was found dead in his boat, washed up on the shoreline of Stubbs I. No one was ever convicted for the murder, nor is it known where the crime took place or why, exactly, his name became associated with this particular feature. The island, owned in the early 2000s by diver and historian Rod Palm, is home to the Strawberry Isle Research Society, which monitors marine ecosystems in Clayoquot Sd and promotes public interest in the marine environment.

Striae Islands (54°05'00" 132°15'00" W side of McIntyre Bay, off mouth of the Otun R, N side of Graham I, QCI). Named by geologist George M Dawson in 1878 for their striated appearance. "Striae," in geological terms, are narrow grooves or scratches worn into the surface of rocks when other rocks or fragments have been dragged over them by glaciers. The outer Striae island is called Gway-tu-wuns, or "unfinished island," by the Haida people, according to QCI historian Kathleen Dalzell. A formation there, supposedly home to a supernatural being, is known as Wind Rk. Someone wanting a particular wind could tap the rock with a small stone, indicating the direction from which the desired wind should blow. *D*

Strombeck Bay (55°23'00" 129°46'00" Just SE of Granby Peninsula, Observatory Inlet, S of Stewart). Named by the hydrographic service in 1970 after John Walford Strombeck (1858–1938), who staked his first mining claims in the Alice Arm area in 1908. John worked with his brother Charles Gustaf "Gus" Strombeck (1871–1955) in a partnership known as the Strombeck Bros. Their main claims were the Alice, Toric and Vanguard groups in the Kitsault R valley. The Toric property, sold to the Consolidated Homestake Mining & Development Co about 1926, became one of the best silver producers in Canada, operating for several years in the late 1920s and then again, 1949–58, as the Torbrit Mine. John Strombeck retired to Prince Rupert, while his brother Gus died at Vancouver.

Strom Cove (52°12'00" 128°10'00" Head of Kynumpt Hbr, N end of Campbell I, just NW of Bella Bella), **Strom Point** (52°04'00" 128°04'00" N side of Hunter I, just S of Bella Bella). Fred Strom (1872–1926) and his wife, Cora (1884–1937), originally from Portland, Oregon, settled at the cove in 1912 after working for two years at Ocean Falls. They homesteaded on the flat, fertile isthmus known as Green Neck, between Strom Cove and Norman Morison Bay, and also fished for a living. Fred's bachelor brother, Charles

Strom, lived in the Bella Bella area for many years as well. Many signs of the old Strom homestead were still visible in the early 2000s, and Fred and Cora are both buried there. The name for the cove was submitted by Robert Sandilands, regional field superintendent of the Institute of Ocean Sciences, in 1984. Kynumpt Hbr is referred to locally as Strom Bay. Strom Point was formerly known as Charles Point but was changed by the hydrographic service in 1946 to avoid duplication.

Strongtide Islet (48°26'00" 123°15'00" Just N of the Chatham Is, E side of Baynes Channel, E of Oak Bay, off SE tip of Vancouver I). This name was applied by RN surveyor Capt George Richards to his 1862 chart of the area. In the *Vancouver I Pilot* of 1864, also by Richards, he notes that "the ebb tide runs very strongly past it, nearly six knots at springs."

Strouts Point (53°48'00" 130°14'00" N side of McCauley I, N entrance to Petrel Channel, S of Prince Rupert). Pilot Officer Frederick Stanley Strouts, DFC, a native of Winnipeg and resident of New Westminster, served in England with No 109 Squadron. He flew 31 bombing and mining sorties over Germany with de Havilland Mosquitoes before he was killed in action Mar 26, 1943, aged 26. Strouts is commemorated on the Runnymede Memorial, near Windsor, England.

Stuart Anchorage (53°51'00" 130°05'00" W of Bonwick Point, NE side of Pitt I), **Stuart Bay** (48°56'00" 125°31'00" E side of Ucluelet Inlet near entrance, E of Hyphocus I, W side of Barkley Sd, W side of Vancouver I), **Stuart Bight**

Stuart Channel from De Courcy Island. *Andrew Scott*

(53°49'00" 130°01'00" SE of Stuart Anchorage, NE side of Pitt I), **Stuart Channel** (49°00'00" 123°42'00" Between SE Vancouver I and De Courcy Group, Thetis I, Kuper I and NW Saltspring I, Gulf Is), **Stuart Point** (49°10'00" 123°55'00" E side of Protection I, Northumberland Channel, off Nanaimo and SE Vancouver I). Charles Edward Stuart (1817–63) was born at Bristol, England, and came to Ft Vancouver in the PNW in 1842 as 1st mate of the HBC vessel *Columbia*. He also served as mate of the *Cadboro* and the *Vancouver* before becoming master of the *Una*, which he sailed out from England in 1850, and the *Beaver*, 1851–52. In 1853, Gov James Douglas sent Stuart to the QCI to act as pilot for Cdr James Prevost and HMS *Virago*. He was put in charge of the HBC's Nanaimo post, 1855–59, and also served as magistrate for the area until discharged, according to one historian, for "chronic drunkenness." The following year Stuart established a trading post at Ucluelet and became the first European settler in that area. He died of bronchitis on board the sloop *Red Rover* off Sangster I and was buried in Nanaimo's old cemetery. Stuart Anchorage and Stuart Point were named by HBC officials in 1853, Stuart Channel and Stuart Bay by Capt George Richards (in 1858 and 1861, respectively). Stuart Bight was formerly known as False Stuart Anchorage. Canal de Haro is recorded as an old Spanish name for the N end of Stuart Channel. *W*

The Stuart Island store in 1962. *Courtesy Tim Woodland*

Stuart Island (50°23'00" 125°08'00" Mouth of Bute Inlet, N of Campbell R). Stuart I and Bute Inlet were both named in 1792 by Capt George Vancouver after Scottish nobleman John Stuart, 3rd Earl of Bute, who was British PM in 1762–63. *See* Bute Inlet for more biographical detail. The island, which was first settled in the early 1900s—and which has been home continuously since then to a handful of loggers and fishermen—has two small communities: the main one at Big Bay (qv) on the W side, and a smaller one at the SW end, known as Stuart I (and briefly, in the 1920s, as Bruce's Landing, after George Bruce, who ran a general store there, bought furs and fish, and served as postmaster). Between the two are the Yuculta Rapids, one of BC's best-known navigational hazards. In recent years Stuart I has become a sport-fishing mecca, home to several luxurious resorts and mega-mansions, including one with a private airstrip and aircraft hangar, and another with a nine-hole, PGA-certified, private golf course. *E*

Stubbs Island (49°09'00" 125°56'00" Between Tofino and Vargas I, Clayoquot Sd, W side of Vancouver I). Capt Napoleon Fitzstubbs (d 1903), a British Army officer whose surname was often written Fitz Stubbs, was an early PNW tourist, coming to BC in 1860 aboard the *Athelstan* with his friend Charles Barrett-Lennard (*see* Lennard I). The pair brought with them, as deck cargo, a small yacht named the *Templar*, which they unloaded at Victoria and sailed around Vancouver I. Barrett-Lennard returned to England and wrote a book, but Fitzstubbs enjoyed the frontier life and stayed on, joining the provincial civil service and working as a government agent, stipendiary magistrate and gold commissioner at Hazelton and, from 1891, Nelson in the W Kootenays. Stubbs I, known locally as Clayoquot I, was named by RN surveyor Capt George Richards in 1861. It became the site of a modest trading post in the 1850s and by the turn of the century was the main commercial settlement on the W coast of Vancouver I, with a store, hotel, school and government offices (police, post, telegraph, etc). Tofino, with its road access, eventually overtook Clayoquot as the regional centre, and the island community suffered a decline, though its popular hotel and pub operated until 1964. Stubbs I changed hands several times before 1989, when it became the privately owned Clayoquot Island Preserve, which opens its marvellous gardens and grounds to the public once a year in May.

Stubbs Island (50°36'00" 126°49'00" S of E end of Malcolm I, SE end of Queen Charlotte Str). Named about 1860 after Lt Edward Stubbs, who served on the Pacific Station aboard HMS *Alert*, 1860–61. He retired from the RN in 1872 and reached the rank of capt, retired, in 1878. Jim Borrowman's Stubbs Island Whale Watching, the first whale-watching company in BC, founded in 1980, took its name from this feature.

Stubbs Point (51°59'00" 128°13'00" S side of Dodwell I, off S side of Campbell I, SW of Bella Bella). Lt Cdr John Hamilton Stubbs, DSO, DSC (1913–44), was born at Kaslo and raised in Victoria. He joined the RCN in 1930 and trained in Britain, returning to Canada in 1935 as navigator of HMCS *Skeena*, a destroyer. During WWII he was appointed CO of the *Assiniboine*, another Canadian destroyer, and spent most of 1941–42 on N Atlantic convoy escort duty, during which time he and his crew attacked and sank a German submarine, *U-210*. In 1943 he became CO of the destroyer *Athabaskan*, and the following year, along with sister ship *Haida*, helped sink

the German destroyer *T-29*. Three days later, on Apr 29, 1944, in another action against enemy destroyers with the *Haida*, the *Athabaskan* was struck by a torpedo and sank, with the loss of 128 men. Lt Cdr Stubbs apparently died in the water while assisting injured crew members, having declined rescue by the *Haida*. He is buried at Plouescat Communal Cemetery in France. This feature was named by the hydrographic service in 1944.

Sturgeon Bank (49°11'00" 123°14'00" Off W side of Sea I and Lulu I, at mouth of the Fraser R, E side of Str of Georgia). Named in 1792 by Capt George Vancouver, "in consequence of our having purchased of the natives some excellent fish of that kind, weighing from 14 to 200 pounds each." Vancouver probably bought white sturgeon (*Acipenser transmontanus*), which grow to a huge size in the Fraser (a 629-kg monster was caught at New Westminster in 1897) and can live well over 100 years. The rare and endangered green sturgeon (*Acipenser medirostris*) is also occasionally found in the Fraser R.

Sturgess Bay (54°02'00" 132°14'00" SW side of Masset Hbr, N side of Graham I, QCI). Named in 1907 by Capt Frederick Learmonth of HMS *Egeria* after the *Susan Sturgis*, a US schooner that was pillaged and burned near here by the Masset Haida in 1852. *See* Susan Bank, which was named by Learmonth at the same time, in association with the bay.

Sturt Bay (49°46'00" 124°34'00" NE side of Texada I, Malaspina Str, just S of Powell R), **Sturt Point** (Just N of Sturt Bay). Lt Henry Evelyn Sturt (1841–85), of the Royal Marine Light Infantry, arrived in BC with his wife in 1870 and served with the joint military garrison that occupied San Juan I during the boundary dispute between Britain and the US. After the garrison disbanded in 1872, Sturt apparently retired from the army with the rank of capt and remained in BC. He first became interested in Texada's iron ore and marble deposits about 1876 and two years later received one of the earliest Crown land grants on Texada I. Several articles in the Victoria *Colonist* refer to Sturt's attempts to finance and develop mines and quarries on Texada, but his efforts all seem to have fallen through. The timber resources of Cortes I and Quadra I also intrigued Sturt, and shortly before he died at Nanaimo he is believed to have entered into a logging partnership of some kind with Moses Ireland. Sturt Bay is known locally as Marble Bay. The creek that flows into it is named after the bay. It is very likely that **Sturt Island** (50°14'00" 125°08'00" One of the Settlers Group, S of Maurelle I, NE of Campbell R) is also named for this entrepreneur.

Subtle Islands (50°07'00" 125°05'00" In Sutil Channel, N end of Str of Georgia, NE of Campbell R). This name, a translation of the Spanish word *sutil*, honours the 18th-century Spanish naval vessel commanded by Dionisio Alcalá-Galiano. The *Sutil* and its consort, the *Mexicana*,

The floating community of Sullivan Bay. *Peter Vassilopoulos*

passed through the region in 1792, in company with Capt George Vancouver's vessels. *See* Cape Sutil for more information. The feature was formerly known as Camp I, and appears as such on an Admiralty chart dated 1865, but was renamed by the hydrographic service in 1945 in order to avoid duplication.

Sue Channel (53°42'21" 128°56'04" N side of Hawkesbury I, between Douglas Channel and Devastation Channel, SW of Kitimat). According to former UBC anthropologist Jay Powell, this is an anglicization of Sawi, the Haisla First Nation name for the channel. Its meaning, however, is not known.

Sullivan Bay (50°53'00" 126°49'00" On Sutlej Channel, N side of N Broughton I, NE of Port McNeill), **Sullivan Point** (50°53'00" 126°48'00" E of Sullivan Bay on N Broughton I). Records at BC's Geographical Names Office suggest that the bay was named after T J Sullivan, from Ireland, an early settler in the area (a Crown grant was issued to Thomas J Sullivan in 1913). Bruce and Myrtle Collinson established a store and post office in the bay in the mid-1940s, with a fuel station that became an important floatplane depot for an emerging coastal airline industry in the 1950s. The entire settlement consists of floating structures, many of which the Collinsons purchased from Fred Petersen at nearby Kinnaird I, where the area's previous store and post office (named O'Brian Bay) had been located. Later owners at Sullivan Bay added rudimentary resort facilities for sport fishing. *E*

Sulphur Passage (49°24'00" 126°04'00" E of Obstruction I, S of Shelter Inlet, Clayoquot Sd, W side of Vancouver I). Named by the hydrographic service in 1945 for HMS *Sulphur*, which in 1835 embarked on a lengthy surveying

expedition under Capt Edward Beechey to the W coasts of N and S America, accompanied by HMS *Starling* under Lt Cdr Henry Kellett. The 340-tonne, 10-gun *Sulphur* had been launched in 1826 as a bomb or mortar ship, then converted to a survey vessel in 1835. Beechey had to be invalided home in 1836 and was replaced as expedition leader by Cdr Edward Belcher, who visited Nootka Sd in 1837 as part of his duties and also explored the islands of the S Pacific and participated in the British attack on Canton in 1841. Belcher and the *Sulphur* finally arrived back in England in 1842, having circumnavigated the globe. The ship was relegated to harbour service in 1843 and decommissioned in 1857. Sulphur Passage Provincial Park, established in 1995, protects a 2,300-ha wilderness area around the passage and nearby Shelter Inlet. *See also* Belcher Point.

Sunderland Channel (50°28'00" 125°53'00" N of Hardwicke I and Johnstone Str, NW of Campbell R). After RN officer John Wellbore Sunderland Spencer, on the Pacific Station in 1859–63. *See* Spencer Ledge. Spanish explorer Dionisio Alcalá-Galiano stopped here in 1792 and called his anchorage the Fondeadero de Bauza, after Felipe Bauzá, cartographer on Alejandro Malaspina's expedition of 1789–94.

Sunnyside Beach (49°18'00" 122°52'00" N side of Port Moody, just E of Vancouver). The Dockrill family settled at Dockrill Point (qv) in 1883 and established a homestead and shingle mill. Their wharf, called Dockrill's Landing at first, became better known as Sunnyside Landing, and this later name became attached to the nearby beach.

Sunshine Coast (50°00'00" 123°45'00" Between Howe Sd and Desolation Sd). The Union Steamship Co borrowed this name from local pioneer Harry Roberts about 1925 to promote its holiday excursions to Sechelt and Selma

The Sunshine Coast, with the Trail Islands in the foreground and Sargeant Bay in the distance. *Peter Vassilopoulos*

Park. The original phrase, which Roberts had painted in large letters on the freight shed at the Roberts Ck steamship dock, was "Sunshine Belt." The company also called the region "the Gulf Coast Riviera" in its brochures. The original Sunshine Coast stretched between Howe Sd and Jervis Inlet, roughly the same piece of shoreline that now forms the southern boundary of the Sunshine Coast Regional District, which was incorporated in 1967. Today the Powell R area (sometimes known as the N or Upper Sunshine Coast) is usually included. While not an official name—and thus not normally eligible for inclusion in this work—the Sunshine Coast appears here partly because the origin of the name is of historic interest, and partly as an indulgence to the author, who lived at Halfmoon Bay and Sechelt for many years. The area, incidentally, receives only slightly more sunshine than Vancouver does—and far less than Victoria. *E*

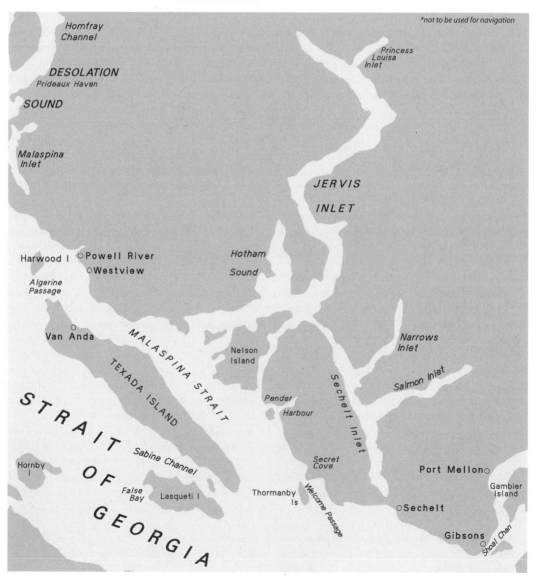

The Sunshine Coast and offshore islands. *Reproduced with the permission of the Canadian Hydrographic Service*

Suquash (50°38'00" 127°15'00" Just NW of Port McNeill, NE end of Vancouver I). Suquash is an adaptation of a Kwakwala term meaning "where seals are butchered." The name was adopted by HBC officers after the first coal discovery on Vancouver I was made here in 1835. Some primitive mining took place about 1850, but better coal was found at Ft Rupert and Nanaimo. Despite its inferior quality, coal was extracted here commercially in 1908–14 and 1920–22 by Pacific Coast Coal Mines Ltd. Another brief attempt to establish a colliery was made as late as 1952. Suquash Ck flows into Queen Charlotte Str at this location. *W*

Surf Inlet (52°57'00" 129°01'00" W side of Princess Royal I). This remote fjord once led to one of BC's most productive gold mines. The name reflects the inlet's direct exposure to Caamaño Sd and the open Pacific; its waters can get rough, especially near the entrance. Princess Royal's gold, silver and copper reserves are located at the N end of the island but were more easily exploited from Surf Inlet. The deposits were first explored about 1900, but it was not until 1917 that Belmont Surf Inlet Mines Ltd began production. The operation was a complex one with several extraction sites. After the ore was crushed and concentrated it travelled via electric tramway and then by barge along a series of lakes to a loading facility and townsite at tidewater. The lakes were modified with a large dam to create an efficient transport route. The initial phase of mining ended in 1926, but Surf Inlet Consolidated Gold Mines Ltd reworked the area in 1935–42 and 1945–46. At its height in the 1920s, the camp at the head of the inlet had 200 workers, a large hydroelectric power plant, hospital, school, recreation hall, store and post office. Nearly 400,000 oz of gold were produced over the years, worth more than $325 million at 2009 prices. The ruined wharf and camp buildings were still visible in the early 2000s. Surf Inlet was formerly known as Port Belmont. The Surf R enters into and is named after the inlet. *E*

Surge Narrows (50°14'00" 125°09'00" SE end of Okisollo Channel, between Quadra I and S end of Maurelle I, NE of Campbell R), **Surge Point** (50°13'00" 125°08'00" Just E of Surge Narrows). The current in these tidal rapids can reach 12 knots (22 km/h) at peak flows. Surge Narrows Provincial Park, established in 1996, protects a 488-ha zone surrounding the rapids, which are noted for their rich marine ecosystem. Surge Narrows is also the name of a small settlement on the W side of Read I that got its start about 1912, when John Jones became the first postmaster. Robert and Margaret Tipton arrived in 1918, established a farm and store and attracted a small group of other homesteaders. A school was built and Tipton was appointed justice of the peace. (The school, in updated quarters, was still open in the early 2000s, as was the post office, though the store closed in 2007.) *E*

Surgeon Islets (50°53'00" 126°52'00" NW of N Broughton I, N end of Wells Passage, NE of Port McNeill). After Thomas Atkinson, an RN assistant surgeon on the Pacific Station, 1864–66. *See* Atkinson I.

Surprise Island (50°03'00" 127°18'00" N of Union I, Crowther Channel, Kyuquot Sd, NW Vancouver I), **Surprise Reef** (49°07'00" 125°56'00" S of Wickaninnish I, SW of Tofino, Clayoquot Sd, W side of Vancouver I). The *Surprise* was a well-known early trading and sealing schooner on the BC coast, owned by capts William Spring and Hugh McKay. They acquired this 40-tonne vessel, built on Puget Sd, in 1859 and traded with it on the W coast of Vancouver I. In 1868 one of their skippers, James Christiansen, had the idea of loading several dugout canoes on board the *Surprise*, along with a group of Tla-o-qui-aht (Clayoquot) First Nation hunters, and taking them out to the sealing grounds instead of merely buying skins from shore-based sealers. The hunters liked this idea too, as it was safer to hunt offshore from a larger vessel and they weren't away from their families for such long periods. The first year Christiansen tried out his new method, it was a failure; only 27 skins were secured. In 1869, however, with a First Nation crew from Port San Juan and smaller canoes, he got 900 skins, and the offshore or pelagic sealing industry was born. The *Surprise* was wrecked off Sooke Hbr in 1874, with John Peterson in command. Surprise Reef was named in 1862 by Capt George Richards of HMS *Hecate*, in association with McKay Reef. *See also* Christiansen Point, McKay Reef *and* Spring Cove. *W*

Surrey (49°07'00" 122°45'00" S side of the Fraser R, between Delta and Langley, SE of Vancouver), **Surrey Islands** (49°30'00" 123°59'00" Between N and S Thormanby Is, NW entrance to Welcome Passage, just NW of Sechelt and Vancouver). The name of the sprawling suburb was chosen by a group of pioneer farmers, mostly British immigrants, at the time the district was incorporated in

The tidal rapids at Surge Narrows. *Andrew Scott*

1879. There are conflicting reports about who originally came up with the idea. Most sources agree, however, that the early settlers named their new home because it lay S of New Westminster, across a river, just as the county of Surrey in England lay S across the R Thames from old Westminster in London. Today Surrey has outgrown its agricultural origins to become BC's second-largest city. The Surrey Is are also named after the English county, but for far less nostalgic reasons. Surrey is home to Epsom Downs, the track that hosts the Derby, one of England's most famous horse races. RN capt George Richards and his wager-loving officers aboard the survey vessel *Plumper* gave the area many horse-racing names in 1860 after hearing happy news of that year's Derby. *E*

Susan Bank (54°02'00" 132°12'00" In Masset Hbr, N side of Graham I, QCI), **Susan Sturgis Point** (53°00'00" 132°20'00" N side of Hibben I, Inskip Channel, Kuper Inlet, NW side of Moresby I). The 150-tonne *Susan Sturgis* was a US schooner that first came to Kuper Inlet in the spring of 1852, following rumours of a gold discovery. Capt Matthew Rooney and his crew found nothing, however, and returned home with a load of spars, much to the indignation of Gov James Douglas, who protested that this was "a liberty that no British vessel would be permitted to take on the American coasts" and took advantage of the incident to extend British control over the region. The *Sturgis* returned that fall, again found no gold, and continued up the E coast of the QCI to trade and prospect. At Skidegate, Chief Edensaw came aboard to pilot the ship along the N shore of Graham I, where it was hijacked, looted and burned by the Masset Haida. Contemporary accounts of the event differ: some say that Edensaw saved the lives of the crew by persuading the Massets to exchange them for ransom; others claim he helped plan the attack and shared in the plunder. Sturgess Bay (qv) in Masset Hbr is also named after this unfortunate vessel. *D*

Susan Rock (52°17'00" 128°30'00" In Milbanke Sd, W of Cecilia I, NW of Bella Bella). Named for Susan Frances Pemberton, the sister of Joseph Pemberton, Vancouver I's first colonial surveyor gen. A native of Ireland, she came out to Victoria about 1855 with her uncle, Augustus Pemberton, and lived with her brother at Gonzales, the large Pemberton estate in SE Victoria. She became the first principal of newly constructed Angela College, an early Victoria school for girls, in 1866 (this institution had previously been located elsewhere in Victoria and known as the Anglican Collegiate for Girls). Susan returned to England in 1869 in poor health and died the following year near Paris. Susan Rk was formerly known as White Rk.

Susan Sturgis Point. *See* Susan Bank.

Sutil Channel, Sutil Mountain, Sutil Point. *See* Cape Sutil.

Sutlej Channel (50°53'00" 126°44'00" NE sides of Broughton I and N Broughton I, NE of Port McNeill), **Sutlej Point** (52°22'00" 126°48'00" S side of N Bentinck Arm, just W of Bella Coola), **Sutlej Rock** (49°18'00" 125°57'00" In Whitepine Cove, E side of Herbert Inlet, Clayoquot Sd, W side of Vancouver I). HMS *Sutlej*, a powerful steam frigate with 35 guns and a complement of 510, was the flagship on the Pacific Station, 1863–66. At 75 m and 3,470 tonnes, it was one of the largest vessels that had been based at Esquimalt up until that time. It was commanded by Capt Matthew Connolly and carried the flag of Rear Adm John Kingcome, the station's cdr-in-chief, until Apr 1864; after that date, Capt Trevenen Coode and Rear Adm Joseph Denman took over. Named after a river in India, the *Sutlej* had been launched as a wooden sailing vessel in 1855, then converted to steam in 1860; it was broken up in 1869. While posted to BC it saw considerable action, taking Kingcome to N Bentinck Arm in 1864 in pursuit of the killers of several white settlers, an incident associated with the so-called Chilcotin War, which was prompted by the massacre of 14 roadbuilders at the head of Bute Inlet. Later that year the frigate carried Denman to Clayoquot Sd to investigate the destruction of the trading sloop *Kingfisher* and the murder of its crew by the Ahousaht. His ships shelled and burned nine First Nation villages but failed to capture Chapchah, the Ahousaht chief involved in the piracy. All three features were named in 1864 by Lt Daniel Pender of the *Beaver*.

The Sutton Islets in Skookumchuck Narrows. *Andrew Scott*

Sutton Islets (49°46'00" 123°56'00" In Skookumchuck Narrows, N end of Sechelt Inlet, E side of Jervis Inlet, NW of Vancouver). After Capt John Sutton of the RN, who commanded the 74-gun ship of the line *Egmont* at the 1797 Battle of Cape St Vincent off Portugal, in which Sir John Jervis defeated a much larger Spanish fleet. He later commanded HMS *Superb*. Sutton was promoted to rear adm in 1804 and ended his career as a knight and a vice adm. Named in 1945 by the hydrographic service, in association with nearby Egmont Point.

Sutton Rock (48°56'00" 125°32'00" Just NW of entrance to Ucluelet Inlet, W side of Barkley Sd, W side of Vancouver I). William John Sutton (1859–1914) and James Edward Sutton (b 1863) were pioneer entrepreneurs at Ucluelet in the late 1880s. Through their company, Sutton Lumber & Trading, the brothers established a sawmill and general store on the NE side of the harbour and also had many mining interests. Their English father, William Sutton (1828–96), a former sheriff of Bruce County, Ont, had brought his family to BC in 1875 and built a sawmill on the Cowichan R. He also helped set up the Ucluelet operation. William John was a metallurgist, a graduate of the Columbia School of Mines at Cornell, and initially worked for the BC government as an assayer in Victoria. He married Helen Annie Fox (1862–1932) in 1892 and became a mineralogist for Robert Dunsmuir's many mining interests. Sutton Pass, N of Sproat Lk, is named for him as well. James, who married Ada Walker, managed his father's Cowichan sawmill before the mill at Ucluelet was established. He was appointed a justice of the peace at Ucluelet in 1896. Both brothers were involved in turn-of-the-century efforts to extract placer gold from the black beach sands of Florencia Bay, an initiative that proved less than successful. Sutton Mill Ck on Meares I is named after the large sawmill built at Mosquito Hbr in 1905; the Sutton brothers were not directly involved in this mill, having sold their timber interests in the area in 1904 to a US company. The new owners kept the old corporate name for the mill, but it failed several years later.

Suwanee Rock (50°54'00" 127°49'00" Shadwell Passage, between Hope I and Vansittart I, off N end of Vancouver I). The USS *Suwanee*, launched at Chester, Pennsylvania, in 1864, during the US Civil War, was an iron-hulled, sidewheel gunboat designed for river use, with a shallow draft and front-and-rear rudders. On its way to Alaska in 1868, with Victoria pilot James Cooper aboard, the 934-tonne naval vessel became grounded on this previously uncharted rock. As the tide dropped, the ship broke in half and was completely destroyed. Cdr Richard Law and his crew survived, and salvage operations retrieved the guns, ammunition and machinery. Nearby First Nation groups claimed the food and most of the smaller articles. The wreck has been a popular dive site for years, and artifacts from the *Suwanee* adorn the homes and gardens of a number of local recreational divers. *W*

Suzette Bay (52°24'00" 128°26'00" SW side of Dowager I, Milbanke Sd, NW of Bella Bella). After Josette Legacé, a pioneer resident of colonial Victoria and the wife of senior HBC official John Work. She often appears in the historical record as Suzette Legacé, though whether this is an alternative personal name or an error is uncertain. *See* Legace Bay.

Swaine Point. *See* Cape Swaine.

Swan Bay (52°20'00" 131°18'00" S side of Burnaby I, off SE side of Moresby I, QCI), **Swan Islands** (Entrance to Swan Bay). James Gilchrist Swan (1818–1900) was commissioned by the Smithsonian Institution in 1883 to tour the QCI and collect Haida First Nation artifacts for the museum. He also prepared reports for the US Fish and Fisheries Commission and for the Bureau of Ethnology. Haida artist Johnny Kit Elswa, from Tanu, acted as his guide and interpreter. Swan was born in Massachusetts but went W during the California gold rush and had an amazingly varied career: customs inspector, shipwright, oysterman, secretary, journalist, lawyer, judge, teacher and school superintendent, railroad promoter, naturalist and ethnographer. He lived for many years at Port Townsend, and his several books include the first ethnographic studies of the Makah people, a First Nation group living at Neah Bay in NW Washington. In 1875, Swan travelled to Alaska, where he purchased First Nation poles, a war canoe and an entire lodge for the 1876 Centennial Exhibition at Philadelphia. Both geographical features were named by the hydrographic service in 1962.

Swan Rock (51°32'00" 127°47'00" S of Addenbroke Point, N entrance to Darby Channel, E side of Fitz Hugh Sd, SE of Bella Bella). The 35-tonne steam tug *Swan* was built at Victoria by W J Stevens in 1893 for Robert Draney, owner of the first Rivers Inlet cannery. Draney later used the *Swan* at his Namu cannery, then sold it to Capt John Cates, who developed Bowen I as a holiday destination for Vancouver vacationers. The vessel had a long history as a cannery tender on the BC coast and was owned by Northern BC Fisheries Ltd in 1919. Swan Rk was named in 1897 by Capt John Walbran, the noted coastal mariner and historian.

Swanson Bay (53°01'00" 128°31'00" E side of Graham Reach, opposite Princess Royal I), **Swanson Channel** (48°46'00" 123°20'00" W of N Pender I, E of Prevost I, Saltspring I and Moresby I, Gulf Is), **Swanson Island** (50°37'00" 126°42'00" N of Hanson I and Blackfish Sd, SE end of Queen Charlotte Str), **Swanson Passage** (50°37'00" 126°41'00" Between Swanson I and Crease I), **Swanson Point** (53°01'00" 128°31'00" N entrance to Swanson Bay). Capt John Swanson (1827–72) was one of the HBC's most reliable early shipmasters in the PNW. He was born in Rupert's Land, probably at Moose Factory on James Bay, where his father, William A Swanson, also worked as an HBC mariner (and, according to HBC records, had 20 children with three different wives). John arrived at Ft Vancouver in 1842 and served as an apprentice sailor on the *Cadboro*, *Vancouver* and *Columbia*, then as a seaman on the *Cowlitz*, working his way up to 2nd mate by 1849. He is listed as mate of the *Mary Dare*, 1852–54, and must have received his master's accreditation in 1854, as he appears in HBC records as master of the *Otter* (1854–56), *Beaver* (1856–58), *Labouchere* (1859–66) and *Enterprise*

Shifting Features

Geographic features have a quality of permanence about them. One doesn't expect a mountain or island to change. In reality, though, the geography of the planet is in constant flux. Rivers alter course; rocks are eroded by wind and ice; beaches form and wash away. Nature, over the long term, is the instigator of such changes, but humankind is making its mark with increasing, relentless frequency. And as the shape and form of the land change, so must the names that we give to its places.

Esquimalt Harbour, for instance, has undergone numerous renovations over the past 150 years, resulting in the loss or alteration of many geographical features. There used to be a Thetis Island in the harbour, off the south shore of Constance Cove. It was marked "Naval Store" on an 1861 Admiralty chart but was joined to Vancouver Island during the construction of Esquimalt's first drydock, in 1887. Forty years later, a much larger drydock was opened near Admirals Road, completely wiping from the charts a feature that had been known for years as Skinner Cove, named after Thomas Skinner, who came to Victoria in 1853 to manage the farm that the Hudson's Bay Company established beside Constance Cove.

Nearby, in Victoria Harbour, was Coffin Island, which was used as a First Nation cemetery. Bodies were left in wooden boxes but not buried, sometimes attracting relic hunters, vandals and arsonists. There are several lurid 19th-century accounts in the Victoria *Colonist* of brush fires that swept through the coffins. In the 1970s, landfills altered the shoreline to such an extent that the island became joined to Vancouver Island, and in 1976 the name was changed to Coffin Island Point. Lone Rock on the west side of Indian Arm, now Lone Rock Point, has been similarly changed by human development. Other features, such as Gowing Island in the Queen Charlottes—joined by a causeway to much larger Moresby Island when the instant mining town of Tasu was built in the early 1960s—are technically no longer islands but still retain their original names.

A separate category of human changes would include rocks that were blown up because they were a danger to shipping. The most famous of many examples is Ripple Rock in Seymour Narrows, responsible for dozens of shipwrecks and hundreds of deaths. It was blasted to smithereens in 1958 in one of the largest non-nuclear explosions in history. Ripple Rock, though decidedly shorter in stature, is still listed by that name on the charts. However, Romulus Rock in Porlier Pass—named after the German steamship that first struck it in 1893—was renamed Romulus Reef after being reduced by blasting in 1972.

Some features are completely new and have been added to the coastal landscape purely through human effort. Elsje Point in front of the Vancouver Maritime Museum is an example. This artificial breakwater was named for Elsje Armstrong, who played key leadership roles with the Vancouver Museums and Planetarium Association and the Vancouver Academy of Music. The name was officially adopted in 1984.

Nowhere in BC have there been more geographical changes in the last century, both natural and constructed, than in the lower reaches of the Fraser River. About 13 million cubic metres of silt (more than enough to completely fill BC Place twice) are added every year to the Fraser delta, which is further modified by extensive dredging and hundreds of kilometres of dikes and training walls. In the last century the estuary's marshes expanded by 625 hectares. More than three metres of deposits have been added in many areas.

An 1860 Admiralty chart by Captain George Richards shows Sparrowhawk Shoal where Barber Island now sits. Annacis Island was once much smaller; its northeast section was separate and known as Robson Island after its owner, who went on to become a premier of BC. Mitchell Island under the Knight Street bridge was originally three islands: Mitchell, Twigg and Eburne. Sand dredged from shipping channels was used to join the properties in 1937. Elsewhere around the estuary, several other islands—Rowling, Tree, Dinsmore, Wood and Pheasant—appeared as separate features on early maps. All have now joined the mainland or are part of Lulu or Sea islands.

Mitchell Island under the Knight Street bridge was originally three islands. *Andrew Scott*

Ruins at Swanson Bay, site of BC's first pulp mill. *Andrew Scott*

(1866–72). He died at Victoria. Swanson Bay, site of BC's first pulp mill in 1909—and later a fisheries station and flying-boat base until abandoned in the early 1940s—was named by HBC mariner Capt Charles Dodd about 1844. Swanson Channel was named by Capt George Richards of HMS *Plumper* in 1859, Swanson I by Lt Daniel Pender of the *Beaver* in 1867. *E W*

Swanton Bank (54°12'00" 133°02'00" Off Cloak Bay, S side of Langara I, off NW end of Graham I, QCI). Linguist and anthropologist John Reed Swanton (1873–1958), from Maine, came to the QCI for a year in 1900–1901 and recorded much of the classic Haida narrative poetry. Strongly influenced by Franz Boas, he took his PhD at Harvard Univ and was employed by the Bureau of American Ethnology for almost 40 years. Swanton's early work was mostly in the PNW, and he published several influential compilations of Haida and Tlingit stories and myths in 1905 and 1909. He then turned his attention to the Muskogean-speaking First Nations of Texas, Louisiana and Oklahoma, writing numerous books on the Chickasaw, Choctaw and Creek people. Swanton was president of the American Anthropological Assoc in 1932 and editor of *American Anthropologist* in 1911 and 1921–23. The Haida name for Swanton Bank, according to QCI historian Kathleen Dalzell, is Th'careway, or "kelp bed and breakers."

Swartz Bay (48°41'17" 123°24'25" N end of Saanich Peninsula, N of Victoria), **Swartz Head** (Extreme NE tip of Saanich Peninsula, just E of Swartz Bay). John Aaron Swart purchased 34 ha of land in the vicinity of the bay from John Otto in 1876. His brother Lansing Otis Swart appears to have lived on the property as well. The Swart brothers were originally from Cranesville, NY, and migrated to California in the 1850s. Their name was incorrectly spelled when Swartz Bay was adopted by the hydrographic service in 1934. Attempts by the province's chief geographer in 1968 to have the name changed to Swarts Bay were rebuffed by BC Ferries officials "because of the vast amount of changes

The BC Ferries terminal at Swartz Bay. *Kevin Oke*

that would be necessary in the printed items" and "also in the degree of confusion that might be created in the minds of people, particularly tourists." Swartz Bay has seen use as a ferry dock since 1930, when the *Cy Peck* began 30 years of service to Fulford Hbr on Saltspring I. In 1960 a modern terminal and highway were built to connect Victoria to the BC mainland, as well as to the Gulf Is.

Swiftsure Bank (48°34'00" 124°59'00" Entrance to Juan de Fuca Str, off SW Vancouver I between Barkley Sd and Port San Juan). HMS *Swiftsure*, a 14-gun steam-powered battleship that was also rigged for sail, served as the flagship on the Pacific Station in 1882–85 and 1888–90 and was largely based at Esquimalt. Rear Adm John Baird was the station's cdr-in-chief for the first period, while the ship's cdr was Capt Henry Aitchison; during the second commission, Rear Adm Algernon Heneage was cdr-in-chief and Capt James Hammet was cdr of the *Swiftsure*. The 6,267-tonne, 85-m vessel was launched in 1871 and saw early service in the Mediterranean. It was classified as a stores hulk in 1901, renamed HMS *Orontes* and sold in 1908. The annual Swiftsure International Yacht Race, first held in 1930, takes its name from the fact that the boats used to race from Victoria out to the US Coast Guard lightship on Swiftsure Bank, then back again. This vessel, which had "Swiftsure" written on its sides in large letters, indicated the entrance to Juan de Fuca Str until 1961 but was then deemed unnecessary and removed. Since that time a temporarily anchored RCN ship has marked the race's turning point. The bank, 13 km offshore with a least depth of 34 m, is an important commercial fishing area.

Swindle Island (52°32'00" 128°35'00" S of Princess Royal I, NW of Bella Bella), **Swindle Point** (52°28'00" 128°28'00"

S

E side of Swindle I). The origin of this intriguing name, unfortunately, is unknown. It first appears on an Admiralty chart dated 1867, though not on a chart of the same area dated 1865. The island is home to Klemtu, a fishing settlement founded about 1875 by the Kitasoo and Xai'xais First Nations, who moved to the area from their respective traditional territories in order to be closer to coastal shipping routes.

Swiss Boy Island (48°55'00" 125°08'00" E side of Imperial Eagle Channel, W of Tzartus I, Barkley Sd, W side of Vancouver I). The US brig *Swiss Boy*, under Capt Weldon, was en route from Puget Sd to San Francisco in 1859 with a load of lumber when it sprang a leak and had to put in to Barkley Sd for repairs. The vessel was boarded by members of the Ohiaht and Tseshaht First Nations, who stripped it of everything valuable, right down to the sails, rigging and masts. According to Weldon, the lives of the crew—who were able to make their way onto another schooner, the *Morning Star*—were preserved only by the intervention of Wha-latl (more commonly known as Swell or Swale), a visiting Makah First Nation chief from Neah Bay. Capt James Prevost and HMS *Satellite* investigated the incident and apprehended several suspects, who were taken to Victoria but later released. Prevost, who believed that forbearance and diplomacy were better policies than force when dealing with First Nation groups, recommended that Gov James Douglas appoint an Indian agent for the region, a suggestion that was later put into effect. The island was named by RN surveyor George Richards of HMS *Plumper* about 1860. *W*

Switzer Cove (52°44'00" 129°17'00" In Borrowman Bay, NW side of Aristazabal I). John William Switzer (1858–1925), a native of NZ, came to BC in 1870 and married Margaret Catherine Wilson (1865–1937) at Victoria in 1886. In the 1901 census he is listed as the owner, with a partner named McClusky, of the Regent Saloon on Douglas St. Switzer is believed to have taken part in the Victoria old-timers' reunion of 1924 (*see* Adams Bay).

Swordfish Island (48°19'00" 123°35'00" Off SW side of Rocky Point, off S tip of Vancouver I). The 660-tonne British sailing ship *Swordfish*, under Capt J S Handley, ran aground here in 1877 and was completely wrecked. The vessel was on its way from San Francisco to Burrard Inlet when it drifted onto the rocks in the middle of the night and was holed and dismasted. All hands made it to shore safely and were taken to Victoria by the RN sloop-of-war *Opal*. The unfortunate ship was consigned to BC's receiver of wrecks and sold for its salvage value. The island appears as Cliff I on an Admiralty chart dated 1872 but was renamed by the hydrographic service in 1934.

Sydney Inlet (49°26'00" 126°15'00" NW side of Flores I, NW of Clayoquot Sd, W side of Vancouver I), **Sydney River** (49°31'00" 126°18'00" Flows S into the head of Sydney Inlet). RN surveyor George Richards named the inlet in 1861, but the derivation of the name is not known. It has been the site of several fish-processing and mining operations. A herring saltery, established at the head of the inlet by ex-sealer Capt George Heater and destroyed in a severe storm in the winter of 1920–21, became quite a local attraction when its owner brought 20 young women from Scotland to work there and housed them in an old converted sealing schooner named the *Favourite*. A pilchard reduction plant operated in the 1920s and '30s, and a copper mine was active intermittently from 1907 to 1939. A post office, misspelled Sidney Inlet for most of its life, operated in 1917–27 and 1936–48. In 1979 the inlet was in the news when the *Samarkanda*, used by Colombian drug traffickers to smuggle tonnes of marijuana into the US, took shelter there to repair an engine problem and was seized by the RCMP. Sydney Inlet Provincial Park, 2,774 ha in area, was established in 1995 to protect one of the best examples on Vancouver I of a wilderness fjord. Nearby Sydney Cone takes its name from the inlet. *E*

Sykes Island (49°49'00" 124°05'00" St Vincent Bay, Jervis Inlet, NW of Vancouver). Named by Capt George Richards of HMS *Plumper* about 1860 after John Sykes (c 1760–1841), an RN seaman and coxswain, and a faithful follower of Adm Lord Nelson. Sykes was present at most of Nelson's great victories and was seriously injured at Cadiz after the 1797 Battle of Cape St Vincent while protecting Nelson in fierce hand-to-hand fighting. He later owned a fishmonger's shop at Greenwich. He is not to be confused with the John Sykes who was a master's mate on HMS *Discovery*, after whom Capt George Vancouver named a point in Behm Canal, Alaska. *W*

Sylvester Point (52°38'00" 127°02'00" W side of Dean Channel, NW of Bella Coola). John Berg Sylvester (1868–1923) was one of the intrepid Norwegian colonists who settled the Bella Coola valley in the mid-1890s. He received several Crown grants of land there, in 1901, 1903 and 1909, and married Karen Thorsen in 1921, only two years before he died. The point was named by the hydrographic service in 1958.

Syren Point (49°53'00" 124°02'00" NE side of Hotham Sd, Jervis Inlet, E of Powell R). Named by the hydrographic service in 1945 after HMS *Syren*, in association with Hotham Sd (qv). About 1756, while still a lt, William Hotham commanded the 20-gun *Syren* in a spirited engagement with the larger, 26-gun French frigate *Télémaque*. This initiative was noted by his superiors, as were other daring actions against larger enemy vessels, and Hotham was soon promoted to capt and the command of frigates himself. He went on to become a noted adm and cdr-in-chief of the Mediterranean fleet.

Ta-aack Rock (51°00'00" 127°40'00" SE of the Storm Is, W end of Queen Charlotte Str). The Nak'waxda'xw people of Seymour Inlet, members of the Kwakwaka'wakw First Nation, have two reserves on the precariously situated (but well named) Storm Is that were used as fishing camps. Ta-aack Rk was named by the hydrographic service in 1947 after one of those reserves.

Taaltz Point (51°02'00" 126°42'00" S entrance to Salmon Arm, Frederick Sd, off SE Seymour Inlet, NE of Port McNeill). Named after a former Nak'waxda'xw settlement on Salmon Arm. The Nak'waxda'xw people of Seymour Inlet, members of the Kwakwaka'wakw First Nation, moved to Blunden Hbr in the mid-1800s to be closer to coastal shipping routes, then moved again, to Port Hardy, in the 1960s. Formerly known as Bluff Point but renamed by the hydrographic service in 1949. Taaltz Ck, which flows S into Salmon Arm, is also named after this First Nation village.

Tahini Cove (49°26'00" 124°10'00" SE end of Lasqueti I, E of Young Point, Str of Georgia). This name was suggested in 1985 by Vancouver architect Wilfred Buttjes, who owned land beside Young Point, after his boat, the *Tahini*. The proposal was supported by a petition of local residents and adopted in 1986. Tahini can be translated as "river of the king salmon" (from the Tlingit First Nation words *tá*, for king salmon, and *héen*, for river). The Tahini R flows S across the BC-Alaska border to join the Chilkat R, which ends up in Lynn Canal.

Tahsis (49°55'00" 126°40'00" Head of Tahsis Inlet), **Tahsish Inlet** (50°06'00" 127°07'00" NE extension of Kyuquot Sd, NW side of Vancouver I), **Tahsish River** (50°08'26" 127°06'19" Flows S into head of Tahsish Inlet), **Tahsis Inlet** (49°43'00" 126°37'00" Extends N from Nootka Sd, W side of Vancouver I), **Tahsis Narrows** (49°52'00" 126°42'00" Between Tahsis Inlet and Hecate Channel, NE end of Nootka I), **Tahsis River** (49°55'00" 126°40'00" Flows S into head of Tahsis Inlet). The name Tahsis is a modification of a Nuu-chah-nulth First Nation word meaning "way"

"Wet launching" from *Uchuck III* in Tahsis Inlet. *Andrew Scott*

or "passage," and refers to an ancient but important trade route across Vancouver I that led up the Tahsis R to Woss Lk and Nimpkish Lk. Another trail across the island (one that Lt Philip Hankin and Dr Charles Wood of HMS *Hecate* took in 1862) led from Tahsish Inlet in Kyuquot Sd up the Tahsish R and overland to Nimpkish Lk. Several versions of the name are recorded, including Tah-cease and Tashees. In the late 18th century, the head of Tahsis Inlet was the site of an important Mowachaht First Nation winter village. Chief Maquinna entertained Capt George Vancouver and Juan Francisco de la Bodega y Quadra in lavish fashion there in 1792. Today's village of Tahsis was founded in 1945, when the Gibson brothers built a sawmill. It has been a sawmill community ever since and was not connected by road to the rest of Vancouver I until 1972. Tahsis Inlet was originally named Tasis Canal; that was changed to Tahsis Canal in 1938 and to its current form in 1947. Tahsish Inlet was formerly known as Tahsish Arm. Tahsish Lk and Tahsis Mtn are also named after the respective rivers. *E W*

Takelley Cove (52°42'00" 131°41'00" W end of Atli Inlet, Lyell I, off E side of Moresby I, QCI). "Takelley" was the old telegraph code for the Kelley Logging Co, which grew

T

to become one of the largest logging operators in the QCI. Thomas Kelley, a civil engineer from the US, came to the QCI as early as 1908 and worked as a timber cruiser. After WWI he became a logging contractor, working at first for the Whalen Pulp & Paper Co, which owned the pulp mill at Swanson Bay. Later he became associated with the Powell R Co, which ultimately bought his company. Kelley's logging methods were not always the soundest. He completely destroyed the salmon run on Lyell I's Gate Ck, for instance, by sluicing logs down the stream. Takelley Cove was named by the hydrographic service in 1948. *D*

Taleomey Narrows (52°01'00" 126°41'00" Near head of S Bentinck Arm, S of Bella Coola), **Taleomey River** (52°02'00" 126°41'00" Flows W into S Bentinck Arm near Taleomey Narrows). Taleomey is a modification of the name of the Talhyumc (or Talyumc) people, a subgroup of the Nuxalk First Nation, who once inhabited S Bentinck Arm (*see below*). They knew the arm as Ats'aaxlh and had a large winter village, called Talyu, at the river's mouth. Substantial log-booming grounds are located nearby. The narrows take their name from the river, as do the Taleomey Glacier and Taleomey Tower.

Tallheo Point (52°19'00" 126°57'00" E entrance to S Bentinck Arm, just W of Bella Coola). Tallheo is the name of the dialect spoken by the Talhyumc (or Talyumc) people, who traditionally lived on S Bentinck Arm (*see above*). The Tallheo Cannery and steamship landing, however, was located on the N side of N Bentinck Arm, just NE of Custom House Point. Originally known as the Nieumiamus Cannery, it was built in 1917 by Bella Coola entrepreneur Fillip Jacobsen with the financial backing of R V Winch, then transferred to Northern BC Fisheries Ltd. In 1925 the Canadian Fishing Co was the proprietor. After 1951 the plant was turned into a gillnet camp. In the early 2000s a private owner restored some of the buildings and opened them as the Tallheo Cannery Inn. The Tallheo Hot Springs are located on S Bentinck Arm.

Talunkwan Island (52°50'00" 131°45'00" Between Selwyn Inlet and Dana Inlet, off E side of Moresby I, QCI). Named by geologist George M Dawson in 1878 after the Haida First Nation name for the E end of the island (now known as Heming Head). Two quite different meanings for the word have been advanced: QCI expert Kathleen Dalzell states that it refers to the marine bioluminescence that is very noticeable at that location; BC historians Helen and Philip Akrigg translate it as "to slice something that is fat." The island saw a great deal of prospecting activity for copper in the early 1900s. Thurston Hbr on its N side was an important "aeroplane spruce" camp during WWI and continued to be a logging centre for many years thereafter. *D*

Tangent Island (53°34'00" 129°56'00" N of Anger I, W side of Pitt I), **Tangent Point** (53°34'00" 129°57'00" SW

end of Tangent I). These features were named by a coast triangulation party under A E Wright, a surveyor with the BC Lands Service, in 1921. A tangent is a mathematical ratio between the sides opposite and adjacent to an angle in a right-angled triangle and is used in surveying to measure gradients and distances. Other nearby features (Azimuth I, Cosine Bay, Cosine I, Cosine Point, Logarithm Point, Sine I, Sine Point) are also named after surveying terms.

Tangil Peninsula (52°47'00" 131°43'00" Between Dana Inlet and Logan Inlet, E side of Moresby I, QCI). The name of this long narrow feature, applied by the hydrographic service in 1957, is the Haida First Nation word for tongue, as listed by geologist George M Dawson in the appendix to his 1880 monograph "On the Haida Indians of the QCI."

Tangle Cove (52°20'00" 131°21'00" SW entrance to Burnaby Str, SE side of Moresby I, QCI). George Mercer Dawson anchored at this location in the small schooner *Wanderer* on his 1878 geological expedition around the QCI. He named the cove after the tangle of vegetation he found there, both in the water and along the shoreline.

Tanu Island, site of the famed Haida village of T'aanuu. *Andrew Scott*

Tan Island (50°06'00" 125°00'00" In Gorge Hbr, SW side of Cortes I, N end of Str of Georgia). Tan I was formerly known as Brown I. In 1945 it was renamed by the hydrographic service—in one of its less-inspired moments—in order to avoid unnecessary duplication.

Tanu Island (52°45'00" 131°40'00" Between Logan Inlet and Richardson Inlet, off E side of Moresby I, QCI), **Tanu Passage** (52°45'00" 131°44'00" Between Tanu I and Richardson I), **Tanu Point** (52°44'00" 131°42'00" SW end of Tanu I), **Tanu Rock** (52°46'00" 131°36'00" Off E end of Tanu I). Geologist George M Dawson named the island Tanoo in 1878, after the famous Eagle crest village on its eastern shore. While the preferred spelling today is T'aanuu, the variants Tannu, Tahnoo and Tanoo have all been widely used in the past. The word can be translated as "sea grass" or "eelgrass" and refers to the subtidal marine plants that grow near the village site. Tanu was also known as Klue's village, after the hereditary name of the powerful and influential town chief (*see* Klue Passage). "When we visited this village," wrote Dawson, "we found it to be the most flourishing of any on the Charlottes. Sixteen well-built lodges ring the shoreline and 30 finely carved poles proclaim the artistry of its residents." HBC officer John Work counted 545 people there in 1840. In 1887, after the ravages of TB and smallpox had reduced the population to 80, the remaining inhabitants moved to New Kloo on the N end of Louise I. *D W*

Tar Islands (52°40'00" 131°25'00" Off E side of Lyell I, E of Moresby I, Hecate Str, QCI), **Tar Rock** (52°39'00" 131°25'00" Just SE of Tar Is). George Mercer Dawson applied the name Tar Is in 1878 to the entire chain that forms the E side of Gogit Passage. His Haida informants had told him of the bituminous substance that oozed to the surface on the islands' shorelines. Later geologists also found evidence of tar-like matter on the shores of nearby Ramsay, House and Agglomerate islands. *D*

Tarr Inlet (59°04'00" 137°03'00" NW extension of Reid Inlet and Glacier Bay, NW corner of BC on the BC-Alaska boundary). Named about 1912 by Lawrence Martin, of the US Geological Survey, after Ralph Stockman Tarr (1864–1912), a geographer who taught at Harvard and Cornell universities, 1890–1912, and wrote on glaciology, geology and earthquakes. He visited the area in 1911 while on a National Geographic Society expedition. The inlet is of great interest as a geographical anomaly. The glaciers of Glacier Bay in Alaska have receded dramatically—more than 100 km—over the past 250 years. They were only 6 km from Capt George Vancouver's ships when he sailed past the ice-choked mouth of the bay in 1794. By 1860 the retreating floes had reached the entrances to Reid Inlet and Muir Inlet. Tarr Inlet and Johns Hopkins Inlet, farther to the NW, did not emerge from their deep coverings of glacial ice until the 1890s. By 1925 the shrinking Grand Pacific Glacier had crossed the international border and uncovered the head of Tarr Inlet—revealing a large patch of ocean and a strip of flat land in BC territory. J P Forde, district engineer with Canada's Dept of Public Works, was sent to investigate and later reported that, because the glacier had reached shore, icebergs were no longer calving and Tarr Inlet had become fairly free of ice. "Navigation in these waters is now practically safe during daylight," he wrote. "So far as the recession of the ice opening up a new route into northern BC and the Yukon is concerned, this is still impracticable but may prove of value in the years to come." It took about two decades for entrepreneurs to see the possibilities. BC's northernmost ice-free harbour was at Stewart, 550 km to the SE, but here was a potential new port—a gift of nature—that could replace Skagway and Haines, both in a foreign country, as gateways to the Yukon and open up an entire new territory

for mineral exploitation. Soon, though, it was discovered that the Grand Pacific Glacier had stalled, then reversed, its northward flight. It crossed back over the BC-Alaska boundary about 1950 and continued S until stalling again about 1995. Scientists pointed out that the glacier had a history of relatively rapid movement changes and fluctuations, and that putting a port in its path would be nothing short of madness. Tarr Inlet today, in fact, is not a BC geographical feature at all, but an Alaska one.

Tarte Island (52°44'00" 129°17'00" Borrowman Bay, W side of Aristazabal I). Capt James Wright McKnight Tarte (1849–1920), a native of England, came to Esquimalt with his family in 1863 and found work on a sloop that ferried people between Victoria and Esquimalt harbours. His father, John F Tarte (1824–1905), had managed a coal mine in England and soon became involved in the PNW coal trade. In 1869 the Tartes moved to Bellingham in Washington state, where John supervised the loading of ships for a US coal company and later bought land at Blaine and went into the hotel business. James worked as mate on a number of small vessels, eventually becoming master of the steamship *Eliza Anderson*, which ran from Bellingham to New Westminster and Port Moody. He married Mary Eleanor Smith, also from England, in 1879. In the early 1890s, James operated the *Evangel* between Seattle, Port Angeles and Victoria, then the *Brick* on the mail route between Blaine and Bellingham. His brothers Whitfield (b 1858) and Alfred (b 1865) were also well-known mariners in Whatcom county.

Tasu Head (52°44'00" 132°07'00" S entrance to Tasu Sd), **Tasu Narrows** (52°45'00" 132°06'00" Entrance to Tasu Sd), **Tasu Sound** (52°47'00" 132°03'00" W side of Moresby I, QCI). The sound, known as Tasoo (or Tassoo) Hbr in the early days, apparently takes its name from a longer Haida phrase meaning "lake of plenty." Early US fur traders knew it as Port Montgomery, after Maj Gen Richard Montgomery, an Irish native, who was killed in the unsuccessful US attack on Que in 1775. There were many Haida habitation sites on Tasu Sd, including the large winter village of Singa on Lomgon Bay; ancient trails connected the sound to Kootenay Inlet farther N and to Sewell Inlet on the E side of Moresby I. The first prospectors arrived at Tasu about 1907, and more trails were built, to Crescent Inlet and Lockeport to the SE. Falconbridge Nickel Mines Ltd established the Wesfrob iron-ore operation on Tasu Mtn in 1962 and built a modern townsite on Gowing I, complete with indoor swimming pool and gymnasium. More than 400 people lived at Tasu until the huge open-pit mine closed in 1983. In the 1970s the Canadian government allowed Russian fishing vessels to use Tasu Sd as a base in return for staying out of the Vancouver I fishing grounds (the crews were not allowed ashore). Tasu Ck, which flows into the head of Newcombe Inlet, takes its name from the sound. *D E*

T

Tatchu Point (49°51'00" 127°09'00" NW entrance to Esperanza Inlet, W side of Vancouver I), **Tatchu Rocks** (49°53'00" 127°11'00" NW of Tatchu Point). According to pioneer Roman Catholic missionary Augustin Brabant, this name derives from a First Nation word meaning "to chew." The beach near Tatchu Point was a well-established fishing and feasting site for people of the Ehattesaht First Nation, who are members of the Nuu-chah-nulth Tribal Council. Nearby Tatchu Ck takes its name from the same source. The point was named by RN surveyor Capt George Richards in 1861. *W*

Tate Cove (52°44'00" 129°16'00" In Borrowman Bay, W side of Aristazabal I). Charles Montgomery Tate (1852–1933), from Blyth, England, came to BC via Panama in 1870 in search of gold but arrived too late for the Cariboo rush. He got a job instead at Nanaimo, working in a coal mine, and became associated with the Methodist church, teaching at Native mission schools in Nanaimo and Vancouver and eventually being ordained as a Methodist minister in 1879. That same year he married Caroline Sarah Knott (1842–1930), also from England—and also a strong Methodist—whom he met while she was teaching at Port Simpson. Later the Tates lived and worked at Chilliwack, where they established the Coqualeetza Industrial School for First Nation students in about 1888, and at Bella Bella, Rivers Inlet and Clayoquot. Charles was something of a linguist, translating Bible texts into Native tongues, several of which he learned. In 1889 he published a book on Chinook jargon, written "for the use of traders, tourists and others who have business intercourse with the Indians." The Tates retired to Victoria in 1910 and are believed to have taken part in the Victoria old-timers' reunion of 1924 (*see* Adams Bay).

Tate Lagoon (52°22'50" 128°13'20" Don Peninsula, W side of Spiller Channel, N of Bella Bella). Flight Sgt George Douglas Watson Tate, from New Westminster, was killed in action June 27, 1943, age 21, when his Vickers Wellington medium bomber was shot down during a night raid. He was serving with RCAF No 432 Squadron, based at York, England. His name is inscribed on the Runnymede Memorial near Windsor, UK.

Tatsung Rock (52°33'00" 131°20'00" SE of Ramsay I, N entrance to Juan Perez Sd, off E side of Moresby I, QCI). The name is an adaptation of the Haida word for hat and was adopted by the hydrographic service in 1962. The spelling is taken from the Haida vocabulary listed in the appendix to George M Dawson's 1880 monograph "On the Haida Indians of the QCI."

Tattenham Ledge (49°31'00" 123°59'00" Off N end of S Thormanby I, NW entrance to Welcome Passage, SE end of Malaspina Str, NW of Sechelt). Tattenham Corner, where the horses turn into the final straightaway, about 800 m from the finish line, is a famous location on a famous racecourse: Epsom Downs in Surrey, England. It was here in 1860 that Thormanby won the Derby, much to the delight of Capt George Richards and his fellow officers, who finally heard the news later that year while doing survey work with HMS *Plumper* near the Thormanby Is. They gave the area many names related to horse racing and Epsom Downs. *W*

Taylor Bank (50°50'00" 127°16'00" Between Numas I and the Deserters Group, N side of Queen Charlotte Str, NE of Port Hardy). Flying Officer Edward Arthur Thomas Taylor, DFC, of Victoria, was killed in action on May 25, 1944, age 21. He was serving with No 252 (RAF) Squadron, which was based in Egypt and Libya for much of its history, and is credited with shooting down two enemy planes with his twin-engined Bristol Beaufighter while attacking shipping and coastal targets in the E Mediterranean. Taylor is commemorated on the Alamein Memorial in Egypt.

Taylor Bay (49°12'00" 123°51'00" NW end of Gabriola I, Gulf Is). George William Taylor (1854–1912) was a British mining engineer and naturalist who moved to Victoria in 1879. He was persuaded by Bishop George Hills to study for the Anglican clergy, was ordained in 1884 and the following year married Elizabeth A Williams (1860–95), headmistress at the Girls Central School and organist at the Anglican cathedral. The Taylors moved to the coalfields at Wellington, where George ministered to the miners, often going down into the pits when accidents occurred in order to help injured men. He also pursued his other interests, studying local marine life and collecting moths and butterflies. After the death of his wife, he settled on Gabriola I, on land he had been given by a grateful coal company executive, and continued to work as a clergyman. In 1905, Taylor was appointed to the BC Fisheries Commission. He helped persuade the federal government to establish the Pacific Biological Station at Departure Bay, and in 1908 became its first curator, but he suffered a severe heart attack in 1910. Alfred J T Taylor, the engineer who developed the British Properties subdivision in W Vancouver and built the Lions Gate Bridge, was one of his five children.

Taylor Bight (53°06'00" 129°12'00" S side of Gil I, N end of Campania Sd, W of Princess Royal I). Flying Officer Richard Winter Taylor, DFC, of Victoria, was killed in action Mar 14, 1943, age 22. He was serving with No 161 Squadron, a hush-hush RAF group that was primarily used by Britain's Special Operations Executive to drop and collect secret agents and equipment behind enemy lines in Europe. Taylor's Handley Page Halifax heavy bomber crashed while flying an undercover team into Czechoslovakia. He is buried at Durnbach War Cemetery in Germany.

Taylor Cove (48°54'00" 123°22'00" E side of Galiano I, Gulf Is). George Taylor acquired a Crown grant for land at this location in 1892. The name, which had become well established locally, was submitted by the Gulf Is Branch of the BC Historical Assoc in 1968.

Taylor Point (48°46'00" 123°08'00" W of Bruce Bight, S side of Saturna I, Gulf Is). Scottish stonemason George Grey Taylor (1858–1933) came to Canada with his wife, Annie (b 1864), and family in 1882. Ten years later they moved W to BC and pre-empted land at Potato Bay on Plumper Sd. George soon found work at Warburton Pike's sandstone quarry, located near what is now Taylor Point. Under his management the quarry produced stone for a number of prominent Victoria buildings, including the armouries, the public library, Craigdarroch Castle and Metropolitan Methodist Church. Additional stone went to Winnipeg and other prairie cities.

Tcenakun Point (53°09'00" 132°35'00" NW end of Chaatl I, W end of Skidegate Channel, between Graham I and Moresby I, QCI). The name was adopted from an 1897 map drawn by ethnologist Charles Newcombe, who combined versions of two Haida words, *tce* and *nakun*, and translated them as "salmon point." This feature was formerly called Skidegate Point (and is still known locally by that name) but was changed by the hydrographic service in 1946. It is marked by a navigational light.

Teakerne Arm, where Captain George Vancouver and his colleagues anchored for almost three weeks in 1792. *Peter Vassilopoulos*

Teakerne Arm (50°11'00" 124°52'00" E of Lewis Channel, W Redonda I, NE of Campbell R). The derivation of the name is not known, but the fact that it appears as Tea-kerne in the 1864 *Vancouver I Pilot* by Capt George Richards and as Teak-Erne in the 1909 gazetteer has led some writers to suspect that it may have a First Nation origin. Capt George Vancouver anchored here for almost three weeks in the summer of 1792, along with his new Spanish friends Dionisio Alcalá-Galiano and Cayetano Valdés, while they

surveyed the surrounding area with the ships' boats. For Vancouver the area presented "as gloomy and dismal an aspect as nature could well be supposed to exhibit ... dull and uninteresting ... [with] dreary rocks and precipices." Archibald Menzies, however, the expedition's naturalist, described the setting as "wild" and "romantic." He found "a number of new plants never before discovered" on W Redonda and appears to have enjoyed bathing with his colleagues in the warm waters of nearby Cassel Lk, which is connected to Teakerne Arm by a lovely waterfall (this area was preserved in 1989 as a 128-ha provincial park). Vancouver, though, remained depressed. "Our residence here was truly forlorn," he wrote in his journal. "An awful silence pervaded the gloomy forests, whilst animated nature seemed to have deserted the neighbouring country." The arm was the location of a logging camp for many years and still serves as a booming ground and aquaculture site.

Teece Point (48°45'00" 123°10'00" E side of S Pender I, Gulf Is). Named by the hydrographic service in 1969 for Lance Cpl Philip S Teece, of S Pender I, who was killed in action Aug 26, 1944, during the Battle of Normandy. He served with the Black Watch (Royal Highland Regiment) of Canada and is buried at Bretteville-sur-Laize Canadian War Cemetery, S of Caen in France. Formerly known as Tantallon Point.

Tee Island (53°59'00" 132°35'00" In Naden Hbr, off mouth of Lignite Ck, N side of Graham I, QCI). The name is apparently an adaptation and abbreviation of the Haida word for "kill." It could be translated as Death I.

Telegraph Cove (48°28'00" 123°17'00" N of Cadboro Bay, SE side of Saanich Peninsula, NE of Victoria). Victoria's first telegraph cable came ashore here in 1866, brought across Haro Str from San Juan I by the RN gunboat *Forward*, which had been hired by the Collins Overland Telegraph Co and especially equipped to lay the line. A later cable was laid through the cove in 1904 by the Pacific States Telephone Co, with one circuit going to Bellingham and one to Vancouver. In the early 1880s an explosives plant was constructed at this site by the Giant Powder Co of California; it was eventually relocated to James I. The cove was formerly known as Telegraph Bay, and the road that leads to it is still named Telegraph Bay Rd. The Songhees First Nation name for the feature was Kohnguksen, meaning "tide rip running around a point."

Telegraph Cove (50°33'00" 126°50'00" NE side of Beaver Cove, SW entrance to Johnstone Str, E of Port McNeill, NE side of Vancouver I). A lineman's station was built at the cove in 1912 when the federal government completed a telegraph line between Campbell R and Port Hardy. The spot was named by Albert Wastell, who was managing a sawmill and box factory for the BC Fishing & Packing Co at nearby Alert Bay at the time. He constructed the

The boardwalk village of Telegraph Cove. *Andrew Scott*

lineman's cabin and later bought a tract of timber around the cove. In the mid-1920s, Wastell and some Japanese partners built a chum salmon saltery and primitive box mill at Telegraph Cove. The operation soon closed, but Albert's son, Fred Wastell, resurrected the mill in 1929, expanded it and ran it, with partner Alex Macdonald, for the next 45 years. A small village eventually circled the tiny cove, complete with school, store, post office and community hall, much of it built on pilings over the water and connected by boardwalks. Today Telegraph Cove is a tourist destination, home to Jim and Mary Borrowman's Stubbs Island Whale Watching, the first company in BC dedicated to this popular pastime. *E*

Telegraph Passage (54°02'00" 130°06'00" E side of Kennedy I, S entrance to the Skeena R, S of Prince Rupert). This name commemorates part of the route taken in 1866 by the *Mumford*, a sternwheeler under the command of Capt Horace Coffin, to transport cable and supplies from Victoria for the construction of the Collins Overland Telegraph. Coffin, the first steamship captain on the Skeena, had been partway upriver the two previous years with the small sternwheeler *Union* but was driven back by strong currents. The underpowered *Mumford* was also unable to proceed beyond the junction with the Kitsumkalum R (now the site of Terrace), but Coffin made three trips to that point in 1866 and had his cargo transferred to canoes and paddled to the junction of the Skeena and Bulkley rivers (now Hazelton), where parties of linemen working W from the Fraser R were able to collect it. The telegraph line was intended to run from New Westminster, up the Fraser, Bulkley and Skeena rivers to Telegraph Ck on the Stikine R, and thence to the Yukon, Alaska and Russia. In 1867, however, the overland route was abandoned after it was learned that a line had successfully been laid across the Atlantic the year before. *W*

Telescope Passage (49°45'00" 124°09'00" Between Nelson I and Hardy I, just S of Jervis Inlet, SE of Powell R). Named

by the hydrographic service in 1945, in association with nearby Nelson I (qv), to celebrate a famous incident at the 1801 Battle of Copenhagen. RN cdr Horatio Nelson, a vice adm at the time and second-in-command of the British forces, was attacking the Danish-Norwegian fleet when his cdr, Adm Sir Hyde Parker, who was farther offshore and unable to see the progress of the battle clearly, gave the signal for recall, knowing that the unorthodox Nelson would ignore it if things were going well. For his part, Nelson famously held a telescope to his blind eye and told his flag captain that he could not see any signal to withdraw. The RN attack proved successful, enabling the British to secure a favourable peace treaty with the Danes, and Nelson was named a viscount.

Templar Channel (49°08'00" 125°55'00" Between Esowista Peninsula and Wickaninnish and Lennard islands, just S of Tofino, Clayoquot Sd, W side of Vancouver I), **Templar Rock** (48°24'00" 123°20'00" Gonzales Bay, off S side of Victoria). Charles Barrett-Lennard, an early (and wealthy) British tourist, brought the 18-tonne cutter *Templar* out to BC with him from Britain in 1860 as deck cargo on the *Athelstan*. He was accompanied by his friend Capt Napoleon Fitzstubbs. Together the pair made the first yachting trip around Vancouver I, taking two and a half months. Barrett-Lennard then sold the *Templar* to the Victoria merchants Robert Burnaby and William Henderson and returned home, publishing an account of his expedition, *Travels in British Columbia, with the Narrative of a Yacht Voyage Round Vancouver's Island*, in 1862. The *Templar*, while on a trading cruise off Vancouver I that same year, was driven ashore in Gonzales Bay in a storm and totally wrecked. *See also* Lennard I *and* Stubbs I. *W*

Tenas Island (52°42'00" 128°33'00" E side of Tolmie Channel, N of Swindle I, NW of Bella Bella). Tenas was the word for "small" or "few" in the Chinook jargon used on the W coast by First Nation groups and early traders and settlers. There are numerous other features named Tenas in BC, including two creeks, a hill, a lake, a peak, a narrows (on Little Lillooet Lk) and the Tenas Tikke Glacier N of Tarr Inlet.

Tenedos Bay (50°07'00" 124°42'00" E side of Desolation Sd, NE end of Str of Georgia, E of Campbell R). The RN sloop *Tenedos* was on the Pacific Station, based at Esquimalt, 1872–76, under Capt Edward Ray (1872–74) and Capt Edwin Pollard (1874–76). The 6-gun, 1,592-tonne steam vessel, named for the historic Turkish island of Tenedos near the entrance to the Dardanelles, was launched at Devonport dockyard in 1870, converted to a corvette in 1876 and broken up in 1887. After leaving Esquimalt it served at the Cape of Good Hope and off the W coast of Africa, then was based on the N America and W Indies Station. Tenedos Bay was formerly known as Deep Bay but was renamed by the hydrographic service in 1945. It has

Tenedos Bay in Desolation Sound. *Peter Vassilopoulos*

become one of the most popular anchorages in Desolation Sd Marine Provincial Park.

Ten Mile Point (48°27'15" 123°16'00" Just N of Cadboro Point, E side of Saanich, just NE of Victoria). If one followed the course a ship would take, this feature is exactly 10 nautical miles from Esquimalt Hbr. The point has a long history of alternating names on hydrographic charts with Cadboro Point, just to the S. Most local residents now use Ten Mile Point to refer to the entire peninsula E of Cadboro Bay. *W*

Tent Island (48°56'00" 123°38'00" Off S end of Kuper I, W of N end of Saltspring I, Gulf Is). This feature, a Penelakut First Nation reserve, was leased to BC for many years as a provincial marine park. The lease was not renewed, however, and while the island, with its beautiful beaches and warm waters for swimming, is still popular with visitors, the Penelakut band must grant permission for camping. The name appears on an Admiralty chart published in 1865, based on an 1860 survey by Capt George Richards in HMS *Plumper*. It is much older, therefore, than any park-related designation. Perhaps crew members from the *Plumper* also camped there.

Termagant Point (50°29'00" 125°49'00" E entrance to Topaze Hbr, Sunderland Channel, N of Hardwicke I and Johnstone Str, NW of Campbell R). HMS *Termagant*, under Capt Robert Hall, escorted the two small RN gunboats *Forward* and *Grappler* to Esquimalt in 1860. The 24-gun steam frigate, 64 m long and 2,180 tonnes, was launched at Deptford dockyard in 1847 and named after a villainous character who often appeared in medieval morality plays, usually dressed in a turban and gown (it was only later that the word came to mean a quarrelsome, scolding woman). The vessel saw service during the Crimean War, conveying French troops to the Baltic and bringing prisoners back, then was stationed in the W Indies. After visiting Victoria,

Termagant was based at Coiba, off Panama, until 1863. It was sold in 1867. RN surveyor Lt Daniel Pender named this feature Aguilar Point in 1863; the hydrographic service renamed it in 1946, however, to avoid duplication with Aguilar Point (qv) on the W coast of Vancouver I.

Testlatlints Rock (54°11'00" 132°59'00" Off SE side of Langara I and NW end of Graham I, QCI). This unusual and much-photographed feature is a large, roughly spherical boulder with half a dozen old, stunted conifers growing off its top surface. The name is an adaptation of a Haida phrase meaning "round-topped rock." It has many alternative local names, including Egg Shaped Rk, Flower Pot Rk, Plum Pudding and Princess Rk. According to QCI historian Kathleen Dalzell, this latter name refers to a figure in a Haida legend who was buried there after dying of grief when her lover was drowned. There is, apparently, a shaman's grave on the rock. *D*

Testlatlints Rock, a Haida Gwaii landmark. *Andrew Scott*

Texada Island (49°40'00" 124°24'00" E side of Str of Georgia, S of Powell R). Spanish naval officer José Narváez, who explored the Str of Georgia in 1791 (the first European to do so) with the *Santa Saturnina*, originally gave the name San Felix to what is now Texada I, probably because he was there on July 12, the feast day of this 3rd-century Christian martyr from Milan. Confusingly, Narváez applied the name Isla Texada to today's Lasqueti I. These names appear on the chart drawn by Juan Pantoja y Arriaga, the pilot aboard the *San Carlos*, the other vessel in the 1791 expedition. Francisco Eliza, the overall expedition cdr, shifted the names around on his official chart, changing San Felix to Texada and giving Lasqueti its current name. Felix de Tejada (Texada) was a prominent Spanish naval officer at the time of Eliza's expedition; he later became a capt-gen, responsible for the navy's northern dept, based at the important port and shipbuilding centre of El Ferrol in Galicia. Capt George Vancouver adopted the name on his 1792 expedition but mistakenly spelled it Favida in his journal and Feveda on his chart, an error that was corrected on subsequent editions. The 287-sq-km island, which had a population of about 1,100 in the early 2000s, has a long history as a mining centre, with gold, iron ore and limestone all important exports. There are three small communities, Van Anda, Gillies Bay and Blubber Bay, the last of which is connected by ferry to Powell R. The Sechelt First Nation knows the island as Lháwtíkán and Spílksen. *E*

Thames Shoal (48°25'00" 123°17'00" NE of Gonzales Point, E of Mouat Channel and Victoria, SE of Oak Bay). The steamship *Thames*, purchased for Edward Stamp's Alberni Saw Mill Co, arrived at Victoria, under Capt Echte, via Hawaii in 1862. The 40-m, 270-tonne vessel had been built in Holland and used in the cattle trade between Hamburg and London for a number of years. The *Thames* steamed mostly between Alberni and Victoria, under Capt John Henderson, carrying workers and lumber, and also towed larger sailing ships up Alberni Inlet to load at the mill and then back out to sea. It was used to salvage the ship *Elizabeth Kimball* at the Trial Is in 1865. In 1866 the *Thames* was taken by Capt John Devereux to Nagasaki, Japan, where it was sold and employed in the Japanese coastal trade. The little steamer came to a tragic end several years later when it was driven ashore during a storm, causing the deaths of more than 150 passengers. *W*

The Cut, between Thetis and Kuper islands. *John Lund*

The Cut (48°59'05" 123°39'40" Between Thetis I and Kuper I, Gulf Is). This artificial canal allows small boats to pass between Thetis I and Kuper I, which would normally be joined at low tide, and to approach Telegraph Hbr from the E. The passage, originally dug in 1905 and dredged regularly, is sometimes incorrectly referred to as The Gut. The islands were rejoined with a bridge after The Cut was created, but this was removed in 1945, partly (and unsuccessfully) to prevent cattle from Kuper I coming across and ravaging vegetable gardens on Thetis I.

The Gorge. *See* Gorge Waters.

The Naze (48°26'00" 123°17'00" S of Cadboro Bay, N of Oak Bay, just E of Victoria). This point was named after a headland on the E coast of Essex, an important area for migrating birds. The English feature is eroding severely, threatening a historic tower built as a shipping landmark. The Naze was not officially adopted as a BC name until 1981, though it appears on T N Hibben & Co's 1913 map of Victoria. The name derives from *ness*, the Old English word for a headland. Several other promontories in the Cadboro Bay area commemorate English E coast landforms.

Theodore Point (50°08'00" 127°32'00" W side of Ououkinsh Inlet, Checleset Bay, NW side of Vancouver I). Lt Theodore Izard of the RCN was killed in action in the sinking of HMCS *Athabaskan* off the coast of France in 1944. *See* Izard Point.

Theresa Rock (53°53'00" 130°31'00" Near entrance to Porcher Inlet, S of Prince Rupert). Named for the sealing schooner *Theresa* (or *Teresa*, as the name is also recorded), based out of Victoria from about 1887 until the early 1900s. It was owned by P A Babbington in 1894 and commanded by Capt Fred Gilbert. Capts Myers, John Dodd, J J Whiteley, John Steele, J Anderson, A Sighorst, Owen Thomas and Ernest Lorenz also served as the vessel's skippers.

Thetis Anchorage (52°56'00" 132°09'00" Head of Mitchell Inlet, Kuper Inlet, NW side of Moresby I, QCI), **Thetis Cove** (48°27'00" 123°26'00" E side of Esquimalt Hbr, W of Victoria), **Thetis Island** (49°00'00" 123°41'00" W of N end of Galiano I, Gulf Is). The RN frigate *Thetis*, 36 guns and 1,382 tonnes, was launched at Plymouth dockyard in 1846. Named after a Greek sea nymph who was one of the Nereids and the mother of Achilles, it served in the Mediterranean and off the E coast of S America before joining the Pacific Station, 1851–53, under Capt Augustus Kuper. In 1852 it was sent to the QCI, after the discovery of gold at Mitchell Inlet, to survey the region and maintain the peace. The following Jan the crew of the *Thetis* were involved in one of the earliest RN actions against a First Nation group on the BC coast. The frigate's launch, barge and pinnace were towed by the HBC's *Beaver* (as a large sailing ship, the *Thetis* could not safely navigate the narrow, uncharted passages off SE Vancouver I) as part of a large force, led by Gov James Douglas, that went to Cowichan

Thetis Island is at the left and in the distance, with Telegraph Harbour in the foreground. Kuper Island lies to the right. *Peter Vassilopoulos*

Bay to apprehend the suspected murderers of Scottish shepherd Peter Brown. In 1854 the vessel was exchanged for two small paddle steamers and became a seamen's training ship for the Prussian navy. Thetis Anchorage was originally named Thetis Cove by the ship's officers in 1852; Thetis I and Thetis Cove at Esquimalt were named in 1858 by Capt George Richards. Thetis I, 26 sq km, is home to a small recreational and retirement community with a population of about 250; it was joined to Kuper I in the early days but was separated by The Cut, a small, artificial, boat channel, in 1905. Another Thetis I used to exist in Esquimalt Hbr, on the S side of Constance Cove, but became part of Vancouver I in 1887 when the original graving dock (drydock) was constructed; it appears on an 1861 Admiralty chart, marked "Naval Store." Thetis Lk near Victoria is also named for this vessel. *D E W*

The Trap (52°02'00" 127°57'00" Between Hunter I and Clayton I, Fisher Channel, SE of Bella Bella). This alarming name merely indicates a drying cove that could conceivably cause an anchored vessel to ground. Several similar names offer related cautions for BC mariners: **Trap Islands** (53°08'00" 129°44'00" Off N side of Trutch I, Estevan Group, SE of Banks I), **Trap Rock** (50°41'00" 126°41'00" W side of Bonwick I, Dusky Cove, E end of Queen Charlotte Str) and **Trap Rocks** (53°09'00" 129°42'00" Just NE of the Trapp Is).

Thiepval Channel (48°54'00" 125°21'00" NE of Turret I, Broken Group, Barkley Sd, W side of Vancouver I).

Named after HMCS *Thiepval*, a 324-tonne, 44-m *Battle*-class trawler, built at Kingston, Ont, in 1917, that struck a rock in the middle of this channel and sank in Feb 1930, under Lt Cdr Harold Tingley (*see* Tingley Rock). The vessel was equipped as a minesweeper in WWI and was transferred in 1920 to BC, where it served as a patrol and fisheries inspection vessel. In 1924 it was sent to Japan and Petropavlovsk in Russia with fuel and spare parts for Stuart McLaren's ill-fated round-the-world flight. His Vickers Viking flying boat crashed on takeoff in Russia, and the trawler brought the pilot, co-pilot and wreckage to Vancouver. The wreck of the *Thiepval*, located in only 14 m of water, is popular with sport divers; the vessel's deck gun has been salvaged and put on display in nearby Ucluelet. *Thiepval* is a village in northern France, site of a WWI battle and a major memorial to the more than 73,000 British and Commonwealth soldiers who died in the First Battle of the Somme and have no known grave.

Thieves Bay (48°46'00" 123°19'00" W side of N Pender I, Gulf Is). According to a reminiscence by Mary Hamilton in *Gulf Islands Patchwork*, the feature got its name in the 1890s when a pair of sheep thieves were spotted killing and salting down sheep at this site to sell to Fraser R fishermen. The local police constable deputized a group of farmers, and the squad rowed over to the bay and apprehended the criminals. The special deputies then left for home, letting the thieves row themselves to Mayne I, where the jail was located, under the careful supervision of the policeman. They managed to elude their captor, however, when he stepped out of the boat onto the dock, by quickly pushing off and hightailing it to the US.

T

Third Beach (49°18'00" 123°09'00" Just N of Ferguson Point, W side of Stanley Park, Burrard Inlet, Vancouver). The name refers to the fact that as one moves N along the shoreline away from the W End, this is the third main beach encountered. The mostly rocky area was not developed until the late 1920s and '30s, when dressing rooms and a concession stand were constructed, and extensive sand deposits were not added until 1962.

Third Beach (49°43'05" 126°56'00" Between Skuna Bay and Ferrer Point, NW end of Nootka I, off W side of Vancouver I). A Bible camp was set up at Tongue Point on Nuchatlitz Inlet in the late 1940s, and campers frequently visited the nearby beaches. The "first" and "second" beaches were close to the camp, but the "third" beach, farther away, had to be reached by boat. Many years later, when the Nootka Trail was developed along the W coast of Nootka I, the "third" beach became a favoured rendezvous or drop-off spot for hikers, and the name began to appear on hiking maps. It was officially adopted in 2005 as a well-established local name.

Thistle Passage (52°38'00" 128°45'00" E side of Hastings I, S side of Princess Royal I). The Canadian Hydrographic Service acquired the 11-m motor launch *Thistle* from the RCN in 1922. It saw service on the W coast until 1928, when it was destroyed by fire. Hydrographer H L Leadman arrived from Ottawa in 1923 to take charge of the vessel, along with the houseboats *Somass* and *Fraser*. The *Thistle* was employed primarily by camping parties and was used to survey these waters in 1925. It is not to be confused with an earlier, larger vessel named *Thistle*, which became the private steam yacht of Lt Gov James Dunsmuir and caught fire at the mouth of Queen Charlotte Str in 1907. The passengers, including Dunsmuir, were returning to Victoria from a hunting adventure; all 17 persons aboard were able to safely abandon the doomed ship, which was a total write-off.

Thistleton Islands (52°30'12" 129°02'49" Entrance to Weeteeam Bay, SW end of Aristazabal I). Lance Cpl James Thistleton (1837–83) was a member of the Columbia detachment of Royal Engineers, which served in BC 1858–63. In 1862, at New Westminster, he married Eliza Whitehouse (1840–1917), a dressmaker, who had recently arrived in BC with her family from England. Thistleton remained in the colony after the contingent was disbanded and was working as a tanner and currier at Sapperton in 1863. He and his wife later moved to Victoria, where she filed for divorce in 1879. Thistleton was listed in the 1881 BC census as a hotel steward and in the 1882 Victoria directory as an employee of Sir Matthew Baillie Begbie. Named by regional hydrographer Henri Parizeau in 1927.

Thomas Island (50°04'00" 127°29'00" SE of the Bunsby Is, Checleset Bay, NW side of Vancouver I). Named by

the hydrographic service in 1947 for Welsh sealing capt Owen Thomas (1852–1924), who went to sea aged 15 and arrived at San Francisco in 1873, joining Capt James Warren's sealing schooner *Thornton*. Thomas moved to Victoria at some point and spent two seasons in the *Pathfinder* and two in the *Favorite*. In 1889, as skipper of the *Black Diamond*, he was apprehended by the US revenue cutter *Richard Rush* for hunting in US waters and ordered to Sitka. Thomas went to Victoria instead, telling the single seaman placed on board by US authorities that the ship's First Nation hunters would kill all the white crew members if the vessel headed to Alaska. The incident received widespread news coverage but did no harm to Thomas's career, which continued with stints on the *Kate*, *Alfred Adams* and *Theresa*. Thomas I was formerly known as Whiteface I.

Thomas Islet (52°54'00" 128°08'00" Mussel Inlet, E of Princess Royal I). Named by the hydrographic service in 1965 after Able Seaman John Thomas, a crew member aboard HMS *Discovery* during Capt George Vancouver's expedition to the PNW, 1791–95. Thomas was one of several members of a survey team, under Lt James Johnstone and Midshipman Robert Barrie, who ate tainted mussels for breakfast while working in this area with the ship's boats. John Carter, another seaman in the *Discovery*, died as a result, but Thomas and John McAlpin, while both made seriously ill by paralytic shellfish poisoning, recovered after drinking heated seawater, which acted as an emetic.

Thompson Sound (50°47'00" 126°03'00" E side of Tribune Channel, E of Gilford I, just N of southern Knight Inlet). The origin of the name is not known, though Spanish explorer Dionisio Alcalá-Galiano called this feature the Brazo de Balda and stated in his account of his 1792 voyage that Juan Vernaci, 2nd officer of the *Mexicana*, had been the first European to visit it. A large logging camp was located at the head of the inlet in the 1970s, complete with a post office.

Thomsen Rock (50°53'00" 128°05'00" W of Cape Sutil, off N end of Vancouver I). Peter Thomsen was one of four founding Danish colonists who came to the Cape Scott area in the mid-1890s and signed a land application to the BC government in 1896. He and his colleagues persuaded James Baker, the minister of Immigration, to provide free land and build roads, a dike and a school, provided that 75 settlers arrived over the first four years. Although the requisite number of colonists came, the community was not a success, partly because the government failed to follow through on its promise to build roads. The rock was named by the hydrographic service in 1946; it was formerly known as Skinner Rk, and also as Hecate Rk, after HMS *Hecate*, a survey vessel on the BC coast in the early 1860s.

Thomson Cove (48°36'00" 123°29'00" E side of Saanich Inlet, NE of Henderson Point, NW of Victoria), Thomson Island (52°44'00" 129°17'00" In Borrowman Bay, NW side of Aristazabal I). William Thomson (1829–1908), from Forfarshire, Scotland, was one of the earliest white settlers in central Saanich. He was a shipwright who went to California for the gold rush, then came to BC in 1854 aboard the *William*, which was wrecked near Pachena Point on the W coast of Vancouver I. The survivors, including Thomson, stayed with Ditidaht First Nation members for several months before being delivered safely to Sooke. After working as a farmhand for the HBC, he moved in 1855 to the Mt Newton area of Saanich and built a cabin, eventually carving a farm named Bannockburn from the surrounding forest. The following year Thomson married 15-year-old Margaret Dyer (1841–1920, *see* Dyer Cove), who would bear him 15 children. The Thomsons were influential Saanich pioneers, donating land for a church and school (and helping build them), founding the Saanich Agricultural Society, building and maintaining roads, and providing hospitality and assistance to new settlers.

Thomson Point (52°57'00" 129°36'00" W entrance to Pemberton Bay, S side of Dewdney I, Estevan Group, N side of Caamaño Sd). Named after Thomas Thomson, who is believed to have served as master of the salvage tug *William Jolliffe*, 1911–13, while it was under contract to the federal government's fisheries protection service.

Thorenson Point (52°19'00" 127°34'00" N side of Dean Channel, just SE of Ocean Falls). This feature was named, but misspelled, by the hydrographic service in 1953 after Peder H Thoreson, one of the original Norwegian colonists in the Bella Coola valley in 1894. While the early Scandinavian settlers often altered or anglicized their names, Thoreson's signature or written surname is clearly visible on several of the colony's early documents and agreements, as well as on surveyor Peter Leech's land allocation map. He was a member of the colony's first managing committee, which was elected back in Minnesota before the settlers had even emigrated.

Thormanby Islands (49°30'00" 124°00'00" Just W of S end of Sechelt Peninsula, W side of Welcome Passage, Str of Georgia, NW of Vancouver). The islands were named in 1860 by Capt George Richards of the RN survey vessel *Plumper* after hearing that the British racehorse Thormanby had won the famous Epsom Derby earlier that year. Richards and his officers applied numerous race-related names to the area's features, suggesting that they may have had a guinea or two riding on the winning horse. Most of the S island was pre-empted by Calvert Simson, storekeeper at Vancouver's pioneer Hastings sawmill, in the early 1890s. He built a cabin and let his friends do likewise, and later developed a farm, which he ran with

The Thormanby Islands, looking southwest, with Buccaneer Bay and its fine beaches in the centre. *Peter Vassilopoulos*

tenants. The Simson family donated much of the island as a provincial park in 1982. Another provincial park is located on a fine beach at the S end of N Thormanby I. Elsewhere on this smaller island is Vaucroft Beach, where the BC Telephone Co maintained a hotel and summer camp for its employees in the 1920s. The Sechelt First Nation name for the islands is Sxwélap. *E W*

Thornbrough Bay (49°27'00" 123°27'00" W side of Gambier I near S end), Thornbrough Channel (49°29'00" 123°28'00" W of Gambier I, W side of Howe Sd, NW of Vancouver). The channel was named in 1859 by RN surveyor Capt George Richards after Adm Sir Edward Thornbrough (1754–1834). Richards named dozens of features in Howe Sd after the officers and ships that participated in Adm Howe's greatest victory—the 1794 English Channel naval battle known as the Glorious First of June. Thornbrough, for instance, at that time capt of the 38-gun frigate *Latona*, was stationed so as to repeat the adm's signals, but he later plunged into the thick of the fight to assist the line-of-battle ships. He had joined the RN early, at age seven, as a servant to his naval officer father, and much later in his career had several important commands: cdr-in-chief on the coast of Ireland, 1810–13 (as a vice adm), and cdr-in-chief at Portsmouth, 1817–19 (as an adm). *W*

Thorndike Shoal (51°19'00" 127°50'00" Between Irving Passage and Radar Passage, entrance to Smith Sd, NW of Port Hardy). This feature was probably named for the schooner *Thorndike* (often written *Thorndyke*), which was attacked by a Lekwiltok First Nation group in 1863 while sailing N through Johnstone Str. Some crew members were apparently rescued by the crew of another schooner, the *Nanaimo Packet*, while others were killed. One suspected perpetrator, Quamish, was tried at Nanaimo in 1865.

Thorn Reef (49°07'00" 125°55'00" W side of Templar Channel, SW of Tofino, Clayoquot Sd, W side of Vancouver

T

I). Jonathan Thorn (1779–1811) was the autocratic capt of the fur-trading barque *Tonquin*, which was attacked in Clayoquot Sd by Tla-o-qui-aht First Nation warriors in 1811. He was born at Schenectady, NY, joined the US Navy as a midshipman at age 11 and distinguished himself in the Mediterranean during the First Barbary War by helping Lt Stephen Decatur burn a captured US frigate in Tripoli Hbr. As a young lt, Thorn became the first cdr of the NY Navy Yard in 1807. He was granted a leave of absence in 1810 to take John Jacob Astor's barque *Tonquin* to the mouth of the Columbia R and establish Ft Astoria. Two months after arriving in the PNW, Thorn took his ship N to Clayoquot Sd on a trading voyage but managed to so insult Nuukmiis, a Tla-o-qui-aht chief, that his vessel was attacked and he was killed, along with most of his crew. For a more detailed account of the destruction of the *Tonquin, see* Tonquin I. Thorn Reef was formerly known as Village Rk but was renamed by regional hydrographer Henri Parizeau in 1933.

Thorn Rock (52°57'00" 132°11'00" In Mitchell Inlet, Kuper Inlet, off NW side of Moresby I, QCI). This hazard, identified by Capt Augustus Kuper of HMS *Thetis* in 1852, is thought to be named after Charles Thorn (or Thorne), an engineer on the HBC's small steamship, the *Otter*. Thorn helped bring the venerable vessel out from England in 1853 and is frequently mentioned in its logbook, often because of his drinking habits. The Oct 1, 1854, entry is typical: "Mr Thorne, 1st engineer, in a furious state of intoxication during all the day endeavouring to quarrel with and insult every person on board."

Thornton Islands (49°58'00" 127°20'00" One of the Barrier Is, SW of Union I, entrance to Kyuquot Sd, NW side of Vancouver I). The *Thornton* was one of the earliest sailing vessels on the BC coast. Built in 1861 at Dungeness, Washington, the tiny, 26-tonne, 16-m sloop was owned by Capt James Warren (*see* Warren Rks) of Victoria, who traded along the W coast of Vancouver I and later became deeply involved in BC's sealing and steamship industries with his partner Joseph Boscowitz. In 1868, according to Warren, the *Thornton* was assaulted by an armed First Nation group while becalmed in Queen Charlotte Sd; in the ensuing shootout, 15 of the attackers were killed. In 1871 the sloop was converted to a sealing schooner; 10 years later, steam power was added. The *Thornton* helped set off a 25-year controversy in 1886 when it and two other sealing schooners were seized by US authorities for hunting in areas of the Bering Sea claimed by the US. All three vessels were left to rot on an Unalaska beach in the Aleutian Is, and inflated claims for damages were later submitted to an international tribunal.

Thorp Point (50°35'00" 127°37'00" S side of Holberg Inlet, SW of Coal Hbr, NW Vancouver I). Soren Thorp (b 1871) and his wife, Christiane (b 1871), were members of the Danish colony that settled and farmed Cape Scott at the NW tip of Vancouver I in the late 1890s. Their daughter Ellen was born there in 1899. Soren also received a Crown grant for land situated between Holberg and San Josef Bay in 1906 and may have become part of the short-lived community that flourished near the bay in the years before WWI.

Thrasher Cove (48°33'00" 124°28'00" N side of Port San Juan, SW side of Vancouver I). This feature was probably named after Abram Thrasher, who received a Crown grant of land near here in 1917.

Thrasher Rock (49°09'00" 123°39'00" Gabriola Reefs, E of Gabriola I, Gulf Is). The *Thrasher*, a sturdy new US ship, was wrecked on this rock in 1880 while being towed by the steamers *Etta White* and *Beaver*. It was en route from Nanaimo to San Francisco at the time, under Capt F Bosworth, with 2,300 tonnes of coal. J F Engelhart of Victoria purchased the wreck for $500 and the coal cargo for $50. A subsequent salvage lawsuit turned into a major constitutional challenge, known afterwards as "the *Thrasher* case," with the Supreme Court of BC questioning the province's authority to regulate the sitting of the court and to dictate where judges should reside.

Thrumb Islet (54°15'00" 133°05'00" Off W side of Langara I, N of NW end of Graham I, QCI). US fur trader Joseph Ingraham gave the name Thrumb Cap to a headland on SW Langara I on one of the charts he made of the area in 1791–92. The hydrographic service named Thrumb It to keep alive that historic designation, though the origin of the word is unknown.

Thulin Passage (50°01'00" 124°49'00" Between Copeland Is and Malaspina Peninsula, NE end of Str of Georgia, NW of Lund and Powell R). Charles August Thulin (1863–1932) left Sweden in 1887 and made his way across the US to BC, where he worked at first for the CPR. By 1889, when his younger brother Frederick Gotfrid Thulin (1872–1935) joined him, he was handlogging on the Sunshine Coast. Both brothers pre-empted land N of Powell R and received Crown grants in 1894 and 1903. They opened a store and a hotel, and a small village sprang up, which they named Lund after their ancient hometown in Sweden. Charles married another Swedish immigrant, Maria Josephine Johanson (1866–1958), at Vancouver in 1892; Frederick married twice, to Vera May Palmer in 1900 and Ida Amelia Vainia (1883–1952) in 1920. In 1903 the brothers crossed the Str of Georgia and bought land in the heart of what would became the town of Campbell R. They built the Willows Hotel and, a discreet distance away, its famous "Loggers' Annex"; a store and wharf soon followed. In 1909, a much larger and more impressive Willows replaced the old hotel, and the extended Thulin clan went on to play key roles in the development of the district. Thulin Passage was named by the hydrographic service in 1945; nearby

Thulin Ck and Thulin Lk also honour these hard-working Scandinavian pioneers. *E*

Thurgate Rock (52°37'00" 129°12'00" NW of Clifford Bay, W side of Aristazabal I). Little is known about Sapper Frederick Thurgate other than that he was a member of the Columbia detachment of Royal Engineers, which served in BC 1858–63.

East Thurlow Island's Shoal Bay was the largest community in the area in 1901, when this photo was taken. *BC Archives D-08207*

Thurlow Islands (50°25'00" 125°35'00" Between Hardwicke I and Sonora I, N side of Johnstone Str, NW of Campbell R), **Thurlow Point** (50°25'00" 125°20'00" E end of E Thurlow I, NE of Hemming Bay). The islands (E Thurlow and W Thurlow) were named by Capt George Vancouver in 1792 after Baron Edward Thurlow (1731–1806), a lawyer and Tory politician who served as lord chancellor of GB, 1778–92. Before that he had been solicitor gen and attorney gen. The islands were first logged in the 1880s and saw considerable mining activity the following decade. Commercial fishing and tourism have also been important in the area. A cannery and sawmill operated at Blind Channel (qv) on W Thurlow, while the community of Shoal Bay (qv, also known simply as Thurlow) on E Thurlow was first settled in the 1880s and has been the site of a landmark hotel and lodge. Another early E Thurlow settlement, Channeton, was briefly located on Bickley Bay. *E W*

Thurston Bay (50°22'00" 125°19'00" W side of Sonora I, Nodales Channel, N of Campbell R). Robert Jabez F Thurston (1867–1929) and Aird Flavelle (1888–1973), both from Ont, established the Thurston-Flavelle Lumber Co about 1912 and constructed a series of sawmills at Port Moody (where Thurston and his wife, Elizabeth Lillian, also built one of the town's finest homes) and elsewhere in the Lower Mainland. Their company was sold to Canadian Colliers Resources Ltd in 1955 and ultimately became part of Weldwood of Canada Ltd. The bay was the regional centre for the BC Forest Service's marine dept from 1914 to 1941, with maintenance facilities for its fleet

Thurston Bay, former BC Forest Service marine depot. *Peter Vassilopoulos*

of patrol boats. A number of workers and other settlers homesteaded around the bay in the 1920s and '30s, and a school and post office opened (the post office was named Nodales, after adjacent Nodales Channel). The area was designated a 389-ha provincial marine park in 1970. *E*

Thurston Harbour (52°50'00" 131°44'00" Talunkwan I, S side of Selwyn Inlet, off E side of Moresby I, QCI). Named in the early 1900s after the 24-m *Nellie G Thurston*, which was active in nearby waters, 1902–6, fishing for halibut. According to QCI historian Kathleen Dalzell, the 80-tonne vessel was built in Gloucester, Massachusetts, in 1883 and fished in the Atlantic until 1897, when it was chartered for a trip, via Cape Horn, to the Klondike gold rush. In 1906 the venerable schooner was purchased by New Westminster businessman Capt E J Fader and used as a receiving boat. Thurston Hbr became an important forestry centre during WWI, a collection depot for "aeroplane" (Sitka) spruce, run by the Imperial Munitions Board. A hospital was built, along with a store, post office, offices and even a YMCA building. Three large sawmills were under construction when the end of the war brought a stop to everything, and the entire operation was sold for a pittance. The harbour continued as a base for private loggers, including Whalen Pulp & Paper and Frank Beban Logging, until the 1970s. *D E*

Thynne Peninsula (50°29'00" 125°46'00" Between Bessborough Bay and Forward Hbr, just NE of Hardwicke I, N of Johnstone Str), **Thynne Point** (50°29'00" 125°47'00" W end of Thynne Peninsula). In 1865, RN surveyor Daniel Pender named a number of features around Forward Hbr after the family of Lt Cdr Horace Lascelles, who served on the BC coast, 1861–65, as cdr of the gunboat *Forward* (*see* Lascelles Point) and later returned to Victoria as a businessman, dying there suddenly in 1869. Thynne Peninsula honours his mother, Lady Louisa Thynne (d 1859), who became Countess of Harewood after marrying Henry Lascelles, 3rd Earl of Harewood. Thynne Point, formerly known as Church Point, was renamed by the hydrographic service in 1946, presumably to reduce the duplication of place names.

Tian Bay (53°46'00" 133°04'00" Just NW of Port Louis, W side of Graham I, QCI), **Tian Head** (53°47'00" 133°07'00" W of Tian Bay), **Tian Islets** (53°45'00" 133°05'00" SW of Tian Bay), **Tian Rock** (53°46'00" 133°07'00" SW of Tian Head). All these features derive their names from the Haida village of Tian (also written Teaen and Ti-ahn), which was located on Tian Bay. It was a rich vicinity for sea otter hunting, and QCI historian Kathleen Dalzell has suggested "good hunting" as the name's meaning. George F MacDonald, however, in his *Haida Monumental Art*, translates Tian as "slaughter village" and speculates that the animal mainly hunted was the sea lion. HBC official John Work recorded 10 houses and 196 inhabitants at Tian about 1840, but by 1913, when an application was made for a First Nation reserve at this site, only one house was still standing. According to Dalzell, the reserve was not designated until 1928 because a petroleum and coal licence had been granted in the area. A test hole was, in fact, drilled right in the village in 1911, reaching a depth of 370 m. Then WWI began, development money ran out and the venture was abandoned. *D*

Tibbs Islet (49°14'00" 126°06'00" Just NE of Tofino, Russell Channel, Clayoquot Sd, W side of Vancouver I). Frederick Gerald Tibbs (1886–1921), from England, came to Canada as a young man, worked on farms and for the railroad, and ended up on the W coast of Vancouver I in the early 1900s. He pre-empted land on Wickaninnish Bay and then on White I (as Tibbs It was known until 1934), receiving a Crown grant in 1913. Tibbs completely logged his island except for one tall spruce tree, which he limbed and cropped and then built a platform on top with a ladder up to it. There he used to sit and enjoy the view and sometimes play a cornet. Tibbs also built a wooden, castle-style home on the island, but never quite finished it. He served overseas during WWI, then returned to Clayoquot Sd where he drowned after becoming separated from his boat while tending the coal-oil lights on the harbour buoys and attempting to swim to shore.

Tilbury Island (49°09'00" 123°01'00" S side of Gravesend Reach, S of Lulu I, SW of Annacis I, lower Fraser R), **Tilbury Slough** (49°08'00" 123°02'00" Between Tilbury I and the S side of the Fraser R). The English port towns of Gravesend and Tilbury are on opposite banks of the Thames R between Westminster and the sea. RN surveyor Capt George Richards named Tilbury I and Gravesend Reach (qv) in association with their English counterparts because of their location between New Westminster and the Str of Georgia. The original Tilbury, in Essex, got its start as a 16th-century fort guarding the Thames and was the site of an ancient cross-river ferry to Gravesend. Its Fraser R equivalent is really an overgrown mud flat that has become attached at its E end to the N shore of the municipality of Delta. The island was developed as an industrial park in the late 1970s, with much of the

slough being filled in; by 2008 more than 650 businesses, including gigantic Canadian Autoparts Toyota, called Tilbury home.

Tildesley Point (52°36'00" 128°56'00" SE side of Aristazabal I, W side of Laredo Sd). Land surveyor Cyrus Ellerton Tildesley (1883–1956) was born and educated in London, England, worked in Uganda for a rubber company 1907–9 and immigrated to Canada in 1910. He married Margaret Annette Dorsey (1880–1972) at Victoria in 1912 and was registered as a BC surveyor the following year. With the exception of the WWI years, when he served with the Canadian Engineers, and a brief stint working in Trinidad for an oil company in 1919, Tildesley spent his entire career with the BC provincial surveys branch before retiring in 1948. He was noted for several technical publications he prepared concerning geographical co-ordinates and triangulation problems. The point was formerly known as Schooner Point.

Tillicum Bay (49°32'00" 123°46'00" E side of Sechelt Inlet, N of Four Mile Point, NW of Vancouver). Tillicum was the word for "person" or "relative" in the Chinook jargon used on the W coast by First Nation groups and early traders and settlers. Later it was also widely used to mean "friend." There are many places with this name in BC, including a creek, a lake, two mountains and a neighbourhood in Victoria. The Sechelt First Nation name for the bay is Chichxwalish.

Tilly Point (48°44'00" 123°12'00" S tip of S Pender I, Gulf Is). The origin of this name, which was applied as early as 1858 by RN surveyor Capt George Richards and which appears on an 1859 chart, is unknown. An alternative name for the feature, given about 1886 by island residents Arthur Spalding and Leonard Higgs, was Bilk Point. According to the memoirs of early S Pender resident Winifred Grey, the pair "were 'bilked' or fooled into rushing out in a boat, after dark, to rescue someone who was not in any danger; merely showing a light! They crept back, hoping they had not been seen." Land at the point was pre-empted by Elijah Pollard, who farmed there, served as a school trustee and built most of S Pender's roads.

Tingley Cove (53°41'00" 132°57'00" S side of Port Louis, W side of Graham I, QCI). The brothers Brydone Lorne "Bert" Tingley (1879–1974) and Elias James Tingley (1881–1964) built a comfortable cabin on this bay in 1910–11 for use while prospecting in the region with their 8-m boat, the *Little Johnny*. The cabin was later borrowed by the hydrographic service during its 1912–15 survey of Port Louis; in gratitude, the surveyors of CGS *Lillooet* named the cove after their hosts. The Tingley brothers had come to BC from NB as youngsters with their family about 1887 and lived at Ladner, Mission, Vancouver and Victoria. Eli went N to the Klondike in 1898 and worked as a prospector and roadhouse owner in the Yukon. In 1908 he determined to establish a townsite at Port Clements (qv). He was joined in this endeavour by Bert, who built a hotel and store there. Eli married Ruth Hilda Wood (1894–1982) at Victoria in 1913 and became part owner of the Port Clements sawmill. In the early 1920s the brothers left the QCIs; Eli pursued business interests in Victoria while Bert became a fisherman. Tingley Cove was later the site of an unsuccessful exploratory well drilled by the Union Oil Co of Canada in 1971. *D*

Tingley Rock (52°03'00" 128°29'00" W entrance to Golby Passage, Queens Sd, SW of Bella Bella). Formerly known as Middle Rk but renamed by the hydrographic service in 1944 after Lt Cdr Harold Reed Tingley (1894–1964), a native of NS. He became a cadet in 1911, then served with the RN during WWI aboard HMS *Melampus*, a destroyer. In 1925 he married Lillian Gertrude Ambridge (1894–1977), from Ottawa. Tingley served with the RCN on the BC coast, 1928–30, and was in command of HMCS *Thiepval* when it struck an unmarked rock and sank in 1930 (*see* Thiepval Channel). During WWII he was harbourmaster at Esquimalt and also in charge of compass adjustments and the chart depot. He died at Saanich.

Tinson Islands (50°59'00" 127°32'00" Part of the Southgate Group, NW side of Queen Charlotte Str, N of Port Hardy), **Tinson Point** (49°12'00" 123°51'00" N end of Gabriola I, W of Pilot Bay, Gulf Is). Lt Charles Wills Tinson (b 1883) was involved in re-surveying these vicinities as an officer aboard HMS *Egeria*, 1901–8. Both features were named by Cdr John Parry, the *Egeria*'s cdr, 1903–6. Tinson was transferred to HMS *Merlin*, another survey vessel, in 1908 and was later involved with surveys in Australia and SE Asia. In 1928, by now a cdr, he was a co-author of the *Australia Pilot*. Tinson Point appeared as Rocky Point on an Admiralty chart dated 1860.

Titul Island (52°47'00" 131°34'00" N of Kunga I, off E side of Moresby I, QCI). This small wooded feature with low limestone cliffs was named by geologist George Mercer Dawson in 1878 after the Haida word for loon.

Tlell (53°34'00" 131°56'00" E side of Graham I, S of the mouth of the Tlell R, QCI). The small community of Tlell is named after the Tlell R, but the meaning of the name, a Haida word, is uncertain. QCI historian Kathleen Dalzell records two meanings for it: "place of big surf" and "land of berries." The area was first settled by William Thomas Hodges, or "Mexican Tom," in 1904. He built up a homestead, now known as the Richardson Ranch, on the banks of the river, and an early hotel was established nearby. *D E*

Tlupana Inlet (49°43'00" 126°28'00" Extends N from Nootka Sd, E side of Nootka I, W side of Vancouver I),

Tlupana River (49°45'00" 126°23'00" Flows SW into Nesook Bay on Tlupana Inlet). The powerful Mowachaht First Nation chief Tlupana was second in importance only to Maquinna at Nootka Sd at the time of European contact. Capt George Vancouver, who spelled Tlupana's name Clewpaneloo, visited him at his winter village of Moutcha (or Mooacha) on Tlupana Inlet in 1794, along with Spanish official José Manuel de Álava. The inlet was named Fondo de Clupananul on the 1791 chart of Alejandro Malaspina—and this spelling, according to PNW cartography expert Henry Wagner, "much more accurately" reflected the pronunciation of the chief's name. Dionisio Alcalá-Galiano and Cayetano Valdés, meanwhile, transcribed the name as Brazo de Tlupananulg on their 1795 chart. (*Fondo* is Spanish for "anchorage," *brazo* for "arm.") On early Admiralty charts the inlet also appears as Hapana Reach and Tlupana Arm. *W*

Toba Inlet, northeast of Campbell River. *Peter Vassilopoulos*

Toba Inlet (50°25'00" 124°35'00" Extends NE from N end of Str of Georgia, NE of Campbell R), **Toba River** (50°30'00" 124°21'00" Flows SW from Toba Glacier into head of Toba Inlet). Toba Inlet, the traditional territory of the Klahoose First Nation, was explored in 1792 by Spanish naval officers Dionisio Alcalá-Galiano and Cayetano Valdés. They named it Boca de las Tablas after several large, carved, painted planks or boards (*tablas* in Spanish) that they found there, which may have been from the front of a Klahoose house. This name appears on Alcalá-Galiano's 1793 chart but was altered to Brazo de Toba on the 1795 edition. This change was thought by early historians to be a draftsman's error; then PNW cartography expert Henry Wagner pointed out that it was probably intended to honour Antonio de Toba y Arredondo (1760–1825), one of Alejandro Malaspina's officers. Toba was a competent astronomer and cartographer with considerable New Spain naval experience when he was invited to join the Malaspina expedition as second-in-command of the *Atrevida*. He suffered from ill health later in life but still managed to hold several important posts, including that of naval cdr at Bilboa. The Klahoose, whose main villages were at the head of Toba Inlet (Tl'émtl'ems, meaning "many houses," was occupied until the 1950s) and on Brem Bay (Kw'ikw'tichenam, or "having lots of pink salmon"), eventually moved to a reserve at Squirrel Cove on Cortes I. Toba Inlet has been extensively logged; one camp on Brem Bay was large enough to have a post office from the 1940s to the '60s. In 2007 the E Toba R was chosen as the site of a controversial run-of-the-river hydroelectric complex, projected to generate 196 MW of electricity by 2010. Nearby Toba Glacier, Toba Mtn and Toba Peak are all named after the inlet. *E W*

Tobey Point (54°18'00" 130°23'00" E side of Digby I, just W of Prince Rupert). As an assistant engineer with the GTP, William Homer Tobey (1880–1959) was one of the dignitaries present when the railway's last spike was driven just E of Ft Fraser on Apr 7, 1914. He had a long career with the GTP and CNR in BC between 1906 and 1940, working successively as a construction engineer, maintenance engineer, divisional engineer and superintendent of the Smithers division. Later Tobey was appointed gen manager of the PGE.

Tod Inlet (48°34'00" 123°28'00" E side of Saanich Inlet, just S of Brentwood Bay, NW of Victoria), **Tod Rock** (48°26'00" 123°17'00" E of Oak Bay and Victoria). Early HBC official John Tod (1794–1882) was a significant figure in the colonial history of BC. He was born in Scotland and worked in a Glasgow cotton warehouse before coming to Canada in 1811 as a clerk with the Earl of Selkirk's Red River settlers, arriving at York Factory in the *Edward and Ann*. Tod, who was not liked by HBC gov George Simpson, spent the next 35 years working at isolated trading posts, including Trout Lk, Severn House, Island Lk, Ft George and Nelson R. Although considered a "highly meritorious officer" and "a man of excellent principle," he was also thought, by one senior HBC official, at least, to have "vulgar manners." He was the clerk in charge at McLeod Lk for a decade, 1824–33, before finally being promoted to chief trader in 1835. After two leaves of absence, during which he returned to the UK, Tod passed another decade in BC's southern Interior, managing Ft Alexandria, 1839–42, and Ft Kamloops, 1842–49. A series of wives, of both First Nation and European heritage (Catherine Birstone, Eliza Waugh, Sophia Lolo), enlivened his exile, as did numerous children; Mary Tod I (qv) off Oak Bay is named for one daughter, Emmaline Bank and Mohun Shoal (qv) in Milbanke Sd for another. In 1850, in poor health, he retired from the HBC and settled near Ft Victoria on a fine 40-ha holding at Oak Bay, which he called Willows Farm (and later expanded to 165 ha). Gov Richard Blanshard named him to Vancouver I's legislative council in 1851, and he served until 1858; James Douglas made him a justice of the peace. Tod's 1851 Oak Bay home, a designated heritage house, is one of the oldest surviving buildings in western Canada. Tod Ck, which flows into Tod Inlet, is also named for him, as is Mt Tod in the Kamloops area. The traditional Wsanec (Saanich) First Nation name for the inlet is Snitcetl, meaning "place of the blue grouse." *E W*

Tofino, on Clayoquot Sound. *Peter Vassilopoulos*

Tofino (49°07'00" 125°53'00" At S entrance to Clayoquot Sd, NW end of Esowista Peninsula, W side of Vancouver I), **Tofino Inlet** (49°09'00" 125°40'00" SE side of Clayoquot Sd). Tofino Inlet was named in 1792 by the Spanish explorers Dionisio Alcalá-Galiano and Cayetano Valdés to honour Vicente Tofiño de San Miguel (1732–95), a Spanish naval officer and renowned astronomer and mathematician. He served as Spain's chief hydrographer, 1784–88, and was appointed director of the country's naval academies in 1787. The town of Tofino was named in association with the inlet. The first settlers arrived on the Esowista Peninsula in the 1890s, and a store opened where Tofino is today in 1901. The townsite that sprang up over the next few years came to be known as Tofino, and the name was confirmed when a post office opened in 1909. The community was incorporated as a village in 1932. Fishing, logging and mining were all important to Tofino's development in its early days, but since the creation of Pacific Rim National Park Reserve in 1970 and the paving of the road to Port Alberni, the district has become a major tourism destination. Tofino Ck takes its name from the inlet. *E*

Tolmie Channel (52°48'00" 128°33'00" Between Sarah I and Princess Royal I, NW of Bella Bella), **Tolmie Point** (52°53'00" 128°32'00" N end of Tolmie Channel, opposite Sarah Head). William Fraser Tolmie (1812–86) was an important HBC official in the PNW and also an influential early BC politician. He was born at Inverness, Scotland, and studied medicine at the Univ of Glasgow, though without becoming a fully qualified physician. He also studied botany, in which he was greatly interested, under the famed William Hooker, and it was Hooker who recommended Tolmie to the HBC, which offered him a contract in the PNW as a clerk and medical officer. He arrived at Ft Vancouver on the Columbia R in 1833 in the HBC supply ship *Ganymede* and was immediately sent to Ft Nisqually on Puget Sd. From there, six months later, he went to Ft McLoughlin, near today's Bella Bella, and from 1836 to 1841 was stationed at Ft Vancouver. James Douglas wrote to his HBC superiors: "I have had none here who discharged the laborious duties of his two stations of Surgeon and Trader of this place with such zeal and attention." Tolmie returned to London in 1841 and also spent time in Paris, then decided to sign up with the HBC again; by 1843 he was back at Ft Nisqually, this time in charge—a position he filled until 1859, when he moved to Victoria. By this time he was a chief factor and one of the most senior officials in the HBC's western dept; he was also married to Jane Work (c 1827–80, *see* Jane I), daughter of John Work, another top HBC officer. Tolmie was elected to Vancouver I's colonial legislative assembly, 1860–66, and was a member of its first board of education, 1865–69. He was a strong supporter of Confederation, temperance and women's right to vote and was elected to the BC legislature, 1874–78. The Tolmies settled at Cloverdale, their large farm in Saanich, and raised five daughters and seven sons, one of whom was Simon Fraser Tolmie, premier of BC, 1928–33. William continued to pursue interests in botany (at least eight plants are named for him) and First Nation languages (he published, with co-author George Mercer Dawson, *Comparative Vocabularies of the Indian Tribes of BC* in 1884). His journals were published in 1963. Historian John S Galbraith praised his "amazing capacity to endure irritations with calmness and courage, which won him the reluctant admiration of his most hostile critics." Mt Tolmie in Saanich, also named after him, appears on Admiralty charts as early as 1847 (though initially misspelled as Mt Tolme); its Songhees First Nation name was Pkaals. *E W*

Tom Islet (50°33'00" 126°12'00" N of Hull I, Havannah Channel, E of E Cracroft I, N of Johnstone Str). Formerly known as Green I but renamed by the hydrographic service in 1955 in association with nearby Hull I, which commemorates RN hydrographer Cdr Thomas Arthur Hull. *See* Hull I.

Tomkinson Point (53°25'48" 128°54'17" S entrance to Bishop Bay, E side of Ursula Channel, S of Hawkesbury I and Kitimat). Lt Edward Philip Tomkinson served on the BC coast, 1871–75, aboard HMS *Boxer*, under Lt Cdr William Collins. As part of their duties, the officers of

the *Boxer* reported on inlets that might be suitable for a transcontinental railway terminus. In 1875, members of a CPR land survey team named a number of features on Ursula Channel after them.

Tomlinson Point. *See* Mt Tomlinson.

Tom Point (48°40'00" 123°16'00" E tip of Rum I, W side of Haro Str, Gulf Is). Named in 1858 by the officers of the RN survey vessel *Plumper* after Thomas Pamphlet, early master mariner on the BC coast, who was known familiarly as "Capt Tom." He was becalmed off this point in his schooner *Violet* when a party from the *Plumper* decided to go and visit him. *See* Pamphlet Cove for a more detailed biography.

Tongass Passage (54°45'00" 130°39'00" W of Wales I, on BC-Alaska boundary, N entrance to Portland Canal, NW of Prince Rupert). The Tongass First Nation, whose members live in the southernmost part of the Alaska panhandle, are part of the larger Tlingit cultural and linguistic family. A number of features in Alaska are named after them.

Tonquin Island (49°07'00" 125°55'00" W side of Templar Channel, SW of Tofino, Clayoquot Sd, W side of Vancouver I). The *Tonquin*, built in NY in 1807, was owned by John Jacob Astor's Pacific Fur Co and brought to the PNW in 1810–11 to establish Ft Astoria at the mouth of the Columbia R. Its capt was Jonathan Thorn, a young naval officer known for his arrogance and dictatorial behaviour (*see* Thorn Reef). Several months after arriving, Thorn took the 29-m, 263-tonne ship N to Clayoquot Sd on a fur-trading venture, accompanied by one of the company's partners, Alexander McKay, who had been Alexander Mackenzie's deputy on his historic overland journey to the Pacific coast in 1793. Thorn managed to deeply insult Nuukmiis, a Tla-o-qui-aht chief, who returned with his followers and succeeded in storming the vessel and killing most of the crew, including Thorn and McKay. A few survivors, after driving off their attackers, abandoned ship in a canoe and were later killed on shore. Only one wounded man remained aboard, but he apparently managed to lay a trail of gunpowder to the ship's magazine, which he later lit when a large number of warriors had returned to pillage the vessel. In the explosion that followed, more than 100 people are alleged to have died. The story of the *Tonquin* is based on the testimony of a First Nation pilot who somehow escaped the carnage and made his way back to Astoria. Much effort has been expended over the years on a search for the wreck of the ship, presumed to be located in the vicinity of Tonquin I (formerly known as Village I), and this quest was still ongoing in 2009.

Topaze Harbour (50°31'00" 125°48'00" Off Sunderland Channel, N of Hardwicke I and Johnstone Str). HMS *Topaze*, a steam frigate of 51 guns and 3,551 tonnes, was launched at Devonport dockyard in 1858 and served on the BC coast from 1859 to 1863, under Capt John Spencer. In 1863, when the Lamalcha, a First Nation group from Kuper I accused of killing two Gulf Is settlers, were tracked down and captured (*see* Lamalchi Bay), Spencer, as one of the region's senior officers, played a major role. The *Topaze* was too large to participate in the hunt directly, but its launches and seamen provided substantial support. In the early 1860s, RN surveyor Capt George Richards named a number of features in the vicinity of Topaze Hbr after Spencer and his family. The vessel, reduced to 31 guns, was back on the Pacific Station in 1866–69, under Capt Richard Powell. One of the duties the crew undertook was to place a plaque on a peak in the remote Juan Fernández Is, off the coast of Chile, in 1868. This commemorated the lonely vigil of Alexander Selkirk, who lived there in solitude, 1704–9, and was probably the inspiration for Daniel Defoe's *Robinson Crusoe*, published in 1719. Between 1871 and 1877 the *Topaze* served on detached or "flying" squadrons, an RN innovation designed to reduce the number of ships on remote stations and thus save money. Detached squadrons, under the command of a rear adm, undertook long worldwide cruises designed for training and for showing the flag at foreign ports and far-flung colonies. The frigate's last commission was in 1878, for Coast Guard duty; it was broken up in 1884. *W*

Topping Islands (52°40'00" 131°40'00" In Darwin Sd, just NW of Lyell Bay, E of Moresby I, QCI). Eugene Sayre Topping (1844–1917), a native of NY, was the founder and first mayor of the city of Trail. He began his working life as a seaman, became a railroad labourer, then spent a number of years in Wyoming, building roads and running a boat on Yellowstone Lk. By 1890 he had moved to BC and was serving as Nelson's deputy mining recorder when Joe Moris and Joe Bourgeois recorded a number of claims on Red Mtn near Rossland. Topping agreed to pay the recording fees ($12.50) in exchange for ownership of one claim, the Le Roi. With Frank Hanna he also purchased land where Trail Ck joined the Columbia R, speculating that it would later become an important townsite. Red Mtn turned out to be fabulously rich in gold and copper—with the Le Roi claim, in particular, eventually producing almost $30 million in gold. Topping's Trail Ck property also panned out; in 1895 a smelter was built there, and the city of Trail soon grew up around it. Topping visited the QCI in 1906–7 with James Johnstone and claimed that they had found Lynch's Ledge, a famous "lost mine" on McLellan I in Cumshewa Inlet. The pair soon had a mining promotion in play, selling out to an English syndicate in 1910. Much development work was done on the island but no mine resulted. Topping married Mary Jane Hanna, his former partner's widow, in 1906. He died at Victoria. *D*

Toquart Bay (49°01'20" 125°20'30" N side of Barkley Sd, SW of Port Alberni, W side of Vancouver I), **Toquart River**

(49°02'00" 125°21'00" Flows S into Toquart Bay). Named after the Toquaht First Nation, a member of the Nuu-chah-nulth Tribal Council, whose traditional territories are on the N and W sides of Barkley Sd. The main Toquaht village, abandoned for many years but re-inhabited in the mid-1980s, is Macoah, situated on Macoah Passage, just W of Toquart Bay. According to *Ha-shilth-sa*, a Nuu-chah-nulth newspaper, Toquaht means "people from a situated area." Other translations that have been recorded include "people of the narrow channel" and "people of the narrow, rocky beach." Nearby Toquart Lk is also named after this First Nation.

Torrance Islet (50°55'00" 127°33'00" W of Kent I, Walker Group, Queen Charlotte Str, N of Port Hardy). William Beveridge Torrance (1889–1965), born in Manitoba of Scottish heritage, pre-empted land in this area in 1914 and received a Crown grant in 1920. He had come as a child, in 1895, to the Comox district, where his parents, Mary Anne and Arthur Stewart Torrance, were pioneer farmers. William Torrance died at Golden. The feature was formerly known as Green I.

Torrens Island (53°15'00" 131°59'00" NE of Image Point, Skidegate Inlet, just off Skidegate and SE Graham I, QCI). Capt Robert Williams Torrens (d 1887) was a former British Army officer who came to Victoria in 1859 and was hired as a colonial civil servant. Gov James Douglas sent him to the QCI the year he arrived, along with William Downie, to look for further evidence of gold; he later served as the clerk of Vancouver I's colonial assembly and as a gold commissioner, justice of the peace and stipendiary magistrate at Clayoquot and Lillooet. Torrens died in England. Formerly known as Bare I but changed by the hydrographic service in 1945. *D*

Tortoise Islets (48°43'00" 123°22'00" Off SE Portland I, NE of N end of Saanich Peninsula, Gulf Is). The origin of this name, which appears on an 1861 Admiralty chart, is uncertain, though it has been suggested that HMS *Tortoise* was the source. This seems unlikely, though, as the venerable *Tortoise*—which was built for the E India Co in 1789 and spent much of its life as an RN coal hulk, convict transport and store ship at Ascension I—was never anywhere near the PNW. Reginald MacKenzie acquired a Crown grant for the islets in 1912.

Totem Inlet (53°46'00" 130°25'00" S side of Dolphin I, S of Porcher I and Prince Rupert). The whole of Dolphin I is a Tsimshian First Nation reserve, home to the village of Kitkatla, the principal settlement of the Gitxaala people. The hydrographic service named the inlet in 1952 in recognition of the region's long-standing First Nation heritage.

Tow Hill (54°05'00" 131°48'00" Mouth of the Hiellen R, E side of McIntyre Bay, NE end of Graham I, QCI). This

Legendary Tow Hill on Graham Island. *Andrew Scott*

133-m formation of columnar basalt, the most distinctive landmark for miles around, has a well-known blowhole at its base and is associated with numerous Haida First Nation legends. The name Tow originally rhymed with "cow" but has come to be pronounced *toe*. It is supposedly derived from a Haida word meaning "place of food," and the area's rich razor clam beds did indeed support a small cannery in the 1920s. QCI historian Kathleen Dalzell tells the story of a supernatural being named Tow who lived on top of the hill, terrorizing local residents and eating their children. The crippled outcast Hopi promised to vanquish Tow in return for the hand of the chief's gorgeous daughter. His offer was ridiculed by other tribe members, of course, but Hopi succeeded in irritating Tow so severely with his whistle and drum that the monster jumped off the hill in pursuit of his tormentor and fell to his death. Hopi became an important—and happily married—community member. Geologist George M Dawson gave "eulachon grease" as a meaning for Tow and added the name to his charts in 1878. Prior to that the feature had been known as Nagdon Hill and Macroon Hill. The area is now part of Naikoon Provincial Park. *D E*

Towner Bank (52°42'00" 129°35'00" W of Moore Is, off W side of Aristazabal I, Hecate Str), **Towner Bay** (48°40'00" 123°28'00" NE side of Saanich Inlet, NW of Victoria). William Towner (1840–1925), from Kent, England, immigrated to Ont in 1858 and arrived on Vancouver I from California in 1864, reportedly bringing with him the colony's first hop plants. He and Isaac Cloake bought 130 ha of land in N Saanich, established a farm and soon had a large area in hops. They also built BC's first oast houses or hop kilns in 1871. N Saanich, in fact, was the hop centre of BC until about 1900, when a parasite infestation took its toll and the Fraser Valley emerged as the main growing area. Towner may have taken part in the Victoria old-timers' reunion of May 1924 (*see* Adams Bay).

Townley Islands (50°01'28" 124°50'26" W of Bliss Landing on Malaspina Peninsula, NE Str of Georgia, E of Campbell

R). Charles Robert Townley (1861–1925), from Orillia, Ont, had a background in mining but came to BC in the early 1900s as a purchasing agent for the CPR's steamship operations to the Orient. He soon became involved in real estate, and in 1904 married Alice Ashworth (1862–1941), whose brother George Ashworth had become infatuated with the idea of turning Savary I into a summer holiday resort. George formed a business partnership with Townley and Harry Keefer and proceeded to buy, subdivide and develop much of the island, promoting it vigorously as the "Catalina of the north." The Townleys built a choice home on Savary, naturally, and spent much of the rest of their lives there. The Townley Is were formerly known as the Double Is but were renamed by the hydrographic service in 1945.

Townsend Point (52°12'00" 128°30'00" N end of Wurtele I, off W side of Athlone I, W of Bella Bella). Charlotte Townsend (1834–1929) arrived at Victoria in 1862 aboard the brideship *Tynemouth*, with her older sister Louisa, and worked briefly as a music teacher. In 1864, to the confusion of genealogists, she married an unrelated man with the same surname, Alfred Allatt Townsend (1817–84), who had come to BC from England in 1858 and worked as a hotel and saloon keeper. Charlotte gave birth to colonial Victoria's first twins—Susan Emma and Harriet Elizabeth—in 1867. She is believed to have attended the grand 1924 Victoria old-timers' reunion (*see* Adams Bay). Her sister Louisa married Victoria architect Edward Mallandaine (*see* Mallandaine Point).

Towry Head (50°40'00" 125°31'00" E side of Loughborough Inlet, S end of Cooper Reach, NW of Campbell R), **Towry Point** (51°04'00" 126°54'00" S side of Seymour Inlet, W of Miles Point, N of Queen Charlotte Str and Port McNeill). After Lt Henry Towry Miles Cooper of the Royal Marines, who served in BC 1859–66. Capt George Towry, cdr of HMS *Diadem* at the 1797 Battle of Cape St Vincent, was apparently an ancestor. *See* Cooper Reach.

Tozier Rock (48°37'00" 123°31'00" W side of Saanich Inlet, NE of McPhail Point, NW of Victoria). Capt Dorr Francis Tozier (1843–1926), from Georgia, who had joined the US Marine Revenue Service while working in Maine, was in command of the revenue cutter *Grant* when it struck this uncharted rock in 1901. In the proud tradition of honouring the unfortunate skipper who first "discovers" an unknown rock, the feature was named that same year by the Geographic Board of Canada. Tozier, based at Port Townsend, was a keen collector of First Nation artifacts and amassed more than 10,000 items, including 3,000 baskets. His reputation was tainted, however, by persistent reports that he had used his quasi-military position to force reluctant owners to sell. After he retired and moved to LA in 1907, there were bitter struggles over the sale of his material, with much of it

T

eventually going to the Museum of the American Indian and the Smithsonian Institution.

Trahey Inlet (52°42'00" 128°47'00" S end of Princess Royal I, just W of Laredo Inlet). James W Trahey (d 1868), a native of NS, came to Victoria via California in 1858 and established a shipyard on the W side of Victoria Hbr. Here he built BC's first sternwheelers, the *Caledonia* (1858) and the *Governor Douglas* (1859), before moving his operation to Laurel Point and constructing the *Colonel Moody* (1859). A series of notable steamboats followed, including the *Maggie Lauder* (1861, later renamed the *Union*), *Hope* (1861), *Reliance* (1862), *Onward* (1863), *Lillooet* (1863), *Alexandra* (1864) and *Isabel* (1866). Most of them operated on the lower Fraser R. Trahey also produced sternwheeled river and lake vessels for the BC Interior. The *Enterprise*, built at Four Mile Ck near Alexandria in 1863, and the *Victoria*, completed at Quesnel in 1868, ran on the upper Fraser. He constructed the *Marten*, which was the first steamship on the Thompson R and served on Shuswap Lk as well, at Savona in 1866.

Trail Bay (49°28'00" 123°45'00" E side of Str of Georgia, S of Sechelt, NW of Vancouver), **Trail Islands** (49°27'00" 123°48'00" W side of Trail Bay, just SW of Sechelt). Named after the ancient First Nation trail that once crossed the isthmus between Porpoise Bay and the Str of Georgia, a distance of 1 km. The trail is indicated on an early Admiralty chart, published in 1863 and based on a survey conducted by Capt George Richards in 1860. This chart also names the Trail Is. A road replaced the trail in 1896. Sechelt First Nation chief Paul Policeman grazed his sheep on the Trail Is in the 1880s and repeatedly tried to pre-empt or buy them. Those rights, however, were reserved only for white settlers. The islands were eventually purchased in 1892 by Arthur Pritchard for $1 an acre. The Sechelt First Nation name for the Trail Is is Lhílhknách.

Transit Island (53°12'00" 132°01'00" E of Maude I, S side of Skidegate Inlet, QCI). The island is one of many BC geographical features named after surveying terms and devices. The transit, invented in 1831, is a specialized instrument, similar to a theodolite, used for measuring angles. Efficient, rugged and economical, it became the preferred tool for surveyors working in the wilds of BC. Early models measured only horizontal angles, but later ones could also take vertical readings. Transit I was originally named Leading I by Lt Daniel Pender when he surveyed Skidegate Inlet in 1866. He noted that a line extending from the W side of the island through the E side of Torrens I provided a safe route into Skidegate Inlet, allowing skippers to easily clear the dangerous bar that extends N of Sandspit and the equally hazardous Bar Rks. As several other coastal features were also called Leading I, the hydrographic service changed the name to Transit I in 1946. **Transit Head** (50°54'00" 125°34'00" NE of Ahnuhati

Point, W side of Knight Inlet), **Transit Point** (50°32'00" 126°16'00" E side of Port Harvey, E Cracroft I, N of Johnstone Str) and **Transit Point** (53°17'00" 129°05'00" N entrance to Home Bay, NW side of Princess Royal I) were also presumably named for their associations with the surveying process. *D*

Trap Islands, Trap Rock, Trap Rocks and **Trap, The**. See The Trap.

Treat Bay (52°04'00" 131°01'00" E side of Kunghit I, at the S end of the QCI). This boulder-dotted cove is named for John B Treat, who served as a furrier on the *Columbia Rediviva*'s initial voyage to the PNW, 1787–89.

Treble Island (53°13'00" 132°13'00" In Kagan Bay, off S side of Graham I, QCI), **Treble Islands** (48°56'00" 125°17'00" W of Nettle I, Broken Group, Barkley Sd, W side of Vancouver I). Treble I in Kagan Bay was shown as three islets on the chart produced by Lt Daniel Pender after his 1866 survey of the area but is now considered to be one feature. The Treble Is in Barkley Sd—marked Treble I (singular) on the manuscript chart prepared by Capt George Richards and the officers of HMS *Hecate* in 1861—were changed to Treble Is (plural) on the 1865 published chart. The feature consists of a compact group of one small island and three islets. There are also two Treble mountains in BC, one SE of Stewart and the other between Phillips Arm and Frederick Arm, both presumably named for their triple peaks.

Trematon Mountain (49°28'30" 124°16'53" S side of Lasqueti I, Str of Georgia). RN surveyor Capt George Richards named the mountain in 1860 because its profile resembled that of Trematon Castle in Cornwall. This ancient hilltop fort had a house within its ruined walls that was home to the Tucker family, and several family members associated with the RN have features named for them in BC—all more or less in the shadow of Trematon Mtn. Nearby Jervis I (qv), for instance, is named after Adm John Jervis Tucker, Jedediah I (qv) after Jedediah Stevens Tucker, and Tucker Bay (qv) after Benjamin Tucker. Trematon Ck and Trematon Lk are named after the mountain. Trematon Castle is currently owned by Prince Charles, the Duke of Cornwall, and was not open to the public in the early 2000s. *W*

Tremayne Bay (54°15'00" 130°24'00" S side of Digby I, just SW of Prince Rupert). Named in 1908 for Dr Henry Ernest Tremayne (1873–1942), who was hired by the GTP as Prince Rupert's first physician. He was born at Milton, Ont, and married Annie Evelyn Fletcher (1877–1950) at Barrie in 1903 before becoming the medical officer at nearby Metlakatla for the Dept of Indian Affairs in 1906. When an isolation hospital for new immigrants was built across Prince Rupert Hbr on Dodge I in 1912, Tremayne also filled the post of quarantine officer. After serving overseas during WWI he returned to Prince Rupert and practised there for many years. He died at Kelowna.

Trevan Rock (52°10'00" 131°06'00" In Houston Stewart Channel, E of Rose Inlet, off S end of Moresby I, QCI). Henry Trevan (1808–80), the surgeon aboard HMS *Virago*, was a medical doctor, trained at St Bartholomew's hospital in London, and joined the RN as an assistant surgeon in 1836. He served on the Pacific Station, 1852–55, and retired with the rank of fleet surgeon in 1861. The journal he kept while on the BC coast was an important source for the book *HMS Virago in the Pacific*, by BC historians Philip and Helen Akrigg. Capt James Prevost and the crew of the *Virago* surveyed Houston Stewart Channel in 1853.

Trevenen Bay (50°01'00" 124°44'00" W side of Malaspina Inlet, W of Coode Peninsula, NW of Powell R). After Capt Trevenen Penrose Coode, an RN officer on the Pacific Station, 1864–66. *See* Coode I, which was named in association with the bay, along with Penrose Bay and Coode Peninsula.

Trevor Channel (48°52'05" 125°07'30" E side of Barkley Sd, W side of Vancouver I). Frances Hornby Trevor (1769–1845), from Somersetshire, England, was raised in Ostend, Belgium, where her father was the rector of a Protestant church. She married Charles Barkley (1759–1832), a ship's capt with the E India Co, there in 1786 and four weeks later accompanied him on his early fur-trading voyage to the PNW with the *Imperial Eagle* (*see* Barkley Sd). She is believed to have been the first European woman to see the BC coast. After selling his furs at Macao, Barkley sailed to Mauritius, where Frances bore her first child, then to India, where his vessel was confiscated in a disagreement with the E India Co, before finally returning to England. Frances continued to travel with her husband, bearing another child in a gale while rounding the Cape of Good Hope and sailing with Charles to Alaska in 1792 aboard the *Halcyon*. She twice circumnavigated the world. Her memoirs, written in her mid-60s and discovered at the BC Archives, were published in 1978 as *The Remarkable World of Frances Barkley*, edited by Beth Hill. (Two diaries, kept at the time of her journeys and used as source material by historian John Walbran, were apparently destroyed by fire in 1909.) Nearby Hornby Rk is also named for her. Trevor Channel was originally called Eastern Channel but was renamed by the hydrographic service in 1931.

Trevor Islet (48°47'45" 123°12'15" In Lyall Hbr, W side of Saturna I, Gulf Is). In 1968 the hydrographic service submitted the name Page It for this feature to the Canadian Permanent Committee on Geographical Names. It was intended to commemorate Herbert Joseph Page (b 1890), who settled on Saturna I about 1910 after immigrating to

Canada from England. He died in action during WWI on Feb 15, 1916, when his Royal Naval Air Service Short 827 seaplane went down in a storm while on patrol over the N Sea. A request that the feature be named instead after Trevor Page, Herbert's son, was made in 1969 by Hazel W Stretton, Trevor's mother and Herbert's widow, who had long since remarried and was living in Victoria. She suggested that the feature had been known locally as Trevor's It for many years. The committee acceded to her request and changed the name accordingly.

Trial Islands, off Victoria. *Peter Vassilopoulos*

Trial Islands (48°23'53" 123°18'20" S of McNeill Bay, off SE end of Vancouver I, just SE of Victoria). According to some sources, this name originates in a trial run that naval vessels under repair at Esquimalt would take out to these islands and back when they were tested for seaworthiness. The problem with this interpretation is that the name is a very old one and long predates the appearance of repair facilities in Esquimalt Hbr. The Trial Is appear on a plan of Victoria district dated about 1848 and on several maps and charts from the 1850s. RN ships only began anchoring at Esquimalt in the late 1840s. Rudimentary hospital huts were erected in 1855, but the first steps toward establishing a dockyard were not taken until the early 1870s. An alternative explanation for the name makes more sense. Rounding the islands by sail and entering Juan de Fuca Str—especially on a flood tide or in a prevailing westerly—has always represented a fine trial of a skipper's navigation skills, and it was this shade of meaning, according to a notation at BC's Geographical Names Office, that probably accounted for the name. Dangerous currents swirl round the 23-ha Trial Is, and a series of vessels have wrecked there over the years, including the tugs *Velos*, *Des Brisay* and *George McGregor*. Many lives have been lost. A hermit lived on the main island in the 1890s, and a lighthouse was built at the S end in 1906; today it is also home to several local radio station antennas. The first lightkeeper, Harrold O'Kell, kept a cow at his station, rowing it over on a handmade raft to provide fresh milk for his child. In 1970, when a new concrete light tower was constructed,

T

the old lens and lantern house were dismantled and reassembled in Victoria's Bastion Square. The islands were made an ecological reserve in 1990; more endangered plant species are protected there than in any other reserve in the province. The Songhees First Nation name for the main island was Tlikwaynung, or "beach peas."

Triangle Island ecological reserve. *Russ Heinl*

Triangle Island (50°52'00" 129°05'00" Westernmost of the Scott Is, W of Cape Scott, off NW end of Vancouver I). According to coastal historian Capt John Walbran, the island is named for its shape, but as the surface area is only vaguely triangular, the reference is probably to the feature's vertical appearance, which is somewhat conical when seen from a ship. The name first appears on an Admiralty chart dated 1863. The island was home to BC's highest and most powerful lighthouse from 1910 to 1920; horrific weather conditions and constant high winds soon forced its abandonment. Today Triangle I is one of BC's most important ecological reserves and the site of a seabird research station. It is home to the world's largest nesting population of Cassin's auklets and the largest colony of tufted puffins S of Alaska. *E*

Triangular Hill (48°25'03" 123°30'40" W of Royal Roads and Victoria, S end of Vancouver I). This feature is one of many on the BC coast that derive their names from the surveying trade. George Aitken, BC's chief geographer for many years and the province's long-serving representative on the Geographic Board of Canada, noted that the name was "suggested, no doubt, from early triangulation of land district boundaries" in the vicinity. Triangulation is a process of determining a location by measuring angles to it from known points at either end of a fixed baseline. While colonial surveyor gen Joseph Pemberton did not name this hill on his 1855 map of SE Vancouver I, he did triangulate the positions of nearby Metchosin Mtn and Mt McDonald from its summit.

Tribal Group (52°03'00" 128°19'00" S of Horsfall I, N side of Queens Sd, SW of Bella Bella). Named by the hydrographic service in 1944 after the *Tribal* class of destroyers that served in the RCN during WWII. Twenty-seven of these vessels were constructed, beginning in 1936, for the RN, RCN and Royal Australian Navy. They were designed as a response to new, heavily armed destroyers built by Japan, Italy and Germany, and had more guns than their predecessors but fewer torpedo launchers. For details on individual vessels *see* Athabaskan I, Haida Is, Huron I *and* Iroquois I.

Tribune Bay (49°30'59" 124°37'38" SE side of Hornby I, W side of Str of Georgia), **Tribune Channel** (50°48'00" 126°12'00" NE and NW sides of Gilford I, NE of Port McNeill), **Tribune Point** (50°38'00" 126°29'00" S side of Gilford I, Knight Inlet), **Tribune Rock** (50°51'00" 127°34'00" N of Hurst I, Gordon Channel, SW Queen Charlotte Str). HMS *Tribune*, a 2,034-tonne steam frigate, served two commissions on the Pacific Station, 1859–60 and 1864–66, after which it was broken up. The 60-m vessel was built at Sheerness dockyard in 1853 with 31 guns, though that number was later reduced to 23. During the Crimean War it was stationed in the Baltic and Black seas; in 1857 it took part in the 2nd Anglo-Chinese War. The *Tribune* originally arrived in BC from China, under Capt Geoffrey Hornby, to provide support to British forces in the San Juan Is boundary dispute. Hornby was the son of Adm Phipps Hornby, who had been cdr-in-chief on the Pacific Station, 1847–51, and after whom Hornby I is named; about 1860, surveyor George Richards decided to extend the tribute to the father by naming a number of features around Hornby I after the son and his ship and officers (*see also* Mt Geoffrey). The K'omoks (Comox) First Nation name for Tribune Bay is Lhekep and may mean "almost joined together"; the NE side of the bay is a midden site. A provincial park was established on Tribune Bay in 1978; its white sand beach is one of the finest in the Str of Georgia. Tribune Channel—which the Spanish pilot Juan Vernaci explored in 1792 and Dionisio Alcalá-Galiano named Canal de Baldinat—was given its current name in 1865 by Lt Daniel Pender of the *Beaver*. Tribune Point was formerly known as Leading Point, Tribune Rk as Grey Rk. The channel and point were named in association with nearby Gilford I, as Viscount Gilford (Capt Richard Meade) was cdr of the *Tribune* during its second posting to BC. *W*

Trickey Islands (52°45'00" 129°18'00" E side of Beauchemin Channel, off NW Aristazabal I). William Trickey (1851–1937), a native of Devon, England, came to Victoria in 1870 and settled in the S Saanich area, where he farmed. In 1878 he married Mary Ann Marwick (1856–1921), who was born and raised in Victoria. William, who was listed as an expressman in the 1892 Victoria directory, is believed to have taken part in the famous Victoria old-timers' reunion of 1924 (*see* Adams Bay).

Trincomali Channel from Galiano Island. *Katherine Johnston*

Trincomali Channel (48°58'00" 123°35'00" Between Galiano I and Saltspring I, Gulf Is). HMS *Trincomalee* (as it is more commonly spelled), a 24-gun, 1,312-tonne frigate under Capt Wallace Houstoun, served on the Pacific Station, 1853–56. This venerable wooden sailing ship, named after a city and important RN base in Ceylon (now Sri Lanka), was built of Malabar teak at Bombay in 1817. It was modelled on the French frigate *Leda* and originally carried 46 guns. The vessel was stored from 1819 to 1845 but then refitted and put back into service in the W Indies and the Nfld region before sailing to PNW waters. In 1856 its crew was part of a large force gathered by Gov James Douglas and taken to the Cowichan Valley to apprehend Chief Tathlasut of the Somenos band for shooting an English settler. By 1861 the *Trincomalee* had been converted to a drill ship for the RN reserve, but in 1897, slated for demolition, it was bought privately, renamed the *Foudroyant* and converted to a training vessel for sea cadets. In 1987 the historic frigate, now the second-oldest ship afloat (after the USS *Constitution*), was transported to Hartlepool, England, for a complete, 14-year restoration and renamed *Trincomalee* once again. Today it is a major tourist attraction. The channel was named by RN surveyor Capt George Richards of HMS *Plumper* in 1858.

Trinity Bay (49°20'00" 123°22'00" SE side of Bowen I, Howe Sd, NW of Vancouver). Named about 1907 by members of the Cowan family (*see* Point Cowan) for Trinity Hall, Ethel Bryant's old school in Southport, Lancashire, UK, established in the 1870s to educate girls from Methodist families. Bryant (1888–1980) was born in S Africa and came to Vancouver from England in 1898,

after the deaths of her parents, to live with her widowed grandmother, Annie Malkin, whose three sons had formed a successful wholesale grocery business, W H Malkin & Co, in the city (one of the brothers, William Malkin, was mayor of Vancouver, 1929–30). The Malkins owned land at Point Cowan on Bowen I and were part of the community there (they later bought more land on the W side of Bowen; *see* King Edward Bay). Bryant was sent to Trinity Hall, 1902–6, then returned to Vancouver, taught school and married Wallace Wilson (1888–1966), a local physician, in 1921. She began writing in the 1930s and, as Ethel Wilson, published five novels and many short stories, gradually developing a reputation as one of Canada's best fiction writers. The Wilsons purchased their own summer retreat on Bowen about 1940 and later donated the property to UBC. Life on Bowen I was chronicled in Ethel's 1949 biographical novel, *The Innocent Traveller*.

Triquet Island (51°48'00" 128°15'00" S of Spider I, W of S entrance to Kildidt Sd, S of Bella Bella). Col Paul Triquet, VC (1910–80), was born in Que and joined the Royal 22nd Regiment (the "Van Doos") in 1927. He was awarded the VC (and the French Légion d'honneur) in Dec 1943 for his actions at Casa Berardi, Italy. A capt at the time, he led his company in capturing and holding a key German strongpoint, despite heavy casualties and a determined enemy counterattack. Triquet left active service in 1947 with the rank of maj and became district sales manager for a forest products company, but re-enlisted with the Canadian Army Reserve and was promoted to col in command of the 8th Militia Group. He eventually retired to Florida. Triquet I was formerly known as Fan I but was changed in 1944 by regional hydrographer Henri Parizeau, who applied many WWII-related names to surrounding features. With its beautiful beaches and bird-rich lagoon, the island is a popular wilderness kayaking destination.

Triumph Bay (53°28'00" 128°42'00" Extends S from W end of Gardner Canal, S of Kitimat), **Triumph Point** (52°45'00" 131°48'00" N entrance to Crescent Inlet, N end of Darwin Sd, E side of Moresby I, QCI), **Triumph River** (53°27'00" 128°41'00" Flows N into Triumph Bay). Named after the small trading sloop *Triumph*, built at Cowichan in 1872, which carried geologist James Richardson (*see* Richardson Head) on his explorations of the BC N coast. In 1872 he sailed to Skidegate Inlet to prepare a report on the recently abandoned Cowgitz coal mine, which its owners were hoping to reopen. In 1874, Richardson and the 15-tonne *Triumph* were at Gardner Canal, assisting CPR deputy engineer Marcus Smith, in the *Otter*, in his search for a suitable railroad terminus. The vessels anchored in Triumph Bay, which was named that year by the CPR surveyors. A different, larger schooner named *Triumph* made a name for itself in the Victoria-based sealing trade in the 1880s and '90s. The Triumph R and nearby Triumph Lk are named for the bay. Triumph Point

T

was originally called White Point by geologist George Dawson in 1878 but was renamed by the hydrographic service in association with nearby Richardson I. *W*

Trivett Island (50°49'00" 126°33'00" E side of Broughton I, Penphrase Passage, NE of Port McNeill), **Trivett Point** (53°18'00" 129°02'00" McKay Reach, N end of Princess Royal I), **Trivett Rock** (50°49'00" 126°33'00" Just E of Trivett I, S of Wishart Peninsula). John Frederick Trivett, listed in 1838 as an honorary lt in the RN reserve, was an early ship's capt for the HBC. He was in charge of the supply barque *Princess Royal*, 1856–58 and 1859–61, sailing back and forth between London and Victoria, and also brought the company's new paddle steamer *Labouchere* out to the PNW from England in 1858–59. Adm John Kingcome's nephew William Kingcome worked as an officer under Trivett and eventually succeeded him as cdr of the *Princess Royal*. In 1866, Lt Daniel Pender named the island, probably because of its proximity to Kingcome Inlet. Coast historian John Walbran speculated that the point, also surveyed that year by Pender, appears on the chart because Trivett's vessel and Princess Royal I had the same name. The island, of course, commemorates the much earlier trading sloop of Charles Duncan. Trivett resigned from the HBC in 1861, stating that he had been "advised by my friends and medical men to remain on shore for a short time, the sudden changes of temperature which I experience during these long voyages, having much tried my constitution." He wrote an article about his travels that appeared in 1861 in the *Mercantile Marine Magazine*. *W*

Trollope Point (48°23'00" 123°42'00" E side of Sooke Hbr, SW of Billings Point, S end of Vancouver I). RN officer Henry Trollope (1815–79) served in BC waters in 1846–47 as 2nd lt of HMS *Herald*, under Capt Henry Kellett, who named this feature in 1846. He was from a naval family with a number of adms to its credit and had joined the service in 1828. In 1853–54, as cdr of HMS *Rattlesnake*, he overwintered at Port Clarence in Bering Str while bringing supplies to the vessels searching for missing Arctic explorer Sir John Franklin. Trollope spent considerable time travelling in the region and meeting the local Inuit, and his journal for the period contains much useful cultural and geographic detail. He was promoted to capt in 1860, retired from the RN in 1868 and reached the rank of rear adm, retired, in 1876.

Trotter Bay (52°53'00" 131°53'00" NE side of Moresby I, facing Selwyn Inlet, opposite SW end of Louise I, QCI). Named by the hydrographic service in 1945 for William Waddington Trotter (1891–1961), who was manager of the nearby Lagoon Bay Cannery in 1943 and reported several dangerous rocks in the vicinity when the area was surveyed. He was from N Yorkshire and immigrated to Canada after working for the British post office and

serving in WWI. In BC he found employment with the Bank of Montreal and the provincial government. Trotter, who married Hilma Anna Justina Swanson at Vancouver in 1928, eventually joined the Canadian Fishing Co and managed a series of salmon canneries, including Margaret Bay in Smith Inlet and the Gulf of Georgia at Steveston. He retired in 1956 and died at Coquitlam. Trotter Bay was formerly known as Goose Bay. *D*

Trounce Inlet (53°10'00" 132°19'00" Skidegate Channel, between E Narrows and W Narrows, S side of Graham I, QCI), **Trounce Point** (54°34'00" 130°20'00" S of Grace Point, NW side of Work Channel, N of Prince Rupert). Thomas Trounce (1813–1900) was chairman of the Queen Charlotte Coal Co, which operated the unsuccessful Cowgitz Mine, 1864–72. A native of Cornwall, he studied architecture before immigrating to Tasmania and later joining the Australian gold rush. He was in San Francisco in 1849 for the California gold rush and then in BC for the Fraser and Cariboo stampedes, where he apparently made good money. Trounce, a staunch Methodist, then settled in Victoria with his wife, Jane (1815–88), and returned to his first interest, designing residential, commercial and religious buildings in and around the capital city, including, surprisingly, St Paul's Anglican church in Esquimalt. He drew up plans for missionary Thomas Crosby's first church at Port Simpson, which was constructed in 1874 and could seat 800. Trounce was also one of Victoria's most prominent contractors and constructed dozens of office buildings and homes; in 1859, in a dispute with the city and other landowners, he built Trounce Alley as a private-access route to stores on his downtown property. He was elected a Victoria alderman, 1875–77, and also served as Grand Master of BC's main Masonic society. After Jane's death he married Emma Richards (1839–1902) at San Francisco in 1888. Trounce Inlet, which is connected to Long Inlet by an ancient Haida trail, was originally named North Arm by geologist George Mercer Dawson in 1878 but was renamed by the hydrographic service in 1945. *D*

Troup Bank (54°04'00" 132°11'00" N of Entry Point, off E entrance to Masset Hbr, N side of Graham I, QCI). Named in 1907 by Capt Frederick Learmonth of the RN survey vessel *Egeria* after one of the ship's officers, Lt James Andrew Gardiner Troup (1883–1975), who participated in the survey of this area. Nicknamed "Jaggers," Troup went on to a significant naval career, serving as capt of the cruiser *Cairo*, 1926–28, and the battleship *Revenge*, 1930–32. He also held a number of specialized posts: director of the navigation school at Portsmouth, 1928–30; director of the tactical school, 1933–34; and, as a rear adm, director of naval intelligence, 1935–38. He came out of retirement during WWII and served, with the rank of vice adm, as flag-officer-in-charge at Glasgow. Troup was knighted in 1943.

Troup Narrows (52°17'00" 128°00'00" NE end of Troup Passage), **Troup Passage** (52°15'00" 128°04'00" Between Chatfield I and Cunningham I, just N of Bella Bella). Capt James William Troup (1855–1931) was born at Vancouver, Washington, and learned the steamboat trade on the Columbia R. After marrying Frances Julia Stump (1860–1938) he came to BC in 1883 to join the Canadian Pacific Navigation Co, but returned three years later to manage the steamship arm of the Oregon Rwy & Navigation Co. His next move was to eastern BC, about 1892, where John Irving put him in charge of the Columbia & Kootenay Steam Navigation Co, which operated steamers on Kootenay and Arrow lakes and was bought by the CPR in 1897. Troup was back on the W coast in 1901 and appointed gen manager of the CPR's BC Coast Steamship Service, a position he held until 1928. He created the company's *Princess* fleet, expanding it to a modern line of 19 vessels that carried nearly 800,000 passengers and more than 30,000 vehicles the year he retired. Troup's gravestone in Victoria's Ross Bay Cemetery reads "Last Anchorage." A CPR station was also named for him on the W Arm of Kootenay Lk. Troup Passage was formerly called Thornton Passage, after Sir Henry Thornton, president of the CNR, 1922–32. It was then changed to Deer Passage, a name by which it is still known locally, before being given its current title by the hydrographic service in 1925. *E*

Trueworthy Bight (48°46'00" 123°11'00" SW side of Saturna I, Gulf Is). Charles Trueworthy was one of Saturna I's first settlers. He homesteaded on property adjacent to this bay in 1873 and acquired almost 600 ha of land on the island over the next decade or so. He had come to Canada from Wales with his brother William, who settled on Orcas I across the border in the US. In 1884, Charles, in poor health, sold much of his estate to Warburton Pike and Charles Payne and moved to California. The name was submitted by the Gulf Is Branch of the BC Historical Assoc in 1968. The bight has also been known locally as Billys Bay.

Trutch Island (53°06'00" 129°41'00" Part of the Estevan Group, SE of Banks I). Joseph William Trutch (1826–1904) was born and educated in England but spent his childhood on his father's Jamaican estates. Trained as an engineer, he immigrated in 1849 to San Francisco and later worked as an assistant to John Preston, Oregon's first surveyor gen. In 1855 he married Julia Elizabeth Hyde (1827–95), Preston's sister-in-law, who was originally from NY. The Trutches moved first to Illinois, where Joseph was assistant superintendent of the Illinois & Michigan Canal, and then, in 1859, to BC. Trutch found steady employment in the new colony as an engineer, building sections of the Cariboo Rd and—his finest achievement—the Alexandra suspension bridge. He bought land on Vancouver I and entered politics, winning election to the Vancouver I legislative assembly, 1861–63. In 1864 he replaced Col Richard

Moody as BC's chief commissioner of Lands and Works, in which capacity he was responsible for First Nation reserves. Trutch was noted for his racist and contemptuous attitudes toward BC's aboriginal population. He refused to negotiate land claims or recognize title, arguing that Native people had no valid rights to land and should simply make room for white colonizers. The reserves he did set aside were minimal, and many existing reserves were reduced in size, with arable lands being offered to settlers. Trutch's dismissal of First Nation concerns left a bitter legacy for future generations to deal with, but he was popular at the time, a member of BC's legislative council from 1866, a strong supporter of Confederation and one of three officials named to arrange the terms of union with Ottawa. After serving as BC's first lt gov, 1871–76, Trutch returned to England until appointed dominion agent for BC, 1880–89, with special responsibility for the transcontinental railway. He was knighted in 1889 and retired "home" (which for Trutch was always England). Mt Trutch on the BC-Alberta border N of Golden is also named for him, as are Trutch Ck and the community of Trutch in the Peace R district. Julia Trutch died at Victoria while she and Joseph were making a rare return visit to BC. Hyde Point and Lady Trutch Passage (qv) are named for her. Trutch I, formerly known as North I, was home to a radar and radio communications facility for many years; its massive antennas were perched on the higher of the two Musgrave Peaks. The station was supplied via a dock and helipad at Ethelda Bay on nearby Barnard I. *E*

Tsamspanaknok Bay (54°40'00" 130°06'00" S side of Khutzeymateen Inlet, NE of Prince Rupert). This adaptation of the feature's Tsimshian First Nation name was given by the hydrographic service in 1955. It supposedly means "abode of a supernatural being."

Tsawwassen, home to a major BC Ferries terminal. *Peter Vassilopoulos*

Tsawwassen (49°01'00" 123°05'00" N portion of Point Roberts peninsula, W side of Boundary Bay, S of Delta and Vancouver), **Tsawwassen Beach** (49°00'00" 123°05'00" W side of Point Roberts peninsula, between BC-US border and BC Ferries causeway). This Halkomelem (Central

Coast Salish) word is the name of the First Nation that traditionally occupied this area. It means "facing the sea," according to anthropologist Wilson Duff. Dozens of different spellings have been recorded over the years, including Sewathen, Cheahwassen, Pswwassan and Tshewass-an. The correct pronunciation of the name is *sa-WOSS-en*. The area is now a residential suburb, part of the municipality of Delta, and home to the huge Tsawwassen ferry terminal, which serves Vancouver I and the Gulf Is. In 2007, Tsawwassen First Nation members signed BC's first modern-day urban treaty. *E*

Tsehum Harbour (48°40'00" 123°24'00" NE side of Saanich Peninsula, N of Victoria). According to ethnologist William Newcombe, Tseycum First Nation members, who lived on the harbour before moving to their current reserve on Patricia Bay, took their name from a type of clay that was found in the area and used to remove lanolin from mountain goat wool. The feature is also known locally as Shoal Hbr or Shoal Bay, but that name was officially changed in 1939 by the hydrographic service at the request of local residents. The harbour's current name is often spelled Tseycum, and this version is also commonly used to refer to the First Nation (though members prefer the spelling Wsikem) and to a creek that enters Patricia Bay on the W side of the peninsula. Tsehum Hbr is home to a number of recreational marinas.

Ts'im K'ol'hl Da oots'ip (55°00'10" 129°38'15" N side of lower Nass R, near Laxgalts'ap, or Greenville, NE of Prince Rupert). This feature, pronounced *sim-kol DAW-AW zip*, was formerly known as Fishery Bay, a name identified in the report of the 1916 Royal Commission on Indian Affairs. It was one of 34 official names adopted in 2000 as part of the Nisga'a First Nation treaty and can be translated as "behind the fortress." A huge rock at this location was apparently used as a defence against enemy raids. The bay has an important history as an eulachon harvesting and processing site, used by other First Nations in the region as well as the Nisga'a. Eulachon, a small smelt-like fish, produced an oil, or "grease," that was much valued as a food condiment and became a staple item for trade.

Tsimpsean Peninsula (54°22'00" 130°15'00" Extending NW from Prince Rupert, between Chatham Sd and Work Channel). Adopted in 1927 to recognize the First Nation people who have traditionally occupied this territory— and whose name is more commonly spelled Tsimshian today. The word is pronounced *SIM-shin* and has had many spellings over the years, including Chimsain, Tsimp-Sheean and Chimsyan. It can be translated as "inside the Skeena R," Skeena being an adaptation of the Tsimshian term *k'shian*, meaning "water of the clouds." Most Tsimshian First Nation members are now based at Prince Rupert, though the large community of Lax Kw'alaams (Port Simpson) still flourishes on the peninsula. *E*

Tsinga Point (52°43'00" 131°34'00" N side of Lyell I, N of Atli Inlet, off E side of Moresby I, QCI). Named by the hydrographic service in 1957 for its tooth-like shape on the chart. Tsinga is an adaptation of the Haida word for tooth, taken from the vocabulary list in George Mercer Dawson's 1880 monograph "On the Haida Indians of the QCI." *D*

Tsowwin Narrows (49°47'00" 126°39'00" At mouth of the Tsowwin R, Tahsis Inlet, opposite E side of Nootka I, W side of Vancouver I), **Tsowwin River** (49°47'00" 126°38'00" Flows W into Tsowwin Narrows). Named for the Mowachaht reserve located just N of the narrows, once the site of Tsawun, an important Nuu-chah-nulth First Nation village. The narrows have been formed by a gravel bar created where the river, once known locally as the Sandspit R, enters Tahsis Inlet. A logging camp and booming ground are situated just S of the narrows.

Tsuquanah Point (48°40'00" 124°51'00" W entrance to Nitinat Narrows, SE of Barkley Sd, SW side of Vancouver I). Named after Tsuxwkwaada, the preferred spelling for the nearby Ditidaht First Nation reserve, once the site of a significant village. The inhabitants of Tsuxwkwaada were noted whalers, fur-seal hunters and halibut fishers. There were five large houses at the settlement when the 96-ha reserve was marked out in 1892.

Tsusiat Falls (48°41'00" 124°55'00" At mouth of the Tsusiat R), **Tsusiat Point** (48°41'00" 124°55'00" E of Pachena Point, SW side of Vancouver I), **Tsusiat River** (Flows SW into the Pacific Ocean, E of Pachena Point). According to BC historians Helen and Philip Akrigg, Tsusiat is a Ditidaht First Nation word meaning "water pouring down"—ie, a waterfall. The Tsusiat R pours over a wide ledge directly onto the beach and into the ocean, making spectacular Tsusiat Falls one of the most photographed and popular campsites on the W Coast Trail. Tsusiat Lk takes its name from the river and falls. A dramatic sea arch at Tsusiat Point, called Hole in the Wall, has given this nearby feature an alternative local name: Hole Point.

Tucker Bay (49°30'00" 124°16'00" N side of Lasqueti I, Sabine Channel, Str of Georgia). Named by Capt George Richards of the survey vessel *Plumper* in 1860 after Benjamin Tucker (1762–1829), secretary to Adm Sir John Jervis, Earl St Vincent. He first served as purser of several RN vessels, but from 1798 on, his career was closely associated with that of the adm. Tucker was appointed a commissioner and 2nd secretary of the RN before Jervis retired. In 1808 he became surveyor gen of the duchy of Cornwall. It is likely, from its location, that **Tuck Rock** (49°30'00" 124°17'00" In Tucker Bay) was named in association with the bay (though much later, in 1945, by the hydrographic service). Several other features in the area commemorate the Tucker family as well; *see* Jedediah I, Jervis I *and* Trematon Mtn. *W*

Tuck Inlet, north of Prince Rupert. *John Alexander*

Tuck Inlet (54°25'00" 130°18'00" NW extension of Prince Rupert Hbr), **Tuck Island** (54°15'00" 130°22'00" S entrance to Prince Rupert Hbr), **Tuck Narrows** (54°24'00" 130°15'00" Between Tuck Inlet and Prince Rupert Hbr), **Tuck Point** (54°24'00" 130°15'00" W entrance to Tuck Inlet). Civil engineer Samuel Parker Tuck (1837–1916), from St John, NB, was educated at Harvard Univ and married Sarah Matilda Morse (1848–1930) in 1873 in NB. He built railways in NB before coming to BC in 1880, where he served as divisional construction engineer for the CPR, under Andrew Onderdonk, on the section of line between Lytton and Spences Bridge and was later employed as a provincial land surveyor. The name Tuck Inlet was adopted on an 1896 Admiralty chart after Tuck made a preliminary survey of the area in 1892. At that time the inlet included what is now Prince Rupert Hbr. In 1906, after Kaien I was chosen as the GTP's western terminus, hydrographer G Blanchard Dodge divided the inlet into two portions; the SW part became Prince Rupert Hbr and the NE part remained Tuck Inlet. Samuel Tuck moved to the Kootenays in 1892, worked as a surveyor at Nelson and Kaslo, and was appointed the region's sheriff in 1899. He died at Nelson. Sarah Tuck seems to have preferred life in Victoria, where she ran the Roccabella, a genteel boarding house or "family hotel," for 40 years. Tuck Lk near Cowichan Lk on Vancouver I was also named for Samuel after he made a number of surveys in the Nitinat valley for the BC government in 1890. Tuck I was formerly known as Mink I. *W*

Tuft Islets (52°42'00" 131°24'00" E of Lyell I, off E side of Moresby I, QCI). The hydrographic service named this feature in 1957, presumably because of the tufts of vegetation that grace the summit of the largest islet. Geologist George Mercer Dawson had originally given the name Tuft I to nearby Skaga I (qv), just to the SE, in 1878.

Tuga Point (52°09'00" 131°14'00" W side of Louscoone Inlet, S end of Moresby I, QCI). The point was named by the hydrographic service in 1962 after the Haida First Nation village of Chuga (or Tc'uga), which was located

across the peninsula on the W side of Moresby I, just S of Cape Freeman. The name can apparently be translated as "to go for cedar planks." *D*

Tugboat Passage (50°25'00" 125°12'00" Between Dent I and Little Dent I, Cordero Channel, N of Sonora I and Campbell R). Despite the passage's islets, shoals and confused currents, this is the route often preferred by tugs towing log booms. "Local knowledge is advised," states *Sailing Directions*. The alternative is Dent Rapids, just to the W, where dangerous overfalls and eddies form and currents can reach 9 knots (17 km/h). At the S entrance to the rapids is Devils Hole, famed for its violent whirlpools.

Tugwell Island (54°20'00" 130°30'00" Entrance to Metlakatla Bay, Chatham Sd, W of Prince Rupert), **Tugwell Reef** (54°18'00" 130°30'00" Off S end of Tugwell I). Rev Lewen Street Tugwell (1835–98) and his wife, Harriet Leah (née Greenwood), were sent to BC from England by the Anglican Church Missionary Society and joined William Duncan at Ft Simpson in 1860. They assisted with the mission there and were in the process of moving to Duncan's new model Christian settlement at Metlakatla when Lewen became ill. In 1861 he and his wife returned to England, where he worked as a curate, then moved to Spain, where Lewen became the British chaplain at Seville. Tugwell I was named by RN surveyor Capt George Richards of HMS *Hecate* in 1862.

Tuite Point (52°52'00" 128°41'00" S entrance to Fifer Cove, Laredo Inlet, Princess Royal I). Peter Tuite, who had come to Victoria from the US in 1858 with the early Fraser R gold seekers, was appointed deputy postmaster of Victoria that year, at a salary of £200 per annum. Alexander C Anderson served as collector of customs, postmaster gen and treasurer of the colony of Vancouver I in those early days, but Tuite performed the actual work of the city's post office, which was at that time located in a one-storey wooden building on Government St between Yates St and Bastion St. He resigned and left Victoria in 1859 when Gov James Douglas refused his request for a £100 raise.

Tully Island (50°21'00" 125°19'00" Cameleon Hbr, W side of Sonora I, N of Campbell R). Many features in Cameleon Hbr were named after officers who served aboard HMS *Cameleon* in 1863, during the naval pursuit of a First Nation group from Lamalchi Bay, on Kuper I, that was suspected of murdering two Gulf Is settlers (*see* Lamalchi Bay). John Handfield Tully was master of the vessel at that time, under Cdr Edward Hardinge. He was promoted to staff cdr in 1870. Nearby Handfield Bay was also named for him. The 17-gun sloop had several commissions on the BC coast: 1861–63, 1867–69 and 1870–74.

Tumbo Channel (48°47'00" 123°05'00" Between Tumbo I and E end of Saturna I, Gulf Is), **Tumbo Island** (48°48'00"

Tumbo Island, just north of Saturna Island. *Kevin Oke*

123°04'00" Just N of E end of Saturna I), **Tumbo Point** (48°48'00" 123°03'00" E end of Tumbo I), **Tumbo Reef** (48°48'00" 123°03'00" Just N of E tip of Saturna I, S end of Str of Georgia). The origin of this unusual name, which first appears on an 1860 Admiralty chart surveyed by Capt George Richards, had stumped historians until the mystery was solved in 1991 in a neat piece of detective work by Victoria journalist Peter Murray. US writer Bryce Wood, in a 1980 book on the place names of San Juan I, had revealed that Lt Charles Wilkes, who led a US naval exploring expedition around the S Pacific, 1838–42, was in the Gulf and San Juan Is in 1841 and had named a number of places, including "Tumbow I" off Saturna. Capt Richards seems to have changed all of Wilkes's names in BC, though Tumbow he only altered slightly, to Tumbo, perhaps to give it more of a Spanish flavour, in keeping with Saturna I. He also named Tumbo Channel on his 1860 chart. The meaning or derivation of the word, however, was still unknown. But Murray's research showed that Wilkes had been working on his charts of the Fiji Is just before his PNW visit, and he deduced that Tumbow had been named after Tumbou, a village on the Fijian island of Lakemba. The fact that Wilkes had given Fijian names to two other features in nearby Bellingham Bay confirmed Murray's hunch. Tumbo I, at 121 ha, is one of the last unspoiled examples of what all the Gulf Is might have looked like a century and a half ago. Even Tumbo has seen some primitive development over the years, though. A log-cabin homestead beside an ancient field may date back to the 1880s, when Tumbo was Crown-granted to Charles Gabriel and Isaac Tatton. A century-old coal mine, worked by Japanese colliers, shut down after two men were killed in an explosion. Later industrial efforts included fur and oyster farms. Fortunately, the island was purchased from its California owner for $3.7 million in 1997 and is now part of the Gulf Is National Park Reserve. Its Sencoťen (Coast Salish) name is Temosen, which has been translated as "becoming a good fishing tide." Tumbo Point was labelled Race Point on the 1860 chart surveyed by Capt Richards; its current name, and that of Tumbo Reef, do not appear until the chart's 1911 edition.

Tunis Point (52°40'00" 128°35'00" N entrance to Alexander Inlet, Princess Royal I). After Harold R L G Alexander, 1st Earl of Tunis, Canada's 17th gov gen, 1946–52. *See* Alexander Inlet.

Tunstall Bay (49°21'00" 123°25'00" SW side of Bowen I, Howe Sd, NW of Vancouver). George Christie Tunstall (1867–1950) was vice-president and one of the founders of Western Explosives Ltd, which built a dynamite factory at this location in 1909. Before that the bay had been a base for the Lipsett Whaling Co in the late 1860s, while the surrounding area, originally purchased by Joseph Mannion in 1885, had been owned by logging companies. According to Bowen I historian Irene Howard, the explosives plant, which had a staff of 80 and its own post office, was a dangerous place to work. A number of white and Asian employees were killed in a series of detonations before the factory was sold to Canadian Explosives Ltd in 1911. The operation was closed down in 1913 and moved to James I. Tunstall, wealthy by then and married to Marguerite M Duchesnay, retired to Savona and later moved to Kamloops. He claimed in a letter to the chief geographer at Ottawa that the bay was not named for him at all, but for his father, also George Christie Tunstall (1836–1911). Tunstall Ck, NE of Nelson, commemorates the senior Tunstall as well. Originally from Que, he had come to BC with the Overlanders of 1862, married Annie Morgan and served as government agent, court registrar, returning officer and gold commissioner at various locations around the province: Kamloops (1879), Granite Ck (1885), Yale (1886), Revelstoke (1890) and back to Kamloops, where he was also city assessor. The area around Tunstall Bay saw a great deal of subdivision after WWII and is now luxuriously residential.

Tupper Rock (49°20'00" 122°54'00" In Indian Arm, SW of Racoon I, just NE of Vancouver). Named after politician Charles Hibbert Tupper (1855–1927), son of Conservative PM Charles Tupper. He was born and raised in NS, took a law degree at Harvard Univ and married Janet McDonald (1858–1935), daughter of NS politician James McDonald, at Halifax in 1879. Three years later he was elected MP for Pictou; in 1888, PM Sir John A Macdonald made him minister of Marine and Fisheries, the youngest Canadian, at 32, to serve in cabinet up to that time. Tupper was knighted in 1893 for his work on the Bering Sea sealing dispute. He later served in various cabinets as minister of justice and solicitor gen, then moved to BC in 1897 to practise law. He continued to take a keen interest in Conservative politics, both federally and provincially, but eventually fell out with his old friend PM Sir Robert Borden. An attempt in 1923 to form a new provincial party in BC was a failure. Charles Reef in Indian Arm is named for him as well. *See also* Hermit I, which was bought in 1926 by his son and law partner, Reginald Hibbert Tupper. *E*

Turgoose Point (48°36'00" 123°23'00" E side of Saanich Peninsula, NW side of Saanichton Bay, N of Victoria). William Turgoose (1830–85), a native of Lincolnshire, England, immigrated to Illinois in the US before 1861 and came to BC, via California, to participate in the Cariboo gold rush. He ended up buying land in the Saanichton area about 1865 and eventually farmed more than 200 ha, specializing in shorthorn cattle. His property was known as the Fronton Farm. William married Emma Pope (1844–1922), daughter of Abraham and Sarah Pope, also Saanich pioneers. After William's death, she married Edmund Sadler, another Saanichton farmer. The Turgoose post office, named after William's son Frederick, who served as postmaster, 1892–1912, became Saanichton post office in 1922.

Turnagain Island (49°32'00" 123°58'00" W of Secret Cove, W side of Sechelt Peninsula, NE entrance to Welcome Passage, NW of Vancouver). The name first appears on an Admiralty chart published in 1865 but based on a survey conducted by Capt George Richards and HMS *Plumper* in 1860. According to an old story, the crew of one of the *Plumper*'s boats were attempting to circumnavigate the island but could not get around the N side, where a very narrow passage dries at low tide. The boat's cdr ordered his oarsmen to "turn again," and thus the island got its name.

Turnback Point (50°25'00" 125°08'00" N end of Stuart I, SE entrance to Arran Rapids, N entrance to Bute Inlet, N of Campbell R). A note at BC's Geographical Names Office states that this name has its origins in the fact that boats attempting a western passage through the Arran Rapids against the tide are usually forced to turn back at this point. It could just as easily be a warning message, however, to unwary mariners. Currents in the Arran Rapids can reach 9 knots (17 km/h).

Turnbull Cove (50°57'00" 126°50'00" N side of Kenneth Passage, N of Watson I and N Broughton I, NE of Port McNeill), **Turnbull Reef** (48°44'00" 123°21'00" Off NE Portland I, W side of Moresby Passage, NE of Saanich Peninsula, Gulf Is). Alexander Turnbull was assistant surgeon aboard HMS *Topaze*, under Capt John Spencer, and served on the Pacific Station, 1859–63. He was appointed a deputy inspector-gen of hospitals and fleets in 1889 and, after retirement, became an inspector-gen of hospitals and fleets (the second-highest medical rank in the RN, equivalent to a rear adm) in 1896. The reef was named by Capt George Richards of HMS *Plumper* about 1860, the cove by Lt Daniel Pender of the *Beaver* in 1865.

Turnbull Inlet (51°46'00" 128°02'00" W side of Nalau I, just N of Hakai Passage, S of Bella Bella). Civil engineer John Moncrieff "Jake" Turnbull (1877–1982), born at Montreal and educated at McGill Univ, is believed to have been part of a land survey party that worked in this area

in the early 1920s. He had come W in 1897 and worked at mines near Revelstoke and Rossland. His wife, Kathleen Gladys Herbert (1886–1968, née Jarvis), soon joined him in BC. Turnbull turned his attention in the early 1900s to the lead-zinc-silver deposits of the E Kootenays, in the Kimberley-Cranbrook region. In 1915 he became a member of UBC's first faculty and founded the dept of mining and metallurgy, teaching and serving as dept head until he retired in 1945. Before he died, in Vancouver, at the age of 104, Turnbull was the univ's last living original faculty member (he had given a lecture when he was 101), the oldest member of the Canadian Institute of Mining and Metallurgy, and registrant number five in the Assoc of Professional Engineers of BC. He wrote several books on BC's mining heritage. Mt Turnbull in the Kootenays is also named for him.

Turner Point (53°42'00" 132°58'00" N entrance to Port Louis, W side of Graham I, QCI). Probably named for James Alexander Turner, who was born at Montreal in 1891, graduated from the Royal Military College and studied civil engineering in Toronto. In 1913 he came out to BC and worked for the hydrographic service as a junior hydrographer on the Hecate Str survey. Regional hydrographer Lt Cdr Philip Musgrave named Turner Peak, on the S end of Graham I, for him during the course of the survey; Turner Point was named by Musgrave at approximately the same time. Turner enlisted and went overseas in the fall of 1914 as a lt with the First Canadian Expeditionary Force. He later joined the Royal Scots Regiment, rose to the rank of lt col, in command of the 2nd battalion, and was awarded the DSO and MC before being killed in action July 26, 1918, during the 2nd Battle of the Marne. He is buried at Vauxbuin French National Cemetery.

Turner Reef (54°10'00" 133°07'00" W of Lepas Bay, off NW end of Graham I, QCI). Named in 1907 by Capt Frederick Learmonth of the survey vessel *Egeria*, after James Turner, 2nd mate of the *Queen Charlotte*, which passed along this coastline in 1787 under Capt George Dixon. Dixon was an early fur trader and one of the first Europeans to realize that the Queen Charlottes were not part of the mainland. He named the archipelago after his ship.

Turner Rock (52°36'00" 129°08'00" At head of Clifford Bay, W side of Aristazabal I). Lance Cpl George Turner (1836–1919), from London, joined the Royal Engineers in 1855 and was posted to the Ordnance Survey of GB. In 1859 he came out to the PNW with the Columbia detachment, which served in BC until 1863, and worked in the survey office at the engineers' camp in Sapperton. His name appears on many early maps and plans made by the engineers. Turner remained in BC when the contingent disbanded and established a surveying partnership with his friend Sgt William McColl. He worked for the CPR and on various government surveys for townsites and

T

roads, including the wagon road between Yale and Boston Bar, and parts of the Dewdney Trail. McColl died in 1865, leaving a widow and six children, and in 1869, Turner and Ann McColl (1832–1913, née Baseley) were married at New Westminster. From 1869 to 1871 he tried his hand at the saloon business, running the London Arms in New Westminster, then returned to surveying, working on the Yale Rd from New Westminster to Hope in 1874 and the road from Cowichan to Nanaimo. He purchased several properties in the New Westminster land district and also received a military land grant, given to all Royal Engineers who decided to settle in BC. In the early 1880s, Turner, Charles Woods and Francis Gamble formed a survey firm that laid out many of the first subdivisions in Port Moody, Vancouver and New Westminster. Turner was one of 82 surveyors authorized by the province in 1891, the year the profession was regulated. He retired about 1906.

Turnour Bay (50°35'00" 126°27'00" S side of Turnour I), **Turnour Island** (50°36'00" 126°27'00" Between W Cracroft I and Gilford I, mouth of Knight Inlet, E of Port McNeill), **Turnour Point** (50°35'00" 126°31'00" SW side of Turnour I), **Turnour Rock** (50°35'00" 126°28'00" Clio Channel, entrance to Turnour Bay). Capt Nicholas Edward Brook Turnour (b 1827) served on the Pacific Station, 1864–68, as cdr of the RN steam corvette *Clio*. He entered the navy in 1843 and was wounded, as a midshipman aboard ḤMS *Vixen*, at the storming of Ft Serapequi, Nicaragua, in 1848. Turnour was promoted to cdr for his bravery and initiative during the Indian Rebellion of 1857–58 (Sepoy Mutiny). In 1865, Turnour and the *Clio* were dispatched to Ft Rupert on northern Vancouver I to arrest three Kwakwaka'wakw First Nation members suspected of killing a man from Nahwitti. When the Ft Rupert chief refused to surrender them, Turnour and his crew completely destroyed the village and about 50 large canoes. *W*

Signs commemorate some of the boats that made it past Turret Rock.
James and Jennifer Hamilton

Turret Rock (51°06'00" 127°30'00" Nakwakto Rapids, entrance to Seymour Inlet, N of Port Hardy). While the name is simply descriptive of the islet's shape, this famous feature deserves a fuller mention. It sits right in the mouth of the Nakwakto Rapids (qv), the fiercest tidal currents on the BC coast, and is said to actually shake and shudder from the action of the rushing waters. Locally it is known as Tremble I and was formerly called Grave I. *Sailing Directions* warns that "tidal streams in Nakwakto Rapids attain a maximum of 11.5 knots (21 km/h) on the flood and 14.5 knots (27 km/h) on the ebb, one of the highest rates in the world, their main strength impinging on Turret Rk. Duration of slack is about six minutes." Despite its remote location, Turret has become a magnet for kayaking and scuba-diving daredevils; nailed to the trees that cover the rock are dozens of placards commemorating boats that have braved the rapids.

Turtle Head (49°19'00" 122°56'00" SE side of Indian Arm, E of Vancouver). Named for its shape by RN hydrographer Capt George Richards on his 1859–60 survey of Burrard Inlet in HMS *Plumper*.

Tuwanek Point (49°33'00" 123°47'00" E side of Sechelt Inlet, S of Salmon Inlet, NW of Vancouver). The word is a modification of Téwánkw (or Tahw-ahn-kwuh), the name of one of the four subgroups of the Sechelt First Nation. The traditional territories of the Téwánkw people included the inner waters of Sechelt, Salmon and Narrows inlets. They had their main winter village at the head of Narrows Inlet. That settlement is believed to have been damaged by a rock slide in the early 1800s, and many of its residents moved to Slahlt, a reserve on the E side of Porpoise Bay. Today Tuwanek also refers to a residential suburb of Sechelt just S of the point.

Tuzo Islands (52°47'00" 129°19'00" S of Rennison I, Beauchemin Channel, off NW Aristazabal I), **Tuzo Rock** (48°25'32" 123°22'30" Just off Songhees Point, Victoria Hbr, SE end of Vancouver I). Henry Atkinson Tuzo (1832–90) was born in Que and earned his medical degree there in 1853. He joined the HBC as a clerk that year and came out to Ft Vancouver, moving to Victoria in 1858. Tuzo (whose family name was originally spelled Touzeau) left HBC service in 1870 and became the Victoria manager of the Bank of BNA. He was also appointed a justice of the peace. Two years later the bank sent him to NY as a senior manager. In 1876, Tuzo and his family moved to England, where Henry died. Several other place names in BC are named after his children, who both returned to Canada. Mt Tuzo in Kootenay National Park honours his alpinist daughter, Henrietta Laetitia Tuzo (1874–1955, later Henrietta Wilson), the first person to climb this peak. She was also a president of Canada's National Council of Women. Tuzo Ck and Tuzo Lk, E of Penticton, commemorate his son, John Atkinson Tuzo (1875–1918), who was an assistant engineer during the construction of the Kettle Valley Rwy and died on active service in

German E Africa in WWI. Tuzo Rk was formerly known as Otter Rk.

Tweedsmuir Point (53°22'00" 129°46'00" S entrance to Buchan Inlet, SW side of Pitt I). Sir John Buchan, 1st Baron Tweedsmuir of Elsfield, was gov gen of Canada, 1935–40. *See* Buchan Inlet.

Twigg Island. *See* Mitchell I.

Twin Islands (50°02'00" 124°56'00" Off SE side of Cortes I, N end of Str of Georgia). Regional hydrographer Henri Parizeau's 1945 initiative to change a number of names in the vicinity backfired when local residents lobbied BC's chief geographer to have the old names reinstated. Mink I (qv) had been changed to Repulse I, the Martin Is to the Tory Is and the Twin Is to the Ulloa Is. Twin Is is a purely descriptive name (though the islands are in fact joined by a drying bank and a short causeway). Parizeau chose Ulloa Is as a name because of nearby Cortes and Marina islands; according to historian John Walbran, the Veracruz fortress of San Juan de Ulloa (or Ulúa) was where Spanish conquistador Hernán Cortés first met the beautiful Aztec slave Marina (also known as La Malinche), who later became his mistress and interpreter. In 1962, after a petition opposing the new names had been successfully circulated by the owner of Mink I—and after it had been clearly demonstrated that local residents were still using the old names—Canada's geographic board relented, and the original designations reappeared on the charts. "A resort hotel is located on Ulloa Is," the chief geographer noted, "and it is still advertised in the papers as 'Twin Is Resort.'" In the 1970s the islands were owned by Prince Philip's nephew, Prince Max von Baden, and it was here that the royal yacht *Britannia* brought Queen Elizabeth for a day during her 1971 Canadian tour. She was entertained at the property's spacious log cabin-style lodge, with its seven bedrooms and five bathrooms.

Twiss Point (48°54'00" 123°20'00" SE side of Galiano I, Gulf Is). Crawford O Twiss (1885–1982) was employed as an Okanagan teamster when he married Alice Edith Gilmour at Vernon in 1913. The newlyweds moved to Galiano I and began their long association with the island by renting a cottage from Max Enke for $2.50 a month. Crawford worked on island road construction and made deliveries for the Burrills' general store. Every summer for three decades he travelled N to the Skeena R and put in four months at the N Pacific Cannery. The Twisses were still living on Galiano in 1968, when this name was submitted by members of the Gulf Is Branch of the BC Historical Assoc. Crawford died at New Westminster.

Tyee Bank (54°11'00" 129°59'00" N side of the Skeena R, S of the McNeil R mouth, N of Port Essington, SE of Prince Rupert), **Tyee Point** (49°23'00" 123°16'00" N entrance to Horseshoe Bay, Howe Sd, just NW of Vancouver), **Tyee Point** (50°23'00" 125°47'00" W end of W Thurlow I, Johnstone Str, NW of Campbell R), **Tyee Spit** (50°03'00" 125°15'00" S entrance to the Campbell R, Discovery Passage, just N of District of Campbell R). Tyee was the word for "chief" in the Chinook jargon used on the W coast by First Nation groups and early traders and settlers. In the 1920s the word was adopted as a name for a spring or chinook salmon weighing more than 13.5 kg (30 lb). To join the Tyee Club of BC, formed by a group of Campbell R sport fishers, one had to catch a salmon of this size while using light tackle and fishing from a non-motorized boat. Many features in the BC Interior also sport this name: Tyee Butte, two Tyee creeks, Tyee Glacier, two Tyee lakes and Tyee Mtn. There's also a Tyhee Ck and a Tyhee Lk. Tyee Point on Howe Sd was changed in 1929 to Robertson Point, after 19th-century Vancouver pilot Capt George Robertson, but was changed back again in 1949. *E*

Tyler Rock (48°57'00" 125°02'00" Mouth of Alberni Inlet, N side of Barkley Sd, W side of Vancouver I). After a master mariner named Tyler, from Kildonan, who reported this rock in 1924.

Tynemouth Rock (51°18'00" 128°03'00" Sea Otter Group, S of Calvert I, entrance to Smith Sd). The *Tynemouth* was one of several "brideships" that brought young, unmarried women from England to Vancouver I in the 1860s to work as domestic servants and governesses— and to serve as future wives for BC's predominantly male population. This immigration scheme was sponsored by English missionary societies and feminists for a variety of reasons: to help civilize colonial social and cultural life; to provide jobs and opportunities for both poor and middle-class women; and to reduce the number of unsanctified unions that white male settlers were supposedly forming with First Nation women. The 77-m *Tynemouth*, a three-masted barque with steam propulsion, built at Newcastle upon Tyne in 1853, brought 59 closely chaperoned women to Victoria in 1862. A troopship in the Crimean War, the *Tynemouth* had been refitted in 1860, but only with 2nd- and 3rd-class accommodation, and it must have offered an uncomfortable environment for passengers on its 14-week journey round Cape Horn to BC. Thirty-six more women arrived early the next year in the *Robert Lowe*. Most of these immigrants did stay in BC, where they worked, married and often made major contributions to pioneer life. *E*

Tyne Point (49°12'00" 123°56'00" NW end of Newcastle I, Departure Bay, SE side of Vancouver I). Named in 1904 by Cdr John Parry of HMS *Egeria* while re-surveying Departure Bay. He chose Tyne Point because Newcastle I, with its valuable coal reserves, had earlier been named for the ancient English coal-mining centre of Newcastle upon Tyne.

Tzartus Island (48°55'00" 125°05'00" N of Bamfield at NE end of Imperial Eagle Channel, E side of Barkley Sd, W side of Vancouver I). Author George Clutesi, a member of the Tseshaht First Nation, translated this Nuu-chah-nulth name as "place of a seasonal or intermittent waterfall" in 1960. BC historians Helen and Philip Akrigg recorded "water flows inside at the beach." Various spellings appear on old maps, including Tsartoos, Tzartoos and Tzaartoos. The feature was known as Copper I for many years, as shown on an 1863 Admiralty chart based on a survey by Capt George Richards. William Banfield, the government agent in the area before 1862, considered a hill on the island to be "one solid mass of copper ore," but early efforts to develop the resource proved disappointing. Capt William Spring established a pioneer trading post on Tzartus in the 1860s and '70s. The Huu-ay-aht First Nation (Ohiaht) reserve on the island, called Nuchaquis, was once used as a base for harvesting dogfish. A luxurious fishing resort, Canadian King Lodge at Shahowis, was located on Tzartus I in the early 2000s.

Tzoonie Narrows (49°43'00" 123°47'00" In Narrows Inlet, E of Sechelt Inlet, NW of Vancouver), **Tzoonie Point** (49°42'00" 123°47'00" S side of Narrows Inlet, just SW of Tzoonie Narrows). The Sechelt First Nation name for Narrows Inlet is Stl'íxwim, and this name is also applied to the reserved lands at the inlet's head, where the Tzoonie R, known to the Sechelt people as Kékaw, joins the sea. This location was once the site of an important winter village, home to the Téwánkw people (*see* Tuwanek Point), one of the main subgroups of the Sechelt Nation. Another winter village, Chichkwat, was located farther up the Tzoonie R. Both river and inlet have great spiritual importance for the Sechelt Nation and figure largely in its origin myths and other legends. The word Tzoonie is probably a variation of Ts'únay (or Tsonai), the name for another of the Sechelt subgroups, whose members were based at Deserted Bay on Jervis Inlet. The name may have migrated as the result of population transfer or it may have been incorrectly associated with Narrows Inlet. Sháshíshálem language specialist Ronald Beaumont has suggested "sheltering tree" as a translation for Ts'únay. Other spellings recorded for Tzoonie include Tyzoone, Tzoonye, Tsoome and Tzoone.

Tzoonie Narrows on Narrows Inlet, an arm of Sechelt Inlet. *Peter Vassilopoulos*

U

Uchucklesit Inlet (49°00'00" 125°00'00" Just N of entrance to Alberni Inlet, NW of Barkley Sd, on W side of Vancouver I). This is the traditional territory of the Uchucklesaht First Nation, whose members live at Elhlateese, a village at the head of the inlet, and are part of the Nuu-chah-nulth Tribal Council. While many explanations for the name have been recorded, *Ha-shilth-sa*, the official Nuu-chah-nulth newspaper, translated it as "people of the inside harbour" in 2003. Older alternative spellings have included Howchuk-lis-aht, Hautcu'k'les'ath, Howchucklus-aht and Howchuklisat. The first salmon cannery on the W coast of Vancouver I was built on the inlet's shores in 1903. Known as Kildonan (qv), it closed down in 1946 and burned down in 1962. In the early 2000s a fishing lodge was located there instead.

Ucluelet Inlet on Barkley Sound. *Peter Vassilopoulos*

Ucluelet (48°56'32" 125°32'44" On SW side of Ucluelet Inlet), **Ucluelet Inlet** (48°57'21" 125°33'39" NW side of Barkley Sd, W side of Vancouver I). Named after the Ucluelet (Yuu-tluth-aht) First Nation, whose members are part of the Nuu-chah-nulth Tribal Council. In 2003 the Nuu-chah-nulth newspaper, *Ha-shilth-sa*, translated the name as "people with a safe landing place for canoes." Capt Charles Stuart was the first white settler on the inlet, building a trading post there in 1860. A small community

evolved based on logging and, mainly, commercial fishing; tourism and aquaculture became important in later years. A First Nation village, known today as Ittatsoo, is located on the NE side of the inlet. Ucluelet Inlet was formerly called Ucluelet Arm, a name that first appeared on Admiralty charts in 1863, but was changed by the hydrographic service in 1934. *E W*

Ucluth Peninsula (48°57'00" 125°35'00" W of Ucluelet Inlet, NW of Barkley Sd, W side of Vancouver I). The ancient Ucluelet First Nation village site of Ucluth (now a reserve) is located on the ocean side of the peninsula, at the N end. The word is related to the name Ucluelet (*see* Ucluelet) and may have a similar meaning of "a safe landing place." Whether the original landing place was located at Ucluth village or somewhere else is not clear, however. RN surveyor Capt George Richards adopted the name in 1861.

Uganda Passage (50°05'00" 125°02'00" Between Marina I and Cortes I, E of Sutil Channel, N end of Str of Georgia), **Uganda Point** (51°49'00" 127°54'00" S of Warrior Cove, E side of Fitz Hugh Sd, SE of Bella Bella). Named in 1945 for HMCS *Uganda*, a former British light cruiser that had been acquired by the RCN the year before. The 8,712-tonne, 169-m vessel was launched in 1941 as HMS *Uganda* and commissioned in 1943. It served at first on convoy and escort duty, then participated in the invasion of Sicily. In Sept 1943 the *Uganda* took a direct hit from a glider bomb, which killed 16 crew members; it had to be taken to the US for repair. After transfer to the RCN the cruiser was posted to the Pacific, where it participated in the Battle of Okinawa and several other major actions. HMCS *Uganda* was stationed at Esquimalt, 1945–47, then deactivated until 1952. That year the ship was recommissioned as HMCS *Quebec* and served two tours in the Korean War theatre. It was eventually scrapped in Japan in 1961.

Ulric Point (52°50'00" 129°16'00" N end of Aristazabal I). After hydrographer Joseph Ulric Beauchemin. *See* Beauchemin Channel. Formerly known as Devils Point.

U

Umme Point (51°43'00" 127°59'00" NE entrance to Goldstream Hbr, Hecate I, W side of Fitz Hugh Sd, SE of Bella Bella). Umme is an adaptation of a Heiltsuk or Kwakwala word meaning "small" or "little." The name was adopted from the 1884 *Comparative Vocabularies of the Indian Tribes of BC,* by William Fraser Tolmie and George Mercer Dawson. Formerly known as Kelp Point.

Una Point (52°57'00" 132°11'00" SW side of Mitchell Inlet, Kuper Inlet, NW side of Moresby I, QCI). The 170-tonne brigantine *Una,* built at NB in 1849, arrived in the PNW in 1850 to serve as a coastal trading vessel for the HBC. It was a major participant in BC's earliest gold rush. In 1851, after the presence of the precious metal had been reported at Mitchell Inlet in the QCI (or Gold Hbr, as the area was unofficially known), Capt William Mitchell and HBC chief factor John Work visited the discovery site but took only a few samples. Later that year Mitchell and the *Una* brought chief trader William McNeill and a party of miners to the inlet, where they got into an undignified clash with the Haida and left hastily with a small shipload of ore. On its way back to Victoria, the *Una* ran aground at Neah Bay and was pillaged and burned by members of the Makah First Nation. The crew and the miners were rescued by the US schooner *Susan Sturgis,* but the gold was lost. *D W*

Underhill Island (51°46'00" 128°04'00" Between Stirling I and Nalau I, N side of Hakai Passage, S of Bella Bella). The early firm of Underhill & Underhill conducted numerous land surveys in central and northern BC in the years after WWI. Many coastal features were named by the survey parties, often after their own members. The company was formed in 1913 by Frederic Clare Underhill (1890–1982) and his brother James Theodore Underhill (1892–1976). They had come out to BC from England with their parents in 1894, and both took engineering degrees at McGill Univ. Both also served overseas during WWI; James saw action at Gallipoli and Passchendaele, while Frederic was in France. James became president of the Assoc of BC Land Surveyors in 1931. He was involved with the W Coast Rangers militia in WWII and was very active in later years with the Canadian Figure Skating Assoc. Frederic was president of the Assoc of BC Land Surveyors in 1940 and 1952, and served as a lt col with the Canadian Field Artillery Reserve during WWII. Both brothers were also keen rugby players and officials. Over the years, other family members joined the firm, which was known in 2009 as Underhill Geomatics Ltd.

Union Bay (49°35'00" 124°53'00" SE of Comox Hbr, E side of Vancouver I), **Union Point** (49°36'00" 124°53'00" N side of Union Bay). In 1888, BC industrialist Robert Dunsmuir established a townsite at Union Camp, 18 km NW of Union Bay. The camp was originally named after Dunsmuir's Union Colliery Co, which developed the mines in this rich new coal district, but the community soon changed its name to Cumberland. A railway connected the mines to Union Bay, where BC's largest deep-sea loading dock was built in 1889. Coke ovens and a brickyard were soon part of the Union Bay complex, and a village sprang up that flourished until the late 1940s, when the collieries went into decline. The wharves were dismantled in 1966, but several heritage buildings from the coal era have been preserved. Patricia Bay on Saanich Inlet was also known as Union Bay for many years. *E*

Union Cove (49°20'00" 123°22'00" SE side of Bowen I, Howe Sd, NW of Vancouver). The cove was given this name in 1907 because it was used jointly by the Cowan and Malkin families, who had summer homes nearby. It was formerly known as Lee's Landing, after Harry Lee, the original owner of District Lot 1412 at the S end of Bowen I. George Cowan (*see* Point Cowan), who eventually acquired more than 400 ha in the area, sold a small piece of land to William Malkin around the turn of the century. Lee Ck, which flows into Union Cove and was named after Harry Lee, was the dividing line between the Cowan and Malkin properties.

Unkak Cove (50°03'00" 125°14'00" W side of Quadra I, N of Quathiaski Cove and Campbell R). Unkak is a modification of a Kwakwala word meaning "goose." The name was adopted from the 1884 *Comparative Vocabularies of the Indian Tribes of BC,* by William Fraser Tolmie and George Mercer Dawson. Formerly known as Goose Ck.

Unsworth Point (50°01'00" 127°14'00" E side of Union I, Kyuquot Sd, NW side of Vancouver I). After Clara Ann Unsworth Crowther, an early resident of Kyuquot. *See* Crowther Channel.

Upper Harbour (48°25'57" 123°22'26" Between Johnson St bridge and Bay St bridge, Victoria Hbr, SE end of Vancouver I). Victoria Hbr (qv) consists of five sections: Inner Hbr, Upper Hbr, Selkirk Water, Gorge Waters and Portage Inlet. Upper Hbr, which appears on maps of the city as early as 1917, was adopted by the hydrographic service in 1946 as a well-established local name, in use by residents and shipping agencies.

Upsowis Point (50°06'00" 127°30'00" SE tip of Bunsby Is, W entrance to Malksope Inlet, NW of Kyuquot Sd, NW side of Vancouver I). Named after the nearby Checleset (Che:K'tles7et'h') First Nation reserve of Upsowis, just to the N. This ancient summer habitation site, more commonly known as Opsowis (also Apsuwis), became the Checleset's main year-round village from the late 1880s until they moved to Aktis I at Kyuquot in the 1950s. Opsowis was also known as Hollywood, and lodge posts carved in the shapes of human figures were still visible there in the 1970s. The Checlesets, located on the boundary between the great

Nuu-chah-nulth and Kwakwaka'wakw confederacies, were traditionally bilingual; they amalgamated with the Kyuquot (Ka:'yu:'K't'h) First Nation in 1963.

Upward Rock (51°27'00" 128°01'00" SE of Stafford Point, off S side of Calvert I, S of Bella Bella). Named in 1947 after R A Upward, a hydrographer on CGS *William J Stewart*, 1946–48, who worked on surveys of the Inside Passage, Queen Charlotte Sd and Smith Sd. Formerly known as Bird Rk.

Upwood Point (49°29'00" 124°07'00" SE tip of Texada I, Str of Georgia). In June 1792, Capt George Vancouver named this feature Point Upwood "in remembrance of an early friendship." NZ historian John Robson has suggested that Thomas Upwood, who lived at Lovell's Hall, Terrington St Clements, just W of Vancouver's childhood home of King's Lynn, may have been the source of the name.

Uren Point (53°04'00" 129°07'00" Barnard Hbr, NW side of Princess Royal I). Mary Adams Kelly (1867–1945) was one of the first girls born at Barkerville. Her parents, Andrew Kelly and Elizabeth Hastie, from Scotland, were Cariboo pioneers, running several Barkerville businesses, including the Kelly Hotel, the Kelly Store and the Wake Up Jake Cafe. In 1889, Mary married another BC pioneer, James Bottrell Uren (1862–1916), who had been born at Hope. Mary, who died at Kimberley, is believed to have taken part in the Victoria old-timers' reunion of 1924 (*see* Adams Bay). Uren Lk in the Lillooet area and Mt Uren, N of Kamloops Lk, are both named after James Uren's father, also James B Uren (1831–86), who was an early freighter on the Cariboo Rd and also the ferryman at Savona. His wife, Malvina Jane (c 1831–84), noted for her fine cooking, ran hotels at Clinton and Savona.

Urquhart Point (53°34'00" 130°11'00" S end of Dixon I, Principe Channel, between McCauley I and Banks I). Flying Officer Robert Alexander Urquhart, DFC, born at Moose Jaw but a resident of Vancouver, was a member of the famous RAF "Dambusters" squadron (No 617), which bombed and damaged several German dams on the nights of May 16 and 17, 1943. He was killed in action on May 17, aged 24, when the Lancaster bomber he was navigating was shot down while returning from an attack on the Eder dam. Urquhart had been awarded his DFC in 1942 after flying 28 bombing sorties as a pilot officer with No 50 (RAF) Squadron. He is buried at Reichswald Forest War Cemetery in western Germany.

Ursula Channel (53°25'02" 128°54'46" E side of Gribbell I, N of Princess Royal I, S of Kitimat). According to anthropologist Jay Powell, a former UBC professor, this 17-km channel is divided into five traditional Haisla First Nation stewardship zones named, from N to S, Wiilaxdels, Slacu, T'lekemalis, Wawagelisla and Luq'wayac'i. The part of the channel between Egerton Point and Angler Cove is known to the Haisla as Ogwiwalis.

Ursula Rock (49°46'00" 124°34'00" Sturt Bay, E side of Texada I, NW Malaspina Str). Named in 1899 by BC master mariner and coastal historian Capt John Walbran. According to Walbran, he was prompted to come up with this name when the leadman in the bow of his vessel, asked if the objects in the water up ahead were rocks, replied that they were "but they look like little black bears." As the Latin word for bear is *ursus*, Walbran decided that this would be a good time to commemorate Ursula Helen Davies (1877–1962), daughter of Cdr Robert Watts Davies of the RN, and niece of Sir Louis Davies, Canada's minister of Marine and Fisheries, 1896–1901 (*see* Watts Narrows *and* Davies Bay for further information). Ursula, born at Hull, Yorkshire, married Archibald William Douglas (1870–1955) in 1902. He was a clergyman who served as an RN chaplain in WWI and was appointed dean of Ecclesfield, 1921–41, and canon of Sheffield Cathedral, 1932–41. She and her husband both died at Sherborne, Dorset. *W*

Ursus Point (52°29'00" 128°13'00" N entrance to Salmon Bay, Mathieson Channel, W side of Don Peninsula, N of Bella Bella). *Ursus* is the Latin word for bear, and Bear Point was the former name of this feature. It was changed by the hydrographic service in 1948. More than 90 official place names in BC feature the word "bear," so, naturally, duplication has been quite an issue over the years. Even the word "ursus" has found its way into six other official BC place names.

Useless Bay (54°03'00" 130°33'00" NW side of Porcher I, just SW of Prince Rupert), **Useless Point** (W side of Useless Bay). The bay is "choked with sand," according to the 1923 *BC Pilot*. Drying rocks and shoal water extend some distance from nearby Useless Point, where a navigation light is situated. Useless Ck flows into the bay.

Useless Inlet (48°59'00" 125°03'00" N of Seddall I, NE side of Barkley Sd, W side of Vancouver I). *Sailing Directions* states that the inlet, which is home to several aquaculture operations, "is accessible only to small craft because the entrance is foul."

Ustas Point (52°42'50" 131°34'30" N side of Lyell I, off E side of Moresby I, QCI). The point was named by the hydrographic service in 1957 after a supernatural being from the creation myths of the Haida First Nation. Ustas (also known as Nang Kilsdlaas or Nang Ttl Dlstlas) was the uncle of Raven and responsible for creating the first land that other supernatural creatures could settle on after the great flood.

V

Valdes Bay (49°44'00" 126°29'00" E side of Hisnit Inlet, Nootka Sd, W side of Vancouver I), **Valdes Island** (49°05'00" 123°40'00" Between Galiano I and Gabriola I, Gulf Is). Spanish naval officer Cayetano Valdés y Flores (1767–1835) was a member of Alejandro Malaspina's 1789–94 round-the-world voyage. He had been recommended for the post by his uncle, Antonio Valdés y Bazán, who served as Spain's minister of marine and capt-gen of the navy. In 1792, Valdés and Dionisio Alcalá-Galiano left the expedition at Mexico (New Spain) and were dispatched instead to BC to continue the Spanish search for the Northwest Passage. Alcalá-Galiano, in command of the *Sutil*, and Valdés, in the smaller *Mexicana*, charted the Inside Passage and made a historic circumnavigation of Vancouver I. En route, they met Capt George Vancouver off Point Grey and explored with him for several weeks. After returning to Europe, Valdés fought at the Battle of Cape St Vincent, as capt of the *Pelayo*, and at Trafalgar, where he was seriously wounded, with the *Neptuno*. He was appointed gov and capt-gen of Cadiz and became involved in politics, for which initiative he was imprisoned and then exiled to England for his liberal views. In the early 1820s he was part of the revolutionary Cadiz *junta*, which briefly ruled Spain. Cayetano Point on Valdes I is also named for him. Valdes I, named by surveyor Capt George Richards in 1859, has no ferry service and is one of the least developed of the Gulf Is. It is the traditional territory of the Lyackson First Nation, whose members are part of the Hul'qumi'num (Central Coast Salish) treaty group and who once had three villages there. Quadra I, Sonora I and Maurelle I, which were originally thought to be one large land mass N of Campbell R, were also known as Valdes (or Valdez) I. When it was realized, in the 1870s, that there were three islands, they were called the Valdes Is or Valdes group. It was not until 1903 that they received individual names. *E W*

Cayetano Valdés, a posthumous portrait. *Mexicana Museo Naval, Madrid*

Vadso Island, Vadso Rocks (55°23'00" 129°45'00" SW of Larcom I, Observatory Inlet, SE of Stewart). The steamship *Vadso* was built in Sweden in 1881 as the *Bordeaux* and brought out to BC in 1907 by the Boscowitz Steamship Co. It carried only 50 passengers and operated mostly as a freighter to the new gold-mining centre at Stewart and also to the northern canneries. In 1911 the Boscowitz company was sold to the Union Steamship Co, and the 824-tonne, 59-m *Vadso*, named after a town in northern Norway, was part of the deal. The ship had its share of misfortunes on the W coast, running aground off Cape Lazo in 1908, "finding" the Vadso Rks by striking them in 1910 and suffering heavy damage in 1913 at Reef Point in Baynes Sd. In 1914, in a blinding snowstorm, the old steamer hit another uncharted rock at the mouth of Nass Bay, and its load of oil drums caught fire. Crew members somehow managed to get clear of the doomed, blazing wreck and row to Arrandale cannery.

Valencia Bluffs (48°42'00" 124°58'20" W of mouth of the Klanawa R, SE of Barkley Sd, SW side of Vancouver I). The wreck of the steamship *Valencia* holds the tragic distinction of being the worst maritime disaster on the

The steamship *Valencia* on its last voyage before wrecking off Pachena Point in 1906 in BC's worst maritime accident. The tragedy claimed 126 lives. *BC Archives D-06923*

became more important, and today the area is home to many retirees. The post office was originally established, in 1897, as Vananda, and that version of the community name has been the one most commonly encountered over the years. Members of the Texada I Heritage Society, however, mounted a spirited campaign in the late 1980s to change the spelling to Van Anda. Local residents were surveyed and found to cherish an overwhelming preference for the two-word format, and Van Anda was officially adopted in 1992. *E*

Sturt Bay at Van Anda on Texada Island. *Andrew Scott*

BC coast. (The loss of the CPR's *Princess Sophia*, in which 343 people died, took place in Alaska. *See* Locke I.) The 1,450-tonne, 77-m passenger vessel, built in 1882 at Philadelphia, came to the W coast in 1888 and was owned in the late 1890s by the Pacific Steamship Co, which used it to transport prospectors to the Klondike gold rush. On Jan 12, 1906, en route from San Francisco to Puget Sd under Capt O M Johnson, the *Valencia* overshot the entrance to Juan de Fuca Str and ran aground E of Pachena Point. Several rescue attempts failed in the rough weather, and onlookers watched in horror as 126 passengers and crew were flung into the sea and drowned. There were only 38 survivors, all men. The *Valencia* tragedy prompted the building of the W coast lifesaving trail. In 1933 one of the ship's lifeboats was found, in relatively good condition, floating in Barkley Sd. *E*

Van Anda (49°45'30" 124°33'00" NE side of Texada I, Malaspina Str, just S of Powell R), **Van Anda Cove** (49°45'35" 124°33'10" NE side of Texada I), **Van Anda Point** (49°45'40" 124°33'05" SE entrance to Van Anda Cove). Seattle mining man Edward Blewitt named both his son and his business (the Van Anda Copper & Gold Mining Co) after a friend, Carl Vattel van Anda (1864–1945), who worked for the NY *Sun*, 1884–1904, and was managing editor of the NY *Times*, 1904–32. Blewitt's company owned 340 ha on NE Texada and established the first mine in the area—the Copper Queen—in 1897. Within five years the boomtown of Van Anda had formed, complete with hotels, a hospital, opera house, newspaper and sawmill. A smelter operated on and off from 1898 to 1919. As mining wound down in the 1950s, tourism

Vancouver (49°15'00" 123°07'00" S of Burrard Inlet, E side of Str of Georgia), **Vancouver Harbour** (49°18'00" 123°06'00" Burrard Inlet, E of First Narrows). The RN officer who gave his name to BC's largest city and made the first comprehensive charts of the coast of NW America led a surprisingly short and unhappy life. George Vancouver (1757–98) was born at King's Lynn, Norfolk, and, as a young midshipman, joined Capt James Cook's second (1772–75) and third (1776–80) voyages to the S Pacific and the Antarctic. In the 1780s, as a lt, he served in HMS *Martin*, *Fame* and *Europa*, mostly in the W Indies, and was recommended by Commodore Alan Gardner, cdr-in-chief at Jamaica, to be second-in-command of a new scientific expedition planned to the PNW, led by Capt Henry Roberts (*see* Roberts Bank). The voyage was postponed, Roberts reassigned and Vancouver, promoted to cdr, got the top job instead. He left England in Apr 1791 in HMS *Discovery*, together with the armed tender *Chatham*, under Lt William Broughton, and travelled via S Africa, Australia, NZ, Tahiti and Hawaii, arriving in BC waters in Apr 1792. That summer he and his crew made a detailed coastal survey from Puget Sd to Fitz Hugh Sd, meeting the Spanish explorers Dionisio Alcalá-Galiano and Cayetano Valdés en route and travelling with them part of the way. Before spending the winter in Hawaii, Vancouver joined Francisco de la Bodega y Quadra at Nootka to resolve details of the Nootka Sd Convention, a treaty designed to allow Britain access to the PNW and to secure the return of confiscated fur-trading vessels. He was not successful

235

50   50

C. Swaine

Calverts I.

Smiths Inlet
C. Caution
Queen Charlottes Sd.

Scotts Is.
C. Scott

Princess Royal Islands

Quadra and Vancouvers Island

Johnstones Sd.
Pt. Chatham

Woody Pt.

Howes Sd.
Pt. Grey

The Gulf of Georgia

Noatka Sd.
Arch.º de Clayoquot

Arch.º de Niliuat
Pt. of Gonza.

Supposed Strait of Juan de Fuca

C. Flattery

Flattery Rks.
Pto. de los Angelos
Port Discovery
Mt. Olympus

Hoods Canal

Destruction I.

Pt. Grenville

Puget's Sd.

Pt. Brown
Grays Harb.
Pt. Hanson

CAPTAIN VANCOUVER'S
CIRCUMNAVIGATION OF
VANCOUVER ISLAND

- - - - - Vessels track Northward
-·-·-·- Vessels track Southward

C. Disappointment
Pt. Adams

The River Columbia

C. Lookout

Longitude East from Greenwich   233

Bartholomew, Edin.

Captain George Vancouver made his famous circumnavigation of "Quadra and Vancouvers Island" in 1792. *VMM BCP 45*

Captain George Vancouver. *BC Archives PDP02252*

in this initiative but formed a useful friendship with the Spanish cdr. In the summer of 1793 he continued the coastal survey from Burke Channel to SE Alaska, using the ships' boats to laboriously explore every inlet and passage, then charted the California coast to San Diego before spending a second winter in Hawaii. Vancouver completed his meticulous survey of the Alaska coast in 1794, travelling from W to E, and finally extinguished any lingering European hopes that a navigable passage might exist across N America. After another visit to Nootka Sd he sailed to Chile for repairs and then to England via Cape Horn and St Helena, arriving back in poor health, but raised in rank to capt, in Sept 1795. The expedition had been a great success (only one sailor died during the four-year trip), but Vancouver's strict discipline, frequent illnesses and depressive temperament had caused dissent among his officers, and he was accused on his return of mistreating his crew. Conflicts with naturalist Archibald Menzies and midshipman Thomas Pitt, a deranged young nobleman who had been sent home from Hawaii, further damaged his reputation. From 1796 to 1798, helped by his brother John, Vancouver prepared the text for his *Voyage of Discovery to the N Pacific Ocean and Around the World*, which was published only months after his untimely death. The city of Vancouver, which pays to maintain the great explorer's grave at St Peter's, Petersham, in England, was named in 1886 at the suggestion of William van Horne, gen manager of the CPR. The area around the Hastings sawmill had been known earlier as Granville and Gastown; in 1911 the city's boundaries were extended to include the townsite of Hastings, and in 1929 Vancouver amalgamated with the municipalities of South Vancouver and Point Grey. *E W*

Vancouver Bay (49°55'00" 123°52'49" E side of Prince of Wales Reach, Jervis Inlet, NW of Vancouver), **Vancouver Bay** (50°25'14" 125°09'26" W side of Cordero Channel, entrance to Bute Inlet, N of Campbell R), **Vancouver Island** (49°30'00" 125°30'00" SW BC, separated from the mainland by Queen Charlotte, Georgia and Juan de Fuca straits), **Vancouver Point** (48°35'00" 124°41'00" SE of Bonilla Point, W of Port San Juan, W side of Vancouver I), **Vancouver Rock** (52°21'00" 128°30'00" W of Lady Douglas I, Milbanke Sd, NW of Bella Bella). These features are all named after Capt George Vancouver (*see* Vancouver). Vancouver I, the largest island on the W coast of N America at 31,284 sq km, was originally called Gran Isla de Fuca by the Spanish. In 1792, when Vancouver was negotiating the terms of the Nootka Sd Convention, his Spanish counterpart, Francisco de la Bodega y Quadra, entreated him to name a feature after the two of them, to commemorate their friendship. Vancouver suggested that the major island recently circumnavigated by both English and Spanish vessels be called Quadra and Vancouver, and this somewhat unwieldy name appeared on early charts. As Spanish influence in the region waned, however, it was soon abbreviated to Vancouver's I, a version in regular use by the HBC in the 1820s, and finally, by the 1860s, to its current form. Vancouver Bay on Jervis Inlet was named by Capt George Richards in 1860 because its namesake had camped there for a night in June 1792 while exploring the area; the Sechelt First Nation know the bay as Skwákwiyám. The Vancouver R flows into the bay. Vancouver Rk was named in 1866 by Lt Daniel Pender because Vancouver, in 1793, had particularly noted it in his journal as a "very dangerous sunken rock." The Vancouver I Ranges, which run the length of Vancouver I, are also named for the intrepid explorer.

Vanguard Bay (49°45'00" 124°06'00" S side of Jervis Inlet, N side of Nelson I, SE of Powell R). HMS *Vanguard* was the flagship of Rear Adm Sir Horatio Nelson at the 1798 Battle of the Nile. Eleven of 13 French vessels, including the 120-gun flagship *L'Orient*, were captured or destroyed in this decisive victory over a superior force. The 74-gun, 1,460-tonne *Vanguard* was built in 1787 at Deptford dockyard. After the Nile battle the ship was stationed at Jamaica, under capts James Walker and Andrew Evans; it captured the French man-of-war *Duquesne* after a brief engagement and assisted with an evacuation at Santo Domingo in 1803. The *Vanguard* was converted to a prison ship at Plymouth in 1812 and became a powder hulk in 1814. It was broken up in 1821. The bay was named by RN surveyor Capt George Richards of HMS *Plumper* about 1860. *W*

Van Inlet (53°16'00" 132°34'00" NE side of Cartwright Sd, SW side of Graham I, QCI), **Van Point** (53°15'00" 132°38'00" W entrance to Van Inlet). The origin of this name is not known with certainty. It may be an abbreviation for Vancouver. The long, narrow inlet appears on Capt Absalom Freeman's 1912 chart as Van Hbr. The Haida people knew it as Ki-ow or Xi'ao. An iron-copper deposit at its head has never been developed. *D*

Van Nevel Channel (49°09'00" 125°56'00" N of Templar Channel, E of Stubbs I, Clayoquot Sd, W side of Vancouver I). Oblate Fr John Adolphe van Nevel (b 1855), a native of Belgium, was based at the Tla-o-qui-aht village of Opitsat on Meares I, 1895–1900, as the Roman Catholic missionary and teacher for Clayoquot Sd. He had arrived in BC by 1880; before being posted to the W coast he served as assistant pastor at St Joseph's in Esquimalt, with Fr Pierre Rondeault at Cowichan and as rector of Victoria's Catholic cathedral. Van Nevel also worked extensively in Victoria as a teacher and principal at St Louis College, a Catholic boys' school established in 1864. In the 1900s he made a long trip back to Europe but returned to Victoria and was still living there as late as 1913.

Vansittart Island (50°54'58" 127°48'07" E of Hope I, between Bate Passage and Shadwell Passage, off N end of Vancouver I), **Vansittart Point** (50°23'00" 125°45'00" S side of W Thurlow I, Johnstone Str, NW of Campbell R). Capt Nicholas Vansittart (1820–59) entered the RN at the tender age of 12 and was a lt by 22. He spent much time in E Asia, serving with distinction in the Opium Wars and also in Borneo. He was capt of HMS *Magicienne* during the Crimean War and the 2nd Opium War, and died at Shanghai after suffering severe injuries in an unsuccessful attack on the Hai R forts. Vansittart never served in BC waters, though RN chief hydrographer Capt George Richards, who named Vansittart I in 1864, may have known him in the early 1840s, when both officers took part in the 1st Opium War. Mt Vansittart, on W Thurlow I, and the Nicholas Is just N of Vansittart I are also named for him. *W*

Vantreight Cove (48°30'00" 123°18'00" E end of Margaret Bay, just W of Gordon Head, SE side of Saanich Peninsula, N of Victoria), **Vantreight Island** (48°26'00" 123°15'00" One of the Chatham Is, E side of Baynes Channel, E of Oak Bay and Victoria). John Vantreight (1841–96), from Dublin, Ireland, settled in the Gordon Head area in 1884 and established a bulb-growing operation. His son, Geoffrey Arthur Vantreight (1881–1959), developed the business in the 1920s and '30s, and was known as BC's "Strawberry King." Geoffrey's son, also Geoffrey Arthur Vantreight (1924–2000), was active in Saanich community and business affairs, and was known especially as a car-racing and sports fanatic. He helped invent the "Daffodil Day" fundraising campaign, used successfully for more than 50 years by the Canadian Cancer Society. In the early 2000s, fourth-generation family member Ian S Vantreight, former president of several BC agricultural associations, was running the 300-ha flower and produce farm, still

located in S Saanich, with the help of his son Ryan and daughter Corina. Vantreight I was formerly known as Camp I; its Songhees First Nation name was Tiappas. *E*

Kayakers on Vargas Island, Clayoquot Sound. *Greg Shea*

Vargas Cone (49°05'33" 125°52'03" SE of Cox Bay and Tofino), **Vargas Island** (49°11'10" 125°59'00" Just NW of Tofino, Clayoquot Sd, W side of Vancouver I). Vargas I was originally named Isla de Teran, after an unidentified Spanish official, by naval officer Francisco Eliza in 1791. This name was mistakenly adopted by Capt George Vancouver as Feran I. Dionisio Alcalá-Galiano changed it the following year to Vargas I, but it is not certain which particular Vargas he had in mind. Coastal historian John Walbran has suggested Diego de Vargas (1644–1704), gov of New Mexico from 1688 to 1696 and in 1703–4. PNW cartography expert Henry Wagner proposed a more likely candidate: José Vargas y Ponce (1755–1821), a noted Spanish naval officer, geographer, historian and cartographer. This Vargas helped Vicente Tofiño, Spain's chief hydrographer, prepare a famous atlas of the Spanish coast and wrote its introduction. Vargas also drew up instructions for several scientific expeditions to New Spain and was the author of a number of works on the history of Spanish exploration and the geography of the country's far-flung colonies. The 28-sq-km island was the site of the main summer village of the Ahousaht First Nation and was settled briefly by British homesteaders in the 1910s. Today its splendid beaches, much loved by wilderness kayakers, are protected as a provincial marine park. *E W*

Varney Bay (50°33'00" 127°31'00" E of Quatsino Narrows, just SE of Coal Hbr, N end of Vancouver I). Thomas Henry Varney (1869–1952), his wife, Ethel (1870–1959), and their two children emigrated from England in 1896 and arrived the following year at Quatsino Sd. There they pre-empted land at the head of this bay, established a homestead and raised a large family, receiving a Crown grant for their property in 1911. Varney, whose stylish calling cards apparently identified him as "The Queen's Messenger," seems an unlikely pioneer, and the family saw more than its fair share of tragedy. Several of the Varney children died young; Philip and James Varney drowned at the mouth of Quatsino Sd in 1930 when their launch, the *Swastika*, foundered; and Fred Varney, aged 60, was killed in the 1955 crash of a DC-3 at Port Hardy. Nevertheless, the Varneys remained on their farm for more than 50 years. Henry died at Varney Bay, while Ethel died at Port Alice. Their youngest daughter, Dinah, who never married, remained with them at the homestead and operated a fishing lodge there after her parents' deaths. A noted cougar hunter, she eventually moved to Port Hardy, where she died in 1982. The name of the bay was originally adopted as Verney in 1927; this mistake was corrected by the hydrographic service in 1936. Varney Bay was also known in the early days as Marble Bay, after the Marble R, which joins the sea there after flowing NW through Victoria Lk and Alice Lk.

Veitch Point (54°09'00" 130°03'00" S side of the Skeena R, W of Port Essington, SE of Prince Rupert), **Veitch Rock** (Just S of Veitch Point). The point is named after Lt James Richard Veitch (d 1886), who served on the BC coast, 1874–78, as navigating lt of HMS *Daring*, under Cdr John Hanmer. Veitch was navigating sub-lt on board HMS *Galatea* in 1867–70 during that vessel's world tour under the Duke of Edinburgh (Prince Alfred), who was an RN capt at the time. The *Daring* surveyed the entrance to the Skeena R in 1877, and Hanmer named a number of places in the vicinity after the ship and its officers.

Venn Passage (54°20'00" 130°26'00" Connects Metlakatla Bay and Prince Rupert Hbr, just W of Prince Rupert). Named by Anglican missionary William Duncan after Rev Henry Venn (1796–1873), secretary and guiding light of the Anglican Church Mission Society, 1841–73. The society was founded in 1799 by members of the Clapham Sect, an activist, evangelical offshoot of the Church of England. Overseas mission work began in Africa in 1804 but spread rapidly to NZ, Canada, Asia Minor, Greece, Malta, Turkey and the W Indies. Under Venn's direction, the CMS established a large HQ in London and also expanded into China. The name of the passage was adopted by Capt George Richards in 1862 as Venn Ck (creek being an old geographical term for a small inlet). It was changed to its current form in 1911. W

Venn Shoal (53°34'00" 130°37'00" SW of Norway Inlet, off NW Banks I, Hecate Str). Moses Venn (d 1890) was a Tsimshian First Nation chief who became an Anglican lay preacher at Metlakatla during the late 19th century. He also worked at Kitkatla. He and Betsy Venn were married at Metlakatla in 1872. Moses probably chose his Christian surname in honour of Church Mission Society secretary Henry Venn (*see above*).

Venture Banks (54°05'00" 132°08'00" W side of McIntyre Bay, N of Masset, off N side of Graham I, QCI), **Venture Point** (50°18'00" 125°20'00" S side of Sonora I, Okisollo

SS *Venture* in Vancouver Harbour, July 1925. *BC Archives A-07621*

Channel, N of Campbell R). There were two W coast steamers named *Venture*, both originally constructed for the Boscowitz Steamship Co. In 1907, Capt Frederick Learmonth of HMS *Egeria*, while conducting a survey of the region, named the banks after the first *Venture*, which had grounded there the previous year. This 47-m, 736-tonne vessel was built at Victoria in 1902 and destroyed by fire in 1909 at the Inverness cannery on the Skeena R. The next year a larger and more versatile *Venture*, with 60 berths, 500 tonnes of cargo capacity and a licence to carry 186 passengers, was built in Britain. In 1911 the Union Steamship Co acquired the Boscowitz firm, and the *Venture* embarked on a long, productive and remarkably accident-free career as a Union steamer, running mostly to the N coast salmon canneries on the Nass and Skeena rivers. In 1946 the 55-m, 917-tonne vessel was sold to a Chinese company and renamed the *Hsin Kong So*; within six months this carefully maintained steamship had caught fire twice, at Honolulu and Hong Kong, and been damaged beyond repair. The point was named after the second *Venture*. Venture Mtn, N of Bute Inlet, was named in 1985 by members of an RCN climbing party after HMCS *Venture*, the shore-based officer-training centre in Esquimalt, which took its name from an earlier HMCS *Venture*—an RCN sail-training schooner based at Halifax before and during WWII.

Verbeke Reef (48°53'00" 125°23'00" W end of Coaster Channel, Broken Group, Barkley Sd, W side of Vancouver I). Fr Francis R Verbeke (1860–1937), from Belgium, was a Roman Catholic missionary and teacher, at Barkley Sd in the early 1880s and afterwards at Alberni. He came first to St Leo's, the mission to the Huu-ay-aht (Ohiaht) First Nation on Numukamis Bay, and then built a church, residence and school at Dodger Cove on Diana I in 1890. Verbeke moved on to become the Catholic pastor at S Wellington, near Nanaimo, in the early 1900s and was at Kelowna, 1908–17. He died at Victoria. Verbeke Reef was formerly known as Shag I, after the cormorants that congregate there.

V

Verdia Island (49°39'00" 126°34'00" One of the Spanish Pilot Group, SW of Bligh I, Nootka Sd, W side of Vancouver I). José Antonio Verdia was 2nd pilot of the *San Carlos*, under Gonzales López de Haro, in 1789, the year that López de Haro and Estéban Martínez occupied Nootka Sd and established a Spanish garrison there. That Oct he sailed the *North West America*, one of the vessels seized at Nootka by Martínez (and renamed *Santa Gertrudis la Magna*), to Mexico. In 1790 he returned to Nootka Sd as 2nd pilot aboard the *San Carlos*, this time under the command of Francisco Eliza. The following year Verdia accompanied Eliza and José Narváez on their historic exploration of the Str of Georgia. He and Narváez—in the *San Carlos's* longboat and the *Santa Saturnina*, respectively—became the first Europeans to sail round the San Juan Is; they also charted the southern Gulf Is before rejoining Eliza on the S side of Juan de Fuca Str.

Verdier Point (48°38'00" 123°32'00" W side of Saanich Inlet, S of Mill Bay, NW of Victoria), **Verdier Shoal** (52°43'00" 129°27'00" NW of Moore Is, W of N Aristazabal I, S approach to Caamaño Sd, Hecate Str). Francis Verdier (1865–1947), a farmer, timber cruiser and member of a pioneer Saanich family, marked out the original route of the Malahat hwy from Mill Bay to Goldstream. He was born on the Saanich Peninsula and married US-born Anna St Louis (b 1878) at Victoria in 1897. They later divorced and he married Julia Michell (b 1885), from Que, at Victoria in 1927 (this marriage also ended in divorce, in 1929). Verdier is celebrated for felling the timber in what is now downtown Vancouver; he also cleared much forest in the Sooke area, hauling the logs with a team of 24 oxen. He maintained a 65-ha farm in the Brentwood Bay area, where he grew fruit trees and raised cattle and poultry, and is believed to have taken part in the Victoria old-timers' reunion of 1924 (*see* Adams Bay). Verdier died at Victoria. The point appeared on early Admiralty charts as Camp Point but was renamed in 1935.

Vere Cove (50°23'00" 125°46'00" W end of W Thurlow I, Johnstone Str, NW of Campbell R). Named in 1899 in association with nearby Dorothy Rk by Cdr Morris Smyth, in charge of the RN survey vessel *Egeria*, 1898–1900. Dorothy and Vera Thurlow were his nieces, the daughters of Maj Reginald Thurlow of the Royal Welsh Fusiliers. It is not known if these Thurlows were related to Lord Edward Thurlow, the 18th-century British lord chancellor after whom the Thurlow Is are named, or how Vera became changed to Vere. A record at BC's Geographical Names Office notes that, while Vere is a spelling error, it is "too well established now to change."

Vernaci Island (49°38'00" 126°35'00" One of the Spanish Pilot Group, SW of Bligh I, Nootka Sd, W side of Vancouver I), **Vernaci Point** (49°01'00" 123°35'00" SE end of Valdes I, Gulf Is). Juan Vernaci (or Vernacci) y

Retamal, of Italian heritage, was 1st lt of the *Mexicana*, under Cayetano Valdés. Valdés and Dionisio Alcalá-Galiano, in the *Sutil*, explored much of the BC coast between Rosario Str and Queen Charlotte Sd in 1792 and made a historic circumnavigation of Vancouver I. En route, they encountered Capt George Vancouver off Point Grey and explored with him for several weeks. Vernaci led many trips in the ships' boats to examine and survey inlets and side channels in the region. Alcalá-Galiano named Knight Inlet after him (Brazo de Vernaci). Vernaci was well qualified for his position. In the early 1770s he had worked under noted Spanish hydrographer Vicente Tofiño (who also taught him astronomy) on a major survey of the Spanish coast. He was later involved in a survey of the Argentine coast. After his time in BC, Vernaci took part in surveys of Central America and was also stationed at Manila on behalf of the Royal Philippines Co. He died about 1810. Vernaci I was formerly known as House I. Vernaci Point was named in 1905 by Cdr John Parry of HMS *Egeria* while re-surveying Porlier Pass.

Verney Passage. *See* Mt Verney.

Vertical Point (52°54'00" 131°37'00" E side of Louise I, off NE Moresby I, QCI). Geologist George M Dawson named this feature Point Vertical in 1878 "from the attitude of the limestone beds, some of which are over 300 ft [90 m] high." The scenic spot has long been a popular habitation and campsite, both for the Haida people, who once had a village called Xa'lanit there, and for more recent homesteaders, including handloggers in the 1930s and NY artist Benita Saunders, who built a cabin near the point in the 1970s. *D*

Veruna Bay (48°49'00" 123°12'00" NW side of Saturna I, Gulf Is). The *Veruna* was a small schooner owned by Harold Digby Payne (1872–1954), who had followed his older brothers Charles and Gerald out to BC in 1891 (*see* Digby Point *and* Payne Point). The Paynes were a wealthy English family whose members bought property on the Gulf Is (especially Saturna) and at Oak Bay and Sidney. Harold, who had been an RN cadet for five years and done a great deal of sailing, built a store on Saturna and was the island's first postmaster, 1894–97, rowing over to Mayne I once a week to collect the mail. After serving in the Boer War, he raised sheep on Saturna, then moved to Oak Bay and, finally, N Saanich. His wife, Ruth Maude (*see* Ruth I) of Mayne I, died young and he remarried in 1916, to Jessie Ryle. The name was submitted by the Gulf Is Branch of the BC Historical Association in 1968.

Vesuvius Bay (48°53'00" 123°34'00" W side of Saltspring I, N of Booth Bay, Gulf Is). This feature was named in 1859 by RN surveyor Capt George Richards in association with Osborn Bay (qv), which is located on the opposite side of Stuart Channel, on Vancouver I. RN officer and

V

Arctic specialist Sherard Osborn served on the Pacific Station, 1843–46, before going on to a distinguished naval career. In 1855, when he was a cdr, he was put in charge of HMS *Vesuvius*, a 6-gun, 1,164-tonne paddle sloop launched at Sheerness dockyard in 1839. The vessel had a varied career, serving mostly in the Mediterranean but also in the W Indies and off W Africa; under Osborn, during the Crimean War, it was stationed on the Black Sea. The *Vesuvius*, which was never in BC waters, was decommissioned in 1866. Vesuvius Bay became home to groups of black and Portuguese settlers in 1859–60; Estalon Bittancourt, from the Azores, built a store there in 1873 that became the focal point of a small community. Today Vesuvius Bay is the terminus of a ferry to Crofton on Vancouver I. *E W*

Vesuvius Bay, Saltspring Island, in the 1920s. *BC Archives A-09781*

Victoria (48°26'00" 123°22'00" SE end of Vancouver I), **Victoria Harbour** (48°25'16" 123°23'34" Between Victoria and Esquimalt). The largest city on Vancouver I is named after Queen Victoria (1819–1901), who succeeded to the British crown in 1837. The HBC's main depot in the PNW in the early 1800s was at Ft Vancouver on the Columbia R. Anticipating that the border between the region's British and US territories would eventually be farther N, the company began looking for a new HQ in the mid-1830s. A favourable report by Capt William McNeill in 1837 encouraged chief factor James Douglas to choose the SE end of Vancouver I as the site for a new trading post in 1841. The following year he surveyed the area between Oak Bay and Esquimalt Hbr, and in Mar 1843 decided to locate the latest HBC fort on the E side of Victoria Hbr, in the vicinity now bounded by Wharf, Broughton and Government streets and Bastion Square. Local First Nation groups knew Victoria Hbr as Camosack or Camosun—a word that referred more specifically to the tidal rapids at the Gorge and has been translated as "rush of water." Victoria was called Ft Camosun by a few early visitors, and also Ft Albert, as chief trader Charles Ross, in charge of construction, was under the impression that the new post should honour Prince Albert, Queen Victoria's consort. After clarification from head office, the correct name of Ft Victoria was ceremoniously adopted in Dec 1843 with the firing of an official salute. In 1849 the post became HQ of the HBC's Columbia Dept and capital of the colony of Vancouver I (until 1866). A townsite, given the name Victoria, was laid out next to the fort in 1852. Victoria was incorporated as a city in 1862, two years before the old fort was demolished, and became capital of the colony of BC in 1868. It has always been the capital of the province of BC, from Confederation in 1871 to the present day. Capt Henry Kellett of HMS *Herald* first surveyed Victoria Hbr in 1846; it was re-surveyed in 1858 by Capt George Richards of HMS *Plumper*. The harbour comprises five sections: the Inner Hbr, which extends from Juan de Fuca Str to Johnson St bridge; the Upper Hbr, between Johnson St and Point Ellice bridges; Selkirk Water, from Point Ellice Bridge to Chapman Point; Gorge Waters, from Chapman Point to Craigflower Bridge; and Portage Inlet, N of Craigflower Bridge. Several other geographic features in BC are also named after Queen Victoria, including Mt Victoria at the head of Queens Reach on Jervis Inlet, and Mt Victoria and Victoria Lk in Yoho National Park. *E W*

Victoria Harbour, about 1905. *Courtesy Tom Woodland*

Victoria Rock (48°55'00" 123°31'00" W side of Trincomali Channel, E of Fernwood Point, off NE side of Saltspring I, Gulf Is), **Victoria Shoal** (Just NE of Victoria Rk). The 1,367-tonne British steamship *Victoria*, under Capt Laurence Casey, struck this uncharted hazard in 1902, en route from Ladysmith to Juan de Fuca Str with a cargo of coal. While relatively unharmed by the mishap, the *Victoria* met a worse fate the following year, when it was totally wrecked at sea, laden with timber, off the coast of China. The rock was named by the Geographic Board of Canada in 1902.

Victor Island (49°40'00" 126°09'00" In Muchalat Inlet, N of mouth of the Jacklah R, E of Nootka Sd, W side of Vancouver I). Maj Frederick Victor Longstaff (1879–1961) received a Crown grant to this island in 1913. He was born in Yorkshire and came to Victoria in 1911, where he served as an army officer and also worked as an architectural draftsman, helping design St John's Anglican church and the James Bay Anglican Hall. He married Jennie Long McCulloch (1880–1957) at Victoria in 1921. Longstaff had a strong interest in military history and the Anglican church, and wrote books on Christ Church Cathedral and the Esquimalt naval base. He was also a fellow of the Royal Geographical Society, a mountaineer and an associate of the Maritime Museum of BC in Victoria. The island was formerly known as Salmon I.

Vigilant Island (54°20'00" 130°18'00" Prince Rupert Hbr, N of Kaien I). Named by the hydrographic service in 1908 after the fisheries protection vessel *Vigilant*, built by the Polson Iron Works Co of Toronto Ltd in 1903–4 and employed on the Great Lks by the federal government. The 54-m *Vigilant* is regarded as the first modern armed vessel constructed in Canada: a fast, all-steel gunboat that could also be used for defensive patrols in wartime. It was converted to a coal barge in 1935. Vigilant I had a number of earlier names: Anderson I, given by GTP surveyor Fred Ritchie in 1905; Bacon I, probably after GTP harbour engineer James Bacon (Bacon Cove is located nearby); and Pig I, possibly named in association with Bacon Cove but without realizing the latter name's significance.

Village Bay (48°51'00" 123°19'00" W side of Mayne I, Gulf Is), **Village Bay** (50°09'00" 125°11'00" E side of Quadra I, N of Campbell R, N end of Str of Georgia). There are 20 place names in BC with the word "village" in them—mostly on the coast and mostly referring to First Nation settlements. The area around Helen Point on Mayne I, for instance, between Naylor Bay and Village Bay, is a Tsartlip First Nation reserve (the Tsartlip people, who are part of the Wsanec or Saanich cultural family, are based today at Brentwood Bay on the Saanich Peninsula). Archeological excavations have revealed that the point was occupied more than 5,000 years ago, making it the oldest known settlement in the Gulf Is region. Village Bay on Quadra I was also the site of a sizable community and is currently a reserve of the Cape Mudge people, whose members are part of the Kwakwaka'wakw First Nation. An old trail and a stream link the bay to Quadra's network of interconnected lakes. Loggers once floated logs down this stream, ruining it for salmon and angering the residents of Yakwen, the village on the bay. To preserve their fish stocks they blew up the dam that had been built at the lake exit.

Village Channel (50°37'00" 126°38'00" S side of Crease I and the Indian Group, W of Village I), **Village Island** (50°37'00" 126°32'00" NW side of Turnour I, S of Gilford I, mouth of Knight Inlet, N of Johnstone Str). Village I is the site of Mamalilaculla (qv), the main winter settlement of the Mamaleleqala-QweqwaSot'Enox people, a branch of the Kwakwaka'wakw First Nation. The village had a population estimated at 2,000 in the 1830s, but that number had shrunk to 90 by 1911. A school and TB sanatorium were established on the island in 1920 and operated by Anglican missionary Kathleen O'Brien until 1945. Mamalilaculla, with its beautiful setting and atmospheric ruins, was abandoned in the 1960s but has seen a resurgence of visitors in recent years. *E*

Village Island with ruins of Mamalilaculla. *Andrew Scott*

Village Islands (48°20'00" 123°36'00" E side of Becher Bay, S tip of Vancouver I). These islands, themselves a Scia'new First Nation reserve, are named for their proximity to the main Scia'new village sites on the E and N sides of Becher Bay. The Scia'new people are also known as the Beecher Bay First Nation (note the slight spelling variation between the name of the bay and that of the First Nation group). The islands were known before 1934 as the Gleed Is, after Thomas Gleed (1818–80), a Cornish miner who came out to Vancouver I from England with his wife, Rachel (1824–1909), in 1852 and became an early farmer and landowner in this vicinity. The Gleeds received a Crown grant for their property in 1876. After her husband's death, Rachel managed the farm with the help of her nephew, Thomas Stothard, and also served as Metchosin's first postmaster, 1881–91.

Village Point (50°47'00" 126°30'00" W end of Denham I, Burdwood Group, off NW side of Gilford I, NE of Port McNeill), **Village Point** (54°11'00" 132°59'00" SE side of Langara I, off NW end of Graham I, QCI). There are at least five former Kwakwaka'wakw village sites in the Burdwood Group, according to local fisherman and writer Bill Proctor. One is located beside the beach at scenic Village Point, a popular camping site. Village Point on Langara I refers to Dadens, a flourishing Haida community in the 18th century. Early fur trader William Douglas, visiting in 1789, called the village Tartanee (other European names for the site include Tadents and Tadense). A fire apparently destroyed Dadens after Douglas's visit, and a majority of residents migrated to Haida settlements in SE Alaska. *D*

Village Reef (48°53'00" 125°17'00" N of Effingham I, Broken Group, Barkley Sd, W side of Vancouver I). Effingham I (qv), formerly known as Village I, was once a major summer habitation site for the Tseshaht First Nation, whose members belong to the Nuu-chah-nulth Tribal Council. Capt Charles Barkley of the *Imperial Eagle* traded at this village in 1787, and his wife, Frances, described it in her journal. The settlement was abandoned in the early 1900s. The Tseshaht reserve on Effingham I is called Omoah.

Villaverde Islands (49°40'00" 126°34'00" NW of Bligh I, Nootka Sd, W side of Vancouver I). Named after Fr José Joaquin Villaverde, chaplain of the *San Carlos* in 1791. That year the *San Carlos* and its crew sailed from Mexico to Nootka Sd and then, under the command of Francisco Eliza, into the Str of Georgia, accompanied by José Narváez in the *Santa Saturnina*. They were the first European explorers to see these inside waters. Formerly known as the Junction Is.

Viner Point (50°08'00" 125°08'00" S point of Read I, NE of Campbell R, N end of Str of Georgia), **Viner Sound** (50°47'00" 126°24'00" NW side of Gilford I, NE of Port McNeill). After Capt William Viner Read, an assistant in the RN's hydrographic dept in the 1860s. Viner Lk on Gilford I is also named for him. *See* Read I. Viner Sd was once the site of a large Kwakwaka'wakw First Nation village. George O'Brien operated a railway logging camp at the head of the sound, 1924–32.

Virago Point (49°01'00" 123°35'00" S side of Porlier Pass, NW end of Galiano I, Gulf Is), **Virago Rock** (In Porlier Pass, just NW of Virago Point), **Virago Sound** (54°05'20" 132°31'24" Entrance to Naden Hbr, N side of Graham I, QCI). HMS *Virago*, a 6-gun paddle sloop, served on the Pacific Station in 1852–55. The 1,510-tonne vessel, launched at Chatham in 1842, had three cdrs during its Pacific posting: William Houston Stewart (in 1852), James Prevost (1852–54) and Edward Marshall (1854–55). Stewart had handed the ship over to Prevost at Valparaiso,

Chile, after recapturing the southern penal colony of Punta Arenas from a group of rebels. Prevost took it to the QCI to investigate the plundering of the US schooner *Susan Sturgis* and to maintain order in the region. En route, in Porlier Pass, the *Virago* struck the rock named for it, previously unknown to mariners. It got free of the hazard after seven hours but later had to be repaired on the beach at Port Simpson. (The 32-m tug *Point Grey* was less fortunate; it spent 14 years stuck on Virago Rk after wrecking there in 1949.) With the assistance of George Inskip, the *Virago*'s master, Prevost spent much time in 1853 doing survey work along the NW coast of Graham I, in Houston Stewart Channel and at Port Simpson. (A book by BC historians Philip and Helen Akrigg, *HMS Virago in the Pacific 1851–55*, is based on George Inskip's journal.) In 1854, during the Crimean War, Cdr Marshall and the *Virago* took part in an unsuccessful British and French attack on Petropavlovsk on Russia's Kamchatka Peninsula. Virago Sd, named by Cdr Prevost in 1853, had originally been called Puerto Mazarredo by Spanish explorer Jacinto Caamaño in 1792, after noted Spanish naval officer José María de Mazarredo y Salazar; the name was adopted by Capt George Vancouver as Port Maseredo. The sloop went on to serve in S America, the English Channel, the W Indies and Australia before being broken up in 1876. *D W*

Virgalias Cove (53°42'00" 132°55'00" Head of Port Louis, W side of Graham I, QCI). Victor Virgalias was a Scandinavian prospector who came to the QCI in 1905 from Alaska, where, among other activities, he had apparently run a successful dance hall. He was hired to stake oil claims at Tian Point, just N of Port Louis, and also to blaze a rough trail from the point to Naden Hbr whaling station, 45 km away. Virgalias spent the next few years prospecting around Haida Gwaii and found gold in the black sands off Fife Point, at the NE tip of the QCI, but not in commercial quantities. The cove was named by fellow prospector and QCI pioneer Eli Tingley. *D*

Virgin Rocks (51°16'00" 128°12'00" SW end of the Sea Otter Group, Queen Charlotte Sd). These dangers to navigation were named by early fur trader James Hanna of the *Sea Otter* in 1786, on his second voyage to the PNW. They are thus one of the earliest European place names to have survived on the BC coast. Capt George Vancouver corrected the chart position of the hazardous rocks in 1792.

Virtue Rock (48°25'00" 123°15'00" SW of Discovery I, Plumper Passage, E of SE tip of Vancouver I). John Alexander Virtue (1860–1929) was a prominent resident and hotelier at Oak Bay. A native of Que, he was married to Irish-born Sidney Scott (1865–1905) and became manager of the new Mt Baker Hotel at Oak Bay in 1893. This landmark was destroyed by fire in Sept 1902, but Virtue built a new facility, the Oak Bay Hotel, in 1905.

Rudyard Kipling stayed there in 1907 and supposedly immortalized the place with a bit of winsome doggerel. The hotel changed hands over the years and was known as the Old Charming Inn when it was torn down, in 1962, to make way for the then luxurious Rudyard Kipling apartments. Virtue also owned Mary Tod I (qv) in Oak Bay; he bequeathed this property to Oak Bay municipality on condition that nothing should ever be built there. Virtue Rk was named by the hydrographic service in 1934.

Viscount Island (50°41'00" 126°13'00" SE side of Gilford I, NW entrance to Knight Inlet). After Capt Richard Meade, Viscount Gilford, cdr of HMS *Tribune* on the Pacific Station, 1862–64. *See* Gilford I.

Viscount Point (53°47'00" 130°32'00" S side of Goschen I, SW of Porcher I and Prince Rupert). After British parliamentarian and naval official George Joachim Goschen. *See* Goschen I.

Vivian Rock (51°55'00" 128°30'00" W of Duck I, Goose Group, Queens Sd, SW of Bella Bella). Named in 1945 by the hydrographic service after Maj David Vivian Currie, a VC recipient and hero of WWII. *See* Currie It. Formerly known as West Rk.

Entrance to Von Donop Inlet's saltwater lagoon. *Andrew Scott*

Von Donop Inlet (50°11'00" 124°58'49" Drains NW into Sutil Channel, NW end of Cortes I, NE of Campbell R).

Victor Edward John Brenton von Donop served as a midshipman aboard HMS *Charybdis*, under Capt George Keane. The vessel arrived at Esquimalt in 1862 in the wake of the Trent Affair, in which two Confederate diplomats were removed by force from the British mail packet *Trent* by a Union warship capt during the US Civil War. The incident caused a certain amount of international sabre-rattling, and Britain responded by strengthening its Canadian naval bases. The diplomats were later released. As a lt cdr, Von Donop had charge of the RN gunboat *Cromer* in 1875–77. His promising naval career ended prematurely in 1881 when he was swept from the bridge of HMS *Decoy* in a violent storm off W Africa and drowned. The inlet was originally known as Von Donop Ck in 1867 (creek being an old surveying term for a small inlet) and was also mistakenly spelled Van Donop Inlet in the late 1940s. A 1,277-ha area surrounding the inlet was protected in 1993 as Háthayim (Von Donop) marine park. *W*

Voss Point (48°50'00" 125°12'00" S end of Diana I, W side of Trevor Channel, Barkley Sd, W side of Vancouver I). Victoria resident John Claus Voss (c 1851–1922) made a famous voyage in 1901–4 in a remodelled, sail-equipped, 10-m dugout canoe, the *Tilikum*. He was accompanied partway across the Pacific by Norman Luxton, a journalist, who left the expedition at Fiji and was replaced by a series of other crewmen, including one who was washed overboard and lost. Voss eventually reached Margate, England, via Australia, S Africa, Brazil and the Azores, after an extraordinary voyage of 16,000 km. He returned to Victoria, where he married Mary Anna Welde in 1906 and briefly co-owned a hotel, then returned to sea as a sealer (working as a skipper on Japanese-owned vessels, 1908–11), finally publishing his memoirs in 1913. The *Tilikum*, left to rot on the Thames R, was brought home in the 1920s by the Vancouver I Publicity Bureau, restored and displayed at Victoria's Thunderbird Park for several decades. It found a permanent home in 1965 at Victoria's Maritime Museum of BC. Norman Luxton's story was eventually told by his daughter Eleanor Luxton in a 1971 book, *Tilikum: Luxton's Pacific Crossing*. Voss Point got its name because the adventurer apparently took his final PNW departure from Diana I after being stormbound for several weeks in Barkley Sd, during which time he socialized with the storekeeper at Dodger Cove.

Waddington Bay (50°43'00" 126°37'00" NE side of Bonwick I, Broughton Archipelago, E end of Queen Charlotte Str, NE of Port McNeill), **Waddington Channel** (50°13'00" 124°43'00" Between E Redonda I and W Redonda I, SW of Toba Inlet, NE of Campbell R), **Waddington Harbour** (50°55'00" 124°50'00" Head of Bute Inlet). Alfred Pendrell Waddington (1801–72) was born at London, England, son of a merchant banker, and educated in France and Germany. After several business failures he immigrated to California in 1850 for the gold rush and ended up co-owning a successful San Francisco wholesale grocery firm. Waddington came to BC in 1858, opened a branch office in Victoria and became involved in politics. That Nov he wrote *The Fraser Mines Vindicated*, believed to be the first book published in BC. He was elected to Vancouver I's legislative assembly in 1860–61 but resigned to pursue a bold transportation venture: a road from the head of Bute Inlet that Waddington believed would expedite the arduous journey to the Cariboo goldfields. Gov James Douglas granted him the right to charge tolls for 10 years, and a work party was sent to cut a route along the Homathko R. In Apr 1864, 14 members of his crew were killed by Tsilhqot'in First Nation warriors opposed to this incursion into their territory. This was the beginning of the so-called Chilcotin War, during which the attackers were tracked down and captured. Five were eventually tried and executed. The road project had to be abandoned, and Waddington, in financial distress, became Vancouver I's first superintendent of schools, 1865–66. From 1867 until his death in Que from smallpox, he vigorously promoted a transcontinental railroad scheme through Edmonton and Yellowhead Pass to a port at the head of Bute Inlet. Waddington Channel and Waddington Hbr were named by Capt George Richards of HMS *Hecate* in 1862. A number of other BC geographical features also commemorate him, including Waddington Canyon, Waddington Glacier, Waddington Peak, the Waddington Range and Mt Waddington—at 4,016 m the third-highest mountain in BC (but the highest entirely within provincial boundaries) and the highest peak in the Coast Range. Pendrell Sd (qv) may possibly be named for him as well. *E W*

Wadhams (51°31'00" 127°30'00" E side of Rivers Inlet, SE of Bella Bella). A large salmon cannery was built here in 1897 by Edmund Abraham Wadhams (1833–1900), who was born in NY state and travelled W in 1849, then followed the various gold rushes from California to the Cariboo. At Victoria, in 1864, he married Bertha Rosamond Wilson (1846–85), who had come out to BC in 1862 in the famous brideship *Tynemouth*. The Wadhams settled at Astoria on the Columbia R in the early 1870s, and Edmund learned the cannery trade. About 1883, together with partner Marshall English, he started up a cannery on the Fraser R, which he sold in 1890 to the Anglo-BC Packing Co. His next cannery venture, in 1891, was in Washington state, on the E shore of Point Roberts; this one he sold to the Alaska Packers' Assoc in 1893. In 1902, after Edmund's death at Portland, Oregon, his Rivers Inlet venture was taken over by the BC Packers Assoc; his son William Wadhams supervised the association's northern district, including his father's cannery, for many years. Equipment to make cans was installed at the Wadhams cannery in 1916, but production ceased in 1942, after a serious fire, though the site continued to operate as a fishing camp. A Red Cross outpost station, known as the Darby Medical Centre, was located there in the 1950s, and a post office named Wadhams served the area in 1903–67.

Waglisla (52°09'42" 128°08'37" At Bella Bella, NE side of Campbell I, on Lama Passage). The main Heiltsuk First Nation community on Campbell I has had several names over the years and has also changed location slightly, from McLoughlin Bay, where the HBC established a post, Fort McLoughlin, 1833–45, to its present site just to the N, formerly known as New Bella Bella and since 1974, when the post office was renamed, as Waglisla. (*See also* Bella Bella, a name that generally embraces settlements on both sides of Lama Passage.) According to BC historians Helen and Philip Akrigg, Waglisla is a Heiltsuk name meaning "estuary" or "river delta" and refers specifically to a creek mouth just S of the village; it has also been translated as "river on the beach."

Waiatt Bay (50°16'00" 125°15'00" NE side of Quadra I, N of Campbell R). This bay, with its rich marine resources, was an important First Nation habitation site, both for the Klahoose (Coast Salish) people and for the Lekwiltok (Kwakwaka'wakw), who controlled the area in later years. An old portage trail crosses Quadra from the bay to Small Inlet. There are fine examples on Waiatt Bay of what are known today as "clam gardens," an early form of aquaculture in which clam beds were seeded and tended. The name is usually translated as "place where herring spawn" and should be pronounced *WU-ad*, according to First Nation informants. It appeared on Admiralty charts for many years as Wyatt Bay, which was also the post office name, 1913–46. Moses Ireland, a well-known logger in the region, bought land there in 1884. A general store was in operation on one of the nearby Octopus Is prior to WWI and lasted until about 1940. A few handloggers lived in the area, as well as a boatbuilder and the manager of the Wyatt Bay Fish Oil and Fertilizer Co. The S shore of the bay is part of 760-ha Octopus Is Provincial Park, established in 1974. *E*

Wain Rock (48°41'00" 123°29'00" W of Deep Cove, off NW Saanich Peninsula, NW of Victoria). Henry Wain (1826–1914), from Kent, left England in 1849 to work for the HBC as a carpenter, arriving in BC in 1850 in the supply ship *Norman Morison*. He travelled back and forth several times between England and Victoria, bringing his wife, Sarah (1828–1906, née Davis), out with him in 1857, and later pre-empted land in N Saanich, on the S side of Deep Cove, receiving a Crown grant in 1872. Wain grew hops on his property, established an early tavern there and helped build the district's community hall and school (he also did much finishing work on the old Craigflower school). He ran a horse-powered stage to Victoria, transporting the early mails, and was briefly postmaster at the N Saanich post office. Descendants of the Wain family still live in the region. The name Norris Rk has appeared on some maps for this feature as well.

Wainwright Basin (54°15'00" 130°17'00" S end of Kaien I, just S of Prince Rupert). Named in 1908 after William Wainwright (1840–1914), 2nd vice-president and chief lobbyist of the GTP. He was also 1st vice-president of the Grand Trunk Rwy of Canada, the GTP's parent company. Born at Manchester, England, he rose to become gen manager of the Sheffield & Lincolnshire Railroad before immigrating to Canada in 1862 to take the position of chief clerk in the Grand Trunk's accounting dept. He served as gen manager of the N Shore Rwy, 1883–85, as well, and died in the US at Atlantic City. This feature was formerly known as Lk Wainwright, Lk Bacon and Salt Lk No 2. The town of Wainwright, Alberta, was also named for this railroad official in 1908.

Wakash Point (52°10'00" 127°54'00" SE side of Cunningham I, just E of Bella Bella). Named in 1924 by the hydrographic service after Wakash (or Wacash), who is described in the 1834 journal of HBC fur trader and medical officer William Tolmie as the most powerful of the Heiltsuk First Nation chiefs from that era. Formerly known as Fanny Point.

Wakas Point (51°17'00" 127°38'00" NE end of Indian I, W entrance to Takush Hbr, Smith Sd, N of Port Hardy). Named after a Gwa'sala First Nation chief from Takush Hbr. The Gwa'sala people, the most northerly of the Kwakwaka'wakw nations, once had an important winter village on the S side of Indian I, where the Nathlegalis reserve is located today. Wakas Point was formerly known as North Point.

Wakely Rock (52°36'00" 129°26'00" In Wright Passage, SW of Moore Is, off W side of Aristazabal I, Hecate Str). Sapper Samuel Wakely was a member of the Columbia detachment of Royal Engineers, which served in BC 1858–63. Little is known about him, unfortunately, and he seems to have left BC sometime before 1907.

Wakeman River (51°03'00" 126°32'00" Flows S into Wakeman Sd), **Wakeman Sound** (50°59'00" 126°30'00" N side of Kingcome Inlet, NE of Broughton I and Port McNeill). The sound was named in 1866, by Lt Daniel Pender of the *Beaver*, after William Plowden Wakeman (1829–72), who came out to Victoria from London, England, in 1862, in the *Tynemouth*. He worked as a clerk in the naval dockyard at Esquimalt, 1866–72, and died in the naval hospital there. A Kwakwaka'wakw village on the Wakeman R was abandoned in the 1920s, shortly before the Powell R Co began railway logging in the river valley. Twenty John Birch Society members from the US, fearing a communist takeover in their homeland, made a short-lived attempt to settle in the Wakeman valley in the fall of 1962.

Walbran Island (51°31'00" 127°37'00" NW side of Rivers Inlet, SE of Bella Bella), **Walbran Point** (53°46'00" 128°51'00" Devastation Channel, NE end of Loretta I, SW of Kitimat), **Walbran Rock** (52°03'00" 127°56'00" NE end of Hunter I, Fisher Channel, SE of Bella Bella). Capt John Thomas Walbran (1848–1913), a native of Ripon, Yorkshire, trained for the British merchant service at HMS *Conway*, a "school ship" for boys, and was licensed as a master mariner in 1881. He initially arrived at Victoria in 1888 as 1st officer of the steamship *Islander*, which had been built on the Clyde for the Canadian Pacific Navigation Co, and was joined in 1893 by his wife, Anne Mary (1849–1907), and two daughters. Walbran served as capt of the CPN's *Danube* for several years, then, in 1891, joined the federal Dept of Marine and Fisheries. His first job was to supervise the construction of the government steamship *Quadra* at Paisley, Scotland, and then bring the vessel out to the W coast. Except for

Captain John T Walbran, author of *British Columbia Coast Names*, in the 1880s. *BC Archives A-02521*

a seven-month period in 1892, he commanded it until 1903. The *Quadra* was primarily a lighthouse, buoy and fisheries tender, but it visited every corner of the coast to fulfill a wide range of duties. Its capt was also a magistrate, for instance, and represented the long arm of the law in remote areas, and Walbran twice carried govs gen and their parties on official cruises. He had a deep interest in local history and named many coastal features. After retiring in 1904, he devoted himself to writing the book he is noted for, *British Columbia Coast Names, 1592–1906*, which was published in 1909. This estimable volume, with its detailed naval histories and marvellous accumulation of anecdotes—many of them gathered first-hand by the author from old RN officers and Victoria pioneers—was reissued in 1971 and can fairly be called a bestseller. It is also the foundation upon which all other books about BC's coastal place names, including this one, have been based. Walbran I and Walbran Rk were named in 1890 and 1894, respectively, by Admiralty surveyors, Walbran Point by the Geographic Board of Canada in 1898. Mt Walbran and Walbran Ck on SW Vancouver I commemorate this literary mariner as well. *E W*

Wale Island (52°50'00" 129°01'00" Head of Racey Inlet, W side of Princess Royal I). William John Wale (1842–1930), from London, England, immigrated to Victoria in 1853 in the HBC supply ship *Norman Morison* with his mother and stepfather, Amelia Rebecca and Edmund Williams. Edmund worked on HBC farms and then established his own farms at Cadboro Bay and Royal Oak. William was employed at first as a cattle herder and also joined the gold rush before settling down as a farmer at Elk Lk and marrying Ann McHugh (1848–1915) at Victoria in 1872. She was a native of NZ and had come to Canada with her family in 1861. About 1882 the Wales bought Yew Tree Farm, N of Colwood, then went back to Saanich to take over property belonging to Ann's family. They made several more moves: to Colwood Farm, where William was appointed a justice of the peace; to the Millstream district; to NZ; back to Millstream; and then back to Yew Tree Farm. After his wife's death, William made one last move, to Victoria, where he took part in the famous old-timers' reunion of May 1924 (*see* Adams Bay).

Wales Harbour (54°46'00" 130°35'00" NW side of Wales I), **Wales Island** (54°45'00" 130°29'00" Entrance to Portland Inlet, BC-Alaska boundary, N of Prince Rupert), **Wales Passage** (54°48'00" 130°28'00" Between Wales I and Pearse I), **Wales Point** (54°42'00" 130°29'00" S end of Wales I). Capt George Vancouver named Wales Point in 1793 after the astronomer and mathematician William Wales (1734–98), his "much esteemed friend," who had accompanied Capt James Cook on his second voyage to the S Pacific (1772–75) and taught navigation skills to the expedition's young officers, including Vancouver. His "kind instructions ... enabled me to traverse and delineate these lonely regions," Vancouver noted in his journal. Wales was one of four scientists engaged in 1767 to calculate navigation tables for the British government's new *Nautical Almanac*. The Royal Society then sent him, in 1768–69, to Hudson Bay to observe the transit of Venus. On his return from the S Pacific in 1775, he was appointed mathematical master at Christ's Hospital, a position he occupied until his death. Wales I was named in 1871 by the RN hydrographic office, in association with the point. It was claimed by the US as part of Alaska until 1903, when the boundary dispute went to arbitration and a tribunal drew the border down Pearce Canal, just N of Wales I, thus determining that this feature was part of Canada. W

Wales Point (48°40'43" 123°24'58" N side of Tsehum Hbr, just N of Sidney, NE end of Saanich Peninsula, N of Victoria). Charles Wales (1844–1906), a former English sailor, came to Canada in 1871 and worked as a fisherman and farmer. He built a log cabin at the head of Tsehum Hbr about 1885 and rigged a fish trap in the vicinity—a row of stakes in the mud that the fish could go over at high tide but could not escape from when the water level fell. In 1884, Wales and another man formed all the lumber needed to build N Saanich's Holy Trinity Church into a raft and transported it from Cowichan Bay to Patricia Bay. The name was submitted by local residents and adopted in 1965.

Walkem Islands (50°22'00" 125°31'00" E end of Johnstone Str, off W end of E Thurlow I, NW of Campbell R), **Walkem Point** (53°29'00" 128°43'00" S side of Gardner Canal, E of Triumph Bay, S of Kitimat). The Walkem Is, formerly known as the Pender Is, were renamed by the Geographic Board of Canada in 1905 on the suggestion of Capt John Walbran. George Anthony Boomer Walkem (1834–1908) was born in Ireland and came to Canada with his family in 1847. He was educated at McGill Univ and became a lawyer, then moved to BC in 1862 and established a law practice in the Cariboo, where he was elected to BC's legislative council, 1864–70, and also appointed a magistrate. After Confederation, Walkem was elected MLA for the Cariboo (until 1882) and served as chief commissioner of Lands and Works in BC's first provincial administration, as attorney gen in the second one and as premier of BC, 1874–76 and 1878–82. With a reputation for pragmatism and even wiliness, he has been viewed both as BC's "first modern politician" and, by Supreme Court justice Henry Crease, as a "little trickster." Walkem sat on the BC Supreme Court himself from 1882 to 1903, after which he retired. Walkem Point, formerly known as Richardson Point, after James Richardson of the Geological Survey of Canada, was renamed in 1946. Walkem Cone on Broughton I also commemorates this BC politician. *E W*

Walker Hook (48°54'00" 123°30'00" S of Fernwood Point, E side of Saltspring I, Gulf Is), **Walker Rock** (48°55'00" 123°29'00" S of Retreat Cove, Trincomali Channel, off W side of Galiano I, Gulf Is). Edward Walker (1826–1902), from Durham, England, arrived at Vancouver I in 1851 to work for the HBC's marine dept and became a pioneer resident of Nanaimo. He co-owned and operated several early sailing vessels, including the *T T Stephens* (renamed the *Nanaimo Packet*), the *Merlin* (renamed the *Victoria Packet*), the *Flora* and the *Alpha* (first ship built at Nanaimo). Walker spent much of 1860 in the *Nanaimo Packet*, carrying construction materials to Fisgard I, at the entrance to Esquimalt Hbr, for BC's first lighthouse. That year he also married fellow Nanaimo pioneer Selena Sage (1846–1908), who had arrived in BC in 1854 in the *Princess Royal* with her coal-miner family. Walker owned land on Saltspring and was part of a failed attempt to develop a townsite on the E coast of the island, to be named Grantville. He later constructed and repaired wharves for coal baron Robert Dunsmuir. The Walkers eventually moved to Cumberland, where they both died; Edward is listed there as a carpenter in the 1901 census. He brought Walker Rk to the attention of RN surveyor Capt George Richards in 1859. *W*

Walker Island (52°06'00" 128°07'00" Off SW side of Denny I, S of Alarm Cove, just S of Bella Bella). In 1917–18, Lt Cdr Wilfred Tyrell Walker (1888–1967) of the RCN was listed as CO of the torpedo boat *Grilse* (the former motor yacht *Winchester*), operating out of Halifax, and also as CO of HMCS *Acadia*, a patrol and survey vessel. He may have served briefly with HMCS *Rainbow* and *Shearwater* on the Pacific coast as well. During WWII he came out of retirement to take on the role of DEMS (Defensively Equipped Merchant Ship) officer at Esquimalt. Walker I was known before 1944 as Camp I.

Walker Point (51°55'00" 127°54'00" N entrance to Burke Channel, Fitz Hugh Sd, SE of Bella Bella). Named in 1793 by Capt George Vancouver, who led a surveying expedition through this area with the ships' boats while HMS *Discovery* and *Chatham* were anchored at Restoration Bay. William Walker was the surgeon aboard HMS *Chatham*, under Lt Peter Puget.

Wallace Bay (52°17'00" 127°45'00" E side of Cousins Inlet, SW of Ocean Falls, N of Dean Channel). According to Bruce Ramsey, author of *Rain People: The Story of Ocean Falls*, this feature is named after James Wallace, whose NY firm designed and constructed the new pulp mill at Ocean Falls in 1911.

Wallace Island, now a provincial marine park. *Kevin Oke*

Wallace Island (48°57'00" 123°33'00" Trincomali Channel, off NE side of Saltspring I, Gulf Is). The island was named in 1905 by Cdr John Parry of HMS *Egeria*, in association with nearby Houstoun Passage (qv). Capt Wallace Houstoun had served on the Pacific Station in 1853–56. Another RN surveyor, Capt George Richards of HMS *Plumper*, originally named this feature Narrow I, in 1859. Jeremiah Chivers (*see* Chivers Point) gave up a 20-year search for gold to settle on the long sliver of land in the 1880s. He acquired a Crown grant for most of the island in 1889 and homesteaded there for 28 years, planting a large orchard and making his living as a fisherman. In 1946, photographer David Conover (*see* Conover Cove) and his wife, Jeanne, purchased the 80-ha property and created a summer resort. Most of Wallace was sold to a group of Seattle teachers in 1967; it became a provincial marine park in 1990. *E*

Wallace Point (48°44'00" 123°14'00" S end of N Pender I, Gulf Is). Peter William Wallace (d 1875) was assistant surgeon on HMS *Satellite*, under Capt James Prevost, when it was posted to the Pacific Station in 1857. He was appointed to the rudimentary naval hospital at Esquimalt as medical officer, 1857–65, after which he was promoted to surgeon. The feature was named by RN surveyor Capt George Richards about 1860; nearby Peter Cove (qv) also commemorates him. In the early 1900s, Wallace Point was the site of a regular Gulf Is agricultural ritual. Several times a year the semi-wild sheep that roamed the long peninsula at the S end of N Pender I would be driven to the point, where corrals were built for shearing and for separating the lambs for market. After the work was done, the hungry herders and their families would consume a substantial picnic.

Wallace Rocks (54°00'00" 130°48'00" In Hecate Str, W of Porcher I, SW of Prince Rupert). Named in 1895 for Wallace C Langley (1866–1946), from NS, who enjoyed a varied career as a sea and river capt in the PNW and the Far N. In 1892, at Victoria, he married Louise Elizabeth Brinn (1872–1944), who was born on Saltspring I. Langley was employed for a time by the Canadian Pacific Navigation Co as skipper of the *Transfer*, a Fraser R sternwheeler, and the *Thistle*, chartered by the CPN to run freight and passengers along the W coast of Vancouver I in 1895. In the 1900s, however, he worked mostly in Alaska in the summers and lived in Seattle in the off-season. He and his brother Horace owned the Alaska Rivers Navigation Co and ran steamships on the Kuskokwim and Tanana rivers, including the *Tana*, *Quickstep*, *Northwestern*, *Wilbur Crimmin* and *Wallace Langley*, Alaska's last wood-burning sternwheeler, which operated until 1952. In 1911 an unusual notice appeared in the Victoria *Colonist* stating that the capt was seeking a divorce, as "a $7,000 home, $150 monthly allowance and an automobile awaiting its mistress's approval could not wean Mrs Elizabeth Langley away from frequenting the cafés of Seattle and remaining out late at night."

Waller Bay (53°18'30" 130°07'00" S of Wreck Is, SW side of Banks I). William M Waller was an able seaman aboard Capt George Vancouver's HMS *Discovery* on the historic expedition to the PNW, 1791–95. Waller Ck and Waller Lks on Banks I are also named for him.

Wall Islands (52°52'00" 129°21'00" Off N end of Rennison I, Caamaño Sd, W of Princess Royal I). William Henry Wall (1857–1932) emigrated in 1864 from England to Vancouver I, where his family ran a hotel at S Wellington. He married BC-born Naomi Malpass (1865–1915) at Nanaimo in 1880; her parents had come to Nanaimo in the *Princess Royal* in 1854 to mine coal for the HBC. William worked as a mechanic at the Nanaimo collieries, rising to the position of chief engineer at the New Vancouver Coal & Land Co in 1892. He reportedly crafted BC's first telephones, in 1877, working from scratch and basing his makeshift models on diagrams published in a *Scientific American* magazine; the line ran from Wellington to the mine's loading dock at Departure Bay. In 1903, when New Vancouver was sold to the Western Fuel Co of San Francisco, the Walls moved to Vancouver and William worked as a machinist for the Vancouver water board. In 1913 he built a shingle mill and charcoal kiln on land he owned at Craig Bay near Parksville, and in 1916 he was listed as manager of the Diamond Vale Colliery near Merritt. William and Naomi had 11 children, many of whom served overseas during WWI, including several daughters, who were nurses. After Naomi died, William married Mary Ann Shaw (1869–1931) at Vancouver in 1926. He is believed to have taken part in the 1924 Victoria old-timers' reunion (*see* Adams Bay).

Wall Islets (52°44'00" 129°18'00" In Beauchemin Channel, W of Borrowman Bay, off W side of Aristazabal I), **Wall Rocks** (52°44'00" 129°19'00" Just W of Wall Its). Named after Hannah and Edmond Wall, Vancouver I pioneers. The islets commemorate Hannah, who was born Hannah Elizabeth Elliott (c 1853–1948) at San Francisco. She arrived in the colony of Vancouver I in 1858 with her parents, who settled in Saanich's Mt Douglas district. Her first husband, an RN officer named Smith, died at sea, and she married Edmond James Wall (1851–1932) in 1876. The rocks honour Edmond, who was born at Waterford, Ireland, and came to Victoria with his family in 1861. He worked as a grocer and wine merchant, and was co-proprietor of Erskine, Wall & Co. Edmond also took a keen interest in local history, serving as president of the BC Pioneer Society. He died at Essondale, Hannah at Victoria. They both took part in the grand Victoria old-timers' reunion of 1924 (*see* Adams Bay).

Wallis Point (49°16'00" 124°06'00" NE entrance to Nanoose Hbr, E side of Vancouver I, NW of Nanaimo). Richard Pateman Wallis (b 1867), from England, was a farmer and landowner in this vicinity. He came out to BC in 1888, purchased the 900-ha Notch Hill ranch in 1897 and two years later married Eliza Mary Marriott (1863–1914). Wallis was appointed a justice of the peace and served briefly as the Conservative MLA for Alberni in 1918. Nearby Richard Point is named for him as well. Wallis Point, which is also known locally as Berry Point, was named by Cdr John Parry, who re-surveyed Nanoose Hbr with HMS *Egeria* in 1904. *W*

W

Walsh Rock (52°38'00" 128°57'00" SW entrance to Laredo Channel, off E side of Aristazabal I). Sapper Thomas Walsh (1831–89), born in Ireland, was a member of the Columbia detachment of Royal Engineers, which served in BC 1858–63. A tailor by trade, he arrived at Victoria in the *Thames City* in 1859 with the main contingent of men, accompanied by his wife, who gave birth to a son during the long voyage. Sadly, the boy died in BC and was buried at Ft Langley. Walsh stayed on in the colony with his family when the detachment disbanded, acquired land and set up a tailoring firm in New Westminster. One of Walsh's specialties, not surprisingly, was supplying uniforms to the local militia. His business, carried on under the name Walsh & Sons, was still in operation in 1909. Walsh Rk was formerly known as Beaver Ledge.

Walskakul Point (54°41'00" 130°06'00" N side of Khutzeymateen Inlet, N of Prince Rupert), **Walskakul Shoal** (54°41'00" 130°07'00" Just W of Walskakul Point). A possible translation for this Tsimshian First Nation name is "place of narrow passage."

Walter Bay (48°51'00" 123°29'00" S side of Ganges Hbr, E side of Saltspring I, Gulf Is). Edward Walter (1855–1933), who came to Canada from England in 1885, purchased a large block of land adjacent to this bay. He was an active member of the Islands Farmers' Institute and also logged and made charcoal on his property. In 1897, at Vancouver, he married Florence Sarah M Lowther (1860–1954), who had arrived in BC from England two years earlier. Walter produced a pamphlet for the farmers' institute in 1902, designed to attract English settlers possessed of "a moderate income coupled with a love of a country life, who would be glad, untrammelled by conventions, to make a home for themselves by work, bring up their children to a healthy, independent life, and gratify those tastes for shooting and fishing which their means will not permit in the Old Country." The bay, a rich clam-harvesting area, is protected by a sand spit that may once have been the site of a First Nation village.

Walters Cove (N side of Walters I), **Walters Island** (50°02'00" 127°22'00" NE of Aktis I, N entrance to Kyuquot Sd, NW side of Vancouver I). A fishing village is located on Walters I that is the commercial centre of Kyuquot, a maritime community spread out over several small islands and the adjacent shore of Vancouver I, where the Ka:'yu:'K't'h/Che:K'tles7et'h' (Kyuquot/Checleset) First Nation settlement of Houpsitas is situated. The island was settled by Scandinavian fishermen in the 1920s when the nearby whaling station of Cachalot closed. The origin of the name is uncertain. *E*

Wanderer Island (52°25'00" 131°24'00" N entrance to Burnaby Str, off SE side of Moresby I, QCI), **Wanderer Point** (52°24'00" 131°25'00" NE entrance to Skaat Hbr,

just SW of Wanderer I on Moresby I). Wanderer I was named in 1878 by George Mercer Dawson after the 20-tonne trading schooner *Wanderer*, with which he and his younger brother Rankine made a detailed geological exploration of the QCI. The vessel had a crew of three and left Victoria in May 1878, returning in Oct. Dawson described it as "a good craft, with plenty beam, and built originally for a pilot boat." John Sabiston, whom Dawson found "a little opinionative," was the skipper; he was the son of Nanaimo harbourmaster John Flett Sabiston (*see* Sabiston I). The elder Sabiston had taken the *Wanderer* sealing in the early 1870s, under charter for Capt William Spring. The schooner returned to the sealing trade in the 1880s and '90s but was damaged in a storm in 1896, then washed ashore and wrecked in San Josef Bay. The point was named by the hydrographic service in 1962, in association with the island. *D*

Wannock Cove (51°39'00" 127°30'00" N side of Rivers Inlet, W of Moses Inlet), **Wannock River** (51°40'20" 127°15'35" Connects Owikeno Lk to the head of Rivers Inlet). According to BC historians Helen and Philip Akrigg, this name means "river spirit" in the Oowekyala language spoken by the region's First Nation inhabitants, the Oweekeno people. John Walbran, an earlier coastal historian, mistranslated the word as "poison," because "visitors to the tribe, evidently unwelcome, had the reputation of dying suddenly." The name has had quite a variety of spellings, including Wanuck, Whannock, Wannuck, Wharnock and Wannick. Wannock Cove, where a cannery was built in 1884 by the Wannock Packing Co, takes its name from the river. This cannery, which was abandoned in 1934, was acquired by the Victoria Canning Co in 1892 and eventually became part of the BC Packers empire. The cove was the site of the first summer hospital on Rivers Inlet and also featured a pioneer post office called Wanborough, 1896–1903. Another cannery, the earliest in the region, was built at the mouth of the Wannock R in 1882 by Robert Draney and Thomas Shotbolt. Known as the Rivers Inlet or Oweekayno cannery, it was bought by the BC Canning Co in 1888 and was also later owned by BC Packers. After it ceased operating in 1933, it was used as a fishing camp for many years. There is no relationship between Wannock and Whonock (or Whonnock) in the Fraser Valley. The name Whonnock is from Halkomelem, a completely different First Nation language, and is usually translated as "place of many humpback salmon."

Warner Bay (51°02'00" 127°06'00" S side of Seymour Inlet, N of Port McNeill). While the origin of the name is not certain, the bay has long been a centre for logging operations in the region. A sizeable camp was located there in the late 1960s by the Nalos Logging Co Ltd, and the community even had its own post office in 1968–69. In the early 2000s the bay was used primarily as a log sort and booming ground.

Warner Rock (48°57'00" 125°21'00" Loudoun Channel, SW of Lyall Point, Barkley Sd, W side of Vancouver I). Orlando Warner (1841–99), from Pugwash, NS, worked in Victoria as a ship's carpenter and acquired a Crown grant of land NW of Toquart Bay in 1892. His wife, Jane, born in Ireland, died at Victoria in 1911. The Warners raised as their own daughter the orphaned Lucy Sophia Musters (*see* Muster Rk), who married, in 1901, the family boarder, a young realtor from Ont named Arthur Currie. He went on to become cdr of the Canadian Expeditionary Force in WWI and a hero of Vimy Ridge. When Arthur was knighted in 1917, Lucy became Lady Currie.

Warren Rocks (50°04'00" 127°13'00" S of Moketas I, Kyuquot Sd, NW side of Vancouver I). James Douglas Warren (1837–1917) was born in PEI and came to Victoria in 1858. He bought the small sloop *Thornton* and began trading on the BC coast with First Nation groups in the 1860s. In 1868, Warren and the *Thornton* were involved in a notorious shootout with First Nation attackers in Queen Charlotte Sd: 15 people died. Warren, who was also a towboat industry pioneer, teamed up in 1871 with another early Victoria entrepreneur, Joseph Boscowitz (*see* Boscowitz Point), in the pelagic sealing business. Before they became entangled in an interminable legal and financial dispute, Warren and Boscowitz owned the largest fleet of sealing schooners in the Pacific and employed the first steam vessels in the hunt. The partners' economic and legal woes were greatly multiplied in 1886–87 when their sealing ships were seized by US authorities for hunting in US territory. Warren was a principal in the Boscowitz Steamship Co, which operated a coastal passenger and cargo service in the PNW and did well during the Klondike era carrying thousands of eager prospectors and their supplies to the goldfields. It was sold to the Union Steamship Co in 1911. The Warren Rks were formerly known as the Channel Rks but were renamed by the hydrographic service in 1947 to avoid duplication. *E*

Warrior Cove (51°50'00" 127°52'00" E side of Fitz Hugh Sd, S of Kiwash Cove, SE of Bella Bella). Named in 1946 after HMCS *Warrior*, Canada's first aircraft carrier, which sailed that year from England to Halifax. The 212-m, 16,600-tonne ship was built at Belfast, N Ireland, without heaters, for use in the Indian Ocean in WWII, and was originally to be called HMS *Brave*. The war was over by the time it was completed, and the vessel was transferred to the RCN as the *Warrior*. Not surprisingly, it was ill-suited to frigid N Atlantic weather conditions and had to be returned to the RN in 1948 and traded for HMCS *Magnificent*. As HMS *Warrior*, the carrier took part in the Korean War and was involved with the first British hydrogen bomb tests in the S Pacific. The ship was sold to Argentina in 1958, renamed *Independencia* and eventually scrapped in 1971. Warrior Mtn on the BC-Alberta border was named after a different warship, HMS *Warrior*, a heavy cruiser that was sunk by German forces at the 1916 Battle of Jutland.

Warrior Point (48°40'00" 123°28'00" E side of Saanich Inlet, N entrance to Patricia Bay, NW of Victoria). Wsanec (Saanich) First Nation members are believed to have maintained a lookout post at this site so that the alarm could be raised when hostile tribes approached from the N. Formerly known as Boulder Point but renamed in 1934.

Warspite Rock (50°05'00" 125°18'00" Discovery Passage, E of Middle Point, just N of Campbell R). In proud hydrographic tradition, this hazard was named after the ship that first struck it—in this case HMS *Warspite*, a 96-m, 7,620-tonne armoured cruiser that served as flagship at Esquimalt in 1890–93 and 1899–1902. The vessel, under Capt Hedworth Lambton, was returning to base after making a journey around Vancouver I in 1892 when the accident, which was not serious, occurred. The *Warspite* was built at Chatham dockyard, launched in 1884 and spent the years between its PNW postings as a guard ship at Queenstown, Ireland. Rear Adm Charles Hotham was flag officer for the cruiser's first sojourn in BC, while Rear Adm Lewis Beaumont (1899–1900) and Rear Adm Andrew Bickford (1900–1902) were in charge during its second commission. *W*

Washington Rock (52°07'00" 131°08'00" SE entrance to Houston Stewart Channel, off S end of Moresby I, QCI). The 90-tonne sloop *Lady Washington* left Boston in 1787 under the command of Capt Robert Gray and arrived at Nootka Sd one year later, part of the first US fur-trading expedition to the PNW, led by John Kendrick in the *Columbia Rediviva*. Gray traded successfully off the QCI in 1789, then took the *Columbia* to China that summer with a cargo of furs. Kendrick, a bullying, ineffectual leader, sailed the *Lady Washington* back to Haida Gwaii and managed to ruin white-aboriginal relations in the region by deeply insulting the powerful Haida chief Koya and turning him into a dedicated enemy. After selling his furs in China and visiting Japan (the first US ship capt to do so), Kendrick returned to the QCI with the *Lady Washington*, now refitted as a brig, in 1791 and rebuffed an attack by Koya with great loss of Haida life. After this defeat the vengeful chieftain spun out of control, inflicting a reign of terror on the region until killed by John Boit and the crew of the *Union* in 1795. The *Lady Washington* was wrecked off the Philippines in 1798. A replica ship, built in 1989 for the Washington state centennial, has travelled widely in the PNW and appeared in several films. The rock was named by the hydrographic service in 1962. *D*

Waskesiu Passage (52°09'00" 128°25'00" Between Athlone I and Princess Alice I, N end of Queens Sd, W of Bella Bella). HMCS *Waskesiu* was the first RCN frigate built at Esquimalt by the Yarrows shipyard. It was commissioned in June 1943 and taken directly to Halifax for service in the N Atlantic. In Feb 1944; under Lt Cdr James Fraser, the frigate sank a German submarine, *U-257*, after forcing it to the surface with depth charges and then destroying it with gunfire. The 92-m, 1,660-tonne vessel was decommissioned in 1946 and transferred to the Indian navy in 1950 as the *Hooghly*. It was named after Waskesiu Lk in Prince Albert National Park, Sask; the word means "elk" in Cree. The passage was named by the hydrographic service in 1944.

Wastell Islets (Just NW of Wastell Point), **Wastell Point** (50°33'00" 126°49'00" W entrance to Bauza Cove, just E of Beaver Cove, S side of Johnstone Str, E of Port McNeill). Albert Marmaduke "Duke" Wastell (1872–1962) was born at Haliburton, Ont, and learned the box-making trade at a nearby lumber mill. He came to BC in the mid-1890s and worked at the Barnet sawmill in N Burnaby. In 1898 his fiancée, Mary Elizabeth "Mame" Sharpe (1871–1951), came to BC also and married Albert at New Westminster. After returning to Ont and then coming back to BC, the Wastells and their son Fred moved to Alert Bay in 1909, where Duke managed a sawmill and box-making factory for the BC Fishing & Packing Co. He was also appointed the district magistrate. In the mid-1920s he and a group of Japanese partners built a chum salmon saltery and primitive box mill at Telegraph Cove, where Wastell had earlier acquired some timber holdings. When the Alert Bay box factory closed in 1928, Fred Wastell and Alex Macdonald expanded the Telegraph Cove (qv) mill and founded a small community there. *E*

Waterfall Inlet (51°38'00" 127°43'00" N side of Fish Egg Inlet, between Fitz Hugh Sd and Rivers Inlet, SE of Bella Bella). This local name was submitted by Sidney's Institute of Ocean Sciences in 1985. The waterfall is halfway along the E shore of the inlet.

Waterman Point (53°22'00" 129°16'00" At the junction of Douglas Channel and Grenville Channel, SW of Kitimat). Flight Lt Thomas John Davies Waterman, DFC, who had enlisted at Victoria, was killed in action Sept 3, 1943, aged 23, while flying Lancaster heavy bombers with No 207 (RAF) Squadron. Only two weeks before he was killed, Waterman had taken part in Operation Hydra, a raid on the V-2 rocket plant at Peenemunde, Germany, that delayed production of the deadly missiles for about two months. His name is inscribed on the Runnymede Memorial in Surrey, UK. Waterman Point was formerly known as Camp Point but was renamed in 1950.

Wathus Island (53°41'00" 132°29'00" W side of Masset Inlet, Graham I, QCI). This feature was first charted by geologist George Dawson in 1878 as Wat-hoo-us, its Haida First Nation name. In 1907 it was called Young I by the Graham Steamship, Coal & Lumber Co, after John Young, who was a timber cruiser for the firm in 1906–7.

Both names were in use until the 1920s, but Wathus I has long since prevailed as the official, gazetted name. *D*

Watson Island (50°56'00" 126°49'00" N of N Broughton I, entrance to Mackenzie Sd, NE of Port McNeill), **Watson Island** (54°14'00" 130°18'00" E side of Porpoise Hbr, just S of Kaien I and Prince Rupert), **Watson Point** (50°57'00" 126°51'00" W side of Watson I, N of N Broughton I). Alexander Watson (1831–92), from Scotland, came to Victoria in 1859 as a cashier for the Bank of BNA. In 1863 he married Jessie McKenzie (1844–82), second daughter of Kenneth McKenzie, manager of the HBC's Craigflower Farm (*see* Jessie Point). Watson was appointed treasurer of the colony of Vancouver I in 1866 and later became gen inspector of the Bank of BC. In 1871 he announced in the Victoria *Colonist* that the family was moving to Leith, Scotland, where he would be managing a "large manufacturing estate," but the Watsons must have subsequently moved to California, as both Alexander and Jessie died at Oakland. The southern Watson I was named in 1866; Watson Point was formerly known as George Point. Watson I at Prince Rupert is an unofficial name (though widely used); the feature is actually a peninsula. It is home to the Skeena Cellulose pulp mill and connected to Kaien I by a CNR bridge.

Watson Rock (53°55'00" 130°10'00" Off W side of Gibson I, N end of Grenville Channel, S of Prince Rupert). Christopher Robert Watson was assistant paymaster aboard HMS *Malacca* on the Pacific Station in 1866–67, under Capt Radulphus Oldfield. He was promoted to paymaster in 1877 and reached the rank of fleet paymaster, retired, in 1889. Named by Lt Daniel Pender of the hired vessel *Beaver* in 1867.

Wattie Point (52°37'00" 127°02'00" E side of Dean Channel, NW of Bella Coola). Named in 1958 for two brothers, James (1829–1907) and William Wattie (1842–1918), who were among the Overlanders of 1862—a group of stalwart gold seekers and immigrants who crossed the Canadian prairies by cart and horseback from Ft Garry via Ft Edmonton to the headwaters of the Fraser R. James was born at Aberdeen, Scotland, and came to N America with his parents in 1838; he spent three years in California, 1852–55. William was born in Canada and apprenticed as a machinist at Montreal. In BC, the Watties and William Fortune, curious about the country, rafted down the Fraser R and hiked from Alexandria to Bella Coola later in 1862, then travelled to Victoria by canoe and steamship. The following year they returned to the Cariboo and did well at Williams Ck, where James was foreman on John Cameron's profitable gold claim. The brothers left the goldfields in the mid-1860s, and James later managed wool mills in Que and Massachusetts, where he apparently invented and patented numerous devices designed to improve the operation of weaving machinery.

Watt Islet (49°43'20" 124°11'00" Blind Bay, S entrance to Jervis Inlet, NW of Vancouver). Motor Mechanic John Arthur Watt of the RCNVR, from Vancouver, died while on active service on Feb 14, 1945, aged 23. He was a member of the 29th Canadian Motor Torpedo Boat Flotilla, which was virtually destroyed during an accidental fire at Ostend harbour, Belgium. Sixty-three Canadian and British sailors were killed in the disaster. Watt is commemorated on the Halifax Memorial. The name was adopted in 1990.

Watt Point (48°20'00" 123°33'00" S side of Pedder Bay, S tip of Vancouver I). Dr Alfred Tennyson Watt (1868–1913), born at Meaford, Ont, was in charge of the quarantine station at nearby William Head, 1897–1913. He had graduated from Univ of Toronto in 1890 and practised medicine at Victoria, becoming secretary to the provincial board of health and making important contributions to the Health Act and to public health work in BC. In 1913, Watt quarantined a vessel arriving from Asia, the CPR's *Monteagle*, which had two cases of smallpox on board. First-class passengers, unaccustomed to the station's relatively primitive living conditions, mounted a well-publicized protest at their confinement, much of which was directed at Dr Watt personally, and managed to set in motion a commission of inquiry. Watt, who was dealing with a range of problems at the time, committed suicide (and was posthumously cleared of any wrongdoing). His wife, Margaret Rose Watt, OBE (1868–1948, née Robertson)—more familiarly known as Madge Robertson Watt—was a Canadian writer and feminist, a founder of the Federation of Women's Institutes in Canada, member of the UBC senate and leader of several international women's movements. Watt Point was known in the early days as Shoal Point.

Watts Narrows (53°49'00" 129°57'00" Entrance to Baker Inlet, Grenville Channel, opposite NE Pitt I). After Robert Watts Davies (1843–1903), born at Charlottetown, PEI, who served with the RN as a midshipman on the BC coast, 1860–62, before being promoted to lt in 1864 and cdr in 1878. He married Fanny Ramsbotham (1852–1945) in Sussex, England, in 1872, and died in Oxfordshire (*see* Griffon Point, as well). Robert's brother, Sir Louis Davies, became Canada's minister of Marine and Fisheries, 1896–1901 (*see* Davies Bay). Robert was also the father of Louis R Davies (1879–1964), who joined the Canadian Hydrographic Service in 1906 and spent his entire career as a surveyor on the BC coast, retiring in 1947, at which time he was in charge of chart production and distribution at Victoria (*see* Louis Is).

Watts Point (49°39'00" 123°13'00" E side of Howe Sd, NW of Britannia Beach, NW of Vancouver). This feature, which first appears on Admiralty charts in 1863, is possibly named after Isaac Watts (1797–1876), who was the RN's chief ship designer for many years (he had the

titles assistant surveyor, 1848–59, and chief constructor, 1859–63). Watts occupied his important position at a time of great technological change. He designed the first ironclads, for instance—the largest, most powerful and heavily armed warships ever built—including HMS *Warrior*, *Black Prince*, *Achilles*, *Agincourt*, *Minotaur* and *Northumberland*.

Watun River (53°54'00" 132°05'00" Flows NW into Masset Sd, Graham I, QCI). An early settlement, complete with a church and school, was established at the mouth of this river by J B McDonald, a Roman Catholic priest, in 1912. It was originally known as Woden R (a version of the Haida name Watun), and also as the Holy City because of its religious orientation. The area was later the site of a Seventh Day Adventist community, a hotel, boatbuilding sheds and a cannery. When the cannery closed in 1930 the place was abandoned. The origin of the Haida name is not known. *D E*

Wearing Point (52°18'00" 127°45'00" W side of Cousins Inlet, Dean Channel, SW of Ocean Falls). According to a note at BC's Geographical Names Office, this feature was named after the engineer who built the dam across the outlet to Link Lk in 1910–11, thus providing the pulp and paper town of Ocean Falls with its essential source of hydroelectric power.

Wearmouth Rock (52°53'00" 129°08'00" Entrance to Surf Inlet, W side of Princess Royal I). Named by regional hydrographer Lt Cdr Philip Musgrave after Cecil Wylam Wearmouth (1880–1941), who was skipper of several GTP steamships that served the QCI in the 1910s. He was master of the *Prince Albert* in 1910–11, then took over the *Prince John* for several years. Wearmouth married Kate Brand (b 1892) at Prince Rupert in 1914.

Webber Island (52°55'00" 129°08'00" Entrance to Chapple Inlet, W side of Princess Royal I). John Webber (1751–93), born at London of Swiss heritage, was the official artist on Capt James Cook's third voyage to the S Pacific, 1776–80. He was apprenticed to Johann Ludwig Aberli, a leading landscape artist, at Berne. After further training at Paris, he returned to London and studied at the Royal Academy, where his work was noticed by Daniel Solander, the botanist on Cook's first voyage. Solander recommended him to the Admiralty, and Webber was offered a place in Cook's HMS *Resolution*, which he accepted. He was an excellent choice, making about 200 superb drawings and paintings, including 29—the earliest representations of BC coastal life—that depicted Nootka Sd and its inhabitants. Back in England, Webber supervised production of the engravings that illustrated Cook's published journals and also made and sold his own prints from the voyage. He was elected to the Royal Academy as an associate in 1785 and a full member in 1791, and undertook a series of painting

John Webber made the first detailed drawings of BC's coastal First Nation people, at Nootka Sound in 1778. He accompanied Captain James Cook on his third great expedition. *BC Archives PDP00228*

tours to France, Switzerland, England and Wales. Sadly, just as his reputation was growing, Webber died of kidney disease. He never married. There are public collections of his work at the Anchorage Museum of History and Art in Alaska, Bishop Museum in Honolulu, Yale Univ Art Gallery, British Museum, Mitchell Library in Sydney and elsewhere. Hydrographers at the Victoria office had originally proposed to name this feature Jeffreys I in 1944, after Unity Theodora Jeffreys Baile, a young staff member, but were overruled by officials in Ottawa and reprimanded for using "too many names of your office staff ... without reasonable discretion." *E*

Webb Island (53°35'00" 130°34'00" W side of Rawlinson Anchorage, off NW end of Banks I), **Webb Rock** (Just N of Webb I). W H Webb and A V Webb returned from overseas service with the Canadian Expeditionary Force in WWI and were working as sounders on board the W coast survey vessel *Lillooet* in 1921. The island is named for W H, the rock for A V, which suggests that they were probably brothers.

Wedgborough Point (51°39'00" 127°57'00" NE side of Calvert I, W side of Fitz Hugh Sd, S of Bella Bella). Samuel Wedgborough accompanied the fur-trading expedition to the PNW led by James Strange in 1786. His exact role is uncertain, though he was obviously an influential figure on board the *Experiment*, under Capt John Guise, the smaller of Strange's two vessels. Wedgborough may have been a supercargo or owner's representative; he made charts of the voyage, some of which were later engraved. Capt George Vancouver stated in his journal that Wedgborough was in command of the *Experiment* and had named

Queen Charlotte Sd, but most historians believe that he was mistaken in these observations.

Weeolk Passage (51°32'00" 127°42'00" NW of Welch I, Darby Channel, entrance to Rivers Inlet). According to BC historians Helen and Philip Akrigg, when Rivers Inlet was re-surveyed in the late 1930s, a number of names were bestowed to honour the family of Methodist medical missionary Dr George Darby, who operated a summer hospital on the inlet for many years while based at Bella Bella. Weeolk was a Heiltsuk First Nation nickname given to one of the Darby children.

Weeteeam Bay (52°31'00" 129°01'00" SW side of Aristazabal I). Named after a reserve and former fishing camp on the NW corner of this bay belonging to the Kitasoo First Nation, a Tsimshian-speaking people who settled at Klemtu on Swindle I in the 1870s. This is probably the Bay of Disappointment of US fur trader Joseph Ingraham, so named in 1791 because it proved to be uninhabited and an inferior anchorage.

Weewanie Creek (53°41'27" 128°47'11" Flows SW into Devastation Channel opposite N end of Hawkesbury I, S of Kitimat), **Weewanie Hot Springs** (53°41'48" 128°47'20" Just N of Weewanie Ck). The name comes from the Haisla First Nation word *wiwaa*, meaning "many creeks." The remains of a logging operation are still visible at the mouth of Weewanie Ck. In 2004 the hot springs were designated a 35-ha provincial park; a bathhouse is provided for the enjoyment of weary visiting boaters.

Weinberg Inlet (53°08'00" 129°32'00" NW side of Campania I, NE end of Estevan Sd, S of Pitt I). Jack Leonard Weinberg (d 1990) was 1st officer of the W coast survey vessel *William J Stewart* in the early 1940s. He was a native of Finland and initially earned his living as a fisherman, later becoming a ship's officer and eventually qualifying as a BC coast pilot. Weinberg married Marie Irene Canonica (1909–2007) at Victoria in 1930 and lived mostly in that city and Vancouver. The inlet was named in 1944.

Weir Beach (48°21'00" 123°32'00" On Parker Bay, S of Parry Bay, near S tip of Vancouver I), **Weir Point** (48°20'00" 123°33'00" N side of Pedder Bay, S end of Vancouver I). Robert Weir (1809–94), hired by HBC bailiff Kenneth McKenzie as head stockman or "land steward" on the Craigflower Farm, came to Vancouver I in 1853 in the HBC supply ship *Norman Morison*. He was accompanied by five of his sons: William, John, James, Hugh and Adam. The Weirs acquired land at William Head in the 1850s and '60s, and when their terms of service with the HBC were concluded, they developed a substantial farm in the area. By the 1870s they were the largest landowners in Metchosin, with more than 400 ha of property, where they raised sheep and, later, dairy cattle (and trained border collies, as well). The younger Weirs also pursued interests in mining and logging. Descendants of the Weir family still live in the district. Robert Weir was an unsuccessful candidate for Esquimalt in the 1875 BC provincial election. Weir Point, named by the hydrographic service in 1934, was formerly known as Turn Point.

Welbury Bay (48°51'00" 123°26'00" E side of Saltspring I, E of Ganges Hbr, Gulf Is), **Welbury Point** (SW entrance to Welbury Bay). Named by Cdr John Parry of HMS *Egeria*, while re-surveying Ganges Hbr in 1905, after Welbury House at Bradford, Yorkshire. Welbury was a former residence of Saltspring farmer William Scott (*see* Scott Point), who owned the land around Welbury Bay in those early days.

Welch Rock (52°14'00" 128°27'00" Off NW side of Athlone I, Milbanke Sd, NW of Bella Bella). Matilda Welch (1840–1905) came to Canada from Ireland in 1860 and married Michael Muir (1835–88), a son of Vancouver I pioneer John Muir, in 1862. The Muir family had immigrated to BC in 1849 to work at the HBC's Ft Rupert coal mines (*see* Muir Cove). They later settled at Sooke and farmed. The Muirs also operated an early sawmill and ran a small steamship, the *Woodside*, to Victoria, where John and his sons established a lumber yard. Michael Muir served as district magistrate and coroner, and was also Sooke postmaster from 1872 to 1888.

Northwest view of Welcome Passage. *Peter Vassilopoulos*

Welcome Beach (49°29'00" 123°54'00" E side of Welcome Passage), **Welcome Passage** (49°30'00" 123°56'00" Between Thormanby Is and SW end of Sechelt Peninsula, Str of Georgia, NW of Vancouver). In 1860, Capt George Richards, who was conducting a coastal survey with HMS *Plumper*, applied a number of horse-racing names in this vicinity. He and his officers appear to have been betting men, as they "welcomed" the news that the racehorse Thormanby had won the famous Epsom Derby earlier that year. The small community located on nearby Halfmoon

Bay was known as Welcome Pass in the early days; this was the official name of its post office from 1894 to 1915. Welcome Beach is named after Welcome Passage. Nearby Reception Point (qv) was originally called Welcome Point; it was named in association with the passage in 1898, when the shoal off the point was examined and marked with a buoy, but was changed in 1944.

Welcome Harbour. *See* Adams Hbr.

Weld Cove (52°48'00" 128°46'00" W side of Laredo Inlet, S part of Princess Royal I). According to a record at BC's Geographical Names Office, Samuel Weld was an English lawyer who immigrated to the US in the 1850s and worked in Chicago before coming to BC. In 1862, Gov James Douglas appointed him magistrate of the Stikine territory.

Welde Rock (50°53'00" 126°56'00" Entrance to Drury Inlet, N side of Queen Charlotte Str, NE of Port McNeill). Named by the hydrographic service in 1958 after Donald Welde, who had recently drowned while trying to run nearby Roaringhole Rapids in a speedboat. The rock is noted for its marine life and is a popular dive site.

Welgeegenk Point (54°44'00" 130°13'00" N entrance to Khutzeymateen Inlet, N of Prince Rupert). This Tsimshian First Nation name may mean "a warm spot" or "place where it is warm."

Wellbore Channel (50°27'00" 125°45'00" E of Hardwicke I, between Chancellor Channel and Sunderland Channel, NW of Campbell R). After Capt John Wellbore Sunderland Spencer, who served on the RN's Pacific Station, 1859–63. *See* Spencer Ledge. This was the Canal de Nuevos Remolinos ("new whirlpools") of Spanish explorer Dionisio Alcalá-Galiano.

Wellington Rock (52°12'00" 128°09'00" N of Ormidale Hbr, Campbell I, just N of Bella Bella). According to Capt John Walbran, who examined and named this feature in 1902 while master of the lighthouse tender *Quadra*, the rock commemorates the steamship *Wellington*, which "grazed" the unmarked hazard earlier that year. The 83-m, 1,150-tonne collier, built at Newcastle, England, in 1883 and owned by coal baron and BC premier James Dunsmuir, was en route from Ladysmith to Juneau, under Capt Colin Salmond, when the incident occurred. The *Wellington* was somewhat prone to accidents: in 1892 it lost power and drifted for four days before being rescued and towed to San Francisco; six months later the vessel again spent several days adrift in the open ocean after suffering a broken shaft.

Wells Cove (52°21'00" 131°33'00" Just S of Gowgaia Bay, SW side of Moresby I, QCI). Named about 1912 by Capt Absalom Freeman after one of the mates of the *Celestial*

Empire, a steam halibut trawler owned by the Canadian Fishing Co that often operated off the W coast of the QCI.

Wells Islet (53°35'00" 130°35'00" Off W side of Banks I, SW of Griffith Hbr), **Wells Rocks** (52°45'00" 129°29'00" W of Anderson Is, off NW side of Aristazabal I, Hecate Str). John Wells (1890–1975) served aboard the W coast survey vessel *Lillooet* in the 1920s. He was coxswain of the starboard launch in 1921, when the islet was named, and was promoted to 1st officer in 1923. The rocks, previously known as the Gull Rks, were named for him about 1925. The Muriel Rks (qv), farther S, are named after his wife, Muriel Mary Wells (1904–85, née Church), whom he married at Victoria in 1926. The Wells were long-time residents of Victoria.

Wells Passage (50°51'00" 126°55'00" W side of N Broughton I, NE side of Queen Charlotte Str, N of Port McNeill). Named in 1792 by Capt George Vancouver, who explored the area that summer with his ships' boats while anchored for a week at Simoom Sd. RN officer John Wells (1763–1841) was appointed a capt in 1783 and gained distinction while commanding HMS *Lancaster* at the Battle of Camperdown, a 1797 British victory over the Dutch. He was knighted in 1820 and promoted to adm the following year. *W*

Welsford Islands (50°13'00" 125°08'00" Part of the Settlers Group, N end of Hoskyn Channel, between Read I and Quadra I, NE of Campbell R). The Liverpool shipping firm of J H Welsford & Co Ltd bought control of BC's Union Steamship Co in 1911. James Hugh Welsford (1864–1917), the principal owner, was a dynamic figure in British shipping circles. By age 36 he had acquired a fleet of nine cargo vessels and carried cotton from Galveston, Texas, to Liverpool under the name Gulf Transport Line. In 1911 he also purchased the Leyland Shipping Co, which was active in the W Indies and Central America, and the Canadian Mexican Line, hoping that the soon-to-be-open Panama Canal would link his companies together in a beneficial way. Welsford tried three times, quite unsuccessfully, to get elected to the British Parliament as a Conservative MP. His son, Richard A H Welsford, who became president of the company following his father's premature demise, had an even shorter lifespan, dying in 1931 at the age of 35. In 1937 a group of Vancouver businessmen bought out the majority Welsford interest and returned ownership of the Union Steamship Co to BC.

Werner Bay (52°29'00" 131°28'00" W side of Juan Perez Sd, E side of Moresby I, QCI), **Werner Point** (52°30'00" 131°28'00" N entrance to Werner Bay). Named in 1878 by George Dawson of the Geological Survey of Canada after Abraham Gottlob Werner (1749–1817), an eminent German geologist. He studied law and mining, and became instructor of mineralogy at the small but important Freiberg Mining Academy in 1775. Werner's grand theory, known as Neptunism, held that the Earth was once completely covered by an ocean that precipitated all the rocks and minerals in the planetary crust and gradually receded to its present boundaries. He then divided the crust into five formations or layers, depending on certain characteristics. While Werner's ideas have today been completely abandoned, he was, in his time, the most influential geologist in Europe. Werner Point was named by the hydrographic service in 1962. Nearby Abraham Point and Gottlob Point are also named for him. Marshall Inlet and Matheson Inlet, which extend W and SW from the bay, were known by local fishermen for many years as N and S Werner Bay, respectively. *D W*

Weser Island (50°52'00" 128°02'00" At W entrance to Goletas Channel, E of Cape Sutil, off N end of Vancouver I). RN surveyor Capt George Richards named this feature about 1862 in association with Commerell Point (qv, now Sutil Point), after HMS *Weser*, one of the commands of British naval officer John Edmund Commerell. He was in charge of this iron paddleboat, originally built for the Prussian navy in 1851 and named the *Salamander*, in 1855, when he won the VC for a daring commando attack on a Russian supply depot on the Sea of Azov. Commerell, a cdr at the time, went on to become an adm, a knight and a lord of the Admiralty. The 490-tonne, 4-gun *Weser* saw service in the Mediterranean and had a brief S American posting to the River Plate, where it was found to be quite unsuitable. The vessel was decommissioned in 1873. *W*

Wesley Island (50°15'00" 125°10'00" In Okisollo Channel, N of Surge Narrows, between Maurelle I and Quadra I, N of Campbell R). After Lt Col Cyrus Wesley Peck, VC, DSO, politician and WWI hero. *See* Peck I.

West Bay (48°26'00" 123°24'00" Victoria Hbr, N of Work Point, SE end of Vancouver I). Named by Capt Henry Kellett of HMS *Herald*, who surveyed the S coast of Vancouver I in 1846–47, and marked on Joseph Pemberton's 1855 map of SE Vancouver I. In the 1930s, because of the duplication of place names with West in them, regional hydrographer Henri Parizeau tried hard to get the feature renamed Bolduc Bay, after pioneer Roman Catholic missionary Jean Baptiste Bolduc, and even went so far as to introduce the new name on a chart without authorization. The Geographic Board of Canada turned down his request, however. An Ottawa mandarin reminded Parizeau of "the Board's first and most important rule for nomenclature," which was "that old and well-established names should be retained," especially ones "so close to the capital and ... well known." Fr Bolduc, who came to Ft Victoria with James Douglas and other HBC officials in 1843, had a mountain NE of Port Renfrew named for him instead.

West Bay (49°20'00" 123°13'00" N side of Burrard Inlet, E of Sandy Cove, W Vancouver). In 1929 this feature was officially named Patterson Cove, after pioneer Vancouver pilot Capt Donald Patterson (d 1913). The original local name, however, was West Bay, and this designation continued in popular use to such an extent that the new name had to be abandoned. West Bay was made official in 1953.

West Bedford Island. *See* Pim Head.

Westcott Point (50°59'00" 127°28'00" N side of Shelter Bay, NW side of Queen Charlotte Str, N of Port Hardy). Able Seaman James Herbert Westcott, of Victoria, died on active service, Nov 6, 1939, aged 29, while aboard the *Fraser*, an RCN destroyer, at Halifax. He is buried at Esquimalt's Veterans Cemetery. HMCS *Fraser* was later lost off the coast of France in 1940 after it collided in rough weather with HMS *Calcutta*.

West Cracroft Island. *See* Cracroft Inlet.

Wester Point (52°46'00" 131°59'00" NW tip of Botany I, Tasu Sd, W side of Moresby I, QCI). George Wester (b 1859), a native of Norway, came to California in 1880 as a seaman on the *Three Brothers* and worked out of San Francisco for a number of years. In 1887 he sailed from that port in the sealing schooner *Lillie L*, which was seized by a US revenue cutter; the crew members were left to fend for themselves at Sitka. Wester later served as mate and hunter on other sealers, including the *City of San Diego*, *Rosie Olsen*, *James Hamilton Lewis* and *Mary Ellen*. By 1892 he was master of the *Emma Louise*, and in 1893–94 he had charge of the *Allie I Alger* out of Seattle. Later in his career, Wester commanded the five-masted barquentine *Kate G Pedersen*, which hauled lumber from the PNW to Australia, and the barque *Pactolus*, which took a National Geographic expedition to Alaska's Katmai National Park in 1919.

Westham Island (49°05'00" 123°09'00" Mouth of the Fraser R, S of Vancouver). It has been suggested by Westham residents that this name derives from the island's westerly location in the delta of the Fraser R. A more likely explanation, however, is that it is named after West Ham in Essex, now part of greater London, which was the original home of early settler Harry Trim, who had a varied career as a fisherman, whaler and prospector. Henry Mitchell was one of the first to farm on the island, in the 1870s. The Westham landscape is still completely agricultural, though the NW part of the island is now also an important bird refuge, home to the Alaksen National Wildlife Area and the George C Reifel Migratory Bird Sanctuary, which occupies neighbouring Reifel I as well. *E*

West Kinahan Island. *See* Kinahan Is.

Westminster Point (52°04'00" 128°05'00" W entrance to Cooper Inlet, Lama Passage, N side of Hunter I, SE of Bella Bella). Named in association with nearby Harbourmaster Point and Cooper Inlet (qv) by Lt Daniel Pender in 1866. Capt James Cooper was harbourmaster of the colony of BC, based at New Westminster, from 1860 to 1868. In 1864, when Pender was surveying the area around Sand Heads at the mouth of the Fraser R, Cooper marked the channel for him with beacons and wooden buoys, as the permanent metal buoys had not yet arrived from England.

West Race Rocks. *See* Race Passage.

The salmon cannery at Redonda Bay on West Redonda Island.
BC Archives D-09320

West Redonda Island (50°13'00" 124°53'00" At entrance to Toba Inlet, NE of Campbell R). Spanish naval officers Dionisio Alcalá-Galiano and Cayetano Valdés named Isla Redonda (Spanish for "round") in 1792, not realizing that it consisted of two islands. They anchored near Teakerne Arm at W Redonda I for several weeks with Capt George Vancouver's two vessels while exploring the region in small boats. Over the years the 280-sq-km Redondas have seen some mining (iron ore) and quarrying (limestone); a substantial salmon cannery; fruit, vegetable, hog, shellfish and fur farming; lots of logging; and tourism. A small but vibrant community used to exist at Redonda Bay (qv), while the one at Refuge Cove (qv) still thrives. *E*

West Thurlow Island. *See* Thurlow Is.

West Vancouver (49°22'00" 123°10'00" N side of Burrard Inlet, just NW of Vancouver). W Vancouver was incorporated as a district municipality in 1912, when the W Capilano District seceded from the municipality of N Vancouver. The name was in use before that, however, as John Lawson was operating a ferry service, called the W Vancouver Transportation Co, across Burrard Inlet as early as 1910. The community got its start in the 1880s, when Vancouver residents began building summer cottages there. As it developed over the years to become one of

W

Canada's wealthiest suburbs, W Vancouver managed to carefully preserve its residential character. It is part of the traditional territory of the Squamish First Nation. *E*

Weyburn Rock (52°01'00" 128°26'00" Off N end of Goose Group, Queens Sd, SW of Bella Bella). The corvette HMCS *Weyburn*, under Lt Cdr Thomas Golby (*see* Golby Passage), struck a mine and sank in the Mediterranean off Cape Espartel, E of Gibraltar, while on convoy duty in Feb 1943. Seven crew members, including Lt Cdr Golby, were killed. The 63-m, 862-tonne vessel was built at Port Arthur, Ont, and launched in 1941. It had a speed of 16 knots and a complement of six officers and 79 crew. The rock was named in 1944. Mickey I (qv), in the entrance to Howe Sd, used to be called Weyburn I, also after this vessel, from the mid-1940s until 1951.

A homemade photoview postcard of Whaletown, dated 1913.
Author's collection

Weynton Island (50°34'00" 126°47'00" Off W side of Hanson I, NW end of Johnstone Str, E of Port McNeill), **Weynton Passage** (50°35'00" 126°49'00" Between the Pearse Is and Plumper Is, W of Hanson I, SE of Malcolm I). Stephenson Weynton was working for the HBC at Ft Rupert on N Vancouver I in 1860, the year RN surveyor Capt George Richards visited the fort and named the passage after him. The Weyntons were an HBC family: Stephenson's father, Alexander Weynton (d 1847), was the company's marine superintendent in London and a member of its governing committee; his brother, Alexander John Weynton, was master of the HBC barque *Cowlitz*, 1846–51. Company officials at Ft Rupert helped Capt Richards obtain the release of a First Nation woman, the mother-in-law of Jack Dolholt (*see* Jack Point), who had been captured near Nanaimo and was being held in the Ft Rupert area. In 1865, at Victoria, Stephenson married Emma Jane O'Brien, a native of New Orleans, who died at San Francisco in 1869, aged 19. *W*

Whalen Point (53°37'00" 130°18'00" W side of McCauley I, W of Table Hill, Principe Channel, S of Prince Rupert). Flight Lt James Henry Whalen, DFC, of Vancouver, was killed in action on Apr 18, 1944, while flying Hawker Hurricane fighters with No 34 (RAF) Squadron. He had earlier served with No 411 and No 129 (Mysore) squadrons, where he flew Spitfires. Whalen was an RCAF air ace, with six German and Japanese kills to his credit. He is buried at the Kohima War Cemetery in India, near the Burmese border.

Whaler Bay (48°53'00" 123°20'00" SE side of Galiano I, Gulf Is). Cdr John Parry of the RN survey ship *Egeria* applied this local name in 1903 when he was re-surveying Active Pass. Small whaling vessels supposedly used the western end of the bay for anchorage.

Whaletown (On Whaletown Bay), **Whaletown Bay** (50°06'00" 125°03'00" W side of Cortes I, N end of Str of

Georgia). James Dawson of Victoria's Dawson Whaling Co established a whaling station on the bay in 1869–70, where he and Abel Douglas supervised the rendering of whale blubber in large kettles or try-works. Dawson moved his operation to Whaling Station Bay on Hornby I in 1870 (*see below*), but he and Douglas, using the schooner *Kate*, had largely eradicated the local whale population by 1872 (another bout of whaling in the early 1900s finished off the Str of Georgia's humpbacks). A steamship landing, store and post office were built at Whaletown in the mid-1890s and a small community grew up around them. Today the village is the site of a BC Ferries terminal, which provides a link between Cortes I and Heriot Bay on Quadra I.

Whaling Station Bay (49°32'00" 124°36'00" NE side of Hornby I, W side of Str of Georgia). After moving their whaling base from Cortes I (*see* Whaletown) to Hornby I in 1870, James Dawson and Abel Douglas joined forces with the Lipsett Whaling Co to form the BC Whaling Co. By 1872 they had almost completely depleted the stock of humpback whales in the Str of Georgia. That year the entire assets of the BC Whaling Co were sold at auction, including the *Kate* and a "pre-emption claim on Hornby I of 100 acres, with well-built wharf, frame building, cooper's shop, sheds, etc." The Hornby station probably only operated during the 1871 season.

Whidbey Point (51°43'00" 127°53'00" E side of Fitz Hugh Sd, N of Kwakume Inlet, SE of Bella Bella), **Whidbey Reach** (53°21'00" 127°59'00" Toward E end of Gardner Canal, SE of Kemano R, SE of Kitimat). Joseph Whidbey (1755–1833) played an important role in the exploration of the BC coast. As master of Capt George Vancouver's HMS *Discovery*, he did a lot of the actual survey work, leading numerous exhausting journeys with the ships' small boats along the convoluted shorelines. A master, in Vancouver's day, was the senior warrant or non-commissioned officer and was usually responsible for the day-to-day navigation of the vessel (the rank would later be reclassified as navigating lt). Many masters were former merchant skippers, and most were seamen of great experience. Whidbey, for instance, had been an RN master since 1779 and held that position on HMS *Europa*, flagship on the W Indies Station, in 1786, when Vancouver was the ship's 3rd lt. The two men, in fact, collaborated on a survey off Jamaica, and the charts that resulted were published under both their names. Vancouver placed great confidence and trust in Whidbey, and helped him secure an appointment as master attendant at Sheerness dockyard in 1795, when the expedition to the PNW concluded. In 1805, Whidbey was elected a fellow of the Royal Society, primarily for the skill he had shown in raising a sunken Dutch frigate, the *Ambuscade*; Sir Joseph Banks himself read an account of the feat before the society's assembled members. In 1806, when Whidbey was master attendant at Woolwich dockyard, he and two colleagues designed a breakwater for Plymouth Sd. Construction finally began in 1812 with Whidbey as superintending engineer—a position he would hold until his retirement in 1830 (the breakwater was not finished until 1841). He died at Taunton. Whidbey Reach was named in 1907, when Capt Frederick Learmonth re-surveyed Gardner Canal. Whidbey I, across the US border in Puget Sd, commemorates him as well. *W*

Whiffin Spit (48°21'00" 123°45'00" At entrance to Sooke Hbr, S end of Vancouver I). John George Whiffin (1826–92) was a clerk aboard HMS *Herald*, under Capt Henry Kellett, on the BC coast in 1846–47. He served with the *Herald* for six years, accompanying Kellett to the Arctic on his search for the missing Sir John Franklin, and was appointed to the rank of paymaster in 1851. During the Crimean War he was assigned to HMS *Gladiator* and present at numerous actions in the Baltic, the Black Sea and off Turkey. Whiffin was promoted to paymaster in chief, retired, in 1873, and five years later became secretary of the Royal Indian Engineering College. Today the 1-km-long spit is a regional park and a favourite walking trail. *W*

Whirlwind Bay (51°52'00" 127°52'00" Namu Hbr, E side of Fitz Hugh Sd, SE of Bella Bella). Named for the violent gusts that blow down off the mountains in this vicinity. According to *Sailing Directions*, "during autumn and winter months, anchorage ... is not recommended."

Whiteaves Bay (53°11'00" 132°02'00" SW of Alliford Bay, N end of Moresby I, QCI). Joseph Frederick Whiteaves (1835–1909) was an eminent paleontologist and zoologist who immigrated to Canada from England in 1862. From 1863 to 1875 he was curator and secretary of the Natural History Society of Montreal, where he studied marine and freshwater invertebrates as well as the region's fossils. He then joined the Geological Survey of Canada, becoming GSC zoologist in 1883, and was a founding fellow of the Royal Society of Canada in 1882. Whiteaves wrote more than 100 papers, several of which concern late

19th-century fossil collections from BC, including those specimens brought back from the Skidegate Inlet region by George M Dawson in 1878. In 1921, geologist Dr G H McLearn visited Skidegate Inlet and named the point just to the NE of this bay—an excellent fossil site—after Whiteaves, though the name was never officially adopted. The bay was finally named in 1985, after a submission by Glenn Woodsworth of the geological survey's Vancouver office. Mt Whiteaves on the BC-Alberta border N of Golden also honours this distinguished scientist. *D*

Whyte Islet, part of Whytecliff Park, West Vancouver. *Andrew Scott*

White Cliff Point (49°22'00" 123°18'00" Westernmost point in W Vancouver, SE side of Howe Sd, just NW of Vancouver), **Whytecliff** (49°22'00" 123°17'00" W of Horseshoe Bay, W Vancouver), **Whyte Cove** (Just E of White Cliff Point), **Whyte Islet** (Just S of White Cliff Point). White Cliff Point was named for its weathered appearance by RN surveyor Capt George Richards about 1859. It was known locally as Copperhouse Point in the 1870s and '80s, after Howe Sd Copper Mines Ltd opened a short-lived mine there. In 1907, real-estate promoter Col Albert Whyte (1847–1939) and lawyer Sir Charles Tupper bought land nearby and began to develop a summer cottage complex called Whytecliff Park Resort. When the PGE was built through the area in 1914, the well-connected Col Whyte persuaded his friends at the railway to name the local station Whytecliff instead of White Cliff, and when a post office opened in 1920, it too was called Whytecliff. Finally, in 1937, the hydrographic service played along, changing White Cliff Point to Whytecliff Point, and the transformation of district nomenclature was complete. While Col Whyte's bid for immortality has been mostly successful—the neighbourhood still goes by the name of Whytecliff, after all, and a nearby creek and lake are also named for him, as are the cove and the islet—the hydrographic dept came to its senses in 1945 and changed the name of the point back to its original form, as labelled on the early Admiralty charts. The post office name was changed to Horseshoe Bay in 1942. Today most of Whytecliff is either parkland or an expensive residential area. Canada's first marine protected area lies just offshore. *E*

Whiteley Island (50°01'00" 127°12'00" E of Union I, Kyuquot Sd, NW side of Vancouver I), **Whiteley Point** (53°52'00" 130°31'00" S side of Porcher I, S of Prince Rupert). These features commemorate two brothers, both master mariners in the Victoria-based sealing trade. The island is named for William Henry Whiteley (1862–1922), the point for John Joseph Whitely (1867-1945). William, a native of Labrador, arrived in BC about 1885 and began sealing with the schooner *Labrador*. He later brought the *Mermaid* out to Victoria from the E coast and operated that vessel mostly off Japan, where he was celebrated for hitting a whale in a violent storm and seriously damaging his ship. "That night," he reported, "there was the ugliest sea that I have ever seen, but still the old stem held. If she had not been built as she was, we all would have gone to the bottom." After four days the *Mermaid* limped into Yokohama for repairs. William married Ont-born Caroline Alberta Strycher (1872–1946) in 1899 at Port Simpson, where she was working as a missionary nurse. He later commanded the *Otter* and *Princess Ena* for the CPR's BC Coast Steamship Service and was also a harbour pilot for the port of Victoria. John Whiteley, who was born in Que, came to Victoria in 1889, after learning his trade in the Nfld coastal fishery. He first joined the schooner *Theresa*, then took over the *Labrador* after his brother had transferred to the *Mermaid*. John married Joanna Augusta Gissleman (1871–1933) at Victoria in 1895. The two brothers and their families shared a house on Vancouver St.

White Point (54°00'00" 133°07'00" S of Beresford Bay, NW side of Graham I, QCI). Named in 1907 by Capt Frederick Learmonth of the RN survey vessel *Egeria* after George White, who served as 3rd mate aboard the *Queen Charlotte* on Capt George Dixon's historic fur-trading voyage to the PNW in 1786–87. Dixon was the first European to trade extensively with the Haida.

White Rock (49°01'00" 122°48'00" E side of Boundary Bay, SE of Vancouver). This beachside community, now part of greater Vancouver, got its start as a summer cottage area for city residents. The Great Northern Rwy opened a station there in 1909, and a steamship pier was built in 1914. The name, which appears to date from about 1889 when the first subdivisions were being laid out, comes from a large whitish rock on the beach that was prominent enough to have served as a navigation mark. According to First Nation legend, the rock was thrown there by a sea god, either as a sign of his strength or because he and his bride had agreed that they would establish a new home wherever the rock landed. The city of White Rk, incorporated in 1957, has grown rapidly since the 1970s and become a popular destination for retirees. *E*

Whitmore Islands (52°38'00" 129°26'00" SW of Moore Is, off W side of Aristazabal I, Hecate Str). Cpl Henry Whitmore was a cavalry non-commissioned officer who accompanied the Columbia detachment of Royal Engineers to BC. He and another cavalry man, Sgt John Smith, both members of the 15th Hussars, were sent to organize and train any volunteer cavalry squadrons that might be needed in BC. Whitmore travelled in the *Thames City* with the main contingent of men, arriving at Esquimalt in 1859. It was soon obvious that a country with no roads, few horses and thick, impenetrable forests was not well suited to cavalry, and Col Richard Moody, cdr of the engineers, appointed Whitmore assistant postmaster at New Westminster instead. Soon after, Warner Spalding, the magistrate at New Westminster and chief postal official for the colony of BC, complained about Whitmore's "frequent and continued irregular conduct" and "the enmity he has raised against himself amongst the inhabitants here." While the cause of his offence is not known, Whitmore was punished with a term of imprisonment and a reduction in rank to private. He then seems to disappear from the historical record.

Whitney-Griffiths Point (48°23'00" 123°31'00" W end of Witty's Lagoon, N end of Parry Bay, Metchosin, W of Victoria). Named in 1972 after the Whitney-Griffiths family, whose members have lived in the area since 1907. The Capital Regional District acquired a 3-ha parcel of land at this site from the family in 1971 and added it to Witty's Lagoon Regional Park. Brothers Charles Eustatius (c 1886–1953) and William L Griffiths (c 1886–1977) established a flourishing 50-ha farm, The Grange, overlooking Parry Bay in the early 1900s and added Whitney to their surnames to avoid confusion with another family. Charles was president of the Metchosin Farmers' Institute for many years and ran unsuccessfully as a Liberal candidate for Esquimalt in the 1933 and 1937 provincial elections.

Whittaker Point (48°34'00" 123°29'00" Just SW of Willis Point and Smokehouse Bay, E side of Squally Reach and Saanich Inlet, NW of Victoria). Samuel Whittaker (1861–

White Rock beach and pier in 1924. *Harbour Publishing collection*

W

1955), from Manchester, England, immigrated to the US with his father in 1866 and lived at Rhode I and LA before coming to Victoria about 1878. In 1884 he married Christina Irvine (1858–1913), who was born on the HBC's Craigflower Farm, and they lived at Smokehouse Bay (also known locally as Whittaker Bay) for nearly 30 years. Whittaker operated a barber shop in Victoria for four decades and then spent 12 years with the BC Provincial Museum as a taxidermist. He also lived at Dawson City in the Yukon for a brief period during the Klondike gold rush.

Whittaker Point (51°40'00" 128°05'00" SW end of Hecate I, between Calvert I and Hunter I, S of Bella Bella). Henry Whittaker (1886–1971) was born in Brazil and came to Victoria in 1913. He found a job as a draftsman with BC's Public Works dept, becoming supervising architect in 1916 and chief architect in 1934, a position he held until 1949. He was a prolific designer, travelling throughout the province and drawing up plans for everything from bungalows for WWI returnees to hospitals, schools and courthouses. His work, according to architect and historian Donald Luxton, was "solid, monumental and competent, suiting exactly the tenor of the times and the needs of government." After leaving public service, Whittaker practised privately with Donald Wagg until 1957, specializing in hospitals.

Whittle Point (53°35'00" 130°33'00" E side of Griffith Hbr, NW end of Banks I). Levi George Whittle (1887–1965) served overseas during WWI and was working as an oiler on the W coast government survey vessel *Lillooet* in 1921. He married Maud Amelia Henvis (1880–1976) at Victoria in 1919.

Whyac Point (48°40'00" 124°51'00" E entrance to the Nitinat R, SE of Barkley Sd, SW side of Vancouver I). This well-protected site, which is virtually impregnable against attack, was once home to the principal village of the Ditidaht First Nation. Robert Brown, leader of the Vancouver I Exploring Expedition, visited "Why-ack" in 1864 and was impressed with its size and fortifications. According to BC historians Helen and Philip Akrigg, the word refers to the resemblance between the nearby canyon entrance and the opening of a fish trap, and could be translated as "open mouth." The translation "high hill" is also often encountered in early writings. *W*

Whytecliff, Whyte Cove, Whyte Islet. *See* White Cliff Point.

Wiah Island (53°40'00" 132°30'00" W side of Masset Inlet, N of Shannon Bay, Graham I, QCI), **Wiah Point** (54°07'00" 132°19'00" N side of Graham I, between Virago Sd and Masset Hbr). Wiah (or Wiiha), the hereditary name of the chief of the Haida town of Masset, is more commonly spelled Weah. Both features are named after the popular Henry Weah (1852–1932), who became Masset's headman

in 1883. His uncle, who had been one of the first Haida to be baptized a Christian—and had taken the name Stephen in 1882, the year before he died—was the previous Chief Weah. This was the Masset chief who pillaged the US schooner *Susan Sturgis* in 1852; he also constructed the largest traditional-style building in the QCI, at Masset, called Monster House. Henry Weah's successor as chieftain was his nephew William Matthews. Wiah Point, which was designated in 1907 by Capt Frederick Learmonth of the RN survey vessel *Egeria*, is known locally as Seven Mile Point. The Haida knew it as Mi-ah Kwun (Meagwan), named for its proximity to the old village site of Mi-ah. Wiah I was named in 1910. *D*

Long Beach looking south toward Wickaninnish Bay. *Jacqueline Windh*

Wickaninnish Bay (49°03'00" 125°44'00" Between Portland Point and Quisitis Point, SE of Tofino, W side of Vancouver I), **Wickaninnish Island** (49°08'00" 125°56'00" W side of Templar Channel, SE of Vargas I). Wickaninnish is the hereditary name of the principal chief of the Tla-o-qui-aht (Clayoquot) First Nation. According to the writer George Clutesi, who was a member of the neighbouring Tseshaht First Nation, the word came from the Kwakwala language and originated farther N, at Kyuquot. It is usually translated as "having no one in front of him in the canoe." Many other spellings have been recorded, including Waikaninish, Wick-a-nook, Huiquinanichi, Quiquinanis and Wakennenish. The name was sometimes used to refer to the Tla-o-qui-aht people in general, or even to the confederation of regional First Nations known as the Nuu-chah-nulth. The Chief Wickaninnish who was active in the late 1700s held great power in the Clayoquot region, where he was the undisputed ruler, and had numerous interactions, not always friendly, with such early fur traders as John Meares, Robert Gray and James Colnett. Meares noted that "it was very much in our interest to conciliate his regard and cultivate his friendship." Wickaninnish Bay, which appears to have originally been named Wickinanish's Sd by trader Charles Barkley in 1787, was also known for many years as Long Bay. *See* Guaquina Point as well. *E W*

Wiebe Island (48°54'00" 125°17'00" E side of the Broken Group, Barkley Sd, W side of Vancouver I). Victor Wiebe (1908–87), a graduate of the Univ of Sask, was employed as a junior hydrographer on the Pacific coast, 1930–37. He participated in surveys on the W side of Vancouver I, 1930–34, and off the QCI, 1935–36. Wiebe went on to work for the Standard Oil Co of BC, where he became a refinery manager, vice-president and director. He was also president of the Burnaby Board of Trade and very active in the boy scout movement, serving as chief scout of BC and assistant commissioner of the Boy Scouts Assoc of BC. In 1932, regional hydrographer Henri Parizeau recommended that the name Wiebe I replace Randall I, which had appeared on Admiralty charts since 1865. When questioned about the need for this change, he responded that it was because Randall I was duplicated elsewhere on the coast. "You could look back as far as any discovery or any exploration," he wrote in exasperation. "It has always been the privilege of the chiefs of parties to name features after their assistants and helpers ... why should an exception be made in my case?"

Wigen Shoal (51°25'00" 128°08'00" N end of the Sea Otter Group, SW of Calvert I, Queen Charlotte Sd). Named in 1947 after Sydney O Wigen (1923–2000), who graduated from UBC as a civil engineer in 1945 and joined the Canadian Hydrographic Service. He participated in surveys of Seymour Narrows, the Inside Passage and Queen Charlotte and Smith sounds, 1945–47, and later became tidal superintendent for the Pacific region of the CHS, responsible for tide and current research in the Pacific and western Arctic. Wigen was an expert on tsunamis and the first associate director of the International Tsunami Information Centre in Honolulu, 1975–77; he travelled widely around the Pacific Rim pursuing the improvement of tsunami warning programs. After retiring in 1984 he was the Canadian advisor at the 1985 International Tsunami Symposium held at Victoria. He took great delight in choral music and sang with choirs at Saltspring I (where he lived after retirement), Victoria and Honolulu.

Wilbraham Point (49°31'00" 123°58'00" E side of Welcome Passage, W of Halfmoon Bay, Sechelt Peninsula, NW of Vancouver). Named in 1944 after Lt Cdr Frederick Wilbraham Egerton, who served on the BC coast, 1869–72. *See* Egerton Point *and* Boxer Cliff. Formerly known as Gowlland Point.

Wilby Point (52°34'00" 128°49'00" W entrance to Kitasu Bay, W side of Swindle I, NW of Bella Bella), **Wilby Shoals** (49°59'00" 125°08'00" SE of Cape Mudge and Quadra I, NW end of Str of Georgia). Lt Col Arthur William Roger Wilby, CBE (1875–1942), was the Victoria agent of the Dept of Marine and Fisheries in the 1920s and '30s—the dept's senior official on the Pacific coast. He served as a

young soldier in the Boer War. In 1908, at Victoria, he married Jersey-born Marie Elise Gaudin (1874–1918), the eldest daughter of James Gaudin, who was the agent of the Dept of Marine and Fisheries on the W coast from 1892 to 1911. By 1914, before going overseas in WWI, Wilby was district engineer of the dept at Victoria, under agent George Robertson. After Marie's death, he married Eva Mary Blathwayt (1885–1934) in England in 1919. The point, formerly known as Low Point, was named in 1925, the shoals in 1945.

Wilfred Point (50°08'00" 125°21'00" W side of Discovery Passage, SW entrance to Seymour Narrows, NW of Campbell R). Named about 1860 by Capt George Richards of the RN survey vessel *Plumper* after Capt Wilfred Collingwood, brother of Vice Adm Baron Cuthbert Collingwood, cdr of the RN's Mediterranean fleet in the early 1800s. Richards wanted to associate the point with Seymour Narrows, which had earlier been named after Rear Adm Sir George Seymour, cdr-in-chief of the Pacific Station, 1844–48. HMS *Collingwood*, named after the vice adm, was Seymour's flagship. Wilfred Collingwood was appointed capt of HMS *Rattler* in 1784 and served on the W Indies Station until 1787, when he died aboard his vessel. *W*

Wilf Rock (49°08'15" 125°58'30" Off S end of Vargas I, W of Tofino, Clayoquot Sd, W side of Vancouver I). After George Wilfrid La Croix, who was a junior hydrographer aboard CGS *Lillooet* in 1933 when Henri Parizeau, his CO, named this feature. *See* La Croix Group.

Wilhelm Point (48°42'00" 123°24'00" SE end of Piers I, just NE of N end of Saanich Peninsula, N of Victoria). After Wilhelm Schmidt, an early owner and homesteader of Piers I. *See* Schmidt Point.

Wilkie Point (51°08'00" 127°43'00" Burnett Bay, W of Belize Inlet, SE of Cape Caution, NW entrance to Queen Charlotte Str). Able Seaman Claude Osmond Wilkie, of Victoria, died at Comox on July 11, 1940, aged 31, while serving aboard HMCS *Armentières*, which functioned as an RCN patrol and examination boat on the BC coast during WWII. He is buried at Esquimalt's Veterans Cemetery.

Wilks Island (52°44'00" 129°17'00" Just W of Turtish Hbr, off NW side of Aristazabal I). James Wilks was a BC pioneer who came to the province about 1870. He is believed to have worked as a liquor vendor in N Vancouver and may have taken part in the Victoria old-timers' reunion of May 1924 (*see* Adams Bay). Information on him is sketchy, however, and it is difficult to determine which of several early James Wilkses in the province might be commemorated here.

W

Willemar Bluff (49°40'00" 124°54'00" E of Comox Hbr, NE of Goose Spit, E side of Vancouver I). Named in 1945 by the hydrographic service after Rev Jules Xavier Willemars (1843–1935), the first Roman Catholic priest in the Comox district, who later joined the Anglican church. He was born in France and immigrated to Canada in 1867, arriving in the Comox valley in 1871 as a missionary to the First Nations. Willemars was a revered figure in the region, "a quiet sincere kind of man," according to Bishop George Hills, who was "most useful to his parishioners." In 1880 he married Mary Isabel Munro (1856–1942), who was born in Scotland; he retired in 1913. Nearby Willemar Ck and Willemar Lk are also named for him. The feature was marked White Bluff on an 1864 map.

Willes Island (50°53'00" 127°51'00" W end of Nigei I, Bate Passage, off N end of Vancouver I). This is the island, according to BC coastal historian John Walbran, where the bodies of two of the murdered deserters from the ship *England* were found in 1850—a discovery that precipitated a series of RN actions against members of the Nahwitti First Nation (*see* Deserters Group). The origin of the name, unfortunately, is not known.

Willey Point (48°49'00" 123°19'00" W side of N Pender I, Gulf Is). John Willey (1859–1935), who came to Canada from England in 1886, arrived on N Pender about 1890 and farmed in this vicinity. He married Medora Ann Percival (1854–1933) at Victoria in 1903. Descendants of the Willey family were still living on N Pender in the early 2000s. The Gulf Is Branch of the BC Historical Assoc submitted this place name in 1968.

Chinese immigrants arriving at William Head quarantine station about 1917. *BC Archives G-01591*

William Head (48°21'00" 123°32'00" S end of Parry Bay, SW of Victoria, S end of Vancouver I). Named in 1846 by Capt Henry Kellett of HMS *Herald* after Rear Adm Sir William Parry, the famed Arctic explorer. *See* Parry Bay for biographical details. The promontory of William Head was the site of a quarantine station, 1894–1958, where passengers and crew from arriving vessels (especially from Asia) were screened for infectious diseases. The quarantine facilities, while not exactly the last word in comfort, did feature a small golf course for the enjoyment of first-class passengers. The institution was converted into a minimum-security prison in 1959. *E*

William Island (54°02'00" 130°42'00" S of Edye Passage, NW side of Porcher I, SW of Prince Rupert). After RN officer Capt William Henry Edye, who was on the BC coast in 1869. *See* Edye Passage.

Williams Island (48°57'00" 125°16'00" N of the Broken Group and Sechart Channel, Barkley Sd, W side of Vancouver I). Named in 1950 after Mary Isabella Williams (b 1890, at Victoria), who received a Crown grant for the island in 1908. She was the daughter of pioneer Victoria stationer Robert T Williams, who came to Canada in 1859 and was the manager of the Victoria News Co in 1901. She married William Arthur Davis in 1912 at Oak Bay.

Williams Island (49°38'00" 124°03'00" Pender Hbr, SE side of Malaspina Str, NW of Vancouver). The source of this name is uncertain but may refer to a midshipman named Williams who served on the Pacific Station aboard HMS *Tribune* about 1860.

Williams Islet (53°14'00" 129°19'00" Entrance to Crane Bay, W side of Gil I, Lewis Passage, N of Caamaño Sd). Wing Cdr Edwin Mountford "Ted" Williams, AFC, from Victoria, was killed in action on Jan 28, 1945, aged 28. He was born in Hong Kong and educated at Brentwood College near Victoria and the Royal Military College in Kingston. At the time of his death, Williams was serving with the RCAF's No 424 Squadron, which operated Handley Page Halifax heavy bombers on night offensives over Germany. He had been awarded the AFC in 1942, while with No 10 Squadron, at which time he had already made 187 convoy patrols and reconnaissance sorties over the N Atlantic. Williams is buried at Stonefall Cemetery in Harrogate, Yorkshire.

Williamson Island (49°06'00" 123°06'00" Mouth of the Fraser R, between Kirkland I and Barber I, S of Vancouver), **Williamson Slough** (W of Williamson I). John Andrew Williamson (1867–1929) owned this island and, from 1907 on, managed a Canadian Fish Products Co plant there that processed fish heads and entrails from the surrounding canneries for oil and fertilizer. It was known as the "Oilery" and was renowned for its odour (a similar factory had operated on nearby Kirkland I in the 1890s). Williamson was born in Ont and moved in the late 1890s to Whonnock, BC, where his sister and brother-in-law ran a general store. He married Mary Henderson (1875–1951) at Whonnock in 1898; he later became a councillor for the municipality of Delta, 1916–19, and served as reeve, 1920–22. Over the years the channel between Williamson I and Gunn I, immediately to the S, has silted in, so today the two islands are partly joined together, especially at low tide and at the E end. Williamson I was formerly known as Watts I.

Williamson Passage (49°39'00" 126°23'00" Muchalat Inlet, N of Gore I, just E of Nootka Sd, W side of Vancouver I). Named after RN officer John Williamson (d 1798), who visited Nootka Sd with Capt James Cook in 1778 as 3rd lt of HMS *Resolution* and returned to England in 1780 as 1st lt of HMS *Discovery*, the consort vessel on Cook's third expedition. Described by his shipmates as "a wretch," a "very devil" and "a great tyrant," he had a most unfortunate career. When Cook was attacked and killed in Hawaii in 1779, Williamson was standing offshore, in charge of the *Resolution*'s launch, and was accused by his fellow officers of cowardice in not coming to the capt's aid. Later in life, as a capt and in command of HMS *Agincourt* at the 1797 Battle of Camperdown, he was found guilty of disobedience and failure to do his duty, "placed at the bottom of the list of post-capts" and "rendered incapable of ever serving on board of any of His Majesty's ships." *W*

Williamsons Landing (49°27'00" 123°28'00" W side of Thornbrough Channel, W side of Howe Sd, NW of Vancouver). George Edward Williamson (1865–1932) was a Vancouver building contractor and the first person to build a summer home at this location. He was born at Orillia, Ont, served as a soldier in the NW Rebellion and came out to Vancouver in 1888. Williamson constructed many buildings in the Mt Pleasant area, including the beaux-arts-style former postal station at 15th and Main. He served as a Vancouver alderman in 1911–12 and fought overseas during WWI. Williamsons Landing has been the site of the YMCA's Camp Elphinstone since 1907.

Willie Island (53°01'00" 132°28'00" Entrance to Kaisun Hbr, N side of Englefield Bay, NW side of Moresby I, QCI). After Capt William Mitchell, who made several visits to this area in 1851–52 on behalf of the HBC in search of gold. *See* Mitchell Bay.

Willis Passage (52°42'00" 129°27'00" NW of Moore Is, W of N end of Aristazabal I, Hecate Str). Named in 1926 after Walter King Willis (1891–1962), who was at that time a junior hydrographer on the Pacific coast for the Canadian Hydrographic Service. He was born at St John, NB, and studied engineering at the Univ of NB, joining the CHS in 1913. After working on the Great Lks, 1913–16, he transferred to the W coast for a year and then served in England during WWI as a hydrographer at the Admiralty dept. Willis married New Westminster native Grace Isobel Phillips (1897–1981) in 1918 and took part in a multitude

of W coast surveys between 1919 and 1946, spending much time in Hecate Str, on the W coast of Vancouver I and in the Str of Georgia. He was in charge of the W coast's main survey vessel, the *William J Stewart*, 1939–45, and was then appointed regional hydrographer, 1946–53, succeeding Henri Parizeau.

Willoughby Rocks (50°53'45" 127°27'39" NE side of the Deserters Group, Ripple Passage, Queen Charlotte Str, N of Port Hardy). These rocks were originally known as the Twin Its but were renamed by the hydrographic service in 1951, supposedly after a stowaway sailor or "deserter" from the HBC ship *Norman Morison*, who was killed off the N end of Vancouver I in 1850 along with two of his fellows. *See* Deserters Group for a fuller account of this confusing incident, which resulted in two RN attacks on Nahwitti First Nation villages. According to a note at BC's Geographical Names Office, a report by Capt R Brown of the *England*, where the deserters were initially hidden, to John Helmcken, the magistrate at Ft Rupert, stated that one of the stowaways was named A Willoughby. Helmcken, however, who wrote a lengthy account of the whole affair (albeit many years later, in 1890), claimed that the deserters' names were Charles and George Wishart and Fred Watkins. *See also* Wishart I.

Willow Point (49°58'00" 125°12'00" N of Ocean Grove, S end of city of Campbell R, E side of Vancouver I). The name first appears on an 1860 Admiralty chart that was based on a survey by Capt George Richards. There are fossils on the point, and evidence of ancient First Nation village sites. The Lekwiltok people knew this area as Kahushian, Kwakwala for "place of bad waters." A small community of white settlers grew up there at the end of the 19th century. Charles and Frederick Thulin were originally going to buy land and erect their pioneer hotel at Willow Point, but in 1903 they chose a spot in what is now downtown Campbell R instead; they still named their establishment The Willows, however, after this location. In 1911 the steamship *Cottage City*, en route to Alaska with a passenger list that included 30 chorus girls, foundered on the reef beyond the point. In the 1940s a store, garage and community hall were built at Willow Point, and the area gradually became the southernmost suburb of the growing city of Campbell R.

Willows Beach (48°26'00" 123°18'00" NW side of Oak Bay, just E of Victoria, SE end of Vancouver I). HBC officer John Tod retired to Oak Bay in 1850 and called his large estate Willows Farm. The waterfront portion of the farm became known as Willows Beach. A popular watering hole, the Willows Hotel, was built in 1864 at the corner of Cadboro Bay Rd and what is today Eastdowne Rd. In 1891, when the BC agricultural exhibition relocated from Beacon Hill Park, Willows fairground was established between Cadboro Bay and Foul Bay roads. A grand exhibition hall was constructed next to Oak Bay's old horse-racing track (the Driving Park); livestock buildings, a midway and a hockey arena were added later. The fairgrounds served as a staging area for Canadian troops heading overseas during WWI. All the buildings were torn down by 1948, and the area was turned into the Carnarvon Park subdivision in the early 1950s. The pioneer Willows Hotel never recovered from BC's Prohibition era (1917–21) and was converted into a private school for boys, Cranleigh House, in 1923. Willows Beach was the site of a former Songhees First Nation village named Sitchanalth, a word that refers to drift logs and other debris that become lodged in the sand.

Wilman Point (53°16'00" 129°30'00" Entrance to Tuwartz Inlet, S end of Pitt I). Named in 1944 after Arthur Wilman, coxswain aboard the W coast survey vessel *William J Stewart* in 1943.

Wilson Creek (49°27'00" 123°43'00" Just E of Mission Point, SE of Sechelt, E side of Str of Georgia, NW of Vancouver). There is confusion over the naming of Wilson Creek. A record at BC's Geographical Names Office states that it commemorates the district's earliest settler, William Simpson, who pre-empted land there in the 1880s (Wilson is supposedly a combination of the first three and last three letters of his name). Canon G H Wilson of St Michael's Anglican Church in Vancouver, who built a cottage in the vicinity in 1914, has also been considered a possible namesake. The true source of the name, however, appears to be James Wilson, a blacksmith for the Burns & Jackson Logging Co, which was formed in 1923 and had a camp at Wilson Ck in the 1930s and '40s. A small settlement grew up at the mouth of the creek (which was also, at some point, known as Freamer Ck), and steamships called. The mouths of Wilson Ck and nearby Chapman Ck, which have shifted over the years, were named Rio de la Aguada—"river of freshwater supplies"—by Spanish naval officer José Narváez, the first European to explore the Str of Georgia, who stopped there with the *Santa Saturnina* in 1791 to replenish his drinking water. The creeks flow through Tsawcome (Ts'úkw'um), an important reserve of the Sechelt First Nation. *E*

Wilson Inlet (53°34'00" 129°53'00" N of Anger I, S entrance to Petrel Channel, W side of Pitt I). According to surveyor Philip Monckton, the inlet was named after a member of the BC Lands Service triangulation party that worked along the W coast of Pitt I in 1921. The group travelled in a small vessel named the *Ala* and was under the leadership of land surveyor Alfred Wright.

Wilson Point (50°21'00" 125°20'00" N of Edward Point, W side of Sonora I, N of Campbell R). George Wilson of nearby Hemming Bay was "the oldest living resident of the area," according to a 1969 letter at BC's Geographical

Names Office from a BC Forest Service ranger at Thurston Bay. Wilson is believed to have lived in the vicinity until sometime in the 1960s.

Wilson Rock (52°40'00" 128°58'00" S end of Laredo Channel, between Aristazabal I and Princess Royal I). There are at least two different Victoria pioneers who could be the source for this name. One is William Wilson (1841–1924), a plumber, who was born at Que, migrated to Victoria in 1864 and married Elizabeth West (1841–1923) in 1868. The other is a land registry officer named William N Wilson (1843–1920). This candidate, whose wife was named Emily (1851–1922), came to Canada from England in 1860. The feature was formerly known as Channel Rk.

Wimble Rocks (54°02'00" 132°11'00" S end of Masset Hbr, N side of Graham I, QCI). Named in 1907 by Capt Frederick Learmonth of the RN survey vessel *Egeria*, after the vessel's artificer engineer.

The Winchelsea Islands, off east Vancouver Island. *Peter Vassilopoulos*

Winchelsea Islands (49°18'00" 124°05'00" NE of entrance to Nanoose Hbr, between Nanaimo and Parksville, off E side of Vancouver I). Capt George Richards of the RN survey vessel *Plumper* named these islands in 1860, probably after Winchelsea in E Sussex, an important English port during the 12th and 13th centuries. It was destroyed by a massive flood in 1287 and rebuilt on higher ground, beside the R Brede. Winchelsea was part of the Confederation of Cinque Ports, a string of seaport towns that were granted special privileges in return for providing coastal defence services.

Windsor Cove (51°56'00" 127°53'00" SW end of King I, N of Sagen 'It, SE of Bella Bella). The Windsors are a prominent Heiltsuk First Nation family at Bella Bella.

Windy Bay (52°41'25" 131°27'03" E side of Lyell I, off E side of Moresby I, QCI). A Haida First Nation village named Hlkia or Hlk'yah, meaning "falcon town," was once located on this bay. In 1985, when the old-growth

W

forests in the watersheds of Windy Bay and Gates creeks were threatened by logging, the area became the focus of peaceful protests by Haida elders and environmentalists that blocked roads and gained widespread media attention. A traditional longhouse, Looking Around and Blinking House, was designed and built at the bay by Haida carver and leader Guujaaw to honour the battle to preserve the area. Gwaii Haanas National Park Reserve was established in 1987 to protect the S Moresby region and its offshore islands.

Wingate Point (52°36'00" 128°45'00" SW entrance to Meyers Passage, Laredo Sd, NW end of Swindle I, NW of Bella Bella). Lt Walter Wingate of the RCNVR was listed in 1916–17 as CO of HMCS *Grilse*, a motor yacht (the former *Winchester*) that was converted to a torpedo boat and operated out of Halifax. In 1918 he appears as a lt cdr with HMCS *Niobe*, at that time a depot ship at Halifax. Wingate may also have served briefly in HMCS *Rainbow* at Esquimalt during WWI. After the war he is believed to have worked as a master mariner with the Coast Guard.

Wingen Islets (49°10'00" 125°40'00" Off SW end of McCaw Peninsula, Tofino Inlet, Clayoquot Sd, W side of Vancouver I). Named by regional hydrographer Henri Parizeau in 1934 after Thomas Wingen (1864–1931), who pre-empted land on Grice Bay in 1896 and received a Crown grant for his property in 1920. He married Julia Christine Hansen (1869–1941) at Victoria in 1894 and operated a small sawmill on Grice Bay at the mouth of Kootowis Ck. Wingen became a building contractor and boatbuilder at Tofino and established the Tofino Machine Shop, which his son Hjalmar and other family members later took over. The Wingen Its were formerly known as the Trunk Its, a name that first appears on Admiralty charts in 1898.

Winnifred Rocks (52°48'00" 132°02'00" Entrance to Newcombe Inlet, Tasu Sd, W side of Moresby I, QCI). The hydrographic service named these rocks in 1962 after the sealing schooner *Winnifred* (sometimes spelled *Winifred*), which operated out of Victoria in the early 1880s. It was one of the vessels seized in the Bering Sea in 1892 by the US revenue cutter *Richard Rush* during the long-running dispute between Canada and the US over northern seal-hunting rights and territories. Capt Gustave Hansen, a notorious seal poacher, was in command at the time, and US authorities imprisoned him and his two mates at Sitka for almost a year before trying them. The *Winnifred* was confiscated and taken to Unalaska in the Aleutian Is.

Winstanley Point (48°53'00" 123°24'00" W side of Galiano I, Gulf Is). Edward George W Winstanley (1856–1926) was born in Australia and came to Canada with his parents in 1859. He settled at first in Manitoba, where he and his Ont-born wife, Janet or "Jennie" (1860–1926), farmed

and raised a family. The Winstanleys arrived on Galiano I in 1890 and farmed there also. Edward helped build the first school at the S end of the island. He apparently made several successful prospecting trips to the Yukon, both during the Klondike gold rush and afterwards. The name was submitted by the Gulf Is Branch of the BC Historical Assoc in 1968.

Winter Harbour, off Quatsino Sound. *Peter Vassilopoulos*

Winter Harbour (50°32'00" 128°00'00" Head of Forward Inlet, NW side of Quatsino Sd, NW end of Vancouver I). Forward Inlet and Winter Hbr provide an important sanctuary for vessels rounding or heading for N Vancouver I, especially in winter, when storms are more frequent and violent. The community of Winter Hbr, originally called Queenstown, got its start in the early 1900s, when a clam cannery was built. Albert Moore established a floating logging camp there in 1936, and logging continues to be important in the area, as well as aquaculture and commercial fishing. The name Winter Hbr appears in the 1864 *Vancouver I Pilot* written by Capt George Richards. To avoid duplication with Winter Hbr (now Winter Inlet) on Pearse I, farther N, it was changed by the hydrographic service to Leeson Hbr in 1927, after area pioneer Jobe Leeson (*see* Leeson Point). In 1947, at the request of local residents, the name was changed back again to agree with the post office name, which had been established as Winter Hbr in 1935. *E*

Winter Rock (53°53'00" 130°34'00" E of Gurd I, Kitkatla Inlet, SW of Porcher I and Prince Rupert). After Rev Robert Winter Gurd, missionary to the Tsimshian First Nation at Kitkatla. *See* Gurd Inlet.

Wishart Island (50°53'00" 127°29'00" One of the Deserters Group, W of Deserters I, N of Port Hardy, Queen Charlotte Str). Named after a pair of stowaway sailors or "deserters" from the HBC ship *Norman Morison*, who were killed off the N end of Vancouver I in 1850 along with a third man. *See* Deserters Group for a fuller account of this incident, which resulted in two RN attacks on Nahwitti First Nation villages. According to a note at BC's Geographical Names Office, a report by Capt R Brown of the *England*, where the deserters were initially hidden, to John Helmcken, the magistrate at Ft Rupert, stated that one of the stowaways was named James Wishart. Helmcken, however, who wrote a lengthy account of the whole affair (albeit many years later, in 1890), claimed that the deserters' names were Charles and George Wishart and Fred Watkins. *See also* Willoughby Rks.

Wishart Peninsula (50°50'00" 126°32'00" E of Broughton I, S of entrance to Kingcome Inlet, NE of Port McNeill). David Durham Wishart (1816–68), from Middlesex, was an HBC ship's capt who commanded the supply vessel *Norman Morison* on its three early voyages between London and Ft Victoria, 1849–53. He married Eliza Deborah Broughton, a widow (née Hardwicke), in 1849, and that year was also made an honorary lt in the RN reserve. The *Morison* brought out many of Vancouver I's first colonists, including Dr John Helmcken, who reported in his journal that "Wishart was not a social man—he had been soured somehow or other—but nevertheless he was kind and good to all and a thorough seaman ... no matter how bad the weather, he would remain on deck night and day and was always ready at a moment's notice." It is not known if Charles and George Wishart, who jumped ship from the *Morison* and were later murdered off N Vancouver I, were his relatives (*see* Wishart I). In 1854–55, Wishart was master of the *Princess Royal*, which also sailed between England and the PNW, bringing 24 miners and their families to Nanaimo to work the area's rich coal deposits. Named by Lt Daniel Pender of the hired survey vessel *Beaver* about 1864. *W*

Witherby Point (49°29'00" 123°28'00" W side of Howe Sd, N of Gibsons, NW of Vancouver). After Percival Witherby, who received a Crown grant for land at this location in 1897. According to a record at BC's Geographical Names Office, he was a talented man, an excellent writer and speaker, and a good linguist, who spoke and read French, Spanish, Portuguese and German fluently.

Witty's Lagoon (48°23'00" 123°31'00" N end of Parry Bay, W of Albert Head, SW of Victoria). Named for John Frederick Witty (d 1873), who purchased the Bilston Farm adjacent to the lagoon in the mid-1860s. This property, established in 1851 by Thomas Blinkhorn and Capt James Cooper, and later owned by Robert Burnaby, was the first farm in Metchosin and one of the earliest on Vancouver I. John and his First Nation wife, Charlotte Aaroniaton (1842–1900), who was born at Nanaimo, had migrated from San Juan I to Vancouver I in 1863 when it appeared that the San Juans might become part of the US. They and their descendants were influential residents in the Metchosin district, donating land for a school, cemetery and the church of St Mary the Virgin, and helping build

Metchosin Hall. The area surrounding the lagoon is now a 56-ha regional park. This feature was formerly known as Metchosin Lagoon.

Woden River. *See* Watun R.

Wollan Islets (49°10'00" 125°39'00" S of McCaw Peninsula, Tofino Inlet, Clayoquot Sd, W side of Vancouver I). Paul J Wollan (1854–c 1913), a native of Norway, immigrated to Canada in 1891 and pre-empted land S of Grice Bay in 1896. He was listed as a labourer and farmer in the 1901 BC census and received a Crown grant to his property in 1903. Formerly known as the Flat Top Its.

Woodcock Islands (52°36'00" 129°11'00" W of Clifford Bay, off W side of Aristazabal I). Cpl John Woodcock (b 1830), a native of Birmingham, was a member of the Columbia detachment of Royal Engineers, which served in BC 1858–63. He arrived at Victoria aboard the *Thames City* with the main contingent of men in 1859 and spent much of his time helping supervise the construction of the Old Cariboo Road, especially between Lillooet and Clinton. Woodcock was apparently a keen actor and was favourably mentioned numerous times in newspaper reviews of performances put on by the RE's dramatic club. He may have been a blacksmith by trade, as he and fellow engineer George Hand took over a blacksmith's business in New Westminster in 1863, after the Columbia detachment was disbanded. It seems that Woodcock didn't remain long in BC, however, as he appears to have joined his brother in Scotland later in the 1860s.

Wood Cove (50°09'00" 127°19'00" W side of Kashutl Inlet, N of Easy Inlet, Kyuquot Sd, NW side of Vancouver I), **Wood Islets** (49°12'00" 125°47'00" S end of Mosquito Hbr, E of Meares I, Clayoquot Sd, W side of Vancouver I). Dr Charles Bedingfield Wood was the surgeon aboard the RN surveying vessel *Hecate*, under Capt George Richards, on the BC coast in 1860–62. In July 1860 he and Lt Richard Mayne travelled by foot from Jervis Inlet to the Squamish valley, scouting a potential overland route to the interior of BC. In 1862, Wood and Lt Philip Rankin went by land from Kyuquot Sd to the mouth of the Nimpkish R on Queen Charlotte Str and made one of the first European explorations of that part of Vancouver I (*see* Expedition Its). Wood accidentally drowned in the Mediterranean, along with several other RN officers, in 1865, while surgeon of HMS *Orlando*, when one of the ship's cutters was upset in a squall while returning from a picnic. Bedingfield Bay in Clayoquot Sd and the Bedingfield Range, N of Tofino, are also named for him, as is Mt Wood near Shawnigan Lk. *W*

Woodfibre (49°40'00" 123°15'00" NW side of Howe Sd, S of Squamish, NW of Vancouver). A pulp mill opened here in 1912 at the mouth of Mill Ck, on the site of an old sawmill. It was originally known as the Mill Ck mill—and

Woodfibre pulp mill on Howe Sound. *Andrew Scott*

also appeared on early maps as Britannia West or Britannia West Landing. The Whalen Pulp & Paper Co bought the mill in 1917 and expanded it, adding more houses for workers and their families; the isolated site was served by steamship and, in the early days, by a small ferry from Horseshoe Bay. When the community applied for postal services, about 1919, the name Mill Ck was apparently deemed unacceptable, as Millstream and Mill Bay post offices already existed in BC. A school competition was held to select a new name, and Cathy Haar won a $50 prize for coming up with Woodfibre. BC Pulp & Paper Co Ltd took over the mill in 1925, after Whalen went bankrupt. The townsite was demolished in the 1960s; most employees lived in Squamish by then and commuted to work by ferry from Darrell Bay. The plant's final owner, Western Forest Products Inc, shut it down permanently in 2006. Nearby Woodfibre Ck and Woodfibre Lk are named after the mill. *E*

Woodlands (49°20'00" 122°55'00" W side of Indian Arm, NE of Burrard Inlet and Vancouver). This summer cottage community was probably named after Hugh Myddleton Wood (1849–1937), a minister in the Catholic Apostolic Church and former farmer who immigrated to Ont from England in 1870. He married Louisa Elizabeth Brisley (1852–1937). The Woods were the original owners of the waterfront at this location. The site was bought in 1909 by Percy and Zellah Ward and later subdivided among Ward family members. Woodlands was served for many years by the small vessels of the Harbour Navigation Co. Unlike other Indian Arm settlements, however, it is also connected to Deep Cove by a steep, narrow road.

Woodruff Bay (51°58'00" 131°02'00" SE end of Kunghit I, S of Moresby I, QCI). Samuel Woodruff (b 1743), a native of Connecticut, was present on the BC coast in 1778 as a gunner's mate with HMS *Discovery*, on Capt James Cook's last great voyage, 1776–80. In 1787, by now an experienced seaman and navigator, he signed on as 1st mate with the *Columbia Rediviva*, under Capt John Kendrick, for

the first US fur-trading voyage to the PNW. Kendrick, who was infamous for his belligerent, tyrannical style of leadership, soon made life intolerable for Woodruff and had apparently reduced him to the post of ship's cook by the time the expedition arrived at the Cape Verde Is. After being subjected to further indignities, Woodruff quit the *Columbia* at Cape Verde, along with Roberts, the ship's surgeon. *D*

Woods Islands (49°00'00" 123°49'00" Ladysmith Hbr, SE of Nanaimo, SE side of Vancouver I), **Woods Rock** (51°01'00" 127°34'00" NW of Southgate I, off NW side of Queen Charlotte Str, N of Port Hardy). Named in 1904 by Cdr John Parry of the RN survey vessel *Egeria*, after Artificer Engineer James J Woods, who served aboard the ship that year on the BC coast.

Woods Shoal (52°46'00" 129°27'00" W of Anderson I, off NW Aristazabal I, Hecate Str). Helen Katherine Woods (1853–1937) was born in Ireland and immigrated to Canada in 1865. She worked as a teacher at Victoria and married John Alexander Andrew (1839–91) there in 1882. He had been born in Ceylon (now Sri Lanka) and was employed as an accountant by the HBC. Helen is believed to have participated in the Victoria old-timers' reunion of May 1924 (*see* Adams Bay).

Woodward Island (49°06'00" 123°09'00" At W end of Woodward Reach), **Woodward Reach** (49°07'00" 123°06'00" S of Lulu I, near mouth of the Fraser R), **Woodward Slough** (49°07'00" 123°07'00" S of Lulu I, between No 3 and No 5 rds). Nathan Woodward (1824–96), a native of England, and his son Daniel, who was born in Ont about 1856, settled on Lulu I near the S end of today's No 5 Rd in 1874. Nathan was a keen hunter and trapper, and also a skilled boatbuilder, who constructed a number of Fraser R fishing skiffs. Dan farmed and later served as a Richmond councillor and school trustee; he developed the Woodward property into a valuable holding before selling it in 1909 and moving to Vancouver I. A boat dock and warehouse were built, and the area came to be known as Woodward (or Woodwards) Landing; steamers stopped there, and a car and passenger ferry crossed the Fraser from Woodward to Delta. The site eventually became a BC Ferries maintenance and repair depot. From 1922 to 1928 a training wall was built along the N side of Woodward I to stabilize the course of the Fraser's main shipping channel. It was extended in the mid-1930s and is now almost 4 km long. Mud flats have built up S of the wall in recent years, expanding the size of the island, which is an important wildlife habitat area. Woodward Slough was formerly known as Horseshoe Slough. *E*

Woodward Point (48°22'00" 123°43'00" E side of Sooke Hbr, N of Whiffin Spit, S end of Vancouver I). Thomas Woodward was an RN paymaster aboard HMS *Herald*,

W

under Capt Henry Kellett, on the Pacific Station in 1846, when Kellett named this feature. The *Herald* was sent to the Arctic in 1848–50 to assist in the search for missing explorer Sir John Franklin. Woodward contracted a serious illness while in the N and died during the ship's return voyage to England in 1851.

Woody Point. *See* Cape Cook.

Wootton Bay (50°05'00" 124°43'00" N end of Lancelot Inlet, E of Gifford Peninsula, just S of Desolation Sd, NW of Powell R), **Wootton Islet** (52°16'00" 128°20'00" Entrance to Berry Inlet, NW side of Seaforth Channel, NW of Bella Bella). The bay was named by Lt Daniel Pender about 1863 for colonial official Henry Wootton (1826–75); the islet is named for his wife, Eliza Wootton (1826–1918, née Yardley). Henry, a native of Kent, came to Victoria from England in 1859 as 2nd officer of the new HBC paddle steamer *Labouchere*, under Capt John Trivett. Eliza joined her husband at Victoria in 1860. He resigned from HBC service and received a series of colonial civil service appointments: clerk of the Supreme Court of Vancouver I, postmaster and harbourmaster of Victoria and deputy postmaster gen of BC. After Confederation he served as Victoria postmaster and senior postal official in BC until his death. According to BC historian John Walbran, Wootton Bay was named Brazo de Bustamente in 1792 by Spanish explorer Cayetano Valdés, after Josef Bustamente, capt of the *Atrevida*, one of Alejandro Malaspina's two vessels. PNW cartography expert Henry Wagner, however, identifies nearby Theodosia Arm as the Brazo de Bustamente. *W*

Work Bay (52°46'00" 128°29'00" E side of Sarah I, off NW end of Roderick I, Finlayson Channel, NW of Bella Bella). Sarah Work (1829–1906) was the second daughter of John Work and Josette Legacé (*see below*), and the wife of senior HBC official Roderick Finlayson (1818–92, *see* Finlayson Arm), whom she married at Ft Victoria in 1849. She was born at Ft Colville in today's Washington state and attended school at Ft Vancouver and at the Methodist mission on Oregon's Willamette R. Just N of downtown Victoria the Finlaysons built a palatial mansion named Rock Bay, which they trimmed with imported California redwood and extensively landscaped; Sarah, a keen gardener, raised a family of 11 children and was noted for her Oriental poppies. Work Bay was named by the hydrographic service in 1948 in association with Sarah I, which also commemorates this PNW pioneer, as do nearby Sarah Head and Sarah Passage, Sarah Ck and Sarah Lk NE of Prince Rupert, Sarah Point near Port Simpson, and Mt Sarah on Swindle I.

Work Channel (54°28'00" 130°13'00" NE side of Tsimpsean Peninsula, just NE of Prince Rupert), **Work Island** (48°25'00" 123°24'00" Just S of Work Point, Victoria

Hudson's Bay Company official John Work. *BC Archives A-01823*

Hbr), **Work Island** (53°10'00" 128°40'00" Just off Butedale, S end of Fraser Reach, off NE side of Princess Royal I, S of Kitimat), **Work Point** (48°25'00" 123°24'00" W side of Victoria Hbr, SE end of Vancouver I), **Work Point** (52°58'00" 132°13'00" NE tip of Josling Peninsula, Kuper Inlet, NW side of Moresby I, QCI). John Work (c 1792–1861) was present at many defining moments in PNW history. He was born John Wark in Derry, Ireland; Wark became Work on his HBC contract and he adopted that spelling for the rest of his life. After joining the HBC in 1814, he served at a series of trading posts—York Factory, Severn House, Trout Lk, Island Lk—before being sent to the Columbia district in 1823. There, with the rank of clerk, he was posted to Spokane House, Flathead House and Ft Colville. In 1824, Work and James McMillan explored the lower Fraser R; the following year he helped establish Ft Vancouver. In 1830 he was promoted to chief trader, put in charge of the Snake country brigade and led significant trapping and trading expeditions throughout Idaho, Oregon and California. His wife, Josette Legacé (c 1809–96, *see* Legace Bay), daughter of a French-Canadian trapper and a Spokane Native American woman, bore him 11 children and often accompanied him on his extensive travels. In 1834, Work succeeded Peter Skene Ogden as manager of BC's coastal trade and spent much of the next two decades at Ft Simpson. From there he made important surveys of the QCI and in 1851 investigated the Mitchell Inlet gold discovery (hence the name Work Point). He was promoted to chief factor in 1846 and sat on the Columbia district's board of management. Work established Ft Rupert on N Vancouver I in 1849 and moved his family that year to Victoria, where he bought land and built Hillside, a country estate. By 1859 he owned 800 ha on Vancouver I and was the colony's largest land holder. Gov James Douglas appointed him to Vancouver I's colonial legislative council, 1853–61. Six of John and Josette Work's daughters married HBC officers (including William Fraser

Tolmie and Roderick Finlayson) or other prominent early residents of Victoria. HBC gov George Simpson described Work as "a queer-looking fellow, of clownish manners and address; indeed there is a good deal of simplicity approaching to idiocy in his appearance; he is nevertheless a shrewd sensible man, and not deficient in firmness when necessary." Work Channel, Work I in Fraser Reach and Work Point in Victoria Hbr were all originally named Wark—the channel by HBC officials about 1837, while Work was stationed at Ft Simpson; the island by Capt Charles Dodd of the *Beaver* about 1845; and the point by HBC officers at Ft Victoria (the name was adopted in 1846 by Capt Henry Kellett of HMS *Herald* while making the first survey of Victoria Hbr). Mt Work, NW of Victoria, also honours this stalwart fur trader. *E W*

Worlcombe Island (49°21'00" 123°27'00" W side of Collingwood Channel, off SW side of Bowen I, entrance to Howe Sd, just NW of Vancouver). While the precise origin of this name is not known, it is believed to have been applied by Capt George Richards of the RN survey vessel *Plumper* about 1859–60. Worlcombe may be a misspelling of Woolcombe or Woollcombe and perhaps refers to an RN officer of that name, possibly Vice Adm George Woollcombe (b 1795). The 13-ha island was a base for First Nation and early European whaling efforts in the Str of Georgia. Bowen I historian Irene Howard reported that it was known to the Squamish people as Swus-pus-tak-kwin-ace, or "where whales are caught." A group of Seattle sportsmen acquired it at the end of WWII, built a nine-bedroom fishing lodge there in 1949 and then promptly defaulted on their mortgage. The next owner was shipping magnate Jock MacInnes, who sold in 1960 to Jack Terry, president of Northland Navigation Ltd. Capt Jack built a large breakwater and made a beach with sand that had come to BC as ballast from the Riviera. In 1967, when he, in turn, sold, his realtor let it be known that prospective purchasers would be vetted, as "we don't want to see [the island] developed as a honky-tonk." Hungarian architect Peter Kaffka and his wife, Elizabeth, passed muster; the $80,000 purchase price included the lodge, a cottage, cabin, power plant, water tower and cabin cruiser. Today Worlcombe is home to half a dozen recreational properties.

Worsfold Bay (54°34'00" 130°18'00" E side of Work Channel, N of Prince Rupert). Cuthbert Coleman Worsfold (1866–1950) was an assistant engineer at the New Westminster office of the federal Dept of Public Works in 1898, the year that Louis Coste, the dept's chief engineer from Ottawa, was taken on a N coast tour aboard CGS *Quadra* by Capt John Walbran. Worsfold had come to BC from England in 1888 and married BC-born Catharine Charles (1866–1949) at Victoria in 1898. He accompanied the expedition, which examined several northern inlets and the mouth of the Stikine R while looking for a suitable

terminus for a proposed railroad to the Yukon. The young engineer assisted Walbran in making a survey of Work Channel, and the capt suggested that this feature be named for him. *W*

Wouwer Island (48°51'45" 125°21'25" SW end of Broken Group, Barkley Sd, W side of Vancouver I). Alidor Vanden Wouwer (b 1867), a native of Belgium, came to Canada in 1889 and was naturalized in 1894. He received Crown grants for several properties in Barkley Sd between 1900 and 1925, including nearby Turret I in 1911; in the 1901 BC census he is listed as a farmer living at Port Renfrew. According to Barkley Sd historian R Bruce Scott, Wouwer later lived at Bamfield under the surname Vanden. He married Wilhelmine Muller at Vancouver in 1919. The feature appeared on an 1865 Admiralty chart as Storm I but was renamed in 1934 by regional hydrographer Henri Parizeau to avoid duplication. Wouwer I was a Tseshaht First Nation summer village site and base for hunting whales and sea lions.

Wreck Beach (49°15'00" 123°15'00" Just NE of Point Grey, W tip of Vancouver). Vancouver's famous nude beach is named after a derelict ship that lay in the mud just offshore in the late 1940s and '50s. There are also several wrecked barges in the vicinity. The name didn't become official until 1982, though clothing has been optional here since the early 1970s. *E*

Wren Islet (50°05'00" 125°14'00" Gowlland Hbr, W side of Quadra I, just NE of Campbell R). Cdr Cortland Simpson of the RN survey vessel *Egeria* named a number of features in the vicinity after animals in 1900.

Wright Inlet (53°31'00" 129°51'00" W side of Pitt I, E of Anger I), **Wright Island** (53°33'00" 130°05'00" Off S end of McCauley I, Principe Channel, between Pitt I and Banks I), **Wright Narrows** (53°31'00" 129°52'00" Between Wright Inlet and Ala Passage), **Wright Passage** (52°37'00" 129°25'00" S of Moore Is, off NW Aristazabal I, Hecate Str). Alfred Esten Wright (1885–1927), a surveyor with the BC Lands Service, had a varied career on the N coast. He was born at Toronto, educated at Royal Military College in Kingston and worked at first for BC's Crow's Nest Pass Coal Co. After marrying Dora Denison, also from Toronto, in 1911, he moved to Prince Rupert, where he set up a surveying practice. Wright worked on the upper Nass R in 1913, and in 1918 made detailed triangulation surveys of NW Moresby I; Fairfax Inlet on the S side of Tasu Sd was originally named for him but was changed in 1951. He was in charge of a triangulation party off the coast of Pitt I in 1921, using the small vessel *Ala*, and in 1926 was employed by the Dept of Indian Affairs in the vicinity of Aristazabal I. His health failed that year and he moved to Victoria, then Toronto, where he died prematurely at age 42.

Wriglesworth Point (52°44'00" 129°18'00" W of Borrowman Bay, NW side of Aristazabal I). Joseph Wriglesworth (1841–1933), from Devon, England, came to Victoria in 1862 and set up in business as a grocer. He was a volunteer fireman in the 1860s and rose to become chief of Victoria's Union Hook and Ladder Co No 1. Joseph married Sarah Elizabeth Wakefield (1855–1907), a native of Yorkshire who had come to Canada with her parents in 1859. He was elected a Victoria alderman, 1881–84. Later in life he established a second business, the Saanich Lime Co, which supplied plaster, cement and other building materials. Wriglesworth, who was a noted water diviner and located 150 wells on S Vancouver I, took part in the grand old-timers' reunion held at Victoria in May 1924 (*see* Adams Bay).

Wurtele Island (52°10'00" 128°30'00" Off SW end of Athlone I, Milbanke Sd, W of Bella Bella). Named in 1944 after Cdr Alfred Charles Wurtele (1897–2000) of the RCN, who served on the W coast, 1932–39, and was CO at the HMCS *Naden* shore establishment during WWII. Born at Kingston, Ont, he became a cadet at the Royal Naval College of Canada in 1913 and, as a sub-lt aboard HMS *Swift*, was present in 1918 at the surrender of the German fleet. After retiring from the RCN in 1945, he was elected a municipal councillor at Esquimalt and served as reeve of Esquimalt, 1952–65. At the time of his death, Wurtele was Canada's oldest naval officer.

Wya Point (48°58'00" 125°37'00" SE end of Florencia Bay, W of Barkley Sd, W side of Vancouver I). Named after Wya or Wayi, a nearby Ucluelet First Nation reserve. The word can be translated from the Nuu-chah-nulth language as "safe place."

Wymond Point (48°35'00" 123°16'00" SE end of Sidney I, N of Victoria, Gulf Is). After Wymond Hamley, Victoria's collector of customs for many years. *See* Hamley Point.

Yaculta (50°01'00" 125°12'00" SW side of Quadra I, N end of Str of Georgia), **Yaculta Bank** (50°01'00" 125°14'00" Near S end of Discovery Passage, just E of Campbell R). The Lekwiltok village of Yaculta, whose occupants are known as the We-wai-kai, is often referred to locally as Cape Mudge (qv). This area was visited by Capt George Vancouver and naturalist Archibald Menzies in 1792, when it was home to the Northern Coast Salish people, who occupied a village just to the S of present-day Yaculta. In the mid-1800s the Lekwiltok, who are a branch of the Kwakwaka'wakw First Nation—and were known as the "Vikings of Vancouver I" for their frequent attacks on southern tribes—moved S from Knight Inlet and gained control of the region. The name Yaculta, which is an anglicized form of Lekwiltok, began to appear on Admiralty charts in the 1860s. Yuculta (*see* Yuculta Rapids) has the same derivation, and many other versions of Lekwiltok are found, including Euclataw, Laich-kwil-tacks, Li-kwil-tah, Ne-cul-ta, Tah-cul-tus and Yukletas. It may mean "unkillable" and might refer to a sea worm that can survive even if cut into pieces. The Kwakiutl Museum was opened at Yaculta in 1979 to hold potlatch artifacts and regalia repatriated from institutions in eastern N America.

Yadus Point (52°34'00" 131°21'00" E side of Ramsay I, S of Lyell I, off E side of Moresby I, QCI). The Yadus people are one of the families of the Stustas, the great Haida Eagle clan. They migrated across Dixon Entrance to Prince of Wales I sometime in the 18th century and are now part of the Kaigani Haida, who live in SE Alaska.

Yakan Point (54°04'00" 131°50'00" Just W of Tow Hill, N side of Graham I, QCI). Named after the Haida First Nation reserve and former village of Yagan, which was located at this site. Yagan was an Eagle crest community that, at the time of geologist George Mercer Dawson's 1878 visit, was only occupied seasonally, when fishing for halibut and dogfish took place.

Yakaskalui Point (54°47'30" 130°12'10" NE side of Somerville I, Portland Inlet, N of Prince Rupert). The feature was named by the hydrographic service in 1955, after a Tsimshian First Nation word that may refer to the alders growing at this site.

Yakoun Bay (53°40'00" 132°13'00" SE side of Masset Inlet, Graham I, QCI). Named in 1910 by regional hydrographer

The Coast Salish village of Tsqulotn, just south of today's Yaculta, drawn by midshipman William Sykes of HMS *Discovery* in 1792. *MCR 18089*

Lt Cdr Philip Musgrave after the Yakoun R, which flows N into this bay. QCI historian Kathleen Dalzell gives three possible translations for the Haida First Nation word: "straight point," "in the middle" or "on the east." The river is the largest in the QCI, with major salmon and steelhead runs, and was once covered with majestic forests, now extensively logged. The Yakoun valley was the site of the famed 300-year-old Golden Spruce, an unusual, yellow-needled variety that was cut down by a vandal in 1997. Nearby Yakoun Lk is also named for the river. The alternative spellings Yakun and Yah-koon are sometimes seen for these features. The bay is an important sanctuary for waterfowl. *D E*

Yarrow Point (48°38'00" 123°29'00" W side of Coles Bay and Saanich Peninsula, NW of Victoria). Named in 1946 to recognize the war work done by Yarrows Ltd, Esquimalt's largest shipyard. In the years leading up to WWI, Sir Alfred Yarrow (1842–1932), owner of a famous shipyard on the R Clyde at Glasgow, sought to acquire a plant in N America. He ended up buying the BC Marine Rwys Co (more commonly known as Bullen's) in 1913 for $300,000; the fact that there was a government drydock at Esquimalt helped clinch the deal. Sir Alfred's second son, Norman Alfred Yarrow (1891–1955), managed the operation with Edward Izard. He married Ada Hope Leeder at Victoria in 1915 and became a well-known local figure who loved luxurious automobiles and dabbled in aviation. The company built hundreds of large vessels over the years, including steamships, ferries, barges and tankers. During WWII, Yarrows employed more than 4,300 workers and constructed dozens of freighters, as well as a large number of frigates, corvettes and minesweepers for the RCN and RN. The firm was taken over by Burrard Dry Dock Ltd (formerly Wallace Shipyards) in 1946 but continued to operate under its old name until it closed in 1994. *E*

Yates Island (52°10'00" 128°05'00" Between Saunders I and Rainbow I, Lama Passage, just NE of Bella Bella). Named in 1925, possibly after Alfred E Yates, who built the sternwheeler *Vedder* at New Westminster in 1909 and ran it as a ferry on the Fraser R. The *Vedder* used the engines from another sternwheeler, the *John P Douglass*, which was destroyed by fire at the mouth of the Harrison R. In 1914 the *Vedder* went to Wrangell, Alaska, to join the Stikine R trade, but it was demolished in a blaze as well. Yates I was formerly known as Tree I, and also as Payne I, after Sub-Lt Charles Harold C Payne (1884–1949), an RCNVR paymaster during WWI.

Yates Point (48°20'00" 123°36'00" N side of Becher Bay, NE of Arden It, S tip of Vancouver I). James Yates (1819–1900), from Scotland, joined the HBC as a ship's carpenter in 1848 and travelled to York Factory on Hudson Bay in the *Prince Rupert*. He also married Mary Powell (d 1898) that year. The couple came to Ft Victoria in 1849 in the *Harpooner*,

and James worked as a shipwright on various HBC vessels. Emma Frances, James and Mary's daughter, was one of the first white children born at Victoria, in 1850. James left HBC service in 1851 and went into trade, achieving success as a Victoria tavern owner and liquor vendor and buying key properties in the downtown area, where Yates St is named for him. When land prices skyrocketed after the Fraser R gold rush, Yates found himself one of the young city's wealthiest residents. He served on Vancouver I's first colonial legislative assembly, 1855–59, where he was part of a faction that lobbied for electoral reform and loudly opposed the HBC connections of Gov James Douglas. He and his family returned to Britain in 1860, but Yates was out in Victoria again in 1862–64, dealing with his business ventures. He retired to Edinburgh but actively managed his BC investments through agents and was still listed in 1891 as one of Victoria's largest landowners; only the HBC, CPR, W H Oliver, Roderick Finlayson and the estates of James Douglas and Robert Dunsmuir had more valuable holdings. His sons, who were born in BC, came back in the 1880s and lived at Victoria (*see* Yates Shoal). Yates Point was formerly known as Rocky Point but was renamed by the hydrographic service in 1934.

Yates Point (49°16'00" 126°03'00" SE end of Flores I, Clayoquot Sd, W side of Vancouver I). Thomas N Yates pre-empted land on Esowista Peninsula in 1912. Yates Point was formerly known as Base Point but was renamed by the hydrographic service in 1934.

Yates Shoal (52°51'00" 129°33'00" W of Rennison I, entrance to Caamaño Sd, Hecate Str). James Stuart Yates (1857–1950) was born at Victoria, a son of HBC pioneer James Yates (*see* Yates Point), but was raised and educated at Edinburgh, where he studied law. He returned to BC about 1883 and practised law at Victoria for 62 years. In 1890 he married Annie Austin (1868–1948), who was also born in BC. James was involved with his father's BC business interests, served as a city alderman in 1900–1903 and 1906, and was also a director of the Royal Jubilee Hospital; he ran unsuccessfully as a candidate in the 1898 and 1900 BC elections but was nevertheless appointed chief commissioner of Lands and Public Works in the short-lived 1900 cabinet of Premier Joseph Martin. Both he and his wife took part in the Victoria old-timers' reunion of 1924 (*see* Adams Bay), and both played major roles with the Native Sons and Native Daughters of BC, organizations dedicated to the preservation of early provincial history.

Yeatman Bay (50°14'00" 125°11'00" E side of Quadra I, NW of Surge Narrows, N of Campbell R). Frederick Charles Yeatman (1862–1903), from England, came to Quadra I in 1894 with his Welsh wife, Emma (1863–1937), and bought an 80-ha farm just N of Quathiaski Cove from Tom Bell. They homesteaded, logged, fished and

Y

raised a large family. Fred disappeared on a hunting trip to Vancouver I. His rifle was found beside a river bank, and it was assumed that he had fallen in the water and drowned; his remains were found several years later. The Yeatmans had more than their fair share of tragedy; two of their sons, Sam and Fred, drowned on Heriot Bay in 1921, aged 28 and 27, respectively. Yeatman Bay was named by the hydrographic service in 1924.

Yellow Point (49°02'00" 123°45'00" W side of Stuart Channel, NE of Kulleet Bay, SE of Nanaimo, SE side of Vancouver I). The point is apparently named for the yellow stonecrop rock plants (*Sedum* species) that bloom along the shore in spring. It is the site of historic Yellow Point Lodge, founded in the mid-1930s by Gerry Hill. The original main lodge building burned down in 1985 but was rebuilt the following year. The popular resort was still operated by the Hill family in 2009.

Yeo Cove (52°18'00" 128°11'00" SW side of Yeo I), **Yeo Island** (52°21'00" 128°08'00" Between Spiller Channel and Bullock Channel, N of Bella Bella), **Yeo Islands** (49°18'00" 124°08'00" W side of Ballenas Channel, N of Nanoose Hbr, NW of Nanaimo, off E side of Vancouver I), **Yeo Point** (48°48'00" 123°23'00" E side of Saltspring I, Gulf Is). Dr Gerald Yeo (d 1887) was the surgeon aboard HMS *Ganges* and served on the Pacific Station, 1857–60, when the *Ganges* was flagship of station cdr-in-chief Rear Adm Robert Baynes. He became a fellow of the Royal College of Surgeons in 1864, was appointed to the Royal Naval College in 1866 and retired in 1875 with the rank of fleet surgeon. Gerald I in Ballenas Channel and Gerald Point on Yeo I are also named for him. The Yeo Is were named about 1860 by Capt George Richards in HMS *Plumper*, Yeo I by Lt Daniel Pender in 1866 and Yeo Point by Cdr John Parry, while re-surveying Ganges Hbr with HMS *Egeria* in 1905. Yeo Lk on Yeo I takes its name from the island. *W*

Yestalton Bay (53°40'00" 132°24'00" S side of Masset Inlet, Graham I, QCI). While the name of this feature sounds as if it should commemorate an RN officer, it is believed, instead, to be an adaptation of a Haida First Nation word for a nearby former campsite. The camp was on the spit at the mouth of the stream that runs into the head of the bay.

Yorke Island (50°27'00" 125°59'00" At the junction of Johnstone Str and Sunderland Channel, NW of Campbell R). Capt George Richards named this island in association with nearby Hardwicke I in 1862, after the family name of the British earls of Hardwicke. Mt Yorke on Hardwicke I was named at the same time. During WWII, two 4.7-inch guns, searchlights and other facilities were installed on the island. Yorke I's location was strategic, as any southbound vessel headed down the Inside Passage toward Vancouver had to pass it at a distance of less than 4 km, and it had a clear field of view. The post was upgraded to two 6-inch

guns (taken from the battery at Stanley Park) in 1942; 260 men were eventually quartered there. The site's isolation and unenviable living conditions earned it the nickname "Little Alcatraz."

York Point (53°05'00" 129°10'00" SE side of Gil I, Whale Channel, off NW Princess Royal I). Joseph York (1835–1924), a native of Northamptonshire, immigrated to Victoria from England in 1862 and established himself as a dry goods merchant. In 1882 he had a partnership with fellow merchant Moses Lenz, and in 1901 he ran unsuccessfully as a Victoria alderman. York travelled back and forth to England several times; in 1875 he married Martha Dickens (1843–1917) there, and the entire York family returned to Britain for the period 1885–94. These Victoria pioneers, however, spent most of their lives on Vancouver I.

York Rocks (48°53'00" 123°20'00" In Whaler Bay, between E Galiano I and Gossip I, Gulf Is). Named after a pioneer settler on Saturna I, as submitted by the Gulf Is Branch of the BC Historical Association in 1968.

Young Bay (49°25'41" 126°13'27" E side of Sydney Inlet, NW of Clayoquot Sd, W side of Vancouver I). Robert Orr Bruce Young (1907–85) was born in Ont, raised in Alberta and received a civil engineering degree from UBC in 1928. He joined the Canadian Hydrographic Service the following year as an assistant hydrographer on the survey vessel *Lillooet*, and he served in that vessel and in the *William J Stewart* until 1938. Young, who married Norma Mavis Neill at Vancouver in 1929, was involved with some of the first aerial photography done on the Pacific coast, in 1930. He worked on the W coast of Vancouver I, 1930–34, and conducted surveys in Sydney Inlet in 1932, when Young Bay, formerly known as East Bay, was named for him. In 1939–41 he was officer in charge of the houseboat *Pender*, and from 1941 to 1945 he served as senior assistant aboard the *William J Stewart*, carrying out wartime surveys for the Dept of National Defence as well as regular surveys. After WWII he was appointed hydrographer-in-charge of the *Stewart*, a position he held until he became regional hydrographer, responsible for the work of five vessels on the Pacific and Arctic coasts, in 1953. Young retired in 1968.

Young Point (53°12'00" 132°17'00" W entrance to Long Inlet, W end of Skidegate Inlet, QCI). This feature was named by Lt Daniel Pender after William Alexander George Young (c 1827–85), BC's colonial secretary, to whom Pender reported after his 1866 survey of Skidegate Inlet. Young was a rising RN capt when he was appointed secretary of the British boundary commission in 1857 and came to Victoria to co-ordinate the survey of the 49th parallel. He became friends with Gov James Douglas, and in 1858, Young married Douglas's niece, Cecilia Eliza

Cowan Cameron, the stepdaughter of Chief Justice David Cameron. Douglas appointed Young colonial secretary of BC in 1858 and then acting colonial secretary for Vancouver I, as well, and Young soon became indispensable to the gov, who wrote to London that "no other person is so extensively acquainted with the business of the two colonies or so capable of carrying out the general line of policy and the system of government." Young served on the executive and legislative councils of Vancouver I and was also elected to the legislative assembly in 1863–64. He remained, with short interruptions, the senior civil servant of both colonies (which were united in 1866) until 1868, when he left the PNW to become financial secretary of Jamaica. He returned to England in ill health, 1872–77, then was knighted and named gov of the Gold Coast colony in Africa, where he died. *E*

Yovanovich Bight (53°10'15" 132°26'20" Dawson Hbr, SW end of Graham I, N of Skidegate Channel, QCI). Named in 1986 after William Yovanovich (1924–84), a well-known handlogger in the QCI, who lived on the bight for many years. Fish boats frequent this location because of the protection it provides in foul weather and the availability of fresh water.

Yuculta Rapids between Stuart and Sonora islands. *Peter Vassilopoulos*

Yuculta Rapids (50°23'00" 125°09'00" Between Sonora I and Stuart I, N of Campbell R). These well-known hazards to navigation have currents that can run up to 10 knots (18.5 km/h). *Sailing Directions* warns of "strong tidal streams with overfalls and at times violent eddies and whirlpools," and a number of marine disasters have occurred in this vicinity. The name, which is usually pronounced *YUK-le-taw*, refers to the Lekwiltok people, a branch of the Kwakwaka'wakw First Nation, who moved S from Knight Inlet into this area in the mid-1800s. The word Yaculta (qv) has the same derivation, and many other versions of Lekwiltok are found, including Euclataw, Laich-kwil-tacks, Li-kwil-tah, Ne-culta and Tah-cul-tus. The name may mean "unkillable" and might refer to a sea worm that can survive and regenerate even if cut into pieces. *E*

Yuquot (49°36'00" 126°37'00" Just N of Yuquot Point), **Yuquot Point** (49°35'00" 126°37'00" SE tip of Nootka I, W side of Vancouver I). The word means "windy place" in the Nuu-chah-nulth language. Yuquot (or Yucuatl) village was a traditional summer residence of the Mowachaht people, who are part of the Nuu-chah-nulth tribal confederacy. Archeologists have dated signs of habitation back at least 4,200 years. The village became the main point of contact and interaction between First Nation and European cultures in the PNW in the late 18th century. Capt James Cook visited the site in 1778 and was followed by a stream of traders eager to secure valuable sea otter furs. The name Friendly Cove, applied by James Strange in 1786, became synonymous with Yuquot, and Mowachaht chief Maquinna, well known to all the early traders, managed to control much of the fur business in the region. British trader John Meares built a post at Yuquot in 1788 and constructed the *North West America* there; it was the first European vessel built in the PNW. The Spanish occupied the sound the following year and established a fort beside Yuquot that they operated until 1795. They set off an international dispute later in 1789 by seizing several British trading vessels. A lighthouse station was built nearby in 1911. Yuquot was inhabited more or less permanently by the Mowachaht until 1968, when all but one family moved to a reserve at the mouth of the Gold R. The historic site is still visited by tourists and used for ceremonies. *E W*

Zanardi Rapids (54°14'44" 130°17'55" Between Kaien I and Watson I, just S of Prince Rupert). Carlo Zanardi-Landi (1876–1953), an Austrian count, was a member of a GTP survey team in this vicinity about 1910. At around the same time he met Caroline Maria Kühnelt (c 1879–1935, née Kaiser), who had separated from her husband in Que in 1908. The couple lived together in Vancouver for several years before they married, in 1914, at London, England. Shortly after her marriage, Caroline published a book, *The Secret of an Empress*, in which she claimed that she was an unacknowledged daughter of Elizabeth of Bavaria, or "Sisi," the wife of Emperor Franz Josef of Austria. A daughter by her first husband was Elissa Landi, screen actress and novelist, who died in 1948. The rapids, which are crossed by overhead power cables and a railway bridge, have violent currents during large tides.

Zayas Island (54°36'15" 131°04'36" W of Dundas I, E end of Dixon Entrance, NW of Prince Rupert). Named in 1792 by Spanish explorer Lt Jacinto Caamaño, who was sent by Francisco de la Bodega y Quadra to survey the N coast of BC on either side of Dixon Entrance and search for the Str of Fonte, a navigable sea passage that supposedly crossed N America at this latitude. Juan Martínez y Zayas was 2nd pilot on Caamaño's vessel, the *Aránzazu*. He led an expedition in the *Aránzazu*'s boats up Verney Passage to Devastation Channel and Gardner Canal that helped disprove the existence of the fictitious strait. In 1793, Zayas, in command of the *Mexicana*, explored the Oregon coast to Neah Bay and investigated Grays Hbr and the lower reaches of the Columbia R. He had originally accompanied Francisco Eliza and the *Activa* on this voyage but became separated from them. Capt George Vancouver adopted the name Zayas I on his charts in 1793.

Zeballos (49°59'00" 126°51'00" Head of Zeballos Inlet), **Zeballos Inlet** (49°57'00" 126°49'00" N of Esperanza Inlet, E of Espinosa Inlet, W side of Vancouver I). The

The community of Zeballos in 1938. *Courtesy Tim Woodland*

inlet (formerly known as Zeballos Arm) was named by Alejandro Malaspina after Ciriaco Cevallos y Bustillo (c 1767–1816), one of the officers on his global circumnavigation, who explored the area in 1791. Cevallos had joined the Malaspina expedition as a cartographer earlier in 1791, at Acapulco. He was born in northern Spain and entered the naval college at Cartagena in 1779. Six years later, aboard the *Santa María de la Cabeza*, he helped Antonio de Córdoba chart the Str of Magellan. After Malaspina and his ships returned to Spain, Cevallos continued to work on the charts of the voyage; later, he was also involved with the mapping of the Gulf of Mexico. About 1808, for reasons unknown, he left the Spanish navy and moved to New Orleans, where he died. Nearby Zeballos Lk, Zeballos Peak and the Zeballos R are all named after the inlet. The village of Zeballos sprang up as a result of a localized gold rush to the area in 1935–36. The Privateer Mine and other operations produced $13 million worth of gold over the next decade. An iron ore mine operated in the 1960s; then Zeballos became mainly a logging centre. *E*

Zero Rock (48°31'00" 123°17'00" E of Cordova Bay, in Haro Str, off SE Vancouver I). The name apparently comes from the feature's deceptively small size. A navigation light on the rock warns mariners, as does a light on nearby Little Zero Rk, which is also hazardous.

Zorro Bay (49°36'00" 123°15'00" W side of Howe Sd, SW of Britannia Beach, NW of Vancouver). A large "Z" was spray-painted on the rock face in this bay in the 1970s. Zorro Bay was submitted as a well-established local name by an assistant *Sailing Directions* officer in 1981.

Zuciarte Channel (49°38'00" 126°30'00" E side of Nootka Sd, E of Bligh I, W side of Vancouver I). This name, despite its spelling and geographic location, is not of Spanish origin. According to coastal historian Capt John Walbran and pioneer Roman Catholic missionary Augustin Brabant, it is an adaptation of the name of a Muchalaht First Nation clan whose members were traditional enemies of Mowachaht chief Maquinna (both groups were part of the Nuu-chah-nulth tribal confederacy). Zuciarte or Ze-sa-at is also believed to have been the hereditary name of the clan's chieftain. *W*

LIST OF DETAIL MAPS

Harbour Publishing Co. Ltd.
P.O. Box 219, Madeira Park, BC, V0N 2H0
www.harbourpublishing.com

Editor: Audrey McClellan
Proofreading: Amelia Gilliland, Helen Godolphin, Rebecca Hendry, Lenore Hietkamp,
   Alicia J. McDonald, Hugh Morrison, Peter A. Robson, Patricia Wolfe
Photo research: Peter A. Robson
Text design and layout: Roger Handling, Terra Firma Digital Arts
Cover design: Anna Comfort
Maps reproduced with the permission of the Canadian Hydrographic Service
Additional photo credits: Front dustjacket, Ninstints Point, Haida Gwaii, Russ Heinl photo.
   Back dustjacket, Telegraph Cove, Rachel Talibart photo.
   Page 1, Race Rocks Lighthouse, John Lund photo. Pages 2–3, Captain James Cook's *Resolution* and
   Discovery, anchored in what would be named Resolution Cove, 1778, Gordon Miller painting.
   Pages 4–5, Mount Denman towers over Desolation Sound, Boomer Jerrit photo.

Printed on 30% PCW recycled stock using soy-based inks
Printed and bound in Canada

Canada Council   Conseil des Arts
for the Arts   du Canada

BRITISH
COLUMBIA
ARTS COUNCIL
Supported by the Province of British Columbia

Harbour Publishing acknowledges financial support from the Government of Canada through the Book Publishing Industry Development Program and the Canada Council for the Arts, and from the Province of British Columbia through the BC Arts Council and the Book Publishing Tax Credit.

Library and Archives Canada Cataloguing in Publication

Scott, Andrew, 1947-
      The encyclopedia of raincoast place names : a complete reference to coastal British Columbia
/ Andrew Scott.

ISBN 978-1-55017-484-7

      1. Names, Geographical—British Columbia—Pacific Coast. 2. Pacific Coast
(B.C.) —History, Local. 3. Pacific Coast (B.C.) —Biography. I. Title.

FC3806.S37 2009   917.11'10014   C2009-903496-4

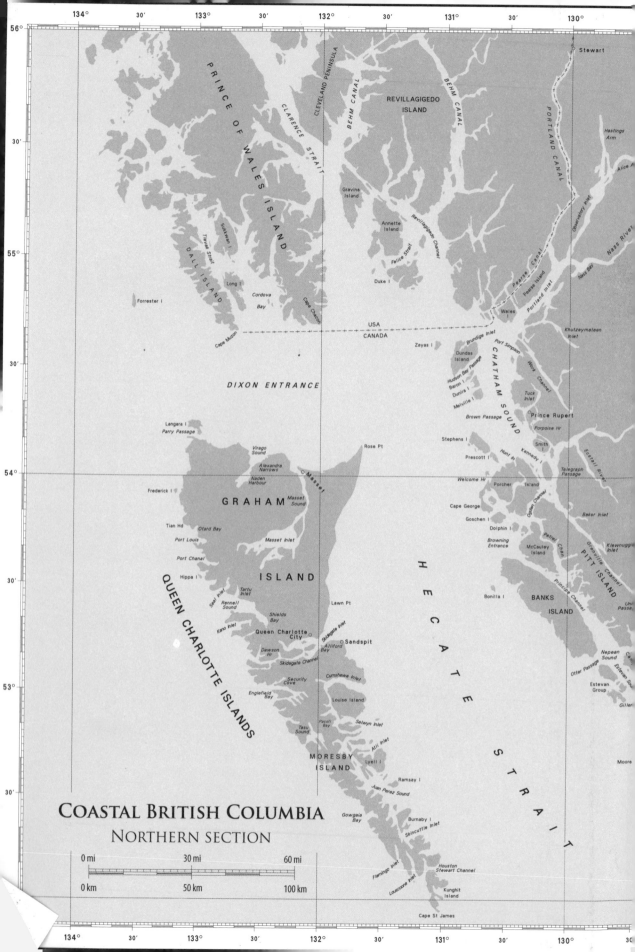

COASTAL BRITISH COLUMBIA

NORTHERN SECTION

0 mi   30 mi   60 mi

0 km   50 km   100 km